Scotland

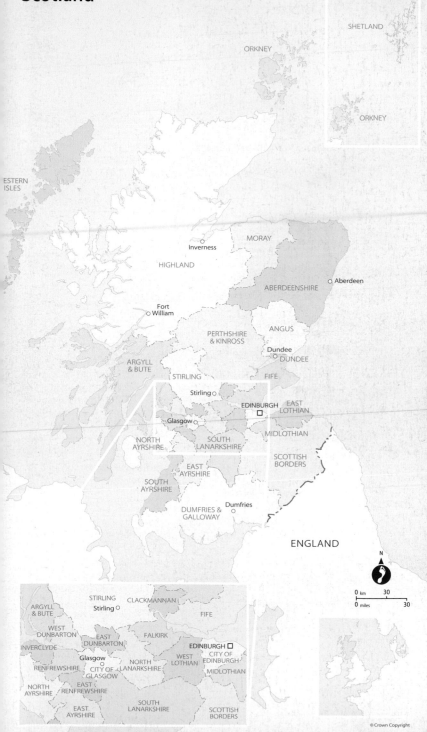

© Crown Copyright

Scotland Handbook
© Footprint Handbooks Ltd 2000

Published by Footprint Handbooks
6 Riverside Court
Lower Bristol Road
Bath BA2 3DZ. England
T +44 (0)1225 469141
F +44 (0)1225 469461
Email discover@footprintbooks.com
Web www.footprintbooks.com

ISBN 1 900949 56 3
CIP DATA: A catalogue record for this book
is available from the British Library

In USA, published by
NTC/Contemporary Publishing Group
4255 West Touhy Avenue, Lincolnwood
(Chicago), Illinois 60712-1975, USA
T 847 679 5500 F 847 679 2494
Email NTCPUB2@AOL.COM

ISBN 0-658-00370-4
Library of Congress Catalog Card Number
on file

® Footprint Handbooks and the Footprint
mark are a registered trademark of
Footprint Handbooks Ltd.

Neither the black and white nor coloured
maps are intended to have any political
significance.

Maps based upon Ordnance Survey
1:50,000 Landranger mapping with the
permission of the Controller of Her
Majesty's Stationery Office © Crown
Copyright. Licence number 43501U.

Illustrations by Sahra Carter

Credits
Series editors
Patrick Dawson and Rachel Fielding
Editorial
Senior editor: Sarah Thorowgood
Maps: Sarah Sorensen
Production
Pre-press Manager: Jo Morgan
Typesetting: Richard Ponsford and
Emma Bryers
Maps: Kevin Feeney, Robert Lunn,
Claire Benison and Map Creation Ltd
Proof reading: Grant Gillespie and
Felicity Laughton

Design
Mytton Williams

Photography
Front cover: Eye Ubiquitous
Back cover: Pictor International
Inside colour section: Duncan MacArthur;
IMPACT Photos (Alan Donaldson); Robert
Harding Picture Library; The Travel Library;
Scotland in Focus; Edinburgh
Photographic Library.

Printed and bound
in Italy by LEGOPRINT

Every effort has been made to ensure that
the facts in this Handbook are accurate.
However, travellers should still obtain
advice from consulates, airlines etc about
current travel and visa requirements
before travelling. The authors and
publishers cannot accept responsibility
for any loss, injury or inconvenience
however caused.

Footprint Scotland Handbook

The travel guide

Alan Murphy

"Breathes there the man, with soul so dead, who never to himself hath said, this is my own, my native land".

Sir Walter Scott

Contents

Left: McLennan Galleries, Sauchiehall Street, Glasgow.

Right: Neist Point Lighthouse, Isle of Skye.

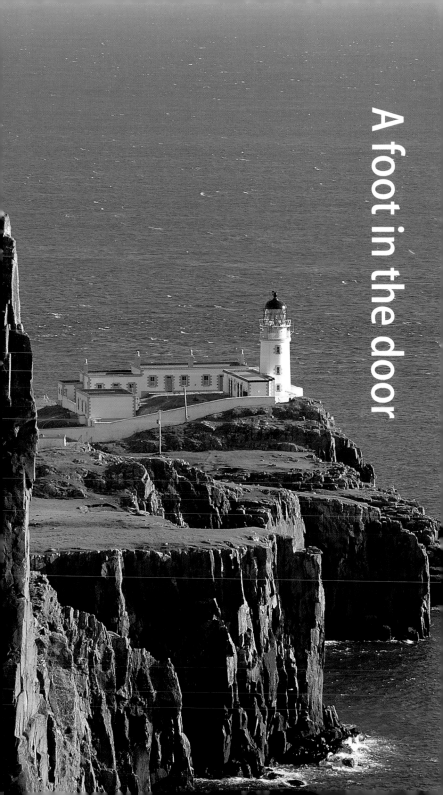

A foot in the door

Right: The perenially photogenic harbour at Crail in Fife.
Below: Croft house on the Isle of Skye.

Above: Forth Rail Bridge.
Right: ferry from Armadale on Skye to Mallaig.

Highlights

There's much more to Scotland than tartan and bagpipes. This is one of Europe's most varied and fascinating countries. An astoundingly beautiful place, with a range of attractions broad enough to make any rival tourist destination stamp its feet in frustration and then storm out of the room protesting unfair competition. Medieval castles, dynamic cities, remote islands, mysterious stone circles, rare wildlife, any number of outdoor sports, superb cuisine, and that famous hospitality all combine to make Scotland an extremely tempting proposition. In fact, about the only thing Scotland doesn't have is a dependable climate, so if you want to lie on a beach all day soaking up rays, then you really ought to go somewhere else.

The last wilderness

Scotland is also one of the least densely populated countries in Europe. It is not much smaller than England but has only one tenth of its population, most of whom are crammed into the narrow central belt, leaving two-thirds of the country unspoiled. The northwest Highlands are Europe's last great wilderness: one of the few places in this increasingly cluttered continent where you can really get away from it all. People come here for peace and quiet and an unequalled variety and quality of landscape: white beaches, turquoise seas, heather-clad mountains, magical glens, towering waterfalls and deep, mysterious lochs.

When the rain stops falling and the mist clears there is no more beautiful place on Earth. Around every bend in the roads that wend their way through this vast region is a sight that leaves you testing the limits of your vocabulary in search of yet another appropriate adjective. The less eloquent amongst you may be reduced to a disbelieving grunt at the sheer wonder of it all. More emotional souls may even be reduced to tears. If there is a heaven, then it must look like the Scottish Highlands, but let's hope the petrol's cheaper.

Culture shock

The Scottish mainland is surrounded by hundreds of islands, each one with its own distinct history and culture. Crossing to these islands doesn't just feel like a different country, it can feel like entering another time zone. Where else could you find a police station using gerbils as paper shredders, or the swings in the playground padlocked to ensure strict observance of the Sabbath?

Lying off the west coast are the Hebridean islands, home of the Gaelic culture, where the road signs include English spellings almost as an afterthought and the local people speak Gaelic as their native tongue. And off the northern tip of the mainland is Orkney, an archipelago of 70 islands, which was a part of Norway until the 15th century. Likewise the Shetland Isles, which are so far north they can only be included on maps as an inset. In fact, they still don't seem a part of Britain: the nearest mainland town is Bergen, in Norway, and Norwegian is taught in the schools.

Scotland the rave

There's nothing the Scots love more than a good party, preferably involving lots of alcohol, singing and dancing. Music and dancing is an intrinsic part of Scottish culture and you're never too far from a *ceilidh* (pronounced "kay-lee"), a kind of Scottish knees-up, which is somewhere between a barn dance and a rugby scrum. One of the most unforgettable experiences of a Scottish trip is to find yourself in a pub in the back of beyond, consuming copious quantities of whisky with the locals and then hurling a bunch of total strangers around the room, to the accompaniment of a fiddle and accordion. By the time you reach the top of the nearest mountain the following day, you'll have forgotten all about the hangover.

Cities of culture

Few cities make such a strong impression on the visitor as Edinburgh. Scotland's capital is one of the most beautiful and elegant cities in Europe, with a unique architectural heritage, but one of the first things that strikes you about Edinburgh is its wide open spaces. It makes you feel small. Everything here seems huge: the medieval tenements, the Georgian terraces, the hills, the sky. The urban bits are separated not just by parks and gardens, but by cliffs and rocks and grassy hills – even an extinct volcano! This is real nature rather than the manicured stuff which is all you get in most other cities. The views around Edinburgh have to be seen to be believed: from the top of Arthur's Seat as far as the Perthshire Highlands to the north; from Calton Hill down the length of Princes Street; and from the castle ramparts you can see over the New Town and across the Firth of Forth to Fife.

Something to celebrate Edinburgh's good looks are backed by impressive cultural credentials. Every year the city plays host to the world's biggest arts festival and bursts into life in a riot of entertainment. Edinburgh during its Festival has been variously described as "simply the best place on Earth" and "the cultural hub of the world". There's a unique buzz about the place as over a million tourists descend on the city to experience a mind-blowing variety of performances. Not content with this, Edinburgh also hosts a Science Festival, an International Children's Festival, plus Jazz and Blues and Beer, to name but a few. On top of all this, its New Year's Eve party is now the biggest in Europe.

In keeping with its status as one of the great European cities, Edinburgh's many excellent museums and art galleries boast the finest collections outside London. Edinburgh is obviously well aware of its own status, and the arrival of the brand new Scottish parliament at the dawn of the 21st century has only added to that confidence.

Designs on success If Edinburgh's tourist trappings become too much, take a trip to Glasgow, Scotland's largest city, which has long been ignored by visitors in favour of its great rival. Now Glasgow is emerging as major attraction in its own right and is successfully wooing visitors with its fascinating blend of style, culture, energy and excitement.

A decade ago, much to Edinburgh's chagrin, Glasgow was chosen as European City of Culture, and has never looked back since. The Kelvingrove and Burrell galleries boast two of the finest art collections in Britain, and Glasgow is also home to both Scottish opera and Scottish ballet, as well as having some of the most exciting theatre companies in the country. In 1999, it received another top accolade: City of Architecture and Design. Now, the many Victorian architectural treasures of the "Second City of the Empire" are being given the attention they deserve, and can stand alongside the internationally-acclaimed creations of Charles Rennie Mackintosh.

The friendly city Art and architecture may be at the forefront of Glasgow's revival, but the city has other attractions. It has a thriving continental-style café culture, many stylish bars and bistros and was recently voted the UK's top city outside London for the choice and quality of its restaurants. But it is the people of Glasgow who really set it apart. Its atmosphere is infused with those vital ingredients missing from so many large urban centres – warmth and humour. Glasgow is without doubt the friendliest of Britain's large cities.

Left: the the Clyde auditorium, better known as the "Armadillo", from Bell's Bridge over the River Clyde, Glasgow.
Below: view of Edinburgh's skyline from Calton Hill.

Above: street performers at the Edinburgh Festival.
Left: St George's Mansions, Glasgow.
Next page: ruin of St Andrews Cathedral.

Outdoor life

Scotland's greatest appeal is to those who love the outdoor life. There are mountains galore to climb or ski down, lochs to fish and wildlife to watch, or you can just sit back and take in all that stunning scenery.

In the Highlands and Islands in particular, there are countless opportunities to leave civilisation a long way behind. You could explore Scotland's long distance footpaths which snake through some of the country's finest scenery. These include the West Highland Way which starts in Glasgow and ends at Fort William, the less well known Speyside Way, which passes through the heart of whisky country, and the Southern Upland Way, which runs from coast to coast through Dumfries and Galloway and the Borders.

The more adventurous can try their hand (or feet) at 'Munro Bagging', which is not some dubious public school practice but the name given to the popular pursuit of climbing Scotland's 284 mountains higher than 3,000 feet. This offers the chance to explore wild areas of unparalleled beauty such as Glen Coe, Torridon, Kintail or the Cairngorms, though not without the proper clothing, even in summer.

In winter, the snow turns the Munros into major expeditions, but also brings the opportunity for downhill skiing. Resorts such as Glenshee, the Nevis Range, Glencoe, the Lecht and the Cairngorms are open from December to April and on a good day offer some superb skiing.

Wildlife spotting Scotland's wide open spaces are rich in wildlife. In October the heather-clad mountains ring to the clashing antlers of rutting red deer and, depending on the time of year and on where you are, you might see ptarmigan, buzzards, golden eagles, wild goats, otters or even pine marten. Wildlife-spotting tours are growing in popularity and the animals on view range from the ubiquitous seals to Britain's only herd of wild reindeer in the Cairngorms and, in the Moray Firth, Europe's largest colony of bottlenosed dolphins. In Orkney you can go on "puffin patrols" and in the waters off the northwest coast minke whales are not an uncommon sight. Less common are killer whales, which have been spotted in the wild Atlantic seas around the Outer Hebrides, and, if you're really lucky, you may just catch a glimpse of Scotland's most sought-after resident – the Loch Ness Monster.

Festivals You'd have to be very unlucky not to experience at least one local festival. The calendar is bursting with them. Many have their roots in pagan ceremonies, such as Lammas Day, which was originally the feast of the Sun God, Lugh. It is still held in St Andrews and Inverkeithing in August. Around the same time a bizarre ritual takes place in South Queensferry, when the Burryman, a kind of human bush, makes his way from house to house receiving gifts. During the summer festivities in the Borders town of Jedburgh, they play the Jedburgh Hand Ba' game – a cross between basketball, rugby and mud wrestling. (The ball in question was originally the head of an Englishman.)

Amongst the most colourful events are the Highland Games, traditional gatherings involving dancing and various sporting competitions, the sound of massed pipe bands and acres of tartan (well, it had to feature somewhere). Much of the time is taken up by large, hairy men in kilts throwing around heavy objects of varying size and shape, but there are also track events and the prestigious individual piper's competition. There are over one hundred of these gatherings held in towns and villages up and down the country during the summer months. They range from large, glitzy affairs such as the Braemar Gathering, which is often attended by the Royal Family, to smaller meetings which are more authentic, and often more enjoyable.

Left: Castle Stalker, Argyll.
Below: Curling on Pulney Loch, Dunkeld, Perthshire.

Above: Lonely Croft house in Glen Torridon.
Left: puffin patrol on Orkney.
Next page: Charles Rennie Mackintosh's famous library in Glasgow School of Art.

Essentials

2

18

Essentials

Planning your trip

Where to go

Which parts of Scotland you choose to visit will be determined by your own particular interests, as well as by the length of your stay and the size of your wallet. It goes without saying (but I'll say it anyway), that a longer trip will allow you to visit the wild, remote and beautiful parts of the country and get much more out of your holiday.

It is easy enough to visit the main towns and tourist sights by bus or train, but getting off the beaten track without your own transport requires careful planning and an intimate knowledge of rural bus timetables. Even if you're driving, getting around the remote Highlands and Islands can be a time-consuming business as much of this region is accessed only by a sparse network of tortuous, twisting, single-track roads. Be sure to allow plenty of time for getting around the Highlands and Islands, especially for the countless impromptu stops you'll be making to admire the views, and book ferries in advance during the busy summer season. All this is covered in greater detail in 'Getting around' (see page 39).

Scotland is a small country but there's a lot to see and trying to cram everything into a first visit can be very frustrating. There are many, many places of great natural beauty and the country's long, turbulent history has left a rich heritage of medieval castles, cathedrals, palaces, abbeys and historic towns and cities. Where do you begin?

Most people start in **Edinburgh**, the capital, and it's hard to disagree with that decision. It is one of the world's truly great cities and deserves at least a few days to explore its castle, palace, medieval streets, fine Georgian architecture, art galleries and museums. Edinburgh is a must.

One week trip If you only have a week and you want to see some Highland scenery, it's only a short drive north from Edinburgh to **Perthshire**. Though not as dramatic as the northwest, the mountains, rivers, lochs and glens of the Perthshire Highlands are very beautiful and easily accessed. If you also want a slice of history thrown in, then you could make a round trip from **Perth** to the historic town of **Stirling**, with its important castle, and return via **Callander** and the **Trossachs**. Also near Perth is the medieval town of **St Andrews**, home of Scotland's oldest university and the world's most famous golf course. From St Andrews, it's an easy day trip to the charming fishing villages of the **East Neuk of Fife**. Also in Fife is the historic town of **Dunfermline**, the ancient capital of Scotland, and the perfectly preserved medieval village of **Culross**.

Two week trip A two week trip would allow you to include a visit to **Glasgow**, Scotland's largest city, renowned for its elegant Victorian architecture, its culture and style and the warmth and humour of its people. A short distance away is **Loch Lomond**, gateway to the Western Highlands and a beautiful introduction to the spectacular sights which lie in wait farther north. From Loch Lomond you should head north through **Glencoe**, one of the main highlights of a visit to Scotland, to **Fort William**, the main tourist centre for the Western Highlands. From Fort William there are two routes to another of Scotland's most popular attractions, the **Isle of Skye**. The quickest route is by road and bridge, via **Kyle of Lochalsh**, but by far the most romantic and scenic route is by **train** from Fort William to **Mallaig**, and by **ferry** from there to **Armadale**. You should then leave at least three days to explore the island, or more if you plan to do any **walking**.

An alternative to Fort William and Skye, or in addition if you have more time, would be to head from Glasgow or Edinburgh to **Oban**, the main ferry port of the west coast, and make the short trip to the beguiling **Isle of Mull**, which tends to be attract fewer visitors than Skye in the summer months. Or you could head south from Oban,

Essentials

Essentials

👉 *British Tourist Authority offices abroad*

The BTA represents the STB abroad. More information can be obtained from their Website (www.bta.org.uk), or from the offices listed below:

Australia *Level 16, The Gateway, 1 Macquarie Pl, Circular Quay, Sydney NSW 2000, T02-93774400, F02-93774499.*

Belgium and Luxembourg *306 Ave Louise, 1050 Brussels, T2-6463510, F2-6463986.*

Canada *111 Avenue Rd, Suite 450, Toronto, Ontario MR5 3J8, T416-9256326, F416-9612175.*

Denmark *Montergade 3, 1116 Copenhagen K, T33-339188, F33-140136.*

France *Maison de la Gran-Bretagne, 19 Rue des Mathurins, 75009 Paris, T1-44515620, F1-44515621.*

Germany, Austria and Switzerland *Taunustrasse 52-60, 60329 Frankfurt, T69-2380711.*

Ireland *18/19 College Green, Dublin 2, T1-6708000, F1-6708244.*

Italy *Corso Vittorio Emanuele II No 337, 00186 Rome, T6-68806821, F6-6879095.*

Netherlands *Stadhouderskade 2 (5e), 1054 ES Amsterdam, T20-6855051, F20-6186868.*

New Zealand *17th Flr, Fay Richwhite Building, 151 Queen St, Auckland 1, T09-3031446, F09-3776965.*

South Africa *Lancaster Gate, Hyde Park Lane, Hyde Park 2196, Johannesburg, T011-3250342.*

USA *7th Flr, 551 Fifth Ave, New York, NY 10176-0799, T212-986-2200/ 1-800-GO-2-BRITAIN. 10880 Wilshire Blvd, Suite 570, Los Angeles, CA 90024, T310-4702782.*

through **Argyll**, with its many **prehistoric sites**, and take a ferry to the little-visited islands of **Islay**, famous for its **malt whiskies**, and **Jura**. Both are great places for **walking** holidays. Also within reach of Argyll, or Ayrshire, is the island of **Arran**, described as 'Scotland in miniature' and ideal for walking or **cycling**.

Three to four week trip If you have three or four weeks at your disposal then you can make the stunningly beautiful trip north from Kyle of Lochalsh, along the coast to **Ullapool**. Most visitors don't make it north of Ullapool but those who do are rewarded with the most spectacular landscapes of the northwest. You can also sail from Ullapool across to the fascinating **Outer Hebrides**, a long, narrow archipelago stretching from **Lewis** and **Harris** in the north to **Barra** in the south. When planning your trip, note that most of the islands are fiercely religious and transport is non-existent on a Sunday.

If you're fortunate enough to be spending even more time in Scotland, you could include a trip to the **Orkney Islands**, with their many Stone Age ruins, or the culturally-distinct **Shetland Isles**, which are so far north of the mainland that they can only be included on maps as an inset.

Sights **Museums, galleries and monuments** Most of Scotland's tourist attractions, apart from the large museums and art galleries in the main cities, are open only from Easter to October. Full details of opening hours and admission charges are given in the relevant sections of this guide.

Over 100 of the country's most prestigious sights, and 185,000 acres of beautiful countryside, are cared for by the *National Trust for Scotland* (NTS), 26-31 Charlotte Square, Edinburgh EH2 4ET, T0131-2265922, www.nts.org.uk. National Trust properties are indicated in this guide as 'NTS' and entry charges and opening hours are given for each property. If you're going to be visiting several or more sights during your stay, then it's worth taking annual membership. This costs £26, £10 if you're aged under 26 and £42 for a family and gives free access to all NTS and NT properties. The *National Trust Touring Pass* costs £16 per adult and £26 for a family, and gives free

Scottish tourist boards

Scottish Tourist Board Central Information Department 23 Ravelston Terr, Edinburgh EH4 3EU, T0131-3322433, info@stb.gov.uk, www.holiday.scotland.net.
In London 19 Cockspur St, London SW1 5BL, T020-79308661.
Scottish Area Tourist Boards
Aberdeen & Grampian Tourist Board 27 Albyn Pl, Aberdeen AB10 1YL, T01224-632727, tourism@agtb.org, www.agtb.org.
Angus & City of Dundee Tourist Board, 7-21 Castle St, Dundee DD1 3AA, T01382-527527, www.angusanddundee.co.uk.
Argyll, the Isles, Loch Lomond, Stirling & Trossachs Tourist Board 7 Alexandra Pde, Dunoon, Argyll PA23 8AB, T01369-701000, info@scottish.heartlands.org.
Ayrshire & Arran Tourist Board Burns House, Burns Statue Square, Ayr KA7 1UP, T01292-288688, ayr@ayrshire-arran.com.
Dumfries & Galloway Tourist Board 64 Whitesands, Dumfries DG1 2RS, T01387-253862, info@dgtb.demon.co.uk, www.galloway.co.uk.
Edinburgh & Lothians Tourist Board 3 Princes St, Edinburgh EH2 2QP, T0131-473-3800, esic@eltb.org, www.edinburgh.org.

Greater Glasgow & Clyde Valley Tourist Board 11 George Square, Glasgow, G2 1DY, T0141-204-4400, tourismglasgow@ggcvtb.org.uk.
The Highlands of Scotland Tourist Board Peffery House, Strathpeffer IV14 9HA, Overseas T+44-0-1479-810363, UK T0870-5143070, info@host.co.uk, www.host.co.uk.
Kingdom of Fife Tourist Board Tourist Information Centre, 70 Market St, St Andrews KY16 9NU, T01334-470021, www.standrews.co.uk.
Orkney Tourist Board 6 Broad St, Kirkwall, Orkney KW15 1NX, T01856-872856, orkneytb@csi.com, www.orkneyislands.com.
Perthshire Tourist Board Lower City Mills, West Mill St, Perth PH1 5QP, T01738-627958, perthtouristb@perthshire.co.uk, www.perthshire.co.uk.
Scottish Borders Tourist Board Tourist Information Centre, Murray's Green, Jedburgh TD8 6BE, T01835-863435, info@scot-borders.co.uk.
Shetland Islands Tourism Market Cross, Lerwick, Shetland ZE1 0LU, T01595-693434, www.shetland-tourism.co.uk.
Western Isles Tourist Board 26 Cromwell St, Stornoway, Isle of Lewis HS1 2DD, T01851-703088, witb@sol.co.uk, www.witb.co.uk.

Essentials

admission to its properties for seven days. A 14-day pass costs £24 and £42 respectively. YHA and HI members and student-card holders get 50 percent discount on NTS admission charges.

Historic Scotland (HS), Longmore House, Salisbury Place, Edinburgh EH9 1SH, T0131-66808800, www.historic-scotland.gov.uk, manages more than 330 of Scotland's most important castles, monuments and other historic sites. Historic Scotland properties are indicated as 'HS' and admission charges and opening hours are also given in this guide. Historic Scotland offer an *Explorer Ticket* which allows free entry to 70 of their properties including Edinburgh and Stirling castles. It costs £13.50 per adult and £28 for a family for seven days, and £18/£36 for 14 days. It can save a lot of money as entry to Edinburgh castle alone is £6.50 per adult.

Many other historic buildings are owned by local authorities and admission is cheap, or in many cases free. Most municipal **art galleries and museums** are free, as well as most state-owned museums, including those in Edinburgh and Glasgow. Most fee-paying attractions give a discount or concession for senior citizens, the unemployed, full-time students and children under 16 (those under five are admitted free everywhere). Proof of age or status must be shown. Many of Scotland's **stately homes** are still owned and occupied by the landed gentry, and admission charges are usually between £4 and £5.

When to go

The **high season** is from May to September and this is when Scotland receives the vast majority of visitors. Though the weather tends to be better during the summer months, prices for accommodation are higher in the high season and hotels and guesthouses in the most popular places need to be booked in advance. It's also a good idea to make reservations - at this time - on ferries to the islands, especially to Skye and Mull. A major advantage to visiting in the summer months is the long hours of daylight, especially farther north, where the sun doesn't set till around 2200 or later in June and July.

During the **low season**, from October to Easter, many tourist sights are closed and travelling around the Highlands and Islands can be difficult as public transport services are limited. Many of the smaller tourist offices are also closed during the low season. Though some hotels and guesthouses close during the low season, the majority are now open all year round, as are most restaurants. Taking everything into consideration, May and September are probably the best months to visit Scotland, though Glasgow and Edinburgh are worth visiting at any time of the year.

Climate   The Scottish climate is notoriously unpredictable, especially on the west coast, where a bright, sunny morning can turn into a downpour in the time it takes to butter your toast. Predicting the weather is not an exact science and tables of statistics are most likely a waste of time. There's an old saying in Scotland that if you don't like the weather, then wait 20 minutes, and this just about sums up the climate.

The west coast receives far more rain than the rest of the country and the east coast gets more sunshine. The west coast is also milder in the winter due to the relatively warm waters of the Gulf Stream. Winters in the north can be very harsh, especially in the mountains and glens, making hiking conditions treacherous. Winter storms also make it difficult to travel around the islands as ferry services are often cancelled.

Generally speaking, May to September are the warmest months, with an average summer high of around 18-19°C, and though they are often the driest months, you can expect rain at any time of the year, even in high summer. So, you'll need to come prepared, and remember the old hikers' adage that there's no such thing as bad weather, only inadequate clothing. For a seven-day weather forecast service, call *Weather Check*, T0891-3331111 plus 101 for the northwest, 102 for the northeast, and 103 for Glasgow, Edinburgh and southern Scotland.

Essentials

Useful websites

The official Scottish Tourist Board site and the various area tourist board sites listed on page 21 contain information on accommodation, transport and tourist sights as well as outdoor activities such as walking, skiing, fishing etc. Other useful sites include:

www.scotland-info.co.uk Good for local information on hotels, shops and restaurants.
www.aboutscotland.co.uk Useful for accommodation.
www.travelscotland.co.uk Run in conjunction with STB, with magazine-style features and reviews.
www.ski.scotland.net Information on ski conditions at all centres, updated daily. Also **www.skihotline.com** and **www.snowhunt.demon.co.uk.**
www.golfscotland.co.uk Everything you need to know on golf in Scotland.
www.edinburgh-galleries.co.uk Lists all exhibitions taking place in the capital.
www.clyde-valley.com/glasgow Covers all Glasgow sights and regularly updated.
www.hebrides.com Comprehensive site for the islands.
www.geo.ed.ac.uk/home/scotland/ scotland/html Background information on history, politics and geography.
www.ceolas.org Celtic music site with lots of information and sounds.

Organized tours

There are many companies offering general interest or special interest tours of Scotland. Travel agents will have details, or you can check the small advertisements in the travel sections of newspapers or contact the *British Tourist Authority* or *Scottish Tourist Board* for a list of operators (see boxes for contact details).

Two recommended British companies aimed at the more mature traveller are *Saga Holidays*, Saga Building, Middelburg Square, Folkestone, Kent CT20 1AZ, T0800-300500 and *Shearings Holidays*, Miry Lane, Wigan, Lancs WN3 4AG, T01942-824824.

Saga also operates in the USA, 222 Berkeley Street, Boston, MA 02116; and in Australia, Level 1, 10-14 Paul Street, Milsons Point, Sydney 2061. Other **specialist tour operators in the USA** are *Abercrombie & Kent*, T1-800-3237308, www.abercrombiekeny.com, *Especially Britian*, T1-800-8690538, *Prestige Tours*, T1-800-8907375 and *Sterling Tours*, T1-800-7274359, www.sterlingtours.com. *Cross-Culture*, 52 High Point Dr, Amherst MA01002-1224, T800-4911148, www.crosscultureinc.com.

Golfing tours are organized from the USA by *Golf International Inc*, T1-800-8331389 and *Jerry Quinlan's Celtic Golf*, T1-800-5356148, www.jqcelticgolf.com.

Finding out more

The best way of finding out more information for your trip to Scotland is to contact the British Tourist Authority (BTA) in your country or write (or email) direct to the head office of the Scottish Tourist Board (STB). (See boxes above for contact details). The BTA and STB can provide a wealth of free literature and information such as maps, city guides, events calendars and accommodation brochures. Travellers with special needs should also contact their nearest BTA office. If you want more detailed information on a particular area, you should contact the **area tourist boards**.

Essentials

 British embassies abroad

Australia High Commission: Commonwealth Ave, Yarralumla, Canberra, ACT 2600, T02-62706666, www.uk.emb.gov.au.
Canada High Commission: 80 Elgin St, Ottowa, K1P 5K7, T613-2371530, www.bis-canada.org.
France 9 Ave Hoche, 8e, Paris, T01-42663810.
Germany Friedrich-Ebert-Allee 77, 53113, Bonn, T0228-234061.
Ireland 29 Merrion Rd, Ballsbridge, Dublin 4, T01-2053700.

Israel 192 Hayarkon St, Tel Aviv, T3-7251222, www.britemb.org.il/
Netherlands Koningslaan 44, 1075AE Amsterdam, T20-6764343.
New Zealand High Commission: 44 Hill St, Wellington, T04-4726049, www.brithighcomm.org.nz.
South Africa High Commission: 91 Parliament St, Cape Town 8001, T21-4617220.
USA 3100 Massachusetts Ave NW, Washington DC 20008, T202-4621340, www.britain-info.org.

Before you travel

Visas Visa regulations are subject to change, so it is essential to check with your local British Embassy, High Commission or Consulate before leaving home. Citizens of all European countries – except Albania, Bosnia, Bulgaria, Macedonia, Romania, Slovakia, Yugoslavia and all former Soviet republics (other than the Baltic states) – require only a passport to enter Britain and can generally stay for up to three months. Citizens of Australia, Canada, New Zealand, South Africa or the USA can stay for up to six months, providing they have a return ticket and sufficient funds to cover their stay. Citizens of most other countries require a visa from the commission or consular office in the country of application.

The **Foreign Office's website** (www.fco.gov.uk) provides details of British immigration and visa requirements. Also the **Immigration Advisory Service** (IAS) offers free and confidential advice to anyone applying for entry clearance into the UK: County House, 190 Great Dover Street, London SE1 4YB, T020-73576917, www.vois.org.uk.

Longer stays & work permits For **visa extensions** contact the Home Office, Immigration and Nationality Department, Lunar House, Wellesley Road, Croydon, London CR9, T020-86860688, before your existing visa expires.

Citizens of **Australia, Canada, New Zealand, South Africa** or the **USA** wishing to stay longer than six months will need an Entry Clearance Certificate from the British High Commission in their country.

Citizens of **European Union** (EU) countries can live and work in Britain freely without a visa, but **non-EU residents** need a permit to work legally. This can be difficult to obtain without the backing of an established company or employee in the UK. Visitors aged between 17 and 27 may apply for a **Working Holiday-Maker Entry Certificate**, which entitles you to stay in the UK for up to two years and work on a casual basis. These certificates are only available from British embassies and consulates abroad and you must have proof of a valid return or onward ticket, as well as means of support during your stay.

In **North America**, **full-time students** can obtain temporary work or study permits through the Council of International Education Exchange (CIEE), 205 E 42nd Street, New York, NY 10017, T212-8222600, www.ciee.org. Also, **Commonwealth** citizens with a parent or grandparent born in the UK can apply for a **Certificate of Entitlement to the Right of Abode**, allowing them to work in Britain.

Overseas consulates in Scotland

The following consulates are all in
Edinburgh (Phone code: 0131):
Australia 37 George St, T6243333.
Canada 30 Lothian Rd, T2204333.
Denmark 4 Royal Terr, T5564263.
France 11 Randolph Cres, T2257954.
Germany 16 Eglinton Cres, T3372323.
Italy 32 Melville St, T2263631.
Japan 2 Melville Cres, T2254777.
Netherlands 53 George St, T2203226.
Spain 63 North Castle St, T2203226.

Sweden 22 Hanover St, T2206050.
Switzerland 66 Hanover Pl, T2265660.
USA 3 Regent Terr, T5568315.

The following consulates are in Glasgow
(Phone code: 0141):
Germany 158 West Regent St, T2210304.
Italy 24 St Enoch Square, T2263000.
Norway 80 Oswald St, T2041353.
Spain 389 Argyle St, T2216943.
Sweden 16 Robertson St, T2217845.

Essentials

For more details, contact your nearest British embassy, consulate or high commission, or the Foreign and Commonwealth Office in London, T020-72701500.

Customs regulations & tax

Visitors from EU countries do not have to make a declaration to customs on entry into the UK. The limits for **duty-paid goods** from within the EU are 800 cigarettes, or 1kg of tobacco, 10 litres of spirits, 20 litres of fortified wine, 90 litres of wine and 110 litres of beer. There is no longer any duty-free shopping. Visitors from non-EU countries are allowed to import 200 cigarettes, or 250g of tobacco, two litres of wine, and two litres of fortified wine or one litre of spirits.

There are various import restrictions, most of which should not affect the average tourist. There are tight **quarantine restrictions** which apply to animals brought from overseas (except for Ireland).

For more information on British import regulations, contact HM Customs and Excise, Dorset House, Stamford Street, London, SE1 9PJ, T020-79283344, www.hmce.gov.uk.

Many goods in Britain are subject to a **Value Added Tax** (VAT) of 17.5 percent, with the major exception of books and food. Visitors from non-EU countries can save money through the Retail Export Scheme, which allows a refund of VAT on goods to be taken out of the country. Note that not all shops are participants in the scheme and that VAT cannot be reclaimed on hotel bills or other services.

Insurance

It's a good idea to take out some form of travel insurance, wherever you're travelling from. This should cover you for theft or loss of possessions and money, the cost of all medical and dental treatment, cancellation of flights, delays in travel arrangements, accidents, missed departures, lost baggage, lost passport and personal liability and legal expenses.

Insurance companies

There are a variety of policies to choose from, so it's best to shop around to get the best price. Your travel agent can also advise you on the best deals available. *STA Travel* and other reputable student travel organizations often offer good value travel policies. Travellers from North America can try the *International Student Insurance Service* (ISIS), which is available through *STA Travel*, T1-800-7770112, www.sta-travel.com. Some other recommended travel insurance companies in North America include *Travel Guard*, T1-800-8261300, www.noelgroup.com, *Access America*, T1-800-2848300, *Travel Insurance Services* (1-800-9371387), *Travel Assistance International*, T1-800-8212828 and *Council Travel*, 1-888-COUNCIL, www.counciltravel.com. Another company worth calling for a quote is *Columbus Direct*, T020-73750011. **Older travellers** should note that some companies won't cover people over 65 years old, or may charge high premiums. The best policies for older travellers are offered by *Age Concern* (T01883-346964).

Points to note: you should always read the small print carefully. Some policies exclude 'dangerous activities' such as scuba diving, skiing, horse riding or even trekking. Not all policies cover ambulance, helicopter rescue or emergency flights home.

Find out if your policy pays medical expenses direct to the hospital or doctor, or if you have to pay and then claim the money back later. If the latter applies, make sure you keep all records. Whatever your policy, if you are unfortunate enough to have something stolen, make sure you get a copy of the police report, as you will need this to substantiate your claim.

What to take You'll be able to find everything you could possibly need for your trip in Scottish cities, so you can pack light and buy stuff as you go along. Given the climate, however, you should bring warm and waterproof clothing, whatever the time of year. Also bring light clothes in the summer, preferably long-sleeved to protect you from the midges.

If you're planning on doing some hill-walking you should come properly prepared as the weather can change rapidly in the mountains (for more details, see 'Walking and climbing' on page 53). It's worth treating your boots with a waterproofing agent as some of the trails cross boggy ground.

A **sleeping bag** is useful in hostels. A **sleeping sheet** with a pillow cover is needed for staying in *Scottish Youth Hostel Association* (SYHA) hostels to save you the cost of having to hire one. A padlock can also be handy for locking your bag if it has to be stored in a hostel for any length of time.

Other useful items include an alarm clock (for those early ferry departures), an adaptor plug for electrical appliances, an elastic clothes line and, if you're hill-walking or camping, a Swiss Army knife, torch (flashlight) and compass.

Getting there

Air

There are good air links to Scotland, with direct flights from European cities to Edinburgh, Glasgow, Aberdeen, Prestwick, Inverness and Shetland, and from North America to Glasgow. There are no direct flights from North America to Edinburgh; these are usually routed via London or Dublin. There are also daily flights from Dublin and Belfast to Aberdeen, Edinburgh, Glasgow and Prestwick, and regular flights to most Scottish airports from other parts of the UK. There are limited flights to Africa, the Middle East and Asia. There are no direct flights to Scotland from Australia or New Zealand. You will have to get a connection from London.

Generally speaking, the cheapest and quickest way to travel to Scotland from the rest of Europe is by plane. Those wishing to also visit England should note that it is generally cheaper to fly to Scotland from the rest of Britain if you use an Airpass bought in your own country. This is offered by **British Airways** and **British Midland**. Airpasses are valid only with an international scheduled flight ticket.

Buying a ticket There is a mind-boggling number of outlets for buying your plane ticket and finding the best deal can be a confusing business. **Fares** will depend on the season. Ticket prices to Scotland are highest from around early June to mid-September, which is the tourist high season. Fares drop in the months either side of the peak season – mid-September to early November and mid-April to early June. They are cheapest in the low season, from November to April, when very few visitors are willing to brave the Scottish winter. The exception is during Christmas and New Year when seats are at a premium and prices rise sharply. It's also worth noting that flying at the weekend is normally more expensive.

Scottish airports

Glasgow, T0141-8871111. The main departure point in Scotland for flights to North America and the Caribbean. There are also regular flights to many European destinations, and domestic flights to and from London, Manchester, Bristol and Belfast. Terminal facilities include car hire, bank ATMs, currency exchange, left luggage, tourist information, T8484440, and shops, restaurants and bars. There's also an SPT Travel Centre, T8484330, in the UK Arrivals concourse, (open daily 0800-2200 in summer and till 1800 in winter) and a Thomas Cook Hotel & Travel Reservations desk in the International Arrivals concourse, T8877220.

Edinburgh, T0131-3331000. There are flights to Edinburgh from all over Europe, Ireland and the UK. Edinburgh airport has all facilities, including a tourist information desk, Bureau de Change, ATMs, restaurants and bars (first floor) and shops (ground floor and first floor). For car hire, Avis, Budget, Europcar, Hertz and National car hire desks are located in the terminal in the main UK arrivals area.

Scotland's other airports include **Aberdeen**, T01224-722331, **Inverness**, T01463-232471, **Prestwick**, T01292-722331 and **Dundee**, T01382-643242. There are regular daily flights to Aberdeen from other parts of the UK as well as several European destinations. There are daily direct flights to Inverness from London Gatwick and London Luton and to Dundee from London City Airport. There are also flights to Prestwick from London Stansted.

Essentials

It is always worth spending a bit of time researching the various options available and starting early, as some of the cheapest tickets have to be bought months in advance and the most popular flights sell out early.

One of the best ways of finding a good deal is to use the internet. There are a number of sites where you can check out prices and even book tickets. You can search in the travel sections of your web browser or try the sites of the discount travel companies and agents listed in this section.

Cheap flight tickets fall into two categories; official and unofficial. Official tickets are called budget fares, Apex, super-Apex, advance-purchase tickets, or whatever a particular airline chooses to call them. Unofficial tickets are discounted tickets which are released by airlines through selected travel agents. They are not sold directly by airlines. Discounted tickets are usually as low or lower than the official budget-price tickets.

Return tickets are usually a lot cheaper than buying two one-way tickets. **Round-the-World** (RTW) tickets can also be a real bargain and may even work out cheaper than a return fare. RTW prices start at around £900 (US$1,500), depending on the season. Note that it's easy to include London on a Round-the-World itinerary, but a stop in Scotland may be harder to arrange and may involve backtracking. It may be cheaper and easier to buy the London to Scotland leg separately or to travel overland to Scotland from London.

When trying to find the best deal, make sure you check the route, the duration of the journey, stopovers allowed, any travel restrictions such as minimum and maximum periods away, and cancellation penalties. Many of the cheapest flights are sold by small agencies, most of whom are honest and reliable, but there may be some risks involved with buying tickets at rock-bottom prices. You should avoid paying too much money in advance and you could check with the airline directly to make sure you have a reservation. You may be safer choosing a better-known travel agent, such as STA, which has offices worldwide, or Trailfinders in the UK, or Council Travel in the USA. These and other reputable discount companies and agents are listed above.

👉 *Airlines in Britain and Ireland*

Aer Lingus, Ireland T01-8444777; UK T0645-737747, www.aerlingus.ie, flies from Dublin to Glasgow (£79) and Edinburgh (£89). It also flies from Cork, Donegal and Shannon to Edinburgh and Glasgow.

British Airways, T0345-222111, www.british-airways.com, flies from the three main London airports to Edinburgh, Glasgow and Aberdeen for £59; also from Bristol, Belfast City and International, Birmingham, Cardiff and Manchester. They also fly from Gatwick to Inverness, Leeds/Bradford to Aberdeen, and from Jersey to Edinburgh and Glasgow.

British Midland, T0345-554554, www.iflybritishmidland.com, flies from London Heathrow to Edinburgh and Glasgow for £69; from Manchester to Aberdeen for £92, and to Edinburgh and Glasgow for £91; from East Midlands to

Edinburgh, Glasgow and Aberdeen; and from Amsterdam to Edinburgh.

EasyJet, T0870-600-000, www.easyjet.com, flies from London Luton to Aberdeen, Edinburgh, Glasgow and Inverness for £29 one way.

Go, T0845-605-4321, www.go-fly.com, is BA's low-cost airline which flies from London Stansted to Edinburgh for £70.

KLM AirUK, T0990-074074, www.klm.com, flies from London Stansted to Glasgow and Aberdeen for £78 return, and from London City to Edinburgh. Also from Amsterdam to Edinburgh, Glasgow and Aberdeen.

Ryanair, T0541-569569; Ireland T01-609-7800, www.ryanair.com, flies from London Stansted to Glasgow (Prestwick) for £60 and from Dublin for £65.

Scot Airways, T0870-6060707, flies from London City airport to Dundee.

Discount travel agents in Britain and Ireland

Council Travel, 28a Poland St, London, W1V 3DB, T020-7437-7767, www.destinations-group.com.

STA Travel, 86 Old Brompton Rd, London, SW7 3LH, T020-73616161, www.statravel.co.uk. They have other branches in London, as well as in Brighton, Bristol, Cambridge, Leeds, Manchester, Newcastle-upon-Tyne and Oxford and on many University campuses. Specialists in low-cost student/youth flights and tours,

also good for student IDs and insurance. *Trailfinders*, 194 Kensington High St, London W8 6FT, T020-79383939.

Usit Campus, 52 Grosvener Gardens, London SW1 0AG, T020-77303402, www.campustravel.co.uk. Student/youth travel specialists with branches also in Belfast, Brighton, Bristol, Cambridge, Manchester and Oxford. The main Ireland branch is at 19 Aston Quay, Dublin 2, T01-6021777 or 6778117.

Departure tax is built into the price of air tickets. For economy fare flights within the UK and from EU countries it is £10 (£5 from April 2001). For all other flights it is £20. From April 2001 taxes on first or club class flights will be £10 for UK and EU and £40 for other destinations.

Flights from Britain, Ireland & Europe
Details of the current best deals are given above, but note that prices may change by the time you read this

There are direct flights to Scotland's three main airports – Glasgow, Edinburgh and Aberdeen – almost hourly from London Heathrow, Gatwick, Stansted and Luton airports. There are also daily flights from provincial UK airports and from Dublin. To fly on to the smaller airports, you'll need to change planes (see page 39 for more details on domestic flights). The cheapest flights usually leave from Luton or Stansted. They are often subject to rigid restrictions but the savings can make the extra effort worthwhile. Cheaper tickets usually have to be bought at least a week in advance, apply to only a few mid-week flights and must include a Saturday night stayover. They are also non-refundable, or only partly refundable, and non-transferable. A standard flexible and refundable fare from London to Glasgow or Edinburgh will cost at least £200 return.

Airlines flying from North America

Air Canada, T1-888-2472262,
www.aircanada.ca.
American Airlines, T1-800-4337300,
www.americanair.com.
British Airways, T1-800-2479297; in
Canada T1-800-6681059,
www.british-airways.com.
Continental Airlines , T1-800-2310856,
www.flycontinental.com.
Delta Airlines, T1-800-2414141,
www.delta-air.com.
TWA, T1-800-8924141, www.twa.com.
United Airlines, T1-800-5382929,
www.ual.com.
Virgin Atlantic Airways, T1-800-8628621,
www.fly.virgin.com.

Discount travel agents in North America

Air Brokers International, 323 Geary St,
Suite 411, San Francisco, CA94102,
T1-800-8833273, www.airbrokers.com.
Consolidator and specialist on RTW and
Circle Pacific tickets.
Council Travel, 205 E 42nd St, New York,
NY 10017, T1-888-COUNCIL,
www.counciltravel.com. Student/budget
agency with branches in may other US
cities.
Discount Airfares Worldwide On-Line,
www.etn.nl/discount.htm. A hub of
consolidator and discount agent links.
**International Travel Network/Airlines of
the Web**, www.itn.net/airlines. Online air
travel information and reservations.
STA Travel, 5900 Wiltshire Blvd, suite 2110,
Los Angeles, CA 90036, T1-800-7770112,
www.sta-travel.com. Discount
student/youth travel discount company
with branches in New York, San Francisco,
Boston, Miami, Chicago, Seattle and
Washington DC.
Travel CUTS, 187 College St, Toronto, ON
M5T 1P7, T1-800-6672887,
www.travelcuts.com. Specialist in student
discount fares, IDs and other travel
services. Branches in other Canadian cities.
Travelocity, www.travelocity.com. Online
consolidator.

Specialist agencies such as *Usit Campus or STA* (see above) offer Domestic Air Passes on *British Airways* flights to travellers under 26 years old. These give you substantial discounts on 'Hopper' flights to Inverness and the Hebrides.

There are flights from Edinburgh, Glasgow and Aberdeen to major cities in **Continental Europe** and some regional centres. Discount charter flights are often available to young travellers aged under 26 and holders of ISIC cards through the large student travel agencies listed above. The London listings magazine *Time Out* is a good place to look for cheap fares, as well as free magazines such as *TNT* which you can find outside train and tube stations in London.

There are several daily non-stop flights to **Glasgow** from many US and Canadian cities, including Boston, Calgary, Chicago, Denver, Las Vegas, Los Angeles, Miami, Montreal, New York, Philadelphia, San Francisco, Seattle, Toronto, Vancouver and Washington. Transatlantic carriers are listed above. Flights to **Edinburgh** go via London or Dublin. Because of the much larger number of flights to London, it is generally cheaper to fly there first and get an onward flight (see 'Airlines in Britain and Ireland' box for the best deals). **Flights from North America**

For low season Apex fares expect to pay around US$400-600 from New York and other East Coast cities and around US$500-700 from the West Coast. Prices rise to around US$700-900 from New York and up to US$1,000 from the West Coast in the summer months. Low season Apex fares from Toronto and Montreal cost around CAN$600-700, and from Vancouver around CAN$800-900, rising to $750-950 and $950-1150 respectively during the summer.

Essentials

Essentials

 Airlines flying from Australia and New Zealand

Air New Zealand, T09-3573000,
www.airnz.co.nz.
Britannia Airways/Airtours,
T02-92474833.
British Airways, T02-89048800;
New Zealand T09-3568690,
www.british-airways.com.
Gulf Air, Australia, T02-92442199.
Japanese Airlines (JAL), Australia,
T02-92721111;
New Zealand, T09-3799906.
Korean Air, Australia, T02-92626000;

New Zealand, 09-3073687.
Qantas , T131313; New Zealand
T09-3578900, www.qantas.com.au.
Singapore Airlines, Australia, T131011;
New Zealand T09-3793209.
Thai Airways, Australia, T1300-651960;
New Zealand, T09-3773886,
www.thaiair.com.
United Airlines, Australia T131777; New
Zealand, T09-3793800, www.ual.com.
Virgin Atlantic, Australia, T02-92442747,
www.flyvirgin.com/atlantic/.

Discount travel agents in Australia and New Zealand

Flight Centres, 82 Elizabeth St, Sydney,
T13-1600; 205 Queen St, Auckland,
T09-3096171. Also branches in other
towns and cities.
STA Travel, T1300-360960,
www.statravelaus.com.au, 702 Harris St,
Ultimo, Sydney, and 256 Flinders St,
Melbourne. In New Zealand: 10 High St,

Auckland, T09-3666673. Also in major
towns and cities and University campuses.
Travel.com.au, 80 Clarence St, Sydney,
T02-92901500, www.travel.com.au.
UK Flight Shop, 7 Macquarie Place,
Sydney, T02-92474833,
www.ukflightshop.com.au. Also branches
in Melbourne and Perth.

Flights from Australia & New Zealand There are no direct flights to Scotland from Australia or New Zealand. You will have to get an onward flight from London. The cheapest scheduled flights to London are **via Asia** with *Gulf Air* or *Thai Airways*. They charge A$1300-1500 in low season and up to A$1800 in high season, and involve a transfer en route. Flights via **Africa** start at around $2000 and are yet more expensive via **North America**. Flights to and from Perth via Africa or Asia are a few hundred dollars cheaper.

The cheapest deal currently on offer is with *Britannia Airways/Airtours*, charter flights from Australia or New Zealand to London Gatwick or Manchester via Singapore and Bahrain. It's a 'no-frills' service which only runs between November and March. Fares start at around $1100 in low season and up to $1750 in high season. For more details contact the *UK Flight Shop* (see above).

The cheapest scheduled flights from **New Zealand** are with *Korean Air, Thai Airways* or *JAL*, all of whom fly via their home cities for around NZ$2000-2300. The most direct route is via North America with United Airlines, via Chicago or Los Angeles. Fares range from around NZ$2800 in low season to NZ$3200 in high season. Britannia Airways' charter flights from Auckland cost from around NZ$1600 in low season to NZ$2100 in high season.

A **Round-the-World** (RTW) ticket may work out just as cheap as a return ticket. Good deals are offered by *Qantas/British Airways*. As with North America, it may be cheaper to buy the London to Scotland leg of the trip separately.

By train

Rail enquiries *National Rail Enquiries*, T0345-484950, www.railtrack.co.uk, for information on rail services and fares. For advance credit/debit card bookings, T0345-550033. *GNER*, T0345-225225; *Virgin*, T0345-222333; *ScotRail*, T08457-550033, www.scotrail.co.uk.

Services

There are fast and frequent rail services from London and other main towns and cities in England to Glasgow, Edinburgh, Aberdeen and Inverness. Two companies operate direct services from London to Scotland: *GNER* trains leave from Kings' Cross and run up the east coast to Edinburgh, Aberdeen and Inverness; and *Virgin* trains leave from Euston and run up the west coast to Glasgow. Journey time from London is about four hours 30 minutes to Edinburgh, five hours to Glasgow, seven hours to Aberdeen and eight hours to Inverness. *Scotrail* operate the **Caledonian Sleeper** service if you wish to travel overnight from London Euston to Aberdeen, Edinburgh, Glasgow, Inverness and Fort William. This runs nightly from Sunday to Friday.

Eurostar, T01233-617575, www.eurostar.com, operates high-speed trains through the channel tunnel to London Waterloo from Paris (three hours), Brussels (two hours 40 minutes) and Lille (two hours). You then have to change trains, and stations, for the onward journey north to Scotland. If you're driving from continental Europe you could take **Le Shuttle**, which runs 24 hours a day, 365 days a year, and takes you and your car from Calais to Folkestone in 35-45 minutes. Fares range from £84 to £165 per carload, depending on how much in advance you book or when you travel.

Fares

The system of rail ticket pricing is very complicated. There are a series of discounted fares, but restrictions are often prohibitive, which often explains the long queues and delays at ticket counters in railway stations. The cheapest ticket is a **Super Apex**, which must be booked at least two weeks in advance. Next cheapest is an **Apex** ticket which has to be booked at least seven days before travelling. Other discount tickets include a **Saver** return, which can be used on all trains, and a **Super Saver**, which costs slightly less but cannot be used on a Friday or during peak times.

For example, a **GNER London-Edinburgh Saver** return costs £79, a **Super Saver** £69, an **Apex** £49 and a **Super Apex** £36. All discount tickets should be booked as quickly as possible as they are often sold out weeks, or even months, in advance, especially Apex and Super Apex tickets. The latter tickets guarantee seat reservations, but Saver and Super Saver tickets do not. These can be secured by paying an extra £1. A **Caledonian Sleeper Apex** return ticket to Edinburgh or Glasgow costs £79.

For details of various **discount rail passes** and rail services within Scotland, see 'Getting around' (page 39).

Bus

Road links to Scotland are excellent and a number of companies offer express coach services day and night. This is the cheapest form of travel to Scotland. The two main operators between England and Scotland are ***National Express***, T0990-808080, www.nationalexpress.co.uk, and its sister company ***Scottish Citylink***, T0990-505050, www.city.link.co.uk.

There are direct buses from most British cities to **Edinburgh, Glasgow, Aberdeen** and **Inverness**. Tickets can be bought at bus stations or from a huge number of agents throughout the country. Fares from London to Glasgow and Edinburgh with *National Express* are between £25 and £30 for an economy advance return. Fares to Aberdeen and Inverness are a little higher. The London to Glasgow/Edinburgh journey takes around eight hours, while it takes around 11-12 hours for the trip to Aberdeen and Inverness.

Slow Coach, T020-73773-7737, www.straytravel.com, run budget backpacker tours of the whole of the UK, leaving from London and stopping in Scotland at Edinburgh, Glasgow and Stirling. This can be a cheap way of getting to Scotland. ***Haggis Backpackers*** run a similar service (see 'Getting around', page 40).

Bus travel passes

Full-time students or those aged under 25 or over 50, can buy a **Coach Card** for £8 which is valid for one year and gets you a 30 percent discount on all fares. A **Family card** costs £15 and allows two children to travel free with two adults, but children

Essentials

Ferries from Northern Ireland

Larne to Cairnryan/Stranraer: *P&O European Ferries*, T0990-980777, *has several crossings daily to* **Cairnryan**. *The journey takes two hours and costs around £25 for foot passengers and £190 for two adults with a car.* **Stena Line**, *T01232-747747, operates ferries to* **Stranraer**.
Belfast to Stranraer: *Stena Line run numerous ferries (three hours) and high-speed catamarans (one hour 30 minutes). The one-way journey costs £25 for foot passengers and £170 for two adults with a car. There are also* **SeaCat**, *T0990-523523, catamarans on this route.*
Ballycastle to Campbeltown: *The* **Argyll and Antrim Steam Packet Company**, *T0990-523523, runs twice daily from mid-June to September. The crossing takes about three hours and costs £25 for foot passengers and £163 for two adults with a car.*

normally travel for half price. See 'Getting around' (page 40) for details of bus passes for travel within Scotland. The **Tourist Trail Pass** offers unlimited travel on all *Scottish Citylink* and *National Express* services throughout Britain. Passes cost from £49 for two days' travel out of three up to £187 for 14 days' travel out of 30. They can be bought from major travel agents, at Gatwick and Heathrow airports, as well as from bus stations in Scottish towns and cities. In **North America** these passes are available from *British Travel International*, T1-800-3276097, www.britishtravel.com, or from *US National Express*, T502-2981395.

Car

There are two main routes to Scotland from the south. In the east the A1 runs to Edinburgh and in the west the M6 and A74(M) runs to Glasgow. The journey north from London to either city takes around eight to 10 hours. The A74(M) route to Glasgow is dual carriageway all the way. A slower and more scenic route is to head off the A1 and take the A68 through the Borders to Edinburgh. See 'Getting around' for more details of driving conditions in Scotland and for information on hiring vehicles.

There's an *Autoshuttle Express* service to transport your car overnight between England and Scotland and vice versa while you travel by rail or air. London Luton to Edinburgh or Glasgow costs £350 return or £200 single. For further information T0990-133714; reservations T0990-502309.

Ferry

To Northern England There are regular ferry services from European ports to Newcastle or Hull in Northern England, which are within easy reach of the Scottish border. The main operators are: *P&O North Sea Ferries*, T01482-377177; Zeebrugge and Rotterdam to Hull; *Color Line*, T0191-7961313; Bergen and Stavangar to Newcastle; *Scandinavian Seaways*, T0191-2936262; Hamburg, Gothenburg and Ijmuiden (Amsterdam) to Newcastle.

To Scotland The only direct route to Scotland from Europe is on the *Smyril Line* (Aberdeen T01224-572615; Faroe Islands T01-5900) service to **Lerwick** (Shetland) from Norway (Bergen), Iceland (Seydisfjordur) and the Faroe Islands (Torshavn). It sails from mid-May to early September only once a week and takes 12 hours. A sleeping berth one way from Norway and Faroe Islands costs £63 in high season. You then have to get from Lerwick to Aberdeen. *P&O Scottish Ferries* (T10224-572615) sail Monday-Friday from Lerwick to Aberdeen (14 hours; £55 per passenger in high season).

Money

The British currency is the pound sterling (£), divided into 100 pence (p). Coins come in denominations of 1p, 2p, 5p, 10p, 20p, 50p, £1 and £2. (And a £5 coin is proposed for late 2000.) *Bank of England* banknotes are legal tender in Scotland, in addition to those issued by the *Bank of Scotland*, *Royal Bank of Scotland* and *Clydesdale Bank*. These Scottish banknotes (bills) come in denominations of £1, £5, £10, £20, £50 and £100 and are legal tender in the rest of Britain, though some shopkeepers south of the border may be reluctant to accept them.

Travellers' cheques

The safest way to carry money is in travellers' cheques. These are available for a small commission from all major banks. *American Express (Amex)*, *Visa* and *Thomas Cook* cheques are widely accepted and are the most commonly issued by banks. You'll normally have to pay commission again when you cash each cheque. This will usually be one percent, or a flat rate. No commission is payable on *Amex* cheques cashed at *Amex* offices. Make sure to keep a record of the cheque numbers and the cheques you've cashed separate from the cheques themselves, so that you can get a full refund of all uncashed cheques should you lose them. It's best to bring sterling cheques to avoid changing currencies twice. Also note that in Britain travellers' cheques are rarely accepted outside banks, so you'll need to cash them in advance and keep a good supply of ready cash.

Credit cards & ATMs

Most hotels, shops and restaurants in Scotland accept the major credit cards (*Access/MasterCard*, *Visa* and *Amex*), though some places may charge for using them. They may be less useful in more remote rural areas and smaller establishments such as B&Bs which will often only accept cash. You can withdraw cash from selected banks and ATMs (or cashpoints as they are called in Britain) with your cash card. Your bank or credit card company will give you a list of locations where you can use your card.

Visa card holders can use the *Bank of Scotland*, Clydesdale Bank, *Royal Bank of Scotland* and *TSB* ATMs; *Access/MasterCard* holders can use the *Royal Bank* and *Clydesdale*; *Amex* card holders can use the *Bank of Scotland*.

If you have an account with a High Street bank in England or Wales, you can use your cashpoint card in Scotland. Bank of Scotland and *Royal Bank* take *Lloyds* and *Barclays* cash cards; *Clydesdale* takes *HSBC/Midland* and *National Westminster* cards. *Bank of Scotland*, *Clydesdale* and most building society cashpoints are part of the Link network and accept all affiliated cards.

Banks

Most towns and villages in Scotland have a branch of at least one of the big four High Street banks – *Bank of Scotland*, *Royal Bank of Scotland*, *Clydesdale* and *TSB Scotland*. In small and remote places, and on some islands, there may only be a mobile bank which runs to a set timetable. This timetable will be available from the local post office.

Bank opening hours are Monday-Friday from 0930 to between 1600 and 1700. Some larger branches may also be open later on Thursdays and on Saturday mornings. Banks are usually the best places to change money and cheques. Outside banking hours you'll have to use a **bureau de change**, which can be found in most city centres and also at the main airports and train stations. **NB** Some *bureaux* charge high commissions for changing cheques. Those at international airports, however, often charge less than banks and will change pound sterling cheques for free. Avoid changing money or cheques in hotels, as the rates are usually very poor.

Money transfers

If you need money urgently, the quickest way to have it sent to you is to have it **wired** to the nearest bank via *Western Union* (T0800-833833) or *Moneygram* (T0800-894887). Charges are on a sliding scale; ie it will cost proportionately less to wire out more money.

Money can also be wired by *Thomas Cook* or *American Express*, though this may take a day or two, or transferred via a bank draft, but this can take up to a week.

Costs Scotland can be an expensive place to visit, though there is plenty of budget accommodation available and backpackers will be able to keep their costs down. Edinburgh is the most expensive city and prices are also higher in more remote parts of the Highlands and Islands. Petrol in particular is very expensive in the Highlands and Islands, where it can cost up to 10p per litre more than in the central Lowlands. Accommodation and restaurant prices also tend to be higher in more popular destinations and during the busy summer months.

The minimum daily budget required, if you're staying in hostels or cheap B&Bs, cycling or hitching, and cooking your own meals, will be around £20 per person per day. If you start using public transport and eating out occasionally that will rise to around £30. Those staying in slightly more upmarket B&Bs or guesthouses, eating out every evening at pubs or modest restaurants, and visiting tourist attractions, such as castles or museums, can expect to pay around £40-45 per day. If you also want to hire a car and use ferries to visit the islands, and eat well, then costs will rise considerably and you'll be looking at least £70-75 per person per day. Single travellers will have to pay more than half the cost of a double room in most places and should budget on spending around 60 percent of what a couple would spend. If you're visiting Edinburgh and want to enjoy the city to the full then you'll need at least £50-60 per day, without being extravagant.

Youth & student discounts There are various official youth/student ID cards available. The most useful is the **International Student ID Card** (ISIC), which soon pays for itself through a series of discounts, including most forms of local transport, cheap or free admission to museums, theatres and other attractions, and cheap meals in some restaurants. US and Canadian citizens are also entitled to emergency medical coverage, and there's a 24-hour hotline to call in the event of medical, legal or financial emergencies.

If you're aged under 26 but not a student, you can apply for a **Federation of International Youth Travel Organisations** (FIYTO) card, or a **Euro 26 Card**, which give you much the same discounts. If you're 25 or younger you can qualify for a **Go-25 Card**, which gives you the same benefits as an ISIC card. These discount cards are issued by student travel agencies (see pages 29 and 30 for addresses) and hostelling organizations (see page 37).

Tipping Tipping in Scotland is at the customer's discretion. In a restaurant you should leave a tip of 10-15 percent if you are satisfied with the service. If the bill already includes a service charge, you needn't add a further tip. Tipping is not normal in pubs or bars. Taxi drivers will expect a tip for longer journeys; usually of around 10 percent. As in most other countries, porters, bellboys and waiters in more upmarket hotels rely on tips to supplement their meagre wages.

Touching down

Tourist information Tourist offices, or Tourist Information Centres, can be found in most Scottish towns. Their addresses, phone numbers and opening hours are listed in the relevant sections of this book. Opening hours vary depending on the time of year, and many of the smaller offices are closed during the winter months. All tourist offices provide information on accommodation, public transport, local attractions and restaurants, as well as selling books, local guides, maps and souvenirs. Many also have free street plans and leaflets describing local walks. They can also book accommodation for you (see page 36), for a small fee. Addresses of the main office of the *Scottish Tourist Board* and the *Area Tourist Boards* are given on page 21.

Touching down

Electricity The current in Britain is 240V AC. Plugs have three square pins and adapters are widely available.

Emergencies For **police**, **fire brigade**, **ambulance** and, in certain areas, **mountain rescue** or **coastguard**, dial 999.

Laundry Most towns have coin-operated launderettes. The average cost for a wash and tumble dry is about £3. A service wash where someone will do your washing for you, costs around £4-5. In more remote areas, you'll have to rely on hostel and campsite facilities.

Time Greenwich Mean Time (GMT) is used from late October to late March, after which time the clocks go forward an hour to British Summer Time (BST). GMT is five hours ahead of US Eastern Standard Time and 10 hours behind Australian Eastern Standard Time.

Toilets Public toilets are found at all train and bus stations and motorway service stations. They may charge 20p but are generally clean with disabled and baby-changing facilities. Those in town centres are often pretty grim.

Weights and measures Imperial and metric systems are both currently in use. Distances on roads are measured in miles and yards, drinks are poured in pints and gills, but generally nowadays, the metric system is used elsewhere.

Essentials

Disabled travellers

For travellers with disabilities visiting Scotland independently can be a difficult business. While most theatres, cinemas and modern tourist attractions are accessible to wheelchairs, **accommodation** is more problematic. Many large, new hotels do have disabled suites, but will charge more, and most B&Bs, guesthouses and smaller hotels are not designed to cater for people with disabilities. **Public transport** is just as bad, though newer buses have lower steps for easier access and some *ScotRail* intercity services now accommodate wheelchair-users in comfort. Taxis, as opposed to minicabs, all carry wheelchair ramps, and if a driver says he or she can't take a wheelchair, it's because they're too lazy to fetch the ramp.

Wheelchair users, and blind or partially-sighted people are automatically given 30-50 percent discount on train fares and those with other disabilities are eligible for the **Disabled Person's Railcard**, which costs £14 per year and gives a third off most tickets. There are no reductions on buses, however.

Information and organizations If you are disabled you should contact the travel officer of your national support organization. They can provide literature or put you in touch with travel agents specializing in tours for the disabled. The Scottish Tourist Board produces a guide, *Accessible Scotland*, for disabled travellers and many local tourist offices can provide accessibility details for their area. For more information, contact *Disability Scotland*, Princes House, 5 Shandwick Place, Edinburgh EH2 4RG, T0131-2298632. The *Royal Association for Disability and Rehabilitation (RADAR)*, Unit 12, City forum, 250 City Road, London, EC1V 8AF, T020-72503222, www.radar.org.uk, is a good source of advice and information and produces an annual guide on travelling in the UK (£7.50 including P&P). The *Holiday Care Service*, 2nd floor, Imperial Building, Victoria Road, Horley, Surrey RH6 7PZ, T-1293-774535, provides free lists of accessible accommodation and travel in the UK.

Gay & lesbian travellers

Scotland is generally tolerant of homosexuality, though overt displays of affection outside 'gay' venues are not advised. Edinburgh in particular has a flourishing gay scene and is a relatively easy place for gay travellers to feel safe and comfortable. *Gay Scotland* magazine, T0131-5572625, is a good source of information and *The List*, the Edinburgh and Glasgow listings magazine, is also useful. For more information contact the *Gay Switchboard*, T0131-5564049 or the *Lesbian Line*, T0131-5570751. Details of gay pubs and clubs are given for Glasgow (on page 179) and Edinburgh (on page 119).

Essentials

Accommodation price codes

Accommodation prices in this book are graded with the letters below and are based on the cost per person for two people sharing a double room with en suite bathroom during the high season. Cheaper rooms with shared bathrooms are available in many hotels, guesthouses and B&Bs. Many places, particularly larger hotels, offer substantial discounts during the low season and at weekends. All places listed are recommended as providing good quality and value within their respective price category. Note that price codes for youth hostels are not given in the accommodation listings, as they all cost under £15 per person per night.

L £80 plus   **A** £66-80
B £46-65   **C** £36-45
D £26-35   **E** £16-25
F £15 and under

Where to stay

Hotels and other places to sleep are identified by a ■ symbol on maps.

Accommodation in Scotland will be your greatest expense. It ranges from hostels and cheaper Bed and Breakfasts (B&Bs) to upmarket hotels, many of which are converted castles and country mansions.

Tourist offices will help find accommodation for you. They can recommend a place within your particular budget and give you the number to phone up and book yourself, or will book a room for you. Some offices charge a small fee (usually £1) for booking a room, while others ask you to pay a deposit of 10 percent which is deducted from your first night's bill. Most tourist offices also offer a **Book-a-Bed-Ahead** service, which reserves accommodation for you at your next destination. This costs £3 per booking and is particularly useful in July and August, or if you'll be arriving in a town late.

Note that single rooms are in short supply and many places are reluctant to let a double room to one person, even when they're not busy. Single rooms are usually more than the cost per person for a double room and in some cases cost the same as two people sharing a double room.

Hotels, guesthouses and B&Bs

Regional tourist boards publish accommodation lists which include campsites, hostels, self-catering accommodation and STB approved hotels, guesthouses and B&Bs. Places participating in the STB system will have a plaque displayed outside which shows their grading, determined by a number of stars ranging from one to five. These reflect the level of facilities, as well as the quality of hospitality and service. However, do not assume that a B&B, guesthouse or hotel is no good because it is not listed by the tourist board. They simply don't want to pay to be included in the system and some of them may offer better value.

Hotels   At the top end of the scale, there are some fabulously luxurious hotels, often in spectacular locations. Many of them are converted baronial mansions or castles and offer a chance to enjoy a taste of aristocratic grandeur and style. At the lower end of the scale, there is often little to choose between cheaper hotels and guesthouses or B&Bs. The latter often offer higher standards of comfort and a more personal service, but many smaller hotels are really just guesthouses, and are often family-run and every bit as friendly. Note that some hotels, especially in town centres or in fishing ports, may also be rather noisy, as the bar can often be the social hub. Rooms in most mid-range to expensive hotels almost always have bathrooms en suite. Many upmarket hotels offer excellent room-only deals in the low season.

Youth Hostel Associations

Australia Australian Youth Hostels Association, 422 Kent St, Sydney, T02-92611111.
Canada Hostelling International Canada, Room 400, 205 Catherine St, Ottowa, ON K2P 1C3, T800-6635777.
England & Wales Youth Hostel Association (YHA), Trevelyan House, 8 St Stephen's Hill, St Albans, Herts AL1 2DY, T01727-855215, www.yha/england/wales/org.uk.
France FUAJ, 7 Rue Pajol, 75018 Paris, T1-4498727.
Germany Deutsches Jugendherbergswerk, Hauptverband, Postfach 1455, 32704 Detmold, T5231-74010.

Ireland An Oige, 61 Muntjoy St, Dublin 7, T01-8304555, www.irelandyha.org.
New Zealand Youth Hostels Association of New Zealand, PO Box 436, Christchurch 1, T03-379970.
Northern Ireland Youth Hostel Association of Northern Ireland, 22 Donegal Rd, Belfast, BT12 5JN, T01232-324733.
Scotland Scottish Youth Hostel Association (SYHA), 7 Glebe Cres, Stirling FK8 2JA, T01786-451181, www.syha.org.uk.
USA Hostelling International-American Youth Hostels (HI-AYH), 733 15th St NW, Suite 840, PO Box 37613, Washington DC 20005, T202-7836161, www.hostel.com.

Guesthouses

Guesthouses are often large, converted family homes with up to five or six rooms. They tend to be slightly more expensive than B&Bs and though they are often less personal, usually provide better facilities, such as en suite bathroom, colour TV in each room and private parking. In many instances, they are more like small budget hotels. Many guesthouses offer evening meals, though this may have to be requested in advance.

Bed & breakfasts

B&Bs provide the cheapest private accommodation. At the bottom end of the scale, you can get a bedroom in a private house, a shared bathroom and a huge cooked breakfast for around £14-18 per person per night. Small B&Bs may only have one or two rooms to let, so it's important to **book in advance** during the summer season and on the islands where accommodation options are more limited. More upmarket B&Bs have en suite bathrooms and TVs in each room and usually charge from £20-24 per person per night. In general, B&Bs are more hospitable, informal, friendlier and offer better value than hotels. Many B&B owners, particularly in the Highlands and Islands, are a great source of local knowledge and can even provide OS maps for local walks. B&Bs in the Outer Hebrides also offer dinner, bed and breakfast, which is useful as eating options are limited, especially on a Sunday.

Some places, especially in ferry ports, charge room-only rates, which are slightly cheaper and allow you to get up in time to catch an early morning ferry. However, this means that you miss out on a huge **cooked breakfast**. If you're travelling on a tight budget, you can eat as much as you can at breakfast time and save on lunch as you won't need to eat again until evening. This is particularly useful if you're heading into the hills, as you won't have to carry so much food. Many B&B owners will even make up a packed lunch for you at a small extra cost.

Hostels

For those travelling on a tight budget, there is a large network of hostels offering cheap accommodation. These are also popular centres for backpackers and provide a great opportunity for meeting fellow travellers. Hostels have kitchen facilities for self-catering and some include a continental breakfast in the price or provide cheap breakfasts and evening meals. **Advance booking** is recommended at all times, and particularly from May to September and on public holidays.

Scottish Youth Hostel Association (SYHA)

The SYHA is separate from the YHA in England and Wales. It has a network of over 80 hostels which are often better and cheaper than those in other countries. They offer bunk-bed accommodation in single-sex dormitories or smaller rooms, kitchen and laundry facilities. Prices range from £4 for juniors (under 18) and £5 for seniors (over 18) for the cheapest up to £11.25 for juniors and £12.75 for seniors for the most expensive. Those in large towns and cities and main tourist centres are more expensive. The average cost is £7-9 per person per night. Though some rural hostels are still strict on discipline and impose a 2300 curfew, those in larger towns and cities tend to be more relaxed and doors are closed as late as 0200. Some larger hostels provide breakfasts for around £2.50 and three-course evening meals for around £4.

The SYHA produces a handbook (free with membership) giving details of all their youth hostels, including transport links. This can be useful as some hostels are difficult to get to without your own transport. You should always phone ahead, as many hostels are closed during the day. Phone numbers are listed in this guide. Many hostels are closed during the winter. Details are given in the *SYHA Handbook*.

For Scottish residents, adult membership costs £6, and can be obtained at the SYHA National Office (see box for address), or at the first SYHA hostel you stay at. SYHA membership gives automatic membership of **Hostelling International** (HI). Youth hostel members are entitled to half-price entry to all National Trust for Scotland properties. The SYHA also offers an **Explore Scotland** and **Scottish Wayfarer** ticket, which can save a lot of money on transport and accommodation, especially if you're not a student (see 'Getting around').

Independent backpackers hostels

The *Independent Backpackers Hostels of Scotland* is an association of over 90 independent hostels/bunkhouses throughout Scotland. They charge between £6 and £15 per person per night, though the average is around £7.50-9.50. They tend to be more laid-back, with fewer rules and no curfew. They all have dormitories, hot showers and self-catering kitchens. Some include continental breakfast, or provide cheap breakfasts. All these hostels are listed in the *Independent Hostel Guide*, which is available from tourist offices or send an A5 SAE to: Pete Thomas, Croft Bunkhouse & Bothies, Portnalong, Isle of Skye, IV47 8SL. They also have a **website**: www.hostel-scotland.co.uk.

Camping, self-catering and campus accommodation

Camping

There are hundreds of campsites around Scotland. They are mostly geared to caravans and vary greatly in quality and level of facilities. The most expensive sites, which charge up to £10 to pitch a tent, are usually well-equipped. Sites are usually only open from April to October. If you plan to do a lot of camping, you should buy *Scotland: Camping & Caravan Parks* (£3.95), available from most tourist offices. It lists around 150 camping and caravan parks graded by the STB.

North Americans planning on camping should invest in an **international camping carnet**, which is available from home motoring organizations, or from *Family Campers and RVers* (FCRV), 4804 Transit Road, Building 2, Depew, NY 14043 (T1-800-2459755). It gives you discounts at member sites.

Self-catering

There is plenty of STB-approved self-catering accommodation available, ranging from remote farmhouse cottages to city centre apartments. The minimum stay is usually one week in the summer peak season, or three days or less at other times of the year. Expect to pay at least £150 per week for a two-bedroom cottage in the winter, rising to £250 in the high season. Places in the city range from around £200 to over £700 per week. A good source of self-catering accommodation is the STB's guide (£5.95), which lists over 1,200 properties and is available from any tourist office.

The *National Trust for Scotland* owns many historic properties which are available for self-catering holidays. Prices start at around £250 per week in high season. Contact them at 5 Charlotte Square, Edinburgh EH2 4DU, T0131-2265922. For something a bit different, *Highland Hideways* has a range of more individual self-catering properties, mainly in the Highlands and Islands. For a free brochure write to them at 5-7 Stafford Street, Oban, Argyll PA34 5NJ, T01631-526056.

Many Scottish universities open their halls of residence to visitors during the summer vacation (late June to September), and some also during the Easter and Christmas breaks. Many rooms are basic and small bedrooms with shared bathrooms, but there are also more comfortable rooms with private bathrooms, twin and family units and self-contained apartments and shared houses. Full board, half board, B&B and self-catering options are all available. Prices for bed and breakfast tend to be roughly the same as most B&Bs, but self-catering can cost as little as £50 per person per week. Local tourist offices have information, or contact the *British Universities Accommodation Consortium*, T0115-9504571 for a brochure. Details are given in this guide under the relevant travel section.

Campus accommodation

Essentials

Getting around

Public transport is generally good and efficient. Most places in the Central Lowlands, between Glasgow, Edinburgh and Dundee, are easily reached by bus and train. Services in the north and south of Scotland are less efficient and it can be a slow and difficult process getting to more remote parts of the Highlands and Islands and Argyll. Public transport can also be expensive, but there's a whole raft of discount passes and tickets which can save you a lot of money. To get off the beaten track, you may have to consider hiring a car, but with a combination of buses, trains, ferries, walking, hiring a bike, plenty of time and careful planning, you can get almost anywhere.

Air

As well as the main airports of Glasgow, Edinburgh and Aberdeen, Scotland has many small airports, many of them on islands (one of them, on Barra, uses the beach as an airstrip). Internal flights are expensive, however, and not really necessary in such a small country, unless you are short of time and want to visit the Outer Hebrides or Orkney and Shetland. For example a return flight from Edinburgh or Glasgow to Shetland costs over £250. There are discounted tickets available, such as Apex fares, which must be booked at least 14 days in advance, and special offers on some services. *BA's* **Highland Rover** costs £189 and allows you to take any five flights within seven days (except inter-island flights within Orkney or Shetland).

The majority of flights are operated by *British Airways/Loganair*, T0345-222111, www.british-airways.com. For inter-island flights in Shetland, you should book direct through *Loganair*, T01595-840246. Other carriers are *Gill Air*, T0191-214666, and *British Midland*, T0345-554554, www.iflybritishmidland.com.

For information on flight schedules, call the airports listed on page 27, or *British Airways*. The *British Airports Authority* (BAA) publishes a free *Scheduled Flight Guide*.

NB From April 2000 there will be no departure tax on flights form Highlands and Islands airports.

Train

The rail network in Scotland is limited and train travel is comparatively expensive, but trains are a fast and effective way to get around and also provide some beautifully scenic journeys. The West Highland line to Fort William and Mallaig and the journey from Inverness to Kyle of Lochalsh are amongst the most beautiful rail journeys in the world

☞ *Railcards*

There are variety of railcards which give discounts on fares for certain groups. Cards are valid for one year and most are available from main stations. You need two passport photos and proof of age or status.

Young Person's Railcard: for those aged 16-25 or full-time students in the UK. Costs £18 and gives 33 percent discount on most train tickets and some ferry services.

Senior Citizen's Railcard: for those aged over 60. Same price and discount as above.

Disabled Person's Railcard: costs £16 and gives 33 percent discount to a disabled person and one other. Pick up application form from stations and send it to: Disabled Person's Railcard Office, PO Box 1YT, Newcastle-upon-Tyne, NE99 1YT. It may take up to 21 days to process, so apply in advance.

Family Railcard: costs £20 and gives 33 percent discount on most tickets (20 percent on others) for up to four adults travelling together. Up to four accompanying children pay a flat fare of £2 each.

and well worth doing. Services in the central belt, between Glasgow, Edinburgh, Stirling, Perth, Dundee and Aberdeen are fast and frequent, and there are frequent trains to and from Inverness.

ScotRail operates most train services. For information on fares and timetables, contact **National Rail Enquiries**, T0345-484950, open 24 hours. You can buy train tickets at the stations, from major travel agents, or over the phone with a credit/debit card. For advance credit/debit card bookings call T0345-550033, or www.scotrail.co.uk. For busy long-distance routes it's best to reserve a seat. Seat reservations to Edinburgh, Glasgow, Aberdeen or Inverness are included in the price of the ticket when you book in advance. If the ticket office is closed, there's usually a machine on the platform. If this isn't working, you can buy your ticket on the train. Details of the different rail passes and railcards available are given below. Details of the different types of tickets are on page 30.

Cyclists should note that reservations for bikes (£3.50) are required on many services and that taking a bike on a train seems to be regarded as a major hassle by many people.

Rail passes Eurorail passes are not recognized in Britain but *ScotRail* offers a couple of worthwhile travel passes. The most flexible is the **Freedom of Scotland Travelpass**, which gives unlimited rail travel within Scotland. It is also valid on all *CalMac* ferries on the west coast, many *Citylink* bus services in the Highlands, some regional buses and Glasgow Underground. It also gives 33 percent discount on *P&O Ferries* from Scrabster to Orkney and 20 percent discount on *P&O Ferries* from Aberdeen to Orkney and Shetland. It costs £69 for four days' travel out of eight consecutive days, £99 for any eight out of 15 consecutive days and £119 for any 12 out of 15 consecutive days. The **Highland Rover** is more limited. It allows unlimited rail travel in the Highlands region, plus the West Highland line from Glasgow and travel between Aberdeen and Aviemore. It also allows free travel on *Citylink* buses between Oban, Fort William and Inverness. It costs £49 for any four out of eight consecutive days. The **Festival Cities Rover** covers the central region and costs £29 for any three out of seven days.

Holders of **Senior Citizen's** or **Young Person's Railcard** get a 30 percent discount on these passes.

Bus

Travelling around Scotland by bus takes longer than the train but is much cheaper. There are numerous local bus companies but the main operator is *Scottish Citylink*, T0990-505050, www.citylink.demon.co.uk, part of the *National Express* group. Bus services between towns and cities are good but far less frequent in more remote rural areas. Note that long-distance express buses are called coaches.

There are a number of discount and flexible tickets for bus/coach travel in Scotland. If you're under 26, a full-time student or 50 or over, a **National Express Discount Coach Card** or a **Scottish Citylink Smart Traveller's Discount Card** saves you 30% on adult fares on all *Scottish Citylink* services and costs £8 for one year. The *National Express* **Explorer Pass** offers unlimited travel within a specified period on *Scottish Citylink* buses. It is available to overseas visitors but must be bought outside Britain. It costs £59 for three days travel within a five-day period, £110 for seven days in a 21-day period and £170 for 14 days in a 30-day period. Smart Card and Discount Coach Card holders can get a 30% discount on these prices. If you're also travelling in England and Wales, you may be better off with a **National Express Tourist Trail Pass** (details on page 31).

Passes & discounts

The SYHA sells its own **Explore Scotland** bus pass, which allows free travel on *Citylink* services. It costs £155 for five days and £250 for eight days and includes seven nights hostel accommodation, free SYHA membership and free entry to many *Historic Scotland* properties. They also sell a **Scottish Wayfarer** ticket which is similar but also includes rail travel, *CalMac* ferries and discounts on many *P&O Ferries*. It costs £160 for four days, £270 for eight days and £299 for 12 days.

Many rural areas, particularly in the Highlands and Islands, can only be reached by Royal Mail postbuses. These are minibuses that follow postal delivery routes and carry up to 10 fare-paying passengers. They set off early in the morning from the main post office and follow a circuitous route as they deliver and collect mail in the most far-flung places. It's a very slow method of getting around but you get to see some of the country's most spectacular scenery and it is useful for walkers and those trying to reach remote hostels or B&Bs. A free booklet of routes and timetables is available from *Postbus Services*, Royal Mail, Strothers Lane, Inverness IV1 1AA, T01463-256273, or from the Scottish Tourist Board (see page 21).

Postbus services

A great and cheap way to get around Scotland is on one of the **jump-on-jump-off** backpacker bus tours. These leave from Edinburgh daily, except Sunday, and stop off at independent hostels in Perth, Pitlochry, Inverness, Loch Ness, Isle of Skye, Fort William, Glencoe, Oban and Glasgow. You can hop on and off whenever you please and you don't need to stay at any of the hostels. Prices range from around £55 to £85 for a complete circuit. The main operators are *Haggis Backpackers*, 11 Blackfriars Street, Edinburgh EH1 1NB, T0131-5579393, www.haggis-backpackers.com; *Go Blue Banana*, T0131-5562000, www.gobluebanana.com and *Macbackpackers*, T0131-5589900, www.macbackpackers.com. *Haggis Backpackers* also run trips from London to Edinburgh, calling in at several tourist sights in England en route.

Bus tours

These companies also run excellent-value Highland tours, leaving from Edinburgh. Prices start at £75 for three days, up to around £139 for six days. Prices do not include accommodation or food. Several other companies run similar tours, including *Rabbie's Trail Burners*, 207 High Street, Edinburgh, T0131-2263133, www.rabbies.com. There's also a variety of coach tours available with *Lothian Regional Transport* (LRT) in Edinburgh, T0131-5556363.

Ferry

There are around 60 or so inhabited islands off the coast of Scotland, and nearly 50 of them can be reached by a scheduled ferry service. Most ferries carry vehicles and can be booked in advance. If you're travelling to the islands by car, it's a good idea to book ferries in advance whatever the time of year, particularly to the more popular islands.

Essentials

☞ *Ferry companies*

Caledonian MacBrayne, *The Ferry Terminal, Gourock, PA19 1QP, T01475-650100, Reservations T0990-650000, reservations@calmac.co.uk, www.calmac.co.uk.*
John O'Groats Ferries, *T01955-611353.*

Orkney Ferries, *Shore St, Kirkwall, KW15 1LG, T01856-872044, www.orkneyislands.com.*
P&O Scottish Ferries, *PO Box 5, Jamieson's Quay, Aberdeen AB11 5NP, T01224-572615, www.poscottishferries.co.uk.*
Western Ferries, *T0141-3329766.*

The majority of ferry services on the west coast are operated by *Caledonian MacBrayne*, or *CalMac* as they're more commonly known. They sail from **Oban**, **Mallaig** and **Ullapool** to over 20 islands in the **Inner** and **Outer Hebrides**. They also run services on the **Firth of Clyde**. Fares are expensive, especially with a car, but if you're planning on using ferries a lot, you can save a lot of money with an **Island Hopscotch** ticket, which offers reduced fares on 17 set routes. The ticket is valid for one month and you need to follow your set itinerary, though this can be changed en route without too much fuss. For more details and some sample fares, see under the relevant destination. A more flexible option is the **Island Rover**, which offers unlimited travel on *CalMac* ferries for a set period, though you still need to make reservations. An eight-day pass costs £41 per passenger and £199 for a car, and a 15-day pass costs £59 per passenger and £299 for a car. *CalMac* schedules are complicated, but fares and frequency of sailings are given under each relevant destination in this guide. *Western Ferries* runs services between **Gourock** and **Dunoon** and **Islay** and **Jura**.

P&O Scottish Ferries run car ferries to **Orkney** and **Shetland**. Ferries to Orkney depart from **Aberdeen** once or twice weekly and take eight to 10 hours, or from **Scrabster**, near Thurso, a few times daily and take two hours. Fares from Aberdeen are about £80 return for passengers and £140 for a car; from Scrabster it costs £30 per passenger and £80 for a car. There's also a passenger ferry from **John O'Groats** to Orkney which sails daily during the summer only (May-September) and is run by *John O'Groats Ferries* (see above).

P&O Ferries run an overnight ferry from **Aberdeen** to **Shetland** daily except Saturday during the summer months. The journey takes 14-20 hours. Fares are around £115 per passenger and £175 for a car. You should also book in advance on these routes if you're travelling by car.

The **Orkney** islands are linked by services run by *Orkney Ferries*, T01856-872044, while **Shetland's** inter-island ferries are run by *Shetland Islands Council*, T01806-244234. There are also numerous small operators offering day-trips to various islands. Details of these are given in the relevant chapters.

Car

Travelling with your own private transport allows you to cover a lot of the country in a short space of time and to reach remote places. The main disadvantages are traffic congestion and parking, which can be a problem in Glasgow and Edinburgh. Roads in Scotland are generally a lot less busy than those in England and driving is relatively stress-free, especially on the B-roads and minor roads. In remote parts of the country, in the Highlands and Islands in particular, many roads are **single track**, with passing places indicated by a diamond-shaped signpost. These should also be used to allow traffic behind you to overtake. Remember that you may want to take your time to enjoy the stupendous views all around you, but the driver behind may be a local doctor in a hurry. Don't park in passing places. A major driving hazard on single track roads are the huge

Car hire companies

Britain Arnold Clark, T0800-838245; Avis, T0990-900500; Budget, T0800-181181; EuroDollar, T01895-233300; Europcar, T0345-222525; Hertz, T0990-996699; Holiday Autos, T0990-300400; National Car Rental, T0990-365365; Thrifty, T0990-168238. **North America** Alamo, T800-5229696, www.goalamo.com; Avis, T800-3311084, www.avis.com; Budget, T800-5270700, www.budgetrentacar.com; Dollar, T800-4216868, www.dollar.com; Hertz, T800-6543001, www.hertz.com; Holiday Autos , T800-4227737, www.holiday/colauto.com; National, T800-CAR-RENT, www.nationalcar.com; Thrifty, T800-3672277, www.thrifty.com. **Australia** Avis, T1800-225533; Budget, T1300-362848; Hertz, T1800-550067. **New Zealand** Avis, T09-5262847; Budget, T09-3752222; Hertz, T09-3676350.

numbers of sheep wandering around, blissfully unaware of your presence. When confronted by a flock of sheep, slow down and gently edge your way past. Be particularly careful at night, as many of them sleep by the side of the road (counting cars perhaps). Also note that petrol in the Highlands and Islands is a lot more expensive than in other parts of the UK and that petrol stations and garages are few and far between.

Rules & regulations

To drive in Scotland you must have a current driving licence. Foreign nationals also need an **international driving permit**, available from state and national motoring organizations for a small fee. Those importing their own vehicle should also have their vehicle registration or ownership document. Make sure you're adequately insured. In all of the UK you **drive on the left. Speed limits** are 30 miles per hour (mph) in built-up areas, 70 mph on motorways and dual carriageways and 60 mph on most other roads.

Motoring organizations

It's advisable to join one of the main UK motoring organizations during your visit for their **24-hour breakdown assistance**. The two main ones in Britain are the *Automobile Association* (*AA*), T0800-448866, www.theaa.co.uk, and the *Royal Automobile Club* (*RAC*), T0800-550550, rac.co.uk. One year's membership of the *AA* starts at £46 and £39 for the *RAC*. They also provide many other services, including a reciprocal agreement for free assistance with many overseas motoring organizations. Check to see if your organization is included. Both companies can also extend their cover to include Europe. Their **emergency numbers** are: *AA* T0800-887766; *RAC* T828282. You can call these numbers even if you're not a member, but you'll have to a pay a large fee. In remote areas you may have to wait a long time for assistance. Also note that in the Highlands and Islands you may be stranded for ages waiting for spare parts to arrive.

Car hire

Car hire/rental is expensive in Scotland and you may be better off making arrangements in your home country for a fly/drive deal through one of the main multi-national companies. The minimum you can expect to pay is around £150 per week for a small car. Small, local hire companies often offer better deals than the larger multi-nationals. Most companies prefer payment with a credit card, otherwise you'll have to leave a large deposit (£100 or more). You'll need your driver's licence and to be aged between 21 and 70. **Motorcycle hire** is very expensive, ranging from around £200 up to £350 per week.

Hitching

As in the rest of the UK, hitching is never entirely safe, and is certainly not advised for anyone travelling alone, particularly women travellers. Those prepared to take the risk should not find it too difficult to get a lift, especially in the Highlands and Islands, where people are far more willing to stop for you. Bear in mind, though, that you will probably have to wait a while to actually see a vehicle in remote parts.

Keeping in touch

Postal services Most **post offices** are open Monday-Friday 0900 to 1730 and Saturday 0900 to 1230 or 1300. Smaller sub-post offices are closed for an hour at lunch (1300-1400) and many of them operate out of a shop. Post offices keep the same half-day closing times as shops.

Stamps can be bought at post offices, but also from vending machines outside and also at many newsagents. A first-class letter to anywhere in the UK costs 26p and should arrive the following day, while second-class letters cost 20p and take between two to four days. Airmail letters of less than 20g cost 30p to Europe. To the USA and Australia costs 43p for 10g and 63g for 20g. For more information about *Royal Mail* postal services, call T0345-740740.

Telephone services
Operator: T100
International operator: T155
Directory enquiries: T192
Overseas directory enquiries: T153

Most public **payphones** are operated by *British Telecom* (*BT*) and are fairly widespread in towns and cities, though less so in rural areas. *BT* payphones take either coins (10p, 20p, 50p and £1) or **phonecards**, which are available at newsagents and post offices displaying the *BT* logo. These cards come in denominations of £2, £3, £5 and £10. Some payphones also accept credit cards.

For most countries (including Europe, USA and Canada) calls are cheapest between 1800 and 0800 Monday-Friday and all day Saturday and Sunday. For Australia and New Zealand it's cheapest to call from 1430 to 1930 and from midnight to 0700 every day.

Phone codes for towns and cities are given in the margin by the town's heading throughout this book. You don't need to use the area code if calling from the same area. Any number prefixed by 0800 or 0500 is free to the caller; 0345 numbers are charged at local rates and 0990 numbers at the national rate.

To **call Scotland** from overseas, dial 011 from USA and Canada, 0011 from Australia and 00 from New Zealand, followed by 44, then the area code, minus the first zero, then the number.

To **call overseas from Scotland** dial 00 followed by the country code. Country codes include: **Australia** 61; **Ireland** 353; **New Zealand** 64; **South Africa** 27; **USA** and **Canada** 1.

Internet Many hotels now have email access. Some hostels also offer Internet access to their guests. Websites and email addresses are listed where appropriate in this guide. The Scottish Tourist Board and area tourist boards have their own websites and these are given on page 21. **Cybercafés** are also listed under each relevant section. Most of these can be found in Edinburgh and Glasgow. In the absence of any cybercafés listed under a particular town try the public library for internet access or ask at the tourist office.

Media **Newspapers and magazines** The main British daily and Sunday newspapers are widely available in Scotland and some of them publish special Scottish editions, among them the *Scottish Daily Mail*, *Scottish Daily Express* and Rupert Murdoch's notorious scandal sheet, *The Sun*.

The **Scottish press** produces two main 'quality' newspapers, the liberal-leaning *The Scotsman*, published in Edinburgh, and *The Herald*, published in Glasgow, is the oldest daily newspaper in the English-speaking world, dating from 1783. The biggest-selling daily is the *Daily Record*, a tabloid paper. The Sunday equivalents of the dailies are *Scotland on Sunday* from the *Scotsman* stable, the *Sunday Herald* and the *Sunday Mail*, published by the *Daily Record*. Provincial newspapers are widely read in Scotland. The two biggest-selling titles are the parochial *Press and Journal* from Aberdeen and *The Courier & Advertiser*, published by Dundee's giant DC Thomson group, who also produce *The Beano* and *Dandy* kids' comics. DC Thomson publish Scotland's most successful Sunday newspaper, the *Sunday Post*, which is fascinating to read but seems incongruous in the 21st century as it has changed little in the last 50 years. In the highlands, the main papers are the weekly *Oban Times* and the radical, crusading *West Highland Free Press* published on Skye. Visitors to Glasgow and Edinburgh should buy a copy of the fortnightly listings magazine, *The List*, with lively features and previews and reviews of all events in both cities.

Foreign newspapers and magazines, including *USA Today* and *International Herald Tribune*, are available in larger newsagents, especially in central Edinburgh and Glasgow. *Time* and *Newsweek* are also available in larger newsagents and bookstores.

TV and radio There are five main **television channels** in Scotland; the publicly-funded BBC 1 and 2, and the independent commercial stations, Channel 4, Channel 5 and ITV. The ITV network in Scotland is formed by STV, which serves central Scotland and parts of the West Highlands, the Aberdeen-based Grampian TV which produces a lot of Gaelic programmes, and Border TV which covers Dumfries and Galloway and northwest England.

The BBC network also broadcasts several **radio channels**, most of which are based in London. These include: *Radio 1 aimed at a young audience; Radio 2* targeting a more mature audience; *Radio 3* which plays mostly classical music; *Radio 4* which is talk based and features arts, drama and current affairs; and *Radio 5 Live* which is a mix of sport and news. *Radio Scotland* (92-95FM, 810MW) provides a Scottish-based diet of news, sport, current affairs, travel and music. It also provides a Gaelic network in the northwest and local programmes in Orkney and Shetland.

There is also a large number of local **commercial radio stations**, stretching from Shetland in the north to the Borders. The local Glasgow station is *Clyde 1* (102.5FM), while in Edinburgh it is *Radio Forth* (97.3FM).

Essentials

Food and drink

While Scotland's national drink is loved the world over, Scottish cooking hasn't exactly had a good press over the years. This is perhaps not too surprising, as the national dish consists of a stomach stuffed with diced innards and served alongside root vegetables, in other words **haggis** served with mashed tatties (potatoes) and neeps (turnips). Not a great start. And things got even worse when the Scots discovered the notorious deep-fried Mars bar.

Places to eat are marked on maps in this book with the symbol ●

But Scottish cuisine has undergone a dramatic transformation in recent years and Scotland now boasts some of the most talented chefs, creating some of the best food in Britain. The heart of Scottish cooking is local produce, which includes the finest fish, shellfish, game, lamb, beef, vegetables and a vast selection of traditionally-made cheeses. What makes Scottish cooking so special is ready access to these foods. What could be better than enjoying an aperitif whilst watching your dinner being delivered by a local fisherman, knowing that an hour later you'll be enjoying the most delicious seafood?

Modern Scottish cuisine is now a feature of many of the top restaurants in the country. This generally means the use of local ingredients with foreign-influenced culinary styles, in particular French. **International cuisine** is also now a major feature on menus all over the country, influenced by the rise of Indian and Chinese restaurants in recent decades. Indeed, so prevalent are exotic Asian and Oriental flavours that curry has now replaced fish and chips (fish supper) as the nation's favourite food.

Anyone staying at a hotel, guesthouse or B&B will experience the hearty **Scottish breakfast**, which includes bacon, egg, sausage and black pudding (a type of sausage made with blood), all washed down with copious quantities of tea, Scotland's staple drink. Although coffee is readily available everywhere, do not expect *cappuccinos* and *café lattes*: filter coffee is the staple 'tea-substitue' in most hotels and B&Bs. You may also be served kippers (smoked herring) or **porridge**, an erstwhile Scottish staple, which is now eaten by few people. Porridge is made with oatmeal and has the consistency of

Essentials

☞ *Eating categories*

*In this book places to eat are divided into three categories: **expensive** (over £20 a head); **mid-range** (£10-20 a head); and **cheap** (under £10 a head). These prices are based on a two-course meal (main course plus starter or dessert) without drinks. We have tried to include an equal number of choices in each category, though this is not always possible. **All places listed are recommended as offering relatively good value, quality and standards of service within their respective price category**.*

Italian polenta. It is traditionally eaten with salt, though heretics are offered sugar instead. **Oatcakes** (oatmeal biscuits) may also be on offer, as well as potato scones, baps (bread rolls), bannocks (a sort of large oatcake) or butteries (butter-laden bread similar to a croissant). These local baked goodies can be spread with marmalade, brought to the world's breakfast tables by the city of Dundee (see page 340).

After such a huge cooked breakfast you probably won't feel like eating again until **high tea**, taken between 1700 and 1800. This national institution consists of a cooked main course (usually fish and chips) and a *smorgesbord* of scones and cakes, washed down with pots of tea.

Scottish dishes Fish, meat and game form the base of many of the country's finest dishes. Scottish **beef**, particularly Aberdeen Angus, is the most famous in the world and has escaped the worst of the recent BSE scares. This will, or should, usually be hung for at least four weeks and sliced thick. **Game** is also a regular feature of Scottish menus, though it can be expensive, especially **venison** (deer), but delicious and low in cholesterol. **Pheasant** and **hare** are also tasty, but **grouse** is, quite frankly, overrated.

Fish and **seafood** are fresh and plentiful and if you're travelling around the northwest coast you must not miss the chance to savour local mussels, prawns, oysters, scallops, langoustines, lobster or crab. **Salmon** is, of course, the most famous of Scottish fish, but you're more likely to be served the fish-farmed variety than 'wild' salmon, which has a more delicate flavour. Trout is also farmed extensively, but the standard of both remains high. **Kippers** are also a favourite delicacy, the best of which come from Loch Fyne or the Achilitibuie smokery. **Arbroath smokies** (smoked haddock) are a tasty alternative.

Haggis, has made something of a comeback and small portions are often served as starters in fashionable restaurants. Haggis is traditionally eaten on *Burns Night* (25 January) in celebration of the great poet's birthday, when it is piped to the table and then slashed open with a sword at the end of a recital of Robert Burns' *Address to the Haggis*. Other national favourites feature names to relish: **cock-a-leekie** is a soup made from chicken, leeks and prunes; **cullen skink** (my own favourite) is a delicious concoction of smoked haddock and potatoes; while at the other end of the scale of appeal is **hugga-muggie**, a Shetland dish using fish's stomach. There's also the delightfully-named **crappit heids** (haddock heads stuffed with lobster), **partan bree** (a soup made form giant crab's claws, cooked with rice) and **stovies**, which is a mash of potato, onion and minced beef. Rather more mundane is the ubiquitous **Scotch broth**, made with mutton stock, vegetables, barley, lentils and split peas.

Waist-expanding **puddings** or desserts are a very important part of Scottish cooking and often smothered in butterscotch sauce or syrup in order to satisfy a sweet-toothed nation. There is a huge variety, including **cranachan**, a mouth-watering mix of toasted oatmeal steeped in whisky, cream and fresh raspberries, and **Atholl Brose**, a similar confection of oatmeal, whisky and cream.

Eaten before pudding, in the French style, or afterwards, are Scotland's many home-produced **cheeses**, which have made a successful comeback in the face of mass-produced varieties. Amongst the tastiest examples are **Lanark Blue**, made from unpasteurized ewe's milk and similar to Roquefort, and **Teviotdale** and **Bonchester**, which both come from the Borders. Many of the finest cheeses are produced on the islands, especially Arran, Mull, Islay and Orkney. **Caboc** is a creamy soft cheese rolled in oatmeal and is made in the Highlands.

There are places to suit every taste and budget. In Edinburgh and Glasgow in particular you'll find a vast selection of eating places, including **Indian**, **Chinese**, **Italian** and **French** restaurants, as well as **Thai**, **Japanese**, **Mexican**, **Spanish** and, of course **Scottish**. More and more restaurants, however, are moving away from national culinary boundaries and offering a wide range of **international** dishes and flavours, so you'll often find **Latin American**, **Oriental** and **Pacific Rim** dishes all on the same menu. This is particularly the case in the many continental-style **bistros**, **brasseries** and **café-bars**, which now offer a more informal alternative to traditional restaurants. It is becoming increasingly irrelevant to talk of a particular nationality of cooking and for this reason places to eat in this guide are grouped according to price and location instead of nationality. Not surprisingly, other parts of Scotland do not offer the same choice as Edinburgh and Glasgow, two cities with the greatest selection of places to eat in the UK outside London. **Vegetarians** are increasingly well catered for, especially in the large cities, where exclusively vegetarian/vegan restaurants and cafés are often the cheapest places to eat. Outside the cities, vegetarian restaurants are thin on the ground, though better quality eating places will normally offer a reasonable vegetarian selection.

Where to eat

Essentials

For a **cheap** meal, you're best bet is a **pub**, **hotel bar** or **café**, where you can have a one-course meal for around £5 or less, though don't expect gourmet food. The best value is often at lunch time, when many restaurants offer three-course **set lunches** or business lunches for less than £10. You'll need a pretty huge appetite to feel like eating a three-course lunch after your gigantic cooked breakfast, however. Also good value are the **pre-theatre dinners** offered by many restaurants in the larger towns and cities (you don't need to have a theatre ticket to take advantage). These are usually available from around 1730-1800 till 1900-1930, so you could get away with just a sandwich for lunch.

The biggest problem with eating out in Scotland, as in the rest of the UK, is the ludicrously limited serving hours in most pubs and hotels. These places only serve food between 1230 and 1400 and 1700 and 1900, seemingly ignorant of the eating habits of foreign visitors, or those who would prefer a bit more flexibility during their holiday. In small places especially, it can be difficult finding food outside these strictly-enforced times. Places which serve food all day till 2100 or later are restaurants, fast-food outlets and the many chic bistros and café-bars, which can be found not only in the main cities but increasingly in smaller towns. The latter may not be to everyone's taste, but they often offer very good value and above-average quality.

Those who prefer to eat to live, rather than the other way round, need never spend more than £5-6 for lunch and £7-10 for dinner, excluding drinks. It is generally not difficult to find a **cheap** meal, though on many of the islands and in parts of the northwest Highlands, there is less choice and prices tend to be higher. Also, if you're on a tight budget avoid those restaurants at visitor centres or other such tourist traps, as they tend to charge exorbitant prices for very average food.

At the other end of the scale, there are many excellent **restaurants**. Outside Edinburgh and Glasgow, these are often found in hotels, where you can enjoy the finest of Scottish cuisine, often with a continental influence. You can expect to pay from around £25 a head up to £40 or £50 in the very top establishments. Many of the best restaurants in the country are included in the *Taste of Scotland* guide (£7.99), which is better than most eating guides (though restaurants have to pay to be included) but certainly not comprehensive.

Essentials

👉 *How malt whisky is made*

Malt whisky is made by first soaking dry barley in tanks of local water for two to three days. Then the barley is spread out on a concrete floor or placed in cylindrical drums and allowed to germinate for between eight and 12 days, after which it is dried in a kiln, heated by a peat fire. Next, the dried malt is ground and mixed with hot water in a huge circular vat called a 'mash tun'. A sugary liquid called 'wort' is then drawn from the porridge-like result and piped into huge containers where living yeast is stirred into the mix in order to convert the sugar in the wort into alcohol. After about 48 hours the 'wash' is transferred to copper pot stills and heated till the alcohol vaporizes and is then condensed by a cooling plant into distilled alcohol which is passed through a second still. Once distilled, the liquid is poured into oak casks and left to age for a minimum of three years, though a good malt will stay casked for at least eight years.

Drinks

Beer is the staple alcoholic drink in Scotland. The most popular type of beer is lager, but connoisseurs should sample one of the many excellent types of **heavy**, which is a thick, dark ale served at room temperature with a full, creamy head. Types of heavy are graded by the shilling, which indicates its strength; the higher the number the stronger the beer. The usual range is 60 to 80 shillings (written 80/-). The best ales are hand-pumped from the cask under pressure. Beer is served in pints, or half pints, and you'll pay between £1.50 and £2.20 for a pint, depending on the brew and location of the pub.

The market is dominated by the large brewers – *Youngers*, *McEwan's*, *Scottish & Newcastle* and *Tennet's*. They produce smooth, strong beers, but the country's best seller is, strangely enough, *Tartan Special*, which is weak and tasteless by comparison. For the best of Scottish beers, however, you should try one of the small **local breweries**. Edinburgh's *Caledonian* produces a wide range of excellent cask ales. Others worth trying are *Belhaven*, brewed in Dunbar near Edinburgh, *Maclays*, brewed in Alloa, and the very wonderful *Greenmantle*, brewed in the Borders.

Whisky No visit to Scotland would be complete without availing oneself of a 'wee dram'. There is no greater pleasure on an inclement Highland evening than enjoying a malt whisky in front of a roaring log fire whilst watching the rain outside pelt down relentlessly. The roots of Scotland's national drink (*uisge beatha*, or 'water of life' in Gaelic) go back to the late 15th century, but it wasn't until the invention of a patent still in the early 19th century that distilling began to develop from small family-run operations to the large manufacturing business it has become today. Now more than 700 million bottles a year are exported, mainly to the United States, France, Japan and Spain.

There are two types of whisky: **single malt**, made only from malted barley; and **grain**, which is made from malted barley together with unmalted barley, maize or other cereals, and is faster and cheaper to produce. Most of the popular brands are blends of both types of whisky – usually 60-70 percent grain to 30-40 percent malt. These **blended** whiskies account for over 90% of all sales worldwide and most of the production of single malts is used to add flavour to a blended whisky. Amongst the best known brands of blended whisky are *Johnnie Walker*, *Bells*, *Teachers* and *Famous Grouse*. There's not much between them in terms of flavour and they are usually drunk with a mixer, such as water or soda.

Single malts are a different matter altogether. Each is distinctive and should be drunk neat to fully appreciate its subtle flavours. Single malts vary enormously. Their distinctive favours and aromas are derived from the peat used for drying, the water used for mashing, the type of oak cask used and the location of the distillery.

Which whisky?

*Opinions vary as to what are the best single malts and as to when you should drink them. As a rough guide, I would recommend a Speyside malt such as Glenmorangie or Glenlivet **before dinner** and one of the Islay malts – Ardbeg, Bowmore, Bunnahabhain (pronounced 'bun-a-haven'), Lagavulin, or the very wonderful Laphroaig (pronounced 'la-froig') – **after dinner**.*

If the Islays are not to your taste, then you could try instead Highland Park from Orkney or perhaps Tamdhu or Aberlour from Speyside. Those eternal favourites, Glenfiddich and The Macallan, can be enjoyed at any time.

Single malts fall into four groups: Highland, Lowland, Campbeltown and Islay. There are over 40 distilleries to choose from, most offering guided tours. The majority are located around Speyside, in the northeast. The region's many distilleries include that perennial favourite, *Glenfiddich*, which is sold in 185 countries. A recommended alternative is the produce of the beautiful and peaceful Isle of Islay, whose malts are lovingly described in terms of their peaty quality. Scots tend to favour the 10 year-old *Glenmorangie*, while the most popular in the USA is *The Macallan*.

Pubs & bars

As in the rest of Britain, **pubs** are the main focus of social life and entertainment for most Scots. These vary greatly, from traditional old inns full of character (and often full of characters) to chic and trendy bars where you can order *foccacia* bread with sundried tomatoes washed down with your bottle of continental lager whilst you dance to DJs. Most city pubs are owned by the large breweries and only serve their own particular beers. There is also a growing number of chain pubs appearing on the high streets of many towns.

In remote parts of the Highlands and Islands the local hotel bar is often the only watering hole for miles around and many pubs close for a couple of hours between 1400 and 1600, which can be very annoying on a wet afternoon. Pubs generally are open from 1100 till 2300 Monday-Saturday and Sunday from 1100-1200 till 2230. In towns and cities many pubs are open till 2400 or 0100 on Friday and Saturday nights, or even later in Edinburgh, which has more relaxed licensing laws.

Shopping

The shelves of gift shops in every tourist attraction from John O' Groats to Jedburgh are stuffed full of dreadful tartan tat such as 'See-you-Jimmy' wigs and bonnets, Loch Ness monster replicas and those scary-looking tartan dolls with flickering eyelashes. All very harmless (except for the dolls which give you nightmares), but not doing much for Scotland's image. But amongst all this tourist kitsch are many excellent high-quality goods on offer.

See also individual towns' Essentials sections for tips on local bargains

Scottish **textiles**, especially the tartan variety, are popular and worth buying. Everything from a travelling rug to your own kilt outfit. Shops up and down the country, and especially in Edinburgh and Inverness, can tell which clan your family belongs to and make you a kilt in that particular tartan. For the full outfit, including kilt, sporran, jacket, shoes and *skeann dhu* dagger expect to pay in the region of £600, or more if you want more elaborate accessories. There are mill shops making tweeds and cloths in many parts of Scotland. Most are in the Borders, though it is not necessarily cheaper to buy at source. **Harris Tweed** is also a good buy and you can watch your cloth being woven on the Hebridean islands of Harris and Lewis.

Knitwear is also good value and sold throughout Scotland, though the cashmere industry in the Borders is suffering from high trade tariffs. Shetland is a good place to

Essentials

find high-quality wool products. Note that Aran jumpers are not from the island of Arran, but from Aran (with one 'r') in Ireland. **Jewellery** is another popular souvenir and there are many excellent craft shops throughout the Highlands and Islands making beautiful jewellery with Celtic designs. **Glassware** is also popular, particularly Edinburgh crystal and Caithness glass, as well as **pottery**.

Food is another good souvenir and not just the ubiquitous shortbread is sold in tartan tins. If you haven't far to travel home, **smoked salmon**, or any other smoked product, is good value. One of the best places for food products is the island of **Arran**, where you can buy their delicious local mustards and preserves, smoked fish and game, and cheeses. And, of course, there's **whisky**. Most distilleries will refund the cost of their guided tour in the form of a discount voucher on a bottle of their brand whisky.

Shopping hours Shop hours in Scotland are generally Monday to Saturday from 0900-1730 or 1800. In larger towns and cities, many shops also open on Sundays and late at night, usually on a Thursday and Friday. Large supermarkets and retail complexes found outside large towns are open till 2000 or later Monday-Saturday and till 1600 on Sunday. In the Highlands and Islands, few shops are open on Sunday, most notably in the Outer Hebrides, when nothing is open on a Sunday. Also note that in many rural areas there is an early-closing day when shops close at 1300. This varies from region to region, but the most common day is Wednesday.

Holidays and festivals

Bank holidays Most Bank Holidays in Scotland are not general public holidays but simply days when the banks are closed. They include **2 January**, **Good Friday**, the first and last Monday in **May**, the first Monday in **August** and **Christmas Day** and **Boxing Day**. Christmas Day, Boxing Day, New Year's Day and 2 January are the only national public holidays. There are also local public holidays in spring and autumn. Dates vary from place to place.

Events & entertainment
Details of local festivals are given in the Essentials sections of individual towns

There is a huge range of organized events held throughout Scotland every year, ranging in size and spectacle from the Edinburgh Festival, the largest arts festival in the world, to more obscure traditional events featuring ancient customs dating back many centuries. The Scottish Tourist Board (STB) publishes a comprehensive list, *Events in Scotland*, twice a year. It's free and is available from the main tourist offices.

The most popular tourist events are the **Highland Games** (or Gatherings), a series of competitions involving lots of kilts, bagpipes and caber-tossing which are held across the Highlands and Islands, northeast and Argyll from **June to September**. The best known is the **Braemar Gathering** (see page 375), which is attended by various members of the Royal Family. Those at Oban and Dunoon are large events, but smaller gatherings are often more enjoyable and 'authentic'. **Folk festivals** are also great expressions of Celtic culture and a list of the best and most popular is given on page 680.

Entertainment Scotland has its own national ballet, opera and orchestra as well as many fine theatres up and down the country. Glasgow and Edinburgh have lively **club scenes**, but you'll also find nightclubs outside the major cities. For a comprehensive guide to what's on in Glasgow and Edinburgh, look out for the fortnightly listings magazine *The List*. **Celtic culture** is alive and well in many parts, particularly in the Highlands and islands, and you'll be able to hear traditional folk music in many pubs. At weekends you may also happen across a **ceilidh** in the local village hall or hotel. These traditional dances can be raucous affairs but great fun, even if you don't have a clue what you're doing. Ask for details at the local tourist office.

Calendar of events

New Year's Day *A variety of ancient local celebrations take place, including the Kirkwall Ba' Game, a mixture of football and mud wrestling.*

Up-Helly-Aa *Re-enactment of the ancient Viking fire festival held on Shetland on the **last Tuesday in January** (see page 583).*

Celtic Connections *Huge celebration of Celtic music from around the world, held in various venues throughout Glasgow over two weeks in **January**.*

Burns Night *Burns suppers held on **25th January** all over the country to celebrate the poet's birthday. Lots of haggis, whisky and poetry recitals.*

Scottish Grand National *Held at Ayr racecourse in **April**.*

Rugby Sevens *Seven-a-side rugby tournament held throughout the Borders.*

Scottish FA Cup Final *Held at Hampden Park in Glasgow in **May**.*

Riding of the Marches *Horse riding, parades, brass bands etc commemorating the wars between the Scots and the English. Held in various towns in the Borders from **June to August** (see page 607).*

Royal Highland Show *Scotland's largest agricultural show, held at Ingliston, near Edinburgh, in **June**.*

International Jazz Festival *Held in Glasgow in **July**.*

T in the Park *Scotland's largest outdoor music festival featuring many of the best pop and rock bands. Held at Balado Airfield at Kinross in **July**.*

Edinburgh International and Fringe Festival *The greatest arts extravaganza on the planet for three weeks of **August**.*

Edinburgh Military Tattoo *Massed pipe bands and military pageantry on the esplanade of Edinburgh Castle. Held over three weeks in **August**.*

World Pipe Band Championships *Held in Glasgow in **August**.*

Spirit of Speyside Whisky Festival *Held on Speyside in **October**.*

Braemar Highland Gathering *Attended by the Royal Family in **September**.*

National Mod *Competitive Gaelic music festival held at various locations in **October** (check with the Tourist Board).*

Tour of Mull Rally *The highlight of the Scottish rally season, run over the island's public roads (no wonder they're in such appalling condition) in **October**.*

Aberdeen Alternative Festival *The northeast's major arts and culture fest, held in **October**.*

Hogmanay *Old year's night and the most important national celebration. Possible derivations of the word include Holag Monath, Anglo Saxon for 'holy month' and Hoog min dag, which is Dutch for 'great love day'. Edinburgh's huge street party is the largest such celebration in the northern hemisphere.*

Sport

Football (soccer) is Scotland's most popular spectator sport. The *Scottish Football League*, established in 1874, is the main competition, with four divisions of 10 teams each, though this is due to change next season (2000-2001). Scottish football is dominated, and always has been, by the two main Glasgow teams, *Rangers* and *Celtic*, known collectively as the 'Old Firm' (see page 180), who regularly attract crowds of over 40,000. For a brief period in the 1980s this stranglehold was broken by *Aberdeen* and *Dundee United*, but events since have proved this an aberration rather than a trend. Money is the main reason for this and Rangers in particular have seemingly endless pots of the stuff, which is why they have been able to fill their team with expensive foreign imports and win most of the domestic competitions in the last decade. Their bitter rivals Celtic have fared poorly in recent times by comparison, which is particularly galling for their fans as they were once the dominant force in Scottish football and also the first British side to win the European Cup, in 1967. Rangers have never managed to repeat this feat.

Football

Scotland's top 10 teams make up the Premier League, which has become a battle between the big two for the championship and a struggle between the rest to avoid relegation to the lower divisions. Teams in the lower divisions mostly exist on a shoestring budget, though the other major competition, the Scottish FA Cup, still throws up occasional upsets, such as Celtic's recent defeat at the hands of lowly *Inverness Caledonian Thistle*.

The **national** team play at the recently-renovated Hampden Park in Glasgow. Their passionate supporters, known as the 'Tartan Army', have gained something of an international reputation for their fun-loving attitude and self-deprecating humour in the face of defeat. This has stood them in good stead over the years, for despite qualifying for every World Cup final save one since 1974, Scotland have never managed to reach the second round, failing against such footballing giants as Iran and Costa Rica along the way.

The domestic football **season** runs from early August to mid-May. Most matches are played on Saturdays at 1500, and there are often games through the week, on Tuesday and Wednesday evenings at 1930. There is usually a match on a Sunday afternoon, which is broadcast live on satellite TV. **Tickets** range from £10 up to £20 for big games.

Rugby Union   Rugby is one of the major sports of the country but lags a long, long way behind football in terms of popularity. The national team plays at Murrayfield in Edinburgh and during match weekends there's always a great atmosphere in the city. Every year, in February and March, Scotland takes part in the **Six Nations Championship**, along with the other home teams, plus France and Italy. The most important game, though, is the clash with the 'Auld enemy', England. Tickets for games are hard to come by, but you can contact the *Scottish Rugby Union* (*SRU*), T0131-3465000, for details of upcoming home fixtures and where to find tickets.

The club rugby scene is in a state of disarray, with many of the top players having moved to England or France. One area of the country where rugby is still strong is the Borders. The Borders town of Melrose is home of **seven-a-side rugby**, a variation of the 15-a-side game, and the **Melrose Sevens**, is the biggest tournament of the year in Scotland. The club rugby season runs from September to May.

Shinty & Curling   **Shinty** (or *camanachd* in Gaelic) is an amateur sport similar to Ireland's hurling. It's a physical game played at a fast and furious pace, and is a bit like hockey, but with more blood. The game is played mostly in the Highlands and the highlight of the season is the **Camanachd Cup Final**, which attracts a large crowd and is televized on STV.

Curling is nothing to with hairdressing, but is in fact a winter game which involves sliding smooth circular granite stones across the ice as close to the centre of a target as possible, while your team-mates use brooms to sweep away the loose white flakes (a bit like hairdressing, in fact). It is still played on frozen ponds occasionally (see photograph page 15) but more commonly played in indoor ice rinks.

Outdoor activities

Scotland is a great country for outdoor activities and many visitors come specifically to enjoy the magnificent scenery as they walk in the hills, cycle through forests, ski down mountains or head off in search of rare wildlife. The coastline, lochs and rivers are ideal for fishing and offer plenty of opportunities for a whole range of watersports, including windsurfing, sailing and scuba diving, and there are lots of beautiful beaches, especially on the northwest coast and the islands.

Munros, Corbetts and Grahams

Essentials

There are 284 mountains over 3,000ft (914m) in Scotland, known as 'Munros', after Sir Hugh Munro, first president of the Scottish Mountaineering Club (SMC), who published the first comprehensive list of these mountains, in 1891. In the 1920s a further list was published, of the 221 summits between 2,500 and 3,000ft, by J Rooke Corbett, and these became known as 'Corbetts'. A third list, of summits between 2,000 and 2,500ft was compiled by Fiona Graham and published in 1992. This list was subsequently revised and corrected and now all peaks of between 2,000 and 2,500ft are called Grahams.

Scotland is a walker's paradise. Throughout the country there are numerous marked trails, ranging from short walks to long-distance treks from one side of the country to the other. Whatever your taste or level of fitness and experience, you'll find plenty opportunities to get off the beaten track and explore the countryside.

Walking & climbing
Walking routes are denoted in the text by a foot symbol in the margin.

The best time is usually from May to September for hiking in the mountains, though in the more low-lying parts, April to October should be safe. Winter walking in the Highlands requires technical equipment such as ice axes and crampons and a lot of experience. July and August are the busiest times, though only the most popular routes, such as Ben Nevis, get really crowded. Another problem during these months are midges (see page 54). May to mid-June is probably the most pleasant time overall, as the weather can often be fine and the midges have yet to appear. September is also a good time, though it can be a lot colder.

Access Scotland has a long tradition of generally free responsible access to mountain and moorland. This free access, of course, relies on walkers behaving responsibly and recognizing that the countryside is a place of work as well as recreation. Most land in Scotland is privately owned and at certain times of the year, such as the main shooting seasons, walkers may be asked to respect certain restrictions on access. The main **deer stalking** season runs from mid-August to 20 October and the **grouse shooting** season is between 12 August (referred to as the 'Glorious Twelfth') and 10 December. For more information on this, see Heading for the Scottish Hills which is published by the Mountaineering Council of Scotland (see below) and the Scottish Landowners Federation and gives estate maps and telephone numbers to call for local advice. There may also be restricted access during the lambing season (March-May).

It is not an offence to walk over someone's land in Scotland but, especially during the stalking and shooting seasons, you may be asked to take a different route, though this rarely happens. There are no national parks in Scotland, but there is free access at all times of the year to areas owned by the *National Trust for Scotland* (address on page 20). These areas include Torridon and Glencoe. There is also free access to most land owned by the *Forestry Commission*, and there is good public access to land owned by the *John Muir Trust, Scottish Natural Heritage*, the *Royal Society for the Protection of Birds* (address on page 59) and the *Woodland Trust*, though these areas are not marked on *Ordnance Survey* (OS) maps. Also not shown on OS maps are **Rights of Way**, which are signposted by the Scottish Rights of Way Society's green metal signs. The society publishes maps of rights of way, many of which follow ancient 'drove roads' through the hills.

Information and advice The *Scottish Tourist Board* is a useful source of information for walkers (address on page 21). Local tourist offices have details of interesting local walks. The organizations listed opposite are also useful sources of information.

Essentials

👉 *The midge*

The major problem facing visitors to the Highlands and Islands of Scotland during the summer months is Culicoides Impunctatus – or the midge, as it's more commonly known. These tiny flying creatures are savage and merciless in the extreme and hunt in huge packs. No sooner have you left your B&B for a pleasant evening stroll, than a cloud of these bloodthirsty little devils will attack from nowhere, getting into your eyes, ears, nose and mouth – and a few places you forgot you even had. The only way to avoid them is to take refuge indoors, or to hide in the nearest loch.

Midges are at their worst in the evening and in damp, shaded or overcast conditions and between late May and September, but they don't like direct sunlight, heavy rain, smoke and wind. Make sure you're well covered up and wear light-coloured clothing (they're attracted to dark colours). Most effective is a midge net, if you don't mind everyone pointing and laughing at you. Insect repellents have some effect, particularly those with DEET, but herbal remedies such as bog myrtle, lavender, citronalla or eucalyptus are considered equally effective. Once you've been attacked the best treatment is antihistamine creams or dock leaves – and don't scratch the bites!

Many walk descriptions and maps are given in this guidebook, but these should ideally be used in conjunction with a good map, such as the *Ordnance Survey* (OS) *Landranger* series. The relevant map numbers have been listed, where possible, with the route description. OS maps can be found at tourist offices and also at **outdoor shops**, which are usually staffed by experienced climbers and walkers who can give good advice about the right equipment. The best equipped shops are *Tiso*, www.tiso.co.uk, who have branches in the main towns and cities and *Nevisport* in Fort William. For a list of recommended **walking guidebooks and maps**, see page 61.

Long distance walks There is a network of long walking trails across Scotland which are carefully prepared to provide ideal walking conditions together with sufficient places for accommodation and supplies en route. These walks can be attempted in full or sampled in part by less experienced walkers. Area tourist boards and local tourist offices can provide information and advice for their own particular sections. Two of the three main trails, the **Southern Upland Way** (see page 600) and the **Speyside Way** (see page 383) are covered in the relevant sections of this guide.

The best known, and busiest, long distance trail is the **West Highland Way**, which runs for 95 miles from Milngavie (pronounced 'mull-guy'), just north of Glasgow, to Fort William. The route progresses steadily from the lowlands, along the eastern shore of **Loch Lomond** and the traverse of the western edge of **Rannoch Moor**, to enter **Glencoe** at White Corries. It continues along the Devil's Staircase, past Kinlochleven, and through **Glen Nevis** to Fort William. Many walkers finish off with an ascent of **Ben Nevis** (4,406ft), the highest mountain in Britain (see page 430). **Further information**, including a trail leaflet with accommodation and facilities guide, is available from *West Highland Way Ranger Service*, Balloch Castle, Balloch, G53 8LX, T01389-758216.

There are several other long distance trails, including **St Cuthbert's Way** (see page 600) and the **Pilgrim's Way** in southern Scotland. Two trails which are not yet fully completed are the **Clyde Walkway**, which will eventually run from the heart of Glasgow to New Lanark, and the **Fife Coastal Path**, which will run for 60 miles along the Fife coastline, from North Queensferry, at the foot of the Forth Bridge, to the Tay Bridge at Dundee. The section from North Queensferry to Pittenweem (39 miles) is complete. Leaflets covering both trails are available from the Greater Glasgow and Clyde Valley and Fife area tourist boards (addresses on page 21).

Organized walks

There are plenty of operators offering guided walks and walking holidays. A selection of companies is given below and the STB has a comprehensive list.

In Britain

Assynt Guided Holidays, Birchbank, Knockan, Elphin, Sutherland, T/F01854-666215.

Avalon Trekking Scotland, Bowerswell Lane, Kinnoull, Perth, PH2 TDL, T/F01738-624194.

C-N-Do Scotland, Unit 32, STEP, Stirling, FK7 7RP, T/F01786-445703, www.btinternet.com/-cndo.scotland.

Glen Coe Mountain Sport, 37 Park Rd, Ballachulish, Glen Coe, Argyll, PA39 4JB, T01855-811472, www.glencoe-mountain-sport.co.uk.

Lomond Walking Holidays, 34c James St, Riverside, Stirling, FK8 1UG, T/F01786-447752, www.biggar-net.co.uk/lomond.

North-West Frontiers, 18A Braes, Ullapool, IV26 28Z, T/F01854-612628, www.nwfrontiers.com.

Ossian Guides, Sanna, Newtonmore,

Inverness-shire, PH20 1DG, T/F01540-673402.

Rua Reidh Lighthouse, Melvaig, Gairloch, Wester Ross, T/F01445-771263, ruareidh@netcomuk.co.uk.

Scottish Border Trails, Drummore, Peebles, EH45 8RL, T01721-720336.

In North America

Above the Clouds Trekking, T800-2334499, www.gorp.com/abvclds.htm.

British Coastal Trails, T800-4731210, www.bctwalk.com.

Himalayan Travel, T800-2252380, www.gorp.com/himtravel.htm.

In Australia and New Zealand

Adventure Specialists, 69 Liverpool St, Sydney, T02-92612927.

Adventure Travel Company, 164 Parnell Rd, Parnell, East Auckland, T09-3799755. New Zealand agents for Peregrine Adventures.

Peregrine Adventures, 258 Lonsdale St, Melbourne, T03-96638611, www.peregrine.net.au; also branches in Brisbane, Sydney, Adelaide and Perth.

Essentials

Short walks

Many of the most popular short walks, including the ascent of Ben Nevis, are described in this guidebook. These range from gentle strolls through forest glades to strenuous hikes, steep hills and mountains, and also include some beautiful coastal trails. One of the most popular pastimes in Scotland is Munro-bagging (see page 53), which involves climbing as many peaks over 3,000ft as possible. The best area for this is the **Highlands**, which provide many challenging peaks, and it's possible to climb several in a day. Many of these hills are straightforward climbs, but many also require a high level of fitness and experience, and all require proper **clothing** (see 'Safety' below). You should never attempt walks beyond your abilities.

Other good areas for walking include the **Isles of Arran**, **Mull**, **Islay** and **Skye**, **Perthshire**, **Stirling** and the **Trossachs** and **Galloway**. The mighty **Cairngorms** are better known as a winter ski area, but provide excellent year-round hill-walking and climbing. This is extremely wild terrain, however, and suitable only for experienced walkers. There are many opportunities for less experienced walkers in Rothiemurchus Estate and Glenmore Forest Park around **Aviemore**. Other areas which are best left to serious climbers are **Torridon**, **Kintail** and **Glencoe**, though the latter also offers a few more straightforward walks through spectacular scenery (see page 435).

Climbing

The Cairngorms and Cuillins on Skye offer the most challenging climbing in Scotland, as do Glencoe and Torridon. For a list of climbing **guidebooks**, see page 61. For more detailed information, contact the Mountaineering Council of Scotland, 4a St Catherine's Road, Perth, T01738-638227. A recommended rock climbing and mountaineering instructor is Gary Latter, Kinalty Cottage, By Kirriemuir, Angus, DD8 5LY, T01575-530308.

Essentials

👉 *Cycling organizations*

Cyclists' Touring Club (CTC), Cotterell House, 69 Meadrow, Godalming, Surrey, GU7 3HS, T01483-417217, www.ctc.org.uk. The largest cycling organization in the UK, providing a wide range of services and information on transport, cycle hire and routes, from day rides to longer tours.
Forestry Enterprise, 21 Church St, Inverness, IV1 1EL, T01463-232811. Provides information on Scotland's extensive network of forest trails.

The Scottish Cyclists' Union (SCU), The Velodrome, Meadowbank Stadium, London Rd, Edinburgh, EH7 6AY, T0131-6520187, www.btinternet.com/~scottish.cycling. Produces an annual handbook and calendar of events for road racing, time trialling and mountain biking.
SUSTRANS, 53 Cochrane St, Glasgow, G1 1HL, T0141-5720234, www.sustrans.co.uk. Provides information on new cycle trails.

Mountain safety Visitors to Scotland should be aware of the need for caution and safety preparations when walking or climbing in the mountains. The nature of Scottish weather is such that a fine sunny day can turn into driving rain or snow in a matter of minutes. Remember that a blizzard can be raging on the summit when the car park at the foot of the mountain is bathed in sunshine. It is essential to get an up-to-date weather forecast before setting off on any walk or climb. A **weather phone-line** service is available from the following numbers: East Highlands T0891-333197; West Highlands T0891-333198.

Whatever the time of year, or conditions when you set off, you should always carry or wear essential items of clothing. A basic list for summer conditions would be: **boots** with a good tread and ankle support and a thick pair of socks; **waterproof jacket and trousers**, even on a sunny day; **hat and gloves** are important if the weather turns bad; **warm trousers** should be worn or carried, tracksuit bottoms are okay if you also have waterproof trousers; **spare woolly jumper or fleece jacket** will provide an extra layer; **map and compass** are essential to carry and to know how to use. Other essentials are **food and drink**, a simple **first aid kit**, a **whistle** and a **torch**. A small 25-30 litre rucksack should be adequate for carrying the above items. Also remember to leave details of your route and expected time of return with someone, and remember to inform them on your return.

In the winter extra warm clothing is needed, as well as an **ice axe** and **crampons** (and the ability to use them). The skills required for moving over ice or snow should be practised with an experienced and qualified mountain guide/instructor.

Cycling & mountain biking The bicycle was invented in Scotland, near Dumfries, so it seems appropriate that travelling by bike is one of the best ways to explore the country. Most towns and cities, however, are not particularly cycle-friendly. Very few have proper cycle routes and there's the added problem of security. It's best to stick to rural backroads, especially unclassified roads and country lanes, which are not numbered but are signposted and marked on OS maps. There are also forest trails and dedicated routes along canal towpaths and disused railway tracks. The main problem in rural areas, though, is the availability of spare parts.

The **south of Scotland** is particularly good for cycle touring due to the gentle gradients and large number of B&Bs and pubs. The wild and remote **Highlands** are popular with cyclists but this is also walking country, and cyclists should stick to tracks where a right to cycle exists and be considerate towards walkers. The *Forestry Commission* has 1150 miles of excellent off-road routes up and down the country. These are detailed in a series of *Cycling in the Forest* leaflets, which are available from Forestry Enterprise offices (see above) and from most tourist offices. These are best used by **mountain bikes** with multi gears, though easier routes can be attempted on hybrid or standard bikes.

Cycle tour companies

Bespoke Cycle Tours, *the Bothy, Camusdarach, Arisaig, Inverness-shire, PH39 4NT , T01687-450272, www.scotland-info.co.uk/tours.*
Scottish Border Trails, *Venlaw High Rd, Peebles, EH45 8RL, T01721-722934,*

arthur@trails.scotborders.co.uk.
Scottish Cycle Safaris, *29 Blackfriars St, Edinburgh, EH1 1NH, T0131-5565560.*
Scottish Cycling Holidays, *87 Perth St, Blairgowrie, Perthshire, PH10 6DT, T01250-876100, www.sol.co.uk/s/scotcycl/.*

You can cut down on the amount of pedalling you have to do by **transporting your bike** by train. Bikes can be taken free on most local rail services on a first come-first served basis (call ScotRail bookings, T0845-550033). On long-distance routes you'll have to make a reservation (£3.50 charge) and pay a small charge. Space is limited on trains so it's a good idea to book as far in advance as possible. **Bus and coach** companies will not carry bikes, unless they dismantled and boxed. **Ferries** transport bikes for a small fee and **airlines** will often accept them as part of your baggage allowance. Check with the ferry company or airline about any restrictions.

Bike rental is available at cycle shops in most large towns and cities and tourist centres. Expect to pay from around £6 to £15 per day, or from £50 a week, plus a refundable deposit. There's also the option of a **cycling holiday package**, which include transport of your luggage, prebooked accommodation, route instructions and food and backup support. A list of specialists is given above.

Information The STB publishes a free booklet, *Cycling in Scotland*, which is useful and suggests routes in various parts of the country, as well as accommodation and repair shops. Many area tourist boards also provide cycling guides for their own areas. A list of useful **cycle guides and books** is given on page 61.

Scotland has over 400 golf courses, with more being built all the time, and, therefore **Golf** has more courses per head of population than any other country in the world. Any decent sized town in Scotland will have a golf course nearby and most, if not all, are available for play. There are many public courses, which tend to be both cheap and extremely busy often have excellent layouts. The majority of private clubs allow visitors, although many have restrictions as to what days these visitors can play. Weekends are usually reserved for club competitions for the members and it is best to try to play on a weekday. All private clubs have a dress code and it is inadvisable to turn up for a round in a collarless shirt and jeans. These minor caveats aside, you are more than likely to receive a warm and courteous welcome.

One of the unique attractions of golf in Scotland is the accessibility of its famous venues. The average football fan will never get the chance to play at Wembley Stadium, likewise the club tennis player is unlikely to play a few sets on the Centre Court at Wimbledon, but any golfer can, for example, play at Carnoustie or St Andrews. This represents a unique opportunity to follow in the footsteps of golf's legendary players and compare your own game, however unfavourably, with theirs. **Green fees** for one of the top championship courses will cost from around £40 upwards. Many clubs offer a daily or weekly ticket. A **Golf Pass Scotland** costs between £46 and £70 for five days (Monday-Friday), depending on the area. *Golf in Scotland* is a free brochure listing 400 courses and clubs with accommodation details. For a copy contact the *Scottish Tourist Board*. The *British Tourist Authority* (BTA) has a very useful *Golfing Holidays* booklet which provides details of golfing holidays and major golf tournaments in Britain. (BTA and STB address on page 21). For a list of recommended golf books, see page 61.

Skiing Conditions in Scotland are not as good or reliable as anywhere in the Alps, but on a clear, sunny day, and with good snow, you can enjoy some decent skiing. However, at weekends, in conditions like these, expect the slopes to be very busy. Scotland offers both **alpine** (downhill) and **nordic** (cross-country) skiing, as well as the increasingly-popular **snowboarding**. The high season is from January to April, but it is possible to ski from as early as November to as late as May. Ski packages are available but it's easy to arrange everything yourself and there's plentiful accommodation and facilities in and around the ski centres.

There are **five ski centres** in Scotland. The largest are **Glenshee**, which has the largest network of lifts and selection of runs, as well as snow machines, and **Cairngorm**, which has almost 30 runs spread over an extensive area. **Glencoe** is the oldest of the ski resorts, and the **Nevis Range**, at Aonach Mor near Fort William, has the highest ski runs and only gondola in Scotland, as well as a dry slope. **The Lecht** is the most remote centre and is good for beginners and families and for nordic skiing. Access to all five centres is easiest by car. Each resort has a ski patrol and facilities for snowboarding.

Costs Ski equipment and clothing can be hired at all resorts but lessons should be booked in advance. Prices vary from centre to centre, but on average expect to pay around £13 per day for hire of skis, sticks and boots, and around £12 per day for ski clothes. Snowboard hire is around £16-17 per day for board and boots. Lift passes cost around £18-20 per day, or £68-80 for five days. Ski lessons are around £18 for four hours. Packages including ski hire, tuition and lift pass cost from around £125 to £155 for five days. These prices are for adults; prices for juniors are less.

Information Details for each of the five resorts, including phone numbers, are given in the appropriate place in the main text. For further general information contact the **Scottish Tourist Board** for its *Ski Scotland* brochure and accommodation list, or visit their website, www.ski.scotland.net, which is updated daily. Or you can contact the **Scottish National Ski Council**, T0131-3177280, www.snsc.demon.co.uk. They produce a useful *Snowsport Scotland Handbook*.

The **Ski hotline** weather-report service gives the latest snow and weather conditions plus a five-day forecast. Phone 0891-654 followed by: 655 for Cairngorm; 656 for Glenshee; 657 for The Lecht; 658 for Glencoe; 660 for Nevis Range; and 659 for cross country skiing.

Fishing Scotland's rivers, streams, lochs and estuaries are among the cleanest waters in Europe and are filled with salmon, trout (sea, brown and rainbow) and pike. Not surprisingly, then, fishing (coarse, game and sea) is hugely popular in Scotland.

There is no close season for **coarse fishing** or **sea angling**. For **wild brown trout** the close season is early October to mid-March. The close season for **salmon** and **sea trout** varies from area to area and between net and rod fishing. It is generally from late August to early February for net fishing, and from early November to early February for rod fishing.

No licence is required to fish in Scotland, but most of the land and rivers are privately owned so you must obtain a **permit** from the owners or their agents. These are often readily available at the local fishing tackle shop and usually cost from around £15, though some rivers, such as the Tweed, can be far more expensive.

The STB's booklet *Fish Scotland* is a good introduction and a source of all kinds of information. It is available free from tourist offices, or by post (see page 21). Also contact the **Scottish Federation of Sea Anglers**, Brian Burn, Flat 2, 16 Bellevue Road, Ayr, KA7 2SA, T01292-264735, or **Scottish National Anglers Association**, David Wilkie, Administration Office, Caledonia House, South Gyle, Edinburgh, EH12 9DQ, T0131- 3398808.

Pony Trekking is a long-established activity in Scotland and miles of beautiful coastline, lochsides, and moorland are accessible on horseback. There are numerous equestrian centres around the country catering to all levels of riders.

The Scottish Tourist Board produces a *Trekking & Riding* brochure listing riding centres around the country, all of them approved by the *Trekking and Riding Society of Scotland* (*TRSS*) or the *British Horse Society* (*BHS*). Centres offer **pony trekking** (leisurely strolls at walking pace for novices), **hacks** (short rides at a fast pace for experienced riders) and **trail riding** (long distance rides at no more than a canter). The **Buccleuch Country Ride** is a four-day route through the Borders, using private tracks, open country and quiet bridleways. For more information, contact the *Scottish Borders Tourist Board*, T01835-863435. For general information contact the *TRSS*, Horse Trials Office, Blair Atholl, Perthshire, T01796-481543, or the *BHS*, British Equestrian Centre, Stoneleigh Park, Kenilworth, Warwicks CV8 2LR, T01203-414288.

Scotland is great for birdwatching. Over 450 species have been recorded, including vast colonies of seabirds, birds of prey and many rare species. Among the best places in Scotland to see birds are **Handa Island**, off the coast of Sutherland, and the **Treshnish Islands**, off Mull, where you'll see colonies of shags, razorbills, guillemots and puffins. Details of how to get there are given in the relevant sections. Other excellent places for birdwatching include **Caerlaverock**, near Dumfries, the **Isle of May**, off the coast of Fife, the **Bass Rock** off North Berwick, **Fowlsheugh**, near Stonehaven, and **Loch Garten**, by Boat of Garten, where you can see ospreys. Many of the Hebridean islands, such as **Islay** and **Mull**, are home to a rich variety of seabirds and you can also see golden eagles.

Orkney and **Shetland** are famous for their rich variety of birdlife and are home to large colonies of seabirds and migratory birds. There are puffins, kittiwakes, fulmars, shags, razorbills, guillmeots and even auks.

Organizations and information Further information can be obtained from the *Royal Society for the Protection of Birds*, 17 Regent Terrace, Edinburgh EH7 5BT, T0131-5573136, the *Scottish Ornithologists Club*, 21 Regent Terrace, Edinburgh EH7 5BT, T0131-5566042, *Scottish Natural Heritage*, 12 Hope Terrace, Edinburgh EH9 2AS, T0131-4474784 and the *Scottish Wildlife Trust*, Cramond House, Cramond Glebe Road, Edinburgh EH4 6NS, T0131-3127765, which owns and runs over 100 nature reserves.

There are thousands of dive sites around Scotland's shores with a rich variety of marine life and plenty of wrecks to explore. The **West Coast** offers the best diving, as the water is warmed by the effects of the Gulf Stream and is not cold, even without a dry suit. Among the best sites are the **west coast of Harris**, the **Summer Isles** and the remote island of **St Kilda**. There are lots of wrecks in the **Sound of Mull** and the chance to find a Spanish Galleon off **Tobermory**. **Scapa Flow** in Orkney is world renowned as the burial site of the German World War I fleet.

On the **East Coast**, there is a great marine reserve off **St Abb's Head**, near Eyemouth, with some spectacular rock formations.

Information Contact *Scottish Sub Aqua Club*, 40 Bogmoor Place, Glasgow, G51 47Q, T0141-4251021; or *British Sub Aqua Club* (*Scottish Federation*), 67 Moredun Park, Gilmerton, Edinburgh EH17, T0131-6644381. A recommended dive operator is *Dive Scotland*, T0131-4412001, in Edinburgh.

Scotland has some of the best surfing beaches in Europe. This is no Hawaii, with its sunbleached hair and bronzed bodies: surfing in Scotland is strictly for the hardy, with water temperatures rarely above 15°C and often as low as 7°C. A good wet suit is therefore essential. The waves, though, make up for the freezing waters and compare with those in Hawaii and Australia. The main season is September to December.

The best beaches on the **West Coast** are to be found at the northern tip of the **Isle of Lewis** and at **Machrihanish**, down near the Mull of Kintyre. On the **North Coast** the top spot is **Thurso**, especially at Dunnet Head to the east of town. Another recommended place is **Strathy Bay**, near Bettyhill, halfway between Thurso and Tongue. On the **East Coast** the best beaches are **Pease Bay**, south of Dunbar, near Cockburnspath on the A1, and **Nigg Bay**, just south of Aberdeen, between Montrose and Arbroath.

There is a bi-monthly surf magazine, *Surf*, which is a good source of information. Also try the surf shops, which sell equipment and provide information on the best breaks. **Glasgow**: Clan, 45 Hyndland Street, Partick, T0141-3396523, *Boardwise*, 1146 Argyle Street, T0141-3345559. **Edinburgh**: *Momentum*, 22 Bruntsfield Place, T0131-2296665. **Aberdeen**: *Granite Reef*, 45 Justice Street, T01224-621193.

Canoeing Scotland's rivers, lochs and deeply indented coastline offer great opportunities for canoeing or kayaking. For information, contact the *Scottish Canoe Association*, Caledonia House, South Gyle, Edinburgh EH12 9DQ, T0131-3177314, www.scot-canoe.org. They organize tours, including introductory ones for beginners. Also try *Splash Rafting* of Aberfeldy, splashraft@compuserve.com.

Paragliding If you fancy getting high during your visit, you can try your hand at the exciting sport of paragliding. Courses and flights are offered by *Parapente Ecosse* in Edinburgh, T0700-0782589, paraglide_scotland@compuserve.com, and *Flying Fever*, No 2 coastguard House, Kildonan, Isle of Arran, T01770-820292, www.arran.uk.com/kildonan/flyingfever.

Health

Medical emergency: dial 999 or 112 (both free) for an ambulance

No vaccinations are required for entry into Britain. Citizens of **EU** countries are entitled to free medical treatment at National Health Service hospitals on production of an E111 form. Also, Australia, New Zealand and several other non-EU European countries have reciprocal health-care arrangements with Britain.

Citizens of other countries will have to pay for all medical services, except accident and emergency care given at Accident and Emergency (A&E) Units at most (but not all) National Health hospitals. Health insurance is therefore strongly advised for citizens of non-EU countries.

Pharmacists can dispense only a limited range of drugs without a doctor's prescription. Most are open for normal shop hours, though some are open late, especially in larger towns. Local newspapers will carry lists of which are open late.

Doctors' surgeries are usually open from around 0830-0900 till 1730-1800, though times vary. Outside surgery hours you can go to the casualty department of the local hospital for any complaint requiring urgent attention. For the address of the nearest hospital or doctors' surgery, T0800-665544.

You should encounter no major problems or irritations during your visit to Scotland. The only exceptions to this are the risk of **hypothermia** if you're walking in the mountains in difficult conditions (see page 56), and the dreaded **midge** (see box page 54).

Further reading

The books listed below are non-fiction and reference guides. For a list of the best in Scottish fiction and poetry, see **Scottish Writers**, on page 675.

The best general overview of Scottish social history is given by Professor Chris Smout in his excellent *A History of the Scottish People (1560-1830)* and *A Century of the Scottish People (1830-1950)*.

History, politics & culture

For a more emotive and subjective view of highland history, read any of John Prebble's books, including *1,000 years of Scotland's History, The Lion in the North, Glen Coe, Culloden* and *The Highland Clearances* (Penguin), or Nigel Tranter's *The Story of Scotland*. Two excellent biographies of the most romantic figures in Scottish history are Antonia Fraser's *Mary, Queen of Scots* (UK Mandarin) and Fitzroy Maclean's *Bonnie Prince Charlie* (Canongate). A highly entertaining account of 16th-century life in the Borders is given in *The Steel Bonnets* by George MacDonald Fraser (Harper Collins). An entertaining account of Scotland's often turbulent relationship with England is given by Sir Ludovic Kennedy's *In Bed with an Elephant*. Tom Nairn's *The Break-up of Britain* gives a radical perspective of Scottish independence and *Scotland's Story* (Fontana) is also insightful. A comprehensive guide to Scottish culture is David Daiches' *The New Companion to Scottish Culture* (Arnold).

If you only read one, then make it James Boswell & Samuel Johnson's *A Journey to the Western Islands of Scotland* (UK Penguin). Other notables include *In Search of Scotland* by HV Morton (Methuen), *A High and Lonely Place* and *Gulfs of Blue Air – A Highland Journey* (Mainstream) by Jim Crumley and Elizabeth Grant of Rothiemurchus, *Memoirs of a Highland Lady* (Canongate). One of the best known Highland memoirs is *A Ring of Bright Water* by Gavin Maxwell; a tale of otters and other wildlife set in Glenelg. *A Last Wild Place* by naturalist Mike Tomkies is a fascinating account of life in a remote West Highland croft. Also interesting is *Queen Victoria's Highland Journal*, edited by David Duff (UK Hamlyn).

Travelogues & memoirs

There are numerous **walking guides** available and this is only the briefest of selections. Two of the best are *Great Walks Scotland* by Hamish Brown and *100 Best Routes on Scottish Mountains* by Ralph Storer. Two helpful hill-walking guides published by the Scottish Mountaineering Trust are *The Munros* by Donald Bennett and *The Corbetts* by Scott Johnstone et al. The SMT also publishes a range of district guides listing mainly high level walks. Also useful are *The Munro Almanac* and *The Corbett Almanac* by Cameron McNeish. A healthy antidote to all those climbing anoraks is Muriel Gray's entertaining and clean-shaven *The First Fifty: Munro Bagging without a Beard* (UK Corgi). Those wishing to attempt one of the long distance walks should read *The West Highland Way* or *The Southern Upland Way*, both highly informative guides by Roger Smith (HM Stationery Office).

Outdoor activities

An excellent guide for both walkers and **mountain bikers** is Ralph Storer's *Exploring Scottish Hill Tracks*. Other recommended cycling guides include: *The Scottish Cycling Guide*, by Brendan Walsh; *Cycling in Scotland and NE England: 50 Great traffic-free routes*, by Philip Routledge (Stigma Press); *101 Bike Routes in Scotland*, by Henry Henniker (Mainstream); *Cycling in Scotland* by John Hancox (Collins Pocket Reference, Harper Collins); and *Cycling in Great Britain: Bicycle Touring Adventures in England, Scotland and Wales*, by Tim hughes & Jo Cleary (Bicycle Books, US).

For a comprehensive guide to Scotland's **golf courses** try: *Scotland – Home of Golf*, a Pastime publication produced by the Scottish Tourist Board; and *The Scottish Golf Guide* by David Hamilton (Canongate Press). An outsider's view of golf in Scotland can be found in American Michael Bamberger's highly entertaining book *To the Linksland* (Mainstream Publishing), ideal if the Scottish weather keeps you from playing!

A good **birdwatching** guide is *Where to Watch Birds in Scotland*, by Michael Madders and Julia Welstead (UK Christopher Helm).

Miscellaneous The Collins pocket guides to *Clans and Tartans*, *Scottish Surnames* and their *Scots Dictionary* are handy and informative. For more detailed genealogical study, look at *Tracing your Ancestors*, by Cecil Sinclair (HM Stationery Office). *Exploring Scotland's Heritage* is a beautifully-illustrated series of books on historic buildings and archaeological sites in different regions of Scotland (HM Stationery Office). Those wishing to bone up on their malt whiskies should refer to the *Malt Whisky Companion*, by Michael Jackson (UK Dorling Kindersley). An excellent Scottish recipe book is the *Claire MacDonald Cookbook*, by Lady Claire MacDonald (UK Bantam) who runs a hotel on Skye.

Maps

You'll find a good selection of maps of Scotland in many bookshops and at the main tourist offices. **Road atlases** can be bought at most service stations. The best of these are the large-format ones produced by the *AA*, *Collins* and *Ordnance Survey* which cover all of Britain at a scale of around three miles to one inch and include plans of the major towns and cities. The *Michelin* and *Bartholomew* fold-out maps are also excellent, as are the official regional tourist maps published by *Estate Publications*, which are ideal for driving and which are available from most tourist offices.

The best detailed maps for walking are the *Ordnance Survey* maps, which are unsurpassed for accuracy and clarity. These are available at different scales. The *Landranger* series at 1:50,000 (1¼ inches to a mile) covers the whole of Britain and is good for most walkers. The new *Explorer* and *Outdoor Leisure* series are 1:25,000 and offer better value for walkers and cyclists. An excellent source of maps is *Stanfords* at 12-14 Longacre, London WC2E 9LP.

Edinburgh

3

Edinburgh

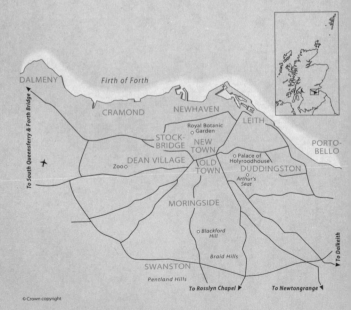

© Crown copyright

Few cities make such a strong impression on the visitor as Edinburgh. The most immediate impact of the city is the huge amount of space it offers. It is open – generously so – almost to the point of seeming empty, and makes you feel small. Everything here is bigger than strictly necessary: the streets, the buildings, the hills, the sky. Scotland's capital is without doubt one of the most beautiful and elegant cities in Europe and its urban bits are separated by parks and gardens and, most stunning of all, cliffs and rocks and grassy hills – even a few dormant volcanoes! This is real nature rather than the manicured stuff, which is all you get in most other cities.

The views around Edinburgh have to be seen to be believed: down from the castle across the Georgian New Town; from the New Town out across the Firth of Forth; from Arthur's Seat across the surrounding moors; and the most dramatic cityscape in Europe, from Calton Hill down the length of Princes Street to the castle. Edinburgh is so spectacular it has an almost unreal quality. The great novelist, Robert Louis Stevenson, born and bred here, described the city as a "profusion of eccentricities, this dream in masonry and living rock", and went on to express his astonishment that it was "not a dropscene in a theatre, but a city in the world of everyday reality".

The city centre is divided in two. North of Princes Street is the elegant Neo-classical New Town, built in the late 18th and early 19th centuries to improve conditions in the city. South of Princes Street, across the beautiful Princes Street Gardens, is the Old Town, a rabbit warren of narrow alleys and closes, inhabited by the ghosts of Edinburgh's seamy past, and inspiration for Stevenson's famous Dr Jeckyll and Mr Hyde. This medieval Manhattan of high-rise tenements runs from the castle down to the Palace of Holyroodhouse. Overlooking the palace is Edinburgh's largest and most impressive volcano, Arthur's Seat, an authentic piece of mountain wilderness within a stone's throw of the city centre.

Fittingly, such a spectacular setting provides the stage for the Edinburgh International Festival, the largest cultural event on the planet, which attracts more than a million visitors over three weeks in August and September. In keeping with its status as one of the great European cities, Edinburgh has many excellent museums and art galleries – and they're mostly free. The National Gallery of Scotland, the Scottish National Gallery of Modern Art and the Museum of Scotland all boast the finest collections outside London. As if that weren't enough, Edinburgh is cultivating an enviable culinary reputation, and is the easiest place in Britain to get a drink, with over 700 bars, many of which are open well into the wee small hours. Edinburgh folk may have a reputation for being cold and stuffy, but they obviously know how to enjoy themselves, every bit as much as the visitors who flock here every year.

Ins and outs

Air Edinburgh international airport, T3331000 general enquiries, T3443136 airport information, is eight miles west of the city centre on the A8 Edinburgh-Glasgow road. Two bus services, *Airline 100* and *Guide Friday*, run between the airport and the main train station at Waverley Bridge. From Waverley Bridge, buses start at 0600 and then run every 15 minutes from 0715 till 1955, and then every 30 minutes till 2155. From the airport the first bus is at 0630, then every 15 minutes till 2100, and then every 30 minutes till 2230. The main pick up/drop off points in town are at the West End of Princes Street and Haymarket train station. A single ticket costs £3.30-3.60 and a return £5-5.50. Tickets can be bought from the driver, at the Tourist Information Centre or at the *Guide Friday* Tourism Centre (see Tours of Edinburgh, page 72). The journey time is 25 minutes, though this will be longer during the rush hours. To the city centre from the airport, one of the white airport taxis will cost £15, while a black taxi cab will cost around £12. Journey time is roughly 20 minutes.

Edinburgh airport has all facilities, including a tourist information desk, Bureau de Change, ATMs, restaurants and bars (first floor) and shops (ground floor and first floor). For **car hire**, *Avis*, *Budget*, *Europcar*, *Hertz* and *National* car hire desks are located in the terminal in the main UK arrivals area. For **flight information**, see page 26.

Train All trains to Edinburgh go to Waverley station, T5562477, off Waverley Bridge at the east end of Princes Street. This is where the main ticket booking office is. Note that during peak periods a wait of 30-40 minutes is not unusual. Leave at least 10 minutes to buy tickets for immediate travel at other times. Taxis collect passengers from the station concourse, but if the queue is depressingly long, there's another taxi rank on Waverley Bridge. All trains to the north and to the west coast, including Glasgow, also stop at Haymarket station. For timetable and ticket enquiries: T0345-484950.

Bus St Andrews Coach station is at the northeast corner of St Andrews Square (see 'New Town' map), only a few minutes' walk from Waverley station. This is the terminal for all coaches from England, from other towns and cities around Scotland and also for local services to outlying towns and villages. At the southeastern corner of the bus station is the SMT Bus Shop, where you can pick up timetables and buy tickets for any one of the vast number of private operators, T6639233; open Mon-Sat 0840-1700, except Wed 0900-1700.

Car Edinburgh is one of the least car-friendly cities in Britain. The main routes into town have been turned into Greenways, which give buses priority, and on-street parking is limited to 10 minutes. The centre of town is a complicated system of one-way streets designed to ease congestion. The privatized traffic wardens are ruthless in their dedication to duty. Free parking in most of Central Edinburgh is limited to resident parking permit holders only, Mon-Fri 0830-1800, and the police have powers to tow away illegally parked cars. For details of car rental companies based in the city, see page 126.

Bicycle This is just about the best way to get around the city, despite the hilly terrain. Many of the main roads have cycle lanes and there are plenty of cycle routes around the town and out into the countryside. The local cycling association, *Spokes*, T3132114, publishes a very good cycle map (£3, available at the tourist office). For details of rental companies, see under 'Cycle hire', page 126. If you've brought your own bike and need spares, you'll find everything you'll need at *Edinburgh Bicycle Co-op*, 8 Alvanley Terr, T2281368; open Mon-Fri 1000-1900, Sat/Sun 1000-1800.

Getting there
Population: 440,000
Phone code: 0131
See also 'Transport', on page 125.

Edinburgh

Getting around
Traveline runs a public transport information service for Edinburgh, East Lothian and Midlothian: T0800-232323 (local calls), or T0131-2253858 (national calls); Mon-Fri 0830-2000. Their enquiry office is at 2 Cockburn St, near Waverley station.

See also 'Transport' page 125.

Bus Public transport in the city is almost entirely by bus. There are two main companies: *Lothian Regional Transport* (*LRT*) operates maroon and white double deckers and has the most extensive city routes, as well as serving the main towns outside Edinburgh; and *FirstBus* runs the green buses to out-of-town destinations as well as city routes. Most of the city bus services terminate on or near Princes Street, the main thoroughfare at the southern end of the New Town, while most of the out-of-town services leave from and terminate at St Andrews Coach station (see **Ins and outs**, page 67).

The City Council has produced a free map with all the different bus routes around Edinburgh. This is available from the **Tourist Information Centre** (see below) or from the **LRT ticket centres** at 31 Waverley Bridge, T2258616, or 27 Hanover St, T5544494.

Orientation & information Although Greater Edinburgh occupies a large area relative to its population of less than half a million, most of what you'll want to see lies within the compact city centre which is easily explored on foot. The centre is clearly divided in two, with the main thoroughfare, Princes Street, and its gardens, running between them. The **Old Town** is a medieval maze of cobbled streets, wynds and closes on or around the Royal Mile,

Edinburgh & surroundings

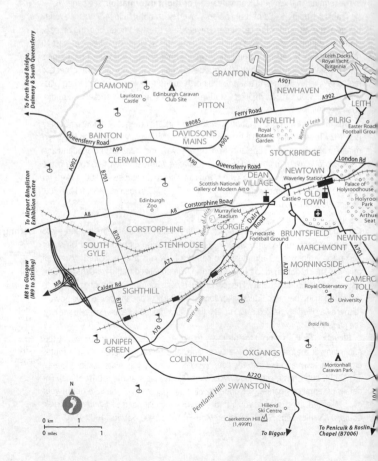

which runs from the castle down to the palace. The **New Town** is the symmetrical lay-out of wide streets lined with elegant Georgian buildings which runs north from Princes Street. Though most of the main sights are within walking distance of each other, Edinburgh is a hilly city and a full day's sightseeing can leave you exhausted. An excellent way to see the sights and avoid wearing out shoe leather is to take one of the **city bus tours** (*Guide Friday* or *LRT*). With a day ticket, you can hop on and off any bus at any time, and there's a tour bus every 15 minutes. For information on bus tours, and the other organized tours in and around Edinburgh, see the 'Tours of Edinburgh' box on page 72.

The city's main **tourist office** is at 3 Princes Street, on top of Waverley Market at the east end of Princes Street, T4733800, F4733881, www.edinburgh.org. Open Apr and Oct Mon-Sat 0900-1800, Sun 1100-1800; May and Sep Mon-Sat 0900-1900, Sun 1100-1900; Jun Mon-Sat 0900-1900, Sun 1000-1900; Jul and Aug Mon-Sat 0900-2000, Sun 1000-2000; Nov-Mar Mon-Sat 0900-1800, Sun 1000-1800. It gets very busy during the peak season and at festival time, but has the full range of services, including currency exchange, and will book accommodation, provide travel

Edinburgh

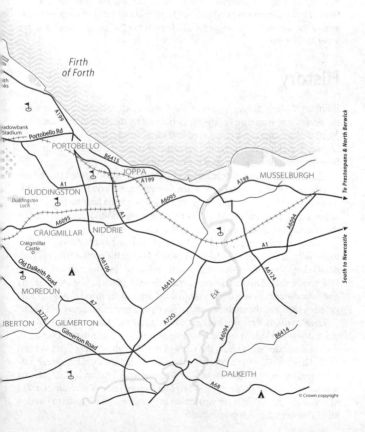

Edinburgh

☞ *Edinburgh's Weather*

To describe Edinburgh's weather as changeable would be a huge understatement. The popular refrain states that if you don't like the weather, then just wait 20 minutes. Perhaps Robert Louis Stevenson best summed up the climatic conditions in his home town, "The weather is raw and boisterous in winter, *shifty and ungenial in summer, and downright meteorological purgatory in spring". So, before you leave your hotel or guest house, be sure to pack your rain jacket, sunglasses, sunblock, thermals, gloves, woolly hat and snow shoes – and maybe an ice axe and crampons in case you fancy a walk up Arthur's Seat.*

information and book tickets for various events and excursions. They also stock a wide range of guides, maps and leaflets for all of Scotland. There's also a tourist information desk at the **airport**, in the international arrivals area, T3332167. It's open Apr-Oct Mon-Sat 0830-2130, Sun 0930-2130; Nov-Mar Mon-Fri 0900-1800, Sat 0900-1700, Sun 0930-1700.

Another useful tourist information resource is the **Backpackers Centre**, 6 Blackfriars St, T5579393 next to *Haggis Backpackers*. They provide information about hostels and tours and will book coach and ferry tickets.

Various **maps of the city** are available, including the Tourist Board's useful foldout map, the very handy Edinburgh Popout Map (£1.50) and the Aero-Plan Map and Guide (£1). A much more detailed and comprehensive map for those wishing to really explore the nooks and crannies of the Old Town is the Ordinance Survey *Edinburgh Street Atlas* (£5.99).

History

Edinburgh's early history begins on the Castle Rock, which was occupied in the Bronze and Iron Age. Following a brief visit by the Romans, the Angles of Northumbria came, saw, conquered and hung around for a while. In the 7th century, their king, Edwin, rebuilt the earlier fortress of Dun Eadain – the Fortress on the Slope – and changed the name to Edwin's Burgh.

The town only began to develop beyond the fortress during the 11th century and the pace of growth quickened when the new king, David I, moved his capital from Dunfermline to Edinburgh in 1124. Four years later he founded his abbey at Holyrood and the Burgh's continued progress was marked in 1329 by the granting of a charter by Robert the Bruce.

During the reigns of James II to IV (1437-1513) the city flourished. The first town wall was built in 1437 (the Wellhouse Tower at the northern foot of Castle Rock is the only remaining trace), followed by the construction of Holyrood Palace. This Renaissance period also saw much patronage of the arts and education, including the granting of a charter to the Royal College of Surgeons in 1506, and the establishment of Scotland's first printing press in 1508.

The Renaissance era was brought to a sudden end, however, by the disastrous defeat at Flodden in 1513, and there followed more than a century of darkness and despair. During the years of the "Rough Wooing", in 1544 and 1547, Henry VIII, never a man to cross, devastated the city. Edinburgh suffered further on Mary, Queen of Scot's return from France, in 1561, during seven turbulent and tragic years. When Mary's son, James VI, became James I of England with the Union of Crowns in 1603, he moved his court to London and Edinburgh slipped into obscurity.

Obscurity did not bring peace, however. The bitter and bloody religious struggle that began in Mary's short reign reached its climax in the 17th century. First, the National Covenant was signed at Greyfriars in 1638, then Cromwell occupied the city in 1650, and in the same year Montrose was executed. Meanwhile, witches continued to be burned on the castle esplanade and over 100 Covenanters were martyred in the Grassmarket.

At the beginning of the following century Edinburgh fared little better. Charles II had rebuilt Holyrood Palace during the Restoration but this proved a false dawn. With the Act of Union of 1707 the city became even less important as a capital. Then came an almost surreal moment, in 1745, with the Jacobite Rebellion, when the Young Pretender held court at Holyrood following his victory at Prestonpans, while the castle remained in government hands.

Towards the end of the 18th century the city's fortunes suddenly changed for the better with the florescence of the Arts and Sciences during the Scottish Enlightenment. Adam Smith, David Hume, Goldsmith, Sir Walter Scott, Robert Louis Stevenson and Allan Ramsay are only a few of the many prominent and brilliant names to feature during the 18th and 19th centuries. Also at this time, the city began to spread outside the confines of its cramped Castle Rock tenements. With the bridging of the Cowgate, building spread southwards beyond the Flodden Wall.

More significantly, the city spread northwards over the next 70 years or so with the building of the most distinguished and extensive area of Georgian architecture in Britain. Two of the most noteworthy landmark events of this period happened in 1818 and 1822. In 1818, Sir Walter Scott instigated a search of the castle for the Scottish regalia, which had been forgotten since 1707. Then, in 1822, he organized the highly successful visit by George IV, the first royal visitor for over a century. The royal visit not only breathed life back into Holyrood Palace, but also revived a feeling of national pride and brought to an end the prevailing mood of despair which had engulfed the nation after defeat at Culloden.

The Industrial Revolution was to affect Edinburgh less than any other city in Britain and it remained essentially professional rather than an industrial. But, though 20th-century development on the whole left the best areas of old and Georgian Edinburgh untouched, the city underwent massive urban expansion, swallowing up many smaller burghs, including the port of Leith.

Since the war Scotland's capital city has gained international recognition as the home of the **Edinburgh International Festival**, and now, at the beginning of the new millenium, is set to take its place on the European political stage with the building of the new **Scottish Parliament**, due to open in 2001 opposite Holyrood.

Sights

The best place to start a tour of Edinburgh is the medieval Old Town, where you'll find most of the famous sights, from the **castle**, down through the **Royal Mile**, to the **Palace of Holyroodhouse**. South of the Royal Mile is the **Grassmarket**, the **Cowgate** and **Chambers Street**, site of the **University of Edinburgh** and two of its best museums, the **Royal Museum of Scotland** and the recently-opened **Museum of Scotland**. The **New Town** also deserves some serious exploration, in particular the excellent **National Gallery**, **Royal Scottish Academy** and **National Portrait Gallery**. A bit further out from the centre are the **Royal Botanic Garden** and the **Gallery of Modern Art**. Though in theory you could "do" the Old Town in a day, you really need several days to do it justice, and to leave yourself enough energy to explore the rest

Edinburgh

☞ **Tours of Edinburgh**

One of the best ways to see the city sights is to take a **guided bus tour** on board an open-top double decker bus. These depart from Waverley Bridge every 15 minutes, the first one leaving around 0900 and the last one between 1730 and 2000, depending on the time of year. The complete tour lasts an hour, stopping at the main tourist sights, but tickets are valid for the full day and you can hop on and off any of the company's buses at any of the stops. The Guide Friday tours are recommended and cost £8 per person (students £6.50/children £2.50). For more information contact the Guide Friday Tourism Centre, 133-135 Canongate, Royal Mile, T5562244, info@guidefriday.com www.guidefriday.com. Lothian Regional Transport (LRT) run similar guided bus tours. These cost £6.50 (students £5.50/children £2.50). Tickets and further information from their city centre offices (see Ins and outs, page 67).

There are various **guided walking tours** of Edinburgh, which fall into roughly two categories: historical tours of the medieval closes and wynds of the Royal Mile during the day, and spooky, nocturnal tours of the city's dark and grisly past. The latter tours also include a visit to the 200 year-old haunted vaults hidden deep beneath the city streets. There are several versions of these tours,

but two of the main operators are Robin's Tours, T/F5579933, whose tours begin outside the tourist office, and Mercat Tours, T/F2256591, who leave from the Mercat Cross by St Giles Cathedral. There are also guided walking tours of **Arthur's Seat** with Geowalks, T5555488, info@geowalks.demon.co.uk, www.geowalks.demon.co.uk.

Most of these guided walking tours last around two hours and cost £5-6 per person.

During the Festival in August the Edinburgh Voluntary Guides take small group of tourists on **free guided tours** from the Castle Esplanade down to the Palace of Holyroodhouse. Just turn up at Cannonball House (by the entrance to the esplanade) between 1000 and 1100 and 1400 and 1500, or call T6647180/ 5568854.

Those who prefer a little libation with their guided tour should try the highly-acclaimed **Edinburgh Literary Pub Tour**, a witty exploration of the city's distinguished literary past, which starts at the Beehive Inn in the Grassmarket. The two-hour tour costs £7 per person (students £5). Tickets can be booked at the tourist office or direct from The Scottish Literary Tour Company, T2266665/7, F2266668, info@scot-lit-tour.co.uk, www.scot-lit-tour.co.uk.

of the city. You should also leave enough time to enjoy the wild, open country-side of **Holyrood Park** and take a stroll up **Arthur's Seat**, from where you get stupendous views of the whole city and beyond.

Edinburgh Castle

The city skyline is dominated by the castle, Scotland's prime tourist attraction and the most-visited sight in Britain outside London. The castle sits on top of an extinct volcano, protected on three sides by steep cliffs, and is well worth a visit, if only for the great views over the city from the battlements.

History Not surprisingly, such a strategic site has been the focus of much attention over the centuries. The Picts, Scots, British (Welsh) and Angles disputed ownership of the Castle Rock until the Scots finally came out on top. Edinburgh then went on to become established as Scotland's capital but, due to its proximity to England, was under constant threat of invasion from south of the border. Since 1174, when it was held by the English for 12 years, the castle defences have

Edinburgh Castle

Edinburgh

hardly had a moment's rest. In 1296 King Edward I occupied this prime piece of real estate, then, in 1314, the Earl of Moray famously climbed the north face and drove out the English incumbents to reinstate King Robert the Bruce. The castle has withstood many sieges since then – the longest from 1570 to 1573, in defence of Mary, Queen of Scots – but has also been breached on a few occasions. In 1650 it succumbed to Cromwell's New Model Army, and in 1689, when the Duke of Gordon tried, but failed, to hold out against the Protestant army of William of Orange.

Today, the castle is still "invaded" on a regular basis, this time by crowds of rather more benign tourists. You can easily wander round the castle yourself, but for a more colourful introduction to its eventful past, you can join one of the first-rate guided tours.

Around the castle

The castle is entered from the top of the Royal Mile, via the **Esplanade**, which was built in the 18th and 19th centuries as a parade ground. During the Festival, the Esplanade is the setting for the Military Tattoo (see page 120) and from the south wall there are excellent views across to the Pentland Hills. Dotted around the Esplanade are various memorial plaques to members of the Scottish regiments who fell in overseas wars, and several military monuments, including one of Field Marshall Earl Haig, one of the city's most notorious sons, whose insane trench warfare strategy in the First World War led to such horrific casualties.

A drawbridge, the last ever built in Scotland, leads to the 19th century **Gatehouse**, which is flanked by modern statues of Sir William Wallace and Robert the Bruce. The main path then leads steeply up, through the **Portcullis Gate**, to the **Argyll Battery** then the **Mill's Mount Battery**. Every day (except Sundays, Christmas Day and Good Friday) since 1851, the 'One o' clock gun' has been fired from the Mill's Mount Battery as a time-check for the city's office workers. From both batteries there are wonderful views across Princes Street, the New Town and the Firth of Forth.

The steep and winding road continues up past the **Governer's House** and the **New Barracks**, both built in the 18th century (many of the buildings within the castle walls date from the 18th century or later). Then the road turns once more, through Foog's Gate, to the summit of Castle Rock and **St Margaret's Chapel**, the oldest surviving building in the castle, and probably the city itself. The tiny, simple yet beautiful building is said to have been built by Margaret herself, but the Norman style suggests it was constructed later, most likely as a memorial by her son, King David I. Following Cromwell's capture of the Castle in 1650, the chapel was used as an ammunition store, until Queen Victoria had it restored and it was eventually rededicated in 1934. In front of the chapel is the **Half Moon Battery**, which offers the best panoramic views of the city.

South of the chapel is **Crown Square**, the most secure and most important section of the entire complex. The eastern side is taken up by the **Palace**, begun in the 15th century and remodelled in the 16th century for Mary, Queen of

Edinburgh

Scots. Above the main doorway are the initials of Mary and her husband Henry, Lord Darnley. Here, in 1566, the Queen gave birth to James VI, later to become James I of England. Rumour has it that her child was stillborn, and the newborn baby of a serving maid was put in its place, but like much else in Scottish history, the truth will remain elusive.

Later, in 1617, the Palace buildings were extended with the addition of the **Crown Room**, where the **Honours of Scotland** are now displayed – the royal crown, the sceptre and the sword of state. There is no more potent a symbol of Scottish nationhood than these magnificent crown jewels, which were last used for the coronation of Charles II in 1651, an event which incurred the wrath of one Oliver Cromwell, who made repeated unsuccessful attempts to get rid of them. Then, in 1707, the crown jewels were locked away in a chest and forgotten. They were presumed lost for over a century, until Sir Walter Scott initiated a search and rediscovered them in 1818. The oldest of the Honours is the **sceptre**, bestowed on James IV by Pope Alexander VI and later

Central Edinburgh

▲ Sights

1 Assembly Rooms & Music Hall	7 Georgian House	13 National Monument
2 Canongate Tolbooth Museum	8 George Heriot's School	14 Nelson Monument
3 City Chambers	9 John Knox House	15 National Portrait Gallery
4 Dynamic Earth	10 King's Theatre	16 Old Royal High School
5 Festival Theatre Filmhouse	11 Museum of Childhood	17 Parliament House
	12 Museum of Scotland	18 Playhouse Theatre
		19 Ross Open Air Theatre

remodelled for James V. The even more impressive **sword of state** was presented to James IV by Pope Julius II in 1507. The jewel-encrusted **crown** contains the circlet of gold with which Robert the Bruce was crowned at Scone in 1306, and was remade for James V in 1540. Also housed in the Crown Room is the recently-installed **Stone of Destiny** (see below), the seat on which the ancient kings of Scotland were crowned. However, no one knows if this "profoundly uninteresting object" is, in fact, the real stone.

On the south side of the square is James IV's **Great Hall**, once the seat of the Scottish Parliament and later used for state banquets. It now houses a display of arms and armour. On the west side of the square is the 18th century **Queen Anne Barracks**, which now contains the **Scottish United Services Museum**. On the north side stands the neo-Gothic **Scottish National Monument**, designed by Sir Robert Lorimer and a dignified testament to the many tens of thousands of Scottish soldiers killed in the First World War.

From the western end of Crown Square you can descend into the **Vaults**, a series of dark and dank chambers, once used as a prison for French captives during the Napoleonic Wars. One of the rooms contains **Mons Meg**, the massive iron cannon forged here in the reign of James IV (1488-1513). It was said to have had a range of nearly a mile and a half and was used for salutes on royal occasions. It was taken to the Tower of London in 1754, where it stayed until Sir Walter Scott persuaded George IV to return it during the latter's state visit to Scotland in 1822. ■ *T2251012. Apr-Sep daily 0930-1800, Oct-Mar 0930-1700. Last ticket sold 45 minutes before closing. £6.50, £2 children.*

Royal Mile

Running through the heart of the medieval Old town, from the castle down to the **Palace of Holyrood-house**, is the **Royal Mile**, where you'll find a greater concentration of historic buildings than almost anywhere else in Britain. This street was described by Daniel Defoe (who lived in Edinburgh at the beginning of the 18th century) as "perhaps the largest, longest and finest Street for buildings, and Number of Inhabitants, not in Britain only, but in the world". It is also now one of the busiest tourist thoroughfares in the world, especially during the Festival. Consequently, it's full of shops selling tacky souvenirs, but nothing can detract from its sheer magnificence.

Edinburgh

Stone of Destiny

Edinburgh Castle is the home of the famous Stone of Destiny, the subject of much controversy and rumour throughout the country's troubled past.

According to legend, the Stone of Destiny was the biblical "Jacob's Pillow", on which he dreamed of a ladder of angels leading from earth to heaven. The stone is said to have arrived in Scotland from the Holy Land, via Spain and Ireland. The king, Kenneth MacAlpin, moved it to Scone, near Perth, where the ancient coronation custom continued. Rumour has it that the supposed original, stolen by Edward I in 1296, which remained under lock and key in Westminster Abbey until 1996, is a poor substitute of Perthshire sandstone, and that the real article was hidden, to reappear when Scotland regained her sovereignty. Some say Bruce was crowned on it, after which it went with his great ally, Angus Og of the Isles, to Islay for safekeeping.

Students removed the stone from Westminster in 1950 and returned it, briefly, to Scotland. Thereafter, unfolds a farcical tale of substitutes, replicas, claims and counter-claims. Some say the real stone was discovered around 100 years ago buried in Macbeth's ruined fort on Dunsinnan. Could this be the hiding place chosen by the monks of Scone in 1296, or did Macbeth hide it centuries earlier? If the stone – returned so ceremoniously from Westminster to Scotland in 1996 in a vain attempt to restore flagging Tory fortunes north of the border – is a fake, where is the real one? Somebody knows and isn't telling.

The 1,984 yards of the Royal Mile, from the Castle Keep to the Palace, comprises four separate streets: (from top to bottom) **Castlehill**, **Lawnmarket**, the **High Street** and the **Canongate**. Branching out from these is a honeycomb of wynds and closes, entered via archways known as pends. A close is the entrance to a "land" or high-rise tenement block, and wynds are the narrow and winding alleyways giving access to the main street. These were the scene of many important – and sinister – events over the centuries and are certainly worth exploring in detail.

Here, the city's aristocracy, gentry, merchants and commoners lived together, often in the same building, with the upper classes at the bottom and the *hoi polloi* at the top. Until the end of the 18th century, the Old Town was the hub of fashionable society. Indeed, such was the concentration of talent that John Amyat, the King's chemist, remarked that he could stand at the Mercat Cross and "in a few minutes take 50 men of genius by the hand".

At the turn of the 19th century the Old Town was gradually abandoned by the Great and the Good of Edinburgh life, who moved lock, stock and barrel to the New Town in what was called "The Great Flitting". The Old Town deteriorated into an overcrowded slum. People would throw their refuse and sewage out of the tenement windows onto the street, shouting to the passers-by, below with the traditional warning of "Gardyloo" (from the French *garde a l'eau*). Not surprisingly, such a place of filth and squalor was highly vulnerable to epidemics and it is only in the past century that the Royal Mile has been cleaned and turned into one of the most fascinating and picturesque streets in the world.

Castlehill The narrow uppermost part of the Royal Mile nearest the castle is known as Castlehill. Just below the Castle Esplanade is an iron fountain which marks the spot where more than 300 Edinburgh women were burned as witches between 1479 and 1722. Behind the fountain rise Ramsay Gardens, a distinctive and picturesque late 19th century apartment block which grew around the octagonal Goose Pie House, home of 18th century poet Allan Ramsay, author of *The Gentle Shepherd*. The highly desirable apartments were designed by Sir Patrick

Geddes, a pioneer of architectural conservation and town planning, who created them in an attempt to regenerate the Old Town.

At the corner of Castlehill and Castle Wynd is **Cannonball House**, which takes its name from a cannonball embedded in the west wall. According to legend, the cannonball was fired from the Castle during the '45 rebellion, but in fact it marks the high water level of the city's first piped water supply in 1681. Next door is **The Scotch Whisky Heritage Centre**, 354 Castlehill, where you can find out everything you ever wanted to know about Scotland's national drink. The tour consists of a couple of short films explaining the production and blending processes and a ride in a "barrel" through a series of historical tableaux. The best part is the bond bar, where you can sample some of the vast range of malt whiskies on offer before buying a bottle in the gift shop. ■ *Daily Jun-Sep 0930-1800, Oct-May 1000-1730, £4.95, children £2.50, students £3.50, T2200441, www.whisky-heritage.co.uk.*

Across the street is the **Edinburgh Old Town Weaving Company**, which has a real working mill where you can see tartan being woven and a small exhibition. ■ *T2261555. Daily 0900-1730. Free entry to Mill and a small charge for the exhibition.*

A few doors further down, on the corner of Ramsay Lane, is the **Outlook Tower**, which has been one of the capital's top tourist attractions since a **camera obscura** was set up in the hexagonal tower by an optician, Maria Theresa Short, in 1854. The device consists of a giant camera which sweeps around the city and beams the live images onto a tabletop screen, accompanied by a running commentary of the city's past. There's also an exhibition of photographs taken with a variety of home-made pinhole cameras and the rooftop viewing terrace offers fantastic views of the city. ■ *T2263709. Daily Apr-Oct 0930-1800 (later in Jul/Aug), Nov-Mar 1000-1700, £3.95, children £1.95, students £3.10.*

A little further down, on the opposite side of the street is the **Tolbooth Kirk**, whose distinctive spire is the highest in the city and a distinctive feature of the Edinburgh skyline. This impressive Victorian Gothic church was designed by James Gillespie Graham, with the spire and superb interiors by Augustus Pugin, famed for his work on the House of Commons in London. The building was originally intended to house the General Assembly of the Church of Scotland, but they moved across the street in the 1850s. The Tolbooth Kirk was where the city's Gaelic speakers used to worship, until it was closed, in 1981. It has recently been converted into **The Hub**, which houses a café (see 'Cafés', page 112) and the ticket centre for Edinburgh International Festival (see 'Festival information', page 121). It's a great eating, meeting and drinking place during the Festival.

Opposite is the neo-Gothic **New College and Assembly Hall**. Built in 1859, it is the meeting place of the annual General Assembly of the Church of Scotland and also used during the Festival to stage major drama productions.

The Tolbooth Kirk and Assembly Hall mark the top of the Lawnmarket, a much broader street named after the old linen market which was held here. At the northern end is **Milne's Court**, built in 1690 and skilfully renovated in 1971 as student residences. Next comes **James Court**, a very prestigious address, where the philosopher David Hume lived and where Boswell entertained Dr Johnson in 1773.

Back on the Lawnmarket itself is **Gladstone's Land**, 477b Lawnmarket, the most important surviving example 17th century tenement housing in the Old Town, where the cramped conditions meant that extension was only possible in depth or upwards. The magnificent six-storey building, completed in 1620, contains remarkable painted ceilings and was the home of an Edinburgh

Lawnmarket

burgess, Thomas Gledstanes. The reconstructed shop booth on the ground floor has replicas of 17th century goods and the first floor of the house has been refurbished as a typical Edinburgh home of the period. If you like what you see, then you can also stay here (see page 20). ■ *1 Apr-31 Oct Mon-Sat 1000-1700, Sun 1400-1700, £3.20, concession £2.20, T2265856.*

Further down, steps lead down to Lady Stair's Close, where you'll find **Lady Stair's House**, another fine 17th century house, though restored in pseudo-medieval style. It is now the home of the **Writer's Museum**, dedicated to the three giants of Scottish literature, Burns, Scott and Stevenson. ■ *T5294901. Mon-Sat1000-1700, Sun 1400-1700 during the Festival only. Free.*

Opposite Gladstone's Land is **Riddle's Court**, another of David Hume's residences. Here also is the late 16th century house of Bailie McMorran, who was shot dead by pupils of the Royal High School during a riot in 1595 against the proposed reduction in school holidays. Further down the street on the same side is **Brodie's Close**, named after the father of one of Edinburgh's most nefarious characters, Deacon Brodie. He was an apparent pillar of the community by day and a burglar by night, until his eventual capture and hanging in 1788. Robert Louis Stevenson co-wrote a play about his life, which was to provide the inspiration for *Dr Jeckyll and Mr Hyde*.

High Street Across George IV Bridge, at the top of the High Street, stands the **High Kirk of St Giles**, the only parish church of medieval Edinburgh and the home of Presbyterianism, where the firebrand preacher John Knox launched the Scottish Reformation. The Kirk is mistakenly called St Giles Cathedral. This is because Charles I called it so when he introduced bishops into the Church of Scotland and the name stuck, even after Presbyterianism was re-established. The church was given a major face-lift in the 19th century, covering most of its Gothic exterior, but parts of the original medieval building still survive, most notably the late 15th century crowned tower. The four huge octagonal pillars which support the central tower are thought to date back to the previous Norman church, built in 1120 and razed by English invaders in the late 14th century.

The church has had a colourful past ever since medieval times when the Scottish Parliament met here. It was the launchpad for the Reformation, as mentioned above. Then, around the turn of the 16th century, it was divided up and used as law courts, the town clerk's office, a school and a prison. When the High Kirk returned to its religious function it was partitioned into four different churches, each serving its own congregation, finally being reunified after its Victorian restoration.

One of the most celebrated incidents in the church's history happened in 1637, when an attempt to read from the English prayer book so incensed Jenny Geddes, a humble stallholder, that she launched her stool at the bishop's head, shouting (according to tradition): "False thief, will ye no say mass about my lug?", which roughly translates as "stop saying mass". A plaque marks the spot where it hit and records the ensuing riot. Such disturbances led to the National Covenenant of 1638, establishing the Presbyterian Church of Scotland in defiance of Charles I. This in turn led to Civil War, during which many Covenanters were imprisoned in the church. Two of the most famous figures of the war, the royalist Marquis of Montrose and the convenanting Marquis of Argyll, were both executed outside the church and now lie entombed within its walls, facing each other from opposite aisles.

There have been many additions to the High Kirk since its restoration. One of these is the very beautiful **Thistle Chapel**, the Chapel of the Most Ancient and Most Noble Order of the Thistle (Scotland's foremost order of chivalry). It was designed by Sir Robert Lorimer and built in 1911. The elaborate

24 hours in Edinburgh

For those unlucky enough only to have a day to spend in Edinburgh, the following itinerary should give a taste of why it is the most visited British city outside London.

*Start the day at the Castle, after which you'll need a breather and a well-earned coffee break at the Elephant House, on George IV Bridge. Afterwards, head across the road to the excellent **Museum of Scotland** in Chambers Street.*

If you're feeling peckish, take a wee stroll down to Black Bo's on Blackfriars Street for a superb vegetarian lunch.

*Then head down towards Princes Street and pop into the **National Gallery of Scotland**, the city's finest art gallery. If you've still got plenty of energy, head up The Mound and down the Royal Mile to the **Palace of Holyroodhouse**.*

If the weather's fine, you may fancy a walk up to Calton Hill for the wonderful views, then head down to the nearby Pivo Caffe for a drink.

Then it's into a taxi and down to Leith for a superb seafood dinner at Fishers.

ornamentation and fine carvings are exquisite (look out for the angel playing the bagpipes). There are also several Pre-Raphaelite stained glass windows in the church, and above the west door is a memorial window to Robert Burns, rather surprising given that the great bard was hardly an upholder of Presbyterian values. There's a good café in the church crypt (see 'Cafés', page 112).

Outside the High Kirk of St Giles, on **Parliament Square**, is an imposing equestrian statue of King Charles II and, nearby, a flat stone bearing the legend "I.K. 1572" marks the reputed burial place of John Knox. In front of the west door of the church is the site of the city Tolbooth, demolished in 1817. The Tolbooth entrance is marked by a heart-shaped pattern in the cobblestones, known as the **Heart of Midlothian**, and made famous by Sir Walter Scott in his eponymous novel. Should you see passers-by spitting on it, it's not a sign of disrespect, but supposed to bring good luck. Behind the church is the **Mercat Cross**, where public proclamations are traditionally read. The present cross is a replica, gifted to the city by the then prime-minister, WE Gladstone.

The rest of Parliament Square is formed by the Law Courts, Parliament House and the Signet Library. The **Law Courts**, where Sir Walter Scott practised as an advocate, were originally planned by Robert Adam (1728-1792), who contributed so much to the grace and elegance of the New Town, but due to lack of funds, built to designs by Robert Reid (1776-1856). On the west side of the square is the **Signet Library**, centre for the Society of Her Majesty's Writers to the Signet, an organization that originated from the 15th century Keepers of the King's Seal, or signet. It boasts one of the finest neo-Classical interiors in the city, but unfortunately can only seen by prior written application, except on very occasional open days. **Parliament House**, facing the south side of St Giles, was the meeting place of the Scots Parliament between 1639 and 1707. It is now used by the city's lawyers in between court sittings, but is readily accessible during the week. The most notable feature is the magnificent Parliament Hall with its wonderful 17th century hammerbeam roof. There's also a fine collection of portraits and statuary.

On the opposite side of the High Street is **Edinburgh City Chambers**, designed by John Adam (brother of Robert) and built in 1761 as the Royal Exchange. However, it proved not to the liking of the city's traders, who preferred to conduct their business in the street, so in the early 19th century it became the headquarters of the city council. Beneath the city chambers is **Mary King's Close**, closed off for many years after the 1645 plague and now open to guided tours (see 'Tours of Edinburgh', on page 72). A little further down is

Edinburgh skyline

Anchor Close, where the first editions of *Encyclopaedia Britannica* and of Robert Burns' poems were printed at the printing works of William Smellie.

At the junction of the High Street and South Bridge is the **Tron Kirk**, founded in 1637, and now more famously known as a favourite Hogmanay rendezvous. The church was named after the Tron, a public weighing beam which stood close by and which was a popular place for merchants to sell their wares. If they were found guilty of selling short measures, they were nailed to the Tron by their ears. The church was built to accommodate the Presbyterian congregation ejected from St Giles during the latter's brief period as a cathedral and continued in use until it was closed in 1952. It now houses the Old Town tourist information centre, and recent excavations have revealed sections of Marlin's Wynd, which ran from the High Street down to the Cowgate.

Past the junction of the North and South Bridges, on the north side of the High Street, is **Carruber's Close**, where Sir James Simpson, the discoverer of chloroform, ran a medical dispensary in the 1860s. Above the entrance to **Paisley Close** is the bust of a boy saved from beneath the rubble when the tenement collapsed in 1861, killing 35 inhabitants, an incident which helped to hasten the much-needed improvement of the Old Town's buildings. The memorial bears the inscription, "Heave awa', chaps, I'm no dead yet", shouted by the boy as he was dug out of the rubble by rescue workers.

In Chalmers Close, just to the west, is **Trinity Apse**, a sad reminder of the Holy Trinity Church, one of Edinburgh's finest pieces of Gothic architecture, demolished in 1848 to make room for the railway line to Waverley. The stones from the original were carefully numbered for rebuilding on the present site, but pilfering depleted the stock so much that only the apse could be reconstructed, in 1852, on the present site. It is now a **Brass Rubbing Centre**, where you can make your own rubbings from the materials supplied. ■ *Mon-Sat 1000-1700; also Sun 1200-1700, during the Festival only, free, T5564364.*

On the opposite side of the High Street, in Hyndford's Close, is the **Museum of Childhood**, the "noisiest museum in the world" which is full of kids screaming with excitement at the vast collection of toys, dolls, games and books, and nostalgic adults yelling "I used to have one of those!". There's even a video history of the various Gerry Anderson TV puppet series such as *Thunderbirds* and *Fireball XL5*. The museum also covers the serious issues of childhood, such as health and education, but that doesn't spoil the sheer fun of the place. ■ *Mon-Sat 1000-1700 and Sun 1400-1700 during the Festival, free, T5294142.*

Almost directly opposite is the early 16th century **Moubray House**, thought to be the oldest inhabited building in Edinburgh, though closed to the public. This is where Daniel Defoe was based when he came to Edinburgh in 1706 as an English agent to help negotiate the Act of Union. Next door is **John Knox's House**, dating from the late 15th century and added to in the 16th century. It is one of the Royal Mile's most distinctive buildings, with its crow-stepped gable, overhanging wooden galleries and outside staircases to different levels of the house. It's not known for sure whether or not the Calvinist preacher actually lived here, but the house did belong to James Mossman, goldsmith to Mary, Queen of Scots. Today, the house is a museum to the life and career of John Knox. ■ *T5569579/2647. Mon-Sat 1000-1700 (in Aug also Sun 1200-1700). £1.95, students £1.50, children 75p.*

Canongate

The High Street ends at the junction of St Mary's Street and Jeffrey Street, where the city's eastern gate, Netherbow Port, once stood. The remaining part of the Royal Mile, the Canongate, was a separate burgh for over 700 years, taking its name from the canons (priests) of Holyrood Abbey. As it was near the Palace of Holyroodhouse, the area developed as the court quarter with several fine residences being built there. Though the Canongate went into decline once the court moved to London in the early 17th century, it could still boast an impressive number of aristocrats among its inhabitants, even in the late 18th century.

Many of the buildings in the Canongate have been ambitiously restored in recent decades. These include **Chessel's Court**, where Deacon Brodie was finally caught, and, opposite, **Morocco Land**, named after a 17th century adventurer who retired here after a career of piracy among the Moors. Further east is **Moray House**, the most lavish of Canongate's mansions, built in 1628 for the daughter of Lord Darnley. Charles I visited here on several occasions and Cromwell used it as his headquarters in 1648. And if that weren't enough historical significance, in 1707 the Treaty of Union was signed in a summerhouse in the garden. More recently, the building has been used as the centre for Moray house College of Education, one of Scotland's leading teacher-training establishments.

A little further east is the 16th century **Huntly House**, the city's main local history museum. Among its displays from Edinburgh's past is a collection of old shop signs. Also on view is the original copy of the National Covenant of 1638. ■ *T5294143. Mon-Sat 1000-1700 and Sun 1400-1700 during the Festival. Free.*

Opposite Huntly House is the late 16th century **Canongate Tolbooth**, the original headquarters of the burgh administration, as well as the courthouse and burgh prison. It now houses **The People's Story**, a genuinely interesting museum which describes the life and work of the ordinary people of Edinburgh from the late 18th century to the present day. The museum is filled with the sights, sounds and smells of the past and includes reconstructions of a prison cell, a workshop and a pub among others. ■ *T5294057. Mon-Sat 1000-1700 and Sun 1400-1700 during the Festival.*

Next door to the Tolbooth is the **Canongate Kirk**, built in 1688 to house the congregation expelled from Holyrood Abbey when it was taken over by James VII (II of England) to be used as the chapel for the Order of the Thistle. The church is built in a cruciform plan, unusually for the Protestant religion. More interesting, though, is the churchyard, burial place of many famous people. Among the list of notable names is Adam Smith, the father of political economy, who lived in Panmure House nearby, the philosopher Dugald Stewart and Robert Fergusson, arguably Edinburgh's greatest poet who died tragically at the tender age of 23 after being forced into the local madhouse during a bout of depression. Robert Burns, who was greatly inspired by Fergusson's poetry, donated the headstone in 1787, inscribed with his own personal tribute. Beyond the Canongate Kirk is the little-known "mushroom garden", a walled garden laid out in 17th-century style.

Further east, on the south side of the Canongate, is **Queensberry House**, former home of the second Duke of Queensberry, who accepted a bribe of £12,000 to push through the Treaty of Union in 1707, thus ending Scotland's independence.

At the foot of the Canongate, is **White Horse Close**, restored in 1964 and named after Mary, Queen of Scots' white palfrey. The stables for Holyroodhouse are thought to have been located here, and later the coaching inn from where stagecoaches began the journey south to London.

The last few yards of the Royal Mile, which forms the approach to the precincts of Holyrood Abbey and Palace, is known as the **Abbey Strand**. The strange little turreted 16th century building here is known as **Queen Mary's Bath House**, where, legend has it, Mary, Queen of Scots bathed in sweet white wine. However, it is more likely that it was a summer pavilion or dovecot.

Opposite the main gates of the Palace of Holyroodhouse is the site of the new **Scottish Parliament** building, due to open in 2001. At present (Spring 2000), the parliament sits in the Church of Scotland headquarters, on The Mound.

Holyrood

At the foot of the Royal Mile lies Holyrood, Edinburgh's royal quarter. According to legend King David I, son of Malcolm Canmore and St Margaret, was out hunting on this site one day in 1128, when he was charged by a huge stag and thrown from his horse. The stag then tried to gore him, and the king grabbed hold of its antlers to protect himself, only to find that he was instead holding a crucifix set between the horns. The stag then disappeared, leaving the crucifix in his hands. That night in a dream he was commanded to build a "house for Canons devoted to the Cross", and so he founded an Augustinian abbey of the Holy Rood (another word for Cross) on the site of his miraculous escape.

The Palace of Holyroodhouse began life as the abbey guest house, until James IV transformed it into a royal palace at the beginning of the 16th century. The only remaining part of the Renaissance palace is the northwest tower, built as the private apartments of his son James V. Most of the original building was damaged by fire in 1543 and further in 1650 during its occupation by Cromwell's troops, never the most considerate of guests.

The present palace largely dates from the late 17th century when the original was replaced by a larger building for the Restoration of Charles II, although the newly-crowned monarch never actually set foot in the place. It was built in the style of a French chateau, around a large arcaded quadrangle and is an elegant, finely-proportioned creation. Designed by William Bruce, it incorporates a castellated southwest tower that balances perfectly the northwest original.

Inside, the oldest part of Holyroodhouse is open to the public and is entered through the **Great Gallery**, which takes up the entire first floor of the north wing. Here, during the '45 rebellion, Bonnie Prince Charlie held court, and it is still used for big ceremonial occasions. The walls are adorned with over one hundred portraits of Scottish Kings, most of them mythical, beginning with 'Fergus I, BC 330' and ending with James VI. Commissioned from the Flemish artist, Jacobus de Wet, they have been described as "paltry daubings [...] painted either from the imagination, or porters hired to sit for the purpose". They certainly make for some amusing viewing.

The **Royal Apartments**, in the northwest tower, are mainly of note for their association with Mary, Queen of Scots and in particular for the most infamous incident in the palace's long history. It was here that the queen witnessed the brutal murder, organized by her husband, Lord Darnley, of her much-favoured Italian private secretary, David Rizzio. He was stabbed 56 times, on a spot marked by a brass plaque and, until it was removed quite recently, by a distinctly unsubtle fake bloodstain.

The later parts of the palace, known as the **State Apartments**, are less interesting, though decorated in Adam Style, with magnificent white stucco ceilings, particularly the Throne Room and Dining room. These are associated with later monarchs, such as George IV, who paid a visit in 1822, dressed in flesh-coloured tights and the briefest of kilts, rather appropriately perhaps, given the length of time he actually spent here. But it was Queen Victoria and Prince Albert who returned the palace to royal favour, as a stopover on their way to and from Balmoral. This custom has been maintained by her successors and the present queen still spends a short while here every year at the end of June and beginning of July. ■ *Daily; 1 Apr-31 Oct 0930-1800 and 1 Nov-31 Mar 0930-1630. Guided tours only take place from Nov-Mar. Closed to the public during state functions and during the annual royal visit in the last two weeks of Jun and first week in Jul, £5.50, children £2.70, family £13, T5561096.*

In the grounds of the palace are the wonderfully romantic ruins of Holyrood Abbey, said to have inspired Mendelssohn's opening movement of his "Scottish Symphony" during a visit in 1829. The only surviving part of King David's Norman church is a doorway in the far southeastern corner. Most of the remains date from the early 13th century.

Holyrood Abbey

The abbey was, at its height, a building of great importance and splendour, and this is hinted at in the surviving parts of the west front. Much of it was destroyed, as were many of the county's finest ecclesiastical buildings, during the Reformation. During the reign of Charles I it was converted to the Chapel Royal and later to the Chapel of the Order of the Thistle, but it suffered severe damage once more, this time during the 1688 revolution. Some restoration work was attempted in the 18th century, but this only caused the roof to collapse in 1768, and since then the building has been left as a ruin. In the Royal Vault beneath the abbey are buried several Scottish Kings, including David II (son of Robert the Bruce), James II, James V and Lord Darnley, "King Consort" to Mary, Queen of Scots.

Holyrood Park Edinburgh is blessed with many magnificent green, open spaces, and none better than Holyrood Park – or Queen's Park – a 650-acre rugged wilderness of mountains, crags, lochs, moorland, marshes, fields and glens – all within walking distance of the city centre. This is one of the city's greatest assets, and it's easy to wander around till you're lost from the eyes and ears of civilization.

The park's main feature, and the city's main landmark, is **Arthur's Seat**, the igneous core of another extinct volcano, and the highest of Edinburgh's hills (822ft). It is probably named after Arthur, Prince of Strathclyde, rather than King Arthur of legend, as many believe. Another dominating feature of the Edinburgh skyline is the precipitous **Salisbury Crags**, lying directly opposite the south gates of the palace.

The best walk in the city is to the summit of **Arthur's Seat**, from where you get the very best view of the city, as well as the Pentland Hills to the south, the Firth of Forth and Fife to the north, and, on a clear day, to the Highland peaks, 70 or 80 miles away. The walk to the top is a popular one, and easier than it looks. If you want to avoid the crowds during summer, then make an early start before breakfast and watch the sun rise over East Lothian.

There are several different routes, all of which take less than an hour, but a good circular one that takes in the wilder bits and the lochs, starts from **St Margaret's Loch**, little more than artificial pond, at the far end of the park from the palace. To reach the loch, follow Queen's Drive east (left) from the palace for about two thirds of a mile (1 km) and it's on the right. Leave the car park beside the loch and head around the loch up towards the 15th century ruin of **St Anthony's Chapel**. Pass the ruined chapel on your right and after a few hundred yards you'll see the main summit towering above you on the right. Keeping the summit to your right, climb over a saddle which joins the path up from **Dunsapie Loch**, which you can see below you on the left, and continue up a rocky path to the top.

Dunsapie Loch is overshadowed by **Dunsapie Hill**, which makes a great place for an evening picnic and from here it's an easy drop down to **Duddingston Village**, just outside the park boundary, and one of the most attractive and unspoilt of the old villages that have become part of the city suburbs. The village **Kirk** dates back to the 12th century and the *Sheep Heid Inn* (see 'Bars', on page 116) is a great place to stop off for some liquid sustenance and a bite to eat. Adjoining the village, on the south side of Arthur's Seat, is **Duddingston Loch**, the largest of the park's lochs, which is a sanctuary for waterfowl. It can also be reached via Queen's Drive, heading right from the palace for about four miles.

There are other routes to the top of Arthur's Seat. One starts opposite the palace car park and winds up by the foot of Salisbury Crags, This is the **Radical Road**, built in 1820 and so called because Sir Walter Scott suggested it be constructed by a group of unemployed weavers from the west, who were believed to hold radical political views. This is where James Hutton is said to have dreamt up the idea of geology by looking at the rock formations. The road traverses the ridge below the crags and continues on grass through "Hunter's Bog" and up to the summit. You can also walk along the top of the crags, though there is no path.

South of the Royal Mile

The Royal Mile is the main tourist attraction, but there are some interesting, and sometimes even quiet, corners of the Old Town to be found not so very far away from the hordes.

Holyrood Road runs from the palace back to the Old Town, running parallel to and south of the Canongate. Close to the palace is one of the city's newest attractions, and now one of its most popular, **Dynamic Earth**. This is one of many Millenium Projects funded by National Lottery funds and has proved one of the most successful. The visitor is taken on a fascinating journey of discovery from the very beginnings of time right through to the future. Using the state-of-the-art technology and special effects, you'll experience every environment on Earth and encounter many weird and wonderful creatures. An absolute must if you've kids in tow and you're guaranteed to find out things you never knew. ■ *Daily Apr-Oct 1000-1800, Nov-Mar 1000-1700, £5.95, children £3.50, T5507800, www.dynamicearth.co.uk.*

Holyrood to the Cowgate

Holyrood Road continues west till it's crossed by the Pleasance and becomes the **Cowgate**, one of Edinburgh's oldest streets and once one of its finest. It runs almost parallel to the High Street, but on a much lower level, and when the South and George IV bridges were built over it, linking the Old and New Towns, it was half-buried below street level and reduced to a dark, desolate canyon of neglect and decay. In recent years the Cowgate has become one of the city's best night-life streets, with many good pubs and clubs, but it attracts few tourists, and remains a spooky place to wander in alone after dark.

There are, however, a couple of very notable and very interesting buildings here. At the corner of Niddry Street is the exquisite **St Cecilia's Hall**, built in 1763 for the Edinburgh Musical Society. The interior, modelled on the opera house at Parma, is stunningly beautiful, with an oval music hall and concave elliptical ceiling. In the 18th century it was the city's main concert hall, and since its restoration in 1966 has again been used as a venue for concerts, especially during the Festival (see also 'Entertainment', on page 118). The Hall also houses the **Russell Collection** of early keyboard instruments for Edinburgh's University's Music Department. ■ *Wed and Sat 1400-1700. £3.*

Further west along the Cowgate is **Magdalen Chapel**, founded in 1541. The unremarkable façade is Victorian but the fine interior is Jacobean and worth a look, in particular to see the only pre-Reformation Scottish stained glass still in its original position. ■ *Mon-Fri 0930-1630. Free.*

The Cowgate passes beneath George IV bridge to become the Grassmarket, a wide cobbled street closed in by tall tenements and dominated by the castle looming overhead. The Grassmarket, formerly the city's cattle market, has been the scene of some of the more notorious incidents in the city's often dark and grisly past. The public gallows were located here and over a hundred hanged Covenanters are commemorated with a cross at its east end. It was in the Grassmarket, in 1763, where Captain Porteous was lynched by an angry mob after he had ordered shots to be fired at them as they watched a public execution. At the west end, in a now vanished close, is where **Burke and Hare** lured their hapless murder victims, whose bodies they then sold to the city's medical schools. The gruesome business finally came to an end, when Burke betrayed his partner in crime, who was duly executed in 1829. Today, the Grassmarket is one of the main nightlife centres, with lots of busy restaurants and bars lining its north side. One of these, the *White Hart Inn*, was patronized by Robert Burns.

Grassmarket to George IV Bridge

Edinburgh

At the northeastern corner of Grassmarket are the few remaining buildings of the old **West Bow**, which once zig-zagged up to the Royal Mile. It was swept away in the early 19th century and replaced with **Victoria Street**, an attractive two-tiered street with arcaded shops below and a pedestrian terrace above. This curves up from the Grassmarket to **George IV Bridge** and the **National Library of Scotland**, founded in 1682 and one of the largest public libraries in the UK. It holds a rich collection of early printed books and manuscripts, historical documents and the letters and papers of notable national literary figures, which are displayed for the public. ■ *Mon-Sat 1000-1700. Free.*

Greyfriars & around

At the southwestern end of George IV Bridge, at the top of Candlemaker Row, is the statue of **Greyfriars Bobby**, the faithful little Skye terrier who watched over the grave of his master John Gray, a shepherd from the Pentland Hills, for 14 years until his own death in 1872. During this time Bobby became something of a local celebrity and was cared for by locals who even gave him his own collar (now in the Huntly House Museum, see page 81), and every day, on hearing the one o'clock gun, he would go to the local pub (now named in his honour) to be fed. By the time of his death, his fame had spread to such an extent that Queen Victoria herself suggested that he be buried beside his master. The little statue, modelled from life and erected soon after his death, is one of the most popular, and sentimental, of Edinburgh's attractions, thanks to a number of tear-jerking movies of the wee dog's life.

The grave that Bobby watched over is the nearby **Greyfriars Kirkyard**, one of Edinburgh's most prestigious burial grounds. Here lie the poet Allan Ramsay, the architects John and Robert Adam, the philanthropist George Heriot (see below), James Douglas, Earl of Morton and Regent of Scotland during James VI's minority, and the poet Duncan Ban McIntyre (1724-1812) whose epic *Beinn Dorain* is considered one of the greatest poems in the Gaelic language. Some of the memorials are protected with metal lattices. This was to defeat the efforts of body-snatchers. One woman was buried here while in a trance and awoke when body-snatchers tried to remove the rings from her fingers.

Greyfriars is particularly associated with the long struggle to establish the Presbyterian church in Scotland. The kirkyard was the first place where the National Covenant was signed, on 28 February, 1638. Later, in 1679, over 1,200 Covenanters were imprisoned in a corner of the kirkyard for three months, and many died of exposure and starvation.

Greyfriars Kirk, somewhat overshadowed by the graveyard, dates from 1620 and was the first church to be built in Edinburgh after the Reformation. It's an odd mix of styles, with Gothic windows and buttresses taken from the nearby Franciscan Friary and a second church joined on to the west end in 1722 in place of the spire which was destroyed in 1718. In 1938 the dividing wall between the two churches was removed, creating one long spireless church.

West of Greyfriars Kirkyard, and reached from Lauriston Place, is **George Heriot's Hospital School**, one of the finest pieces of Renaissance architecture in Scotland. It was founded as a school for the teaching of "puir fatherless bairns" in 1659 by "Jinglin' Geordie" Heriot, James VI's goldsmith, although it had previously been used as a hospital by Cromwell during the Civil War. It is now one of Edinburgh's most prestigious fee-paying schools. You can't go inside but you can wander round the quadrangle and admire the towers, turrets and carved doorways of this fine palatial building.

West of George Heriot's, leading north off Lauriston Place, is the **Vennel**, a narrow passage of steps that descends to the Grassmarket. On the eastern side is the best surviving section of the **Flodden Wall**, the old city wall built in the wake of Scotland's disastrous defeat at Flodden in 1513.

Across the road from Greyfriars Bobby, running between George IV Bridge and South Bridge, is Chambers Street, home of two of the best museums in Scotland. On the corner of Chambers Street and George IV Bridge is the **Museum of Scotland**, a striking contemporary building housing a huge number of impressive Scottish collections which were transferred from the National Museum of Antiquities. The museum is a veritable treasure trove of intriguing and important artefacts, including Roman gold and silver, Pictish and Gaelic carved stones and medieval armour. One of the most popular exhibits is "The Maiden", Edinburgh's once-busy guillotine. The Museum also contains an excellent rooftop restaurant, *The Tower* (see 'Eating', on page 107). ■ *Mon-Sat 1000-1700 (Tue 1000-2000), Sun 1200-1700, £3, concession £1.50, children free, (free admission on Tue 1630-1800). Admission to the Museum of Scotland includes access to the Royal Museum (see below), T2474422, www.nms.ac.uk.*

Further east along Chambers Street, on the same side, is the **Royal Museum of Scotland**. The extensive and eclectic range of collections on display include everything from Classical Greek sculptures to stuffed elephants, from whale skeletons to Native North American totem poles. It's all here, beautifully-presented in a wonderful Victorian building, designed by Captain Francis Fowkes of the Royal Engineers (architect of the Royal Albert Hall in London) and built in 1888 in the style of an Italianate palace. Of particular note is the largely hands-on technology section which features a dazzling collection of machinery of the Industrial Revolution. The magnificent atrium soars high above and makes a very impressive entrance to what is probably the most complete museum in the country. To cap it all, there's a great café (see 'Cafés', page 112). ■ *Same opening hours and admission prices as the Museum of Scotland, which is included on the combined-entry ticket, T2257534.*

Alongside the Royal Museum is the earliest surviving part of the **University of Edinburgh**, the **Old College**, although only a few departments are now housed there. Edinburgh University is the largest in Scotland (the oldest is St Andrews), founded in 1582. The Old College, built between 1789 and 1834, was originally designed by Robert Adam, but on his death in 1792 very little had been completed and his grandiose plans had to be abandoned due to lack of funds. WH Playfair was later commissioned to finish the job, in 1815. The final building is a single large court, instead of Adam's two, and its finest section is the **upper library**, a magnificent architectural achievement, which is now used for mainly ceremonial occasions. Another of Playfair's fine galleries, the upper museum hall, once housed the Royal Museum before it moved to its present site, and now is the home of the **Talbot Rice Gallery**, which features the University's collection of Renaissance European painting as well as several temporary exhibitions every year. ■ *Tue-Sat 1000-1700 (daily during the Fesitval), free, T6502210. There are also free lunchtime guided tours of the Old College, from 19 Jul-28 Aug, Mon-Sat, starting at 1300 at the reception, T6506379.*

The main University campus is further south, around **George Square**. Among the most notable buildings there is the Faculty of Music's **Reid Concert Hall** (see also 'Entertainment', on page 118), built in 1858 in Italian Renaissance style. The University's chief ceremonial centre is the **McEwan Hall**, a huge Italian-style basilica completed in 1897.

Chambers Street and the University

Edinburgh

The New Town

The neo-classical New Town, one of the boldest schemes of civic architecture in the history of Europe, is what makes Edinburgh a truly world-class city, every bit as impressive as Paris or Prague, Rome or Vienna. Built in a great burst of creativity between 1767 and 1840, it was the product of the Scottish Enlightenment. Even today, it is still inconceivable how, in the words of one historian, "a small, crowded, almost medieval town, the capital of a comparatively poor country, expanded in a short space of time, without foreign advice or foreign assistance, so as to become one of the enduringly beautiful cities of western Europe."

The New Town was essentially conceived by Edinburgh's forceful Lord Provost (Lord Mayor), **George Drummond**, who wanted his city to be a tribute to the Hanoverian-ruled United Kingdom, which he had helped create. His plan was to extend the city northwards onto a rectangular plateau known as Barefoot Parks, on the far side of the Nor' Loch (north loch) under the castle rock. Work began on draining the loch in 1759, to make way for Princes Street Gardens, and, five years later, construction began on the North Bridge, which would give access to the New Town. The following year a competition was announced for the plans and the winner was an unknown 22 year-old architect, **James Craig**. His design symbolized the union of Scotland and England, reflected in many of the street names. The grand central thoroughfare of the First New Town, as the area came to be known, is **George Street**, named in honour of the king. It links two great civic squares, **St Andrew** in the east and St George's (later to become Charlotte) in the west. On either side of George Street, and running parallel to it, are two long lanes, **Thistle Street** and **Rose Street**, symbolizing the national emblems of the two countries. Traversing George Street are **Hanover Street** and **Frederick Street**.

The grid-iron pattern is a model of unity, simplicity and regularity, but its overriding success is the use made of the available space. Princes Street and Queen Street are both singles terraces, facing respectively south to the Castle and north towards the Firth of Forth. The beautiful symmetry of the plan and great views on offer were exploited fully by architect Robert Adam, who contributed greatly to the later phases of the work with many elegant neo-Classical buildings.

The speed with which the New Town was built is astonishing, considering the quality of the building. By the end of the century most of George Street, Castle Street, Frederick Street and Princes Street was in place as well as **Register House**, the north side of **Charlotte Square**, the **Assembly Rooms and Music Hall**, and **St Andrew's Church**.

Princes Street The southernmost terrace of the New Town plan was never intended to be the most important, but Princes Street has developed into the city's main thoroughfare and principal shopping street. It is also one of the most visually spectacular streets in the world, because the south side has remained undeveloped, allowing superb uninterrupted views of the Castle Rock, across the valley now occupied by Princes Street Gardens. The north side of the street has lost any semblance of style and is now an undistinguished jumble of modern architecture. Princes Street may be Edinburgh's equivalent of Oxford Street in London, but at least the magnificent view makes walking its length a more pleasant experience.

Everything worthwhile in Princes Street is on the south side, with a few notable exceptions. At the far northeast end of the street is **Register House** (1774-1834), one of Adam's most sumptuous and glorious buildings and now the headquarters of the Scottish Record Office, which stores historical and legal documents – including birth, marriage and death certificates, wills and census records – dating as far back as the 13th century. Unfortunately, the effect of such a superb building is somewhat marred by the **St James Centre**, a huge modern shopping complex that rears its ugly head behind and serves as an unhappy testament to the city's single greatest planning blunder.

Directly opposite is **North Bridge**, built originally in the 1760s as the main artery between the Old and New Towns and completely rebuilt in the late 19th century to span Waverley station. North Bridge runs between the city's main post office and the **Balmoral Hotel**, one of the most luxurious of the city's hotels and a major landmark. Beside the hotel, the **Waverley Market** is a tasteful modern shopping complex, sunk discreetly below street level, and in stark contrast to the St James Centre. The roof gives access to the Tourist Office and forms a nice open-air piazza.

Running along most of the south side of Princes Street are the sunken **Princes Street Gardens**, which were formed by the draining of Nor' Loch in the 1760s and are now a very pleasant place to sit and relax during the summer. Standing in East Princes Street Gardens, is the towering **Scott Monument**, over 200ft high and resembling a huge Gothic spaceship, and built in 1844 as a fitting tribute to one of Scotland's greatest literary figures. It was designed by a self-taught architect called George Meikle Kemp, who tragically drowned in a canal shortly before the monument was completed. Beneath the archway is a statue of Sir Walter Scott, and there are also 64 statuettes of characters from his novels. The monument is open to the public, and a 287-step staircase climbs to a platform near the top of the spire, from where you get wonderful views. ■ *Mar-May and Oct daily 1000-1800; Jun-Sep Mon-Sat 0900-2000, Sun 1000-1800; Nov-Feb 1000-1600. £2.50.* Opposite the Scott Monument is the other notable building on the north side of Princes Street, the elegant 19th century department store, **Jenners**, Edinburgh's answer to Harrods.

A little further west, Princes Street gardens are divided in two by **The Mound**, a huge artificial slope that runs from George IV Bridge in the Old Town down to Princes Street, and was formed by dumping the earth excavated during the building of the New Town. At the junction of The Mound and Princes Street are two of Edinburgh's most impressive neo-classical public buildings, the **Royal Scottish Academy** and the **National Gallery of Scotland**, both designed by William Playfair between 1822 and 1845 in the style of Greek temples. The oldest of the two is the Royal Scottish Academy, which presents an annual exhibition by its members from April to July and special exhibitions during the Festival. To the rear of the RSA, the National Gallery of Scotland houses the largest permanent collection of Old Masters outside London, many of which are on loan from The Duke of Sutherland. There are paintings by Raphael, Rubens, El Greco, Titian, Goya, Vermeer and Rembrandt. Also featured are Gaugin, Cezanne, Renoir, Degas, Monet, Van Gogh and Turner, and the Scottish collection is unrivalled with important works by Raeburn, Ramsay, Wilkie and James Drummond. Around the galleries is a wide space which has long been used as Edinburgh's version of Hyde Park Corner. During the Festival it becomes one of the prime street performing venues, with bands, magicians, fire eaters, escapologists, comedians and string quartets, among others. ■ *Both galleries are open Mon-Sat 1000-1700, Sun 1400-1700. Admission to the National Gallery is free, whilst prices vary for the Royal Academy.*

On the other side of The Mound is **West Princes Street Gardens**, beautifully-located right under the steep sides of Castle Rock. At the entrance is the world's oldest Floral Clock, which is laid out every year with over 20,000 plants. Further west is the **Ross Open Air Theatre**, used for various musical events, particularly during the Festival and at Hogmanay. Behind it a footbridge crosses the railway line and a path leads to the ruined **Wellhouse Tower**, one of the oldest buildings in the city, dating from the reign of David II (1329-71).

At the far western corner of Princes Street Gardens, below the junction of Princes Street and Lothian Road, is **St Cuthbert's Church and Churchyard**. This is the oldest church site in the city, dating back to the reign of Malcolm III, though the present church was mostly built in the 1890s. The churchyard is worth visiting and a peaceful refuge from the Princes Street traffic. Here lies Thomas de Quincey (1785-1859), author of *Confessions of an English Opium Eater*, a classic account of drug addiction in the early 19th century. De Quincey spent the last years of his life in Edinburgh, the city featured in *Trainspotting*, the late 20th century tale of drug addiction.

George Street Running to the north and parallel to Princes Street is George Street, a bustling thoroughfare of shops, banks, offices and trendy new bars. At the eastern end is **St Andrew Square**, which began life as a fashionable residential area. The most impressive building, on the eastern side of the square, is the headquarters of The Royal Bank of Scotland. This handsome 18th century town house was originally the home of Sir Laurence Dundas, but was remodelled in the 1850s when the wonderful domed ceiling was added. The Royal Bank was only one of many banks, insurance, business and legal firms to occupy premises here and it is now one of the wealthiest business squares in the world. In the centre of the square is the massive 100ft pillar, carrying the statue of the lawyer and statesman Henry Dundas, first Viscount Melville (1742-1811), chief ally of William Pitt the Younger and once described as the "absolute dictator of Scotland".

A few hundred yards along George Street is the **Assembly Rooms and Music Hall** (1787) once the social hub of the New Town and now a major Fringe venue. Opposite is the oval-shaped St Andrew's Church, now known as the **Church of St Andrew and St George**. The church is famous as the scene of the "Great Disruption" of 1843, when the Church of Scotland was split in two. The "evangelicals", led by Thomas Chalmers, went on to form the Free Church of Scotland, which proclaimed a much stricter but more democratic form of Presbyterianism.

At the western end of the street is **Charlotte Square**, designed by Robert Adam in 1791 and considered by most to be his masterpiece. Like its counterpart, St Andrew Square, Charlotte Square was originally purely residential, but is now the heart of the city's financial community, home to bankers, investment-fund managers, stockbrokers, corporate lawyers, accountants and insurance executives. Edinburgh, in fact, is the largest financial centre in Europe apart from the City of London.

Charlotte Square has long been the most prestigious address in the city, particularly the **north side**, the oldest part and the best preserved. Number six is the official residence of the Secretary of State for Scotland and the National Trust for Scotland has its head offices at number five. The upper floors of number seven are the official residence of the Moderator of the General Assembly of the Church of Scotland, while the lower floors are open to the public as the **Georgian House**, which gives a fascinating insight into how Edinburgh's gentry lived in the late 18th century. The house has been lovingly restored by the NTS and is crammed with period furniture and hung with fine paintings, including portraits by Ramsay and Raeburn. In the basement the wine cellar and kitchen are also authentically reconstructed. ■ *1 Apr-31 Oct Mon-Sat 1000-1700, Sun 1400-1700, £4.40, concession £2.90, T2263318.*

On the west side of the square is St George's Church, originally designed by Adam but following his death in 1792 the plans were abandoned on grounds of cost and the building you see today was built in 1811 by Robert Reid. In the 1960s it was refurbished as **West Register House** (part of the Scottish Record Office). It is open to the public and features displays of historical documents. ■ *Mon-Fri 1000-1600, free.*

Parallel to George Street, and slightly downhill from it, is Queen Street, the **Queen Street** most northerly terrace of James Craig's New Town plan, bordered by Queen Street Gardens to the north. This was a prime residential area of the New Town, with excellent views across the Firth of Forth to Fife, and the air of exclusivity has been maintained, in that the gardens are accessible only to key holders who live nearby.

The only public building of interest here is the **Scottish National Portrait Gallery**, at the far eastern end of the street, a huge late-19th century red sandstone building, modelled on the Doge's Palace in Venice. The gallery contains a huge range of pictures of notable Scots from the 16th century to the present day. It also has a good café (see 'Cafés', page 111). ■ *T6246200. Mon-Sat 1000-1700, Sun 1400-1700. Free.*

Calton Hill

In the first few decades of the 19th century there were major extensions to the original New Town, spreading to the north, west and east, and all in keeping with the neo-Classical theme. Perhaps the most interesting of the New Town extensions is the area around Calton Hill, another of Edinburgh's dead volcanoes, which grew beyond the east end of Princes Street.

The slopes of Calton Hill are covered with many fine buildings, which probably earned Edinburgh the epithet "Athens of the North". You could take a circular route, clockwise right round the hill, starting from Leith Walk and heading along **Royal Terrace, Calton Terrace, Regent Terrace, Regent Road** and **Waterloo Place**, which leads into the east end of Princes Street. The best of the buildings are to be found in the magnificent sweep of Regent Terrace, hailed as the most beautiful of all Regency terraces in Britain, with fantastic views across to Arthur's Seat and Salisbury Crags.

On Regent Road, 200 yards east of the junction with Regent Terrace, is the former **Royal High School**, perhaps the finest of all Edinburgh's Greek temples. It was built in 1825-29 by Thomas Hamilton, a former pupil of the school and architect of the **Robert Burns Monument**, which stands on the opposite side of the road. The Royal High is the oldest school in Scotland, dating back to the 12th century (the previous premises were near the Cowgate in the Old Town), and its long list of famous former pupils includes Robert Adam, Sir Walter Scott and Alexander Graham Bell. The school was moved in 1970 to the western outskirts and the building's future remains a matter of debate.

Further west on Regent Road, on the south side, is **St Andrews House**, a massive Art Deco structure housing government offices, built on the site of **Calton Jail**. Until 1864, public executions were carried out on top of the jail, watched by crowds who stood opposite on the slopes to the south of the City Observatory (see below). The only part of the jail that remains is the castellated **Governor's House**, which looks onto the **Old Calton Burial Ground**, on the south side of Waterloo Place. The slightly spooky cemetery contains Robert Adam's tower built for the great empiricist David Hume, Thomas Hamilton's obelisk to the political martyrs of 1793 and a memorial to the Scottish-American soldiers who fought in the American Civil War, complete with a statue of Abraham Lincoln. You may come across a mausoleum to Robert Burns, but this is for the architect of the Nelson Monument (see next page) and not to be confused with the poet Robert Burns.

Another of the absolute musts for visitors to Edinburgh is to climb to the top of **Calton Hill**, via the stairs at the east end of Waterloo Place. The views from the top are simply stunning, especially up the length of Princes Street and the sweep of the Forth Estaury. Calton Hill is also the site of anarchic pagan

Edinburgh

Carlton Hill
Acropolis

Edinburgh

festivities at the feast of **Beltane** in May, and at night it's a popular cruising area for the nearby gay community.

On the west side of the hill, overlooking the St James Centre, is the old **City Observatory**, built by Playfair in 1818 for his uncle, a renowned mathematician and philosopher. It was abandoned in 1895 when light pollution became too great and relocated to Blackford Hill (see page 129). The observatory equipment is still used by students and the small, domed pavilion now houses the **Edinburgh Experience**, a 20-minute 3-D presentation of the city's history viewed through special glasses. ■ *Daily Apr-Oct 1000-1700, £2, children £1.20.* The observatory complex also contains the **Old Observatory**, a fantasy Gothic castle and the last surviving building of James Craig, the designer of the New Town.

Calton Hill is full of monuments of all shapes and sizes. Southwest of the observatory is the **Monument to Dugald Stewart** (1753-1828), a Playfair construction commemorating an obscure University professor. A little further south, overlooking Regent Road, is **Nelson's Monument**, a 108ft tower built in 1816 to commemorate Nelson's victory at the Battle of Trafalgar. It's a strange-looking structure, built in the shape of an upturned telescope, and every day, at precisely one o' clock, a large ball is still dropped from the mast at the top to mark the time for ships out in the Firth of Forth. It's worth climbing to the top of the monument, for the panoramic views are even better. ■ *Apr-Sep Mon 1300-1600, Tue-Sat 1000-1600; Oct-Mar Mon-Sat 1000-1500, £2.*

Standing beside Nelson's monument is the bizarre yet romantic **National Monument**, an over-ambitious project begun in 1822 by Playfair as a memorial to those who fell in the Napoleonic Wars. The intention was to build a replica of the Parthenon in Athens, incorporating catacombs for the burial of Scotland's greatest figures, but the money ran out and it never got further than what you can see today – twelve huge columns which have come to be known as 'Edinburgh's Disgrace'.

The West End and Dean Village

The western extension of the New Town followed a couple of years after the eastern extension and spread southwest from Shandwick Place, along West Maitland Street to **Haymarket**, whose railway station was built in 1840 as the original terminus of the line from Glasgow, before it was extended east to Waverley. It also spread northwest along Queensferry Street towards **Melville Street**, the most impressive thoroughfare in the West End. At its western end in Palmerston Place, is **St Mary's Cathedral**, the second largest church in Scotland, designed by George Gilbert Scott in Gothic style, and featuring a set of murals by Phoebe Traquair (see next page).

A walk along the Water of Leith

One of the best ways to escape the traffic fumes is to take a stroll along the Water of Leith, Edinburgh's picturesque river, which can be walked along for most of its length. The walkway runs from Roseburn, past the Gallery of Modern Art, through Dean Village, past the Royal Botanic Garden, then a short walk along the road at Canonmills before passing Warriston cemetery and on down to Leith docks.

Particularly charming is the walk upstream from Stockbridge, into the verdant gorge under the Dean Bridge, where the running water blocks out any traffic noise. At Dean Village you can either continue up the riverside towards the Gallery of Modern Art, or turn right, up the steep slope of Dean Path, once the main road out of Edinburgh, to Dean Cemetery.

Edinburgh

Queensferry Street follows the old coaching route to South Queensferry (see page 133) and soon reaches the wooded valley of the **Water of Leith**, the little river which flows from the Pentland Hills to the port of Leith where it enters the Firth of Forth. The road crosses the steep valley along the 100ft high **Dean Bridge**, a remarkable feat of engineering, built by Thomas Telford in the 1830s. At one time, the Water of Leith powered over 70 mills and below the bridge is **Dean Village**, a picturesque old milling community which has been revitalized with the conversion of some of the mills into designer flats. From here you can walk along the river into neighbouring Stockbridge (see next page), past **St Bernard's Well**, a mineral spring covered by a mock Doric temple. It has recently been restored and is sometimes open to the public, but take note that the waters were once described as having "a slight resemblance in flavour to the washings of a foul gun barrel".

At the north end of Dean Bridge, to the west of Trinity Church, is **Dean Cemetery**, one of Edinburgh's finest places of final rest. The cemetery houses the graves of the likes of architect William Playfair, pioneering photographer Octavius Hill, and Dr Joseph Bell, who is said to have been the flesh-and-blood inspiration for Arthur Conan Doyle's character Sherlock Holmes. It also contains many excellent examples of 19th-century sculpture.

About 10 minutes' walk from Dean Village, set in spacious wooded grounds along Belford Road, is The Scottish National Gallery of Modern Art, which is definitely worth visiting, even if you know *nada* about Dada. It opened to the public in 1984 as the first ever gallery in Britain devoted to 20th century art. The hugely-impressive permanent collection features everything from the Impressionists to Hockney and is now second in Britain only to the Tate in London. It is particularly strong on Expressionism, with works by Picasso, Cezanne, Matisse, Magritte, Mondrain, Henry Moore, Kandinsky, Klee, Giacometti and Sickert all displayed, among many other important names, including many contemporary Scottish artists. There are also frequent temporary exhibitions, and don't miss the excellent café, especially if the sun is shining (see 'Cafés', on page 113). ■ *T6246200. Mon-Sat 1000-1700, Sun 1400-1700. Free. To get there, take a 13 bus from George St, or walk 10 minutes from Dean Village or Palmerston Place.*

The Scottish National Gallery of Modern Art

Across the street is the new **Dean Gallery** (same opening hours as above and also free), featuring the work of Edinburgh-born artist Sir Eduardo Paolozzi. It also houses a major Dada and Surrealist collection and exhibitions of contemporary art.

The Northern New Town

The earliest of the New Town extensions, begun in 1803, was the Northern New Town, which extends downhill from Queen Street Gardens, as far as Fettes Row to the north and bounded to the west by the Water of Leith and Broughton Street to the east. This area is the best preserved of the New Town extensions and has retained its residential character.

The latest, and finest, part of the northern development, begun in 1822, is the **Moray Estate**, to the east of Queensferry Street, designed by James Gillespie Graham, another of Edinburgh's architectural geniuses. This part of the New Town is characterized by gracious curves and circles, none finer than **Moray Place**, a magnificent twelve-sided circus. From Moray Place you can head east into **Heriot Row**, the southernmost avenue of the Northern New Town, where Robert Louis Stevenson spent most of his life (at number 17).

To the northwest, straddling both sides of the Water of Leith to the east of Dean Bridge, is the old village of **Stockbridge**, a fascinating bazaar of antique shops, second-hand bookstores and various other bohemian-type outlets, with a fair number of good restaurants and trendy bars (see 'Shopping', on page 122). The residential streets on the far side of the river were developed by the painter Henry Raeburn. The most notable of these is **Ann Street**, named after his wife and described by the poet Sir John Betjeman as "the most attractive street in Britain". It is now one of the most prestigious addresses in the city and is the only street in the New Town whose houses each have a front garden. Nearby is **Danube Street**, once home to Edinburgh's most notorious brothel, and now the height of middle-class decency.

The eastern "boundary" of the Northern New Town is formed by **Broughton Street**, which, along with the area around the Playhouse Theatre, is the centre of the city's thriving gay scene (see page 119), with numerous trendy bars, clubs, cafés and restaurants. On the corner of Broughton Street and East London Street, is **Mansfield Place Church**, a late 19th century neo-Norman edifice, now famous as the site of an amazing scheme of Pre-Raphaelite murals by **Phoebe Traquair**, a leading light in the Scottish Arts and Crafts Movement. These murals were created by her over eight years (1893-1901), working alone seven days a week without pay. They have suffered badly due to years of neglect but will hopefully be restored in the near future. Her work can also be seen on the walls of the Song School at **St Mary's Cathedral** (see above). The basement of Mansfield Place Church is currently used as a club (see *Café Graffiti*, page 118) but is due to close in 2000 and be turned into offices.

Royal Botanic Garden Further north, beyond the northern boundary of the New Town and the Water of Leith, is the district of Inverleith, where you'll find Edinburgh's gorgeous Royal Botanic Garden. Contained within its 72 acres is a mind-boggling variety of plants and trees, as well as walkways, ornamental gardens, various hothouses and huge open spaces, with not a dog poo in sight. Many of the exotic species you can see were discovered by Scottish collectors during their expeditions around the globe. There's an awful lot to enjoy, but particularly notable are the outdoor rock garden, the huge Victorian Palm House, the amazing Glasshouse Experience and the new Chinese Garden, featuring the largest collection of Chinese wild plants outside China. At the southern end of the gardens, at the highest point, is **Inverleith House**, a fine Georgian mansion which used to house the Scottish National Gallery of Modern Art. There's also a café with outdoor terrace (see 'Cafés', page 111). The views from the house across the New Town to the castle are stupendous. ■ *Inverleith Row, T5527171. Daily* *from 0930-1600 Nov-Jan; till 1700 Feb, Sep and Oct; till 1800 Mar; till 1900 Apr-Jun; till 2000 Jul and Aug. Free, but voluntary donation of £2.50 recommended. Take buses 7a, 8, 23, 27 and 37 from city centre.*

Essentials

Sleeping

As you'd expect in Scotland's major tourist city, Edinburgh has a huge selection of places to stay, more than any other place in Britain outside London. Many of the **hotels** are concentrated in the New Town and the West End, particularly around Princes Street, Calton Hill and the streets north of Haymarket station. There are also hundreds of **guest houses** and **B&Bs** dotted all over the city. There are several areas which have a particularly high concentration, all within about two miles of the centre and all on main bus routes, such as Bruntsfield and Newington, both south of the centre, Pilrig, east of the city centre heading towards Leith, and west from Haymarket along the Corstorphine Road. Many hotels offer good deals during the low season, especially at weekends, and also offer a standby room rate throughout the year. This can save a lot of money but can also involve a lot of frustrating legwork.

There are also four official **SYHA hostels** and several **independent hostels**, most of which are convenient, and a couple of **campsites** which are not too far from the centre. Most of the universities and colleges offer **campus accommodation**, but this is neither cheap nor centrally-located. Another option, if you're staying a week or more, is **self-catering**, which is cost-effective, or you can **rent** a room or flat (see page 104).

If you arrive in Edinburgh without a reservation, particularly during the festival, or at Hogmanay, the chances are you won't find a room anywhere near the centre. It pays to **book well in advance.** The **tourist office** (see page 68) sends out its accommodation brochure for free so that you can book a place yourself, or their Central Reservations Service, T4733855, centres@eltb.org, will make a reservation for you, for a non-refundable fee of £5. *Thomas Cook* have a hotel reservations service which also charges £5 for bookings. They have three branches, at Waverley Steps, near the TIC, T5570905, at Waverley station, T5570034, and at the airport, T3335119. They are open 0700-2230 (bookhotel@cordex.co.uk).

New Town

L *Albany Hotel*, 39-43 Albany St, T5560397, F5576633. 21 rooms. New Town Georgian elegance only a few minutes from Princes Street. Its excellent basement restaurant, *Haldane's* is listed under 'Eating'. **L** *Balmoral Hotel*, 1 Princes St, T5562414, F5573747. 184 rooms. Located above Waverley station, this city landmark is superior in every sense. Its main restaurant, *The Grill*, is excellent and the brasserie, *Hadrian's*, is listed under 'Eating'. **L** *The Howard*, 34 Great King St, T5573500/3152220, F5576515, reserve@thehoward.com. 15 rooms. Beautiful Georgian townhouse famous for its chintzy luxury. Its basement restaurant, *36*, is one of the city's finest and is listed under 'Eating'. **L** *Parliament House Hotel*, 15 Calton Hill, T4784000, F4784001. 54 rooms. Smart, new and centrally-located townhouse close to east end of Princes Street. Continental breakfast only. Has rooms for disabled visitors. **L** *Royal Terrace Hotel*, 18 Royal Terrace, T5573222, F5575334. 110 rooms. Exquisitely-furnished rooms, most with whirlpool spa. The last word in decadent over-indulgence.

A *Channings*, South Learmonth Gdns, T3152226/3323232, F3329631, reserve@channings.co.uk. 48 rooms. Cosy and stylish sister hotel to *The Howard*. Formed from five traditional townhouses, with great views from the top floor. Its brasserie is also highly-rated. **A** *Roxburghe Hotel*, 38 Charlotte Square, T2253921, F2202518. 75 rooms. Lovely Georgian building in Edinburgh's financial heart and on its loveliest square.

New Town

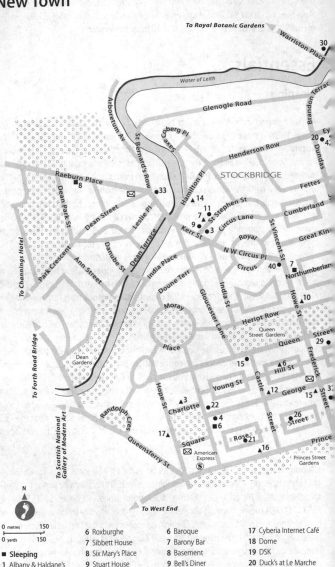

To Royal Botanic Gardens

Warriston Place

30

Water of Leith

Glenogle Road

Brandon Terrace

Arboretum Av

St Bernard's Row

Saxe Coburg Pl

Ey

20 4

Dundas

Henderson Row

STOCKBRIDGE

Fettes

Raeburn Place

8

Dean Park St

Dean Street

Leslie Pl

33

Hamilton Pl

14

11

7 St Stephen St

9 3

Kerr St

Circus Lane

St Vincent St

Cumberland

Great Kin

To Channings Hotel

Park Crescent

Danube St

Ann Street

Dean Terrace

India Place

Doune Terr

Royal

Circus

N W Circus Pl

40 7

Northumberlan

India St

Gloucester Lane

Howe St

10

To Forth Road Bridge

Moray

Place

Dean Gardens

Heriot Row

Queen Street Gardens

Street

29

15

Hill St 6

Castle Street

Queen

Frederick Street

George

15 3

To Scottish National Gallery of Modern Art

Randolph Cres

Queensferry St

Hope St

Young St

3

Charlotte

22

4

6

Rose

26 Street

17

Square

American Express

S

21

16

Prince

Princes Street Gardens

To West End

N

Scale: 0 metres 150 / 0 yards 150

■ **Sleeping**
1 Albany & Haldane's Restaurant
2 Balmoral & Hadrian's Brasserie
3 Howard & 36 Restaurant
4 Parliament House
5 Princes Street Backpackers

6 Roxburghe
7 Sibbett House
8 Six Mary's Place
9 Stuart House

● **Eating**
1 Abbotsford
2 Baan Erawan & Erawan Oriental
3 The Baillie Bar
4 Bar 38
5 Bar Napoli

6 Baroque
7 Barony Bar
8 Basement
9 Bell's Diner
10 Blue Moon
11 Blue Parrot Cantina
12 Café Royal Oyster Bar, Circle Bar & Bistro Bar
13 Cask & Barrel
14 Catwalk Café
15 Cosmo
16 Cumberland Bar

17 Cyberia Internet Café
18 Dome
19 DSK
20 Duck's at Le Marche Noir
21 Erawan Express
22 Est Est Est
23 Glass & Thompson
24 Guildford Arms
25 Henderson's Salad
26 Kenilworth
27 Kweilin

Edinburgh

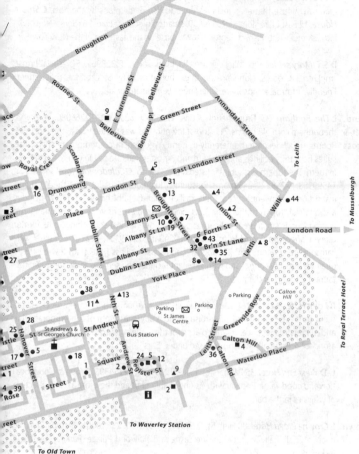

To Leith & Umberto's Restaurant

Broughton Road

Rodney St

E Claremont St

Bellevue Pl

Bellevue St

Green Street

Annandale Street

9 ■

Bellevue

Scotland Sd

Royal Cres

Drummond

16 ●

Place

London St

East London Street

5 ●

31 ●

13 ●

▲4

●44

To Leith

Walk

To Musselburgh

To Leith

Leith St

London Road

London Road

To Musselburgh

■3

reet

27 ●

Dublin Street

Barony St

10 ● 7 ●

Albany St Ln 19 ■

6 ● Forth St

43 ●

▲2

Union St

Albany Street

32 ● Br'n St Lane

■1

35 ●

8 ● 14 ●

▲8

York Place

Dublin St Lane

38 ●

▲13

11 ▲

Nth St

Parking

St James

Centre

⊠

o Parking

Parking

Greenside Row

Calton Hill

To Royal Terrace Hotel

28 ●

25 ●

St Andrew's &

St George's Church

✝

St ANDREW

Bus Station

Leith Street

Calton Hill

▲4

Hanover Street

17 ●

5 ●

18 ●

1 ●

Andrew

Square

24 ● 5 ●

2 ● Register St

12 ●

9 ●

36 ●

Calton Rd

Waterloo Place

stle

4 ● 39 ●

Rose

Street

2 ■

ℹ

To Waverley Station

To Old Town

© Crown copyright

28 Laigh Bake House
29 Le Café St Honoré
30 Loon Fung
31 Lost Sock Diner
32 Mathers
33 Maison Hector
34 Mussel Inn
35 Outhouse
36 Pivo Caffé
37 Po-Na-Na
38 Queen Street Oyster
   Bar

39 Rose Street Brewery
40 Siam Erawan
41 Tampopo
42 Tapas Olé
43 Tapas Tree Table &
   Henderson's Bistro
44 Valvona & Crolla

▲ **Other**
1 Assembly Rooms &
   Music Hall
2 Edinburgh Workshop
   Printmaker's & Gallery
3 The Georgian House
4 Gilded Balloon at the
   Palladium
5 Graffiti
6 Hill Street Theatre
7 Jazz & Blues Festival
   Office
8 Playhouse Theatre
9 Register House

10 Robert Louis
   Stevenson's House
11 Scottish National
   Portrait Gallery
12 Sir Walter Scott's
   House
13 The Stand Comedy
   Club
14 Theatre Workshop
15 Thomas Cook
16 Waterstone's
   Bookshop &
   Starbucks Café
17 West Register House

C *Sibbett House*, 26 Northumberland St, T5561078. 5 rooms. Friendly, intimate Georgian townhouse that even includes the odd skirl o' the pipes by the host. **C** *Stuart House*, 12 East Claremont St, T5579030, stuarto@globalnet.co.uk. 6 rooms. No smoking. Tastefully refurbished Georgian townhouse on the east side of the New Town.

D *Six Mary's Place*, 6 Mary's Place, Raeburn Place, T3328965, ECT-social-firms/ smpl.htm. 8 rooms. Non-smoking guest house on busy Stockbridge main street. Friendly, informal atmosphere. Offers good vegetarian cooking.

West End, Haymarket & Tollcross
L *The Bonham*, 35 Drumsheugh Gdns, T2266050/6236060, F2266080, reserve@ thebonham.com. 48 rooms. This trio of townhouses was turned into a hotel in 1998. Rooms are all decorated differently in trendy, yet elegant contemporary styles. The suites have lofty ceilings and the bath and 3-poster beds are so big you could get lost in them. The superb restaurant is listed under 'Eating'. **L** *Caledonian Hotel*, Princes St, T4599988, F2258221. 246 rooms. Prestigious, luxurious and salubrious, this West End institution underwent a recent multi-million pound refurbishment and now includes a sports club (open to the public). Its excellent and expensive main restaurant, *The Pompadour*, is still a great culinary experience but has lost something of its former glory. **L** *Sheraton Grand Hotel*, 1 Festival Square, T2299131, F2284510, rachel_williamson@ittsheraton.com. 261 rooms. Enormous business hotel with few aesthetic qualities but very central and with excellent facilities and service. Their *Grill Room* restaurant is highly-acclaimed.

B *Point Hotel*, 34 Bread St, T2215555, F2219929. 95 rooms. This former Co-op department store has been stylishly refurbished and is now the height of contemporary chic and minimalist elegance. Handily placed for the castle and Royal Mile. Its bar and grill, *Mondobbo*, is equally stylish and listed under 'Bars'.

C-D *West End Hotel*, 35 Palmerston Place, T2253656, F2254393. 8 rooms. Good location and good value. Popular with visiting Highlanders and therefore a good selection of whiskies in the bar.

Old Town
L *Crowne Plaza Hotel*, 80 High St, T5579797, F5579789. 238 rooms. Slap bang in the heart of it all, halfway between the castle and Holyrood Palace. Parking, gym and indoor pool.

A *Ibis Hotel*, 6 Hunter Square, T2407000, F2407007. 99 rooms. Part of the *Accor* group. Modern hotel handy for everything. Breakfast extra. Low season discounts.

B *Apex International Hotel*, 31-35 Grassmarket, T3003456, mail@ apexhotels.co.uk. 168 rooms. Large, recently converted former University building in the heart of the Old Town. Good value, though top floor rooms with castle views are more expensive. **B** *Bank Hotel*, 1 South Bridge, T5569043. 9 rooms. Well-situated on the corner of the Royal Mile and good value. Lively bar downstairs (*Logie Baird's*).

C-D *Thistle Inn*, 94 Grassmarket. T2202299. 29 rooms. Basic but close to the action and ideal for those who stay out late.

Southside, Marchmont & Bruntsfield
L *Prestonfield House Hotel*, Priestfield Rd, Prestonfield, T6683346, F6683976. Magnificent 17th century mansion with period features, set in its own 13 acres of gardens below Arthur's Seat with Highland cattle and peacocks strutting around. All this only five minutes from Princes Street. A new wing was added recently, increasing the number of rooms to 31. The expensive restaurant is not the best around by any means, but dining here is something special.

A *The Bruntsfield Hotel*, 69 Bruntsfield Place, T2291393, bruntsfield@queensferry-hotels.co.uk. 50 rooms. Large, comfortable hotel in a quiet area overlooking Bruntsfield Links, one mile south of Princes Street. Its restaurant, *The Potting Shed*, serves excellent modern Scottish cuisine.

C *Teviotdale House Hotel*, 53 Grange Loan, T6674376, teviotdale.house@btinternet.com. 7 rooms. No smoking. Quiet refinement, great value and wonderful breakfasts.

West End, Haymarket & Tollcross

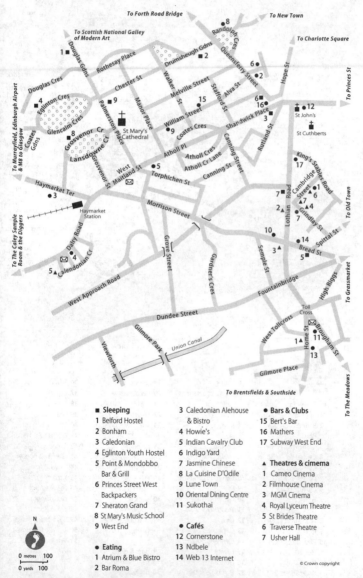

Edinburgh

■ Sleeping	3 Caledonian Alehouse	● Bars & Clubs
1 Belford Hostel	& Bistro	15 Bert's Bar
2 Bonham	4 Howie's	16 Mathers
3 Caledonian	5 Indian Cavalry Club	17 Subway West End
4 Eglinton Youth Hostel	6 Indigo Yard	
5 Point & Mondobbo	7 Jasmine Chinese	▲ Theatres & cinema
Bar & Grill	8 La Cuisine D'Odile	1 Cameo Cinema
6 Princes Street West	9 Lune Town	2 Filmhouse Cinema
Backpackers	10 Oriental Dining Centre	3 MGM Cinema
7 Sheraton Grand	11 Sukothai	4 Royal Lyceum Theatre
8 St Mary's Music School		5 St Brides Theatre
9 West End	● Cafés	6 Traverse Theatre
	12 Cornerstone	7 Usher Hall
● Eating	13 Ndbele	
1 Atrium & Blue Bistro	14 Web 13 Internet	© Crown copyright
2 Bar Roma		

D *Sherwood Guest House*, 42 Minto St, T6671200, sherwdedin@aol.com. 5 rooms. Non-smoking Georgian townhouse in a street full of guest houses and B&Bs. Minto Street continues into Mayfield Gardens, where there's also plenty of places to stay, including the very good **D** *International Guest House*, at number 37, T6672511. **D** *The*

Edinburgh Old Town

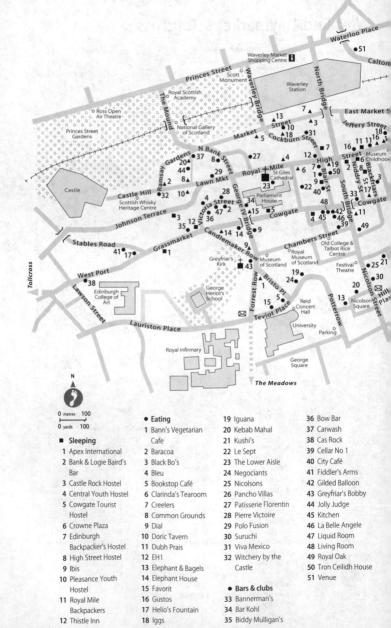

Edinburgh

| 0 metres | 100 |
| 0 yards | 100 |

■ **Sleeping**
1 Apex International
2 Bank & Logie Baird's Bar
3 Castle Rock Hostel
4 Central Youth Hostel
5 Cowgate Tourist Hostel
6 Crowne Plaza
7 Edinburgh Backpacker's Hostel
8 High Street Hostel
9 Ibis
10 Pleasance Youth Hostel
11 Royal Mile Backpackers
12 Thistle Inn

● **Eating**
1 Bann's Vegetarian Cafe
2 Baracoa
3 Black Bo's
4 Bleu
5 Bookstop Café
6 Clarinda's Tearoom
7 Creelers
8 Common Grounds
9 Dial
10 Doric Tavern
11 Dubh Prais
12 EH1
13 Elephant & Bagels
14 Elephant House
15 Favorit
16 Gustos
17 Helio's Fountain
18 Iggs

19 Iguana
20 Kebab Mahal
21 Kushi's
22 Le Sept
23 The Lower Aisle
24 Negociants
25 Nicolsons
26 Pancho Villas
27 Patisserie Florentin
28 Pierre Victoire
29 Polo Fusion
30 Suruchi
31 Viva Mexico
32 Witchery by the Castle

● **Bars & clubs**
33 Bannerman's
34 Bar Kohl
35 Biddy Mulligan's

36 Bow Bar
37 Carwash
38 Cas Rock
39 Cellar No 1
40 City Café
41 Fiddler's Arms
42 Gilded Balloon
43 Greyfriar's Bobby
44 Jolly Judge
45 Kitchen
46 La Belle Angele
47 Liquid Room
48 Living Room
49 Royal Oak
50 Tron Ceilidh House
51 Venue

Town House, 65 Gilmore Place, T2291985. 5 rooms. No smoking. Very nice Victorian guest house in a street full of similar accommodation, such as **D** *Cruachan Guest House*, No 53, T/F2296219 and **D-E** *Armadillo Guest House*, No 12, T/F2296457.

© Crown copyright

Pilrig & Leith

A *Malmaison Hotel*, 1 Tower Place, Leith, T4685000, F4685002, edinburgh@malmaison.com. 60 rooms. Award-winning designer hotel in the hip waterfront quarter. Sleek sophistication and cool, contemporary chic. Its stylish brasserie and café-bar are firm favourites with local celebs and are listed under 'Eating'. **D** *Ecosse Internatinal*, 15 McDonald Rd, T5564967. 5 rooms. Cosy guest house close to the New Town. Their warm welcome includes a wee dram. **E** *Balquhidder Guest House*, 94 Pilrig St, T5543377. 5 rooms. Victorian former church manse with lots of character, 10-15 minutes' walk from Princes Street.

Near the airport

L *Norton House Hotel*, T3331275, F3335305. Country house set in 55 acres of parkland one mile from the airport. **A** *Stakis Edinburgh Airport*, T5194400, F5194466. 134 rooms. You couldn't get any closer to the airport. If you've time, you can make use of their health and fitness club.

Hostels

E *Cowgate Tourist Hostel*, 112 Cowgate, Old Town, T/F2262153. 42 rooms. **F** in low season. Basic but good facilities and location and no curfew. **F** *Belford Hostel*, 6-8 Douglas Gardens, West End, T2216209 (bookings T0800-0966868). 98 beds in small dorms, also double rooms (**E**). About a mile from the West End near Dean Village and the Gallery of Modern Art. Plenty of entertainment and facilities and no curfew. It may be a converted church, but don't expect any quiet reflection! **F** *Bruntsfield Youth Hostel*, 7 Bruntsfield Crescent, T4472994. Reliable and well-run SYHA hostel in quiet area overlooking the links, but within easy reach of the centre (takes buses 11, 15 or 16 from south side of Princes St). Doors locked at 0200. Book ahead at peak times. **F** *Castle Rock Hostel*, 15 Johnston Terr, Old Town, T2259666, castle-rock@scotlands-top-hostels.com. Prime location below the castle. Vast building with 150 beds in various dorms. Same group

▲ **Other**

1 Bedlam Theatre
2 Camara Obscura
3 City Art Centre & Café
4 City Chambers
5 Festival Box Office
6 Festival Fringe Office
7 Fruitmarket Gallery & Café
8 Gladstone's Land
9 Greyfriar's Bobby
10 International Festival Centre & Café Hub
11 James Thin Bookshop
12 John Knox House
13 LRT Travel Shop & Tattoo Office
14 Magdalen Chapel
15 National Library
16 Netherbow Theatre
17 St Cecilia's Hall
18 Stills Gallery
19 Tron Kirk & Old Town Information Centre
20 Writers' Museum

Edinburgh

as the High Street and Royal Mile Hostels below. **F** *Edinburgh Backpackers Hostel*, 65 Cockburn St, Old Town, T2201717/2210022. Just off the Royal Mile, therefore busy and noisy. **E** in private rooms. No curfew. **F** *Eglinton Youth Hostel*, 18 Eglinton Cresent, West End, T3371120. SYHA hostel in a quiet street about one mile west of the centre, near Haymarket train station. 160 beds, most in dorms but also 12 rooms for four. Includes continental breakfast. Doors closed at 0200 and hostel closed in Dec. There are two other SYHA hostels, which are only open from 1 Jul-1 Sep: *Central Youth Hostel*, 4 Robertson Close, Cowgate, and *Pleasance Youth Hostel*, 5/2 New

Southside, Marchmont & Bruntsfield

N

0 metres 100
0 yards 100

■ **Sleeping**
1 Armadillo Guest House
2 Bruntsfield Youth Hostel
3 Cruachan Guest House
4 The Bruntsfield Hotel
5 The Town House

● **Eating**
1 Ann Purna
2 Buffalo Grill
3 California Coffee Company

Arthur Place (near the Pleasance Theatre), both are **F**, or **E-F** in Aug. For bookings, call the Eglinton number, or Edinburgh District Office, T2298660. **F** *High Street Hostel*, 8 Blackfriars St, Old Town, T5573984, high-street@ scotlands-top-hostels.com. Cheap, lively and right in the heart of things. No curfew. Long-established backpacker hang-out. Close by is its wee sister, **F** *Royal Mile Backpackers*, at 105 High St, Old Town, T5576120, which is also lively and great value. They also have hostels in Inverness, Fort William, Oban, Glasgow and on Skye. **F** *Princes Street Backpackers*, 5 West Register St, T5566984. Behind Burger King at the east end of Princes St and near the

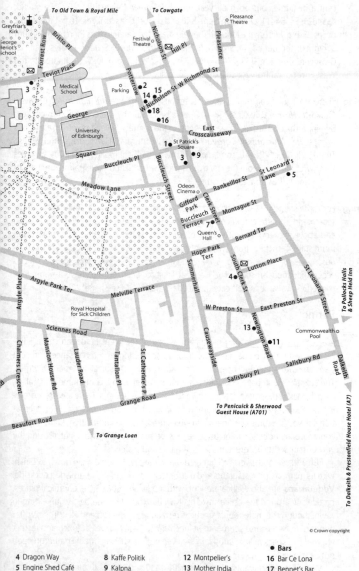

© Crown copyright

Edinburgh

4 Dragon Way	8 Kaffe Politik	12 Montpelier's	● **Bars**
5 Engine Shed Café	9 Kalpna	13 Mother India	16 Bar Ce Lona
6 Howie's	10 Mango & Stone	14 Phenecia	17 Bennet's Bar
7 Isabel's Café	11 Metropole	15 Susie's Diner	18 The Pear Tree

bus station. Cheap, basic and very popular. Great value breakfast and free Sun dinner. The same people also run **F** *Princes Street West Backpackers*, 3-4 Queensferry St, West End, T/F2262939, princes.west@cabinet.co.uk. With bar, cable TV and email facilities. Also free Sun dinner and 7th consecutive night is free!

Campus accommodation C-D *Pollock Halls*, Holyrood Park Rd, T6670662, Hotel.Services@ed.ac.uk. Open Mar-Apr and Jun-Sep. Main halls of residence less than 2 miles from the centre, near the Commonwealth Pool and Holyrood Park. Huge numbers of rooms. **D** *Heriot-Watt University Riccarton Campus*, T4513669, ecc@hw.ac.uk. Six miles west of the city centre in Currie, but open all year round. **E** *Napier University*, 219 Colinton Rd, 4554621, F4554411. Open Jun-Sept. B&B and use of sports facilities. To get there take buses 23 and 27 from the Mound. They also have self-catering flats for rent (minimum 3 nights); for details T4554331. **E** *Queen Mary's Music School*, Coates Hall, 25 Grosvener Crescent, T5387766, F4677289. Open Jul-Aug only. Well-situated in the West End, not far from Haymarket station. Includes continental breakfast.

Camping There are 2 good campsites within a short bus ride of the centre. *Edinburgh Caravan Club Site*, Marine Drive, T3126874. Open all year. Run by the Caravan Club of Great Britain, with good facilities. Five miles east of the centre in Silverknowes. Take a 14 bus from town. *Mortonhall Caravan Park*, 38 Mortonhall Gate, Frogston Rd East, T6641533, MHallCP@ aol.com. Open Mar-Oct. Well-equipped site about six miles southwest of town. From the city bypass take the Lothianburn or Straiton junction, or take a 7 or 11 bus from Princes Street.

Self-catering For those spending several days in the city there's the alternative option of renting a self-catering apartment. Prices range from around £200 per week right up to £800 and above, depending on the type of accommodation, and there's usually a minimum stay of anything from two nights up to one week. For a detailed list of the various types of self-catering accommodation on offer, see the tourist office's accommodation brochure. The National Trust for Scotland also have a number of properties available for self-catering holidays, (for details see page 20).

Eating

In keeping with its growing reputation as one of the great European cities, Edinburgh's restaurant scene has gone through something of a renaissance in recent years and the capital now boasts a wide range of places, to suit all tastes and budgets. The culinary scene has a distinctly cosmopolitan feel, with a large number of Italian, French, Mexican, Spanish, Indian, Thai and Chinese restaurants. There are also a growing number of eateries offering fusion cooking, which combines a range of international flavours. Scottish cuisine is also well represented, from traditional fare to more contemporary eclectic cuisine using various international influences, but all using the very best of Scottish ingredients such as game and seafood.

Fish and seafood lovers will not be disappointed and should head down to **Leith**, with its many stylish restaurants and bistros located around the refurbished dockside. **Vegetarians** are also well catered for, with a selection of good, economical places, particularly around the University. This is where you'll find the best value eating in town, though the more tourist-oriented restaurants in the Old and New Towns offer good value two-course set menus at lunch-time. If you eat well at lunch and restrict yourself to a snack or light supper in the evening, then dining out in Edinburgh need not be expensive.

Most of the restaurants serve from 1200-1430 and 1800-2200 and are closed on Sundays, though times are listed below. If you don't want to be restricted by these eating times, then try some of the many excellent **bistros**, which are often better value and many of which serve food daily until around 0100. The city's countless bars also serve reasonably-priced food, and the cheapest lunches are often found in the city cafés, which are listed below in a separate section. Note that a seat in one of the more upmarket restaurants can be hard to come by during busy periods, such as the Festival, so it's best to book whenever possible. **NB** BYOB is a commonly-used abbreviation meaning bring your own bottle.

Expensive *Café Royal Oyster Bar*, 17a West Register St, T5564124. An Edinburgh institution and much-loved by numerous celebrities. The ornate tiles and stained glass windows create an atmosphere of Victorian elegance and opulence – just make sure you look at the prices! There are better seafood restaurants in town but none are as classy. Open daily 1200-1400, 1900-2200. The adjoining bar is just as impressive (see under 'Bars'). *Cosmo*, 58a North Castle St, T2266743. Elegant and expensive Italian restaurant that's superior in every sense. Excellent food (especially the fish), excellent wine list and excellent service. Popular with the city's more distinguished visitors (Sean C is shaid to have dined here). Booking essential. Open Mon-Fri 1230-1415, 1900-2245, Sat 1900-2200. *Duck's at Le Marche Noir*, 2-4 Eyre Place, T5581608. Classic French provincial cooking in sumptuous surroundings. Perhaps Edinburgh's finest French? Complemented by an extensive wine list. Open Mon-Fri 1200-1400, 1900-2200, Sat 1900-2230, Sun 1830-2130. *Haldane's*, 39 Albany Street, T5568407.

New Town

Edinburgh

Leith

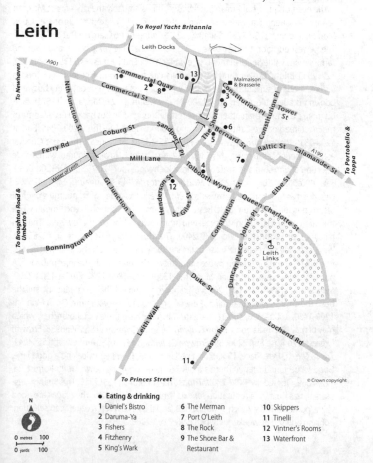

© Crown copyright

● Eating & drinking

1 Daniel's Bistro	6 The Merman	10 Skippers
2 Daruma-Ya	7 Port O'Leith	11 Tinelli
3 Fishers	8 The Rock	12 Vintner's Rooms
4 Fitzhenry	9 The Shore Bar &	13 Waterfront
5 King's Wark	Restaurant	

0 metres 100
0 yards 100

Smart Scottish country house cuisine in the centre of town. Excellent value set lunch. No smoking. Open Mon-Thur 1200-1400, 1800-2130, Fri till 2200, Sat 1800-2230, Sun 1800-2130. *Hadrian's*, 2 North Bridge (under the *Balmoral Hotel*), T5575000. Excellent modern Scottish cuisine with nouvelle-ish tendencies, soothing and well-designed modern surroundings. Superb value for money. Open daily 1200-1430, 1830-2230 (Sun 1230-1500). *DSK*, 32 Broughton Street, T4787246. Enterprising modern Scottish cooking in a mellow, candlelit setting. The set evening meal is great value. Open Tue-Thur 1800-2130, Fri/Sat till 2200. *Le Café Saint-Honoré*, 34 Thistle Street Lane, T2262211. Tucked away in a little side street, this place couldn't be any more French. An authentic corner of Paris in the heart of Scotland's capital. The food is seriously French, too, and seriously priced, but seriously wonderful. Seriously! Open Mon-Fri 1200-1415, 1900-2200, Sat 1900-2200 only. *36*, 36 Great King Street, T556-3636. Basement restaurant of the *Howard Hotel* (see under 'Sleeping'). One of *the* places to eat in the capital. The very best of modern Scottish cuisine in contemporary, minimalist surroundings. Open Sun-Fri 1200-1400, 1900-2200, Sat 1900-2200. No smoking.

Mid-range *Bell's Diner*, 7 St Stephen St, T2258116. The best burgers and steaks in town. This diner is popular with locals, students and tourists alike who come for its honest, filling and great value food in an informal atmosphere. Open Mon-Fri 1800-2300, Sat/Sun 1200-2300. *Blue Parrot Cantina*, 49 St Stephen St, T2252941. Set in the heart of quasi-bohemian Stockbridge, this is arguably the city's finest Mexican restaurant, offering a varied selection of dishes in a relaxed atmosphere. Open Mon-Fri and Sun 1700-2230, Sat 1300-2230. *Canteen*, 4-6 Glanville Place, T2255553. The newest addition to the *Howie's* range of bistros. Chic yet informal and with the same superb value Scottish menu (see under 'West End'). *Est Est Est*, 135a George St, T2252555. Bright, buzzing and bustling Italian trattoria serving excellent value food in a sleek, modern surroundings. Popular with business types so it gets very busy and booking is advisable. Open daily 1200-0100. *Kweilin*, 19-21 Dundas St, T5571875. A bit more expensive than other Chinese restaurants in town but backed up by some of the most imaginative Cantonese cooking around. Open Tue-Thur 1200-2245, Fri/Sat 1200-2315. *Loon Fung*, 2 Warriston Place, T5561781. Still one of the great Oriental eating experiences in town, this Cantonese restaurant is an old favourite, with a wide selection of dim sum and seafood dishes. Open Mon-Thur 1200-2330, Fri 1200-0030, Sat 1400-0030, Sun 1400-2330. *Maison Hector*, 47-49 Deanhaugh St, T3325328. Described as Stockbridge's answer to Central Perk, this is one of Edinburgh's original bistros but still one of the best. Restaurant serves a fine Scottish/French menu while the café-bar area is just brill for weekend brunch. Open Mon-Wed 1100-2400, Thur/Fri till 0100, Sat 1030-0100, Sun 1030-2400. *The Mussel Inn*, 61-65 Rose St, T2255979. What could be better than a huge pot of steaming fresh mussels and a bowl of fantastic chips? Not much, judging by the popularity of this place, in the heart of pub-land. A must for seafood-lovers. Open Mon-Thur 1200-1500, 1800-2200, Fri/Sat 1100-2200. *Siam Erawan*, 48 Howe St, T2263675. Edinburgh's original Thai restaurant and still the best. The cosy basement ambience encourages you to take your time. Open Mon-Sat 1200-1430, 1800-2300, Sun 1800-2230. They now have three other branches, which may or may not be as good: *Baan Erawan*, 14 South St Andrew St, T5568558; *Erawan Express*, 176 Rose St. T2200059; *Erawan Oriental*, 14 South St Andrew St, T5564242. *Tapas Olé*, 10 Eyre Place, T5562754. Excellent tapas, friendly service and a good vibe. Good value lunch menu. There's a new branch in the Old Town, at 4a Forrest Rd, T2257069. Open daily 1100-2300. *Tapas Tree*, 1 Forth St, T5567718. This Spanish restaurant, has built up a reputation for excellent food and service. Their tapas are good value, particularly the lunch-time specials, and they even offer a vegetarian selection. Booking advised at weekends. Open daily 1100-2300.

Cheap *Bar Napoli*, 75 Hanover St, T2252600. Basic Italian which offers much the same as the others in the street but which has the added advantage of offering the best-value set lunch and it stays open late. Open Mon-Thur and Sun 1200-0200, Fri/Sat 1200-0400. *Henderson's Salad Table*, 94 Hanover St, T2252131. This basement vegetarian self-service restaurant is the oldest in the city and still one of the best. It can get very busy but manages to combine efficiency with comfort. Excellent value two-course set lunch. Open Mon-Sat 0800-2230. Upstairs is their deli and takeaway, and round the corner, at 25 Thistle St, is *Henderson's Bistro*, T2252605, which provides the same excellent food but in more intimate surroundings, with table service and at only slightly higher prices. *The Lost Sock Diner*, 11 East London St, T5576097. Relaxed by day and buzzing by night, this bistro offers a huge range of dishes at unbeatable value. Open Mon 0900-1600, Tue-Sat 0900-2200, Sun 1000-1700. *Tampopo*, 25a Thistle St, T2205254. Japanese fast-food at its best. Always busy with takeaway trade, so if you're after a quick, healthy, tasty and economical snack, this is the place for you. Try the sushi. Open Mon 1200-1500, Tue-Sat 1200-1500, 1800-2100.

Expensive *Iggs*, 15 Jeffrey St, T5578184. Serves the best tapas in town at lunch, then in the evening changes to a contemporary Scottish restaurant with a formidable reputation. *The Tower*, Museum of Scotland, Chambers St, T2253003. A relative newcomer to the restaurant scene but fast becoming the place to be seen amongst the smart set. Unpretentious Scottish menu is big on seafood and steaks. The views across the city skyline from the rooftop terrace are simply magnificent, and the food ain't bad either. No smoking. Open daily 1200-2300. *The Witchery by the Castle*, 352 Castlehill, T2255613. Dining doesn't get much more atmospheric than here in one of Edinburgh's finest, on the Royal Mile. Downstairs, in a converted schoolyard, is the impossibly romantic *Secret Garden*, a real hidden gem. Both restaurants share the same glorious Scottish menu. This was formerly a meeting place for Satanists, so go on, be a devil. Open daily 1200-1600, 1730-2330.

Old Town

Mid-range *Bann's Vegetarian Café*, 5 Hunter Square, T2261112. Just off the Royal Mile by the Tron Kirk. A popular street performance place during the festival so perfect for an al fresco lunch. Busy but laid-back and offering an adventurous range of dishes. Great value. Open daily 1000-2300. *Black Bo's*, 57-61 Blackfriars St, T5576136. Vegetarian restaurant that is one of the city's truly great culinary experiences. So good even the most fanatical carnivore might even give up meat. Supremely imaginative use of various fruits gives the exotically delicious dishes a real splash of colour. Their lunch is in the **cheap** category and superb value. Don't miss it! Bar next door serves the same food. Open Mon-Sat 1200-1400, 1800-2230, Sun 1800-2230. *Bleu*, 36-38 Victoria St, T2261900. No traditional separate courses here, just a wide range of truly delicious French tapas dishes, guaranteed to set the taste buds a-tingling. There's another branch in Union Street, opposite the Playhouse. Open daily 0900 till late. *Creelers*, 3 Hunter Square, T2204447. Wonderfully fresh seafood and a great location beside the Tron church, with outdoor seating in the summer. You can push the boat out in the more formal restaurant at the rear or save your pennies in the busy bistro at the front, where the cheap two-course lunch is great value. *The Dial*, 44-46 George IV Bridge, T2257179. Basement restaurant that is as notable for its cool design as for its top-notch modern Scottish cuisine. Menu features some old favourites as well as more unusual Caledonian culinary incarnations. Open Mon-Sat 1200-1500, 1800-2300, Sun 1200-1500, 1900-2300. *The Doric Tavern*, 15/16 Market St, T2251084. Very near Waverley station. Upstairs bistro offering great food and the perfect place to while away an entire afternoon without realizing the time. Open Mon-Sat 1200-0100, Sun 1230-0100. *Dubh Prais*, 123b High St, T5575732. Small basement restaurant in the heart of the Royal Mile offering the best of traditional Scottish cooking, as well as more contemporary innovations. Dinner is à la carte, but you can enjoy a two-course set lunch for a tenner. Open

Edinburgh

Tue-Sat 1200-1400, 1830-2230. *Le Sept*, 7 Old Fishmarket Close, T2255428. Down a steep, cobbled close off the High Street below St Giles. This lively little restaurant is famed for its superb crêpes but also has a 3-course set menu offering good French bistro-type food. Separate no smoking room. Open Mon-Thur 1200-1345, 1800-2200, Fri 1200-2300, Sat 1200-2230, Sun 1200-2130. *Negociants*, 45-47 Lothian St, T2256313. Is it a bar, is it a bistro? Both, actually. Great for a relaxing lunch-time beer or coffee and popular with students and professionals alike. At night it's a fave late-night watering hole with DJs and dancing downstairs. The menu is international in flavour, excellent value and available till 0230. Good place for a relaxing Sun brunch. See also under 'Bars'. Open daily 0900-0300. *Nicolsons*, 6a Nicolson St, T5574567. Large, airy bistro, done out in 1930s Art Deco style and attracting a hip crowd. Great for a bottle of wine or a martini (shaken not shtirred, of courshe) and the food's good, too; Mediterranean-style with a Far Eastern tinge. Open Mon-Fri 1200-1500, 1700-2300, Sat/Sun 1200-2400. *Pancho Villas*, 240 Canongate, T5574416. Ay, Chihuahua! If you want to stuff yourself on the finest Mexican food and have a fun time in the process, then look no further. Open Mon-Thur 1200-1430, 1800-2230, Fri 1200-2230, Sat 1200-2300, Sun 1800-2230. *Pierre Victoire*, 10 Victoria St, T2251721. This is the original of the French brasserie chain which fell on hard times. It's been given a new lease of life and is better than ever. There are several other branches dotted around the city and many more up and down the country, but quality varies. Open daily 1100-1500, 1730-2300. *Polo Fusion*, 503 The Lawnmarket, T6627722. Specializes in fusion cooking, which is very much the flavour of the month. This combines different flavours and ingredients from around the globe to create wonderfully original tastes. Substantial portions and a lively atmosphere. Open Mon-Thur 1200-1400, 1800-2200, Fri/Sat till 2230. *Suruchi*, 14a Nicolson St, T5566583. Opposite the Festival Theatre and upstairs. A cut above the average curry house offering varied southern Indian cuisine with a strong vegetarian emphasis. Their set lunch and pre-theatre dinner are particularly good value. Menu is written in Scots, which some might find amusing and others simply tiresome. Open Mon-Sat 1200-1400, 1730-2330, Sun 1730-2330. *Viva Mexico*, 41 Cockburn St, T2265145. This Mexican restaurant has been around longer than most and it's easy to see why. Definitely one of the top two in town. Open Mon-Sat 1200-1430, 1830-2230, Sun 1830-2200.

Cheap *Baracoa*, 7 Victoria St, T2255846. Cuban bar/restaurant offering two for the price of one meals before 1900 and various cheap drink deals. Fantastic value and a lively spot, especially in the early evenings. Open daily 1100-0100. *EH1*, 197 High St, T2205277. Slap bang in the heart of it all. Outside seating so great for people-watching, comfortable and stylish interior. Relaxed atmosphere is conducive to a lazy late breakfast. At night it's popular with pre-club trendies (see under 'Bars'). Open daily 0930-0100. *Helio's Fountain*, 7 Grassmarket, T2297884. Small, self-service veggie café founded on Steiner principles. Good for an economical lunch or just a quiet break from the hustle and bustle. No smoking. Open Mon-Sat 1000-1800, Sun 1200-1700. *Iguana*, 41 Lothian St, T2204288. Next door to *Negociants*. Fashionable café-bar/bistro that attracts students by day and pre-club ravers by night but still manages to be friendly and unpretentious. The food is excellent and the menu imaginative, but it gets busy at night, so book if you want to be sure of a table. See also under 'Bars'. Open daily 0900-0100. *Kebab Mahal*, 7 Nicolson Square, T6675214. No frills café-restaurant serving good kebabs and curries for under a fiver. What more could you ask? Try the delicious *lussis* (yoghurt drinks). Open daily 1200-2400, Fri/Sat till 0200. *Khushi's*, 16 Drummond St, T5568996. The city's first ever Indian restaurant has been serving simple, tasty curries to poor students for many decades. Basic decor but you can't argue with such great value. Several vegetarian options. BYOB and no corkage charge. Open Mon-Thur 1200-1430, 1700-2030, Fri/Sat till 2100.

Expensive *The Atrium*, 10 Cambridge Street (same building as the Traverse Theatre), T2288882. Award-winning Scottish cooking in elegant modern surroundings. This outstanding restaurant is one of the best in town, but by no means the most expensive. Open Mon-Fri 1200-1430, 1800-2230, Sat 1800-2230. Upstairs is its stylish sister bistro, *blue*.

West End, Haymarket & Tollcross

Mid-range *Bar Roma*, 39a Queensferry Street, T2262977. Traditional Italian serving a huge variety of pasta and pizza to huge numbers of late night revellers in a fun atmosphere. Open Mon-Thur and Sun 1200-2400, Fri/Sat till 0100. *blue*, 10 Cambridge Street (upstairs from *The Atrium*), T2211222. The stylish and minimalist interior of this leading city bistro attracts the arty and media types as well as the more sober suits. Sister to the outstanding *Atrium*, so not surprisingly the food on offer is a substantial cut above the rest. Also a great place for a drink, its well-stocked bar boasts a satisfying selection of malts and excellent service. Open Tue-Sat 1200-0100, Sun and Mon till 1200. *Caledonian Alehouse & Bistro*, 1-3 Haymarket Terr, T3371006. Upstairs bistro offering genuine Scottish cuisine at decent prices. Set lunch is excellent value. Open Mon-Thur 1200-1500, 1800-2100, Fri/Sat till 2200, Sun 1800-2200 only. *Howie's*, 63 Dalry Rd, T3133334. Something of an Edinburgh institution, this chain of bistros hits the spot every time with imaginative Scottish food that is always tasty and great value (BYOB policy), in an informal atmosphere. The others are in the New Town and Southside. Open Mon 1800-2200, Tue-Sun 1200-1400, 1800-2200. *The Indian Cavalry Club*, 3 Atholl Place, T2283282. Classy and exclusive Indian in 'Last days of the Raj' style, and with a deserved reputation for outstanding food. Popular for business lunches, which are great value. Smart dress advised. Open daily 1200-1400, 1730-2330. *Indigo Yard*, 7 Charlotte Lane, T2205603. This converted and covered-over courtyard has been transformed into an immensely popular bar and restaurant. The menu is cosmopolitan (Thai, Mexican, French, Italian etc) and the food excellent. Serves lunch, dinner and late supper. See also 'Bars'. Open daily 0830-0100. *Jasmine Chinese Restaurant*, 32 Grindlay St, T2295757. Handy for the theatres and cinemas, this stylish and modern Chinese restaurant is better value than most and something a little bit different. Open Mon-Thur 1200-1400, 1700-2330, Fri till 0030, Sat 1400-0030, Sun 1400-2230. *Lune Town*, 38 William St, T2201688. Varied and exciting Chinese food served in a cosy, friendly atmosphere. Good dim sum and excellent value set lunch. Open Mon-Thur 1200-1430, 1800-2330, Fri till 2400, Sat 1500-2400, Sun 1600-2300. *Restaurant at the Bonham*, 35 Drumsheugh Gardens, T6239319. This is part of the eponymous hotel and every bit as stylish. Scottish cuisine with a Californian touch and better quality than you could expect at these prices. Open Mon-Fri 1200-1400, 1830-2130, Sat/Sun 1200-1400, 1830-2200. *Sukothai*, 23 Brougham Place, T2291537. This busy little Thai restaurant is very handy for theatres and cinemas so ideal for a quick pre-show bite. Their "all-you-can-eat" Sun buffet is excellent value.

Cheap *La Cuisine D'Odile*, 13 Randolph Crescent, T2255685. Hidden away in the French Institute, this is genuine quality French cuisine at amazingly low prices. Great views from the terrace in the summer. Open Tue-Sat 1200-1400 only. *Oriental Dining Centre*, 8-16 Morrison Street, T2211288. Dim Sum bar (open daily 1200-0300), Noodle Shack (open Mon-Sat 1730-0200) and Chinese restaurant (daily 1200-2400) all rolled into one. Good vegetarian selection and fresh seafood daily.

Mid-range *Ann Purna*, 45 St Patrick's Square, T6621807. Well-respected and popular vegetarian/vegan restaurant specializing in southern Indian and Gujerati cooking. Understated elegance and great value. No smoking. Open Mon-Fri 1200-1400, 1730-2300, Sat/Sun 1730-2300. *Buffalo Grill*, 12-14 Chapel St, T6677427. This is beef central. The steaks are high quality and limitless in this small and intimate diner decked out in Wild West style. It's not all burgers and steaks, but that's why people keep coming.

Southside, Marchmont & Bruntsfield

Edinburgh

Open Mon-Fri 1200-1400, 1800-2215 (Sat 1800-2215 only), Sun 1700-2000. *Dragon Way*, 74 South Clerk St, T6681328. If you can get past the completely OTT decor, the food in this Cantonese restaurant is actually very good. Good value set lunch and dinners. Open Mon-Fri 1200-1430, 1700-2400, Sat 1700-2400 only, Sun 1800-2400. *Howie's*, 75 St Leonards St, T6682917. Another branch of the highly-acclaimed Edinburgh bistro chain. Also at 208 Bruntsfield Place, T2211777. (See under 'West End' above). *Montpeliers*, 159-161 Bruntsfield Place, T2293115. Bruntsfield's favourite bistro serves meals or snacks at pretty much any time of the day or night. Stylish and relaxed it's popular with locals for lunch and young trendies are attracted by their pitchers of cocktails at night. Open daily 0900-0100. *Mother India*, 10 Newington Rd, T6629020. Sister restaurant of the famous Glasgow establishment. Downstairs is more studenty and laid-back while upstairs is altogether more formal, but both offer excellent Punjabi cooking. Set lunch and pre-theatre dinner are great value. Open Mon-Sat 1700-2230 (Fri also 1200-1400), Sat till 2330, Sun 1500-2230. *Phenecia*, 55-57 West Nicolson St, T6624493. Spanish/North African dishes served in a relaxed atmosphere. Cheap lunches so it gets busy at lunch-times. BYOB policy makes it good value for dinner. Open Mon-Sat 1200-1400, 1800-2300, Sun 1800-2200.

Cheap *The Engine Shed Café*, 19 St Leonard's Lane, T6620040. Tucked away in a residential area off St Leonard's St, this little vegetarian café provides just about the best value lunch in town. Bread is baked on the premises and can be bought separately. Bakery and café provides work experience for adults with learning difficulties. No smoking. Open Mon-Thur 1030-1530, Fri till 1430, Sat till 1600, Sun 1100-1600. *Isabel's Café*, 83 Clerk St, T6624014. Tiny vegetarian restaurant at the back of the *Nature's Gate* health food shop. The vegetarian and vegan menu has non-dairy and non-wheat options. Ridiculously cheap meals and snacks served in a laid-back atmosphere. No smoking. Open Mon-Sat 1130-1830 (Tue and Sat till 1530). *Kalpna*, 2-3 St Patrick's Square, T6679890. This popular and imaginative Indian vegetarian is one of the best of its kind in the UK, using fantastically inventive and sophisticated sauces. Buffet lunch is a bargain at £4.50, but not quite the same as the full dinner experience. Don't leave town without trying it. No smoking. Open Mon-Fri 1200-1400, 1730-2300, Sat 1730-2300. *Susie's Diner*, 51-53 West Nicolson St, T6678729. Self-service vegetarian/vegan diner offering a broad range of dishes, including Mediterranean and Middle Eastern. Popular with students and lecturers from the nearby University. Also belly dancing nights and live music at weekends. Good food and atmos. Open Tue-Sat 0900-2100, Mon till 2000, Sun 1200-1900.

Leith **Expensive** *Fishers*, 1 The Shore, T5545666. Tony Blair came here, and left a generous tip (we presume), for this is one of Edinburgh's finest fish restaurants, in an area packed full of them. It's housed in the tower at the end of The Shore. Open daily 1215-2230. *Fitzhenry*, 19 Shore Place, T5556625. This stylish warehouse brasserie is one of only two city eateries to receive a Michelin Red M (the other is *The Atrium*) for its genuinely original and excellent Scottish cooking. Open Mon-Thur 1230-1430, 1830-2230, Fri/Sat till 2230. *The Rock*, 78 Commercial St, T5552225. One of many converted warehouse waterfront restaurants, this stands out from the rest for its sheer quality. The charcoal-grilled steaks are a major attraction but there's a much wider à la carte menu. Mick Jagger is said to have dined here and left satisfied. Open Tue-Sat 1200-1400, 1830-2200. *Skippers*, 1a Dock Place, T5541018. Many in the know would say this is the best place to eat seafood in town. This nautical bistro is small and intimate, and very popular, so you'll need to book. Open Mon-Sat 1230-1400, 1900-2200. *The Vintners Rooms*, 87 Giles Street, T5546767. These former wine vaults dating from the 17th century now house a restaurant and bar, both lit by candlelight and oozing historic charm and romance. The food is French provincial and excellent, as is the service. Meals in the bar at lunch-times are cheaper. Open Mon-Sat 1200-1400, 1900-2230.

Mid-range *Daruma-Ya*, 82 Commercial St, T5547660. Japanese cuisine in elegant 19th century surroundings and served by friendly, helpful staff. Sounds an unlikely combination but come and check it out for yourself. Set lunches and dinners are great value. Open Mon 1830-late, Tue-Sat 1200-1400, 1830-late. *Malmaison Brasserie*, 1 Tower Place, T468-5000. Attached to the acclaimed Malmaison Hotel (see 'Sleeping'). Excellent French brasserie food in stylish surroundings. Open Mon-Fri 0700-1000, 1200-1400, 1800-2230 (Sat from 0800, Sun till 2200). *The Shore*, 3-4 The Shore, T5535080. One of the city's best fish restaurants with a real fire and huge windows overlooking the Water of Leith. No smoking. You can eat from the restaurant menu in the adjoining bar. Open Mon-Sat 1100-2400, Sun 1230-2300. *Tinelli*, 139 Easter Rd, T6521932. This out of the way Italian is one of the city's best and well worth the effort of finding it. Genuine Italian cooking of the highest quality and fantastic value. It's small and gets busy so book ahead. Open Mon-Sat 1200-1430, 1830-2300. *Umberto's*, 2 Bonnington Road Lane (off Broughton Rd), T5541314. Very good Italian food with a Scottish flavour at one of the most children-friendly restaurants in town. A great place for kids and, in the evening, you can pig out and eat and drink as much as you can for £15. Open Mon-Sat 1200-1430, 1700-2200, Sun 1200-1800. *The Waterfront*, 1c Dock Place, T5547427. Great for fish or just for a relaxing drink. Seating in the conservatory or cosy booths. See also 'Bars'. Open Mon-Thur 1200-2300, Fri/Sat till 2400, Sun 1230-2230.

Cheap *Daniel's Bistro*, 88 Commercial St, T5535933. Classic French food with an Alsace influence at unbeatable prices. Friendly atmosphere and always busy. Open daily 1000-2200.

Cafés

Sightseeing can be a tiring business in Edinburgh. Listed below are the pick of the city's coffee houses and tearooms, where you can recharge the batteries with that essential caffeine kick, or simply put your feet up and enjoy a nice cup of tea in pleasant surroundings. Many cafés also offer the best value for lunch or a snack.

Blue Moon, 1 Barony St, T5562788. Gay café in the city's "pink triangle". Good selection of cakes, also snacks and meals. Gets busy later in the evening with pre-clubbers. Open Mon-Fri 1100-0030, Sat/Sun 0900-0030. *Cyberia*, 88 Hanover St, T2204403. One of the city's best internet cafés that's hugely popular with surfers and non-surfers alike. Open Mon-Sat 1000-2200, Sun 1200-1900 (see also under 'Internet cafés'). *Glass & Thompson*, 2 Dundas St, T5570909. Coffee shop and deli with the emphasis on quality food. Popular with local residents who know a good thing when they see (and taste) it. Open Mon-Fri 0830-1830, Sat 0830-1730, Sun 1100-1630. *The Laigh Bake House*, 117a Hanover St, T2251552. Downstairs from the hustle and bustle is a quiet little corner of the Orkneys and Edinburgh's oldest coffee house. Nothing to disturb the peace and stillness save the ticking of the clock, the rustling of newspapers and the occasional squeal of delight from someone tasting the indescribably delicious hazelnut meringue gateau for the very first time. The food is made from purely organic ingredients. Open Mon-Sat 0830-1700. *The Queen Street Café*, The Scottish National Portrait Gallery, 1 Queen St, T5572844. The best scones and caramel shortcake in town, not to mention excellent value snacks and light meals, served in grand surroundings. No smoking. Open Mon-Sat 1000-1630, Sun 1400-1630. *Starbucks*, Waterstone's, 128 Princes St, T2263610. Features the usual wide range of coffees but the reason it merits inclusion is the wonderful view of the castle. Popular with browsers, shoppers and as a meeting point. No smoking. Open Mon-Sat 0800-2000, Sun 1030-1800. *Terrace Café*, Royal Botanic Garden, Inverleith Row, T5520616. Set in the grounds next to Inverleith House, this is little more than a school canteen, but the

New Town

Edinburgh

views of the castle, Old Town and Arthur's Seat take some beating. No smoking. Open daily 0930-1800. *Valvona & Crolla*, 19 Elm Row, T5566066. More authentically Italian than almost anything you'd find in New York. Great home cooking and the best cappuccino in town. Needless to say, somewhere this good is very, very popular. No smoking. Open Mon-Sat 0800-1700.

Old Town *The Bookstop Café*, 4 Teviot Place, T2255298. Small and friendly bookshop and café where you can relax with a book and a good cup of coffee. And if you buy a book you get the coffee free! Popular with students and nurses from the local hospital. Also filled rolls made to order. Open Mon-Sat 1000-1930, Sun 1130-1930. *Café Couronne*, Royal Museum of Scotland, 2 Chambers St, T2474111. Elegant patisserie in the museum foyer serving good coffee and great cakes and pastries. No smoking. Open Mon-Sat 1000-1600, Sun 1200-1600. At the back of the museum, next to the Lumiere cinema, is *Petite Couronne*, a self-service café-bar offering good value snacks. No smoking. Open Mon-Thur 1000-1630, Fri/Sat 1000-1630, 1700-2030, Sun 1200-1630, 1700-2030. *Café Hub*, Castle Hill, T4732015. From the people who brought you the *Atrium* and *blue*, this chic new café at the top of the Royal Mile looks set to rival the *Assembly Rooms* as the place to eat, meet and drink during the festival and plays host to the Festival Club, as well as housing the ticket centre for the International Festival. Outside terrace seating in summer. No smoking. Open daily all day. *Café Lucia*, Festival Theatre, 13-29 Nicolson St, T6621112. Light, airy and contemporary café with a relaxed feel. Usual array of light snacks on offer. No smoking. Open from 1000 till half an hour after the show (from 1600 on Sun). *City Art Centre Café*, 1 Market St, T2203359. Good coffee and cakes and an affordable selection of main dishes in a spacious environment with helpful staff. No smoking. Open Mon-Sat 0830-1700, Sun (only during exhibitions) 1100-1700. *Clarinda's Tearoom*, 69 Canongate, T5571888. Cosy, traditional tearoom serving home-baked scones, shortbread and lots of waist-enhancing cakes. Good stopping-off point on the way to Holyrood Palace. No smoking. Open Mon-Sat 0900-1645, Sun 1000-1645. *Common Grounds*, 2-3 North Bank St, The Mound, T2261416. American-style café with a vast range of coffees and teas. A nice place to relax and take a break from shopping or sightseeing. Cakes, sandwiches and a vegetarian-friendly menu. Smoking only downstairs, where you can hear live music most nights. *Elephant House*, 21 George IV Bridge, T2205355. Very studenty – a great place to linger over coffee and bagels or one of many cheap snacks and main courses. Mellow vibe and lots of elephants (on the walls, not at the tables). Café bar by evening with live music. Open Mon-Fri 0800-2300, Sat/Sun 1000-2300. *Elephants & Bagels*, 37 Marshal St, T6684404. Continuing the elephant theme, and lots more bagels from the same stable. Good coffee, too. Open Mon-Fri 0800-1800, Sat/Sun 1000-1700. *Favorit*, 19-20 Teviot Place, T2206880. Café/bar/deli with an Italian-American look. A cool place to stop for a quick coffee and sandwich at any time of the day or night. Open daily 0830-0300. *Fruitmarket Café*, Fruitmarket Gallery, 45 Market St, T2261843. One of the coolest cafés in town with windows large enough to guarantee being seen. A great place for a quick, cheap and tasty lunch, or just for coffee and chat. No smoking. Open Mon-Sat 1100-1700, Sun 1200-1700. *Gustos*, 105 High St, T5583083. A very popular tourist spot near John Knox house on the Royal Mile. Open daily 1000-1800 upstairs and 0800-1800 downstairs. *The Lower Aisle*, St Giles Cathedral, High St (entrance via Parliament Square), T2255147. This self-service café underneath the cathedral is popular with the legal profession. Good for a cheap light lunch. Open Mon-Fri 0930-1630, Sun 0900-1400. *Patisserie Florentin*, 8 St Giles St, T2256267. Large and lively place to stop for a coffee, a filled croissant and a generous slice of Edinburgh life. Open Sun-Fri 0700-2100, Sat 0700-2200.

Café Q, Queen's Hall, 87 Clerk St, T6683456. Spacious and peaceful. Good value, wholesome food that's strong on vegetarian choices. No smoking. Open Mon-Sat 0930-1700. *California Coffee Company*, a new and growing range of former police boxes, just like the Tardis, now serving excellent coffee to go with a personal touch. At St Patrick's Square (open Mon-Fri 0745-2100, Sat/Sun 1000-2100), Middle Meadow Walk/Teviot Place (Mon-Fri 0745-2100, Sat 0800-2100, Sun 0900-2100), Hope Park Crescent (Mon-Fri 0745-2100, Sat 0800-2100, Sun 0900-2100). *Kaffe Politik*, 146-148 Marchmont Road, T4469873. Stylish surroundings, healthy, vegetable-based food, excellent home baking and good coffee. At its best on a lazy Sun, enjoying brunch with the newspaper. Open daily 1000-2200. *Mango & Stone*, 165a Bruntsfield Place, T229-2987. More of a juice bar than a café. Excellent juices which are not cheap but healthy and substantial. Try the Detox as a hangover cure. No smoking. Open Mon-Sat 0800-1800, Sun 0900-1800. *Metropole*, 33 Newington Rd, T6684999. Stylish and trendy converted bank boasting a wide range of teas and coffees and cappuccino to rival the best. Also a good range of snacks and sandwiches. No smoking. Open daily 0900-2200.

Southside, Marchmont & Bruntsfield

Cornerstone Café, St John's Church, 3 Lothian Rd, T2290212. In the church vaults, a quiet refuge from the Princes Street traffic offering cheap and tasty vegetarian meals. *The Gallery Café*, The Scottish Gallery of Modern Art, 74 Belford Rd, T3328600. There are few better ways to spend a couple of hours on a sunny afternoon than to sit outside in the walled sculpture garden enjoying a coffee and cake, a light snack, or something more substantial washed down with a glass of wine. This is one of the city's great delights. Open Mon-Sat 1000-1630, Sun 1400-1630. *Ndbele*, 57 Home St, T2211141. A real taste of southern Africa in the Tollcross. Huge selection of filling sandwiches with some unusual fillings such as smoked Ostrich. Nice, friendly atmosphere. Open daily 1000-2200. *Web 13*, 13 Bread St, T229-8883. Another internet café (see 'Internet cafés') that's good enough to include here. A great place to hang out and surf, or just hang out and enjoy their good value food. Open Mon-Fri 0900-2200, Sat 0900-2000, Sun 1100-2000.

West End, Haymarket & Tollcross

Bars

Edinburgh has more bars per square mile than any other European city. That may just be the drink talking, but the city does boast an inordinate amount of watering holes, from centuries-old pubs brimming with history, to the latest in contemporary chic. There's a bar for everyone in this town. And if that weren't enough, the city is blessed with liberal licensing laws, which are relaxed even further during the Festival in Aug and over Christmas and New Year. It is not a problem finding bars open till past midnight any night of the week and some are open till 0300 at weekends. Edinburgh may not be quite the city that never sleeps, but it's doing pretty well in the insomnia stakes.

A good area for bars is around the **Grassmarket**, in the Old Town, which gets very lively at weekends and is particularly popular with students, as are the bars in the **Southside**, near the University. There are also lots of bars around the **Tollcross**. Those looking for more hip and happening places should head for the cluster of cool bars around **Broughton Street**, at the east end of the New Town. This is in the 'pink triangle', the centre of the city's gay scene, but many of the bars are not exclusively gay, so relax. An area with a diverse mix of drinking holes is **Leith**. Here you'll find everything from the roughest spit-and-sawdust joints to the trendiest waterside warehouse conversions. Edinburgh's most famous drinking street is **Rose Street**, a narrow pedestrianized lane between Princes Street and George Street, but it has seen better days and only one or two of its many hostelries are worthy of note.

An excellent way to explore some of the city's more notable pubs is to take the **Edinburgh Literary Pub Tour** (see under 'Tours of Edinburgh', on page 72). Or, if you want to investigate the strange smell that permeates the city, then head along to Edinburgh's own independent **Caledonian Brewery**, 42 Slateford Road, T6238066, where you can take a tour and see traditional techniques and equipment in use and sample some of their fine ales. *Mon-Fri at 1100, 1230, 1400. £5.*

The other breweries are the giant Scottish and Newcastle, who produce *McEwan's* and *Younger's*, and the tiny Rose Street Brewery, which has its own pub.

Old Town *Bannerman's*, 212 Cowgate, T5563254. Huge, cavernous cellar-type pub that was once a real ale favourite but has now been taken over by young trendies. Still a good place to relax by the fire or have a big Sun fry-up. Open till 0100 daily. *Bar Kohl*, 54 George IV Bridge, T2256936. Trendy bar with 250 types of vodka on offer. Open Mon-Sat till 0100. *Biddy Mulligan's*, 96 The Grassmarket, T2201246. One of the most popular bars on the Grassmarket drinking strip, and that's saying something. Packed with students during term time and huge groups of lads and lassies at weekends, when it tends to get raucous. Open daily till 0100. *The Bow Bar*, 80 West Bow (halfway down Victoria St), T2267667. No nonsense, no frills pub for real ale enthusiasts and those who long for the days before mobile phones and sun-dried tomatoes. A dependable pint in an ever changing world. Open Mon-Sat till 2330, Sun till 2300. *Carwash*, 1-13 North Bank St, T2200054. Stepping inside is like reliving the Seventies, except that the prices have gone up. Makes you wish you'd packed the flares and permed wig. Open Mon-Sat 1200-0100, Sun 1800-0100. *Cellar No 1*, 1 Chambers St, T2204298. Basement cellar bar that attracts a wide variety of people and gets lively at night. Good value pub food and a good selection of wines. Features DJs Tue-Thur and live jazz Fri and Sat nights. Open Mon-Sat 1200-0100, Sun 1800-0100. *City Café*, 19 Blair St, T2200125. Style bar done out like an American diner with chrome-topped bar and booth seating. It's the major pre-club bar in town, especially on Sat nights. Downstairs is *City Café 2* which has DJs at weekends. Open daily till 0100. *EH1*, 197 High St, T2205277. Comfortable and stylish bar that's popular by day with tourists sitting in the sun and at night it's full of pre-club trendies (see also 'Eating'). Open daily 0930-0100. *Fiddler's Arms*, 9 The Grassmarket. Traditional bar that hasn't changed in centuries. Real fiddling on Mon nights. Open till 2400 (till 0100 at weekends). *Gilded Balloon*, 233 Cowgate, T2262151. Hugely popular during the festival with drunken comedians (professional and amateur). Gets unbearably busy at times. Open till 0300 at weekends. *Greyfriar's Bobby*, 24 Candlemaker Row, T2258328. Old-style bar named after the brave wee Skye Terrier who died waiting for a taxi to stop on a Sat night. Very popular with tourists and students, who come for the cheap bar meals. Open daily till 0100. *Iguana*, 41 Lothian St, T2204288. Fashionable café-bar/bistro that attracts students by day and pre-club ravers by night. See also under 'Eating'. Open daily 0900-0100. *Jolly Judge*, 7 James Court, T2252669. Turn off the High Street just down from the castle, down a narrow close, then down the stairs to reach this cosy, intimate wee place. Live folk music and good value bar food. Open Mon/Sun till 2300, Tue-Sat till 2400. *The Living Room*, 235 Cowgate, T2254628. Dark and dingy place that attracts the city's hipsters. If you don't like the music then you're probably too old. Open daily till 0100. *Negociants*, 45-47 Lothian St, T2256313. Next door to *Iguana*. Civilized late night drinking and eating with table service. DJs and dancing downstairs. See also 'Eating' page 108. Open daily 0900-0300. *The Royal Oak*, 1 Infirmary St. If it's a late-night session of traditional folk music you're after, then look no further. Every night around 2200 there's a spontaneous outbreak of singing and fiddle playing, washed down with copious quantities of whisky and beer. Open daily till 0200.

New Town *The Abbotsford*, 3 Rose St, T2255276. Big, old reliable pub in a street that's largely lost its drinking appeal. Good, solid pub lunches and a restaurant upstairs that's open in the evenings. Open Mon-Sat till 2300. *The Baillie Bar*, 2 St Stephen St, T2254673. Dark, smoky basement bar in bohemian Stockbridge. Attracts a more mature clientele (the *auld yins*, in other words). Serves above-average pub food. *Bar 38*, 126-128 George St, T2206180. Large, elaborately-decorated and popular with the after-work, young professional crowd. And, yes, those toilets are worth checking out! Open Mon-Sat till 0100, Sun till 2400. *Barony Bar*, 81-85 Broughton St, T5570546. Stylish and lively place where you won't feel like you've gatecrashed your young nephew's party. Very busy at weekends. Good bar food. Open till 2400, weekends till 0030. *Baroque*, 39-41 Broughton St, T5570627. Brightly-coloured décor that's not quite as loud as the young party lovers who frequent this popular bar. Usual range of trendy pub grub and a great selection of juices. Open daily till 0100. *The Basement*, 10-12a Broughton St, T5570097. This Broughton Street original feels like it's been around for ever and is just as hip and happening as ever. Good bistro food with a mainly Mexican flavour. Open daily 1200-2400. *Café Royal Circle Bar*, 19 West Register St, T5564124. You can't help feeling spoiled in these elegant and civilized surroundings. Adjacent to the famous *Café Royal Oyster Bar* (see 'Eating'). Treat yourself to the seafood menu while enjoying the sumptuous splendour. Open Mon-Wed 1100-2300, Thur till 2400, Fri/Sat till 0100, Sun till 2300. Next door upstairs is the *Café Royal Bistro Bar*, a big favourite with the Rugger fraternity. *Cask and Barrel*, 115 Broughton Street, T5563132. Set in the increasingly hip Broughton Street part of the New Town, but very different from many of the other, more glamorous places. Real Ale, brass taps and wooden fittings, try the local Deuchar's IPA. *Catwalk Café*, 2 Picardy Place, T4787771. So hip it hurts. Popular with the young and beautiful who come to pose and laugh at anyone with last week's haircut. Expensive trendy bar food. Very busy at weekends when DJs turn the tables. Open daily till 0100. *The Cumberland Bar*, 1 Cumberland Street, T5583134. Classic New Town bar that oozes refinement and respectability. Fine selection of real ales, a beer garden and some decent nosh. A good place to kick back and while away an hour or several. Open Mon-Wed till 2330, Thur-Sat till 2400, Sun till 2200. *The Dôme*, 14 George Street, T6248624. Large, grand and rather imposing bar with high ceiling. Bistro area at the back serves good bistro food. Wicker chairs and assorted greenery give it a slightly colonial feel that's disturbed only by the high percentage of irritating mobile phone users. *The Guildford Arms*, 1 West Register St. Ornate Victorian bar with an excellent selection of good ales. Open Sun-Wed till 2300, Thur-Sat till 2400. *The Kenilworth*, 152 Rose St, T2264385. Beautiful old bar serving good quality pub food. Special children's menu. Open Mon-Thur and Sun till 2300, Fri/Sat till 0100. *Mathers*, 25 Broughton St, T5566754. A welcome respite from the unremitting cool of this part of the city. Just a plain and simple bar serving good beer and unpretentious food in relaxed surroundings. Open Mon-Thur till 2400, Fri/Sat till 0030, Sun till 2300. *The Outhouse*, 12a Broughton St Lane, T5576668. Chic, minimalist and trendy bar that's always buzzing. Good beer garden in the summer months. The only place in the city that sells absinthe, the lethal green lubricant that makes the mind go wander. Open daily 1200-0100. *Pivo Caffé*, 2-6 Calton Rd, T5572925. At the top of Leith Walk opposite the St James Centre. Formerly St James Oyster Bar, now revamped as a slice of Prague, with pictures of the old city adorning the walls. Impressive brass bar. Open daily till 0100. *Po-Na-Na*, 43b Frederick St, T2262224. Done out like an Arabic souk with many nooks and crannies in which to get up to no good. Transforms into a club later on with much madness and mayhem. And it all goes on till 0300 every night. *Queen Street Oyster Bar*, 16a Queen St. One of the venerable chain of oyster bars serving fine cask ales and half a dozen Loch Fyne oysters for around a fiver. This one is more intimate and has live music at weekends. The others in the chain are the *West End Oyster Bar*, 28 Maitland St, and the *Leith Oyster Bar*, 10 Burgess St. All open daily till 0100. *Rose Street Brewery*, 55 Rose St, T2201227. One of the best pubs in this street. Brews its own ales on the premises and these are on tap in the ground-floor bar. Food served upstairs in the restaurant. Open Mon-Thur till 2300, Fri/Sat till 2400.

Edinburgh

West End,
Haymarket &
Tollcross

Bert's Bar, 29-31 William St, T2255748. A better class of rugby bar which attracts the more refined aficionado as well as the occasional Charlotte Street mafiosi. A pie and a pint doesn't get much better than this. Open Mon-Wed till 2300, Thur-Sat till 2400. *Blue Blazer*, 2 Spittal St. Traditional howff pub with wooden fixtures and fittings and a good selection of real ales. Open till 2400. *The Caley Sample Room*, 58 Angle Park Terr, T3371006. Sells the full range of ales from the nearby Caledonian Brewery. Popular with rugby and footie fans enjoying a pre- or post-match pint with their pie and chips (both Murrayfield rugby stadium and Tynecastle football ground are close by). *The Diggers* (*The Athletic Arms*), 1 Angle Park Terr. You could be 'marooned' here on match days, but console yourself with what is reputed to be the finest pint of 80 shilling in Edinburgh. Open till 2400 Mon-Sat. *Filmhouse Café Bar*, 88 Lothian Rd, T2295932. Comfortable place to relax whether or not you're catching a movie. Busy at lunchtimes and evenings with a wide mix of people who come for coffee and chat or to enjoy the excellent value vegetarian food. A good place for star-spotting during the film festival. Open Sun-Thur till 2330, Fri/Sat till 0030. *Indigo Yard*, 7 Charlotte Lane, T2205603. This old courtyard covered with a huge glass canopy is an immensely popular bar and restaurant (see also 'Eating'). Open daily 0830-0100. *Mather's*, 1 Queensferry St. Good real ale pub with a gorgeous interior. Open Mon-Thur till 2400, Fri/Sat till 0100. *Mondobbo*, 34 Bread St, T2215555. Part of the supremely stylish *Point Hotel*, and don't it show. Popular with local office workers for a sophisticated light lunch or after work for happy hour cocktails. Open Mon-Thur and Sun till 2400, Fri/Sat till 0100. *Traverse Bar Café*, Traverse Theatre, 10 Cambridge St, T2285383. Very stylish bar that's popular with luvvies, suits and students. Excellent and affordable food served at all times and regular special drinks offers. Open Mon till 2300, Tue-Thur and Sun till 2400, Fri/Sat till 0100.

Southside,
Marchmont &
Bruntsfield

Bar Ce Lona, 2-8 West Crosscauseway, T6628860. Mediterranean-style bar with civilized table service and al fresco eating. Try their flavoured margaritas or enjoy brunch on a sunny Sun. Live bands and DJs at weekends. Open daily 1100-0100. *Bennet's Bar*, 8 Leven St, T2295143. Next to the King's Theatre. Marvel at the carved wooden gantry, the stained glass windows, the huge mirrors, and the glass-topped tables with inlaid city maps while you enjoy a great pint of beer and perhaps some good old-fashioned (and cheap) food (served in the back room at lunch-times only). One of the city's finest traditional howffs. Open Mon-Wed till 2330, Thur-Sat till 0030, Sun till 2300. *The Canny Man's*, 237 Morningside Road. Part museum/part pub that's been serving good real ale and a vast smorgasbord of sandwiches in most interesting surroundings since Victoria was on the throne, and probably to the same bunch of regulars. A word of caution. If the publican doesn't like the look of you, you'll be out on yer ear. Open Mon-Sat till 2400, Sun till 2300. *The Pear Tree*, 38 West Nicolson Street, T6677533. Near the University, so a favourite student haunt, this was once a focal point for the city's crusties but now the occasional suit can be spotted. Boasts Edinburgh's only decent-sized beer garden, which is not only packed in summer, but populated at other times of the year. Also serves amazingly cheap food. Open Mon-Wed and Sun till 2400, Thur-Sat till 0100. *Sheep Heid Inn*, 43 The Causeway, Duddingston, T6566951. An 18th century coaching inn that makes a pleasant stop for a refreshing drink after a walk over Arthur's Seat. You could make a day of it and include Duddingston Loch and village and lunch here in the restaurant upstairs or in the bar. Either way it's good. In summer there's the added attraction of the open-air barbecue. Open Mon-Wed and Sun till 2300, Thur-Sat till 2400.

Leith

King's Wark, 36 The Shore. T5549260. One of the oldest pubs in Leith, dating back to the early 17th century and it appears not to have changed much. Real historical atmosphere and some damned fine food to boot. Open Mon-Thur 1200-2300, Fri/Sat till 2400, Sun 1100-2300. *The Merman*, 42 Bernard St. Another redoubtable old pub that prefers to ignore the current wave of gentrification that's sweeping Leith. Good range of real ales and a roaring log fire. Open till 2300, Fri/Sat till 2400. *Port O' Leith*, 58 Constitution St. A real piece of old Leith that refuses to change with the times and all the better for it. No fancy bar food but probably some spicy language. Open daily till 0045. *Starbank Inn*, 64 Laverockbank Rd, Newhaven. On the seafront between Newhaven and Leith. Nice old pub where you can enjoy a good pint of real ale and the views across the Forth. Also does bar food. Open Sun-Wed till 2300, Thur-Sat till 2400. *The Waterfront*, 1c Dock Place, T5547427. Great for a relaxing drink sitting in the conservatory or cosy booths. Excellent fish restaurant. See 'Eating'. Open Mon-Thur 1200-2300, Fri/Sat till 2400, Sun 1230-2230.

Entertainment

As host of the World's premiere arts festival, Edinburgh is well endowed with various cultural venues. But don't be mistaken in thinking that when the Festival packs its bags and leaves in early Sep the city hibernates till Aug comes round again. The city's cultural scene is thriving throughout the year, catering equally well for the avid culture vulture or hedonistic night owl. The many fine **theatres** and **concert halls** have full and varied programmes. Club culture in the capital has improved greatly in the last few years and Edinburgh now boasts some of the UK's best club nights, many of which go on until 0400 or 0500. These change frequently but tend to use the same venues, which are listed below. Those who prefer their music live, can take advantage of the liberal licensing laws and check out **jazz**, **folk** and **rock** bands any night of the week in many of city's 700-plus bars. The main live music venues are listed below, but also see under 'Bars'.

The city's vibrant **gay scene** has been centred around the Playhouse Theatre at the top of Leith Walk, the `pink triangle', for many years. It has continued to develop around Broughton Street, with new places constantly opening up, be they exclusively gay or gay-friendly. A large percentage of the city's trendiest bars, cafés and clubs can now be found on or around Broughton Street, making Edinburgh an easy city for the gay tourist to visit.

To find out **what's on** in the city, pick up a copy of *The List*, the fortnightly listings magazine that tells you what's happening and where in both Edinburgh and Glasgow (£1.90). Alternatively, the local evening paper, the *Edinburgh Evening News*, appears daily except Sun and gives details of what's going on the city on that day. Tickets and information on all events are available at the **tourist office**. You can also find flyers (promotional leaflets) for various events at the main concert halls and theatres and in many of the bars and cafés in the centre of town.

Art galleries

Aside from the main galleries mentioned in the 'Sights' section, Edinburgh has several smaller spaces where the work of up-and-coming contemporary artists can be viewed. *City Art Centre*, 2 Market St, T5293993. Houses six exhibition galleries. Home to the city's collection of Scottish art, with works by Peploe, McTaggart, Ferguson and Eardley as well as more contemporary artists such as Blackadder and Paolozzi. Also one of the leading temporary exhibition spaces in the UK. Also has a café. Open Mon-Sat 1000-1700, Sun during the Festival only 1400-1700. Usually free, but charges for selected shows. *Edinburgh Printmakers Workshop and Gallery*, 23 Union St, off Leith Walk, T5572479. Exhibits a huge range of contemporary etchings, lithographs and screenprints. You can buy prints in the shop at reasonable prices and see the workshops. Open Tue-Sat 1000-1800. Free. *The Fruitmarket Gallery*, 45 Market St, T2252383. Near Waverley station. One of the country's major venues for exhibitions of national and international contemporary art. Also has a good bookshop and café. Open Mon-Sat 1100-1800, Sun 1200-1700. Free. *Stills Gallery*, 23 Cockburn St, T622-6200. Scotland's leading photographic gallery, with a stylish new café. Open Tue-Sat 1000-1700. Free.

Edinburgh

Cinemas *The Cameo*, 38 Home St, T2284141. In the Tollcross. Three screens showing new arthouse releases and cult classics. Late showings at weekends and a good bar with video screen showing short films, comfy seating and snacks. Great place for movie buffs to hang out. Bar open Sun-Wed 1230-2300, Thur-Sat till 0100. *The Dominion*, 18 Newbattle Terr, T4474771. A nice old-fashioned cinema down in Morningside. Three screens showing new releases. *Filmhouse*, 88 Lothian Rd, T2282688. Three screens showing a wide range of movies, including new arthouse releases, obscure foreign films and old classics. Good café-bar frequented by a wide range of folk (see 'Bars' above). Hosts the annual Film Festival, so you never know who might bump into. *MGM*, 120 Lothian Rd, T2281638 (information line 229-3030). Mainstream cinema. *Odeon*, 7 Clerk St, T6670971. Five-screen complex showing mainstream releases.

Clubs Many of the clubs will have come and gone by the time you read this, and some are once a week events with no permanent venue. Consult *The List* for the latest information. Most of the clubs listed are in the Old Town and most are open till 0300 (later during the Festival).

The Bongo Club, 14 New St (off the Royal Mile), T5565204. Cabaret-style venue for a wide variety of performing artists. Innovative, eccentric and pretentious in equal measure. *Cavendish*, West Tollcross, T2283252. Hosts *The Mambo Club* upstairs on weekends, playing African/reggae/latin rhythms for a mixed crowd. *Café Graffiti*, Mansfield Place church, on the corner of Broughton St and East London St, T5578003. Great venue that may be closing soon. The *Lizzard Lounge* is a memorable night out for the more mature clubber, playing a soulful mix of jazz, latin, drum and bass and hip hop. *City Café*, 19 Blair St, T2200125. DJs downstairs in *City Café 2* at weekends. Check out *Rebel Waltz* on Fri till 0300. *La Belle Angele*, Hastie's Close (off the Cowgate), T2252774. Various nights featuring soul, latin, hip hop, big beat, house and drum and bass. Also live music venue. *The Liquid Room*, 9c Victoria St (top end), T2252564. Weekly *Diva* on Sat nights is for serious dance fans, while Thur is 70's night. It's also a popular venue for visiting indie bands. *Negociants*, 45-47 Lothian St. Djs and dancing till 0300 down in the basement of this popular bar/bistro (see 'Bars'). *The Subway West End*, 23 Lothian Rd, T2299197. Real student haunt playing a wide mix including indie, 70s cheese and more mainstream dance. Open every night till 0300. *The Venue*, 15 Calton Rd (behind Waverley station), T5573073. One of the longest-running clubs with three levels hosting a variety of different one-nighters, featuring house, funk, hip hop and garage. Top nights to look out for are *Pure*, *Tribal Funktion*, *Motherfunk* (free), *Disco Inferno* and *Scratch*. On weeknights it's one of the main Scottish tour venues for indie bands. *Wilkie House*, 207 Cowgate. Hosts many popular club nights, including *Joy*, *Taste* and *Lovely* (see below).

A popular student haunt, which is more of a late-night bar than a full-on club, is *The Kitchen*, at 237 Cowgate. DJs play hip hop, house, funk and soul Thur to Sat till 0100. Next door is *The Living Room* (see 'Bars'), where you can also dance till 0100, seven nights a week.

Comedy venues Gilded Balloon Theatre, 233 Cowgate, T2262151. One of the main Fringe comedy venues, famous for its riotous *Late'n'Live* slot (see 'Bars'). Here you'll see some of the best, and occasionally some of the worst, young comedians on the circuit. It also puts on regular comedy shows throughout the year. *The Stand Comedy Club*, 5 York Place, T5587272. Showcase for emerging comedy talent seven nights a week. By day it's a popular café-bar serving budget lunches, and on Sun there's free comedy with your lunch. Open Mon-Thur 1200-2400, Fri 1200-1900, 1930-0100, Sat 1930-0100, Sun 1230-2400.

Concert halls Classical music played by one of the national orchestras can often be heard at the main civic concert hall, the *Usher Hall*, Lothian Rd and Grindlay St, T2281155. Smaller classical ensembles, as well as jazz, blues, folk, rock and pop groups, can be heard at *Queen's Hall*, 89 Clerk St, T6682019. Less frequent performances are also staged at *Reid Concert Hall*, Bristo Square, T6504367, and the wonderful 18th century *St Cecilia's Hall*, Cowgate and Niddry St, T6502805. For details of current performances, see *The List* or Sat's *Scotsman* newspaper.

Gay clubs & bars

Blue Moon Café (see 'Cafés' above). Gay-run but straight-friendly café that's always busy. *Café Kudos*, 22 Greenside Place (at the front of the Playhouse Theatre), T5564349. Outside seating in summer. Popular with bright young things. Open daily till 0100. *CC Blooms*, 23 Greenside Place (next to the Playhouse), T5569331. Packed almost every night upstairs and downstairs on the dancefloor. This is where everyone ends up. Open daily till 0300. *New Town Bar*, 26 Dublin St, T5387775. Fairly mixed crowd upstairs. Downstairs is called *Intense* – appropriately named and full-on. Open daily till 0130, weekends till 0230. *Intense* open Thur-Sun. *Nexus Café*, 60 Broughton St, T478-7069. Comfortable and laid-back spot overlooking the garden behind the Gay and Lesbian Centre. Good all-day breakfasts (also vegetarian) and reasonably-priced snacks. Good pre-club meeting place. Open daily 1100-2300. *Planet Out*, 6 Baxter's Place, T5573379. Close to the *Playhouse*. Lively place in the heart of the action. Open daily till 0100. *Wilkie House*, 207 Cowgate. Hosts *Joy*, *Taste* and *Lovely*, three of the biggest gay/gay-friendly club nights in Scotland. *Joy* is held one Sat a month, as is *Taste*, while *Lovely* is held on a Sun.

There are many gay or gay-friendly cafés, bars and restaurants on Broughton Street, and several of these are listed elsewhere in the 'Eating', 'Cafés' and 'Bars' sections.

Live music venues

Good places to catch up and coming young **indie bands** are *La Belle Angele*, *The Liquid Room* and *The Venue*, all of which are listed above under 'Clubs'. Another good venue for little-known indie bands is *Cas Rock*, at 104 West Port, T2294341. Live **jazz** can be heard on Fri and Sat nights at *Cellar No 1* (see 'Bars' above) and on a Sat night at *Nobles Bar*, 44a Constitution St, Leith, T5542024. Here you can also hear folk music on a Thur, and R&B on a Fri, as well as enjoy some good beer and decent food in a lovely old Victorian bar. Occasional jazz concerts, as well as a growing number of top rock and pop gigs, also take place at the *Queen's Hall* (see above). One of the best places to hear authentic grassroots **folk music** is *The Royal Oak* (see under 'Bars'). Another good bet is the *Tron Ceilidh House*, 9 Hunter Square, behind the Tron Kirk, T2201550. Below the ground floor bar are two basement levels, with regular folk sessions and a comedy club. Open Sun-Thur till 2400, Fri/Sat till 0100. Two more popular folk venues are upstairs in the famous *Café Royal* in West Register Street (see under 'Bars') and the *West End Hotel* in Palmerston Place (see under 'Sleeping'). The *West End Hotel* is also a good place to find out where and when ceilidhs are taking place in the city.

When the really big acts come to town (the Rolling Stones, the Pope etc), more ad hoc venues such as *Ingliston Exhibition Centre* and *Murrayfield Stadium* are called into action, and occasionally the *Playhouse Theatre* (see below). And in more recent years, the *Ross Open Air Theatre* in Princes Street Gardens, T2204351, has been used for major music gigs at Hogmanay and during the Festival.

Theatres

Assembly Rooms and Music Hall, 54 George St, T2262428. This is one of the main Fringe venues, hosting a huge variety of mainly higher quality drama productions and more established comedians. It is also used throughout the year, though its future is uncertain at the time of writing. *Bedlam Theatre*, 11b Bistro Place, T2259893. Home of the University's Bedlam Theatre Company. A bit hit or miss but you can always grab a cheap and wholesome bite to eat in the café. *Festival Theatre*, Nicolson St, T5296000. The city's showcase theatre with a hugely varied programme including the world's leading companies. There's also an excellent café (see 'Cafés', page 112). *Hill Street Theatre*, 19 Hill St, T2266522. Homely little venue that's one of the Festival Fringe stalwarts.

Edinburgh

Festival City

Every year Edinburgh plays host to the world's biggest arts festival when the capital bursts into life in a riot of entertainment unmatched anywhere. Edinburgh during its Festival has been variously described as "simply the best place on Earth" and "the cultural hub of the world". There's a unique buzz about the place as over a million tourists descend on the city to experience a mind-blowing variety of performances. Dance groups, opera and theatre companies, orchestras, string quartets, comedians and puppeteers play to audiences in concert halls, theatres, church halls, pubs, clubs, hotels, Masonic lodges and big tents all across the city. Meanwhile, outdoors, the streets, parks and squares are filled with fire-eaters, jugglers, clowns, musicians, trapeze artists and escapologists all vying for your attention and to relieve you of your small change. The best places to see the street performers are the Mound, the High Street and Rose Street.

The Edinburgh Festival is actually a collection of different festivals running alongside each other, from the end of July through to the beginning of September. The **International Festival** tends to be a fairly highbrow affair and features large-scale productions of opera, ballet, classical music, dance and theatre performed in the larger venues. It ends with an open air concert and spectacular fireworks display in Princes Street Gardens. The **Festival Fringe** began life in 1947 as an adjunct to the International, or "official" Festival, but has since grown so large it now overshadows its big brother and threatens to outgrow the city. In 1999 over 500 companies performed in nearly 200 venues; everything from the country's leading comedians at the Assembly Rooms to a group of existentialist students staging "Waiting for Godot" in a draughty church hall – in Mandarin. Over the years the Fringe has been a major showcase for fresh talent and the likes of Billy Connolly, Maggie Smith, Emma Thompson, Rowan Atkinson and Harry Enfield all started out here. The Fringe continues to be the launching pad for many of our greatest actors, comedians, writers and directors as well as pushing back the boundaries of art and entertainment. A good opportunity to preview many of the Fringe performers for free is Fringe Sunday, which takes place in Holyrood Park, at the foot of the Royal Mile.

The **International Jazz and Blues Festival** kicks the whole thing off in July and features some of the world's leading performers, as well as many lesser known ones, playing in just about every pub in the city centre. The **International Film Festival** is the UK's most important film festival and screens many brilliant new movies long before they reach London and the rest of the country. It is also the longest continually running event of its kind in the world. The **International Book Festival**, meanwhile, may look like a just a bunch of tents in Charlotte Square, but the marquees are full of some of the biggest names in literature holding readings, discussions, interviews and a whole range of workshops for adults and children. Although it's a separate event, the **Military Tattoo**, set against the magnificent backdrop of Edinburgh Castle, is very much part of the Festival. It's an unashamedly kilt-and-bagpipes event, featuring Massed Pipes and Drums, display teams, dancers and bands from all over the world.

During the Festival, many of Edinburgh's tourist attractions have longer opening hours. Many of the main Festival venues are used throughout the year and are listed under **Entertainment** (page 50). For details of Festival dates and booking information see **Festival Information**, on page 121.

Edinburgh

Festival Information

Edinburgh International Festival
15 August-4 September. Box office until 1 July: 21 Market St, T4732000, F4732003. Open Monday-Friday 1000-1630. Box office from 5 July: The Hub, Castlehill (same phone and fax). Open July Monday-Friday 1000-1800, Saturday 1200-1500; August Monday-Saturday 0900-2000, Sunday 1000-1700.
Edinburgh Festival Fringe
8-30 August. Box office: 108 High St, T226-5138 (information line T226525) admin@edfringe.com. Open daily 1000-1900, from August 0900-2100.
Edinburgh International Film Festival
15-29 August. Box office: Filmhouse, 88 Lothian Rd, T4732000 (information line T2284051), info@edfilmfest.org.uk.
Edinburgh International Jazz and Blues Festival
30 July-8 August. Box office: 29 St Stephen St, T6677776 (information line T4675200).

International Book Festival
14-30 August. Box office: 137 Dundas St, T2285444, F2284333 (information line T09065-500010), admin@edinbookfest.co.uk.
Edinburgh Military Tattoo
6-28 August. Box office: 32 Market St, T2251188, F2258627, www.edintattoo.co.uk.
For full information about the International Festival events, and for access to the websites of all the Edinburgh Festivals:
www.edinburghfestivals.co.uk.
*For information on the various art exhibitions presented throughout the city, access the Edinburgh Gallery Guide website at **www.edinburgh-galleries.co.uk**. The free daily listings magazine, 'The Guide', is a good way to find out what's on and where. 'The List' and 'The Scotsman' also give comprehensive coverage. Note that dates given are for 1999 and may change for subsequent years.*

King's Theatre, 2 Leven St, T2291201. Refurbished Edwardian theatre showing everything from Shakespeare to panto. *Netherbow Arts Centre*, 43 High St, T5569579. Home to the Scottish Storytelling Centre, with children's shows during the day and Scottish drama for adults in the evenings. *Playhouse Theatre*, 18-22 Greenside Place, T5572950. Vast 3,000-seater theatre where you can catch all the glitzy West End productions as well as the occasional major rock act. Used during the official Festival for dance and opera. *Pleasance Theatre*, 60 The Pleasance, T5566550. One of the top Fringe venues staging comedy and drama. The outdoor cobbled courtyard is a great place to hang out during the Festival for a bit star-spotting. *Royal Lyceum*, 30 Grindlay St, T2299697. Lovely old Victorian theatre staging mainstream drama all year round. *Theatre Workshop*, 34 Hamilton place, T2265425. Small, accessible and amenable theatre down in bohemian Stockbridge with a reputation for innovative and daring productions. *Traverse Theatre*, 10 Cambridge St, T2281404. Internationally-renowned theatre dedicated to encouraging the cream of new writing talent. Consistently good entertainment. Also blessed with the excellent restaurant, *The Atrium*, in the foyer and *blue* bistro upstairs (see 'Eating'), as well as a good bar (see 'Bars').

Festivals

Edinburgh not only hosts the world's greatest arts festival in Aug, but also stages several other notable events throughout the rest of the year. The most renowned of these is **Edinburgh's Hogmanay**, which has grown to become one of the world's major winter events and which was the largest Millenium celebration in the northern hemisphere. It starts on the 29 Dec with a torchlit procession through the city centre followed by four days of various events, including pop and rock concerts. The highlight is the giant street party on the 31st (which is for ticket holders only). Accommodation is always fully booked at this time. For information contact the tourist office, T4733800.

The **Folk Festival**, at the beginning of **April**, is a massive event and draws performers from near and far, T5543092. Also in Apr is the **Science Festival** (Box office: 21 Market St, T4732070, held over two weeks, with exhibitions, workshops, lectures and various hands-on events for adults and children alike. The **Scottish International Children's Festival** is the UK's largest performing arts festival for children and is held at the end of **May** (Box office: 45a George St, T2206602).

At the end of **June** is the **Royal Highland Show**, at the Royal Highland Centre, Ingliston, T3356200. It's a sort of display of the best of rural Scotland, with pedigree livestock competitions, flower shows, craft fairs and showjumping, amongst other things. Also in Jun, around the 1st week, is the **Caledonian Beer Festival**, held at Edinburgh's own Caledonian Brewery on Slateford Road (see 'Bars', on page 113). The event features dozens of real ales, food and live music (mostly jazz) in the brewery's Festival Hall. See local press for details, or T3371286.

The **Filmhouse** (see 'Cinemas', on page 118) also hosts a number of foreign film seasons, most notably French (in **November**) and Italian, in **April**. There's also a gay film season, in **June**. For details, T2282688.

Shopping

Edinburgh's shops are best known for traditional Scottish souvenirs and upmarket goods, food products in particular. The main shopping street is Princes Street, where you'll find all the main department stores such as *Debenhams*, *Frasers*, *BHS*, *Marks & Spencers*. Two independent department stores are *Jenners*, also on Princes Street, and *Aitken & Niven*, at 77-79 George Street. *John Lewis* is in the controversial St James Centre, the ugly shopping complex at the top east end of Princes Street. Waverley Market is another, more pleasant and less obtrusive, shopping complex just above the train station. Good places to look for second-hand and antique art, jewellery and books are around the New Town (St Stephen St, Northwest Circus Place, Thistle St), Broughton Street, Victoria Street and the Grassmarket. Shopping hours are now more relaxed and many of the main city centre outlets are open till 1930-2000 on Thur and on Sun.

Antiques & junk *Byzantium*, 9 Victoria St, T2251768. Two floors of popular collectables from the 40s to the 70s, as well as antiques and hippy chic. Good place to browse with a café on the third floor. Open Mon-Sat 1000-1730, and Sun during the Festival. *Just Junk*, 34 Broughton St, T5576353. Small, reasonably-priced range of stuff from the 50s and 60s. Open Mon-Sat 1100-1800. *Utilities*, 87 Broughton St, T5574385. A real Aladdin's Cave where you could lose hours just browsing. Open Tue-Sat 1030-1830, Sun 1200-1600.

Books *James Thin*, 53-59 South Bridge, T5566743. This venerable Scottish chain has branches across the city and throughout the country, but this particular branch has a good second-hand department. Open Mon-Fri 0900-2200, Sat 0900-1730, Sun 1100-1700. *Waterstone's*, 128 Princes St (West End), T2262666. One of three city branches of this major chain, with a massive range of titles, well-informed staff and a pleasant second-floor café with fantastic views of the castle (see also 'Cafés'). Open Mon-Fri 0800-2100, Sat 0800-2000, Sun 1030-1800. Other branches at 13-14 Princes St, T5563034 and 83 George St, T2253436. *The Cook's Bookshop*, 118 West Bow, T2264445. Owned by celebrity chef Clarissa Dickson Wright with a wide selection of new and second-hand cookery books. Open Mon-Fri 1000-1700, Sat 1030-1700. *West Port Bookshop*, 145 West Port, T2294431. Wonderfully ramshackle, old-fashioned second-hand bookshop. Open Mon-Fri 1030-1730, Sat 1130-1700.

Clothes & shoes *Cruise*, 94 George St, T2263524 (also at 14 St Mary's St, T5562532). Expensive but high-quality range of designer clothes for men and women. Open Mon-Wed and Fri 1000-1800, Thur till 1900, Sat 0900-1800, Sun 1300-1700. *Smiths*, 124 High St,

T2255927. Top British designer menswear. *Jenners* on Princes St stocks a wide range of men's designer labels. *Corniche*, 2 Jeffrey St, T5563707. Stocks all the top names in women's fashion. Open Mon-Sat 1000-1730. *Flip*, 59-61 South Bridge, T5564966. Edinburgh branch of the national chain of second-hand American retro clothing. Open Mon-Sat 0930-1730. *Hand in Hand*, 3 Northwest Circus Place, T2263598. Second-hand women's clothes. *Schuh*, 6 Frederick St, T2200290, and 32 North Bridge, T2256552. The best for trendy footwear. *Barnets*, 7 High St, T5563577. For those who prefer a more classic shoe.

There are more food outlets than any other type of shop in the capital, so you won't have trouble finding your haggis, whisky and shortbread. *MacSweens*, 118 Bruntsfield Place, T4402555. Simply the best place to buy haggis. Open Mon-Fri 0830-1700. *The Scotch Whisky Heritage Centre*, 354 Castlehill (see also 'Sights'). Finding alcohol isn't a problem in Edinburgh, but here you can sample the stuff before parting with your cash. Open daily 0930-1800 (from 1230 on Sun). *Valvona & Crolla*, 19 Elm Row (see also 'Cafés'). Superb Italian deli importing fresh produce direct from Italy. Café at the back where you can linger and savour the delights on offer. Open Mon-Wed and Sat 0800-1800, Thur/Fri till 1930. *Royal Mile Whiskies*, 379 High St, T2253383. Over 300 types of whisky to choose from and all kinds of attractive gift packages. Open Mon-Sat 1000-1900, Sun 1200-1900. *Ian Mellis*, 30a Victoria St, T2266215. An overwhelming selection of cheeses, in every sense of the word. Open Mon-Sat 0930-1730. *Real Foods*, 37 Broughton St, T5571911. The best-stocked vegetarian and vegan grocery shop in town. Open Mon-Wed 0900-1830, Thur and Sat till 1730, Fri till 1900, Sun 1100-1700.

Food & drink

For tartan tack go to the top end of the Royal Mile. Those wishing to hire a kilt, or have one made, should try *McCalls of the Royal Mile*, at 11 High St, T5573979, or *Kinloch Anderson*, on the corner of Dock St and Commercial St, Leith, T5551390. There's also *Hector Russell*, on the High St and on Princes St. For woollies try *Judith Glue* – Orkney Island Knitwear, 64 High St, T5565443. Open Mon-Sat 0930-1800, Sun 1200-1700. Also *The Cashmere Store*, 2 St Giles St, T2254055, and *Number Two*, 2 St Stephen Place, T2256257. Those looking for something a bit different should check out *Round the World*, at 82 West Bow, T2257086, and 15 North West Circus Place, T2257800, or *Eden*, at 37-39 Cockburn St, T2203372. There are a few interesting shops in Raeburn Place, such as *Blackadder Gallery*, at number 5, T3324605.

Gifts & souvenirs

Joseph Bonnar, 72 Thistle St, T2262811. Good range of fine quality antique jewellery. Open Mon-Sat 1030-1700. *Hamilton & Inches*, 87 George St, T2254898. Grand old jewellers with a wonderfully ornate Georgian interior that's worth a peek even if you're not buying. Open Mon-Sat 0900-1800.

Jewellery

Avalanche, 17 West Nicolson St, T6682374, 63 Cockburn St, T2253939, and 28 Lady Lawson St, T2281939. Specializes in new and used vinyl and CDs. The Cockburn St branch is a good place to find out about clubs and gigs. Open daily 1000-1800. *Backbeat*, 31 East Crosscauseway, T6682666. Excellent second-hand record shop with a great selection of jazz, blues and soul. Open Mon-Sat 1000-1730. *Blackfriar's Folk Music Shop*, 49 Blackfriar's St (off the Royal Mile), T5573090. Wide range of traditional Scottish musical instruments. *FOPP*, 55 Cockburn St, T2200133. Another record shop on a street full of them. Good for mainstream, indie and dance music. Open Mon-Sat 0930-1900, Sun 1100-1800.

Music

Blacks Outdoor Leisure, 13-14 Elm Row, T5563491, and 24 Frederick St, T2258686. Good range of clothes and equipment for hikers, skiiers and ramblers. Open Mon-Wed and Fri 0900-1800, Thur 0930-1900, Sat 0900-1730. *Graham Tiso*, 13 Wellington Place and Rose St. Excellent for all kinds of outdoor clothing and sports equipment.

Outdoor & sports

Edinburgh

Edinburgh

Sports

Climbing There's indoor rock climbing at *Alien Rock*, Old St Andrew's Church, Pier Place, New-haven, T5527211. Climbing walls of various degrees of difficulty and a bouldering room.

Football Edinburgh has 2 Scottish Premier League teams, who play at home on alternate Saturdays during the league season. Heart of Midlothian, or Hearts, play at Tyncastle, on the Gorgie Road about a mile west of Haymarket (see map), and Hibernian (Hibs) play at Easter Road, east of the centre near Leith. Rivalry between the two is fierce, but thankfully free from the religious bigotry of their Glasgow counterparts.

Golf There are many fine golf courses around Edinburgh, especially along the coast of East Lothian, but most are private. Public courses in and around the city include the two at *Braid Hills*, T4476666, *Silverknowes*, T3363843, *Torphin Hill*, T4414061, and *Lothianburn*, T4452288. If you plan on playing a lot of golf, then you should buy the *Lothian and Edinburgh Golf Pass*, which costs £5 and allows you to play on 20 courses throughout the region at discounted rates. For details, contact the tourist board, T4733800, www.edinburgh.org/golf.

Pony trekking *Edinburgh & Lasswade Riding Centre*, Kevock Rd, Lasswade, T6637676. *Pentland Hills Icelandics*, Rodgersrigg Farm, Carlops (south of Hillend Ski Centre), Midlothian, T01968-661095. *Tower Farm Riding Stables*, 85 Liberton Drive, T6643375.

Rugby Scotland's national side play at Murrayfield Stadium, a few miles west of the city centre and reached from Corstorphine Rd or Roseburn St. For tickets T3645000, though these are scarce for major internationals.

Skiing *Midlothian Ski Centre*, at Hillend, take the A702 off the City Bypass at the Lothianburn exit (see map), T4454433 (open Mon-Sat 0930-2100, Sun 0930-1900). Artificial ski slope for ski and snowboarding practice and instruction. Also downhill mountain bike trail and chairlift for those who want to admire the view.

Sports centres *Meadowbank Sports Centre*, 139 London Rd, T6615351. The city's main venue for athletics meetings. Indoor and outdoor multi-sports complex with fitness room, squash courts, all weather pitches, velodrome and climbing wall. Open Mon 0930-2300, Tue-Sun 0900-2300. To get there, take bus no 15 or 26 from Princes St (north side) or a no 45 from the Mound. *Craiglockart Tennis and Sports Centre*, 177 Colinton Rd, T4430101. Indoor and outdoor tennis courts, squash, badminton, pulse-centre gym, fitness studio and free weights. Open Mon-Thur 0900-2300, Fri 1000-2300, Sat/Sun 0900-2230. Take bus no 10 from Princes St (south side) or no 27 from the Mound going south.

Swimming pools *Ainslie Park Leisure Centre*, 92 Pilton Rd, T5512400. Swimming pool, sauna, steam room, spa, pulse-centre gym, fitness suite. Open Mon-Fri 1000-2200, Sat/Sun 1000-1800. Take bus no 28 or 29 from the Mound to Crewe Toll, or 27 to Ferry Road. *Leith Waterworld*, 377 Easter Road, T5556000. At the foot of Leith Walk. Good children's facilities. Open Mon-Fri 0900-1700, Sat/Sun 1000-1700 during school holidays. *Royal Commonwealth Pool*, Dalkeith Rd, T6677211. The biggest and most popular in the city, with a 50m pool, flumes, diving pool, children's area, sauna and gym. Open Mon-Fri 0900-2100, Sat/Sun 1000-1600. To get there take a no 14, 21, 33, 82 or 83 bus south from North Bridge. There are also some older, quieter swimming pools at: 6 Thirlestane Rd, Marchmont, T4470052; Glenogle Rd, Stickbridge, T3436376; and 15 Bellfield St, Portobello, T6694077.

Transport

Air There are many flights to Edinburgh from all over Europe, Ireland and from around the UK. Flights from North America arrive via Glasgow. For flight details, see 'Getting there' (page 67). There is one daily flight from Edinburgh to **Inverness**, which takes 45 minutes. Prices from £75 return. For more details, contact *British Airways*, T03450-22211.

Long distance

Bus There are numerous bus services from London and prices are very competitive. There are also links with other English cities, such as Newcastle, Manchester, Birmingham and York. For details of these services, see 'Getting there' (page 67). Buses leave from St Andrew Square bus station to most of the major towns in Scotland. Most west coast towns are reached via Glasgow. There are numerous buses to and from **Glasgow** (£5-7 return fare). There are also regular daily buses to: **Aberdeen** (4 hrs; £13.50 single); **Dundee** (2 hrs 10 mins, or 1 hr 25 mins direct; £6.50 single); **Perth** (1 hr 30 mins, or 1 hr direct; £4.70 single); **Inverness** (4 hrs 30 mins, or 3 hrs 40 mins direct; £12.30 single), via Pitlochry and Aviemore. One of the main operators is *Scottish Citylink*, T0990-505050, with buses to virtually every major town in Scotland. For bus services to and from English towns and cities, contact *National Express*, T08705-010104, www.nationalexpress.co.uk.

Train There are regular daily services to and from London King's Cross. For details of frequency and fares, see 'Getting there' (page 67). *ScotRail* runs regular daily train services to **Inverness** (3 hrs 45 mins), via **Stirling** (45 mins), **Perth** (1 hr 15 mins), **Pitlochry** and **Aviemore** (3 hrs). Also to **Aberdeen** (2 hrs 45 mins), via **Kirkcaldy** and **Dundee** (1 hr 45 mins). There are trains every 30 mins to and from **Glasgow** (50 mins; £8.50 day return). There is also a regular service to **North Berwick** (35 mins). For information on all *ScotRail* services; T0345-484950.

Bus Buses are reasonably frequent during working hours from 0700, but after 1900 and on Sun they are much less so, with some routes stopping completely. Main city centre bus stops have timetables on display and some have clear maps of the bus routes served by that stop and the fares, which are paid to the driver on all buses. Be warned that *LRT* buses are **exact fare only**, and drivers don't give change – ever. *FirstBus* services don't require the exact fare. Fares are much the same for both companies – 50p, 70p and 90p in town, depending on the distance. A **Day Saver** allows unlimited travel around Edinburgh for a day on *LRT* buses and costs £2.40. A one week **Rider Card** costs £10.50 and can also be used on *FirstBus* services after 1900 and on Sun.

Local
See also 'Getting there' page 67.

Taxi The council-imposed city taxi fares are not cheap, costing from around £3 for the shortest of trips up to around £6 from the centre to the outskirts. There are far more people wanting to get home late on Fri or Sat night than there are cabs on the streets, so be prepared to wait, walk or phone. Some of the larger 24-hr companies are: *Capital Castle Taxis*, T2282555; *Central Radio Taxis*, T2292468; *Edinburgh Taxis*, T2288989; *Radio Cabs*, T2259000.

Directory

Airline offices *British Airways/Loganair*, 32 Frederick St, T0345-222111. *British Midland*, T3443302/3. Other carriers are handled by *Servisair*, at Edinburgh Airport, T3443111.

Banks The major **Scottish banks** have branches throughout the city, those with cash dispensers (ATMs) in the centre of town are: *Bank of Scotland*, Canongate, Chambers St, George St, 141 Princes St, 38 St Andrews Square, Shandwick Place, The Mound (head office); *Royal Bank of Scotland*, George St, North Bridge, Princes St, St Andrews Square; *Clydesdale Bank*, 29 George St,

Hanover St, North Bridge. The major **English clearing banks** all have branches in the city, and are open Mon-Fri only (phone for opening times): *Barclays*, 1 St Andrew Square, T0845-6000; *Lloyds/ TSB*, 113 George St, T2264021; *HSBC*, 76 Hanover St, T4653200; *NatWest*, 80 George St, T2266181. For **currency exchange**: *Thomas Cook*, 79a Princes St, T2204039. Open Mon-Fri 0900-1730, Sat 0900-1700. Also have other exchange bureaus in the main tourist office at Waverley Market (open Mon-Sat 0900-2000) and in the accommodation kiosk at Waverley station (see page 95). To change money outside office hours, try the upmarket hotels, though expect to pay a hefty commission. Also *American Express*, 139 Princes St, T2259179. Open Mon-Fri 0900-1730, Sat 0900-1600, Sun (Jul-Sept only) 1000-1600.

Car hire The main national car hire companies can all be found at the airport. The following are local companies which may offer better deals: *Arnold Clark*, Lochrin Place, T2284747; *Condor*, 45 Lochrin Place, Tollcross, T2296333; *Lo-Cost*, 1a Wardlaw Tce (off Slateford Rd), T3132220; *Melville's*, 9 Clifton Terr, Haymarket, T0345-525354, www.melvilles.co.uk. **Communications** **Post office**: central offices at 8-10 St James Centre and 7 Hope St. There is a late collection from the post box at the Royal Mail head office, 10 Brunswick Rd (one third of the way down Leith Walk). A Poste Restante service is available at any post office, providing you have no permanent address in Edinburgh. Envelopes should be marked "Poste Restante" in the top left corner with your name above the address of the office. **Internet access**: there are cybercafés throughout the city, but two of the best are *Cyberia*, 88 Hanover St, T2204403, open Mon-Sat 1000-2200, Sun 1100-2000, prices from £2.50 per half hour (£2 concession) and *Web 13*, 13 Bread St, T2298883, open Mon-Fri 0900-2200, Sat 0900-2000, Sun 1100-2000, prices from £2.50 per half hour at peak times (1200-1700 Mon-Sat) and £3.50 at all other times. Both are also listed under 'Cafés' (see page 111). There are also cybercafés at 66/68 Thistle St, T2255000 and 44 West Preston St, T4467767, www.t2Lg.net. **Consulates** See 'Before you travel', page 25. **Cycle hire** *Central Cycle Hire*, 13 Lochrin Place, T2286333, F2283686. £15/day. Open Mon-Fri 0930-1800, Sat 0930-1730, Sun 1200-1700. *Edinburgh Cycle Hire*, 29 Blackfriars St, T5565560. £10-12/day. Open daily 0900-2100.

Disabled access and facilities Edinburgh is not the most accessible of cities, particularly around the Old Town. All cinemas and permanent theatres have full access. Guide dogs are welcome on public transport and at most Festival venues. The *Lothian Coalition for Disabled People* , T4752360, F4752392, publishes *Access in Lothian*, which they will send out on request. *Artlink* , T2293555, provide an arts access service to Edinburgh residents, so should be able to provide information and access hints. New black cabs can take wheelchairs and the taxi firms listed in the 'Getting around' section (see page 67) all have facilities for disabled passengers. Full details of disabled access on public transport from *Traveline*, T0800-232323. The Fringe Office at 180 High St, T2265257, minicom number T2205594, has a Disability Fact Sheet for further information and holds a list of contacts for each venue. **Drugs information** *Crew 2000* has a walk-in information shop at 32 Cockburn St, T2203404, where volunteers offer impartial information and advice on all aspects of using illicit and non-medical drugs. Open Mon-Wed, Fri and Sat 1300-1700, Thur 1600-2000.

Gay and Lesbian *Gay Men's Health*, T5589444; *Gay Switchboard*, T5564049; *Lesbian Line*, T5570751). **Genealogical research** *Scottish Genealogy Society Library & Family History Centre*, 15 Victoria Terr, T2203677. Open Tue and Thur 1030-1730, Wed 1030-2030, Sat 1000-1700. £5 per session for non-members. *Scottish Roots Ancestral Research Service*, 16 Forth St, T4778214. Open Mon-Fri 0900-1700 by appointment.

Hospitals & medical services Edinburgh's 24-hour walk-in accident and emergency department is at *The Royal Infirmary of Edinburgh*, 1 Lauriston Place, T5361000. If it's not an emergency but you still need to see a doctor look in the *Yellow Pages*, or call the Primary Care department, T5369000. **Alternative medicine**: *Napiers Dispensary and Clinic*, 1 Teviot Place, T2255542, and 35 Hamilton Place, Stockbridge, T3752130. Open Mon 1000-1730, Tue-Sat 0900-1730. Health practitioners providing non-conventional remedies. *The Whole Works*, Jackson's Close, 209 Royal Mile, T2258092. Open Mon-Fri 0900-2000, Sat 0900-1700. *The Edinburgh Floatarium*, 29 North West Circus Place, Stockbridge, T2253350. Open Mon-Fri 0900-2000, Sat 0900-1800, Sun 1000-1600. Natural salt floating tanks, as well as a wide range of beauty therapies and treatments. **Chemist (Pharmacy)**: *Boots the Chemist*, 48 Shandwick Place, T2256757. Open Mon-Sat 0800-2100, Sun 1000-1700. In an emergency outisde these times, go to The Royal Infirmary. **Dental**: *Edinburgh Dental Institute*, Level 7, Lauriston Building, Lauriston

Place, T5364931. Open Mon-Fri 0900-1500. They provide free walk-in emergency treatment though you still need to book an appointment. If it's not an emergency but you need to see a dentist, look in the *Yellow Pages* or call the Primary Care department, as above. **STDs/HIV/AIDS:***The Genito-Urinary Medicine* (GUM) clinic is at Lauriston Building, Lauriston Place (men T5362103; women T5362104). Open Mon-Fri 0830-1700, till 1830 on Thur. Free confidential advice and treatment on sexually transmitted and other diseases.

Laundry *Sundial Laundrettes* offer coin-operated or service washes, full laundry service, ironing, dry-cleaning and alterations. They have several branches at: 7 East London St, T5562743, next to the *Lost Sock Diner* (see 'Eating', page 107); 84 Dalry Rd, T5387002; 17 Roseneath St, T2292137; *Tarvit Laundrette*, 7 Tarvit St, T2296382. **Left luggage** Left luggage lockers at Waverley train station, T5502031, by platform 11, open 0700-2300. Also at St Andrew Square bus station on platform A1 (24 hours) and at Edinburgh Airport, T3331000, in a portakabin next to the new extension, open 0600-2200. **Libraries** *Central Library*, George IV Bridge, T2255884. Open Mon-Fri 0900-2100, Sat 0900-1300. Excellent Scottish and local reference sections. *National Library of Scotland*, George IV Bridge, T2264531. Open Mon-Fri 0930-2030, Sat 0930-1300. Superb copyright library, for research purposes only. Reference facilities at the *Map Room*, 33 Salisbury Place; open Mon-Fri 0930-1700, Sat 0930-1300. **Lost property** Property found and handed in to the police (including property found in taxis) is sent to the **Police HQ** at Fettes Ave, T3113131. It can be collected Mon-Fri 0900-1700. There are lost property departments at **Edinburgh Airport**, T3331000, and **Waverley train station**, T5502711. *Lothian Regional Transport* have a lost property department at Shrub Place, about a third of the way down Leith Walk, on the left-hand side, T5544494. Open Mon-Fri 1000-1330.

Safety Edinburgh is, in general, a reasonably safe and civilized place, but some precautions should be taken. Some areas are best avoided for women walking alone at night. Lothian Road and the Grassmarket are not particularly dangerous but full of beer-soaked revellers who may prove irritating. The Meadows' walkways are lonely at night and potentially risky. The narrow, secluded wynds and closes of the High Street have also been the scenes of assaults in the past. The back streets of Leith are also best avoided at night as they are one of the city's most notorious red-light districts. If you are robbed or assaulted and need to report the crime, call 999. The police information centre is at 188 High St, T2266966, open daily 1000-2200. **Rape crisis centre**: T5569437. For lost property see above. **Shoe repairs** *Master Cobbler*, 5 Waverley Steps, T5573756. *Uppermost Shoe repairs*, 9 North Bridge Arcade, T2264584. *H Robertson*, 21a Castle St, T2263464.

Tour agencies *Campus Travel*, 53 Forrest Rd, T2256111, and 5 Nicolson Square, T6683303. *Edinburgh Travel Centre*, 196 Rose St, T2262019, 92 South Clerk St, T6679488, and 3 Bristo Square, T6682221. Both are youth and student travel specialists. Minibus tours around the Highlands aimed at the adventurous and independent-minded backpackers are offered by *Go Blue Banana*, 12 High St, T5562000, and *Haggis Backpackers*, 11 Blackfriars St, T5579393, info@ haggis-backpackers.com (see 'Getting around', page 31.

Around Edinburgh

Edinburgh's best tourist attractions are not confined to the city centre. Around the suburbs and beyond are some worthwhile sights, all easily reached by public transport, including the Zoo and the Royal Observatory. Not far to the south are the Pentland Hills, with some good walks, and on the northern side of the city the port of Leith is worth exploring. And then there's the Forth Rail Bridge, perhaps the country's greatest feat of engineering, which can be seen in its all its glory from South Queensferry.

Leith

Leith Walk leads from Princes Street down to the port of Leith, which has a distinct flavour all of its own. There has been a settlement here for over 800 years and the harbour has been used commercially since Edward I captured Berwick for England in 1296. Leith became a burgh in its own right in 1833 and only became integrated into the city of Edinburgh in 1920.

Leith is a good 20-minute walk from the top of Leith Walk, or you can take one of the many buses which head that way. Near the top of Leith Walk is a statue of Sherlock Holmes, whose creator, Sir Arthur Conan Doyle, lived nearby.

In its heyday, Leith was Scotland's major port. Ships exported coal, salt, fish, paper, leather and local ale and returned with grain, timber, wine and foreign delicacies, from Northern Europe and as far afield as North America and Australia. Up until the 1950s and 60s, Leith and nearby **Granton** supported large deep-sea fishing fleets and were landing thousands of whales every year. Between the two ports the shoreline was lined with shipyards, dry docks, breaking yards and repair yards. The streets of old Leith were full of shipping agents, chandlers and merchants, plus all the attendant "services" such as pubs, clubs, flophouses and brothels.

When the fishing and shipping trade decanted south, the heart was ripped out of Leith. Much of its old centre was replaced with grim housing schemes and the port area fell into decay. However, the old port's fortunes have changed in recent years and Leith has been turned around. Millions have been spent on restoring many of its fine historic buildings, and it is now one of the best parts of the city for eating and drinking, with scores of fashionable restaurants, bistros and bars (see 'Eating', on page 110, and 'Bars', on page 116). At the same time private developers have been converting old warehouses and office buildings into expensive dockside flats.

The old port still has its rough edges, and you'll need to be careful after dark, but it's worth a visit, especially **The Shore**, the road which follows the last stretch of the Water of Leith before it reaches the Firth of Forth, where you'll find many handsome neo-Classical buildings. In the adjoining streets are some of the most notable buildings to have been given a face-lift, such as the old **Customs House** on Commercial Street, **Trinity House** on Kirkgate and the former **Town Hall** on Constitution Street. Set back from The Shore is **Lamb's House**, a well-preserved Renaissance house, which was the home of Andro Lamb, the merchant with whom Mary, Queen of Scots spent her first night on her return to Scotland in 1561. It is now used as an old people's day centre. Just east of the old Town Hall is **Leith Links**, now a public park but which, it is claimed, was the world's first official golf course, in the 15th century. Indeed, the rules drawn up here in 1744 by the Honourable Company of Edinburgh Golfers, ten years before they were formalized in St Andrews, still form the basis of the game today.

One of Leith's main attractions is the **Former Royal Yacht Britannia**, which is now docked in the harbour, just off Ocean Drive. It's certainly worth visiting, and you'll pick up some interesting royal titbits, but make sure you have a good look around the visitors centre before boarding the ship. ■ *Daily 1030-1800 (last admission 1630), £7.50, children £3.75, T5555566, pre-booking advised by telephone, or at the Tattoo Office, 32 Market St.*

Newhaven A mile west of Leith is the little port of Newhaven, founded by James IV around 1500 as the building place of *The Great Michael*, then the biggest warship on earth and whose construction was said to have used up all the trees in Fife. The grandiose scheme, like so many others, was a failure and following the defeat of the Scottish army at Flodden in 1513, and the death of James IV, the great ship was sold to the French, who left her to rot in Brest harbour.

Newhaven was once a busy fishing community and one of the most colourful and interesting parts of Edinburgh. Tram cars used to ply its bustling main street lined with shops and businesses and millions of oysters were landed every year at the thriving fish market. But the fishing has now gone and though the little fishermen's cottages have been restored, there is no life left in the place, other than the occasional pleasure yacht in the harbour. The village's proud maritime past is told in the excellent **Newhaven Heritage Museum**, 24 Pier Place. The little, one-room museum has hands-on exhibits, a dressing-up box, evocative living history recordings and various activities for children. ■ *Daily 1200-1700, free, T5514165, take buses 10, 16, 22 or C33 from Leith Walk*. Next door to the museum is *Harry Ramsden's*, famous for its fish and chips.

Portobello

To the east of Edinburgh is the Georgian seaside resort of Portobello. This was where the whole of Edinburgh used to come on sunny weekends, to paddle in the Firth of Forth, and stroll along its two miles of promenade. The long, sandy beach is still quite busy on sunny days, and there are the usual amusement arcades, funfairs, chips and ice cream, but now it's more of a relaxing escape from the city centre bustle. There used to be a hugely popular outdoor swimming pool, which was demolished in 1987, and it's a little-known fact that a young Sean Connery worked there as a life guard before he made it big. ■ *Portobello is about five miles east of the city centre and can be reached on buses 15, 26, 42, 66 or X86 from Princes Street*.

The Southern Suburbs

The city also developed south from the Old Town, creating a district which became known as **Southside** and which today forms the heart of the University quarter. Beyond this area, and the open parkland of the **Meadows** and **Bruntsfield Links**, are the residential suburbs of **Merchiston, Marchmont, Newington** and **Morningside**. The latter has traditionally been the home of Edinburgh's elite, or 'crème de la crème', as Miss Jean Brodie might have put it in her Morningside accent, renowned for its "rifained zenzitivity".

Beyond Morningside, Comiston Road leads south past **Blackford Hill** (539ft), at the top of which stands the city's **Royal Observatory**. Visitors can find out all about the mysteries of the solar system, play with various hands-on exhibits and enjoy the panoramic views of the city. ■ *Mon-Sat 1000-1700, Sun 1200-1700, £3, children £2, concession £1.50, T6688405, take buses 40 or 41 from The Mound and get off at Blackford Ave, or it's a short walk from Morningside*.

At the foot of Blackford Hill, on Blackford Glen Road, is the starting point for the **Hermitage of Braid** nature trail, a lovely gentle walk along the Braid Burn. The track is easy to follow and although the hill is within the city, there's a real sense of being out in the countryside. The path takes you to Hermitage House, an 18th century mansion which now serves as an information centre. ■ *Mon-Fri 1000-1600, Sun 1100-1800*. Immediately to the south are the **Braid Hills**, which are mostly occupied by two golf courses, part of a great ring of golf courses that almost completely encircle the city. At this point you may wish to reflect on George Bernard Shaw's pertinent comment on the sport.

The road southeast from Newington passes Craigmillar Castle. It may be in **Craigmillar** ruins and roofless, but it is nonetheless an impressive and well-preserved 15th **Castle** century fortress, despite its proximity to a sprawling council estate. It was once a refuge for Mary, Queen of Scots, who came here in 1566 to grieve the murder of Rizzio at Holyrood and it was also here that the murder of her husband, Lord Darnley, was plotted. The castle encompasses one and a half acres and

Edinburgh

Craigmillar Castle

there's plenty to be seen. The prison in particular is worth seeing. ■ *Apr-Sep daily 0930-1830, Oct-Mar daily 0930-1630 (closed Thur pm, Fri and Sun am), £1.80, children 75p, T6614445. The castle is on Craigmillar Castle Rd, off the Old Dalkeith Rd (A7). Take bus 14, 42 or 46 from the city centre and get off at the junction of Duddingston Rd West and Peffermill Rd.*

The Pentland Hills

South of the Braid Hills, beyond the City Bypass, are Edinburgh's Pentland Hills, a serious range of hills, remote in parts, rising to almost 2,000ft and which stretch some 16 miles from the outskirts of Edinburgh to Lanarkshire. The hills offer relatively painless climbs and you'll be rewarded with magnificent views once you reach the top.

On the northern slopes of the Pentlands is the village of **Swanston**, a huddle of 18th century thatched, whitewashed cottages. The largest of these, Swanston Cottage, was the holiday home of the Stevenson family, where the sickly young Robert Louis spent his summers.

There are many paths up to the various Pentland summits and round the lochs and reservoirs. One of the many walks is described above, but if you want to explore more fully there are many books about the Pentlands, including *25 Walks in Edinburgh and Lothian* (HMSO, 1995). Ordnance Survey Landranger Map no 66 covers the area.

The main access is the A702, which passes the *Midlothian Ski Centre* at **Hillend** (see also page 58). There's a marked walking trail up to the ski slope, or you can take the chair lift. At the top of the slope it's a short walk to **Caerketton Hill** for fantastic panormaic views of Edinburgh, the Firth of Forth and the hills of Fife and Stirlingshire.

Roslin

Seven miles south of Edinburgh, in the county of **Midlothian**, just off the A701 to Penicuik, lies the little village of Roslin, home of the mysterious 15th century **Rosslyn Chapel**. Perched above the North Esk, the magnificent and unique chapel has a richly carved interior full of Biblical representations and pagan and masonic symbols and has been described as "a fevered hallucination in stone". Foundations were laid in 1446 for a much larger church which was never built. What exists is the Lady Chapel, inspiration of Sir William Sinclair, who himself supervized masons brought from abroad who took 40 years to complete it to his design. According to legend, his grandfather, the adventurer Prince Henry of Orkney, set foot in the New World a century before Columbus. This is backed up by the carvings of various New World plants.

Edinburgh

Walking in the Pentlands

A relatively easy walk which provides great views and varied scenery starts at **Boghall Farm***, headquarters of the Pentlands Regional Park, on the A702 to Biggar. There are regular buses from the city centre, including the 4, 15 and 100. The circular walk covers five miles and takes around three hours. There's a map of the route in the car park at Boghall.*

Follow the Farm Trail signs from the corner of the car park, through the gates and along a fenced path. Cross the main track and follow the path past a pond and up Boghall Glen. Cross the burn by a footbridge and continue along the path. Follow the yellow arrows through a gate, up the side of a field and through another gate. Then head left to pick up the main track heading into the hills.

Follow the track steadily upwards, passing through several gates. Then it curves right and climbs to **Windy Door Nick***, the pass between* **Allermuir Hill** *(91,618ft) and* **Caerketton Hill** *(1,499ft). Turn left and follow the clear path to the*

top of Allermuir Hill. The views from here, north to the Forth bridges and beyond, and south to the main Pentland ridge, are magnificent.

From here, retrace your steps to the Nick and continue up Caerketton Hill. The views from the top are equally good, and extend further east to Berwick Law and the Bass Rock. Head east from the summit. Stay by the fence to pass a large cairn, then descend steeply to a fence corner. On your left you can see the Hillend ski slope. At the fence corner, cross the stile and continue down to the wood. Turn right here and you'll see the yellow arrows again, taking you along the top edge of the wood. When the wood ends, walk through gorse to a stile, then across open ground past a large mast and back to the cottage.

Three miles south of Boghall is the **Flotterstone Inn***, which does a decent pub lunch or evening meal from 1800-2000. This is also the starting point for further walks in the Pentlands, most notably the one to Glencorse.*

One of the most fascinating sights in the church, and the most elaborate carving, is the **Prentice Pillar**. Legend has it that while the master mason was away in Rome making additional drawings to complete the pillar, an apprentice finished it for him. On the mason's return he murdered the apprentice in a fury.

Speculation as to the purpose of the chapel dwells on esoteric secrets and a plethora of recent books claims that the Holy Grail, supposedly brought from the East by the Knights Templar, is buried here. Whether or not you believe this, you'll still find its architecture and atmosphere fascinating. Once you've seen the chapel, there are some very pleasant walks in nearby Roslin Glen, from where you get great views of Roslin Castle. ■ *Apr-Oct Mon-Sat 1000-1700, Sun 1200-1645; Nov-Mar Mon-Sat 1000-1700, Sun 1200-1600, £3, T4402159, take one of the regular buses for Penicuik from St Andrews station.*

Other sights around Midlothian

Rosslyn Chapel is the most interesting sight in Midlothian, but there are a few other worthwhile places of interest, especially if you've got kids in tow. **Butterfly and Insect World** is part of **Dobbie's Garden World**, in **Lasswade**, near **Dalkeith**. This large glass enclosure has loads of butterflies fluttering around while you stroll past tropical plants and water features. There are also creepy crawlies, which are thankfully in individual cages in a separate area. There's also a café in the garden centre. ■ *Daily 0930-1730 (1000-1700 in winter), £3.85, children £2.85, T6634932, to get there, leave the city bypass at the Gilmerton exit or Sheriffhall roundabout, or take buses 3, 80 or 80a.*

A mile or so south of Dalkeith is **Newtongrange**, a former mining village whose Lady Victoria Colliery closed in 1981 and has been transformed into the **Scottish Mining Mueum**. Here you can get some idea of what working conditions were like more than 1,500ft below ground during the guided tour led by former miners, and you can see the massive steam engine, the largest in Scotland, which hauled men and coal up and down the pit shaft for 87 years. ■ *Mar-Oct daily 1000-1700, £4, children £2.20, T6637519, there are regular buses from central Edinburgh (3, 30, 82).*

Edinburgh Zoo Three miles west of the city centre, is Edinburgh's zoo, by far the largest in Scotland, set in 80 acres on the side of Corstorphine Hill. Whatever you think of zoos, this one is highly respected for its serious work as well as being an enormous amount of fun. There are over 1,000 animals from all over the world, but the zoo is best known for its penguins – the largest breeding colony of Antarctic penguins anywhere outside Antarctica itself. You can watch the famous penguin parade at 1400 daily (March-October weather permitting) and see them swimming underwater in the world's largest penguin pool. The latest attractions are the endangered Asiatic lions and the Magic Forest, full of marmosets and tamarins. There are also animal handling sessions, available at an extra £1 per person, and afternoon animal talks (ask for details at the zoo entrance). ■ *Daily Apr-Sep 0900-1800; Oct-Mar 0900-1700; Nov-Feb 0900-1630, £6.80, children £3.80, T3349171, www.edinburghzoo.org.uk, there are numerous buses from Haymarket and Princes St.*

Lauriston Castle, Cramond and Dalmeny

About five miles northwest of town is Lauriston Castle, a fine Edwardian country mansion set in lovely grounds overlooking the Firth of Forth. The original tower house is late 16th century, with many neo-Jacobean additions by William Burn in the 19th century. It was once the home of John Law, who founded the first bank in France and obtained sole trading rights in the Lower Mississippi, which he christened Louisiana in honour of the French King. The interior contains fine collections of period furniture and antiques. ■ *Apr-Oct Sat-Thur 1100-1300 and 1400-1700; Nov-Mar Sat/Sun 1400-1600, £4, concession £3, T3362060.*

One mile further west is the lovely little coastal village of **Cramond**, situated where the River Almond flows into the Forth. The 18th century village of whitewashed houses is the site of an ancient Roman fort, a large part of which has been excavated. The most recent discovery was a magnificent sandstone sculpture of a lioness dating from the second century BC. In addition to being steeped in ancient history, Cramond boasts a pleasant promenade, a golf course and a lovely, wooded walk along the banks of the Almond river towards the 16th century **Old Cramond Brig**. And if that weren't enough to tempt you, there's also **Cramond Island**, which can be reached via a raised walkway when the tide is out. Just make sure you keep an eye on the time or you may find yourself stuck there for longer than you anticipated. Tide times are posted on the shore, and are also available from the Tourist Information Centre.

A local passenger ferry service still crosses the river Almond at Cramond. ■ *0900-1300 and 1400-1700 in summer, till 1600 in winter, closed Fri.* From the other side of the river it's a two-mile walk to **Dalmeny House**, the Earl of Rosebery's home for over 300 years. The present house, built in 1815 in Tudor Gothic, contains a superb collection of 18th century French furniture, porcelain and tapestries and paintings, including portraits by Gainsborough,

Raeburn, Reynolds and Lawrence. There is also a fascinating collection of Napoleon Bonaparte memorabilia, assembled by the fifth Earl of Rosebery, a former Prime Minister. ■ *Jul and Aug Sun 1300-1730, Mon and Tue 1200-1730 (last admission 1645), £3.80, children £2, T3311888.*

The house can also be reached via the village of **Dalmeny**, eight miles west of Edinburgh, on the A90 then B924. There's a bus service from St Andrew Square to Chapel Gate, one mile from the house, or you can take a train which stops at the village station. The main point of interest in the village is the wonderful 12th century church.

South Queensferry

Less than a mile from Dalmeny is the ancient town of South Queensferry, which gets its name from the 11th century St Margaret, who used the town as the crossing point during her trips between her palaces in Edinburgh and Dunfermline, which was Scotland's capital at that time. The town's narrow main street is lined with picturesque old buildings, most striking of which is the row of two-tiered shops. If you fancy a drink, or a meal, or perhaps a bed for the night, try the historic *Hawes Inn*, which was featured in Stevenson's *Kidnapped*. The small **museum** on the High Street traces the town's history and the building of the road and rail bridges. ■ *Mon and Thur-Sat 1000-1300 and 1415-1700, Sun 1200-1700, free, to get to South Queensferry from Edinburgh, take buses 43, X43, 47 or 47a from St Andrew Square bus station.*

The town is dominated by the two great bridges that tower overhead on either side, spanning the Firth of Forth at its narrowest point. The massive steel cantilevered **Forth Rail Bridge**, over a mile and a half long and 360ft high and is a staggering monument to Victorian engineering. It was built in 1883-90 and 60,000 tons of steel were used in its construction. Beside it, is the **Forth Road Bridge**, a suspension bridge built between 1958 and 1964, which ended the 900 year-old ferry crossing between South and North Queensferry. The Road Bridge is open to pedestrians and it's worth walking across for the views of the Rail Bridge.

Forth Cruises

From Hawes Pier, right underneath the Rail Bridge, you can take a variety of **pleasure boat cruises** on the Forth. *Jet Boat Tours*, T3314777, have cruises up the River Almond at Cramond, looking out for dolphins, seals and porpoises en route, as well as 'Bridge Tours' and 'Jet-Boat fun rides'. ■ *Prices vary between £5-10 per person. Cruises run Apr/May/Sep/Oct weekends and public holidays 1000-1800; Jun-Aug daily 0930-2000.*

Inchcolm Abbey

There are also Sealife Cruises on board the *Maid of the Forth*, T3314857, as well as Evening Cruises beneath the bridges with jazz and folk accompaniment. The most interesting cruise of all, and the most popular, is the cruise to the island of Inchcolm, whose beautiful ruined **abbey**, founded in 1123 by King Alexander I, is the best-preserved group of monastic buildings in Scotland. The oldest surviving building is the 13th century octagonal chapter house. You can also climb the tower for great views of the island, which is populated by nesting seabirds and a colony of seals. ■ *Cruises to the abbey run from Apr-Sep (daily Jul-Sep, weekends only Apr-Jun). Cruises last three hours and include time ashore to explore the abbey and island, £9, children £4, and include admission to the abbey.*

Hopetoun House

Two miles west of South Queensferry is Hopetoun House, which thoroughly deserves its reputation as "Scotland's finest stately home". Set in 100 acres of magnificent parkland, including the Red Deer park, the house is the epitome of aristocratic grandeur and very recently celebrated its 300th birthday.

Hopetoun House is perhaps the finest example of the work of William Burn and William Adam. It is, in fact, two houses in one. The oldest part was designed by William Bruce and built between 1699 and 1707. In 1721 William Adam began enlarging the house by adding the facade, colonnades and grand State Apartments. It was built for the Earls of Hopetoun, later created Marquesses of Linlithgow and part of the house is still lived in by the Marquess of Linlithgow and his family. The house contains a large collection of art treasures and the grounds are also open to the public. You could come here and pretend you're a member of the aristocracy for the day, then go back to your tiny B&B and weep. ■ *Daily Apr-end of Sep, and every weekend in Oct, 1000-1730, £5, children £2.70, grounds only £2.80, children £1.70, T3312451.*

Glasgow

4

Glasgow

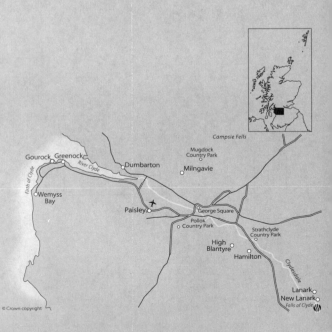

© Crown copyright

There's an old saying that Edinburgh is the capital but Glasgow has the capital. This dates back to the late 19th century, when Glasgow was the "Second City of the Empire". It was a thriving, cultivated city grown rich on the profits from its cotton mills, coal mines and shipyards, and a city that knew how to flaunt its wealth. The heavy industries have long gone, but Glasgow has lost none of its energy and excitement, and its people possess a style and swagger that makes their Edinburgh counterparts look staid and stuffy by comparison.

The legacy of Glasgow's extravagant energy and entrepreneurial past is all around: in the beautiful City Chambers in George Square; in the elegant neo-classical townhouses of the Merchant City; in the sweeping terraces of the West End. This vast commercial wealth is what made Glasgow a centre for the arts. It was the great ship owners whose collections filled the Kelvingrove Art Gallery and the Burrell Collection and paved the way for the city's proudest moment, when it was chosen as European City of Culture, in 1990. The ship owners also built beautiful mansions in the West End and South Side of the city. Many of these architectural treasures lay unnoticed until 1999, when Glasgow was chosen as the City of Architecture and Design.

Glasgow may have ignored its great artists in the past but its present inhabitants are devoted to style. Just take a stroll round the revived Merchant City or along Byres Road in the West End, and sit in one the countless stylish bars and restaurants, and you'll witness a degree of posing that is Continental in its fervency. The licensing laws may not be Continental but they're more liberal *than they are in London and the atmosphere is infused with those vital Glasgow ingredients missing from so many large British cities – warmth and humour. Glasgow is without doubt the friendliest of Britain's large cities. Perhaps that's because it doesn't feel British. Glasgow is often described as European in character; for the remarkable diversity of its architecture, for the accessibility of its art, and for the optimism and openness of its people. It is also compared with North America; for its gridiron street system and for the wisecracking of its streetwise citizens.*

Entertainment in today's Glasgow is far more sophisticated and diverse than the competitive drinking that once held sway. The city has a beautifully restored Victorian theatre in the Theatre Royal, home to both Scottish Opera and Scottish Ballet. The city has a thriving European-style café culture, not surprising given that Glasgow invented the tea room, and it was recently voted the UK's top city outside London for the choice and quality of its restaurants.

Scotland's largest city was not always so well-loved. In the post war years it was misunderstood and misrepresented more than any other city in Britain. If people had looked beyond the stereotyped images of urban poverty and squalor, they would have seen a city of handsome buildings and noble character, of passion, vision, ambition and wit. It was once said that all Glasgow needed was some love, affection and a good scrub. Now the city has cleaned up its act and its buildings and is successfully wooing visitors with its fascinating blend of style, culture and humour.

Ins and outs

Air Glasgow's airport, T8871111, is eight miles west of the city, at junction 28 on the M8. It handles domestic and international flights. To get into town take a bus from outside Arrivals. They leave every 15 minutes to the Buchanan bus station, in the city centre, with drop-off points near the mainline train stations, and take about 25-30 minutes. Single fare costs: *Scottish Citylink* £3, T0990-505050; *Airport Express* £2.70, T5531313. There are also buses to Paisley Gilmour Street train station, from where you can catch a train to Glasgow Central. A taxi from the airport to the city centre costs around £12.

Terminal facilities include car hire, bank ATMs, currency exchange, left luggage, tourist information, T8484440 and shops, restaurants and bars. There's also an SPT Travel Centre in the UK Arrivals concourse, T8484330 (open daily 0800-2200 in summer and till 1800 in winter) and a Thomas Cook Hotel and Travel Reservations desk in the International Arrivals concourse, T8877220.

Bus All long-distance buses to and from Glasgow arrive and depart from Buchanan Bus station, on Killermont St, T3327133, three blocks north of George Square. A number of companies offer express coach services day and night around the country and to most English cities; these include *Citylink Coaches*, T0990-505050, and *National Express* T0990-808080.

Train Glasgow has two main train stations: Central station is the terminus for all trains to southern Scotland, England and Wales; and Queen Street serves the north and east of Scotland. A shuttle bus (40p) runs every 10 minutes between Central station (Gordon Street entrance) and Queen Street, at the corner of George Square. It takes 10 minutes to walk between the two. For information on rail services and fares, call National Rail Enquiries, T0345-484950 (advance credit/debit card bookings T0345-550033).

Getting there
Phone code: 0141
For flight, bus and train details, see 'Transport' (page 181), and 'Getting there' in the Essentials section page 26.

Getting around

The best way to get around the city centre sights is by walking, although some of the hills are very steep. If you want to explore the West End or South Side, you'll need to use the public transport system, which is efficient and comprehensive.

If you're staying for a week or more, it's worth buying a *Zonecard*, which allows unlimited travel on all public transport systems and is valid for a week or a month. Costs depend on the number of zones you wish to travel through. Further details are available from the Strathclyde Travel Centres (see above). The *Roundabout Glasgow* ticket covers all underground and train transport in the city for one day and costs £3.40. The *Roundabout Glasgow Plus* ticket also includes the *Discovering Glasgow* tour buses (see below) and costs £13 for three days. There's also a *Daytripper* ticket which gives unlimited travel on all transport networks throughout Glasgow, the Clyde coast and Clyde valley. It's valid for one day and costs £7 for one adult and two children, or £12.50 for two adults and up to four children.

It's also easy to get around Glasgow by car, especially as the M8 runs right through the heart of the city. Parking is not a problem either. There are sufficient street meters and 24-hour multi-storey car parks dotted around the centre, at the St Enoch Centre, Mitchell Street, Oswald Street, Waterloo Street and Cambridge Street. For car hire companies, see page 182. Taxis are plentiful and reasonably priced and can be hailed from anywhere in the city.

There's an extensive suburban train network which is a fast and efficient way to reach the suburbs south of the Clyde. The best way to get from the city centre to the West End and south of the river is to use the city's Underground, or subway as it's also known, whose stations are marked with a huge orange 'U' sign.

Glasgow city centre covers the large area from **Charing Cross** train station and the M8 in the west to **Glasgow Green** in the east, near the cathedral. It is built on a grid system across some steep hills on the north side of the River Clyde. The heart of the city is

Orientation & information

George Square. Here you'll find the tourist office, and the two main train stations (Central station and Queen Street) and the Buchanan bus station are all within a couple of blocks. Immediately to the east of George Square is the renovated **Merchant City** which, together with the streets west of George Square, forms the commercial and business centre. The main shopping streets in the city centre are **Sauchiehall Street**, which runs parallel to the river, west as far as Kelvingrove Park, the pedestianized **Buchanan Street**, which runs south from the east end of Sauchiehall Street, and **Argyle Street**, at the south end of Buchanan Street.

The **West End** begins on the other side of the M8, which cuts a swathe through the city. This is the home of the University and is the city's main student quarter, with many of its best bars, cafés and restaurants. The West End is well connected with the city centre by the Underground. South of the Clyde are the more sedate suburbs, know as the **South Side**. To the southwest, in Pollock Country Park, are two of Glasgow's main tourist attractions, **Pollock House** and the **Burrell Collection**, which can easily be reached from the city centre by train or bus.

Glasgow & surroundings

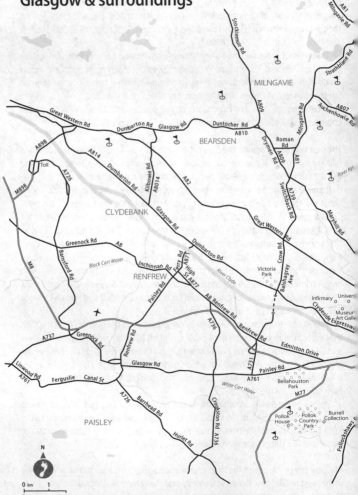

The main **tourist office** is at 11 George Square, T2044400, F2213524, TourismGlasgow@ggctvb.org.uk (open May daily 0900-1800; June & September daily 0900-1900; July & August daily 0900-2000; October-April Mon-Sat 0900-1800). They provide an excellent service, including a wide selection of maps and leaflets and a free accommodation booking service. You can also buy travel passes, theatre tickets, arrange car rental and exchange currency at their *bureau de change*.

South of George Square, in front of the giant St Enoch Centre, is the **Strathclyde Travel Centre**, T2264826 (open Mon-Sat 0830-1730). They can provide maps, leaflets and timetables. Their free *Visitor's Transport Guide* includes a particularly useful map of the city. There are other **travel information centres** at Buchanan Bus station, T3327133 (open Mon-Sat 0630-2230 & Sun 0700-2230), Hillhead Underground Station, on Byres Road, T3333673 (open Mon 0800-1730, Tue-Sat 0830-1730), and at Glasgow airport (see page 139).

There's also a Glasgow **website** at www.citylive.org

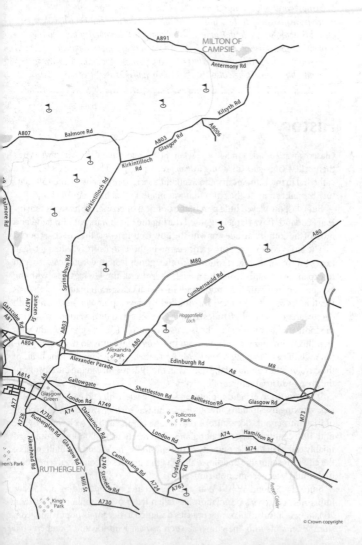

Glasgow

© Crown copyright

Guided Tours

There are various guided walks around the city. The Scottish Tourist Guides Association, T/F01786-447784/0870-607071, offer **Heart of Glasgow** *walks Monday-Friday at 1800 and Sunday at 1030, and the* **Cathedral Walk** *on Wednesday & Sunday at 1415, from 1 May to 30 September. These leave from the James Watt statue in George Square and cost £4 per person (£3 concession). Mercat Tours, T7720022, offer the chilling* **Gruesome Glasgow Tour**, *daily at 1900, and* **Ghosts and Ghouls Tour**, *daily 2100, which leave from outside the tourist office in George Square, from 1 June to 30 September (£5 per person, £4 concession). All these walking tours last one and a half hours. There's also The* **Glasgow Literary Tour**, *T0800-3283024, which is a lot of fun.*

There are sightseeing guided bus tours of the city with **Guide Friday**, *2nd floor, St George's building, 5 St Vincent Place, T2487644, and* **Discovering Glasgow**, *153 Queen St, T2040444. These are on board open-top buses and the all-day ticket allows you to hop on and off as you please. Tours run from April to October, and buses leave from George Square every 20 minutes. (Fares are £6.50 per person per day, £5 children/concession).*

There are also cruises on the Clyde, on board the **P.S. Waverley**, *the world's last ocean-going paddle steamer, from June to August. These leave from the Waverley Terminal, T2218152, (see page 161).*

History

Glasgow was founded in 543 AD when St Mungo built a church in what was then called *Glas-ghu* (meaning "dear green place"). The establishment of a cathedral in the 12th century and Scotland's second university in the 15th century brought status to the city and it was made a royal burgh in 1454.

But Glasgow played little part in the political or economic history of medieval Scotland. It was largely ignored during the bitter wars with England and most of the country's trade was with the Low Countries via the east coast ports.

The city's commercial prosperity came in the 17th century, when it began importing tobacco, sugar, cotton and other goods from the Americas. It began to expand westwards from the medieval centre of the High Street (with the exception of the cathedral, nothing of medieval Glasgow remains). Glasgow's location in the Clyde valley, surrounded by developing coalfields and with deep-water docks only 20 miles from the sea, ensured its development during the Industrial Revolution, in the late 18th century. The city grew rapidly with an influx of immigrants, mainly from the West Highlands, to work in the cotton mills. The deepening of the Clyde up to the Broomielaw, near the heart of the city, and the coming of the railway in the 19th century made the city one of the great industrial centres of the world.

It continued to expand rapidly between the late 18th and early 19th centuries, growing five-fold in only 50 years, and was further swelled by thousands of Irish immigrants fleeing Ireland to escape famine and to seek work. By the mid-19th century Glasgow's population had reached 400,000 and it could justifiably call itself the "second city of the empire". The Victorians built most of the city's most notable buildings, along with the acres of congested tenements that would later become notorious slums.

Since the Second World War and the decline of shipbuilding and heavy industries, Glasgow's population has fallen from over a million to less than 700,000: the result of planning policies designed to decant its population from slum tenements into "new towns" such as East Kilbride and Combernauld outside the city. During the recession of the late 1970s, Glasgow suffered more than most but instead of confronting central government, Glasgow embarked on a bold plan to reinvent itself and shake off the shackles of its industrial past. With its customary energy and wit, the city launched the "Glasgow's Miles Better" promotional campaign in 1983 which led to the 1988 Garden Festival, 1990's year as European City of Culture and, most recently, City of Architecture and Design, in 1999. Glasgow may still suffer the problems of urban deprivation, but it has regained its old confidence and transformed itself into a thriving, post-industrial city with a bright future.

Sights

It's no accident that Glasgow was chosen as both City of Culture and, more recently, UK City of Architecture and Design. Its main attractions are its magnificent Victorian buildings, its museums and its art galleries (most of which are free). Sir John Betjeman, Poet Laureate and architectural enthusiast, described Glasgow as the "greatest Victorian city in Europe" and many examples of its rich architectural legacy can be found in the commercial centre (from George Square west to the M8).

To the east of George Square is the **Merchant City**, where the Palladian mansions of the Tobacco Lords have been cleaned up and reclaimed by the professional classes as a fashionable place to eat, drink and play. Further east, in almost surreal contrast, is the **East End**, a traditional working-class stronghold, and to the north is the oldest part of Glasgow, around the medieval **cathedral**.

West of George Square is **Buchanan Street**, one of the city's principal shopping thoroughfares, along with **Sauchiehall Street**, at its northern end, and the more downmarket **Argyle Street**, at the southern end. From here the streets rise towards **Blythswood Square**, a much quieter area of elegant late Georgian buildings filled with office workers. Beyond **Charing Cross**, across the ugly scar of the M8, is the city's **West End**, an area of grand Victorian townhouses and sweeping terraces and home of some of the city's best **museums**.

On the city's **South Side**, across the River Clyde, is **Pollock Country Park**, home of two of Glasgow's finest museums, the **Burrell Collection** and **Pollock House**. The **River Clyde** itself has been added to the list of visitor attractions. The **Clydeside Walkway**, running from Victoria Bridge in the east to the River Kelvin in the west, is an attempt to direct Glasgow's great river towards a post-industrial future of leisure and tourism.

Perhaps not surprisingly, given the origins of its name, Glasgow boasts quite a few green spaces – more per head of population than any other city in Europe. There are more than 70 parks in all, from **Glasgow Green** in the East End to **Kelvingrove Park** in the West End, and **Queen's Park** and **Pollock Country Park**, both in the South Side.

Several of the sights listed below may be closed for restoration work, and some of the churches are only open during services. For details of opening times, ask at the tourist office in George Square.

George Square and around

The heart of modern Glasgow is George Square, which makes the obvious starting point for a tour of the city centre, as the **tourist office** is located here, on the south side. Amongst the many statues which adorn the square are those of Queen Victoria, Prince Albert, Sir Walter Scott, Robert Burns, Sir Robert Peel and James Watt.

The square is surrounded by fine Victorian buildings, most notable of which is the grandiose **City Chambers**, which fills the east side, a wonderful testament to the optimism and aspiration of Victorian Glasgow. It was designed in Italian Renaissance style by William Young and the interior is even more impressive than its façade. The imposing arcaded marble entrance hall is decorated with elaborate mosaics and a marble staircase leads up to a great banqueting hall with a wonderful arched ceiling, leaded glass windows and paintings depicting scenes from the city's history. One wall is covered by a series of murals by the Glasgow Boys (see page 154). ■ *T2872000. There are free guided tours of the City Chambers, Mon-Fri at 1030 and 1430.*

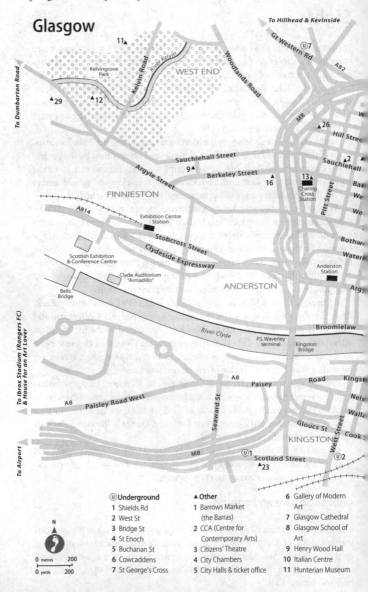

Glasgow

0 metres 200
0 yards 200

On the northwest corner of George Square, opposite Queen Street station, is another fine building, the **Merchants' House**, now the home of Glasgow Chamber of Commerce. ■ *T2218272. Free. Entry by appointment only.*

Just to the south of George Square, facing the west end of Ingram Street, is **Royal Exchange Square**, which is almost completely filled by the Gallery of Modern Art (GOMA). The building dates from 1778, when it was built as the Cunninghame Mansion, home to one of Glasgow's wealthy Tobacco Lords. It passed to the Royal Bank of Scotland in 1817 and ten years later the magnificent portico was added to the front and the building then became the Royal

The Gallery of Modern Art

Glasgow

Exchange, the city's main business centre. It then housed a library, until its reopening in 1996 as one of the city's newest, and its most controversial, art venues, drawing the ire of many a critic for its unashamed eclecticism and populism.

The gallery features contemporary works from artists worldwide over four themed levels: the **Earth Gallery** on the ground floor; the **Fire Gallery** in the basement (where else?); the **Water Gallery**; and the **Air Gallery**. It's a bold, innovative art space, making excellent use of the fabulous original interior. It includes interactive computers and art workshops. There's also a superb top-floor **café**, with great views across the city's rooftops (see page 174). ■ *T2291996. Open Mon-Sat 1000-1700, Sun 1100-1700. Free.*

The Merchant City

The grid-plan of streets to the east of George Square as far as the High Street form the Merchant City, where the Tobacco Lords built their magnificent Palladian mansions. They made Glasgow the most important tobacco trading city in Europe and can also take the credit for it being one of the lung cancer capitals of the world by the mid-20th century.

This part of the city was once a bustling trade centre and money has been poured into the restoration of its 18th century warehouses and homes in an attempt to revitalise and regenerate the city's old historic core. Though many of the buildings are little more than façades, the investment has succeeded in attracting expensive designer clothes shops and a plethora of stylish bistros, cafés and bars, which are packed with the city's young professionals and media types. It's a very pleasant and interesting area to explore, and when all that neo-classical architecture gets too much, you can pop into one of the trendy café-bars for some light relief.

A good place to start is **Hutchesons' Hall**, at 158 Ingram Street, a distinguished Georgian building which is now the National Trust for Scotland's regional headquarters. It was built by David Hamilton in 1805 in neo-classical style with a traditional Scottish "townhouse" steeple. It was once home of the Scottish Educational Trust, a charitable institution founded by the 17th century lawyer brothers George and Thomas Hutcheson which provided almshouses and schools for the city. Their statues gaze down towards the site of the original almshouse in Trongate. Inside is a shop and information room with an audio-visual programme about the history of the Merchant City. ■ *T5528391. Mon-Sat 1000-1700. Free.*

In nearby Glassford Street is Glasgow's oldest secular building, the **Trades Hall**, designed by Robert Adam and built in 1794 as the headquarters of the city's trade guilds. It still serves its original purpose. ■ *T5522418. Entry by appointment only.* At the corner of Ingram Street and Glassford Street is the lavish **Trustee Savings Bank** building, designed by that prodigious talent, JJ Burnet in 1900. Nearby, on Ingram Street, is another fine building, **Lanarkshire House**, designed by his father, John Burnet, along with two more of Glasgow's greatest architects, David Hamilton and James Salmon Jnr. It dates from 1879 and has recently been opened as a combination of bars, restaurants and meeting rooms.

Running off Ingram Street is Virginia Street, whose name recalls Glasgow's trading links with America. Here you'll find a rather dilapidated collection of early 19th century buildings, **Virginia Buildings**. Behind the southernmost of these buildings is **Crown Arcade**, formerly the tobacco and sugar exchange and now beautifully converted to a glass-roofed arcade of antique and craft shops. Parallel to Virginia Street is Miller Street, where you'll find the Merchant City's oldest surviving house (No 42), the **Tobacco Laird's House**, dating from 1775.

Trongate to the East End

The Merchant City is bounded to the east by the High Street and to the south by Trongate. These two streets meet at Glasgow Cross, once the centre of trade and administration and regarded as the city centre, until the coming of the railway in the mid-19th century. In the centre of the intersection stands the 126 feet-high **Tolbooth Steeple**, one of only three crowned steeples in the country. This is the only remnant of the original tolbooth built in 1626, which housed the courthouse and prison (described by Sir Walter Scott in *Rob Roy*). The **Mercat Cross** next to the steeple is a 1929 replica of the medieval original.

The nearby **Tron Steeple** is the only surviving part of St Mary's Church, built in 1637. This church was accidentally burned down by drunken members of the aptly-named Glasgow Hellfire Club in 1793. After a meeting, they went to the church to warm themselves by a fire, which they built up until it got out of control. The steeple has been incorporated into the modern frontage of the **Tron Theatre** (see page 180), and the interior of the replacement church forms the theatre auditorium.

Nearby, at 14 King Street, is the **Sharmanka Kinetic Gallery and Theatre**, which puts on performances by mechanical sculptures made from carved wooden figures and old bits of junk. A great place to take the kids. ■ *T5527080. Gallery open Sat/Sun 1200-1800; free. Performances on Sat/Sun at 1600; £3 (£2 children).*

To the south, on Bridgegate, is the **Merchants' Steeple**, built as part of the **Fishmarket** in 1872. The 164 feet-high steeple, with details in Gothic and Renaissance style, is all that's left of the old Merchants' House, built in 1651-59.

East of Glasgow Cross, Gallowgate and London Road lead into the city's **East End**, only a stone's throw from the Merchant City. It may look shabby and rundown by comparison but this is where you can sample a slice of pure Glasgow, especially in The Barrows ("The Barras"), a huge market spread out around the streets and alleys south of Gallowgate. You could spend days rummaging around through acres of cheap, new and second-hand goods. A lot of it's junk (dodgy computer games, pirate videos etc) but there are plenty of bargains to be found and there's every chance of unearthing some valuable antique. The real attraction, though, is the unique atmosphere of the place and wit and repartee of the market traders. ■ *The market is held every weekend, 1000-1700, and the entrance is marked by the huge red gates on Gallowgate.*

South of The Barras is the wide expanse of Glasgow Green, said to be the oldest public park in Britain. It has been common land since at least medieval times and Glaswegians still have the right to dry their washing here. Bonnie Prince Charlie reviewed his troops here in 1745 before they were hung out to dry by the English at Culloden. The Green has always been dear to the people of Glasgow and some of the city's major political demonstrators have held meetings here, including the Chartists in the 1830s and Scottish republican campaigners in the 1920s. There are various **monuments** dotted around the park, including a 144 feet-high monument to Lord Nelson, erected in 1806, and one to James Watt. Just to the north of the Green are two of the city's oldest churches, dating from the mid-18th century. In St Andrew's Square is **St Andrew's Church**, and nearby is the episcopal **St Andrew's-by-the-Green**, once known as the Whistlin' Kirk because of the introduction of its organ, a radical move in those days.

On the edge of the green, to the east of the People's Palace (see below), is **Templeton's Carpet Factory**, a bizarre structure designed in 1889 by William

Glasgow Cross & around

The Barras

Glasgow Green

Glasgow

Leiper in imitation of the Doge's Palace in Venice. It's Britain's best example of polychromatic decoration (in other words, very colourful). The building is now used as a business centre.

People's Palace On the northern end of the green, approached from London Road, is the People's Palace, opened in 1898 as a folk museum for the East End. The recently refurbished museum gives a real insight into the social and industrial life of this great city from the mid-18th century to the present day. Its galleries display a wealth of artefacts, photographs, cartoons and drawings, and a series of films, music and people's anecdotes. A visit to the People's Palace should be on everyone's itinerary, particularly if you're interested in scratching beneath the city's surface and getting to know it better. Equally recommended is the **Winter Gardens**, a huge conservatory at the rear of the museum, where you can enjoy a cup of tea or coffee in tropical surroundings. ■ *T5540223. Mon-Sat 1000-1700, Sun 1100-1700. Free.*

The Cathedral area

Until the 18th century Glasgow consisted only of a narrow ribbon of streets running north from the river past the Glasgow Cross and up the High Street to the cathedral. Then came the city's rapid expansion west and the High Street became a dilapidated backwater. At the top of the High Street stand the two oldest buildings in the city, **Glasgow Cathedral** and **Provand's Lordship**.

Glasgow The rather severe-looking early Gothic structure is the only complete medieval
Cathedral cathedral on the Scottish mainland. It was built on the site of St Mungo's original church, established in AD 543, though this has been a place of Christian worship since it was blessed for burial in AD 397 by St Ninian, the earliest missionary recorded in Scottish history. Most of the building was completed in the 13th century though parts were built a century earlier by Bishop Jocelyn. The choir and crypt were added a century later and the building was completed at the end of the 15th century by Robert Blacader, the first Bishop of Glasgow.

During the Reformation, the city's last Roman Catholic Archbishop, James Beaton, took off for France with most of the cathedral treasures, just ahead of the townsfolk who proceeded to rid the building of all traces of "idolatry" by destroying altars, statues, vestments and the valuable library. The present furnishings mostly date from the 19th century and many of the windows have been renewed with modern stained glass. The most outstanding feature in the cathedral is the fan vaulting around St Mungo's tomb in the crypt, one of the very finest examples of medieval architecture in Scotland. There's also fine work in the choir, including a 15th century stone screen, the only one of its kind left in any pre-Reformation secular (non-monastic) church in Scotland.

Behind the cathedral looms the **Western Necropolis**, a vast burial ground overlooking the city from the top of a high ridge. It's the ideal vantage point from which to appreciate the cathedral in all its Gothic splendour and many of the tombs are wonderfully-ornate. Interred here are the great and the good (and not so good) of Victorian Glasgow, overseen by a statue of John Knox, the 16th century firebrand reformer. ■ *T5526891. April-September Mon-Sat 0930-1800, Sun 1400-1700, October-March Mon-Sat 0930-1300, 1400-1600, Sun 1400-1600. Free.*

Cathedral In front of the cathedral is the weetabix-coloured **St Mungo Museum of Reli-**
Precinct **gious Life and Art**, which features a series of displays of arts and artefacts representing the six major world religions, as well as a Japanese Zen garden in the

courtyard outside – great for a few moments of quiet contemplation. Highlights include Salvador Dalí's astounding painting *Christ of St John of the Cross*, purchased by the city from the artist in 1951. Don't miss the extremely interesting comments on the visitors' board. There's also a bookshop and café serving hot meals, snacks and drinks. ■ *T5532557. Mon-Sat 1000-1700; Sun 1100-1700. Free.*

Across the street the **Provand's Lorship**, the oldest remaining house in Glasgow, built in 1471 as part of a refuge for the city's poor and extended in 1670. It has also served as an inn of rather dubious repute in its time. Now it's a museum devoted mainly to medieval furniture and various domestic items. ■ *Same phone number and opening hours as above.*

Buchanan Street to Charing Cross

Glasgow's commercial heart is the area between Buchanan Square and the M8 to the west. This vast grid-plan – which inspired town planners in the USA – is home to the city's main shopping streets and arcades, as well as its businesses and financial institutions. It is also where you'll find many of its architectural treasures.

At the bottom (south) end of Buchanan Street is St Enoch Square, dominated by the **St Enoch Centre**, a gigantic glass-covered complex of shops, fast-food outlets and an ice rink. There's also a subway station and transport centre in the square. St Enoch Square looks onto Argyle Street, one of Glasgow's most famous shopping streets. Though its status has been usurped in recent decades by the more fashionable streets to the north, it does boast the **Argyle Arcade**, Scotland's first ever indoor shopping mall, built in 1827 in Parisian style, at the junction with Buchanan Street.

Argyle Street runs west from here under the railway bridge at **Central station**. This bridge has always been known as the 'Heilanman's Umbrella', owing to the local joke that Highlanders would stand under it for shelter rather than buy an umbrella.

A short walk north on Buchanan Street is **Princes Square**, one of the most stylish and imaginative shopping malls in Britain. Even if you're not buying or looking, it's worth going in to admire this beautifully-ornate Art Nouveau creation, or to sit at the top-floor café and watch others spend their hard-earned cash in the trendy designer clothes shops below. A little further north, on the opposite side of the street, is a branch of the famous **Willow Tea Rooms** (see below) with replicas of Mackintosh designs. Almost opposite is **Borders Bookshop**, housed in the huge and impressive former Royal Bank of Scotland (1827), which backs onto Royal Exchange Square.

The Lighthouse

Lovers of architecture should head west into Gordon Street and then south (left) into Mitchell Street, where you'll find The Lighthouse, another of Glasgow's hidden gems. It was designed by the ubiquitous Charles Rennie Mackintosh in 1893 to house the offices of the Glasgow Herald. The Herald vacated the premises in 1980 and it lay empty, until its recent transformation into **Scotland's Centre for Architecture, Design and the City**, a permanent legacy of the Glasgow's role as UK City of Architecture and Design in 1999. This stunning 21st century building also contains the **Mackintosh Interpretation and Orientation Centre**, which features original designs and information on the life and work of the great architect. There's also a shop and café. ■ *T2216362. Admission £2.50.*

Glasgow

Glasgow

👉 *A fishy tale*

Though it is many years since salmon were caught in the Clyde, two appear in the city's coat of arms. Each fish has a ring in its mouth, recalling an old local legend.

The Queen of Strathclyde was given a ring by her husband but then promptly gave it to her lover. The king found the lover wearing the ring as he slept beside the Clyde. He took the ring and threw it

into the water, and then went to his wife and asked her to show it to him. The Queen prayed to St Mungo for help, and immediately, one of her servants miraculously found the ring in the mouth of a salmon he had caught. The king then had to accept his wife's pleas of innocence, despite knowing something fishy was going on.

Buchanan Street north & St Vincent Street

Further north on Buchanan Street, close to Buchanan Street Underground, are two more interesting buildings: **St George's Tron Church**, designed in 1808 by William Stark and the oldest church in the city centre, and the **Athenaeum**, designed in 1886 by JJ Burnet and showing early signs of his later modernism. Running west from George Square, between Argyle Street and Sauchiehall Street, is St Vincent Street, where you'll find two of the city's extraordinary buildings. **The Hatrack**, at No 142, was designed in 1902 by James Salmon Jnr. It's a very tall, narrow building, like many in the city centre, with a fantastically-detailed roof which looks like an old hat stand.

Further along St Vincent Street, near the intersection with Pitt Street, is one of the jewels in Glasgow's architectural crown, the **St Vincent Street Church**, designed in 1859 by Alexander 'Greek' Thomson, the city's "unknown genius" of architecture. Much of his work was destroyed in the 1960s and this is his only intact Romantic Classical church, now on the World Monument Fund's list of the 100 most endangered sites. The Presbyterian church is fronted by Ionic columns like those of a Greek temple and the church also shows Egyptian and Assyrian decoration. The main tower is Grecian in style while the dome could have come straight out of India during the Raj.

A series of streets climb northwards from St Vincent Street up to Sauchiehall Street, another of the city's main shopping thoroughfares. If there's one thing Glaswegians like to do it's spend money and Glasgow is second only to London in the UK in terms of retail spending. The newest of the city's shopping centres is the upmarket **Buchanan Galleries**, next door to the **Royal Concert Hall** (see page 178), at the north end of Buchanan Street, where it meets the east end of Sauchiehall Street.

Sauchiehall Street

There are a few notable places of interest on Sauchiehall Street, including Charles Rennie Mackintosh's wonderful **Willow Tea Rooms**, at No 217, above *Henderson's* the Jewellers. This is a faithful reconstruction on the site of the original 1903 tea room, designed by CRM for his patron Miss Kate Cranston, who already ran three of the city's most fashionable tea rooms, in Argyle Street, Buchanan Street and Ingram Street. The tea room was very much peculiar to Glasgow, promoted by the Temperance Movement as a healthy alternative to the gin palaces, popular throughout the country in the late 19th century, and Miss Cranston's were the *crème de la crème* of tea rooms. They offered ladies-only rooms, rooms for gentlemen and rooms where both sexes could dine together. In addition, her tea rooms offered a reading room, a billiards room for the gentlemen and a smoking room, not forgetting the unrivalled splendour of the decoration.

Mackintosh had already worked with Miss Cranston on her other tea rooms, but Sauchiehall Street was their *tour de force*. Sauchiehall means "alley

Glasgow School of Art

Glasgow

of the willows" and this theme was reflected not only in the name, but throughout the interior. Mackintosh was allowed free rein to design the fixtures and fittings; everything, in fact, right down to the teaspoons. The exclusive Salon de Luxe, on the first floor, was the crowning glory, and the most exotic and ambitious part of the tea rooms, decorated in purple, silver and white, with silk and velvet upholstery.

Visitors today can relive the splendour of the original tea rooms as they relax in the distinctive high-backed chairs with a cup of tea, brought to them by the specially selected high-backed waitresses. ■ *The tea rooms are open from 0930 to 1630 (see also 'Cafés' on page 174).*

A few yards west, on the opposite side of the street, are the **McLellan Galleries**, another fine example of classical architecture. The galleries host a wide of touring and temporary exhibitions. ■ *T3311854. Opening times and admission charges change with each exhibition.*

Further down the street, on the same side, is the **Centre for Contemporary Arts (CCA)**, housed in the Grecian Buildings, a former commercial warehouse designed by Alexander 'Greek' Thomson in 1867-68. The centre presents a changing programme of contemporary theatre, dance and other cultural events. It also has an excellent café-bar (see 'Cafés', page 174). ■ *T3327521. Centre and Café-bar open Mon-Wed 0900-2400; Thur-Sat 0900-2400; Sun 1200-1900. Galleries open Mon-Sat 1100-1800; Sun 1200-1700. Free.*

Glasgow School of Art

A very steep walk up from Sauchiehall Street, at 167 Renfrew Street, is the Glasgow School of Art, one of the city's most important buildings, and one of the most prestigious Art Schools in the country. The building was designed by Charles Rennie Mackintosh, after his proposal won a competition set to find a design for the school, in 1896. It was built in two stages from 1897-1899 and completed in 1907.

Much of the inspiration for his design came from nature and from his drawings of traditional Scottish buildings. He was also influenced by the Art Nouveau style, particularly the illustrations of Aubrey Beardsley. The school is now regarded as Mackintosh's architectural masterpiece and gives full expression to his architectural ideals. It is rooted in tradition, with a thoroughly modern-looking exterior of extreme austerity, and there are medieval, castle-like features such as turrets and curving stair wells.

The interior is both spacious and utilitarian and shows perfectly his desire to create a unified and harmonious working environment for both students and teachers. The studio walls and high ceilings are painted white, with huge windows allowing light to pour into the spaces. The corridors and staircases are decorated with glazed coloured tiles to help guide students and staff around the massive building. In the spectacular two-storey library Mackintosh also designed the light fittings, bookcases and the oak furniture. There are symbols of nature everywhere throughout the building, used to inspire the students to produce their own works of art. And who could fail to be inspired in such a stunning environment.

Entry to the school is by guided tour only which visits the main rooms containing many of the well-known pieces of furniture and includes the famous library. It is still a working art school, so take note of the annual closing. ■ *T3534526, www.gsa.ac.uk Tour times Mon-Fri at 1100 and 1400, Sat 1030. Closed 14 Jun-3 Jul and from Christmas through to New Year. £3.50, £2 students.*

Other Mackintosh buildings Aside from the Mackintosh buildings listed separately, there are a number of his lesser known works scattered around the city centre. These include the **Martyrs' Public School** (1895), at Parson Street, just off the High Street and M8, the **Daily Record Building** (1901), at 20-26 Renfield Lane (external viewing only), the **Royal Fusiliers Museum** (c1903), at 518 Sauchiehall Street, T3320961, open Monday-Friday 0900-1630, and the former **Glasgow Society of Lady Artists' Club** (1908), at 5 Blythswood Square (external viewing only).

For more information on the man and his work, and for details of access to the Martyrs' Public School, contact the CRM Society, at **Queen's Cross Church**, 870 Garscube Rd, Glasgow G20 7EL, T9466600, F9452321.

The Tenement House A few hundred yards northwest of the School of Art, down the other side of the hill, at 145 Buccleuch Street, is the Tenement House, a typical late Victorian tenement flat. This was the home of Miss Agnes Toward, a shorthand typist, for 50 years until she moved out in 1965. It's a fascinating time-capsule of life in the first half of the 20th century and retains most of the original features such as the bed recesses, kitchen range and coal bunker. The whole experience is a little voyeuristic, as the flat includes many of Agnes' personal possessions, and in the parlour the table is set for afternoon tea, lending a spooky atmosphere redolent of the Marie Celeste. On the ground floor is an exhibition on tenement life. The property is owned by the NTS. ■ *T3330183. 31 Mar-31 Oct, daily 1400-1700. £3.20, £2.20 children.*

On the other side of Cowcaddens Road, behind the huge Royal Scottish Academy for Music and Drama, is the **Piping Centre**, at 30-34 McPhater Street. It's a kind of centre for the promotion of the bagpipes and contains rehearsal rooms, performance spaces and accommodation for aficionados of the instrument which divides opinion so sharply. There's also a very fine **café** and a **museum** which features a collection of antique pipes. ■ *Daily 1030-1630. £1.50.*

The West End

On the other side of the M8 is the West End, an area which contains many of the city's major museums, as well some of its finest examples of Victorian architecture. During the course of the 19th century the West End grew in importance as wealthy merchants moved here, away from the dirt and grime of the industrial city. By the middle of the 19th century the **Park Conservation Area** had been established and was described as one of the finest pieces of architectural planning of the century. Perhaps most impressive of all the terraces in the conservation area are **Park Quadrant** and **Park Terrace**, with

Charles Rennie Mackintosh

To say that Barcelona has Gaudi and Glasgow has Rennie Mackintosh is not overstating the case. He is not only one of Scotland's most celebrated architects, but one of the creative geniuses of modern architecture.

Charles Rennie Mackintosh was born in Glasgow in 1868 and at 15 began work as a draughtsman with a local firm of architects. At the same time, he continued to pursue his studies at the Glasgow School of Art where his talent as an artist soon earned him recognition, and his experimental, decorative style brought him into contact with kindred spirits Herbert MacNair and two sisters, Frances and Margaret MacDonald. They became known as 'The Four' and together they developed their unique form of art and design, which became known as the 'Glasgow Style'

Mackintosh was as much an artist and interior designer as an architect but he saw no conflict in this. He considered architecture to be "...the synthesis of the fine arts, the commune of all the crafts", and he used his diverse talents to great effect, designing every detail of a building, down to furniture, carpets and decoration. This can be seen to greatest effect in his most important building, the Glasgow School of Art.

In the late 1890s he began his Argyle Street tea room project for Miss Cranston, and developed his distinctive, elegant high-backed chairs, for which he is probably best known today. In 1900 he married Margaret Macdonald (Herbert MacNair and Margaret's sister were married the previous year) and they began to design the interior of their own flat, creating their distinctive colour schemes of white and grey, pink and purple, and the light and dark interiors representing the masculine and feminine.

Throughout his career, Mackintosh's talents were far better understood abroad than at home, where his designs were often criticised as being iconoclastic and too modern. He was forced to leave Glasgow in 1914 due to lack of work and soon became depressed and alcoholic, and though his fortunes improved after moving to London, he died, a tragic but romantic figure, in 1928.

It is only in the past few decades that his genius has been fully recognised and serious efforts made to preserve his artistic legacy. The restoration of the Willow Tea Rooms, Scotland Street School, Queen's Cross Church and the Mackintosh House at the Hunterian Art Gallery, as well as The Hill House in Helensburgh, are all testimony to his prodigious talents.

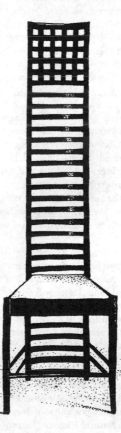

Ladder-back chair

Glasgow

The Glasgow Boys

With the coming of the industrial age, Glasgow had grown rapidly from a small, provincial town into the "Second City of the Empire". This sudden growth in size and wealth led to the beginnings of the famous and long-standing rivalry between Glasgow and Edinburgh, and, by the 1880s, to a new departure from the cultural mainstream, when a group of students nicknamed the Glasgow Boys, united in protest against Edinburgh's dominance of the arts.

This group of five painters – Guthrie, Hornel, Lavery, Henry and Crawhall – rejected the traditional concept of art which was confined to historical melodrama, sentimental "poor but happy" cottagers and grandiose visions of the Highlands inspired by Sir Walter Scott. They referred to these paintings as "gluepots" for their use of megilp, a treacly varnish that lent the paintings a brown patina of age. Instead, they experimented with colour and, inspired by the European Realists, chose earthy, peasant themes. This not only shocked and offended the genteel Edinburgh art establishment, but also scandalized their fellow citizens.

The Glasgow Boys left Scotland to study in Paris, where their work met with great acclaim. Subsequently their art began to fetch high prices from the new rich of Glasgow, eager to buy status through cultural patronage. But once the group had achieved the artistic respect and commercial success its members craved, they sadly lost their freshness.

The influence of the Glasgow Boys cannot be underestimated. They shook the foundations of the art establishment and were the inspiration for the next generation of great Scottish painters, known as the "Colourists".

glorious views across **Kelvingrove Park**. Soon after, in 1870, the **university** also moved west, to its present site overlooking Kelvingrove Park, and in 1896 the Glasgow District Subway was extended west. In 1888 the park was used to stage an international exhibition and the profits were used to build the **Kelvingrove Museum and Art Gallery**, which housed the second international exhibition, in 1901.

The bustling hub of the West End is **Byres Road**, running south from the Great Western Road past Hillhead Underground. It's an area populated mostly by students and full of fashionable shops, bars, cafés and restaurants.

Kelvingrove Museum and Art Gallery Glasgow's greatest art gallery (with the possible exception of the Burrell Collection) is the Kelvingrove Art Gallery and Museum, which stands below the university, on the other side of the River Kelvin, at the most westerly end of Argyle and Sauchiehall Streets, near Kelvingrove Park. This massive sandstone Victorian building houses one of the finest municipal collections of Scottish and European paintings in the country, and should not be missed.

The art gallery and museum, first opened to the public in 1902, can be entered from the "rear", leading to one of the most popular urban myths, that it was mistakenly built back to front and when the architect found out he was so distraught that he jumped from one of the towers. It was actually designed by two architects, Sir JW Simpson and Milner Allen, and is a wonderful structure, especially the breathtaking atrium. At one end of the atrium is a huge set of organ pipes, and recitals are still held here. On the ground floor is the **Scottish Natural History Museum** and, on the opposite side of the main hall, a rather jumbled collection of pottery, porcelain, silverware, costumes, tapestry and a collection of arms and armour.

But it is the art gallery upstairs which makes this such a fascinating attraction. Displayed in a series of rooms are some superb works, including

*Glasgow University
from Kelvingrove
Park*

Botticelli's *Annunciation*, Giorgione's *The Adultress Brought Before Christ* and Rembrandt's *Man in Armour*. There are also outstanding examples of French Impressionism, Post-Impressionism and Dutch schools, including works by Degas, Monet, Turner, Bonnard, Pissaro, Vuillard, Braque and Derain. There are also excellent works by many of Scotland's finest artists, including, Sir Henry Raeburn, Horatio McCulloch and Alexander Naysmith. The Glasgow Boys are also well represented, with works by George Henry, Joseph Crawhall, Sir James Guthrie and Sir John Lavery. There's also a room dedicated to Charles Rennie Mackintosh, featuring a marvellous collection of furniture. ■ *T2872690. Mon-Sat 1000-1700; Sun 1100-1700. Free. There's a cheap self-service café on the ground floor. Also free guided tours most days from the enquiry desk. To get there, take any bus heading for the Dumbarton Rd (Nos 6, 6A, 57, 64A). Nearest Underground station is Kelvin Hall.*

Opposite the Kelvingrove Museum and Art Gallery and behind the **Kelvin Hall**, just off Argyle Street, is the Transport Museum, whose name may lack appeal but which is one of the country's most fascinating museums. There are collections of trams, trains, motor cars, horsedrawn vehicles, bicycles, motorbikes, as well as a whole room dedicated to models of Clyde-built ships. Everything you ever wanted to know about the history of transport but were too disinterested to ask. Well, this place will change all that. There's also a reconstruction of a 1938 cobbled street, an old Underground station and a cinema showing old films of Glaswegians heading "doon the watter". Something for everyone, as they say in the tourist brochures. ■ *T2872720. Mon-Sat 1000-1700, Sun 1100-1700. Free.* | **Transport Museum**

The university's roots go back to 1451 when Pope Nicholas V authorised William Turnbull, Bishop of Glasgow to found a seat of learning in the city. At first there was just an Arts faculty and lectures were held in the cathedral crypt and neighbouring monastery. In the 17th century the university moved to new premises in the High Street, but these became too small and, in 1870, it moved to its present site, on Gilmorehill, overlooking Kelvingrove Park. The Gothic buildings were designed by Sir George Gilbert Scott, though the Lion and Unicorn balustrade on the stone staircase opposite the Principal's Lodging is a | **Glasgow University and the Hunterian Museum** relic of the old High Street colleges, as is the stonework of the lodge gateway. Bute Hall, which is now used for graduation and other ceremonies, was added in 1882. The **university chapel** is also worth seeing.

Contained within the university buildings is the **Hunterian Museum**, named after William Hunter (1718-83), a student at the university in the 1730s. His bequest to the university of his substantial collections led to the establishment of the Hunterian Museum in 1807, Scotland's oldest public museum. It has displays of social history, archaeology and geology and includes Roman relics from the Antonine Wall and one of the largest coin collections in Britain. Beneath the museum is the **University Visitor Centre**, which features interactive displays on the university and a coffee bar. There's also a **Zoology Museum**, housed in the Graham Kerr Building, a few minutes' walk from the main museum. ■ *T3304221, www.gla.ac.uk/Museum Mon-Sat 0930-1700. Free.*

Hunterian Art Gallery & Mackintosh House

Across the road, at 82 Hillhead Street, is the Hunterian Art Gallery, a modern building containing the more interesting part of Hunter's bequest, the fabulous art collection. The gallery holds an important collection of European paintings including works by Rembrandt, Koninck, Rubens, Pissaro and Rodin, as well as 18th century British portraits by Ramsay and Reynolds. There is also a fine collection of Scottish 19th and 20th century paintings including works by McTaggart, Guthrie and Fergusson. The *piece de resistance* is the huge collection of works by the American painter, James McNeill Whistler. There are some 70 paintings and a selection of his personal possessions on show, making it the largest display of his work outside the USA.

Attached to the gallery is the **Mackintosh House**, a stunning reconstruction of the main interiors from 78 Southpark Avenue, the Glasgow home of Charles Rennie Mackintosh and his wife, Margaret MacDonald, from 1906 to 1914. A stairway leads to an introductory display containing numerous drawings and designs, including those for his major buildings, furniture and interiors. From there you are led into the cool, soothing rooms, lovingly reconstructed and exquisitely furnished with some 80 original pieces of his furniture. These give the perfect example of just why this innovative designer and architect is so revered. Among the highlights are the Studio Drawing Room, decorated in white and flooded with natural light, and the guest bedroom from Northampton, a later commission, with its bold and dazzling geometric designs. When George Bernard Shaw, a guest, was asked if the décor would disturb his sleep, he replied, "No, I always sleep with my eyes closed." ■ *T3305431. Mon-Sat 0930-1230 and 1330-1700. Free. To get there take buses 44 and 59 from the city centre (Hope St), or the Underground to Hillhead and walk. Opposite the entrance is the student refectory.*

Botanic Gardens

At the top of Byres Road, where it meets the Great Western Road, is the entrance to the Botanic Gardens, a smallish but perfectly formed park where you can lose yourself along the remote paths that follow the wooded banks of the River Kelvin (see page 160). There are two large hothouses in the park, one of which is the **Kibble Palace**, built as a conservatory for the Clyde Coast home of Glasgow businessman, John Kibble, and then shipped to its present site in 1873. The domed glasshouse, which contains a collection of ferns and palms from around the world, is thought to have been designed by Sir Joseph Paxton who designed the Crystal Palace in London, as well as Kelvingrove Park. The **main glasshouse** is more attractive, with outstanding collections of orchids and begonias. ■ *Gardens open daily 0700 till dusk. Free. Kibble Palace open daily 1000-1645 in summer, 1000-1615 in winter. Main glasshouse open daily till 1645, Sat from 1300 and Sun from 1200-1645 in summer, till 1615 in winter.*

Due east of the Botanic Gardens, at the junction of Garscube Road and
Maryhill Road, is a fascinating piece of architecture, **Queen's Cross Church**,
designed by Rennie Mackintosh (his only church). Beautifully simple, with
echoes of the symbolism of his other buildings, it now functions as the headquarters of the Charles Rennie Mackintosh Society. There's an information
centre, a small display and a gift shop. ■ *T9466600. Mon-Fri 1000-1700, Sat*
1000-1400, Sun 1400-1700. Free, but donation suggested for adults. Buses 21, 61
and 91 from Hope St (west side of Central station), or Underground to St
George's Cross and walk 15 minutes on Maryhill Road.

Nearby is Firhill Park, home of one of Glasgow's *other* football teams, the
much-maligned Partick Thistle. So awful are they, that comedian Billy
Connelly once joked that people outside Scotland thought their full name was
"Partick Thistle nil". Just to the north of Firhill, across the Forth & Clyde
Canal, is **Ruchill Park**, from where you get fantastic views across the whole
city and surrounding hills.

In the far west of the city, near the north mouth of the Clyde Tunnel, is **Victoria Park and Fossil Grove**, which has a glasshouse containing a grove of fossil
tree stumps dating back some 350 million years. Information boards provide
explanations of the scientific importance of the site. ■ *T9599087. Daily*
Apr-Sept 1000-1700 (from 1100 on Sun). Free. Buses 44, 44C and 44D from city
centre to park entrance.

South Side

South of the River Clyde is a part of Glasgow largely unknown to most visiting
tourists, except for two of the city's most notable attractions, the **Burrell Collection** and **Pollock House**, both set in the sylvan surrounds of **Pollock
Country Park**. There are other reasons to venture south of the river, however,
not least of these being to see Charles Rennie Mackintosh's **House for an Art
Lover** in nearby Bellahouston Park. Further east is another stop on the Mackintosh trail, the **Scotland Street School Museum of Education**. To the south,
in Cathcart, is **Holmwood House**, Alexander 'Greek' Thomson's great architectural masterpiece.

Three miles southwest of the city centre is Glasgow's top attraction and a must
on any visit, the Burrell Collection, standing in the extensive wooded park-
lands of Pollock Country Park. The magnificent collection contains some
8,500 art treasures, donated to the city in 1944 by the shipping magnate, William Burrell (1861-1958) who sold his shipping interests in order to devote the
remainder of his life to collecting art. He began collecting in the 1880s, and in
1917 bought Hutton Castle near Berwick-on-Tweed to house his collection.
There it stayed, until the modern, award-winning gallery was built with the
£450,000 donated by Burrell for the purpose of displaying his hugely eclectic
bequest. The building opened to the public in 1983.

The collection includes ancient Greek, Roman and Egyptian artefacts, a
huge number of dazzling oriental art pieces, and numerous works of medieval
and post-medieval European art, including tapestries, silverware, textiles,
sculpture and exquisitely-lit stained glass. There's also an impressive array of
paintings by Rembrandt, Degas, Pissaro and Manet amongst many others.

The gallery is a stunning work of simplicity and thoughtful design, which
allows the visitor to enjoy the vast collection to the full. The large,
floor-to-ceiling windows afford sweeping views over the surrounding woodland and allow a flood of natural light to enhance the treasures on view. Some

Glasgow

Glasgow

Alexander Thomson was the greatest architect of Victorian Glasgow, who did as much to shape the city as the famous Charles Rennie Mackintosh. In the middle of the 19th century, when the "Second City of the Empire" was a growing, dynamic place, he brought a distinctive flair to all manner of buildings: warehouses and commercial premises, terraces and tenements, suburban villas and some of the finest Romantic Classical churches in the world.

Despite his nickname he never visited Greece and was not a conventional Greek Classicist. In fact, he thought the architects of the Greek revival had failed "because they could not see through the material into the laws upon which that architecture rested. They failed to master their style, and so became its slaves". Instead, Thomson evolved a distinctive manner of building using a Greek style but in an unconventional way and incorporating modern inventions such as iron beams and

plate glass. Thomson was struck by "the mysterious power of the horizontal element in carrying the mind away into space and into speculations on infinity". This dominance of horizontality has led to comparisons with Frank Lloyd Wright, though Thomson predates him by 40 years.

Thomson was a truly original and brilliant architect yet was shamefully neglected after his death in 1875. In the 1960s, in a frenzy of destruction, the city planners did their best to wipe out this man's amazing achievements completely. Finally, though, the city paid tribute to one of their most talented sons with a major exhibition about his work as part of the City of Architecture and Design year.

For more information on Alexander "Greek" Thomson and his surviving buildings, see the tourist office's Glasgow architectural guide 1. The only building open to the public is Holmwood House, in Cathcart (see below).

sections of the gallery are reconstructions of rooms from Hutton Castle and incorporated into the structure are carved stone Romanesque doors. There's also a café and restaurant on the lower ground floor. ■ *T6497151. Mon-Sat 1000-1700, Sun 1100-1700. Free. Buses 45, 48A and 57 from the city centre (Union St) pass the park gates on Pollockshaws Rd, also buses 34 and 34A from Govan Underground. From the gates it's a 10-minute walk to the gallery, or there's a twice hourly bus service. There are also regular trains from Central station to Pollockshaws West station. A taxi from the city centre costs £6-7.*

Pollock House & Country Park Also in Pollock Country Park, a 10-minute walk from the Burrell, is **Pollock House**, designed by William Adam and finished in 1752. This was once the home of the Maxwell family, who owned most of southern Glasgow until well into the last century. It contains one of the best collections of Spanish paintings in Britain, including works by Goya, El Greco and Murillo. There are also paintings by William Blake, as well as glass, silverware, porcelain and furniture. The most interesting part of the house are the servants' quarters downstairs, and there's a good tearoom in the old kitchens. ■ *The house is managed by the NTS. T6166410. 1 Apr-31 Oct daily 1000-1700, 1 Nov-31 Mar daily 1100-1600. £3.20 (£2.20 child/concession); Nov-Mar, free.*

If the weather's fine, the park is worth exploring. There are numerous trails through the woods and meadows and guided walks on Sundays with the park rangers. There are two golf courses within the park grounds, as well as a herd of highland cattle. ■ *T6329299. Entry to the park is from Pollockshaws Road, or Haggs Road if you're on foot. Car parking is at the Burrell Collection and costs £1.50.*

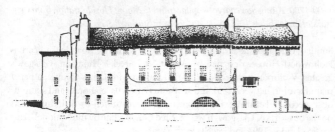

*House for an
Art Lover*

Glasgow

A short distance north of Pollock Park is Bellahouston Park, site of the most **House for** recent addition to the Charles Rennie Mackintosh trail, the House for an Art **an Art Lover** Lover. Although the building was designed in 1901 as an entry to a competition run by a German design magazine, it was not completed until 1996, when it became a centre for Glasgow School of Art postgraduate students, though a number of rooms on the lower floor are open to the public.

Mackintosh worked closely with his wife on the design of the house and there is distinctive evidence of her influence, especially in the exquisite **Music Room** with its elaborate symbolism, particularly the rose motif, which is used throughout. But though the detail is, as ever, intense, the overall effect is one of space and light. The exterior of the house is equally impressive and totally original. On the ground floor is an excellent **café**, which is popular with locals (see 'Cafés' on page 174). ■ *T3534770. Sat and Sun 1000-1700, for weekday access T3534449. £3.50, £2.50 concession. To get there take the Underground to Ibrox station and walk (15 minutes), or bus 91 from Hope St.*

Directly opposite Shields Road Underground is another of Charles Rennie **Scotland Street** Mackintosh's great works, the Scotland Street School, which opened in 1906 **School Museum** and closed in 1979. The entire school has been preserved as a museum of edu- **of Education** cation and is a wonderfully evocative experience. There's a fascinating collection of school memorabilia and reconstructed classrooms from Victorian times up to the 1960s, as well as changing rooms, science room and headmaster's office (straighten your tie and comb your hair before entering).

This was the most modern of Mackintosh's buildings and is notable for its semi-cylindrical glass stair towers, the magnificent tiled entrance hall and his customary mastery of the interplay of light and space. There's also a café, but don't worry, they don't serve authentic school food. ■ *T4291202. Mon-Sat 1000-1700, Sun 1400-1700. Free. Underground to Shields Road, or buses 89, 90, 96 and 97 from the city centre.*

To the east of Pollock Country Park, by Pollockshaws Road, is **Queen's Park**, **East of** named after Mary, Queen of Scots, whose reign ended after defeat here, at the **Pollock Park** Battle of Langside, in 1568. A memorial outside the park marks the site of the battle. It's a pleasant place for a stroll and the views north across the city make it even more enjoyable. Close by, in Mount Florida, is **Hampden Park**, home of Scottish football and once the largest football ground in Britain, with a capacity of 135,000. When full, as was often the case, the famous "Hampden roar" could be heard for miles around. Nowadays, the capacity is a mere 52,000.

Hampden is also the home of the new **Scottish National Football Museum**, which describes the history of the game in Scotland. This may strike some as a rather masochistic idea given some of the more infamous and embarrassing episodes, but there have been highs (Wembley '67 and Lisbon '69) as well as lows (Wembley '66 and Argentina '78). ■ *T2872746. Mon-Sat 1000-1700, Sun*

1100-1700. Admission charge. Regular trains to Mount Florida station from Central station, or buses 12, 12A, 19 and 74 from Stockwell St.

Holmwood House

South of Queens Park and Hampden, at 61-63 Netherlee Road in Cathcart, is Holmwood House, designed by Alexander "Greek" Thomson, Glasgow's greatest Victorian architect. Holmwood was built for James Couper, a paper manufacturer, between 1857 and 1858 and is the most elaborate and sumptuously decorated of all the villas Thomson designed for well-to-do industrialists on the outskirts of Glasgow. It was rescued from decline by the National Trust for Scotland in 1994 and is well worth a visit.

The building is a work of genuine originality and has become a monument of international importance, as Thomson was the first modern architect to apply a Greek style to a free, asymmetrical composition. The house also includes features reminiscent of Frank Lloyd Wright, which pre-date the great American architect by some forty years. Thomson designed everything in the house and conservation work is revealing very beautiful and elaborate stencilled decoration and friezes with Greek motifs. The best description of Holmwood comes from Thomas Gildard who wrote in 1888: "If architecture be poetry in stone-and-lime – a great temple an epic – this exquisite little gem, at once classic and picturesque, is as complete, self-contained and polished as a sonnet". ■ *T6372129. 1 Apr-31 Oct, daily 1330-1730, but access may be restricted at certain times; phone in advance. £2.40, child/concession £1.60. Trains every half hour to Cathcart from Central station, or take buses 44 and 46 from the city centre.*

City walks and cycle routes

As well as the many green spaces, there are several scenic **walkways** and **cycle paths** in and around the city, giving the visitor the opportunity to escape the noise and traffic and to stretch their legs. There are also several long-distance walkways/cycle routes which start in Glasgow. The **tourist office** has a wide range of maps and leaflets detailing these routes, which follow quiet back streets, public parks and disused railways for much of the way. Many of the routes start at Bell's Bridge (by the SECC). For the most up-to-date information on the expanding network of cycle routes in the area, and throughout the country, contact *Sustrans*, 53 Cochrane St, T5720234, www.sustrans.co.uk A useful book is *25 Cycle Routes In and Around Glasgow*, E.B. Wilkie (HMSO). (For **bike hire**, see 'Cycling', on page 182).

The **Kelvin Walkway** follows the River Kelvin from Kelvingrove Park through the northwest of the city to Dawsholm Park, about three miles away. It goes through the Botanic Gardens and under the Forth and Clyde Canal. With the appropriate maps you could follow one waterway out and return by the other. The path starts just west of the Transport Museum, by the bridge on the Dumbarton Road.

The **Forth and Clyde Canal** was opened in 1790 and provided a convenient short-cut for trading ships between Northern Europe and North America, linking both coasts of Scotland. The **towpath** starts at **Port Dundas**, just north of the M8 by Craighall Road, and runs to the main canal at the end of Lochburn Road, off Maryhill road. It then runs east all the way to Kirkintilloch and Falkirk, and west, through Maryhill and Drumchapel to Bowling and the River Clyde. It passes through sections of bleak industrial wasteland, but there are many interesting sights along the way and open, rural stretches. A series of "Walk Cards" are available from *British Waterways*, T3326936.

Glasgow

The **Clyde Coast Cycle Routes** run from Bell's Bridge at the SECC through some of the city's parks and closely follows the old Paisley-Ardrossan Canal to Greenock, Gourock and on to Ardrossan, for ferries to the Isle of Arran. It's 28 miles one way as far as Gourock and the route is covered by the *Glasgow and Clyde Coast Cycle Routes* leaflets; Glasgow to Paisley and Paisley to Greenock sections.

The **Glasgow-Loch Lomond Cycle Way** is for both walkers and cyclists. It runs from the centre of Glasgow, following a disused railway track to Clydebank, the Forth and Clyde Canal towpath to Bowling, then a disused railway to Dumbarton, and finally reaching Loch Lomond by way of the River Leven. The route continues all the way to Killin, in the heart of the Perthshire Highlands, via Balloch, Aberfoyle and Callander.

There's also a new **Glasgow-Edinburgh** route, which incorporates part of the Clyde Walkway (see below). The **West Highland Way** (see page 54) begins in Milngavie, eight miles north of the city centre, and runs for 95 miles to Fort William.

Clyde Walkway

The Clyde Walkway is a 40-mile walking route which is being developed to link the centre of Glasgow to the Falls of Clyde at Lanark, via the Clyde Valley (see page 188). Sections of the waterfront walk are still rather empty and depressing but the central part, between Victoria Bridge and the SECC, is interesting and takes in some of the more distinguished bridges and much of Glasgow's proud maritime heritage.

Start the walk at **Victoria Bridge**, built in 1854 to replace the 14th century Old Glasgow Bridge, and continue past the graceful **Suspension Bridge**, built in 1851 as a grand entrance to the "new town" on the south bank. You can cross from here to **Carlton Place**, whose impressive Georgian façades have been restored and which were designed to front the never-completed "new town".

Back on the north bank is **Customs House Quay** and, further west beyond George V Bridge, **Broomielaw Quay**. From here, Henry Bell's *Comet* inaugurated the world's first commercial passenger steamboat service. This was also the departure point for many Scottish emigrants to North America, and, later, for thousands of holidaying locals heading "doon the watter" to the Firth of Clyde seaside resorts.

Further west, at Anderston Quay, is the **P.S. Waverley Terminal**. The *P.S. Waverley* is the world's last sea-going paddle steamer and still operates on the Clyde (see page 142). Between here and the SECC is the huge 175ft high **Finnieston Crane**, which was once used for lifting railway locomotives at a time when Glasgow was the largest builder of these in the world outside North America. Close by is the **Rotunda** (1890-96) which was once the northern terminal of the complex of tunnels which took horse-traffic and pedestrians under the river, until the building of a new road tunnel in the 1960s. The Rotunda has been restored as a restaurant complex.

You cannot miss the **Scottish Exhibition and Conference Centre (SECC)**, built in 1987 on the site of the former Queen's Dock and now the country's premier rock and pop venue. Next door is the controversial **Clyde Auditorium**, known locally as the "Armadillo", which was designed by Sir Norman Foster and built in 1997.

Beyond the SECC you can continue a short distance west to the **Clyde Maritime Centre**, at Yorkhill Quay, where you can find out exactly how "The Clyde made Glasgow – but Glasgow made the Clyde". ■ *T3390631. 1000-1700. Also café, bar and shop.*

Essentials

Sleeping

Glasgow has a good range of accommodation. Most of the hotels, guest houses, B&Bs and hostels are in the city centre and the West End or south of the river, around Queen's Park. The best area to find good value mid-range accommodation is the West End, around Kelvingrove Park and the university. Many of the hotels and guest houses around here are restored Victorian townhouses This is a good area to stay in, as it's convenient for several of the city's major sights as well as many of the best bars and restaurants.

Finding a decent room for the night can be difficult during the major festivals (see 'Festivals', page 180) and in Jul and Aug and it's best to book ahead at these times. The **tourist office** can help find somewhere to stay and also publishes a free accommodation guide. Many of the expensive business hotels offer substantial discounts at weekends, making them excellent value for a weekend break. Details of these are also available at the tourist office.

City Centre L *Glasgow Hilton*, 1 William St, T2045555, F2045044. 319 rooms. Gigantic, futuristic-looking luxury hotel regarded as one of the city's best. Full facilities include leisure centre and shopping mall. Their restaurant, *Cameron's*, is also widely held to be one of the finest around (see 'Eating' below). **L-A** *Glasgow Moat House*, Congress Rd, T3069988, F2212022. 283 rooms. Massive glass structure next to the SECC and "Armadillo" on the banks of the Clyde. Two excellent restaurants, *Mariner's* and *Dockside No 1*. **L** *Malmaison*, 278 West George St, T5721000, F5721002, glasgow@malmaison. com 72 rooms. Sister hotel of the one in Edinburgh and equally chic and stylish. Superior in every way. Their brasserie is also highly recommended.

A *The Brunswick Merchant City Hotel*, 106-108 Brunswick St, T5520001, F5521551, brunhotel@aol.com 21 rooms. Chic minimalism in the heart of the Merchant City. Ideal for cool dudes wishing to sample the delights of Glasgow night-life. Their bar-restaurant still sets the standard for style and quality (see 'Eating'). **A** *Copthorne Hotel*, George Square, T3326711, F3324264, www.mill-cop.com 150 rooms. Huge 18th century hotel in the heart of the city, next to Queen St station. Some rooms nicer than others. Conservatory bar on the ground floor is good for people-watching.

C *The Art House*, 129 Bath St, T2216789, www.arthousehotel.com. Stylish refurbishment of former education authority building. Well located and good value. Features Scotlands's first Japanese Teppan-yaki grill. **C-D** *Adelaide's*, 209 Bath St, T2484970, F2264247. 8 rooms. Beautiful "Greek" Thomson restoration in the heart of the city centre. **C-D** *Babbity Bowster*, 16-18 Blackfriars St, T5525055. 6 rooms. A local institution and one of the first of the Merchant City townhouses to be renovated. Typical Glaswegian hospitality, a near-legendary pub (see 'Bars' below) and an excellent restaurant (see 'Eating').

D *Cathedral House*, 28/32 Cathedral Square, T5523519, F5522444. 8 rooms. Overlooking the cathedral. Wonderfully-atmospheric old building with comfortable rooms and very good moderately-priced restaurant (open daily 1030-2400). **D-E** *The Merchant Lodge*, 52 Virginia St, T5522424, F5524747. 33 rooms. Renovated old building in quiet side street close to the Merchant City's stylish bars and restaurants. Great value.

E *Greek Thomson Hotel*, 140 Elderslie St, T3326556. 17 rooms. Named after Glasgow's less famous architectural son. More of a guest house, with the service that goes with it,

24 hours in Glasgow

Twenty-four hours in Glasgow is just not enough, but if you're really pushed for time the following suggested itinerary will give a brief indication of why this is now considered one of the most exciting cities in Europe.

*Start the day at the **People's Palace** on Glasgow Green for an introduction to the city's history. Head across to Sauchiehall Street for mid-morning coffee in the **Willow Tea Rooms** and admire the elegant interior design of Charles Rennie Mackintosh. Down to **Princes Square** for a spot of shopping, followed by a walk*

*around the **Merchant City**. Lunch in **Babbity Bowster**.*

*After lunch take the St Enoch subway to Kelvin Hall, for the **Kelvingrove Museum & Art Gallery**, then take a stroll through Kelvingrove Park to the **Hunterian Art Gallery**. Then walk up to the **Botanic Gardens** and enjoy afternoon tea in the **Kibble Palace**. Subway back to Buchanan Street and head to **Rogano** for a drink. Take a taxi to **Café India** for dinner, then finish up with a nightcap at **Café Insomnia** on Woodlands Road.*

and great value. **E-D** *Rennie Mackintosh Hotel*, 218-220 Renfrew St, T3339992, F3339995. 24 rooms. Another homely guest house exploiting a great architect's name, but they also offer friendly service and superb value for money. **E-D** *The Victorian House*, 212 Renfrew St, T3320129, F3533155. 60 rooms. Large, friendly guest house very close to the art college. Superb location and just about the best value in the city centre. There are many other guest houses along Renfrew St, including **E-D** *The Old School House*, No 194, T3327600 and **E-D** *Willow Hotel*, No 228, T3322332/7075.

L *Devonshire Hotel*, 5 Devonshire Gardens, T3397878, devonshire@aol.com 16 rooms. A luxury townhouse with individually designed rooms. Less stylish than its more famous neighbour but with an understated charm. **L** *One Devonshire Gardens*, 1 Devonshire Gardens, T3392001, F3371663. 27 rooms. Highly- acclaimed hotel which is the very last word in style and comfort. There are few, if any, classier places to stay in the country. Their restaurant is sensational and was the only one in Glasgow or Edinburgh to be awarded a Michelin star last year (see 'Eating'). **West End**

B *Kelvin Park Lorne Hotel*, 923 Sauchiehall St, T3149955, F3371659. 100 rooms. Dependable old stalwart and well located for galleries, museums etc.

C *Wickets Hotel*, 52 Fortrose St, T/F3349334. 10 rooms. Overlooking the West of Scotland cricket ground and close to Partick rail station and Underground. Family-run hotel with good restaurant and its own beer garden.

D-E *Botanic Hotel*, 1 Alfred Terr, by 625 Great Western Rd, T3396955, F3371812. 16 rooms. Good value Victorian townhouse close to the West End action. **D** *Jury's Glasgow Hotel*, Great Western Rd, T3348161, F3343846. 137 rooms. Nothing too fancy, but comfortable rooms and good facilities including pool, sauna and gym. Free parking. Very good value. **D-E** *Kelvin Hotel*, 15 Buckingham Terr, Great Western Rd, T3397143, F3395215. 33 rooms. Comfortable guest house in lovely Victorian terrace near Byres Road and Botanic Gardens. In the same terrace is the smaller **D-E** *Lomond Hotel*, T3392339. **D** *Kirkland House*, 42 St Vincent Crescent, T2483458, kirkland@ gisp.net 5 rooms. Small, family-run guest house with that little bit extra. Close to Kelvingrove Park. A few doors down, at No 36, is **D** *Number Thirty Six*, T2482086. **D** *Kirklee Hotel*, 11 Kensington Gate, T3345555, F3393828. 9 rooms. Lovely Edwardian townhouse with beautiful garden. Close to bars and restaurants on Byres Road and the Botanic Gardens. **D-E** *The Sandyford Hotel*, 904 Sauchiehall St, T3340000,

Glasgow

Glasgow city centre

Glasgow

Sleeping
1 Adelaide's
2 Babbity Bowster
3 Baird Hall
4 Brunswick Merchant City
5 Copthorne
6 Glasgow Hilton
7 Malmaison
8 Merchant Lodge
9 Old School
10 Rennie Mackintosh
11 Victorian House
12 Willow

Eating
1 Amber Regent
2 Axiom
3 Baby Grand
4 Bargo
5 Buttery
6 Café Cossachock
7 Café Gandolfi
8 Café Gandolfi @CCA
9 City Merchant
10 Fratelli Sarti
11 Froggies
12 Glasgow Noodle Bar
13 Granary
14 Green Room (Royal Concert Hall)
15 Ho Wong
16 Ichiban Japanese Noodle Bar
17 Le Bouchon
18 Loong Fung & Canton Express
19 Mojo
20 Pattaya
21 Pierre Victoire
22 Rogano
23 Schottische
24 Tex Mex
25 Thirteenth Note
26 Tun Ton
27 Wee Curry Shop

Cafés & bars
28 Balsa & De Quincy's
29 Bar 10
30 Bar 91
31 Blackfriars
32 Café Roberta

Glasgow

© Crown copyright

33 Caffe Latte, Café
   Delmonica's & Polo
   Lounge
34 Cask & Still
35 Gate
36 Griffin
37 Guido's Coronation
38 Havana
39 Horse Shoe Bar
40 Jenny Tea Rooms
41 Lounge
42 Mitre Bar
43 O'Neill's
44 Rab Ha's
45 Scotia Bar

46 Toast
47 Variety Bar
48 Victoria Bar
49 Willow Tea Rooms

▲ **Other**
1 Archaos
2 Arches
3 Barrow Market
   (The Barras)
4 Bennet's
5 CCA
6 Citizens' Theatre
7 City Chambers

8 City Halls & ticket
   office
9 Gallery of Modern Art
   & Royal Exchange
   Square
10 Garage
11 Glasgow Film Theatre
12 Glasgow School of Art
13 Hutcheson's Hall
14 Italian Centre
15 King's Theatre
16 King Tut's Wah Wah
   Hut
17 Lighthouse
18 McLellan Galleries

19 Nice 'n' Sleazy
20 Pavilion Theatre
21 People's Palace
22 RSAMD
23 Sub Club
24 Trades House
25 Tenement House
26 Theatre Royal
27 Tobacco Exchange
28 Tolbooth Steeple
29 Tron Theatre
30 Tunnel

F3371812. 60 rooms. Comfortable and good value hotel convenient for the SECC and art galleries. **D-C** *The Townhouse*, 4 Hughenden Terr, T3570862, F3399605. 10 rooms. Just off the Great Western Rd. Lovely Victorian townhouse offering comfort, hospitality and great value. **D-E** *The Townhouse Hotel*, 21 Royal Crescent, T3329009, F3539604. 20 rooms. Yet another elegantly-restored Victorian townhouse (is there no end to them?), set back off Sauchiehall Street. Good value and handy for the SECC and Kelvingrove Park.

E-D *Hillhead Hotel*, 32 Cecil St, T3397733, hillhotel@aol.com 11 rooms. Small, friendly hotel ideally placed for the Byres Rd nightlife and close to Hillhead Underground. **E** *Hillview Guest House*, 18 Hillhead St, T3345585, F3533155. 10 rooms. Friendly, good value B&B close to university and Byres Rd.

Glasgow West End

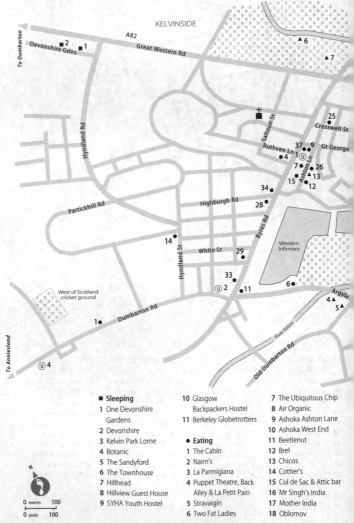

■ **Sleeping**
1 One Devonshire Gardens
2 Devonshire
3 Kelvin Park Lorne
4 Botanic
5 The Sandyford
6 The Townhouse
7 Hillhead
8 Hillview Guest House
9 SYHA Youth Hostel
10 Glasgow Backpackers Hostel
11 Berkeley Globetrotters

● **Eating**
1 The Cabin
2 Nairn's
3 La Parmigiana
4 Puppet Theatre, Back Alley & La Petit Pain
5 Stravaigin
6 Two Fat Ladies
7 The Ubiquitous Chip
8 Air Organic
9 Ashoka Ashton Lane
10 Ashoka West End
11 Beetlenut
12 Brel
13 Chicos
14 Cottier's
15 Cul de Sac & Attic bar
16 Mr Singh's India
17 Mother India
18 Oblomov

A-B *The Ewington*, Balmoral Terr, 132 Queen's Drive, T4231152, ewington@
aol.com 45 rooms. Friendly and comfortable hotel in a secluded terrace facing Queen's
Park. Their restaurant, *Minstrels*, is superb value and worth a visit in its own right.

D *Boswell Hotel*, 27 Mansionhouse Rd, T6329812. Just to the south of Queen's Park,
off Langside Rd. Lively and informal hotel better known for its excellent pub where
you can hear live folk and jazz.

E *Reidholme Guest House*, 36 Regent Park Square, T4231855. Small, friendly guest
house in a quiet side street near Pollockshaws Rd.

Glasgow

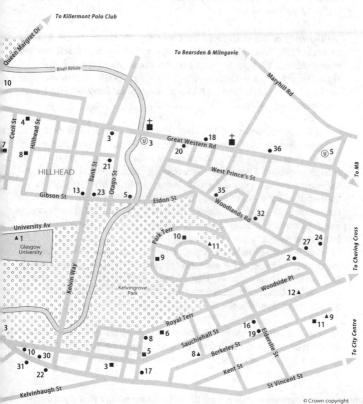

© Crown copyright

19 Asha	29 University Café	2 Kelvinhall	5 Kelvin Hall Sports
20 The Bay Tree	30 The Brewery Tap	3 Kelvinbridge	Arena
21 Café Alba	31 Firebird	4 Partick	6 Botanic Gardens
22 Murphy's Pakora Bar	32 The Halt Bar	5 St George's Cross	7 Kibble Palace
23 Sal e Pepe	33 The Living Room		8 Henry Wood Hall
24 Vegville	34 Tennent's	▲ **Other**	9 Mitchell Library &
	35 Uige Beatha	1 Hunterian Museum	Theatre
● **Cafés & bars**	36 Wintergills	2 Hunterian Gallery &	10 BBC Studios
25 Brasserie Metro	37 Curlers	Mackintosh House	11 Goethe Institut
26 Grosvener Café		3 Kelvingrove Museum	12 Internet Café
27 Insomnia	Ⓤ **Underground**	& Art Galleries	13 Grosvenor Cinema
28 Tinderbox	1 Hillhead	4 Transport Museum	

Hostels & **F** *SYHA Youth Hostel*, 7/8 Park Terr, T3323004. 144 beds. This former hotel has been
campus converted into a great hostel with dorms for 4-6, many with en suite facilities. Price
accommodation includes continental breakfast. It gets very busy in Jul/Aug so you'll need to book
ahead. Open till 0200. It's a 10-minute walk from Kelvinbridge Underground station,
or take bus 44 or 59 from Central station and get off at the first stop on Woodlands Rd,
then head up the first turning left (Lynedoch St). Close by is **F** *Glasgow Backpackers
Hostel*, 17 Park Terr, T3329099. 90 beds. Open 3 Jul-23 Sep. Independent hostel
housed in university halls of residence. Also very popular, and cheaper than the *SYHA*.

F *Berkeley Globetrotters*, 63 Berkeley St, Charing Cross, T2217880/2045470. 30 beds.
Open all year, very cheap and popular, so phone ahead to book. It's just past the
Mitchell library, on the other side of the M8 heading west from Bath St. Take a 57 bus
from the city centre. Next door is the *Blue Sky Hostel*, T2217880, which is also open all
year and slightly more expensive.

The *University of Glasgow*, contact the Conference and Visitor Services, 81 Great
George St, T3305385, consf@ gla.ac.uk www.gla.ac.uk Has a range of **self-catering**
accommodation, available Jul-Sep. *Cairncross House*, 20 Kelvinhaugh Place, off
Argyle St near Kelvingrove Park, costs from £78 per week, and flats at Kelvinhaugh St
cost from £150 per week. It also has **B&B** accommodation at *Dalrymple Hall*, **E**, available Mar-Apr and Jul-Sep.

The *University of Strathclyde*, T5534148, RESCAT@mis.strath.ac.uk. www.strath.ac.
uk/department/rescat/sales/index.htm A wide range of **B&B** accommodation in its
various halls of residence across the city, mostly available Jun-Sep, though a few are
open all year round. **E** *Baird Hall*, 460 Sauchiehall St. Open all year. 185 rooms (all
shared bathrooms). The pick of the bunch. A beautiful Art Deco high-rise building in a
great location. Also cheaper than most of the others. **E-D** *Chancellors Hall*, Rottenrow
East (on campus). 231 en suite rooms. **E** *Clyde Hall*, 318 Clyde St. 128 rooms (mostly
en suite). Central location, almost overlooking the Clyde near St Enoch bus terminal.
E-D *Garnett Hall*, Cathedral St (on campus). 124 rooms. Also self-catering from £250
per week. **E-D** *Murray Hall*, Collins St (on campus). 70 rooms. Farther out of town, but
the cheapest of the lot, is **F-E** *Jordanhill Campus*, 76 Southbrae Drive. 189 rooms.
Take a 44 bus from Central station. More salubrious accommodation is available at the
C *Strathclyde Graduate Business School*, 199 Cathedral St, T5536000, F5536137. 107
en suite rooms. Open all year.

There are also **self-catering** flats (**E-F** per person per night) for 4-6 people, available
all year round, at the *YMCA Aparthotel*, David Naismith Court, 33 Petershill Drive,
T5586166, DNC@cqm.co.uk It's a rather characterless tower block three miles northeast of the city centre.

Camping The only campsite anywhere near the city is *Craigendmuir Park*, Campsie View,
Stepps, T7794159/2973. It's four miles northeast of the city centre and a 15-minute
walk from Stepps station.

Eating

Glasgow's culinary renaissance continues unabated. The last few years has seen a proliferation of classy restaurants combining the finest of cuisine with all the style and
cool you'd expect from this most design-conscious of cities. Glasgow has always
boasted a wide selection of ethnic eateries, particularly **Indian**, **Chinese** and **Italian**
restaurants, and these have been joined by a growing number of cuisines from
around the globe. **Scottish** cuisine is also well represented, reflecting the growing

trend of marrying traditional Scottish ingredients with continental and international flavours and styles. **Vegetarians** are also well catered for. Though there aren't too many exclusively vegetarian or vegan restaurants, most places now offer substantial and imaginative vegetarian menus.

Glasgow also reflects the move away from strict culinary national boundaries and towards a more international style. Its many bistros and brasseries feature wide-ranging menus which incorporate everything from Mediterranean cooking to Pacific Rim specialities. They also tend to be more lively and informal places to eat, as well as offering good value for money. And this is one of the city's great strengths. Compared to other cities (ie London), you can eat well and in some style without breaking the bank.

The greatest concentration of eating places is around **Byres Road** in the West End, which is heavily populated by students and therefore the best area for cheap, stylish places to eat. The **Merchant City** contains most of the designer brasseries, which are more expensive, but many of the **bars** serve good food at reasonable prices. Some of the places listed below also appear in the **Bars** section. **Cafés** are often good value places to eat, and these are also listed separately below.

For those on a tight budget, many city restaurants offer cheap business lunches. Pre-theatre dinner menus also provide an opportunity to sample some of the finest food at affordable prices, if you don't mind eating before 1900. Also note that many of Glasgow's restaurants are open seven days a week. **NB** BYOB means bring your own bottle.

Expensive *The Buttery*, 652 Argyle St, T2218188. Victoriana abounds in this old **City Centre** favourite with its clubby atmosphere. Consistently rated as one of the best in the city, with an emphasis on the finest Scottish fish, seafood and game. Good high-quality wine list. Open Mon-Fri 1200-1430, 1900-2230; Sat 1900-2230. Downstairs is the much cheaper and less formal *The Belfry*, open Mon-Fri 1200-1500, 1700-2300; Sat 1700-2300. *Cameron's*, 1 William St, T2045555. In Glasgow's *Hilton Hotel*. Sublime Scottish cuisine. Pricey but well worth it. No smoking area. Open Mon-Fri 1200-1400, 1900-2200; Sat 1900-2200. *Ho Wong*, 82 York St, T2213550. Tucked away just off Argyle St, this Chinese restaurant doesn't look much from the outside but inside awaits a memorable Cantonese culinary experience and the city's finest Szechuan food. Not cheap but worth every penny. BYOB. Open Mon-Sat 1200-1400, 1800-2330; Sun 1800-2330. *Rogano's*, 11 Exchange Place, T2484055. A Glasgow culinary institution. Designed in the style of the Cunard liner, *Queen Mary*, and built by the same workers. Looks like the set of a Hollywood blockbuster and you'll need a similar budget to pay the bill, but the seafood is truly sensational. Open daily 1200-1430, 1830-2230. Downstairs is *Café Rogano*, which offers a less stylish alternative, but it's a lot easier on the pocket. Open Sun-Thur 1200-1430, 1830-2230.

Mid-range *Amber Regent*, 50 West Regent St, T3311655. Plush and very upmarket restaurant serving classic Chinese cuisine. Those on a tight budget can also indulge themselves, with half price main courses before 1900 Wed-Sat and all night Mon/Tue. BYOB. Open Mon-Thur 1200-1415, 1730-2300; Fri 1200-1415, 1730-2330; Sat 1200-2400. *Axiom*, Lancefield Quay, 154 Hydepark St, T2212822. Newly established and already one of the city's finest. Wide-ranging menu featuring contemporary Scottish dishes. Superb value. Open Mon-Sat 1100-2300. *Baby Grand*, 3-7 Elmbank Gardens, T2484942. Chic jazz-café offering good bistro-style food when most other places have shut up shop. Enjoy late night drinks and food and soothing jazz piano. Open Mon-Thur 0730-2400; Fri 0730-0200; Sat 1000-0200; Sun 1000-2400. *Brunswick Café Bar*, 106-108 Brunswick St, T5520001. Part of the hotel (see page 162) and equally stylish and design-conscious. The food is every bit as appealing as the décor and ambience and reasonably-priced. Open daily 0800-2400. *Café Cossachock*, 10

Glasgow

King St, T5530733. Near the Tron Theatre. Cosy, authentic-feeling Russian restaurant with a relaxed, informal atmosphere. Art gallery upstairs. More than just a good meal, it's an entire cultural experience. Open Mon-Sat 1030-late; Sun 1600-late. *Café Gandolfi*, 64 Albion St, T5526813. The first of Glasgow's style bistro/brasseries back in 1979, which almost makes it antique by today's contemporary design standards. Still comfortably continental, relaxed and soothing. Good place for a snack or a leisurely late breakfast. Open Mon-Sat 0900-2330. *City Merchant*, 97-99 Candleriggs, T5531577. The best of Scottish meat and game but it's the fish and seafood which shine. Absolutely superb. It's at the top end of this price range but their two- and three-course set menus are more affordable and excellent value (available 1200-1900). Very popular and a good atmosphere. BYOB. No smoking area. Open Mon-Sat 1200-2300, Sun 1700-2300. *Fratelli Sarti*, 121 Bath St, T2040440. Everything you'd expect from a great Italian restaurant, and a lot more besides. Exceptional value food washed down with the best value bottle of wine in the city. No wonder it's always busy. No smoking area. Open Mon-Sat 0800-2300; Sun 1200-2300. *Froggies*, 53 West Regent St, T5720007. French café-bistro featuring spicy, mouth-watering Cajun specialities. Excellent value three-course pre-theatre dinner and two-course lunch. BYOB. No smoking area. Open Mon-Sat 1200-1500, 1700-2400; Sun 1700-2400. *The Green Room*, Glasgow Royal Concert Hall (see 'Entertainment'), 2 Sauchiehall St, T3323163. Much more than a good place to eat before the show. A superb restaurant in its own right where you can indulge in the finest of Scottish produce at reasonable prices. Good vegetarian selection. No smoking area. Open Mon-Sat 1200-1430, 1730-2130; also Sun (performance days only). *Le Bouchon*, 17 King St, T5527411. A genuine Parisian bistro offering classic French dishes at unbeatable value. Their cheap lunchtime set menu is hugely popular with local professionals. They also do a cheap two-course pre-theatre supper. Open Mon-Thur 1200-1400, 1730-2400; Fri/Sat 1200-1430, 1700-0100. *Loon Fung*, 417 Sauchiehall St, T332-1240. Classic city Cantonese restaurant and a perennial favourite with locals, including the Chinese community. Wide variety, including vegetarian. Open Mon-Sat 1200-2330; Sun 1130-2330. *Mojo*, 158a Bath St, T3312257. Comfortable, intimate city bistro serving usual classics as well as Japanese specialities. Excellent value pre-theatre menu (1700-1900). Popular with pre-club set later in evening (see 'Bars'). Open Mon-Sat 1200-2400; Sun 1800-2400. *Pattaya*, 437 Sauchiehall St, T5720071. Top-class, well-presented Thai cuisine in calm, casual surroundings. Good value. Open Mon-Thur 1200-1400, 1730-2330; Fri/Sat 1200-1400, 1730-2400; Sun 1800-2330. *Schottische*, 16-18 Blackfriars St, T5527774. Upstairs from the legendary *Babbity Bowsters* (see below). The best of Scottish food at very affordable prices. Leave room for their diet-busting puddings. Open Mon-Sat 1230-1530, 1830-2100. *Tex Mex*, 198-200 Bath St, T3328338. Refreshingly different take on the rather tired old Mexican theme. Vast portions of delicious Tex Mex standards and a good selection of veggie options. Entertaining and efficient service is also refreshing. Attracts a lively younger crowd who also frequent its adjoining bar. Open daily 1200-2400. *Tron Theatre*, Chisholm St, T5528587. Refurbished restaurant offers a dining experience that's worth applauding. The two-course set lunch is exceptional value. No smoking area. The effortlessly stylish bar is perfect for that pre-prandial tipple. Open Mon-Sat 1200-2200; Sun 1030-1600, 1800-2200. *Tun Ton*, 157 Hope St, T5721230. Fusion food seems to be the flavour of the moment and this is a tasty example. Imaginative menu has something for everyone and is matched by the cool, stylish décor. Cheap lunch options and an excellent-value pre-theatre dinner menu. No smoking area. Open Mon 1200-1500, 1730-2200; Tue-Thur till 2230; Fri/Sat till 2245; Sun 1730-2200.

Cheap *Babbity Bowster*, 16-18 Blackfriars St, T5525055. You can't get away from this place, and why would you want to? Buzzing café-bar housed in a magnificent 18th-century building in the heart of the Merchant City. Traditional Scottish and French dishes served with flair. Outrageously good value. The bar is one of the city's perennial favourites (see 'Bars'). Open Mon-Sat 0800-2400; Sun 0900-2400. *Bargo*, 80 Albion St, T5534771. Impressively stylish designer bar serving excellent value bar snacks and meals of superior quality. Definitely a place to be seen in (see 'Bars'). Open Mon-Sat 1100-2400; Sun 1200-2400. *Café Gandolfi @ CCA*, 350 Sauchiehall St, T3327864. From the people who brought you *Café Gandolfi* (see above), a new café-bar in the Centre for Contemporary Arts (see 'Sights'). Excellent vegetarian cuisine at affordable prices. No smoking area. Open Mon-Wed 0900-2300; Thur-Sat 0900-2400; Sun 1200-1800. *Canton Express*, 407 Sauchiehall St, T3320145. No-frills, cheap and filling Chinese fast food at any hour of the day or night. Open daily 1200-0500. *Glasgow Noodle Bar*, 482 Sauchiehall St, T3331883. Oriental fast food eaten from disposable containers with plastic chopsticks or forks. Very cheap chow and great after a heavy night on the town. Open daily 1200-0500. *The Granary*, 82 Howard St, T2263770. Behind the St Enoch Centre. Serves good, honest and wholesome vegetarian food. Big portions, big value, fast counter service. Popular with office workers and shoppers at lunchtimes. No smoking area. Open Mon-Sat 0900-1730; Sun 1100-1700. *Ichiban Japanese Noodle Café*, 50 Queen St, T2044200. Excellent value, healthy Japanese specialities in cool, modern surroundings. BYOB. No smoking. Open Mon-Fri 1200-1600, 1730-2300; Sat 1200-2300; Sun 1300-2200. *Pierre Victoire*, 165 Hope St, 2219131. Cheap and cheerful French grub. Superb value three-course lunch. BYOB. Mon-Thur 1200-2230; Fri 1200-2300; Sat 1200-0100. *The Thirteenth Note*, 50-60 King St, T5531638. Cheap and tasty vegan food upstairs and live indie music downstairs in the sweaty basement (see 'Live music venues'). Goes without saying, that it attracts a mixed crowd (but we're saying it, anyway). Friendly, relaxed atmosphere by day; by night I'm back in my cheap B&B writing up my notes. Open Mon-Sat 1200-2400; Sun 1230-2330. *Wee Curry Shop*, 7 Buccleuch St, T3530777. Son of *Mother India* (see below). Small in every sense except flavour and value. Quite simply the best cheap curry this side of Bombay, in a cosy, relaxed atmosphere. Good vegetarian options and incredible value three-course buffet lunch. BYOB. Open Mon-Sat 1200-1430, 1730-2300; Sun 1730-2300.

Expensive *The Cabin*, 996-998 Dumbarton Rd, T5691036. If you're idea of a good night out is piles of the finest Scottish food followed by a post-dinner cabaret by Wilma, the legendary singing waitress, then this is the place for you. A truly one-off experience and great fun. Not to be missed. The only drawback is there's only one dinner sitting, at 1930. BYOB. Closed Mon/Sun. *Nairn's*, 13 Woodside Crescent, T3530707. Much-hyped restaurant run by TV chef Nick Nairn, but deserving of all the praise. Exceptional cuisine and superb value. Open daily 1200-1400, 1800-2200. *One Devonshire Gardens*, 1 Devonshire Gardens, T3392001. Part of the eponymous hotel (see 'Sleeping'). The only restaurant in Glasgow or Edinburgh to have been awarded a Michelin star in 1999. Enough said. No smoking. Open Sun-Fri 1230-1400, 1915-2200; Sat 1915-2200. *La Parmigiana*, 443 Great Western Rd, T3340686. This sophisticated Italian restaurant is one of Glasgow's finest eating establishments. Recommended for a special occasion. Open Mon-Sat 1200-1430, 1800-2300. *Puppet Theatre*, 11 Ruthven Lane, T3398444. Very stylish, very intimate dining. Menu is Scottish with an international flavour. Good value set lunches. Open Sun and Tue-Fri 1200-1430, 1900-2230; Sat 1900-2300. *Stravaigin*, 28-30 Gibson St, T3342665. Hard to define but difficult to resist. An eclectic mix of exotic Asian flavours and prime Scottish ingredients to produce the most sublime results. Expensive but you won't get better value for money in this category and totally justifies its many awards. Upstairs is a café-bar where you can sample some of that fabulous food at more affordable prices. Open Mon-Thur 1200-1430, 1700-2230; Fri/Sat 1200-1430, 1700-2300; Sun 1700-2230. *Two Fat Ladies*, 88 Dumbarton Rd, T3391944. Fantastic fish and seafood in the humblest of surroundings, tucked away in an unfashionable corner of the West End. Open Tue-Thur 1800-2215; Fri/Sat 1200-1400, 1800-2215. *The Ubiquitous Chip*, 12 Ashton

West End

Glasgow

Lane, T3345007. A ground-breaking, multi award-winning restaurant and still the city's favourite place for Mctastic Scottish food, especially venison and seafood. All served in a plant-filled, covered courtyard patio. Open Mon-Sat 1200-1430, 1730-2300; Sun 1230-1430, 1830-2300. Upstairs is their bistro, *Upstairs at the Chip*, which doesn't make you feel quite as special but is much easier on the wallet. Open daily 1200-2300.

Mid-range *Air Organic*, 36 Kelvingrove St, T5645200/5201. Ultra-cool bistro. The type that could only really exist in Glasgow. Styled on Miami International Airport and serving organic and orgasmic food. Try their Thai or Japanese offerings. No smoking area. Open Mon-Thur and Sun 1100-2300; Fri/Sat 1100-2400. *Ashoka Ashton Lane*, 19 Ashton Lane, T3371115. First-class Indian restaurant, part of the famous west coast chain. Very popular with students and Byres Road trendies. Open Mon-Thur 1200-2400; Fri/Sat 1200-0030; Sun 1700-2400. *Ashoka West End*, 1284 Argyle St, T3393371. The oldest in this ever-popular chain of excellent Indians. Great value and a vegetarian-friendly menu. Open Mon-Thur 1200-1400, 1700-0030; Fri 1200-0100; Sat 1700-0100; Sun 1700-0030. *Back Alley*, 8 Ruthven Lane, T3347165. Firm West End favourite and it's easy to see why. The right ambience, good value eclectic menu and very child-friendly. Their superb burgers are reckoned to be the best in town. Open Mon-Sat 1200-2400; Sun 1100-2300. *Beetlenut*, 142 Dumbarton Rd, T3371145. Imaginative, international-flavour food served in a relaxed atmosphere. Good at any time of the day and child-friendly. New addition to the West End's already busy cuisine scene but manages to fill a gap. Open Mon-Sat 1100-0100; Sun 1200-0100. *Brel*, 39-43 Ashton Lane. Another stylish continental eating establishment in Glasgow's hippest culinary quarter. This time it's Belgian. Great food and great value, especially during the half price happy hour (1700-1900). Open Mon-Thur and Sun 1000-2300; Fri/Sat 1000-2400. *Café India*, 171 North St, T2484074. Cavernous Indian restaurant that's big on style and has a deserved reputation for fine food. Good value buffet downstairs. No smoking area. Open Mon-Thur 1200-2400; Fri/Sat 1200-0030; Sun 1500-2400. *Chicos*, 52 Bank St, T339-5407. Next to Glasgow University Union. Relatively new but already a firm favourite with the Italian community. Caters for the more discerning palate. Nice friendly atmosphere. Open daily 1200-2300. *Cottier's*, 93-95 Hyndland St, T3575825. Very elegant Latin American restaurant housed in a converted church. The food is heavenly and the ambience spiritually rewarding. These dear souls are also great with kids, bless them. Stylish bar and theatre downstairs on the ground floor where you can often hear live music (see 'Live music venues' below). Open Mon-Thur 1700-2230; Fri/Sat 1700-2400; Sun 1200-2230. *Cul de Sac*, 44-46 Ashton Lane, T3344749. Effortlessly fashionable, laid back and oh, so boho. A great place to sit back, soak up the atmosphere and enjoy good French-style food. Their famous crêpes are half price between 1700 and 1900, as are the tasty burgers and pasta. Good vegetarian choices, too, and it's a great place to work of last night's excesses with a hearty Sun brunch. Open Sun-Thur 1200-2300; Fri/Sat 1200-2400. *Gingerhill*, 1 Hillhead St, T9566515. Well off the beaten track in posh Milngavie, but well worth the trip. By day it's a café and by night one of Glasgow's best seafood restaurants. It's an awfy wee place so you'll have to book well in advance. Open Mon-Sat 1100-1600; Thur-Sat 1930-2400. No smoking. BYOB (no corkage charge). *Killermont Polo Club*, 2022 Maryhill Rd, T9465412. An exclusive, elegant Indian restaurant that offers a genuinely new culinary experience with their astonishing Dum Pukht (slow-cooked) menu. A bit out of the way, but worth it for something out-of-the-ordinary. Open Mon-Sat 1200-1400, 1700-2300; Sun 1700-2300. *Mr Singh's India*, 149 Elderslie St, T2040186. Imagine good Punjabi cooking brought to you by kilted waiters with a background wallpaper of disco music. If that sounds like your cup of char then get on down here and join in the fun. Many celebs have, so you never know who might pop in for a popadum. BYOB. Open Mon-Thur 1100-2330;

Fri/Sat 1100-2400; Sun 1430-2330. *Mother India*, 28 Westminster Terr, Sauchiehall St, T2211663. Exquisite Indian cooking at affordable prices. Friendly and informal atmosphere. Strong vegetarian selection. Cheap set lunch and pre-theatre menus. BYOB (no drinks licence). Open Mon-Thur 1200-1400, 1730-2300; Fri 1200-1400, 1700-2330; Sat 1200-2330; Sun 1700-2300. *Oblomov*, 372-374 Great Western Road, T3399177. A deliciously decadent slice of Eastern Europe. The dark, sumptuous decor and classic cuisine are enhanced by an accompanying string quartet. Open Sun-Thur 1100-2300; Fri/Sat 1100-2400. *Stazione*, 1051 Great Western Rd, T5767576. Housed in a converted Victorian train station, this is most definitely the "rail" thing. Stylish and comfortable, excellent Mediterranean food and great service. Good vegetarian selection, too. No smoking area. Open daily 1200-1400, 1700-late.

Cheap *Asha*, 141 Elderslie St, T2217144. Vegetarian Indian restaurant with a vegan slant. One of the friendliest and one of the best. Open Mon-Thur 1200-1430, 1730-2330; Fri/Sat 1200-1430, 1730-2400; Sun 1700-2330. *The Bay Tree*, 403 Great Western Rd, T3345898. Rather basic self-service café serving rather basic vegan/vegetarian food with a Middle Eastern emphasis. No smoking area. Open Mon-Sat 0930-2100; Sun 1000-2000. *Café Alba*, 61 Otago St, T3372282. Vegetarian café that's another popular student haunt, therefore great value. All the old meat-free staples are there, plus delicious home-baked goodies. Nice, cosy atmosphere. No smoking area. Open Mon-Sat 1000-1700. *The Canal*, 300 Bearsden Rd, T9545333. Stylish and upmarket American diner beside the Forth and Clyde Canal. Good grub, and beer from its very own microbrewery on the premises. Open Sun-Thur 1200-2200; Fri/Sat 1200-2300. *Murphy's Pakora Bar*, 1287 Argyle St, T3341550. As you can tell from the name, superb quality and great value. A mind-boggling variety of pakora, including haggis. Great as a snack with your pint in the bar or as a full-blown meal. Special kiddies menu and the weans eat for free on Sun. Open Mon-Thur 1200-2400; Fri/Sat 1200-0100; Sun 1230-2400. *Sal e Pepe*, 18 Gibson St, T3410999. This little Italian is one of those places you just can't stop talking about (or writing about). It is, quite simply, perfect in every sense. And as if that weren't enough, there are half price pizza and pasta offers weekdays between 1500 and 1800. What more could you want? Open Mon-Sat 0930-1100; Sun 1200-2300. *Vegville*, 93 St George's Rd, T5721160. Popular vegetarian restaurant with its finger on the pulse. Wide-ranging and imaginative menu makes it tempting to even the most committed of carnivores. Now incorporates a bar which makes it even more of an attractive proposition. Open Mon-Sat 1000-0100; Sun 1230-2300.

Mid-range *Ashoka Southside*, 268 Clarkston Rd, T6370711. Small and intimate Southside version of this venerable chain of Indian restaurants. Open Mon-Sat 1700-2400; Sun 1700-2300. *Cul de Sac Southside*, 1179 Pollockshaws Rd, T649-1819. Wee sister to the West End original (see above). Same excellent food and atmosphere. Open Mon-Thur 1200-1430, 1700-0100; Sat/Sun 1200-0100. *The Wok Way*, 2 Burnfield Rd, Giffnock, T6382244. Spectacular Chinese cooking in this very popular tiny venue. Gets very lively at weekends! Booking essential at all times. Open Tue/Wed 1700-2400; Thur 1200-1400, 1700-2400; Fri 1200-2400; Sat/Sun 1700-2400.

South Side

Cheap *Buongiorno*, 1021 Pollockshaws Rd, T6491029. The best pizza in Glasgow – at these prices? Impossible, surely. Well, check it for yourself. Impeccable Italian family cooking, with cosy ambience to match. They even have a pre-theatre two-for-one deal! Are they crazy? Simply unbeatable, so book ahead. Open Mon-Sat 0900-2300; Sun 1000-2200.

Cafés

Glasgow prides itself on its café society and many of the new, trendy designer cafés make it seem more like Barcelona or Greenwich Village than the west coast of Scotland. Glasgow is also full of authentic Italian cafés where you can enjoy a cheap fry-up washed down with frothy cappuccino. Whatever your preference, you won't have any trouble finding the right place for that essential caffeine shot during a hard day's sight-seeing or shopping. Glasgow is also the home of the tearoom and those who insist on their mid-afternoon infusion won't be disappointed. The cafés listed below also serve food and are often the most economical option for a midday snack or meal, while some others have a drinks licence and make pleasant alternatives for a civilized evening out.

City Centre *Borders*, 98 Buchanan St, T2227700. Inside *Borders* bookshop. Browse while you enjoy some good coffee (free refills) and delicious cakes and scones, or a fresh fruit smooth-ie, or a light snack. Also live jazz bands on Fri nights (see 'Entertainment'). No smoking area. Open Mon-Sat 0800-2300; Sun 1100-2130. *Café Cosmo*, 12 Rose St. Part of the Glasgow Film Theatre (see 'Entertainment') and definitely worth knowing about, even if you're not a movie buff. It's a great cheap lunch venue, especially for vegetari-ans. Open daily 1200-2100. *Caffe Latte*, 58 Virginia St, T5532553. Another cool Mer-chant City hang-out. More of a café-bar, with a relaxed feel about it, and popular with young professionals (see also 'Gay clubs and bars'). Does good, cheap bar-type food as well as wines, beers and cocktails. Happy hour 1700-2000. No smoking area. Open Mon-Sat 1100-2400; Sun 1200-2400. *Café Roberta*, 84 Gordon St. Opposite Central station. Great little Italian coffee house serving good espresso and cappuccino, light snacks and cheap, tasty pasta dishes. Open Mon-Fri 0800-1800; Sat 1000-1800; Sun 1200-1700. *Costa*, Royal Exchange Square. Part of the reputable chain which has sev-eral other outlets in the city. Good quality coffee and a good range of snacks, salads and meals. Open daily 0800 till late. Also at 68 Gordon St (open Mon-Fri 0700-1900; Sat 0800-1900; Sun 1000-1800) and in *Waterstones* bookshop, at 153-157 Sauchiehall St (open Mon-Fri 0800-2130; Sat 0800-1900; Sun 1030-1800). *Gallery of Modern Art*, Royal Exchange Square, T2217484. The ideal place to sit and relax and admire the art-work on display or the fine views across the city. Or have lunch here. Good value menu with half-price kiddies' portions. No smoking. Open daily 1000-1630. *Guido's Corona-tion*, 55 Gallowgate. Traditional Italian café serving fish and chips and good home-made ice cream. Handily placed for a late meal after a gig at the *Barrowland* (see 'Entertainment'). *Jenny Tea Rooms*, 18-20 Royal Exchange Square, T2044988. Opposite the Gallery of Modern Art but nothing modern about this wee slice of tradi-tionalism cocking a snook at trendy modernism. Tea and scones, soup and snacks and Scottish breakfasts of epic proportions. Outside seating in the summer. No smoking area. Open Mon-Sat 0800-1830; Sun 0800-1800. *Toast*, 84-86 Albion St, T5523044. Big, bright and popular Merchant City café offering a vast range of coffees and teas and a varied sandwich menu. Great all-day breakfasts, but also loads of healthy options. Outside seating on the summer. Open Mon-Sat 0800-2000; Sun 1000-1800. *Willow Tea Rooms*, 217 Sauchiehall St, T3320521. A recreation of the original Miss Cranston's Tearooms, designed by Charles Rennie Mackintosh and filled with many of his original features. Most visitors come here for the interior design, but they also offer a good selection of reasonably-priced teas, sandwiches, cakes and scones, as well as hot meals. There's also a sister branch at 97 Buchanan St (T2045242), which is licensed. No smoking area. Open Mon-Sat 0930-1630; Sun 1200-1615.

West End Brasserie Metro, 8 Cresswell Lane, T3388131. Big and bright West End café/deli just off Byres Road that's popular with students. Wide-ranging menu makes it a good, cheap choice for lunch. No smoking area. Open Mon-Sat 0800-1800; Sun 0900-1800. *Grosvener Café*, 31 Ashton Lane, T3391848. Behind Hillhead Underground. A perennial favourite with local students who come for the wide selection of cheap food (filled rolls, soup, burgers, pizzas, etc). Cosy and friendly atmosphere. Good Sun brunch, and Thai food in the evenings. Open Mon 0900-1900; Tue-Sat 0900-2300; Sun 1030-1730. *Insomnia*, 38-42 Woodlands Rd, T5641700. 24-hour café/deli where the menu changes with the mood. Still the best place for late-night refuelling, whether it's a caffeine kick, herbal infusion or a cheap bite to eat. BYOB. No smoking area. Open daily. *La Petit Pain*, 239 Byres Rd, T3371118. Long-established continental-style café/deli with a wide variety of sandwiches to eat in or take away. Open Mon-Fri 0830-1800; Sat 1000-1800; Sun 1200-1800. *Tinderbox*, 189 Byres Road, T3393108. Coffee shop which looks and feels more like a style bar. Great coffee, good magazines to read and a large no smoking, child-friendly area. Open daily 0800-2200. *University Café*, 87 Byres Rd, T3395217. A gloriously authentic Italian Art Deco café, where grannies and students sit shoulder-to-shoulder enjoying real cappuccino, great ice cream and good, honest and cheap mince and tatties, pie and chips, sausage rolls, gammon steak and all the other golden oldies. Open Mon-Fri 0900-2200; Sat 0900-2230; Sun 1000-2200.

South Side *Art Lovers' Café*, Bellahouston Park, Drumbreck Rd, T3534779. Housed in CRM's exquisite House for an Art Lover. A nice place to chill and a good selection of light snacks and hot and cold meals. Also live jazz on Sat nights in the bar. No smoking. Open Sun-Fri 1000-1700; Sat also 1830-2400. *Café Blankitt*, 378 Cathcart Rd, T4235172. Out-of-the-way but worth knowing if you're in the area. Very comfortable and relaxing place to enjoy a coffee or a snack. Also does more substantial meals in the evenings (cheap-Mid-range). Open Tue-Thur 1000-2000; Fri/Sat 1000-2300; Sun 1100-2000. *Chisholm's*, 145 Kenmure St. No-nonsense traditional caff serving very cheap filled rolls and fry-ups to a grateful public. Open Mon-Fri 0900-1730; Sat 0930-1700; Sun 1100-1700.

Bars

Forget all the tired old clichés about Glasgow and Glaswegians, a night out in Scotland's largest city is a memorable experience – for all the right reasons. There are bars and pubs to suit all tastes, from ornate Victorian watering holes to the coolest of designer bars, where you can listen to thumping dance beats before heading off to a club. Even the trendiest of places, though, are saved from being pretentious by the never-ending warmth and humour that pervades this city.

The city centre is packed full of bars of every description, from the continental style of the **Merchant City**, to the authentic spit-and-sawdust of the **East End**. One of the best areas for the sheer number and variety of pubs and bars is the **West End**, with its large student population.

Glasgow's famously liberal licensing laws have unfortunately been repealed and there now exists a restrictive **curfew**. At the time of writing, most pubs and bars open till 2400, though a few are open later, and many of them close at 2300 on weekdays and Sun.

Note that there's bound to be some overlap between bars, cafés, bistros and restaurants. Many of the bars listed below, especially those in the Merchant City and West End, serve very good food at reasonable prices, and the best of these are also included in the 'Eating' section. Similarly, many of the **cafés** and **bistros** listed under their respective sections are among the best places to enjoy a drink. Also note that many bars feature regular **live bands** and **comedy nights**, and the most notable of these are listed separately (see 'Comedy' and 'Live music venues' below).

City Centre Babbity Bowster, 16-18 Blackfriars St. Prime Merchant City pub that has everything; lively atmosphere, wide selection of real ales and good food (see also 'Eating'). *Balsa*, 71 Renfield St. Revamped and restyled and attracting a young, hip pre-club crowd in the evenings. By day it serves cheap and imaginative food (1200-1500). Upstairs is *De Quincey's*, which attracts a more mature, refined clientele in keeping with its sumptuous interior. *Bar 10*, 10 Mitchell St. This converted warehouse is Glasgow's original style bar and still as cool as ever. Good food on offer and a popular pre-club meeting place at weekends with regular DJs. *Bar 91*, 91 Candleriggs. Another cool style bar, but comfortable and relaxed and a good place to eat. Happy hour specials 1700-2000. *Bargo*, 80 Albion St (see also 'Eating'). Stylish and spacious Merchant City bar/bistro with surprisingly good food and a high posing quotient. *Blackfriars*, 36 Bell St. Merchant city favourite which pulls in the punters with its vast range of international beers and lagers. Also a wide range of excellent grub, live music and comedy at weekends and that inimitable Glasgow atmosphere (see also 'Comedy' and 'Live music venues' below). *The Cask and Still*, 154 Hope St. Formerly the *Pot Still* and famous for its massive range of malts (around 500 of them). They also have a selection of cask ales and decent pub grub. Closed Sun. *The Gate*, 408 Sauchiehall St. New addition to the long list of style bars and another popular pre-club place. Cool and intimate at the same time and great value for lunch. Happy hour is 1200-2000 (!) and DJs pump up the volume Thur-Sat. *The Griffin*, 226 Bath St. Opposite the King's Theatre. Turn of the century pub (not the most recent one) recently renovated but losing none of its style. Still the best place in the city for pie and chips and a drink (only £2.75!). Other traditional dishes, plus vegetarian, at amazing value. *Havana*, 50 Hope St, T2484466. Is it a bar, is it a restaurant, or is it a club? All three, in fact. Latin grooves, Latin food and Latin spirit, all rolled into one. Coming here is like stepping into a Bacardi advert. Ay, Caramba! (See also 'Nightclubs'). Open Mon-Wed and Sun 1200-2400; Thur-Sat 1200-0100. *The Horse Shoe Bar*, 17 Drury Lane, between Mitchell St and Renfield St, near the station. Classic Victorian Gin Palace that is still one of the city's favourites. Its much-copied island bar is the longest continuous bar in the UK, so it shouldn't take long to get served, which is fortunate as it gets very busy. Incredibly good-value lunch served till 1430, then all day till 1900 upstairs and perhaps the cheapest pint in town. If you only visit one pub during your stay, then make sure it's this one. *The Lounge*, 142 West Regent St. Stylish, yet comfortable basement bar that's very popular with city suits due to its great value lunch specials. *The Mitre Bar*, 12-16 Brunswick St. A great traditional Glasgow pub in the midst of the Merchant City's cool designer bars. Good *craic*, cheap grub and fine ales. *Mojo*, 158a Bath St. One of Glasgow's funkiest bars with cool sounds for that pre-club drink. Good food served through the back in a more intimate atmosphere (see 'Eating'). *O'Neill's*, 457 Sauchiehall St. Yes, it's another of those dreaded Irish theme bars, but stop and look at the opening hours. This place has a disco licence and you dance the night away till the wee, small hours. Entry is free Sun-Tue and around £3-4 the rest of the week. There's also a free buffet from 1700 on Fri, be Jaisus! Open Sun-Wed till 0230; Thur-Sat till 0300. *Rab Ha's*, 83 Hutcheson St. This old Merchant City stalwart still packs 'em in. It has an enviable reputation for its food and is above the restaurant of the same name. *The Scotia Bar*, 112 Stockwell St. This old East End pub also claims to be the oldest in town, and its low ceilings and wooden beams support a convincing argument. Its also the best place in town for folk music (see 'Live music venues' below), and much-frequented by writers, poets and drinking thinkers (or thinking drinkers). *Variety Bar*, 401 Sauchiehall St. A strange combination of old-fashioned décor and young, hip clientele. Various drinks promos and happy hours and good music. *The Victoria Bar*, 159 Bridgegate. Real traditional howff in one of Glasgow's oldest streets. Seemingly unchanged since the late 19th century and long may it stay that way. One of the city's great pubs, where entertainment is provided free, courtesy of the local wags. Their bar food is so cheap it's almost complimentary.

The Attic, 44-46 Ashton Place. Above the *Cul de Sac* restaurant (see 'Eating'). Stylish **West End**
designer bar where you can enjoy tasty tapas and a bottle of plonk in cool, calm surroundings. Also good for a sandwich and fresh fruit smoothie at lunchtime. *The Brew-*
ery Tap, 1055 Sauchiehall St. Classic student haunt, within skiving distance of the
university. Convivial atmosphere, cheap food and a good selection of ales on tap are
all major attractions, as are the weekday happy hour (1700-1900) and regular live
music sessions (see 'Live music venues' below). *Firebird*, 1321 Argyle St. Yet another
of the city's never-ending stream of new style bars, but this one has the distinct
advantage of providing excellent food, especially their pizzas. Happy hour 1700-1900
daily and DJs Thur-Sun. *The Halt Bar*, 160 Woodlands Rd. T5641527. This erstwhile
tram stop (hence the name) is one of Glasgow's great unspoiled pubs with many of
the original Edwardian fixtures intact. Also a good place to see live music two or three
times a week (see 'Live music venues' below). *The Living Room*, 5-9 Byres Rd. Near
Kelvinhall Underground. Cool, relaxing space with good music and a wide choice of
food throughout the day. Plenty of drinks promos, a happy hour, and DJs five nights a
week are other reasons to pay a visit. *Lock 27*, 1100 Crow Rd. If the weather's fine (and
it sometimes is), there are few nicer places to enjoy a spot of al fresco eating and drinking than this place by the Forth and Clyde Canal in Anniesland. Good food served until
2100 and kids are made welcome. You could take a stroll along the towpath afterwards. *Tennent's*, 191 Byres Rd. Big, no-nonsense, old West End favourite, serving a
range of fine ales to a genuinely mixed crowd. It's also a great place for a chat (no loud
music) and some very cheap food. *Uisge Beatha*, 232 Woodlands Rd. The "water of
life" is one of those pubs you go into for a wee drink and you're still there many hours
later, the day's plans in ruins around your feet. Looks and feels like a real Highland hostelry. Cosy and welcoming and serving ridiculously cheap food. Scottish in every
sense, right down to the effigy of Mrs T's head strung up by a tartan scarf (if only it
were real!). *Wintersgill's*, 226 Great Western Rd. Nothing fancy or out-of-the-ordinary,
but well placed for hostels and B&Bs and one of the few places you can get a decent
cheap meal at any time on a Sun.

Boswell Hotel, 27 Mansionhouse Hotel. Lively Queen's Park favourite with a good **South Side**
selection of real ales and regular live music sessions. Noted for its good food; also has
rooms (See also 'Sleeping'). *The Church on the Hill*, 16 Algie St. Popular Southside bar
housed in an old church. Stained glass windows, beer garden, contemporary menu
and DJs preach to the converted at weekends. *Heraghty's Free House*, 708
Pollockshaws Rd. The best pint of Guinness in Glasgow in an old-style Irish pub with
old-style hospitality and old-style prices (no need for happy hours here). And they
even have a ladies' toilet, proving that everything comes to those who wait! *Samuel
Dow's*, 69-71 Nithsdale Rd. Or Sammy Dow's as it's known by its many Shawlands regulars. A friendly Southside local serving good ale and cheap bar food. Also regular live
folk music nights. *The Stoat and Ferret*, 1534 Pollockshaws Rd. No-nonsense real ale
pub also serving traditional food all day. *The Taverna*, 778 Pollockshaws Rd. Popular
Southside venue near the Tramway Theatre and Queen's Park. Nice, bright Mediterranean look and feel which extends to their love of kids. Good selection of ales and European beers and good value food, especially their pre-theatre dinner. Next door is a
good Greek restaurant.

Entertainment

It's been a few years now since Glasgow was chosen as 'City of Culture' but the legacy
lives on and the city continues to enjoy a wide span of art, theatre, film and music. The
majority of the larger **theatres, concert halls** and **cinemas** are concentrated in the
city centre, though its two most renowned theatres, the Citizens' and the Tramway,
are to be found south of the Clyde.

Details of all the city's events are listed in the two local newspapers, *The Herald* and the *Evening Times*. Another excellent source of information is the fortnightly listings magazine *The List* (£1.90), which also covers Edinburgh and which is on sale in most newsagents. To book **tickets** for concerts or theatre productions, call at the Ticket Centre, City Hall, Candleriggs (open Mon-Sat 0900-1800; Sun 1200-1700). Phone bookings T2874000 (Mon-Sat 0900-2100; Sun 0900-1800). Note that some of the **live music venues** don't have their own box office. For tickets and information go to Tower Records, on Argyle St, T2045788.

When it comes to **nightlife**, Glasgow is a city of energy and passion. Its **club scene** is amongst the most vibrant in the UK, despite the imposition of a curfew, barring entry to nightclubs after a certain time. This changes frequently, so check on the latest "rules" at the tourist office. Most of the nightclubs are clustered around the main shopping streets of the city centre, within easy walking distance of each other, and are open from 2230/2300 to between 0300 and 0400. Expect to pay around £5-10 entry on Fri and Sat nights, and around £3-5 on week nights and Sun. Club nights and venues often change, so check current details in *The List* and also look for flyers in bars and pubs.

Art galleries Apart from the large, main galleries listed under 'Sights', there are many small, independent galleries showcasing contemporary local, Scottish and international artists. The *Glasgow Galleries Guide*, free from any of the galleries, lists all current exhibitions. The following galleries are amongst the most interesting. *Art Exposure Gallery*, 19 Parnie St (behind the *Tron Theatre*), T5527779. Open Mon-Sat 1200-1700. *Collins Gallery*, 22 Richmond St, T5482558. Part of Strathclyde University campus. Open Mon-Fri 1000-1700; Sat 1200-1600. *Compass Gallery*, 178 West Regent St, T2216370. Open Mon-Sat 1000-1730. *Cyril Gerber Fine Art*, 148 West Regent St, T2213095/2040276. Open Mon-Sat 0930-1730. *Fireworks*, 35a Dalhousie St, T3324969. Open Tue-Sat 1000-1800. Ceramic gallery and workshop. *Glasgow Print Studio Gallery*, 1st floor, 22 King St, T5520704, www.gpsart.co.uk Open Tue-Sat 1000-1730. Opposite is *The Original Print Shop*. *Street Level Gallery*, 26 King St, T5522151. Open Tue-Sat 1000-1730.

Cinemas There are mainstream multiplexes throughout the city, such as *Odeon Cinema*, at 56 Renfield St, T3323413 and The Quay, Paisley Rd, T4180111. For more discerning film-goers, there's the *Glasgow Film Theatre* (*GFT*), at 12 Rose St, T3326535, with an excellent programme of art-house movies and a good bar for discussion later. In the West End is the *Grosvener*, in Ashton Lane, off Byres Rd, T3394928. An old two-screen cinema showing art-house and mainstream films.

Comedy venues *Blackfriars*, 36 Bell St, T5525924. Regular slots on Sun nights. Also live jazz (see below). *Curlers*, 256 Byres Rd, T3386511. Next to Hillhead Underground. Real student hole which claims to be the oldest pub in the city. Live comedy on Wed nights, also live bands (see below) and DJs at weekends. *The State Bar*, 148 Holland St, T3322159. Good comedy club on Thur nights. Also live blues on Tue and a good selection of real ales. Not a bad pub, actually. *Waxy's*, 20 Candleriggs, T5528717. In the Merchant City. Comedy on Thur nights, and added attractions such as cheap cocktails and mega-cheap lunches.

Concert halls *City Halls*, Candleriggs, T2875024. Smaller-scale classical music events. Home of the Scottish Chamber Orchestra. *Henry Wood Hall*, 73 Claremont St, T2044540/2263868. HQ of the Royal Scottish National Orchestra. *Royal Concert Hall*, 2 Sauchiehall St, T3326633. Prestigious venue for orchestras and big-name rock, pop and soul acts. *The Royal Scottish Academy of Music and Drama*, 100 Renfrew St, T3324101. Varied programme of international performances. *Theatre Royal*, Hope St, T3329000. The home of the generally excellent Scottish Opera and Scottish Ballet, also regularly hosts large-scale touring theatre and dance companies and orchestras.

Glasgow's gay scene has grown around the trendy bars and cafés of the Merchant City, especially Virginia St, Wilson St and Glassford St. *Austins*, 183a Hope St, T3322707. Basement bar outside the scene and popular with older crowd. Open daily till 0100. *Bennet's*, 80 Glassford St, T5525761. Glasgow's main gay club. Wed-Sun till 0300. Tue night is straight night. *Café Delmonica's*, 68 Virginia St, T5524803. Stylish bar attracting a friendly, lively crowd. DJs at weekends and free passes for the nearby *Polo Lounge*. Open daily till 2400. Next door is *Caffe Latte*, which has the same owners but is more laid-back (see 'Cafés'). *Polo Lounge*, 84 Wilson St, T5531221. Very classy bar with a comfortably exclusive air. Open till 0100. Disco downstairs thumps away till 0300. *Waterloo Bar*, 306 Argyle St, T2217539. Attracts a more mature clientele. Also *Sadie Frost's*, 8 West George St, in front of Queen St station.

Gay clubs & bars

Barrowlands, Gallowgate, T5524601. Famous old East End ballroom and now Glasgow's liveliest and best-loved gig venue. Popular with acts just breaking through and big names trying to rediscover what it's all about. *Blackfriars* (see 'Comedy venues' above). Bar featuring live jazz in the basement Thur-Sat. *Curlers* (see above). Student bar with live bands on Tue nights. *The Brewery Tap*, 1055 Sauchiehall St, T3390643. Popular West End featuring live jazz/funk/blues on Sat nights (see also 'Bars'). *Cottier's Theatre*, 93-95 Hyndland St, T3575825. Good venue for more esoteric music acts, also jazz and blues (see also 'Eating'). *The Garage*, 490 Sauchiehall St, T3321120. Medium-sized venue for bands on the verge of a breakthrough. *The Halt Bar*, 160 Woodlands Rd, T5641527. Popular bar featuring live indie/pub rock bands two or three times a week (see also 'Bars'). *King Tut's Wah Wah Hut*, 272a St Vincent St, T2215279. Glasgow's hallowed live music venue. Many a famous band has made the break in this cramped, sweaty club. Good bar downstairs for a pre-gig drink. Tickets on sale in the bar or at *Tower Records* in Argyle St. *Nice 'n' Sleazy*, 421 Sauchiehall St, T3330900. Don't be put off by the name. This is a straightforward indie hang-out, with regular underground bands playing in the basement (where else?) and a juke box playing those essential sounds. *Pavilion Theatre*, Renfield St, T3321846. A good place to see fairly well-known pop and rock acts. *The Scotia Bar*, 112 Stockwell St, T5528681. Home of Glasgow's folk scene, with live sessions on Wed nights and at weekends (see also 'Bars'). *Scottish Exhibition and Conference Centre* (*SECC*), Finnieston Quay, T2483000. Gigantic multi-purpose venue with all the atmosphere of a disused aircraft hangar. Plays host to the likes of Robbie Williams and Pavarotti. *The Thirteenth Note*, 50-60 King St, T5531638. Another major player on the alternative live music scene. Popular and lively venue for up-and-coming indie/rock bands. Also good veggie food in the bar upstairs (see 'Eating').

Live music venues

Archaos, 25 Queen St, T2043189. Huge nightclub sprawling over three floors with state-of-the-art lighting. House, garage, hip-hop and disco all featured at weekends and cheap student nights through the week. *The Arches*, 30 Midland St, T2219736. Cavernous space under Central station. Glasgow's finest and always at the cutting edge of the UK dance scene. Featuring the legendary *Slam* on Fri nights. *Fury Murry's*, 96 Maxwell St, T2216511. Behind the St Enoch Centre. An eclectic crowd get down to a mix of dance and student faves. *Babaza*, Royal Exchange Square. Good mix of nights, with student cheese through the week and funk, hip-hop, garage and house at weekends. *The Garage*, 490 Sauchiehall St, T3321120. Downbeat, sticky student haunt featuring the usual cheesy retro stuff that they seem to love, and cheap drinks, which always go down well. Occasional live bands. More of an old-fashioned getting bevvied up and copping off kind of place. *Havana*, 50 Hope St, T2484466 (see also 'Bars'). More of a bar with dancing, and only open till 0100 at weekends, but they play the hottest Latin grooves you can find. *The Lime*, 5 Scott St, T3320712. Frankie says it's 80s student faves through the week. At weekends it's down to some serious dance, garage, hip-hop, hard house and hardcore. *The Sub Club*, 22 Jamaica St, T2484600. Been around for donkeys but cool

Nightclubs

Glasgow

☞ **The Old Firm**

As Glasgow enters the 21st century with its image greatly enhanced, there remain a few skeletons in the cupboard, not least of which is the unfortunate anachronism that is its 'Old Firm' rivalry. The Old Firm is the name given to the city's two main football teams, Rangers and Celtic, who have between them totally dominated Scottish football for decades.

Rangers are a team with Protestant traditions based in the South Side near the Govan shipyards, while Celtic were founded by Irish immigrants in the East End and therefore have Catholic traditions.

Now, to the casual observer, religion may have little to do with football, but try telling that to the respective sets of bigots – sorry, supporters. This bitter rivalry, fuelled by religious intolerance, has caused more trouble between the fans than anyone would care to remember, leading to injury, and even death. And it's not just off the field that problems have occurred. Even several of the sides' foreign imports have lost control in the hate-filled cauldron of an Old Firm contest, and have been involved in some unsavoury incidents.

and funky as ever. House and techno beats at weekends for serious clubbers. *The Tunnel*, 84 Mitchell St, T2041000. A new Millenium and still going strong as one of the city's prime club venues. *The Arc and Triumph* are major-league house nights on the UK scene. *The Velvet Rooms*, Sauchiehall St, T3320755. Small and studiously hip bar/club playing funk, hip-hop, house and garage.

Theatre The Arches, 30 Midland St, T2219736. In the railway arches under Central station. Presents more radical and experimental theatre. Also home to one of the city's major clubs (see 'Nightclubs' above). *Centre for Contemporary Arts* (CCA), 350 Sauchiehall St, T3327521. Hosts contemporary dance and theatre, as well as staging various art exhibitions. Great café (see 'Cafés' above). *Citizens' Theatre*, 119 Gorbals St, T4290022. Just across the river. Home to some of the UK's most exciting and innovative drama. Main auditorium and two smaller studios. Big discounts for students and the unemployed. *King's Theatre*, 294 Bath St, T2485153. The city's main traditional theatre presenting musicals, panto and that kind of thing. *Mitchell Theatre*, 3 Granville St, T2874855. At Charing Cross. Stages various drama productions as well as occasional jazz concerts. *Theatre Royal* (see 'Concert Halls' above). Primarily a concert hall but also stages high-brow theatre, darling. *Tramway Theatre*, 25 Albert Drive, T4222023. Just off Pollockshaws Rd. Internationally-renowned venue with varied programme of innovative and influential theatre, dance, music and art exhibitions. *Tron Theatre*, 63 Trongate, T5524267. Major contemporary theatre productions. Also musical performances and big-name comedy acts. Home to a very fine bar and restaurant (see 'Eating').

Festivals

Glasgow doesn't like to be overshadowed by Edinburgh, and has a few notable festivals of its own. Things kick off in the last two weeks of **January** with the **Celtic Connections** music festival, featuring artists form around the world. It is held in the *Royal Concert Hall* (T3326833). The city's biggest festival is the **West End Festival**, two weeks of music, theatre and various free events held over two weeks in **June** (T3410844). Other festivals include the **Royal Scottish National Orchestra Proms**, at the Royal Concert Hall in **June**, the **Glasgow International Jazz Festival** (T5523552) in **July**, and the **World Pipe Band Championships** (T2215414) which are held on Glasgow Green in **mid-August**. For further information, contact Glasgow City Council's events department (T2872000).

Shopping

Bookshops *Borders*, 98 Buchanan St, T2227700. Gigantic bookstore, with café and sells international newspapers and magazines. *John Smith's*, 57 St Vincent St, T2217472; also at 252 Byres Rd, T3342769. Stocks a wide range of books and maps, including foreign language books and magazines. *Waterstone's*, 153 Sauchiehall St, T3329105. Huge bookstore with internet café and *Costa coffee* shop, where you can relax in pleasant surroundings. **Camping and outdoor equipment** *Tiso's*, 129 Buchanan St, T2484877. *Black's*, 254 Sauchiehall St, T3532344. **Clothes shops** *Cruise*, 47 Renfield St, T2482476 (Men's); *Slater's*, 165 Howard St, T5527171 (Men's). *Italian Centre*, John St, for Armani, Versace etc. *Cruise*, 180 Ingram St (Women's); *Moon*, Ruthven Lane, West End, T3392315 (Women's); *Mello*, 2659 Virginia St, T5525656; *Flip*, 68 Queen St, T2212041. The best place for designer clothes are the shops in the Princes Square shopping mall on Buchanan St.

Transport

Air Glasgow is the main departure point in Scotland for flights to North America and the Caribbean. There are also regular flights to many European destinations, and domestic flights to and from London Luton, London Stansted, Heathrow, Gatwick, Manchester, Bristol and Belfast (City and International). **Airport enquiries** T8871111. For airline addresses and phone numbers, see 'Directory' below.

Long distance
See also 'Ins and outs' (page 139) and 'Getting there' (page 26).

Ryanair flies from London Stansted to Prestwick airport, T01292-722331, 30 miles southwest of Glasgow city centre. Flight tickets include train travel (every 30 minutes) to Glasgow Central station (40 minutes).

Bus A number of companies offer express coach services day and night. There are numerous buses to and from London, and fares are very competitive (£25-30 return). The journey takes around 8 hours. *National Express* (T0990-808080) has several services daily, with links to other major English cities, including: **Manchester** (4 hours, £18 return); **Birmingham** (5 hours 30 minutes, £30 return); **Newcastle** (4 hours, £18 return) and **York** (6 hours 30 minutes, £21 return).

Scottish Citylink (T0990-505050, Info@Citylink.demon.co.uk) has buses to most major towns in Scotland: there are buses to **Edinburgh** every 15 minutes (1 hour 15 minutes, £4.50 single); hourly buses to **Stirling** (45 minutes, £3.20 single) and **Inverness** (4 hours, £11.50 single); 15 buses daily to **Aberdeen** (4 hours, £13.50 single); 4 daily to **Oban** (3 hours, £10 single); 4-5 daily to **Fort William** (3 hours, £10 single); 3 daily to **Portree** (7 hours, £17 single); and hourly to **Perth** (1 hour 35 minutes, £7 single) and **Dundee** (2 hours 15 minutes, £7 single). There are also buses to **St Andrews** with *Fife Scottish* (T01592-261461). *Midland Bluebird* (T01324-613777) runs buses to **Milngavie**, at the start of the West Highland Way (30 minutes, £1.45 single).

Train There is a fast and efficient rail service from England and Wales to Glasgow. There are several daily trains to and from Glasgow Central to **London Euston/King's Cross** (5 hours, £30 return). There are also daily services to **Birmingham** (4 hours, £25 return) and **Manchester** (3 hours 30 minutes, £18 return). The prices listed are the cheapest deals available, with *Virgin Trains* (T0345-222333). For information on current deals, also try *GNER* (T0345-225225). *Scotrail* operates the Caledonian Sleeper service if you wish to travel overnight from London Euston.

Scotrail also operates the West Highland line from Queen Street north to **Oban** (3 daily, 3 hours), **Fort William** (3 daily, 3 hours 40 minutes) and **Mallaig** (3 daily, 5 hours 15 minutes). ScotRail also run services to **Edinburgh** (every 30 minutes, 50 minutes, £7.10 single), **Perth** (hourly, 1 hour), **Dundee** (hourly, 1 hour 20 minutes), **Aberdeen** (hourly, 2 hours 35 minutes), **Stirling** (hourly, 30 minutes) and **Inverness** (3 daily, 3 hours 25 minutes). For information on rail services and fares, call National Rail Enquiries T0345-484950 (advance credit/debit card bookings T0345-550033).

Local Bus Bus services are operated by *First Bus* under the names *Greater Glasgow* and *Kelvin Buses*. Routes are shown on the *Visitor's Transport Guide*. For short trips in the city fares are 65p. On most buses you'll need to have exact change. After midnight, till 0400, there's a limited night bus service (more frequent at weekends). Full details from Travel Centres. A good way to get around town is to buy a ticket for one of the **guided bus tours**.

Taxi There are taxi ranks at Central and Queen Street train stations and Buchanan bus station. To call a cab, try *Glasgow Wide TOA* (T3326666/7070), who also run city tours. Minimum fare around the city centre is £1.50-2. To the Burrell collection from the city centre (about three miles) should cost around £6-7.

Train Trains leave from **Glasgow Central** mainline station to all destinations south of the Clyde, including to Greenock (for ferries to Dunoon), Wemyss Bay (for ferries to Rothesay), Ardrossan (for ferries to Arran) and to Prestwick airport. There's a low-level station below Central station which connects the southeast of the city with the northwest. This cross-city line serves the SECC and a branch runs north to Milngavie, at the start of the West Highland Way. There's also a line from **Queen Street** which runs west all the way to Helensburgh, via Partick and Dumbarton. Branches of this line run to Balloch, at the south end of Loch Lomond, and Milngavie.

Underground Locals affectionately call it the "Clockwork Orange", as there's only one circular route serving 15 stops and the trains are bright orange. It's easy to use and there's a flat fare of 65p, or you can buy a day ticket for £2. A multi-journey ticket costs £5.40 for 10 journeys or £10 for 20 journeys. Trains run roughly every 5-8 minutes from approximately 0630 till 2235 Mon-Sat and from 1100 till 1750 on Sun.

Bicycle hire *Dales*, 150 Dobbies Loan, T3322705. Close to Buchanan bus station. *West End Cycles*, 16 Chancellor St, T3571344, at the south end of Byres Rd. £12 per day for mountain bikes, £50 per week. ID and £50 deposit required.

Car hire *Arnold Clark*, 10-24 Vinicombe St, T3349501 (also at the airport, T8480202). *Avis*, 161 North St, T2212877 (also at the airport, T8872261). *Budget*, 101 Waterloo St, T2264141 (also at the airport, T8870501). *Hertz*, 106 Waterloo St, T2487736 (also at the airport, T8877845). *Melvilles Motors*, 555 Sauchiehall St, 192 Battlefield Rd, Langside and at airport, T0345-525354.

Directory

Airlines *Aer Lingus*, 19 Dixon St, T0645-737747. *British Airways*, 66 Gordon St, T0345-222111 (Glasgow Airport T889-1311). *Icelandair*, Glasgow Airport, T0345-581111. *Lufthanasa*, 78 St Vincent St, T0345-737747. *Qantas*, 395 King St, T0345-747767.

Banks *Bank of Scotland*, 235 Sauchiehall St, 110 Queen St, 55 Bath St and 63 Waterloo St. *Royal Bank of Scotland*, 98 Buchanan St, 22 St Enoch Square, 140 St Vincent St and 393 Sauchiehall St. *Clydesdale Bank*, 14 Bothwell St, 7 St Enoch Square, 30 St Vincent Place, 344 Argyle St and 120 Bath St. **English banks** include *Barclays*, 90 St Vincent St and *Lloyds TSB*, 12 Bothwell St. **Exchange:** *American Express*, 115 Hope St, T2214366, open Mon-Fri 0830-1730, Sat 0900-1200. *Thomas Cook*, Central station, T2044496, open Mon-Wed & Sat 0800-1900, Thur & Fri 0800-2000, Sun 1000-1800.

Communications The main **post office** is at 47 St Vincent St, T0345-222344. Services include poste restante, currency exchange and cash withdrawal at the *German Savings Bank*. Open Mon-Fri 0830-1745, Sat 0900-1900. Also branches at 85-89 Bothwell St, 216 Hope St and 533 Sauchiehall St. Post offices in some supermarkets are open on Sun. **Cyber cafés**: *The Internet Café* is at 569 Sauchiehall St, T5641052. It charges £2-2.50 per half hour on line. *Internet Exchange*, 136 Sauchiehall St, T3530535. *Cafe Internet*, 153-157 Sauchiehall St, T3532484.

Football *Celtic Football Club* are based at Celtic Park, 95 Kerrydale St, T5562611, off the London Rd in the East End. Their bitter opponents, *Rangers*, play at Ibrox Stadium, 150 Edmiston Drive, T4278500, in the South Side. Tickets for league matches start at around £12.

Gay & lesbian contacts Lesbian and Gay Switchboard, T3328372, open daily 0700-2200.

Hospitals and medical services *Glasgow Royal Infirmary* is at 84 Castle St, T2114000, near the cathedral. The *Southern General Hospital* on Govan Rd, T2011100, is the main South Side hospital. For **dental emergencies** go to the *Glasgow Dental Hospital*, 378 Sauchiehall St, T2119600. **Pharmacies**: *Superdrug*, Central station, T2218197; open Mon-Wed & Sun till 2000, Thur-Sat till 2100. *Munroes'*, 693 Great Western Rd, T3390012; open daily till 2100.

Left luggage There's an office at Buchanan bus station, open daily 0630-2230. Also lockers at Central and Queen Street train stations (£2 per day).

Police 945 Argyle St, T5323200. Free emergency numbers are T999 or T112.

Travel agents *Campus Travel*, The Hub, Hillhead St, T3570608; and 122 George St, T5531818. *Glasgow Flight Centre*, 143 West Regent St, T2218989.

Around Glasgow

Glasgow is surrounded by a series of drab satellite towns, once major centres of coal and steel, or shipbuilding, which are struggling to recover their identity. It's tempting to pass through this depressed hinterland, especially as the delights of the West Highlands lie just beyond the city's boundary, to the northwest, but there are some hidden gems waiting for those with the time or the inclination. The 18th century model community of **New Lanark** and the spectacular **Falls of Clyde** nearby are well worth the trip from Glasgow, and there are a couple of interesting historical sights near Hamilton, namely **Bothwell Castle** and **Chatelherault**.

Within easy reach of the city, north of the suburb of Milngavie (pronounced 'Mullguy'), is **Mugdock Country Park**, sitting between Glasgow and the **Campsie Fells** (see Stirling section, page 295). It offers some fine walking along marked trails and includes the first section of the **West Highland Way**, which starts in Milngavie (see page 54). There are regular trains from Central station to Milngavie. You can either walk from here for three miles across Drumclog Moor or take the Mugdock bus from the station.

Paisley

West of Glasgow, close to the airport, is the town that gave its name to the famous fabric design copied from Kashmiri shawls. Paisley grew up around its 12th century roots and by the 19th century was a major producer of printed cotton and woollen cloth, specializing in the production of the eponymous imitation shawls.

Phone code: 0141
Population 78,000

Sights In the town centre, opposite the town hall, is **Paisley Abbey**, founded in 1163 but destroyed during the Wars of Independence in the early 14th century. It was rebuilt soon after, but fell into ruin from the 16th century. Successive renovations took place, ending with a major restoration in the 1920s. The façade doesn't do justice to the wonderfully spacious interior, which includes exceptional stained glass windows and an impressive choir. Also of note is the 10th century Barochan Cross, at the eastern end of the north nave. The best time to visit is during one of their open days, held one Sat a month (phone the tourist office for details), when the 150-feet high tower is open to the public. The views form the top are great. ■ *T8897654. Mon-Sat 1000-1530. Free. To get there, follow Gilmour St from the train station to The Cross, then turn left into Gauze St and cross the river.*

In the High Street is the **Museum and Art Gallery**, with a huge collection of the world famous Paisley shawls and an interesting display of the history of weaving. ■ *T8893151. Tue-Sat 1000-1700, Sun 1400-1700. Free.* Also on the High Street is another imposing ecclesiastical monument, the **Thomas Coats Memorial Church**, built by the great Victorian thread maker and one of the grandest Baptist churches in Europe. ■ *T8899980. Mon, Wed and Fri 1400-2000, May-Sept.*

Above the High Street, on Oakshaw Street, is the **Coats Observatory**, which has some interesting displays on climate, seismology and astronomy. ■ *T8892013. Tue-Sat 1000-1700, Sun 1400-1700. Free. Public telescope viewing Thur 1930-2130 between Oct and Mar.* Another interesting sight is the **Sma' Shot Cottages**, in George Place, off New Street. These are fully restored and furnished 18th century weavers' cottages, with photographs and various artefacts. There's also a tearoom with home baking. ■ *T8891708. Open Wed and Sat 1300-1700 Apr- Sep.*

To the south of Paisley is the **Gleniffer Braes Country Park**, which is a great place for a walk in the hills. ■ *To get there, take the B775 south of town.*

Essentials The **tourist office** is in the Lagoon Leisure Centre at the junction of Mill St and Christie St (T8890711). To get there from the train station, head down Gilmour St, turn left into Gauze St and you'll see the leisure centre on your right. It's open Apr and May Mon-Fri 0900-1300 & 1400-1700; Jun-Sep Mon-Sat 0900-1800.

The tourist office will help you find accommodation, though there's no reason to stay in Paisley as it's so close to Glasgow. If you must stay, then the best bet is **D** *Makerston House*, 19 Park Rd, T8842520. 11 rooms. This lovely Tudor-style mansion offers friendly guest house accommodation and good food.

There are frequent **trains** to Paisley's Gilmour St station from Glasgow Central (£1.85 single). There are also frequent **buses**, which stop at the abbey. Buses depart from Gilmour St station every 10 minutes for Glasgow Airport, two miles north of town.

The Firth of Clyde

West of Glasgow, the banks of the Clyde are still lined with the hulking ghosts of this great river's shipbuilding heritage. West of the **Erskine Bridge**, which connects the north and south banks of the Clyde, is **Port Glasgow**, the first of a series of grim towns which sprawl along the southern coast of the Firth of Clyde. It was developed as the city's first harbour in the late 17h century, but there's little to detain visitors today. Just before Port Glasgow, however, at Langbank, just off the M8/A8, is **Finlaystone Estate**, a Victorian mansion house set in sprawling grounds and featuring a walled garden, visitor centre and conservatory tearoom. ■ *T01475-540285. Gardens open all year daily 1030-1700. Tearoom open daily Apr-Sep 1100-1630. House open Apr-Aug (Sun tours at 1430 and 1530).*

About 30 miles west of Glasgow, Greenock was the first dock on the Clyde, back in the early 18th century and was the birthplace, in 1736, of James Watt, whose development of the steam engine contributed so much to the Industrial Revolution. Greenock today doesn't look particularly appealing, but it has its attractions. On the quay is the **Customs House Museum**, housed in the 19th century neo-classical former Customs House, where Robert Burns and Adam Smith were once employees. The museum charts the history of the Customs and Excise service, which is a lot more interesting than it sounds. ■ *T726331. Open Mon-Fri 1000-1600. Free.* While you're here, you should also visit the **McLean Museum and Art Gallery**, at 15 Kelly St, near Greenock West station. The museum contains a collection of items belonging to the town's most famous son, James Watt, and the small gallery on the ground floor has works by the Glasgow Boys as well as Fergusson, Cadell and Peploe. ■ *T723741. Mon-Sat 1000-1700. Free.*

A recommended walk near Greenock is to the **Greenock Cut**, a 19th-century aqueduct built to supply water to the town's mills. Follow the A78 south from town and turn off at the sign to Cornalees Bridge Visitor Centre. From the centre walk along the lochside to Overton (3 miles), and the path is signed from here. South of here is **Muirshiel Country Park**, which is a great place to stretch the legs and grab a few lungfuls of fresh air. It's accessed via the A761 south from Port Glasgow, then take the B786 south to Lochwinnoch.

Greenock
Phone code: 01475
Population: 50,000

Essentials There's a **tourist office** in Greenock, at 7 Clyde Square, near the High Street behind the town hall (T722007). It's open all year, Mon-Fri 0830-1645, Sat 0930-1230. The tourist office will book accommodation, should you, for some reason, wish to spend the night here. The best hotel for miles around is the superb **A** *Gleddoch House Hotel*, T540711, at Langbank (see above) near Port Glasgow. This former home of the Lithgow shipping family is extremely comfortable, with marvellous views across the Clyde and a reputation for excellent cuisine. There are a few decent and cheap places to eat in Greenock itself, including *Bennick's Brasserie*, at 49 West Blackhall St, and *Aldo's*, at 121 West Blackhall St. There are regular **trains** to Greenock from Glasgow Central and **buses** every hour from Buchanan bus station.

Three miles west of Greenock is the shabby old seaside resort of Gourock. Midway between Greenock and Gourock, on the rail line, is **Fort Matilda** station. It stands at the foot of **Lyle Hill**, which is worth the climb for the fantastic views over the Firth of Clyde. Gourock is the terminal for the **CalMac ferry** to **Dunoon**, on the Cowal peninsula (see page 194). Ferries leave frequently every day on the 20-minute crossing. For details call *CalMac* T650100. **Western Ferries**, T01369-704452, also runs a ferry service (every half hour) between Gourock and Dunoon. They leave from McInroy's point, two miles from the train station, from where *Citylink* buses also depart. **Clyde Marine**, T721281, runs a frequent passenger-only ferry service to **Kilcreggan** (10 minutes, £1.55) and a less frequent service (40 minutes, £1.55) to **Helensburgh** (see page 192), Mon-Sat. *Clyde Marine* also run **cruises** on the Firth of Clyde, to Brodick on Arran, Tighnabruaich, or Tarbert on Loch Fyne. Note that these leave from Princes Pier in Greenock.

Gourock

Gourock train station is next to the *Calmac* ferry terminal. Trains and buses to Glasgow are the same as for Greenock.

Eight miles south of Gourock is Wemyss Bay, departure point for ferries to **Rothesay**, on the Isle of Bute. Every summer this place used to be packed full of holidaying Glaswegians heading "doon the watter" to Rothesay, and the magnificent Victorian train station is a proud legacy of those days. *CalMac*

Wemyss Bay

Glasgow

ferries, T01700-502707, run frequently (see page 197), and trains run every hour to Glasgow.

Dumbarton
Phone code: 01389

Once the capital of the ancient Britons of Strathclyde, Dumbarton dates back as far as the fifth century, when it was an important trading centre and of strategic importance. Today, though, it's a pretty awful place, and of little importance to tourists. It's best to avoid the town and head straight for the spectacular **Dumbarton Castle**, perched on top of Dumbarton Rock, which is surrounded by water on three sides and commands excellent views over the Clyde estuary. This has been a strategic fortress for 2,000 years, though most of the current buildings date from the 18th century or later. ■ *T732167. Apr-Sep Mon-Sat 0930-1800, Sun 1400-1800; Oct-Mar Mon-Wed and Sat 0930-1200 and 1330-1600, Thur 0930-1300, Sun 1400-1600. £1.50.*

If you're interested in shipbuilding then you should visit the **Scottish Maritime Museum**, on Castle St. It has a working ship model experiment tank; the oldest one in the world, in fact. ■ *T763444. Open Mon, Tue, Fri and Sat 1000-1600. £1.50.*

The **tourist office**, T742306, is out of town, on the A82, which runs north to Balloch and Loch Lomond. It's open daily Jun-Sep 0930-1800; Oct-May 1000-1700. **Trains** to Dumbarton Central and Dumbarton East stations run every half hour from Helensburgh and Balloch, and every 15 minutes from Glasgow Queen Street. Get off at Dumbarton East station for the castle.

The Clyde Valley

The River Clyde undergoes a series of changes as it begins the journey from its source, 80 miles southeast of Glasgow, through the orchards and market gardens of pretty Clydesdale and the abandoned coal mines of North Lanarkshire on its way to the former shipyards of Glasgow. The M74 motorway follows the course of the river, straddled by the valley's two largest towns, **Hamilton** and **Motherwell**, the latter still reeling from the recent closure of its steelworks. Sandwiched between them is **Strathclyde Country Park**, a huge recreational area which features a 200-acre man-made loch and is massively popular with water-sports enthusiasts. The M74 then turns south towards the border with England, while the A72 takes up the task of shadowing the river to **Lanark**, the most interesting focus of this area, standing as it does beside the fascinating village of **New Lanark**.

Blantyre
Phone code: 01698
Population: 18,500

This town, now more of a suburb of Hamilton, is famous as the birthplace of **David Livingstone**, the notable Victorian missionary and explorer, who felt the white man's burden more than most and took off to Africa in 1840 to bring Christianity to the natives. He was born in the humble surroundings of a one-roomed tenement, in 1813, and worked in the local cotton mill before educating himself and taking a medical degree. The entire tenement block, at 165 Station Road, has been transformed into the **David Livingstone Centre**, which tells the story of his life, including his battle against slave traders and that famous meeting with Stanley. There's also an African-themed café, gift shop and garden. The centre is a short walk from the train station. ■ *T823140. Open Mon-Sat 1000-1700, Sun 1230-1700. £2.95, £1.95 children/concession.*

A 30-minute walk down the river towards Uddingston brings you to the substantial red sandstone ruin of **Bothwell Castle**. This is commonly regarded as the finest 13th century stronghold in the country and was fought over repeatedly by the Scots and English during the Wars of Independence. It has

withstood the ravages of time well and is still hugely impressive. ■ *T816894.*
Open Apr-Sep Mon-Wed and Sat 0930-1800, Thur 0930-1330, Sun 1400-1800;
Oct-Mar Sat-Wed 0930-1600, Thur 0930-1230. £1.80, £1.30 children.

Transport Trains to Blantyre leave from Glasgow Central every half hour. It's a
20-minute journey and costs £2.40-3 return. *Kelvin Central* buses run regularly from
Buchanan bus station; take nos 63 or 67 for Blantyre and nos 55 or 56 for Bothwell.

Hamilton has the longest history of any town in the area, with associations
with Mary, Queen of Scots, Cromwell and the Covenanters, who were defeated
by Monmouth at nearby Bothwell Bridge, in 1679. The town today is unremarkable but a mile or so south, at Ferniegair, are the gates to **Chatelherault**,
an extensive country park and impressive hunting lodge and summer house,
built in 1732 by William Adam for the Dukes of Hamilton. There are ornamental gardens and 10 miles of trails to explore along the deep wooded glen of
the Avon, past the 16th century ruins of **Cadzow Castle** and into the surrounding countryside. The Ranger service offers guided walks around the
park. ■ *T426213. Visitor centre open Mon-Sat 1000-1700, Sun 1200-1700.*
Free. House open Mon-Thur and Sat 1000-1630, Sun 1200-1630. Free.

Hamilton
Phone code: 01698
Population: 51,500

Within the bounds of nearby Strathclyde Park is the **Hamilton Mausoleum**, a huge burial vault of the Hamilton family. It's an eerie place with an
amazing 15-second echo: the longest in Europe, Europe, Europe......■ *Mausoleum tours Apr-Sep on Wed, Sat and Sun at 1500; also at 1900 in Jul and Aug.*
£1.05, children 75p.

Lanark and New Lanark

The little market town of Lanark sits high above the River Clyde. Most people
come here to visit the immaculately-restored village of **New Lanark**, one of the
region's most fascinating sights, a mile below the town, beside the river. The
community was founded in 1785 by David Dale and Richard Arkwright as a
cotton-spinning centre, but it was Dale's son-in-law, Robert Owen, who took
over the management in 1798 and who pioneered the revolutionary social
experiment. He believed in a more humane form of capitalism and believed
the welfare of his workers to be crucial to industrial success. He provided them
with decent housing, a co-operative store (the forerunner of the modern
co-operative movement), adult educational facilities, the world's first day
nursery and the social centre of the community, the modestly-titled **Institute
for the Formation of Character**. Here, in the **Visitor centre** you can see an
introductory video about New Lanark and its founders. Amongst the other
former mill buildings open to the public is the **Annie MacLeod Experience**,
which sounds like a folk group, but is actually a high-tech and highly effective
audio-visual odyssey of village life in 1820 through the eyes of an imaginary
10-year old mill girl. You can wander through the village and see the 1920s
shop, a restored mill-worker's house and even **Robert Owen's House**. There's
also a tearoom and gift shop. ■ *T661345. Visitor centre open daily 1100-1700.*
£3.75, £2.50 children. Access to the village at all times.

Population: 9,000
Phone code: 01555

Just beyond the village lies the wooded **Falls of Clyde Nature Reserve**, managed by the Scottish Wildlife Trust (SWT). You can visit the **SWT Wildlife Centre**, housed in the old dyeworks, which provides information about the history
and wildlife of the area. ■ *T665262. Apr-Sep Mon-Fri 1100-1700, Sat and Sun*
1300-1700; Feb, Mar and Oct-Dec Sat and Sun 1300-1700. £1, 50p children.

Glasgow

Walk to the Falls of Clyde

You can walk from the village to the stunning **Corra Linn** waterfalls and beyond. Starting from the village, walk past the SWT centre and up the stone steps into the nature reserve above Dundaff Linn, the smallest of the three waterfalls on the walk. A riverside boardwalk takes you past a 200-year-old weir, and just beyond the end of the boardwalk go right at a junction to pass Bonnington power station.

Steps then lead up to a viewing platform above the dramatic Corra Linn, the highest falls on the Clyde, where the river plunges 90 feet in three stages. Continue up the steps and follow the path through woodlands to reach another set of falls at **Bonnington Linn**.

You can retrace your steps back to the village, or extend the walk by crossing the weir at Bonnington Linn and turning right down the track on the opposite bank, taking a narrow path on the right after a few hundred yards. Take care here as the path is very close to the lip of the gorge! After about a mile, the path leads you to the crumbling ruin of Corra Castle. To return to Bonnington Linn, retrace your steps for about 100 yards and then follow the vehicle track on the right.

The total distance, including the extension, is about five and a half miles. Allow three to four hours there and back and wear boots or strong shoes as some parts can be muddy.

Sleeping

There's a **tourist office** in Lanark, in the Horsemarket, 100 yards west of the train station, T661661. It's open May-Sep Mon-Sat 1000-1800, Sun 1200-1700, Oct-Apr Mon-Sat 1000-1700. They can book accommodation and there's plenty to choose from, though the most interesting places to stay are in New Lanark. The **F** *New Lanark Youth Hostel*, T666710, is beautifully situated in Wee Row by the river. It's open all year and includes continental breakfast. There's also the **D** *New LanarkMill Hotel*, T667200, which has a restaurant and serves moderately-priced lunches and dinners.

Eating

There are plenty of place to eat in Lanark, including the usual hotels and pubs, cafés, chip shops and Indian restaurants. The best place is *Ristorante La Vigna*, at 40 Wellgate, T630351, a moderately-priced Italian of some renown. It's open daily for lunch and dinner, but is popular, so book in advance. If you're in town on a Mon, which is market day, it's well worth trying the *Market Bar and Restaurant*, at Lanark Market on Hyndford Rd.

Transport

Lanark is 25 miles southeast of Glasgow. There are hourly trains from Central station. There's an hourly bus service from Lanark train station to the village, but the 20-minute walk is recommended for the wonderful views. The last bus back uphill from the village leaves at 1700. To book a taxi, call *Clydewide*, T663221. Lanark is home to Scotland's largest residential **horse riding centre**, at the *Race Course Stables*, T01470-532439.

Craignethan Castle

Five miles northwest of Lanark is the village of **Crossford**, from where you can visit Craignethan Castle, an ornate tower-house standing over the River Nethan. It was built by Sir James Hamilton for James V, in 1530, and was last major castle to be built in Scotland. Mary, Queen of Scots left from here to do battle at Langside (at Queen's Park in Glasgow), where she was defeated and fled to France before her eventual imprisonment. The castle, like so many others in Scotland, is said to be haunted by her ghost. ■ *Apr-Sep Mon-Sat 0930-1630, Sun 1400-1630, Mar and Oct Mon-Wed, Sat and Sun 0930-1630, Thur 0930-1230. £1.50. To get there, take a bus from Lanark to Crossford, then it's a 15-minute walk.*

Argyll

5

Argyll

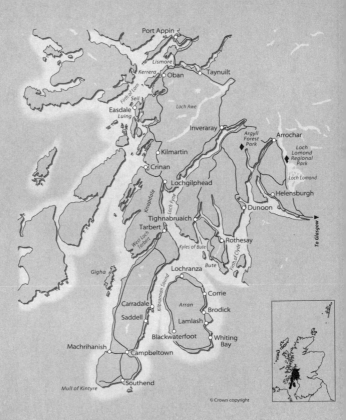

© Crown copyright

Stretching north from the Mull of Kintyre almost to Glencoe and east to the shores of Loch Lomond, the region of Argyll marks the transition from Lowland to Highland. It's a region of great variety, containing all the ingredients of the classic Scottish holiday: peaceful wooded glens, heather-clad mountains full of deer, lovely wee fishing ports, romantic castles and beautiful lochs.

Argyll also has its own particular attractions in the shape of its numerous prehistoric sites. Much of the region was once part of the ancient **Kingdom of Dalriada**, established by the Irish Celts (known as the Scotti, hence Scotland) who settled here in the fifth century. Their capital was at **Dunadd**, near Lochgilphead, from where they gained ascendancy over the native Picts. Argyll has since been ruled by Norse invaders, then by Somerled, whose successors, the powerful MacDonalds, Lords of the Isles, were in turn dislodged by the Campbells, allies of Robert the Bruce. They became the **Dukes of Argyll**, and even today are still one the largest landowners in the region.

Despite its proximity to the massive Glasgow conurbation, Argyll is sparsely populated. Its largest town, **Oban**, has only 8,000 inhabitants. Oban is also the main ferry port for Argyll's Hebridean islands.

This chapter covers mostly mainland Argyll, plus the smaller coastal islands. Also included are the Firth of Clyde islands of **Bute** and **Arran**, the most accessible of Scotland's more southerly islands, and the most popular. Bute is actually part of Argyll and Bute, created in the recent regional government reorganization, while Arran was tacked onto Ayrshire to form Ayrshire and Arran.

Ins and outs

Getting there Most visitors' approach to Argyll is west from Glasgow. At Dumbarton there's a choice of route: the more popular one is north on the busy A82 along the west bank of **Loch Lomond** (see page 296); the other route is along the north shore of the Firth of Clyde, through **Helensburgh** and along the shores of **Gare Loch** and **Loch Long**. Both routes converge at **Arrochar**, the gateway to the real Argyll. The latter road is much quieter but is not exactly a scenic alternative, as it passes through an industrial wasteland that includes the submarine base at Faslane and the oil tanks at Finnart.

Getting around Public transport is limited in much of Argyll, though the main towns are served by buses. The main bus operators are *Scottish Citylink*, T0990-505050, and *Oban & District Buses*, T01631-562856. The Oban to Glasgow rail line passes through the northern part of the region. For rail enquiries, T0345-484950. For general public transport enquiries contact Argyll & Bute Council, T01546-604695. Times of local buses and trains can also be checked at local tourist offices.

Most **ferries** to the islands and remote peninsulas are run by *CalMac*, T01475-650100, www.calmac.co.uk. If you're planning on taking more than one or two ferries, especially with a car, it may be more economical to buy an **Island Hopscotch** ticket. They can be used on a variety of route combinations and are valid for one month. They require advance planning but are better value than buying single tickets. For example, the Bute-Cowal-Kintyre Hopscotch ticket allows you to travel by ferry from Wemyss Bay to Rothesay, from Rhubodach to Colintraive and from Portavadie to Tarbert for £5.85 per passenger plus £27.50 for the car. During the peak summer months it's essential to book ferry tickets in advance.

Information Most of this chapter is covered by the *Argyll, the Isles, Loch Lomond, Stirling & Trossachs Tourist Board*, F01369-706085, info@scottish.heartlands.org, www.scottish.heartlands.org. The main offices, which are open all year round, are in **Oban**, **Inveraray**, **Dunoon**, **Rothesay** and **Campbeltown**. There are smaller seasonal offices in **Lochgilphead**, **Tarbert**, **Ardgarten** and **Helensburgh**. The island of **Arran** is covered by the *Ayrshire & Arran Tourist Board*, T01292-262555, F269555, ayr@ayrshire-arran.com, www.ayrshire-arran.com.

When to go As with the rest of the west of Scotland, the weather is highly unpredictable. It rains a lot on the west coast of Argyll and the summer months are no guarantee of good weather. It's best to avoid the busiest months of July and August, when the single-track roads can become frustrating and accommodation is harder to find. You'll also have more chance of avoiding the dreaded midge (see page 54).

Firth of Clyde

Helensburgh

Phone code: 01436
Colour map 2, grid A1
Population: 14,000

Twenty three miles northwest of Glasgow on the A814, overlooking the Clyde estuary, is the town of Helensburgh, its wide, grid-plan streets lined with elegant Georgian houses. The town boasts a few very notable connections; both **Henry Bell**, originator of the steamship, and **John Logie Baird**, who invented the television, were born here.

Helensburgh is more famously known, though, for its connection with the great Glasgow architect, **Charles Rennie Mackintosh**. In the upper part of the town, on Upper Colquhoun Street, is **Hill House**, one of the best examples of

Mackintosh's work. The house was designed for Glasgow publisher, Walter Blackie in 1902-04, and is now owned by the NTS. The house is a masterpiece of balanced perfection and artistry and there's much to admire. The attention to detail, the use of natural light and the symbolism of the floral patterns and use of light and dark, hallmarks of his personal Art Nouveau style, are all very much in evidence. After exploring the house, you can visit the kitchen, which has been tastefully converted into a tearoom (open 1330-1630). For more on Charles Rennie Mackintosh, see page 153. ■ *T673900. Daily 1330-1730 Apr-Oct. £6, child £4. To get there from the central train station, walk about a mile and a half up Sinclair St, then turn left at Kennedy St and follow the signs. From Helensburgh Upper station (see 'Transport' below) it's a five-minute walk.*

Tourist office In the clock tower on the waterfront, T672642. ■ *Apr to mid-May daily 1000-1700; mid-May to Jun daily 0930-1800; Jul-Sep daily 0930-1900; early Oct Mon-Fri 1000-1630, Sat-Sun 1000-1700.*

The most upmarket place to stay is **D-C** *The Commodore Hotel*, 112-117 West Clyde **Sleeping** St, T676924, F677112. Forty five rooms. West Clyde Street overlooks the loch and is where you'll find most of the hotels and guest houses, including **E** *Ardmore Guest House*, T673461. There are lots of B&Bs, including **E** *Ava Lodge*, 44 Glasgow St, T677751.

Helensburgh has 2 **train** stations. The Central station has a regular service (every ½ hr) **Transport** to and from **Glasgow** (45 mins), while the Upper station serves **Oban** (3 times daily; 2 hrs 15 mins) and **Fort William** (4 times daily Mon-Sat, 3 times on Sun; 3 hrs). For times, contact *Scotrail*, T0345-484950.

There's a daily passenger-only **ferry** service from Helensburgh to **Gourock** (see page 185) and **Kilcreggan**.

The Cowal Peninsula

The Cowal peninsula reaches out into the Firth of Clyde, framed by Loch Fyne and Loch Long. This is the most visited part of Argyll, due to its proximity to Glasgow, but despite the summer hordes, much of it is undisturbed. Most people head straight for **Dunoon**, the main ferry port and one of the major Clyde seaside resorts, leaving more adventurous souls to enjoy the forests and mountains of **Argyll Forest Park** in the north or the peace and tranquillity of the southwest coastline.

North Cowal

The northern part of the peninsula is largely covered by the sprawling **Argyll** *Colour map 3, grid C6* **Forest Park** which extends from Loch Lomond south to Holy Loch. This area contains the most stunning scenery in Cowal, and includes the **Arrochar Alps**, a range of rugged peaks north of Glen Croe which offer some of the best climbing in Argyll. The most famous of these is Ben Arthur (2,891 feet), better known as "**The Cobbler**", but this, and the other "Alps" are only for the more serious hill walker. Rather less imposing are the hills south of Glen Croe, between Loch Goil and Loch Long, in an area known as **Argyll's Bowling Green** (not because it's flat, but an English corruption of the Gaelic *Baile na Greine*, meaning "Sunny Hamlet"). There are also numerous footpaths and cycle tracks threading their way through the park, and details of these can be found in the Forestry Commission leaflets available at the **tourist office** in Ardgarten (see below).

Arrochar
Phone code: 01301
Colour map 3, grid C6

The gateway to Cowal sits at the head of Loch Long on the main A83, only a few miles west of Tarbet and the shores of Loch Lomond. It's a small, unremarkable place but the setting is dramatic, with The Cobbler towering overhead.

Arrochar shares a **train station** with Tarbet, on the main west coast line. Trains heading north to Oban (1 hour 45 minutes) or Fort William (2 hours 30 minutes) or south to Glasgow (1 hour 15 minutes) stop 3-4 times daily. Scottish Citlink **buses** between Glasgow and Oban stop off at Arrochar (1 hour 10 minutes to Glasgow; 1 hour 40 minutes to Oban), three times daily in each direction (twice on Sunday). There are plenty of **hotels** and **B&Bs**, including **D** *The Village Inn*, T702279, F702458, which also serves decent grub, and the very friendly **E** *Lochside Guest House*, T/F702467, which also serves food and which is very close to the village's main pub.

Ardgarten, Glen Croe & Lochgoilhead

A few miles beyond Arrochar, on the shores of Loch Long, is **Ardgarten**, where there's a Forestry Commission **campsite**, T702293; open Easter-October, an **SYHA youth hostel**, T702363; open February-December, and a **tourist office and visitor centre**, T702342; open daily April-October 1000-1700, till 1800 in July and August, which provides useful advice and information on hill-walking and wildlife, as well as organizing various activities.

From Ardgarten the A83 climbs steeply up **Glen Croe** to reach one of Scotland's classic viewpoints at the top of the pass, the **Rest and be Thankful**. The hordes of like-minded tourists, eager for that memorable photograph, cannot detract from the majestic views of the surrounding craggy peaks.

Here the road forks. The A83 continues towards **Inveraray** (see page 201) and the single-track B828 heads southwest to meet the B839, which runs down to the village of **Lochgoilhead**, in a beautiful setting on Loch Goil. There are several **hotels** and **B&Bs** as well as an unsightly village of self-catering holiday chalets next door. At the end of the road, several miles down the west side of Loch Goil, are the ruins of 15th century **Castle Carrick**.

Glen Kinglas & Cairndow

The A83 meanwhile runs down through **Glen Kinglas** to reach the village of **Cairndow**, at the head of Loch Fyne. Nearby is the **Ardkinglas Woodland Garden**, which contains an impressive collection of exotic rhododendrons, as well as the largest conifers in Europe, over 120 feet high and 30 feet in girth. ■ *T01499-600263. Daily dawn till dusk. £2.*

A mile or so further on towards Inveraray, at **Clachan**, at the head of Loch Fyne, is the highly-acclaimed *Loch Fyne Oyster Bar* (see page 202).

Loch Eck & around

Just before Cairndow, the A815 branches left and runs south down the eastern shore of Loch Fyne. At **Strachur** it turns inland and heads down to **Loch Eck**, a very beautiful and narrow freshwater loch, popular with trout fishermen. At the southern end of Loch Eck, at **Benmore**, is **Younger Botanic Garden**, a lovely woodland garden and offshoot of the Royal Botanic Garden in Edinburgh. Its 140 acres are laid out with over 250 species of rhododendrons and feature an avenue of Giant Redwoods. ■ *T01369-706261. 1 Mar-31 Oct daily 0930-1800. £3.*

Dunoon

Phone code: 01369
Colour map 2, grid A1

The largest town in Cowal, and indeed the largest in Argyll, with 13,000 inhabitants, is Dunoon, one-time favourite holiday destination for Glaswegians, who came in their hordes on board the many paddle steamers that sailed "doon the watter" from Glasgow. Dunoon still attracts visitors, albeit in much smaller numbers, but the town has fallen on desperately hard times with the recent closure of the US nuclear submarine base on nearby Holy Loch, which was the town's life blood.

Nevertheless, the town still comes to life during the **Cowal Highland Gathering**, held on the last weekend of August. This is the world's largest Highland Games and culminates in a spectacular march of massed pipes and drums through the streets. Dunoon also hosts the Gaelic music festival, The Mod, in 2000.

Tourist office Cowal's main tourist office is on Alexandra Parade, T703785. ■ *Apr Mon-Fri 0900-1700, Sat 1100-1730, Sun 1100-1500; May Mon-Fri 0900-1730, Sat-Sun 1000-1700; Jun and Sept Mon-Fri 0900-1800; Jul-Aug Mon-Sat 0900-1900; Oct Mon-Fri 0900-1730.*

Sights

There's not much to keep you in Dunoon, but if the weather's bad and you need to kill time, you could head for the **Castle House Museum**, on Castle Hill, which dominates the town centre, where you can bone up on Cowal's often grisly past. ■ *Open Easter-Oct 1030-1630 Mon-Sat, 1400-1630 Sun. £1.50 (children free).* A mile northwest, along the A855 to Sandbank, is the **Cowal Bird Garden**, an aviary with exotic birds such as parrots and macaws and a small rare-breeds farm. ■ *Easter-Oct daily 1030-1800, Nov-Easter Sun only 1100-1600. £3 (children £2).*

Sleeping & eating

There are more than enough **hotels** and **guesthouses** to choose from. One of the best is the **A** *Enmore Hotel*, Marine Parade (near Hunter's Quay), T702230, F702148, enmorehotel@btinternet.com. A small, family hotel in its own grounds overlooking the sea and with a reputation for good food (restaurant open to non-residents; mid-range-expensive). Also good is **B** *Ardfillayne House*, a mile south of town on the Innellan Rd, T702267, F702501. A Victorian country house offering fine Scottish/French cooking (booking required). Three miles north of Dunoon, on the A815, is **C** *The Anchorage Hotel & Restaurant*, T/F705108, ach2811@aol.com. Also has a reputation for fine food (lunch moderate; dinner expensive). There's lots of **B&B** accommodation, which can be booked at the tourist office (see below), and there are 2 **campsites** nearby: *Cot House Caravanan & Campsite* is at Kilmun, a few miles north of town, on the shores of Holy Loch, T840351; open Apr-Oct; and a few miles further north, at the southern end of Loch Eck, is *Stratheck Caravan Park*, T/F840472; open Mar-Dec.

Aside from the hotels listed above, the best food can be found at *Chatters*, at 58 John St, T706402, an informal and outstanding little restaurant offering French-style Scottish cuisine (lunch mid-range; dinner mid-range-expensive). Open Mon-Sat.

Sport

Cycle hire *Highland Stores*, 156 Argyll St. **Pony trekking** *Velvet Path Riding & Trekking Centre*, Rowan House, Innellan, by Dunoon, T830580.

Transport

There are 2 **ferry** crossings to Dunoon from Gourock. The most popular is the *CalMac* car and passenger ferry which makes the 20-min trip daily all year round every 30 mins. The first leaves Gourock at 0620 and the last returns from Dunoon at 2105. For times and details of **train** connections from **Gourock** to **Glasgow**, T01475-650100. There's also a *Western Ferries* service every 30 mins which arrives at Hunter's Quay, a mile north of the town centre, T01369-704452. There are **buses** to **Colintraive** 2-3 times daily Mon-Sat (40 mins), to **Inveraray** (on Tue, Fri-Sat; 1 hr 15 mins) and to **Lochgoilhead** (Mon and Fri; 1 hr 15 mins). For times, contact *Western Buses*, T01700-502076.

Argyll

Southwest Cowal

Colour map 1/2

One of the most beautiful parts of Argyll is the southwest of Cowal, particularly the route down to the little village of **Tighnabruaich**. The A8003 runs down the west side of Loch Riddon and there are few lovelier sights than the view from this road across the **Kyles of Bute**, the narrow straits that separate Cowal from the island of Bute.

Tighnabruaich
Phone code: 01700
Colour map 5, grid A3

Tighnabruaich gets busy in the summer with visitors who come here to enjoy some of the best sailing on the west coast. Much of the accommodation is booked up by those enrolled at the **Tighnabruaich Sailing School**, T811717, which offers dinghy sailing and windsurfing courses at all levels. There is a bank in the village and buses leave from here to **Portavadie** (one to three times daily; 25 minutes), **Colintraive** (see below) and **Rothesay** (one to two times daily Monday-Thursday; one hour).

Sleeping The **SYHA youth hostel**, T811622, open Apr-Sept, sits high above the village with great views across the Kyles and is often full. There's also **D** *The Royal Hotel*, T811239, F811300, royalhotel@btinternet.com, on the waterfront, with a multi-gym and sauna and excellent restaurant serving cheap lunches and mid-range-expensive dinners. There are a couple of cheap **B&Bs** in the village, including **E-F** *Ferguslie*, T811414, open Apr-Sept. In neighbouring **Kames**, there's the **D** *Kames Hotel*, T811489, F811283, with great views and live music in the bar.

It's also possible to reach **Bute** from southwest Cowal. The A8003 turns off the main A883, which runs right down the west of the peninsula and the east side of Loch Riddon to **Colintraive**, at the narrowest point in the Kyles, only a few hundred yards wide. A small car and passenger *CalMac* ferry crosses to **Rhubodach** on Bute (for details, see Bute, 'Ins and outs' next page). There are buses from **Colintraive** to **Tighnabruaich** (one to two times daily Monday-Thursday; 35 minutes), and to **Dunoon** (see previous page).

South of Tighnabruaich

A few miles southwest of Kames, is **Portavadie**, on the west coast of Cowal. A *CalMac* car and passenger **ferry** sails from here to **Tarbert**, on the Kintyre peninsula, saving a lot of time if you're heading for the islands of **Islay**, **Jura** or **Colonsay**. The ferry to Tarbert makes the 25-minute crossing, every hour, daily, from 0830 (0945 on Sunday) till 1945 in the summer months (till 1745 in the winter). The one way trip costs £2.50 per passenger and £12 per car.

About 10 miles further up the deserted west coast of Cowal is **Otter ferry**. There used to be a ferry link from here to Lochgilphead, but not for the small, amphibious mammals. It gets its name from the gravel bank that juts out into Loch Fyne (*An Oitir* means gravel bank in Gaelic). It's still worth stopping here, if only for the excellent oyster bar and pub, *The Oystercatcher*, T01700-821229, which overlooks the lovely sandy beach.

Isle of Bute

Barely a stone's throw off the south coast of Cowal is the island of Bute, another favourite holiday destination for people from Glasgow and Ayrshire, who come here in droves during the busy summer months. But though the island is small (15 miles long by five miles wide), it's deceptively easy to escape the hordes, who tend to congregate around the east coast resort of Rothesay, leaving the delights of the sparsely populated west coast free for those who enjoy a bit of peace and quiet.

Phone code: 01700
Colour map 5, grid A3
Population 7,500

Bute has been a popular place since late Victorian times, when a gaggle of Glasgow grannies could be seen being pushed along the promenade in their bath-chairs under tartan blankets, taking the invigorating sea air. Now, the island is successfully reinventing itself as a haven for walkers and cyclists. Some of the island's walks are described below.

Ins and outs

Bute is easily accessible from Glasgow. Take a **train** from Glasgow Central to the ferry terminal at Wemyss Bay (1 hr 10 mins), and from there it's a 35-min crossing to Rothesay. **Ferries** sail daily every 45 mins from 0800 till 1945 (later on Fri, Sat-Sun). For times, T01700-502707. The one-way trip costs £3.05 per passenger and £12.10 per car. There's also a ferry to Rothesay from Brodick on Arran (2 hrs), once a day on Mon, Wed and Fri in the summer only. Bute can also be reached from the Cowal peninsula. A small car/passenger ferry makes the five-minute crossing from Colintraive to Rhubodach, at the northern end of Bute, daily every half hour or hour; from 0530-2055 Mon-Sat and 0900-2055 Sun in the summer (26 Apr-28 Aug). The one-way trip costs £0.90 per passenger and £6.20 per car. There are also **buses** to Rothesay from Tighnabruaich in Southwest Cowal (see above) once or twice a day Mon-Thur (1 hr). For times, contact *Western Buses*, T502076).

Getting there

The *Western Buses* service around Bute is fairly good, though limited on Sun. **Buses** connect with the arriving ferries at Rothesay and run to: Mount Stuart (hourly; 15 mins), Kilchattan Bay (4 daily Mon-Sat, 3 on Sun; 30 mins) and Rhubodach (1-2 daily Mon-Sat; 20 mins).

Getting around

The best way to see Bute is by **bicycle**. The island is fairly flat and the roads are quiet and in good condition. For cycle hire try *Mountain Bike Centre*, 24 East Princes St, Rothesay, T503554, open daily 0800-2000 Apr-Sept, or at *Mount Stuart House*, T502333.

Rothesay

The sole town on Bute is Rothesay, which, like Dunoon, is a hugely popular holiday destination. There the similarity ends, however, for Rothesay is a genteel and tasteful Victorian seaside resort, with its handsome period mansions lining the broad sweep of bay, its elegant promenade lined with palm trees and the distinctive 1920s **Winter Gardens**, now refurbished and housing a cinema and restaurant.

Tourist office   15 Victoria St (opposite the pier). ■ *T502151. Apr and Oct Mon-Fri 0900-1730, Sat 1000-1730, Sun 1100-1500; May Mon-Fri 0900-1730, Sat-Sun 1000-1700; Jun and Sept Mon-Fri till 1800; Jul-Aug Mon-Sat till 1900; Nov-Mar Mon-Thur 0900-1730, Fri 0900-1700.*

One thing you must do before leaving Rothesay is spend a penny in the palatial **Victorian public toilets**. Rather more than that (£300,000 to be exact) has already been spent on restoring this architectural gem to its former glory.

Sights

Gents get the best deal but the ladies can also take a peek. ■ *Daily Easter-Oct 0800-2100, Nov-Easter 0900-1700. 10p.*

Rothesay Castle is also worth visiting. Built around the 12th century, the castle was attacked by Vikings, before becoming a favourite with the Stewart kings. It fell into English hands during the Wars of Independence and was retaken by Robert the Bruce in 1311. It was also occupied by Cromwell's New Model Army after the Civil War and partly dismantled, but restoration work has helped preserve much of this impressive circular, moated ruin. ■ *Apr-Sep Mon-Sat 0930-1830, Sun 1400-1830; Oct-Mar Mon-Sat 0930-1630, Sun 1400-1630 (closed Thur-Fri pm). £1.50, children 75p. To get there, follow the signs from the pier.*

Behind the castle is **Bute Museum**, which features interesting displays covering the island's history, wildlife and archaeology. ■ *Oct-Mar Tue-Sat 1430-1630; Apr-Sep Mon-Sat 1030-1630, Sun 1430-1630. £1.20, children 40p.*

Around Bute

One of Bute's main attractions is **Mount Stuart**, a unique Victorian Gothic house set in 300 acres of lush woodland gardens, three miles south of Rothesay. This magnificent architectural fantasy reflects the Third Marquess of Bute's passion for astrology, astronomy, mysticism and religion and the sheer scale and grandeur of the place almost beggars belief. This is truly one of the great country houses of Scotland and displays breathtaking craftsmanship in marble and stained glass, as well as a fine collection of family portraits and Italian antiques. Much of the existing house dates from 1877, and was built following a terrible fire which destroyed the original, built in 1719 by the Second Earl of Bute.

Equally impressive are the **landscaped gardens** and woodlands, established by the Third Earl of Bute (1713-92), who advised on the foundation of Kew Gardens in London. It's worth spending a whole day here in order to take in the amazing splendour of the house and to explore the beautiful gardens. And if the weather's fine, why not bring a picnic and enjoy the wonderful sea views. ■ *T503877, www. mountstuart.com. Easter weekend and 1 May-17 Oct, daily except Tue and Thur. Gardens open 1000-1700; House open 1100-1630. Admission to House/gardens £6, children £2.50; gardens only £3.50/£2. A regular bus runs from Rothesay to the gates of the House (see 'Getting around' above).*

Isle of Bute

Just before Mount Stuart is the tidy little village of **Kerracroy**, designed by the wife of the Second Marquess of Bute and featuring an interesting mix of building styles. South of Mount Stuart and the village of Kingarth is **Kilchattan Bay**, an attractive bay of pink sands and the start of a fine walk down to Glencallum Bay, in the southeastern corner of the island (see below). There's accommodation at Kilchattan Bay, at **E** *St Blane's Hotel,* T/F831224.

Rothesay Castle

Argyll

Southwest of Kilchattan Bay is **St Blane's Chapel**, a 12th century ruin in a beautifully peaceful spot near the southern tip of the island. The medieval church stands on the site of an earlier monastery, established in the sixth century by St Blane, nephew of St Catan, after whom Kilchattan is named. The ruin can be reached by road from Rothesay, or as part of the walk from Kilchattan Bay (see below).

Four miles north of St Blane's, on the west coast, is **Scalpsie Bay,** the nicest beach on the island and a good place for seal-spotting. A little further north is **St Ninian's Point**, looking across to the island of Inchmarnock. At the end of the beach are the ruins of a sixth-century chapel, dedicated to St Ninian.

Walks on Bute

The Highland-Lowland dividing line passes through the middle of Bute at **Loch Fad**, which separates the hilly and uninhabited northern half of the island and the rolling farmland of the south. The highest point on the island is **Windy Hill** (913 feet) in the north, from where there are great views across the island. A less strenuous walk is up **Canada Hill**, a few miles southwest of Rothesay, above Loch Fad. Walk along Craigmore promenade and turn off at the old pier to Ardencraig Gardens. Then continue uphill along the golf course to the top of the hill for great views of the Firth of Clyde.

A longer walk is the circular route from **Kilchattan Bay** south to **Glencallum Bay** and back, via **St Blane's chapel.** Follow the signpost for 'Kelspoke Path' beside Kiln Villas and take the track which climbs steadily before turning sharply back on itself. Go through a gate and shortly before the next gate turn right. Follow the rough track, which swings right, then left over open ground to the ruins of **Kelspoke Castle**.

The route is waymarked, but if you want to take a map, it's OS Landranger sheet 63

Continue along the grassy path, past a reservoir on your right, then cross the stile and go down and across a small burn. Turn left and follow the burn, before heading right to join the shore path and follow this past the lighthouse on your left and around the headland to Glencallum Bay. Continue round the shoreline and at the far end of the bay follow the waymarks as the path climbs to cross the headland. The path then levels out and from here there are great views across to the mountains of **Arran**.

The path then reaches the col above **Loch na Leighe**. Drop down to the loch and follow the waymarks south over open ground. Before reaching a farm called 'The Plan', go right over two footbridges, then left below a low ridge. Keep to the right of the buildings, following the waymarks across open ground to the stile that crosses to the ruins of St Blane's Chapel (see above).

Leave the chapel by the gap in the boundary wall and go through a gate, turning left on a clear track which climbs steadily to a stile. Cross the stile and turn right, following the edge of the field down to a gate. Walk uphill on the left side of the field to Suidhe Hill. At the top of the field, cross the fence and keep going, turning right at the corner of the fence. Go through a gate at the next corner and look for a waymark about 100 yards downhill. Follow the path steeply downhill, passing through a kissing gate and staying close to the wall. You then reach a drying green at the foot of the hill; turn left and follow a path around the buildings and back onto the road at Kilchattan.

The walk is five miles in total. Allow about three hours. For buses to and from Rothesay, see 'Getting around' above.

Essentials

Sleeping Most of the island's accommodation is in and around Rothesay, and the tourist office will book your hotel or B&B. Convenient for the ferry is **D** *Cannon House Hotel*, Battery Pl, T502819, F505725. A comfortable Georgian townhouse. Also central is **E** *The Commodore*, 12 Battery Pl, T/F502178. One of the nicest guest houses. There are lots of other guest houses and B&Bs on Battery Place. North of town, in **Ardbeg**, is the **D-C** *Ardmory House Hotel & Restaurant*, T502346, F505596, with a restaurant open to non-residents. Three miles south of town, at **Ascog**, is the excellent value **F-E** *Ascog Farm*, T503372.

Eating The best place to eat on the island is the *New Farm Restaurant*, T831646, which is 6 miles south of Rothesay, near Mount Stuart House and Gardens (see below). This whitewashed cottage farmhouse is set on a working sheep farm and dairy and uses local produce to great effect. The atmosphere is friendly and informal. Booking is essential for lunch (mid-range) and dinner (expensive). They also offer B&B (**E**, or **D** including dinner).

In town, there's *Fowler's*, housed in the Winter Gardens, T500505, offering good value lunches and dinners. It is an absolute culinary must while you are on Bute to sample the superb fish and chips at the award-winning *West End Café*, 1-3 Gallowgate, T503596. It's open for takeaways all year round, and for sit-down meals Easter-Sep 1200-1400 and 1600-2400 (closed Mon).

Festivals The island holds its own **Highland Games** on the last weekend in Aug. There's also the **Isle of Bute International Folk Festival** and **World Ceilidh Band Championships**, a massive festival of music and dance held over the third weekend in Jul, and the **Isle of Bute Jazz Festival**, during the May Bank Holiday weekend.

Sport **Golf** *Rothesay Golf Course*, T503554, scenic 18-holes with great views at Canada Hill. **Pony trekking** *Rothesay Riding Centre*, at Ardbrannan Farm, Canada Hill, T504791. **Sailing** *Bute Sailing School*, Cannon House, Battery Pl, T502819. Open Mar-Nov. Runs all RYA courses, as well as cruises on their own luxury yacht.

Inveraray

Inveraray is the classic 18th-century planned village, with its straight wide streets and dignified Georgian houses, and enjoys the most stunning of settings, on the shores of Loch Fyne. It was rebuilt by the third Duke of Argyll, head of the Campbell clan, at the same time as he restored the nearby family home, which now attracts hordes of summer visitors. As well as its natural beauty and elegance, and fine castle, Inveraray has several other notable attractions in and around the town and you could quite happily spend a few days here, whatever the weather.

Phone code: 01499
Colour map 3, grid C6
Population: 700

Ins and outs

Inveraray is on the main Glasgow-Oban and Glasgow-Campbeltown bus routes and *Scottish Citylink* **buses** from Glasgow (1 hr 45 mins) stop in Front St, 6 times daily Mon-Sat (4 times on Sun). Three of these buses (2 on Sun) continue to Oban (1 hr 5 mins), and 3 continue (2 on Sun) to Lochgilphead and Campbeltown (2 hrs 30 mins). For times, T0990-505050.

Getting there

Argyll

Sights

Tourist office Front St. ■ *T302063. Open Apr Mon-Fri 1000-1700, Sat-Sun 1200-1600; May-Jun Mon-Sat 0930-1700, Sun 1100-1700; Jul-Sep Mon-Sat 0900-1830, Sun 0900-1700; Oct Mon-Sat 0930-1800, Sun 1200-1600; Nov-Mar Mon-Fri 1100-1600, Sat-Sun 1200-1600.*

One of Argyll's most famous castles, Inveraray has been the clan seat of the Campbells for centuries and is still the family home of the Duke of Argyll. The present neo-Gothic structure dates from 1745, and its main feature is the magnificent armoury hall, whose displays of weaponry were supplied to the Campbells by the British government to quell the Jacobite rebellion. The elaborately furnished rooms are also on display, as is the fascinating and troubled family history in the Clan room. There are extensive grounds with fine walks, particularly up to the hill-top folly. ■ *T302203. Apr-Jun, Sep-Oct Mon-Thur and Sat 1000-1300 and 1400-1745, Sun 1300-1745; Jul-Aug Mon-Sat 1000-1745, Sun 1300-1745. £4.50, children £2.50.*

Inveraray Castle

In the old stables in the castle grounds is the unusual **Combined Operations Museum** which relives the time when Inveraray was used as a secret training ground for Allied troops ahead of the D-Day landings in Second World War. ■ *For opening times contact the tourist office, or T500218.*

The Georgian prison and courthouse in the centre of the village has been brilliantly restored as a thoroughly fascinating museum that gives a vivid insight into life behind bars from medieval times up till the 19th century. You can sit in on an 1820 courtroom trial, then visit the cells below and learn all about some of the delightful prison pursuits, such as branding with a hot iron, ear nailing and public whipping. The whole experience is further enhanced by the guides, who are dressed as warders and prisoners. Makes you want to stay on the right side of the law, though, thankfully, conditions have improved – as you will see for yourself. ■ *T302381. Daily Apr-Oct, 0930-1800, Nov-Mar 1000-1700. £4.50, children £2.20.*

Inveraray Jail

Inveraray Maritime Museum Another worthwhile diversion, especially if you've got kids in tow, is the *Arctic Penguin*, one of the world's last iron sailing ships, which is moored at the loch-side pier. Below decks are lots of interesting displays on Clyde shipbuilding and the Highland Clearances, as well as various 'hands-on' activities. ■ *T302213. Daily Apr-Sep 1000-1800, Oct-Mar 1000-1700. £3, children £1.50.*

All Saints Church One sight which has great appeal is the **Bell Tower** of All Saints Church, which attracts campanologists from near and far to ring the second heaviest set of church bells in the world. It's worth a visit, not just to dangle from the end of a rope, but to climb the tower and admire the panoramic view of the town below. ■ *Daily mid-May to end-Sep 1000-1300 and 1400-1700. £2, children 75p.*

Argyll Wildlife Park A few miles southwest of town, on the A83 to Lochgilphead, Argyll Wildlife Park is another great place for kids. Amongst the native wildlife wandering around the forest-clad hills are pine martens, badgers, foxes, deer, wildcats, wild goats, a variety of wildfowl and birds of prey, racoons and wallabies, though the more informed of you will have noted that the last two are not native to Scotland. There's also the obligatory tearoom and gift shop. ■ *T302264. Daily 1000-1700. £3.50.*

Auchindrain Township Three miles beyond Argyll Wildlife Park is Auchindrain, a complete reconstruction of an original West Highland village. The thatched cottages, barn and smiddy have all been perfectly restored and are all furnished and equipped to give a real insight into what rural life must have been like in the Highlands before the Clearances. There's also an informative visitor centre, with a bookshop and tearoom. ■ *T500235. Daily 1 Apr-30 Sept 1000-1700. £3, children £1.50.*

Crarae Gardens Four miles further down the A83 is one of Scotland's very best public gardens, dramatically set in a deep wooded glen on the shores of Loch Fyne. There are marked woodland walks winding their way through a spectacular array of rhododendrons, azaleas and numerous other exotic plants towards the tumbling waterfalls of the "Himalayan Gorge". May is a good time to see the gardens in full bloom, as is Autumn for the vast variety of deciduous trees, but any time of year is worth it. ■ *T01546-886614/886388. Mar-Oct 0900-1800, from dawn till dusk in winter. £2.50, children £1.50.*

Essentials

Sleeping There are several good **hotels** to choose from, such as the historic **C** *Argyll Hotel*, Front St, T302466, F302389, formerly the *Great Inn*, or the **C** *Fernpoint Hotel*, T302170, F302366, a lovely Georgian house overlooking the loch. Also good is the **C** *Loch Fyne Hotel*, just of town on the A83, T302148, F302348, and the **D** *George Hotel*, T302111.

There's also lots of **B&Bs** in town, including **E** *Newton Hall*, Main St, T302484, a converted church, open Mar-Dec, as well as a *SYHA Youth Hostel*, Dalmally Rd, T302454, open mid-Mar to end-Oct, and a **campsite**, at *Argyll Caravan Park*, T302285, 2½ miles south of town on Loch Fyne, with excellent facilities.

Eating The best place to eat for miles around is the *Loch Fyne Oyster Bar*, T600264/217, about 9 miles east of town on the A83 near Clachan. This restaurant, shop and smokehouse attracts customers from miles around to enjoy their famous oysters and other "Fyne" foods such as the renowned smoked kippers. Open daily all year 0900-1800 Nov-Mar, 0900-2100 from mid-Mar onwards (booking essential at weekends). The *George Hotel* in town offers good, cheap bar food and good ale in a lively atmosphere. The *Loch Fyne Hotel* also does good food, but is a bit more expensive.

Argyll

Pony trekking *Argyll Riding & Activities*, Dalchenna Farm, T302611.

Loch Awe and Loch Etive

North of Loch Fyne is Loch Awe, the longest freshwater loch in Scotland and, further north, the beautiful Loch Etive. There's enough here to justify a couple of days exploration, particularly the little-visited west shore of Loch Awe, but if you're pressed for time, there are a few conveniently placed sights along the A85 from Glasgow to Oban.

Colour map 3, grid B/C 6

The A819 north from Inveraray joins the A85 at the northeastern tip of Loch Awe, between the villages of of **Dalmally** and **Lochawe**. Just west of the junction is the romantic ruin of **Kilchurn Castle**, on a promontory jutting out into the loch. ■ *Daily, it can be visited by boat from the pier in Lochawe village.*

There's a good selection of places to stay in Dalmally and Lochawe. A place with an especially nice view is the **D** *Loch Awe Hotel*, T01838-200379, open Feb-Dec. Both Dalmally and Lochawe are on the Glasgow-Oban rail and bus routes. **Trains** in either direction stop 3 times daily and there are several *Scottish Citylink* **buses** daily. These buses also stop at **Inveraray** (see above) and **Taynuilt** (see below) en route from Glasgow to Oban and vice versa.

A few miles west of Lochawe, and almost a mile inside Ben Cruachan (3,695 feet) is the underground **Cruachan Power Station**, or "Hollow Mountain". From the visitor centre on the shores of Loch Awe, a guided bus trip takes you deep into the heart of the mountain through massive tunnels until you reach the generating room. ■ *T822618. Apr-Nov 0930-1700; Jul-Aug 0930-1800. £3, children £1.50.*

Colour map 3, grid B6

Between Loch Awe and Loch Etive runs the River Awe, which squeezes through the dark and ominous **Pass of Brander**, so steep and narrow that legend has it that it was once held against an entire army by an old woman brandishing a scythe.

Further west, and 12 miles east of Oban, is the tiny village of Taynuilt, near the shore of Loch Etive. Just before the village, at **Bridge of Awe**, is a sign for **Inverawe Fisheries, Smokery & Country Park**, T822274, where you can take fishing lessons, learn about traditional smoking techniques, or wander along a series of nature trails. If the weather's fine, you can buy some of their delicious smoked products and have a picnic.

The main attraction though, is **Bonawe Iron Furnace**, north of the village on the shores of Loch Etive. Founded in 1753 by a group of Cumbrian ironmasters, Bonawe used the abundant woodlands of Argyll to make charcoal to fire its massive furnace. At its height, it produced 600-700 tons of pig-iron a year. This was then shipped out to the forges of England and Wales. Iron production ceased at Bonawe in 1876 and it has now been restored as an industrial heritage site, with displays explaining the whole production process. ■ *T822432. Daily Apr-Sep, Mon-Sat 0930-1830, Sun 1400-1830. £2.30.*

Beyond the Bonawe Heritage Site is the pier from which **Loch Etive Cruises** depart. The loch is inaccessible except by boat, and the three-hour cruise of one of Scotland's great hidden treasures is definitely worth it. You'll see the mountains of Glencoe, seals on the rocks, deer on the hillsides and maybe even a golden eagle flying above, and you won't stop talking about it for weeks, or months. ■ *T822430. Cruises depart at 1030 and 1400 (except Easter-30 Apr, Sat-Sun, 1-14 Oct, at 1400 only). £8, children £4, no booking necessary but arrive in plenty of time.*

Kilchurn Castle

Running south from the village is the very lovely and very quiet **Glen Lonan**. About four miles along the Glen Lonan road is **Barguillean's Angus Garden**, one of Argyll's youngest and smallest gardens, but also one of the most peaceful and evocative, set around the shores of little Loch Angus. It was created in 1957, in memory of Angus MacDonald, a journalist and writer killed in Cyprus in 1956. ■ *T822333/822381. Daily 0900-1800. No admission charge but there's an honesty box.*

Sleeping & eating There's a good selection of accommodation in and around Taynuilt. On the main road is the welcoming **D-E** *Taynuilt Hotel*, T822437, F822721, and there are also several B&Bs. The most luxurious places to stay, and the best places to eat, are in **Kilchrenan**, south of Taynuilt on the shores of Loch Awe. **L** *Ardanaiseig Hotel*, T833333, F833222, postbox@ardanaiseig-hotel.com. Three miles east of Kilchrenan village on an unclassified road. Open Feb-Dec. Offers opulence and style, beautiful surroundings and views and exquisite food (lunch mid-range; dinner expensive). **B** *Taychreggan Hotel*, T833211/833366, F833244. Not as grand as the *Ardanaiseig Hotel*, but with equally wonderful views and superb cuisine (lunch mid-range; dinner expensive).

Walking around Loch Awe

These routes are all outlined, with accompanying maps, in the Forestry Commission leaflet, 'A Guide to Forest Walks and Trails in North Argyll', available at tourist offices.

A single-track road runs southwest of Kilchrenan, along the shores of Loch Awe, to the tiny villages of **Dalavich** and **Ford**, through the very beautiful **Inverinan Forest**, a Forestry Commission property which has a series of undemanding marked trails running through the hills overlooking the loch.

The first walk starts out from the little hamlet of **Inverinan**. Red waymarkers lead you from the car park into the woods surrounding the gorge of the river Inan. Part of the route follows the old drove road along which cattle were driven from the Highlands down to the markets in south and central Scotland. The walk is three miles long and should take around an hour and a half.

Further along the road, half a mile north of Dalavich, is a car park at **Barnaline Lodge**, the starting point for a nine-mile bike route, a waymarked walk through the **Caledonian Forest Reserve** and a couple of other woodland walks. The longest of the walks is the five-mile route that leads along the river Avich, then along the shores of Loch Avich before returning to the lodge.

Two and a half miles south of Dalavich is a car park, which marks the starting point for a blue waymarked walk along the shores of Loch Awe. The route passes through **Mackenzie's Grove**, a sheltered gorge containing some of the largest conifers on the west coast. The route then runs along the shores of the loch, from where you can see the remains of a *crannog*, one of over 40 of these Iron-Age settlements on Loch Awe. The route then heads back to the car park; about three miles in total.

Oban

Oban lies at the centre of the northerly part of Argyll, known as Lorn, which stretches north as far as Appin, south to Ardfern and east to the shores of Loch Awe. It also comprises several relatively peaceful islands, including Lismore, Kerrera, Seil and Luing. It's is a busy little place: not only is it the largest port in northwest Scotland and the main departure point for ferries to the Hebrides, it is also the main tourist centre in Argyll. Not surprisingly, it gets very crowded in summer, with passing traffic and people using it as a base for exploring the region. It has a wide range of hotels, guest houses, B&Bs, restaurants and shops and a number of tourist attractions, which is useful to know if you're stuck here in bad weather. The town lies in the beautiful setting of a wide, crescent-shaped bay, backed by steep hills, with the island of Kerrera, just offshore, providing a natural shelter. It has been a favourite with tourists since Victorian times, when Queen Victoria pronounced it as 'one of the finest spots we have ever seen'. More recent royal comments, however, made in relation to the drinking habits of the local populace, have been less than flattering.

Phone code: 01631
Colour map 3, grid B5
Population: 8,500

Argyll

Ins and outs

Oban is reasonably well served by **buses** and **trains** from Glasgow, Fort William and Inverness, and there are a number of west coast local bus services to and from Lochgilphead, Dalmally and Kilmartin. See transport section page 209 for details.

Getting there

There are regular local buses around town and around Lorn, including to Clachan Seil, North Cuan, Isle of Luing, North Connel, Dalavich, Bonawe, and Ganavan Sands. These are mostly operated by *Oban & District Buses* or *Royal Mail Postbuses*, T01463-256200.

Getting around

Sights

Tourist office The Tourist Information Centre is on Argyll Square. ■ *T563122. It's opening hours are: 1-5 Apr 0900-1700 Mon-Fri, 1200-1700 Sat; 6-26 Apr 0900-730 Mon-Fri, 1000-1700 Sat; 27 Apr-14 Jun 0900-1730 Mon-Sat, 1000-1700 Sun; 15 Jun-28 Jun 0900-1830 Mon-Sat, 1000-1700 Sun; 29 Jun-30 Aug 0900-2100 Mon-Sat, 0900-1900 Sun; 31 Aug-13 Sept 0900-1830 Mon-Sat, 0900-1700 Sun; 14 Sep-27 Sept 0900-1700 Mon-Sat, 1000-1700 Sun; 28 Sep-25 Oct 0900-1730 Mon-Fri, 1000-1600 Sat-Sun; 26 Oct-31 Mar 1000-1700 Mon-Fri, 1200-1600 Sat-Sun.*

The town's great landmark is **McCaig's Folly**, an incongruous structure that resembles Rome's Coliseum and which dominates the skyline. The tower was built by local banker John Stuart McCaig in the late 19th century, as a means of providing work for unemployed stonemasons. Unfortunately, McCaig died before the project was complete, and to this day no one is quite sure of his intentions. There's not much to see, apart from the exterior walls, but the views of the town and bay are quite magnificent and well worth the climb up. There are various routes on foot, but the most direct is to go up Argyll Street and on the left beside the church climb the set of steps, known as Jacob's Ladder, which lead to Ardonnel Terrace. Turn left here and the tower soon comes into view and is well signposted.

Oban

© Crown copyright

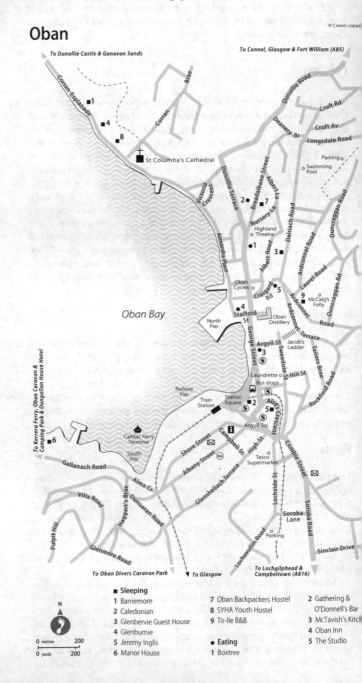

To Dunollie Castle & Ganavan Sands

To Connel, Glasgow & Fort William (A85)

Corran Esplanade

Corran Brae

Dunollie Road

Croft Rd

Deanery Br

Croft Av

Longsdale Road

St Columba's Cathedral

Victoria Crescent

Dunollie Terrace

Breadalbane Street

Albert La

Nursery La

Dalriach Road

Parking

Swimming Pool

Alexandra Place

Highland Theatre

Albert Road

Ardonnel Road

Laurel Road

Duncraggan Road

Oban Cycles

Craigard Rd

Ardconnel

McCaig's Folly

Oban Bay

Stafford St

Oban Distillery

Ardconnel Terrace

Road

North Pier

George Street

Argyll St

Jacob's Ladder

Tweedale St

Tailors Brae

To Kerrera Ferry, Oban Caravan & Camping Park & Dungallan House Hotel

Railway Pier

Hill St

Rockfield Road

Train Station

Station Square

Bus stops

Laundrette

Alma's Crescent

CalMac Ferry Terminal

South Pier

Argyll Sq

Shore Street

Campbell St

High St

Lochside St

Combie Street

Gallanach Road

Albany Street

Pol

Glenshellach Terrace

Tesco Supermarket

Villa Road

Haggart's Brae

Dunuaran Road

Alma Cr

Soroba Lane

Soroba Road

Pulpit Hill

Glenmore Road

Lochavullin Road

Parking

Sinclair Drive

To Oban Divers Caravan Park

To Glasgow

To Lochgilphead & Campbeltown (A816)

N

0 metres 200
0 yards 200

■ **Sleeping**
1 Barriemore
2 Caledonian
3 Glenbervie Guest House
4 Glenburnie
5 Jeremy Inglis
6 Manor House

7 Oban Backpackers Hostel
8 SYHA Youth Hostel
9 Tir-Ile B&B

● **Eating**
1 Boxtree

2 Gathering & O'Donnell's Bar
3 McTavish's Kitch
4 Oban Inn
5 The Studio

Argyll

Another good walk is to the ruins of **Dunollie Castle**, north of town on the Corran Esplanade towards Ganavan, from where there are also wonderful views. The castle was built on the site of an ancient stronghold of the King of Scots, and was then taken over in the 13th century by the MacDougalls, Lords of Lorn.

The principal seat of the MacDougalls was **Dunstaffnage Castle**, three miles north of Oban, off the A85. The 13th-century fort is built on an impressive site and much of the huge curtain wall remains intact. The ruins of the little chapel nearby are worth a look. The castle served as a temporary prison for Flora Mac-Donald. ■ *Apr-Sep daily 0930-1830, Oct-Mar 0930-1630. T562465. £1.80.*

Two miles east of Oban along the Glencruitten Road is the **Rare Breeds Farm Park**. It's a fun place, especially for kids, with lots of strange-looking, yet familiar animals native to these shores. The animals are in pens, or roam free, and are very friendly and approachable. ■ *T770608. Daily late Mar to late Oct 1000-1730 (till 1930 mid-Jun to end of Aug) £4. There are three buses daily Mon-Fri to and from Oban train station.*

If the weather's bad you can take a tour round the **Oban Distillery**, at the end of Stafford Street, which is opposite the North Pier. ■ *T572004. Mon-Fri 0930-1700, and Sat 0930-1700 from Easter to Oct (Jul-Sep Mon-Fri 0930-2030). £3.*

Another worthwhile rainy day activity is a trip to **A World in Miniature**, seven miles south of town on the A816 to Lochgilphead. Here you'll find an extraordinary collection of miniature rooms full of furniture, models and dioramas, all worked in intricate detail. Not for the long-sighted, though. ■ *T01852-316202. Daily Easter-Oct 1000-1700. £3, children £2.50.*

Boat trips can be made from Oban, to **Mull, Iona, Staffa,** and **The Treshnish Islands** with *Gordon Grant Tours*, on Railway Pier, T562842. There are other boat operators around the harbour, on the North, South and Railway Piers. You can also rent boats from *Borro Boats*, Dungallan Parks, Gallanach Road, T563292.

Essentials

There's no shortage of **hotels**, **guest houses** and **B&Bs**, most of which are very reasonably priced, and many of which are on or near the seafront. There are also lots of B&Bs in the streets below McCaig's Folly. Though it shouldn't be a problem finding a room for the night, Oban is the main ferry port for the islands and gets very busy in the summer with through traffic. It's often a good idea, therefore, to get the tourist office to find a place, which costs a little more, but can save a lot of time and effort.

A *Caledonian Hotel*, Station Sq, T563133, F562998. 70 rooms. Huge old Victorian Gothic building which is hard to miss. Full of 'character', which hides a multitude of sins, but it's very handily placed for the ferry and train station.

B *Manor House Hotel*, Gallanach Rd, T562087, F563053. 11 rooms, open Feb-Dec. Overlooking the bay on the road south out of town towards the Kerrera ferry. Offers comfort, style and superb cuisine.

C *Dungallan House Hotel*, Gallanach Rd, T563799, F566711. 13 rooms, open Jan, Mar-Oct and Dec. A Victorian house set in 5 acres of woodland, offering great views, hospitality and fine food. **D** *Barriemore Hotel*, Corran Esplanade, T/F566356. 13 rooms, open Mar-Nov, more of a guesthouse, and a superior one at that, Victorian style and elegance coupled with great views and a friendly atmosphere mean that this is much more than all right.

Sleeping
■ *on map*
Price codes:
see inside front cover

Argyll

D *Glenburnie Hotel*, Esplanade, T/F562089. 15 rooms, open Apr-Oct, another very good guesthouse along the seafront, which is lined with more upmarket guest houses and small hotels. **E** *Glenbervie Guest House*, Dalriach Rd, T564770, F566723. 8 rooms, lovely Victorian house high above the town on a street full of good quality accommodation, very good value.

There are dozens of **B&Bs** on Ardconnel Rd, including the excellent value **F** *Tir-Ile*, T566654.

The official *SYHA youth hostel*, T562025, open all year from Mar, is on Corran Esplanade, just beyond St Columba's cathedral. Cheaper and more central is the independent hostel, *Oban Backpackers*, T562107, on Breadalbane St. Open all year and where you can get breakfast for £1.40. Cheaper still is the much smaller *Jeremy Inglis Hostel*, T565065/563064, at 21 Airds Cres, opposite the TIC. There are 2 campsites nearby: the *Oban Divers Caravan Park*, T/F562755, open Mar-Nov, on the Glenshellach Rd, about 1½ miles south of the ferry terminal; and the *Oban Caravan & Camping Park*, T562425, F566624, open Apr to mid-Oct, on Gallanach Rd, 2 miles south of town near the Kerrera ferry.

Eating **Expensive** The best food in Oban can be found at the excellent *Manor House Hotel* (see above).

Mid-range *The Boxtree*, 108 George St, T563542. Very good bistro-style lunches and dinners and a wide vegetarian selection, open daily 1130-2200 in summer. *The Studio*, Craigard Rd, T562030. Good value 3-course set dinner and good à la carte menu, popular with locals, so you'll need to book, open daily 1700-2200 (cheap 'early bird special' served 1700-1830). A few miles south at Lerags, is *The Barn Bar*, T564618. Good pub food and children-friendly, open daily 1100-2100 Apr-Oct. *The Gathering*, Breadalbane St, T564849/565421/566159. Good, honest home cooking in one of Oban's oldest restaurants. Downstairs is *O'Donnell's* (see below).

Cheap There are numerous cheap options around town, none of which are particularly memorable. Bar meals are available at pubs and hotels, and there are the ubiquitous fish and chip shops, the best of which is *Onorio's* on George St. Perhaps the best place in this category is the much-publicised *McTavish's Kitchens*, at 34 George Street, T563064. There's a self-service cafeteria downstairs (open from 0900) and the restaurant upstairs (open 1200-1400 and 1800-2230) has a 'Scottish Show' (see below).

Bars & The town is not exactly the party capital of Scotland, so don't expect much in the way
entertainment of late night diversion. Your best bet is *O'Donnell's*, an Irish pub which has live music most nights, including ceilidhs, serves bar meals till 2300 and stays open till 0100. There's also Scottish music and dancing every night at *McTavish's Kitchens* 0830-2230 May-Sep (£3 admission, £1.50 if dining). Otherwise, there's the *Oban Inn*, by the north pier, which is the nicest pub in town and serves bar food.
The local cinema, confusingly called *The Highland Theatre*, is at the north end of George St, T562444, and shows most of the popular current releases.

Festivals At the end of **Apr/beginning of May** is the **Highlands & Islands Music & Dance Festival**. At the beginning of **Jun** is the **Oban Mod**, and at the beginning of **Aug** it's the **Lorn Agricaltural Show**. The **Argyllshire Gathering** (Oban Games) is held at the **end of Aug** in Mossfield Park. The precise dates change annually, so check the latest details at the tourist office.

Cycling You can rent bikes from *Oban Cycles*, 9 Craigard Rd, T566966. For details of cycle routes through the forests of Argyll, see the Forest Enterprise leaflet, *Cycling in the Forest*, available free at the tourist office. **Diving** *Puffin Dive Centre*, Gallanach Port, Gallanach Rd, T566088. Diver training centre and facilities (open 0800-2000). **Fishing** Excellent trout and coarse fishing on Loch Awe and Avich. Permits and boat hire from *The Angler's Corner*, 2 John St, T566374 (open daily 0930-1700). **Golf** *Glencruitten Golf Club*, T562868/564115, is an 18-hole course on the edge of town; £16 per round per day. **Pony Trekking** *Melfort Riding Centre*, Melfort Village, Kilmelford by Oban, T01852-200322. Also at *Achnalarig Farm*, Glencruitten, T562745. **Swimming** *Atlantis Leisure*, Dalriach Rd, T566800. **Walking** The *Oban Walkers* organize walks throughout Argyll and beyond every fortnight. For more details contact the tourist office, where you can also pick up the Forestry Commission guides to *Forest Walks and Trails in North Argyll and Knapdale, Kintyre & Kilmichael*. **Windsurfing** *Oban Windsurfing* at Ganavan, T564380, also at *Linnhe Marine Watersports Centre* at Lettershuna (see under North of Oban below).

Sport

Car hire *Flit Van & Car Hire*, Glencruitten Rd, T/F566553. From £20 per day. *Practical Car & Van Rental*, Robertson's Motor Repairs, Lochavullin Industrial Estate, T570900. From £30 per day. *Hazelbank Motors*, Lynn Rd, T566476, F566783. From £30 per day.

Transport

Argyll

Train There are 3 trains daily to **Glasgow**, via Crianlarich, where the Oban train connects with the Mallaig/Fort William-Glasgow train. For times, contact *Scotrail* (T0345-484950).

Bus There are regular daily buses to and from **Fort William**, via Benderloch and Appin (1 hr 45 mins) with *West Coast Motors*, T01586-552319, *Highland Country Buses*, T01463-233371 and *Oban & District Buses*, T562856. There's a regular daily service to and from **Glasgow** (3 hrs) with *Scottish Citylink Coaches*, T0990-505050, and to **Inverness** (1 hr 15 mins). There are regular daily buses to and from **Dalmally**, via Cruachan Power Station, Lochawe and Taynuilt Hotel, operated by *Oban & District*, *Scottish Citylink*, *Awe Service Station*, T01866-822612 and *LF Stewart*, T01866-833342. There's a service to **Lochgilphead**, via Kilmartin, a couple of times a day (Mon-Sat), operated by *Oban & District*, *Scottish Citylink* and *West Coast Motors*.

Ferry Oban is the main ferry port for many of the Hebridean islands. The *CalMac* ferry terminal, T566688 is on Railway Pier, to the south of the town centre. Only a hundred yards away is the train station, T563083, which is next to the bus terminal. Details of ferries out of Oban are on page 236. For ferries to Lismore, see page 211.

Banks All the major banks have branches in the town centre and you can also change foreign currency at the tourist office.

Directory

Isle of Kerrera

A good place to get away from the crowds and enjoy some peace and quiet and some fine walking is the island of Kerrera, which protects Oban Bay. It's only five miles by two, so can be explored easily on foot or by bike.

Phone code: 01631
Colour map 3, grid C5

The highest point on the island is 600 feet, from where there are great views across to Mull, the Slate Islands, Lismore and Jura. Otherwise, there's a good trail down to the ruins of **Gylen Castle**, built by the MacDougall's in 1582, which is perched on a cliff-top on the south coast. Near the castle is the F *Kerrera Bothy*, T570223, which has six beds, is open April-September, and can also arrange a lift to and from the ferry. There's also a tearoom here, which serves tea, coffee, juices, cakes and snacks.

The ferry lands at the spot where King Alexander II was mortally wounded while defeating the Vikings in battle, in 1249. A mile northwest of here is **Slatrach Bay**, a nice sandy beach and a great place for a picnic.

Getting there The departure point for ferries to Kerrera is 1½ miles along the Gallanach Road. They leave several times daily between 0845 and 1800 (between 1030 and 1700 on Sun). The trip takes 5-10 minutes and costs £2.50 return (£1.50 for children and 50p for bikes), T563665.

North of Oban

Phone code: 01631
Colour map 3, grid B5

Five miles north of Oban an impressive steel cantilever bridge carries the A828 across the mouth of Loch Etive at **Connel**. It's worth stopping here to see the **Falls of Lora**, a wild tide-race created by the narrow mouth of the sea loch and the reef that spans most of it, thus restricting the flow of water. The result is the impressive rapids, which are best seen from the shore in the village or from halfway across the bridge. There are several cheap **B&Bs** in Connel village, should you wish to stay, but the nicest place is the **D** *Ards House*, T710255, which offers good food.

Five miles east of Connel Bridge, on the north shore of Loch Etive, **Archattan Priory Garden** is worth a detour if the weather's fine. You can wander amongst the 13th century priory ruins and the gardens, which are at their best between July and September, though Spring is also a good time. There's also a tearoom. ■ *T750274. 1 Apr-31 Oct 0900-1800.*

At **Benderloch**, a few miles north of Connel Bridge, a road turns west (signed South Shian) to the *Tralee Dive Centre*, T/F720262, where you can charter boats for fishing. Nearby is *Tralee Rally Karting*, T720297, which is open daily July-September 1000-1800.

Continue on this road to reach **Barcaldine Castle**, built by the Campbells in the late 16th century. The tower house is still occupied by Campbells, having been sold in the mid-19th century and the bought back as a ruin 50 years later. It's now open to the public and though there are no real treasures, there are interesting stories to be told, secret passages to explore, a dungeon (with ghost) and a tearoom where you can try Mrs Campbell's home baking. You can also spend the night: there are two **D-E** rooms for B&B. ■ *T720598. 11-17 Apr and 2 May-2 Oct daily 1100-1730; 21-30 Apr and 6-29 Oct 1100-1700 Tue, Wed-Thur only. £3.25.*

If the thought of a night in a haunted castle doesn't appeal, there are several **B&Bs** in the village of Benderloch. If money's no object, then treat yourself to the luxurious **L** *Isle of Eriska Hotel*, T720371, F720531. 17 rooms. Argyll's only five-star hotel, situated on its own private 300-acre island off the northern point of Benderloch.

Near Barcaldine Castle, on the main A828, is the **Oban Sealife Centre**, on the shore of Loch Creran. It's enormous fun and also environmentally-friendly as they rescue seals and other aquatic life and then release them back into the wild at the end of the season. You can see lots of strange underwater creatures at close quarters and even touch some of them. It's the ideal place to come with kids, or if it's raining. There's also a self-service restaurant. ■ *T720386. Daily 0900-1800 (1000-1700 in the winter months). £5.50, children £3.50. Buses to Fort William pass by the Sealife Centre (see under 'Oban Transport' above).*

The road runs around Loch Creran and enters the district of Appin, made famous in Robert Louis Stevenson's *Kidnapped*, which was based on the 'Appin Murder' of 1752. A road turns southwest off the main Fort William road to Port Appin, on the western tip of the peninsula, the departure point for the passenger ferry to **Lismore.**

Sleeping There are a couple of hotels in this attractive little fishing village, the best of which is the superb **L** *Airds Hotel*, T730236, F730535. 12 rooms, this classy little roadside hotel boasts one of the very best restaurants in the whole country and is recommended in all the best guide books. There's also the **C** *Pierhouse Hotel*, T730302, F730400. Sitting right by the tiny pier, this cosy little hotel has a deserved reputation for excellent, moderately-priced local seafood. If your budget doesn't stretch that far, then there's the **E** *Fasgadh Guest House*, T730374.

To the north of Port Appin is the irresistibly photogenic Castle Stalker. Standing on its own tiny island with a background of islands and hills, it's probably second only to the famous Eilean Donan, in its portrayal of Scotland's romantic image. It was built in the 16th century by the Stewarts of Appin before falling into Campbell hands after the ill-fated 1745 rebellion. The current owners open it to the public for a limited period in July and August. Check opening times at the tourist office in Oban.

Castle Stalker

At **Lettershuna**, just beyond Port Appin, is the **Linnhe Marine Watersports Centre**, where you can hire motor boats, sailing dinghies or windsurfing boards, take sailing or windsurfing lessons, or try water-skiing, pony trekking or even clay pigeon shooting. ■ *T730227, Cell 0421-503981. May-Sep 0900-1800.*

The island of Lismore lies only a few miles off the mainland, in Loch Linnhe, yet feels a world away. It makes an ideal day trip and offers great opportunities for walking and cycling, as well as wonderful views across to the mountains of Morvern and Mull, the Paps of Jura to the south and Ben Nevis to the north. It's a fertile little island (the name *leis mór* is Gaelic for "the big garden") and once supported a population of 1,400, though the present population is about a tenth of that.

Lismore has a long and interesting history. It was the ecclesiastical capital of Argyll for several centuries and a cathedral was founded there in the 12th century, about a mile north of Clachan (see below). All that remains is the choir, which is now used as the parish church. The **Cathedral of St Moluag** occupies the site of a church founded by the Irish saint, who established a religious community on the island about the same time as St Columba was busy at work in Iona. Legend has it that the two saints were racing to the island, in an attempt to be the first to land and found a monastery. Such was Moluag's religious zeal that he cut off his finger and threw, onto the shore, thus claiming possession.

Not far from the church, is the 2,000-year-old **Broch of Tirefour**, one of the best-preserved prehistoric monuments in Argyll with surviving circular walls up to 16 feet high. Other interesting sights include **Castle Coeffin**, a 13th-century fortress built by the MacDougalls of Lorn, on the west coast, and in the southwest of the island, the 13th century **Achadun Castle**, built for the Bishops of Argyll. It's a short walk from here to **Bernera Island**, which can be reached at low tide (but don't get stranded).

The *CalMac* car ferry from Oban lands at **Achnacroish**, about halfway up the east coast (2-4 daily Mon-Sat; 50 mins). A passenger ferry leaves from Port Appin pier to the island's north point (daily every 1-2 hrs; 10 mins).

Getting there

Essentials There are a couple of **B&Bs** on the island, including **E-F** *The Schoolhouse*, T760262, beyond Clachan, 1½ miles north of the ferry pier. There's also a shop and post office at Clachan. There's a limited postbus service which runs Mon-Sat (see the *Lorn Area Transport Guide* for times), or you can hire bikes from *Mary MacDougall*, T760213).

South Lorn and the Slate Islands

Phone code: 01852
Colour map 3, grid C4/5

Eight miles south of Oban the B884 turns west off the A816 to a small group of islands known as the Slate Islands. At their peak in the mid-19th century, the island's slate quarries exported millions of roofing slates every year.

Ins and outs

Getting there A passenger **ferry** sails from Ellanbeich on Seil to Easdale, making the 5-min trip at regular intervals between 0745 and 2300 Mon-Sat (between 0930 and 1750 on Sun), partly to schedule, partly on request. Check times at Oban tourist office.

A car ferry to Luing (South Cuan) sails from South Cuan on Seil (5 mins), Mon-Sat every 15-30 mins from 0745 to 1830 (later in summer) and on Sun every 30 mins from 1100-1800. Check times at Oban tourist office. Note that it can be a rough crossing and times are subject to sailing conditions.

Getting around A *Postbus* service runs from Oban train station to Clachan Seil, Balvicar, Ellenbeich and North Cuan on Seil. There's also a circular postbus service on Luing, from South Cuan to Cullipool and Toberonochy. Check times at Oban tourist office.

Isle of Seil

Phone code: 01852

The most northerly of the Slate Islands is Seil, which is reached from the mainland across the impressive Clachan Bridge, better known as the 'Bridge over the Atlantic', built in 1792, with its elegant, high arch to allow ships to pass beneath. Beside the bridge is an old inn, *Tigh an Truish*, or 'House of the Trousers', where islanders would have to swap kilt for trousers in order to conform to the post-1745 ban on the wearing of Highland dress.

Two miles south, at **Balvicar**, the road turns right and climbs up and over to the main village of **Ellanbeich**, an attractive wee place with rows of white cottages around the harbour. This was once a tiny island itself until the intensive slate quarrying succeeded in silting up the narrow sea channel. The village is also, rather confusingly, known by the same name as the nearby island of **Easdale**, so renowned was the latter for its slate deposits. Another road runs south from Balvicar to **North Cuan**, from where the car ferry sails across the treacherous Cuan Sound to **Luing** (see below).

Sleeping There's **B&B** accommodation on Seil, at *Mutiara* , T300241, open May-Nov, and *The Haven*, T300468; open Apr-Sep, both **E** and both in Clachan Seil.

Isle of Easdale
Phone code: 01852

Easdale is separated from Seil by a 500-yard-wide channel which has to be dredged to keep it open. The island, only 800 yards by 700 yards, was the centre of the slate industry and the old dilapidated workers' cottages can still be seen, lending an air of melancholy to the place. There was once a population of over 450 here, but the quarries were flooded during a great storm in 1881 and the industry collapsed. The present population numbers around 50. The old quarries can still be seen, filled with water, with the derelict work buildings standing forlorn as the surrounding vegetation takes over. The fascinating

Argyll

Atlantic Bridge,
Clachan,
Isle of Seil

Argyll

history of the island is explained at the **folk museum** near the main square in the village. ■ *T300370. Apr-Oct daily 1030-1730. £2.*

There are no roads on the island, which only takes about half an hour to walk around. There's a tearoom by the pier and some of the old cottages have been modernized and turned into self-catering accommodation (details from the tourist office in Oban).

Isle of Luing

Phone code: 01852

The long, thin island of Luing (pronounced 'Ling') once had a population of around 600 which was drastically reduced during the Clearances to make way for cattle. The island is still well known for its beef and is the home of a successful new breed named after it.

The island is small, six miles by two, and mostly flat, making it ideal for exploring by bike. Bikes can be hired in the pretty little village of **Cullipool**, a mile or so southwest of the ferry (contact *Isle of Luing Bike Hire*, T314256). There's also a tearoom, post office and general store. On the road to Cullipool is the island's only B&B, **E-F** *Bardrishaig Farm*, T314364.

The only other village is **Toberonochy**, three miles from Cullipool on the east coast. It's another village of attractive white cottages built for slate workers and nested below a ruined church.

South Lorn

South of the turn-off to the Slate Islands is **Arduaine Garden**, a beautiful place and an absolute must for all gardening enthusiasts. The 20-acre garden, now owned by the NTS, is best visited in May and June when you can enjoy the spectacular rhododendrons, but there are also beautiful herbaceous borders, ponds filled with water lilies, woodland and sweeping lawns to admire, as well as great views across to Jura and the Slate Islands. T200366. ■ *Daily all year 0930 till sunset. Admission £2.50.*

Arduaine
Phone code: 01852

Sleeping If you want to stay around here, there's the superb **B-A** *Loch Melfort Hotel*, T01852-200233, F200214, lhotel@aol.com. Twenty six rooms. Open Mar-Dec and New Year. It enjoys great views and a reputation for the finest seafood. If you can't afford such luxury, there's a **campsite** nearby, or **B&B** at **E-F** *Willow Cottage*, T200202.

Craignish
Peninsula
Phone code: 01852

This is boating country, and just south of Arduaine, on the northern coast of the Craignish peninsula, is surreal **Croabh Haven**, a yachting marina, built in the style of a reproduction 18th century fishing village. You can go for comfort and stay at the **D-E** *Buidhe Lodge*, T500291, or opt for the faded charm of **E-F** *Lunga*, T500237, F500369.

South of Croabh Haven is another yachting marina at **Ardfern**, where there's a hotel and B&B accommodation, a popular pub, restaurant and delicatessen. You can arrange boat trips from Ardfern around Loch Craignish and to the offshore islands with *Ruby Cruises*, T/F500616.

Mid-Argyll

The area south of Oban and north of Kintyre is commonly known as Mid-Argyll, a very attractive region of sea lochs, rolling hills and the huge forest of Knapdale, which offers some fine walking. The greatest attraction in Mid-Argyll, though, is Kilmartin Glen, which is littered with Neolithic, Bronze Age and Iron Age monuments, and is one of the most interesting and least known prehistoric sites in Europe.

Ins and outs

Getting around Public transport is thin on the ground, but with a little time and patience it is possible to explore the area by bus. *Scottish Citylink*, T0990-505050, runs a daily service from Glasgow to Campbeltown which stops in Lochgilphead. There are buses from Lochgilphead to Cairnbaan, Crinan, Achnamara and Tayvallich several times daily Mon-Sat. There are buses and shared taxis to Oban via Kilmartin (Mon-Sat) and a postbus to Inveraray (Mon-Sat). There's also a local service to and from Ardrishaig. You can find out times of buses at the tourist office in Lochgilphead (see below), or pick up a free copy of Argyll & Bute Council's Mid-Argyll timetable. For details of shared taxis, or to book a taxi, contact *Mid Argyll Taxis*, 4 Slockavullin, Kilmartin, T01546-510318.

Lochgilphead

Phone code: 01546
Colour map 3, grid C5

The main town in the area, and administrative centre for the entire Argyll & Bute region, is Lochgilphead, a sleepy little place at the head of Loch Gilp, an arm of Loch Fyne. Lochgilphead started life as a planned town, but the industries came and went, leaving it with the customary grid plan of wide streets but little else. Today, it serves as a useful base for exploring the area, with a decent range of accommodation, a bank, supermarket and **tourist office** on Lochnell St. ■ *T602344. Apr-Oct.*

South of Lochgilphead and almost a continuation of the town, is the village of **Ardrishaig**, where you'll find the *Castle Riding Centre*, at Brenfield Estate & Farm, T603274. Here you can enjoy cross country horse riding, beach gallops, pub rides or hire mountain bikes, sail boards, boats, or even try clay pigeon shooting and archery. There's a nice easy walk from the car park at **Kilmory Castle Gardens**, about a mile east of town, up to **Kilmory Loch**. It takes about an hour there and back and is well marked. The gardens also make a pleasant stroll and there are other marked walks, including up to Dun Mór (360 feet).

If it's raining, you could pass the time visiting the pottery workshop of *Highland Porcelain*. ■ *T602044. Tours are at 1030 and 1400 Mon-Fri and cost £2, children 50p.*

There are several hotels, guesthouses and B&Bs in and around Lochgilphead. Best of the bunch is **B** *Cairnbaan Hotel*, T603668, F606045, a lovely 18th-century coaching inn overlooking the Crinan Canal in the village of Cairnbaan, just north of Lochgilphead.

Sleeping & eating

In the town itself is **E** *The Argyll Hotel* on Lochnell St, T602221, F603576, which has a moderately-priced restaurant and lively bar. Just outside of town, at Bank Park, is a **caravan park**, where you can pitch a tent. It has the full range of facilities and also hires out mountain bikes, T602003.

In **Ardishaig** is the recently refurbished **F-E** *Grey Gull Inn*, T606017, F606167, which is very good value and serves snacks and meals all day. A cheaper alternative for eating out is *The Stables*, or the bar of the *Stag Hotel*, both on Argyll St. If you fancy a picnic, then try the *Alba Smokehouse*, an excellent deli in Kilmory, just east of town.

Cycle hire *Crinan Cycles*, The Pier, Ardrishaig, T603511. Also *Lochgilphead Caravan Park* (see above).

Sport

Banks *Bank of Scotland*, Poltalloch St.

Directory

Kilmartin Glen

Phone code: 01852
Colour map 3, grid C5

North of Lochgilphead, on the A816 to Oban, is Kilmartin Glen, an area of Neolithic and Bronze Age chambered and round cairns, stone circles, rock carvings, Iron Age forts and duns, Early Christian sculptured stones and medieval castles. Most notable of all is the **linear cemetery**, a line of burial cairns that stretch southward from Kilmartin village for over two miles. The largest and oldest of the group is the Neolithic cairn, **Nether Largie South**, which is over 5,000 years old and big enough to enter. The other cairns, **Nether Largie North**, **Mid Nether Largie** and **Ri Cruin**, are Bronze Age and the huge stone coffins show carvings on the grave slabs. Nearby are the **Temple Wood Stone Circles**, where burials took place from Neolithic times to the Bronze Age.

On the other side of the A816, and visible from the road, is a group of monuments which can all be reached from **Dunchraigaig Cairn**. This is a huge Bronze Age cairn with some of the covering stones removed to reveal three stone coffins. From here a path is signed to **Ballymeanoch Standing Stones**, the tallest of which is 12 feet high. Two of the stones are decorated with cup marks, prehistoric rock carvings that can be found at numerous locations throughout the Kilmartin area. There's also a henge monument in the same field. These were generally round or oval platforms with an internal ditch and it's thought they were used for ceremonial purposes.

The best example of rock carvings is at **Achnabreck**, near Cairnbaan village, the largest collection anywhere in Britain. The purpose and significance of these cup- and ring-marked rocks is still a matter of debate.

Before exploring this fascinating area, it's a good idea to stop off at **Kilmartin House**, the multi award-winning interpretive centre, housed in the old manse next to the parish church in the village of Kilmartin. The imaginative and interesting museum helps to explain the bewildering array of prehistoric sites lying all around and includes artefacts from the various sites and prehistoric music. Upstairs is an audio-visual display which tells the story of this unique corner of Scotland. The café/restaurant does not disappoint either and serves cheap snacks and meals, using local produce, and excellent coffee from 1230 till 1700. ■ *T510278. Daily all year 1000-1730. £3.90, children £1.20.*

Kilmartin

Next door in the church graveyard are the **Kilmartin crosses**, dating from as far back as the 9th and 10th centuries. Also within the graveyard is one of the largest collections of medieval grave slabs in the West Highlands.

Argyll

Two miles north of Kilmartin, sitting high above the A816, is **Carnasserie Castle**, an imposing 16th century tower house built by John Carswell, Bishop of the Isles, who translated *The Book of the Common Order* in 1567, the first book to be printed in Gaelic. Entry to the castle is free, but it's a little way from the car park.

Dunadd A few miles south of Kilmartin village is the Iron Age hill fort of Dunadd, which stands atop a rocky outcrop and dominates the surrounding flat expanse of Moine Mhór (Great Moss), one of the few remaining peat bogs in the country and now a Nature Reserve. Dunadd Fort became the capital of the ancient kingdom of Dalriada around 500 AD and is one the most important Celtic sites in Scotland. The views from the top are wonderful and worth the visit alone, but you can also see carved out of the exposed rock, a basin and footprint, thought to have been used in the inauguration ceremonies of the ancient kings of Dalriada. There's also an inscription in *ogham* (a form of early writing from Ireland) and the faint outline of a boar, possibly of Pictish origin.

Sleeping & eating If you want to spend more time exploring Kilmartin Glen, there are a few accommodation options. Opposite the church is **D** *Kilmartin Hotel*, T510250, F606370, which is comfortable and serves meals all day. There are also a couple of cheaper B&Bs to choose from, including **E** *Burndale*, T510235 and **F-E** *Tibertich*, T/F810281, a working sheep farm just north of the village. A good place for lunch is the café at Kilmartin House (see above), otherwise, there's *The Cairn* restaurant, T510254, which serves very good, moderately-priced Scottish and European dishes using local produce (open 1100-1500 and from 1830).

Crinan Canal

Colour map 3, grid C5 Kilmartin Glen is bordered to the south by the Crinan Canal, a nine-mile stretch of waterway linking Loch Fyne at Ardishaig with the Sound of Jura. It was designed and built by Sir John Rennie in 1801, with the assistance of the ubiquitous Thomas Telford, to allow shipping to avoid the long and often hazardous journey round the Mull of Kintyre and to help stimulate trade in the islands. These days, you're more likely to see pleasure yachts and cruisers sailing on the canal than the cargo vessels which once transported coal and other goods to the islands and returned with livestock. You don't need to come in a boat to appreciate the canal. You can walk or cycle along the towpath that runs the entire length of the canal, from Ardrishaig to Crinan, and watch boats of all shapes and sizes negotiating a total of 15 locks. The best place to view the canal traffic is at **Crinan**, a pretty little fishing port on Loch Crinan at the western end of the canal. Here you can take a boat trip with *Gemini Cruises*, based at Crinan harbour, T/F01546-830238. They offer two-hour wildlife spotting cruises round Loch Craignish (£9 per person), or longer trips out to the Gulf of Corrievreckan.

Sleeping & eating Crinan boasts one of Scotland's finest hotels, the **L** *Crinan Hotel*, T01546-830261, F830292, nryan@crinanhotel.com. Not only is this one of the most beautifully-located hotels in the country, but its celebrated restaurants are amongst the best on the west coast. The bar next to the *Lock 16* restaurant on the top floor offers cheaper lunches, for those who can't afford such indulgence. A cheaper **B&B** alternative is **E-D** *Tigh-Na-Glaic*, T830245, F830243.

Knapdale

Running south from the Crinan Canal down to Kintyre is Knapdale, a forested, hilly area that gets its name from its Gaelic description, *cnap* (hill) and *dall* (field). It's an area worth exploring, for there are many walking trails and superb views from the west coast across to the Paps of Jura.

Phone code: 01880
Colour map 5, grid A2

Immediately south of the canal is **Knapdale Forest**, which stretches from coast to coast over hills dotted with tiny lochs. The Forestry Commission has marked out several lovely trails. Three fairly easy circular trails start from the B8025 which runs south from **Bellanoch**, just east of Crinan. One sets out from the car park at the Barnluasgan Interpretation Centre and runs up to a point beyond Loch Barnluasgan, with great views over the forest and the many lochs. It's a mile in total. A second trail, also a mile long, starts from a car park a little further along the B8025 and heads through the forest to the deserted

Knapdale

© Crown copyright

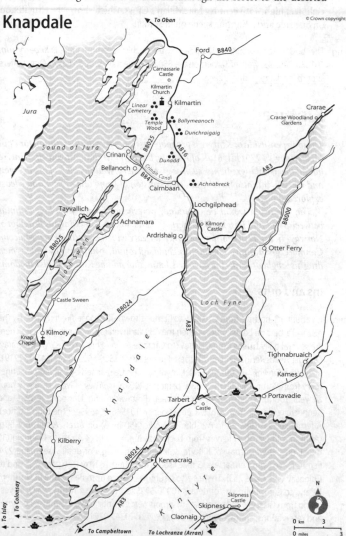

Argyll

township of Arichonan. The third trail starts out from the car park between the starting points for the first and second trails. It runs right around Loch Coille-Bharr and is three miles long. A more strenuous walk starts from a car park about 100 yards into the forest, off the B841, about half a mile west of Cairnbaan, and climbs up to the peak of **Dunardy** (702 feet).

At the Barnluasgan Interpretation Centre a little side road turns south down the eastern shore of beautiful **Loch Sween**, past the village of **Achnamara**, to the 12th century **Castle Sween**. First impressions of the castle, situated on the shores of the lovely loch with the forested hills all around, are completely ruined by the criminally distasteful caravan park nearby. Unfortunately, the caravans were not there when Robert the Bruce attacked the castle, otherwise he might have done us all a favour by razing them.

Three miles south is the ruined 13th century **Kilmory Knap Chapel**. A new glass roof protects the carved stones inside. The most notable of these is the eight feet high, 15th century MacMillan's Cross, which shows the Crucifixion on one side and a hunting scene on the other.

Sleeping The best place to stay in Knapdale is the highly recommended **D** *Kilberry Inn*, T01880-770223, west of Tarbert on the B8024. Three rooms, open Easter-Oct, it offers superb food and perfect peace.

Kintyre

Colour map 5, A/B2 *The long peninsula of Kintyre is probably best known as the inspiration for Paul McCartney's 1970s hit, Mull of Kintyre, but don't let that put you off. Kintyre has all the usual ingredients, such as great scenery, wildlife, bags of history, golf and whisky, but also has the added attraction of being one of Scotland's least explored spots.*

The peninsula would be an island, were it not for the mile-long isthmus between West and East Loch Tarbert, a fact not lost on King Magnus Barefoot of Norway. In the 11th century, he signed a treaty with the Scottish king, Malcolm Canmore, giving him all the land he could sail round, so he promptly had his men drag his longboat across the narrow isthmus, thus adding Kintyre to his kingdom.

Ins and outs

Getting there It's about a 3-hr drive from Glasgow to Campbeltown. The most direct route is by the A82 to Tarbert on Loch Lomond, then the A83 via Inveraray and Lochgilphead. There are several daily **buses** from Glasgow to Campbeltown (4 hrs 20 mins), via Inveraray, Lochgilphead, Kennacraig and Tarbert. For details: T01586-552319 or 0141-3329191, or *Scottish Citylink* (T0990-505050). Kintyre can also be reached by car and passenger **ferry** from Portavadie on the Cowal peninsula (20 mins). They leave daily every hour all year round. There are buses between Portavadie and Dunoon, Tarbert and Kennacraig (details from Argyll & Bute Council, T01546-604695, or the tourist office). A ferry leaves Ardrossan in Ayrshire to Brodick (50 mins) on Arran. A summer ferry (April to mid-October) leaves from Lochranza in the north of Arran, to Claonaig (30 mins), on the west coast of Kintyre, south of Kennacraig. For details, see page 224. Ferries leave from Kennacraig, 5 miles south of Tarbert, to Islay (see page 255 and to Colonsay (see page 253). There's also a summer service from Ballycastle in Northern Ireland to Campbeltown; for details T0990-523523. There are 2 **flights** daily, all year round from Glasgow to Machrihanish airport near Campbeltown (35 mins). For times and reservations, contact *British Airways Express*, T0345-222111.

Getting around Kintyre without your own transport requires time and patience. **Getting around**
There's a **bus** service running up and down the west coast (see above), and also a limited service from Campbeltown to places around the peninsula (see page 222). There
are also buses from Kennacraig and Tarbert to Claonaig and Skipness (2-3 daily
Mon-Sat), and from **Tarbert** to **Kennacraig** (several times daily Mon-Sat). If you want
to hire a car, there's *Campbeltown Motor Company*, T01586-552030 or *Fona taxis &
minibuses*, T01586-554001/551000.

Tarbert

The fishing village of Tarbert sits at the head of East Loch Tarbert, in a shel-   *Phone code: 01880*
tered bay backed by forested hills, and is one the most attractive ports on the   *Colour map 5, grid A3*
west coast. Tarbert (the name derives from the Gaelic *An Tairbeart* meaning
"isthmus") has a long tradition of fishing and in the 18th and 19th centuries
was a major herring port. Today, prawns and other shellfish are the main catch
and though there is still a sizeable fleet, fishing has declined in importance to
the local economy. Tourism, meanwhile, is a growing source of income, and
Tarbert attracts its fair share of yachties, particularly in May, when the village
hosts the second largest racing series in the UK, after Cowes, attracting hundreds of boats and thousands of visitors. The town also hosts an excellent **folk
music festival**, over a weekend at the end of September (for details, T820343).

Overlooking the harbour is the dramatically-sited ruin of **Robert the Bruce's**
14th-century castle. There's not much left to see, other than the five-storey
15th-century keep. It's unsafe to investigate the ruins too closely, but the view
alone is worth the walk. There are steps leading up to the castle, next to the *Ann
Thomas Gallery*, on Harbour Street. Behind the castle, there are several marked
trails leading up into the hills, with great views over Loch Fyne and the islands.
Less strenuous is the short walk at the end of Garvel Road, on the north side of
the harbour, which leads to the beach. At the end of East Pier road, beyond the
Cowal Ferry, is another interesting walk, to the Shell Beaches. You can also
explore the lovely gardens at Stonefield Castle Hotel (see 'Sleeping' below).

Just south of town, on the main A83, is the **An Tairbeart Heritage Centre**,
which tells you all you need to know about the area's fascinating history, as well
as providing a whole host of activities such as woodturning and sheep shear-
ing. There's also a good, moderately-priced restaurant offering local specialities such as venison and oysters. ■ *T820190, www.an-t.co.uk. Easter till early
Jan daily 1000-1900. Free.*

Tourist office Harbour St. ■ *T820429. 1-26 Apr Mon-Fri 1000-1700,
Sat-Sun 1200-1700; 27 Apr-28 Jun Mon-Sat 1000-170, Sun 1100-1700; 29
Jun-13 Sept Mon-Sat 0930-1800, Sun 1000-1700;14 Sep-25 Oct Mon-Sat
1000-1700, Sun 1200-1700.*

Three miles north on the A82 to Lochgilphead is the sumptious **A** *Stonefield Castle* **Sleeping**
Hotel, T820836, F820929, a magnificent Baronial Victorian mansion set in 60 acres of
beautiful woodland garden, with great views across the loch and an acclaimed restaurant to boot.

There's a good selection of places to stay in Tarbert itself, including the **C** *Columba
Hotel*, T/F820808, on East Pier Rd. 10 rooms. This refurbished and comfortable Victorian hotel is on the waterfront and features fine cooking. The restaurant is moderately
priced and the popular bar offers cheap, imaginative meals.

Just outside the village is the **D** *West Loch Hotel*, T820283, F820930, a traditional
18th-century coaching inn on the main A83 overlooking West Loch Tarbert. There's
also plenty B&B accommodation, mostly **E**, and a **campsite**, at Escart Bay in a
secluded spot overlooking West Loch Tarbert, T820873.

Argyll

Eating As you'd expect with a place popular with yachties, Tarbert boasts some very fine restaurants. Pick of the bunch is *The Anchorage*, on Harbour St, T820881. Wonderful food, particularly the local seafood and fish, and mid-range prices. Small and cosy so book in advance. Otherwise the best food is available at the hotels. There's the above-mentioned *Columba and Stonefield Castle Hotels* but also recommended is the *Victoria Hotel*, T820236, aliatvic@aol.com, which is on the right as you enter the village from Lochgilphead.

Shopping *Earra Gael Craft Shop*, T820428, in the old Weighbridge on Harbour St. Open daily Apr-Oct 1000-1730. *Ann Thomas Gallery*, Harbour St, T820390. Good selection of books, local prints and stationery; open daily (Mon-Sat 0900-1830, Sun 1100-1830 in summer).

Directory **Banks** *Bank of Scotland* and *Clydesdale Bank* are both on Harbour St, and both have ATMs.

Isle of Gigha

Population: 120
Phone code: 01583

The small island of Gigha (pronounced "Gee-a" with a hard "g") translates from Norse as "God's Island". A grand claim, perhaps, but there's no question that this most accessible of islands is also one of the loveliest and most romantic. It's only a 20-minute ferry ride away, and only six miles by one mile, so it can be visited easily in a day, which is just about enough time to appreciate why the Vikings loved it so much. Like so many of the Hebridean islands, Gigha has had a long list of owners, including various branches of the MacNeils and, more recently, in 1944, Sir James Horlick, he of bedtime drink fame.

It was Horlick who created the island's single greatest attraction, the wonderful **Achamore Garden**, one mile south of the ferry terminal. Thanks to Gigha's mild climate, the 50-acre woodland garden has an amazing variety of tropical plants, including rhododendrons, azaleas, camellias as well as other, more exotic, species. There are two marked walks through the gardens, which start out from the walled garden. The gardens are best seen in early summer, when the rhodies are in full bloom. ■ *T505254, F505244. Daily all year 0900 till dusk. £2.*

Walks on the island The island's other delights include some good **walks**, white sandy **beaches** and fantastic views across to Jura on one side and Kintyre on the other. One of the best walks is to take the path left after the **nine-hole golf course**, signed Ardaily, past Mill Loch to the Mill on the west shore. The views from here are just magnificent. Another good idea is to walk, or cycle (see below for bike hire) to the peninsula of **Eilean Garbh** at the north of the island. About half a mile beyond Kinererach Farm a path leads left to the peninsula where two crescent-shaped beaches are separated by a thin spit of land. And if the weather's good enough for a picnic, make sure you try some of the island's famously distinctive cheese.

Sleeping & eating The ferry port and only village is **Ardminish**. Here you'll find the **C** *Gigha Hotel*, T505254, F505244, open Mar-Oct, which offers comfort, great views and good bar food. Another option is the **E** *Post Office House*, T505251, a short walk from the ferry. The McSporrans also run the post office and general store, provide good home cooking and even rent out bikes.

A good alternative to staying on the island, at the ferry port of **Tayinloan**, is the **C** *Tayinloan Inn*, T441233, a small and cosy 18th-century coaching inn offering the best food south of Tarbert.

Transport The small *CalMac* car and passenger ferry leaves from Tayinloan to the ferry pier at Ardminish, daily all year round (hourly 0900-1800 Mon-Sat, 1100-1700 Sun). The return trip costs £4.45 per passenger and £17 per car (a car is unnecessary).

Campbeltown

At the southern end of the Kintyre peninsula is the "metropolis" of Campbeltown, originally called Kinlochkilkerran (*Ceann Loch Cille Ciaran*) but renamed in the 17th century by the Earl of Argyll, who was, of course, a Campbell. This may be the largest town by far in this part of Argyll, but it has a real end-of-the-line feel, due in part to its geographical isolation, but also because the town has long since lost its *raison d'être* – whisky.

Population: 6,500
Phone code: 01586
Colour map 5, grid B2

There was once a lot of whisky distilled in Campbeltown. So much so, in fact, that local fishermen were able to smell their way home. That may be apocryphal but there's no doubting that the place did inspire tartan crooner Andy Stewart (a man responsible for such dubious classics as *Donald, Whar's yer Troosers*) to sing *Campbeltown Loch I wish you were whisky*. But even Andy Stewart might have had problems trying to consume the total production of the town's whisky at its 1886 peak; no fewer than two million gallons.

It's not only whisky that's in decline; shipbuilding and fishing have also suffered. But it's hoped that the new car ferry link to Ballycastle in Northern Ireland will help to stimulate the local economy.

Tourist office on the Old Quay. ■ *T552056. Apr Mon-Fri 0900-1730; May-Sep Mon-Fri 0900-1730, Sat-Sun 1100-1700; Oct Mon-Fri 0930-1730, Sat-Sun 1000-1600; Nov-Mar Mon-Fri 1000-1600.*

Campbeltown's whisky production was such that the town even has its own particular regional subgroup of single malt named after it, but of the 34 distilleries once in production, only one remains, the **Springbank distillery**. This family-run distillery is in Well Close, off Longrow, and guided tours are by appointment only, T552085. Whisky aficionados should also pay a visit to **Eaglesome** on Longrow South, where you can choose from over 400 single malts.

Sights

To find out more on the town's history, you can visit the **Campbeltown Heritage Centre**, housed in the former Lorne Street church, or "Tartan Kirk" as it is known locally, due to its distinctive facade of alternating stone and red brick. ■ *On the Southend Rd. Apr-Oct Mon-Sat 1100-1700, Sun 1400-1700. £2.*

The most interesting sight in town is the wonderfully evocative **"Wee Picture House"**, on Hall Street, first opened in May 1913. This rare art deco treasure was closed in 1983, but such was the storm of local protest that it was lovingly refurbished and reopened in 1989. No visit to Campbeltown would be complete without witnessing the glories of a bygone era in the oldest surviving cinema in Scotland. Films are shown six nights a week (Friday night is bingo night).

If the weather's good, it's worth taking a walk up to **Beinn Ghulean**, which overlooks the town and loch. Follow the signs for the A83 to Machrihanish until you reach Witchburn Road. After passing the creamery on your left, turn left into Tomaig Road and continue till you come to a wooden gate. Cross over the stile and follow the track through the fields, crossing two more stiles, before you reach the Forest Enterprise sign which marks the start of the walk. It's about four miles there and back from the end of Tomaig road.

Excursions

One of the most popular day trips is to the uninhabited **Davaar Island**, connected to the peninsula by a tidal breakwater. Here you can see the cave painting of the Crucifixion, completed in secret by a local artist in 1877. The island can be visited at low tide from Kildalloig Point, a couple of miles east of town. Check tide times at the tourist office before setting out.

There's plenty of accommodation in town. There's the comfortable **C** *Ardshiel Hotel*, T552133, F551422, on Kilkerran Rd, or the **D** *White Hart Hotel*, T552440, F554972, on

Sleeping & eating

Argyll

Main St. Pick of the bunch is the **D** *Balegreggan Country House*, T/F552062, which is out of town on Balegreggan Rd. There are also several cheap **B&Bs**. Aside from the aforementioned hotels, the culinary scene is not worth mentioning.

Festivals If you're around at the end of **August**, don't miss the **Mull of Kintyre Music Festival**, 3 days of the best in traditional Celtic music, held in various venues throughout the town, with numerous impromptu pub sessions.

Sport **Horse riding** *Mull of Kintyre Equestrian Centre*, Homeston Farm (2 miles south on the B842 to Southend), T552437. Dinner, bed and breakfast also available.

Transport There are buses from Campbeltown to **Machrihanish** (hourly Mon-Sat, 3 on Sun; 15 mins), to **Carradale** (45 mins) and **Saddell** (4 daily Mon-Sat, 2 on Sun; 25 mins), to **Southend** (several daily; 25 mins), and also to the **airport** (2 daily Mon-Fri; 10 mins).

Machrihanish

Argyll

Phone code: 01586
Colour map 5, grid B2

Six miles from Campbeltown, on the west coast of Kintyre, is Machrihanish, site of Campbeltown's airport and a magnificent beach. Five miles of glorious unspoiled sand backed by dunes and washed by gigantic Atlantic breakers. Not surprisingly, this is a cracking place for **windsurfing** and **surfing**, one of the very best in the country. It also boasts a dramatic 18-hole championship golf course, whose first hole was described by Jack Nicklaus as the world's greatest opening hole. The beach can be approached either by walking north from the village, or south from the car park on the main A83 to Tayinloan and Tarbert, where it leaves the coast.

Sleeping There are a couple of options if you wish to stay here, the best of which is **D** *Ardell House Hotel*, overlooking the golf course, T/F810235. Open Mar-Oct, 10 rooms. Cheaper and simpler is **E** *Kilgour House*, T/F810233, which has a lively bar/restaurant next door. There's also a **campsite** at East Trodigal, T810366; open Mar-Sep, with full facilities. It's on the right just before the village heading west from Campbeltown.

Southend and the Mull of Kintyre

It's only a short drive south from Campbeltown to the tip of the peninsula, the Mull of Kintyre, eulogised by one-time resident Paul McCartney in the irritating eponymous hit single. There's nothing much to see in this bleak, storm-battered place, apart from the coast of Ireland, a mere 12 miles away and clearly visible on a good day. The road out to the lighthouse, built in 1788 and remodelled by Robert Stevenson, grandfather of Robert Louis, is pretty hairy, to put it mildly. It's possible to walk from here up to Machrihanish (about 10 miles), past the ruined township of Balmavicar and the Largiebaan Bird Reserve. The views are great and there's a chance of seeing Golden Eagles.

The southernmost village on Kintyre is **Southend**, a bleak, windswept place with a wide sandy beach. At the east end of the beach, jutting out on a rocky promontory, are the scant remains of **Dunaverty Castle**, once a MacDonald stronghold, where 300 Royalists were brutally massacred in 1647 by the Covenanting army of the Earl of Argyll, despite having already surrendered. To the west of Southend, below the cliffs, is the ruined 13th-century **Keil Chapel**, which is said to mark the spot where **St Columba** first set foot on Scottish soil, before heading north to Iona. Close by is a pair of footprints carved into the rock, known as **Columba's footprints**.

Should you wish to spend time here, there are a couple of good **B&Bs** in Southend, including **E** *Ormsary Farm*, T830665, open Apr-Sep.

The east coast

The slow and winding single track B842 meanders up the east coast from Campbeltown to Skipness and Claonaig, departure point for the ferry to Arran (see below). The scenery en route is gentle and pleasant with nice views of Arran, and there are some worthwhile places to stop, but public transport is somewhat limited (see Campbeltown 'Transport' above).

Ten miles up the coast are the idyllic ruins of **Saddell Abbey**, a Cistercian establishment, founded by Somerled in 1160. The abbey fell into ruin in the early 16th century and much of the stone was used in the building of Saddell Castle for the Bishop of Argyll. Though little remains, there are some impressive medieval grave slabs, depicting knights, monks, ships, animals and other images.

A few miles further north is the village of Carradale, the only place of any size on the east coast, nestling in the sandy sweep of beautiful Carradale Bay. There are several pleasant marked walks through the woods between the B842 and the shore. The shortest of these walks (with green waymarkers) starts from the Network Centre (see below) and is a mile long. There's a three-mile walk with red waymarkers which starts at the Port Na Storm car park and follows the forest road to the left. After 150 yards the route turns left again at the road junction. A mile further on, you turn right off the road and follow the track up to the summit of Cnoc-nan Gabhor, from where there are great views of Kintyre and across to Arran. A third walk (six miles; blue waymarkers) also starts from the Port Na Storm car park. This time the route heads right at the junction 150 yards beyond the car park and then runs north along the shore, with a chance of seeing dolphins and basking shark. The path then swings west towards the road, then turns south with views of Carradale Glen.

If the weather's bad, there's the **Network Carradale Heritage Centre**, which features displays of fishing, farming and forestry. ■ *Easter to mid-Oct Mon-Sat 1030-1700, Sun 1230-1600.* A little further north is the **Grogport Tannery**, which produces organically tanned, naturally coloured sheepskins. ■ *Daily 0900-1800.*

Twelve miles north of Carradale the B842 ends at **Claonaig**, which is actually nothing more than a slipway for the ferry to Arran (see below). From here, the B8001 heads west to meet the A83 near the Kennacraig ferry pier. A dead-end road runs north for a few miles to the tiny village of **Skipness**, where you can visit the substantial ruins of the 13th century **Skipness Castle** and nearby chapel. You might want to stop here and enjoy some fresh seafood or good home baking at the *Seafood Cabin*, T01880-760207, open daily end May-end September 1100-1800.

Carradale

Phone code: 01583
Colour map 5, grid B2

Argyll

Sleeping There are a couple of hotels in Carradale, including the **D** *Carradale Hotel*, T/F431223, which offers excellent food and a lively bar with a good selection of local malts and cask ales. There are also several **B&Bs** and a **campsite** at Carradale Bay with full facilities T431665; open Easter-Sep.

Isle of Arran

Phone code: 01770
Colour map 5, grid B3

In the wedge of sea between Ayrshire and Kintyre lies the oval-shaped and very beautiful island of Arran. It manages to combine the classic features of the North-west Highlands with the more sedate pleasures of the Southern Lowlands, thus earning the sobriquet, "Scotland in Miniature". This obvious appeal, coupled with its easy accessibility, makes Arran a very popular destination, but it remains unspoiled and at 25 miles long, is big enough to never feel crowded.

The island attracts all sorts of visitors: hill-walkers and climbers come to tackle the 10 summits over 2,000 feet and dozens of ridge routes; golfers are driven by their desire to play on no fewer than seven courses; the beaches of the southeast are popular with the bucket and spade brigade; and the island is a big hit with geology students, who come here in droves to marvel at the unique rock formations.

Although tourism has become Arran's main income earner, the island is large enough to sustain a relatively stable population of around 4,500, only slightly more than the number of red deer which roam wild in the beautiful mountain glens. Arran was tacked onto North Ayrshire in the recent local government reorganisation, but its geological, historical and cultural links are with the Highlands and Islands, hence its inclusion here.

Ins and outs

Getting there The main **ferry** route to Arran is from the distinctly unappealing Ayrshire town of Ardrossan to the island's main town, Brodick. The *CalMac* car/passenger ferry makes the 55 min journey 6 times daily Mon-Sat, 4 times on Sun. A 1-way fare costs £4.10 per passenger and £23.15 per car. A 'Day Saver' return (available Apr-Oct) costs £63 for a car and up to 4 passengers. There's a train connection between Ardrossan and Glasgow Central (5 times daily Mon-Sat, 4 times on Sun). There's also a bus connection to/from Edinburgh twice daily Mon-Sat. By **car**, from the south the main route to Arran is from the M74 motorway, on to the A71 via Kilmarnock, to Irvine and Ardrossan. For more ferry information, contact *Ardrossan ferry office*, T01294-463470, or *Brodick*, T01770-302166. There's also a car/passenger ferry to Brodick from **Rothesay**, on the island of Bute, a 2-hour journey. It sails once a day on Mon, Wed and Fri, in the summer only.

The other **ferry** route to Arran is from Claonaig, near Tarbert on Loch Fyne (see page 218), to Lochranza in the north of the island. The non-bookable car/passenger ferry makes the 30-min trip 8-11 times daily during the summer (Apr-Oct). A 1-way journey costs £3.80 per passenger and £17.15 per car. A 'Day Saver' return costs £42.50 for a car and up to 4 passengers. For ferry times, T0990-650000. For details of **bus** services to Claonaig, see page 218, or T01546-604695.

Getting around Fifty seven miles of main road run right around the coastline and pass through every village, making it easy to see much of the island by **car** in a short space of time. There are also two roads, "The String" and The Ross Road, which bisect the island. Arran is best appreciated on a **bike**, however, and for details of bike hire, see below under Brodick.

It's possible to explore the island using public transport, as there are regular **bus** and postbus services. There are regular daily buses from Brodick to Blackwaterfoot (30 mins) via "The String"; to Lamlash (10 mins) and Whiting Bay (25 mins) and on to Blackwaterfoot (1 hr 10 mins); to Corrie (20 mins), Sannox (25 mins), Lochranza (45 mins), Catacol (50 mins), Pirnmill (1 hr), Machrie (1 hr 10 mins) and Blackwaterfoot (1 hr 20 mins). There's also a postbus service from Brodick to Corrie, Sannox, Lochranza, Catacol, Pirnmill, Machrie, Blackwaterfoot and back to Brodick; and from Brodick to Lamlash, "The Ross", Kildonan, Whiting Bay and back to Brodick.

A rural daycard gives you unlimited travel on Arran for £3. For bus times and more information contact the tourist office in Brodick, where you can pick up a free copy of the *Arran Transport Guide*, or contact *Western Buses*, T302000, or *Royal Mail*, T01463-256200.

Brodick

The largest and busiest settlement on Arran, and main ferry port, is Brodick, lying in a wide bay (hence its Norse name *breidr vik*, meaning "broad bay") backed by a range of steep crags. It's not the most attractive village on the island, and consists of little more than one long street that sweeps round the bay, but you'll find a wide range of tourist facilities and services here. Brodick also makes a convenient base from which to explore the island, particularly if you intend climbing Goatfell, Arran's highest mountain, or walking in Glen Rosa (see page 230).

Tourist office Beside the ferry pier and bus terminal. ■ *T302140/302401, F302395. May-Sep Mon-Sat 0900-1930, Sun 1000-1700; Oct-Apr Mon-Sat 0900-1700.*

Sights A few miles north of town is the impressive **Brodick Castle**, one of the island's top sights and a flagship NTS property. Until recently, this was the family seat of the Dukes of Hamilton, erstwhile owners of the island. The oldest part of the

Argyll

Arran

castle dates from the 13th century, with extensions added in the 16th, 17th and 19th centuries. The hour-long tour of the sumptuously-furnished rooms and huge kitchens is very interesting and can perfectly rounded off with a visit to the Castle restaurant, where you can enjoy cheap and tasty, home-cooked meals or light snacks and excellent home baking. On a good day you even sit outside on the castle terrace and have lunch whilst admiring the views over Brodick Bay. The walled garden is also worth a look and the surrounding country park includes 11 miles of way-marked trails. ■ *T302202. Castle and restaurant open 1 Apr-30 Jun and 1 Sep-31 Oct, daily 1100-1630; 1 Jul-31 Aug, daily 1100-1700. Garden and country park open all year, daily 0930-sunset. £5 (£2.50 child); garden and country park only £2.50 (£1.70).*

Halfway between the village and the castle is the **Arran Heritage Museum**, which consists of a pile of old tools and furniture in a converted 18th century farm. Strictly for the enthusiast or the terminally bored. ■ *3 Apr-end of Oct, Mon-Sat 1000-1700. £1.50, 75p child.*

Sleeping Brodick boasts some pretty high-class accommodation, the best of which is the **B** *Kilmichael Country House Hotel*, T302219, F302068. 9 rooms. Take the road north to the castle, turn left at the golf course and follow the signs for about a mile. Refined elegance and gracious living in the heart of the countryside in the island's oldest house. Their award-winning restaurant is quite simply the best on the island, and that's really saying something, and booking is essential for non-residents.

Just beyond the turning to Kilmichael is the road leading to **B-C** *Auchrannie Country House Hotel*, T302234, F302812. 28 rooms (also self-catering and time-share lodges). May lack the charm of *Kilmichael* but makes up for it with superb facilities and state-of-the-art leisure complex. Their *Garden Restaurant* is also highly-rated and the popular *Brambles Bistro* offers less expensive bar meals.

There are several hotels closer to the ferry along the seafront, and best of these is the **D** *Dunvegan House Hotel*, T/F302811, which offers good quality cooking for residents only. There is also plentiful **B&B** accommodation, including the secluded **E** *Glen Cloy Farmhouse*, Glen Cloy Rd, T302351, open Mar-Oct, which is a cut above the rest, or the consistently-good **E** *Tigh-na-Mara*, on the seafront, T302538, open Apr-Oct. The nearest **campsite** is *Glen Rosa*, T302380, open Apr-Oct, two miles from town on the road to Blackwaterfoot.

Eating Aside from the hotels, and the castle restaurant, mentioned above there's the excellent *Creelers Seafood Restaurant*, at the Home Farm, a mile or so north of town on the road to the castle, T302810. Some of the best seafood in the whole country served in an informal atmosphere. Taste their Scandinavian smoked salmon and die. Cheap lunch specials and moderate 3-course dinners on Tue only. For a cheaper alternative try the *Brodick Bar*, behind *Wooley's bakery* and opposite the post office. Superior pub grub served in the bar or restaurant next door at cheap-mid-range prices.

Shopping Arran has an enviable reputation for producing fine foods and at *Home Farm*, just north of the village, are a couple of places you won't want to miss if you're looking for a tasty souvenir. The *Island Cheese Company*, T302788, produces a range of cheeses for sale, including soft cheeses, flavoured cheddars and the famous Arran Blue Cheese. You can also watch the whole process of cheese making. On the opposite side of the courtyard is *Creelers Smokehouse*, T302797, where you can find a vast range of delicious smoked fish, shellfish, poultry and game, and an excellent restaurant (see Eating above). Next door is *Arran Aromatics*, T302595, open daily 0930-1730, which produces a wide range of unique and beautifully-packaged natural soaps and body care products. A rare treat for the olfactory organ.

On the main street is the excellent *Wooley's of Arran*, a highly-acclaimed bakers producing great rolls and their own oatcakes. For more basic provisions, there's the *Co-op supermarket* near the ferry terminal.

Cycle hire *Mini Golf Cycle Hire*, T302272, F302903, *Brodick Cycles*, T/F302460, and *Brodick Boat & Cycle Hire*, T302868, are all on the seafront and all charge around £9 per day for mountain bikes. **Sport**

Banks The *Bank of Scotland* and *Royal Bank* are both on the seafront, both with ATMs. **Directory**
Communications Post office: Just off the seafront, opposite the petrol station and pharmacy.

The South

The south of Arran is a fertile landscape of rolling hills and pretty little seaside villages. Here you'll find the bulk of the island's population and tourists.

A few miles south of Brodick is Lamlash, a quiet and attractive place set in a wide, sheltered bay but with an unappealing mud beach. Lying just offshore is the humpbacked **Holy Island**, which is owned by a group of Scottish Buddhists (or MacBuddhists), who have retired here for peace and meditation. A ferry runs to and from the island several times daily from 1 May to 4 September (limited service 5 September to 30 October), and costs £6 return. The first ferry departs Lamlash at 1000 and the last one returns at 1700, leaving you just enough time to climb up to the highest point, **Mullach Mór** (1,030 feet). Boats can be hired for **fishing trips** from the pier, T600998 or 600349. For fishing supplies or information on **scuba diving**, contact *Johnson's Marine Stores* at the Old Pier, T600333. **Lamlash**

The main reason for visiting Lamlash is the excellent *Arran Fine Foods*, at the Old Mill, at the southern entrance to the village, T600606. Here you'll find a mouth-watering selection of locally-produced mustards, preserves and chutneys. Don't leave Arran without them!

Sleeping & eating The **C** *Glen Isle Hotel*, T600559, does a good, moderately-priced 3-course dinner. Otherwise there's the **D** *Lilybank Guest House*, T600230, which also serves good food. There are several cheaper **B&B** options and also a **campsite** T600251, open mid-Apr to mid-Oct, a short way south of town.

The best place to eat by far is the superb *Carraig Mhor Restaurant*, T600453, whose Austrian chef specializes in local seafood. Open for dinner only (1900-2130), closed Sun. Booking is essential. Moderate-expensive.

Down in the southeast of Arran, Whiting Bay enjoys a beautiful setting and makes a pleasant alternative to Brodick as an island base with some good accommodation and restaurants. Whiting Bay is also the starting point for the lovely walk up to **Glenashdale Falls** (see page 231230). **Whiting Bay**

Sleeping & eating **C-B** *Argentine House Hotel*, T700662, F700693, argentine.hotel@ arrandial.pipex.com. Five rooms, on the seafront and easily recognisable by the flags flying outside, Swiss owners are friendly, hospitable and professional, excellent cooking with a continental touch. Dinner is also available to non-residents but booking is essential. **C-D** *Burlington Hotel*, T700255, F700232, burlhotel@aol.com. Nine rooms, open Easter-Oct, comfortable rooms and a reputation for superb seafood, moderately-priced set 3-course dinner in dining room or a la carte in bistro.

There are also **B&Bs** and **guesthouses**, such as the lovely **D** *Grange House*, T/F700263; open mid-Mar to end-Oct, and a *SYHA Youth Hostel* on the seafront by the bridge, T700339; open end-Feb to end-Oct.

A cheaper alternative to the hotels mentioned above is the *Coffee Pot* on Golf Course Rd, T700382, where you can enjoy tasty but cheap snacks and home baking. Open daily Easter-Oct, 1000-1700 (Jul/Aug 1000-1900).

Transport Car hire/taxis/island tours *Whiting Bay Garage*, T/F700345. **Cycle hire** *Whiting Bay Hires*, on the jetty, T700382.

South of Whiting Bay The main road runs south from Whiting Bay, then swings west along the south coast of Arran, with great views south across to the distinctive mound of Ailsa Craig, lying off the coast of South Ayrshire.

There are some good sandy beaches along this stretch, particularly at **Kildonan**, a village set back off the main road and with a ruined castle looking out to the island of **Pladda**. Anyone with a sudden urge to throw themselves off the nearest cliff can try their hand at **paragliding**, at *Flying Fever*, No 2 Coastguard House in Kildonan, T820292. A half day course costs £30 and full day is £50.

About four miles west of Kildonan are the tiny villages of **Torrylinn**, **Lagg** and **Kilmory**, where you can stop off at the **Torrylinn Creamery** to buy some excellent local cheese and watch it being made, T/F870240, open daily 1000-1600. You can stay here at the **C** *Lagg Hotel*, T870255, an 18th century coaching inn set in acres of woodland by the river, or at the local **campsites**, at *Breadalbane Lodge*, T820210, and *Kildonan Hotel*, T820207, where there's also a **bunkhouse**.

Just beyond these villages the Ross Road branches off northeast up Glen Scorrodale to Lamlash. The A841 meanwhile continues north to Blackwaterfoot, on the southwest coast.

Blackwaterfoot The little fishing village of Blackwaterfoot is set round an attractive bay with a tiny harbour – smaller than some people's jacuzzis. The village maintains its quiet charm, even at the height of the summer, and is the ideal place to escape the crowds and enjoy some peace and quiet.

There's plenty to do around these parts. Two miles north along the coast are the **King's Caves**, where, according to legend, Robert the Bruce watched a spider try, try and try again and was thus inspired to secure his own and Scotland's destiny. It's a 20-minute walk from where you leave the car to the cathedral-like main cave which has an iron gate to keep out wandering sheep.

There's also **pony trekking** at *Cairnhouse Riding Centre*, T860466, which caters for beginners and experienced riders, and **fly fishing**, at *Port-Na-Lochan Fishery* (contact the *Kinloch Hotel*, see below).

A couple of miles northeast of Blackwaterfoot, at **Shiskine**, on the "String Road" which cuts across the middle of the island to Brodick, is the **Balmichael Visitor Centre**, it's a good place to bring the kids, with a motor museum, adventure playground and a quad bike track. ■ *T860430. Mon-Sat 1000-1700, Sun 1200-1700.*

Four miles north of Blackwaterfoot, off the main coast road, is **Machrie Moor**, site of the most impressive of Arran's Bronze Age **stone circles**. Park by the Historic Scotland sign and then walk for one and a half miles along the farm track to reach an area boasting no fewer than six stone circles. Many of them are barely visible above the ground, but the tallest is over 18 ft high.

A few miles further on, just south of the turn-off to Machrie village, is another Historic Scotland sign, this time for **Moss Farm Road Stone Circle**, which lies about a half mile walk along the farm track. There's another Bronze Age site nearby, at **Auchagallon**.

Sleeping There are a couple of options should you wish to stay here. **B-C** *Kinloch Hotel*, T860444, F860447, Kinloch@cqm.co.uk. The largest hotel on the island with 51 rooms and full leisure facilities including swimming pool, sauna, gym and squash court. The are also plenty of **B&Bs**, which are cheaper and of rather more modest proportions, including **E** *Morvern House*, T860254.

The North

The north half of Arran contrasts sharply with the southern part. It looks and feels more like the Scottish Highlands – desolate, unspoiled and much of it accessible only to the serious hill-walker. But though the north is scenically more spectacular, it attracts relatively few visitors.

Six miles north of Brodick is Arran's loveliest village, Corrie; a row of perfect, whitewashed fishermen's cottages lining the seafront. Corrie has a couple of hotels and B&Bs, a good pub, and makes an attractive alternative to Brodick as a starting point for the ascent of Goatfell (see page 230230).

    The main coastal road continues north from Corrie to **Sannox,** with its sandy beach, then it cuts inland and climbs steeply northwest towards Lochranza. It's worth taking your time on this part of the road to admire the wonderful views of the mountains and on the other side of the pass, in **Glen Chalmadale**, you can see red deer heading down to the shore at dusk.

Corrie

Sleeping **D** *Tigh-na-Achaidh*, T810208. Three rooms, superior B&B with sea views. **E** *Corrie Hotel*, T810273. Friendly, unassuming and good value with a lively bar. **E** *Blackrock Guest House*, T810282. Open Mar-Oct.

The most spectacular introduction to Arran is to arrive at Lochranza, the most northerly village and second ferry port. This charming village is guarded by its ruined 13th-century castle and backed by looming mountains. **Lochranza Castle** can be visited free of charge (the key is available from the Lochranza Stores).

    Lochranza is also the site of Scotland's newest distillery, **Isle of Arran Distillers**, which opened in 1995 and is the first legal whisky distillery on the island for over 150 years. There are guided tours of the distillery, followed by the obligatory dram, and also an excellent restaurant (see below). ■ *T830264, www.arranwhisky.com. Daily 1000-1700 Apr-Oct. £3.50, £2.50 child*.

    A couple of miles southwest of Lochranza is the tiny village of **Catacol**, whose whitewashed cottages are know as 'The Twelve Apostles'. Here, the bar of the *Catacol Bay Hotel* serves good, cheap pub food and also puts on live music, as well as hosting a week-long **folk festival** in early June.

Lochranza

Sleeping & eating Lochranza has a decent selection of places to stay, best of which is **D** *Apple Lodge*, T/F830229. A lovely country house with four double rooms, offering high quality home cooking (for residents only). Around the same price but lacking the charm, is **D** *Lochranza Hotel*, T830223, whose bar is the social hub of the village. A cheaper option is **E** *Castlekirk*, T830202, a converted church opposite the castle, or the slightly austere **E** *Benvaren*, T830647. Cheaper still is the *SYHA Youth Hostel*, T830631, open Feb-Dec, overlooking the castle. There's a beautifully-situated **campsite** next to the golf course, with full facilities, T820273, office@ lochgolf.demon.co.uk, open Apr-Oct.

    The best place to eat is *Harold's Restaurant*, T830264, arranvc@aol.com, on the upper floor of the distillery visitor centre. Here you can enjoy innovative Scottish/Caribbean cuisine in bright, modern surroundings. Open till 2100. Mid-range prices (cheap lunch menu). The only alternative is the *Lochranza Hotel* which does cheap bar meals.

𝄐 Walks on Arran

OS map No 69 covers these walks. Ask local advice during the deer stalking season (late Aug to late Oct).

Arran is a hill walker's paradise. The north part of the island boasts ten peaks of over 2,000 feet and dozens of ridge walks while the gentler south features a variety of less strenuous forest walks.

Note that you should only attempt these routes in good weather and avoid climbing any rockfaces. Some ridge walks (A'Chir, Witches Step, Suidhe Fherghas and Cioch Na Oighe) involve quite a lot of scrambling and should only be attempted by fit and experienced climbers.

Goatfell Arran's most popular peak, Goatfell, is also its highest, at 2,866 feet. There's a path leading up from Corrie, but most people begin the walk from the car park at **Cladach sawmill**, near Brodick Castle. The path is well marked, easy to follow and, apart from the final section, relatively easy. It runs initially through the **Brodick Country Park**, then follows the **Cnocan burn** as it rises steadily through woodland before crossing the **Mill burn**. Beyond the burn is a deer fence which runs across the entire island to keep the deer from the north away from the farming in the south. Above the deer fence the landscape changes to heather moorland and the path begins to climb the flanks of the mountain. The final 650 feet up to the top is steep and rocky and the path is not always clear. The last section requires some scrambling on loose scree but the views that greet you at the top on a clear day are magnificent, stretching right across from Ireland to Mull.

The walk to the summit and back should take about five hours. Though it's considered a fairly straightforward ascent, remember that this should be treated with the same caution and respect as any Scottish mountain. You should be dressed and equipped appropriately and be prepared for any sudden change in the weather. There are also numerous ridge walks around Goatfell as well as other high peaks to climb.

Glen Rosa Many of the walks start from **Glen Rosa Farm**. One of these takes in the three Bheinns; **Beinn Nuis**, **Beinn Tarsuinn** (2,681 feet) and **Beinn A'Chliabhain**. Start at Glen Rosa Farm and go up the Wood Road to the High Deer Gate, then to Torr Breac and the 'Y' junction at the top of the Garbhalt and on to the path which runs round the Three Beinns. This is a full day's walk.

Another excellent walk is from Glen Rosa to the head of the Glen; then take the path up into the **Coire Buidhe** and onto the ridge between **Cir Mhor** (2,617 feet) and **A'Chir** (known as the **Ceems Ridge**). Then follow the path around the west side of A'Chir. This is not easy to find, but takes you around the back of A'Chir to **Bowman's Pass** and the north end of **Beinn Tarsuinn**. From here take the path to **Beinn A'Chliabhan** and down to the foot of **Garbhalt Ridge** and back down to Glen Rosa.

Cir Mhor can also be climbed from Glen Rosa. Before going over into Glen Sannox take the steep path straight up. On the way back down, head into Coire Buidhe and back down the glen. You can also continue from the top of Cir Mhor and take the path around the west side of A'Chir to the north end of the Bowman's Pass up onto Beinn Tarsuinn and along the ridge to Beinn Nuis, then down the path to the Garbhalt Bridge.

Finally, you can also climb **Caisteal Abhail** (2,818 feet) from Glen Rosa. Go straight up into Coire Buidge on to the Ceems Ridge. Then take the path round the west side of the A'Chir through the Bowman's Pass and on to Beinn A'Chliabhain down the side of the Garbhalt to Glen Rosa.

There are also several walks in and around lovely Glen Sannox. It's a pleasant walk just to head up the head of the Glen and return the same way. You can walk up the Glen to beyond the old mine then make your way up towards the **Devil's Punchbowl** until you reach the main path and follow that down into the Coire. Take the main path back down into Glen Sannox instead of trying to climb out of the Devil's Punchbowl. You can also walk from **Glen Sannox** to **Glen Rosa**, which takes around four hours.

Glen Sannox

This is one of the most popular walks on the island. It's a steady, easy climb through woodland with the considerable incentive of a beautiful waterfall at the end of it. Both walks can be done together and should take around two to three hours in total, though you should allow some time to enjoy the falls. If you want to take a picnic, then pop into the Village Shop which has a wide range of deli-type foods and local cheeses.

The Giants' Graves & Glenashdale Falls

The trail starts by the bridge over **Glenashdale Burn**, next to the Youth Hostel. There's a map board here showing the route. Walk up the track alongside the burn till you see the sign for the path leading to the left up to the **Giants' Graves**. It's about 40-45 minutes up to the graves and back to this point, but it's a stiff climb up a steep staircase of 265 steps. At the top continue left along a path through the trees, which then curves right till you reach a clearing and the graves, which are chambered tombs, believed to be around 5,000 years old. Depending on the light, this can be a very eerie, but almost magical place.

Return back down the steps, and head left along the main path as it climbs steadily above the burn, past smaller falls, till you reach the main falls. The setting is stunning and the falls are spectacular as they plummet 140 feet into the pools below. You can rest and have a picnic at the top of the falls, or follow the paths down to the pools below which you can swim.

The path back down to **Whiting Bay** passes the scant remains of an **Iron Age fort**, then turns back uphill to reach a broad track. Turn right, cross a small burn by stepping stones, then follow the track downhill all the way to the main road, a short way along from the car park.

Glenashdale Falls & Giants' Graves

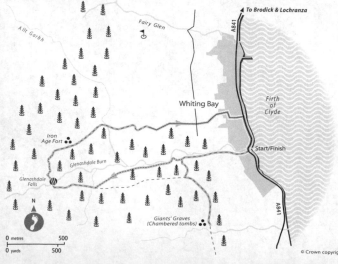

Argyll

Inner Hebrides

6

Inner Hebrides

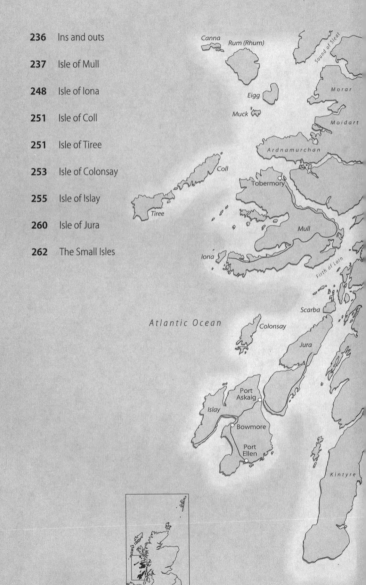

Canna
Rum (Rhum)
Sound of Sleat
Eigg
Morar
Muck
Moidart
Ardnamurchan
Coll
Tobermory
Tiree
Mull
Firth of Lorn
Iona
Scarba
Atlantic Ocean
Colonsay
Jura
Port Askaig
Islay
Bowmore
Port Ellen
Kintyre

© Crown copyri

The Inner Hebrides comprise the great swathe of islands lying off the western coast of Scotland – east of the Outer Hebrides, south of Skye and west of the Kintyre peninsula. Each is very different in appearance and atmosphere and each has its own unique appeal.

The most accessible of the islands is **Mull**, a short ferry ride from Oban. It's also the most popular by far, and with some justification. The variety of scenery on offer is astounding and its capital, Tobermory, is the most attractive port in western Scotland. A stone's throw from Mull is tiny **Iona**, one of the most important religious sites in Europe, whose abbey attracts hordes of pilgrims all year round. Boat trips can be made from Mull or Iona to the dramatic island of **Staffa**, looming out the sea like a great cathedral and the inspiration for Mendelssohn's 'Hebrides Overture'. Further west, windswept **Coll** and **Tiree** offer miles of unspoilt beaches and some great windsurfing and, to the south, **Colonsay** is a stress-free zone that makes Mull seem hectic.

Those who enjoy a good malt whisky should head for **Islay**. There are over half a dozen distilleries on this attractive island, as well as a rich variety of wildlife, while neighbouring **Jura**, famous for its three shapely mountains, the Paps of Jura, is a wild and beautiful place, perfect for some off-the-beaten-track hiking. If you're after some peace and quiet on Jura then you're in good company, for this where George Orwell came to write '1984'. Furthest north are the "small islands" of **Eigg**, **Muck**, **Rùm** and **Canna**, reached from Mallaig, but ignored my most tourists. People come here for the fine bird watching and superb walking.

Ins and outs

Getting there There are flights from Glasgow to Port Ellen (**Islay**): 2 daily Mon-Fri and 1 on Sat (40 mins), all year round. From Glasgow to **Tiree**: 1 flight daily Mon-Sat (45 mins) all year round. For flight times, call *British Airways Express*, T0345-222111, the local **tourist offices**, or Port Ellen airport, T01496-302022, and Tiree airport, T01879-220309.

CalMac car and passenger **ferries** sail to and from Mull, Islay, Coll, Tiree, Colonsay and Gigha, and passenger-only ferries sail to Iona and the Small Isles (Eigg, Muck, Rùm and Canna). Ferry times change according to the day of the week and time of the year, so they aren't listed in full below. Services listed below under each separate island are for the summer period (2 Apr-16 Oct). For full details see the *CalMac* Ferry Guide or call *CalMac*; T0990-650000, reservations@calmac.co.uk (reservations) T01475-650100, www.calmac.co.uk (general enquiries). Car space is limited during the summer months, so it's advisable to book ahead. For details of bus connections from Oban to Glasgow, contact *Scottish Citylink*, T0990-505050. For train services from Mallaig to Fort William and Glasgow, contact *Scotrail*, T0345-484950. See also 'Essentials', page 41.

The departure point for ferries to Mull, Coll, Tiree and Colonsay is **Oban**. There are regular daily **train** and **bus** services from Glasgow. For full details, see under Oban (page 205), or contact the tourist office in Oban, T01631-563122. The departure point for ferries to Islay (and on to Jura), and some ferries to Colonsay, is **Kennacraig**. There are daily bus services from Glasgow, via Tarbert (see page 218). **Mallaig** is the ferry port for the Small Isles of Eigg, Muck, Rùm and Canna. There are regular bus and train services from Glasgow, via Fort William (see page 443).

For bus, train and ferry times, pick up a copy of Argyll & Bute Council's free *Area Transport Guides* to Lorn, Mull and *Islay & Jura*, which is available at most tourist offices. For times of buses and trains to Mallaig, for the Small Isles, see the *South Highland Public Transport Travel Guide* which costs £1 and is available at main tourist offices. For details on how to get around the Inner Hebrides by public transport, see under the relevant island destination.

Getting around **Island Hopscotch Tickets** are a cheaper way to get around the islands with a **car**. There are various route options and tickets give you 30 days unlimited travel on each route. For example, a ticket for the Oban-Craignure Tobermory-Kilchoan Mallaig-Armadale route, allowing you to visit Mull and Skye, costs £8.30 per passenger and £50 per car. See the *CalMac* guide or call the numbers above for full details of the Island Hopscotch Tickets, and the **Island Rover Ticket**, which gives unlimited travel on most *CalMac* routes for 8 or 15 days.

Orientation & information There are **Tourist offices** in Oban (see page 205), Craignure and Tobermory (Mull), Bowmore (Islay), and Mallaig (see page 443). Oban tourist office has information on all the islands covered in this chapter, with the exception of the Small Isles, information on which can be got from Mallaig tourist office.

Isle of Mull

The island of Mull is the third largest of the Hebridean islands and, after Skye, the most popular. Everyone has their own particular favourite island, but Mull has enough going for it to appeal to most tastes: spectacular mountain scenery, 300 miles of wild coastline, castles, wildlife, a narrow-gauge railway, some of the best fishing in Scotland and some of the prettiest little villages, all in an area roughly 24 miles from north to south and 26 miles from east to west. It's worth spending time on Mull to really appreciate its pleasures, and take advantage of the great hospitality of an island where people don't lock their doors at night.

Colour map 3, grid B3/4

Ins and outs

Mull is one of the most accessible of the Hebridean islands and well served by **ferry** services. From Oban to Craignure (40 mins) 6-8 times daily Mon-Sat and 5 times daily on Sun. One way ticket costs £3.35 per passenger and £23.35 per car. *CalMac* offices: Oban, T01631-566688, and Craignure, T01680-812343. From Kilchoan to Tobermory 7 times daily Mon-Sat and 5 times daily on Sun (Jun-Aug). One way ticket costs £3.20 per passenger and £17.15 per car. From Lochaline to Fishnish (15 mins) hourly 0700-1910 Mon-Sat and 0900-1800 Sun. One way ticket costs £2 per passenger and £9.15 per car. Some ferries from Oban to Coll and Tiree call in at Tobermory.

Getting there

You can get to most parts of the island by **bus**. Services given below are for Apr-Oct. Winter services are less frequent. There's a bus from Tobermory post office to Dervaig and Calgary, 5 times a day Mon-Fri and twice on Sat (operated by *RN Carmichael*, T01688-302220). The Craignure to Tobermory via Salen service runs 5 times a day

Getting around

Inner Hebrides

Mull

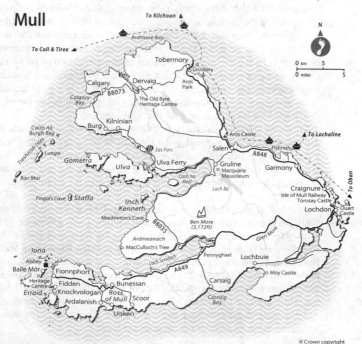

© Crown copyright

Mon-Fri, 8 times on Sat and 3 times on Sun (operated by *Bowman's Coaches*, T01680-812313, and *Highlands & Islands Coaches*, T01680-812510). There's a bus from Craignure to Fionnphort (for Iona) 6 times a day Mon-Fri, 4 times on Sat and 1 on Sun (Bowman's and Highlands & Islands). There's also a postbus service from Salen to Burg (Kilninian) via the Ulva Ferry twice a day Mon-Sat (*Royal Mail*, T01463-256200). For bus times, contact the operators or pick up a free copy of the *Mull Area Transport Guide* at the tourist office in Oban, Tobermory or Craignure. This also includes ferry times.

The island's 140 miles of **roads** are almost all single-track and mostly in poor condition, so allow plenty of time to get from place to place. The best sections are from Craignure to Salen and the few miles south from Tobermory towards Salen. Petrol stations are few and far between, so it's best to fill up before leaving Oban, on arrival in Craignure, or in Tobermory. Another point worth noting is that the sheep on Mull are even more fearless and stubborn than in other parts of the Highlands & Islands and regard the roads very much as their own, which can slow you down even more.

Cycling is a good way to get around and there are a number of places to rent bikes. In Tobermory there's *Tom-a' Mhuillin* on the Salen Rd, T01688-302164, or try the youth hostel (see page 242). In **Salen** there's *On Yer Bike*, T01680-300501, which also has a shop by the ferry terminal in **Craignure**, T01680-812487. Expect to pay around £8-10 per day.

Climate The best time to visit is generally May and Jun and late Aug to Sept. At these times midges and clegs (horse flies) are not so much of a problem. But Mull is the wettest of the Hebridean islands and rain can fall at any time, even in the summer months, so you'll need to come prepared.

History and background

Like many of the Hebridean islands, the people of Mull, or *Muileachs*, suffered greatly during the Clearances, when they were forced off their land to make way for sheep. The subsequent decline in population was exacerbated by the terrible potato famine of 1846 and the population fell dramatically from a peak of 10,600 in 1820. Numbers have stabilized to around 2,500 in recent years, mainly through the replacement of native islanders by English and Scottish incomers, known as 'White Settlers'. This is something of a sore point and the locals sarcastically refer to their island as 'The Officer's Mess', when the resident population rises to around 8,000 during the summer.

With around 600,000 visitors a year, tourism is an important contributor to the island's economy, supplementing the traditional fishing, crofting and whisky distilling. Despite the numbers, Mull remains unspoiled, though the main roads become congested at the height of the season and accommodation can be hard to find, as there are few large hotels or campsites on the island.

Festivals & events on Mull A great time to be on Mull is during the annual **Mull Music Festival**, held on the last weekend of April, when you can enjoy a feast of Gaelic folk music. The focus of the festival is the bar of the *Mishnish Hotel* in Tobermory (for details T01688-302383). Another great musical event is the **Mendelssohn on Mull Festival**, held over ten days in early July to commemorate the famous composer's visit here in 1829. On 22 July are the **Tobermory Highland Games**. Rally enthusiasts should not miss the **Tour of Mull Rally** held in early October, which is part of the Scottish Championship. Anyone who's complained about the state of Mull's roads (and who hasn't?) should watch the professionals hurtle around the island at over 60 miles per hour!

Craignure and around

The arrival point for most visitors is Craignure, little more than a row of houses scattered along the seafront. Directly opposite the pier is the **tourist office**, T812337, in the same building as the *CalMac* office. ■ *Easter-end Oct Mon-Thur and Sat 0900-1900 (Sat till 2015 in Jul/Aug), Fri 0900-1700, Sun 1030-1700 (till 1900 Jun-Aug).*

Phone code: 01680

Not far from the pier, on the main road heading south, is **D** *Craignure Inn*, T812306. Three rooms, open all year, it's cosy bar serves decent cheap-moderately priced food and is a good place to seek refuge on a wet day. There are also several **guesthouses** and **B&Bs** around Craignure, all in the **E** category (details from the tourist office). A little further south of the *Craignure Inn*, on the opposite side, is the turning to *Shielings Holiday Campsite*, T812496, which is beside the terminal for the little steam railway to Torosay Castle (see below). As well as a campsite with full facilities, there's accommodation in self-catering "shielings", which are carpeted cottage tents (**F**).

On the north side of the ferry pier is the *Ceilidh Place* restaurant, T812471, a general store and post office. Next to the tourist office is a craft shop where you can rent cars or bikes, and there's also a garage on the road to Torosay Castle.

Three miles south of Craignure, at Lochdon, is **D** *Old Mill Guest House & Restaurant*, T/F812442. Three rooms, their cosy little restaurant has a deserved reputation for fine cuisine, so you'll need to book in advance.

Sleeping & eating

One and a half miles south of Craignure is **Torosay Castle**, more of a baronial family home than a full-blown castle. Inside everything is informal and, refreshingly, there are invitations to sit down, or touch things, or even look through old family scrapbooks. There is some fine Edwardian furniture and paintings by Landseer and Sargent. The real attraction is though, the fabulous garden, designed by Lorimer, especially the Italianate statue walk. In the castle grounds you can watch traditional weaving methods at the **Isle of Mull Weavers**, or visit the gallery and workshops of **Kells gold and Silversmiths**, T812526, open daily 0900-1800. You can walk to the castle along a forest path starting just to the south of Craignure, but the best way to arrive at the castle is by the **Mull and West Highland Railway**. The little steam and diesel engine pulls the miniature carriages along the narrow-gauge track on the 20 minute journey from Craignure. ■ *The castle is open Easter-mid Oct daily 1030-1730. T812421. Gardens open all year daily 0900-1900. Admission to house and gardens £4.50, £1.50 child; gardens only £3.50, child £1. Free parking, tearoom and shop. Isle of Mull Weavers open daily all year 0900-1700. Free. Mull and West Highland Railway open Easter-mid Oct (T812494 for times). Fares: £2.30 adult single, £3.30 return.*

Torosay & Duart Castles

A couple of miles east of Torosay is **Duart Castle**. The 13th century ancestral seat of the Clan Maclean stands imperiously at the end of a promontory, commanding impressive views over Loch Linnhe and the Sound of Mull. The castle's main feature is the tower house, built in the late 14th century when it became the main residence of the Macleans of Duart. Mull belonged to the clan until it was forfeited when the Macleans supported young Prince Charles Edward Stuart, who was defeated at Culloden in 1746. The castle was deserted for the next century and a half, then in 1911, Colonel Sir Fitzroy Donald Maclean, chief of the clan, bought the castle from Murray Guthrie of Torosay and restored it as the clan chief's residence. Today, it's a fascinating place to visit, with many relics and artifacts on display. There's also an excellent tearoom serving delicious home-baked scones. ■ *May-mid Oct daily 1030-1800. T812309. £3.50, £1.75 child.*

Salen

Phone code: 01680

Midway between Craignure and Tobermory on the main A849 is the pretty wee village of Salen. It stands on the east coast at the narrowest point on the island, and is only three miles from the west coast, making it a good base from which to explore the island. Bicycles can be hired from *On Yer Bike* (T300501) for around £10 per day.

There are a couple of interesting sights around Salen. Just to the north, overlooking the bay, is the ruin of **Aros Castle**, built in the 14th century and one of the strongholds of the Lords of the Isles. Tradition holds that the treasure of the Spanish galleon sunk in Tobermory Bay in 1588 (see page 240) was recovered by the Macleans and still lies buried beneath the ruins of Aros Castle.

Four miles southwest of Salen, near **Gruline** and **Loch Ba**, is the **MacQuarrie Mausoleum**, which houses the remains of Major-General Lachlan MacQuarrie (1761-1824). He took over as Governer-General of New South Wales from the unpopular William Bligh, formerly of the *Bounty*, and became known as the "Father of Australia". The mausoleum is maintained by the National Trust of Scotland, on behalf of the National Trust of Australia.

Wildlife tours can be made from Aros, just to the north of Salen, with Richard Atkinson at *Island Encounter Wildlife Safaris*, Arla-Beag, Aros, T300441. Full-day wildlife safaris with a local guide cost £22 including lunch. You'll see golden eagles, white-tailed sea eagles, hen harriers, divers, merlins, peregrine falcons, seals and porpoises to name but a few.

Sleeping & eating

The best place by far is **A** *Killiechronan Hotel*, set in its own 5,000 acre estate, 3 miles west of Salen on the shores of Loch na Keal, T300403, F300463. Six rooms, open Mar-Oct, includes dinner, this old lodge house is the last word in comfort and elegance, and the food isn't bad either. In the village itself is **D-E** *Salen Hotel*, T300324, F300599. Eleven rooms, open all year. Near the MacQuarrie Mausoleum, at Gruline, is **D-E** *Gruline Home Farm*, T300581, F300573. There are also several **B&Bs** in and around Salen, mostly in the **E** category. About 5 miles south, just before the turn-off to the Fishnish to Lochaline Ferry, is *Balmeanach Park Caravan & Campsite*, with full facilities, and *Cynthia's Tearoom*, T300342, which serves snacks, lunches and a cheap to mid-range 3-course dinner. In the village itself is *The Puffer Aground*, T300389; closed Sun and Mon, which does very good cheap meals and snacks.

Tobermory

Phone code: 01688
Population: 800

There is no prettier port in the west of Scotland than Tobermory, Mull's main village, which is set on the side of a steep hill in a wooded, sheltered bay. The brightly-painted houses that line the harbour front date from the late 18th century when the British Fisheries Society built Tobermory as a planned herring port. It never really took off as a fishing port, however, and nowadays you're more likely to see pleasure yachts anchored in the protected waters of the natural harbour. Lying at the bottom of the harbour is a galleon of the Spanish Armada (the *San Juan de Sicilia* or *Florencia*). In 1588, the galleon was blown up and sank in mysterious circumstances, along with its treasure of gold doubloons, which has eluded salvage crews ever since.

Tourist office In the same building as the *CalMac* ticket office, at the far end of Main St. ■ *T302182. Apr Mon-Fri 0900-1700, Sat-Sun 1000-1700; May-Jun Mon-Fri 0900-1730, Sat-Sun 1000-1700; Jul-Sept Mon-Sat 0900-1800, Sun 1000-1700; Oct Mon-Sat 0900-1700, Sun 1000-1600.*

Sights

The harbour front – known as **Main Street** – is where you'll find most of what you want: hotels, guesthouses, restaurants, pubs and shops and the tourist office. Mercifully, though, it's free from the tartan tat that blights so many other tourist hot-spots. Here you'll find the **Mull Museum**, housed in an old bakery. It's worth visiting on a rainy day and you'll learn all about the island's history. ■ *Mon-Fri 1030-1630, Sat 1030-1330. £1.* At the foot of the main road down to the harbour is the tiny **Tobermory Distillery** which offers a guided tour rounded off with a sampling of the island's single malt. ■ *T302645. Easter to end-Oct, Mon-Fri 1000-1700; £2.50.* At the top of Back Brae, on Argyll Terrace, is **An Tobar**, the new arts centre housed in an old schoolhouse and featuring a varied programme of exhibitions, music and workshops. Or you can just have a coffee and admire the view. ■ *T302211/302218. Mon-Sat all year 1000-1800.*

Tobermory

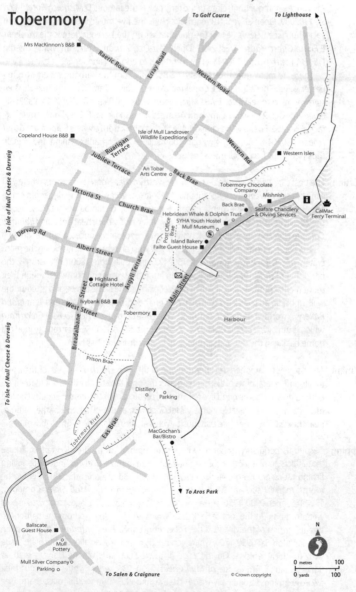

Inner Hebrides

Sleeping

The tourist office can book you into a B&B for a small fee.

The accommodation on Main Street tends to be a bit more expensive than that in the higher part of the village, but it saves you the steep walk uphill after the obligatory night in the *Mish* (see below).

L *Western Isles Hotel*, T302012, F302297. 23 rooms. Open all year, the biggest and grandest hotel on the island, set high above the harbour with great views from the comfortable rooms, has 3 excellent restaurants, including the lovely conservatory bar.

C *Tobermory Hotel*, 53 Main St, T302091, F302254. Good value and great location. Also on the harbour front, close to the ferry port is the famous **D** *Mishnish Hotel*, Main St, T302009. Open all year, 10 rooms. Its bar is the live music focus of the town and social hub (see below). Best of the guesthouses on the harbour front is the excellent **E** *Failte Guest House*, T/F302495. Open Mar-Oct, 7 rooms. Also on Main St is the **F** *SYHA Youth Hostel*, T302481. Open end-Feb to end-Oct and rents out bikes.

There are many **guesthouses** and **B&Bs** uphill from the harbour, which are often better value. These include: **E** *Copeland House*, Jubilee Terr, T302049/302422. 3 en suite rooms with seaviews. **E** *Mrs Mackinnon*, 'Ardsorn' Raeric Rd, T302214, F302148. Open Apr-Oct, 2 en suite rooms with great seaviews, parking. **F-E** *Ivybank*, Argyll Terrace, T302250. Friendly and comfortable. A short walk from town is **E** *Baliscate Guest House*, T302048, F302666. 4 en suite rooms. They also organize fishing and wildlife trips (see 'Trips from Tobermory' below).

Eating

The best eating in town is to be had in the *Western Isles Hotel* (see above), where you can choose between three restaurants. A 3-course à la carte in the dining room or the oriental *Spices Bistro* is expensive to mid-range, while cheap bar meals are served in the excellent *Conservatory Bar*. Not so stylish or tasty, but cheaper is the *Highland Cottage Hotel* on Breadalbane St, which does a moderately-priced 4-course dinner.

The harbour front is filled with places where you can fill yourself, including the moderately-priced *Back Brae Restaurant*, T302422, open daily from 1800. Cheaper still is the bar of the *Mishnish Hotel*, where you can attempt to munch your way through their monumental portions and, if you're not sleeping on the same street, also attempt the walk uphill on an over-filled stomach. Also on the harbour front is the excellent *Island Bakery*. A worthwhile detour is to walk to the edge of town to the excellent *Green Barn* which is run by *Isle of Mull Cheese* (see 'Shopping' below). Here you can enjoy good old home baking in the unusual surroundings of a plant-filled glass barn.

Entertainment

An absolute must when in Tobermory is a night in the *Mish*. After one of their pub meals and several pints of ale, bending over the pool table is an effort, not to mention getting down to some good live folk music. For the sake of choice, other pubs and live music venues are available, namely *MacGochan's*, at the other end of the harbour, near the distillery. There are also music events at *An Tobar* (see 'Sights' above).

Shopping

Despite its popularity, Tobermory hasn't succumbed to the dreaded tartan disease that afflicts so many other tourist hot-spots. You're more likely to find shops selling fishing tackle or diving gear than tacky souvenirs and the ones that do cater for the tourist market, such as *Mull Pottery* , T302057, and the *Mull Silver Company*, T302345, open 0900-1730, are tastefully done and enjoyable places to browse in on a wet afternoon. At the foot of Back Brae, which leads steeply up from the harbour to the upper part of the village, is the *Tobermory Chocolate Company*, T302526, open Mar-Jan Mon-Sat 0930-1700, where you can try out their speciality of chocolate made with the local whisky . On the edge of town, 500 yards off the Dervaig road, at Sgriob-Ruadh Farm, is *Isle of Mull Cheese*, T302235, where you can savour their award-winning traditionally-made cheese and their wonderful glass barn (see 'Eating' above). Open Apr to end-Sept Mon-Fri 1000-1600.

Things to do on Mull when it's wet

It rains a lot on Mull, but luckily there's a fairly large number of indoor options to keep you nice and dry until the weather changes. If you've just arrived off the ferry from Oban and it's chucking down, then head straight for **Torosay Castle**, just to the south of Craignure. And if the weather changes whilst exploring the interior, don't miss the gardens. Nearby is Mull's greatest fortification, **Duart Castle**, which is also worth a peek. If all that history gets too much then you could do worse than hole up in the bar of the **Craignure Inn** and

relax in front of their roaring log fire.

In the north of the island, the most appealing option by far is the **Old Byre Heritage Centre**, not far from the picturesque village of Dervaig. When in Tobermory do as the locals do, and get yourself down to the bar of the Mish, though you shouldn't really need the excuse of inclement weather. Meanwhile, over in Fionnphort, the departure point for the pilgrimage to Iona, you can seek spiritual assistance with a wee dram in the cosy **Keel Row Bar**.

Whale and dolphin watching trips can be made from Tobermory with *Sea Life Surveys*, T302787. A full-day tour costs £42 (£45 in Jul/Aug), and there's a maximum of 12 people per trip. Proceeds from the trips go to the *Hebridean Whale and Dolphin Trust*, a charity which aims to protect the marine environment through education. You can visit the trust at 28 Main Street, Tobermory, T302620, F302728, hwdt@sol.co.uk, www.gn.apc.org/whales. Mon-Fri 1000-1700, Sat/Sun 1100-1600.

Trips from Tobermory

Fishing trips can be made on the *Silver Swift*, leaving from the ferry pier 1200-1500 and 1800-2100. Trips cost £12.50 per person (tackle supplied). Book at the tourist office or after hours T302182, paul@scotshop.demon.co.uk, www.silverswift.co.uk. The *Silver Swift* can also be chartered for £300 per day, T302390. Fishing trips are also available with *Amidas Sea Fishing & Wildlife Trips*, based at Baliscate House (see 'Sleeping' above), or book at *Tackle & Books*, T302336.

Fishing permits for trout fishing are available from *A. Brown & Son*, 21 Main Street, Tobermory, T302020, F302454. For more details pick up the *Tobermory Angling Association* leaflet from the tourist office.

Diving trips and courses are available with *Seamore Diving*. Book through *Seafare Chandlery & Diving Service*, Main Street, Tobermory, T/F302277.

Wildlife expeditions with *Isle of Mull Landrover Wildlife Expeditions*, at Ulva House Hotel, T302044 (David Woodhouse). Full day tour costs £24.50/£18.50 per person.

Banks Mull's only permanent bank is the *Clydesdale Bank* on Main St. There's also a mobile bank which tours the island; for details T0345-826818.

Directory

The West Coast

Mull's west coast is where you'll find some of the island's most stunning scenery. The B8073 winds its way anti-clockwise from Tobermory in a series of tortuous twists and turns as it follows the contours of the deeply-indented coastline. It starts off in terrible condition and soon deteriorates into something resembling a poorly-maintained farm track.

The road climbs west from Tobermory then makes a dramatic descent, with innumerable hairpin bends, to Dervaig. This section of road is closed to the public for the annual car rally in October. Dervaig is a lovely wee village of whitewashed cottages, where the old folk still converse in Gaelic, beautifully situated at the head of Loch Cuin.

Dervaig
Phone code: 01688

Inner Hebrides

It has two very notable features (quite a lot for such a tiny place). One is **Kilmore church**, which has a very unusual pencil-shaped spire (the only other one in Scotland is at Dunfermline in Fife). Dervaig's real claim to fame, though, is the **Mull Little Theatre**, the smallest professional theatre in Britain, with only 43 seats. It puts on an impressive programme of plays throughout the summer (May-September), and common sense dictates that advance booking is essential (T400245).

One mile beyond Dervaig take the turn-off to Torloisk to reach the **Old Byre Heritage Centre**, which stands out as one of the few genuinely interesting examples of these places. It also features a video of Mull's history and an excellent tea-room (see below). ■ *T400229. Easter to end-Oct daily 1030-1830. £2.*

Sleeping & eating Dervaig has a wide choice of places to stay. The nicest is **A** *Druimard Country House Hotel*, T400291, T/F400345. Six rooms, open end Mar-Oct, this Victorian country house offers peace and comfort in beautiful surroundings and is right beside the *Mull Little Theatre*, the room rate includes dinner in the excellent restaurant. They offer a pre-theatre 4-course dinner for non-residents (expensive). **E-D** *Ardbeg House Hotel*, T/F400254. Four rooms, open all year, not as stylish as the *Druimard* but with plenty of charm. There are several **B&Bs** and **guesthouses** in and around the village, including the excellent **E** *Cuin Lodge*, overlooking Loch Cuin, T400346, open Mar-Oct.

Aside from the *Druimard Country House*, probably the best food around is at the *Old Byre Heritage Centre* (see above), whose tearoom serves delicious but cheap snacks and home baking. There's also the 16th century *Bellachroy Hotel*, where you can get decent bar meals. Opposite is *Coffee and Books*, for good coffee and, funnily enough, books.

Calgary Bay Five miles west of Dervaig is Calgary Bay, Mull's most beautiful beach, ringed by steep wooded slopes and with views across to Coll and Tiree. Any Canadians reading this, may be interested to note that the large city in Alberta was named after the former township. Many emigrants were forcibly shipped to Canada from here during the Clearances.

Nearby is the wonderfully peaceful and relaxing **D** *Calgary Farmhouse Hotel*, T01688-400256. Nine rooms, open April-October. This restored farmhouse is one of Mull's gems and the adjoining *Dovecote Restaurant* serves excellent, moderately-priced food using the best of local seasonal produce. There's also a tea-room, *The Carthouse*, which offers cheap and delicious light lunches and home baking. There can be no better end to a day than dinner at the *Dovecote* followed by a stroll along the beach at sunset.

The road down the west coast passes through a series of tiny settlements before reaching the turn-off to Ulva Ferry. A couple of miles before the turning, it's worth stopping at **Eas Fors**, a spectacular waterfall that tumbles straight into the sea from under the road bridge. There's a path down to the bottom and you can swim in the sea, below the falls.

Isle of Ulva
Colour map 3, grid B3

If you have the time and need to escape the hectic bustle of Mull, then take a day out on idyllic Ulva (meaning 'wolf island' in Norse), just off the west coast. You won't see any wolves around, but you're almost guaranteed to spot deer, golden eagles, buzzards and seals offshore. There are several well-marked walks that criss-cross the island, including one to the southwest where there are basalt columns similar to those on Staffa. Or you can cross to its smaller neighbour **Gometra** by a causeway.

It's hard to believe, but the island once sustained a population of over 850, until they were completely cleared between 1846 and 1851. The derelict crofts can still be seen around the island, along with the lovely little church, which still holds services for the remaining population of around 20. For more information on the island walks and on its history, visit the *Boathouse Heritage Centre* close to the ferry slip on Ulva. There's also a licensed tea-room where you can try the local oysters with Guinness. ■ *T01688-500241/264, ulva@zetnet.co.uk. Easter-Oct Mon-Fri 0900-1700 and Sun Jun-Aug only. £2.50, children £1.50.*

Transport A small bicycle/passenger-only ferry makes the 2 min crossing on demand from Ulva Ferry, Apr-Oct Mon-Fri 0800-1700, and on Sun from June-Aug, £2.50 return (50p for bikes). At other times, phone to make arrangements, T500226. No accommodation but ask the ferry operators about camping.

The tiny uninhabited island of Staffa, five miles off the west coast of Mull, is one of the most spectacular sights not just in Scotland but anywhere in the world. It consists of immense, hexagonal, basalt pillars which loom up out of the sea, like a giant pipe organ. Staffa was formed 60 million years ago by the slow cooling of Tertiary basalt lavas. These have been carved by the pounding sea into huge cathedral-like caverns such as the mightily impressive **Fingal's Cave**. The sound of the sea crashing against the black crystalline columns made such an impression on Felix Mendelssohn in 1829 that he immortalized the island in his *Hebrides Overture*. The composer was obviously aware of its original name in Gaelic, which means 'The Melodious Cave'.

> **Isle of Staffa**
> *Colour map 3, grid B3*

You can land on the island – if the weather is good enough – and walk into the cave via the causeway; an experience not be missed. But even if the seas are too rough, it's worth making the 90-minute boat trip just to witness the huge columns and gaping black hole of the cave.

Most boat trips to Staffa include a memorable tour of the uninhabited Treshnish Isles to the northwest. The two most northerly islands, **Cairn na Burgh** and **Cairn na Burgh Beg** have ruined castles, while another, **Bac Mór**, is better known as **Dutchman's cap** because of its curious shape. The largest island, **Lunga**, is the main bird sanctuary and a haven for thousands of sea-birds, including razorbills, guillemots, kittiwakes, shags, fulmars, skuas and puffins so tame you'll need to tread carefully to avoid them. In the surrounding seas there are seals, dolphins, minke whales, porpoises, and maybe even basking sharks and killer whales! Most boat trips include time ashore on Lunga and all are dependent on sea conditions.

> **Treshnish Isles**
> *Colour map 3, grid B3*

Boat trips to Staffa and the Treshnish Isles leave from Oban, Dervaig, Ulva Ferry, Iona or Fionnphort, weather permitting. A full day cruise including Staffa and the Treshnish Isles costs £25-30 per person (half fare for children); a cruise to Staffa only costs around £12.50. *Turus Mara* leave from Ulva Ferry, T/F01688-400242/297 (mobile 0831-638179), turus.mara@dial.pipex.com. *Inter-island Cruises* leave from Croig near Dervaig, T/F01688-400264. They're a little bit more expensive than the others, but also have trips to Coll and Muck. *Gordon Grant Marine* leave from Fionnphort and Iona, T01681-700338. *Staffa Trips* sail to Staffa on the *MB Iolaire* from Iona and Fionnphort, T01681-700358.

> **Boat trips to Staffa & the Treshnish Isles**

From Ulva Ferry the B8073 heads east along the north shore of **Loch na Keal** then enters a wide flat valley, where the road forks east to Salen (see page 240) and west along the south shore of Loch na Keal. This part of Mull is dominated by **Ben More** (3,170 feet), the island's highest mountain. All around is a

> **Ben More & the Ardmeanach peninsula**

spectacular region of high jutting mountains and deep glens, extending west to the **Ardmeanach peninsula**. The road passes Dishig, the best point from which to begin the steep walk to the summit (see page 247), then cuts through the towering Gribun cliffs, with the tiny island of **Inch Kenneth** lying offshore. There are also great views of Ulva, Staffa and the Treshnish Isles. The road then turns south across peninsula as it climbs over the pass and down to Loch Scridain, where it joins the A849 which runs through the beautiful and dramatic **Glen More** to Craignure.

The peninsula may look impenetrable but with the proper walking gear can be explored on foot. On the north coast, about a mile from the road, is the massive entrance to **MacKinnon's Cave**, which runs for about 100 yards back under the cliffs. Make sure to visit only at low tide and also watch out for the evil spirits who live inside and who are said to have caused the deaths of an entire party of adventurous – or foolish – men. The area around the headland, now owned by the National Trust for Scotland, is known as '**The Wilderness**'. Near the headland is **MacCulloch's Tree**, a remarkable fossilized tree 40 feet high and thought to be 50 million years old, which was discovered in 1819. The tree is only accessible by a seven mile footpath which begins at Burg farm. You should call in at the farm to let them know of your intentions and also to get directions. You should have a good map of the area and also time your arrival with low tide.

The Ross of Mull

Phone code: 01681 Mull's southernmost peninsula stretches west for 20 miles from the head of Loch Scridain as far as Iona. Most visitors use it merely as a route to Iona, but if you've got the time and the weather's good, there are a couple of interesting little detours along the way. The Ross of Mull also makes a sensible alternative to trying to find a bed for the night on Iona.

The first village is **Pennyghael**, which has two hotels overlooking the loch, **D** *Pennyghael Hotel*, T704288, F704205, which is open Easter-October and has an excellent restaurant, and **D** *Kinloch Hotel*, T704204, which serves cheap bar meals. A tortuous, twisting side road leads south from Pennyghael over the hills and down to **Carsaig Bay**, from where you can head east or west along the shore for some dramatic coastal scenery. For a description of these walks, see 'Walks on Mull' (page 247).

The next village is **Bunessan**, fairly unappealing, but the largest place around with a wide range of inexpensive B&B accommodation and very convenient for an early ferry to Iona. There are also a couple of superb hotels around Bunessan. In the village itself is the excellent **A-B** *Assapol House Hotel*, T700258, F700445. Five rooms, open Easter-October. A few miles west of Bunessan is the turning to **B** *Ardfenaig House*, T/F700210. Five rooms, open April-October, the former shooting lodge offers style and elegance and expensive but superb food.

You can find out everything about local history and culture at the **Ross of Mull Historical Centre**, on Pier Road. ■ *T70065. Daily 1000-1630. £1.*

A mile east of Bunessan is the **Isle of Mull Angora Rabbit Farm**, where you can cuddle the cute fluffy bunnies, watch them being shorn and then listen to someone rabbiting on about the history of angora. ■ *Easter to end-Oct daily 1100-1770 (except Sat); £2.*

Two roads lead south from Bunessan. One leads to **Scoor**, near where is a great beach at Kilveockan. The other road splits near the coast: the left branch leads to **Uisken Bay**, where there's a nice beach; the righthand branch leads to **Ardlanish Bay**, which also has a good beach. You can spend the night at Uisken Bay at the idyllic **E** *Uisken Croft*, T700307, open April-October.

The road ends at **Fionnphort**, the departure point for the small passenger-only ferry to Iona, just a mile across the Sound of Iona. The village is little more than a car park, a row of houses, a pub and a shop, but there are several inexpensive B&Bs for those arriving too late to make the crossing. Even if you're not staying, it's worth stopping off in the village to visit the **Columba Centre**, a museum which relates the saint's life story, ■ *mid-May to end-Sept, Mon-Sat 1000-1800, Sun 1100-1800. £2, children £1.*

Just before the village is **E** *Achaban House*, T700205, F700649. Seven rooms, this former manse is comfortable and well-furnished and also offers dinner. **E-F** *Burnside*, T700208. One room, 2 mins from the ferry with a great view of Iona. North of Ffionnphort, in Kintra, is **E-F** *Dail An Inbhire*, T/F700509. Two rooms, open Mar-Sept, great views and organic food.

Eating options are limited to the *Keel Row Bar & Restaurant*, where you can get moderately-priced meals and enjoy a drink by the fire in the cosy bar.

Sleeping & eating

A road runs south from Fionnphort a mile to a **campsite** at *Fidden Farm*, T700427. Further south is **Knockvologan**, opposite **Erraid island**, which is accessible at low tide. The island has literary connections, for it was here that Robert Louis Stevenson is believed to have written *Kidnapped*. **Balfour Bay** on the south of the island is named after the novel's hero who was shipwrecked here.

Further south

Walks on Mull

Mull presents numerous walking opportunities, ranging from gentle forest trails to wild and dramatic coastal routes, or even a spot of Munro-bagging for the more interpid.

OS Landranger Nos 47, 48 & 49

With the exception of the Cuillins on Skye, Mull's highest peak (3,169ft) is the only Munro not on the mainland. The trail starts at a lay-by on the B8035, at Dishig, and is fairly clear, though it can be tricky near the top. Return the same way or more experienced climbers could continue down the narrow ridge to the eastern summit, **A'Chioch**, then descend the eastern face to the road that skirts **Loch Ba**. The views from the top are magnificent, across the other Hebridean islands and even as far as Ireland. If it's a cloudy day, it's worth postponing the ascent until there's clear weather. Allow around six hours for the round trip.

Ben More

There are a couple of excellent coastal walks which start out from Carsaig Bay. A good path heads west along the shore to **Carsaig Arches** at Malcom's Point. The path runs below the cliffs out to the headland and then around it, and after about a mile reaches **Nun's Cave**, a wide and shallow cave where the nuns of Iona took refuge after being expelled during the Reformation. The path continues for another mile or so, but becomes a bit exposed in places and traverses a steep slope above a sheer drop into the sea. The famous arches are columnar basalts worn into fantastic shapes. One is a free-standing rock stack and another is a huge cave with two entrances. You'll need to allow about four hours in total plus some time at the arches.

Coastal walks

Heading east from Carsaig Bay is a spectacular four and a half mile walk to **Lochbuie**, past Adnunan stack. It starts out through woodland, then follows the shore below the steep cliffs, with waterfalls plunging straight into the sea. It's easy at first but then gets very muddy in places and there's quite a bit of wading through boggy marsh, so make sure you've got good walking boots. Allow about five to six hours in total.

Inner Hebrides

Forest walks There are a few marked trails through Forestry Commission land on Mull. For detailed maps and more information pick up the free *Guide to Forest Walks and Trails in North Argyll* leaflet at any tourist office.

The first walk is to **Aros Park**, on the south side of Tobermory Bay. Start out from the car park near the distillery in Tobermory and follow the shoreline for about a mile to Lochan a'Ghurrabain, which is good for trout fishing (see page 243). From here there is also a marked path around the loch (1 mile).

A longer walk is to **Ardmore Bay**, three miles north of Tobermory. The trail/cycle path starts at the car park by the road that runs northwest from Tobermory. From here, it runs out almost to Ardmore point and back again, passing a couple of ruined villages on the way. There's a good chance of seeing seals and lots of sea birds in Ardmore Bay. The trail is four miles in total.

Four miles north of Craignure is the car park and picnic site at **Garmony Point**, where a two-mile trail leads to the Ferry terminal at **Fishnish**, hugging the shore all the way. Another trail (four miles) runs out to Fishnish Point and back through the forest to the car park by the old harbour.

Isle of Iona

Phone code: 01681
Colour map 3, grid C3
Population: 130

Iona is a small island – barely three miles long and a little over a mile wide – but its importance to Christianity is out of all proportion to its size. Iona's place in religious history was guaranteed when **St Columba** arrived with his 12 disciples and founded a monastery there in AD 563. The Irish monk then set about converting practically all of pagan Scotland and much of northern England. Iona went on to become the most sacred religious site in Europe and has been a place of pilgrimage for several centuries. Today that pilgrimage has turned into more of an invasion, with hordes of daytrippers making the five-minute ferry trip from Mull to visit the abbey. Few, however, venture beyond the main village, **Baile Mór**, and it's easy to find a quiet spot, particularly on the west coast with its sparkling silver beaches washed by turquoise sea. It's worth spending a day or two here to soak up the island's unique spiritual peace, so well conveyed in the words of Dr Johnson: "that man is little to be envied whose…piety would not grow warmer among the ruins of Iona".

Ins and outs

Getting there Passenger-only **ferry** only from **Fionnphort**, Mull, (5 mins) frequently T0845-1815 Mon-Sat and hourly 0900-1800 Sun; return trip £3.10.

History

St Columba (*Colum Cille* in Gaelic), a prince of Ireland and grandson of the Irish King, Niall of the Nine Hostages, came to Scotland, not as a missionary, but as an act of self-imposed penance for his actions. He stubbornly refused to hand over his copy of the Gospels, illegally copied from St Finian's original, which led to a bitter dispute with the king. This ended in a pitched battle, in which Columba's supporters prevailed, but he was so overcome with remorse at the bloodshed he had caused that he fled Ireland, finally settling on Iona, as it was the first place he found from where he couldn't see his homeland.

Columba, however, was not retiring into obscurity. His missionary zeal drove him to begin work on building the abbey. He also banished women and cows from the island, declaring that "where there is a cow there is a woman, and where there is a woman there is mischief". Workers at the abbey had to leave their womenfolk on nearby Eilean nam Ban (Women's Island). Not content with that, he also banished frogs and snakes from Iona, though there are plenty on Mull. He is even said to have pacified the Loch Ness Monster during a visit to Inverness.

He went on to found the Celtic Church, or the Church of the Culdees, with centres throughout Scotland, which differed in many ways from the Church of Rome. Iona became known as 'Cradle of Christianity in Scotland' and was a centre of the arts, the monks producing elaborate carvings, manuscripts, ornate gravestones and Celtic crosses. Their greatest work was the beautiful *Book of Kells*, which dates from 800 and which is now on display in Dublin's Trinity College. This proved to be the high point of the church's history. Shortly after, came the first of the Viking raids, in 806, when many monks were slaughtered at Martyrs' Bay, followed by another in 986 which destroyed the work of many years. The relentless pressure from the established church ended with the suppression of the Celtic Church by King David in 1144.

In 1203 Iona became part of the mainstream church with the establishment of a nunnery for the Order of the Black Nuns as well as a Benedictine Abbey by Reginald of the MacDonalds of the Isles. Iona became overshadowed by the royal city of Dunfermline and its final demise came with the Reformation, when buildings were demolished and all but three of the 360 carved crosses destroyed.

The abbey lay in ruins until in 1899 the island's owner, the 8th Duke of Argyll, donated the buildings to the Church of Scotland on condition that the abbey church was restored for worship. Then in 1938 the Rev George Macleod founded the Iona Community as an evangelical Church of Scotland brotherhood, with the abbey buildings as its headquarters, and by 1965 had succeeded in rebuilding the remainder of the monastic buildings. Now the abbey complex has been completely restored and the island of Iona, apart from the abbey buildings, is owned by the NTS.

The Abbey

The present abbey dates from around 1200, though it has been rebuilt over the centuries and completely restored in the 20th century. The oldest part is the restored **St Oran's Chapel**, to the south of the abbey on the right, plain and unadorned save for its splendid 11th century Norman doorway. It is said that Columba was prevented from completing the building of the original chapel until a living person had been buried in the foundations. His friend Oran volunteered and was duly buried. Columba later asked for the face to be uncovered so that he could bid a final farewell to his friend, but Oran was found to be alive and claimed he had seen Heaven and Hell, describing them in such blasphemous terms that Columba ordered he be covered up immediately!

Surrounding the chapel is the **Reilig Odhrain**, the sacred burial ground, which is said to contain the graves of 48 Scottish kings, including Macbeth's victim, Duncan, as well as four Irish and eight Norwegian kings. The stones you see today are not the graves of kings but of various important people from around the West Highlands and Islands. The most recent is that of **John Smith**, leader of the British Labour Party from 1992 until his untimely death in 1994.

Beside the **Road of the Dead**, which leads from the abbey church to St Oran's Chapel, stands the eighth century **St Martin's Cross**. This is the finest of Iona's Celtic high crosses and is remarkably complete, with the Pictish serpent-and-boss decoration on one side and holy figures on the other. Standing in front of the abbey entrance is a replica of **St John's Cross**, the other great eighth century monument. The restored original is in the **Infirmary Museum**, at the rear of the abbey, along with a fine collection of medieval gravestones.

Inner Hebrides

No part of St Columba's original buildings survives, but to the left of the main entrance is **St Columba's Shrine**, the small, steep-roofed chamber, which almost certainly marks the site of the saint's tomb. You get a good view of the whole complex from the top of the small grassy knoll opposite the abbey entrance. This is **Torr an Aba**, where Columba's cell is said to have been. The **Abbey** itself has been carefully restored to its original beautiful simplicity and inside, in a side chapel, are marble effigies of the eighth Duke of Argyll and his third wife, Duchess Ina. ■ *The abbey is open all year and at all times. Admission is free but you're asked to give a £2 donation at the entrance where you can pick up a plan of the abbey.*

Baile Mór

The passenger ferry from Fionnphort on Mull lands at Baile Mór, Iona's main village, which is little more than a row of cottages facing the sea. There are several places to stay, but as demand far exceeds supply during the busy summer, it's best to book in advance at one of the tourist offices on Mull, or in Oban. There's also a post office, a very good craft shop and general store in the village.

Just outside the village, on the way to the abbey, are the ruins of the **Augustinian nunnery**. Just to the north, housed in the parish church manse, built by Thomas Telford, is the **Iona Heritage Centre**, which features displays on the island's social history. ■ *Apr-Oct Mon-Sat 1030-1630. £1.50.* Nearby stands the intricately-carved 15th century **Maclean's Cross**.

Sleeping & eating **B-C** *Argyll Hotel*, T700334, F700510. 17 rooms, open Apr-Oct, this is the better of the island's two upmarket hotels and its very good restaurant serves cheap lunches and mid-range-expensive 4-course dinners. There are a couple of **B&Bs** in and around the village, including **E** *Bishop's House*, T/F700306, open Mar-Oct, overlooking the Sound of Iona. There's also **E** *Finlay Ross (Iona) Ltd*, T700357/365, F700562. Fifteen rooms, open all year, they also have a gift shop where you can rent mountain bikes for £8 per day. **Camping** is possible but ask permission first.

Apart from the *Argyll Hotel*, there's the *Martyrs' Bay Restaurant*, which serves soup and snacks. Opposite the abbey is a coffee house run by the Iona Community (open Mon-Thur 1100-1630, Fri 1200-1630, Sat 1130-1630, Sun 1200-1600), serving soup, filled rolls and cakes.

Around the island

Do yourself a real favour by taking the time to explore the island and enjoy its natural beauty as well as its spiritual peace. On the west coast, are some lovely beaches of white sand and colourful pebbles.

The best of the lot is the **Bay at the Back of the Ocean**, beside the golf course, and only a mile and a half walk from the ferry. This was one of John Smith's favourite places and it's easy to see why. At the southern tip of the island is another sandy beach at **St Columba's Bay**, believed to be the spot where the saint first landed. The small cairns here are said to have been built by the monks as penance for their sins. They obviously had a lot on their conscience. Around the corner, at Rubha na Carraig-géire on the southeastern tip, is the **marble quarry**, disused since 1915. The rusting remains of the cutting equipment is still lying around.

Another good walk is to the top of **Dun I**, the only real hill, which rises to a height of 300 feet. Continue on the road north from the abbey, past MacDougal's Cross, then go through a gate to the right of Bishop's Walk Farm and follow the fence up to where you join a footpath up to the top. It's only about half an hour up and down and there are great views from the top of the entire island and the coastline of Mull.

Isle of Coll

The low-lying, treeless and windswept island of Coll offers the simple pleasures in life and is so peaceful and quiet that it makes some of the more popular islands appear crowded by comparison. There's little to do here other than stroll along the magnificent, deserted beaches and enjoy the relatively long hours of sunshine. Tourism, though, remains low on the list of priorities here and those who do come prefer it that way. Even by Hebridean standards there are few facilities and accommodation is scarce.

Phone code: 01879
Colour map 3, grid B3
Population: 170

Getting there There's a **ferry** from Oban to Coll (2 hrs 40 mins) and Tiree (55 mins) once daily on Mon, Tue, Wed, Fri and Sat. One way ticket to Coll or Tiree costs £10.80 per passenger and £61 per car; from Coll to Tiree costs £2.70 and £15.80.

Getting around The *CalMac* ferry from Oban calls in at Coll's only village, Arinagour, where half of the island's population live and where you'll find the post office and a few shops. There's no petrol station but that's probably a hint to leave the car behind. The island is only 13 miles long by four miles wide and the best way to get around is on foot or by bike.

Around the island The best of Coll's beaches are on the west coast, at **Killunaig**, **Hogh Bay** and **Feall Bay**. The latter is separated from the nearby **Crossapool Bay** by giant sand dunes up to 100 feet high. These are now owned by the RSPB to protect the resident corncrake population. Nearby, at the head of Loch Breachacha, is the restored medieval **Breachacha Castle**, built by the Macleans of Coll and once owned by them but now used as an adventure-training school for young overseas aid volunteers. The castle is sometimes open to the public; check with the tourist office in Oban for details. The dilapidated 18th century mansion nearby is where Boswell and Dr Johnson stayed when they were stranded here for 10 days during their grand Highland tour in 1773.

It's worth taking a walk up **Ben Hogh** (341 feet), the island's highest point, overlooking Hogh Bay on the west coast, to get a good overview. The east coast, north from Arinagour to **Sorisdale**, is an uninhabited wilderness which is ideal for some gentle hill-walking.

Sleeping & eating In Arinagour is the **D** *Coll Hotel*, T230334, F230317. A wee family hotel with a good restaurant and which is the social hub of the island. Also in the village is **E** *Taigh Solas*, T/F230333. A few miles to the west is **E-F** *Achamore*, T230430. A lovely old farmhouse. Down in the southwest, at Breachacha Bay, is **E** *Garden House*, T/F230374. Nearby, in the walled garden of the castle, is the island's **campsite** (open Apr-Oct; phone as for *Garden House*). The only alternative to hotel or guesthouse food is the trendy bistro in Arinagour.

Isle of Tiree

Tiree claims to be the sunniest place in Scotland, and has a comparatively low average rainfall, but it's also one of the windiest places in the country. So windy, in fact, that Tiree has become the windsurfing capital of Scotland and is known as the 'Hawaii of the North'. International windsurfers are attracted by the huge Atlantic rollers that break on the island's countless, long, clean and silver beaches.

Phone code: 01879
Colour map 3, grid B2
Population: 800

Inner Hebrides

Compared to Coll, Tiree is heavily populated, with over 800 inhabitants. It's also much greener and more fertile than its neighbour. Tiree was once known as the breadbasket of the Hebrides and its Gaelic name, *tir-iodh*, means 'Land of Corn'. The island supported a population of 4,450 in 1831, but was ruthlessly cleared by its owner, the Duke of Argyll, so that by 1881 the population had been halved. Not content to stop there, he even drafted in the marines, in 1885, to evict those crofters who dared to protest. Today, Tiree enjoys relative prosperity and crofting is the mainstay of the economy, with cattle and sheep grazing the miles of rich machair. Tourism is also a major contributor and during the height of the season, the island's population approaches the levels of the early 19th century.

Getting there Tiree has an **airport** and there are regular daily flights (except Sun) all year round from Glasgow. The airport is at The Reef, Crossapol (T220309). For full details, see page 236.

There are *CalMac* car and passenger **ferries** to the island from Oban, via Coll and, occasionally, Tobermory. The ferry port is at Scarinish (T220337). From Oban to Tiree (55 mins) once daily on Mon, Tue, Wed, Fri and Sat. One-way ticket to Tiree costs £10.80 per passenger and £61 per car; from Coll to Tiree costs £2.70 and £15.80.

Getting around There's a **shared taxi** service which operates on request Mon-Fri 0930-1500 (limited service on Sat), also Mon-Wed and Fri 1600-1730. There's also a Tue evening service for arriving ferries, but only in the summer. For private taxi hire call *Island Cabs*, T220344 (evenings and weekends only). There's a **postbus** service around the island, including to and from the airport. The timetable is available at Scarinish Post Office. **Bicycle hire** is available at the *Tiree Lodge Hotel* (see below), or contact Mr N Maclean, T220428.

Around the Tiree is a low, flat island, only about 11 miles long and six miles across at its
island widest, and is also known by the nickname *Tir fo Thuinn*, or "Land below the waves". When seen from a distance most of it disappears below the horizon save its two highest hills, **Ben Hynish** (462 feet) and **Beinn Hough** (390 feet), on the west coast. Being flat and small, it obviously makes good sense to explore it by bicycle, but remember that the constant wind varies from strong to gale force.

The ferry port is at **Gott Bay**, half a mile from **Scarinish**, the island's main village and home to a *Co-op* supermarket, post office and bank (there's a garage at the pier head). About four miles from Scarinish, is Vaul Bay, where the well-preserved remains of **Dun Mor**, a Pictish Broch built around the first century AD, stand on rocky outcrop to the west of the bay. A few miles west of here is the **Clach a'Choire**, or 'ringing stone', a huge glacial granite boulder covered in Bronze Age cup marks which makes a metallic sound when struck. Legend has it that should it ever shatter, or fall off its pedestal, then Tiree will sink beneath the waves.

The island's main road runs northwest from Scarinish, past the beautiful beach at **Balephetrish Bay** to **Balevullin**, where you can see some good examples of restored traditional thatched houses. Just to the south, at **Sandaig**, is the **Thatched House Museum** which tells of the island's social history. ■ *Jun-Sept, Mon-Fri 1400-1600.*

In the southwestern corner of the island is the most spectacular scenery of all, at the headland of **Ceann a'Mara**, or Kenavara. The massive sea cliffs are the home of thousands of sea birds and you can see seals on the rocky shore. East from here, across the golden sands of Balephuil Bay, is the island's highest hill, **Ben Hynish**, topped by a radar-tracking station resembling a giant golf ball. Despite this, it's worth the climb to the top for the magnificent views over the island and, on clear days, across to the Outer Hebrides. Below Ben Hynish, to the east, is the village of **Hynish**, where you'll find the **Signal Tower Museum**, which tells the fascinating story of the building of the **Skerryvore Lighthouse** (1840-44) by Alan Stevenson, an uncle of Robert Louis Stevenson. This incredible feat of engineering was carried out from Hynish, where a dry dock/reservoir was built for shipping materials by boat to the Skerryvore reef, ten miles to the southwest.

Best of the 2 hotels is **D** *Tiree Lodge*, T220368, F220994, at Gott Bay. The other is the **E** *Scarinish Hotel*, T220308, F220410, in the village itself. There are several **guesthouses** and **B&Bs**, the best of which is the wonderful **E** *Kirkapol House*, T/F220729, in a converted Victorian church overlooking Gott Bay. It's possible to **camp** free on the island, but ask for permission first.

Sleeping & eating

The best food on offer is at the moderately-priced *The Glassary*, T/F220684, at Sandaig. It also offers accommodation (**D-E**). There's also the option of bar lunches and suppers at the *Tiree Lodge* and *Scarinish Hotels*. For afternoon tea or coffee you're limited to the *Alan Stevenson Centre* in Hynish, open 1430-1630, or *Glebecraft* in Scarinish.

Windsurfing tuition is available at Loch Bhasapol, T220559 (summer only). The major windsurfing event is the **Wave Classic**, held annually in Oct.

Sports

Isle of Colonsay

Colonsay is the epitome of the island haven: remote, tranquil and undemanding. It has abundant wildlife (150 species of resident or migrant birds), beautiful plants and flowers (over 500 species) and glorious beaches. All this has become accessible to daytrippers, with a ferry round trip (see below), leaving you six hours ashore. This does scant justice to the island's peculiar charms, however, and judging by the ever-growing number of holiday homes and self-catering accommodation on Colonsay, it's a view shared by many.

Phone code: 01951
Colour map 3, grid C3
Population: 100

There are **ferry** sailings from Oban (2 hrs) 1 daily Wed, Fri and Sun, arriving at Scalasaig on the east coast. From Kennacraig there is 1 sailing (3 hrs 35 mins) on Wed from Port Askaig 1 sailing (1 hr 10 mins) also on Wed. 1-way Oban/Kennacraig-Colonsay costs £9.60 per passenger and £45.50 per car; Port Askaig-Colonsay £3.35 and £17.75. Ferries need to be booked well in advance during the summer months.

Getting there

There's a limited **bus** and postbus service around the island Mon-Sat, for those without their own transport. On Wed in the summer, a tour bus meets the ferry and takes visitors round the island. As the island is only 8 miles long by 3 miles wide, you might want to consider hiring a bicycle. **Bike hire** from *A McConnel*, T200355.

Getting around

Colonsay's population lives in the three small villages, the largest of which is **Scalasaig**, the ferry port. The island's only hotel is here and there's also a restaurant, a post office/shop, a petrol pump and a heritage centre by the pier. A few miles north of the ferry, in the middle of the island, is **Colonsay House**, dating from 1772. The house was sold, along with the rest of the island, in 1904 to Lord Strathcona, who had made his fortune in Canada with the Hudson Bay Company and went on to found the Canadian Pacific Railway. The house is not open to the public but the lovely gardens and woods, full of rhododendrons, giant palms and exotic shrubs, are worth a stroll. The estate cottages are now self-catering holiday homes.

Around the island

Inner Hebrides

The island is rich in archaeological and historical remains. There are several standing stones, the best of which are **Fingal's Limpet Hammers**, at Kilchattan, southwest of Colonsay House. There are also Iron Age forts, such as **Dun Eibhinn**, next to the hotel in Scalasaig (see below). Colonsay is also home to a wide variety of **wildlife**. You can see choughs, one of Britain's rarest birds, as well as corncrakes, buzzards, falcons, merlins and perhaps even the odd golden eagle or sea eagle. There are also otters, seals and wild goats (said to be descended from the survivors of the Spanish Armada ships wrecked in 1588).

The jewel in the island's crown, though, lies six miles north of Scalasaig, past Colonsay House, at **Kiloran Bay**. The beach here is described as the finest in the Hebrides, and who could argue? The magnificent half mile of golden sands, backed by tiers of grassy dunes, with massive breakers rolling in off the Atlantic is worth the two-hour ferry crossing alone.

Sleeping & eating

Apart from one hotel and a couple of B&Bs, all accommodation is self-catering. Also note that caravans and camping are not allowed on the island.

Accommodation on Colonsay is limited and must be booked up well in advance. **B** *Isle of Colonsay Hotel*, T200316, F200353. A few hundreds yards from the ferry, 11 rooms, a cosy 18th century inn with a friendly bar and excellent food, they also arrange various trips around the island. Attached to the hotel is *Viragos*, a coffee house and well-stocked bookshop. A cheaper option is the excellent **E** *Seaview*, T200315, at Kilchattan, near the standing stones. Open Apr-Oct. There's also a **B&B** near the hotel, at **E** *Smiddy Cottage*. Aside from the hotel bar, you can eat at *The Pantry*, T200325, near the ferry pier. It is open Mon-Sat and offers simple home cooking as well as teas and cakes.

Isle of Oronsay

Just off the southern tip of Colonsay is the island of Oronsay, two miles square with a population of six and one of the highlights of a visit to Colonsay. The name derives from the Norse for 'ebb-tide island', which is a fitting description as Oronsay can be reached on foot at low tide, across the mud flats known as 'The Strand'. It takes about an hour to walk from the south end of Colonsay to the ruins of 14th century **Augustinian Priory**. This was the home of some of the most highly-skilled medieval craftsmen in the Western Highlands. A surviving example of their work is the impressive Oronsay Cross and the beautifully-carved tombstones, on display in the **Prior's House**.

Legend has it that St Columba first landed here after leaving his native Ireland, but he could still see his homeland from the top of Ben Oronsay and so decided to continue north to Iona, where he founded the community that was to become the centre of Christianity in northern Britain (see page 248).

Make sure you take wellies for the walk across The Strand and check on the **tides**. Tide tables are available at the hotel or shop. Spring tides (new and full moon) allow about three to four hours to walk across and back, which is just enough time to see the priory but little else. If there's time, you can pop into *The Barn*, T200344, for home cooking and crafts.

Isle of Islay

Phone code: 01496
Colour map 5, grid A1

Islay (pronounced eye-la), the most southerly of the Hebridean islands and one of the most populous, with around 4,000 inhabitants, has one very important claim to fame – single malt whisky. Islay produces a very distinctive, peaty malt and connoisseurs are in for a treat, as the island has no fewer than six working distilleries. Aside from whisky, people also come here to watch birds. The island is something of an ornithologists paradise and from October to April plays host to migrating barnacle and white-fronted geese flying down from Greenland in their thousands for the winter.

If that leaves you cold, then there's always the spectacular coastal scenery, from the wild Mull of Oa to the glorious beach at Laggan Bay. Compared to other islands like Skye, Mull or Arran, Islay receives few visitors, mainly due to its distance from the mainland, giving it a really isolated feel. And because the island is partially Gaelic-speaking the road signs are bilingual.

Ins and outs

Islay can be reached by **air** from Glasgow (for flight details, see page 236). The airport is at Glenegedale, a few miles north of Port Ellen on the road to Bowmore.

The **ferry** to Islay (and Jura) from Kennacraig to Port Ellen (2 hrs 10 mins) sails 1 daily on Mon and Sun and 2 daily on Tue, Thur, Fri and Sat and to Port Askaig (2 hrs) 1 daily on Tue, Wed, Thur, Fri and Sat and 2 daily Mon. 1-way to Port Ellen/Port Askaig costs £6.65 per passenger and £35.50 per car. The ferry from Oban to Port Askaig sails on Wed (4 hrs 15 mins); 1-way £9.60 per passenger and £45.50 per car. From Colonsay to Port Askaig (1 hr 10 mins) there is a sailing on Wed; 1-way £3.35 and £17.75. *CalMac* offices: Kennacraig, T01880-730253; Port Ellen, T01496-302209.

It takes about 2½ hrs to **drive** to Kennacraig from Glasgow, and there's a daily **bus** from Glasgow to Kennacraig (with *West Coast Motors*) which connects with the ferry to Islay (for bus times, contact Buchanan Street bus station, T0141-3327133).

Getting there

For those without their own transport, there's a regular bus service around the island, with *Islay Coaches*, T840273, and *Royal Mail Postbuses*, T01463-256200. There are buses from Portnahaven to Port Ellen, via Port Charlotte, Bridgend, Bowmore and the airport; from Port Askaig to Port Ellen via Ballygrant, Bridgend, Bowmore and the airport; from Port Ellen to Ardbeg, Bowmore, Port Askaig and Portnahaven, and also a **postbus** to Bunnabahain. Buses run hourly at least from Mon-Sat, but only once on Sun. For bus times, pick up a copy of the *Islay & Jura Area Transport Guide* from the tourist office in Bowmore, Tarbert, Lochgilphead or Oban.

For **car hire** there's *D&N Mackenzie* at Glenegedale, T302300, and *Bowmore Engineering*, T810206. **Taxi hire** at *Carol's Cabs*, Frederick Cres, Port Ellen, T302155. **Bicycle hire** at *Macauley & Torrie*, Frederick Cres, Port Ellen, T302053, and Mick Stuart, Lennox St, Port Ellen, T302391, who is also a wildlife guide.

Getting around

Port Ellen

Port Ellen is the largest place on Islay and the main ferry port, yet it still has the feel of a sleepy, wee village. It was founded in 1821 by the laird, Walter Frederick Campbell, and named after his first wife. There are shops, hotels, B&Bs, restaurants, bank, a couple of filling stations, a post office and an information centre of sorts, based in a caravan beside the *White Hart Hotel*, making Port Ellen a good base from which to explore the delights of the southern half of Islay.

Around Port Ellen

There are a number of excellent day trips from Port Ellen. A road runs east out to **Ardtalla**, where it ends. Along the way, it passes three distilleries, first **Lapgroaig**, then **Lagavulin** and lastly, **Ardbeg**, all of which offer guided tours (see 'The Whisky Trail'). Between the Lagavulin and Ardbeg distilleries is the dramatically-sited 16th century ruin of **Dunyvaig Castle**, once the main naval base and fortress of the Lords of the Isles (see also page 259). A mile further on is the impressive **Kildalton Cross**, standing in the graveyard of the ruined 13th century chapel. The eighth-century cross is remarkably well preserved and one of Scotland's most important Early Christian monuments, and the carvings depict biblical scenes. At the end of the road is Ardtalla, from where you can begin the ascent of **Beinn Bheigeir** (1,609 feet), the island's highest hill, with spectacular views from the summit.

Southwest of Port Ellen a road runs out to a little, rounded peninsula known as **The Oa**, an area of varied beauty, both wild and pastoral, and with a wonderful coastline. The road runs as far as **Upper Killeyan**, from where it's about a mile uphill to the spectacular headland at the **Mull of Oa**. Here you'll see the strange-looking **American monument**. The obelisk commemorates the shipwrecks offshore of two US ships, the *Tuscania* and the *Ontranto*, both of which sank in 1918 at the end of the war. There's a great walk north from the Mull of Oa up to Kintra, but it's best to start out from Kintra (see below).

A turn-off from the road to The Oa leads north to **Kintra**, at the south end of **The Big Strand** at Laggan Bay, with five miles of glorious sands and dunes.

Islay

© Crown copyright

The Whisky Trail

Though the whisky distilling process is basically the same everywhere, some distilleries have more beautiful locations and more interesting tours. Islay's six distilleries enjoy the most scenically stunning settings and are full of character and history. Islay also offers the unique opportunity to visit several of Scotland's most impressive distilleries in one day, and their distinctive peaty malts are considered to be among the finest.

Laphroaig *(pronounced 'la-froyg') is the closest to Port Ellen and its wonderful setting is summed up by its name, meaning "The beautiful hollow by the broad bay" in Gaelic. According to many (including me) this is the ultimate in malt whisky and is at its best after dinner. The distillery's tours are by appointment only, T302418.*

Lagavulin *(pronounced 'laga-voolin') is a mile along the shore by the romantic ruin of Dunyveg Castle. Their 16-year-old single malt is one of the classics and also makes the ideal after-dinner tipple. They also offer a very interesting tour, Monday-Friday by appointment only, T302400.*

Ardbeg *distillery is a mile further east and produces a robust and powerful single*

malt. Established in 1815, it was closed for a while, but was recently acquired by Glenmorangie and runs tours Monday-Friday from 1030 till 1530, and also on Saturday and Sunday June-August, T302244.

Bowmore *is the oldest distillery on Islay and still uses all the old traditional methods to produce its fine single malt, also at its best after dinner. Their hour-long tours are the most professionally done and even include a video. Tours all year round from Monday-Friday at 1030 and 1400, in the summer months at 1030, 1130, 1400 and 1500, T810441.*

Caol Ila *(pronounced 'coal-eela') was founded in 1846 and lies close to Port Askaig with great views across the Sound of Islay to Jura. Unlike most of its island peers, this single malt is best before dinner. Tours of the distillery all year round by appointment only, T840207.*

Bunnahabhain *(pronounced 'bun a havan') is the most northerly of the distilleries, set in a secluded bay with great views across to Jura. Tours are also by appointment only, T840646.*

There's a restaurant and accommodation here, and it's a great place for camping (see 'Sleeping & eating' below). The restaurant is at the end of the road, with the beach on one side and on the other a wild and spectacular coastal walk to the **Mull of Oa**. There's a detailed map of the route in the restaurant. Just to the north of Kintra is the **Machrie golf course**, a memorable golfing experience. The *Machrie Hotel* does golfing packages (see 'Sleeping & eating' below).

Sleeping & eating

The places listed below are in and around Port Ellen. Four miles to the north, overlooking Laggan Bay, is **A** *Machrie Hotel*, T302310, F302404. Eighteen rooms, this golfing hotel is right by a great beach and a great golf course,. The bar and restaurant make the perfect end to 18 perfect holes. Also by the golf course is the excellent **B-C** *Glenmachrie*, T/F302560. Five rooms, a genuine farmhouse offering genuine hospitality and superb food. The price includes dinner, but you'd be crazy to book B&B only and deny yourself the pleasure. Nearby is **D** *Glenegedale House Hotel & Restaurant*, T302147, F302210, which is very handy for the airport. At Kintra beach (take the Oa road and follow the signs for Kintra) is **E-F** *Kintra Farmhouse*, T302051. Open Apr-Sept, 3 rooms. Also an independent hostel, the **F** *Kintra Bunk Barns Hostel* and a very good restaurant (see below). This is a great place for camping and there's a **campsite** with full facilities (open Apr-Sept).

There are several places to stay in the village itself. **E** *The Trout-Fly Guest House*, T/F302204, is right beside the ferry terminal and has a decent restaurant (for residents only). **E** *The Bothy*, 91 Lennox St, T302391. Run by the versatile Mick Stuart who also hires out bikes and acts as a wildlife guide. Keen divers might want to try the *Islay Dive Centre*, 10 Charlotte St, T302441, which has apartments to rent (**E**).

Apart from the places mentioned above, there's very good, cheap food available at the *Old Granary* at Kintra Farm (open 1730-2300, Jul/Aug 1200-2300).

Bowmore

The A846 runs north from Port Ellen, straight as a pool cue, to Bowmore, the island's administrative capital and second largest village. Founded in 1768 by the Campbells, it's an appealing place, laid out in a grid plan with the main street running straight up the hill from the pier to the unusual **round church**, designed to ward off evil spirits, who can hide only in corners. Thankfully, the nice spirit stayed behind and can be found at the **Bowmore Distillery**, just to the west of Main Street. This is the oldest of the island's distilleries, founded in 1779, and the most tourist-friendly.

Tourist office Islay's only official tourist office is in Bowmore, T810254. ■ *Apr-Jun Mon-Fri 0930-1730 (and Sun 1400-1700 in Jun); Jul-Sept Mon-Sat 0900-1745, Sun 1100-1700; Oct-Mar Mon-Fri 1000-1600. They'll find accommodation for you.*

Sleeping & eating **D** *Harbour Inn*, Main St, T810330, F810990. Four rooms, completely refurbished to a high standard, great views across the bay and superb food in their acclaimed restaurant (mid-range-expensive). **D** *Lochside Hotel*, Shore St, T810244, F810390. Eight rooms, friendly and good value hotel with a mind-boggling selection of single malts. On the road between Bowmore and Port Charlotte, at Bridgend, is **C** *Bridgend Hotel*, T810212, F810960. Ten rooms, nice and peaceful and good bar meals, there are also several B&Bs in Bowmore.

The Rinns of Islay

North of Bowmore, at **Bridgend**, the A846 joins the A847 which runs west to the hammerhead peninsula known as the Rinns of Islay ("rinns" is derived from the Gaelic for promontory). A few miles west of Bridgend the B8017 turns north to the **RSPB Reserve** at **Loch Gruinart**. The mudflats and fields at the head of the loch provide winter grazing for huge flocks of barnacle and white-fronted geese from Greenland, arriving in late October. There's an RSPB visitor centre at **Aoradh** (pronounced "oorig") which houses an observation point with telescopes and CCTV, and there's a hide across the road. In total there are about 110 species of bird breeding on Islay, including the rare chough and corncrake. Keen bird watchers can stay close by at **E** *Loch Gruinart House*, T/F850212 (**D** including dinner).

The coastal scenery around the Rinns is very impressive, particularly at **Killinallan Point**, a beautiful and lonely headland at the far northeast of Loch Gruinart. Also impressive is **Ardnave Point**, west of Loch Gruinart, and further west along the north coast, **Sanaigmore.** The best beaches are at **Saligo** and **Machir Bay** on the west coast, past Loch Gorm. Both are lovely, wide, golden beaches backed by high dunes, but swimming is forbidden due to dangerous undercurrents.

You can stay at **Kilchoman**, near Machir Bay, at the excellent **E-D** *Kilchoman House*, T850382, F850277, a former Georgian Manse with a reputation for fine cooking. Open April-October, book in advance.

Port Charlotte Port Charlotte is without doubt the most charming of Islay's villages, with rows of well-kept, whitewashed cottages stretched along the wide bay. It, too, was founded by the prolific Walter Frederick Campbell, in 1828, and named after the other important woman in his life, his mother.

But Port Charlotte is not just a pretty face. The **Islay Wildlife Information and Field Centre** is a must for anyone interested in flora and fauna. It's very hands-on, with good displays on geology and natural history, a video room and reference library. It's also a great place for kids and has activity days when staff take tours of the surrounding area. ■ *Easter-Oct Tue and Thur 1000-1700, Fri and Sun 1400-1700. £1.50.*

Also worth visiting is the compact **Museum of Islay Life**, to the east of the village, where you can find out all about illegal whisky distilling on the island. ■ *Easter-Oct Mon-Sat 1000-1630, Sun 1400-1630. £1.60.* Across the road is the **creamery**, where you can see the local cheeses being made. There are also a few good beaches around.

Sleeping & eating Accommodation is somewhat limited in Port Charlotte. The best place to stay is the **C** *Port Charlotte Hotel*, T850361, F850361. Ten rooms, restored Victorian inn with gardens and conservatory on seafront, their restaurant features local seafood and is the best around. There's also a **B&B** run by *Mrs Wood* (T850225), **E**, open April-October, and a *SYHA youth hostel* (T850385; open Mar to end-Oct), next to the Wildlife Information Centre.

Aside from the hotel, the best place to eat is the *Croft Kitchen* (T850230). It's a coffee and gift shop by day and moderately-priced restaurant by night, open Mar-Oct daily 1000-2030, best to book in season.

At the southern end of the Rinns is the picturesque little fishing and crofting **Portnahaven** village of Portnahaven, its Hebridean cottages rising steeply above the deeply-indented harbour. A mile south is Portnahaven's twin settlement, **Port Wemyss**, also named after the laird's wife, would you believe (she was a daughter of the Eighth Earl of Wemyss).

Sleeping Amenities are few and far between in this remote corner. If you want to stay, you can find a bed at **E** *The Old School House*, in Portnahaven, T860242.

Around Port Askaig

The A846 runs east from Bridgend out to Port Askaig passing a couple of inter- **Ballygrant** esting sights on the way. A mile and a half beyond Bridgend is the **Islay Woollen Mill**, which was established in 1883 on the site of a 17th century mill. The road then passes through **Ballygrant**, just to the south of **Loch Finlaggan**. Here, on two crannogs (artificial islands) were the headquarters of the Lords of the Isles, the ancestors of Clan Donald. The MacDonalds ruled from Islay for nearly 350 years, over a vast area covering all of the island off the west coast and almost the whole of the western seaboard from Cape Wrath to the Mull of Kintyre. There's a new **visitor centre** to the northeast of the loch, where you can learn more about the history of the site and see some of the archaeological remains. ■ *Easter-Oct, Tue, Thur and Sun 1430-1700. £1.50.* You can walk across the fen to **Eilean Mor**, where there's a collection of carved gravestones near the ruins of a medieval chapel. A smaller island, **Eilean na Comhairle** ('The Council of the Isle'), is where the Lords of the Isles met to decide policy.

Sleeping There's accommodation at the superb **D** *Kilmeny Farmhouse*, T/F840668. Comfort, style, excellent food and a warm, friendly atmosphere. The only drawback is that there are only three rooms, so book well in advance. Otherwise, there's the **D** *Ballygrant Inn*, T/F840277, which is comfortable and serves great pub grub.

Inner Hebrides

Port Askaig Port Askaig is Islay's other ferry port, with connections to the mainland and to the islands of Jura and Colonsay. It's little more than a dock, a car park and a few buildings huddled at the foot of a steep, wooded hillside. If you're arriving by the late ferry, there's accommodation at **C-D** *Port Askaig Hotel*, T840245.

A short walk north along the coast is the **Caol Ila distillery** and a couple of miles further north, at the end of the road which branches left before you enter Port Askaig, is the beautifully-situated **Bunnahabhain Distillery**.

Isle of Jura

Phone code: 01496
Colour map 5,
grid A1/2

The words 'wild' and 'remote' tend to get overused in describing the many Hebridean islands, but in the case of Jura they are, if anything, an understatement. The short ferry crossing from neighbouring Islay takes you into another world, pervaded by an almost haunting silence. Jura has one road, one hotel, six sporting estates and 5,000 red deer, which outnumber the 200 people by 25:1, the human population having been cleared to turn the island into a huge deer forest. Rather appropriately, the name Jura derives from the Norse 'dyr-ey', meaning deer island.

Ins and outs

Getting there A small car and passenger **ferry** makes the regular 5-min crossing daily from Port Askaig on Islay to Feolin Ferry. For times, contact *Western Ferries*, T01496-840681. A 1-way ticket costs £5.75 per car and 80p per passenger.

Getting around Amazingly enough, there is a **bus** service on Jura, which runs from Feolin Ferry to Craighouse several times a day, Mon-Sat. A few buses continue to Lagg and Inverlussa and return to Craighouse. Note that some journeys are by request only and must be booked the day before, T820314. For bus times, see the *Islay & Jura Area Transport Guide*, available free at tourist offices.

Around the island

The Paps Jura is one of the last, great wildernesses in the British Isles and perfect for some real off-the-beaten-track walking. Its main attractions are the beautiful **Paps of Jura**, three breast-shaped peaks that dominate not only the island itself but also the view for miles around. From Kintyre, Mull, Coll and Tiree, and from the mountains of mainland Scotland from Skye to Arran, they can be seen on the horizon. The Paps provide some tough hill walking and require good navigational skills, or a guide. It takes a good eight hours to cover all three peaks, though during the Paps of Jura fell race they are covered in just three hours. A good place to start is by the three-arch bridge over the Corran river, north of **Leargybreack**. The first pap you reach is **Beinn a'Chaolais** (2,408 feet), next is the highest, **Beinn an Oír** (2,571 feet) and the third is **Beinn Shiantaidh** (2,476 feet). To find out about guides, ask at the hotel in Craighouse (see below). The island's west coast is completely uninhabited and inaccessible to all but the hardiest and most dedicated of walkers.

Corryvreckan whirlpool & the north One of the island's main draws is the Corryvreckan whirlpool at the very northern tip, between Jura and the uninhabited island of **Scarba**. The notorious whirlpool, the most dangerous tide race in Scotland, is best appreciated one hour after low tide and its awesome roar can be heard long before you reach it. It is named after a Viking, Bhreacan, who anchored his boat here for

Inner Hebrides

three days and nights by a rope woven from the hair of virgins. Unsurprisingly, the rope parted under the strain, casting doubt on the status of one of the contributors, and Bhreacan drowned. To get there, follow the rough track from **Ardlussa** to **Kinuachdrach**, or get someone to drive you, then it's a two-mile walk. Before setting out, ask at the hotel for information and directions.

Also in the north of the island is **Barnhill**, the completely isolated and forlorn-looking cottage where **George Orwell** wrote *1984* between 1946 and 1948 (hence the book's title). Though the house attracts literary pilgrims, it remains closed.

The only village on Jura is Craighouse, eight miles from Feolin Ferry on the southeast coast. Here you'll find the **Jura distillery** which welcomes visitors. Tours are by appointment, T820240. Beside the distillery is the island's one and only hotel, the **C** *Jura Hotel*, T820243, F820249, overlooking the lovely small isles bay. They'll provide information on island walks and the pub is the social hub. There's cheaper accommodation with **E** *Mrs Boardman*, T820379, open April-September.

Craighouse

Three miles south of the village, at **Ardfin**, is **Jura House**, with its beautiful walled garden, filled with wild flowers and Australasian plants and trees. ■ *Daily during daylight hours. £2.*

Jura

Inner Hebrides

The Small Isles

Phone code: 01687   *The Small Isles is the collective name given to the four islands of Eigg, Muck, Rùm and Canna, lying south of Skye. Seen from the mainland, they look a very tempting prospect, especially the jagged outline of Rùm and the curiously-shaped Eigg. But visiting the islands is not easy, as ferry transport is purely designed for the inhabitants and not geared towards the convenience of island-hopping tourists. Furthermore, the island populations are small and accommodation and facilities are limited. But the determined traveller with time on their hands will be well rewarded, particularly on mountainous Rùm, with its superb walking and abundant wildlife.*

Getting there   A *CalMac* passenger-only **ferry** sails from Mallaig to all four islands. From Mallaig to **Eigg** (1 hr 30 mins) on Mon, Tue, Thur and Sat; Mallaig to **Muck** (2 hrs 30 mins) on Tue, Thur and Sat; Mallaig to **Rùm** (1 hr 45 mins-3 hrs 30 mins) on Mon, Wed and Sat; Mallaig to **Canna** (3 hrs) on Mon, Wed, Fri and Sat. One way Mallaig to: Eigg £4.45; Muck £6.85; Rùm £6.70; Canna £7.70. There are also ferries between Eigg, Muck, Rùm and Canna; for details contact the *CalMac* office in Mallaig, T01687-462403. On Sat in the summer a ferry leaves at 0500 and sails Mallaig-Canna-Rùm-Muck-Eigg, allowing those with limited time to at least see the islands from close up. A second ferry leaves on summer Sat, making it possible to spend either 9½ hrs on Canna, or 7½ hrs on Rùm, or 5 hrs on Muck, or 3½ hrs on Eigg. At Eigg, Muck and Rùm passengers are transferred to small boats as there are no suitable piers. Also from May-Sept the *CalMac* ferries from Mallaig are supplemented by cruises from Arisaig with *Arisaig Marine* , T01687-450224.

Eigg

Colour map 3,   Little Eigg has had something of a chequered past. In 1577 it was the scene of
grid A/B 4   one of the bloodiest episodes in the history of Clan warfare, when 395 MacDonalds, almost the entire population, were trapped in a cave and suffocated by a raiding party of Macleods from Skye, who lit a fire at the entrance. More recently it has been at the heart of a bitter land ownership debate. Having endured a succession of absentee landlords, ranging from the merely eccentric to the criminally negligent, the 65 remaining islanders seized the moment and bought the island themselves, in conjunction with the Scottish Wildlife Trust. Now everyone can enjoy the island's wildlife, which includes otters, seals, eagles and many other birds, such as the Manx shearwater, guillemots and black-throated divers.

The island is dominated by **An Sgurr**, a 1,289 feet flat-topped basalt peak with three vertical sides. It can be climbed easily by its western ridge and there's a superb view from the summit. Sitting in the shadow of the Sgurr, at the southeastern corner, is the main settlement, **Galmisdale**. This is where the ferries drop anchor (passengers are transferred to a smaller boat), and there's a post office, shop and tearoom, all by the pier. At the northern end is the small township of **Cleadale**, on the Bay of Laig. Just to the north are the "**Singing Sands**", a beach that makes a strange sound as you walk across it.

Sleeping   Two croft houses at Cleadale offer **B&B**: **D** *Lageorna*, T482405, also offers full board and caters for vegetarians; and **D** *Laig Farm*, T482437. There's also an independent **hostel** with 24 beds, *The Glebe Barn*, T482417.

Muck

Tiny Muck is the smallest of the four islands and is flat and fertile, with a beau-   *Colour map 3, grid B3*
tiful shell beach. It has been owned by the MacEwan family since 1879. The
island gets its unfortunate name (*muc* is Gaelic for pig) from the porpoises, or
"sea pigs", that swim round its shores. The ferry drops anchor near **Port Mór**,
and you can stay at **D** *Port Mór House*, T462365. The price includes dinner
which is also available to non-residents. Alternatively, you can ask permission
to camp at the tearoom, which does snacks and sells fresh bread.

Rùm

Rùm, or Rhum (the extra 'h' was added to avoid alcoholic associations) is the   *Colour map 3, grid A3*
largest of the islands and the most wild, beautiful and mountainous. Though it
looks like a wilderness, Rùm once supported a population of 300. Most of
them were shipped off to Canada in the mid-19th century, leaving behind an
uninhabited deer forest for sporting millionaires. One of these, John Bullough,
bought it in 1888 and passed it on to his son, Sir George Bullough, who built
the extravagant and extraordinary **Kinloch Castle**. No expense was spared on
this massive late-Victorian mansion, constructed of red sandstone from Arran
in a bizarre combination of styles. To describe it as over-the-top would be a
gross understatement. The fantastic folly is now a hotel (see below) but it is
also open to the public and the caretakers are happy to show visitors around.
Tours coincide with the arrival of the ferry. The castle stands at the head of narrow Loch Scresort by the little hamlet of **Kinloch**, where you'll find a
well-stocked shop, a post office and a coffee shop in the community hall.
Ferries are anchored in the loch and passengers are transferred to a smaller
craft and dropped a few minutes' walk along the shore from Kinloch.

The Bullough family mausoleum, built in the style of a Greek Doric temple,
stands incongruously on the west coast at **Harris Bay**. It's an interesting seven
and a half mile walk across to the mausoleum from Kinloch.

The island is owned and run by Scottish Natural Heritage as an enormous
outdoor laboratory and research station, and most of the 30 or so inhabitants
are employed by them. Studies of the red deer population is one the most
important areas of their work and access to parts of the island is restricted. This
is not prohibitive, though, and there are many marked nature trails, walks and
bird-watching spots. The island is a haven for wildlife and perhaps its most
notable resident is the magnificent white-tailed sea eagle, successfully
re-introduced onto Rùm in the 1980s and now spreading beyond the island.
Rùm is also home to golden eagles, Manx shearwaters and, less appealingly,
millions of midges. The island is the wettest of the Small Isles and a haven for
the little pests.

Rùm's other great attraction is its mountain range, which rivals that of the
Cuillins of Skye. The highest point is **Askival** (2,664 feet), which can be
reached by the main ridge from **Hallival**, though the route involves some rock
scrambling and is only advised for fit and experienced walkers. Before setting
out, you'll need to ask permission from the manager of the reserve office at the
White House (T462026).

Accommodation on the island is limited and most people visit on a day trip. If you   **Sleeping**
plan to stay longer, then book well in advance. **B** *Kinloch Castle*, T462037, is open
Mar-Oct and lets out a few of its opulent rooms which feature amazing bathrooms.
The old servants' quarters down below have been turned into cheap hostel

Inner Hebrides

accommodation, and there's also bistro which does a good, moderately-priced 3-course dinner (no lunches). Aside from the castle, there are a couple of cheap and basic **bothies** (F), and **camping** is allowed at Kinloch. For both, contact the reserve manager, T462026.

Canna

Colour map 3, grid A3
There are no shops on
Canna, so you'll need to
bring your own supplies.

Canna is the most westerly of the Small Isles and is owned by the National Trust for Scotland. The population of twenty mostly work on the island's farm. Canna was gifted to the National Trust by its benevolent owner, Dr John Lorne, a notable Gaelic scholar who still lives there. The island continues to be run as a single working farm and, since it was sold in 1938, has been an unofficial bird sanctuary with 157 recorded bird species, including Manx shearwater and puffins.

It's a small island, five miles long by one mile wide, bounded by cliffs and with a rugged interior, fringed by fertile patches. It's attached to its smaller neighbour, **Sanday**, by a narrow isthmus which is covered, except at low tide. The main attraction for visitors is some fine walking. It's about a mile from the ferry jetty up to the top of **Compass Hill** (458 feet), so called because its high metallic content distorts compasses. The highest point on the island is **Carn a' Ghaill** (690 feet).

During the summer, a day trip from Mallaig allows you over nine hours in which to explore Canna and enjoy the fantastic views across to Rùm and Skye. Those wishing to stay put, can **camp** rough, with permission from the NTS, or rent out their self-catering cottage, T0131-2265922.

Inner Hebrides

Perthshire and Stirling

7

Perthshire and Stirling

© Crown copyright

These two historically important regions straddle the **Highland Boundary Fault**, *the dividing line between the heavily-populated Central Lowlands and the wild, remote Highlands. As the main access route between the Highlands and Lowlands, Perthshire and Stirling have been at the very heart of the main events which have shaped the country's destiny. Many of the most important battles have been fought here and the region is littered with remnants of the past.*

Standing between Edinburgh and Glasgow, yet only a short distance from some of the country's most beautiful scenery, is the ancient town of **Stirling**, *its magnificent castle perched on a rocky crag above medieval streets, like a smaller version of Edinburgh. Two of Scotland's most famous and important battles were fought here and the town is synonymous with the country's two greatest historical heroes,* **Robert the Bruce** *and* **William Wallace**. *Stirling is the gateway to the* **Trossachs**, *a beautiful area of mountains, forests, lochs and steep-sided glens that stretches west from* **Callander**. *This part of the country was eulogized and popularized by* **Sir Walter Scott**, *who also dramatized the life of local hero,* **Rob Roy** *MacGregor, Scotland's answer to Robin Hood.*

Northeast of Stirling is the ancient town of **Perth**, *erstwhile capital of Scotland and surrounded by stunning countryside. At nearby* **Scone Palace** *Kenneth MacAlpin united the Scots and the Picts in 846 and every Scottish king was crowned there – all 42 of them. Numerous* **castles** *are scattered around the glens of Perthshire, including* **Blair Castle**, *one of the country's top attractions and home to the only legitimate private* army in Britain. Of the many myths and legends which abound in these parts, the most startling comes from the tiny village of **Fortingall**, near **Loch Tay**. Here, it is claimed, is the birthplace of **Pontius Pilate**.

The region has other attractions, not least of which is the spectacular and varied landscape, ranging from the gentle pleasures of **Strathearn** to the rugged peaks of the **Grampian Mountains**. There are Munros aplenty for the bagging, and in the far west of the region, on the eastern shores of **Loch Lomond**, is the **West Highland Way**, Scotland's most popular long-distance hike. There are numerous **cycle trails** through the forests and glens, and a long-distance cycleway runs from Glasgow, through the Trossachs and along the shores of Loch Tay to Pitlochry. There's also **skiing** in Glenshee, **salmon fishing** on the river Tay, **watersports** on Loch Earn and **golfing** at glorious Gleneagles, all within easy reach of Edinburgh and Glasgow.

Ins and outs

Getting around

Though the more remote northerly parts of Perthshire and Stirling are difficult to reach by public transport, much of the region is easily accessible. The towns of Perth and Stirling are transport hubs and one of the country's main train lines, from Glasgow to Inverness, passes through the region. A good network of intercity and local buses connects all the main towns and villages. The main road north to Inverness, the A9, runs through the eastern part of the region, and the main route north from Glasgow, the A82, forms its western boundary.

Information

Stirling, Falkirk, parts of the Ochils, the Campsies, the Trossachs and Loch Lomond are all covered by the *Argyll, the Isles, Loch Lomond, Stirling & the Trossachs Tourist Board*, info@scottish.heartlands.org, www.scottish.heartlands.org, with tourist offices in Aberfoyle, Alva, Balloch, Callander, Drymen, Dunblane, Falkirk, Killin, Stirling, Tarbet and Tyndrum.

The rest of the region, from Kinross in the south to Blair Atholl in the north and from Glenshee in the east to Rannoch Moor in the west, is covered by the *Perthshire Tourist Board*, www.perthshire.co.uk, perthtouristb@perthshire.co.uk, with tourist offices in Aberfeldy, Auchterarder, Blairgowrie, Crieff, Dunkeld, Kinross, Perth and Pitlochry.

Both tourist boards can provide information and literature on accommodation and various outdoor activities such as walking, cycling, golf and fishing. Two good walking guides are Bartholomew's *Walk Perthshire* and *Walk Loch Lomond and the Trossachs*.

Perth

Perth and Stirling

'The Fair City' of Perth is aptly named. Situated on the banks of Scotland's longest river, the Tay, Perth and its surrounding area boasts some of the most beautiful scenery in the country. From the 12th century, Perth was the capital of Scotland and here are many interesting sights to visit (most of which are free). The jewel in Perth's crown, though, is undoubtedly Scone (pronounced 'scoon') Palace, on the outskirts of town. Scone was the home of the Stone of Destiny for nearly 500 years and the site where every Scottish king was crowned.

*Phone code: 01738
Colour map 4, grid C3
Population: 42,000*

The town makes a convenient and very pleasant base for exploring this beautiful Highland region. There are many colourful parks and historic buildings, excellent shopping opportunities and plenty of places to eat, drink and relax. Perth also has a proliferation of leisure and sporting facilities – and not many towns can boast a golf course on an island in the middle of a river.

Ins and outs

Getting there

Perth is easy to get to from almost anywhere in the country. It's only 1½ hrs from Edinburgh or Glasgow, and half an hour from Dundee, by road, and on the main train lines to these cities, as well as on the main lines north to Aberdeen and Inverness. The **train** and **bus stations** are almost opposite each other at the west end of town, where Leonard St meets Kings Pl.

Getting around

The town centre is very compact and lies on the western bank of the Tay, between 2 large parks; North Inch and South Inch. It's easy to get around on foot, but Scone Palace and many of the B&Bs are on the eastern bank of the river, so you may wish to take a bus. **Local buses** are run by *Stagecoach*, T629339. For a **taxi**, call *Ace Taxis*, T633033. An enjoyable way to see the sights is to use the *Guide Friday* bus tour of Perth. Tour tickets are valid all day, so you can get on and off as often as you please and you can join the tour at various locations throughout the city. T0131-5562244 for more details, or contact the tourist office.

Tourist information The Tourist Information Centre is housed in the Lower City Mills, West Mill St, T638353. It is open Apr-Jun, Sept and Oct Mon-Sat 0900-1800, Sun 1100-1600; Jul and Aug Mon-Sat 0900-2000, Sun 1100-1800; Nov-Mar Mon-Sat 0900-1700.

Sights

Town centre The heritage of Perth is easy to trace as it holds so many interesting historical sites within walking distance of each other. Standing on the river Tay ensured that Perth became a busy trading port which still has a bustling harbour, the only inland harbour in Britain. In years gone by, salmon and wool were major exports from Perth, while claret was imported from Bordeaux in France.

Between the High Street and South Street is **St John's Kirk**, still standing on its original site. It was founded in 1126, though most of the present church dates from the 15th century. In 1559, firebrand preacher John Knox gave one of his trademark sermons, inspiring the good folk of Perth to destroy the local monasteries. The church gave the town its original name of 'St John's town', a name upheld in the local football team, St Johnstone.

A few minutes walk north, on North Port, is the **Fair Maid's House**, the fictional home of Sir Walter Scott's virginal heroine in his novel, *The Fair Maid of Perth*. The novel was set in the 14th century, at the time of the Battle of the Clans, which took place on the North Inch, just to the north, across Charlotte Street. Close by, at the corner of Charlotte Street and George Street is the **Museum and Art Gallery**, with displays on local history, art, archaeology, natural history and whisky. ■ *Mon-Sat 1000-1700, free, T632488.*

In the 18th century, the world famous Black Watch regiment was raised in Perth and the **Black Watch Museum**, housed in the 15th-century Balhousie Castle, is well worth a visit even to the most un-military minded. The museum is on Hay Street, on the edge of the North Inch, to the north of the town centre. ■ *May-Sept Mon-Sat 1000-1630; Oct-Apr Mon-Fri 1000-1530, free, T621281.* Back in the town centre, in West Mill Street (also home of the tourist office), is **Lower City Mills**, a restored and working 19th-century oatmeal mill powered by a huge water wheel.

Perth's other museum contains the excellent **Fergusson Gallery**, a display of works by the renowned Scottish colourist, John Duncan Fergusson. The gallery is found at the south end of Tay Street, near South Inch, in a splendid neo-classical building which was once Perth's waterworks. ■ *Mon-Sat 1000-1700, free, T441944.*

Those with souvenirs to buy may be interested in a visit to the **Caithness Glass** factory, on Inveralmond Industrial Estate, a mile north of town on the A9, where you can also watch the glass-blowing process. ■ *Apr-Oct Mon-Sat 0900-1700, Sun 1000-1700; Nov-Mar Mon-Sat 0900-1700, Sun 1200-1700, free, T637373.*

For those of you with more horticultural leanings, **Branklyn Garden**, at 116 Dundee Road, has been described as 'the finest two acres of private garden in the country'. With an impressive collection of rare and unusual plants, it includes superb examples of Himalayan poppies. Well worth a visit at any time of year, many of the plants grown there are on sale in the potting shed shop. ■ *Mar-Oct daily 0930-sunset, £2.50, £1.70 child/concession, T625535 (NTS).*

Kinnoull Hill Woodland Park is a beautiful wooded area on the outskirts of the city. The trip to the top of Kinnoull Hill (783ft) itself affords an astounding view across Perth, down to the Tay estuary and through Fife to the Lomond hills. To the north, the views sweep from Ben More in the west to Lochnagar in the northeast.

There are four walks through the Woodland Park – Nature Walk, Tower Walk, Jubilee Walk and Squirrel Walk – and each of these is graded according to how difficult it is and what type of conditions the walker can expect. However, none of the walks are extremely strenuous, though the Squirrel Walk is most suitable for the less able. If you're feeling particularly energetic, cycling and horse riding take place in specific zones in the park, principally in the Deuchny Wood area. There is a *Countryside Ranger Service* in the park and they will be happy to answer any questions you may have about their work or the park itself. Also ask at the tourist office in town for details.

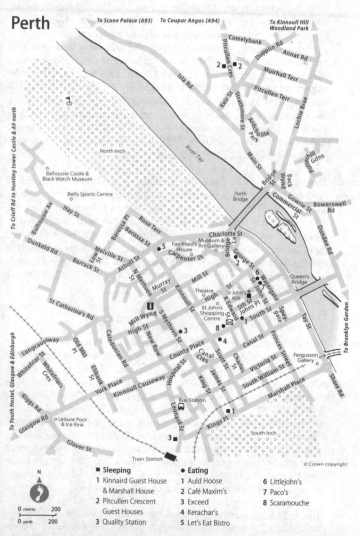

Perth

Perth and Stirling

To Scone Palace (A93)   To Coupar Angus (A94)   To Kinnoull Hill Woodland Park

© Crown copyright

■ Sleeping	● Eating	
1 Kinnaird Guest House & Marshall House	1 Auld Hoose	6 Littlejohn's
2 Pitcullen Crescent Guest Houses	2 Café Maxim's	7 Paco's
	3 Exceed	8 Scaramouche
3 Quality Station	4 Kerachar's	
	5 Let's Eat Bistro	

Scone Palace Situated a few miles outside Perth on the A93 Braemar Road, is the unmissable **Scone Palace**, one of the most historically important places in the whole country. The home of the Earls of Mansfield, Scone has a long and fascinating history. It was the capital of the Pictish Kingdom in the sixth century and home of the Celtic church. Here, Kenneth MacAlpin united Scotland and in 838AD placed the stone of Scone (or 'Stone of Destiny') on the Moot Hill, opposite the palace entrance. This became the ancient crowning place of Scottish kings, including Macbeth and Robert the Bruce. The Royal City of Scone became the seat of government and the kings of Scotland resided at the Palace of Scone before their coronations. The coronation stone was removed to Westminster by that most hated foe, Edward I, in 1296, and only recently returned to Scotland in a desperate, but failed, Conservative attempt to win back support north of the border. The famed 'Stone of Destiny' currently resides in Edinburgh Castle (see page 76). In 1651 the last coronation in Scotland took place when King Charles II was crowned by the Scots on the Moot Hill. The ceremony was attended by Lord Stormont, forefather of the present occupier, Lord Mansfield. Part of the church where this took place still remains.

Aside from its hugely impressive history, the palace also houses beautiful collections of porcelain, needlework, royal furniture, clocks, ivories and many other absorbing artefacts. You could also spend a few hours walking in the magnificent 100-acre gardens, filled with bluebells, rhododendrons, roses and rare trees, strutting peacocks and Highland cattle roaming around. There's also a maze, picnic park and adventure playground for the kids, plus a gift shop and coffee shop with delicious home baking. ■ *T552300. Early Apr to late Oct, daily 0930-1715 (last admission 1645). Palace and grounds £5.60, £4.80 concession; grounds only £2.80, £2.40 concession.*

Huntingtower Castle Though not as impressive as Scone, Huntingtower Castle, three miles west of Perth on the A85 to Crieff, is worth a visit. It consists of two complete towers, dating from the 15th and 16th centuries, linked by a 17th-century range, and features some fine 16th-century painted ceilings. The castle, once owned by the Ruthven family, has some interesting history of its own. Prior to the building of the range, a daughter of the house once leapt between the two towers to avoid being caught in her lover's bedroom. ■ *T627231 (HS). Apr-Sept daily 0930-1830; Oct-Mar Mon-Wed and Sat 0930-1630, Thur 0930-1200, Fri and Sun 1400-1630. £1.80, £1.30 concession.*

Essentials

Sleeping There are numerous places to stay in and around Perth. Pick of the bunch is the **A** *Ballathie House Hotel*, at Kinclaven, near Stanley, 2 miles north of Perth, just off the A9, T01250-883268, www.ballathiehousehotel.com. 28 rooms, this elegant, award-winning 19th-century former hunting lodge has a reputation for superb Scottish cuisine (expensive). Another excellent option is the **B** *Huntingtower Hotel*, T583771, F583777, 1 mile west of Perth off the A85 to Crieff. 34 rooms, elegant country house hotel in its own landscaped gardens, good food in the dining room (mid-range) and bar meals in the conservatory (cheap). Next to the train station, on Leonard St, is the **B-C** *Quality Station Hotel*, T624141, admin@gb628-u-net.com. 70 rooms, a grand old Victorian edifice close to the town centre. **D-C** *Sunbank House Hotel*, 50 Dundee Rd, T624882, F442515. 9 rooms, lovely little hotel overlooking the river Tay and close to Branklyn Garden and Kinnoull Hill, great value.

There are **B&Bs** and **guesthouses** all over town. You'll find lots of them along Dunkeld Rd, heading north out of town towards the A9, including: **E** *Almond Villa Guest*

House, No 51, T629356, almondvilla@compuserve.com; **E** *Clark Kimberley*, No 57-59 (T637406); **E** *The Gables Guest House*, No 24, T/F624717; and **E** *Strathcona*, No 45, T626185. There are also several places on Marshall Pl, which overlooks the South Inch, including the highly recommended **E** *Kinnaird Guest House*, No 5, T6280121, www.yell.co.uk/sites/kinnaird-ph-2. Next door at No 6 is **E** *Marshall House*, T442886. The best place to look is Pitcullen Cres, on the A94 Coupar Angus road, where almost every house on the street offers B&B. The most recommended include **E** *Achnacarry Guest House*, No 3, T621421; **E** *Adam Guest House*, No 6, T/F627179; **E** *Clunie Guest House*, No 12, T/F623625; and **E** *Pitcullen Guest House*, No 17, T626506.

The excellent *SYHA Youth hostel* is at 107 Glasgow Rd, T623658, open Mar-Oct, about half a mile west of the town centre (take bus No 7). There's a **campsite** at *Cleeve Caravan Park*, T639521, open Apr-Oct, on Glasgow Rd, near the ring road, about 2 miles from town. There's also the *Scone Palace Camping & Caravan Club Site*, T552323, open Mar-Oct.

Perth is packed with pubs and restaurants to suit all tastes. Restaurant-wise, quite a few come with glowing references from diners. *Let's Eat Bistro*, T643377, on Kinnoull St, is a very classy establishment which provides a modern Scottish menu with Mediterranean influences, all meals cooked fresh to order. *Exceed*, T621189, at 65 South Methven St, has a more general menu but it's just as appetizing, as is the menu at *Café Maxim's*, T567056, at 80 George St, close to the museum. For something a little more expensive, try *Kerachar's*, T449777, at 168 South St, which specializes in delicious fish and game. *Paco's*, T622290, 16 St John's Pl, has a more 'Tex-Mex' feel to it, serving fajitas, enchiladas, steaks and a fine line in chicken dishes, while also serving up a children's menu of burgers and pizzas. *Littlejohn's*, T639888, 24 John St, covers a lot of bases, from pizza to Tex-Mex.

Eating & drinking

Of the **pubs** in town, *The Auld Hoose*, (T624136) on the corner of South St and King Edward St, does a nice bar lunch, as does *Mucky Mulligan's*, T636705, at 97 Canal St. *Scaramouche*, T637479, 103 South St, is a very popular bar, as is the *Cherrybank*, T624349, at 210 Glasgow Rd, where the bar lunches and suppers come very highly recommended.

Perth Theatre, 185 High St, T621031, is a beautiful Victorian-era theatre with an excellent reputation for high-class productions. The *Playhouse* **cinema** at 6 Murray St, T623126, offers a dose of escapism on the big screen. For the younger (and young at heart) traveller, there are 2 **nightclubs** in Perth; *Curly Lloyd's* at 40-48 Canal St, T630503, and the *Ice Factory* at 6 Shore Rd, T630011.

Entertainment

The **Perth Highland Games** are held on the second Sun in Aug, T627782, on the same weekend as the **Perth Show**, which takes place on South Inch. There are also regular **jump racing** events during the summer at **Perth Racecourse**, near Scone Palace, T551597.

Festivals & events

Outdoor equipment *Mountain Man Supplies*, 133 South St, T632368.

Shopping

For sports and leisure, Perth takes a bit of beating. Four sports centres in the city ensure there's no excuse for 'couch-potato' inactivity. *Perth Leisure Pool*, T635454, open daily 1000-2200, west of the town centre on the Glasgow Rd, claims to have the best leisure swimming pool in Scotland. Next door is *Dewar's Rinks*, T624188, where the visitor can curl, ice skate or bowl. *Bell's Sports Centre*, on Hay Street, T622301, open daily 0900-2200, covers virtually every sport and leisure activity imaginable.

Sports

Scotland is famed for its superb fishing and Perth, handily situated in Scotland, has more than its fair share of **game and course fishing** facilities. Too many, in fact, to

Perth and Stirling

detail here, so we'll mention just one which is recommended: the *Sandyknowes fly-fishery* at Bridge of Earn, T813033, a few miles southeast of Perth. Located between the rivers Earn and Tay, there are facilities for the novice, right up to the most experienced angler with great fishing in a beautiful landscape. The season runs from Mar-Dec and currently costs £10 per day. Details of all the Perthshire fisheries are available from the Tourist Information Centre at West Mill Street.

Another sport Scotland is renowned for is **golf**, and Perth is particularly worthy of mention in this respect as it has a golf course in the middle of the river Tay! Moncrieff Island is worth playing a round on, if only to be able to tell your friends that the golfers don't shout 'fore' on this course, they shout 'ahoy there!' Details from the Tourist Information Centre, or contact *King James VI Golf Club*, T625170.

Perth is also well-placed for other outdoor activities such as **walking**, **cycling** and **skiing**. *Glenshee ski centre* is on the A93 north of Blairgowrie and easily reached from Perth (see page 282). The tourist office can provide suggested cycle routes and stocks the *Cycle Routes in Highland Perthshire* booklet. For walkers, two recommended guidebooks are *Perthshire, Angus and Fife Walks* which details 28 routes, and Bartholomew's *Walk Perthshire* which describes 45 routes.

Transport *Scottish Citylink* **buses** (T0990-505050) run frequently to **Glasgow** (1 hr 15 mins; £6.80), **Edinburgh** (1 hr 30 mins; £4.50), **Dundee** (35 mins; £3), **Aberdeen** (2 hrs 30 mins; £9) and **Inverness** (2 hrs 30 mins; £9). *Stagecoach* (T629339) run local buses to Dunkeld, Pitlochry, Aberfeldy and Crieff, and *Strathtay Scottish* (T01382-228054) buses serve Blairgowrie, Alyth and Dundee.

There's an hourly **train** service (Mon-Sat; 2 hourly on Sun) to **Glasgow Queen St** (1 hr; £11.40), and frequent trains to **Edinburgh** (1 hr 20 mins; £9.10). There are also hourly trains to **Stirling** (30 mins; £7.10), **Dundee** (25 mins; £4.30) and **Aberdeen** (1 hr 40 mins) and several daily to **Inverness** via **Pitlochry** (30 mins; £7.80) and **Aviemore**.

Car hire *Arnold Clark*, St Leonard's Bank, T442202.

Directory **Medical facilities** *Perth Royal Infirmary*, Taymount Terr, T623311.

North of Perth

The A9 runs north from Perth and is the main route to **Inverness** and the **Highlands**. There are a number of attractions along the route, which is served by regular trains and buses.

Dunkeld and Birnam

Phone code: 01350
Colour map 4, grid B3

Twelve miles north of Perth is the attractive village of Dunkeld, standing right on the Highland line. Dunkeld is surrounded by beautiful scenery offering excellent **walking** opportunities, details of which are available from the **tourist office** at The Cross, T727688, in the heart of the village. ■ *All year round: Apr-Jun, Sept and Oct Mon-Sat 0930-1730, Sun 1100-1600; Jul and Aug Mon-Sat 0900-1930, Sun 1100-1900; Nov and Dec Mon-Sat 0930-1330.*

Sights It's definitely worth making a stop here, if only to admire the **cathedral**, in the most idyllic situation on the banks of the fast-flowing, silvery Tay. Half of it is still in use as a church and the other half is in ruins. The oldest part of the cathedral is the 14th-century choir which now forms the parish church, while the 15th-century nave and tower are also still standing. Much of the original was damaged during the orgy of ecclesiastical destruction that sadly accompanied the Reformation, then it was damaged again in the Battle of Dunkeld, in 1689, fought between supporters of the protestant William of Orange and the Stuart monarch James VII. ■ *Apr-Sept 0930-1830 (HS), free.* On your way to the cathedral you'll pass a collection of lovely little whitewashed cottages, beautifully restored by the NTS. More details are available at the Ell Shop nearby.

Across the bridge from Dunkeld is **Birnam**, made famous by Shakespeare's *Macbeth*, though the play's protagonist was in reality a very different character from the evil villain portrayed by the Bard. Birnam was the inspiration for another famous literary figure, **Beatrix Potter**, who spent her childhood summers here. Visitors can explore the origins of the *Peter Rabbit* stories in the **Beatrix Potter Garden**.

A short distance north of Dunkeld on the A9, is the turning to **The Hermitage**. A marked woodland walk starts from the car park and follows the river Braan to the Black Linn Falls, overlooked by Ossian's Hall, an 18th-century folly built by the Duke of Atholl. It's a lovely spot, which has inspired the likes of Wordsworth and Mendelssohn. Further on is Ossian's Cave. Buses to Pitlochry (see below) stop at the turning for The Hermitage.

A few miles northeast of Dunkeld, off the A923 to Blairgowrie, is the **Loch of the Lowes Visitor Centre**, managed by the Scottish Wildlife Trust. There's a hide with binoculars for viewing a pair of ospreys which breed here and which can be seen on the loch from early April to early September. ■ *Apr-Sept daily 1000-1700, free (donation advised), T727337.*

Sleeping & eating

The top hotel in the area is **L** *Kinnaird House*, at Dalguise, about 8 miles north via the A9, T01796-482440. The setting, the style and the service are all unbeatable. In the village is the luxurious **L** *Stakis Dunkeld*, T727771, former home of the Duke of Atholl, now with full leisure and outdoor activity facilities. More modest options include **D** *Atholl Arms Hotel*, T727219, by the bridge, or **B&B** at **E-D** *The Pend*, 5 Brae St, T727586, www.thepend.com, and **E** *Birnam Guest House*, 4 Murthly Terr, Birnam, T727201. There's also a **hostel**, the *Western Caputh Independent Hostel*, at Caputh, 5 miles east of Dunkeld, on the A984 to Coupar Angus, T01738-710617. It has 18 beds and is open all year. **Eating** options are mostly limited to the hotels. The best bar meals are offered by the *Atholl Arms* (see above) and the *Birnam House Hotel*, T727462, on the main road through Birnam.

Transport

Citylink **buses** between Perth and Inverness stop at the train station by Birnam several times daily in either direction. *Stagecoach* buses from Perth to Pitlochry and Aberfeldy stop in Dunkeld, and *Strathtay Scottish* buses between Blairgowrie and Aberfeldy also stop in the village (twice daily Mon-Sat). There are several **trains** daily, T0345-484950, to and from Perth and Inverness.

Pitlochry

Despite being one of the busiest Highland tourist towns in the summer, Pitlochry's lovely setting on the shores of the river Tummel, overlooked by Ben y Vrackie makes it a pleasant base for exploring this beautiful area. The town also has a few worthwhile attractions of its own.

Phone code: 01796
Colour map 4, grid B3
Population: 2,500

The **tourist office** is at 22 Atholl Road, T472215. ■ *Apr to mid-May and Oct Mon-Sat 0900-1800, Sun 1200-1800; mid-May to Sept daily 0900-2000; Nov-Apr Mon-Fri 0900-1700, Sat 0900-1330.*

There are two whisky distilleries to visit. The larger of the two is Bell's **Blair Atholl Distillery**, at the southern end of town, heading towards the A9 to Perth. ■ *T472234. Easter-Sept Mon-Sat 0900-1700, Sun 1200-1700; Oct-Easter*

Sights

Mon-Fri only, tours every 10 mins. £3. A couple of miles east of town, on the A924, is the **Edradour Distillery**, the smallest in Scotland. ■ T472095. Mar-Oct Mon-Sat 0930-1700, Sun 1200-1700; Nov and Dec Mon-Sat 1000-1600. Free.

Pitlochry's main attraction is the **fish ladder**, part of the **power station and dam** which formed man-made **Loch Faskally** when it was constructed on the river Tummel. The ladder allows salmon to swim up to their spawning grounds and you can watch them leap spectacularly in the spring and summer. The best months are May and June. The fish ladder is across the river, a short distance from the *Pitlochry Festival Theatre* (see below).

Walks around Pitlochry

The tourist office sells a useful leaflet *Pitlochry Walks* (50p), which describes four long local walks, but there are many other fine walks in the surrounding area. The Bartholomew series *Walk Perthshire* (£4.99) describes the walks below, plus 43 others, with clear route maps.

OS Landranger maps Nos 43 & 52 cover all the walks and the OS Explorer map No 21 (Pitlochry and Loch Tummel) covers them in greater detail.

The greatest walking attraction is **Ben y Vrackie** (2,758ft), a steep six-mile walk (there and back) from the tiny hamlet of Moulin, a mile north of Pitlochry on the A924 (turn left at the Moulin Inn). The path is well trodden and the going is relatively easy, across bleak moorland, until the steep final ascent on scree. On a clear day the views from the summit of the Trossachs are wonderful, so it's best not to attempt this on a cloudy day. In spite of its proximity to Pitlochry, you need to be properly equipped and take the usual safety precautions (see page 56).

Another excellent walk from Pitlochry, described in the tourist office leaflet, leaves town on the north road and turns left past the boat station. It then crosses the Cluanie footbridge and follows the road to Loch Faskally and up the river Garry to Garry Bridge over the **Pass of Killiecrankie** (see page 277). The path returns to Pitlochry along the west banks of the river Garry, before turning west up the river Tummel, passing close by the **Linn of Tummel**, then crossing the Tummel and following the west shore of Loch Faskally to the dam and fish ladder.

Sleeping

There's plenty of accommodation to choose from. The best hotel in town is the superb **B** *Pine Trees Hotel*, Strathview Terr, T472121. This Victorian country house is set in 10 acres of gardens away from the tourist bustle. Its *Garden Restaurant* has a fine reputation. A few miles north of Pitlochry, in the village of Killiecrankie, is the **B-C** *Killiecrankie Hotel*, T473220, www.btinternet.com/~killiecrankie.hotel/index.html. Open Mar-Dec, 11 rooms, it's a quiet, cosy country house hotel which offers quite possibly the very finest food in the area. Another top-class hotel is the **C-D** *Dunfallandy Country House Hotel & Restaurant*, T472648, dunfalhse@aol.com, a mile out of town on the Logierait road. 9 rooms, this Georgian mansion offers great views, peace and quiet and superb cuisine, no smoking, excellent value.

There are numerous guesthouses and B&Bs, far too many to list here. The tourist office will provide a full list. Among the most recommended are **D-E** *Craigroyston House*, 2 Lower Oakfield, T472053, **E** *Arrandale House*, Knockfarrie Rd, T472987, and **E** *Comar House*, Strathview Terr, T473531. There's an *SYHA Youth Hostel*, T472308, open all year, on Knockard Rd overlooking the town centre.

Eating

The *Killiecrankie Hotel* (see above) is expensive but the best place to eat. The best restaurant in town is *Port-na-Craig Inn & Restaurant*, T472777, which is just below the Festival Theatre on the banks of the river Tummel. It offers great Scottish cooking at mid-range prices in a bistro ambience. Another good choice is the *Old Smiddy*, at 154 Atholl Rd, T472356, which is moderately priced and open daily till 2100. A couple of miles south of Pitlochry on the old A9 road is the *East Haugh Country House Hotel & Restaurant*, T473121, www.world-traveller.com/scotland.east.html, a 17th-century country house with excellent and elegant dining and great bar lunches (lunch mid-range; dinner expensive). A few miles north of Pitlochry, at Moulin on the A924 is the wonderful *Moulin Inn*, T472196, which serves good, hearty and cheap pub food, fine real ales (try their 'Braveheart') and a great atmosphere. Food daily till 2130.

The *Pitlochry Festival Theatre*, T472680, is across the river from the town centre. It stages a different play every night for 6 nights a week during its season from May to Oct. **Entertainment**

MacNaughton's, Station Rd. A vast range of everything tartan and lots more besides. Come here first. **Shopping**

The **bus** and **train stations** are on Station Rd, south of the main street. *Scottish Citylink* **buses** run almost every hour between **Glasgow** (2 hrs 15 mins; £6.80), **Edinburgh** (2 hrs 45 mins; £6.30) and **Inverness** (2 hrs; £7) via Pitlochry. Stagecoach buses run daily except Sun to **Aberfeldy**, **Dunkeld** and **Perth**. Pitlochry is on the Perth-Inverness rail line and there are several daily **trains** (Mon-Sat; fewer on Sun) to Perth (30 mins; £7.10). **Transport**

    Cycle hire *Escape Route*, 8 West Moulin Rd, T/F473859. Touring and off-road bikes for £14 per day. **Taxi** *Elizabeth Yule Transport*, T472290.

Around Pitlochry

Four miles north of Pitlochry the A9 cuts through the **Pass of Killiecrankie**, a spectacular wooded gorge which was the dramatic setting for the Battle of Killiecrankie in 1689, when a Jacobite army led by Graham of Claverhouse, Viscount 'Bonnie Dundee', defeated the government forces under General Hugh Mackay. One government soldier evaded capture by making a jump of Olympic gold medal-winning proportions across the river Garry at **Soldier's Leap**. An NTS **visitor centre** has displays on the battle and the local natural history. ■ *T473233. Apr-Oct daily 1000-1730. Free (honesty box; £1 donation advised).*

Seven miles from Pitlochry, and a mile from the village of Blair Atholl, is Blair Castle, traditional seat of the Earls and Dukes of Atholl. This whitewashed, turreted castle dates from 1269 and presents an impressive picture on first sight. This is the headquarters of Britain's only private army, the Atholl Highlanders, and one of them usually pipes in new arrivals. Thirty-two rooms in the castle are open for public viewing and are packed full of paintings, furniture, armour, porcelain and much else besides, presenting a startling picture of aristocratic Highland life in previous centuries. The most outrageously sumptuous of the rooms are the Tapestry Room and the ballroom. The surrounding landscaped grounds are home to peacocks and Highland cattle, and there are woodland walks and a walled Japanese water garden to enjoy. ■ *T481207. Apr-Oct 1000-1800 (last admission 1700). £5.50, plus £2 parking charge.*

Blair Atholl & Blair Castle
Phone code: 01796
Colour map 4, grid B3

    There's a **caravan park** within the castle grounds, T481263, open April-October, with good facilities. A very good **walk** starts from the caravan park and heads up into **Glen Tilt**. It's about 10½ miles there and back along estate roads, though this can be shortened by four miles or lengthened by six miles. A leaflet describing the routes is available from the castle or caravan park.

Sleeping There's a selection of accommodation in Blair Atholl village. The **C-D** *Atholl Arms Hotel*, T481205, near the train station does B&B and serves bar meals.

Transport Not all **trains** stop at Blair Atholl. *Elizabeth Yule Transport* (see Pitlochry Transport above) runs a service between Pitlochry and Blair Atholl, via Killiecrankie, a few times daily, except Sun (£1.10 each way). You can **hire bikes** from *Atholl Mountain Bikes*, T473553, for £10-12 per day. They have a leaflet listing various cycle routes, including the Glen Tilt route above.

Falls of Bruar Eight miles from Blair Atholl, just off the A9, are the Falls of Bruar. There's a short walk from the car park to the lower falls, but it's worth continuing to the more dramatic upper falls, which are less visited. A well-maintained path leads from the lower falls along the gorge of the Bruar River to the upper falls and back down the other side. It's a 1½ mile round trip. An information panel at the start of the walk shows the route. Close by is the excellent **House of Bruar**, a huge shopping emporium designed like a Victorian hunting lodge where you can buy just about any kind of souvenir and enjoy some very fine Scottish cooking.

Loch Tummel & The B8019 turns off the B8079 road from Pitlochry to Blair Atholl and runs
Loch Rannoch west along the shores of beautiful lochs Tummel and Rannoch, best seen in the
Phone code: 01796 autumn when the trees change their colours. At the eastern end of Loch
Colour map 4, grid B2 Tummel is **Queen's View**, a spectacular viewpoint which looks down the loch and across to Schiehallion. There's a **visitor centre** here, with displays and audio-visual programmes about the area. ■ *T473123. Apr-Oct daily 1000-1730. Free, but £1 parking charge.*

Schiehallion (3,552ft) is one of Scotland's best-loved mountains whose distinctive conical peak made it ideal for use in early experiments in 1774 to judge
OS sheet No 51 the weight of the earth. These were not an unqualified success, but led to the invention of contour lines as an aid to surveying the mountain. The walk to the summit is fairly straightforward, except for the very rocky final stretch. You'll need to be properly clothed and equipped (see page 56) and take a map and compass. The route to the summit starts at the car park on the B846 Kinloch Rannoch to Aberfeldy road, near Braes of Foss.

Kinloch Beyond Loch Tummel is the little village of Kinloch Rannoch, where back-
Rannoch packers can stock up on supplies before heading into the hills. There are a few
Colour map 4, grid B2 **places to stay** in the village, including the characterful **C** *Dunalastair Hotel*, T01882-632323, and **E** *Bunrannoch House*, T01882-632407, a former Victorian shooting lodge which offers good cooking.

Sixteen miles west of the village the road ends at Rannoch station, where you can catch trains north to Fort William or south to Glasgow. Beyond the west end of Loch Rannoch is bleak Rannoch Moor which extends all the way to Glen Coe. By the station is the **E-D** *Moor of Rannoch Hotel*, T01882-633238, which does good, moderately priced meals. There's a daily (except Sunday) **postbus** service, T472386, from Pitlochry to Rannoch station, via Kinloch Rannoch, or check with *Elizabeth Yule Transport* (see Pitlochry **Transport**).

Aberfeldy

Phone code: 01887 The little town of Aberfeldy stands on the banks of the river Tay, on the A827
Colour map 4, grid B2 which runs between the A9 and Loch Tay. It's well placed geographically for
Population: 2,000 exploring the northern part of Perthshire, though Pitlochry has better tourist facilities. The **tourist office** is housed in an old church on The Square, in the centre of town. ■ *T820276. Apr-Jun, Sept and Oct Mon-Sat 0930-1730, Sun 1200-1600; Jul and Aug Mon-Sat 0900-1900, Sun 1100-1800; Nov-Mar Mon-Fri 0930-1700, Sat 0930-1330.*

The river Tay is spanned by **Wade's Bridge**, built by General Wade in 1773 Sights
during his campaign to pacify the Highlands. Overlooking the bridge is the
Black Watch Monument which commemorates the famous regiment
becoming part of the British Army's peacekeeping force here, in 1739. In Mill
Street is the **Aberfeldy Water Mill**, built in 1825 and restored in 1983 to produce stone-ground oatmeal in the traditional Scottish way. ■ *Easter-Oct
Mon-Sat 1000-1700, Sun 1100-1700, £2.*

A mile west of Aberfeldy, across the Tay at Weem, is **Castle Menzies**, an
impressive, restored 16th-century, 'Z-plan' fortified tower house and former
seat of the chief of Clan Menzies. ■ *T820982. Apr-Oct Mon-Sat 1030-1700,
Sun 1400-1700. £3, £2.50 concession.*

A popular local walk is to the **Falls of Moness**, through the famous **Birks of
Aberfeldy**, forever associated with the poet Robert Burns who was inspired by
the birks (birch trees) to write his eponymous song. It's a fairly easy walk along
a marked trail (see map) up to the impressive falls and the views of Strathtay
and the surrounding hills on the descent also make it worthwhile. It's about
four miles there and back.

There are several hotels in and around town, the best of which is the magnificent **Sleeping &**
15th-century **L-A** *Farleyer House Hotel* in Weem, T820332, 100127.222@ **eating**
compuserve.com. Also recommended is **B-C** *Guinach House*, T820251, a family-run
country house hotel in a lovely setting by the Birks and with a superb restaurant
(expensive); and the very friendly **C** *Weem Hotel* T820381, in Weem, about a mile
west of Aberfeldy on the B846 to Strathtummel. There are many **guesthouses** and
B&Bs, including **D-E** *Fernbank House*, Kenmore St, T820345, **E** *South Lodge*,
T820115, by Castle Menzies and **E** *Tigh'N'Eilean Guest House*, T820109, on Taybridge
Drive, all of which are recommended and offer good value.

There's not a great deal of choice for **eating**, other than the hotels in town or a bar
lunch in one of the pubs. The *Breadalbane Bakery*, at 37 Dunkeld St on the way out of
town, is recommended for home baking and their Aberfeldy Whisky Cake.

Stagecoach **buses** run regularly (Mon-Sat) to **Pitlochry** (45 mins; £2.50), **Dunkeld** (1 **Transport**
hr 15 mins) and **Perth** (1 hr 45 mins; £3.75). *Strathtay Scottish* has twice daily (except
Sun) buses to **Blairgowrie**, via Dunkeld. There's also a **postbus** service to **Killin** and
another to **Glen Lyon** once a day, except Sun, T01463-256200.

Around Loch Tay

The 14 mile-long Loch Tay is surrounded by some of the loveliest scenery in *Colour map 4, grid B2*
Perthshire and is well worth exploring, though public transport around its
shores is limited to one postbus service a day. At the northeast end of Loch Tay
is **Kenmore**, a neat little village of whitewashed cottages dominated by a huge
archway which stands at the gateway to Taymouth Castle, built by the Campbells of Glenorchy in the early 19th century and now a very fine **golf course**,
T830228. Near the village, on the southern bank of the loch, is **The Scottish
Crannog Centre**, an authentic reconstruction of a *crannog*, an artificial
Bronze Age island-house built for defensive purposes. ■ *T830583. Apr-Oct
daily 1000-1700, £2.80.*

Loch Tay is a major **watersports** centre and close by the Crannog Centre is **Sleeping &**
Croft-Na-Caber, T830588, Scotland's best watersports and activities centre, where you **sport**
can try water-skiing, windsurfing, sailing, rafting, jet biking, river sledging (!), fishing,
parascending, clay-pigeon shooting, hill walking and Nordic skiing. There's

accommodation at the **D** *Croft-Na-Caber Hotel*, T830236. Also in Kenmore is the *Loch Tay Boating Centre*, T830291, open Apr-Oct, where you can hire speedboats, fishing boats and canoes. The best place to stay in Kenmore is the **C** *Kenmore Hotel*, T830205, which claims to be Scotland's oldest coaching inn, dating from 1572. Whether or not that's true, there's no denying it's full of character and very comfortable. There's also a **campsite** at the *Kenmore Caravan and Camping Park*, T830226, complete with its very own golf course. You can **hire bikes** from *Perthshire Mountain Bikes*, T830291.

Kenmore to Amulree
Colour map 4, grid B2

For those with their own transport, one of the most scenic routes in this part of the country is the spectacular road which winds its way south from Kenmore high up into the mountains, across a bleak and barren plateau and down the other side to the tiny hamlet of **Amulree**. This road is often closed in the winter and there are gates at either end. From Amulree you can continue south to Crieff (see page 282), through the gentler, but equally stunning, scenery of the **Sma' Glen**. Alternatively, you could head north to Aberfeldy and then complete the circuit back to Kenmore.

Fortingall & Glen Lyon
Colour map 4, grid B2

A few miles west of Kenmore an unclassified road turns off the A827, which runs along the north bank of the loch, and heads to Fortingall, a tiny village of classic beauty which features on many a calendar. It's little more than a row of thatched cottages which wouldn't even get a mention were it not for two amazing claims. The 3,000-year-old yew tree in the churchyard is claimed to be the oldest living thing in Europe. More astonishing is the claim that this is the birthplace of **Pontius Pilate**, said to be the son of a Roman officer who was stationed here. Furthermore, it is believed that Pilate returned here to be buried, and a gravestone in the churchyard bears the initials 'PP'. There's **accommodation** in the village at the wonderful, and very popular, **D** *Fortingall Hotel*, T01887-830367, next to the churchyard.

If you have your own transport, make a detour up Glen Lyon, one of the most beautiful of all Scottish glens. On a summer's day, there can be few lovelier places on earth as the river Lyon tumbles through corries and gorges, and through flowering meadows, with high mountain peaks on either side and eagles soaring overhead. It's no surprise that Wordsworth and Tennyson waxed lyrical over its qualities. The road from Fortingall runs all the way to the head of the glen, at Loch Lyon. This is walking and fishing paradise. There are several Munros to 'bag' and fishing permits are available at the *Fortingall Hotel* (see above).

Ben Lawers
Colour map 4, grid B2

The north side of Loch Tay is dominated by Ben Lawers (3,987ft), the highest mountain in Perthshire. Its massif of seven summits includes six Munros which are linked by an eight-mile ridge which can be walked in one day by fit and experienced hill walkers. The best access to the ridge is from Glen Lyon. You'll need OS sheet No 51. The trek to the main summit starts from the **NTS Visitor Centre** (£1 admission), two miles along a track which turns off the main A827 about halfway between Kenmore and Killin (see page 302). This track continues over a wild pass to Bridge of Balgie in Glen Lyon. Leaflets describing the climb are available from the visitor centre. It's a seven-mile walk there and back and though the route is straightforward and easy to follow, it's a very steep, tough climb of 2,700ft from the centre to the summit. Allow five to six hours. You should be fit, properly clothed (see page 56) and have some previous hill-walking experience, but the views from the top on a clear day are amazing, across to the North Sea in the east and the Atlantic Ocean in the west. There's also a much easier one-mile nature trail and an accompanying booklet describing the rare Alpine flora is available at the centre. Near the turn-off to the NTS Visitor Centre is the **E** *Ben Lawers Hotel*, T01567-820436.

Blairgowrie and Glenshee

The other major road running north from Perth is the A93, which passes the Glenshee ski resort on its way to Braemar and then heads east through Deeside to Aberdeen (see page 375).

The respectable town of Blairgowrie, or Blairgowrie and Rattray to give it its full title, lies amidst the raspberry fields of Strathmore and is conveniently placed to serve as an accommodation centre for Glenshee Ski Centre (see below). The **tourist office** is at 26 Wellmeadow in the centre of town. ■ *T872960. All year, Easter-Jun, Sept and Oct Mon-Sat 0930-1730, Sun 1100-1600; Jul and Aug Mon-Sat 0900-1900, Sun 1000-1800; Nov-Easter Mon-Fri 0930-1730, Sat 1000-1400.*

Blairgowrie
Phone code: 01250
Colour map 4, grid B4

There's little of real interest to detain passing tourists but **Keathbank Mill**, off the A93 to Braemar, is worth a look. This huge 19th-century jute mill has an 1862 steam turbine driven by the largest water wheel in Scotland. There's also a heraldry museum, model railway and woodcarving workshops. ■ *T870025. Apr to early Oct daily 1030-1700, £2.95.* Three miles south of Blairgowrie, just off the A93 by **Meikleour**, is a 100ft high **beech hedge**, the highest hedge in the world.

Sleeping There's a good selection of accommodation. Top of the range is the **L** *Kinloch House Hotel*, T884237, 101445.2270@compuserve.com, a luxurious country house 3 miles west of town on the A923 to Dunkeld. It offers excellent cuisine (expensive) and sporting facilities. More affordable is the **C** *Altamount House Hotel*, T873512, on the Coupar Angus Road, which also offers top-class cooking (mid-range-expensive). There are plenty of cheaper options, including **D-E** *Rosebank House*, T872912, on Balmoral Road. **Camping** is available at the *Blairgowrie Holiday Park*, T872941, in Rattray, across the river Ericht.

Twenty miles north of Blairowrie, at **Spittal of Glenshee** is *Gulabin Lodge*, T885256, a **hostel/bunkhouse** run by Cairnwell Mountain sports which rents out skis, boards and mountain bikes and also gives skiing tuition. Nearby is one of the area's top hotels, **B-C** *Dalmunzie House Hotel*, T885224, a grand old Highland sporting lodge set in a 6,000-acre estate and boasting the highest nine-hole golf course in Britain.

Eating There are several decent eating places, best of which is *Cargills*, T876735, a nice-looking bistro housed in a converted mill store by the river. Moderate prices. Closed Mon. The *Angus Hotel* and *Brig o'Blair* pub, both on Wellmeadow, serve decent bar meals, as does the lovely **D-E** *Bridge of Cally Hotel*, T886231, six miles north of town on the A93.

Transport *Strathtay Scottish*, T01382-228054, **buses** run hourly (Mon-Sat; less frequently on Sun) to and from **Perth** (45 minutes; £2) and **Dundee** (one hour; £2.25).

Perth and Stirling

Glenshee Ski Centre

Glenshee ski centre is at the crest of the Cairnwell Pass (2,199ft), the highest main road pass in Britain, on the border of Perthshire and Aberdeenshire. It is the most extensive skiing area in Scotland, with 38 pistes, as well as Nordic skiing. **Ski rental** is around £13 per day (£12 for snowboards) and lessons are £18 for four hours. A day **lift pass** costs £18, or £72 for five days, including tuition and hire. For more information, call Ski Glenshee (T01339-741320, www.ski.scotland.net). For the latest snow and weather conditions, call the Ski Hotline (T0900-1-654656).

The only public transport is a daily **postbus** service (Monday-Saturday only) from Blairgowrie to Spittal of Glenshee, or to the ski resort from Braemar and Ballatar.

Strathearn

Strathearn is the wide valley (or *strath*) of the river Earn, which stretches west from Perth to **Loch Earn**, on the border of the Perthshire and Stirling regions. The Highlands officially begin in the western part of Strathearn and the Highland Boundary Fault runs through right the village of Comrie, near Crieff.

Auchterarder
Phone code: 01764
Colour map 4, grid C3

South of Strathearn is the trim little town of Auchterarder, overlooked by the **Ochil Hills** to the south and surrounded by rich farmland. There's a **tourist office** on the High Street. ■ *T663450. Apr-Jun, Sept and Oct Mon-Sat 0930-1730, Sun 1100-1600; Jul and Aug Mon-Sat 0900-1800, Sun 1100-1700; Nov-Mar Mon-Fri 0930-1330.* The adjacent **heritage centre** tells of the local textile industry which has been going here since the 16th century. Most people come here to play **golf** at the world-renowned L *Gleneagles Hotel*, T662231, www.gleneagles.com, a luxury five-star hotel and leisure resort with three top-class golf courses. If you can afford it, there is no better way to pamper yourself.

Dunning

Five miles east of Auchterarder, and eight miles southwest of Perth, is the historically interesting little village of Dunning, once the capital of the Picts and the place where Kenneth I, king of the Picts and Scots, died, in 860. The village was burned to the ground by the Jacobites in 1716 and the only surviving building is the 12th-century Norman tower of **St Serf's church**. A mile west of the village, by the B8062, is **Maggie Walls Monument**, which commemorates the burning of a local witch in 1657.

There are daily **buses** with *Docherty's Midland Coaches*, T662218, to and from **Dunning**, **Crieff**, **Stirling** and **Perth**.

Crieff and around

Population: 6,350
Phone code: 01764
Colour map 4, grid C2

The well-groomed town of Crieff sits on the slopes of the Grampain foothills overlooking the wide Strathearn valley. It's a popular tourist centre and a good base for exploring the western part of Perthshire and the Trossachs. People have been coming here since Victorian times, when Crieff was a popular spa town, and its position between the Highlands and Lowlands made it an important livestock market in the 18th century, with traders coming from as far afield as the Isle of Skye to buy and sell cattle. The **Crieff Highland Gathering** takes place on the penultimate Sunday in August.

The **tourist office** is in the town hall on the High Street. ■ *T652578. All year Apr-Jun, Sept and Oct Mon-Sat 0930-1730, Sun 1100-1600; Jul and Aug Mon-Sat 0900-1900, Sun 1100-1800; Nov-Mar Mon-Fri 0930-1700, Sat 0930-1330.*

Sights

A mile from town, just off the A85 to Comrie, is **Glenturret Distillery**, Scotland's oldest distillery, established in 1775. It has a good restaurant which serves food all day (lunch cheap-moderate; dinner expensive). ■ *T656565. Mar-Dec Mon-Sat 0930-1800 (last tour 1630), Sun from 1200; Feb Mon-Sat 1130-1600, Sun from 1200; Jan free tours Mon-Fri 1130-1600, guided tours £3.50; tasting tour £7.50.*

Five miles southeast of Crieff, off the B8062, is **Innerpeffray Library**, Scotland's first ever public library (founded in 1680) with a huge collection of rare and ancient books (but don't make too much noise about it). ■ *T625819. Feb-Nov daily (except Thur) 1000-1245 and 1400-1645, Sun 1400-1600, £2.50 with guided tour.* The chapel next door dates from 1508 and is also interesting.

Two miles south of Crieff, on the A822 to **Muthill**, is the turning to the very wonderful **Drummond Castle Gardens**, one of the finest formal gardens in Europe. Even the most horticulturally ignorant of people could not fail to be amazed by the graceful harmony and symmetry, in particular the magnificent parterre celebrating family and Scottish heraldry. If you have the feeling you've seen them before, that's because they were featured in the film *Rob Roy*. ■ *T681257. May-Oct daily 1400-1800 (last entry 1700), £3. To get there, take bus No 47 towards Muthill and get off at the gates, then walk 1½ miles up the castle drive. The castle is closed to the public.* In the village of Muthill itself is an ancient **church bell tower**, which dates from c.1225-50.

Sleeping

There's a good selection of accommodation in Crieff. Most of the hotels are to be found on the Perth Rd or Comrie Rd, but the best place to stay is the enormous **L** *Crieff Hydro*, T655555, which first opened in 1868 as the *Stratheam Hydropathic*. Turn off the High Street at the *Drummond Arms Hotel* then continue uphill and follow the signs. It doesn't sell alcohol (it's owned by the Church of Scotland) but offers a huge range of leisure activities and a fine restaurant.

Crieff

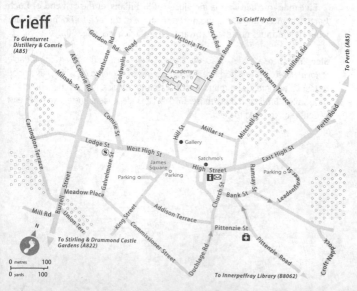

Best of the cheaper accommodation is **E** *Merlindale*, Perth Rd, T655205. Also good is **E** *Comely Bank Guest House*, 32 Burrell St, T653409, bookings@ comelybank.demon. co.uk, and **E** *Sydney Villa Guest House*, 57 Burrell St, T652757.

Eating Other than the hotels in town and the Glenturret Distillery (see above), there isn't a huge choice of decent places to eat. Pick of the bunch is *Satchmo's Restaurant*, 32 High St, T656575, which offers bistro-style modern Scottish food (cheap to mid-range) and a lot of jazz memorabilia.

Shopping *The Strathearn Gallery & Pottery*, 32 West High St, T656100, www.strathearn-gallery.com, open Mon-Sat 1000-1700, Sun 1300-1700.

Transport *Stagecoach* **buses**, T01738-629339, run every hour (Mon-Sat) to **Perth** (45 mins; £2.20) and **Comrie**. Some buses continue to **St Fillans**. There are regular buses to **Stirling**, via **Muthill**, and also to **Auchterarder** via Muthill. *Stagecoach* also runs a special 'Tourist Trail' bus around Perthshire and Stirling, stopping at Pitlochry, Aberfeldy, Dunkeld, Comrie, St Fillans and various other places. **Cycle hire** *Crieff Ski Shop*, 66 Commissioner St, T654667.

Comrie
Colour map 4, grid C2

Five miles west of Crieff is the pleasant village of Comrie, which has the distinction of being the most earthquake-prone place in Britain due to its position on the Highland Boundary Fault. The world's first seismometer was set up here, in 1874, at the **Earthquake House**, which is at The Ross, about a mile west of the village, just off the A85. ■ *Apr-Oct at all times.*

A great place for kids is the **Auchingarrich Wildlife Centre**, a few miles south of Comrie on the B827 on a windy hillside. It has a large collection of wild and exotic animals which you can feed and pet. ■ *T679469. Daily all year 1000 till dusk. £4, £3 child.*

A recommended **walk** from Comrie is to the **Deil's Cauldron**, a spectacular waterfall in **Glen Lednock** which extends six miles into the hills northwest of Comrie. It's a pleasant mile-long woodland walk to the waterfall, and from there you can climb up to **Melville Monument**, at the top of Dunmore Hill (840ft), from where there are excellent views across Strathearn and the Ochil Hills.

Five miles further west is the village of **St Fillans**, at the east end of **Loch Earn**. The A85 runs along the northern shore of the loch to **Lochearnhead**, where it continues northwest towards **Crianlarich** (see page 302).

Sleeping There are a few places to stay in Comrie, including the very comfortable **B** *Royal Hotel* on Melville Square, T679200, www.royalhotel.co.uk, which has a good restaurant and great pub round the back serving real ales. At the other end of the price scale is *Braincroft Bunkhouse*, T670140, an independent hostel two miles east of Comrie on the road to Crieff.

Stirling

As you'd expect with such a strategically important town, Stirling has a long and fascinating history and is packed with major historical sights. The town is best known for its castle, perched high on a rocky crag above the town and every bit as impressive as Edinburgh's. Also the Wallace Monument, a huge monolith high on Abbey Craig to the northeast of town which commemorates William Wallace, portrayed by Mel Gibson in the movie Braveheart.

Phone code: 01786
Colour map 2, grid C2
Population: 37,000

    Being so close to both Edinburgh and Glasgow, the sights of Stirling can be visited in a day from either city, but it's a very pleasant place to stay. It may lack the cosmo-politan feel of Edinburgh but has a lively buzz of its own during the busy summer months and there is a wide range of accommodation and other tourist facilities.

Ins and outs

Stirling is easily reached from Edinburgh, Glasgow, Perth and most other main towns and cities by regular **bus** and **train** services. The **train station** is on Station Rd, near the town centre, and the **bus station** is close by, on Goosecroft Rd, behind the Thistle Shopping Centre.

Getting there

Most of the important sights, except Bannockburn and the Wallace Monument, are within easy walking distance of each other. There's an open-topped 'hop on, hop off' Heritage Bus Tour which runs from Jun to Sept and includes the castle and Wallace Monument. There are tours every 30 mins from 1000 till 1700. A day ticket costs £6. Check details at the tourist office.

Getting around

Perth and Stirling

History

It was once said that whoever controlled Stirling held the key to Scotland. Consequently, the town and its surrounds have witnessed many crucial struggles between the Scots and the English. In fact, its name is derived from 'The Striveling', or place of strife. It was here that the Scots under William Wallace defeated the English at the **Battle of Stirling Bridge**, in 1297. A more famous battle was fought just a few miles away, at **Bannockburn** in 1314, when Robert the Bruce's small army routed Edward II's much larger English force. For the next three centuries, until the Union of Crowns in 1603 and James VI's move to England, Stirling Castle was the favourite residence of the Stuart monarchy and the setting for the coronation, in 1543, of the young Mary, future Queen of Scots.

Sights

The **tourist office** is at 41 Dumbarton Rd in the centre of town. It is the main office for Loch Lomond, Stirling and the Trossachs and stocks a wide range of books, guides, maps and leaflets. It also has information on the various **guided walks** of the town, including the popular **ghost walks** which take place Tue-Sat at 1930 and 2130. Alternatively, there are personal stereo guides available from *Stags Audio Walks*, at 24 Broad St. ■ *T475019. All year Jun and Sept Mon-Sat 0900-1800, Sun 1000-1600; Jul and Aug Mon-Sat 0900-1930, Sun 0930-1830; Oct-May Mon-Sat 1000-1700.*

The obvious place to begin a tour is the immensely impressive castle which stands 250ft above the flat plain atop the plug of an extinct volcano. From the west there's a sheer drop down the side of the rocky crag, making the castle

Stirling Castle

Stirling

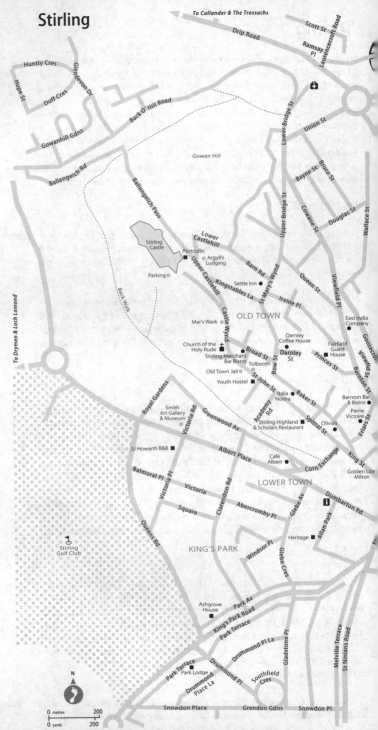

To Callander & The Trossachs

Drip Road

Scott St

Ramsay Pl

Laurencecroft Road

Huntly Cres

Hope St

Glentevon Dr

Duff Cres

Back O' Hill Road

Lower Bridge St

Union St

Gowanhill Gdns

Ballengeich Rd

Gowan Hill

Bayne St

Bruce St

Ballengeich Pass

Cowane St

Douglas St

Upper Bridge St

Wallace St

Stirling Castle

Lower Castlehill

Portcullis

Argyll's Ludging

Barn Rd

Queen St

Viewfield Pl

Parking

Upper Castlehill

Kingstables La

Settle Inn

St Mary's Wynd

Irvine Pl

Back Walk

Mar's Wark

Castle Wynd

OLD TOWN

East India Company

Goosecroft

Church of the Holy Rude

Darnley Coffee House

Fairfield Guest House

Viewfld St

Stirling Merchant Bar Bistro

Broad St

Darnley St

Princes St

Barnton St

Old Town Jail

Tolbooth

Bow St

Baker St

Barnton Bar & Bistro

Youth Hostel

St John St

Italia Nostra

Pierre Victoire

Royal Gardens

Victoria Rd

Greenwood Av

Academy Rd

Stirling Highland & Scholars Restaurant

Spittal St

Olivia's

Friars St

King St

Smith Art Gallery & Museum

Corn Exchange

SJ Howarth B&B

Albert Place

Café Albert

Golden Lion Milton

Balmoral Pl

Victoria

Clarendon Rd

LOWER TOWN

Dumbarton Rd

Square

Abercromby Pl

Glebe Av

Allan Park

Queens Rd

Windsor Pl

Glebe Cres

Heritage

Stirling Golf Club

KING'S PARK

Melville Terrace

St Ninians Road

Ashgrove House

Park Av

King's Park Road

Park Terrace

Gladstone Pl

Drummond Pl La

N

Park Lodge

Park Terrace

Drummond Pl

Southfield Cres

Drummond Place La

0 metres 200

0 yards 200

Snowdon Place

Grendon Gdns

Snowdon Pl

To Drymen & Loch Lomond

Perth and Stirling

seem a daunting prospect to would-be attackers, and now presenting visitors with fantastic views of the surrounding area. There's been a fortress here since the Iron Age, though the current building dates mostly from the 15th and 16th centuries, when it was the favourite residence of the Stuart kings.

On the esplanade is a **visitor centre** which shows an introductory film giving a potted history of the castle. From here you proceed to the **Upper Square**, where you can see the magnificent **Great Hall**, built by James IV and which was recently restored to its original condition. He also built the royal residence known as the **King's Old Building**, which now houses the **museum** of the Argyll and Sutherland Highlanders, which traces the history of this famous regiment from its inception in 1794 to the present day. James V, whose wives were both French, brought masons from France to create the spectacular **Palace** (1540-42), the finest Renaissance building in Scotland. This was where the young Mary, Queen of Scots spent much of her life until her departure for France, in 1548.

The interior of the royal apartments is largely bare but you can still see the **Stirling Heads**, 56 elegantly carved oak plaques which once decorated the ceiling of one of the rooms. Also impressive is the interior of the **Chapel Royal**, built by James VI in 1594 for the baptism of his son. The 16th-century **kitchens** are also interesting and have been restored to recreate the preparations for a royal banquet. ■ *T450000 (HS). Apr-Sept daily 0930-1800; Oct-Mar till 1700, £6 (includes admission to Argyll's Ludging).*

The Old Town The Old Town grew from around the 12th century, when Stirling became a royal burgh, and spread from the castle down the hill towards the flood-plain of the river Forth. Most of the historic sights are clustered around these medieval cobbled streets.

Stirling Bridge

The Old Town was fortified behind massive **town walls**, built in the mid-16th century as protection against Henry VIII's constant attacks in order to force Mary, Queen of Scots to marry his son and unite the kingdoms – the so-called 'Rough Wooing'. These walls are the best surviving in Scotland and can be followed along a path known as the **Back Walk**, which starts near the tourist office in Dumbarton Road and runs around the base of the Castle Rock and back up to the Old Town. On the way the path passes Gowan Hill, site of the **Beheading Stone**, used in numerous executions, most notably that of Murdoch, Duke of Albany, in 1425.

Five minutes walk downhill from the castle is **Argyll's Ludging** (lodging), the finest and most complete surviving example of a 17th-century town house in Scotland. It was built by William Alexander, founder of Nova Scotia, and then, on his death, was bought by the ninth Earl of Argyll. In the 18th century, the house became a military hospital and in the 1960s was used as a youth hostel. It has recently been restored to its former glory and rooms are furnished as they would have been in the late 17th century. ■ *T461146. Same opening hours as the Castle. £2.80, or joint ticket with the Castle.*

Further down Castle Wynd, at the top of Broad Street, is **Mar's Wark**, the ornate façade of a dilapidated town house, started by the first Earl of Mar, Regent of Scotland, in 1569 but left to fall into ruin following his death two years later. It was further damaged during the 1745 Jacobite Rebellion. A little further down Castle Wynd is the medieval **Church of the Holy Rude**, where the infant James VI was crowned in 1567. The oldest parts, the nave and tower, date from 1456 and the church also features one the few surviving 15th-century open-timber roofs. Behind the church is **Cowane's Hospital**, built in 1637 by the wealthy merchant John Cowane as an almshouse for 'Decayed members of the Guild of Merchants'. It now houses a tartan display and computer database for those wishing to trace their roots. ■ *T461146. Apr-Sept Mon-Sat 0900-1700, Sun 1300-1700. Free.*

A short way down St John Street is the impressively refurbished **Old Town Jail**, where the rigours of life behind bars in times gone by is brilliantly illustrated by enthusiastic actors. A glass lift then takes you up to the roof for spectacular views across the town and Forth Valley. ■ *T450050. Apr-Sept daily 0930-1800; Oct daily till 1700; Nov-Mar daily till 1600. £3, £2.25 concession.* Opposite the jail is Broad Street, centre of the medieval town and site of the **Mercat Cross**, which is topped by a Unicorn known locally as the 'Puggy'. Nearby is the **Tolbooth**, built in 1705 as the town's administrative headquarters by Sir William Bruce (who designed the Palace of Holyroodhouse in Edinburgh) and used as a courthouse and jail in the 19th century. At the bottom of Broad Street is **Darnley's House**, where Mary, Queen of Scots' second husband, Lord Darnley, is said to have stayed. It now houses a coffee shop (see Eating below).

At the bottom of Spittal Street, where it joins King Street, turn into Corn Exchange Road and then head west up Dumbarton Road to reach the **Smith Art Gallery and Museum**, which houses some interesting displays about the town's history and culture as well as a fine collection of paintings. ■ *T471917. All year Tue-Sat 1030-1700, Sun 1400-1700. Free.*

At the north end of the town, a good 20-minute walk from the town centre, is the 15th-century **Old Bridge**, which was the lowest crossing point on the Forth, and one of the most important bridges in Scotland, until Kincardine Bridge was built in 1936. The bridge was built to replace earlier structures, including the famous wooden bridge, scene of the battle in 1297 in which William Wallace defeated the English.

Two miles northeast of the town, near the University and Bridge of Allan, is the Wallace Monument, an impressive Victorian Gothic tribute to Sir William Wallace, hero of the successful but hugely inaccurate film, *Braveheart*. Wallace was knighted by Robert the Bruce for his famous victory at Stirling Bridge, but following defeat later at Falkirk he went off to Europe in search of support for the Scottish cause. During his absence he was betrayed by the Scots nobles and on his return found guilty of treason and cruelly hanged, drawn and quartered in London. Ironically, a new statue to Wallace located in the car park met a similar fate when locals decapitated it because it bore too strong a resemblance to Mel Gibson.

Inside the monument are various exhibits including a Hall of Scottish Heroes and Wallace's mighty two-handed sword (5ft 4in in length – about the same size as the actor who played him in the film). There are fantastic views from the top of the 220-ft tower – if you can manage the climb up 246 spiral steps. There's a shuttle bus which runs from the foot of the hill up to the tower every 10 minutes. An open-topped **tour bus** runs to the monument from Stirling Castle every half hour (see 'Ins and outs' above). ■ *T472140. Jan, Feb, Nov and Dec daily 1030-1600; Mar-May and Oct 1000-1700; Jun and Sept 1000-1800; Jul and Aug 0930-1830. £3.25, £2.25 children.*

A mile east of Stirling are the ruins of Cambuskenneth Abbey, founded in 1147 by the prolific David I for Augustinian canons and once one of the richest abbeys in the country. Robert the Bruce held his parliament here in 1326 and King James III (1451-88) and his wife, Queen Margaret of Denmark, are buried in the grounds. The only substantial surviving feature is the 14th-century belfry. The abbey can be reached from Stirling on foot, via a footbridge over the river Forth, and from the Wallace Monument which is just a mile to the north. ■ *Open at all times, free.*

A few miles south of Stirling is the site of Scotland's greatest victory over the English, when Robert the Bruce defeated Edward II's army, on 24 June 1314. It was the **Battle of Bannockburn** which united the Scots and led to the declaration of independence at Arbroath in 1320 (the 'Declaration of Arbroath'). There's not an awful lot to see but the **Bannockburn Heritage Centre** puts flesh on the bones and brings to life the full scale of the battle. Outside is an equestrian statue of Bruce, on the spot where he is said to have commended his forces, and the site of the bore stone, where Bruce planted his standard after victory. What's left of the original bore stone is on display in the visitor centre, safe from souvenir hunters. ■ *T812664 (NTS). Site open all year, Heritage Centre open Apr-Oct daily 1000-1700; Mar and Nov-Dec 1100-1500. £2.50, £1.70 child/concession. To get there, take buses Nos 51 and 52 from Stirling (every 30 mins).*

Essentials

Sleeping
■ *on map*
Price codes:
see inside front cover

B *Stirling Highland Hotel*, Spittal St, T475444, F462929. 78 rooms, converted former school refurbished to high standards with full facilities, including a pool and saunas. Their *Scholars Restaurant* is highly recommended (see Eating below). **B** *Golden Lion Milton Hotel*, 8 King St, T475351, F472755. 71 rooms, large Victorian hotel which is convenient for sights, shops and restaurants. 5 miles east of town on the A91 is **B** *Blairlogie House Hotel*, T/F01259-761441, set in lovely gardens with views of the Wallace Monument and Ochil Hills. **C** *Park Lodge Hotel*, 32 Park Terr, T474862, F449748. 10 rooms, luxurious Georgian/Victorian town house beautifully situated close to town centre, overlooking the park and castle, has a very fine restaurant. **C-D** *The Portcullis*, Castle Wynd, T472290, F446103. 6 rooms, 200 year-old hotel next to castle, some rooms have great views over the town.

There are lots of **B&Bs** and **guesthouses** in the King's Park area, to the south of the tourist office. Near the tourist office is **D-E** *The Heritage*, 16 Allan Park, T473660. An elegant Georgian town house with good views of the castle, its restaurant boasts an impressive reputation for Scottish/French cuisine (see Eating below). A short distance west of the tourist office is **E** *SJ Howarth*, 8 Victoria Pl, T479360, and, just to the south, **D-E** *Ashgrove House*, 2 Park Ave, T/F472640. Close to the train station is **E** *Fairfield Guest House*, 14 Princes St, T472685. A short walk north of the train station is the recommended **E** *Forth Guest House*, 23 Forth Pl, T471020. There are also lots of B&Bs and guesthouses on Causewayhead Rd, which leads to the University. These include **E** *Ravenswood Guest House*, at No 94, T475291.

There's **campus accommodation** at Stirling University, a couple of miles north of the town centre near **Bridge of Allan** (**E**, T467140, open Jan, Feb and Jun-Sept). Also on campus is the **C-D** *Stirling Management Centre*, T451666, open all year, which offers more luxurious B&B accommodation and full board (**A-B**). There are regular buses (Nos 53 and 58) to the campus which leave from Murray Pl.

A cheaper option is the *SYHA youth hostel*, in a converted church on St John St at the top of the town, T473442, open all year. There's an excellent **campsite** at *Witches Craig Caravan Park*, at Blairlogie, 3 miles east of Stirling on the A91, T474947, open Apr-Oct.

Eating

Mid-range *Scholars Restaurant* at the Stirling Highland Hotel (see above) has an excellent reputation for modern Scottish cuisine. Another place with a good reputation is *The Heritage* (see above). *Hermann's*, 32 St John St, T450632, at the Tolbooth on the road up to the castle, is an upmarket choice. It offers excellent Scottish/Austrian cuisine at moderate prices (and cheap set lunch). Also on the road up to the castle is *Stirling Merchant Bar Bistro*, 39 Broad St, T473929, which serves modern Scottish dishes.

Cheap A good place for a cheap set lunch is the Stirling branch of *Pierre Victoire*, at 41 Friars St, T448171. The best curry in town can be had at the *East India Company*, 7 Viewfield Pl, T471330, with a cheaper pakora snack bar upstairs. A good Italian restaurant is the busy *Italia Nostra*, 25 Baker St, T473208, which serves cheap-moderate food daily till 2300. On the same street, at No 5, is *Olivia's Restaurant*, T446277, which offers good Scottish food in an informal atmosphere (cheap to mid-range prices, open Mon-Sat 1200-1430 and 1830-2200). *Café Albert*, is a café-bistro in the Albert Hall on Dumbarton Rd, T446930, and a cheap and relaxing place for lunch (open daily 1000-1700). A firm favourite with students is the *Barnton Bar & Bistro*, opposite the post office on Barnton St, T461698. It's cheap, open daily till 2400 (0100 at weekends) and serves great all-day breakfasts. A good place for coffee and a snack is the elegant *Darnley Coffee House*, 18 Bow St, T474468.

Two of the best **pubs** in Stirling are the *Portcullis*, T472268, on Castle Wynd, below the castle, and the *Settle Inn*, further down on St Mary's Wynd, which is the oldest hostelry in town (1773) and very popular with Stirling's large student population. The lively *Barnton Bar & Bistro* (see above) is also a good place for a drink.

Ceilidhs are held from Jun to Sept in *Cowane's Hospital* at the bottom of Castle Wynd (see 'Sights'). Check details at the tourist office. The *MacRobert Arts Centre*, T461081, on the campus of **Stirling University** shows a good selection of mainstream and arthouse **films** and **drama** productions. Buses run from the town centre (see 'Sleeping').

Scottish Citylink, T0990-505050, **buses** run at least every hour to and from **Edinburgh** (1 hr 30 mins; £5.30) and **Dundee** (1 hr 30 mins) and at least every 30 mins to **Perth** (50 mins) and **Glasgow** (1 hr; £3). There are also regular buses to Inverness (3 hrs 30 mins; £10.30) and **Aberdeen** (3 hrs 30 mins: £12.80) but you'll probably need to change at Perth and Dundee respectively. Local buses are run by *Midland Bluebird*, T01324-613777. There are frequent services to **Dunblane, Doune via Blair Drummond** (30 mins; £2.40), **Callander** (45 mins), **Dollar** (35 mins), **Falkirk** (30 mins) and **Linlithgow** (1 hr), and several daily to **Aberfoyle** (45 mins).

There are *ScotRail* **trains**, T0345-484950, every 30 mins (Mon-Sat; hourly on Sun) to **Edinburgh** (45 mins; £4.70) and **Glasgow** (45 mins; £3.70), and regular services to **Perth** (35 mins), **Dundee** (1 hr) and **Aberdeen** (2 hrs 15 mins).

Car hire *Arnold Clark*, Kerse Rd, T478686. From £16 per day. **Cycle hire and tours** *Wildcat Bike Tours*, Stirling Enterprise Park, Unit 102, John Player Building, T/F464333, www.wildcat-bike-tours.co.uk. **Taxis** *Woodside Taxis*, T450005.

Around Stirling

Four miles north of Stirling is the attractive little town of Dunblane, which was suddenly and horrifyingly catapulted into the media spotlight in 1996 when Thomas Hamilton walked into the local primary school and gunned down 15 children and their teacher. The town has been an ecclesiastical centre since it was founded in the seventh century by St Blane who lived at the nearby dun (fort), hence the name.

There's a seasonal **tourist office** on Stirling Road, T824428, open May-Sept. The main attraction is the beautiful **cathedral**, dating mainly from the 13th century, though the lower part of the tower is Norman. The cathedral was restored to its former glory in the late 19th century. ■ *Apr-Sept Mon-Sat 0930-1830, Sun 0930-1800; Oct-Mar Mon-Sat 0930-1630, Sun 1400-1630 (HS), free.* Close by on the square, housed in the 17th-century Dean's house, is the tiny cathedral **museum**, with display on local history. ■ *May-Oct Mon-Sat 1000-1230 and 1400-1630, free.* Nearby is **Leighton Library**, the oldest private library in Scotland, now open to the public. ■ *May-Oct Mon-Fri 1000-1230 and 1400-1630, free.*

Sleeping There are a couple of very exclusive hotels in and around Dunblane. Overlooking the town is the luxurious Victorian **A** *Dunblane Hydro*, T825403, set in 44 acres of woodland and now run by the Stakis group. 4 miles north of town, near Kinbuck on the B8033, is **L** *Cromlix House*, T822125, one of Scotland's best country house hotels, with its own loch and chapel. Excellent service and cuisine (expensive). It's worth coming here for dinner or Sun lunch. Rather less expensive is the *Sheriffmuir Inn*, T823285, on the wild moors of **Sheriffmuir** south of Dunblane, where the Jacobite Earl of Mar took on the government forces in 1715. The inn dates from the same period and serves fine food and ales and is a wonderful place in the summer.

Transport There are regular **buses** to Dunblane from Stirling (see Stirling Transport), and also frequent **trains** to and from Stirling, Edinburgh and Glasgow.

Doune
Phone code: 01786
Colour map 4, grid C2

Seven miles northwest of Stirling is the quiet village of Doune, which is worth visiting for its well-preserved late 14th-century courtyard **castle**, overlooking the river Teith. Built for the Regent Albany, it passed into the hands of the Earls of Moray (who still live there) following the execution of the Albany family by James I. Its most striking feature is the combination of tower, gatehouse and domestic quarters which includes the Lord's Hall with its carved oak screen and musicians' gallery. ■ *Apr-Sept daily 0930-1830; Oct-Mar Mon, Wed and Sat 0930-1630, Thur 0930-1230, Fri and Sun 1400-1630, £2.30, £1.75 concession).*

Also worth seeing is the **Doune Motor Museum**, about a mile west of the castle on the A84 to Callander. You don't have to be a car nut to appreciate the present Earl of Moray's beautiful vintage collection which includes a Lagonda, Aston Martin and the second oldest Rolls Royce in the world. ■ *T841203. Apr-Nov daily 1000-1700, £3.50.*

A few miles south of Doune, off the A84 to Stirling, is the **Blair Drummond Safari Park**, Scotland's only wildlife park, with lions, tigers, elephants, monkeys, rhinos, giraffes, zebras and various other exotic animals. There's a safari bus for those without their own transport. There are also sea lion shows and numerous other kids' activities. ■ *Mar to early Oct daily 1000-1730, last admission 1630. £8, £4 children.*

Transport There are regular **buses** to Doune from Stirling, via Blair Drummond (see Stirling Transport above).

Falkirk and Linlithgow

Colour map 5, grid A6

Stretching southeast from Stirling along the Firth of Forth is an area noted more for its industry than its scenic beauty, though there are one or two interesting historical sights, most notably **Linlithgow Palace**.

Falkirk
Phone code: 01324

Falkirk is the main town between Stirling and Edinburgh and a busy shopping centre. Its main attraction is **Callendar House**, a huge turreted mansion extensively altered over the years but thought to date originally from the 14th century. The working Georgian kitchens are worth a look. ■ *T503770. Mon-Sat 1000-1700, Sun 1400-1700, £1.80.*

North of Falkirk, near Airth, on the B9124, is **The Pineapple**, one of the most bizarre buildings in Scotland. This 45ft-high pineapple was built in 1761 as a garden folly for the fourth Earl of Dunmore. It is now owned by the NTS. ■ *All year daily from 0930 till sunset. The building can be rented as a holiday home from the Landmark Trust.*

There's accommodation in Falkirk, details of which can be obtained from the **tourist office**, 2-4 Glebe Street. ■ *T620244. Apr and May daily 0930-1700; Jun, Jul, Sept and Oct daily 0930-1800; Aug daily 0930-1900.*

There are regular **trains** from **Stirling**, **Perth**, **Glasgow Queen Street** and **Edinburgh** to Falkirk Grahamston station, which is a five-minute walk from the tourist office.

Linlithgow
Phone code: 01506

Halfway between Falkirk and Edinburgh is the pleasant little West Lothian town of Linlithgow, home of the magnificent Renaissance **Linlithgow Palace**, one of the most romantic and impressive historic buildings in Scotland. It's off the beaten track and relatively little-visited but well worth the detour, for this is a real gem. The 15th-century ruin is set on the edge of Linlithgow Loch and is associated with many of Scotland's main historical players, including James V (1512) and Mary, Queen of Scots (1542), who were both born here. James V was also married here, to Mary of Guise, and Bonnie Prince Charlie popped in for a visit during the 1745 rebellion. One year later the palace was badly damaged by fire during its occupation by General Hawley's troops, prior to their defeat by Jacobite forces under Prince Charles at the Battle of Falkirk. The ruin still conveys a real sense of the sheer scale of the lavish lifestyle of the court, from the ornate fountain in the inner courtyard to the magnificent Great Hall with its massive kitchens. ■ *T842896. Apr-Sept daily 0930-1830; Oct-Mar Mon-Sat 0930-1630, Sun 1400-1630. £2.50, £1.90 concession.*

Next to the palace is **St Michael's Church**, the largest pre-Reformation church in the country, with its controversial crown and spire, added in 1964. On the High Street is the **Linlithgow Story**, which relates the history of the royal burgh. ■ *Mar-Oct Mon and Wed-Sat 1000-1700, Sun 1300-1600, £1.*

West of town, at **Cairnapple Hill**, are ancient stone circles dating from around 2500BC to 500BC. Details of how to get there from the **tourist office**, in the Burgh Halls at the Cross. They will also provide details of accommodation, though Linlithgow is easily reached from Edinburgh and Stirling. The best place in town for a bar lunch (and a good pint of ale) is *The Four Mary's*, on the High Street. ■ *T844600. The tourist office is open May and Sept Mon-Sat 1000-1700; Jun daily 1000-1700; Jul and Aug daily 1000-1800.*

Transport Regular **buses** from Stirling and Edinburgh stop at the Cross. The **train station** is at the southern end of town. There are hourly **trains** to and from **Edinburgh** (20 minutes), **Glasgow Queen Street** (30 minutes) and **Stirling** (35 minutes).

The Ochils

The Ochil Hills rise sharply from the flat flood-plain of the river Forth and stretch northeast, through **Clackmannanshire**, into Perth and Kinross. This unfashionable and little-known range of hills is characterized by the shapely, rounded tops divided by steep-sided glens. There are good walking opportunities and some surprisingly dramatic scenery. At their feet, the pretty little towns and villages known collectively as 'the Hillfoots' were once Scotland's second largest wool-producing region, after the Borders. Today, visitors can explore the region's tweedy heritage on the **Mill Trail**, which starts in **Alva** and links the main mill centres along the A91, which runs east all the way to St Andrews in Fife.

Colour map 4, grid C3

A few miles northeast of Stirling, in the village of **Blairlogie**, is the crumbling 16th-century **Logie Old Kirk** and its ancient graveyard full of fascinating old stones, beautifully located by Logie Burn.

A few miles further east is the little town of **Alva**, home of the **Mill Trail Visitor Centre**, in Glentana Mill, on Stirling Street. Here you'll see what life was like for mill workers in the mid-19th century (pretty grim) and learn about the history of textile production from the Industrial Revolution onwards. ■ *T01259-769696. Jan-Jun and Oct-Dec 1000-1700; Jul-Sept till 1800. Free.*

A fine walk from Alva heads up Alva Glen to the summit of **Ben Cleuch** and then down Mill Glen to **Tillicoultry**. It's a total distance of eight miles and should take around four to five hours. It's mostly on good paths and tracks, but walking boots are recommended, as well as waterproofs, warm clothing, food and drink.

Alva Glen

OS Landranger No 58

Perth and Stirling

Starting from the car park head up the glen, cross the bridge, climb a series of steps and then go under a large pipe and past the water works to reach a gate giving access to the open hill. Follow a clear path across the hill till it reaches a track. Follow this track up to the head of the glen and just before it turns left, leave it and take a path on the right which climbs towards the summit of Ben Buck. First, you'll reach a false summit, from which there are great views north to the mountains of Breadalbane, near Callander and Loch Earn.

Follow the fence line to the right and, after a fence junction, take a clear path up to the rocks at the summit of Ben Cleuch. Having taken in the views, leave the summit along the same fence line. Near a fence junction, keep to the right and take the path which climbs up to **The Law** (2,093ft), from where there is a wonderful view across the Forth. Follow the path which descends steeply and is eroded, taking care especially near the foot of the hill. Cross the burn by the footbridge and, at the path junction beyond, take the right-hand lower path, which winds down the steep-sided **Mill Glen**, re-crossing the burn several times.

Once you reach the road, go down Upper Mill Street till you reach the main road. You can head left into Tillicoultry to catch a bus back to Alva, or enjoy a pint at *The Woolpack*. To continue the walk, head right and take the next right along a rough road heading up to the quarry. Continue straight ahead on a clear track leading up beside the golf course and through woodland till you reach *The Farriers* hotel, restaurant and craft shop complex. At the entrance to the Woodland Park car park, go right and follow a broad path uphill through the trees. The path levels out then crosses the Silver Burn, where silver was mined in the 18th century. Go through a kissing gate and then head back to the start of the walk.

Alloa
Phone code: 01259
Colour map 4, grid C3

A few miles south of Alva is the unappealing brewery town of Alloa, notable only for the beautifully restored **Alloa Tower**, which stands in a park, a short walk from the town centre. The 15th-century tower house, one of the largest surviving medieval tower houses in Scotland, is the ancestral home of the Erskine family, Earls of Mar and Kellie, who were custodians of the young Mary, Queen of Scots. Of particular note is the Italianate staircase, the original oak rood beams and the pit dungeon. There are also excellent views from the parapet walk. ■ *T211701 (NTS). Easter and May-early Oct daily 1330-1730; Oct weekends only 1330-1730, £2.50, £1.70 concession.*

Sleeping Alloa is also worth visiting for **A** *Gean House*, T219275, on Tullibody Rd, a luxurious Edwardian mansion house hotel with a superb restaurant.

Dollar
Phone code: 01259
Colour map 4, grid C3

Top of the bill in these parts is the well-heeled little town of Dollar, 11 miles east of Stirling and well worth a day trip. Looming above the town at the head of magical **Dollar Glen**, is the spectacularly sited **Castle Campbell**, standing between two deep ravines and formerly known as Castle Gloom, until it passed into the hands of the Campbells in the 15th century. The castle was sacked by Cromwell's troops in 1654 but the tower is well preserved and there are fantastic views down Dollar Glen from the parapet. There's an excellent marked

Alva Glen walk

walk from the town up to the castle through the narrow, steep-sided glen, said to be the home of fairies and other woodland spirits. ■ *T742048 (HS). Apr-Sept daily 0930-1830; Oct-Mar Mon-Wed and Sat 0930-1630, Thur 0930-1230, Sun 1400-1630, £2.50.*

Sleeping and eating There's not a huge choice of accommodation, but the **D** *Castle Campbell Hotel*, T/F742519, is comfortable and does good meals. If you're after a sandwich or something for a picnic, then look no further than *Nesbits*, a popular local deli on the main street.

Transport There are regular *Midland Bluebird* **buses** to Dollar from **Stirling**. There are also buses to and from **Alloa**.

The A91 passes through the gloriously named hamlet of **Yetts o' Muckhart**, at the junction with the scenic A823 which runs north through Glen Devon to meet the A9 Stirling-Perth road, near the famous **Gleneagles Hotel** (see page 282). A few miles north of Yetts o' Muckhart, at the village of **Glendevon** is a basic *SYHA Youth Hostel*, T781206, open mid-March to early October, which provides information on walks in the Ochil Hills. South of Yetts o' Muckhart is **Rumbling Bridge**, at the junction of the A823 and A977, from where there are breathtaking views down into a deep gorge.

East of Dollar

The A91 meets the M90 Edinburgh-Perth motorway by the town of Kinross, which is mostly bypassed by tourists speeding north to the Highlands or south to the capital. Kinross is covered by the **Perthshire Tourist Board** and you don't even have to venture too far from the motorway to visit the local **tourist office**, which is next to the service area at Junction 6, T863680. If you're passing by around lunchtime there's a good restaurant only a few hundred yards away, *The Grouse and Claret*, at Heatheryford Country Centre, T864212. They serve game and seafood and also cater for vegetarians (mid-range, open daily except Monday). They also have three rooms for **B&B (D)**. Another good place to eat, and cheaper, is the **D-E** *Muirs Inn*, T862270. To get there, turn off the motorway at Junction 6 and follow the A922 for Milnathort, then turn right at the 'T' junction.

Kinross & Loch Leven
Phone code: 01577
Colour map 4, grid C3

On an island in the middle of Loch Leven, and visible from the M90, is the lonely tower of **Loch Leven Castle**, where Mary, Queen of Scots was imprisoned for almost a year at the behest of Queen Elizabeth. She made a dramatic escape in May, 1568, with the help of her young, impressionable jailer. There's not much left of the 14th-century ruin but it's an evocative place full of romance and history. During the summer a **ferry** leaves from Kinross to the island. ■ *Apr-Sept (HS) Mon-Sat 0930-1830, Sun 1400-1800, £3.*

The Campsies

Running southwest from Stirling to Loch Lomond, and bordered by the broad farmlands of the **Carse of Stirling** to the north and the northern suburbs of **Glasgow** to the south are the **Campsies**. This is an area of gently rolling hills and fertile farmland, comprising the **Fintry, Gargunnock, Strathblane** and **Kilsyth Hills** and the **Campsie Fells**. Other than weekend hikers from Glasgow, the Campsies attract few visitors and this unspoiled peace and beauty is their main attraction. There's a string of picturesque villages nestled in the hills, amongst them **Killearn, Kippen, Gargunnock** and **Balfron**, birthplace of Alexander 'Greek' Thomson, Glasgow's great Victorian architect (see page 158). There's plenty of good walking to be done here. For details of the **Campsie Fells Trail**, contact the **Stirling tourist office**, T01786-475019.

Colour map 4, grid C2

Perth and Stirling

Fintry
Phone code: 01360

Lying at the heart of the Campsies is the attractive little village of Fintry, at the head of the Strathendrick valley, and regular winner of the 'Scotland in Bloom' competition. Two miles east of the village is the 90ft-high **Loup of Fintry** waterfall. There are a few places to stay in Fintry, including the wonderful **B** *Culcreuch Castle Hotel*, T860228, a 14th-century castle set in the 1,600-acre Culcreuch Country Park. A cheaper option is the **E** *Fintry Inn*, T860224, which also offers pub food.

Drymen
Phone code: 01360

At the western end of the Campsie Fells is the village of Drymen, the busiest of the Campsie villages due to its proximity to the eastern shores of Loch Lomond. Drymen also lies on the **West Highland Way** (see page 54). There's a seasonal **tourist office** in the library on The Square. ■ *T660068. May-Sept.* There's a decent selection of **accommodation** in Drymen. Best hotel is the **B-C** *Buchanan Arms Hotel*, T660588. There are lots of **B&Bs**, including **E** *Easter Drumquhassle Farm*, T660893, juliamacx@aol.com, on Gartness Road, and **E** *The Old School*, T660136. A highly recommended place to eat is the moderately priced *Clachan Inn*, T660824, on The Square. You can rent **bikes** at *Lomond Activities*, 64 Main Street, T660066.

Walks

South of **Killearn** on the A81 is the **Glengoyne Distillery**, ■ *Apr-Nov Mon-Sat 1000-1600, Sun 1200-1600; £2.50*, which is the starting point for two excellent walks in the Strathblane Hills, to the top of **Dumgoyne Hill** (1,400ft) and **Earl's Seat** (1,896ft), the highest point in the Campsies.

Further west, on the other side of Strathblane, is **Queen's View** on **Auchineden Hill**, from where there are wonderful views up Loch Lomond as far as Ben Ledi. Queen Victoria was particularly impressed. The path to the top starts from the busy car park on the A809 Bearsden to Drymen road. It takes about 45-50 minutes each way. From the car park a path also leads up to **The Whangie**, a deep cleft in the rock face with sheer walls rising over 30ft on either side. A path runs for 100yd through the narrow gap.

Transport

Midland Bluebird, T01324-613777, runs several **buses** daily to Drymen from Glasgow, via Queen's View. There are also buses through the region from Stirling. A **postbus** service, T01463-256200, leaves from Denny, five miles south of Stirling, to Fintry (Mon-Sat at 0955), from where two buses (Mon-Sat) run to Balfron. There are regular buses to Denny from Stirling bus station.

Loch Lomond

Colour map 4, grid C1

Britain's largest inland waterway, measuring 22 miles long and up to five miles wide, is Scotland's most famous (uninhabited!) loch, thanks to the Jacobite ballad about its "bonnie banks". These same banks are now one of one of the busiest parts of the Highlands, due to their proximity to Glasgow, (only 20 miles south on the congested A82). During the summer the loch becomes a playground for day-trippers who tear up and down the loch in speedboats and on jet skis, obliterating any notion visitors may have of a little peace and quiet.

The **west bank** of the loch, from Balloch north to Tarbet, is one long, almost uninterrupted development of marinas, holiday homes, caravan parks and exclusive golf clubs. The most picturesque village on the west bank, **Luss**, is the setting for the Scottish TV soap *Take the High Road*, and is full of visitors buying souvenir tea towels and hoping to catch a glimpse of one of the 'stars'. The **Loch Lomond Authority Visitor Centre**, T01436-860601, next to the large car park in the village, has information on the loch's natural history, flora and fauna. ■ *Easter-Oct daily 1000-1800.*

At the southern end of the loch is the resort town of **Balloch**, packed full of hotels, B&Bs, caravan parks and any number of operators offering **boat trips** around the loch's overcrowded waters. Try *Sweeney's Cruises*, T752376 or *Mullen's Cruises*, T751481, which both offer a wide range of trips, starting at around £4-5 for an hour. A daily 2½ hour cruise from Balloch to Luss, leaves at 1430 (£7). There's also a **tourist office**. ■ *T753533. Apr-Jun, Sept and Oct daily 1000-1700; Jul and Aug 0930-1930.*

Balloch to Tarbet
Phone code: 01389

North of **Tarbet**, at the narrow northern end of the loch, things quieten down a great deal and the road to **Ardlui**, at its northern tip, is very beautiful and peaceful. The A82 continues north of Ardlui, past **Inverarnan**, to meet the A85 at **Crianlarich** (see page 303). There's a **tourist office** in Tarbet. ■ *T01301-702260. Apr-Oct.*

The tranquil **east bank** of Loch Lomond is a great place for walking. The **West Highland Way** (see page 54) follows the east bank all the way from **Drymen**, through **Balmaha**, **Rowardennan** and **Inversnaid**. Beyond Rowardennan this is the only access to the loch's east bank, except for the road to Inversnaid from the Trossachs. From Rowardennan you can climb **Ben Lomond** (3,192ft), the most southerly of the Munros. It's not too difficult and the views from the top (in good weather) are astounding. There are two routes: the easier one starts from the car park at the end of the road just beyond the *Rowardennan Hotel*; the other route, known as the 'Ptarmigan Route', starts from beyond the youth hostel. You can also go up by one route and return by the other. Allow about five to six hours there and back.

East bank & Ben Lomond
✐
OS Landranger map 58

An easier climb is **Conic Hill**, on the Highland fault line and very close to Glasgow. The route starts from the Balmaha car park. It takes about 1½ hours to reach the top, from where the views of the loch are stunning.

There are numerous hotels and B&Bs in Balloch, Luss, Inverbeg and Tarbet. In **Balloch**, the **D** *Balloch Hotel*, T752579, near the A82, has a good restaurant. Best of the B&Bs is the **E** *Gowanlea Guest House*, T752456, on Drymen Rd. There's a good **campsite** at *Tullichewan Holiday Park*, T759475, on the Old Luss Rd, where you can hire **mountain bikes**. A few miles further on up the west bank, in **Arden**, is *Loch Lomond SYHA Youth Hostel* , T850226, a grand 19th-century turreted mansion complete with the obligatory ghost. A few miles north of Luss, at **Inverbeg**, is the **C-B** *Inverbeg Inn*, T01436-860678, which does good food.

Sleeping & eating

On the **eastern shore** there's an *SYHA Youth Hostel* at **Rowardennan**, T01360-870259, open Jan-Oct. There's also the **C** *Rowardennan Hotel*, T01360-870273, which offers a bit more comfort and serves bar meals. There are a couple of **campsites** on the east bank, at *Milarrochy Bay*, T01360-870236, open end Mar to Oct, near Balmaha, and the Forestry Commission campsite at *Cashel*, T01360-870234, a few miles further north. On the northeast shore, and only accessible by road via the B829 from Aberfoyle, is the splendidly isolated **D** *Inversnaid Hotel*, T01877-386223.

In **Ardlui**, at the northern tip of the loch, is the comfortable **C** *Ardlui Hotel*, T01301-704243. A few miles north, at **Inverarnan**, is the *Drover's Inn*, T01301-704234, the famous Highland watering hole, with smoke-blackened walls, low ceilings, bare floors, open fires, a hall filled with stuffed animals, barman in kilt and a great selection of single malts. The perfect place for a wild night of drinking in the wilderness. It simply doesn't get any better than this.

Scottish Citylink, T0990-505050, **buses** run regularly from Glasgow to **Balloch** (45 mins; £3) and on to **Luss** and **Tarbet** (1 hr 10 mins). Some buses go to **Ardlui** (1 hr 20 mins; £6.30) and on to **Crianlarich**.

Transport

Perth and Stirling

There are 2 **rail** lines from Glasgow to Loch Lomond. One runs to **Balloch** every 30 mins (35 mins; £2.90). the other is the West Highland line to Fort William and Mallaig, with a branch line to Oban. It reaches Loch Lomond at **Tarbet** and there's another station further north at **Ardlui**.

There's a passenger **ferry service** across the loch between **Inverbeg** and **Rowardennan**, T01360-870273, 3 times daily (£4). There are also ferries between **Inveruglas** and **Inversnaid**, T01877-386223.

The Trossachs

Strictly speaking, the Trossachs is the narrow wooded glen between **Loch Katrine** and **Loch Achray**, but the name is now used to describe a much larger area between Argyll and Perthshire, stretching north from the **Campsies** and west from **Callander** to the eastern shore of Loch Lomond. It's a very beautiful and diverse area of sparkling lochs, craggy mountains and deep, forested glens and for this reason is often called the 'Highlands in miniature'. Visit in the autumn when the hills are purple and the trees are a thousand luminous hues, from lustrous gold to flaming scarlet and blazing orange.

The Trossachs was one of the country's first holiday regions, and remains a major tourist destination. Its enduring appeal is due in no small measure to Sir Walter Scott, who eulogized its great natural beauty in his epic poem, *Lady of the Lake*, and whose historical novel, *Rob Roy* brought to public attention the region's other great attraction, Rob Roy MacGregor, one of the great romantic Highland figures.

Ins and outs

Getting around The *Trossachs Trundler* is an old vintage **bus** which makes a circuit of the Trossachs, linking Stirling, Callander, Loch Katrine, Aberfoyle and Port of Menteith and stopping off at various scenic places *en route*. It also connects with departures of the *SS Sir Walter Scott* on Loch Katrine. It runs from Jun-Sept, Mon-Fri and Sun and costs £8.10 for a day ticket. Contact the local tourist office for details.

Walking in the Trossachs

OS Landranger maps 56 and 57

The Trossachs is superb walking country. The two most challenging peaks are **Ben Venue** and **Ben A'an** around Loch Katrine and Loch Achray, about 10 miles west of Callander. **Ben Venue** (2,385ft) is the more difficult climb. It starts from behind the *Loch Achray Hotel* and is waymarked, but it's a strenuous climb which requires hill walking experience, proper clothing and all the usual safety precautions (see page 56). Allow about five hours for the return trip. **Ben A'an** (1,520ft) isn't a giant of a hill but it's a steep climb from the start, from the car park of the former*Trossachs Hotel* (now a timeshare development) on the north bank of Loch Achray, and there's a bit of scrambling involved near the summit. It takes about 1½ hours to the top. The views from both hills are stupendous on clear days, but remember that the weather is as unpredictable in the Trossachs mountains as anywhere else in the Highlands. A useful guide is Bartholomew's *Walk Loch Lomond and the Trossachs*.

Both these mountains lie within the **Queen Elizabeth Forest Park**. This vast and spectacular wilderness of 75,000 acres borders Loch Lomond to the west and incorporates Loch Ard, Loch Achray and Loch Lubnaig, as well as Ben Venue, Ben A'An and **Ben Ledi** which overlooks Callander. The park is run by the Forestry Commission and is criss-crossed by a network of less

Rob Roy

As the tourist board never tires of reminding us, the Trossachs is Rob Roy country. Rob Roy ('Red Robert' in Gaelic) was one of Scotland's most notorious outlaws or one the bravest Highland heroes, depending on your point of view. It is true that he was a freebooter, but he was also defending Highland clan culture and more specifically fighting for the very survival of his own clan against proscription and persecution by government and its supporters.

Rob Roy MacGregor (1671-1734) was born in Glengyle, to the northwest of Loch Katrine. The MacGregors' lands included those previously owned by the rival Campbells but bestowed on the MacGregors for services rendered to Alexander II in his conquest of Argyll. For a long time the clan kept possession of their lands by right of the sword, but the constant attempts by neighbouring clans to displace them led to retaliation by the MacGregors and earned them a reputation for being aggressive. Rob Roy did little to change this image and his bitter feud with the powerful Duke of Montrose led to his being outlawed and eventually captured and sentenced to transportation. He was pardoned and returned to **Balquhidder**, where he stayed for the rest of his life. He now lies buried in the churchyard.

The Rob Roy story was first popularized by Sir Walter Scott's eponymous 19th-century novel and his life continues to be romanticized, most recently in the 1995 film starring Liam Neeson and Tim Roth. Like Robin Hood before him, his courage in refusing to bow to the forces of authority seems to strike a chord with people.

Perth and Stirling

difficult waymarked trails and paths which start from the Queen Elizabeth Park **Visitor Centre**, about half a mile north of Aberfoyle on the A821. Available at the centre are audio-visual displays on the park's flora and fauna and information on the numerous walks and cycle routes around the park. ■ *T01877-382258. Apr-Oct daily 1000-1800; Nov-Mar Sat and Sun only 1000-1600 (parking £1). Full details of the park are available from the* **Forest Enterprise** *in Aberfoyle, (same tel no).*

Aberfoyle

The sleepy little village of Aberfoyle suddenly bursts into life in the summer with the arrival of hordes of tourists. It lies on the edge of Queen Elizabeth Forest Park and, along with Callander to the east, is one of the main tourist centres for the Trossachs. It makes an ideal base for walking and cycling in the surrounding hills. There's plentiful accommodation, though you'll have to book during the busy summer season. The **tourist office** is on the main street. ■ *T382352. Mar-Jun, Sept and Oct daily 1000-1700; Jul and Aug 0930-1900.*

Phone code: 01877
Colour map 4, grid C1

Three miles east of Aberfoyle is the **Lake of Menteith**, the only lake in Scotland (as opposed to loch). On Inchmahome island in the middle of the lake are the beautiful and substantial ruins of **Inchmahome Priory**, the 13th-century Augustinian priory where the four-year-old Mary, Queen of Scots was sent in 1547, safe from the clutches of Henry VIII. A **ferry** takes visitors over to the island from **Port of Menteith**. ■ *T385294 (HS). Apr-Sept Mon-Sat 0930-1830, Sun 1400-1830, £3, £2.30 concession.* The lake is also a popular spot for **fly-fishing** and you can rent boats from *Lake of Menteith Fisheries,* T385664, April-October.

To the north of Aberfoyle is Doon Hill, better known as the **Fairy Knowe**. The tree at the top is said to be the home of the 'People of Quietness' and in 1692 a local minister was less than discreet in telling the world of their secrets. As punishment, he was taken away to fairyland and his spirit has languished there ever since. If you go round the tree seven times, your wish will be granted, but go round it backwards and… well, we won't be held responsible. It's about an hour up and back. Cross the bridge over the Forth River and head past the cemetery, then follow the signs.

Sleeping The best place to stay in the area is the **A-B** *Lake Hotel*, in Port of Menteith, situated on the lakeshore overlooking Inchmahome, T385258. It's stylish, comfortable, very romantic and boasts a fine restaurant (lunch mid-range; dinner expensive). There are dozens of **B&Bs** in and around Aberfoyle, including the comfortable and non-smoking **E** *Craigend*, on Craiguchty Terr, T382716, open Mar-Oct, **E** *Tigh-na-Cruinn*, T382760, open Apr-Sept, and the lovely **D-E** *Creag-Ard House* in Milton, 2 miles west of Aberfoyle overlooking Loch Ard, T382297, with fishing and boat hire available.

Camping is available at *Cobeland Campsite*, T382392, open Apr-Oct, 2 miles south of Aberfoyle on the edge of Queen Elizabeth Forest Park, and the excellent *Trossachs Holiday Park*, T382614, open Mar-Oct, set in 40 acres with **mountain bike hire**.

Eating There are several decent **eating** places in the village. The *Forth Inn Hotel*, T382488, and *The Coach House*, T382822, both on Main St, serve good pub food. Best place to eat is the excellent and very popular *Braeval Old Mill*, T382711, a few miles east on the A873 to Port of Menteith.

Transport There are regular **buses** to and from **Stirling** with *Midland Bluebird*, T01324-613777. There are also daily services from **Glasgow**, via Balfron. There's a **postbus service**, T01463-256200, from Aberfoyle to **Callander** via Port of Menteith (Mon-Fri in the afternoon) and another (Mon-Sat) from Aberfoyle to **Inversnaid** on Loch Lomond (see page 297).

Aberfoyle to Callander The A821 route north from Aberfoyle, through the spectacular **Duke's Pass**, and then east past Loch Achray and Loch Vennachar, is one of the most beautiful routes in the country and not to be missed. There are a couple of worthwhile diversions along the way. About five miles north of Aberfoyle, a track branches to the right and runs through Achray Forest and along the shores of Loch Drunkie, before rejoining the A821 further north. A few miles further on, a road turns left to **Trossachs Pier** on the eastern shore of **Loch Katrine**. This is the departure point for **cruises** on the *SS Sir Walter Scott*, T376316. In the mornings (Sun-Fri) it sails to the remote settlement of **Stronachlachar** on the far western shores of the loch and back. In the afternoons it only sails around the loch for an hour. ■ *Cruises depart end of Mar to end of Oct: Sun-Fri at 1100 to Stronachlachar, returning at 1200, and around the loch at 1345 and 1515; Sat at 1345 and 1515 only. Cruises cost £3.70 (£2.30 morning cruise one way).* There's a road and cycle path around the loch as far as Stronachlachar and you could take the morning cruise there and then cycle back to the pier. **Cycle hire** from *Trossachs Cycle Hire*, T382614, for £6.50-10 per half day and £10-16 per full day.

The road then swings east along the northern shores of luscious Loch Achray and Loch Venachar, past **Brig o' Turk**.

Callander

Callander sits at the eastern end of the Trossachs, 14 miles northwest of Stirling, its wide streets totally and unashamedly devoted to tourism and lined with tea-rooms, restaurants and craft shops. The town's overworked **tourist office** is on the main street, in Ancaster Square. ■ *T330342. Same opening times as visitor centre below.* It shares the same building as the **Rob Roy and Trossachs Visitor Centre** which gives an entertaining account of the life of Rob Roy MacGregor. ■ *Mar-May and Oct-Dec daily 1000-1700; Jun and Sept 0930-1800; Jul and Aug 0900-1900; Jan and Feb weekends only 1000-1700, £2.50.*

Phone code: 01877
Colour map 4, grid C2
Population: 2,500

Callander is also a good base for exploring the Trossachs. A recommended local walk is to **Bracklinn Falls**, reached by a woodland trail which leads from Bracklinn Road. It's about 30 minutes each way. Another trail from Bracklinn Road leads up to **Callander Crags**, from where there are great views of the surrounding area. Allow 1½ hours there and back. The most challenging walk in the area is to the summit of **Ben Ledi** (2,857ft), but it's a tough climb and you'll need to be fit, experienced and prepared (see page 56).

Walks & cycle routes

OS Landranger No 57

Two miles north of Callander, on the A84 route to the Highlands, are the **Falls of Leny**, in the narrow and dramatic Pass of Leny. The falls are accessible from the car park by the roadside or via the **Callander to Strathyre Cycleway**, which follows the old train line to Oban, from Callandar north along the west bank of **Loch Lubnaig**. This forms part of the **Glasgow to Killin Cycleway**, which runs from the centre of Glasgow, via Balloch, Aberfoyle, Callander, Balquhidder and Lochearnhead, to Killin. This is the best way to see the Trossachs. For more details on cycle routes in the area, get a copy of *25 Cycle Routes: Stirling & Trossachs* by Erl B. Wilkie (HMSO), available at the tourist office or good bookshops. You can **hire bikes** in Callander from *Wheels*, Invertrossachs Road (T331100) for £5-12 per day.

If you want something a wee bit special, then head for the **A** *Roman Camp Country House Hotel*, T331533, www.roman-camp-hotel.co.uk. An exquisite 16th-century hunting lodge set in extensive grounds by the river, away from the hoi polloi. Queen Victoria was quite taken with the place. Also superb Scottish cuisine (expensive). For something a bit more down-to-earth, there's a huge selection of **B&B** accommodation, including the highly recommended **C-D** *Arran Lodge*, T330976, open Mar-Oct, on Leny Rd. Also recommended are **D-E** *Brook Linn Country House*, T330103, open Mar-Nov, a fine Victorian house overlooking the town; **D-E** *Arden House*, T/F330235, open Mar-Nov, on Bracklinn Rd; **D-E** *The Priory*, T/F330001, open Easter-Oct, also on Bracklinn Rd; and **D-E** *Dunmor Guest House*, T330756, open Apr-Oct, on Leny Rd.

Sleeping & eating

A couple of miles out of town, along the Invertrossachs Rd, which turns off the A81, is the *Trossachs Backpackers*, T331200, trosstel@aol.com, an independent hostel which also **rents bikes**. There's also **camping** at *Gart Caravan Park*, Stirling Rd, T330002, open Apr to mid-Oct.

The best place to eat is the *Roman Camp Hotel* (see above). Otherwise the hotels and pubs offer bar meals. Most of the places along the main street are overpriced, but the *Ben Ledi Café* offers good-value basic grub. A few miles north of town, at Kilmahog, is the highly-rated *Lade Inn*, T330152.

There are regular **buses** to and from **Stirling** (45 mins; £2.90). There's a *Scottish Citylink* service once daily between Edinburgh and Fort William which stops in Callander. A **postbus** leaves daily, except Sun, at 0915 to **Trossachs Pier** and connects with **cruises** on Loch Katrine (see 'Aberfoyle to Callander' above). There's also a postbus between Callander and **Aberfoyle**, via **Port of Menteith** (Mon-Fri in the afternoon).

Transport

Perth and Stirling

North of Callander

Colour map 4, grid C2 The A84 heads north from Callander, along the east bank of Loch Lubnaig, and beyond towards **Loch Earn**. At the northern end of Loch Lubnaig, in **Strathyre**, is **C-D** *Creagan House*, T384638, a family-run 17th-century farmhouse offering excellent food (mid-range-expensive) and comfortable accommodation.

A few miles further north, a side road branches left to the tiny village of **Balquhidder**, famous as the burial place of Rob Roy. His grave in the little churchyard, where his wife and two of his sons are also buried, is thankfully understated. The road continues west along the north shire of Loch Voil to **Inverlochlarig**, from where there are numerous excellent opportunities for experienced hill walkers. The best place by far to stay in these parts is the small, family-run **C** *Monachyle Mhor Hotel*, T384622, on the road to Inverlochlarig. It offers great views of the loch, peace and quiet and fabulous Scottish/French cuisine (lunch mid-range; dinner expensive).

Lochearnhead
Phone code: 01567

A few miles north of the Balquhidder turn-off, where the A84 meets the A85 from Crieff to Crianlarich, is Lochearnhead, at the western tip of Loch Earn. The loch is a highly popular **watersports centre** and at *Lochearnhead Watersports*, T830330, you can try water-skiing, windsurfing, canoeing and kayaking. Lochearnhead is also a good base for **walking** in the surrounding hills.

Sleeping and eating   **D-E** *Clachan Cottage Hotel*, T830300. Most other options are **self-catering** cabins and caravans and include *Earnknowe*, T/F830238, cottages for rent, from £120-355 per week for up to six people. The best place to eat is the *Four Seasons Hotel*, T685333, at St Fillans, at the east end of the loch.

Killin
Phone code: 01567

In the far northwestern corner of Stirling region, just to the west of Loch Tay, is Killin, a pleasant little village which makes a good base for walkers wishing to explore the wild mountains and glens of the ancient district of **Breadalbane** (pronounced Bread-*al*binn). Killin's picture-postcard setting, with the beautiful **Falls of Dochart** tumbling through the centre of the village, make it a popular destination for tourists.

The **tourist office** overlooks the falls. In the same building is the **Breadalbane Folklore Centre**, which has displays on local clan history and contains the sacred healing stones of the seventh-century missionary, St Fillan. ■ *T820254. Tourist office and Folklore Centre both open Mar-May and Oct daily 1000-1700; Jun and Sept till 1800; Jul and Aug 0930-1830; Feb weekends only 1000-1600. £1.50, £1 concession.*

Sleeping and eating   The best place to stay is the **D** *Dall Lodge Country House Hotel*, T820217, wislon@dalllodgehotel.co.uk, open Mar-Oct, which offers idiosyncratic style and very good food. Next best choice is the **D-E** *Killin Hotel*, T820296. Amongst the dozens of **B&Bs** is **E** *Invertay House*, T820492, invertay@btinternet. com. There's also a **youth hostel**, T820546, open end Feb to end Oct, at the northern end of the village. The **outdoor centre**, T820652, on the main road hires out mountain bikes, as well as climbing equipment.

Transport   There are **buses** to Killin (on schooldays only) from **Stirling** via **Callander** (1 hr 45 mins; £4.75). There's a **postbus** from **Callander** once daily except Sun (1 hr), which continues to **Crianlarich** and **Tyndrum**. There's also a postbus service from **Aberfeldy** (see page 278).

Twelve miles west of Killin is Crianlarich, at the crossroads of the A82 Glasgow-Fort William road and the A85 to Perth, and at the junction of the Glasgow to Fort William and Oban **rail lines**. It is a staging post on the **West Highland Way**. There are many places to stay, including an *SYHA Youth Hostel*, T300260, open all year.

Six miles further north is tiny **Tyndrum**, which shot to prominence recently after the discovery of gold in the surrounding hills. There's a **tourist office**, T400246, in the car park of the *Invervey Hotel*.

There are two **train stations** at Tyndrum. One serves the Glasgow to Oban line and the other the Glasgow to Fort William line. There are **trains** from both villages to **Fort William**, **Oban** and **Glasgow** (T0345-484950). *Scottish Citylink* **buses**, T0990-505050, between **Glasgow** and **Oban** and **Fort William** stop in both villages. There's also a **postbus** service between Crianlarich and Tyndrum and **Killin** (Mon-Sat).

Crianlarich & Tyndrum
Phone code: 01838
Colour map 4, grid C1

Perth and Stirling

Fife

8

Fife

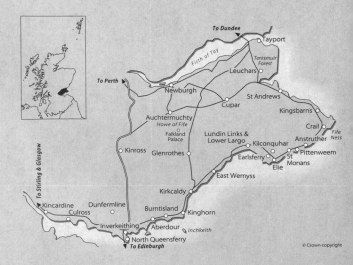

© Crown copyright

Bounded by the firths of Tay to the north and Forth to the south, and the North Sea to the east, Fife was once isolated from the rest of the country, and even since the building of the Forth and Tay bridges, the region has managed to retain a unique flavour. The county has been known as the Kingdom of Fife, ever since it was designated as such by the Picts in the fourth century. The small peninsula juts out into the North Sea like the head of a little terrier dog. Rather apt, given the proud Fifers' fight to preserve the identity of their own 'Kingdom' when it was threatened by local government reorganization in 1975 and 1995.

The Kingdom's eventful past has left it well endowed with places of historical interest: royal palaces, cathedrals, castles, abbeys, medieval churches, even ancient Roman forts are all to be found here. If you like to be beside the seaside, then there are many good, sandy beaches and, quite miraculously, the highest number of hours of sunshine of any part of the British Isles.

For such a small region, Fife is a very diverse place. The difference between the blighted industrial landscape of the southwest and the prosperous-looking rural northeast couldn't be more marked. Northeast Fife consists of **St Andrews** and the **East Neuk** and if you only have a few days in which to visit, then this is what you should see. **St Andrews**, in particular, is important and attractive enough to visit on its own. The ruins of its cathedral and castle bear witness to its former importance, while the Royal and Ancient Golf Club is the sport's spiritual home and stands on the world's most famous links course. It also has the oldest university in

Scotland and some magnificent beaches within easy striking distance. **The East Neuk of Fife** is a string of picture-postcard old fishing villages, from the stately burghs of **Elie** and **Earlsferry**, through **St Monans**, **Pittenweem**, **Anstruther** and on to **Crail**, the loveliest of them all.

Those with more time on their hands could also venture inland to explore **Falkland**, **Cupar** and the **Howe of Fife**. Here, you'll find **Falkland Palace**, one of Scotland's most remarkable historic buildings.

Southwest Fife was the region's industrial heartland and contains the largest towns; Kirkcaldy, Dunfermline and Glenrothes. But this corner of Fife is not without its attractions. **Culross**, west of Dunfermline, is well worth a detour, and **Deep Sea World** is conveniently placed beside the Forth Road Bridge.

Ins and outs

Getting around

The main transport route through the region is the M90 which runs from Edinburgh north to Perth and skirts Fife's western boundary. A more scenic alternative is the beautiful coastal route, which branches east off the M90 just north of the Forth Road Bridge as the A921 to Kirkaldy, the A955 from there to Leven and the A917 from Leven through the East Neuk villages and on to St Andrews. The coastal route also affords easy access into the centre of Fife. The Tay Road Bridge leads south from Dundee into Fife, via the A914 and A919 southeast to St Andrews and the A92 southwest to Glenrothes and Kirkaldy. It meets the A91, which runs east from the M90 and gives access to Falkland Palace, the Scottish Deer Centre, Cupar and also St Andrews.

The **train** line north from Edinburgh follows the coast as far as Kirkaldy and then cuts inland towards Dundee, stopping at Cupar and Leuchars. From Leuchars a **bus** can be taken to St Andrews. It is possible to explore the peninsula using public transport, but it can be a slow and time-consuming business as buses to the more remote parts are few and far between.

Information

The various *Tourist Information Centres* provide free and comprehensive information on all that Fife has to offer, including where to stay. They also sell tickets for events, attractions, trips and tours, provide exchange facilities and stock maps and guide books. Details of the TICs are given under the relevant town. You'll find them in St Andrews, Kirkaldy, Anstruther, Crail, Dunfermline and North Queensferry.

Southwest Fife

Travelling north from Edinburgh across the Firth of Forth, you pass through this industrial corner of the Kingdom. This area was once a major producer of coal, but a succession of pit closures has left a scarred and depressed wasteland. However, the area is not without its attractions. Dunfermline boasts an impressive history and the coastal route takes you through some attractive little villages.

Culross

Pronounced 'kooros', this beautifully restored village contains the finest surviving examples of Scottish vernacular architecture from the 16th and 17th centuries. Culross was then one of the largest ports in Scotland, and enjoyed a flourishing trade in coal and salt with other Forth ports and the Low Countries. Following the industrial revolution, however, the little town went into near-terminal decline until the National Trust rescued it from decay in 1932.

Phone code: 01383
Colour map 4, grid C3

Getting there

Culross lies off the A985, 12 km west of the Forth Road Bridge. Take a *Fife Scottish* No 14/14a bus on the Dunfermline-Glasgow route, T621249. There are also services from Falkirk, and from Glasgow, via Stirling and Alloa.

Sights

To appreciate the town's unique sense of history fully, explore its narrow cobbled streets on foot. A good starting point is the **National Trust Visitor Centre**, in the **Town House**, or Tolbooth, on the main road beside the palace, which dates from 1626. Here you can see an excellent video telling the history of the town.

The **Palace** was built between 1597 and 1611 by local merchant, Sir George Bruce, who made his fortune from coal and salt panning. It's not so much a palace as a grand house, but its crow-stepped gables and pan-tiled roofs give a

Fife

☞ *Golf*

If golf is your bag, then Fife has it all. Here you'll find the very home of golf, St Andrews, and 40 other courses to rival those of Ayrshire or East Lothian. The Kingdom of Fife Tourist Board produces a free guide to Golfing in Fife and this can be picked up at the various Tourist Information Centres, or call

T01334-477685 and ask for the Golf Line.

There are also several tour operators offering specialized golfing holidays. Details are given in the tourist board brochure Holidays and Short Breaks in the Kingdom of Fife and St Andrews. Many hotels in St Andrews and throughout the region will arrange golfing packages.

delightful example of Scottish architecture from this period. Inside, the many small rooms and connecting passageways make it feel much larger than it is. The main features are the wonderful original painted ceilings and wood panelling. The National Trust has filled the house with 17th and 18th century furniture and restored the garden which now features a variety of vegetables, herbs and perennials from the period.

A steep, cobbled street known as **Back Causeway** leads up behind the Town House to a tiny market place, where you'll find another distinctive building, the late 16th-century **Study**, a restored house that takes its name from the small room at the top of the corbelled tower, reached by a turnpike stair.

Further up the steep hill, past the many wonderfully restored little houses, is **Culross Abbey**, founded in 1215 by Cistercian Monks on land given to the church by the Earl of Fife. The original choir and tower are now the site of the parish church, which contains the beautiful family tomb of Sir George Bruce. There is little remaining of the rest of the abbey, but it's worth the climb for the peaceful surroundings and views over the Forth. ■ *T880359. The Palace is open from 1 Apr (or Good Friday if earlier) to 30 Sept, daily 1100-1700 (last admission 1600). The Town House and Study are open the same dates, 1330-1700, and weekends in Oct, 1100-1700. Groups can visit at other times by appointment. A combined ticket for the Palace, Town House and Study is £4.40, £2.90 child/concession, £11.70 Family ticket. T880359. Most of the exhibition and the ground floor of the Palace have wheelchair access, also parking and toilet facilities. Guidebook in French and German, also Braille. Explanatory text in Dutch, French, German, Hebrew, Italian, Japanese and Spanish. Video shown in Town House in French and German.*

West from Culross, the road continues to **Kincardine**, on Fife's westernmost boundary. The town is famous for its bridge, opened in 1936. Like so many other towns in Fife, Kincardine has many buildings showing a Dutch influence. It also shares with most of the coastal burghs an industrial heritage of salt-panning.

East from Culross, along the shore, is the ruin of **St Mungo's Chapel**, built in 1503 by Archbishop Blackadder. It was here, in the sixth century, that St Kentigern was born. Affectionately nicknamed 'Mungo', he went on to build Glasgow Cathedral, around which the city later grew.

About 10 km east of Culross is **Charlestown**, an 18th-century village with a picturesque harbour, built by the 5th Earl of Elgin for sailing vessels trading with Europe. It was the 7th Earl of Elgin who took the ancient Greek marble sculptures from the Parthenon in Athens and sold them to the British Museum in 1816 for £35,000. These became known as the 'Elgin Marbles' and continue to be a bone of contention between Britain and Greece. One and a half kilometres further east lies the charming village of **Limekilns**, which takes its name from the lime kilns that used to be one of its main industries. If you fancy a drink, try the *Ship Inn*, which featured in Robert Louis Stevenson's 'Kidnapped', and *Il Pescatore* restaurant offers good Italian cooking.

E *St Mungo's Cottage*, Low Causeway, T882102. B&B, run by Mrs Jackson, 3 rooms, 1 with bathroom, very good.

> The café in the **Bessie Bar Hall** in the *Palace* (see above) serves home-made food and is open 1030-1630.

Sleeping & eating

Dunfermline

A mere five kilometres inland off the M90, the town of Dunfermline is steeped in history. It was once the capital of Scotland, from the 11th century to the Union of Crowns in 1603, and its great abbey and royal palace still dominate the skyline. Until the late 19th century, Dunfermline was one of Scotland's most important linen producers and a major coal-mining centre. Those traditional industries have long since gone but the town still thrives economically and has grown considerably in size.

Phone code: 01383
Colour map 4, grid C3
Population: 52,000

Ins and outs

Trains from Edinburgh connect with Dunfermline. The train station is a 15-min walk southeast of the centre, halfway down St Margaret's Drive. There's an hourly bus service from Edinburgh, and 2-hourly services from Glasgow, Perth and Dundee. The bus station is in the Kingsgate Centre, on the north side of town, T621249.

History

In the 11th century, Malcolm Canmore, King of Scotland, offered hospitality in his tower in Dunfermline to the English heir to the throne, Edgar Atheling and his family, on their flight from William the Conqueror and the Norman conquest. Edgar's sister, Princess Margaret, a devout Catholic and later 'Saint Margaret', married the King in 1067, and was largely responsible for introducing the religious ideas of the Catholic Church into Scotland. Horrified by the lax ways of the Celtic Church, she began to build a new church which was founded in 1072 (see below).

Sights

Tourist Information Centre is at 13/15 Maygate (next to the Abbot House). ■ *T720999. Mon-Sat 0930-1730, Sun 1100-1600; closed on Sun, Oct-Mar.*

Dunfermline Abbey stands on the site of the Benedictine Priory, built by Queen Margaret in the late 11th century. When she endowed the priory, she set up a shrine, with a relic of the 'True Cross' and encouraged pilgrims to come from miles away to venerate it. Her son, David I, raised the priory to the rank of abbey and began building the new abbey church in 1128, on the foundations of Margaret's church. These foundations were rediscovered in modern times and can now be seen through a grating in the floor. Frequently sacked and burned over the centuries, today's building is a combination of different tastes and styles. Much of the present abbey was built long after King David's death but the superb Norman nave, with its massive pillars, is still there to be admired. The Norman decorations above the west doorway are rare

Abbey & the Royal Palace

examples of such work in Scotland. The north porch, northwest tower, west front and massive buttresses are all the work of William Shaw, Master of works to Anne of Denmark in the 16th century. The other part of the abbey church was added in the 19th century and today serves as the parish church.

Close to the east gable of the parish church are the foundations of the shrine of St Margaret where she and her husband are buried. But they were not the only royal persons to be buried in the abbey. Six Scottish kings also lie there with the grave of Robert the Bruce beneath the pulpit. He was buried in the abbey in 1329 but over the years the exact position of his grave became uncertain. Then, in 1818, when the foundation of the new church was being prepared, Bruce's tomb was rediscovered, the skeleton covered in a shroud of gold and the breast bone severed where his heart had been removed in order to take it to the Holy Land, in accordance with his wishes. Unfortunately, it never made it and now lies in Melrose Abbey. In 1889, Robert the Bruce's descendent, the Earl of Elgin, gifted a memorial brass to mark the tomb. To celebrate the historic find, an over-enthusiastic architect designed the vast inscription round the top of the square tower, which no-one can fail to notice.

The Abbey church stands adjacent to the ruined **monastery** building and the **Royal Palace**, which are linked by a pend or alleyway.

The palace, built when Malcolm and Margaret married, has fallen into ruins, but what little remains still hints at its undoubted magnificence. For centuries, it was a favourite residence of the Kings of Scotland. David II, James I and Charles I were all born here, the latter being the last monarch to be born in Scotland. ■ *T739026. The palace and abbey are open all year (in winter closed Thur afternoons, Fri and Sun mornings). £1.80, £1.30 concession, 75p children. Disabled access.*

Andrew Carnegie Birthplace Museum Dunfermline may have been the home to many Scottish monarchs, but its most famous son was born in more modest surroundings. **Andrew Carnegie** (1835-1919), the son of a humble linen weaver, emigrated to the USA and made a fortune in steel. One of the great philanthropists, he gave away £350mn for the benefit of mankind and was particularly generous to his home town, giving it Pittencrief park, public baths, a library and an annual Festival of Music and Arts. The Andrew Carnegie Birthplace Museum is the small cottage in Moodie Street where Carnegie was born. The rooms are furnished as they

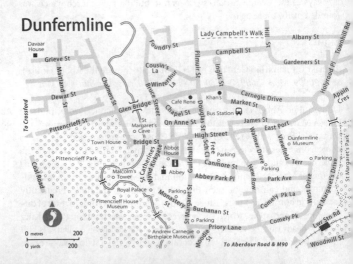

Dunfermline

were in his lifetime and the millionaire himself sits at the his desk in his study. ■ *T724302. Apr-Oct daily (Sun afternoon only), Nov-Mar daily 1400-1600. £1.50, 75p concession, children free.*

The beautiful and lavishly-endowed Pittencrief Park, known locally as 'the **Pittencrief Park** Glen', is opposite the west door of the Abbey. Inside the park is **Pittencrief House Museum**, built in 1610 and also bought by Carnegie for the people of Dunfermline. It features displays of local history, costumes and an art gallery. The glasshouses (free entry) are filled with tropical plants and flowers, and the art deco pavilion has a restaurant. Here also stands the ruin of **Malcolm's Tower**, where King Malcolm and his bride lived before the building of the palace. Dunfermline – which means 'fort by the crooked pool' – takes its name from the tower's location. ■ *T722935. Museum open daily. Free.*

In the Maygate is the **Abbot House**, which was the home of Robert Pitcairn, **Other sights** the post-Reformation Abbot of the Abbey. The house is one of the oldest in Scotland, possibly 14th century, and was restored in 1963. ■ *T733266. Daily. £3, £2 concession, children free.*

The 19th-century **Town House** in Bridge Street was designed in the French and Scottish Gothic style, said to be very fashionable at the time. Among its interesting features are the gargoyles and grotesques, depicting the heads of King Robert the Bruce, King Malcolm, Queen Margaret and Queen Elizabeth.

Incongruously housed in the stone building in Chalmers street car park is the entrance to **Saint Margaret's Cave**. The saintly queen often retired here for moments of secret devotion. Her husband, suspicious of her frequent visits to the cave, followed and discovered her kneeling in prayer. Overjoyed that his suspicions were groundless, he had the cave fitted up for her as a place of devotion. ■ *Daily Easter-end Sept. Free.*

Dunfermline Museum is at Viewfield Terrace, south of the East Port. The Victorian villa has displays concentrating on local history, including the weaving and damask linen industries, for which the town was famous and which greatly contributed to Fife's economic well-being. ■ *T313838. All year, Mon-Fri. Free.*

Essentials

A-C *Garvock House Hotel*, St John's Drive, Transy, T621067, F621168. 12 rooms with **Sleeping** bathroom, elegant country house in woodland setting, short break deals available. ■ *on map* Excellent. **C** *Pitbauchlie House Hotel*, Aberdour Rd, T722282, F620738. 50 rooms with *Price codes:* bathroom, set in landscaped gardens, only a few mins from the M90, with recom- *see inside front cover* mended restaurant. Very good. **B-C** *Davaar House Hotel*, 126 Grieve St, T721886/736463, F623633. 10 en suite rooms, within walking distance of the town centre and bus and rail stations, good restaurant. Very good. **E** *Pitreavie Guest House*, 3 Aberdour Rd, T/F724244. 6 rooms with 2 shared bathrooms, B&B.

A few miles west of Dunfermline, at Crossford, is **B-C** *Keavil House Hotel*, T736258, F621600, www.queensferry-hotels.co.uk. 40 en suite rooms, excellent accommodation and restaurant, leisure club.

Dunfermline offers the usual array of ethnic restaurants, including *Khan's*, 33 Carne- **Eating** gie Drive, for Indian cuisine, and *Blossom's*, 6-8 Chalmers St, for Chinese cooking. There are several restaurants, a café and a fish and chip shop on Carnegie Drive. The best place is *Café Rene*, which offers a good cheap lunch. *The New Victorian*, Hight St, opposite City Chambers, T623798. Old favourite. Wide-ranging and cheap menu. Open daily till 1900.

Fife

Sports Four miles north of the town centre, just off the A823, is *Knockhill Racing Circuit*, T723337, www.knockhill.co.uk, Scotland's national motorsport centre, which stages major car and motorbike racing events between Apr and Oct, usually on Sun. Admission £5-20 depending on the event, children under 16 free, OAP/concession half price. Also rally, race and 4X4 driving courses.

Transport **Buses** run frequently to **Stirling**, **Edinburgh** (30 mins), **Dundee** (1½ hrs) and **Kirkcaldy** (30 mins). *Scottish Citylink*, T0990-505050, runs buses hourly to **Edinburgh** and **Perth**. **Train** to **Edinburgh** every hour (30 mins).

Directory **Banks** There are several banks with ATMs in the High St. **Communications** The *Post Office* is in Pilmuir St, near the bus station.

North Queensferry
Phone code: 01383
Colour map 4, grid C3

Situated at the foot of the Forth Rail Bridge, North Queensferry was originally the northern terminal of the ferry established by Queen Margaret to carry pilgrims to Dunfermline. It remained a ferry terminal until the road bridge was opened in 1964. Now it is home to a yacht marina and provides the ideal vantage point from which to wonder at the fantastic engineering feat of the Forth Rail Bridge. Also here is the popular **Deep Sea World**, Scotland's award-winning national aquarium, which boasts the world's largest underwater viewing tunnel, through which you pass on a moving walkway, coming face-to-face with sharks, conger eels and all manner of strange sea creatures. There is also a display of species from the Amazon rainforest. ■ *T0930-100300. Daily all year. £6.15, £4.25 concession, £3.75 children, under 3 free. Restaurant; disabled access.*

On the north side of the Forth Road Bridge is the **B-C** *Queensferry Lodge Hotel*, T410000, F419708, home of the **Forth Bridges Exhibition** which tells the story of the bridges through models, artefacts and a 40-minute video. ■ *Daily. Free. Disabled access.* The hotel is also home to the **Forth Valley Tourist Information Centre**, T417759, and, surprisingly enough, offers comfortable accommodation in 77 en suite rooms with great views of the Forth and a restaurant.

Trips can be made from North Queensferry to **Inchcolm Island** in the Firth of Forth. Known as the Iona of the East, the island's famous Abbey of St Columba was founded in 1123 for Augustinian monks by King Alexander I. A Columban monk who lived on the island saved the king when his boat foundered on the rocky shore, and building the abbey was his act of gratitude. Although sacked many times by the English and desecrated during the Reformation, the abbey is remarkably well preserved and includes one of Scotland's rare 13th-century octagonal chapter houses and 14th-century cloisters. These are the finest monastic buildings left in the country. ■ *T0131-3314857. Sailings from Easter to Oct. Evening Jazz and ceilidh cruises throughout the summer on Fri, Sat and Sun evenings. Admission to the Abbey £2.50, £1.90 concession, £1 children. Wheelchair access.*

Inverkeithing
Phone code: 01383
Colour map 4, grid C3

The desolate shipbreakers yards at Inverkeithing, a stone's throw from North Queensferry, give no hint that this is one of the oldest Royal Burghs in Scotland. Granted a charter by King William the Lion around 1165, Inverkeithing was for centuries a place of trade and commerce with a small harbour and local coal workings. Behind the busy central square in the High Street, the medieval friary houses the **museum**, which recalls the history of the burgh. This includes the life of Samuel Greig, born in the town in 1735 and often described as the founder of the Russian Navy. The son of a local shipmaster, he initially had a career in the British Navy, but after secondment to Russia, he organized the Russian fleet for Catherine the Great, for which he received a knighthood. ■ *T313595. Thur-Sun 1200-1600. Free.*

Five miles east of the Forth bridges, on the A921, is Aberdour. The **castle** at the southern end of the main street, was built by the Douglas family on lands originally granted to Thomas Randolph, Earl of Moray, by King Robert the Bruce in 1325. The 14th-century tower is the oldest part of the castle, the other buildings having been added in the 16th and 17th centuries, including the unusual Dovecote (pronounced doocot) and the attractive walled garden. Nearby is **St Fillan's Church**, which is part Norman, part 16th century. The church has a peaceful, timeless quality which entices the visitor to linger in quiet contemplation. Note the leper-squint in the west wall, formerly used by sufferers who were not allowed to worship within the church. ■ *Mon-Sat 0930-1830, Sun 1200-1830; closed Thur afternoons, Fri and Sun mornings Oct-Mar. £1.80, £1.30 concession, 75p children. Restaurant, wheelchair access, disabled toilets.*

The town today is a popular tourist resort, with its attractive **silver sands** beach, watersports and golf course. A ferry sails from Hawkcraig Point in Aberdour to **Inchcolm Island** (see under North Queensferry above).

Aberdour
Phone code: 01383
Colour map 4, grid C3/4

Sleeping B *Hawkcraig House*, Hawkcraig Point, T860335. Excellent B&B run by Mrs Barrie, 2 en suite rooms, price includes dinner. **C-D** *Aberdour Hotel*, High St, T860325, F860808, www.aberdourhotel.co.uk. 16 en suite rooms, restaurant.

Transport Trains run hourly to **Kirkcaldy** and **Edinburgh**. There are 2 No 7 **buses** every hour to **Dunfermline**. No 57 bus runs about every 2 hrs to **Edinburgh**.

Three miles east of Aberdour is Burntisland, once famous for shipbuilding but now more popular as a holiday resort. The **Highland Games** held in mid-July are reputed to be the second oldest in the world and take place, like most of the town's summer activities, on the busy seafront Links. The church of **St Columba** was the first to be built in Scotland after the Reformation. The General Assembly of the Kirk of Scotland was held here in 1601, when in the presence of James VI, it was proposed that there should be a new translation of the Bible, the Authorised version, published in 1611. **Rossend Castle** is a 15th-century tower house that was recently restored and is now occupied by a firm of architects. It was here that the impetuous French poet, Chastelard, propositioned Mary, Queen of Scots in 1563, and was promptly beheaded (as a result) – for his impertinence.

Burntisland
Phone code: 01592
Colour map 4, grid C4

Fife

Transport Trains as for Aberdour. Buses run 3 times every hour to Kirkcaldy.

Sleeping B-C *Inchview Hotel*, 69 Kinghorn Rd, T872239, F874866. 12 en suite rooms, restaurant. **B-C** *Kingswood Hotel*, Kinghorn Rd, T872329, F873123. 9 en suite rooms, very comfortable, set in 2 acres of gardens and woodland, views across the Forth, offers good bar meals, high teas and dinners. There are many **B&Bs** along the Links. Particularly good is **E** *Gruinard*, 148 Kinghorn Rd, T873877.

A few miles along the coast from Burntisland, at Kinghorn, you'll pass a monument beside the road in the shape of a Celtic cross. This is where Alexander III was thrown from his horse and killed, an event that completely changed the course of Scottish history. The king had been heading home from Edinburgh to his new wife, whom he had married only six months earlier in an attempt to provide himself with an heir. There was a violent storm that night, but he insisted on being ferried across the Forth before galloping east towards Pettycur, where his still-barren queen was waiting. His horse stumbled on the cliff edge and the king was thrown to his death, thus plunging the country into many years of bitter conflict and power struggles. Today, Kinghorn is a busy

Kinghorn
Phone code: 01592
Colour map 4, grid C4

summer resort with a sandy beach, a golf course and a wide range of guest-houses. Transport details are as for Burntisland above.

Kirkcaldy

Population: 49,570
Phone code: 01592
Colour map 4, grid C4

Fifteen miles east of the Forth bridges is Kirkcaldy (pronounced kirkoddy), called the 'Lang Toon' because of its main street, running along the seafront, is all of four miles long. It's perhaps unkind to say that Kirkcaldy was once famous (or infamous) for its terrible stench, but at the height of its thriving linoleum industry you could smell the place for miles around. Nowadays, the town's economy has diversified and the smell has thankfully gone. Also gone is much of its shipping trade, and the area around the harbour bears witness to a once thriving sea port. Some of the little streets and wynds (steep alley-ways) opposite the harbour are worth exploring, such as Kirk Wynd or Sailor's Walk, which have been lovingly restored by the NTS. Today, the town may be best known as Fife's main shopping centre, but if you're passing through there are other a number of attractions aside from the many high street chain stores.

Sights The **tourist office** is at 19 Whyte Causeway. ■ *T267775. Mon-Fri 1000-1700, Sat 1000-1300 and 1400-1700. They will book accommodation and explain how to get there, which is invaluable as hotels and guesthouses are limited and scat-tered around the outskirts of town.*

The **Museum and Art Gallery** is in the War Memorial Gardens next to the railway station. There is a good archaeological collection and you can learn about the area's social, industrial and natural history. The small art gallery has an excellent collection of Scottish colourists, including work by William McTaggart, Peploe, Lowry, Sickert and Raeburn. There are also displays of the local Wemyss Ware pottery. ■ *T412860. Daily all year (closed Sun afternoons). Free. Disabled access.*

Across from the War Memorial Gardens is the **Adam Smith Centre**, named after one of the town's most famous sons, the pioneer economist and author of *The Wealth of Nations* in 1776. The centre stages live theatre and concerts and also has a cinema and restaurant/bar, T412929. In the High Street among the many shops, you'll find the birthplace of Adam Smith. At the old burgh school there's a plaque recording that both he and Robert Adam, the famous architect, were pupils there in the 1730s, and that Thomas Carlyle, the historian and essayist, taught there nearly 100 years later.

Ravenscraig Castle towers dramatically above the park of the same name, at the east end of the town, on a rocky promontory guarding the wide bay. The ruin dates from 1460, when James II intended it as a dower house for his wife. The castle was the first in Britain to be designed specifically for defence by and against cannon fire and you can see the wide gun loops in the massive thick walls. Near the castle, the steps that lead from the high-rise flats in Nether Road down to the beach should number 39 and are said to have inspired John Buchan to write his famous novel.

Dysart, the eastern suburb of Kirkcaldy, is a little burgh dating back to the 16th century and is full of character, with its delightful little wynds and court-yards and old houses with crow-stepped gables and pan-tiled roofs. Dysart was once a busy trading port with the Netherlands. Now all that remains is the little harbour, perfectly set below the ancient battlements of St Serf's church. The **Pan Ha'**, an area of 17th-century houses, was restored by the NTS, as was the **McDougall Stuart Museum**. This house, dated 1575, was the birthplace of John McDougall Stuart, the first man to cross Australia from north to south, in

1866. The award-winning museum tells of Stuart and his fascinating and often dangerous expedition. ■ *T412860. Daily Jun-Aug, 1400-1700. Free.*

C *Dunniker House Hotel*, Dunniker Park, Dunniker Way, T268393, F642340. 15 en suite rooms set in pleasant grounds, good food. **B-D** *Parkway Hotel*, 6 Abbotshall Rd, T262143, F200433. 35 en suite rooms, comfortable, near the rail station. **D-E** *Royal Hotel*, Townhead, T654112/652109, F598555, Royalhotel@aol.com. 4 en suite rooms, 2 with shared bathroom, in one of Dysart's historic buildings, good food.

Sleeping

Kirkcaldy's **guesthouses** and **B&Bs** are spread throughout the town's residential districts. These can all be booked at the TIC. Among the most recommended is the **E** *North Hall Guest House*, at 143 Victoria Rd, T268864/215059. Run by Norie and Agnes Cairns, 2 mins from the train station; and **E** *Bennochy Bank Guest House*, 26 Carlyle Rd, T200733.

There are lots of unremarkable places to eat in the High St, including the usual array of bakers, pubs, chip shops and Indian and Chinese restaurants. The best restaurant by far is the *Old Rectory*, in Dysart, a few miles east, T657211. It is moderately-priced and open Tue-Sat for dinner; Tue-Sun for lunch. The best fish and chips here, or anywhere else, can be found at *Valente's*, 73 Oventon Rd, east of town centre. A symphony in salt and vinegar. Open till 2300, closed Wed.

Eating

Every Apr, Kirkcaldy's esplanade is closed to traffic for 5 days during the **Links Market**, one of the largest and oldest street fairs in Britain.

Entertainment

The **train** station is in the upper part of town. The **bus** station is 1 block uphill from the High Street. Kirkcaldy is on the main **Edinburgh** to **Dundee** and **Aberdeen** rail line, with regular services each way. Numerous buses run to **St Andrews**, **Dunfermline**, **Edinburgh** and the **East Neuk**.

Transport

Around Kirkcaldy

A few miles east along the coast from Dysart are the villages of **East and West Wemyss**, so called from the many 'weems', or caves, found on this particular stretch of Fife coast. The famous caves lie along the foreshore of East Wemyss, below the ruins of **MacDuff's Castle**, reputed to be the home of Macduff of Shakespeare's *Macbeth*. Within the caves you'll find Britain's earliest picture of a boat, as well as hunting scenes, portrayed by craftsmen of Pictish times. King James IV was so impressed by one of the caves that he held court there and it is now known, not surprisingly, as Court Cave.

The A92 runs from the northeastern outskirts of Kirkcaldy to **Glenrothes**, a sprawling new town, developed since 1950, which was originally designed to meet the housing needs of new colliery workers. Coal mining, however, declined in Fife, and Glenrothes instead attracted the trailblazers of Scotland's new light electronics industries.

In the neighbouring town of **Markinch** is **Balbirnie Craft Centre**, displaying jewellery, knitwear, pottery, furniture and glass. ■ *T01592-756016. Daily.* Two miles east of Glenrothes on the B921 off the A911, is the splendid 14th-century **Balgonie Castle**. This was the 17th-century home of Field Marshall Sir Alexander Leslie, Lord General of the Scottish Covenanting Army and 1st Earl of Leven, and was garrisoned by Rob Roy MacGregor with 200 clansmen in 1716. Restoration continues in this family home and living museum. ■ *Daily 1000-1700, for a personal guided tour.*

Fife

Sleeping **L** *Balbirnie House Hotel*, Balbirnie Park, Markinch, T610066, F610529, balbirnie@ btinternet.com, www.balbirnie.co.uk. This magnificent Georgian mansion is set in 400 acres of country park with its own 18-hole golf course and is the height of luxury, 30 en suite rooms and restaurant.

Falkland, Cupar and the Howe of Fife

In stark contrast to the industrial landscape of Kirkcaldy and Glenrothes, The **Howe of Fife** is a low-lying area of patchwork fields, woodlands and farming communities which runs from the attractive market town of **Cupar** in the east to **Falkland**, at the foot of the **Lomond Hills**. The area makes a worthwhile stopping point on the way to or from St Andrews. It is reached from the M90 and is well served by regular buses to and from Dundee and Kirkcaldy. The main Edinburgh to Dundee and Aberdeen train also stops here, at Cupar.

Falkland

Phone code: 01337
Colour map 4, grid C4

Tucked away at the foot of the Lomond Hills, off the A912, the ancient and beautiful village of Falkland is the most royal of Fife's Royal Burghs and holds a unique place in Scottish history, as it is the site of **Falkland Palace**, the favourite residence of the Stuart monarchs. More than three centuries have passed since the last of the kings left Falkland, but it still retains a delightful charm, thanks to the NTS Little Houses Improvement scheme.

Sights The great **Royal Palace** stands in the heart of the village, which is a surprise in itself as it shows a remarkable lack of class distinction; rare in medieval Scotland. But it is not only the location of the palace that is exceptional. It is one of the grandest buildings in the country and its variety of styles is part of its charm.

Facing the street, the south front is a splendid example of Scottish Gothic with its buttresses, niches and statues of Christ and the saints. The magnificent courtyard frontage in the classical style, with pillars and medallions, strikes an altogether different mood and an air of gracious living. Scotland has few surviving buildings that were in the mainstream of Renaissance architecture, but here is one which is by far the best.

Though the building shows a strong French influence, there is a flavour about it that is unmistakably Scottish. Most of the existing palace was built in the early 16th century by James IV and his son James V. It was designed as a hunting lodge and was much loved by the Stuart kings and queens who came here to hunt deer and wild boar in the surrounding forests. There was also royal (or real) tennis to ease the strains of government. The royal tennis court, built in 1539 and the oldest in Britain, is still in use.

But though the monarchy, from James II to Charles II, spent some of their happiest days at Falkland, the best known event to happen there was the tragic death of King James V. He had come to the palace after his defeat at Solway Moss in 1542 and died of a broken heart on hearing of the birth of a daughter, the future Mary, Queen of Scots. When the news was broken to him he exclaimed "Fareweil, it cam with ane lass and it will pass with ane lass". He then turned his face to the wall and died. The king's bedchamber is one of the many attractions inside the palace, morbid though it may be. A guided tour lasts 40 minutes and includes the Chapel Royal (still used for Mass), the superb Flemish Tapestry Gallery, the King's Bedchamber and Queen's Room, as well as the gardens and Tennis Court. ■ *T857397. The Palace is open daily 1 Apr to 31 Oct, Mon-Sat 1100-1730, Sun 1330-1730. £5, £3.35 children/concession, £13.35 family.*

Falkland is a good base for **walks** in the **Lomond Hills**. A narrow road leads from the village to a pass between East and West Lomond. It's about one hour to the pass and a further 45 minutes to the summit of West Lomond (1,712ft). The views from the top on a clear day are wonderful.

C-D *Covenanter Hotel*, is situated opposite the palace, T857224, F857163, www. covenanterhotel.com. 6 comfortable en suite rooms, excellent food served in the bar downstairs. **E** *Oakbank House*, The Pleasance, T857287. 2 en suite rooms, excellent value. *Youth Hostel*, Back Wynd, T857710. Open mid Mar-early Oct. Good home baking at *Kind Kyttock's Kitchen*, Cross Wynd. Open daily except Mon.

Sleeping & eating

Buses run daily to Kinross and from Perth, Kirkcaldy and Cupar. The nearest train station is 5 miles away at Markinch, on the Edinburgh to Dundee line.

Transport

Cupar

The main centre in the Howe of Fife is Cupar, a thriving market town that was once the administrative centre of Fife. There's an air of relative well-being about the place, verified by an array of shops catering for the connoisseur. In the heart of the burgh is the Castlehill which played a notable part in Cupar's history. There, the Thanes of Fife had their principle residence in ancient times and later it became the home of Sir David Lindsay. Sir David was a dramatist with a devastating wit and his play *Ane Pleasant Satyre of the Three Estaits* earned him considerable fame. It was by far the most popular play of its day and is still popular at the Edinburgh Festival.

Phone code: 01334
Colour map 4, grid C4
Population: 7,610

One of the main reasons for stopping off at Cupar is to visit **Hill of Tarvit**, two miles south of the town and one mile from Ceres (see below). This Edwardian mansion house was beautifully remodelled by Robert Lorimer in 1906. Among the fine collection of treasures inside are Flemish tapestries, Chinese porcelain, Dutch paintings and 18th-century French, Chippendale and vernacular furniture. The gardens are laid out in French style, with box hedges and yews, and there is a woodland walk to a hilltop toposcope with a lovely view of the house. The estate includes the fine **Scotstarvit Tower**, three quarters of a mile west of the mansion house, dating from 1579. The cottage at the foot of the tower can be rented from the NTS for around £250 per week, T0131-2439331.

Sights

Fife

B *Fernie Castle Hotel*, near Letham, 5 miles north of Cupar, T01337-810381, F810422. A beautifully restored 14th-century castle set in 17 acres of grounds with its own loch, 15 comfortable en suite rooms, lovely dining room and bar. **B-C** *Eden House Hotel*, 2 Pitscottie Rd, T652510, F652277, lv@eden.u-net.com. Elegant Victorian town house with 11 en suite rooms and excellent restaurant, also arranges golfing packages. **D-E** *Rathcluan*, Carslogie Rd, T657856/7, reservations@rathcluan.co.uk, www.rathcluan.co.uk. 2 en suite rooms and 3 with shared bathroom, parking and wheelchair access. **C-D** *Lordscairnie*, Lordscairnie near Cupar, T/F01337-870252. Superior B&B with 4 en suite rooms, dinner available on request.

Sleeping

In the town centre there are bakeries, fish and chip shops and the obligatory Indian and Chinese restaurants and takeaways. Particularly good is *Ostler's Close*, 25 Bonnygate, T655574, which does a 3-course lunch for under £20. The best place in the area is the renowned *Peat Inn* (see under St Andrews).

Eating

Robinson Crusoe

In a humble cottage down by the shore at Lower Largo, Alexander Selkirk spent his boyhood. By the age of 15 he was a strapping lad with a fierce temper, and in one particular incident the minister and kirk session were appalled to hear that he had threatened to blow out both his brother's and father's brains.

Young Alex went to sea after that and, in 1704, he set off for the South Seas as a sailing master in the vessel Cinque Ports. Eight months had elapsed when Selkirk had a violent quarrel with the captain and, at his own request, went ashore on the uninhabited island of Juan Fernández, off the coast of Chile.

Four years and four months later, Selkirk saw two ships approaching the island and, lighting a fire to attract their attention, ran along the shore to meet them. He was dressed completely in goat skins. However, by the time he returned home to Lower Largo, he had amassed a small fortune in pirate booty and his clothes were somewhat more elegant. So much so that his mother didn't even recognize him.

This was the story that was related to Daniel Defoe when the two met in a London coffee house in 1715 the fiery-tempered Fifer was immortalized in Defoe's tale of Robinson Crusoe.

Transport Cupar is on the **Edinburgh** to **Dundee** rail line and **trains** depart in each direction roughly every hour, or every 2 hrs on Sun. **Buses** from **Dundee** to **Kirkcaldy** pass through the town, and there are direct buses to **St Andrews** every 20 mins.

Around Cupar

The **Scottish Deer Centre**, three miles west of Cupar on the A91, is both enjoyable and educational. Here you can see many species of deer at close hand, and even feed, stroke or photograph them during a ranger-led tour. There are indoor and outdoor adventure parks for the kids as well as a restaurant and winery. ■ *T01337-810391. Easter to 31 Oct daily 1000-1800, Nov to Easter daily 1000-1700. £3.50, £2 children, £3 concession, £10 family. Disabled access.*

Those who prefer more exotic animals can head a few miles further west on the A91 to the **Fife Animal Park** at Collesie, where you can see ostriches, wallabies, emus, bison and llamas as well as more familiar breeds. ■ *T01337-831830. Mar-Oct daily, Nov-Feb Wed-Sun. £2.75, £2.25 child/concession. Disabled access.*

Once described as the most attractive village in Scotland, **Ceres** lies three miles south of Cupar. Whether or not you agree with that assertion, the village does present an appealing picture with its pan-tiled cottages surrounding a historic village green. Tradition says that the village and ancient cobbled bridge have been there for more than 650 years; that the men of Ceres marched across the bridge on their way to the battle of Bannockburn and on their return celebrated their victory with games on the village green. The **Highland Games** are still an annual event, on the last Saturday in June, with the Ceres Derby the highlight of the day.

Another special feature of Ceres is the **Fife Folk Museum**, housed in part of the 17th-century Tolbooth Weigh House and two adjoining cottages. The award-winning museum displays crafts and trades, costumes, tools and utensils of a bygone age in rural Fife. ■ *T828250. Easter and mid-May to mid-Oct, 1400-1700 (closed Fri). £2, 50p/£1.50 children/concession. Limited wheelchair access.*

Also worth visiting is the **Griselda Hill Pottery**, at Kirkbrae. Here you can see a revival of the production of Wemyss Ware, the best-known Scottish pottery. ■ *T828273. Summer and Christmas Mon-Fri 0900-1630, Sat and Sun 1400-1700, Mon-Fri 0900-1630 in winter. Free. Wheelchair access.*

Before you leave Ceres, don't miss one of Fife's most loveable monuments, **The Provost**. This genial figure surveys the passing traffic at the crossroads and is said to be a caricature of the last ecclesiastical provost of the village.

Three miles southeast of Ceres on the B940 is *Peat Inn*. This is well worth a detour, for here, in the 18th-century building, you can sample perhaps the finest **food** in the country. The proprietors have a Michelin star to verify this and the French-influenced décor and ambience match the culinary excellence.

The East Neuk

Fife was described by King James VI as "a beggar's mantle fringed with gold". The golden fringe to which he referred was the East Neuk (or nook, meaning corner). Here, on Fife's easternmost stretch of coastline are some of the kingdom's greatest attractions. From Largo Bay to Fife Ness lies a string of picturesque villages, each with its own distinctive character and charm. These were once thriving seaports trading with the Low Countries. The Dutch influence lives on in their architectural styles. The red pan-tiled roofs and crow-stepped gables lend a particular continental feel to one of the most attractive corners of Scotland.

Lundin Links and Largo

Lundin Links is the most westerly of the East Neuk villages. It is popular with the golfing fraternity and boasts some fine courses. On the ladies course you can see three large standing stones, reminders of the Bronze Age peoples who once populated this area.

Phone code: 01333
Colour map 4, grid C4

Next door to Lundin Links is **Lower Largo**, best known as the birthplace of Alexander Selkirk, the real-life Robinson Crusoe. His statue can be seen in the main street running behind the *Crusoe Hotel*. This was once an important fishing centre. Now it is a popular holiday resort with its golden crescent of sand and picturesque little harbour, framed by an impressive railway viaduct.

L-C *Old Manor Hotel*, Leven Rd, Lundin Links, T320368, F320911, enquiries@ oldmanorhotel.co.uk, www.oldmanorhotel.co.uk. Overlooking Largo Bay, 24 en suite rooms, restaurant, excellent.

Sleeping

For good bar meals try the *Crusoe Hotel*, by the harbour in Lower Largo. *Scotland's Larder*, T360414, on the road east out of Upper Largo, provides a real insight into Scottish food with its restaurant, shop and cooking demonstrations. Booking for dinner is essential. Open Apr-Nov daily 1000-late, Nov-Mar Sun-Thur 1100-1500, Fri and Sat from 1100.

Eating

Elie and Earlsferry

Heading east from Largo, the next coastal villages are Elie and Earlsferry, which are really two halves of the same place. This is one of Fife's most popular resorts, with a mile of lovely sandy beaches, and is very popular with sailors and windsurfers. There are also two golf courses, a nine-hole and 18-hole.

Phone code: 01333
Colour map 4, grid C5

There is an exclusive air about Elie, which is only enhanced by the tale that, at one time, fish and chips were banned from the town! Like its neighbours, though, it shares the distinctive Dutch-influenced architecture.

The **Lady's Tower**, a short walk from the harbour, recalls a more aristocratic past. The tower was built as a bathing box for Lady Janet Anstruther, a noted beauty of the 18th century. The whole town knew when Lady Janet was bathing, for she sent a bellman round the streets to warn the inhabitants to stay away.

Elie's westerly neighbour is the much older burgh of Earlsferry. There are three caves in the rock face at **Kincraig Point**, the headland at the far end of a broad sandy beach: the Deil's (Devil's) Cave; Doo's (dove's) Cave; and the spectacular MacDuff's Cave, where the Thane (Earl) of Fife is said to have hidden from Shakespeare's Macbeth, until fishermen rowed him across the Forth to safety. Hence the town's name.

Sleeping & eating **B-C** *The Golf Hotel*, Bank St, Elie, T330209, F330381, golf@standrews.co.uk, www.golfhotel.co.uk Very comfortable accommodation, 22 en suite rooms, restaurant, will arrange tee times for St Andrew and local courses. For tasty bar meals and a good pint try the *Ship Inn*, down by Elie harbour. The best place to eat is the highly-acclaimed *Bouquet Garni*, on the High St, T330374. It's open for lunch and 1900-2100; closed Sun. No smoking. Moderate prices.

Kilconquhar
Phone code: 01333

Inland from Elie is Kilconquhar (pronounced Kinneuchar), a timeless and tiny village on the shores of a loch. Here you can see great-crested grebe, pochard, shelduck, swans, moorhen, reed bunting, teal, black-headed gulls, coots, hawks, grouse and barn owls. On the road north out of the village is the *Kilconquhar Estate* & *Country Club*, T340501, F340239, set in 40 acres of landscaped grounds. 11 en suite rooms, restaurant, pub and extensive facilities including heated pool, badminton, squash, golf driving range and stables.

St Monans

Phone code: 01333
Colour map 4, grid C5

Further along the coast, St Monans was once one of Scotland's busiest fishing ports, a fact that is emphasized by the presence of Miller's boatyard by the harbour. This is one of the oldest surviving boat-builders, established in 1747 and still producing traditional fishing boats. Other reminders of the town's sea-faring past remain. The tiny fishermen's church stands so close to the sea that during winter storms the spray rises over the churchyard wall to wash the gravestones in the cemetery. The present foundations of the church date from 1362, but the original church dates from a century earlier.

Pittenweem

Phone code: 01333
Colour map 4, grid C5

This is the home of the East Neuk fishing fleet with a thriving fish market and harbour crammed with fishing boats. It is well worth rising early to come here and witness the landing of the catch. At the east end of the harbour is **The Gyles**, an attractive group of 16th- and 17th-century houses beautifully restored by the NTS and boasting some fine examples of Dutch-style gables.

The oldest house by far in Pittenweem is in **Cove Wynd**, which climbs steeply up to the High Street from the East Shore overlooking the harbour. In the seventh century the early Christian missionary, **St Fillan** lived here in a **cave**, dug deep into the rock. All through the middle ages pilgrims came to visit the cave. This primitive dwelling gave the town its name, for in the Pictish tongue, the word means 'place of the cave'. ■ *T311495. To visit the cave, collect the key from the Gingerbread Horse in the High St.*

The pilgrims who visited the shrine received hospitality at the 12th-century **Priory**, established by Augustinian monks from the Isle of May. The remains can be seen in the Marygate, behind the Episcopal church. Nearby, in the High

Street is the impressive 16th-century Parish church and **Kellie Lodge**, also 16th-century, town house of the Earls of Kellie and an excellent example of the vernacular style.

Three miles inland from Pittenweem, on the B9171, stands **Kellie Castle**, one of the oldest and most magnificent of Scottish castles. This is 16th- and 17th-century domestic architecture at its best, though the oldest part of the castle dates from 1360. Owned by the Oliphants for over 250 years, then by the Earls of Mar and Kellie, the castle was saved from ruin over a century ago by Professor James Lorimer. The interior is notable for its superb plasterwork ceilings, which were then the height of fashion. The castle's 16 acres of beautifully landscaped gardens were designed by Lorimer's son, Robert, who became a well-known architect specializing in restoration. Among his works is the Hill of Tarvit, near Cupar. His grandson, the sculptor Huw Lorimer, is the present custodian and resident. ■ *Easter and 1 May to 30 Sept daily, and weekends in Oct, 1330-1730, £3.90, £2.60 concession/children, £10.40 family. Bus Nos 61A/B runs from St Andrews to Arncroach and passes the castle entrance 4 times daily, except Sun (1 hr).*

Anstruther

Known locally as Anster (pronounced enster), this is the largest of the East Neuk villages. Today, it is best known as the home of the Scottish Fisheries Museum, but it was Scotland's main fishing port at the end of the 19th century, with almost 1,000 boats in its fleet.

Phone code: 01333
Colour map 4, grid C5
Population: 3,270

Like its neighbours, Anster traded with the Low Countries and Scandinavia, before becoming an important centre for herring fishing. This proud heritage has been well preserved in **The Scottish Fisheries Museum**, which faces the harbour on the site of the pre-Reformation St Ayles chapel. The museum, established in 1969, gives a fascinating insight into the life and work of a fishing community and is well worth a visit. There's also a fine collection of actual and model fishing boats, equipment, maps and compasses, as well as an aquarium. ■ *T310628. Apr-Oct Mon-Sat 1000-1730, Sun 1100-1700, Nov-Mar Mon-Sat 1000-1630, Sun 1400-1630. £3.50, £2.50 concession/children. Wheelchair access.* Next to the Fisheries museum is the helpful **Tourist Information Centre**. ■ *T311073. Easter to mid-Sept Mon, Fri-Sat 1000-1700, Tue-Thur 1000-1300 and 1400-1700, Sun 1200-1700.*

Sights

Moored in the harbour opposite the museum is the **North Carr Lightship**. For more than 40 years she did service off Fife Ness and is now a museum where you can picture what life must have been like for the seven-man crew in those cramped conditions for weeks on end.

Three miles north of Anstruther, just off the B9131 to St Andrews at Troy Wood, is **Scotland's Secret Bunker**, one of Fife's most fascinating attractions. This was to have been the government HQ for Scotland in the event of nuclear war and was only opened to the public in 1994. In fact, part of the complex is still operational and remains secret, as do the equivalent centres in England and Wales. The approach is through an innocuous-looking farmhouse, then visitors descend via a huge ramp to the bunker, 30m underground and encased in 5m of reinforced concrete. The bunker could house 300 people and was to be fitted with air filters, an electricity generator and its own water supply. It even had a couple of cinemas, which are now used to show a rather frightening 1950s newsreel giving instructions to civilians on what to do in the event of nuclear attack. Aside from the café and gift shop, the bunker has been left exactly as it was in the 1950s. ■ *1 Apr-end Oct daily 1000-1700. £5.95,*

£3.25 children, £4.95 OAP. T310301. The direct St Andrews to Anstruther bus takes you to the turn-off for Troy Wood, then it's a mile walk.

During the summer months boats from Anstruther visit the **Isle of May**, five miles offshore guarding the mouth of the Firth of Forth. The approach to the island's impressive cliffs is spectacular. The island became a national Nature Reserve in 1956 and is home to a large population of puffins, shags, guillemots, razorbills and kittiwakes as well as seals. The island has an intriguing history. It was home to the Benedictine Priors who came in remembrance of St Adrian, the Christian missionary who was murdered there in 870 AD and the remains of whose chapel can still be seen. The first lighthouse in Scotland, built here in 1636, can also be seen. The present lighthouse was built by Robert Louis Stevenson's grandfather in 1816. ■ *T310103 (24 hours). There are sailings from 1 May-30 Sept, £12, £5 children, £10 concession.*

Sleeping **B-C** *Craw's Nest Hotel*, Bankwell Rd, T310691, F312216. Very good hotel with restaurant and full range of facilties, 50 en suite rooms. There are plenty of good **guesthouses** and **B&Bs**. **E** *Beaumont Lodge*, 43 Pittenweem Rd, T/F310315, reservations@beau-lodge.demon.co.uk. Superior guesthouse with 4 en suite rooms which also serves good evening meals. **D** *The Spindrift*, Pittenweem Rd, T/F310573, spindrift@east-neuk.co.uk, www.east-neuk.co.uk/spindrift. 7 en suite rooms. **E** *The Sheiling*, 32 Glenogil Gardens, T310697.

Eating Several hotels and pubs serve bar meals, including the *Craw's Nest* and the *Smuggler's Inn*, on the High St, while the *Anstruther Fish Bar*, on Shore St, does a mean takeaway fish supper. A restaurant of particular note is *The Cellar*, in East Green, just behind the Fisheries Museum. The seafood here is among the finest in the country and will set you back around £30 for a 3-course dinner.

Transport The No 95 **bus** runs every hour between **Dundee** and **Leven**, via **St Andrews**, **Crail**, **Anstruther**, **Pittenweem**, **St Monans** and **Elie**. There are also daily buses to **Kellie Castle**, **Troy Wood** and **St Andrews**.

Crail

Phone code: 01333
Colour map 4, grid C5

Three miles northeast of Anstruther is the most ancient and picturesque of all Fife's Royal Burghs. Crail was once the largest fishmarket in Europe and for centuries its ships returned from the Low Countries and Scandinavia laden with cargo. Today you're more likely to see tourists than fishermen, but you can still buy fresh lobster and shellfish here.

Sights Centuries ago, the town's rich merchants built their handsome houses round the market place. At the far end of the Marketgate, is the **Collegiate Church of St Mary**, whose origin goes back to the 12th century. During the building of the church the Devil is said to have hurled a great boulder at it from the Isle of May. The boulder split as it flew through the air and one part landed only 30m from the churchyard gate. It still sits there, bearing the Devil's thumbprint.

At the other end of the Marketgate is the **Tolbooth**, dating from the early 16th century, now serving as the town hall. In the striking Dutch tower is a bell dated 1520, cast in Holland. Also in the Marketgate is the **Museum and Heritage Centre** which shows much of the history of the town. ■ *Easter-Jun weekends and public holidays, Jun-Sept daily 1000-1300 and 1400-1700, Sun 1400-1700. Free.* There's also a **Tourist Information Centre** at the Museum and Heritage Centre, 62-64 Marketgate. ■ *T450869. Easter-Sept. Guided walks around the village start from here at 1430 on Sun from 28 Jun-30 Aug. £1, 50p children.*

Crail's real attraction, however, is its beautiful **harbour**, surrounded by whitewashed cottages with pan-tiled roofs and crow-stepped gables. It is one of the most photographed locations in all of Scotland and a favourite with artists. To reach the old harbour you go down the steep, winding Shoregate. At the foot of the Shoregate is the 19th-century customs house.

D *Marine Hotel*, 54 Nethergate, T450207, F451145. 9 en suite rooms, restaurant, good bar meals from £5-9. **E** *Caiplie Guest House*, 53 High St, T/F450564. 3 en suite rooms and 2 with shared bathroom. Excellent 3-course dinner available.

Sleeping & eating

Crail is 10 miles from St Andrews. The **Dundee** to **Leven bus** passes through every hour (30 mins to St Andrews).

Transport

St Andrews

St Andrews is possibly the most visited town in Scotland after Edinburgh. This well-groomed seaside resort on the northeastern coast of Fife is the 'Home of Golf' and a mecca for aficionados of the sport the world over. Here is the headquarters of the game's governing body, the Royal and Ancient Golf Club, and the world's most famous golf course, the Old Course. But it's not all Pringle sweaters and five irons. St Andrews has an air of calm dignity tinged with an inherent sense of history, as you'd expect from a place that was once the ecclesiastical capital of Scotland and the country's oldest seat of learning. Not forgetting the two fine beaches – the West and East Sands – that enclose the town like golden bookends.

Phone code: 01334
Colour map 4, grid C5
Population: 13,000

Ins & outs

St Andrews, 13 miles south of Dundee and 55 miles north of Edinburgh, is not on the **train** line. The nearest station is 5 miles away at Leuchars, on the Edinurgh-Dundee-Aberdeen line. Regular **buses** make the 15-min journey from there to St Andrews. A **taxi** costs around £7. The bus station is on City Road, at the west end of town. There are frequent buses to Dundee (30 mins), the East Neuk villages and Cupar (20 mins). There is also a service to Stirling. Buses run from Edinburgh to St Andrews via Kirkcaldy.

Getting there

If you're driving, parking in the town centre can be difficult at busy times. You need to buy vouchers (30p per hr) from the tourist office or from local shops. Taxis available from *Golf City Taxis*, 13 Argyle St, T477788.

Getting around

History

St Andrews is, of course, synonymous with Scotland's patron saint. Andrew was the first of the disciples and among his many converts was the wife of the Roman Governor of Patras in Western Greece. The governor was so furious and jealous of his wife's conversion that he had Andrew crucified. Andrew asked to be tied to an X-shaped cross so that he would not appear to be emulating Christ – thus giving the Scottish flag its distinctive Saltire Cross.

According to legend, a saintly monk called Rule, or Regulus, who lived in Patras, was divinely inspired to take some of the Apostle's bones and make a journey far to the west. St Rule set off and was shipwrecked on the rocks just to the west of St Andrews harbour. After converting the Pictish king to Christianity, St Rule enshrined the sacred relics on the headland where the ruins of the 12th-century cathedral now stand. The shrine became a place of worship for

Christian pilgrims from far and wide and a special ferry was kept on the river Forth to transport them. St Andrew became Scotland's patron saint and his city the ecclesiastical capital of the country.

Sights

The **Tourist Information Centre** has comprehensive information about St Andrews and Northeast Fife. ■ *70 Market St, T472021. Apr-May Mon-Sat 0930-1800, Sun 1100-1600; Jun Mon-Sat 0930-1900, Sun 1100-1800; Jul-Aug Mon-Sat 0930-2000, Sun 1100-1800; Sept to mid-Oct Mon-Sat 0930-1900, Sun 1100-1800; mid-Oct to Mar Mon-Sat 0930-1700.*

Cathedral St Andrews' street plan has not changed since the Middle Ages. It basically consists of three main streets – North Street, Market Street and South Street – which still converge on the Cathedral standing proudly, overlooking the harbour at the eastern end of the town. Founded in 1160, it was consecrated 160 years later, in 1318, by Robert the Bruce. Medieval pilgrims came in their thousands to pray at its many altars. This explains the exceptional width of North Street, which enabled the vast numbers to proceed to the cathedral. Perched on the cliffs above the harbour are the foundations of the Church of **St Mary of the Rock**, all that remains of the ancient Celtic settlement. It fell into disuse as the church of St Rule and the Cathedral prospered.

Fife

St Andrews

Though devastated over the years by fire and by zealous religious reformers, the Cathedral ruins are still impressive, giving adequate proof that this was by far the largest ecclesiastical building ever to be erected in Scotland. The imposing Romanesque **St Rule's Tower** is where the holy relics of the Apostle were kept until the Cathedral was completed. It's a long hard climb to the top of the tower, but the view on a clear day is well worth the effort.

The Cathedral visitor centre has a fine collection of early Christian sculptured stones from the church of St Mary of the Rock. Of particular interest is the unique eighth century Pictish sarcophagus. ■ *T472563. Apr-Sept daily 0930-1830; Oct-Mar Mon-Sat 0930-1630, Sun 1400-1630. £1.80, 75p children, £1.30 concession. Joint ticket with Castle £3.50, £1.25 children, £2.70 concession.*

Castle

Poised on a rocky headland overhanging the sea stands the ruin of **St Andrews Castle**. It was built at the end of the 12th century as the place and stronghold of the Bishops of St Andrews and has witnessed many violent incidents in the blood-stained history of the Scottish church. Many reformers suffered imprisonment here, including George Wishart, whom the infamous Cardinal Beaton had burnt at the stake in front of the castle in 1546. His initials can be seen picked out in cobble-stones on the roadway near the entrance.

Following the martyrdom of Wishart, a group of avenging Protestants gained entry to the castle disguised as stone masons and brutally murdered Beaton. His body was then hung over the battlements for all to see. After the murder the reformers held the castle against siege for a year until they capitulated to the French fleet. The castle fell into ruin in the 17th century, but two very notable features remain. In the northwest tower is the grim bottle dungeon, hollowed out of solid rock and from which death was the only release. Also of note is the mine and countermine, tunnelled through the rock during the siege that followed Cardinal Beaton's murder. The besiegers started their tunnel, but were thwarted by the defenders who tried to intercept them. Uncertainty about who was where led to its abandonment. A fascinating exhibition in the visitor centre brings the history of the castle to life. ■ *T477196. Opening times as for the Cathedral, £2.50, £1 children, £1.90 concession. Joint ticket with Cathedral available (see above). Wheelchair access.*

University

The University of St Andrews, founded in 1410 by Henry Wardlaw, Bishop of St Andrews, is the third oldest in Britain after Oxford and Cambridge. Among its many fine buildings is the **Church of St Salvator** in North Street. The first of its colleges, St Salvator's was founded by Bishop Kennedy in 1450. The Bishop's niece,

E Scores

Museum of
St Andrews
Preservation
Trust

Cathedral

Kirk Hill

St Rule's Tower

Pier

Harbour

The Pends

Shorehead

East Sands

en Mary's
House

St Leonard's
School

y Walk

To Crail, Anstruther & Grange Inn (A917)

© Crown copyright

Fife

ing

mbles
ntral Bar
vegan
therie & Firkin
etta's
ejohn's

7 New Balaka Bangladeshi
8 Ogston's
9 Peter Michael's
10 The Merchant's House
11 The Vine Leaf
12 Victoria Café

The Home of golf

The Royal and Ancient Golf Club of St Andrews is the ruling house of golf worldwide and a mecca for all who play or follow the game. On any one day during the summer, you'll see many addicts staring reverentially across the most famous stretch of golf course in the world. The imposing 1854 clubhouse overlooks the first and 18th holes and you can enter by invitation only. Anyone, however, can play on the six courses at St Andrews, including the historic Old Course itself.

The citizens of St Andrews have been playing golf on these Links for a very long time, even before 1457 when the Scottish Parliament tried to ban the game. No one in the town took the ban seriously and by 1553 they had an inalienable right to play golf on the Links. The game developed and acquired popularity in the highest circles – even Mary, Queen of Scots was known to indulge in the odd round or two. The new craze was getting out of hand, however, and towards the end of the 16th century there was a spate of church absenteeism caused by people slipping off for a quick 18 holes. Two men were brought before the Kirk session in 1598 for "prophaning of the Saboth day in playing at the gouf eftir nune". As it was a first offence they got off with an admonition.

By the 17th and 18th centuries St Andrews was very much in decline, but exciting things were happening in the world of golf. In 1754 some 22 noblemen, mostly landowners in Fife, decided to move their golfing activities from Edinburgh to St Andrews. And so the exclusive Society of St Andrews Golfers, the forerunner of the Royal and Ancient Golf Club, came into existence. It was that fortunate decision that saved St Andrews turning into a ghost town and it has never looked back since.

The history of this game and the town's intimate association with it, are all to be discovered in the **British Golf Museum**, standing directly behind the R & A Clubhouse on Bruce Embankment. It is the most exciting of its kind, and audio-visual displays and touch activated screens bring the game to life and trace its development through the centuries. T478880, Apr-Oct daily 0930-1730; Nov-Mar Thur-Mon 1100-1500, £3.75, £1.50 children, £2.75 concession, £9.50 family.

Kate, was said to be so beautiful that all the students were in love with her. Today's students still pay homage to her pulchritude in the Kate Kennedy Pageant (see below). The bishop's tomb is in the church, along with a magnificent mace from his time, which is still carried on special occasions. The pulpit is the very one from which John Knox delivered his firebrand sermons in the Parish Church. The initials PH laid in the pavement outside the entrance mark the spot where Patrick Hamilton, one of the early reformers, was burned in 1528.

Other parts of the University include **St Mary's College**, in South Street, founded in 1537 by Archbishop James Beaton, uncle of the notorious cardinal. **Queen Mary's House**, in South Street by the Cathedral, is where the ill-fated queen stayed in 1563. Charles II also stayed here, in 1650. The house was restored in 1927 and is now used as St Leonard's school library. During her stay Queen Mary planted a thorn tree that still flourishes in the quadrangle of St Mary's college. **St Leonard's College**, on Pends Road which leads from the end of South Street down to the harbour, was founded in 1512 but then amalgamated with St Salvator's in 1747. The present buildings now house a girls' private school.

Other sights St Andrews has many other notable historic buildings and monuments. The **West Port** (c.1580) at the west end of South Street, was the main entrance to the old town and is one of the few surviving city gates in Scotland. All that remains of **Blackfriars Chapel**, a small Dominican church, is a single apse.

Rebuilt around 1515, its remains are in South Street, beside Madras College. Opposite the Tourist Information Centre in South Street is the **Holy Trinity Church**, rebuilt in 1410, which was modified in the late 18th century and restored in the 20th century. Inside, Archbishop Sharp's monument graphically records his brutal murder in 1679 on Magus Muir.

History envelops St Andrews; every street, every building has its own story. So it's a real pleasure just to wander aimlessly through its narrow alleyways (or 'closes') that connect the medieval streets and discover its many hidden delights. A good example is **Louden's Close**, between Blackfriars and the West Port. Or stroll down **The Pends** by the Cathedral to the quaint old harbour; here, during term time, you might see the Sunday Parade of University students processing from the chapel in their scarlet medieval gowns that were introduced so that they could be spotted easily when entering the local brothels.

As well as an impressive history, St Andrews has other attractions. There are two fine sandy **beaches**, the **East and West Sands**, at either end of town. The latter provided the setting for the opening sequence in the film *Chariots of Fire*. If you've got kids, then the huge **Sea-Life Centre** is a must. Situated on The Scores, at the west end of town near the Golf Museum (see above), this is where you can legally indulge in any number of piscean pleasures with an array of weird and wonderful sea creatures. ■ *T474786. Daily all year 1000-1800; £4.25, £3.25 children, £3.75 concession, free admission for disabled*. The **Museum of St Andrews Preservation Trust** has a number of fascinating displays including 19th-century shop interiors. ■ *T477629. Easter weekend and 23 May to end Sept, daily 1400-1630. Free*. Also worth a visit is the **St Andrews Museum**, in Kinburn Park near the bus station, which charts the history of the town from earliest times. ■ *T412690. Daily all year. Free*. Two miles west of the town centre on the B939 is **Craigtoun Country Park**. The park has an **Italian Garden**, a **Dutch Village** surrounded by an ornamental lake, a miniature railway, putting green, boating, trampolines a licensed restaurant and picnic area. ■ *T473666. Daily Mar-Oct; £2*. The **Botanic Gardens** on Canongate offer a peaceful retreat, only 10 minutes walk south of South Street. ■ *T477178/ 476452. Daily all year. £1.50*.

Essentials

St Andrews has plentiful accommodation, from humble B&Bs to international class hotels, but advance booking is still advisable during the summer months.

Sleeping
■ *on map*
Price codes:
see inside front cover

L *Old Course Hotel*, T474371, F477668. Internationally renowned golf resort and spa overlooking the 17th hole, 125 en suite rooms, bar and restaurants. **L** *Rufflets Country House Hotel*, Strathkinnes Low Rd, T472594, F478703, www.standrews.co.uk/ hotels/rufflets. Small country house set in 10 acres of grounds on the outskirts of town by the B939, 25 en suite rooms, good restaurant. **L-C** *Rusacks Hotel*, Pilmour Links, T474321, F477896. Recently refurbished, bar and restaurant overlooking the 1st and 18th holes, 48 en suite rooms. There are several hotels lining The Scores, overlooking the bay. At No 40 is **B** *St Andrews Golf Hotel*, T472611, F472188, thegolfhotel@ standrews.co.uk. 22 comfortable en suite rooms, good restaurant with extensive wine list, specialize in golfing breaks. Cheaper but still comfortable is **B-D** *Hazelbank Hotel*, at No 28, T/F472466. 10 en suite rooms.

Most of the **guesthouses** are around Murray Park and Murray Place between The Scores and North Street. Among the most recommended are: **D-E** *Amberside Guest House*, 4 Murray Park, T474644, F850640. **E** *Cameron House*, 11 Murray Park, T472306, F479529. **E** *Doune House*, 5 Murray Pl, T/F475195. **D-E** *Glenderran*, 9 Murray Park,

Fife

The origins of golf

It is a matter of debate as to what Scotland is most famous for in the wider world. Some might say whisky, others bagpipes, still others tartan and some, perhaps, the birthplace of the man who invented television. Certainly, a high proportion, particularly those interested in sport, would say golf. The country and the game have become synonymous and Scotland is widely recognized as the 'home of golf'.

Romantics suggest that the game of golf was begun by a shepherd tending his flock. Bored and with little to do, he turned his crook upside down and whacked a pebble from the ground in front of him, thus hitting golf's very first stroke. Serious historians, however, have other theories. There are those who believe that golf was descended from a game called paganica, played with a feather-stuffed ball and a curved stick, that the Romans brought with them to Britain. Disappointingly, there is no direct evidence that this game survived beyond the departure of the Romans.

Another theory states that golf was a Dutch game called 'het kolven' and there are many paintings by the 18th and 19th century Dutch painters showing a game similar to golf being played on both ice and land. There were close trade links between the Low Countries and the East Coast of Scotland, so it is eminently possible that social pastimes were exchanged. By the time these paintings appeared, however, golf had already been played in Scotland for some three centuries.

Whatever the real origins of the game, it can be stated with certainty that the Scots adopted it with the greatest zeal and created the sport with which we are familiar today.

The earliest known written mention of golf was the famous decree of King James II in 1457; "the fute-ball and golfe be utterly cried down, and not be used". The King was worried about the defence of his Kingdom against the English invasion and was concerned that the populace were neglecting their archery practice in favour of more popular sporting diversions. It is clear from the strong reaction of the King that golf was already well established as a game of the masses and, despite the fact his successors also frowned upon it, the game continued to thrive, until finally winning a royal reprieve when James IV married daughter of Henry VII in 1503 and a peace treaty was signed with the English.

In these early days, golf courses, as we know them today, did not exist. The game was simply played on the links land that bordered Scotland's eastern coasts. This land, formed when the sea receded, was sandy and of no use to agriculture. Thus, apart from being grazed by sheep, it was used by people for recreational purposes.

The first golf course, it is generally agreed, is the Old Course at St Andrews in Fife. It was created without great movements of the earth or complicated landscape architecture. Quite simply, the course evolved from the links land beside the Eden estuary. The rolling fairways were entirely natural and raised areas of land were designated as greens. The early bunkers were simply shallow scrapes, used by sheep to shelter from the fearsome east coast winds. The number of holes varied in the early years (at one point there were 22), before settling with 18; the number which has since become accepted as standard for golf courses everywhere.

T477951, F477908, glenderran@telinco.com. **C-E** *Craigmore Guest House*, 3 Murray Park, T472142, F477963. On North Street are: **D** *Aslar Guest House*, No 120, T473460, F477540, pardoe@aslar.u-net.com. **D** *Deveron House*, No 64, T473513.

Between Jun and Sept, the **university** rents out rooms in various locations throughout the town on a B&B basis, with dinner optional; T462000, F462500, or book through the *Tourist Information Centre*.

Eight miles north of St Andrews, on the road to Dundee, is **L-C** *Drumoig Golf Club & Hotel*, T01382-541800, F542211, drumoig@standrews.co.uk, set beside its own 18-hole championship golf course, with 24 en suite rooms, bar and restaurant. Plans

Indeed, St Andrews was the original blueprint for the majority of courses built in Great Britain and around the world.

St Andrews also became, quite naturally, the administrative centre of the game. The original rules of golf contained 13 articles and were laid down by the Honourable Company of Edinburgh Golfers, who played on the links of Leith, in 1744. Ten years later, the St Andrews Society adopted these rules and, over the next hundred or so years, took over all authority for their administration. This society became known as the Royal and Ancient Golf Club of St Andrews, the governing body of the sport that today sets the rules for all the world's golfers, except those in America. American golfers are governed by the United States Golf Association, which was founded in 1894. Six years earlier, in 1888, golf was first brought to American notice by a Scotsman, John Reid of Dunfermline, who built his own three hole course in Yonkers, New York.

Golf quickly took off in America and native Scots were in great demand as teachers of the game. Many Scottish professionals migrated across the Atlantic and golf was soon thriving in the United States. Scots around the world displayed an almost missionary zeal in transplanting their favourite game to whatever country they found themselves in. It didn't take long for golf to take a firm foothold in almost every corner of the globe.

Scotland also provided the world with the first professional golf championship, a competition that is still played to this day. The Open Championship was first held in 1860 on the Prestwick Links on Scotland's West Coast. The Prestwick Club had

inaugurated an amateur competition in 1857, involving the leading clubs of the time. These clubs then agreed on a subscription to provide a prize for a professional competition. This prize was a red leather Challenge Belt, somewhat resembling those given to boxers today. When young Tom Morris of St Andrews won this belt three times in succession, between 1868 and 1870, he was given it to keep and, since there was no prize to play for, no Open was held in 1871. The following year a silver claret jug replaced the belt as a prize and this famous trophy is still played for today.

After the very first competition, it was decided that the entry requirements were too restrictive and amateurs were allowed to compete against the professionals, in a championship 'open to all the world'. From that date, in 1861, the Open has retained those values and remains the most cosmopolitan of all golf's major championships.

The Open was held in Scotland until 1894, when the competition took place in Sandwich in Kent. England had been one of the first countries outside of Scotland to embrace the game of gold and, as a result, had many fine courses. From that early competition, The Open has shifted from one course to another around the British Isles. At the time of writing, this rota consists of eight courses; three in England and five in Scotland. In 1999, at Carnoustie, Paul Lawrie became the first home-based Scot to win The Open in Scotland since Willie Auchterlonie, at Prestwick in 1893. Lawrie defends his title at St Andrews in July 2000, a singularly appropriate venue for the Millennium.

Fife

for the future include building the Scottish National Golf Centre and the Rhynd Country Sports Centre, with clay pigeon shooting, fishing and horse riding.

There is no shortage of restaurants, cafés and bars, as you'd expect of a town that **Eating** attracts tourists and students alike. The best restaurant in the area, and one of the best in Britain, is the *Peat Inn*, about 7 miles south of St Andrews, on the B940, T840206, -840350. A 3-course meal is very expensive, but it's an unforgettable culinary experience. Also rooms to rent (**L** including dinner).

Another excellent restaurant out of town is *The Grange Inn*, on the Crail Road, near Kinkell Braes overlooking the East Sands, T472670, F462604. Many of the hotels have good restuarants, such as the *St Andrews Golf* and the *Rusacks*. *The Vine Leaf*, 131 South St, T477497, has a well-deserved reputation and high prices. Two of the nicest places for lunch, a light snack or coffee and cakes are *Brambles*, 5 College St beside the Market Square, and *The Merchant's House*, 49 South St. The latter has a good vegetarian selection. The *Victorian Café*, 1 St Mary's Place, is a popular student hang-out, serving snacks and drinks. For a good burger or steak try *Littlejohn's*, at the east end of Market St. The *New Balaka Bangladeshi Restaurant*, T474825, at the corner of St Mary's Place and Alexandra Place, is *the* place to go for a curry. It was recently voted "Best Curry on Scotland".

Mid-range *Ogston's*, 116 South St, T473473, is a good café-bar/bistro serving a wide range of moderate-cheap dishes. The best chip shop is *Peter Michael's* on the coner of Market St and Union St. The best place for ice cream is the wonderful *Janetta's*, at 31 South St, near the Byre Theatre (don't confuse with the smaller branch at the other end of South St). You can choose from 52 flavours, including Irn Bru sorbet.

Bars and pubs There are also a lot of good pubs to satisfy the large student population. The *Central Bar*, on Market St, is a particular favourite. Also popular is the *Featherie & Firkin*, St Mary's Pl, which serves a large selection of real ales. In the basement of the *St Andrews Golf Hotel* is *Ma Belle's*, which attracts students and locals alike and serves cheap bar meals. There's always a warm welcome at the *Dunvegan*, in Pilmour Pl, the most convivial of drinking dens.

Entertainment The *Byre Theatre*, on Abbey St, T476288, stages an excellent range of productions
& events throughout the year and began its life in a cowshed of the old Abbey St Dairy Farm, hence its name. The *Crawford Arts Centre*, in North St, T474610, has a changing programme of art exhibitions, professional theatre and music performances in its drama studio and galleries.

Lammas Fair is Scotland's oldest surviving medieval market, with showmen from all over Britain setting up stalls and booths in the three main streets. This bright, lively carnival is held in early **Aug**. The other main event in the town's calendar is the **Kate Kennedy Pageant**, usually held on the 3rd Sat in **Apr**.

Shopping The main banks are on South St, near the Holy Trinity Church. Shops have half-day closing on Thur, though most stay open during the summer.

Tours There are various organized tours on offer. *The Original St Andrews Witches Tour* (£6, £4 children) and *Mrs Linskill's Saints & Sinners Tour* (£6 per person) both operate all year round, Sun 1830 in the winter, and Thur and Sun 2000 in the summer; T655057. Guided **walks** of the cathedral, castle, university and golf courses are on Wed all year round, and leave from Church Square at 1100; £2.50, £1.50 children (under 8 free), £2 concession, T850638. There is also an open-top bus tour which leaves from Church St, daily from Jun-Sept 1000-1600, T474238 or through the tourist office.

North Fife

Four miles northwest of St Andrews is **Leuchars**, best known as an RAF base, *Colour map 4, grid C4* but in the centre of the village is one of the oldest churches in Scotland. The 12th-century chancel and apse, incorporated into the parish church, are exceptional examples of Norman architecture. A mile east of Leuchars is **Earlshall Castle** built in 1546 by Sir William Bruce, ancestor of the present owners. This is a fine example of a 16th-century Scottish castle, very strongly built with 5-ft thick walls, battlements and gun loops. Mary, Queen of Scots stayed here and you can see her bedroom. The richly fitted main rooms include the long gallery with the magnificently painted ceiling. There is also a display of Scottish weapons as well as a set of bagpipes that were played at Waterloo. The castle is set among beautiful gardens with unusual topiary chessmen.

Just beyond Leuchars is the B945 turning for **Tentsmuir Forest**, on the northeastern tip of Fife. There is an excellent broad sandy beach, the perfect spot for a picnic, as well as a Nature Reserve where you can see wildfowl waders and a large colony of seals sunning themselves on the sands. In 1957, on a site near Morton Farm on the Tentsmuir peninsula, evidence was found of a settlement visited seasonally by fishing and hunting people about 8,000 years ago. This remarkable site is one of the earliest human habitations in Scotland. Finds from the site are in the Dundee Museum and the National Museum of Antiquities in Edinburgh.

Nearby, on the shores of the Tay, is the unremarkable village of **Tayport**, from where a ferry used to cross the river to Dundee. Tayport's church tower is 17th century and a plaque commemorates General Ullysses Grant's visit on his way to see the first Tay Rail Bridge, which was blown down in 1879 while a train was passing over it. A new bridge has been built since, along with the **Tay Road Bridge** (80p toll), which carries you from Fife into the city of Dundee.

Five miles west of the Tay Rail Bridge, off the A914, is **Balmerino Abbey**, on a hill overlooking the river. It was founded in the 13th century by Alexander II, whose mother Ermengarde, widow of William the Lion lies buried there. Little of the abbey remains today. In 1547 it was set on fire by the English Army during the 'Rough Wooing' and in 1559 Knox's Reformers completed the destruction on their way back to St Andrews after 'reforming' Lindores (see below). Some of the pillars and part of the cloisters are still visible and in the orchard is a great Spanish chestnut tree, planted by the monks some 700 years ago. Unfortunately, the buildings are unsafe and inaccessible. ■ *All year. £1.*

Newburgh

Lying on the south shore of the River Tay, close to Fife's western boundary, *Phone code: 01337* Newburgh is a Royal Burgh with a pretty little harbour and a long history. On the hill to the south of the town are the remains of MacDuff's Cross, the legendary place of sanctuary for any MacDuff who had committed a murder in hot blood. To achieve pardon, the murderer had to touch the cross, wash himself nine times at Ninewells nearby and forfeit nine cows, each of which had to be tied to the cross. If you're passing through, it's worth stopping to visit the **Laing Museum**, which shows excellent exhibitions including fossil fish discovered the area, a feature on Scottish emigration and Victorian displays. ■ *T840223. Apr-Sept, Mon-Fri 1000-1700, Sat-Sun 1400-1700; Oct-Mar, Wed, Fri 1200-1600, Sun 1400-1700. Free.*

Standing above the town are the ruins of **Lindores Abbey**, founded in the 12th century by David, Earl of Huntingdon. Not much of the great abbey now

Fife

remains – only the gateway, part of the tower and fragments of the great walls. The abbey never recovered form the devastation visited upon it in 1559 by John Knox and his 'Congregation of the Godly'. Its ruins became a quarry whenever any building stone was needed. The views from the ruins across the Tay are lovely, especially on a summer evening.

The story of Newburgh, however, goes far back beyond its abbey. A thousand years earlier, history was already being made on the eastern outskirts of the town, at Carpow. Here, in 208 AD, the Romans built a great fortress which was to be the base for their campaign against the tribes of Angus and Mearns. Unlike England, Scotland never became Romanized, and the fortress at Carpow was eventually demolished by the Romans when they withdrew to the south. Evidence of human settlement around Newburgh extends even further back in time. People built and lived in the hillfort on top of Norman's Law during the last four centuries BC. Today, its remains are accessible by public footpath from the roads north and south of the Law. Three circles of fortification can be traced clearly.

Northeast Scotland

9

Northeast Scotland

© Crown copyright

The northeast of Scotland is the huge triangle of land that thrusts defiantly into the harsh North Sea and comprises the regions of Aberdeenshire, Moray and Angus, and the cities of **Aberdeen** and **Dundee**, Scotland's third and fourth largest cities respectively. This is a hard-working region based on agriculture, fishing and, more recently, the oil industry and its people typify the stereotype of the dour, determined and thrifty Scot.

The region may lack the sheer drama and majesty of the northwest but the coast and countryside between the Firth of Tay and the Moray Firth have their own, more subtle charms – and better weather. The **Moray Firth**, from the hardy fishing port of Fraserburgh west to the Findhorn community, has some of the country's most dramatic coastal scenery, with perfect little fishing villages clinging for dear life to storm-battered cliffs. There are also long stretches of apricot-coloured beaches, long hours of sunshine, and even **dolphins** frolicking in the waters offshore.

The river Spey flows into the Moray Firth, and its gentle, wooded valley is the centre of Scotland's malt whisky industry. There are more distilleries along its banks than you could shake a still at and the tourist board has not been slow in making capital out of the local industry. Its well-signposted **Malt Whisky Trail** includes some of the most famous names, such as Glenfiddich and Glenlivet.

Another of the region's assets is its rich history and there are relics aplenty to prove it. This is castle country and there are over 70 in Aberdeenshire and Moray alone. Visiting them all would take forever, but the tourist board *has again come to the rescue with the **Castle Trail**, which points out a selection of the best. One of the most famous is **Balmoral Castle**, forever linked to the royal family since Queen Victoria came, saw and purchased in 1852. So strong is the connection that this area is better known as 'Royal Deeside' and visitors can indulge in a bit of royal spotting at the annual **Braemar Gathering**, the local Highland Games.*

*Deeside runs all the way west from Aberdeen to the eastern fringes of the **Grampian Mountains**, which offer opportunites for walking, climbing, skiing and mountain biking. It's possible to walk from Deeside south to the **Angus Glens** along a series of ancient drove roads. The beautiful glens are easily visited from the attractive little towns of Edzell and Kirriemuir. Also in Angus is that other famous royal residence, **Glamis Castle**, the Queen Mother's family home as well as Macbeth's.*

*Another historically important place is **Arbroath Abbey**, site of one of the most significant episodes in Scotland's long and often traumatic relationship with its southern neighbour. To the north of Arbroath is the port of **Montrose**, only a few miles from **Lunan Bay**, one of the loveliest beaches on the entire east coast.*

*The largest settlement is the city of **Aberdeen**, built from grey granite and made rich by North Sea oil. The other city, **Dundee**, is a poor relation by comparison, but is undergoing something of a renaissance and makes a convenient and economical base from which to explore not only the northeast, but also Fife to the south and Perthshire to the west.*

Ins and outs

Dundee and Aberdeen are connected by the fast A90 which runs inland through Angus before linking up with the coastal A92 near Stonehaven. Regular **buses** ply between the two cities, and there's a good **rail** link, connecting Aberdeen and Dundee to Edinburgh. Trains also run northwest from Aberdeen to Inverness, passing through Elgin and other inland towns. There's a fairly good bus service throughout the northeast, as well as a limited network of **postbuses** serving the Angus glens. Only the most remote and mountainous parts of the region cannot be reached by public transport. For more details of transport in Aberdeenshire and Moray, see page 366, and for Dundee and Angus see page 347.

Getting around

Dundee

Scotland's fourth largest city sits on two prominent hills, Balgay and the Law, overlooking the river Tay. Few cities in Britain can match Dundee's impressive setting, seen at its breathtaking best from across the Tay, in Fife. But, despite the common consensus that the views of the city are indeed spectacular, certain guide books have suggested that visitors keep their distance. Which just goes to show how out of touch they are, for Dundee has transformed itself into a vibrant, thriving city and an increasingly popular destination for tourists.

Phone code: 01382
Colour map 4, grid B4
Population: 177,500

One of Dundee's big attractions is Captain Scott's ship, the Discovery, and such is the civic pride engendered by its return home that Dundee has become widely known through its slogan – City of Discovery. There are other, less publicized, attractions, such as the Law Hill, which commands fantastic views over the city and the Tay estuary, and the attractive seaside suburb of Broughty Ferry. Dundee also has a thriving arts scene and plenty of good shops, bars and restaurants. But the city's best kept secret is its people. The accent may at first be somewhat impenetrable but Dundonians have an endearing earthy humour and are the friendliest bunch of people you'll find anywhere on the east coast of Scotland.

Ins and outs

Dundee's **airport**, T643224, is on Riverside Drive, about a 5-min drive west of the city centre. There are no buses to the centre. A taxi will cost around £2. For flight information, see page 347.

Getting there

The **bus station**, T228345, is on Seagate, a few hundred yards east of the City Square. All regional and national buses arrive here (for details, see page 347). **Trains** into Dundee arrive at Taybridge Station, T228046, a few hundred yards south of the High St, across the dual carriageway at the foot of Union St. For details of train services, see page 347.

By **car** the best approach is from the south, across the Tay Road Bridge (80p toll; payable heading south only), which gives a spectacular introduction to the city. Alternatively, the city is reached via the A90, from Aberdeen to the north or Perth to the west. Coming from Perth, turn on to Riverside Drive at the Invergowrie roundabout for the city centre.

Dundee city centre is fairly compact and most of the sights are within walking distance of each other. For outlying sights, the city is served by an efficient bus service. **Buses** heading west along the Perth Rd pass along the High St, stopping at the city square. Heading northwards, buses leave from Albert Square, behind the McManus Galleries, and buses heading east towards Broughty Ferry leave from outside Littlewoods on the High St. The average fare around town is about 80-90p.

Getting around

Northeast Scotland

For information on city buses, phone Dundee District Council Transport Division, T433125. Local services are run by *Travel Dundee*, T201121, and *Strathtay Scottish*, T228054. Day passes (£3) can be bought on board buses or at the Travel Dundee shop at the top of Commercial St.

There are **taxi** ranks on Nethergate and High St, or call *City Cabs*, T566666, or *Tele Taxis*, T889333.

A good way to see the city is to go on one of the tourist office's **bus tours**, which take in all the main sights, including Shaw's Sweet Factory, Claypott's Castle and a visit to the top of the Law. Tours leave from the city centre every hour from 1030 till 1600 during the summer months. There are some doubts as to their continuation during 2000. Call the tourist office for latest information.

Information The very helpful **tourist office** is at 7-21 Castle St, T527527, F527550, www.angusanddundee.co.uk, a short walk from the train station. They provide extensive details and free leaflets for all Dundee's attractions. They also sell bus tickets, book accommodation and have a good souvenir shop. You can pick up a free copy of the monthly *What's On* listings magazine here. Open May-Sept Mon-Sat 0900-1700, Sun 1200-1600; Oct-Apr Mon-Sat 0900-1700.

The two local newspapers, the morning *Courier & Advertiser* and the *Evening Telegraph* (the "Tully") are also good sources of information.

History

The name Dundee is derived from the Gaelic words 'dun' meaning hill or fort and 'daig', who was thought to be an early local chieftain. Dundee has been settled since prehistoric times and Pictish earthworks and chambers can still be seen at Tealing, Ardestie and Carlungie, just beyond the city's boundaries. The city was an important trading port as long ago as the 12th century and it was here that Robert the Bruce was proclaimed King of Scots, in 1309. Its importance, however, made it a prime target for a succession of English invaders. It was captured by Edward I, besieged by Henry VIII, destroyed by Royalists and Cromwell's army during the Civil War, and then again by Viscount Dundee prior to the Battle of Killiecrankie. The young William Wallace, the fiery Scottish patriot, was educated in Dundee, and during its occupation by Edward's forces, Wallace stabbed the son of an English overlord for daring to insult him, and had to flee south. A plaque on the High Street marks the spot where the incident took place.

Dundee is famous within Scotland as the city of the three J's; **Jute**, **Jam** and **Journalism**. These three industries were part of the city's commercial success and the jute mills in particular, from the early 19th century, were the foundation of the city's wealth. Along with Edinburgh, Dundee became a centre for investment trusts which sunk cash into ventures all over the world, particularly the USA. In 1873, Dundee jute man Robert Fleming set up the Scottish Investment Trust to channel money into US cattle ranches, mining companies and railways. The biggest cattle ranch in the USA was run from Dundee until 1951 and the Texas oil industry was largely financed by Dundee jute wealth. The jam-making came about almost by accident, when a ship carrying a cargo of oranges was forced to put into Dundee harbour during a storm. A local grocer bought the oranges, which his wife then made into marmalade, and an industry was born.

Journalism is the only 'J' still in operation in the city. DC Thomson are now the city's largest employers, outside the health and leisure industries, and continue to produce many newspapers and magazines. Perhaps their most famous creations are the children's comics *The Dandy* and *The Beano*, begun in 1937 and 1938 respectively and still going strong. Generations of British children have been brought up on the antics of *Dennis the Menace*, *Desperate Dan*, *The Bash*

A whale of a time

On one famous occasion the whalers did not have to travel very far in search of their quarry. In December 1883 a humpback whale swam into the Tay estuary and foundered on the sandbanks. Large crowds gathered to watch the doomed animal's attempts to return to the sea and it was harpooned on 7 December before finally being landed, completely exhausted, on 8 January the following year. It was put on public display before being sold and the skeleton of the 'Tay whale' now resides in the city's McManus Galleries (see below).

Street Kids et al, and the popularity of these cartoon characters is reflected in the choice of the comic-inspired lettering for Dundee's promotional logo.

While the three 'J's' were undoubtedly important to Dundee, other industries also played a substantial role in the city's history. Dundee was a major centre for shipbuilding and ships were built for both the whaling industry and for the import and export of jute and other cargoes. Dundee has a proud maritime heritage and for many years was the capital of the British whaling industry. In these more enlightened times we may shudder at the decimation of the whale stocks that led to the demise of the industry, but whale oil was a very valuable commodity and the men who sailed the freezing Arctic seas to catch whales suffered terrible privations and hardships.

Sights

Discovery Point

The obvious place to begin your tour of the city is Discovery Point, the impressive riverside location of Dundee's main attraction, the **Royal Research Ship** *Discovery*. This excellent facility, which attracts tens of thousands of visitors each year, is across the road from the train station, next to the Leisure Centre and *Stakis Hotel*. When Dundee was an important shipbuilding centre, its speciality was wooden ships and it was the Royal Geographical Society who commissioned the *Discovery*, which was launched on the Tay on 21 March 1901. She was the first specially designed scientific research ship and spent two winters in the Antarctic, where her wooden hull was able to withstand the enormous pressures of the pack ice. Famous as Captain Scott's ship, the *Discovery* and Scott parted company after his expedition in 1904. Another Dundee-built vessel, the *Terra Nova*, carried Scott to the South Pole in 1911 – the fateful expedition from which he never returned. After being purchased by the Maritime Trust, the *Discovery*, was returned to Dundee in 1986 and moored at its present specially built quay with an excellent **visitor centre** at her side. The state-of-the-art centre presents an entertaining introduction, with audio-visual displays and an exhibition. On board the vessel you can see the cabins used by Scott and his crew and hear some interesting anecdotes from the enthusiastic guides. ■ *T201245. Apr-Oct Mon-Sat 1000-1700, Sun 1100-1700, Nov-Mar till 1600, £5, £3.75 child/concession, or £9 (£6) for joint ticket with Verdant Works.*

A short distance west of *Discovery*, in Victoria Dock, on the other side of the road bridge, is Dundee's other major floating attraction, the **HM Frigate** *Unicorn*. Built in 1824, this is the oldest British warship still afloat, probably because it never fired a shot in anger. It was used variously as a gunpowder store and a training vessel, until it was rescued from the scrapyard in 1968 by a preservation society. A tour of the ship gives some idea of the cramped conditions in which the 300 men had to live and work and the unused cannons are still on display. ■ *T200900. Mar-Oct daily 1000-1700, Nov-Feb Mon-Fri 1000-1600, £3.50, £2.50 child/concession.*

Northeast Scotland

Around City Square The focal point of the city centre is City Square, which is surrounded by shops and cafés, the imposing **Caird Hall**, the city's main concert hall, and the **City Chambers**, scene of much shady dealing in the 1960s and 70s, which led to the demolition of the city's medieval core. The resulting shopping mall, the infamous Overgate, has itself been replaced by a brand new retail complex which should be complete by the time you read this.

The pedestrianized Reform Street leads north from City Square to **Albert Square**, site of the **McManus Galleries**, housed in Gilbert Scott's impressive Victorian Gothic edifice. Inside are some very fine exhibits detailing the city's history from the Iron Age to the Tay Bridge Disaster. The latter event was chronicled by the inimitable William McGonagall, the 'World's Worst Poet', and here you can read his excruciatingly awful verse, along with an equally painful account of the famous 'Tay Whale', the skeleton of which is also on display. Upstairs is the superb **Albert Hall**, which contains various antique collections, and the **Victoria Gallery**, whose 19th- and 20th-century collections include some notable Scottish painters such as McTaggart. ■ *T432020. Mon 1100-1700, Tue-Sat 1000-1700.*

Also in Albert Square are the huge red sandstone offices of local publishing giant, DC Thomson, who have entertained generations of British kids with their *Beano* and *Dandy* comics. Opposite is a medieval burial ground known as the **Howff**, granted to the townsfolk of Dundee by Mary, Queen of Scots, during her visit in 1565.

A five-minute walk west, along Meadowside and Ward Road, across the dual carriageway, and up Guthrie Street, is the excellent **Verdant Works** heritage centre, in West Henderson's Wynd. This former jute mill gives a unique insight into what life was like for mill workers and details the history of the jute industry. ■ *T225282. Apr-Oct Mon-Sat 1000-1700, Sun 1100-1700, Nov-Mar till 1600, £5, £3.75 child/concession, or £9 (£6) for joint ticket with the Discovery.*

After a hard day's sightseeing, why not round things off with a visit to **Shaw's Sweet Factory**, at 34 Mains Loan. Sweet-making demonstrations take place every half hour during opening hours, and afterwards you can sample the finished products. ■ *T461435. Mar-May and Sept-Oct Wed only, 1330-1600, Jun Mon-Fri 1030-1600, Jul-Aug till 1700, £1, 50p child.*

Law Hill The most prominent feature of the city is the Law Hill, a 571ft-high ancient volcanic plug. The views from the summit, over the entire city and south to Fife across the river Tay and its two bridges, are fantastic. It's a steep climb to the foot of the Law from the city centre, up the Hilltown, so it's best to take a bus (Nos 3 or 4) from Albert Square, or even better, visit it as part of the **city bus tour** (see 'Information' above). The 1½-mile-long **Tay Road Bridge** was opened in 1966, while the **Tay Rail Bridge** is over two miles long and the longest railway bridge in Europe. It was built in 1878 but the following year the final section collapsed during a terrible storm. No one could alert the driver of the approaching train and it plunged into the cold, dark waters of the Tay, killing the crew and 75 passengers. A replacement section was built in 1887 and still stands today.

Balgay Hill About a mile west of the Law, is Balgay Hill, site of the **Mills Observatory**, a free public facility which houses a planetarium as well as displays on astronomy and space exploration. ■ *T435846. Apr-Sept Mon-Fri 1100-1700, Sat 1400-1700, Oct-Mar Mon-Fri 1600-2200, Sat 1400-1700. Free. Take bus Nos 2, 36 or 37 to Balgay Road, at the entrance to Balgay Park.*

On Riverside Drive, to the west of the city, is the University of Dundee **Botanic** **Parks & gardens**
Garden, with two large planthouses and an excellent visitor centre. One of the
most popular of the city's many green spaces, is **Camperdown Park**, just off the
Kingsway on the A923 to Coupar Angus. It has a wildlife centre, golf course and
mansion house. The large country park once belonged to Admiral Duncan, best
remembered for his brilliant tactics and seamanship in defeating the Dutch fleet
at the Battle of Camperdown in 1797. In recognition of this, the native
Dundonian was made a peer of the realm and granted the estates which now

Dundee

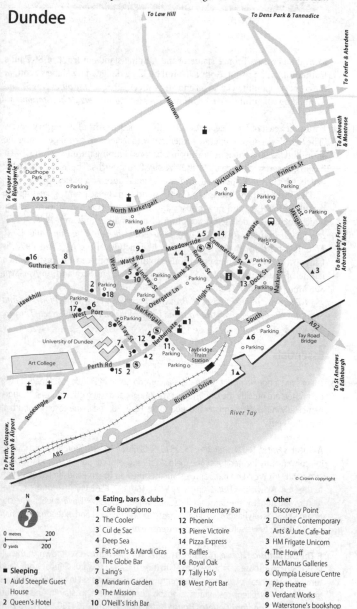

© Crown copyright

Northeast Scotland

● Eating, bars & clubs
1 Cafe Buongiorno
2 The Cooler
3 Cul de Sac
4 Deep Sea
5 Fat Sam's & Mardi Gras
6 The Globe Bar
7 Laing's
8 Mandarin Garden
9 The Mission
10 O'Neill's Irish Bar
11 Parliamentary Bar
12 Phoenix
13 Pierre Victoire
14 Pizza Express
15 Raffles
16 Royal Oak
17 Tally Ho's
18 West Port Bar

▲ Other
1 Discovery Point
2 Dundee Contemporary
   Arts & Jute Cafe-bar
3 HM Frigate Unicorn
4 The Howff
5 McManus Galleries
6 Olympia Leisure Centre
7 Rep theatre
8 Verdant Works
9 Waterstone's bookshop

N

0 metres   200
0 yards   200

■ Sleeping
1 Auld Steeple Guest
   House
2 Queen's Hotel

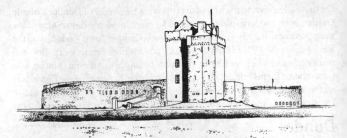

Broughty Castle

form the park. (A bronze statue of the Admiral stands in front of **St Paul's Cathedral**, an imposing Gothic Revival building designed by Gilbert Scott, at the corner of Commercial Street and High Street.) ■ *Strathtay buses Nos 57 and 59 will drop you off at the park entrance. They leave from Seagate bus station.*

Broughty Ferry   Four miles east of Dundee, is the attractive seaside resort of **Broughty Ferry**. 'The Ferry' was once a separate settlement with fishermen's cottages lining the shore and the large villas of wealthy jute barons climbing the hills behind, but it has since been swallowed up by the city's eastern suburbs. There's a long sandy beach, which is sadly polluted, and several good pubs and places to eat.

The 15th-century **Broughty Castle** stands on the seafront, guarding the mouth of the Tay, and now houses an interesting **museum** of local history which includes a detailed description of the whaling industry. ■ *T776121. Mon-Thur and Sat 1000-1300 and 1400-1700, Jul-Sept also Sun 1400-1700. Free.* Just north of Broughty Ferry, at the junction of the A92 and B978, is **Claypotts Castle**, a rather precarious-looking late 16th-century castle, which is one of the most complete Z-plan tower houses in Scotland. ■ *Apr-Sept Sat-Mon 0930-1800. £2.50.*

■ *There are frequent buses to Broughty Ferry with both Travel Dundee and Strathtay Scottish, leaving from outside Littlewoods on the High Street. The fare one way is 80-90p.*

Essentials

Sleeping   There's not a huge amount of top-class accommodation in Dundee and many of the best hotels are outside the city. There are plenty of good value guesthouses, though, particularly in the West End, on and around the Perth Rd, and in the eastern suburb of Broughty Ferry.

A *Queen's Hotel*, 160 Nethergate, T322515, F202668. 47 rooms, perennial old favourite, conveniently located for all the main sights and with car parking round the back, also handy for West End pubs and restaurants, the Rep Theatre and almost next door to the DCA. **A** *Swallow Hotel*, Kingsway West, T641122, F568340. 107 rooms, conveniently situated by the large roundabout where Riverside Drive meets the city ringroad (Kingsway) and A90 to Perth, tastefully refurbished and extended Victorian mansion with full leisure facilities and extensive grounds.

B *The Old Mansion House*, T320366. 8 rooms, 10 miles northwest of town, in the village of Auchterhouse, on the B954 to Alyth (take the A923 towards Coupar Angus and turn off at Muirhead). Luxurious 16th-century baronial house set in beautiful grounds and with an excellent restaurant, probably the best place to stay in and around Dundee. **B-C** *Sandford Country House Hotel*, near Wormit, T541802, F542136. 16

rooms, 5 miles south of the Tay Rail Bridge, just off the A92 Dundee-Kirkcaldy road (take the B946 to Wormit). Secluded mansion set in lovely grounds and with an excellent restaurant. The numerous activities on offer include fishing, clay-pigeon shooting and off-road driving. In Brought Ferry is the **B** *Woodlands Hotel*, 13 Panmure Terr, T480033, F480126. 38 rooms, set in extensive grounds and with pool and gym.

C *Shaftesbury Hotel*, 1 Hyndford St, T669216, F641598. 12 rooms, in a converted jute baron's mansion just off the Perth Rd about a mile from the city centre. Comfy, relaxed, with a decent restaurant.

Most of the **guesthouses** and **B&Bs** are to be found to the east and west of the city centre, but if you want to be smack in the centre of town, then try the **E** *Auld Steeple Guest House*, 94 Nethergate, T/F200302. 11 rooms, nothing fancy but clean and tidy and only a few mins walk from the train station. A short walk north of the city centre is **D-E** *Hillside Guest House*, 43 Constitution St (off Constitution Rd), T/F223443, TildaB@aol.com. Comfortable, friendly and non-smoking. **E-F** *Nelson Guest House*, 8 Nelson Terr (off Victoria Rd), T225354. A 10 min walk from the bus station. In the east, heading towards Broughty Ferry, is **D-E** *Aberlaw*, 230 Broughty Ferry Rd, T/F456929. There are lots of places along the Arbroath Rd, including **D-E** *Anlast*, No 379, T456710, and **E-F** *Ash Villa*, No 216, T450381. There's also a good selection of guesthouses/B&Bs in the West End, including **D-E** *Bracklinn*, 5 Fort St (off Richmond Terr), T/F566563, and **E** *Ashgrove*, 251 Perth Rd, T566175, 106330.2404@compuserve.com. The *University of Dundee* offers B&B accommodation (**E**, shared bathrooms) from Jun-Sept in its halls of residence at *West Park*, 319 Perth Rd, T647181, g.anderson@dundee.ac.uk. It also has self-catering flats for weekly rental, T344039.

Dundee's only **youth hostel** is the independent **F** *Riverview Backpackers Hostel*, 127 Broughty Ferry Rd, T450565. Price includes breakfast (on request), only 17 beds, so it's best to book ahead, 10-min walk east of the bus station, or bus No 75 from High St.

There's a **campsite** at Carnoustie, 10 miles east of Dundee city centre: *Woodlands Caravan Park*, T01241-854430, which is open Apr-Oct.

There's a wide range of places to stay in **Broughty Ferry**. One of the best is **D-E** *Hollies Orchard*, 12 Castelroy Rd, T776403, mediamack@sol.co.uk. Also recommended is the **E-D** *Beach House Hotel*, 22 Esplanade, T776614. Further east towards **Monifieth** is **E** *Auchinean*, 177 Hamilton St, T774782. There are lots of places on Monifieth Rd, including **E** *Invermark House*, No 23, T739430.

There's no shortage of places to eat in Dundee, from the ubiquitous burger bars, pizza parlours, fish and chip shops and takeaways to upmarket continental cuisine. Many of the city's pubs provide excellent value meals. Most of the better restaurants, bars and pubs are to be found in the West End, around the University and Perth Rd, and there's also a wide selection of places to eat in Broughty Ferry. **Eating**

Expensive *Raffles*, 18 Perth Rd, T226344. There was a time when this was *the* place to eat but some say its new trendy image is the victory of style over content, good (and reasonably priced) for Sun brunch, though. Open Tue-Sun. Best of the lot is *South Kingennie House*, T350562, near Kellas, off the B978 which runs north from Broughty Ferry. It's a bit of a schlep from town but well worth it for the superb traditional Scottish cooking. Open daily except Sun evening and Mon, lunch cheap to mid-range; dinner expensive.

Northeast Scotland

Mid-range Another excellent out-of-town place is *11 Park Avenue* in Carnoustie T/F01241-853336. Open Tue-Sat. *Agacan Kebab House*, 113 Perth Rd, T644227. Brightly decorated and cosy Turkish restaurant, nice ambience and tasty grills, open Tue-Sun. *Café Buongiorno*, 11 Bank St, T221179. Small, intimate Italian, popular as a café by day and restaurant by night. *Cul de Sac*, 10 South Tay St, next to the Rep, T202070. Café-bar/restaurant with a cool, laid back atmosphere, open daily 1200-2230. They also run *The Het*, the Rep Theatre's foyer café-bar. *Mandarin Garden*, 40-44 South Tay St, T227733. Excellent Chinese cuisine, served by friendly, efficient staff. Try the house banquet. Open daily except Sun for lunch and 1700-2300. *Pierre Victoire*, 15 Shore·Terr (at the foot of Castle St), T202077. Part of the French brasserie chain, decent French provincial fare at cheap-mid-range prices. *Pizza Express*, 31a Albert Square, T226677. Part of the acclaimed pizza chain, great pizza, elegant surroundings. *Royal Oak*, 167 Brook St, T229440. In an unlikely setting, near Verdant Works and the Hawkhill, great pub food with an Indian emphasis, large portions.

Cheap The best fish and chips in town can be found at the legendary *Deep Sea*, 81 Nethergate. *Jute Café-bar*, 152 Nethergate, in Dundee Contemporary Arts. So stylish you could be in Glasgow, and a great vibe, small but interesting menu. Open daily 1030-2400 (Sun till 2300).

There are lots of restaurants in **Broughty Ferry**, but don't miss a trip to *Visocchi's*, 40 Gray St, T779297. A genuine Italian café serving the best ice cream for miles. Nearby, at 43a, is *Nawab*, T731800, an excellent Indian Balti house that's a cut above the rest.

Bars & clubs Although a fairly large city, Dundee's nightlife is concentrated in a relatively small area of the city centre, based around the West Port and Nethergate. Here you'll find a plethora of pubs and the city's main nightclubs. Being close to the universities means they're popular with the city's large student population.

Bars *Cul de Sac* and the *Jute Café-bar* (see above) are both civilized places to chill, but for something a bit livelier, try any of the busy bars along the Nethergate, especially the *Phoenix* and *Parliamentary Bar*, on opposite sides of the street by the junction with West Marketgait. At the top of South Tay Street is the West Port, where you'll find a clutch of student bars, including *Tally Ho's* and *The Globe*. On the other side of the Hawkhill are the *West Port Bar* and nearby, in Brown St, the *Freelance & Firkin*, which has live music at weekends. Further up the Perth Rd, opposite Duncan of Jordanstone Art College, Roseangle branches left, and here you'll find *Laing's*, which is hugely popular with 20-30s and boasts a beer garden with views across the Tay. It also serves pretty decent grub. If you want a slice of pure, unsullied Dundee, continue up the Perth Rd to the legendary *Taybridge Bar* which has been there as long as its namesake.

In the city centre is the *Mercantile Bar*, at the top of Commercial St. It's popular with suits but has a variety of ales and serves good food. *O'Neill's Irish Bar*, 80 North Lindsay St. Cheap and cheerful pub with a wide range of good value pub food and live folk music.

Broughty Ferry is a good place for a drink on a summer's evening, especially the *Ship Inn*, a cosy old pub right on the seafront with a reputation for fine food. Also recommended is the *Fisherman's Tavern*, 12 Fort St. It's popular with nautical types and is rightly famed for its superb real ales and good pub food.

Clubs There's no shortage of post-pub venues, though the best places are to be found around the West Port area. *Fat Sam's*, at 31 South Ward Rd, attracts a slightly older crowd (ie out of short trousers), and has a large chill-out area. Next door is *Mardi Gras*, a vast club open every night except Tues. It's popular with teenagers. Just around the corner, at 15 Ward Rd, is *The Mission*, where you can hear the very latest sounds. A short distance west, up the Hawkhill, is *The Cooler*, at 3 Session St, a basement club which attracts a mainly student crowd.

Cinema and theatre The *Odeon* multiplex at the Stack Leisure Park, Harefield Rd, Lochee, T400449, shows mainstream movies, as does the *Virgin* multiplex, at Kingsway West near the entrance to Camperdown Park, T0870-9020407. *Dundee Contemporary Arts*, 152 Nethergate, T432000 is Dundee's cultural hub, housed in a superb modern building, with two cinema screens showing current arthouse releases, also exhibition spaces, print studio, visual research centre and the *Jute Café-bar*.

Entertainment

Dundee's excellent *Rep Theatre* is on Tay Square, off South Tay St, T223530. It stages locally produced contemporary theatre and hosts various national touring companies. It is also a jazz venue and has a good café-restaurant in the foyer.

Bookshops *James Thin*, 7 High St. *Waterstone's*, 34 Commercial St.

Shopping

Football Dundee has two Premier League football clubs, the legendary *Dundee FC*, who strut their stuff at Dens Park, T826104, and their bitter rivals *Dundee United* (aka the 'Arabs') who reside at Tannadice, T833166, which is just across the street. **Golf** There are two public courses, at *Caird Park*, Mains Loan, T434706, and Camperdown, in *Camperdown Park*, T432688. *Downfield Golf Club*, on Turnberry Ave, T825595, is a fine private course which allows visitors. Dundee is also within 30 mins drive of *Carnoustie* and *St Andrews*, both of which have famous championship courses. **Leisure centres** *Olympia Leisure Centre*, Earl Grey Place (next to the RRS Discovery), T434888. Pool with water slides and wave machines, also gym, sauna and climbing wall. Open Mon-Fri 0900-2100, Sat-Sun 0900-1700. *Stack Leisure Park*, Harefield Rd. Multiplex cinema and 10-pin bowling.

Sport

Campus Travel, Airlie Place, T200412. *Ramsay Travel*, Crichton St, T200394.

Tour operators

Air There are direct flights to Dundee from **London City Airport**, 4 times daily, with *Scot Airways*, T0870-6060707.

Transport

Bus *National Express*, T0990-808080, runs 4 services daily to and from **London** (10 hrs direct). *Scottish Citylink*, T0990-505050, operates an hourly service to and from **Edinburgh** (2 hrs, £6.50 single) and **Glasgow** (2 hrs 15 mins, £7 single). Most Edinburgh and Glasgow buses stop en route in **Perth** (35 mins, £3). There are also hourly buses to **Aberdeen** (2 hrs, £6.70). Some Aberdeen buses go via **Forfar** (25 mins, £2.50) and others go via **Arbroath** (30 mins, £2.50). *Strathtay Scottish*, T01382-228054, runs buses at least every 30 mins to **Blairgowrie** (1 hr, £2.25), **Forfar** (30 mins, £2.05), **Brechin** (via Forfar, 1 hr 15 mins, £3.30) and **Arbroath** (1 hr, £2.35), and hourly to **Perth** (1 hr, £2.20), **Kirriemuir** (1 hr 10 mins, £2.45) and **Montrose** (1 hr 15 mins).

Train There are trains at least every hour, Mon-Sat, to and from **Glasgow** (1 hr 30 mins, £18.50 single) and **Edinburgh** (1 hr 15 mins, £14). Trains run less frequently on Sun. Trains run every 30 mins to and from **Aberdeen** (1 hr 15 mins, £16.40), via **Arbroath**, **Montrose** and **Stonehaven**. For all rail enquiries, call T0345-484950.

Car hire *Alamo*, 45-53 Gellatly St, T0870-4004508. *Arnold Clark*, 14-22 Trades Lane, T225382. *Hertz*, 18 Marketgait, T223711. **Cycle hire** *Just Bikes*, 57 Gray St, T732100. *Nicholson's*, 2-4 Forfar Rd, T461212.

Banks *Bank of Scotland*, 2 West Marketgait, T317500. Clydesdale Bank, 158 Nethergate, T221464. Lloyds TSB, 96 Albert St, T453535. *Royal Bank of Scotland*, 133 Albert St, T462256.

Directory

Northeast Scotland

Currency exchange: *Thomas Cook*, City Square, T200204. Open Mon-Fri 0900-1730, Sat 0900-1700. Also at the tourist office. **Communications** Internet: *Megabyte Internet Bistro*, 31 Hilltown (behind Wellgate Centre), T200134. **Post office**: 4 Meadowside, T203532. Open Mon-Fri 0900-1730, Sat 0900-1900. **Medical facilities** Hospital: *Dundee Royal Infirmary*, Barrack Rd, T660111. 24-hr accident and emergency. **Pharmacy**: *Boots*, High St. Open Mon-Wed, Fri-Sat 0830-1745, Thur till 1900. Sun opening on rota basis; check local press. **Useful addresses** Police: *Tayside Police HQ*, Bell St, T223200.

Angus

Colour map 4, grid B4/5

The fishing and farming county of Angus was formerly part of the giant Tayside region but is now a separate authority with its own distinct identity. Angus isn't a name that rolls of many tourists' tongues but it has much to recommend it to those prefer to escape the summer hordes. The east coast, from Arbroath north to Montrose, is particularly attractive with its sheer red cliffs punctuated by sweeping bays of golden sand. In the north are the Angus Glens, stretching deep into the heart of the Grampian peaks and offering excellent walking opportunities. The heart of the county is the wide valley of Strathmore with a string of neat market towns. This was part of the ancient Pictish Kingdom and there are still many interesting carved stones scattered around the area.

Ins and outs

Getting around The towns along the main Dundee-Aberdeen routes are easy to get to by bus or train, but public transport to the more remote parts is limited. For more information pick up a copy of Angus Council's *Public Transport Map & Guide*, available from tourist offices, or call the *Transport Team*, T01307-461775, or *Strathtay Scottish*, T01382-228054. For rail enquiries, T0345-484950.

Information Angus is covered by the *Angus & Dundee Tourist Board*, which has offices in Arbroath, Brechin, Carnoustie, Forfar, Kirriemuir and Montrose. They have a website: www.angusanddundee.co.uk.

Arbroath

Phone code: 01241
Colour map 4, grid B5
Population: 23,500

The A92 coast road to Aberdeen bypasses the little coastal town of **Carnoustie**, whose **championship golf course** is revered worldwide, and heads to Arbroath, 17 miles northeast of Dundee. This is the home of that great Scottish delicacy, the **Arbroath smokie** – haddock smoked over oak chips – which you can buy in the tiny smokehouses around the harbour. But though Arbroath was once a thriving fishing and trading port, today it has the look of a place that's down on its luck, with high unemployment and a town centre blighted by insensitive planning.

Despite this, however, Arbroath boasts a long, eventful history and has some interesting sights. The **tourist office** is on Market Place, right in the centre of town. ■ *T872609. Apr-May Mon-Fri 0900-1700, Sat 1000-1700, Jun-Aug Mon-Sat 0930-1730, Sun 1000-1500, Sept Mon-Sat 0930-1730, Oct-Mar Mon-Fri 0900-1700, Sat 1000-1500.*

Sights The chief attraction is undoubtedly **Arbroath Abbey**, on Abbey Street, near the top of the High Street, not far from the tourist office. Founded by William the Lion in 1178 (who's buried here), it went on to become one of the wealthiest monasteries in the country. It is also one of the most important sites in Scottish history. It was here, on 6 April 1320, that the Declaration of Arbroath was issued, asking Rome to reverse its excommunication of Robert the Bruce and recognize him as King, thus asserting Scotland's independence from England. Pope John XXII finally agreed to the claim four years later. You can buy copies of the declaration (the original is in Edinburgh) which contains the stirring words: "For so long as a hundred of us remain alive, we will yield in no least way to English dominion. For we fight, not for glory, not for riches, nor honour, but only for freedom, which no good man surrenders but with his life".

After the Reformation, the abbey suffered badly and, like so many other important ecclesiastical buildings in Scotland, was used as a quarry for the building of the town. However, enough of the abbey survives to give you a good idea of just how magnificent it must have been; in particular the massive west front and the south transept (containing a circular window which was once lit up as a beacon to guide ships). In 1951, the **Stone of Destiny** found a temporary home here following its theft from Westminster Abbey by Scottish Nationalists. It was duly returned, where it stayed until its recent move to Edinburgh Castle (see page 76). ■ *T878756. Apr-Sept Mon-Sat 0930-1830, Sun 1200-1830, Oct-Mar Mon-Sat till 1630, Sun 1400-1630. £1.80, £1.30 concession.*

Beside the harbour is the **Signal Tower Museum**, housed in the elegant Regency building that was once the shore base and family living quarters for the keepers of the Bell Rock Lighthouse, lying 12 miles offshore. The museum has some interesting local history displays, including re-creations of a fisherman's cottage and a schoolroom. ■ *T875598. Mon-Sat 1000-1700, also Sun 1400-1700 in Jul-Aug. Free.*

A mile northwest of the town centre is **St Vigeans**, where the red sandstone church is perched right on top of a hill in the centre of the village. Beside the hill is tiny **St Vigeans Museum**, which contains an excellent collection of Pictish and medieval carved stones. ■ *Apr-Sept Mon-Sat 0930-1830, Sun 1400-1830. Free (collect the key from No 7).*

Five miles north of Arbroath by road is the attractive little fishing village of Auchmithie, perched precariously on the cliff-top with a steep descent to the harbour and quay. Auchmithie is the true home of the smokie, and though Arbroath later took the credit, the village can at least lay claim to the region's best seafood restaurant, the *But'n'Ben* (see Eating below). You can walk to the foot of Auchmithie along a marvellous cliff path which starts at the far end of **Victoria Park**. There are numerous caves to explore and lots of seabirds to see along the three-mile route. You should pick up a free copy of *The Arbroath Cliffs Nature Trail Guide* from the tourist office.

Auchmithie

There are several **B&Bs** around the centre, including the **E** *Harbour Guesthouse*, 4 The Shore, by the harbour, T878047, and **E** *Scurdy Guesthouse*, 33 Marketgate, T872417, near the High St. A mile south of town on the A92 to Dundee and overlooking the golf course, is **D-E** *Five Gables*, T871632.

Sleeping

The best place to eat is the cosy *But'n'Ben* restaurant, T877223, by the harbour in Auchmithie (see above). Their seafood is superb and great value (mid-range). Open daily except Tue 1200-1500 for lunch, 1600-1730 for high tea and 1900-2200 for dinner. Four miles northwest of town, signposted off the A933 Brechin Rd, is the *Letham Grange Resort*, T890373, www.lethamgrange.co.uk, a beautifully restored baronial mansion now functioning as a top-class golf resort hotel. It has a more formal restaurant (mid-range) and a conservatory for lunches and light meals (cheap). It will come as no surprise that Arbroath boasts an excellent fish and chip shop, *Peppo's*, at 51 Ladybridge St, by the harbour (closed Sat).

Eating

Northeast Scotland

Transport The **train** station is on Keptie St, about 5 mins walk from the tourist office. The **bus** station is nearby, on Catherine St, T870646. Arbroath is on the Dundee-Aberdeen rail line and there trains every 30 mins to and from **Dundee** (£3, 20 mins). For rail enquiries call T01382-228046. There are *Scottish Citylink* **buses**, T0990-505050, every 2 hrs to **Aberdeen** (£6.20, 1 hr 30 mins) via **Montrose** and **Stonehaven**, and to **Dundee** (£2.50, 25 mins). *Strathtay Scottish*, T01382-228054, runs regular buses to **Brechin** via **Montrose**, and less frequently to **Auchmithie**.

Montrose

Phone code 01674
Colour map 4, grid B5

Fourteen miles north of Arbroath is the elegant town of Montrose, the most pleasant and interesting of the Angus towns, rich in history and with great beaches to the north and south. It stands at the mouth of a vast tidal basin, covering 2,000 acres and bordered by 17 miles of roads. The basin is home to a multitude of wild birds such as ducks, geese, swans and waders who come here to search for food on the wide expanse of mud flats. The **Montrose Basin Wildlife Centre** is at Rossie Braes, a mile out of town on the A92. They have superb viewing facilities with binoculars and high-powered telescopes as well as remote-control video cameras. There are also guided walks around the reserve. ■ *T676336. Apr-Oct daily 1030-1730, Nov-Mar daily 1030-1600. £2.50.*

Sights Montrose was once a thriving port, trading with various European countries, and the wealthy 18th- and 19th-century merchants built their houses gable-end to the street, in imitation of the Continental style. This earned the townsfolk the nickname of 'gable-endies', which has stuck to this day. The sole remaining gable-ended houses can be seen on the High Street, which is the widest in Scotland. The south end of the High Street is overlooked by a statue of **Sir Robert Peel**, a local man, who was British Prime Minister and founder of the present-day Police Force. From his name came the old slang term for police, 'The Peelers'. Also at the southern end of the High Street is the Old Kirk with its fine steeple and the tiny **tourist office** is next to the library. ■ *T672000. Apr-Jun and Sept Mon-Sat 1000-1700, Jul-Aug 0930-1730.*

A few blocks from the High Street, on Panmure Place is **Montrose Museum and Art Gallery**, housed in a fine neo-classical Victorian building and one of the first purpose-built museums in Scotland. Among the displays are Bronze Age axe-heads, Montrose pottery and silver (the town had its own assay mark, a rose, and pieces are much sought after). The Maritime Gallery has a fleet of model ships, relics of the once thriving whaling industry, and Napoleonic items, including a cast of his death mask. ■ *T673232. Mon-Sat 1000-1700. Free.*

Outside the museum is a lifesize bronze sculpture of a boy by local sculptor, William Lamb (1893-1951). More of his work can be seen at the **William Lamb Sculpture Studio**, on Market Street, where his famous subjects include the Queen, Queen Mother and the great Scots poet Hugh McDiarmid. The studio was left by the artist as his memorial gift to the town. ■ *Jul-Sept Tue-Sun 1400-1700. Free.*

Near the museum, on the same side of the street, up an alley (or close), are **Taylor's Auction Rooms**, T672775. Every second Saturday, people come from far and wide to bid for paintings, jewellery, furniture and many other items. It's well worth a visit, and you might even come away with a piece of locally hall-marked silver. On the A92 heading north out of town is the **Aerodrome Museum**. Montrose was Scotland's first airport, used in both world wars for the training of pilots. The museum documents the lives of many of the men who lost their lives, including the chilling tale of Lieutenant Desmond Arthur whose ghost is said to haunt the former air base. There are also assorted aircraft on display outside. ■ *T675401. Sun 1200-1700, or at other times by appointment.*

Traill Drive leads to the town's impressive **beach**, which stretches all the way north to St Cyrus (see page 367). About four miles south of Montrose, reached by turning off the A92, is the great sweep of **Lunan Bay**, a stunningly beautiful, and usually deserted, sandy beach, once popular with smugglers. Like many beaches on the northeast coast, there are strong currents so do not swim beyond your capabilities. There's a variety of **wildlife** around, including nesting puffins on the red sandstone cliffs. Overlooking the beach is the 12th-century ruin of **Red Castle**, which was originally a royal hunting lodge.

Three miles west of Montrose on the A935 is the House of Dun, built in 1730 for David Erskine, Lord Dun. It is a very attractive Georgian building in the Palladian style, designed by William Adam, who was at the forefront of Scottish architecture between the Jacobite risings of 1715 and 1745, but somewhat eclipsed by his sons Robert and James otherwise. Lady Augusta Kennedy-Erskine, daughter of William IV and the actress Mrs Jordan, also lived there and the house contains many royal mementos. Alas, the huge sword which was driven into a tree in the grounds by one of the Erskines was removed by the present owners, the National Trust, for safety reasons. The courtyard has recently been restored, and *Angus Handloom Weavers*, Scotland's last handloom linen weavers, are based there. Fine linen is for sale by the yard, as well as linen goods. There's an attractive café and shop. ■ *T810264. Easter and 1 May-3 Oct daily 1330-1730, Oct weekends only 1330-1730, £3.70, £2.50 child/concession. Strathtay bus No 30 to Brechin passes the entrance, ask to get off.* **The House of Dun**

C *The Links Hotel*, Mid Links, T671000. A short walk from the beach, comfortable town house hotel offering good Scottish/French cooking at mid-range prices. For **B&B** accommodation try the **E** *Limes Guesthouse*, T677236, thelimes@easynet.co.uk, at 15 King St. For something a bit more scenic, there's **E** *Lunan Lodge*, T01241-830267, b&b@lunanlodge.sol.co.uk. An 18th-century country house in the village of Lunan overlooking Lunan Bay. There's a **campsite** at *Littlewood Holiday Park*, T672973, on the Brechin Rd. **Sleeping & eating**

Apart from the hotels, eating options are limited to the bars and cafés. *Roo's Leap*, by the golf club at the northern end of Traill Drive, serves decent Aussie tucker. *Steeple Computers Systems* is a **cyber café** opposite the Old Kirk, T662160. Open Tue-Sat.

The **train** station is on Western Rd, 1 block from the High St. There are trains every 30 mins to Aberdeen and Dundee. **Buses** stop in the High St. *Bluebird Buses*, T01224-212266, run an hourly service to and from **Aberdeen** (1 hr 45 mins) via **Stonehaven**. *Strathtay Scottish*, T01382-228054, runs regular buses to **Brechin** and **Forfar**. **Transport**

Brechin

Nine miles west of Montrose is Brechin, a quiet little town on the banks of the river South Esk, whose main attraction is its 14th-century **cathedral**, in Bishop's Close off the High Street. There's been a church here since the ninth century though most of the what you see dates from the beginning of the 20th century when major restoration work was carried out. The adjacent 106-ft high **round tower** dates from the 11th century and is one of only two such structures in the country. *Phone code: 01356*
Colour map 4, grid B5
Population: 7,500

The small **Brechin Museum** is housed in the library on St Ninian's Square and is the usual collection of local curiosities and memorabilia. ■ *Mon, Tue, Thur-Fri 0930-1800, Wed 0930-1900, Sat 0930-1700. Free.* Also on St Ninian's

Square is the terminus of the **Caledonian Railway**, which runs steam trains on a four-mile section of line between Brechin station and Bridge of Dun, a mile from the House of Dun (see under Montrose above). ■ *T810318. Trains run six times daily on Sun only, from Jun to early Sept, £4.50 return, £2.50 child/concession.*

Just off the A90, is the **Brechin Castle Centre**, which is a Country Park with garden centre, pets corner, miniature railway (open April-September), picnic areas and waterside walks. There's also a coffee shop. Part of the centre is the newly opened **Pictavia**, which gives a fascinating glimpse into Scotland's Celtic past. You'll help to solve the riddles of the stones, see the mysterious Pictish standing stones and hear the sounds of battle in the Tower of Sound. ■ *T626813. Open all year.*

The **tourist office** is at 10 St Ninian's Place, opposite the library. They have information on hiking in Glen Esk. ■ *T623050. Apr-Jun and Sept Mon-Sat 1000-1700; Jul-Aug Mon-Sat 0930-1730.*

Sleeping Accommodation is limited. There's the **D** *Northern Hotel*, 2 Clerk St, T625505, which also serves moderately priced meals, and **B&B** at **E-D** *Doniford*, 26 Airlie St, T622361.

Transport *Scottish Citylink* **buses**, T0990-505050, run every 2 hrs to **Aberdeen** (1 hr 5 mins, £4.80), **Dundee** (50 mins, £5.30) and **Forfar** (20 mins, £3.30). Buses leave from Panmure St. *Strathtay Scottish*, T01382-228054, has services to **Edzell** several times daily (20 mins, £1.10) and daily every hr to **Montrose** (20 mins), from South Esk St.

Edzell and Glen Esk

Phone code: 01356
Colour map 4, grid B5

Five miles north of Brechin, on the B966, is Edzell, an impossibly neat and picturesque planned village lying at the foot of Glen Esk. At the entrance to the village is the impressive **Dalhousie Arch**, which leads on to the wide main street, lined with quaint little tearooms and shops selling Victoriana.

A mile west of the village is the red sandstone ruin of **Edzell Castle**, a 16th-century tower house which, over the course of its life, has been visited by Mary, Queen of Scots, James VI and, less happily, Cromwell's troops. But it is the magnificent **garden**, or 'Pleasance', which is the real attraction. Created by Sir David Lindsay in 1604, the superb heraldic and symbolic sculpted wall panels are rare examples of European Renaissance Art in Scotland. ■ *T648631. Apr-Sept 0930-1830, Oct-Mar Mon-Wed and Sat 0930-1630, Thur 0930-1200, Fri and Sun 1400-1630, £2.50, £1.90 concession.*

Three miles southwest of Edzell, on either side of the road, are the **Brown Caterthun** and **White Caterthun**, two remarkable Iron Age forts, defended by ditches and ramparts over 900-ft high. These were occupied by the Picts around the first few centuries AD and the views from the top are amazing. To get there, follow the road west of the castle and turn left at Bridgend, then take the left fork. Or take the road southwest from Edzell and take the first right after Dunlappie. There's no public transport. It's an easy walk from the road to either fort.

North from Edzell, the road runs 13 miles to the head of beautiful **Glen Esk**, the most easterly of the Angus Glens and, like the others, quiet and empty. Nine miles north of Edzell along the Glen road is the **Glenesk Folk Museum**, housed in an old shooting lodge known as 'The Retreat'. The museum's extensive local folk history collection gives a fascinating insight into the lives of the Glen's inhabitants. It also has a good tearoom (try their rhubarb jam and home baking). ■ *T670254. Easter-May Sat-Mon 1200-1800, Jun to mid-Oct 1200-1800. £2.*

Northeast Scotland

Four miles further on, beyond Tarfside village, the public road ends at **Mount Keen** **Invermark Castle**. This is the start of one of the Mounth Roads, ancient rights of way leading from the Angus Glens across the mountains to Deeside. This route leads eventually to Ballater or **Glen Tanar**, near Aboyne. For a description of the latter route in reverse, see under **Deeside** (page 376). You can also hike from here to the summit of **Mount Keen** (3,081ft), Scotland's most easterly Munro, but like the Mounth Road, this is a tough walk and you'll need full hill-walking equipment and a map. An easier walk is to the **Queen's Well**, three miles from the car park across the river from Invermark Castle. It's about three hours there and back. Altenatively, you can head west from the castle, past the lovely old church and along the north shore of **Loch Lee.**

OS Landranger No 44

The pleasant **C** *Glenesk Hotel*, T648319, does bar and restaurant meals. There's also **Sleeping &** **B&B** at **E-F** *Inchcape*, T647266, on the High St, and **E-F** *The Gorse*, T648207, on **transport** Dunlappie Rd. For details of buses to Edzell, see Brechin 'Transport' above.

Forfar

Fourteen miles north of Dundee, just off the main A90, is Forfar, the county capital of Angus. Forfar was the ancient capital of the Picts, and though it wouldn't be picked as a top tourist destination today, it is only a few miles from the county's star attraction, **Glamis Castle**. The town is best known for its contribution to Scottish cuisine, the famous **Forfar Bridie**, a gigantic shortcrust pastie filled with mince and onions (see 'Eating' below).

Phone code: 01307
Colour map 4, grid B4
Population: 12,650

The Meffan Gallery & Museum, at 20 West High Street, illustrates the colourful history of town and county, and includes Pictish remains and a grisly account of the witch-hunts of the 17th century. ■ *T464123. Mon-Sat 1000-1700. Free.* Two miles east of town, off the B9113, are the ruins of **Restenneth Priory**. The 12th-century Augustinian priory was chosen by King Robert the Bruce as the last resting place of his son, Prince John. ■ *Open at all times, free.* About four miles southeast, on the road to Letham, is **Dunnichen Hill**, once known as Nechtansmere, scene of a Pictish victory in 685 AD over Ecgfrith, King of the Angles, thus assuring Scotland's independence. The **tourist office** is at 45 East High Street. ■ *T467876. Apr-Jun and Sept Mon-Sat 1000-1700, Jul-Aug Mon-Sat 0930-1730.*

Sights

Five miles northeast of Forfar, along the B9134, is the tiny village of **Aberlemno**, home to some of the country's best **Pictish stones**. In the churchyard, just off the main road, is an eighth-century cross-slab with a Celtic cross, entwined beasts on one side and an elaborate depiction of the Battle of Nechtansmere on the other. There are three other stones with Pictish and early Christian symbols by the roadside. There are plans to move the stones to a protected site, so check with the tourist office before visiting. ■ *Open access except Nov-Mar. Free. Buses from Forfar to Brechin stop in Aberlemno.*

Five miles southwest of Forfar is the county's star attraction, Glamis Castle **Glamis Castle** (pronounced Glamz), the fabulous family home of the Earls of Strathmore and **& village** Kinghorne. Glamis is every inch the archetypal Scottish castle, and one of the most famous. This was the setting for Shakespeare's *Macbeth*, but its royal connection doesn't end there. It was the childhood home of Her Majesty Queen Elizabeth the Queen Mother and the birthplace of Her Royal Highness the Princess Margaret.

Northeast Scotland

The setting matches the impeccable pedigree. As you approach down the long, tree-lined drive, the castle suddenly appears in all its glory, the jumble of turrets, towers and conical roofs rising up against the backdrop of the Grampian Mountains like one of Walt Disney's fairy-tale fantasies. Most of the building you see dates from the 15th century, though the glamorous touches were added in the 17th century.

The five-storey, L-shaped castle grew from its humble beginnings as a mere hunting lodge, used by the Kings of Scotland in the 11th century. In 1372, King Robert II gave it to his son-in-law, Sir John Lyon, whose descendants, the Earls of Strathmore and Kinghorne, have lived here ever since. The 14th Earl was the Queen Mother's father.

Highlights of the tour include the 17th-century drawing room with its impressive plasterwork ceilings, and the ghostly crypt, haunted by Lord Glamis and Crawford who was entombed within its walls as punishment for playing a few hands of gin rummy with the Devil on the Sabbath. The 17th-century chapel, with its biblical frescoes, is also haunted, this time by the 'grey lady', the ghost of the sixth Lady Glamis, who was burnt as a witch by James V. Duncan's Hall is reputedly where King Duncan was murdered by Macbeth, though like much else in the play, this is very doubtful. You can also see the Royal Apartments, including the Queen Mother's bedroom, and the extensive grounds are also well worth exploring. There's a restaurant on site. ■ *T840393. Late Mar to end Oct, daily 1030-1730 (Jul-Aug from 1000), last admission 1645. Guided tours last one hour and leave every 15 minutes. £5.20, £2.70 child/concession. There's a limited bus service from Dundee, Forfar & Kirriemuir. Contact Strathtay Buses, T01382-228054.*

In the village of **Glamis**, just off the square, is the **Angus Folk Museum**. It's housed in a picturesque row of 18th-century cottages which are divided into the domestic and agricultural sections. The changes in living and farming in Angus over the last 200 years are vividly illustrated with the help of a vast collection of local artefacts. ■ *T840233. Easter and 1 May-Sept, daily 1100-1700; weekends only in Oct 1100-1700. £2.40, £1.60 child/concession.*

Sleeping & eating
There are several places to stay in Forfar, but **Kirriemuir** is nicer and equally convenient for Glamis Castle. The best place to eat is *O'Hara's*, 41-43 West High St, T464350. Bar-bistro offering great food with an inventive twist and real ales. Food served Mon-Sat lunch and evening. Also good is the *Chapelbank House Hotel*, at 69 East High St, T463151. They serve a good, cheap lunch daily except Mon, and moderately priced dinner daily except Sun and Mon.

Several bakeries in town sell bridies, but the locals will tell you that the best place to sample this delight is *McLaren's*, next to the *Queen's Hotel* on West High St.

Transport
Scottish Citylink **buses**, T0990-505050, run to and from **Dundee** every 2 hrs (25 mins, £2.80) and **Aberdeen** (1 hr 20 mins, £6.50), via **Brechin** (20 mins). Buses stop opposite the church in East High St. *Strathtay Scottish*, T01382-228054, runs buses every hr to **Kirriemuir** (25 mins, £1.20) and to **Brechin** via **Aberlemno**.

Kirriemuir

Phone code 01575
Colour map 4, grid B4
Population: 5,300

Kirriemuir, or Kirrie as it's known locally, is the ideal spot for those wishing to explore the beautiful Angus Glens, or visit Glamis Castle, only five miles south, or simply for those who wish to get off the tartan trail and stay in a lovely, unspoiled wee town.

Kirrie's claim to fame, though, is as the birthplace of JM Barrie (1860-1937), creator of Peter Pan, the little boy who never grew up. Barrie was the son of a hand-loom weaver and ninth of 10 children. His classic tale of *Peter Pan and the Lost Boys*, written in 1904, is said to have been inspired by the memory of his older brother, who died while still young. Kirrie is the fictional Thrums of Barrie's autobiographical novel, *A Window in Thrums*. **Barrie's birthplace** can be visited at 9 Brechin Road. The humble little weaver's cottage is now managed by the NTS and the upper floor is furnished as it would have been when he lived there. The adjacent house features an exhibition of his literary and theatrical works. The outside wash-house is said to have been his first theatre and the model for the house built for Wendy by the Lost Boys in Never-Never Land. Barrie is also buried in Kirrie, at the nearby St Mary's Episcopal Church. ■ *T572646. Easter and May-Sept, Mon-Sat 1100-1730, Sun 1330-1730. Weekends only in Oct, Sat 1100-1730, Sun 1330-1730. £2, concession £1.30.*

At the top of Kirriemuir Hill is a **camera obscura**, which offers a panorama of the surrounding Strathmore countryside and the glens to the north. At the southern end of town, at Bellies Brae, is the **Aviation Museum**, which houses a large, eclectic collection of Second World War memorabilia. ■ *Apr-Sept Mon-Sat 1000-1700, Sun 1100-1700. Free but donations welcome.*

Birdwatchers should head a few miles west of town, just off the B951, to the **Loch of Kinnordy**, and **RSPB Reserve**, where there are two hides overlooking the loch and wetlands.

The **tourist office** is on Cumberland Close. ■ *T574097. Apr-Jun and Sept Mon-Sat 1000-1700, Jul-Aug Mon-Sat 0930-1730.*

Sleeping

There's not a huge choice of accommodation in Kirrie. Best of all is the **D** *Airlie Arms Hotel*, St Malcom's Wynd, T572847. A converted medieval monastery now a small, comfortable hotel, offers cheap bar meals and decent, moderately priced evening meals. Among the few **B&Bs** is **E** *Woodlands*, at Lisden Gardens, T572582 and **E** *Crepto*, at 1 Kinnordy Place, T572746. Those wishing to stay longer can rent a self-catering cottage next door to Barrie's birthplace, it costs £250-320 per week for up to 4 people, contact the *National Trust for Scotland* head office, 5 Charlotte Square, Edinburgh, EH2 4DU, T0131-2439331, F2439302.

Eating

The best restaurant in the area is the *Lochside Lodge*, by the Loch of Lintrathen, T560340, 6 miles along the B951, then take the turning left for Bridge of Lintrathen. This converted farmstead serves moderately priced modern Scottish cooking and also rents rooms (**D**). In town, the *Airlie Arms* (see above) and the *Thrums Hotel*, Bank St, T572758, both serve decent food. A great café is *Visocchi's* on the main street, which has been serving delicious ice cream since 1953.

Entertainment

Kirriemuir is well known for its **Folk Festival**, held on the first weekend in Sept each year. The best venues for live music are the *Airlie Arms* (see above), the *Roods Bar* nearby, and *Three, Bellies Brae*, which may be an unusual name for a pub, but is a very welcoming watering hole.

Transport

Strathtay Scottish, T01382-228054, runs hourly **buses** (Mon-Sat, less frequently on Sun) to and from **Dundee** (1 hr 10 mins, £2.45). There are also buses every hr to **Forfar** (25 mins, £1.20) and twice a day (except Sun) to **Glamis**. There's a **postbus service**, T01463-256200, from Kirriemuir to **Glen Prosen** (once daily except Sun) and **Glen Clova** (twice on weekdays, once on Sat).

Northeast Scotland

The Angus Glens

Colour map 4, grid B4 Kirriemuir is the gateway to **Glens Isla, Prosen** and **Clova**, three of the Angus Glens. The other two, Glens Lethnot and Esk, are reached via Brechin and described on page 352.

Glen Isla Running parallel to Glen Shee (see page 282), lovely Glen Isla is the furthest west of the Angus Glens and can also be reached from **Alyth**. At the southern end of the glen, five miles north of Alyth by Bridge of Glenisla, is **Reekie Linn**, a series of waterfalls that plunge through a deep, wooded gorge. A path leads for 200 yards from the car park and picnic site on the road between Bridge of Glenisla and Bridge of Lintrathen. Nearby is the excellent *Lochside Lodge* restaurant (see above under Kirriemuir) and *Peel Farm Coffee and Craft Shop*.

Six miles north, at **Kirkton of Glenisla**, on the B951, is the **C-D** *Glenisla Hotel*, T01575-582223, glenislahotel@sol.co.uk, an impossibly cosy 17th-century inn with log fires, real ales, good grub and plenty of local characters. It's worth the trip just to spend a night here. Further north a side road turns off the B951 and runs to **Auchavan**, at the head of the glen. There are paths from here into the wild and mountainous **Caenlochan Forest**. A **postbus** runs Monday-Saturday from Blairgowrie to Auchavan.

At the mouth of the glen, in the tiny village of **Meigle**, home to Scotland's most important collection of early Christian and Pictish carved stones. They are hosued in the superb **Meigle Museum**. ■ *Apr-Sept daily 0930-1830. £1.80.*

Glen Prosen Five miles north of Kirriemuir is the tiny village of **Dykehead**, at the foot of Glen Clova, where a side road branches northwest and runs into Glen Prosen. Both glens penetrate deep into the Grampian Mountains and are blessed with a rugged beauty, but Glen Prosen carries little of the cachet of its neighbour and is consequently a much more peaceful option for hill walkers. The little road runs deep into the glen but it's best explored on foot.

A good walk is the relatively straightforward four-mile **Minister's Path**, which connects the two glens. It starts from behind the kirk in Glenprosen village and heads over the hilly moorland and down to the B955 just before Clova village. You can catch the **postbus** back to Kirriemuir from the *Clova Hotel* (see below). The Kirriemuir to Glen Prosen postbus runs once daily except Sunday.

Glen Clova & Glen Clova is only 30 miles north of Dundee yet you could be in the heart of the
Glen Doll Highlands, with craggy mountains towering overhead and heather-clad slopes populated by deer and grouse. Glen Clova leads north into Glen Doll, from where you can follow the old **drove roads** which lead to Ballater and Braemar
OS Landranger Nos 43 & 44 in Deeside. These ancient routes were used by whisky smugglers, government troops and rebels, as well as cattle drovers, and though they may look straightforward on the map, they can be as treacherous as any of the Scottish mountains. Only fit and experienced walkers should attempt these walks.

One of the best walks in the famous **Jock's Road** to Braemar. The 14-mile route starts from the Glen Doll youth hostel and it's a tough seven-hour hike up to the summit at Crow Craigies (3,108ft) and down to the head of Loch Callater. The descent is very steep and may require crampons in winter. From the loch, the path follows the Callater Burn till it reaches the main A93, two miles from Braemar (see page 375). Another excellent walk is the **Loops of Brandy**, which starts from behind the *Clova Hotel* and climbs up into the mountains, around Loch Brandy and back again. It's a four-hour walk there and back.

Drivers should note that the B955 from Dykehead divides just before the bridge of the river South Esk. The west branch is traditionally used by vehicles heading up the glen, while the east branch should be for traffic returning down the glen. The two roads meet up again six miles further on, at the tiny hamlet of **Clova**, which consists of little more than the **D-E** *Clova Hotel*, T550222, which is a very friendly and popular climbers' retreat. As well as bar meals, the hotel lays on regular barbecues, ceilidhs and a multitude of various activities. There's also an eight-bed bunkhouse outside (**F**) which is open all year. It has a kitchen, but no shower.

Four miles further north, near the end of the road, in Glen Doll, is a **campsite**, T550233, by the bridge. It's open during the summer and has only basic facilities. A few hundered yards north is *Glendoll Youth Hostel*, T550236, open 10 March-31 October. It has 45 beds and boasts a squash court as well as the standard facilities. Note that access is limited to between 1030 and 1700.

There's a **postbus** service to Glen Clova from Kirriemuir twice a day Monday-Friday and once on Saturday. The 0830 departure runs as far as the hostel and the 1500 departure (Monday-Friday only) stops at the *Clova Hotel*. The afternoon service leaves from the hotel at 1530.

Aberdeen

Scotland's third largest city, and Britain's most isolated, is a hard place. Hard because of the grey granite of its buildings, and hard because of the nature of its people, who are industrious, thrifty, proud and uncompromising. First impressions are often determined by the weather: when it rains it's about as appealing as cold porridge. Sometimes leaden skies hang low over a uniform greyness, and a howling gale blows in from the North Sea, but when the clouds do part and the sun shines down, the tiny mica chips, which form a natural part of granite, sparkle and glisten like a display in a jeweller's window. Whatever the impression, it is a place that elicits a strong response. Lewis Grassic Gibbon, the northeast's most famous writer, wrote: "One detests Aberdeen with the detestation of a thwarted lover. It is the one haunting and exasperatingly lovable city in Scotland."

Phone code: 01224
Colour map 4, grid A6
Population: 217,260

Ins and outs

Aberdeen **airport** is 7 miles northwest of the city centre, at Dyce, off the A96 to Inverness. There are regular domestic flights to Scottish and UK destinations, including Orkney and Shetland, as well as international flights to several European destinations. For airport information, T722331. There's car hire and currency exchange at the airport. Buses 27 and 27A run at peak times to and from the city centre (35 mins, £1.35 single). For more information T650065. Alternatively, take a train to Dyce station and a bus (Mon-Fri only) or taxi from there. A taxi from the airport to Dyce railway station costs around £5, and £10 to the city centre.

Getting there
For more details, see 'Transport', page 366

Aberdeen is linked to Lerwick in Shetland and Stromness in Orkney by *P&O* **ferries**, T572615. There are regular sailings from the passenger terminal in the harbour, a short walk east of the train and bus stations.

The **bus** terminal is next to the train station, on Guild St. *National Express* has daily buses from London, T0990-808080, and *Scottish Citylink*, T0990-505050, runs buses to all major Scottish towns. *Bluebird Buses*, T212266, is the main regional operator.

The **train** station is on Guild St. There are regular services from London, and major Scottish towns and cities. For all rail enquiries, T0345-484950.

Aberdeen city centre is compact and the best way to get around is on foot, though you may need to use local buses to reach some of the outlying sights, such as Old Aberdeen and the University. Almost all **buses** pass along Union Street, the city's

Getting around

☞ *City of roses*

Aberdeen is known as the 'Granite City', and Rubislaw Quarry still bears testament to the vast quantities of granite hewn there and used to build its striking Victorian Gothic buildings. But it has a softer side, and is also known as the 'City of Roses'.

There is a profusion of blooming flowers that fill the parks, gardens, traffic islands and roadways, creating a stark contrast to the grey streets and buildings. In fact, flower power is so prevalent here that Aberdeen has been debarred from entering the 'Britain in Bloom' competition, in order to give other places a chance!

main thoroughfare. The most useful services are: Nos 18, 19, 24 and 24A from Union St to Great Western Rd; Nos 6, 20 and 26 to Old Aberdeen; No 14 to the Beach and Footdee; and Nos 17 and 26 to Duthie Park from Union St. A good idea, if you're using public transport frequently, is to buy a prepaid **Farecard** (for £3, £5 or £10), which works like a phonecard. These are available at the tourist office (see below), where you can also pick up the free *Public Transport Guide* which includes a map of bus routes. For information on local bus services, call *First Aberdeen*, T650065, or *Bluebird Buses*, T212266. For a **taxi**, call *Mair's*, T724040.

Information The very helpful **tourist office** is in St Nicholas House, Broad St, just off the east end of Union St, about 10 mins walk from the bus and train stations. As well as the usual accommodation booking service, they also will also book tickets for theatres and events, trips and tours. They have a wide selection of leaflets on walks in Aberdeen and run bus tours (see below). The tourist office also gives out free monthly listings magazines, *Listings Aberdeen* and *What's On*, and has a 24-hr *What's On Line*, T636363. Another good source of information on current events are the local newspapers, the *Press and Journal* and *Evening News*. Open Jun and Sept Mon-Sat 0900-1700, Sun 1000-1400, Jul-Aug Mon-Fri 0900-1900, Sat 0900-1700, Sun 1000-1600, Oct-May Mon-Fri 0900-1700, Sat 1000-1400, T632727, www.agtb.org.

History

Aberdeen lies between two rivers, the Don to the north and the Dee to the south, backed by a fertile hinterland and facing the wild North Sea, which has brought the city great wealth since the discovery of oil in the early 1970s. Its maritime history, however, dates back to its foundation as a Royal Burgh in 1124. In the past, Aberdeen had strong trading links with Scandinavia and the Low Countries. Fast clipper ships built in the city, brought tea from India and other goods from all over the world. Until some years after the Second World War, Aberdeen's lifeblood was fishing and shipping. It was the biggest fish market in the country and still lands considerable catches. Then came the discovery of North Sea oil and gas and Aberdeen became Boom City, flaunting its new-found wealth with an almost unseemly fervour. The glory years of the early 1980s may have gone, but Aberdeen still exudes an air of self-confidence and prosperity rare in other regional UK cities.

Aberdonians also have an inordinate amount of civic pride, which can verge on the overweening. This may have been enhanced in recent years by its new-found status and wealth, but has its roots in the 14th century, when the townsfolk offered protection to Robert the Bruce during the Wars of Independence. In return, Bruce rewarded the town with 'Freedom Lands' for which he had previously received rent. The money saved was diverted into a Common Good Fund, to be spent on amenities. Today, this money is still used

City of oil

When oil was discovered in the North Sea in 1970, it was assumed that 'black gold' would bring nationwide prosperity. But while many in the country would argue that the huge oil revenues flowed south with little benefit accruing to the Scottish people, the people of Aberdeen have a different tale to tell.

Oil transformed Aberdeen from a relatively impoverished northern backwater to a flourishing and prosperous city, where every oil company, exploration firm, tool manufacturer and diving supplier now base themselves. Aberdeen quickly became the oil capital of Europe. Millions were invested in infrastructure, such as the harbour and airport, the population increased rapidly, average earnings soared and unemployment plummeted. Aberdeen was suddenly a city brimming with confidence. New, upmarket restaurants,

bars and shops opened to cater for a population with money to burn. Ironic, really, in a city whose people have a reputation for being less than extravagant with their cash.

But it couldn't last. In the mid-1980s the price of oil slumped from US$80 a barrel to US$10 and recession struck the northeast. Jobs vanished, house prices dropped and Aberdonians woke up to the realization that they were completely dependent on oil for their economic well-being. But predictions of the city's demise were greatly exaggerated. In recent years, oil prices and production have risen to the levels of the early 1980s and house prices are once more on the up. Oil looks set to continue flowing in from the North Sea for a very long time to come. And this time around everyone will surely heed the dangers of the past and learn to be a bit more Aberdonian.

to pay for the upkeep of its many fine parks and to keep the city looking its best. This sense of pride in its parks and public buildings makes Aberdeen an extremely pleasant place to visit. It's also a very lively place, and its many bars, restaurants, nightclubs, theatres and shops are as vibrant and thriving as you'd expect in any city with money in its pockets.

Sights

The main sights can be visited in a couple of leisurely days, and many of them are free. Most of the **museums and art galleries** are clustered around the compact city centre and can be covered on foot. From the centre, it's only a short walk down to the **harbour**, with its bustling fish market and interesting **Maritime Museum**. The outlying sights, such as the suburb of **Old Aberdeen**, **Duthie Park** and the city's superb **beach** can all easily be reached by bus. The best way to get around is to take one of *Grampian Coaches'* open-topped **bus tours** of the city, which leave from the tourist office. These run from June-September and cost £3.50 per person for a 90-minute tour, or £5.50 per person for a full day *Explorer ticket*, which allows you to hop on and off official tour buses as well as use any other buses around the city. Tickets can be bought from the driver, at the sales kiosk in St Nicholas Street, or at the head office at 395 King Street, T650024.

The city centre Aberdeen's main artery is **Union Street**, one mile long and built on pillars (an amazing and expensive engineering feat). The street is a fascinating mix of Victorian Gothic and modern glass and concrete and is perpetually packed with buses, cars and pedestrians. The oldest part of the city is the 13th-century **Castlegate**, at the eastern end of Union Street, now dominated by the 17th-century **Mercat Cross**, which was the focus of Aberdeen's long history as a major market town and trading centre.

Northeast Scotland

Opposite, at the corner of Union Street and King Street, in the Town House, is the **Tolbooth Museum** which dates from the 14th century. Not only did it serve as a collection point for tolls and taxes but it was also used as the Wardhouse, housing prisoners held on remand. Inside its narrow entrance stands the old sandstone Market Cross. You have to be quite nimble to negotiate the narrow spiral staircases complete with rope 'rail'. For the less agile, there's a video of the building. To see the building, you first go through a heavy metal door into a dimly lit interior and climb the steps up to the first chamber where lifelike figures of Jacobite prisoners are shackled to a metal rod. Their muttered conversation sounds very realistic. In an adjoining cell are the figures of Alexander Keith, imprisoned in 1638 and in the process of being helped to escape by his sister Elizabeth. A large iron bound trunk is just discernible in the gloom. A further climb takes you up to another chamber where a girl huddles, moaning. After this dramatic experience, you'll see exhibits including uniforms, robes and portraits. The whole place is packed with history and has a very authentic feel. ■ *T621167. Apr-Sept Tue-Sat 1000-1700, Sun 1400-1700. £2.50, £1.50 children.*

Aberdeen

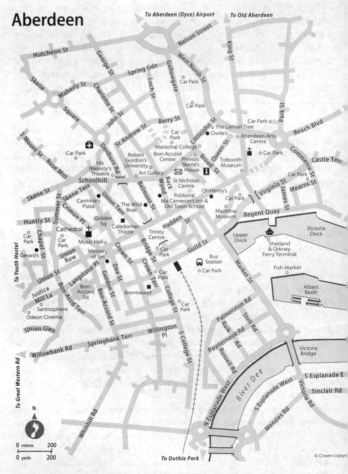

© Crown copyr

A little further west down Union Street is Broad Street, where you'll find the tourist office. 50 yards beyond it, at 45 Guestrow, is Aberdeen's oldest surviving private house, the 16th-century **Provost Skene's House**. Its distinctive style, with boldly pointed stone and little turrets, stands out from the adjacent modern buildings. It was only the intervention of the Queen Mother which saved this little historical gem from the same fate as its neighbours. The interior features a series of ornate tempera-painted ceilings dating from 1622, which somehow survived the orgy of vandalism in the wake of the Reformation. There are also furnished period rooms and an interesting display of memorabilia, including mementos of John Brown, ghillie and companion of Queen Victoria. There is a pocket watch given to him by the widowed queen, also a silver pipe and case from the same donor. ■ *T641086. Mon-Sat 1000-1700, Sun 1300-1600. £2.50, £1.50 concession.*

Across the road from the tourist office is the imposing **Marischal College** (pronounced 'Marshall'), the second largest granite building in the world, after the Escorial in Madrid. This massive neo-Gothic sculpture in loved and loathed in equal measure, but cannot be ignored. Aberdeen was the seat of two universities, the Catholic King's College (see 'Old Aberdeen' below) and the Protestant Marischal College, founded in 1593 by the 5th Earl of Marishcal. The two colleges combined in 1860 to form Aberdeen University. The **museum**, entered through the main quadrangle and up the stairs, is open to visitors and worth visiting. It is divided into two exhibitions, the 'Encylopaedia of the Northeast', which depicts the region's distinctive culture, and 'Collecting the World', which features many wonderfully diverse items collected from around the globe. ■ *T274301. Mon-Fri 1000-1700, Sun 1400-1700. Free.*

From Marischal College, head down Upperkirkgate, past the Bon Accord and St Nicholas Shopping Centres, and up Schoolhill to the city's magnificent **Art Gallery**, a most elegant building of marble steps with a pillared gallery overlooking a central well. At the top of the stairs stands a showcase of lovely Meissen china. There are changing displays of costumes and applied arts. All the big names are here; there's a Degas bronze, and paintings by Dante Gabriel Rossetti, Monet, Pissaro, Millais, Legros, Sargent, Sisley, Russell Flint, Holman Hunt, Landseer, Augustus John, Raeburn, McTaggart, and Sir George Reid, amongst many others. William Roelofs' large oil of *Waterlilies* is a fitting rival to Monet. There are also several works by Joan Eardley, who lived near Stonehaven. A large number of the paintings were bequethed by local granite merchant, Alex MacDonald, in 1900. Downstairs is a white-walled circular room which commemorates the 167 people who lost their lives in the Piper Alpha oil rig disaster in 1988. There's also a well-stocked shop, café and craft gallery. ■ *T646333. Mon-Sat 1000-1700, Sun 1400-1700. Free.*

West of the Art Gallery are the sunken **Union Terrace Gardens**, which make a pleasant escape from the traffic on Union Street. Here, at the end of Union Terrace, stand three buildings at right angles: the Central Library, His Majesty's Theatre and St Mark's Church, always known locally as 'Education, Damnation and Salvation'. They are obligingly pointed out by a huge statue of William Wallace, brandishing his sword.

At the West End of Union Street, Bon Accord Terrace leads south into Justice Mill Lane, home to many of the city's best bars and nightclubs, and also to the **Sartrosphere**, a fun-focused hands-on science and technology discovery centre. ■ *T213232. Apr-Oct Mon-Sat 1000-1700, Sun 1330-1700, Mar-Nov Mon-Fri (closed Tue) 1000-1600, Sat 1000-1700, Sun 1330-1700. £4.50, £2.25 children/concession.*

Anyone interested in military history should not miss the **Gordon Highlanders Museum** at St Luke's in Viewfield Road, which is off Queen's Road (buses 14 or 15 from Union Street). This is a most evocative exhibition, displaying no less than 12 VCs of the 19 awarded to the regiment described by Winston Churchill as the finest in the world. When the Gordons were raised in 1794, Lady Gordon helped her husband in recruiting. There is a lovely painting of her, wearing a tartan bonnet with a white cockade. In an adjoining showcase is the very bonnet. The Gordon Highlanders are now part of the Highlanders, also comprising the Seaforths and the Camerons. ■ *T311200. Apr-Oct Tue-Sat 1030-1630, Sun 1330-1630. £2, £1.50 concession.*

The harbour From the Castlegate, Shiprow, a steep cobbled street, leads down to the harbour and the gleaming glass and steel of the excellent new **Maritime Museum**, which traces Aberdeen's long seafaring history from earliest times up to the present day. In the entrance is a list, up-dated daily, of ships in harbour. The Lloyd's register is there if you ask. As you go up the stairs (there's a lift, if needed), the first things that you will see are the lenses from Rattray Head lighthouse. The sounds are authentic, the cry of seagulls and the crash of the sea on shale. A huge board lists all the ships built in Aberdeen from 1811 until 1991, including the famous fast clippers. Most dramatically, down the stairwell hangs a model of an oil rig. The methods in use in oil and gas exploration and production are explained. The auditorium (which has an induction loop system) features good explanatory videos. There is a hands-on children's area and a layout of bunks. The museum spills over into the adjoining **Provost Ross' House** dating from 1593, the oldest building in the city. There you'll find paintings and models of ships. There's also a shop and a good licensed café. ■ *T337700. Mon-Sat 1000-1700, Sun 1200-1500. £3.50, £2.50 children.*

At the foot of Shiprow is Market Street, which runs the length of the harbour. It's still a busy place and on any one day you'll see a huge variety of vessels from all over the world. Follow your nose and the screech of seagulls down to the **fish market**, where fish has been landed and traded since the 13th century. ■ *The best time to see it is early in the morning, before 0800.*

At the northeast corner of the harbour is the old fishing village of **Footdee** (pronounced 'Fittie'), which is interesting to explore and an easy walk from Market Street, via Regent and Waterloo Quays and York Street, or south from the Beach Esplanade. Ask at the tourist office about guided walks, or pick up one of their leaflets.

At the southern end of Market Street, North Esplanade leads to **Duthie Park**, a 10-minute bus ride from town, on the banks of the Dee. The park features a beautiful rose garden, known as 'Rose Mountain', which is best seen in summer. Also in the park are the Winter Gardens, a gigantic hothouse full of tropical plants and birds. It covers an amazing two acres and is possibly the largest of its kind in Europe.

Old Aberdeen A 20-minute bus ride northwest of the city centre, on the banks of the Don, is the beautifully preserved suburb of Old Aberdeen, with its cobbled streets and peaceful atmosphere. An independent burgh until 1891, Old Aberdeen is clustered around **St Machar's Cathedral**, with its soaring twin spires. The cathedral was founded in the sixth century and is one of the oldest granite buildings in the city, dating from the 15th century. It is also one of the few examples in the country of a fortified cathedral. Legend has it that Machar, a follower of Columba, was sent to establish a church at a place near the sea where the river was shaped like the crook on a Bishop's crozier, hence its site. Inside, the heraldic ceiling is particularly impressive. ■ *T485988. Daily 0900-1700, free, services on Sun at 1100 and 1800.*

Next to the cathedral is the **Cruickshank Botanic Garden**, with beautiful floral displays. ■ *May-Sept Mon-Fri 0900-1630, Sat-Sun 1400-1700, Oct-Apr Mon-Fri 0900-1630. Free.*

A short walk south of St Machar's is **King's College**, founded in 1495 by Bishop Elphinstone. The most notable of the college buildings is the 16th-century **King's College Chapel**, with its distinctive crowned spire. The interior is remarkably well preserved and features some rare and beautiful medieval woodcarving in the ceiling and choir stalls. ■ *T272137. Mon-Fri 0900-1700. Free.* The **King's College Visitor Centre** houses a multimedia display on the university's often turbulent history. ■ *T273702. Mon-Sat 1000-1700, Sun 1200-1700. Free.* The are **guided walks** around the cathedral and University from June-August, leaving from King's College on Wednesday at 1900 and Sunday at 1430. The guides are extremely helpful and well informed.

Just to the north of St Machar's Cathedral, on the banks of the Don, is **Seaton Park**, another of the city's fine open spaces. North of the park, the Don is spanned by the **Brig o' Balgownie**, completed in the 14th century with money from the Common Good Fund. It is the oldest Gothic bridge in Scotland and over the years has charmed the likes of Byron. On the north bank of the Don is **Bridge of Don**, home to the city's two finest golf courses, the Royal Aberdeen and Murcar.

The beach Between the mouths of the rivers Don and Dee, and less than a mile east of Union Street, is Aberdeen's beach, a two-mile stretch of glorious golden sand. But though the northeast gets a large share of Scotland's sunshine, don't expect to sunbathe comfortably as the beach is exposed to the bitter North Sea winds. And as you watch parents coaxing their reluctant children into the water, note that a few miles offshore, oil rig workers are being warned of the dangers of perishing in these freezing seas.

At the southern end of the esplanade is **Aberdeen Fun Beach**, a huge leisure complex, with multi sports facilities, swimming pool, bar and cafés, ice arena, multiplex cinema, nightclub and Scotland's largest permanent fun fair. Nearby is Pittodrie Park, home of Aberdeen FC, once a major force in Scottish football, now more of a major farce. The northern end of the long, long beach is backed by a succession of golf links.

Essentials

Sleeping Aberdeen has plenty of accommodation but its hotels are relatively expensive. Though full of transient oil workers and business people during the week, many hotels offer discounts at the weekend, when prices fall by up to 50%. Note that single rooms are at premium and very poor value. The best value are the B&Bs and guesthouses, many of which can be found on Bon Accord St and Crown St, both running south off Union St, and along Great Western Rd. The cheapest options are the youth hostel and university residences left vacant during summer vacation. There's also a campsite in the suburbs. The tourist office has a free guide and will book accommodation.

L *Caledonian Thistle Hotel*, Union Tce, T640233, F641627. 78 rooms, superior city-centre hotel in a grand old Victorian building. Full facilities, friendly service and good restaurants. **L** *The Marcliffe at Pitfodils*, North Deeside Rd, T861000, reservations@marcliff.com. 42 rooms, this outstanding, luxurious country house hotel on the outskirts of town offers an unbeatable mix of baronial elegance and modern comforts, as well as exceptional hospitality and service, and superb cuisine.

Northeast Scotland

A *Simpson's Hotel Bar/Brasserie*, 59 Queen's Rd, T327777, address@simpsonshotel. com. 37 rooms, very stylish, modern hotel with a Mediterranean look and feel, the attached restaurant has won many plaudits for its excellent Scottish/international cuisine (see 'Eating').

C *Atholl Hotel*, 54 King's Gate, T323505, info@atholl-aberdeen.co.uk. 35 rooms, 1 of many elegant granite mansions in the West End, this one has an excellent reputation for its reliability, service and good food. **C** *Brentwood Hotel*, 101 Crown St, T595440, reservations@brentwood-hotel.demon.co.uk. 65 rooms, good value business hotel and therefore often full on weekdays, on a street full of similar hotels, but better than most, close to the action on Union St and its cellar bar does very good bar meals (see 'Bars'). **C** *Craiglynn Hotel*, 36 Fonthill Rd, T584050, www.craiglynn.co.uk. 8 rooms, intimate and comfortable Victorian house close to the town centre, also has a good reputation for its food. **C** *Mannofield Hotel*, 447 Great Western Rd, T315888, mannofield_hotel@tartan-collection.co.uk. 9 rooms, small, friendly and elegant hotel about a mile west of Union St.

D *Cults Hotel*, 328 North Deeside Rd, T/F867632. 6 rooms, 4 miles from the town centre on the A93 to Deeside and close to *Faraday's* restaurant (see 'Eating' below), good value. **D-E** *Speedbird Inns*, Argyll Rd, Dyce, T772884. 99 rooms, large, purpose-built hotel chain at the airport, good value.

There are many **guesthouses** on Bon Accord St, including: **E** *Applewood Guesthouse*, No 154, T580617, **E** *Crynoch Guesthouse*, No 164, T582743, and **E-F** *Denmore Guesthouse*, No 166, T587751. There are also numerous small, family-run guesthouses along Great Western Rd: **E** *Aberdeen Springdale Guesthouse*, No 404, T316561, **D-E** *Fourways Guesthouse*, No 435, T310218, **E** *Kildonan Guesthouse*, No 410, T316115, and **D-E** *The Noble Guesthouse*, No 376, T313678. Another good place to look is along King St, where you'll find **D-E** *Campbell's Guesthouse*, No 444, T625444, cam44@zetnet.co.uk, and the very highly rated **D-E** *The Jays Guesthouse*, No 422, T638295, jaysguesthouse@clara.net.

F *Aberdeen Youth Hostel* is at 8 Queen's Rd, T646988, a mile west of the bus and train stations (take buses 14 or 15 from the bus station). It's open all year till 0200 and has 116 beds.

Campus accommodation is available at the *University of Aberdeen* **C** *Kings Hall* (open all year) and **C** *Crombie Johnston Hall* (open Mar-Apr and Jun-Sept), both well situated in Old Aberdeen. Contact: conference office, Regent Walk, Old Aberdeen, T272664, j.m.pirie@admin.abdn.ac.uk. *Robert Gordon's University*, T262134, also has self-catering flats throughout the city. For more details check with the tourist office.

The nearest **campsite** is *Hazelhead Caravan Park & Campsite*, T321268, about 4 miles west of town on the A944, with a swimming pool nearby. Take buses 14 or 15 from town. Open Apr-Sept.

Eating There's no shortage of good places to eat in Aberdeen, though prices tend to be higher than elsewhere in the region. Many of the city's pubs and bars serve good value meals, though many of them don't serve food in the evening.

Expensive *Courtyard on the Lane*, Alford Lane, T213795, just off the west end of Union St. Highly rated bistro serving imaginative Scottish/European menu, with a more formal restaurant upstairs. Open Tue-Sat. *Faraday's*, 2 Kirk Brae, Cults, T869666, 4 miles from the town centre but well worth the trip. Superior traditional Scottish dishes served with consummate flair in a converted hydro-electric station, you could say it's a current favourite. Open Tue-Sat for lunch and Mon-Sat 1900-2130. *Gerard's*, 50 Chapel St, T639500. This *très cher* traditional French restaurant has been around for as long as anyone can remember and remains one of the best, the set meal is less of a strain on the bank balance. Open daily. *Silver Darlings Restaurant*, Pocra Quay, North Pier, Footdee, at the southern end of the Beach Esplanade, T576229. Highly recommended as serving the best seafood in town, also a great location overlooking the harbour entrance, best to book in advance. Closed Sat-Sun lunch. *Simpson's*, 59 Queen's Rd, T327777 (see also 'Sleeping'). Designer brasserie serving superb Scottish cuisine with an international flavour. Open daily.

Mid-range *Little Italy*, 79 Holborn St, T515227, near the west end of Union St. Usual pasta and pizza fare. Open late (till 2400 Mon-Wed and till 0200 Thur-Sat). *Owlie's*, Littlejohn St, T649267. French brasserie food with some interesting variations and good vegetarian/vegan options, very popular, so good atmosphere and good value. Open Mon-Sat. *Poldino's*, 7 Little Belmont St, T647777, one of the city's favourite Italian restaurants, so it's always busy. *The Royal Thai*, Crown Terr (off Crown St), T212922. Long-established Thai restaurant with wide-ranging menu. Open daily for lunch and 1900-2300. *The Wild Boar*, 19 Belmont St, T625357. Popular bar-bistro serving good value food, plenty of vegetarian choices, and just look at those cakes! Open daily.

Cheap *Ashvale*, 46 Great Western Rd, T596981. The northeast's most famous, and best, fish and chips, quite simply unmissable, this is the original branch and it's huge, with seating for 300, also takeaway. Open daily till late. Another superb chippie, some say better, is *The New Dolphin* on Chapel St. Mostly takeaway and open till 0100 (0300 at weekends). *Carmine's Pizza*, 32 Union Terr, T624145. Best pizza in town and excellent value 3-course lunches. Open Mon-Sat 1200-1730. *The Lemon Tree*, 5 West North St, T642230. Café inside the excellent arts centre (see also 'Entertainment'). Relaxed and laid-back place for a light vegetarian lunch, or coffee and cakes. Open Wed-Sun 1200-1500.

Like most busy ports, Aberdeen has a large transient population with lots of cash to spend. Consequently, its numerous loud, flashy bars and traditional pubs are usually packed with people out for a good time.

Bars

There are lots of trendy bars in Justice Mill Lane, off the West End of Union St, which fall in and out of fashion, but *Bex* is a perennial fave. *Café Society*, 9 Queen's Rd, opposite the youth hostel. A bit of an oil workers' pick-up joint but has a good beer garden and serves food till 2200. *Cocky Hunters*, 504 Union St. Very popular with students and young professionals and features regular live music. *The Globe*, 13 North Silver St. Down-to-earth café-bar which serves decent food at lunchtime. *Ma Cameron's Inn*, Little Belmont St. The city's oldest pub, though the old bit now constitutes only a small section, serves food at lunch and early evening. In the same street is *The Old Town School*, which is more of a modern theme bar but has a good selection of ales and does food. *O'Neill's*, 9 Back Wynd. An Irish theme pub which serves decent grub, a good selection of Irish beers, stout and whiskeys, and has live folk music at weekends. Wild club upstairs (see below). *The Prince of Wales*, 7 St Nicholas Lane. Just off Union St. Probably the best-known pub in the city, with a great selection of real ales and a real flagstone floor, also does very cheap bar food, gets very crowded. *Under the Hammer*, North Silver Street, along from *The Globe*, a basement wine bar which attracts a more mature crowd. Open evenings only.

Aberdeen also has numerous nightclubs to choose from, most of which close at 0200. Pick of the bunch is *Ministry of Sin*, 16 Dee St, T211661, off Union St. The faithful

Nightclubs

Northeast Scotland

congregate in this converted church for a heavenly mix of cool sounds and atmosphere. Popular with students and oldies. Often has big-name guest DJs and open 7 days. *The Works*, 9 Belmont St. Subterranean and sub-twenties, sweaty and lively kind of a place. Open Thur-Sat till 0200. *Oh'Henry's*, 20 Adelphi Close, just off Union St. Very studenty and therefore very retro (70s and 80s). *The Pelican* at the *Metro Hotel*, Market St. Basement club featuring live indie bands and guest DJs. Open Thur-Sat. *O'Neill's*, 9 Back Wynd. Upstairs in Irish theme pub. Nominal cover charge gets you a wild, raucous night of Irish music till 0200. Lots of stamina needed hence the younger crowd.

Entertainment Details of what's on can be found in the tourist office's free listings guide. Tickets for most plays and concerts can be booked at the **box office**, next to the Music Hall on Union St, T641122. Open Mon-Sat 1000-1800.

Cinema Among the city's mainstream cinemas is *Virgin*, T572228, a huge 9-screen complex on Beach Esplanade, and the *Odeon*, T916422, on Justice Mill Lane.

Theatre *His Majesty's*, Rosemount Viaduct, T637788. Aberdeen's main theatre, with a programme featuring opera, ballet, musicals and panto. *Music Hall*, Union St, T632508. The main venue for classical music concerts, as well as big-name comedy acts. *Capitol Theatre*, 431 Union St, T583141. Venue for smaller touring rock and pop bands. *Aberdeen Arts Centre*, 33 King St, T635208. Stages a variety of theatrical productions and exhibitions, and also shows arthouse movies. *The Lemon Tree*, 5 West North St, T642230. The hub of the city's arts scene with a wide and varied programme of events, including live jazz and folk, comedy and contemporary drama. Also has a good café/bar-restaurant (see 'Eating').

Sport **Swimming pools** *Aberdeen Fun Beach* has a swimming pool with flumes and slides for kids. For serious swimming, try *Bon Accord Baths*, T587920, on Justice Mill Lane.

Tour operators *Grampian Heritage Tours*, T01358-789513, run various day tours around the region, leaving from the tourist office. Tickets also from tourist office. *STA Travel*, 30 Kirkgate, T658222.

Transport **Air** There are domestic flights to and from London Heathrow and Luton, Manchester, Belfast, Orkney and Shetland. Also international departures to the Netherlands, Norway, Denmark, Faroe Islands, Malta, Cyprus, Spain and Portugal. See also 'Ins and outs' (page 357).

Boat *P&O* ferries, T572615, have daily evening departures (Mon-Fri) to **Lerwick** on Shetland. The trip takes 14-20 hrs. From Jun-Aug there are departures on Tue and Sat to **Stromness** on Orkney; Sat only the rest of the year. See also under **Orkney & Shetland** (page 554).

Bus *Scottish Citylink* runs direct buses to **Dundee** (2 hrs, £6.50), **Perth** (2 hrs 30 mins, £9), **Edinburgh** (4 hrs, £13), **Stirling** (3 hrs 30 mins, £12.80) and **Glasgow** (4 hrs 30 mins, £13.30). *Bluebird Buses*, T212266, is the major local bus operator. Service No 10 goes every hour to **Inverness** (£9.50) via **Huntly** and **Elgin**. Service No 201 goes every 30 mins (hourly on Sun) to **Banchory** (£2.40), every hour (Mon-Sat; less frequently on Sun) to **Ballatar** (£5.50) and several times daily to **Braemar**. There are also buses to **Stonehaven** (Service No 103; £2.40), **Alford** (Service No 220; £4.50), **Peterhead** (No 263; £3.50), **Fraserburgh** (Nos 267/268; £4.25) and **Ellon** (Nos 290/291). A Country Bus Rover Ticket gives unlimited travel on *Bluebird Buses* and costs £9.50 for a day. For more details pick up a free copy of the *Aberdeenshire & Moray Public Transport Guide* at the bus station or tourist office, or call the Public Transport Unit, T664581.

Train There are services to **Edinburgh** (2 hrs 30 mins, £32), **Glasgow** (2 hrs 45 mins, £35.10), **Dundee** (1 hr 15 mins, £16.40), **Perth** (1 hr 45 mins, £19.50), **Stirling** (2 hrs 15 mins, £29) and **Inverness** (2 hrs 15 mins, £18.50).

Bike hire *Aberdeen Cycle Centre*, 188 King St, T644542. *Alpine Bikes*, 64 Holburn St, T211455. From £12 per day. Open daily. **Car hire** *Budget*, Powis Terr, Great Northern Rd, T488770; also at the airport, T771777. *Arnold Clark*, Girdleness Rd, T249159. *Thrifty*, 76 Huntly St, T621033.

Airlines *British Airways*, T0345-222111. *British Midland*, T725779. *EasyJet*, T0990-292929. *Gill Airways*, 64 Newlands Cres, T0191-214-6666. *KLMUK*, T0990-750900. *SAS*, T770220. *Servisair*, T722331. **Banks** All the major banks have branches with ATMs on and around Union St. **Currency exchange:** *Thomas Cook*, 335-337 Union St, T212271. Open Mon-Sat 0930-1730; or the tourist office on Broad St. *American Express* office at *Lunn Poly*, 3-5 St Nicholas St, T633119. Open Mon-Fri 0900-1730, Sat 0900-1700. **Communications** Internet facilities at the Central Library, also at *RSC Internet*, 15 Marischal St, T585113. The main **post office** is in the St Nicholas Centre, T633065. **Medical facilities** *Aberdeen Royal Infirmary*, T681818, is on Foresthill, northeast of the town centre. It has a 24-hr A&E. **Pharmacy**: *Boots*, 161 Union St, T211592. Open Mon-Sat 0800-1800. **Useful addresses** Left luggage: 24-hr lockers at the train station. **Police:** Queen St, T639111.

Directory

South Aberdeenshire

The main A90 runs north from Dundee to Aberdeen and passes through the Howe of the Mearns, an agricultural district so evocatively described by local author, Lewis Grassic Gibbon in his brilliant trilogy A Scots Quair. *His home can be visited at Arbuthnott. The coastal route (A92) from Dundee runs north from Montrose and meets the A90 by the little fishing port of Stonehaven, which is close to the dramatic ruins of Dunnotar Castle, one of the area's main attractions. Other places of interest include Fasque House, family home of Victorian prime minister Gladstone.*

Northeast Scotland

Montrose to Stonehaven

North of Montrose on the A92, is the little coastal village of St Cyrus, whose church steeple is seen to great effect for miles around. Thanks to a bequest in the will of one John Orr, in 1844, four local brides benefit each year in the most unusual way. The eldest, the youngest, the tallest and the shortest (all of them carefully measured by the local minister) receive a dowry from the interest on the money which he left for that purpose. Thus they are known as The Dowry Brides. The annual interest is in fact divided in five. The final fifth is used to buy comforts for the poor. The town is also known for its strict enforcement of the 30 mile per hour speed limit (this applies to Kincardine O'Neil on Deeside too). There's a wonderful sandy **beach** here, and the **National Nature Reserve**, complete with marine-life tank and visitor centre, is interesting, T830736, May-Sept.

St Cyrus
Phone code: 01674
Colour map 4, grid B5

Sleeping **E** *Kirkside Bothy*, near the beach, T830780, Apr-Oct. There's also a **camp-site** at *East Bowstrips Caravan Park*, T850328. At Lauriston, turn right at the *Bush Hotel* for Milton Haven.

Transport *Bluebird Buses*, service No 101 between Stonehaven and Montrose, pass through St Cyrus and Johnshaven hourly Mon-Fri (less frequently Sat-Sun).

Johnshaven
Phone code: 01561
Colour map 4, grid B5

A few miles further on is the old fishing village of Johnshaven, a thriving fishing port until quite recently, and in the early 18th century probably the largest in Scotland. The village is unusual because of the great number of people who are called McBay. They are all mostly descended from two cousins, Long Ned and Little Ned, one of whom had seven sons, and the other 10. Johnshaven is a good spot for buying lobster and crab, and its annual **Fish Festival** is getting more and more popular. It takes place on either the first or second Saturday in August. The date depends upon the tides, which have to be suitable for visiting craft. There's accommodation in the village at **E** *Ellington B&B*, Station Place, T362756.

The three-mile walk north along the shore to **Gourdon**, is one of the most pleasant and one of the easiest in the area. Very often, cormorants bask in the sun out on the rocks, spreading their wings to dry. Rather less often dolphins tumble past, their fins cutting a path through the water. In Gourdon you can buy fish from several fish houses on the harbour.

Inverbervie
Colour map 4, grid B6

A few miles further on from Johnshaven lies Inverbervie, birthplace of Hercules Linton, designer of the *Cutty Sark*. The village is probably better known for the *Bervie Chipper* which was recently voted the best fish and chip shop in the UK. You can either eat in or takeaway (either way it's excellent value); just don't leave town without finding out what all the fuss is about.

By decree of King David, son of Robert the Bruce, Inverbervie is a Royal Burgh and residents enjoy several privileges, such as free fishing in the local river. Many anglers know this, but the fish seem to know as well as they are not very plentiful. For full-blooded **fishing** make for either the North Esk River at Edzell (see page 352) or somewhere along its length before it flows out to the sea by the two bridges just north of Montrose. The old bridge in Inverbervie, built in 1799, is the oldest single span bridge in the British Isles. To see it, turn left to the north of the village, just before the memorial to Linton. In the village square is *Mingei*, which has a good selection of Japanese and European antiques.

Just to the south of the village, on the left heading north, is the **Mill of Benholm** (pronounced 'Ben-um'). This is a water mill, powered by the water from the miller's dam. There's also a little tearoom and an easy signed walk nearby.

Transport *Bluebird Buses,* service No 101 between Stonehaven and Montrose, pass through Inverbervie and Kinneff (see below) hourly Mon-Fri (less frequently Sat-Sun).

Arbuthnott
Phone code: 01561
Colour map 4, grid B6

Five miles inland from Inverbervie, between the A92 and A90, is Arbuthnott, birthplace of the amazingly prolific author Lewis Grassic Gibbon (1901-35) and where he spent his formative years. From 1928 till his untimely death at the age of 34, he wrote an astonishing 17 books. *Sunset Song*, the first part of the *Scots Quair* trilogy, is his best-known work. It remains one of the true classics of Scottish literature and is an absolute must for anyone exploring this area. The **Grassic Gibbon Centre**, at the east end of the village, traces his life and points out the places he wrote about. There is also a café and bookshop. ■ *T361668. Apr-Oct daily 1000-1630. £2, £1.25 child/concession.* Grassic Gibbon is also buried here, under his real name of James Leslie Mitchell, in a corner of the churchyard, about half a mile away at the other end of the village. The parish church itself is one of the few intact pre-Reformation churches in Scotland and is notable for its 13th-century chancel. Near the centre is **Arbuthnott House**, a fortified manorhouse dating from the 15th century. ■ *The gardens are open daily all year 0900-1700, the house on certain days in the summer. Details from Bervie Information and Activity Centre in the main street.*

A few miles north of Inverbervie, on the road to Stonehaven, you'll see a sign on the right to the **Old Church**, Kinneff, where the Scottish Crown Jewels – the Royal Regalia – were hidden in 1651 to protect them from Cromwell's greedy paws. Here they lay buried under the church floor for nearly 10 years. It's a mile and a half down to the church, where there's a memorial to the Reverand James Grainger, who hid the treasures and thus saved the 'Honours of Scotland': the crown, sceptre and sword. There are various stories of how they were smuggled out of nearby Dunnottar Castle (see below). In *Tales of a Grandfather*, Sir Walter Scott relates how Christian Grainger, the minister's wife, accompanied by her serving maid, carried them out of Dunnottar in collaboration with the Governor and his wife. Another version tells how they were lowered on ropes down the castle wall. There, on the beach, a fishwife gathering seaweed hid the sword in a bundle of flax and the crown in her creel (used for catching lobsters). So, the 'Honours' were saved and are now displayed in Edinburgh castle.

Kinneff
Colour map 4, grid B6

Just to the north of Kinneff, at **Crawton**, is the **Fowlsheugh RSPB Reserve**. The spectacular 250-ft high cliffs are home to tens of thousands of seabirds, including shags, guillemots, kittiwakes, fulmars, razorbills and puffins. They're best seen in early summer (May-July). You can see them from the top of the cliffs, but take great care. Better still, take a boat trip from Stonehaven (May-July on Tuesday and Friday at 1830).

Stonehaven

The solid and tidy old fishing port of Stonehaven lies 15 miles south of Aberdeen, where the coastal A92 joins the main A90 from Dundee. Nowadays, Stonehaven is better known as a seaside resort attracting a fair few visitors in the summer months. Not least of the town's attractions is its wonderful Olympic-sized, outdoor, heated salt-water swimming pool, one of only two in Scotland (the other is at Gourock). It is kept at a constant 82°F. The pool is open only during the summer, from 1100-1930 (there's also a midnight swim; ask for details at the tourist office). By the harbour is the **Tolbooth**, built around 1600, and the town's oldest building. It now houses a seafood restaurant (see below) and local history **museum**. ■ *Jun-Sept, Mon and Thur-Sat 1000-1200 and 1400-1700, Wed and Sun 1400-1700. Free.* Another attraction is the town's highly respected **folk festival**, held over three days in mid-July.

Phone code: 01569
Colour map 4, grid B6
Population: 9,000

Away from the harbour and old town, is the market square, where you'll find banks with ATMs and most of the shops. Just off the square is *Just Scottish*, an excellent arts and crafts shop (open Monday-Saturday 1000-1730). Everything is quite central, except for the train station, which is a 15-minute walk from the square. The **tourist office** is at 66 Allardyce St, T762806, the main street past the square. ■ *Apr, May and Oct Mon-Sat 1000-1300 and 1400-1700; Jun and Sept Mon-Sat 1000-1300 and 1400-1800, Sun 1300-1800; Jul-Aug Mon-Sat 1000-1900, Sun 1300-1900.*

It's possible to head straight from Stonehaven to **Deeside** by taking the A957 (known as 'The Slug') to **Crathes** (see page 372).

The main reason for coming to Stonehaven is to visit the impressive and impregnable Dunnottar Castle, two miles south of town, just off the A92. Dating from the 12th century, this ancient ruin was a stronghold for the Earls Marischal of Scotland. Standing 160ft high, with the sea on three sides and a huge drop and 'curtain wall' on the fourth, it is not far short of an island. It is worth devoting considerable time to exploring one of the country's most outstanding castles, which is approached by a steep 400-yard walk from the car park. So dramatic is its setting, that it was used as the backdrop for Zeffirelli's

Dunnottar Castle

Northeast Scotland

film version of *Hamlet*, starring Mel Gibson. But the fortress has a dramatic and bloody history all of its own. In 1297, William Wallace (another of Mel Gibson's characters, strangely enough) burnt alive an entire English garrison here; later, in 1685, a large group of Covenanters were imprisoned, tortured and then left to rot in the castle dungeons. The castle was reduced to its present state in 1716, during reprisals for the Earl Marischal's Jacobite activities. ■ *T762173. Easter-Oct Mon-Sat 0900-1800, Sun 1400-1700; Nov-Mar Mon-Fri 0900-1700, £3, £1 children. The castle can also be reached by a footpath from Stonehaven, contact the tourist office for the relevant leaflet.*

Sleeping   The tourist office has a list of accommodation. A couple of recommended places are **C** *Heugh Hotel*, Westfield Rd, T762379, and **D** *Arduthie House*, Ann St, T762381.

Eating   The best place to eat in the area is the superb *Lairhillock Inn & Restaurant*, a few miles north of town at Netherley, on the B979, T01569-730001, www.welcome.to/laihillock. This charming old coaching inn offers excellent local produce in beautifully rustic surroundings at mid-range prices. Also has rooms. In town, the *Tolbooth Restaurant*, T762287, upstairs from the museum on the harbour, is expensive but worth it for the excellent seafood. Open for dinner only, closed Sun. A cheaper alternative is a bar meal in any of the hotels, such as the *Ship Inn* and *Marine Hotel* at the harbour, or the *Royal Hotel* on Allardyce St.

Transport   Stonehaven is on the Aberdeen-Dundee rail line and there are regular **trains** in either direction. It is also served by **buses** 101, 107 and 707 from **Aberdeen**. The 101 continues to **Montrose**, passing through the coastal villages described above.

The Howe of the Mearns to Deeside

Colour map 4, grid B5   Fourteen miles south of Stonehaven, just off the main A90 is **Laurencekirk**. A few miles east, off the tiny B9120, is the **Hill of Garvock** (908ft), which gives great views over the Howe of the Mearns. It is topped by the Tower of Johnston (which lies up a footpath), built to commemorate Britain's victory over Napoleon in the Peninsula Wars. On the other side of the hill is a depression called the **Sheriff's Kettle**. Here, at Baileys Farm, in 1420, disgruntled local lairds boiled the Sheriff and 'supped the brew'.

Four miles west of Laurencekirk on the B9120 is the village of **Fettercairn**, famous for its handsome arch, built in 1861 following a visit from Queen Victoria. A mile west of the village is the **distillery**, one of the oldest in Scotland, with free guided tours and a 'dram' at the end. ■ *T01561-340205. May-Sept, Mon-Sat 1000-1630.* The village holds its annual **Highland Games** on the first Saturday in July. They're authentic and the setting is lovely.

A few miles north on the B974 is the 18th-century **Fasque House**, erstwhile home of four-times British prime minister, William Gladstone. The family still live in the west wing. Closed at the outbreak of the Second World War, and only reopened in the 1970s, the faded grandeur of the place is wonderfully tangible. Though the house is interesting because of its historic connections with the former prime minister, it is also an excellent example of an 'Upstairs-Downstairs' country house and gives a fascinating insight into the lifestyle of a wealthy Victorian landowner. The estate also includes extensive grounds filled with deer. ■ *T01561-340569. May-Sept daily 1100-1730. £3.50, £2.50 concession.*

Beyond Fasque, the B974 wends its way through rich farming country, with its distinctive red soil, up to the **Cairn O' Mount** (1,492ft) and on to **Banchory**. Before you start the actual steep ascent, the road to the right, over a water splash, leads to the **Glen of Drumtochty**. This is a delightful detour,

Northeast Scotland

ending up in the little town of **Auchenblae**. If you decide not to divert and feel like some refreshment, park on the left and climb the steps to the *Clatterin' Brig tearoom*. Opened originally by a Bowes-Lyon, kinswoman of Queen Elizabeth the Queen Mother, it is open all year round. When you eventually reach the summit of the Cairn O' Mount, stop for a moment to admire the view. The cairn dates from 2000 BC. In common with the Devil's Elbow on the A93 between Braemar and Perth, this road was once a testing challenge for early motorists, though nowadays, the ascent is easy.

Deeside

The river Dee rises in the Cairngorms and flows down through the surrounding   *Colour map 4, grid A4-6*
hills, eastwards to the sea at Aberdeen. The valley of the Dee is known as Deeside,
or rather Royal Deeside, for its connections with the royal family, who have
holidayed here, at Balmoral, since Queen Victoria first arrived in 1848. Ori-
ginally, Queen Victoria and Prince Albert were looking for an estate further west,
but were advised that the Deeside climate would be better for Albert's delicate
constitution. The queen fell in love with this area and its people, and following
Albert's death she sought out the company of straight-talking northerners, prefer-
ring their down-to-earth honesty to the two-faced toadies she endured at court.

    Today, Deeside's royal associations have made it the tourist honeypot of the
northeast, but the royal presence has also saved it from mass development.
There's an air of understated affluence and refinement in the villages strung out
along the A93 that runs along the north bank of the Dee and, as well as the obvi-
ous attraction of Balmoral, there are many other fine examples of baronial cas-
tles. Deeside is also a great area for various outdoor activities, such as hiking in
the surrounding mountains, mountain biking, canoeing and skiing.

Ins and outs

All the main tourist attractions on Deeside can be reached by **bus** from Aberdeen.   **Getting around**
Bluebird Bus service No 201, T01224-212266, runs every 30 minutes (Mon-Sat) to Banchory, via Cults and Crathes, and every hour to Braemar, via Aboyne, Dinnet, Ballater and Crathie (for Balmoral). On Sun, the bus runs every hour and two hours respectively. See also under Aberdeen 'Transport' (page 366). If you wish to explore Deeside along a less popular route (though even in the summer, crowds are never great) take the B976 along the south bank of the river Dee.

For details of the **Castle Trail**, **Victorian Heritage Trail** and **Deeside Tourist Route**,   **Information**
contact the tourist office in Aberdeen, or in any of the towns along the way.

Aberdeen to Banchory

The first sight of interest heading west from Aberdeen is **Drum Castle**, three   *Colour map 4, grid A5/6*
miles west of **Peterculter** (pronounced 'Petercooter'). It's a combination of a 13th-century square tower, Jacobean mansion house and later Victorian additions. It was given to one William de Irvine by Robert the Bruce for service rendered at Bannockburn and was in the family's hands for over 650 years, until taken over by the NTS in 1976. There's a beautiful walled garden and a trail through the 100-acre ancient Wood of Drum which forms part of the castle grounds. ■ *T01330-811204. Easter and 1 May-3 Oct, daily 1330-1730, weekends in Oct 1330-1730, gardens same dates daily 1000-1800, grounds all year daily 0930 till dusk. £4.20.*

Northeast Scotland

A few miles southeast of Peterculter is its sister village, **Maryculter** (pronounced 'Marycooter') where you'll find **Storybook Glen**, the northeast's answer to Disneyland. This very attractive and tasteful 'theme park' is a great place to take the kids and features giant tableaux and lifesize characters from many childhood fairy tales and nursery rhymes. ■ *T01224-732491. Daily Mar-Oct 1000-1800, Nov-Feb weekends only 1100-1600. £3.50, £1.75 child.*

Crathes Castle & gardens Fifteen miles west of Aberdeen, where the A93 meets the A957 from Stonehaven, is Crathes Castle, a perfect 'fairytale' castle built over 40 years in the mid-16th century. The turreted tower-house is still furnished with many period pieces and wall hangings, and is notable for its superb painted ceilings.

There are narrow spiral staircases leading to tiny rooms, one of which is said to be inhabited by the obligatory ghost. The castle is well worth exploring but is almost overshadowed by the exceptional gardens which shouldn't be missed. There are no fewer than eight of them, so take your time. There's also a visitor centre, restaurant and shop. ■ *T01330-844525. 1 Apr-31 Oct, daily 1100-1730 (last admission 1645), grounds and garden open all year daily 0900-dusk. £4.80 castle and grounds combined.*

Opposite the castle gates is *The Milton Restaurant*, T01330-844566, serving excellent, moderately priced food daily till 2200 (lunch only on Sunday).

Banchory

Phone code: 01330
Colour map 4, grid A5

Banchory makes a very pleasant base for exploring the area, with the river Dee burbling through, but there's not a great deal to do here, apart from salmon fishing, which is popular in these parts. You can watch salmon leaping spectacularly at the **Bridge of Feugh**, to the south of town. There is a sad tale, though, of a lady-in-waiting who was staying at Balmoral when the royal family were in residence some years ago. She was standing fishing in the river, in quite deep water, and wearing chest-height waders, when the sovereign rode by. Seeing the king, she curtsied, whereupon the water flowed quickly into her waders and she sank beneath the water and drowned.

The **tourist office** is in the local museum, on Bridge Street, behind the High Street. ■ *T822000. Easter-May and Oct, Mon-Sat 1000-1300 and 1400-1700, Sun 1300-1700; Jun and Sept Mon-Sat 1000-1300 and 1400-1800, Sun 1300-1800; Jul-Aug Mon-Sat 1000-1300 and 1400-1900, Sun 1300-1900. It can provide information on walking and fishing in the area.*

Sleeping & eating There are some very fine places to stay in and around Banchory. Three miles north of town on the A980 is the very wonderful **L** *Raemoir House Hotel*, T824884. A country mansion set in 3,500 acres of woods and parkland, 20 rooms.

Another excellent choice is the **A-B** *Banchory Lodge Hotel*, T822625, a sporting lodge-type hotel superbly situated on the banks of the river near the town centre. It's also a great place to stop and have a bite to eat for lunch. The river runs past the lawn and you can watch the salmon leap as you perhaps enjoy the fruits of their labour. Also recommended is the **B** *Tor-na-Coille Hotel*, T822242, tornacoille@btinternet.com, outside town on the Inchmarlo Rd. This tastefully furnished Victorian country house hotel is set in lovely grounds and boasts a considerable reputation for its modern Scottish cooking (lunch mid-range; dinner expensive).

There are also plenty of good **guesthouses** and B&Bs, including **E** *Towerbank House*, at 93 High St, T824798, and **D-E** *The Old West Manse*, 71 Station Rd, T822202. Ten miles northwest of Banchory, near Tornaveen on the B9119, is **F** *The Wolf's*

Hearth, T01339-883460, open all year, an independent hostel in a converted farm steading which makes a great base for walking or cycling in the hills. There's also a **campsite**, *Silver Ladies Caravan Park*, T822800, at Strachan, just outside Banchory.

Aside from the hotels listed above, the best place to **eat** is probably the *Burnett Arms Hotel* on the High St, T824944. There's also *Le Bistroquet*, which has a varied menu.

Adventure Scotland, T850332, dlatham@netcomuk.co.uk, is a Banchory-based com- **Tour operators** pany offering a wide range of adventure activities, including white-water rafting, mountain biking, skiing and hiking.

From Banchory you can head northwest on the A980 to Alford, in the Don Val- **Lumphanan** ley (see page 379). Roughly halfway is the village of Lumphanan, which was *Colour map 4, grid A5* thought to be the burial place of Macbeth, the Scottish king so misrepresented by Shakespeare (he is actually buried on Iona). **Macbeth's Cairn** is instead a pre-historic cairn. Just to the south of the village is the **Peel Ring**, a 12th-century Motte, or castle mound, and one of Scotland's earliest medieval sites.

Thirteen miles west of Banchory, one the A93, is the attractive little village of **Aboyne** Aboyne, where there's modest fishing in a little loch just to the northeast. *Colour map 4, grid A5* There are a couple of very good places to eat in and around Aboyne. In the vil-lage itself is *The Black-faced Sheep*, T01339-887311, a coffee shop with excel-lent home baking. A few miles back down the road to Banchory is *The White Cottage*, T01339-886265, an award-winning restaurant which uses the very best local produce in its creative Scottish cooking (expensive; closed Monday). South of Aboyne, in **Glen Tanar** (see 'Walks in Deeside' below), is *Glen Tanar Equestrian Centre*, T01339-886448, which offers riding in the forests and hills.

A few miles further on is Dinnet. In the **Muir of Dinnet National Nature** **Dinnet** **Reserve** you can explore the Burn o' Vat, a sheltered valley which attracts *Colour map 4, grid A4* many butterflies and dragonflies. During the walk, you'll come to a huge circu-lar stone chamber and, in nearby Loch Kinord, there are crannogs, which are ancient man-made islands.

Ballater and Balmoral

The neat little town of Ballater is proud of its royal connections. You can buy *Phone code: 01339* meat from the butcher with his 'By Royal Appointment' sign, or clothes from *Colour map 4, grid A4* royal outfitters. This is where Lizzie and Phil pop down to the shops for a pint of milk or perhaps to choose a video. Ever since Queen Victoria first arrived by train from Aberdeen in 1848, the royal family have been spending their holi-days here in their summer residence, Balmoral. She was not amused at the prospect of having an unsightly rail station on her doorstep, so the line ended eight miles east, at Ballater. The line has been closed for some time, but you can still visit the old train station, which now houses an elegant tearoom.

The royals are not the only famous summer visitors. The poet Byron (who attended Aberdeen Grammar School) spent many childhood summer holidays at Ballaterach, a few miles east of Ballater. He had a narrow escape when he slipped and nearly fell into the fast flowing stream at the Linn of Dee, beyond Braemar. He was rescued just in time and went on to reminisce in *The Island*,

He who first met the Highlands' swelling blue
Will love each peak which shows a kindred hue.

Those beautiful hills of which Byron waxed poetic are Ballater's other great attraction. The town makes the ideal base for **hiking** (see below) as well as a number of other outdoor activities. Many of the walks set off from **Loch Muick** (pronounced 'Mick'), nine miles southwest of Ballater, at the head of Glen Muick. (For details, see 'Walks in Deeside' below). There's a visitor centre and car park at Spittal of Glenmuick. From here a track leads along the west shore of the loch to the lodge where Queen Victoria met John Brown. For guides and equipment for canoeing, climbing, mountain biking and skiing, contact *Adventure Scotland* in Banchory (see above).

The **tourist office** in Ballater is in Station Square, opposite the old station. ■ *T755306. Easter-May and Oct Mon-Sat 1000-1300 and 1400-1700, Sun 1300-1700; Jun and Sept Mon-Sat 1000-1300 and 1400-1800, Sun 1300-1800; Jul-Aug Mon-Sat 1000-1300 and 1400-1900, Sun 1300-1900.*

Balmoral Castle
Colour map 4, grid A4

Eight miles west of Ballater is the area's main attraction, Balmoral Castle. The 16th-century tower house, formerly owned by the local Gordon family, was bought for Queen Victoria by Prince Albert in 1852 and converted into today's baronial mansion. It has been the royal family's summer retreat ever since. Only the ballroom and the grounds are open to the likes of you and me, and only for three months of the year. **Pony trekking** and **pony cart rides** are available around the estate grounds and are favourite ways of enjoying the wonderful scenery. Opposite the castle gates is **Crathie Church**, which is used by the family when they're in residence. There's a small souvenir shop next to the main gates and a visitor centre which gives a lot of information on the castle and its owners. ■ *T742334. Mid-Apr to end Jul, daily 1000-1700 (closed on Sun in Apr-May). £3.50, £2.50 concession. Buses to Braemar from Aberdeen stop by the gates.*

Sleeping

There's plenty of accommodation in Ballater, from expensive hotels to reasonably priced B&Bs. Pick of the bunch is the **A-B** *Darroch Learg Hotel*, T755443, darroch.learg@exoams.wk.com, half a mile from town, off the A93 heading west to Braemar. 18 rooms, open Feb-Dec, friendly country house hotel with fine views and a reputation for superb food (expensive), good value. **A-B** *Stakis Craigendarroch*, T755858, on the Braemar Rd. 44 rooms, Victorian country house converted into a modern resort hotel with full leisure and sports facilities, 2 good restaurants. **B** *Balgonie Country House Hotel*, T/F755482, on the western outskirts of town, off the A93. 9 rooms, open Feb-Dec, friendly and comfortable country house hotel, excellent food (expensive). **C** *Glen Lui Hotel*, Invercauld Rd, T755402, sgeraud@glen-lui-hotel.co.uk. 19 rooms, another comfortable hotel offering fine food (lunch cheap; dinner mid-range). **E** *Deeside Hotel*, T755420, set back from the A93 heading out of town towards Braemar. Friendly, good value and good food (mid-range).

Among the many B&Bs is the recommended **E** *Inverdeen House*, 11 Bridge Square, T755759. French, German and Polish spoken, great breakfasts, no smoking. Also good is **E** *Moorside House*, T/F755492, on the Braemar Rd. There's a **campsite** at *Anderson Road Caravan Park*, T755727, open Apr-Oct.

Eating

Apart from the hotels listed above, there are lots of places to eat. Best of all is *The Green Inn*, T/F755701, on the green in the town centre. It boasts a well-deserved reputation as one of the very best restaurants in the region, classic Scottish cooking with an imaginative and health-conscious twist, expensive, open daily (closed Sun Oct-Mar), also has 3 rooms upstairs (**B-C** full board). Also good is the *Hayloft Restaurant*, T/F755999, on Bridge Square (lunch cheap-mid-range; dinner mid-range to expensive).

Braemar

Nine miles west of Balmoral, is Braemar, the final town on Deeside, lying at the foot of the awesome, brooding **Cairngorm** massif, which dominates the Eastern Highlands. Even at the height of summer you can see a dab of snow still lying in a hollow in the surrounding mountains, and Braemar is an excellent base for **hiking** (see below), and winter **skiing** at Glenshee (see page 282). It's an attractive little place, much loved by Queen Victoria and much visited during its annual **Braemar Gathering** (or games), which attracts tens of thousands of visitors each year, amongst them members of the royal family. ■ *The games are held on the first Sat in Sept. Booking is essential and tickets can be bought in advance from the Booking Secretary, BRHS, Coilacreich, Ballater, AB35 5UH, T755377. Or contact the tourist office for details.*

Phone code: 01339
Colour map 4, grid A3

Just north of the village, and well signposted, is **Braemar Castle**, dating from 1628. This impressive fortress was used by Hanoverian troops after the Jacobite Rising of 1745. It is L-shaped with a star-shaped defensive wall and a central round tower with a spiral stair. There are barrel-vaulted ceilings and an underground prison. The world's largest cairngorm (a semi-precious stone, a variety of quartz, which is yellow, grey or brown in colour) weighing 52 lbs is on display in the morning room. There's also a piece of tartan worn by Prince Charles Edward, Bonnie Prince Charlie. ■ *T741219. Mid-Apr to end Oct Sat-Thur 1000-1800. £2.50, £1 children.*

The **Braemar Highland Heritage Centre** in Balmoral Mews by the tourist office, includes informative talks (in several languages) on the area, an exhibition and shops. ■ *T741944. Daily Apr-Sept 0900-1800 (Jul-Aug till 2000), Oct-Mar 1000-1700. Free.*

A very scenic side trip from Braemar is to the **Linn of Dee**, six miles west of the village, at the end of the road. Here, the river thunders through a narrow gorge to spectacular effect. There are numerous walks from here along the river, or for the more adventurous, the famous **Lairig Ghru**, which runs through the Cairngroms to Aviemore (see below). Between the Linn of Dee and the tiny settlement of **Inverey**, a mile to the east, there's a very basic **youth hostel** (open mid-May to early October), which has no phone, so book through Braemar hostel (see below). A postbus runs in the afternoon (Monday-Saturday) from Braemar to the Linn of Dee, via the hostel.

The **tourist office** in Braemar is in Balmoral Mews, on Mar Road. ■ *T741600. Daily, Jan-May and Sept-Dec 1000-1700, Jun 0930-1800, Jul-Aug 0930-1900.* For rental of **ski** equipment, try the The *Braemar Ski School Hire*, in Victoria Hall on Glenshee Road.

Accommodation is hard to find before and during the Braemar Gathering, but at other times of the year there's plenty to choose from. Best of all is the **A** *Braemar Lodge Hotel*, T741627, on the outskirts of the village on the road south to Glenshee and Blairgowrie. There's also the **B** *Invercauld Arms Hotel*, T741605, and, on the Glenshee Rd, the **D-E** *Callater Lodge Hotel*, T741275, maria@callater.demon.co.uk, which is small and comfortable. There are plenty of guesthouses and B&Bs, including **E** *Schiehallion House*, T741679, open Jan-Oct, on Glenshee Rd, and **E** *Clunie Lodge*, T741330, on Cluniebank Rd. There's a *SYHA Youth Hostel*, T741659, open all year, at Corrie Feragie on Glenshee Rd, and also *Rucksacks*, 15 Mar Rd, T741517, a cheap and friendly bunkhouse that's popular with hikers and also rents out **mountain bikes**. There's **camping** at *Invercauld Caravan Site*, T741373, open Dec-Oct, on Glenshee Rd.

Sleeping & eating

The only real places to eat are the bars of the larger hotels, which are a bit on the expensive side. Otherwise, try the *Braemar Takeaway*, 14 Invercauld Rd, for some cheap stodge.

Northeast Scotland

Braemar Gathering

There has been a gathering (or games) of some sort at Braemar for 900 years, ever since Malcolm Canmore set contests for the local clans so that he could pick the strongest and bravest of men for his army. These events take place up and down the country throughout the summer but none are as famous, or well attended, as Braemar's. Queen Victoria attended in 1848 and the Gathering is still patronized by the royal family. Crowds come from all over the world to proclaim the monarch as Chieftain of the Braemar Gathering.

At the gathering the visitor will see contests in traditional Scottish events, such as tossing the caber, Highland dancing and bagpipe competitions and displays. There is an inter-services tug o' war championship, a medley relay race and a hill race up Morrone. The sounds of the massed pipes echoing around the encircling heather-clad hills and a plethora of tartan also help to make this a real tourist highlight. The royal connection (and the crowds) apart, many other local communities hold similar games.

Walks in Deeside

Ballater and Braemar are ideal bases for walking in the surrounding Grampian Mountains, and if you feel like 'bagging a Munro' (ie climbing a mountain over 3,000ft), there are some close at hand.

Lochnagar

OS Landranger No 44

The best walk in the area is to the summit of Lochnagar (3,786ft), made famous by Prince Charles in the book he wrote for his brothers when young, *The Old Man of Lochnagar*. The noble and mysterious mountain dominates the Royal Forest of Balmoral and takes its name from a small loch at its foot (it's also known as the White Mounth). This fine granite mass is approached from the car park by the Rangers' **visitor centre** at Spittal of Glen Muick. For information on their free guided walks, T755377. The path to the top is well trodden and well marked, though steep as you near the summit. It's 10 miles there and back, so allow a full day for the climb. You'll need to be properly equipped and take a map.

Northeast Scotland

Cambus o' May & Morrone

OS Landranger No 43

An easier walk is to Cambus o' May, on the river, about four miles east of Ballater. It's a great spot for a picnic, or to swim in the river, or to enjoy a stroll along the riverbank. A good walk from Braemar is to the summit of Morrone (2,818ft), the mountain to the southwest. The walk takes about four hours in total.

Lairig Ghru

A much more strenuous walk is the famous Lairig Ghru, an ancient route through the Cairngorms which passes between Ben Macdui and Braeriach. The route starts from Inverey, heads up Glen Dee and through Rothiemurchus Forest to Aviemore (see page 486).

Glen Tanar to Glen Esk

OS Landranger No 44

Another good climb is the route up **Mount Keen** (3,077ft), the most easterly Munro, which lies between Deeside and Glen Esk, the loveliest of the Angus glens (see page 352). Again, you should allow a whole day for this expedition.

It can be approached from the Visitor Centre in **Glen Tanar**, at the end of the little road that runs southwest off the B976, across the river from Aboyne. You can climb to the summit and return by the same route, but if your party has two cars, it is well worth walking over to Glen Esk, 14 miles away. Drive around to the Invermark car park at the head of Glen Esk and park one car there. From Glen Tanar follow the old drove road which at times runs with the

Mounth road. Skirting the Home Farm with its Arboretum and its dammed lake, the fairly flat track winds along Glen Tanar through the forest for about four miles. Then comes the Halfway Hut, used for rest and repast by former shooting parties. You will pass shooting butts *en route*. The next stretch is through open country with the **Clachan Yell** (626ft) on the left.

The walk proper then begins to take shape. Cross the stone bridge of Etnach, and then the path begins to lead up to the Shiel of Glentanar. The second bridge forks left and the track heads for the summit. The rough path continues along a ridge, the shoulder of Mount Keen. From the summit with its stone marker, Dinnet and its two lakes is visible to the north, and the river Esk glints its way down the valley to the south. Watch out for adders around here. On the descent, you'll pass the **Queen's Well**, used by Queen Victoria when she and her party went down to Fettercairn posing as a wedding party. The well is decorated with a graceful granite crown which was erected in 1861. The royal party covered much of the climb on hill ponies. The stone arch at Fettercairn commemorates this visit. Perhaps the queen saw the stone, dated 1799, in the ancient graveyard by the ruined church at Loch Lee, which reads:

The grave, great teacher, to one level brings
Heroes and beggars, galley slaves and kings.

The Queen's Well

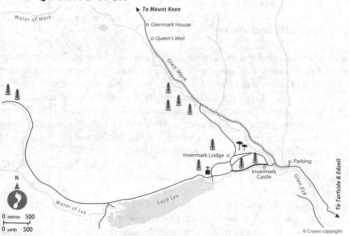

The Don Valley

Colour map 4, grid A4/5

North of Royal Deeside is the lesser-known valley of the Don, Aberdeen's second river. This relatively little-visited corner of the northeast is a historian's and archaeologist's dream, as it's littered with medieval castles, Pictish stone circles and Iron Age hillforts. A quarter of all Britain's stone circles can be found here (if you look hard enough). Local tourist offices have free leaflets on the region's archaeological sites, with background information and details of how to find them. The main sites are included in the tourist board's 'Stone Circle Trail'. There's also a well-signposted 'Castle Trail', which includes the area's main castles. One of these castles, Corgarff, stands at the southern end of the notorious Lecht Road, which runs from Cock Bridge to Tomintoul. This area, known as The Lecht, is one of Scotland's main ski centres.

Ins and outs

Getting around Getting around the Don Valley without your own transport is not easy. There are regular **trains** and **buses** to Inverurie, from Aberdeen and Inverness. *Bluebird Buses*, T01224-212266, No 220 runs regularly every day to Alford (one hour 15 minutes, £4.50), and No 219 runs from Alford to Strathdon (Mon-Sat). Services beyond Strathdon are virtually non-existant.

Inverurie and around

Phone code: 01467
Colour map 4, grid A5

The solid farming town of Inverurie is 17 miles northwest of Aberdeen, on the A96 to Inverness. It makes a useful base for visiting the numerous castles and ancient relics dotted around the area. There's little of specific interest in the town itself, though the **Victoria cinema** is a wonderful throwback to the golden days of the movies. Films are only shown occasionally, T621436. The **Thainstone Mart**, south of town just off the A96, is one of the largest livestock markets in the country and interesting, if you like that sort of thing. It's held Monday, Wednesday and Friday around 1000.

The **tourist office** is in the Town Hall on Market Place. ■ *T518315. Apr-Sept Mon-Sat 1000-1300 and 1400-1800.*

Sights About six miles southwest of Inverurie, off the B993 (turn first left after the village of Kemnay) is the magnificent **Castle Fraser**, built in 1575 by the 6th Earl of Mar and similar in style to Crathes and Craigievar. The interior was remodelled in 1838 and many of the furnishings date from that period. There's a walled garden, tearoom and trails through the estate. ■ *T01330-833463 (NTS). Easter, May-Jun and Sept, daily 1330-1730, Jul-Aug daily 1100-1730, Oct weekends only 1330-1730, garden all year daily 0930-1800, grounds all year daily 0930 till dusk. £4.20, £2.80 child/concession.*

Close by, and signed off the B993, is the 4,000 year-old **Easter Aquhorthies Stone Circle**. This archaeological site is overshadowed by **Bennachie** (1,732ft), by far the best hill in the area and thought to be the site of Mons Graupius, in 83 AD, when the Romans defeated the Picts. It's a straightforward two-hour walk to the summit and the views from the top are great. There are various trails, though the most commonly used route starts from the **Bennachie Centre**, at Esson's car park, a mile beyond **Chapel of Garioch** (pronounced 'Geery'), signposted off the A96 at Pitcaple, and about five miles northwest of Inverurie. ■ *Bennachie Centre, T681470. Apr-Oct, Tue-Sun 1000-1700; Nov-Mar Wed-Sun 1000-1700. For more details of the various*

Castle Fraser

Bennachie Hill walks and the 'West Gordon Way', T794161. Near here is the **Maiden Stone**, a 10-ft high Pictish gravestone with relief carvings showing what looks like an elephant, along with other creatures not normally found around these parts.

A few miles west of the turn-off to Chapel of Garioch, the B9002 heads west off the A96 to the village of **Oyne**, site of the **Archaeolink Prehistory Park**. This state-of-the-art interpretive centre takes you on a journey back in time. It's a great introduction to the numerous ancient sites in the area and explains why the stone circles were built and what the various carved symbols mean. The 40-acre park includes various interesting features such as a reconstructed Iron Age farm, Stone Age settlement and Roman camp, as well as a hilltop Iron Age fort. The Archeodrome features audio-visual presentations which bring to life the ancient history of the area. ■ *T01464-851544, www.archaeolink.co.uk. Daily Apr-Oct 1000-1700, £3.90, £2.35 child/ concession.*

North of the A96, near the village of **Daviot**, off the B9001 from Inverurie, or reached via the A920 west of **Oldmeldrum**, is the **Loanhead of Daviot Stone Circle**. This impressive 6,000 year-old site is 500 yards from the village and consists of two stone circles, the smaller of which encloses a cremation cemetery dating from 1500 BC.

Northeast Scotland

Sleeping & eating

The best place to stay around Inverurie is the magnificent **L** *Pittodrie House Hotel*, near Chapel of Garioch, T681444, www.macdonald.hotels.co.uk. 27 rooms, this fine baronial mansion originally belonged to the Earls of Mar and the 2,000-acre estate was granted to them by Robert the Bruce for their loyalty at the Battle of Bannock-burn. The opulent surroundings are matched by the superb cuisine. **L** *Thainstone House Hotel*, to the south of Inverurie off the A96, T621643, is a luxurious country mansion offering excellent cuisine and leisure facilities.

There's also a decent selection of cheaper **guesthouses** and **B&Bs**, including **E** *Breaslann Guest House*, Old Chapel Rd, T621608.

Alford and around

The main tourist centre on Donside is the little country town of Alford (pro-nounced 'Ah-ford'), 25 miles west of Aberdeen. The principal point of inter-est in town is the **Grampian Transport Museum**, which features a comprehensive and fascinating display of transport history, with collections of cars, buses, trams, steam engines and some more unusual exhibits. ■ *T562292. Daily end Mar to end Oct, 1000-1700, £3, £1.25 children.* Almost

Phone code: 01975
Colour map 4, grid A5

next door is the terminus for the **Alford Valley Railway**, a narrow-gauge passenger steam railway that runs for about a mile to Murray Park and back again (total journey time one hour). ■ *T562811. Apr-May and Sept, Sat-Sun 1300-1700, Jun-Aug daily 1300-1700, £1.50, 80p children.*

The railway station is also where you'll find the **tourist office**. ■ *T562052. Apr-Jun, Sept-Oct, Mon-Sat 1000-1700, Sun 1300-1700; Jul-Aug Mon-Sat 1000-1800, Sun 1300-1800.* Also in town is the **Alford Heritage Centre**, on Mart Road, which has a large display of agricultural and domestic items. ■ *T562906. Apr-Oct Mon-Sat 1000-1700, Sun 1300-1700.*

Alford is close to The Lecht winter ski centre (see below) but you can ski here all year round on the local dry ski slope at the **Alford Ski Centre**, on Greystone Road, T563024. There's also snowboarding, instruction and equipment hire.

Craigievar Castle   Six miles south of Alford is one of the northeast's most gorgeous castles, the classic tower house of Craigievar, with its impressive turrets, balustrades and cupolas. The castle remains much as it was when it was built in 1626 by wealthy local merchant, William Forbes. Unfortunately, though, its popularity led to its deterioration and the NTS now restricts entry to only a small number of visitors at a time to prevent further damage. The castle stands in well-tended grounds. ■ *T01339-883280. 1 May-30 Sept daily 1330-1730 (last admission 1645), grounds open daily all year 0930-dusk. £5.80, £3.90 child/ concession.*

Sleeping & eating   About a mile west, at Bridge of Alford, is the **D** *Forbes Arms Hotel*, T562108, where you can get decent bar food (prices cheap to mid-range). There's also **B&B** accommodation in Alford at **E** *Dunvegan*, 26 Gordon Rd, T563077, and **E** *Bydand*, 18 Balfour Rd, T563613.

West of Alford

Kildrummy Castle
Phone code: 01975
Colour map 4, grid

Six miles west of Alford, the A944 meets the A97 which heads north towards the town of Huntly, on Speyside (see page 383). A few miles south of the junction stand the extensive and impressive ruins of Kildrummy Castle, Scotland's most complete 13th-century castle. Amongst the most infamous events in the castle's long and bloody history was the treacherous betrayal of Robert the Bruce's family to the English during the Wars of Independence. It was the seat of the Earls of Mar and used as an HQ for the Jacobite rebellion of 1715, after which the 6th Earl of Mar ('Bobbing John') fled to exile in France and the castle fell into ruin. ■ *T571331. Daily Apr-Sept 0930-1830. £1.80, £1.30 concession.*

Across the other side of the river from the castle ruins is one of the very best hotels in the northeast, the spectacularly sited **L-A** *Kildrummy Castle Hotel*, T571288, a baronial country mansion set in beautiful grounds (see above). It also has an excellent restaurant.

Strathdon
Phone code: 01975
Colour map 4, grid A4

Ten miles southwest of Kildrummy is the tiny village of Strathdon, famous for its **Highland Games**, known as the *Lonach Highland Gathering*, held on the third Saturday in August, and a healthy blast of authenticity in comparison to the rather more glitzy affair at Braemar on Deeside (see page 376).

As you head west through Strathdon, you'll see a sign which appears to tell you that you're lost, but in fact is pointing the way to the wonderfully named village of **Lost**, four miles north of Strathdon, in the middle of nowhere. Take the turning off the A944 at Bellabeg. This road also leads to the excellent **Lost Gallery**, which shows work by contemporary artists and is well worth visiting. ■ *T651287. Wed-Sun 1100-1700.*

The Lecht

The Lecht is a ski resort for all seasons. It offers dry-slope skiing throughout the year and its snowmaking facilities mean that the winter season can be extended beyond January and February. The Lecht's gentler slopes make it ideal for beginners and intermediates and the emphasis is on family skiing. There's a snowboard fun park with half pipe, log slide, gap jump and table top. However, there are also more difficult runs for the more experienced skier, and extensive off piste skiing.

*A **day ticket** costs £15 for adults, and £8 for children; a half-day ticket costs £12. There's a ski school and equipment hire at the base station, T01975-651440, thelecht@sol.co.uk. For latest snow and weather conditions call the base station, or the Ski Hotline, T09001-654657.*

Five miles west of Strathdon, the A944 meets the A939 Ballater-Tomintoul road. A few miles beyond the junction is the austere **Corgarff Castle**, a 16th-century tower house, later turned into a garrison post, with an eventful and gruesome history. Here Margaret Forbes and her family were burned alive by the Gordons in 1571 during the bitter feud between the two families. In the wake of the ill-fated 1745 rebellion, the government re-modelled the castle, building a star-shaped defensive wall, and garrisoned 60 men to maintain order and communications in this part of the Highlands. Corgarff continued in use into the 19th century when English Redcoats were stationed here in order to prevent whisky smuggling. Today, it's managed by Historic Scotland. ■ *T651460. Daily Apr-Sept 0930-1830, Oct-Mar weekends only. £2.50, £1.90 concession.*

Just before the castle, an old military road leads for about a mile to *Jenny's Bothy*, T651449. Open all year, a basic but wonderfully remote bunkhouse.

Tomintoul

Beside Corgarff is the hamlet of **Cock Bridge**, standing at one end of one the most beautiful and notorious stretches of road in the country. In winter, the Tomintoul to Cock Bridge road is almost always the first road in Scotland to be blocked by snow (you have been warned!). From Cock Bridge, the A939 rises steeply to the Lecht Pass (2,089ft) before dropping dramatically to **Tomintoul**, one of the highest villages in Scotland, at 1,600ft.

Phone code: 01807
Colour map 4, grid A4

Tomintoul is a bit of a one-horse town, and like so many others in this area, is an 18th-century planned village, built by the local laird to keep an eye on his tenants. It lies roughly midway between the Don Valley and Speyside, and is therefore well-placed for both the Whisky and Castle Trails. It is also the nearest settlement of any size to **The Lecht**, one of Scotland's top five ski resorts (see above), and it marks the end of the long-distance **Speyside Way** (see page 392), so is popular with walkers and skiers.

The **tourist office** is in the village square. ■ *T580285. Apr, May and Oct Mon-Sat 1000-1300 and 1400-1730, Sun 1400-1700, Jun and Sept Mon-Sat 1000-1300 and 1400-1800, Sun 1400-1800; Jul-Aug Mon-Sat 1000-1900, Sun 1300-1900.* Also on the Square is the **Museum & Visitor Centre**, which has a display of local history, wildlife, landscape and outdoor activities. ■ *T673701. Jun-Sept Mon-Sat 1000-1600, Oct-May Mon-Fri 1000-1600. Free.*

Sights

Ten miles north of Tomintoul on the B9008 is the **Glenlivet Crown Estate** (see also 'The Malt Whisky Trail', page 385), with an extensive network of hiking paths and cycle trails, as well as lots of wildlife, including reindeer. Information and free maps are available from the **ranger's office** in Tomintoul, T580283.

Northeast Scotland

Sleeping & eating There are a few hotels around the main square, the nicest of which is the **D-E** *Glenavon Hotel*, T580218. It is also the best place for a drink and popular with *après* skiers, tired walkers and locals. There are several **B&Bs**, including **E-F** *Milton Farm*, T580288, open Jan-Nov, just outside the village on the B9008. There's also a *SYHA Youth Hostel*, on Main St, T580282, open mid-May to end Oct.

Other than the hotels, the best place to eat is the *Clockhouse* on the Square.

Transport There are **buses** to Tomintoul from **Keith** via **Dufftown**, (Tue and Sat only), from **Elgin** (Thur only) and from **Aberlour** (on schooldays, with connection to Elgin). For details call *Roberts of Rothiemay*, T01466-711213.

Speyside

Colour maps 2, grid C3/4 — *The river Spey is Scotland's second longest river, rising in the hills above Loch Laggan and making its way northeast to where it debouches at Spey Bay, on the Moray coast. Speyside is one of Scotland's loveliest valleys and is synonymous with two of Scotland's greatest products, salmon and whisky. The upper part, Strathspey, is equally famous for its hiking, skiing and watersports. It is covered in the Highlands chapter (see page 486). This section covers the lower part of the valley and comprises the famous Malt Whisky Trail. There are more malt whisky distilleries in this small area than in any other part of the country, and some of the famous brands include Glenlivet and Glenfiddich.*

It's not all whisky in these parts. There's also some fine walking along the 45-mile Speyside Way, which runs from Spey Bay south to Tomintoul.

Dufftown

Phone code: 01340 Colour map 2, grid C4 — A good place to start your whisky tour is Dufftown, founded in 1817 by James Duff, the fourth Earl of Fife, and the self-proclaimed 'Malt Whisky Capital of the World'. There's more than a grain of truth in that assertion, for there are no fewer than seven working distilleries here. This is indeed the town that was built on seven stills.

Dufftown's **tourist office** is inside the Clock Tower in the centre of the main square. They have maps and information on the whisky trail. ■ *T820501. Apr, May and Oct Mon-Sat 1000-1300 and 1400-1700, Jun and Sept Mon-Sat 1000-1300 and 1400-1800, Sun 1300-1800, Jul-Aug Mon-Sat 1000-1900, Sun 1300-1900.*

Sights Just outside of town, on the A941 to Craigellachie, is the **Glenfiddich Distillery**, the town's most famous distillery and one of the best known of all malt whiskies (see box, page 385). Behind the distillery are the 13th-century ruins of **Balvenie Castle**, built by Alexander 'Black' Comyn, then added to in the 15th and 16th centuries, and visited by Mary, Queen of Scots in 1562. ■ *T820121 (HS). Daily Apr-Sept 0930-1830, £1.20, 90p concession.*

Four miles north of Dufftown, at the junction of the A941 and A95, is the little village of **Craigellachie**, site of the **Speyside Cooperage** (see below) and where you can see Thomas Telford's beautiful bridge over the river Spey. At nearby Aberlour is the home of Walkers Shortbread, T01340-871555.

About eight miles southwest of Craigiellachie, on the A95 to Grantown-on-Spey, is beautiful **Ballindalloch Castle**, a mile west of the village of Marypark. The castle is one of the loveliest in the northeast and has been lived in continuously by its original family, the Macpherson-Grants, since 1546. It houses a fine collection of Spanish paintings and the extensive grounds are home to the

The Speyside Way

The Speyside Way follows the River Spey from its mouth at Spey Bay inland as far as Ballindalloch, then crosses high moorland to Tomintoul. The 45-mile route takes three to five days to complete. Much of it is on an old railway line and passes close to several small villages, meaning that it can easily be broken down into shorter walks. It also passes several distilleries along the way. There are plans to extend the route in the next few years, from Buckie, on the Moray coast, to Aviemore.

There is no guidebook to the Speyside Way, but OS Landranger maps Nos 28 & 36 cover the entire route. Further information and route leaflets are available from the **Moray Council Ranger Service**, at Boat of Fiddich, Craigellachie. The office is open Easter-Oct, daily 0900-1700 (T01340-881266, www.moray.org/area.speyway/ webpages/swhome.htm).

famous Aberdeen-Angus herd of cattle, bred here since 1860. ■ T01807-500206. Easter-Sept daily 1000-1700, £4.50, £2 concession.

Also in Ballindalloch is the **Glenfarclas Distillery**. ■ T01807-500245, www.glenfarclas.co.uk. Apr-Sept Mon-Fri 0930-1700; Jun-Sept also Sat 0930-1630; Oct-Mar Mon-Fri 1000-1600, £3.50, under 18s free.

The best place to stay is the superb **L** *Craig iellachie Hotel*, T881204, in the village of Craig iellachie. Also recommended is the **B** *Minmore House Hotel*, T01807-590378, open May-Oct, 10 miles southwest of Dufftown, in the village of Glenlivet, it stands right beside the distillery and is the former home of the owner. Also in Craig iellachie is the **E** *Highlander Inn*, on Victoria St, T/F881446. Popular and serves decent bar meals. There's a fairly wide selection of accommodation in Dufftown itself. Two good **B&Bs** are **E** *Davaar*, T820464, on Church St, and **E** *Tullich House*, T821008. Both also provide dinner.

Sleeping & eating

The best place to eat is the moderately priced *A Taste of Speyside*, on Balvenie St, T820860. The Fife Arms Hotel, T820220, on the Square does cheap bar meals. As far as entertainment goes, the *Commercial Hotel*, T820313, on Church St has ceilidhs on Thursday nights during the summer.

Bluebird Buses, T01224-212266, runs a daily service from **Elgin** (No 336). There's also a bus (Nos 360 & 361) which connects Dufftown with **Keith** and **Aberlour** (Mon-Fri). For details call W W Smith, T01542-882113.

Transport

Huntly

Ten miles east of Dufftown is the pleasant and prosperous-looking little town of Huntly. Close to the Whisky Trail and on the main Aberdeen to Inverness train route; it makes a convenient base from which to explore this area. It also boasts a lovely little castle all of its own. The 16th-century **Huntly Castle** stands in a beautiful setting on the banks of the river Deveron, on the northern edge of town. It was built by the powerful Gordon family and is notable for its fine heraldic sculpture and inscribed stone friezes, particularly over the main door. ■ T793191 (HS). Apr-Sept daily 0930-1830, Oct-Mar Mon-Wed and Sat 0930-1630, Thur 0930-1200, Fri and Sun 1400-1630. £2.50, £1.90 concession.

Phone code: 01466
Colour map 2, grid C5

Seven miles south of town, near the village of Kennethmont, is **Leith Hall**, an unprepossessing mid-17th-century mansion house. The house contains the personal possessions of successive Leith lairds, most of whom saw military service overseas, but more interesting are the extensive grounds which include

Northeast Scotland

The Malt Whisky Trail

*Speyside is Scotland's most prolific whisky-producing region and the **Malt Whisky Trail** is a well-signposted 70-mile tour around seven of the most famous distilleries, plus the Speyside Cooperage. Most of the distilleries offer guided tours, and most (with the exception of Glenfiddich) charge an entry fee, which can then be discounted, in full or in part, from the cost of a bottle of whisky in the distillery shop. Tours also include a free dram. Those listed below are the most interesting.*

***Strathisla**, in Keith, is the oldest working distillery in the Highlands (1786) and perhaps the most atmospheric, in a beautiful setting on the River Isla. This is a relatively rare malt, which is also used in the better-known Chivas Regal blend. T01542-783044. Open Feb to end Nov, Mon-Sat 0930-1600, Sun 1230-1600. £4 (includes £2 discount voucher).*

***Speyside Cooperage** is near Craig iellachie, four miles north of Dufftown. Here you can watch the oak casks for whisky being made. T01340-871108. Open Jun-Sept Mon-Sat 0930-1630; Oct-May Mon-Fri 0930-1630. £2.25.*

***Dallas Dhu** is a bit off the beaten track, a mile south of Forres, off the A940. It no longer produces whisky but it's a beautifully preserved Victorian distillery which you can explore on your own. T01309-676548. Open daily Apr-Sept 0930-1830; Oct-Mar Mon-Wed and Sat 0930-1630, Thur 0930-1200, Fri and Sun 1400-1630. £2.50.*

***Cardhu** is seven miles west of Craig iellachie, at Knockando on the B9102. This lovely little distillery is now owned*

by United Distillers and their fine malt is one of many used in the famous Johnny Walker blend. T01340-872555. Open Mar-Nov Mon-Fri 0930-1630, Sun 1100-1600; Jul-Sept also Sat 0930-1630 and Sun 1100-1600; Dec-Feb Mon-Fri 1000-1600. £2 (includes £3 discount voucher).

***Glen Grant** is in Rothes, on the A941 to Elgin. This distillery tour has the added attraction of a Victorian garden and orchard, woodland walks by the burn and the rebuilt 'Dram Pavilion'. T01542-783318. Open mid-Mar to end Oct Mon-Sat 1000-1600, Sun 1130-1600; Jun-Sept Mon-Sat 1000-1700, Sun 1130-1700. £2.50 (includes £2 discount voucher).*

***Glenfiddich** is just north of Dufftown, on the A941. Probably the best known of all the malts and the most professionally run operation. It's the only distillery where you can see the whisky being bottled on the premises, and the only major distillery that's free (including the obligatory dram). T01340-820373. Open all Apr to mid-Oct Mon-Sat 0930-1630 and Sun 1200-1630; mid-Oct to Mar Mon-Fri only. Free.*

*The **Glenlivet** is 10 miles north of Tomintoul, on the B9008. This was an illicit whisky until it was licensed in 1824. The distillery was later founded in 1858 and this malt has gone on to become one of the world's favourites. It was then taken over in 1978 by Seagram's. T01542-783220. Open mid-Mar to end Oct Mon-Sat 1000-1600, Sun 1230-1600; Jul-Aug till 1800. £2.50 (includes £2 discount voucher).*

Northeast Scotland

a six-acre garden, 18th-century stables and ice house, two ponds, a bird observation hide and countryside walks. ■ T01464-831594 (NTS). *Easter and 1 May-30 Sept daily 1330-1730; Oct at weekends 1330-1730, garden and grounds open all year, daily 0930-dusk. £4.20, £2.80 child/concession.*

The **tourist office** is on the main square. ■ T792255. *Daily Apr-Oct 1000-1700; Jul-Aug till 1900.* Near the castle is the **Nordic Ski Centre**,

T794428, the only year-round cross-country ski centre in the UK. The centre also hires out ski equipment and mountain bikes.

Sleeping & eating

There's a decent selection of accommodation in and around Huntly. The most impressive place to stay is **C** *The Castle Hotel*, T792696, castlehot@enterprise.net. The former home of the Duke of Gordon, it's approached through the castle entrance and then over the river. Another excellent place is **B-C** *the Old Manse of Marnoch*, at Bridge of Marnoch, T/F780873. This delightful Georgian country house is set in 4 acres of gardens and offers style, comfort and superb cuisine, German spoken. There are several good **B&Bs** in town, including **E** *Greenmount Guesthouse*, 43 Gordon St, T792482 and **E-F** *Strathlene*, on MacDonald St, T792664. The hotels in town serve bar food, as does the *Auld Pit*, which is a good pub. Another good pub, especially for real ale, is the *Borve Brew House*, in Ruthven, a few miles off the A96 to Keith.

The Tap o' Noth
Colour map 4, grid A5

OS Landranger No 37

Eight miles south of Huntly on the A97 is the village of **Rhynie**, where you turn off for one of the best walks in the northeast. The Tap o' Noth (1,851ft) dominates this part of rural Aberdeenshire and the panoramic views from the top make it a worthwhile climb. It's also a fairly easy walk to the conical summit, where there's a vitrified fort.

It's believed that the name derives from the Gaelic *taip a'nochd*, which translates as look-out top. But there's also a local legend that the hill's giant, Jack o'Noth, stole the sweetheart of his neighbour, Jack o'Bennachie. In retaliation, the cuckolded neighbour hurled a huge boulder and flattened Jack on his own hilltop.

Start the walk from the car park at **Scurdargue**, a few miles west of Rhynie, off the A941. Leave the car park and head straight up the track to a gate. Go through the gate and cross some rough pasture into woodland. At the northwest corner of the wood, go through another gate and turn left onto a track. Follow this grassy track uphill beside a fence until you see another area of forestry ahead, with rough pastureland on the right. Follow the faint track across the pasture to the broad track which then climbs up the Tap's western slopes. Follow this all the way to the top, up the tight zig-zag on the southern flank and through the eastern entry to the hillfort, into a large enclosure.

On the way back down look out for a subsidiary path under the fort's western ramparts. This path descends steeply to the left, south of the main track. It then joins the main track and you can retrace your steps back to the car park.

The total distance is three miles. Allow at least two hours there and back.

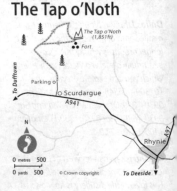

The Tap o'Noth

The Tap o'Noth (1,851ft)

Fort

To Dufftown

Parking

Scurdargue

A941

N

Rhynie

A97

0 metres 500
0 yards 500
© Crown copyright

To Deeside ▼

The Coast

The northeast coast holds some of Scotland's best coastal scenery, particularly the *Colour map 2, grid C3-6*
Moray Coast from Spey Bay to Fraserburgh. Here you'll find some picturesque
little villages clinging to the cliffs like limpets, and miles of windswept, deserted
sandy beaches. Portsoy, Pennan, Gardenstown and Crovie are all well worth vis-
iting, and there are great beaches at Cullen, Lossiemouth, Rosehearty and
Sunnyside. Other highlights in the region include the beautiful Duff House, the
working abbey at Pluscarden and Findhorn, famous worldwide for its alterna-
tive, spiritual community.

Ins and outs

The two largest towns along the coast are the hard-working, no-nonsense fishing   **Getting around**
ports of Peterhead and Fraserburgh, both linked by a regular bus service from
Aberdeen. Fochabers, Elgin and Forres are all on the main Aberdeen-Inverness **bus**
route and served regularly, and **trains** between Aberdeen and Inverness stop at Elgin
and Forres. Otherwise, public transport is somewhat limited and it can be difficult getting to the more out-of-the-way places without your own transport.

Aberdeen to Peterhead

The A90 runs north to Peterhead. Fifteen miles north of Aberdeen is the
turn-off to **Ellon**, and five miles west of Ellon, on the A920 to **Oldmeldrum**,
are **Pitmedden Gardens**. The centrepiece of the property, the Great Garden,
was originally laid out in 1675 by Sir Alexander Seton, and the elaborate,
orderly floral patterns have been lovingly recreated. Also on the 100-acre site is
the **Museum of Farming Life**, where you can see how the estate workers lived.
There's also a visitor centre, tearoom and a woodland walk. ■ *T01651-842352*
(NTS). 1 May-30 Sept, daily 1000-1730. £3.70, £2.50 child/ concession.
     A mile north of Pitmedden, a side road turns left off the B999 to **Tolquhon**
Castle (pronounced 'tee-hon'). This early 15th-century tower was built for the
Forbes family and later extended with a large mansion around a courtyard.
The most impressive feature is the ornamental gatehouse but there are other
interesting original features to discover. ■ *T01651-851286. Apr-Sept, daily*
0930-1830, Oct-Mar weekends only. £1.80, concession £1.30.

Four miles north of Pitmedden, reached via the B9005 from Ellon, is the ele-   **Haddo House**
gant Palladian mansion of Haddo House, one of the most impressive of Scotland's country houses. Designed by William Adam for the 2nd Earl of
Aberdeen in 1732 and later refurbished in the 1880s, the house beautifully
marries graceful Georgian architecture with sumptuous late Victorian interiors. Home of the Gordon family for over 400 years, Haddo is a wonderfully
tasteful legacy of how the other half lived. The house sits in 177 acres of country
park, where you can stroll around the woodland and lakes, home to abundant
wildlife such as deer, red squirrels and pheasants. Haddo also hosts a varied
programme of music, drama and arts events. For details of forthcoming productions, contact the *Haddo Arts Trust,* T01651-851770, or the National
Trust. ■ *T01651-851440 (NTS). Easter and 1 May-30 Sept daily 1330-1730,*
weekends in Oct (last admission 1645), guided tours Mon-Sat, garden and coun-
try park open all year 0930-dusk. £4.20, £2.80 child/concession.

Northeast Scotland

Fyvie Castle　Seven miles west of Haddo House is Fyvie Castle, off the A947 between Oldmeldrum and Turriff. This grandest of Scottish baronial piles is a major feature on the 'Castle Trail' and shouldn't be missed if you're in the vicinity. The castle's five towers are each named after one of the five families who have had the pleasure of living here over the centuries. The last lot only moved out in 1980 so it has a rare lived-in feel to it. The oldest part of the castle dates from the 13th century and, apart from the great wheel-stair and the 17th-century morning room, the extravagantly opulent interior largely dates from the Edwardian era. There's a superb collection of portraits including works by the likes of Raeburn, Batoni, Gainsborough and Hoppner, as well as 17th-century tapestries and collections of arms and armour. The landscaped grounds and Fyvie Loch are also worth exploring and even the tearoom is great. ■ *T01651-891266 (NTS). Easter to 30 Jun and Sept daily 1330-1730, Jul-Aug 1100-1730, weekends only in Oct, grounds open all year daily 0930-dusk. £4.20, £2.80 child/concession.*

Newburgh to Cruden Bay　Eleven miles north of Aberdeen, the A975 turns off the A90 and makes an interesting little detour along the coast before rejoining the A90 a few miles south of Peterhead. The road crosses the mouth of the river Ythan at **Newburgh** and passes the dramatic **Sands of Forvie**, which are now part of the **Forvie National Nature Reserve**, one of Britain's largest dune systems and home to a vast array of birdlife.

Eight miles north is the little town of **Cruden Bay**, at the northern end of a wide sweep of sandy beach. Close by, perched on the clifftop, are the gaunt, storm-lashed ruins of **Slains Castle**, built in 1597 by the Earls of Errol. So eerily evocative is the ruin that it fired the imagination of Bram Stoker and inspired him to write *Dracula* during one of his holiday visits. The castle ruin is a 15-minute walk from Cruden Bay. From the car park at the end of the main street, head along the cliffs.

Three miles north of Slains Castle is the **Bullers of Buchan**, an amazing 245-ft deep circular basin of rocky cliff where the sea boils in through an eroded archway. In spring and summer the cliffs are home to countless thousands of seabirds. You can also reach this point from the A975, via the footpath from the car park. Take great care near the edge of the chasm and watch out for kamikaze seabirds.

Cruden Bay also has a terrific **golf course**, rated as one of the best links courses in the UK, T01779-812285. You can stay in town at the **B** *Red House Hotel*, T01779-812215.

Peterhead

Phone code: 01779
Colour map 2, grid C6
Population: 18,500

Thirty miles north of Aberdeen is the harsh, uncompromising town of Peterhead, Europe's busiest white-fish port. Fish is Peterhead's *raison d'être* and everything revolves around its huge harbour. Local fishermen have not been having it so good in recent years, however, as North Sea fish stocks have become dangerously depleted and EU quotas have threatened livelihoods. The town's alternative sources of income are the power station and the high-security prison.

Peterhead may not be the most appealing prospect, but the town is rightly proud of its seafaring heritage. The **Peterhead Maritime Heritage Museum** is housed in an attractive new building on South Road. It tells the story of the whaling and fishing industries and depicts the life and times of the townsfolk through a series of interactive displays and a video presentation. ■ *T473000. Apr-Oct Mon-Sat 1000-1700, Sun 1200-1700, Nov-Mar Sat 1000-1600, Sun 1200-1600. £2.50, £1.50 children.*

At the north end of town, on Golf Road at the mouth of the river Ugie, is the **Ugie Fish House**, Scotland's oldest working fish house. Salmon and trout have been smoked here since 1585 and you can still see traditional methods being employed, and then purchase the finished product. ■ *T476209. All year Mon-Fri 0900-1700, Sat 0900-1200. Free.*

Nine miles west of town, at Mintlaw, is the **Aden Country Park** (pronounced 'Ah-den'). It's a great place for kids, with numerous walks around the estate, various organized activities and events and the **Aberdeenshire Farming Museum**, which features a semi-circular farmstead built in the early 19th century and a working farm dating from the 1950s. ■ *T01771-622906. May-Sept daily 1100-1700, Apr and Oct weekends only 1200-1630. Free. Bus No 286 daily to and from Peterhead.*

There's no tourist office in town, but the best place to stay is the modern **A** *Waterside Inn*, T471121, on the road heading out of town to Fraserburgh, by the river Ugie. A cheaper option is **E** *Carrick Guesthouse*, T470610, at 16 Merchant St. A good fish and chip shop is the *Dolphin*, on Alexandra Pde by the harbour. **Sleeping & eating**

Bluebird Buses, T01224-212266, run every 30 mins (Mon-Sat; every hour on Sun) from Aberdeen, via **Ellon** (No 260) and **Cruden Bay** (No 263). **Transport**

Fraserburgh

Eighteen miles north of Peterhead, at the very northeastern tip of the northeast coast, is the hardy, windswept fishing town of Fraserburgh. At the northern tip of the town, is **Kinnaird Head Castle and Lighthouse**, which now houses Scotland's **Lighthouse Museum**. This bizarre structure started out as a 16th-century castle which was then converted by the Northern Lighthouse Company in 1787 into one of mainland Scotland's first lighthouses. The museum offers a truly fascinating illumination of the engineering skill and innovation involved in the design and workings of the lighthouse, with displays of the huge lenses and prisms, as well as a history of the Stevenson family (Robert Louis' father and grandfather) who designed many of Scotland's lighthouses. The highlight is the guided tour to the top of Kinnaird Head Lighthouse itself. ■ *T511022. Apr-Oct Mon-Sat 1000-1800, Sun 1200-1800; Nov-Mar till 1600.* The **tourist office** is at 3 Saltoun Square. ■ *T518315. Apr-Jun and Sept Mon-Sat 1000-1300 and 1400-1700, Jul-Aug Mon-Sat 1000-1300 and 1400-1800, Sun 1300-1700.*

Phone code: 01346
Colour map 4, grid C6
Population: 13,000

Accommodation is fairly thin on the ground. There's the **A** *Saltoun Arms Hotel*, T518282, or **B&B** at **E-F** *Clifton House*, 131 Charlotte St, T518365. There's also a **campsite** 5 miles west of town at **Rosehearty**, which has a good beach. The best place to **eat** in Fraserburgh is the very homely *Coffee Shoppe*, 30 Cross St, which serves great home-made soup and cakes. Open Mon-Sat 0900-1630; closed Wed. **Sleeping & eating**

Bluebird Buses, T01224-212266, run regular buses to and from Aberdeen, via Mintlaw, and Peterhead. There are also buses to Banff via Pennan and Gardenstown (No 273; Mon-Sat). **Transport**

Northeast Scotland

Crovie

Pennan, Crovie and Gardenstown

Colour map 2, grid C5/6

Between Fraserburgh and Macduff/Banff lies a trio of charming little coastal villages, clinging hungrily to the sea cliffs like babies to their mothers' breasts. The most easterly is **Pennan**, which shot to fame in 1982 when the hit British movie *Local Hero* was filmed here. The tiny hamlet lies just off the road, at the foot of a very steep hill, and consists of little more than a row of neat, white-washed cottages, bravely challenging the North Sea. The only place to **eat and sleep** is the cheap and cosy E *Pennan Inn*, T01346-561201.

A few miles west, on the other side of Troup Head, is the equally lovely little fishing village of **Gardenstown** (or Gamrie, pronounced 'Game-ree'), whose streets are so precipitous you almost need to be roped up to get around on foot, never mind trying to drive a car. You can also sleep here, at E *The Palace Farm*, T01261-851261, March-Nov, or E *Bankhead Croft*, T01261-851584, both of which provide dinner. A stone's throw away is the even tinier village of **Crovie** (pronounced 'Crivvie'), which is so narrow its residents have to walk sideways.

Banff and Macduff

Phone code: 01261
Colour map 2, grid C5

The road west from Pennan leads on to the busy fishing port of Macduff, separated only by a bridge from neighbouring Banff, whose town centre still retains its faded Georgian elegance.

The great attraction in the area is **Duff House**, on the Banff side of the river Deveron, a short walk upstream from the bridge. This magnificent Georgian mansion, was designed by William Adam in 1735 for local entrepreneur William Duff, who later became Earl of Fife. The house was supposed to act as the capital of Duff's huge estate, but the whole project collapsed after a major disagreement between architect and patron and ended with a lawsuit in 1747. The wings were never built but Duff House remains one of the finest Georgian baroque houses in Britain. After a variety of uses and a period of dereliction, the house has been meticulously restored and reopened as an important outpost of the **National Gallery of Scotland**. The extensive collection on display includes works by Scottish artists Ramsay and Raeburn, as well as an El Greco. ■ *T818181. Apr-Oct daily 1100-1700, Nov-Mar Thur-Sun 1100-1600, £3, £2 child/concession.*

The house is surrounded by extensive grounds with some lovely walks through sylvan settings. The best, though, is along the banks of the river Deveron to the beautiful **Bridge of Alvah**, spanning the river across a deep gorge. It's about four miles there and back from Duff House. Leaflets showing the route are available free from the tourist office in Banff (see below).

A mile southwest from Banff, on the A97 to Huntly, is the **Colleonard Sculpture Garden**, a peaceful space populated by wooden sculptures, carved out of tree trunks, the work of Frank Bruce, who lives in the house and can often be seen around the site. ■ *Daily 0930-1700. Free.*

In Macduff is the **Macduff Marine Aquarium**, at 11 High Shore. Various weird and wonderful specimens from the Moray Firth are displayed in Britain's deepest aquarium tank. ■ *T833369. Daily 1000-1700. £2.75, £1.50 children.* The local **tourist office** is in Banff, at Collie Lodge, opposite the gates of Duff House. ■ *T812419. Apr-Sept daily 1000-1300 and 1400-1700, Jul-Aug Mon-Sat till 1800, Sun 1300-1800.* They offer a free hour-long walkman tour (£1 deposit) which takes you around the elegant Georgian upper town.

Banff C *Banff Springs Hotel*, T812881, is on the western outskirts of town on the A98 to Elgin. It's a friendly, modern hotel with a good restaurant (mid-range). There are several very good **guesthouses** and **B&Bs**, including **E** *Links Cottage*, T812223, Mar-Nov, overlooking Boyndie Bay, **E** *Bryvard Guesthouse*, Seafield St, T818090, bryvard@aol.com, and **E** *The Orchard*, Duff House, T812146, jma6914291@aol.com. There's a **campsite** at *Banff Links Caravan Park*, T812228; open Mar-Oct, on Boyndie Bay.

Macduff D *The Highland Haven*, T832408, on Shore St, and the **D-E** *Knowes Hotel*, T832229, on Market St.

For **places to eat** try the *Market Arms*, on High Shore in Banff, or the highly rated *Fagin's*, a few miles west of Banff, in the little village of Whitehills, T861321. Mid-range prices; open Fri-Sun for lunch and Wed-Sat 1900-2200.

Bluebird Buses, T01224-212266, run services from Banff to **Fraserburgh** (Mon-Sat) via **Gardenstown** and **Pennan**, and from Macduff to **Huntly/Keith** (Mon-Sat). Bus No 305 leaves hourly (Mon-Sat; less frequent on Sun) to **Aberdeen**, and to **Elgin** via **Portsoy**, **Cullen** and **Buckie**.

*Sleeping &
eating*

Transport

Portsoy and Cullen

West of Banff are two of the most attractive towns on the Moray coast, Portsoy and Cullen. Portsoy is particularly lovely, with its 17th-century harbour, restored merchants' houses and narrow streets. The famous Portsoy marble, used in the building of Versailles, was quarried nearby. The best time to visit is in late June, when you can enjoy the town's excellent *Scottish Traditional Boat Festival* and take a dip in the open-air **swimming pool**. ■ *Jun-Aug.*

Six miles west is the town of **Cullen**, dramatically sited beneath a series of striking 19th-century railway viaducts and fronting an impressive sweep of sand. There's a **tourist office** on the main square of the new town. ■ *Jun-Aug, daily 1100-1700.*

Walk east from Cullen harbour along the coast for a few miles to the lovely, deserted beach at **Sunnyside**, overlooked by the lemming-like ruin of **Findlater Castle**. There's another great beach at **Sandend**, between Portsoy and Cullen.

*Phone code: 01542
Colour map 2, grid C4/5*

Northeast Scotland

The best places to stay in **Cullen** are **C** *The Seafield Arms Hotel*, T840791, and **D** *The Bayview Hotel*, T841031, both on 57 Seafield St. There are also several **B&Bs**. The local delicacy (and delicious it is, too) is Cullen Skink, a soup made with smoked haddock and cream. The best places to try it are *The Bayview*, *Seafield Arms*, and the bar of the *Three Kings Inn*, on North Castle St, T840538.

*Sleeping &
eating*

Fochabers and around

Phone code: 01343
Colour map 2, grid C4

The A98 runs inland, bypassing the coastal town of **Buckie**, to reach the pleasant little town of Fochabers, 12 miles west of Cullen. The town is best known as the home of the famous Baxter family, whose name has become synonymous with food, especially soup. The Baxters factory now stands west of the bridge over the Spey, by the A98 and the **Baxter's visitor centre** tells the story of the famous food-producing from 1868, when George and Margaret Baxter opened their grocery shop in Spey Street. There are also factory tours on weekdays, and cooking demonstrations. The Baxter's *Spey Restaurant* serves good cheap meals and snacks. ■ *T820666, www.baxters.com. Factory tours Mon-Fri 1000-1130 and 1230-1600. Free.*

Christie's is a very good garden centre, on the A98 heading east out of town, and *Just Art*, on the main street, is a good place to buy art or ceramics.

Five miles north of Fochabers, at the mouth of the river Spey, is **Spey Bay**, site of the **Tugnet Ice House**, which was built in 1830 to store ice for packing salmon, and now houses an exhibition on the salmon industry and the wildlife of the Spey Estuary. ■ *T01309-673701. May-Sept daily 1100-1600. Free.* Next door is the **Moray Firth Wildlife Centre**, which has an exhibition of the Moray Firth dolphins, as well as other local wildlife, including grey and common seals, otters and ospreys. The centre also houses a research unit studying the resident bottlenose dolphins (for more on the dolphins, see page 408). ■ *T820339. Mfwc@dial.pipex.com. Mar-Dec daily 1100-1630; Jul-Aug 1030-1900. £1.50, 75p concession.*

Fochabers to Spey Bay

There's an excellent walk from Fochabers to Spey Bay, along the first section of the Speyside Way. Start by the old Spey Bridge and follow the B9104 for about 800 yards until you reach the 'Speyside Way' sign which takes you away from the road onto the riverside footpath. Follow this path for two miles, then, as the river swings left, look for the sign on the right showing where you leave the riverside track. Continue along this path for 500 yards, then turn left on to a minor track and, after a further 400 yards, you join a wider track and follow this all the way to Spey Bay.

You can take an alternative route back to Fochabers by turning right at the old railway track (Scottish Wildlife Trust sign) on to a track leading down to the river and then up on to the old railway viaduct and across the river. At the road bridge, take the steps on the left and go up to the road, then turn left and follow this minor road all the way back to the A98, about half a mile west of Baxters.

Instead of turning left at the end of the viaduct, you can make a short diversion into the little village of Garmouth. Here, a plaque marks the spot where King Charles II signed the Solemn League and Covenant in June 1650, thus accepting the proposed Reformation of the Church.

The total distance covered is nine miles, and you should allow between four and five hours. There's no public transport to Spey Bay.

Fochabers to Spey Bay

There's accommodation in town at the **C-D** *Gordon Arms Hotel*, 80 High St, T820508. Fochabers is on the main A96 Aberdeen-Inverness route and there are regular buses to and from various towns *en route*, such as **Elgin**, **Forres** and **Nairn**. There are also *Bluebird Buses*, T01224-212266, to **Banff**, via **Cullen** and **Portsoy**.

Sleeping, eating & transport

Elgin

Nine miles west of Fochabers and 38 miles east of Inverness, is the busy market town of Elgin, which dates back to the 13th century. Elgin has retained much of its medieval streetplan, making it one of the loveliest towns in the country.

Phone code: 01343
Colour map 2, grid C3
Population: 20,000

The **tourist office** is at 17 High Street. ■ *T542666. Apr, May and Oct Mon-Sat 1000-1300 and 1400-1700, Sun 1300-1700; Jun and Sept daily till 1800; Jul and Aug daily till 1900.*

There's a good range of shops, and banks with ATMs, in the town centre. The **bus station** is central, on Alexandra Road, one block north of the High Street. The **train station** is about 750 yards south of town, on Station Road, off Moss Street, which runs south from the High Street.

The main tourist attraction is **Elgin Cathedral**, on North College Street, round the corner from the tourist office. Though partially ruined, the scattered remains still bear testament to what was once a majestic and beautiful cathedral. Founded in 1224, the cathedral was considered the finest in Scotland, until 1390 when it was burned to the ground by the big, bad 'Wolf of Badenoch', the name given to Alexander Stewart, the illegitimate son of Robert II, following his excommunication by the bishop. And if that weren't bad enough, it was rebuilt, only to suffer further damage during the orgy of vandalism that followed the Reformation. There are still some 13th-century features remaining amongst the ruins, particularly the Pictish cross-slab and the octagonal chapterhouse.

Sights

■ *T547171. Apr-Sept Mon-Sat 0930-1830, Sun 1400-1830, Oct-Mar Mon-Wed and Sat 0930-1630, Thur 0930-1200, Sun 1400-1630. £2, £1.50 concession, joint ticket with Spynie Palace (see below) £2.80, £2.10 concession.*

Also in town is **Elgin Museum**, at 1 High Street. It has excellent displays of fossils and Pictish relics, as well as some interesting anthropological collections. ■ *T543675. End Mar-Oct Mon-Fri 1000-1700, Sat 1100-1600, Sun 1400-1700. £1.50, 75p concession.*

Two miles north of Elgin is **Spynie Palace**, the residence of the Bishops of Moray from the 14th century till 1686, when they were abolished in the Scottish Church. The palace is now a ruin, though the massive tower, built by Bishop David Stewart, remains, affording spectacular views over Spynie Loch and the Moray Firth. ■ *Apr-Sept Mon-Sat 0930-1830, Sun 1400-1830, Oct-Mar weekends only till 1630. £1.80, £1.35 concession, joint ticket with Elgin Cathedral available (see above).*

Six miles southwest of Elgin, set in a sheltered valley, is the giant hulk of **Pluscarden Abbey**. The abbey was founded in 1230, but in 1390 became another victim of the incredibly vengeful Wolf of Badenoch (see above). It recovered, but then fell into disrepair after the Reformation, until 1948 when it was rebuilt by an order of Benedictine monks, who still inhabit the abbey, lending it an authentic medieval touch. There are guided tours and services are open to the public. ■ *T890257. Daily 0445-2045. Free.*

There's a wide range of accommodation in Elgin. Best of the hotels is the **A** *Mansion House Hotel*, The Haugh (north of the High St, overlooking the river), T548811. 23 rooms, full leisure facilities and a good restaurant in an elegant and comfortable town

Sleeping

Northeast Scotland

house. Also recommended is the **C** *Mansfield House Hotel*, on Mayne Rd (1 block south of the High St), T540883. 21 rooms, centrally located, elegant town house. Its restaurant is very popular with locals and reputed to be the best in town (expensive).

There are many fine **guesthouses** and **B&Bs**, including the highly rated **D-E** *The Pines Guesthouse*, T542766, kath-pos@hotmail.com, on East Rd, a short walk from the town centre. Also good are **E** *The Lodge*, 20 Duff Ave, T549981, **D-E** *The Croft*, 10 Institution Rd, T546004, and **E** *Ardgye House*, T850618, which is 5 mins' drive from town on the A96 west to Inverness. For something a bit different, there's **D-E** *The Old Church of Urquhart*, T843063, a converted church in the tiny village of Urquhart, 5 miles east of Elgin, off the A96 to Aberdeen.

Eating The best place to eat in town is the *Mansfield House Hotel* (see above). 6 miles south of town, on the A941 to Rothes, is the *Rothes Glen Hotel*, T01340-831254, which is acclaimed for its superb modern Scottish cooking. There are plenty of cheaper places in town, including *Littlejohn's*, 193 High St, a Tex-Mex/Cajun restaurant chain that's child-friendly. Nearby, at 181 High St, is *Ca'Dora*, a fish and chip shop. *Gordon and McPhail*, 50-60 South St, is an excellent deli, with a lip-smacking variety of fine foods and a huge range of malt whiskies. A good pub is *Thunderton House*, in Thuderton Place, off the High St.

Transport Elgin is well-served by public transport. **Trains** run hourly every day to **Aberdeen** and **Inverness**, stopping at **Forres** and **Nairn**. **Buses** *Bluebird Buses*, T01224-212266, run hourly to **Aberdeen** (3 hrs, £6.50) and **Inverness** (1 hr 15 mins, £5.50) via **Nairn** (40 mins) and **Forres** (25 mins). There are buses every 30 mins to **Lossiemouth** (20 mins) and hourly to **Burghead** (Mon-Sat, 30 mins). There are buses along the coast to **Banff** and **Macduff**, hourly to **Dufftown** (1 hr) and to **Findhorn** (Mon-Sat, 20 mins). There's also a bus once a day (schooldays only) to **Pluscarden**, T01542-882482.

Lossiemouth to Burghead

Colour map 2, grid C4 Six miles north of Elgin is Lossiemouth, at the mouth of the river Lossie, funnily enough. The old fishing port is blessed with two fine beaches, to the east and west of town, and an excellent golf course, making it a popular seaside resort in summer. The town's real claim to fame, though, is as the birthplace of James Ramsay MacDonald (1866-1937), Britain's first Labour prime minister.

Between 'Lossie' and Burghead, south of the coast road, is the scattered village of **Duffus**. The old part is home to a ruined 14th-century motte and bailey castle, and an interesting 13th-century church, while the newer part is better known for its close neighbour, **Gordonstoun School**, the public school favoured (but not necessarily loved) by the royal family.

Six miles west of Lossie is the fishing village of **Burghead**, ancient Pictish capital of Moray and site of an important Iron Age fort. The only real surviving feature is the well in King Street (key from No 69 King Street). The village gave its name to the **Burghead Bulls**, a series of remarkable Pictish stone carvings, some of which can be seen in the Elgin Museum (the others are in the Royal Museum in Edinburgh and the British Museum in London). The old Pictish New Year is still celebrated in the village, on 11 January, when a burning tar barrel – the Clavie – is carried around. To the west of the village a wide sweep of sandy beach stretches all the way west to Findhorn (see below). There's a good chance of seeing the Moray Firth's resident population of bottlenose **dolphins** from here.

There are a few **campsites** between Lossiemouth and Burghead. A couple of miles **Sleeping**
east of Burghead is *Hopeman Sands Caravan Park*, T830880, open Apr-Nov, and
overlooking the beach to the west of Lossiemouth there's the *Silver Sands Leisure
Park*, T813262, open Apr-Oct. There are regular **buses** to Lossiemouth and Burghead
from Elgin (see above).

Forres and Findhorn

Twelve miles west of Elgin is the solid little town of Forres. On the eastern edge   *Phone code: 01309*
of town is the 20-ft high **Sueno's Stone**, one of the most remarkable and   *Colour map 2, grid C3*
important Pictish carved stones in Scotland. About six miles south of Forres is
one of the northeast's best-kept secrets, the very beautiful **Randolph's Leap**, a
spectacular gorge on the river Findhorn which is the perfect place for a picnic,
or a swim in the river. To get there, head south on the A940 and just beyond
Logie Steading take the right fork (the B9007) for a half a mile. It's on the right
side of the road as you head south. It's also worth stopping at Logie Steading,
where you can buy good value arts arts and crafts. ■ *Daily May-Oct
1100-1700, weekends from 1200.* A few miles west of Forres is **Brodie Castle**
(see 'Highlands' chapter, page 412).

There's a **tourist office** in Forres, at 116 High Street. ■ *T672938.
Easter-Jun, Sept and Oct Mon-Sat 1000-1300 and 1400-1700, Jul-Aug Mon-Sat
till 1800, Sun 1300-1800.*

There's a surprisingly wide range of accommodation in Forres. Best of the hotels are   **Sleeping**
the excellent **A** *Knockomie Hotel*, T673146, overlooking the town on the A940 south
to Grantown, and the **B** *Ramnee Hotel*, T672410, on Victoria Rd. Both have highly
acclaimed restaurants. Among the many fine **guesthouses** and **B&Bs** are
D-E *Springfield*, T676965, hbain@globalnet.co.uk, on Croft Rd, **D-E** *Sherston House*,
T671087, at Hillhead, and **E** *Tormhor*, T673837, at 11 High St.

Forres is on the main Aberdeen to Inverness bus route and rail line, and there are regu-   **Transport**
lar **buses** and **trains** in either direction. *Bluebird Buses* Nos 310 and 311 run from **Elgin**
to **Forres**, via **Kinloss** and **Findhorn** several times daily (Mon-Sat).

A few miles northeast of Forres is **Kinloss**, site of a major RAF base. The B9011   **The Findhorn**
heads north from Kinloss and past the RAF base; on the right is a sign to the   **Foundation**
'Findhorn Bay Caravan Park'. In the shadow of the RAF base in a landscape of
gorse and pine-clad dunes, the caravan park is the original site and nucleus of
the Findhorn Foundation, a world-renowned spiritual community.

A combination of hard work and serendipity led three hard-pressed caravan dwellers in the early sixties – Peter and Eileen Caddy and Dorothy
Maclean – to establish a garden in the dunes which quickly became renowned
far and wide for its miraculous abundance, owing, they claim, not only to
organic methods but directions from the kingdom of nature spirits. Attracting
the like-minded and curious, it grew into a pioneering community where, with
an emphasis on the spiritual, the philosophy of the ecological movement was
put into practice, following angelic guidance regularly channelled by two of the
founding fathers.

Caravans are slowly being replaced by energy efficient houses using envi-
ronmentally safe building materials, including upturned whisky barrels sal-
vaged from a nearby distillery, with reed bed sewage systems and turf roots. A
strong educational bias brings 4,000 people annually from all over the world to
participate in residential courses in personal development, community living
and ecological building, or to complete a year-long 'foundation course'. In a

Northeast Scotland

vibrant, hot-house atmosphere overshadowed by pine trees, in a warren of densely packed houses, is a community centre and a stone and timber arts centre/café architecturally inspired by the tenets of Rudolph Steiner, all giving shelter against the sea winds in order to promote plant life and greenery.

Extending worldwide by reputation, the influence of the Foundation has also spread locally, attracting kindred spirits to settle in the area and establish initiatives such as native reforestation of the Highlands, a Steiner School and complementary health practices.

All but the most world-weary of cynics will find the Foundation a fascinating, and possibly enlightening, experience. There are guided tours around the site daily at 1400 throughout the summer.

Sleeping and eating You can also join the community as a short-term guest, eating and working on-site and staying at local recommended **B&Bs**, and there's a full programme of courses and residential workshops on spiritual growth and healing etc. For more information, T690311. The excellent on-site **shop/deli** by the car park sells books, new-age paraphernalia and a huge variety of organic food (open Mon-Fri till 1800; weekends till 1700). There's also a very good vegetarian **café**. The caravan park is open to the public and you can **camp** beside the Foundation, T690203, caravan@findhorn.org.

Findhorn A mile north of the Caravan Park is the traditional fishing village of Findhorn, sparkling white under a huge sky, on the eastern shore of Findhorn Bay. The bay provides sheltered waters for boating and watersports, which can all be arranged from the village. On the other side of the bay you can walk on the dunes of Culbin Sands, explore the forest and look for dolphins in the Moray Firth. You may even see an osprey fishing for trout or salmon.

In the village itself is the **Findhorn Heritage Centre**. ■ *Daily (except Tue) Easter, Jun, Jul-Aug 1400-1700; also weekends 1400-1700 in May and Sept.* A good place to eat in the village is the *Kimberley Inn*, T690492, which serves seafood and real ales in a colourful pub atmosphere.

The Highlands

10

The Highlands

The Highlands of Scotland contain some of the most beautiful scenery on earth. Around every bend in the twisting, tortuous roads that snake their way through this vast region is a sight that leaves you (and me) reaching for the thesaurus to find an alternative to 'spectacular', or 'stunning'. Forget nightclubs or multi-screen cinemas. People come here for the beauty and variety of the landscape, the wide, open spaces and tranquility.

The west coast is the part which reflects most perfectly people's romantic image of Scotland. The main town is Fort William, which lies in the shadow of Ben Nevis, Britain's highest mountain. North from here stretches a dramatic shoreline of deep sea lochs and sheltered coves of pure white sand backed by towering mountains and looking across to numerous Hebridean islands. West of Fort William, via the lyrical 'Road to the Isles', is Mallaig, now the main departure point for ferries to Skye. Further north is Ullapool, one of the main ferry ports for the Outer Hebrides and the ideal base from which to explore the wild and near-deserted far northwest.

Inverness is the largest town in the region and 'capital of the Highlands'. It lies at the northeastern end of the Great Glen, which cuts diagonally across the southern Highlands to Fort William, linking deep and mysterious Loch Ness with the west coast and giving access to Glencoe, one of the most beautifully evocative Highland glens and a major climbing and skiing centre. Inverness is also ideally situated for exploring the northeast coast, with its charming old fishing ports, and the storm-lashed north coast, running west from John O'Groats to Cape Wrath, as wild and remote a place as you could ever wish for.

Ins and outs

Getting around Getting around in the Highlands is a lot easier with your own transport, especially in the more remote parts, but it's not difficult to reach the main tourist centres by bus or train. Inverness is linked to the south by the fast A9 from Edinburgh and Perth, to Aberdeen by the A96 and to Fort William by the A82, and is well served by buses. Wick, Thurso, Ullapool and Kyle of Lochalsh can all be reached by bus from Inverness. The rail line from Edinburgh closely follows the A9 to Inverness, and there are connections north to Wick and Thurso, west to Kyle of Lochalsh and east to Aberdeen. Fort William is easily reached from Glasgow by buses and trains, which continue to Mallaig for the ferry to Skye.

By far the most scenic route to the Highlands is the spectacular West Highland Railway, one of the world's great rail journeys, particularly the section from Fort William to Mallaig.

Getting off the beaten track can be a little more complicated, but with forward planning is easily achievable. Much of the time you'll need to rely on the local postbus service, which runs between the various remote post offices throughout the region. Timetables are available at most post offices, or T01463-256228. Tourist offices will also provide local timetables. A good idea is to purchase the Public Transport Travel Guides, for South Highland and/or North Highland and Orkney. These are available at main tourist offices for £1. Note that details of ferries from the mainland ports to Skye, the Outer Hebrides and Orkney are given in the respective island chapters.

Information Roughly speaking, the Highlands cover the northern half of mainland Scotland. This chapter includes the Highland administrative region, minus the Isle of Skye, which has its own chapter. All of this chapter is covered by the **Highlands of Scotland Tourist Board**, T01997-421160, admin@host.co.uk, www.host.co.uk, which publishes free accommodation guides for the region. They will also book accommodation for a nominal fee. Note that many of the smaller offices are closed during the low season. There's also a local website which has lots of information, including maps, at www.cali.co.uk/highexp/.

Climate The beauty of the Highlands is only enhanced by the notoriously unpredictable weather and that ever-present travelling companion, the midge. That's a lie. The midge is the scourge of many a Highland holiday. A ferocious, persistent and unbelievably irritating little beast who will drive you to the edge of insanity. For details on how best to combat this little terror, see page 54.

The only predictable thing about the weather is its unpredictability. You can have blazing sunshine in Apr, pouring rain in Jul and a blizzard in May. So, you'll need to be prepared for everything. Climbers and walkers especially must take heed of all weather warnings. It can be hot enough for bikinis in the car park at the foot of a 2,000-ft mountain, and two hours later near the summit you're faced with driving, horizontal hail, rain or snow and unable to see further than the end of your nose. People die every year on the Scottish mountains, simply because they are ill-prepared, and it is essential to take proper precautions (see page 56). Even those who are not intent on bagging the odd Munro should remember the old adage, that there's no such thing as bad weather, only inadequate clothing.

Inverness

Inverness is the largest town in the Highlands and the busy and prosperous hub of the region. All main routes through the Highlands pass through here at some point, so it's a hard place to avoid. The town's position at the head of the Great Glen and on the shores of the Moray Firth have made it a firm favourite with tourists, who flock here in their legions during the summer months to look for the evasive Loch Ness Monster. Though Inverness has little in the way of major sights, it's a pleasant place to base yourself as you explore the other, more visible attractions on offer in the surrounding area, including the resident population of dolphins in the Moray Firth. The town, though, is not without its own appeal, particularly the leafy banks of the river Ness, which runs through its heart, linking Loch Ness with the Moray Firth.

Phone code: 01463
Colour map 2, grid C2
Population: 42,000

Ins and outs

Inverness is 109 miles from Aberdeen, 161 miles from Edinburgh and 117 miles from Perth. There are daily flights to and from London Gatwick, Glasgow and Edinburgh with *British Airways* (continuing to Kirkwall and Sumburgh), and daily flights to and from London Luton with *EasyJet*. There are also flights to and from Stornoway Mon-Sat with *British Airways Express*. The airport is 7 miles east of the town, at Dalcross (T232471). A twice-daily airport bus to and from the town centre connects with London and Stornoway flights. It takes 20 mins and costs £2.50. A taxi to/from the airport costs £10.

Getting there
For more details of transport services see 'Transport', page 408

   The **train station** is at the east end of Academy St (T238924). There are regular services to Aviemore, Perth, Glasgow, Edinburgh and Kyle of Lochalsh (for Skye). Left luggage lockers at the train station cost £2-4 per 24 hrs. The **bus station** is nearby, just off Academy St (T233371). Left luggage costs £1 per item, open Mon-Sat 0830-1800, Sun 1000-1800.

The **tourist office**, T234353, is on Castle Wynd, near Ness Bridge, 5 mins walk from the train station. It stocks a wide range of literature on the area, can book accommodation and transport and gives out free maps of the town and environs. Tickets for all the tours listed below are available from the tourist office. 1 Apr-28 May Mon-Fri 0900-1700, Sat 0930-1700, Sun 0930-1600; 29 May-20 Jun Mon-Fri 0900-1800, Sat 0900-1700, Sun 0930-1700; 21 Jun-4 Jul Mon-Sat 0900-1800, Sun 0930-1700; 5 Jul-29 Aug Mon-Sat 0900-2030, Sun 0930-1800; 30 Aug-12 Sept Mon-Sat 0900-1800, Sun 0930-1700; 13 Sept-26 Sept Mon-Fri 0900-1800, Sat-Sun 0930-1700; 27 Sept-23 Oct Mon-Fri 0900-1700, Sat 0930-1700, Sun 0930-1600; 24 Oct-Apr Mon-Fri 0900-1700, Sat 1000-1600.

Tourist information

History

One of the town's fist visitors was that much-travelled cleric, St Columba, who came in AD 565 to confront the Pictish King Brude, whose fortress was reputedly at **Craig Phadraig**, a few miles west of Inverness. Around the mid-12th century King David I built the original castle and made Inverness a royal burgh on the strength of its growing importance as a trading port. Furs, hides, wool and timber were all exported as far afield as the Mediterranean. The town's economic prosperity and status as the most important northern outpost, however, made it a prime target for marauding Highland clansmen, and during the Wars of Independence in the 13th century, Inverness was also a regular target for both English and Scots armies.

The Highlands

☞ *Loch Ness Monster Tours*

*There are various **monster-spotting tours of Loch Ness** which leave from the tourist office. Inverness Traction (6 Burnett Road, T239292) run half-day coach trips right round the loch, departing at 0945, returning at 1430. Tickets cost £7 and are available from the tourist office, Thomas Cook booking office at the train station and Skyeways office at bus station. They also run local bus services; phone for details.*

Coach tours, boat cruises and combined coach and cruise trips round the loch are offered by Jacobite Cruises

(T233999, jacobite@cali.co.uk). Half day cruises cost £9, half day coach and cruise trips cost £12.50 (including entry to the Loch Ness Monster Exhibition and Urquhart Castle). Trips run from April-October and leave from Tomnahurich Bridge on Glenurquhart Road, 1½ miles south of the town centre. Free buses leave from the TIC 20 minutes before sailing, if tickets are bought here. Otherwise, to get there take Inverness Traction buses Nos 3, 3A, 4 and 4A every 15 minutes from Church St (75p).

The town's renaissance came with the completion of the Caledonian Canal and rail links with the south in the 19th century. These improved communications heralded something of a tourist boom amongst the wealthy and fashionable who came north to the Highlands to shoot anything that moved in the name of sport. In the mid-19th century Queen Victoria decided to embrace all things Scottish, which only boosted the town's popularity. Over recent decades, Inverness has grown rapidly, not only as a prime base for visiting tourists, but also as the main administrative and commercial centre for the Highlands.

Sights

The town is dominated by its red sandstone **castle**. Built in 1834, this Victorian edifice is very much the new kid on the block in terms of Scottish castles. The original castle dates from the 12th century and was built on a ridge to the east of the present structure. Nothing remains of the old castle, which is unsurprising given its bloody and eventful history. It was here that King Duncan of Scotland was slain by Macbeth, an event dramatically (and erroneously) portrayed in Shakespeare's eponymous work. The castle was occupied three times during the Wars of Independence in the 13th century and when Robert the Bruce recaptured it in 1307, he destroyed it. In the mid-17th century Cromwell ordered his men to build a stone version on the same site. In 1715 James Francis Edward was proclaimed king there, but not long after, it was destroyed by the Jacobites to prevent it from falling into enemy hands following the defeat of Bonnie Prince Charlie at Culloden (see page 422).

The present castle houses the Sheriff Court and also stages the **Castle Garrison Encounter**, where you can sign up as a mid-18th century soldier. New recruits (that's you) pass through the Quartermaster's Store and are introduced to the Sergeant of the Guard, before being accosted by a female camp follower and finally led out through the garrison shop. ■ *T243363. Mar-Nov Mon-Sat (Sun only in Jul/Aug) 1030-1730. £3.*

On the castle terrace is a statue of **Flora MacDonald**, to honour her part in helping the prince to escape (see page 503). Below the castle is **Inverness Museum and Art Gallery**, on Castle Wynd beside the Tourist Information Centre. The museum gives a decent overview of the history of the town and the region, while the gallery is eminently missable. ■ *Mon-Sat 0900-1700. Free.*

Just around the corner, on High Street, is the Gothic-style **Town House**, where Prime Minister Lloyd George held an emergency cabinet meeting in 1921,

Tours of Inverness

An open-top double-decker **Bus Tour** around Inverness and Culloden is run by Guide Friday. Tours leave from Bridge Street near the tourist office at 1000 and then every 45 minutes till 1645, from May to October. Tickets can be bought at their booth in the train station, T224000; open Mon-Fri 0900-1730, Sat 0830-1745, or on board the bus. A full day ticket costs £6.50 (£5 concession).

The Inverness Terror Tour, T07771-768652, leaves from outside the tourist office at 1900 nightly and tells the tale of the town's horrific past, complete with witches, ghosts, torture and murders (£5.50 adult, £5 student, £3 child).

the first ever to be held outside London. Opposite, on the corner of Bridge Street and Church Street, is the **Tolbooth Steeple** which dates from 1791 and which had to be repaired after an earth tremor in 1816. Church Street also boasts the town's oldest building, **Abertarff House** (built around 1592), which is now owned by the National Trust but not open to the public. Almost opposite is the much-restored **Dunbar's Hospital**, built in 1688 as an almshouse for the town's poor. At the end of Church Street, where it meets Friar's Lane, is the **Old High Church**, founded in the 12th century and rebuilt in 1772, though the 14th-century vaulted tower remains intact. In the adjoining graveyard, prisoners taken at Culloden were executed and you can still see the bullet marks left by the firing squads on some of the gravestones. ■ *The church is open on Fri 1200-1400 and during services; guided tour at 1230.*

One of the town's most interesting sights is **Balnain House**, which stands on the west bank of the river, on Huntly Street, over the footbridge. This is the home of Highland music, where you can trace the development of this musical tradition from its earliest days right up to the present, as well as try your hand at playing the bagpipes, the fiddle, or harp. You can sample the wide range of musical styles from the region at CD listening posts. The café downstairs offers traditional regional fare, and there's also a shop and library. Throughout the summer, various musical events take place here. ■ *Tue-Sun 1000-1700 (also Mon in Jul-Aug). £1.50.*

A few minutes' walk south of Balnain House, at the corner of Huntly Street and Ness Bridge, is the **Kiltmaker Centre**, where you can learn everything you ever wanted to know about tartan (including what Scotsmen wear under their kilts). You can also see kilts being made in the factory and, in the shop downstairs, be measured up for one of your own. ■ *T222781, kilts@ russellh.win-uk.net, www.hector-russell.com. Mid-May to end of Sept Mon-Sat 0900-2100, Sun 1000-1700; Oct to mid-May Mon-Sat 0900-1700. £2.*

Nearby, directly opposite the castle, is the neo-Gothic **St Andrews Cathedral** which dates from 1869, and is worth a peek if you're passing by. Continuing south along Ness Bank, past the **Eden Court Theatre** (see 'Entertainment' below), you reach **Bught Park** (see 'Sleeping'), which overlooks the **Ness Islands**, joined by footbridge to both banks. The islands are attractively laid out as a park and are a favourite with local anglers. This also happens to be a lovely place for a peaceful evening stroll.

Essentials

You shouldn't have much trouble finding somewhere to stay in Inverness, though in Jul and Aug it's advisable to book ahead. This can be done through the tourist information centre, or in the train station at the Thomas Cook booth, but you'll be charged a booking fee (see page 36). There are several good quality hotels in and around town

The Highlands

Sleeping
■ *on map*
Price codes:
see inside front cover

and plenty of B&Bs. The best places to look are along both banks of the river south of the Ness Bridge, Old Edinburgh Rd, Southside Rd, Culduthel Rd and Ardconnel St, all to the east of the castle, and on the west bank, behind Balnain House, around Kenneth St and Fairfield Rd. There are also several budget hostels in and around the centre, and a couple of large campsites.

Inverness

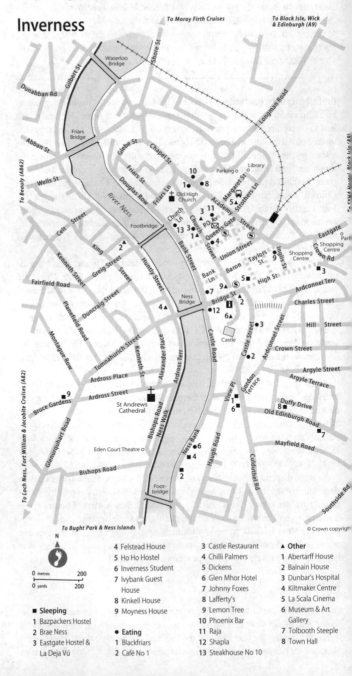

© Crown copyright

To Moray Firth Cruises

To Black Isle, Wick & Edinburgh (A9)

To Beauly (A862)

To Loch Ness, Fort William & Jacobite Cruises (A82)

To Bught Park & Ness Islands

The Highlands

N

| 0 metres | 200 |
| 0 yards | 200 |

■ **Sleeping**
1 Bazpackers Hostel
2 Brae Ness
3 Eastgate Hostel & La Deja Vú

4 Felstead House
5 Ho Ho Hostel
6 Inverness Student
7 Ivybank Guest House
8 Kinkell House
9 Moyness House

● **Eating**
1 Blackfriars
2 Café No 1

3 Castle Restaurant
4 Chilli Palmers
5 Dickens
6 Glen Mhor Hotel
7 Johnny Foxes
8 Lafferty's
9 Lemon Tree
10 Phoenix Bar
11 Raja
12 Shapla
13 Steakhouse No 10

▲ **Other**
1 Abertarff House
2 Balnain House
3 Dunbar's Hospital
4 Kiltmaker Centre
5 La Scala Cinema
6 Museum & Art Gallery
7 Tolbooth Steeple
8 Town Hall

L *Culloden House Hotel*, Milton of Culloden, about 3 miles east of town near the A9. T790461, F792181. 28 rooms, superb Georgian mansion with 1st-class facilities, service and restaurant. **L** *Dunain Park Hotel*, about 3 miles southwest of the town centre, just off the A82 Fort William Rd. T230512, F224532, Dunainparkhotel@btinternet.com. 12 rooms, in an elegant Georgian mansion house with its own grounds, lovely and peaceful with an excellent restaurant (see below) and its own indoor pool.

A *Kingsmills Hotel*, Culcabock Rd, 1 mile south of the town centre near A9, T237166, F225208. 81 rooms, large, modern hotel with excellent rooms, service and facilities.

B *Glenruidh House Hotel*, Old Edinburgh Rd South, 2 miles from the town centre (phone for directions). T226499, F710745, glenruidhhousehotel@btinternet.com. 6 rooms, no smoking. Comfortable and peaceful hotel in secluded setting, with friendly service and excellent food. **B** *Glenmoriston Town House Hotel*, 20 Ness Bank. T223777, F712378. 15 rooms. Recently refurbished and now one of the classiest places in town with a superb Italian restaurant (see below).

D *Moyness House Hotel*, 6 Bruce Gardens. T/F233836, kayjonesmoyness@msn.com. Fine Victorian villa in a quiet area near the theatre, with comfortable rooms and very good food. **D** *Brae Ness Hotel*, Ness Bank. T712266, F231732. 10 rooms, no smoking. Family-run Georgian hotel overlooking the river and Eden Court with a licensed restaurant for residents. **D** *Felstead House*, 18 Ness Bank. T/F231634, jaf@yrl.co.uk. 7 rooms, 4 with bathroom en suite. Comfortable family-run Georgian guesthouse, decent value.

E *Ivybank Guesthouse*, 28 Old Edinburgh Rd. T/F232796. 5 rooms, 3 with en suite bathroom. Georgian house with lots of character, nice garden and friendly welcome. **E** *Kinkell House*, 11 Old Edinburgh Rd. T235243, F225255, clare@kinkell.freeserve.co.uk. 7 rooms, 3 with en suite bathroom. Comfortable Victorian family home with spacious rooms, decent value, £2 charge for credit card payment.

F *Bazpackers Hostel*, 4 Culduthel Rd (at the top of Castle St), T717663. 48 beds in dorms of 4-8, twin and double rooms available, cooking facilities and garden for barbecues, also has laundrette, good atmosphere. **F** *Eastgate Hostel*, 38 Eastgate (above *La Déjà Vu* restaurant). T/F718756. 38 beds in 8 dorms, free tea and coffee and continental breakfast for £1.50. **F** *Inverness Student Hotel*, 8 Culduthel Rd, next door to *Bazpackers*. T236556. 9 dorms with 57 beds, some dorms have good views. Friendly and laid-back atmosphere with all the usual facilities. **F** *SYHA Youth Hostel*, Victoria Drive, off Millburn Rd. T231771, F710349. 166 beds, huge hostel in former school hall of residence. Another cheap option is the *Ho Ho Hostel*, T221225, at 23a High St.

Bught Caravan and Camping Site, Bught Park, on the west bank of the river near the sports centre, T236920. The largest and most centrally located campsite, with good facilities, charges £3-10 per pitch.

Eating There's no shortage of places to eat in Inverness. As you'd expect in a major tourist centre, there's the usual plethora of pubs, cafés and restaurants serving cheap and basic food for the non-discerning palate, but those looking for a higher standard of cuisine won't be disappointed either. There are also loads of takeaways, particularly on Academy St and the Eastgate around the train station, and on Young St, just across the Ness Bridge. A good bakery is *Asher's* in Church St.

Expensive *Dunain Park Hotel* (address as above). Award-winning Scots-French cuisine in elegant surroundings and a superb list of malts, take a stroll in the lovely

The Highlands

gardens afterwards. *Glen Mhor Hotel*, 9-12 Ness Bank, T234308. *Riverview* restaurant at the front is good, especially for seafood. *La Riviera*, at the *Glenmoriston Town House Hotel* (see above). Excellent Italian food.

Mid-range *Café No 1*, 75 Castle St, T226200. Stands head and shoulders above everything else in the town centre in terms of quality and imagination, has nice contemporary décor, good selection of vegetarian options, open for lunch and 1800-2200. *Dickens*, 77 Church St. T713111. Offers a mix of oriental and international dishes with an emphasis on fish, business lunch for £6.50, open 1200-1400 and 1730-2300. *La Déjà vu*, 38 Eastgate. T231075. Very good French provincial cooking in an informal atmosphere, their 3-course business lunch is great value at £7, open daily 1200-1400 and 1700 till late. *Nico's Bistro* at the back is also good for traditional Scottish dishes. *Raja*, behind the post office on Post Office Ave. T237190. Highly rated Indian restaurant. *Shapla*, 2 Castle Rd, T241919. Good Indian restaurant with Tandoori and Balti menu, good views of the river in the upstairs lounge, open till 2330. *Steakhouse No 10*, 10 Bank St. T714884. Specializes in crêpes and steaks, offers reasonably priced snacks 1100-1500, and à la carte lunch and dinner.

Cheap *Castle Restaurant*, 41 Castle St. Glorified greasy spoon serving huge portions of stodgy, filling grub, convenient for backpacker's hostels, open till 2100. *The Lemon Tree*, 18 Inglis St. Located in the pedestrianized town centre, family-run café offering good home baking and basic but filling meals.

The best bet for a cheap lunch or evening meal is one of the city's many pubs and bars, where you can get a main course for £5-6. The most favoured options are *Johnny Foxes*, *Chilli Palmers* and *No 27* (see below).

Bars   At 108 Academy St is the *Phoenix*, one of the best pubs in town and always lively. Next door is an Irish theme pub, *Lafferty's*, which features Scottish/Celtic live music on Fri and Sat. Across the street is *Blackfriars*, which is another good pub. *Gellions*, on Bridge St, has varied live music throughout the week and *Johnny Foxes*, at 26 Bank St, features Irish folk music every night in summer as well as boasting one of the most unusual pub menus around. *Chilli Palmers*, on the corner of Queensgate and Church St, is a trendy new bar offering decent food and a DJ at weekends, and you can enjoy a Jazz Lunch on Sun at *No 27*, on Castle St. A good place to hear traditional folk music is in the basement café of *Balnain House* (see 'Sights').

Entertainment   **Theatre and cinema** *Eden Court Theatre* is on Bishops Rd, overlooking the river Ness. It offers a varied programme of theatre, dance and all kinds of music. There's also a bar and self-service restaurant with good food and views over the river. The attached cinema shows a programme of art-house and newly released movies, for information: T234234. *La Scala* on Strother's Lane, just off Academy St, has 2 screens, and the 7-screen *Warner Village* is on the A96 Nairn Rd, about 2 miles from the town centre. Eden Court prices vary depending on the performance; cinema tickets cost from £4.

Festivals   There are numerous events held in and around Inverness throughout the year. These range from a humble pub ceilidh to a full-blown Highland Games. For details contact the tourist office or visit their website. The best of the local folk festivals are held over the Easter weekend (T01738-623274) and the excellent Highland Festival takes place over 3 days at the end of Jun (T711112, info@highlandfestival.demon.co.uk, www.highlandfestival.demon.co.uk). There's also a festival of folk music in Jul and Aug at Balnain House (see 'Sights' above).

The Highlands

Inverness is a good place to buy a **kilt**, or practically anything else in tartan. To find out your own clan tartan, head for *the Scottish Kiltmaker Visitor Centre* (see 'Sights' above). Other places which sell highland dress and traditional gifts are *Chisholm's Highland Dress*, 47-51 Castle St, T234599, open 0900-1730 and 1900-2130 in Jul and Aug; and *Hector Russell*, 4-9 Huntly St, T222781. At *James Pringle Weavers* (Holm Mills, Dores Rd, T223311) you can see tartan rugs being made in the weaving mill, then spend your cash in their extensive mill shop and eat in the restaurant. The Eastgate Shopping Centre houses all the usual high street branches and the Victorian Market on Church St has a wide range of shops. The largest **bookshop** in town is *James Thin*, 29 Union St, T233500, which has an excellent range of Scottish books and maps. There's also a branch of *Waterstone's*, at 50-52 High St, T717474.

Shopping

Bowling 10-pin bowling at Roller Bowl, 167 Culduthel Rd, 235100. Open Mon-Fri 1200 till late, Sat-Sun 1100 till late. **Cycle hire** *Barney's Bicycle Hire & Shop*, 35 Castle St, T232249. Open 0900-2100. Mountain bike hire from £7 per day. Also bikes for hire from *Bazpacker's Hostel* (see 'Sleeping'). **Golf** The best golf course in the area is at Nairn (see page 411). There's an 18-hole municipal course at Torvean, 2 miles from town on the A82 to Fort William. T711434. **Horse riding** The *Highland Riding Centre* is at Borlum Farm, Drumnadrochit, T/F01456-450358. **Leisure centre** The *Aquadome Leisure Centre* is at Bught Park (T667500). Open Mon-Fri 0730-2200, Sat-Sun 0730-2100. Competition sized pool, flumes, wave machine and kiddies' pool, also health suites, gym and other indoor sports facilities. **Tennis** The *Inverness Tennis and Squash Club* is at Bishop's Rd (T230751).

Sports

Orkney Islands Day Tours leave from Inverness every day throughout the summer. The tour departs daily 1 Jun-5 Sept from Inverness bus station at 0730; returns 2100. Booking essential; £42 per person, under 16 half price. Details from the tourist office, or contact *John O'Groats Ferries*, Ferry Office, John O'Groats, Caithness. T01955-611353, F01955-611301, www.jogferry.co.uk (for tours from John O'Groats, see page 474).

Tours & tour operators
See also box, page 403

Buses There are regular daily buses to **Glasgow** (£11.50 single) and **Edinburgh** (£12.30) via **Aviemore** (£4), **Pitlochry** (£7) and **Perth** (£9) with *Scottish Citylink* (T0990-505050). Change at Perth for **Dundee**. There are regular daily *Citylink* buses to **Ullapool** (£7), connecting with the ferry to **Stornoway**; also to **Fort William** (£6.30) and **Oban** (£9.80). There are daily *Citylink* buses to **Kyle of Lochalsh**, **Portree** (£10.50) and **Uig** (connecting with ferries to **Tarbert** and **Lochmaddy**). There are regular *Citylink* buses to **Fort Augustus** via **Drumnadrochit** and **Urquhart Castle** (also with *Highland Bus & Coach*, T233371), and to **Scrabster**, for the ferry to **Stromness**, via **Wick** and **Thurso** (£9); also with *Morrison's Coaches*, T01847-821241.

Transport

To **Ullapool** via **Gairloch** and **Aultbea**, there are daily buses with *Spa Coaches* (T01997-421311), *Bluebird Buses* (T239292) and *Westerbus* (01445-712255). To **Tain** and **Lairg** there are daily services with *Bluebird* and *Rapson's* (T710555). To **Tain** and **Helmsdale**, via **Dornoch** there are regular daily buses with *Citylink*, *Morrison's* and *Bluebird*. To **Lochinver** via **Ullapool** there's a daily service with *Spa* coaches and *Rapson's* of Brora (01408-621245). To **Durness** via **Lairg** and **Tongue**, or via **Ullapool** (not in winter) there's a daily service with *Royal Mail Postbuses* (T01463-256228). To **Grantown-on-Spey**, daily service with *Highland Country Buses* (T233371) and *Highland Bus & Coach*. *Inverness Traction* and *Highland Country Buses* have services to places around Inverness, including **Nairn**, **Forres**, **Culloden**, **Beauly** and **Dingwall**. Bluebird have regular buses to **Aberdeen**, via **Nairn**.

The Highlands

☞ *Dolphin cruises*

*There are various **dolphin-spotting cruises** around the Moray Firth, but there is a code of conduct for boat operators. Before you choose a cruise, make sure the company is part of the Accreditation Scheme. One such company, based in Inverness, is **Moray Firth Dolphin Cruises**, T717900, morayfirth.cruises@virgin.net. Trips are £10 (£8 concession), last 1½ hours and leave from Shore Street Quay (beyond the roundabout at the far end of Chapel St). Buses run from the tourist information centre 15 minutes before sailings. Also in Inverness are McAuley Charters, Harbour offices, Longman Drive, T717337. Dolphin-spotting cruises also leave from Cromarty (see page 476) and Buckie (see page 392). Buckie is also the home of the **Moray Firth Wildlife Centre**, which houses a **dolphin exhibition**, where you can learn all about these fascinating mammals.*

Ferries For details of connections to Stornoway (Lewis) see page 521, or contact the *CalMac* office in Inverness, T717681. For Scrabster to Stromness, see page 554.

Taxis *Rank Radio Taxis*, T221111/220222; *Tartan Taxis*, T233033.

Trains There are direct trains to/from **Aberdeen** (£17.60), **Edinburgh** via Aviemore (£29.60) and **Glasgow** (£29.60). There are several daily services to/from **London King's Cross**, via Perth and Edinburgh, including a sleeping car service (see page 30). There is also a regular service to **Wick** (£12.50) and **Thurso** (£12.50), via Tain, Lairg and Helmsdale. The journey from Inverness to **Kyle of Lochalsh** (for Skye) costs £14.70 and is one of the most scenic in Britain. There are 3 trains daily (none on Sun). Phone 0345-484950 for all rail enquiries.

Car hire *Avis* is at the airport (T01667-462787); *Budget* is on Railway Terr behind the train station (T713333); *Europcar* has an office at the Highlander service station on Millburn Rd (T235337) and at the airport; *Thrifty* is at 33 Harbour Rd (T224466). Expect to pay from around £30 per day.

Directory **Banks** All the major banks can be found in the town centre. The *Royal Bank* is opposite the post office on Queensgate; the *Bank of Scotland* is opposite the Town House on the High St; the *Clydesdale* is opposite the train station; and *Lloyds TSB* is on Church St. Foreign currency can also be exchanged at the tourist office's bureau de change at 2.5% commission (see below for address and opening hours). Also *Thomas Cook*, 9-13 Inglis St, T711921, Mon-Fri 0900-1700; and *Alba Travel* (American Express agents), 43 Church St, T239188, Mon-Sat 0900-1700. **Communications** Post office: the main branch is at 14-16 Queensgate, T234111. Open Mon-Thur 0900-1730, Fri 0930-1730, Sat 0900-1320. **Internet:** *MTC Internet*, 2 Grant St, T715450. *Invernet* is in the process of moving premises, agrainger@yahoo.com. *The Gate* café bar, opposite the post office, has internet facilities and serves drinks and snacks from 1000-2100. **Cultural centres** Inverness library is just around the corner from the bus station. It has an excellent genealogical research unit. Consultations with the resident genealogist cost £12 per hr; T236463 for an appointment. The library also houses the highland archives, where you can research the history and culture of the region. Open Mon-Fri 1100-1300 and 1400-1700; 1400-1700 only during Oct-May. **Medical facilities** *Raigmore Hospital* is on the southeastern outskirts of town near the A9 (T704000) for accidents and emergencies. **Pharmacies:** *Boots* is in the Eastgate Shopping Centre; open daily 0900-1730, Thur till 1900.

The Highlands

Battle of Culloden

The second Jacobite rebellion of 1745 was ill-fated from the start. Bonnie Prince Charlie's expedition south lacked sufficient support and was turned back at Derby. After their long and dispiriting retreat north, the half-starved, under-strength army, exhausted after an abortive night attack on Hanoverian forces at Nairn, faced overwhelmingly superior forces under the command of the ambitious Duke of Cumberland at Culloden.

The open, flat ground of Culloden Moor was hopelessly unsuitable for the Highlanders' style of fighting, which relied on steep hills and plenty of cover to provide the element of surprise for their brave but undisciplined attacks. In only 40 minutes the Prince's army was blown away by the English artillery and the Jacobite charge, when it finally came, was ragged and ineffective. Cumberland's troops then went on to commit the worst series of atrocities ever carried out by a British Army. 1,200 men were slain, many as they lay wounded on the battlefield. Prince Charlie, meanwhile, fled west where loyal Highlanders protected him until he made his final escape to France.

But the real savagery was to come. Cumberland resolved to make an example of the Highlands. Not only were the clans disarmed and the wearing of Highland dress forbidden, but the Government troops began an orgy of brutal reprisals across the region. Within a century the clan system had ended and the Highland way of life changed forever.

The Moray Firth

Colour map 2, grid C2

East of Inverness along the Moray Firth stretches a long coastline of cliff-top walks, fine beaches, attractive old towns and many historic sites and castles. The busy A96 parallels the coast and the region is well served by public transport. The attractions listed below can be visited as day-trips from Inverness, or *en route* to Aberdeen (see page 357).

The Moray Firth is perhaps best known for its large resident population of **bottlenose dolphins**, the largest dolphins in the world. Over 100 of these beautiful and intelligent mammals live in the estuary, the most northerly breeding ground in Europe, and there's a very good chance of seeing them, particularly between June and August. The Moray Firth dolphins have become a major tourist attraction and several companies run dolphin-spotting boat trips. You can also see them from the shore. Two of the best places are **Chanonry Point**, on the southern shore of the Black Isle (see page 475), and **Fort George**, on the opposite shore (see below). The **Kessock Bridge**, which crosses the Moray Firth to the Black Isle, is another good dolphin-spotting location and also has a **visitor centre**, where you listen in to their underwater conversations.

Culloden

Colour map 2, grid C2

The eerie and windswept Culloden Moor, five miles to the east of Inverness on the B9006, was the site of the last major battle fought on the British mainland. The Jacobite cause was finally lost here, on 16 April 1746, when the army of Prince Charles Edward Stuart was crushed by the superior Government forces, led by the Duke of Cumberland, whose savagery earned him the nickname 'Butcher'. Now owned by the National Trust for Scotland, Culloden is a melancholy place and by far the most painfully evocative of Scotland's battlefields, particularly on a bleak and windy April day.

The Highlands

The battlefield has been restored to its original state (minus the dead bodies). The Visitor Centre is the obvious starting point and gives a graphic audio-visual description of the gruesome episode. From the Visitor Centre paths lead across the field to the clan graves, marked by simple headstones which bear the names of the clans who fought. Next to the Visitor Centre, the restored cottage of Old Leanach – which was used by the Jacobites as a headquarters, and where 30 Highlanders were burnt alive – is now a museum. A memorial cairn, erected in 1881, is the scene each April of a commemorative service organized by the Gaelic Society of Inverness. ■ *Site open daily all year. Visitor Centre open 1 Feb to 31 Mar and 1 Nov to 31 Dec, daily1000-1600; 1 Apr to 31 Oct daily 0900-1800. £3.20, £2.50 child/concession. Wheelchair access, bookshop, restaurant. Highland Country Bus No 12 leaves from Inverness Post Office Mon-Sat, last bus back at 1830; Guide Friday tour bus leaves from Bridge Street, May to Sept from 1030, last bus returns at 1745.*

Clava Cairns This impressive and important Bronze Age site lies only a mile southeast of Culloden and is well worth a short detour. The 5,000 year-old site consists of three large burial cairns encircled by standing stones, set in a grove of trees. The less imaginative visitor may see it as merely a pile of stones but no one can fail to be affected by the spooky atmosphere of the place. This is even more perceptible when no one else is around! ■ *To get there, continue on the B9006 past Culloden Moor, then turn right at the Culloden Moor Inn and follow the signs for Clava Lodge. Look for the sign on the right of the road.*

Fort George

Colour map 2, grid C2 Eleven miles northeast of Inverness and six miles west of Nairn, standing proudly on a sandy spit that juts out into the Moray Firth, is **Fort George**, Europe's finest surviving example of 18th-century military architecture. Begun in 1748, it was the last in a chain of three such fortifications built in the Highlands – the other two being Fort Augustus and Fort William – as a base for George II's army to prevent any potential threats to Hanoverian rule. It was completed in 1769, by which time the Highlands were more or less peaceful, but was kept in use as a military barracks. Today, it remains virtually unchanged and there are even armed sentries at the main gate.

You can walk along the ramparts to get an idea of the sheer scale of the place and also enjoy the sweeping views across the Moray Firth. You may even be lucky enough to see a school of dolphins. Within the fort are the barracks, a chapel, workshops and the Regimental Museum of the Queen's Own Highlanders, which features the fascinating Seafield Collection of arms and military equipment, most of which dates form the Napoleonic Wars. ■ *Daily, Apr-Sept 0930-1830; Oct-Mar, Mon-Sat 0930-1630, Sun 1400-1630. £3. Wheelchair access, café. Highland Bus and Coach No 11 from the Post Office in Inverness, several daily except Sun, also buses from Nairn.*

Cawdor

Cawdor Castle Though best known for its legendary association with Shakespeare's *Macbeth*, Cawdor Castle post-dates the grisly historical events on which the great Bard based his famous tragedy. The oldest part of the castle, the central tower, dates from 1372, and the rest of it is mostly 16th or 17th century. But despite the literary disappointment, the castle is still one of the most appealing in Scotland. The castle has been in the hands of the Cawdor family for over six centuries and each summer they clear off, leaving their romantic home and its glorious

The Highlands

gardens open for the enjoyment of ordinary folks like us. Highlights include the impressive paintings and tapestries, fascinating kitchen and the genuinely witty captions that have visitors laughing all over the castle. There's also a nine-hole golf course.

According to family legend, an early Thane of Cawdor, wanting a new castle, had a dream in which he was told to load a donkey with gold, let it wander around for a day and watch where it lay down, for this would be the best spot for his new castle. He duly followed these instructions and the donkey lay down under a thorn tree, the remains of which can still be seen in the middle of a vaulted chamber in the 14th-century tower. ■ *May to mid-Oct daily 1000-1730. £4.50. Highland Bus No 12 runs to Cawdor from Inverness Post Office several times daily Mon-Sat, the last bus returns around 1800. Also regular buses from Nairn.*

In the village of Cawdor, close by the castle, is the *Cawdor Tavern*, T/F01667-404777, a traditional country pub serving excellent food in a friendly atmosphere. Perfect for lunch or dinner after visiting the castle. Prices are cheap to mid-range.

Just to the west of Cawdor is **Kilravock Castle**, a lovely 15th-century stately home which is closed to the public, but can be visited by prior appointment. The castle (pronounced 'Kilrawk') is still the seat of the Rose family, who now run it as a guesthouse on strictly Christian principles. ■ *T01667-493258. The castle gardens are open to the public Mon-Sat 1000-1600, and worth visiting. Free.*

Nairn

The genteel seaside resort of Nairn claims the driest and sunniest climate in the whole of Scotland. This alone should be reason enough to pay a visit, but there are other attractions besides the sunshine. There are miles of sandy beach stretching east to the Culbin Forest, a **championship golf course** (which hosted the 1999 Walker Cup), and two of the best castles in the country are within easy reach – **Cawdor Castle** (see above) and **Brodie Castle** (see below).

Phone code: 01667
Colour map 2, grid C2
Population: 11,190

Nairn began life as an important commercial centre in the 12th century and by the early 17th century had grown to such an extent that King James VI was able to boast of a town in his northern kingdom so large that people at one end of the High Street didn't understand the language spoken by those at the other end (the different languages being English and Gaelic). The town was a major fishing port in the 19th century and the tiny houses of the **Old Fishertown**, huddled together around the harbour, are very different from the town centre, which is known as **New Fishertown**. Both lie apart from the substantial villas and hotels of the seaside resort that developed with the arrival of the Highland Railway in the mid-19th century.

Today, Nairn is still a tourist favourite with its seafront full of people munching chips and ice cream. There are banks with ATMs in the High Street, a post office in Cawdor Street, a swimming pool on Marine Road and Cinema on King Street. The town hosts its annual **Highland Games** in August.

The **Fishertown Museum** in old Fishertown is interesting and tells of the building of the harbour by Thomas Telford in 1820 and the subsequent decline of the herring industry. The harbour is now mainly used by pleasure craft. ■ *The museum is open from Jun to Aug, Mon-Sat 1000-1700. Free.*

Sights

About two miles east of Nairn, in the little village of **Auldearn**, is a 17th-century doocot (dovecote) from where the royal standard was flown, in 1645, by the victorious troops of Charles I led by the Marquis of Montrose against the Covenanters. Displays in the doocot tell of the battle (entry £1.50).

The Highlands

Sleeping & eating There's lots of accommodation to choose from right across the range. The most luxurious is **B** *The Golf View Hotel*, on Seabank Rd next to the golf course, T452301, scotland@morton-hotels.demon.co.uk. 47 rooms, pool, sauna, spa, gym, tennis courts and fine restaurant. **C** *Clifton House*, Viewfield St, T453119. This genuinely unique hotel offers superb hospitality and a touch of class, every room is different and the place is full of antiques, they also host musical and theatrical evenings and dinner is also quite an event. There are lots of **guesthouses** and **B&Bs**, including the very fine **E** *Bracadale House*, Albert St, T452547, neil.macleod@lineone.net. There's a good **campsite** 1½ miles from town; *Spindrift Caravan & Camping Park*, at Little Kildrummie, T453992, open Apr-Oct.

Aside from the hotels in town, one of the best places to eat is the *Boat House*, T455469, 2 miles east of Nairn in the little village of Auldearn (prices mid-range). If you fancy a fish supper, try *Friar Tuck's*, at 30 Harbour St. For a hot snack there's *Asher's Bakery*, 2 Bridge St, which is recommended and run by the same folk as the one in Inverness.

Sport **Pony trekking** *Heatherfield Riding Centre*, Lochloy Rd, T456682.

Transport There are regular daily **buses** from Inverness (30 mins, £2.60) with *Highland Country Buses* and *Bluebird* (see Inverness Transport above). Nairn is on the **Inverness-Aberdeen** rail line and there are several **trains** daily from Inverness (20 mins, £3.10). **Bike hire**: *The Bike Shop*, 178 Harbour St.

Directory **Tourist office** 62 King St, T452753. Open Easter-May, Sept-Oct Mon-Sat 1000-1700; Jun-Aug daily 0900-1800.

Around Nairn

Dulsie Bridge Ten miles south of Nairn on the A939 to Grantown is Dulsie Bridge, a very popular local beauty spot which is a great place for a summer picnic or to swim in the river Findhorn.

Brodie Castle Eight miles east of Nairn, just off the main A96 to Forres, is one of Scotland's finest castles, still lived in by the Brodie family. The oldest part of the castle, the Z-plan tower house, is 16th-century, with additions dating from the 17th and 19th centuries, giving it the look of a Victorian country house. The interior of the house is the epitome of good taste, with some fabulous ceilings, and you can look round several rooms, including the huge Victorian kitchen. The collections of furniture and porcelain are wonderful but most notable are the outstanding paintings, which include Edwin Landseer and Scottish Colourists. The grounds, too, are a delight, especially in spring when the daffodils are in bloom. There's also a tearoom. ■ *T01309-641371. Apr-Sept Mon-Sat 1100-1730, Sun 1330-1730; Oct weekends only, grounds open all year daily 0930-sunset. £4.40, £2.60 children/concession, £2 (£1) grounds only. Bluebird buses run to Brodie from Inverness, via Culloden and Nairn; 45 mins.*

The Highlands

West of Inverness

West of Inverness, the Moray Firth becomes the **Beauly Firth**, a relatively quiet little corner despite its proximity to Inverness, as most traffic heading north crosses the Kessock Bridge on the main A9. The A862 west to Beauly offers a more scenic alternative, and the chance to visit a **13th-century priory**, and a **distillery**. South of Beauly, the A831 leads to two of Scotland's most beautiful glens, **Glen Strathfarrar**, and **Glen Affric**.

Beauly

The sleepy little market town of Beauly is 10 miles west of Inverness, where the Beauly River flows into the Firth. It's a lovely wee place – hence its name. According to local legend, when Mary, Queen of Scots stayed here, at the priory, in 1564, she was so taken with the place that she cried (in French, of course) "Ah, quel beau lieu!" (What a beautiful place!).

Phone code: 01463
Colour map 2, grid C1

At the north end of the marketplace is the ruin of **Beauly Priory**, founded in 1230 for the Valliscaulian order, but like so much else of Scotland's ecclesiastical heritage, destroyed during the Reformation. ■ *Mid-Jun to Sept daily 0930-1830. From Oct to Mar get the key from the Priory Hotel. £1, children 50p.*

The best place to stay is the **C** *Lovat Arms Hotel*, on the main street, T782313, lovat.arms@cali.co.uk. A relaxed and comfortable place with an excellent restaurant and great bar food, lots of tartan and the occasional ceilidh. Also good is **C** *The Priory Hotel* at the opposite end of the main street, T782309. A cheaper **B&B** option is **F** *Ellengowan*, Croyard Rd, T782273 (open Apr-Oct).

Sleeping & eating

The best food is at the *Lovat Arms Hotel*, which offers cheap meals in the bar or an expensive 4-course dinner in the restaurant. Otherwise, you could try the *Beauly Tandoori* on The Square, T782221, for a cheap curry, or the *Friary* for an even cheaper fish supper.

There are *Inverness Traction* **buses**, T239292, every hour to Beauly, and on to Muir of Ord, from Inverness and from Dingwall. There's also a *Ross's Minibus* service from Beauly 3 days a week, T761250.

Transport

Around Beauly

Four miles east of Beauly, at Balchraggan just off the main Inverness road, is **Moniack Castle Winery**, where you can try a whole range of wines, including elderflower and birch. ■ *Mon-Sat 1000-1700.* Four miles to the north is the **Glen Ord Distillery**, on the outskirts of **Muir of Ord**, just off the A832. ■ *T01463-872004. Mar-Oct Mon-Fri 0930-1700; Jul-Sept also Sat 0930-1700 and Sun 1230-1700. Take a bus from Inverness or the train.*

The river Beauly is one of Scotland's best salmon-fishing rivers, and five miles south of Beauly, at **Aigas**, is a fish lift, where you can watch salmon bypass the dam with the aid of technology. ■ *Mon-Fri 1000-1500.*

Southwest of Beauly are glens Affric and Strathfarrar. Glen Strathfarrar, the lesser known of the two, is unspoiled and considered by some to be the more beautiful. To get there, take the A831 nine miles south from Beauly to **Struy** and follow the signs. Access to the glen is restricted by the owners, Scottish Natural Heritage, to 12 cars at a time and you have to leave by 1900. The glen is also closed from mid-August to October. But once you're in, there is a tremendous feeling of peace and there's good climbing, fishing and walking. The little

Glen Strathfarrar
Colour map 1, grid C6
Most of the walks and cycle routes around glens Strathfarrar and Affric are covered by OS Landranger Nos 25 & 26

The Highlands

ungraded road runs for 14 miles all the way to the impressive Monar Dam at the head of the glen. Glen Strathfarrar can also be reached from Drumnadrochit, via Cannich (see below).

Glen Affric
Colour map 3, grid A6

OS Landranger Nos 25 & 26

The A831 continues south from Struy, through **Strathglass**, to the village of **Cannich**, gateway to glorious Glen Affric, a dramatic and beautiful gorge, with the river Affric rushing through it, and surrounded by Caledonian pine and birch forest (this is one of the few places where you can still see the native Scots pine). There are few, if any, more stunning sights in the Scottish Highlands and it's perfect for walking, or even just to drive through and stop for a picnic on a nice, sunny day.

Glen Affric reaches west into the very heart of the Highlands and is great for a spot of Munro-bagging. Beyond Loch Affric the serious walking starts. From Affric Lodge, nine miles west of Cannich, begins a 20-mile trail west to Morvich, near **Shiel Bridge**, on the west coast near Kyle of Lochalsh (see page 445). This strenuous walk is for experienced hikers only, and takes around 10 hours. You can stop off halfway at one of the most remote **youth hostels** in Scotland, *Glen Affric Youth Hostel*, at Allt Beithe (no phone; open mid-March till end October).

There are also many shorter, easier walks around Glen Affric. There are some short, circular marked trails at the end of the road which runs west from Cannich almost to Loch Affric, and also from the car park at the impressive **Dog Falls**, 4½ miles from Cannich and a great place to stop for a picnic and swim. Cycling in the forests around Cannich is good too – you can hire bikes at *Cannich Caravan and Camping Park*.

Glen Affric can also be reached from **Drumnadrochit** (see page 416) by heading west on the A831 through **Glen Urquhart** to Cannich. Just before Cannich, on the road from Drumnadrochit, a single track road leads left (south), past the Caravan and Camping Park, to the tiny village of **Tomich**. From here, it's a three-mile hike up a woodland trail to a car park. A few hundred yards down through the trees takes you to the lovely **Plodda Falls**. An old iron bridge affords a spectacular view of the waterfall as it plunges 150 yards into the foaming waters below.

Sleeping
There are several options in and around **Cannich**. One of the best hotels in the area is the **B** *Mullardoch House Hotel*, in Glencannich, on the road to Beauly, T/F01456-415460. An excellent **B&B** is **D-E** *Kerrow House*, in Cannich village, T415243, F415425, stephen@kerrow-house.demon.co.uk.

There are also a couple of **hostels**: the *SYHA Cannich Youth Hostel* , T415244, open mid-Mar to end Oct; and the slightly cheaper independent *Glen Affric Backpackers*, T/F415263, which is open all year.

In the village of **Tomich** is **C** *The Tomich Hotel*, T01456-415399, F415469. The price includes dinner, it's a comfortable place with good food and free use of the nearby indoor heated pool, also great for fishing holidays. Near Tomich is the independent hostel *Cougie Lodge*, T01456-415459, which is open Apr-Sept and will pick you up from Tomich or Cannich if you phone ahead.

Transport
Highland Bus & Coach, T01463-233371, runs buses 3 days a week Mon-Fri from Inverness to Cannich and Tomich, via Drumnadrochit. There are also buses from Inverness to Cannich and Tomich, via Beauly (2 on Tue and Fri, and 1 on Sat).

The Highlands

The Great Glen

The Great Glen, which splits the Scottish mainland from Fort William in the south to Inverness in the north, is one of the world's major geological fault lines. The Glen was formed millions of years ago when the northern part of the Caledonian mountains 'slid' more than 60 miles south, leaving behind a massive glen, with four freshwater lochs – **Loch Linnhe, Loch Lochy, Loch Oich** and **Loch Ness**. The most famous of these is Loch Ness, which attracts hordes of visitors eager to catch a glimpse of its elusive monster.

The renowned engineer, Thomas Telford, succeeded in connecting all these lochs when he built the impressive **Caledonian Canal**. The canal took 22 years to complete, and when it was opened in 1822 was the first in Britain to take ships from one coast to the other. It remains the only canal in the country capable of carrying ships of up to 500 tons.

The best way to appreciate the glen is by boat, through the 38 miles of natural lochs and rivers and the 22 miles of canal, and every summer, pleasure craft of all shapes and sizes ply its length. The main A82 runs from Inverness south to Fort William. The southern section, from Fort Augustus, follows the original line of the road constructed in 1727 by General Wade to link the military garrisons at Fort William and Fort Augustus (hence their names). There are regular daily **bus services** between Inverness and Fort William, with additional buses between Invergarry and Fort Augustus.

Another way to travel through the Great Glen is along the excellent **cycle route**, which follows the canal towpaths, forest trails and quiet minor roads to avoid the busy main road. The route is outlined in the Forestry Commission leaflet, available from most tourist offices.

Loch Ness

One of Scotland's biggest attractions is the narrow gash of Loch Ness, Britain's deepest body of fresh water, stretching 23 miles from Fort Augustus in the south, almost to Inverness in the north. The loch is scenic in its own right, with rugged hills rising steeply from its wooded shores, but visitors don't come here for the views. They come every year, in their hundreds of thousands, to stare across the dark, cold waters in search of its legendary inhabitant, the **Loch Ness Monster**. A huge tourist trade has grown up around 'Nessie', as the monster is affectionately known, and every summer, the main A82 which runs along its western shore is jam packed with bus loads of eager monster-hunters, binoculars trained on the loch surface, desperate for one glimpse of the elusive beast.

Colour map 4, grid A1/2

The best way to see the loch is on a cruise from Inverness (see 'Loch Ness Monster Tours', on page 402). There are also boat trips from Drumnadrochit and Fort Augustus (see below). Most of the tourist traffic uses the congested A82, which offers few decent views of the loch. By far the best views of the loch are from the quiet and picturesque B862/852 which runs along its eastern shore, from Fort Augustus up to Inverness. It's possible to make a complete circuit of the loch, which is best done in an anti-clockwise direction heading south from Inverness on the A82, but you'll need your own transport (or take a tour), as there are no buses between Fort Augustus and Foyers.

The Highlands

The Great Monster Hunt

In a country full of myths and legends, the Loch Ness Monster is the greatest of them all. As elusive as a straight answer from a politician, Nessie has single-handedly sold more tins of tartan-wrapped shortbread to foreign visitors than Edinburgh castle.

Tales of Nessie go way back to the sixth century, when St Columba is said to have calmed the beast after she had attacked one of his monks. But the monster craze only really took off with the completion of the A82 road along the loch's western shore in 1933. Since then, there have been numerous sightings, some backed up with photographic evidence, though the most impressive of these – the famous black-and-white movie footage of Nessie's

humps moving through the water, and the classic photograph of her head and neck – have been exposed as fakes.

In recent decades, determined monster hunters have enlisted the help of new technology, such as sonar surveys, but have failed to come up with conclusive evidence. Enter Cyber Nessie, the latest attempt to end the years of rumours, hoaxes and speculation. Nessie's very own website – www.lochness.scotland.net/ camera.htm – is a 24-hour real-time video watch of Loch Ness, and has already produced a couple of claimed sightings. But nothing could compare with the excitement of seeing the monster in the flesh.

Drumnadrochit

Phone code: 01456
Colour map 2, grid C1

The Nessie tourist trade is centred on the village of Drumnadrochit, 15 miles south of Inverness, where the canny locals have cashed in on the enduring popularity of the monster myth. The monster hype is almost overpowering, with two rival Monster Exhibitions and the inevitable souvenir shops selling all manner of awful tartan tack, including those scary-looking tartan dolls with flickering eyelids, the "See-You-Jimmy" tartan bonnet, complete with ginger 'hair' and not forgetting the Loch Ness Monster novelty hat.

Of the two aforementioned Monster Exhibitions, the **Original Loch Ness Visitor Centre** is the least worthwhile. It's a glorified gift shop with a rather amateurish audiovisual show attached. ■ *T450342. daily Apr to end of Oct 1000-1800 (Jul-Aug till 2100). £3.50, child £2.75.*

Those genuinely interested in the fascinating history of the search for 'Nessie' should visit the recently refurbished **Official Loch Ness Monster Exhibition**. Though it's considerably more expensive, it gives a detailed description of the many eye-witness accounts over the years and also explains the recent research projects carried out in the loch. ■ *T450573. Easter-end May 0930-1730; Jun and Sept 0930-1830; Jul-Aug 0930-2030; Oct 0930-1800; Nov-Mar 1000-1600. £6.50, £3.50 students, £2.50 children.*

Loch Ness Cruises operate from the Original Loch Ness Visitor Centre, from March to October and run daily from 1000-1730. They last one hour and cost £8 per person.

If it all gets too much, then fear not, for Drumnadrochit gives easy access to one of the most beautiful corners of Scotland. The A831 heads west from the village, through **Glen Urquhart**, to **Cannich** about 12 miles away, at the head of **Glen Affric**, a great place for walking or enjoying a picnic (see page 414). If the weather's good, hiring bikes in Drumnadrochit (see below) and cycling into Glen Affric makes for a great day out. There's also **pony trekking** at the *Highland Riding Centre*, T450358, at Borlum Farm.

A few miles south of Drumnadrochit are the ruins of Castle Urquhart. The castle bears the scars of centuries of fighting but its setting, perched on a rocky cliff on the loch's edge, is magnificent, and not surprisingly, one of the most photographed scenes in Scotland. Dating from the 14th century, the castle was a strategic base, guarding the Great Glen during the long Wars of Independence. It was taken by Edward I, held by Robert the Bruce against Edward II, and was then almost constantly under siege before being destroyed in 1692 to prevent it from falling into Jacobite hands. Most of the existing buildings date from the 16th century, including the five-storey tower, the best-preserved part of the complex, from where you get great views of the loch and surrounding hills. At the time of writing, there are plans to build a new visitor centre. ■ *T450551. Daily Apr-Sept 0930-1830; Oct-Mar 0930-1630. £3.80, £1.20 child.*

Castle Urquhart

There's a wide range of accommodation on offer in and around the village of Drumnadrochit. If you can afford it, your best bet is to head for **B** *Polmaily House Hotel*, 3 miles from Drumnadrochit on the A831 to Cannich, in Glen Urquhart, T450343, F450813, polmailyhousehotel@btinternet.com. 10 rooms, a comfortable, child-friendly country house far enough away from the madding crowd to offer peace and quiet, many walks nearby, also tennis courts, horse riding and covered pool, good restaurant. In the village itself is **D** *The Benleva Hotel*, T450288, F450781. Small, family-run hotel with bar and dining room. There are numerous **B&Bs**, including the excellent **E** *Drumbuie Farm*, T450634, F450595, a modern farmhouse on the right as you enter the village from Inverness, with its own herd of Highland cattle. Also good value is **E-F** *Heatherlea*, Balmacaan Rd, T450561, tjbeet@globalnet.co.uk, and **E-F** *Gillyflowers*, T/F450641, gillyflowers@cali.co.uk. Cheaper still is the *Loch Ness Backpackers Lodge*, at Coiltie Farmhouse in East Lewiston, T450807, immediately south of Drumnadrochit, on the left. It's open all year, has excellent facilities and arranges boat trips and local walks.

Other than the hotels, which all serve decent bar food, there's the *Glen Restaurant*, T450282, which offers simple fare and, next door, the more upmarket *Fiddler's Bistro*, T450678, where you can also hire **mountain bikes**.

Sleeping & eating

Citylink **buses** between Inverness and Fort William stop at Drumnadrochit several times daily in either direction. Additional services run between Inverness and Urquhart Castle during the summer months. There are also buses from Inverness to Cannich and Tomich, via Drumnadrochit (see page 414).

Transport

Invermoriston

Between Drumnadrochit and Fort Augustus is the tiny village of Invermoriston, probably the nicest spot on the entire Inverness to Fort Augustus stretch of the A82. It's a beautiful little piece of Highland scenery, with a photogenic old stone bridge over foaming river rapids. There are marked woodland trails leading off into the hills past some lovely waterfalls.

At Invermoriston the A887 heads west through **Glen Moriston** to meet the A87 which runs from **Invergarry** (see below) all the way through the rugged and dramatic **Glen Shiel** to the awesome mountains of **Kintail** on the west coast near **Kyle of Lochalsh**. *Citylink* buses between Inverness and Kyle of Lochalsh stop at Invermoriston.

Phone code: 01320
Colour map 4, grid A1

There are several **B&Bs** in the village and, a few miles to the north on the main A82 overlooking Loch Ness, is the *SYHA Loch Ness Youth Hostel*, T351274, open mid-Mar to end Oct. 1½ miles south of Invermoriston, and 6 miles north of Fort Augustus, is the *Loch Ness Caravan & Camping Park*, T351207, right on the shores of the loch with great views and excellent facilities (open Easter-Oct).

Sleeping

Fort Augustus

Phone code: 01320
Colour map 4, grid A1

At the more scenic southern end of Loch Ness stands the village of Fort Augustus, originally set up as a garrison after the Jacobite rebellion of 1715 and headquarters of General Wade's campaign to pacify the Highlands. Today, Fort Augustus is a busy little place, full of monster-hunting tourists and boats using the flight of five locks to enter or leave Loch Ness on their journey along the **Caledonian Canal**.

The village hosts **Highland Gatherings** in late June and July, mid-August and early September, featuring traditional dancing and piping competitions, tossing the caber and sheep dog trials.

The **tourist office** is in the car park next to the petrol station and *Bank of Scotland*. ■ *T366367. Apr-Jun Mon-Sat 1000-1700; Jul-Aug 0900-2000; Sept-Oct 0900-1800.*

Sights

On the shores of Loch Ness is **Fort Augustus Abbey**, a Benedictine Monastery founded in 1876 on the site of the original fort. The abbey closed in 1998 and the adjoining Catholic boys' school is now a **Heritage Centre** which takes you through the history of the Great Glen. The abbey also offers accommodation (see below). ■ *T366233. Daily Easter-Oct 0900-1700; Nov-Mar 1000- 1600. £4, £2 child.*

By the canal locks is **The Clansman Centre**, where young guides in traditional dress provide a lively and entertaining presentation of 17th-century Highland family life in an old turf house. There follows a display of weaponry and a mock sword fight in the garden. You can even have your picture taken wearing traditional highland costume. There's also a craftshop selling the more tasteful kind of souvenirs. ■ *T366444. Daily Apr, May, Jun and Sept 1100-1700; Jul-Aug 1000-1800. £3, £2.50 concession.*

Loch Ness Cruises with *Loch Ness Ferry Co Ltd*, on board the *Catriona* set off from the jetty in the abbey grounds. ■ *T01223-208939. Hourly from 1000 between Apr and Oct. The trip lasts 50 minutes and costs £4 per person. Also boat and bike hire.*

Sleeping & eating

There's a good selection of places to stay in Fort Augustus, but perhaps the best, and certainly the most unique, is the **C-D** *Lovat Arms Hotel*, T366206, F366677. 23 rooms, a beautiful old mansion house standing above the village. Another good bet is **C-D** *The Brae Hotel*, T366289; open Mar-Oct. At the cheaper end, the best value is undoubtedly the *Abbey*, T366233, F366228, abbey@monk.co.uk, which offers basic but cheap guest rooms in the main building (**E-F**). The monks also run a small *Backpackers' Lodge*, with self-catering and laundry facilities, and there's a restaurant, the *Abbot's Table*, which offers cheap, healthy food.

There are lots of **B&Bs** to choose from, including the friendly **E-F** *Kettle House* on Golf Course Rd, T366408; open Feb-Nov, and the wonderfully named **E-F** *Mrs Service*, at *Sonas* on the Inverness Rd, T366291.

Other than the hotels in the village, there's the cosy *Bothy Bite* (T366710) by the canal bridge, which serves cheap meals from 1200-2100. The *Loch Inn*, by the canal, is the best place for a drink, and also serves decent pub grub.

Sport

Pony trekking *Fort Augustus Riding Centre*, Pier House, T366418.

Transport

Fort Augustus is a convenient stopover between Fort William and Inverness and there are several **buses** daily in either direction. It takes 1 hr to both towns and costs £5.80 single. There is an additional service between Fort Augustus and Invergarry (see below) once a day Mon-Sat. **Cycle hire** at *Loch Ness Ferry Co Ltd* (see above).

The Highlands

Fort Augustus to Dores

A worthwhile detour from Fort Augustus is to take the B862/852 up the **east** *Colour map 4, grid A1/2*
shore of Loch Ness on a mostly single-track road that skirts the loch for much
of its length to the village of Dores. It's a much quieter and more scenic route
than the busy A82 and follows General Wade's original (and very straight)
military road which linked Fort Augustus with Fort George. Though it makes a
more interesting alternative to the more popular A82 route from Inverness to
Fort Augustus, it's best done from south to north, if you have the time.

The road winds its way up into rugged hills before returning to the lochside
at **Foyers**, where there's accommodation at **E-F** *Intake-House*, T01456-
482258, open Apr-Oct, and the small independent youth hostel *Foyers House*,
T01456-486623. It's worth stopping here to see the impressive **waterfall**
where the river Foyers plunges into Loch Ness. To get there, follow the steep
(and slippery) track down from opposite the shops.

Three miles further north, at **Inverfarigaig**, is the spooky and sinister
Boleskine House, once home of Alastair Crowley, who is said to have practised Devil worship here. In the 1970s the house was bought by Jimmy Page of
Led Zeppelin, but sold some years later after the tragic death of his daughter.
Those of a nervous disposition may wish to pass on quickly and continue to
the little village of **Dores**, at the northeastern end of the loch, where you can
enjoy a good pint of ale and some decent grub at the *Dores Inn*. You can then
continue to Inverness, or return via the beautiful hill road that leads up to **Loch
Mhor** and back to Fort Augustus via the **Stratherrick** valley. From **Errogie**, at
the northern end of Loch Mhor, there's a dramatic section of road that winds
down to the loch through a series of tight, twisting bends, reminiscent of an
Alpine pass, and great for cyclists. There are also some interesting marked
woodland trails around Errogie.

This route is only possible if you have your own transport. There are buses south from **Transport**
Inverness, but they only run as far as Foyers (3 times Mon-Fri, twice on Sat). Alternatively,
it can be done by **bike**, as a full-day circular trip from Fort Augustus or from Inverness.

Fort Augustus to Fort William

South of Fort Augustus, the A82 leaves behind Loch Ness and runs along the
west shore of **Loch Oich** and then the east shore of **Loch Lochy**, till it reaches
Spean Bridge. Here, the A82 continues south to **Fort William**, while the A86
branches east, through **Glen Spean** to finally join the A9 Perth to Inverness
road at **Kingussie**. All along this route are many opportunities to get off the
beaten track and explore huge chunks of real wilderness, deserted since the
Clearances and soaked in the blood of history.

Invergarry and around

The old village of Invergarry stands where the A82 turns west to meet the A87. *Phone code: 01809*
There's not much to see or do in the village, but the surrounding area merits *Colour map 4, grid A1*
some exploring, particularly the route west through Glen Garry (see next
page), and there are several places to stay.

Inside the entrance to the *Glengarry Castle Hotel* (see 'Sleeping' below) stand **Sights**
the ruins of **Invergarry Castle**, once the stronghold of the MacDonnells of
Glengarry and later destroyed by the Duke of Cumberland as he wreaked

The Highlands

revenge on the Highlands in the aftermath of Culloden (see page 36). The hotel was later built as the main house of the Ellice family, who made their fortune from the *Hudson Bay Company* in Canada and who were the main driving force behind the creation of the Victorian planned village.

A mile or so south of the village, at **North Laggan**, is a monument by the side of the road standing over **The Well of the Seven Heads**. This tells the grisly story of the Keppoch Murders, one of the most infamous clan murders which took place at **Roy Bridge** (see below) in the 17th century. It all began when the chief of the clan MacDonnell died, leaving two young sons, who were sent away to complete their education before returning to Roy Bridge to celebrate the elder brother's accession to the chiefship. Another branch of the clan present at the celebrations started a fight in which both brothers were killed. Believing they had been murdered, one of their cousins persuaded a fellow clan member to raise 50 men and march on the murderers' house at nearby Inverlair. The accused murderers – a father and his six sons – were duly slaughtered and their heads cut off, to be displayed before the local laird at Glengarry. On the way to his lodge, the heads were washed here in this well.

A few miles further south, at **Laggan**, where the A82 crosses to the east bank of Loch Lochy, is the site of one the bloodiest battles in Scottish clan history. The **Battle of the Shirts**, fought in 1544, was so named because it was fought on a hot day and the combatants took off their shirts before proceeding to butcher each other. One side – the Frasers – were almost wiped out and their opponents – a combined force of MacDonalds, MacDonnells and Camerons – suffered less heavy losses and claimed victory. In total, over 1,000 were killed and a plaque beside the canal locks describes the terrible events.

On the east shore of Loch Oich, near North Laggan, is the **Great Glen Water Park**, T501381, an outdoor activities centre offering numerous adventure sports, including white-water rafting, canoeing, mountain biking, rock climbing, sailing, windsurfing, hill walking and water skiing. There are also self-catering lodges for rent.

Sleeping There are various options for sleeping in and around Invergarry, but none can match the splendour of **B** *Glengarry Castle Hotel*, T501254, F501207, castle@glengarry.net, set in 60 acres of woodland running down to Loch Oich. 26 rooms, open Mar-Nov. The hotel has been in the MacCallum family for over 40 years and continues to be one of the best in the Highlands. Rather less luxurious but still comfortable and good value are **D** *Invergarry Hotel*, T501206, F501400, hotel@invergarry.net, **D** *Ardochy Lodge Hotel*, T511232 and **E** *Drynachan Cottage*, T501225, drynachan@aol.com.

South of Invergarry, at South Laggan, is the *SYHA Loch Lochy Youth Hostel*, T501239, open mid-Mar to end-Oct. There are a couple of **campsites** near the village: *Faichem Park*, T501226, open Easter-Oct; and *Faichemard Farm Camping Site*, T501314, open Apr-Oct, which is off the A87.

Tour companies *Glengarry Mini Tours*, T501297 run various minibus day tours around in the Great Glen, Glen Coe and Glen Nevis.

Transport Invergarry is on the Fort William to **Inverness** bus route (see Fort Augustus above). It is also on the main **Fort William** to **Kyle of Lochalsh** (and **Skye**) *Citylink* route and a couple of buses pass through daily in both directions. For times: T0990-505050.

West of Invergarry The A87 leads west from Invergarry, through Glen Shiel to **Shiel Bridge**, on the way to Kyle of Lochalsh on the west coast (see page 445). About seven miles along the A87, past the turning for Kinloch Hourn (see below) is the Glen Garry viewpoint, from where you get one of the most stunning, and famous, of all Highland views. From this angle Loch Garry looks uncannily like a map of Scotland, so get out the camera for that classic holiday snap.

Glen Garry to Kinloch Hourn

A mile or so before the Glen Garry viewpoint, where the A87 begins to leave the shores of Loch Garry, is the turning left for the road through Glen Garry, described as the longest and most beautiful cul-de-sac in Britain. The little single-track road turns and twists for 22 glorious miles along the shores of **Loch Garry** and **Loch Quoich** all the way to **Kinloch Hourn**, at the head of Loch Hourn, a sea loch on the west coast. *Colour map 3, A5/6*

Glen Garry is now virtually deserted but was once home to some 5,000 people who were driven out during the infamous Highland Clearances in the 19th century. The road passes the tiny hamlet of **Tomdoun**, once the junction of the main road to Skye, until the massive post-war hydroelectric schemes changed the landscape. Experienced hill walkers can still follow the old route to Skye, through Glen Kingie, along Loch Hourn and then across the wild **Knoydart peninsula** till they reach the tiny settlement of **Inverie**. From here a little ferry runs twice a day on Mon-Wed and Fri to **Mallaig**.

Beyond Tomdoun the road passes a huge dam, built in the 1950s, which raised the waters of Loch Quoich by over 100ft, flooding many of the old settlements. Also flooded was Glen Quoich Lodge, which can count Edward VII and Sir Edward Landseer among its notable guests. It was reputedly Glen Garry that gave Landseer the inspiration for his famous painting *The Monarch of the Glen*. The road then reaches its highest point, at 1,200ft, before descending to **Kinloch Hourn**, once a thriving fishing village but now remote and isolated. Incredible as it may seem, you can actually stay here. **B** *Skiary*, phone ahead to arrange for a boat to meet you, T01809-511214, open May-Sept. This is perhaps the most remote guesthouse in the Highlands. It is accessible only by boat or foot and has no mains electricity. There are two rooms and prices are for full board. The food is wonderful and the setting is simply magnificent.

Transport There's one **bus** a day (Mon-Sat) between Invergarry and Kinloch Hourn, but a more scenic return would be to take the **ferry** from Kinloch Hourn to **Arnisdale** (summer only; daily by arrangement) and then head to **Glenelg**, from where you can take a ferry across to **Kylerhea** on Skye (see page 510).

Spean Bridge

The main A82 runs down the east shore of Loch Lochy to the village of Spean Bridge, at the head of Glen Spean, beneath the towering Lochaber mountains. The village gets its name from Thomas Telford's bridge across the river Spean. Two miles west are the remains of the old 'Highbridge', built in 1736 by General Wade, and the site of the first clash between Government troops and the Jacobites, three days before Prince Charles raised his standard at Glenfinnan. *Phone code: 01397 Colour map 3, grid B6*

Spean Bridge is only eight miles north of Fort William so gets busy in the summer, but it still makes a more peaceful and attractive alternative base for exploring this astoundingly beautiful part of the Highlands. There's a **tourist office** just off the main road behind the post office. ■ *T712576, F712675. Easter-Oct.* Spean Bridge is also the starting point for the excellent **Grey Corries ridge walk** (OS Landranger Map No 41).

The Highlands

Sleeping There's no shortage of accommodation in Spean Bridge. Pick of the bunch has to be **B** *Old Pines Restaurant with Rooms*, T712324, F712433, goodfood.at.oldpines@ lineone.net, www.lochaber.com/oldpines. 8 rooms, just past the Commando Memorial, on the B8004, price includes dinner. This Scandinavian-style chalet is a great place to stay, especially if you have kids in tow, and is renowned for its exceptional, award-winning Scottish cuisine. Food is available to non-residents (the 5-course dinner is expensive but lunch is much cheaper). **C** *Corriegour Lodge Hotel*, 9 miles north of Spean Bridge on the A82, T712685, F712696. 9 rooms, open Feb-Dec. Lovely Victorian hunting lodge on the shores of Loch Lochy with fine views and an excellent restaurant (non-residents dinner only; expensive). Further south, on the shores of Loch Lochy, is a very good **B&B**, **E** *Invergloy House*, T712681. In the village itself is **E** *Smiddy House*, T712335, F712043. A comfortable guesthouse with a bistro attached, serving good, cheap meals. Also good is the **D-E** *Corriechoille Lodge*, T/F712002, enquiry@ corrie1.demon.co.uk, www.corrie1.demon.co.uk. open Mar-Nov.

There are lots more guesthouses and B&Bs and a couple of **campsites**, north of the village at *Stronaba Caravan & Camping*, T712259, open Apr-Oct, and west towards Gairlochy at *Gairlochy Holiday Park*, T712711, F712712, open Apr-Oct.

Eating There's also a wide choice of places to eat. As well as those listed above, there's the *Old Station Restaurant*, T712535, in a converted railway station. Has a very good reputation, dinner is expensive; lunch by prior arrangement only, open Apr-Oct, Tue-Sun 1800-2100. Also recommended is *The Coach House Restaurant*, T712680, crann_tara@bigfoot.com, which is about 3 miles north of town on the right-hand side, at Glenfintaig. It's a popular place and small, so you'll have to book ahead for lunch (cheap) or dinner (mid-range to expensive), open late Apr to late Oct, daily 1200-1500 and 1800-2100.

Transport There are regular **buses** to and from Fort William and Inverness (£6 single). Spean Bridge is also on the Fort William-Glasgow **rail** line (see Fort William Transport below).

Loch Arkaig

Phone code: 01397
Colour map 3, grid A6

A mile north of Spean Bridge on the A82 is the **Commando Memorial**, which commemorates the commandos who trained here during the Second World War. It's worth lingering for a few moments to appreciate the fantastic views all around. From here the B8004 branches west to **Gairlochy**, crossing the Caledonian Canal, then the B8005 heads north to Loch Arkaig, a long, deep and mysterious loch stretching west through the mountains. Bonnie Prince Charlie passed this way, before and after Culloden, through an area which has, for centuries, been the seat of the Camerons of Lochiel. The Camerons were fervent supporters of the Jacobite cause and when Prince Charles landed at Loch nan Uamh, on the road from Fort William to Mallaig, he called on Cameron of Lochiel to join him at Glenfinnan.

You can find out all about the Camerons and their involvement in the Jacobite rebellion of 1745 in the **Clan Cameron Museum**, in the tiny township of **Achnacarry**, nestled between the shores of Loch Lochy and **Loch Arkaig**. The museum is housed in an old cottage rebuilt after being burned by government troops in 1746. ■ *T712480. Daily Easter to mid-Oct 1330-1700; Jul-Aug 1100-1700. £2, children free.*

Beyond the turn-off to Achnacarry, the single-track road runs through the Clunes Forest and **The Dark Mile**, a long line of beech trees which completely cuts out daylight. At the east end of Loch Arkaig, a stone bridge crosses the Caig Burn. Beside the bridge is a car park, from where a path leads up to the spectacular **Cia-Aig Falls** which tumble into a deep, dark pool known as **The Witch's**

Cauldron. It was here that an old hag was accused of casting her evil eye over Lochiel's cattle, causing them to fall ill and die. But when she fell into the pool and drowned, the cattle miraculously began to recover from their illness.

Beyond the falls is *Highland Icelandic Horse Trekking*, T/F712427, hihot@compuserve.com, which offers one-hour, two-hour and day rides in the surrounding hills. The road runs along the north shore of Loch Arkaig all the way to the head of the loch, from where experienced and well-equipped hill walkers can hike through the glens to Loch Nevis and Knoydart.

Transport There's no public transport beyond Achnacarry, and there's only one **bus** a day to Achnacarry from Lochaber High School in Fort William.

Glen Roy and Loch Laggan

From Spean Bridge, the A86 runs east through Glen Spean to meet the A9 Perth to Inverness road which leads to **Aviemore**, Scotland's main ski centre (see page 487). The road passes through **Roy Bridge**, which is the turn-off for **Glen Roy**, noted for its amazing 'parallel roads'. These are not in fact roads but three gravel ledges etched on to the mountains at different heights. The 'roads' marked the shorelines of a glacial lake formed during the last ice-age. Roy Bridge was also the site of the infamous Keppoch Murders (see page 419).

Phone code: 01397
Colour map 4, grid A/B1

The road continues east towards Loch Laggan. After a couple of miles it passes **Cille Choirille**, an ancient church built by a 15th-century Cameron chief as penance for a life of violence. The church fell into disrepair but was restored and reopened in 1932 and now attracts people of all creeds as it's said to inspire peace and spiritual healing. Further east, at the eastern end of Loch Laggan, is the massive **Laggan Dam**, built in 1933 to provide water for the aluminium smelter at Fort William. The water is piped through tunnels up to 15ft in diameter carved through the core of Ben Nevis. The road runs along the north shore of the loch, past the **Creag Meagaidh National Nature Reserve**, where you can see herds of red deer right by the reserve car park. A track leads from here up to **Lochan a' Choire** (about four hours).

There are several hotels in **Roy Bridge**, including the **C-D** *Stronlossit Hotel*, T712253, F712641, which serves good meals all day from 1100 (cheap lunch; mid-range dinner). There are also 3 independent **hostels**: the *Grey Corrie Lodge*, T712236, F712241, is handy for shops and transport, serves cheap bar meals and also has laundry facilities. A mile and a half from the village is the cheaper *Aite Cruinnichidh* hostel, at Achluachrach, T712315. Five miles east, at Tulloch train station, is *Station Lodge*, T/F732333, which also serves meals (including vegetarian).

Sleeping & eating

Aside from the places listed above, a good place to eat is the *Glenspean Lodge Hotel*, T712223. Lunch served 1230-1430 (cheap) and dinner 1830-2100 (expensive).

Fishing *Fishing Scotland*, T/F712812, info@fishing-scotland.co.uk, www.fishing-scotland.co.uk, runs fishing courses and trips on the surrounding lochs. Loch Arkaig in particular is renowned for its trout fishing. **Hiking and climbing** *Nevis Guides*, Bohuntin, Roy Bridge, T712356.

Sport

There are **buses** from Fort William to Roy Bridge (3 times daily Mon-Fri; 1 on Sat). Roy Bridge is also on the Fort William-Glasgow **rail** line.

Transport

The Highlands

Fort William

Phone code: 01397
Colour map 3, grid B6
Population: 10,774

Fort William is the gateway to the Western Highlands and one of the country's main tourist centres. It stands at the head of Loch Linnhe, with the snow-topped mass of Ben Nevis towering behind. You could be forgiven for assuming that it's quite an attractive place, but you'd be wrong. Despite its magnificent setting, Fort William has all the charm of a motorway service station. A dual carriageway runs along the lochside, over a litter-strewn pedestrian underpass and past dismal 1960s concrete boxes masquerading as hotels.

Ins and outs

Getting there
For more details see 'Transport', on page 428.

Fort William is easily reached by **bus**, from Inverness, Glasgow and Oban, and by **train**, direct from Glasgow via the amazing and beautiful West Highland Railway. The train and bus stations are next to each other at the north end of the High St, on the other side of the dual carriageway. If you're driving, parking can be a problem. There's a big **car park** beside the loch at the south end of town, and another behind the tourist office. You can also walk to Fort William, if you have a week to spare, from just north of Glasgow, along the 95 mile-long **West Highland Way** (see page 54).

Getting around

The town is strung out for several miles along the banks of Loch Linnhe. The centre is compact and easy to get around on foot. Many of the **guesthouses** and **B&Bs**, and a few youth hostels, are in **Corpach**, 1½ miles to the north, but there are frequent buses from the town centre. There are also buses to the youth hostel in **Glen Nevis**. For information on these and on **taxis**, **car hire** or **cycle hire**, see under Transport, page 428.

Tourist information

The busy **tourist office** is on Cameron Square, just off the High St, T703781, F705184. They stock a good range of books, maps and leaflets covering local walks. They will also help arrange transport to more remote Highland parts. ■ *Apr-late May Mon-Sat 0900-1700, Sun 1000-1600; Jun-early Jul Mon-Sat 0900-1800, Sun 1000-1700; Jul-Aug Mon-Sat 0900-2030, Sun 0900-1800; Sept-late Oct Mon-Sat 0900-1800, Sun 1000-1700; Nov-Mar Mon-Fri 0900-1700, Sat 1000-1600, closed Sun.*

Though it's not a pretty sight, Fort William is the largest town hereabouts and has all the services and facilities you'd expect. There are banks with ATMs on the pedestrianized High Street, as well as a couple of good supermarkets and two well-stocked outdoor-equipment shops. Most of the good things about Fort William are outside the town. The surrounding mountains and glens are amongst the most stunning in the Highlands and attract hikers and climbers in their droves. The main attractions are **Ben Nevis** – Britain's highest peak at 4,406ft – and the very beautiful **Glen Nevis**, which many of you may recognize from movies such as *Braveheart* and *Rob Roy*. For more details, see page 429. There's also skiing and snowboarding at nearby **Aonach Mor**, one of Scotland's top ski areas (see page 431), and some good **mountain biking** around the Leanachan Forest (see page 428).

Sights

There's little of real interest in the town, though the **West Highland Museum**, on Cameron Square by the tourist office, is a worthwhile exception. It contains excellent exhibits of Jacobite memorabilia, including a bed in which Prince Charles slept and a 'secret' portrait of the prince which is revealed only when reflected in a cylindrical mirror. There are also fine displays of Highland clans and tartans, wildlife and local history. ■ *T702169. Jun-Sept Mon-Sat 1000-1700; Oct-May 1000-1600; also Sun Jul-Aug 1400-1700. £2, £1.50 children.*

Tours from Fort William

Top of the Pops as far as tours are concerned has to be the **Jacobite Steam Train** to Mallaig. The train runs through some of the West Highlands' most stunning scenery and crosses the historic Glenfinnan viaduct, with great views down Loch Shiel. The train runs from mid-June to September, daily except Saturday. It leaves Fort William at 1035 and returns from Mallaig at 1410. A day return costs £19.25. T703791.

There are several **cruises** which leave from the Town Pier, giving you the chance to spot local marine wildlife, including seals, otters and seabirds. One of the operators is **Seal Island Cruises** (T705589), who run trips of one and a half hours from April to September.

The **Ben Nevis Distillery** is at Lochy Bridge, at the junction of the A82 to Inverness and the A830 to Mallaig. ■ *T700200. Visitor Centre open Mon-Fri 0900-1700 (also Sat in Jul-Aug 1000-1600).* In Corpach is **Treasures of the Earth**, an exhibition of crystals, gemstones and fossils displayed in a huge simulated cave. ■ *T772283. Daily May-Sept 0930-1900, Oct-Apr 1000-1700.*

The **fort** from which the town gets its name was built in 1690 by order of William III to keep the rebellious Scottish clans in order. The garrison fought off attacks by Jacobites during the rebellions of 1715 and 1745 but was then demolished to make way for the railway line. The scant remains of the fort can be seen on the lochside, near the train station.

North of town, just before the turn-off to Mallaig, on the left, are the 13th-century ruins of **Inverlochy Castle**, and at Banavie is **Neptune's Staircase**, a series of eight linked locks on the Caledonian Canal. The locks lower the canal by 90ft in less than two miles between Loch Lochy and Loch Eil and comprise the last section of the canal which links the North Sea with the Irish Sea.

Essentials

Fort William has plentiful accommodation, ranging from large luxury hotels to modest guesthouses and B&Bs. Many of the B&Bs are in **Corpach** and **Banavie** to the north of town (see 'Transport' below). As a main tourist centre, Fort William gets very busy in the high season and you'll need to book ahead at this time. The tourist office will book a room for you, for a small fee, or you can ask for their free *Fort William & Lochaber Visitor Guide* and phone around yourself.

Sleeping
■ *on map*
Price codes:
see inside front cover

L *Inverlochy Castle Hotel*, 3 miles north of town on the A82 to Inverness, T702177, F702953. 16 rooms. One of the best hotels in the country and everything you'd expect to find in a real castle, unsurpassed elegance, impeccable service and superb food, all set in 500 acres of beautiful grounds.

B *Alexandra Hotel*, The Parade, T702241, F705554, sales@miltonhotels.com. 97 rooms, large established hotel right in the centre of town, with restaurant.

C *Glenloy Lodge Hotel*, about 6 miles from town on the B8004 north from Banavie, T/F712700. 9 rooms, open mid-Dec to late Oct. Friendly and comfortable little hotel tucked away in a quiet, secluded location, and with a good restaurant. **C** *The Moorings Hotel*, 3 miles out of town in Banavie, on the road to Corpach and Mallaig, T772797, F772441. 21 rooms. Overlooks 'Neptune's Staircase', well situated and comfortable with an excellent restaurant.

The Highlands

D *Distillery House*, Nevis Bridge, North Rd (opposite the road into Glen Nevis), T700103, F702980. 6 rooms, comfortable, upmarket guesthouse. Across the road is **E** *Glenlochy Guesthouse*, T702909, which is also recommended.

Achintore Rd, which runs south along the loch, is packed with B&Bs and hotels, many of which are large and characterless. More appealing than most is **D-E** *Lawriestone Guesthouse*, T/F700777. Running parallel is **Grange Rd**, which is lined with B&B accommodation. Two of the best are **C** *Crolinnhe*, T702709, open Mar-Nov, and **C** *The Grange*, T705516, open Apr-Oct. There are also plenty of B&Bs which are closer to the **bus and train stations**, mostly on and around Fassifern Rd and Alma Rd. These include **D-E** *Guisachan House*, T/F703797, and **E-F** *Mrs Heger*, 'Finnisaig', T702453, both on Alma Rd, and **E** *6 Caberfeidh*, Fassifern Rd, T703756.

Fort William

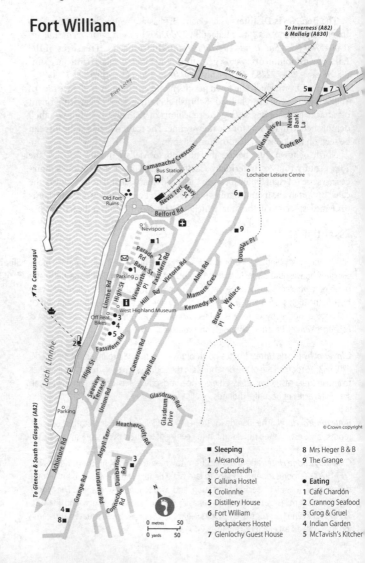

© Crown copyright

■ **Sleeping**
1 Alexandra
2 6 Caberfeidh
3 Calluna Hostel
4 Crolinnhe
5 Distillery House
6 Fort William
  Backpackers Hostel
7 Glenlochy Guest House

8 Mrs Heger B & B
9 The Grange

● **Eating**
1 Café Chardón
2 Crannog Seafood
3 Grog & Gruel
4 Indian Garden
5 McTavish's Kitchen

There are several more places to stay in **Glen Nevis**, including E *Achintee Farm Guesthouse*, T702240, mcy@btinternet.com, by the start of the path to Ben Nevis. For details of how to get there, see 'Transport' below.

There are also cheaper options, in the shape of several **hostels** and a couple of **campsites**. The popular *Fort William Backpackers* is on Alma Rd, 500yd from the train station, T700711. 3 miles out of town in Glen Nevis, near the start of the path up Ben Nevis, is the large *SYHA Youth Hostel*, T702336, which gets very busy in summer. A better bet is the independent *Ben Nevis Bunkhouse*, at Achintee Farm, across the river from the visitor centre (see above). *Calluna*, T700451, F700489, mountain@guide.u.net.com, www.guide.u.net.com, is at Heathercroft, about 15 mins walk from the tourist office (see map). It's run by experienced mountain guide, Alan Kimber. There are 2 hostels in Corpach (see 'Transport' below). *The Smiddy Bunkhouse*, T772467, info@snowgoose.presetel.co.uk, www.highland.mountain.guide.co.uk, is next to Corpach train station with the *Snowgoose Mountain Centre* attached. *Scottish International Backpackers* is at Farr Cottage Activity Centre, T772315, F772247, farrcottage@sol.co.uk, www.fort-william.co.uk\farrcottage, which also organizes hill walking trips and rents out mountain bikes.

Two miles up the Glen Nevis Rd is *Glen Nevis Caravan & Camping Park*, T702191, open mid-Mar to late Oct, which has excellent facilities. Five miles from town on the road to Mallaig, is *Linnhe Caravan & Chalet Park*, T772376, open Christmas to late Oct, also with full facilities.

Fort William isn't exactly the culinary capital of the Highlands, but there are some top quality restaurants and a decent choice across the range. Most of the hotels offer lunch and dinner, and the best of these are the *Inverlochy Castle* and *The Moorings* (see 'Sleeping' above). Otherwise, by far the best option is the excellent *Crannog Seafood Restaurant*, on the Town Pier, T705589, crannogallan@msn.com. Housed in an old smokehouse, the seafood is as fresh as you can get and the surroundings are unpretentious. It gets very busy and service can be slow, so book ahead and take your time (lunch cheap to mid-range; dinner mid-range). Four miles from town is *An Crann*, T772077. Take the A830 to Mallaig, then turn right to Banavie on the B8004. This converted barn is a local favourite and offers good Scottish cooking in a friendly atmosphere. (Mid-range prices.) Lunch 1230-1500, dinner 1700-2100, closed Sun. Open late Mar to mid-Oct. A great place for baguettes, filled rolls and pastries to eat in or takeaway is *Café Chardón*, upstairs at Peter Maclennan's store, in a side lane off the High St, T772077. Fort William boasts a very fine curry house, the *Indian Garden Restaurant*, at 88 High St, T705011. It does a cheap lunch, takeaways and is open late. *The Grog & Gruel*, 66 High St, T705078, is a pub-cum-restaurant offering good value pizza, pasta and Tex Mex and a wide range of superb cask ales. Open till 2400/0100. Also on the High St is *McTavish's Kitchens*, T702406, serving steaks and seafood at mid-range prices. In summer it hosts nightly Scottish music shows, with dancing and bagpipes, from 2030.

In Glen Nevis, near the SYHA hostel, the *Glen Nevis Restaurant*, T705459, serves a cheap-mid-range 2-course lunch and mid-range 3-course dinner. Open 1200-2200, Apr-Oct. Nearby is *Café Beag*, T703601, a cosy place with log fire. Good vegetarian food.

Canoeing There are several good rivers around Fort William, ranging in difficulty from Grade 1 to 6. Canoe courses are run by *Snowgoose Mountain Centre*, which is attached to *The Smiddy Bunkhouse* (see 'Sleeping' above). A useful contact is the *Nevis Canoe Club*, T705388. **Fishing** *Torlundy Trout Fishery*, at Torlundy Farm in Tomacharich, 3 miles north, off the A82, T703015, has 3 lakes filled with rainbow trout and hires out rods. **Hiking and climbing** Fort William is a mecca for hikers and climbers. For information on the climb up Ben Nevis and walks around Glen Nevis, see

Eating

Sports

The Highlands

☛ *The West Highland Railway*

The spectacular West Highland Railway runs from Glasgow via Fort William to Mallaig. It is a magnificent feat of engineering and the most dramatic entrance possible to the West Highlands. The stretch before Fort William is particularly breathtaking as the train crosses the bleak and desolate Rannoch Moor, then skirts Loch Ossian, runs around Ben Nevis and enters Fort William from the northeast, through the Monessie Gorge and the most southerly part of the Great Glen. But this railway line saves the best for last. The final section is even more stunning and must rank as one of the most beautiful railway journeys in Europe.

page 429. If you want to hire a guide, try *Lochaber Walks*, 22 Zetland Ave, T703828, *Fort William Mountain Guides*, T700451, *Alba Walking Holidays*, T704964 and *Snowgoose Mountain Centre* (see 'Sleeping' above). Fort William has 2 excellent outdoor activity equipment shops. *Nevisport*, T704921, is on the High St, and has a huge selection of books, maps and guides, a bureau de change and bar-restaurant. At the other end of the High St is *West Coast Outdoor Sports*, T705777. There's an indoor climbing wall at the *Lochaber Leisure Centre* (see below). **Mountain biking** The Leanachan Forest, below Aonach Mhor, is 4 miles north of Fort William. Access is via the road to the Aonach Mhor ski development. The forest covers a huge area with 25 miles of mountain bike trails, ranging from easy to demanding. There is also the Great Glen Cycle Route, which is mainly off-road and runs all the way from Fort William to Inverness. For the hire, sale or repair of bikes, and good advice on local cycle routes, visit *Off Beat Bikes*, 117 High St and at the Nevis Range Ski Centre, T704008, info@offbeatbikes.co.uk, www.offbeatbikes.co.uk, open only Jul-Aug. **Skiing** The Nevis Range ski centre is at nearby Aonach Mhor. For details, see page 431, and for ski equipment, try *Nevisport* (see above). **Swimming** There's an indoor pool at the *Lochaber Leisure Centre*, off Belford Rd (see map), T704359.

Transport **Local Bus**: There are buses every 10-20 mins to and from **Caol** and **Corpach**, and every hour on Sun and in the evening. There is an hourly service to **Glen Nevis**, Mon-Sat from 0800-2300, Jun to Sept only (less frequent on Sun). There are 4 buses daily to **Aonach Mhor** during the ski season. **Car hire**: *Easydrive*, at Lochy Bridge, T701616, *Volkswagen Rental*, at Nevis Garage, Argour Rd, Caol, T702432, *Budget*, at North Rd, T702500, or *Practical Car & Van Hire*, at Slipway Autos, Corpach, T772404. Prices start from around £35 per day. **Taxis**: You can call a taxi on T706070, or T704000.

Long distance Buses: There are several daily *Citylink* buses to **Inverness** (1 hr, £6.30 single); to **Oban** (1 hr 45 mins, £6 single) via **Glencoe** (30 mins; £2); and to **Uig** (3 hrs 30 mins, £14), via **Portree** and **Kyle of Lochalsh** (1 hr 50 mins). Citylink buses also go several times daily to **Glasgow** (3 hrs 15 mins, £10), via Glencoe and Tyndrum, and to **Edinburgh** (4 hrs, £14), via **Stirling** (3 hrs, £11). There is a bus to **Mallaig** (1 hr 30 mins, £4.50) daily except Sun with *Shiel Buses*, T01967-431272. *Highland Country Buses*, T702373, run several times a day to **Kinlochleven** (50 mins, £2.10) via Glencoe. There is also a *Postbus* service (Mon-Sat) to **Glen Etive**. **Ferries**: There is a passenger-only ferry service to **Camusnagaul**, on the opposite bank of Loch Linnhe, from the Town Pier. It sails several times daily (Mon-Sat) and takes 10 mins. For times etc contact Highland Council, T01463-702695, or ask at the tourist office. **Trains**: There are 2-3 trains daily from **Glasgow** to Fort William (3 hrs 45 mins, £22.70) via **Crianlarich**. These trains continue to **Mallaig** (a further 1 hr 20 mins, £7.20) where they connect with ferries to Armadale on Skye (see page 496). There are no direct trains to Oban; you need to change at Crianlarich. There is a sleeper service from **London Euston** (see page 30), but you'll miss the views. For all rail enquiries, T0345-484950.

Glen Nevis

Only 10 minutes drive from Fort William is one of Scotland's great glens, the classic Glen Nevis. The sparkling Water of Nevis tumbles through a wooded gorge, closed in by steep, bracken-covered slopes, with the massive hulk of Ben Nevis watching over. The whole scene is both rugged and sylvan and the nearest you'll get to a Himalayan valley in the Scottish Highlands. It's not surprising, then, that this is a favourite with movie directors and has featured in films such as *Rob Roy* and *Braveheart*.

Colour map 3, grid B6

There are many walks in and around the glen, not least of which is the trek up to the summit of Britain's highest mountain. Aside from the walks described below, there are several easy, marked forest walks which start from the car park at Achriabhach. There are buses into Glen Nevis, as far as the youth hostel, from Fort William bus station (see 'Transport' above).

A fairly easy low level walk is to the spectacular 300ft-high Steall Falls at the head of the glen. It's a popular walk, especially in the summer when the trail can resemble the queue for the Ladies at a Tom Jones concert, but this doesn't detract from its stunning natural beauty.

Steall Falls

OS Landranger No 41

The path starts at the end of the road, at the second car park. Before setting off, you might like to note the sign by the steep waterfall that cascades down to the edge of the car park. It reads 'Warning! This is not the path to Ben Nevis'. Now, if you need to be warned against attempting to climb up Ben Nevis through a waterfall, you probably shouldn't be left alone in possession of this book, never mind let loose on the Scottish mountains. Once you've shaken your head in disbelief at the apparent mind-numbing stupidity of some of your fellow travellers, follow the track alongside the Water of Nevis. The path climbs steadily through the woods and becomes rocky, with the river thundering below through the steep gorge. It runs close to the river before emerging

Glen Nevis-Steal Falls

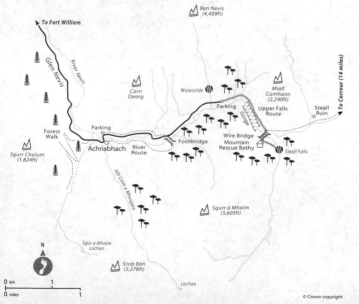

The Highlands

© Crown copyright

from the gorge and opening up into a wide, flower-filled meadow, with a high waterfall at the far end. It's a beautiful, tranquil place and ideal for a picnic.

Follow the path across the valley floor till it crosses the river via a precarious bridge that consists of three ropes of thick wire in a V-shape. The path then leads to the bottom of the falls. You can also head left at the bridge and continue up the valley to some ruins. From here the path leads to **Corrour station**, 14 miles away, but it's for fit and experienced hill walkers only. You can then catch a train back to Fort William. It's a very popular route, and there's even accommodation at the end of it, near the train station, at the *SYHA Loch Lochy Youth Hostel* (T01809-501239; open mid-March to late October).

Walking up Ben Nevis

OS Landranger No 41

Every year many thousands of people make the relatively straightforward ascent of Ben Nevis, and every year a frighteningly high percentage end up injured, or lost, or dead. More people die annually on the 'Ben' than Everest, so this is a mountain that needs to be taken seriously. Though it may be in the eighties in the car park when you set off, the weather changes with alarming speed and you can find yourself in a blizzard at the summit, or, as is usually the case, in a blanket of cloud or hill fog.

It goes without saying that you need to be well prepared. You will need a good, strong pair of boots, warm clothing, waterproofs, food and drink. You should also take a map and a compass. Allow 6-8 hours for the return trip. In the winter the top part of the mountain is covered in snow and you should not attempt the walk unless you are an experienced hill climber. See also page 53.

The main tourist path, built as a pony track to service the now-dilapidated observatory on the summit, starts from the car park at Achintee Farm, on the north side of the river, reached by the road through Claggan. It climbs

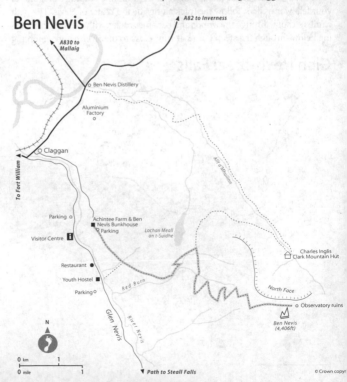

Ben Nevis

© Crown copyr

Nevis Range Ski Centre

The Nevis Range Ski Centre, four miles northeast of Fort William, at Torlundy, is situated on the mountain of **Aonach Mhor** (4,006 feet). It's Scotland's highest ski area and has the longest ski season, running from Christmas to May. It also boasts the country's only cable-car system, built in 1989. The 1½ mile gondola ride is a popular attraction not only with skiers in the winter but also during the summer off-season period, when it's used by hill walkers to gain easy access to the mountains. For most tourists, though, it's an easy way to climb to over 2,000 feet and enjoy the wonderful views from the terrace of the self-service restaurant at the top. There's also a dry slope for summer skiing in July and August (open Sunday-Thursday 1100-1230, £18 including gondola).

The gondola is open all year, except early November to Christmas, 1000-1700 (July-August 0930-1900) and costs £6.50 return (children £4). T01397-705825, nevisrange@sol.co.uk, www.ski.scotland.net.

gradually at first across the flank of Meal an t-Suidhe, before joining the alternative path from the youth hostel. This latter route is shorter but much steeper. The trail continues to climb steadily as it begins to follow the **Red Burn**, until it reaches a junction, with Lochan Meal an t-Suidhe down to the left. Here, an alternative route down from the summit heads left under the north face of the mountain (see below).

This is the halfway point of the main route. The path crosses the Red Burn and then climbs by a series of long and seemingly never-ending zig-zags up to a plateau. The path splits in two, but both paths take you up to the summit, marked by a cairn and emergency shelter, on ruins of the old observatory.

To return simply retrace your steps all the way. If the weather is settled enough and you have time, you can follow the alternative route below the north face. This leads right round the mountain to the Charles Inglis Clark mountain hut, then heads down into the **Allt a' Mhuilinn** glen which leads all the way down to the distillery on the A82, a mile north of the town centre. Note that this route adds an extra three or four miles to the descent and should only be attempted by fit and experienced hill walkers.

Fort William to Glen Coe

The main A82 south to Glasgow runs down the side of Loch Linnhe towards Glen Coe. About eight miles south of Fort William it passes the **Corran Ferry** to **Ardgour** (see page 438). The ferry makes the five-minute crossing every 30 minutes. Foot passengers are free and cars cost £4.20. By the ferry is the **D-E** *Nether Lochaber Hotel*, T821235, which serves decent, cheap pub meals.

Phone code: 01855
Colour map 3, grid B6

Less than half a mile south of the ferry is the turning to **Inchree**, where you'll find cheap lodging at the *Inchree Bunkhouse Hostel*, T821287. There's also a good restaurant nearby, the *Four Seasons Bistro and Bar*, T821393, a friendly and informal place that looks like a log cabin. It's open daily (except Tuesdays) 1800-2130. (Prices mid-range.)

There's an easy 40-minute circular walk up to **Inchree Waterfall**. It starts from the car park at the end of the road beyond the tiny hamlet and is clearly marked. The waterfall is impressive and divided into three sections. The views from the top, down the length of Loch Linnhe, are worth the walk alone. The path continues up past the waterfall to the forest road which leads back downhill to the car park.

Sleeping A mile south of the ferry are the villages of **Onich** and **North Ballachulish**. There's a wide selection of places to stay here, mostly with good views of the loch, which make an attractive alternative to Fort William. Overlooking the loch are **B** *Allt-nan-Ros Hotel*, T821210, allt-nan-ros@zetnet.co.uk, and **B** *The Lodge on the Loch Hotel*, T821237, laurence@mysteryworld.co.uk, open Feb-Dec. Both are high-quality hotels with great views and good restaurants (lunch mid-range; dinner expensive). A cheaper option is **C** *Onich Hotel*, T821214, which also has loch views and serves good meals (cheap-mid-range) in its busy bar. A good place to dine, but for residents only, is **E** *Cuilcheanna House*, T821226; open Easter-Oct, a comfortable guesthouse just off the main road.

Sport *Alfresco Adventure*, T821248, just to the east of North Ballachulish on the B863 to Kinlochleven, offers boat hire and various outdoor activities such as mountain biking and canoeing.

Kinlochleven

Phone code: 01855
Colour map 3, grid B6

The B863 turns east off the A82 at North Ballachulish and heads to Kinlochleven, at the head of Loch Leven. It can also be reached on the same road from Glencoe village, seven miles west. It's an unlikely place to find a huge aluminium factory, but it kept the village alive for many years. Now,

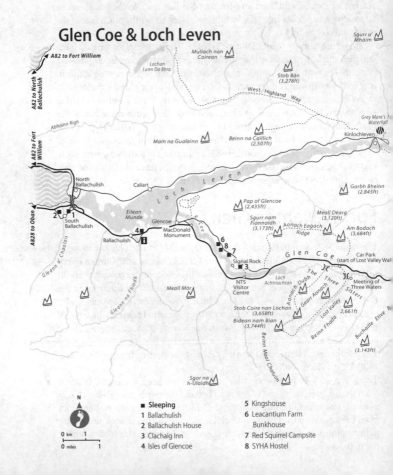

Glen Coe & Loch Leven

■ **Sleeping**
1 Ballachulish
2 Ballachulish House
3 Clachaig Inn
4 Isles of Glencoe

5 Kingshouse
6 Leacantium Farm Bunkhouse
7 Red Squirrel Campsite
8 SYHA Hostel

though, it's threatened with closure and there's talk of Kinlochleven being developed as a major mountaineering centre.

You can find out all about the long, and often tragic, history of aluminium working in Lochaber at **The Aluminium Story**, in the Kinlochleven Visitor Centre and Library, on Linnhe Road. ■ *T831663. Apr-Oct, Tue-Fri 1030-1800, Sat/Sun 1100-1500,*

The West Highland Way passes through the village and many walkers spend the night here before setting out on the last stretch before Fort William. There are also several good walks in the surrounding hills and glens, a few of which are described below.

There's not a huge amount to choose from in the way of accommodation or eating out. The **D** *MacDonald Hotel*, on the Fort William Rd, T831539, open Mar-Dec, serves cheap bar lunches and moderately priced dinners, and the **E** *Tailrace Inn*, on Riverside Rd, T831777, does cheap bar meals all day. There are also several **B&Bs**, as well as an independent hostel, the *West Highland Lodge*, Hostel Brae, T831471.

Sleeping & eating

Highland Country Buses, T01397-702373, runs 6 times a day (Mon-Sat) between Fort William and Kinlochleven (50 mins, £2.10).

Transport

Binnein Mór

Na Gruagaichean (3,461ft)

Loch Eilde Mór

R Leven

Blackwater Reservoir

Dam

West Highland Way

Devil's Staircase

Altnafeadh

Rannoch

A82 TO Crianlarich & Glasgow

■ 5

Moor

Buachaille Etive Mór (Great Shepherd of Etive)

(2,963ft)

(1032ft)

Glen Etive

R Etive

Museum of Scottish Skiing & Climbing

To Glencoe Ski Centre ▶

© Crown copyright

There are some fairly easy short walks from Kinlochleven up the glen of the river Leven, including the one to the impressive **Grey Mare's Tail** waterfall. A fairly easy but rewarding half day walk is to follow the **West Highland Way** south from the village to the top of the **Devil's Staircase**, where it meets the A82 at the eastern end of Glen Coe. The route starts from the British Aluminium Visitor Centre, runs around the side of the aluminium factory, then crosses a wooden bridge and climbs gradually on a dirt jeep-track up to Penstock House, at 1,000ft. At the top, near the house, the track forks to the right and continues on a rough footpath to the Devil's Staircase. The path is marked with the West Highland Way thistle sign, so it's easy to follow, uphill to the top of the pass (1,804ft), from where you get great views of Loch Eilde Mór and the Mamores to the north. The path then descends down the staircase to Glen Coe, with breathtaking Buachaille Etive Mór in front of you all the way.

You'll have to return to Kinlochleven by the same route, or you could carry on to the *Kingshouse Hotel* (see below). The return trip from Kinlochleven should take four to five hours, or you can start out from Glencoe (see below). This section of

Walks around Kinlochleven

OS Landranger No 41

The Highlands

👉 **Glencoe Ski Centre**

The Glencoe Ski Centre is just over a mile from the Kingshouse Hotel, on the other side of the A82, on **Meall A'Bhuiridh** (3,636 feet). This is Scotland's oldest ski centre, established in 1956, and remains one of the best, with the longest single descent. At the base station is the **Museum of Scottish Skiing and Climbing** where you can see the ice axe used by Chris Bonnington, among other things. It's open daily May-September 0900-1700. There's also a restaurant and café. The chair lift operates daily 0930-1700. A full day pass, including lifts, costs £17 (children £9.50). There's also a combined five-day pass for Glencoe and Nevis Range. T851226, glencoe@sol.co.uk, www.ski.scotland.net.

the West Highland Way was once part of the old military road which ran from Fort William to Stirling. The Devil's Staircase was named by the 400 soldiers who had to endure severe hardship while building it in the 17th century.

Another good hike, though more strenuous, is to **Beinn na Callich** (2,507ft). You'll need to be fairly fit for this steep climb and allow around 6-7 hours for the return trip. The route is well marked and starts from the West Highland Way footpath opposite the school, which is on the road heading out of the village towards Fort William.

The path climbs steeply at first, crosses the tarmac road to Mamore Lodge, then continues till it joins General Wade's old military road, which takes the West Highland Way on its final 11miles to Fort William. From here, you'll see the path zig-zagging up the mountain. Continue along the old military road for about 400yd until you cross a wooden bridge. Then follow a path down to another wooden bridge, where the ground is quite boggy. Cross the bridge and the path begins to zig-zag uphill till it levels out onto a plateau, before continuing relentlessly upwards through a long series of zig-zags to the summit, marked by a couple of cairn and a commemorative plaque. The views from the top make the tiring climb worthwhile. You can see down onto Loch Leven, across to Glen Coe and the magnificent Mamores looming close by.

Fit and experienced hill walkers can access the Mamores from the Mamore Lodge road. Once you're up there you have the opportunity to bag several Munros, via a series of excellent ridge walks connecting **Am Bodach** (3,386ft) with **Stob Coire a' Chairn** (3,219ft), **Na Gruagaichean** (3,461ft), **An Gearanach** (3,222ft), **Sgor An Iubhair** (3,285ft), **Sgurr a'Mhaim** (3,606ft) and **Stob Ban** (3,278ft). These peaks and ridges can also be reached from Glen Nevis (see page 429). As well as a good pair of lungs and the proper equipment, take a map and a compass.

Ballachulish

Phone code: 01855
Colour map 3, grid B6

On the southern shore of Loch Leven, a mile or so west of Glencoe village, on the A82, is the old slate quarrying village of Ballachulish. Here you'll find a good range of accommodation and, in the car park just off the main road, the local **tourist office**. As well as the usual accommodation booking service they have displays about the quarries. ■ *T811296. Apr-May Mon-Sat 0900-1700, Sun 1200-1600; Jun-Sept Mon-Sat 0900-1800, Sun 1000-1700; Sept-Oct Mon-Sat 1000-1700, Sun 1000-1600.*

Across the road is the **Highland Mysteryworld**, which attempts to bring to life many of the old Highland myths and legends with some dodgy special effects and ham acting. There's also a gift shop and reasonable café. ■ *T811660. Daily Easter-Oct 0930-1800. £4.95, £3.50 children.*

The Highlands

B *The Isles of Glencoe Hotel*, T811602, F811770, reservations@mysteryworld.co.uk. 39 rooms. A modern hotel and leisure complex next to Highland Mysteryworld, excellent location on the shores of the loch and facilities include heated pool, sauna and gym. The restaurant serves a mid-range to cheap 3-course lunch and expensive to mid-range 3-course dinner. **B-C** *Ballachulish Hotel*, in South Ballachulish by the bridge, T821582, F821463, reservations@mysteryworld.co.uk. 54 rooms, grand old hotel, handily placed for Glen Coe, Fort William or Oban, restaurant serves meals all day (3-course lunch mid-range to cheap; 3-course dinner expensive). **C** *Ballachulish House*, T811266, F811498, open Mar-Oct. 7 rooms, 200yd beyond the *Ballachulish Hotel* on the A828 to Oban. This comfortable and elegant hotel/guesthouse is steeped in history and said to be the most haunted house in Scotland. The seat of the Stewarts of Ballachulish since the 16th century, this was where the final order for the Glencoe Massacre was signed (see below). Hospitality is second-to-none and the food is superb, even if you're not staying you can enjoy the experience of dining here (expensive), but book ahead.

There's also a wide selection of cheaper **B&Bs** and **guesthouses** in the village, including the very good **E** *Fern Villa*, T811393.

Sleeping

Glen Coe

There are many spectacular places in the Scottish Highlands, but few, if any, can compare to the truly awesome scenery of Glen Coe. No one could fail to be moved by its haunting beauty, with imposing mountains, their tops often wreathed in cloud, rising steeply on either side from the valley floor. The brooding atmosphere of the landscape is only enhanced by the glen's tragic history. Once you've heard of the Glen Coe Massacre it sends a shiver down the spine every time you pass this way.

Scotland's most famous glen is also one of the most accessible, with the A82 Glasgow to Fort William road running through it. Much of the area is owned by the National Trust for Scotland and virtually uninhabited, leaving huge tracts of glen and mountain which provide outstanding climbing and walking. There's also skiing, at the **Glencoe Ski Centre** (see below) and canoeing, on the river Coe and river Etive.

There's a small **NTS Visitor Centre** at the western end of the glen, about three miles south of Glencoe village. It shows a short video on the Glencoe Massacre and has a gift shop selling the usual stuff. ■ *T811307/729. Daily, early Apr to mid-May and early Sept to end Oct 1000-1700; mid-May to end Aug 0930-1730. 50p.*

Glencoe Village

At the western entrance to the glen, on the shores of Loch Leven, is Glencoe village, 16 miles south of Fort William, just off the A82. There are several places to stay in and around the village, as well as a general store, post office and the thatched **Glencoe Folk Museum**, which has collections of costumes, military memorabilia and domestic and farm tools and equipment. ■ *Late May to Sept 1000-1730. £1.50.*

Phone code: 01855
Colour map 3, grid B6

About 3 miles south of the village, on the old road which leads from the village to the NTS visitor centre is **D-E** *Clachaig Inn*, T811252, inn@glencoe-scotland.co.uk. 19 rooms. Good-value accommodation and one of the great Highland pubs, it's a favourite haunt of climbers and there's a lively atmosphere as well as some fine real ales and decent cheap food. There are also 3 chalets which can be rented on a weekly basis (phone for details), and mountain bike hire (see below).

Sleeping & eating

The Highlands

Glen Coe

On the same road, about 2 miles from the village, is the excellent *SYHA Youth Hostel*, T811219. It's open all year and is very popular with climbers, so you should book ahead. Nearby are the *Leacantuim Farm Bunkhouses*, T811256, which offer cheap, basic accommodation in 2 bunkhouses and an alpine barn. It also runs the *Red Squirrel Campsite* further along the road, which charges £3.50 per person per night.

There are several **B&Bs** and **guesthouses** in the village itself, including **E** *Scorrybreac Guesthouse*, T/F811354, john@tajones.demon.co.uk, open Dec-Oct, and on the outskirts of the village, at Upper Carnoch, is **E** *The Glencoe Guesthouse*, T811244. To the east of the village, on the shores of Loch Leven, you can camp at *Invercoe Caravans*, T/F811210.

At the east end of the glen, almost opposite the turn-off to the Glencoe Ski Centre, is **D-E** *Kingshouse Hotel*, T851259. 22 rooms. This is Scotland's oldest established inn and such a landmark that it even appears on maps, marked as 'hotel', it's on the West Highland Way and is popular with hikers, climbers and skiers who frequently drop in for a refreshing drink in the bar and some good-value food.

Apart from the places listed above, you can eat in the village at *The Glencoe Hotel*, T811245, which serves cheap bar lunches and moderately priced 3-course dinner.

Guides *Hadrian Mountaineering*, 19b Carnoch, Glencoe, T/F811472, info@glencoe-mountain-sport.co.uk, www.glencoe-mountain-sport.co.uk. *Glencoe Guides*, T811402. *Dave Hanna*, Ardarroch, Ballachulish, T811620.

Transport *Highland Country Buses* run several times daily from **Fort William** to Glencoe village (30 mins). There are *Citylink* buses to **Glasgow** (2 hrs 30 mins, £8.80) and **Fort William** (£2.80).

The daily *Postbus* service from **Fort William** to the Kingshouse Hotel and **Glen Etive** stops at the Glencoe crossroads.

Cycle hire *Glencoe Mountain Bike Centre* at the *Clachaig Inn* (see above); £12 for a full day, £8 for a half day.

🦶 Walks in Glen Coe

OS Landranger No 41   Glen Coe offers some of Britain's most challenging climbing and hiking, with some notoriously treacherous routes and unpredictable weather conditions that claim lives every year. The routes described below are some of the least strenuous but you'll need a map, good boots, warm clothing, food and water, and you should take the usual precautions (see page 53).

The Highlands

The Glen Coe Massacre

Glen Coe is probably best known as the scene of one of the most shameful and notorious incidents in Scottish history. Following his succession to the throne, William III wanted all the clans to swear an oath of allegiance by 1 January 1692. After much hesitation, the Jacobite clans of the West Highlands agreed to do so. However, Maclain of Glencoe, chief of a small branch of the MacDonalds, was not only late in setting off on the journey, but mistakenly went to Fort William to sign, instead of Inveraray. By the time he reached Inveraray it was 6 January and the deadline had passed.

The government decided that the rebellious clan be punished, in order to set an example to other clans, some of whom had not taken the oath. A company of 120 soldiers, under the command of Cambell of Glenlyon, were sent to Glen Coe, and since their leader was related by marriage to Maclain, the troops were billeted in MacDonald homes, in keeping with the long-standing Highland tradition of hospitality.

There they stayed for almost two weeks, until the cold-blooded order came through to '… put all to the sword under seventy'. And so, on a cold winter's night, in the early hours of 13 February 1692, the Campbells ruthlessly slaughtered their hosts. Maclain and 37 men, women and children were slain in their beds, while many others fled into the hills, only to die of hunger and exposure. It was a bloody incident which had deep repercussions and proved to be the beginning of the end of the Highland way of life.

There's a monument to the fallen MacDonalds in the village of Glencoe, where members of the clan still gather on 13 February each year. For a powerful and evocative account of the Massacre, you should read Glencoe by John Prebble (Penguin).

One of the most popular walks is the relatively straightforward hike up to the **Lost Valley**, a secret glen where the ill-fated MacDonalds hid the cattle they'd stolen. Allow around three hours for the return trip. Start from the car park by the large boulder (see map page 432), opposite the distinctive **Three Sisters**. Head down to the valley floor and follow the gravel path which leads down to a wooden bridge across the river Coe. Cross the bridge and follow the path up and over the stile. From here there's a choice of two routes. The less obvious route heads right and offers an easier climb into the valley. This eventually meets the lower, well-worn track, which involves a bit of scrambling but is more exciting as it follows the rushing waters of the **Allt Coire Gabhail**. The upper and lower paths meet a few miles further up and here you cross the river by some stepping stones. Proceed up the steep scree slope till you reach the rim of the Lost Valley, where many of the MacDonalds fled on the night of the infamous massacre. Once in the valley there are great views of Bidean nam Bian, Gearr Aonach and Beinn Fhada and you can continue for a further 20-30 minutes to the head of the valley. From here it's possible to climb Bidean, but you'll need to be fit, experienced and well equipped.

Glen Coe also offers one of the world's classic ridge walks, the **Aonach Eagach**. It's not for the inexperienced or faint-hearted as there are some fairly exposed pinnacles. The ridge runs almost the entire length of the glen, starting at Am Bodach and ending at Sgor nam Fiannaidh. Don't make the mistake of descending from the last summit straight down to the Clachaig Inn. This is not the correct route.

Another difficult route is to the summit of **Buachaille Etive Mór**, one of the most photographed mountains in Scotland and one you'll probably recognize immediately then first time you see it from the A82 on the way to or from Glencoe. The mountain is best viewed from the Kingshouse Hotel and the

The Highlands

route starts from Altnafeadh, a couple of miles west of the hotel. This is also the start or finish point for the fairly easy half-day walk over the **Devil's Staircase**, which is part of the **West Highland Way** (for a description of the route, see page 433).

Glen Etive runs southwest from the hotel. It's a very beautiful and little-visited place and great for wild camping. There's a postbus service once a day from Fort William.

Finally, there are some short, pleasant walks around **Glencoe Lochan**, an artificial loch created in the mid-19th century by Lord Strathcona for his homesick Canadian wife. Take the left turning off the minor road to the youth hostel just beyond the bridge over the river Coe. There's a choice of three walks of between 40 minutes and an hour, all detailed at the car park.

Ardgour, Ardnamurchan and Morvern

Colour map 3, grid B4/5

West of Fort William is one of the most remote parts of the Highland region, stretching south from **Loch Ailort** to the **Morvern peninsula**, and west to the wild and beautiful **Ardnamurchan peninsula**. This lonely, southwestern corner features a dramatic landscape of rugged mountains, desolate moorland and near-deserted glens, fringed by a coastline of sparkling white beaches and clear turquoise seas with wonderful views across to the isles of Mull and Skye. This is one of the least-populated areas in Britain, mainly due to the legacy of the Highland Clearances in the mid-19th century, when whole communities were evicted by landlords in favour of more profitable sheep.

With so few people around, this is an area noted for its wildlife, with a huge variety of birds and animals, such as deer, pine martens, wildcats and eagles. If you have both the time and the energy, it's worth exploring on foot. There's a series of footpaths throughout the area, particularly around Ardnamurchan. 30 such walks are listed in a local guide book available at tourist offices. You should also have OS Map numbers 40, 47 and 49, which cover the area.

Getting around It's an area of few roads. Once you leave the A830 Fort William to Mallaig road, **buses** are few and far between, so it's not easy to get around quickly without your own transport. *Shiel Buses*, T01967-431272, run most of the bus services. There's a bus once a day on Tue, Thur and Sat from Fort William to Lochaline (2 hrs), via the **Corran Ferry**. There's a bus once a day (Mon-Sat) from Fort William to Acharacle (1 hr 30 mins, £4.25), via Lochailort. There's also a bus (Mon-Fri) to Acharacle from Mallaig (1 hr 30 mins). There's a bus once a day (Mon-Sat) from Fort William to Kilchoan (2 hrs 25 mins, £5), via Strontian (1 hr, £2.70), Salen and Glenborrodale.

For details of the **ferry** from Lochaline to Fishnish on Mull and from Kilchoan to Tobermory, see the Inner Hebrides chapter, page 237. If you're travelling by **car**, access is via the A861, leaving the A830 before Glenfinnan or at Lochailort. You can also make the 5-min ferry crossing to Ardgour from the Corran Ferry, about 8 miles south of Fort William on the A82 (see page 431).

Ardgour

The name Ardgour means 'height of the goats', and you can still see feral goats in this huge, sparsely populated wilderness bordered by Loch Shiel, Loch Eil, Loch Linnhe and Loch Sunart. Access is via the A861 south from Kinlocheil, or on the Corran Ferry to the tiny lochside villages of **Corran** and **Clovulin**. There's accommodation here at **D-E** *The Inn at Ardgour*, T01855-841225.

The attractive little village of Strontian on the shores of Loch Sunart gave its name to the element strontium, which was first discovered in the nearby lead mines in 1790. These now-abandoned mines also produced most of the lead shot used in the Napoleonic wars. Strontian is the largest settlement in these parts and has a couple of shops, a post office and a **tourist office**. ■ *T402131. Apr to Oct, Mon-Fri 0900-1700, Sat 1000-1600 and Sun 1000-1400.*

Strontian
Phone code: 01967
Colour map 3, grid B5

About two miles north of the village is the **Ariundle Nature Reserve**, which offers a pleasant two-hour nature trail through the glen and a 40-minute forest walk.

Sleeping Strontian has a couple of good hotels. The luxurious **A-B** *Kilcamb Lodge Hotel*, T402257, F402041, open Mar-Nov, stands in its own grounds on the lochside and serves superb food. A cheaper option is the 18th-century **C** *Horsley Hall Hotel* , T/F402471. There are several **B&Bs**, including the very comfortable **E** *Kinloch House*, T402138, open Jan-Nov.

Morvern

Just east of Strontian the A884 leads south through the bleak, desolate landscape of Morvern to the tiny remote community of **Lochaline** on the Sound of Mull, departure point for the *CalMac* ferry to **Fishnish**.

Phone code: 01967

About three miles before Lochaline is the turning left for the track which leads down the side of Loch Aline to the 14th-century ruins of **Ardtornish Castle**. First you'll come to **Kinlochaline Castle** (keys available at the cottage) and **Ardtornish House**. This house stands on the site of the original house, which was visited on several occasions by Florence Nightingale, who was a family member of the original owners. The author John Buchan spent many summers here in the 1930s. There's a path which leads from the estate office and uphill across open moorland for an hour till it reaches **Loch Tearnait**. In the centre of the loch is a 1,500 year-old crannog, an artificial island built for defensive purposes. This walk is detailed in the tourist board's *Great Walks* leaflet, along with the Ariundle Nature Trail, available from local tourist offices. During the stalking season (1 July-20 October) check at the estate office before setting out.

If you want to stay in Lochaline, there are a couple of **B&Bs** and the **E** *Lochaline Hotel*, T421657, which serves decent bar meals. There's also a scuba diving school at the ferry pier, T421627.

Sleeping

The Ardnamurchan peninsula

The main places of interest in this area are to be found on the rugged Ardnamurchan peninsula, the end of which is the most westerly point on the British mainland.

The winding A861 runs west from Strontian along the north shore of Loch Sunart to **Salen**, where the single-track B8007 branches west and runs all the way out to the tip of the peninsula. The A861 meanwhile turns north to **Acharacle**. There's accommodation at Salen in the **D** *Salen Hotel*, T431661, salenhotel@aol.com, where you can also get food (cheap to mid-range) and information on local walks. A mile or so east of Salen, at **Resipole**, you can pitch a tent at the *Resipole Farm Caravan Park*, T431235. There's also a restaurant and bar on site.

The Highlands

Glenborrodale & Glenmore
Phone code: 01972
Colour map 3, grid B4

The first settlement you reach heading west out to Ardnamurchan Point is Glenborrodale. Before you reach the tiny hamlet look out on the left for the castellated late-Victorian towers of Glenborrodale Castle, once the property of a certain Jesse Boot, who founded a chain of chemist shops which you may have heard of.

Just west of Glenborrodale is the excellent **Glenmore Natural History Centre**, local photographer Michael McGregor's interactive exhibition which features some of his most stunning photographs of local wildlife. The centre is designed to interact with the environment and there's live video action of the surrounding wildlife, including pine martens, birds and even fish in the nearby river. It's a great place for kids, and adults, too. There's also a café serving snacks and a bookshop. ■ *T500254. Apr-Oct 1030-1730 (1200-1730 on Sun). £2.50, £1.20 child.*

A mile to the east is the **RSPB Reserve** where you can see golden eagles, otters and seals. You can take a two-hour wildlife trip to the **seal colonies** – or further afield to Tobermory on Mull or Staffa and the Treshnish Islands – with *Ardnamurchan Charters*, T500208 or T01967-431263.

A few miles west of the centre, the B8007 turns away from the coast. Here, you'll see the beautiful bay of **Camas nan Geall**. It's worth stopping at the car park to admire the fantastic views, or take the path down to the beach. A great place to stay in Glenborrodale is C *Feorag House*, T500248, F500285. Between Glenborrodale and Kilchoan, a road runs to the north coast of the peninsula and the beautiful beaches at **Fascadale**, **Kilmory** and **Ockle**.

Kilchoan
Phone code: 01972
Colour map 3, grid B4

The straggling crofting village Kilchoan is the main settlement on Ardnamurchan. Shortly after passing the sign for the village, you can turn left to the scenic ruin of **Mingary Castle**, built around the 13th century. There's a **tourist office** here which provides information on local scenic walks and will help with accommodation. ■ *T510222. Easter-Oct Mon-Sat 0900-1845, Sun 1030-1715.* A car and passenger **ferry** leaves Kilchoan for Tobermory on Mull. It sails mid-April to mid-October and the crossing takes 35 minutes (see page 237).

Sleeping There's a decent selection of accommodation. **B-C** *Meall Mo Chridhe*, T/F510328. Open Apr-Oct. A beautiful 18th-century converted manse with great sea views and fine cooking. Full board also available (**A**). Dinner available for non-residents (expensive) but booking essential. **C-D** *Far View Cottage*, T510357, www.ardamurchan.com/farview. Open Mar-Nov. Superior and friendly B&B with great views and excellent food (mid-range; also for non-residents but booking essential). A cheaper option is **E** *Doirlinn House*, T/F501209. A few miles beyond the village, on the road to Ardnamurchan Point, is **C-D** *Sonachan Hotel*, T/F510211, darie@sonachan.u-net.com. You can get lunch (1200-1430; cheap) and dinner (1800-2000; mid-range) at the *Kilchoan House Hotel*, T510200.

Ardnamurchan Point & Sanna Bay
Phone code: 01972
Colour map 3, grid B3

Beyond Kilchoan the road leads to the **lighthouse** at mainland Britain's most westerly point, with stunning views (on a clear day) across to the small isles of Rum, Eigg, Muck and Canna, with the Cuillins of Skye rising behind Rum. The former lighthouse was designed by Alan Stevenson, father of Robert Louis, and built in 1849. The buildings have been converted into the **Ardnamurchan Visitor Centre**, where you can learn about the history and workings of lighthouses. There's also self-catering accommodation, a café and gift shop. ■ *T510210. Daily 1 Apr-31 Oct, from 1000-1800 (1700 in Oct). £2.50, £1.20 child.*

A mile northwest of Kilchoan, a road branches to the right to the beautiful long, white beach at **Sanna Bay**. It's worth making the trip here just to walk on the beach, but this is also a good place to spot whales and dolphins. On the road to Sanna Bay is the tiny settlement of **Achnaha**, which is famed for its rare 'ring-dyke' system, a huge, natural rock formation which is the crater of an extinct volcano. You can stay in Achnaha, at **E-F** *Hillview*, T510322.

You'll need your own transport to reach Ardnamurchan Point and Sanna Bay as there are no buses beyond Kilchoan (see 'Getting around' above).

North of Salen on the A861 is the scattered crofting township of Acharacle, at the western end of Loch Shiel surrounded by rolling hills. A couple of miles to the west a road leads to beautiful **Kentra Bay**. Cross the wooden bridge, follow the footpath round the side of Kentra Bay and then follow the signs for Gortenfearn, where you'll find the famous '**singing sands**'. Not only is the beach music to the ears as you walk its length, but the view across to Skye and the small isles is a feast for the eyes.

> **Acharacle & Castle Tioram**
> *Phone code: 01967*
> *Colour map 3, grid B4*

Three miles north of Acharacle is **Loch Moidart**. Here, perched on a rocky promontory in the middle of the loch, is the 13th-century ruin of **Castle Tioram** (pronounced 'Cheerum'), one of Scotland's most romantic and atmospheric castles. This was the seat of the MacDonalds of Clanranald, until it was destroyed by their chief in 1715, to prevent it from falling into Hanoverian hands while he was away fighting for the Jacobites. There are plans to restore the castle, but you can visit it (free) via the sandy causeway that connects it to the mainland at low tide.

Sleeping The village has several shops, a post office, garage and plenty of places to stay. **D** *Loch Shiel House Hotel*, T431224, F431200. 10 rooms. Comfortable and decent bar meals (cheap lunch; mid-range to cheap dinner). Contact them for details of cruises on Loch Shiel. A couple of good **B&Bs** are **E** *Belmont House*, T431266, and **D-E** *Ardshealach House*, T431301; open Apr-Sept. Food is also available at the *Clanranald Hotel*, at Mingarry, T431202.

About five miles east of the village, on a side road off the A861 north to Lochailort and Mallaig, is the very beautiful **D-E** *Dalilea House*, T431253; open Apr-Oct. From Dalilea Pier you can cross to The *Achnanellan Centre*, T431265, an outdoor activities centre on the south shore of Loch Shiel, at the foot of **Beinn Resipol** (2,772ft). They hire out mountain bikes, canoes, sail boats and camping equipment as well as providing cheap, basic bunkhouse accommodation (**F**). It was from Dalilea Pier that Bonnie Prince Charlie left to sail up Loch Shiel to raise his standard at Glenfinnan (see below).

The Road to the Isles

The 46-mile stretch of A830 from **Fort William** to **Mallaig** is known as 'The Road to the Isles'. It's a very beautiful journey, particularly by train (see page 428), through a landscape that resonates with historical significance. This is Bonnie Prince Charlie country, where the ill-fated Jacobite Rising not only began, but also ended, with the Prince's flight to France.

Glenfinnan

It all started on 19 August 1745, at Glenfinnan, 19 miles west of Fort William, at the head of Loch Shiel. Less than a month earlier, Prince Charles Edward Stuart had landed on the Scottish mainland for the first time, on the shores of Loch nan Uamh, between Lochailort and Arisaig (see below). He had come to claim the British throne for his father, James, son of the exiled King James VII of Scotland and II of England.

> *Phone code: 01397*
> *Colour map 3, grid B4*

The clan chiefs had expected French support, but when the Prince arrived with only a handful of men they were reluctant to join the cause. Undeterred, the prince raised his standard and his faith was soon rewarded when he heard the sound of the pipes and Cameron of Lochiel, along with 800 men, came marching down the valley to join them. It must have been an incredible moment.

There's a powerful sense of history here. You don't have to be Scottish to feel a shiver run down the spine and a tear well in the eye as you gaze across stunning Loch Shiel stretching into the distance, veiled by steep mountains. You can almost hear the wail of the bagpipes in the distance. A commemorative **tower** stands proudly at the head of the loch, erected in 1815 by Alexander MacDonald of Glenaladale in memory of the clansmen who fought and died for the Prince. You can climb to the top of the tower (mind your head, though) for even better views down the loch.

On the other side of the road is the NTS **visitor centre**, which has displays and an audio programme of the Prince's campaign, from Glenfinnan to its grim conclusion at Culloden. There's also a café. ■ *T722250. Daily 1 Apr to 18 May and 1 Sept to 31 Oct 1000-1700; 19 May to 31 Aug 0930-1800. £1.50, £1 child.*

A mile away, in Glenfinnan village, is the **Station Museum**, which is housed in the railway station, on the magnificent Fort-William to Mallaig railway line. It has displays of memorabilia from the line's 100-year history. ■ *T722295. Daily Apr-Oct 0930-1630. 50p.* You can also sleep and eat here (see below). The 1,000-ft span of the **Glenfinnan viaduct**, between the visitor centre and the village, is one of the most spectacular sections of the famous **West Highland Railway** (see page 428).

You can take a cruise down Loch Shiel, from Glenfinnan to Acharacle (see above) at its southern end. Contact *Loch Shiel Cruises* at the *Glenfinnan House Hotel* (see below). There are sailings most days from April to October.

Sleeping & eating Just off the main road is **B-C** *Glenfinnan House Hotel*, T/F722235. 17 rooms, open Apr-Oct. Wonderful historic house that oozes charm, dinner is served from 1930 (expensive to mid-range for 4 courses), you can also walk in the vast grounds or fish on the loch. **B-C** *The Prince's House*, T722246, F722307, princeshouse@ glenfinnan.co.uk. 9 rooms, open Mar-Nov. On the main road, half a mile past the monument on the right, heading west. Comfortable old coaching inn which offers good food (mid-range). A much cheaper option is the **F** *Glenfinnan Sleeping Car*, at the train station, T722400. Bunkhouse accommodation for 10 people, also mountain bike hire. You can eat here, too, in the *Glenfinnan Dining Car* (cheap 2-course lunch; mid-range 3-course dinner).

Lochailort
Phone code: 01687
Colour map 3, grid B5

About 10 miles west of Glenfinnan the road passes through the village of Lochailort, where the A861 branches south to the remote Ardnamurchan peninsula (see above). There's accommodation and food here at the **D** *Lochailort Inn*, T470208, open March-October.

A couple of miles further on, is **Loch nan Uamh**, where Prince Charles first landed on the Scottish mainland and from where, a year later, he fled for France following the disastrous defeat at Culloden (see page 409). A path leads down from the car park to the **Prince's Cairn**, which marks the beginning and the end of the Jacobite cause.

Arisaig and Morar

Phone code: 01687
Colour map 3, grid A4

At the western end of the Morar peninsula is the little village of Arisaig, scattered round a sandy bay. This was the birthplace of Long John Silver, who worked on the construction of the nearby lighthouse at Barrahead, which happened to be one of many such lighthouses designed by the father of Robert Louis Stevenson. Silver met Robert Louis on a few occasions, and so impressed the young writer that he immortalized him in his classic novel *Treasure Island*.

There are some nice beaches around and the road west from the village out to the **Rhue peninsula** is great for seal spotting. You can also take a **cruise** from Arisaig to the islands of **Rum, Eigg** and **Muck**. ■ *There are sailings daily Mon-Fri, and also Sat-Sun during the summer months. For details contact Murdo Grant, T450224. Also see the Inner Hebrides chapter, on page 262.*

Between Arisaig and Morar is a string of glorious beaches of white sand backed by beautiful machair, washed by turquoise seas and enjoying magnificent views across to Rum and the Cuillins of Skye. This is one of the most stunning stretches of coastline in Britain, despite the presence of too many ugly holiday bungalows and caravan sites. Eight miles north of Arisaig is **Morar**, where the famous beach scenes from the movie *Local Hero* were filmed – with not a caravan in sight.

This coastline gets very busy in summer, but like so much of the Highlands, it's easy to get away from it all. A single-track road leads up behind the village of Morar to dark, mysterious **Loch Morar**, the deepest inland loch in the country and home of Morag, Scotland's other, lesser-known monster. Two locals reported seeing her in August 1969 and a scientific investigation two years later uncovered a remarkable number of eye-witness accounts. You could always try to elicit further information from the locals over a wee dram in the bar of the *Morar Hotel*. The road runs along the north shore of the loch for three miles till it reaches the pretty little hamlets of **Bracora** and **Bracorina**. Here the road stops, but a footpath continues all the way to **Tarbet** on the shores of Loch Nevis, from where it's possible to catch a boat back to Mallaig (see below). It takes about three hours to walk to Tarbet (where there's now a bothy) and you'll need to get there by 1530 for the boat.

Sleeping & eating

Arisaig has plenty of accommodation and a decent range of services. There are several hotels, including **D** *Arisaig Hotel*, T450210, arisaighotel@dial.pipex.com. They serve moderately priced food 1200-1400 and 1800-2100. A good restaurant is *The Old Library Lodge*, T450651, open Apr-Oct, which also has rooms (**D**).

Mallaig

Phone code: 01687
Colour map 3, grid A4

The end of the road is Mallaig, a busy fishing port and main departure point for the ferry to Skye. It's not a particularly appealing place, but it's always busy with people waiting for the ferry to Skye or the train to Fort William.

Mallaig is a small place, huddled round its harbour, and the train and bus stations and CalMac ferry office are all within a few yards of each other. Also close by are banks with ATMs and the post office. The **tourist office** is also by the harbour. ■ *T462170. Mon-Sat 0900-2000, Sun 1000-1700.*

Sights

If you have some time to kill you could visit **Mallaig Marine World**, an aquarium with indigenous marine creatures as well as displays on the history of the local fishing industry. ■ *T462292. Jun-Sept Mon-Sat 0900-2100, Sun 1000-1800; Oct-May Mon-Sat 0900-1700. £2.77, £1.50 child.* Beside the train station is the **Mallaig Heritage Centre**, with interesting descriptions of the

The Highlands

local Clearances, the railway line and the fishing industry. ■ *May-Sept Mon-Sat 0930-1700, Sun 1300-1700. £1.80, £1.20 child.*

For something a bit more energetic, there are a couple of good walks around the village. An easy one which should take around 45 minutes goes to the little village of **Mallaig Bheag** (Mallaigviag), further east along the coast. Just before the car park at the eastern end of the harbour you'll see a sign, on the right as you head east, which points you towards the old road to Mallaig Bheag. Follow the path up behind the houses and continue into a small glen behind the hill that overlooks the port. The path then rises gradually till you're rewarded with great views Loch Nevis. It continues through Mallaig Bheag then joins up with the main road back to Mallaig. Follow this till the end of the row of houses on your right, turn right and then left and back down to Mallaig bay and the start of the walk.

Sleeping & eating   **D** *Marine Hotel*, T462217, Marinehotel@btinternet. Next to the train station and much nicer inside than it appears. Their restaurant also serves the best food in the town (mid-range). Follow the road round the harbour to East Bay, where you'll find the excellent value **E-F** *Western Isles Guesthouse*, T/F462320, open Jan-Nov, which serves dinner to guests. Nearby is **E** *Glencairn*, T462412; open Apr-Sept. There are lots of other **B&Bs** to choose from. The cheapest place to stay is *Sheena's Backapackers Lodge*, T462764, a friendly, easy-going independent hostel, with dorm beds, double rooms and kitchen facilities.

The *Cabin Seafood Restaurant* serves cheap to mid-range main courses and a great value 'teatime special'. The *Cornerstone Café* also does cheap meals and snacks, but cheapest of the lot is the cafetería in the *Fisherman's Mission* at the pier.

Transport   **Bus** *Shiel Buses*, T01967-431272 run 2 buses daily Mon-Sat from Mallaig to **Fort William** (1 hr 30 mins, £4.50) from Jul-Sept, and on Mon, Thur-Fri the rest of the year.

Ferry *CalMac*, T462403, ferries run throughout the year to **Armadale** on Skye (for full details, see page 496), to **Lochboisdale** and **Castlebay** (see page 521) and to the Small Isles (see page 262). *Bruce Watt Sea Cruises* , T462320, have trips to the remote village of **Inverie**, on the Knoydart peninsula (see below), and **Tarbet** on Loch Nevis (see above). They sail on Mon, Wed and Fri throughout the year, departing at 1015 (to Inverie only) and 1415, and returning at 1155 and 1745. They also sail on Sat (to Inverie) during Jun-Aug, departing at 1030 and returning at 1215. Other departures are to **Loch Scavaig** on Skye (Thur) and to the islands of **Rum** and **Canna** (Tue) from Jun to mid-Sept.

Train The best way to arrive in Mallaig is by train. There are several services daily (1 on Sun) to and from **Fort William**, with connections to **Glasgow** (see page 428). There's also a steam train which runs in the summer months (see page 428).

The Knoydart peninsula

Colour map 3, grid A5   The Knoydart peninsula, the most remote and unspoilt region in Britain and one of Europe's last great wildernesses, literally lies between Heaven and Hell, for it is bordered to the north by **Loch Hourn** ('Loch of Hell') and to the south by **Loch Nevis** ('Loch of Heaven'). It can only be reached on foot or by boat and consequently attracts walkers, who can wander for days around a network of trails without seeing another soul.

The Highlands

Getting there

As mentioned above, the only way in is by boat or on foot. A two-day **hiking** route starts from Kinloch Hourn, reached by bus from Invergarry (see page 419). The trail winds its way around the coast to Barrisdale and on to Inverie. Another route into Knoydart starts from the west end of Loch Arkaig (see page 422) and runs through Glen Dessarry. Both are tough hikes and only for fit, experienced and well-equipped hill walkers.

An easier way in is by **boat**. *Bruce Watt Sea Cruises* sail from Mallaig to Inverie (see above). There's also a ferry service from **Arnisdale** on the north shore of Loch Hourn, to Barrisdale. To arrange a crossing, contact Len Morrison, Croftfoot, Arnisdale, T01599-522352. It's a small open boat which takes five passengers and all sailings are subject to weather.

Inverie
Phone code: 01867

The peninsula's only settlement of any size is tiny Inverie, with just 60 inhabitants. It's the only village in Scotland which can't be reached by road, but still has a post office, a shop, a few places to stay and Britain's most remote pub.

The only **guesthouse** is **E** *Pier House*, T462347, which offers good, old-fashioned hospitality and wonderful local seafood (mid-range prices). A cheaper option is *Torrie Shieling*, T462669. It's a bit more expensive than most other hostels, but is very comfortable and popular with hikers. They also have their own transport for trips around the peninsula and will collect guests from Mallaig by arrangement. The only alternative is the much cheaper, but less appealing *Knoydart Hostel*, T462331, near Inverie House.

Another place to eat is *The Old Forge*, T462267, the most remote pub on mainland Britain. You can enjoy some tasty local seafood and a pint of real ale in front of an open fire. There's even the occasional impromptu ceilidh.

Three or four miles up the peninsula's only road is the highly recommended **C** *Doune Stone Lodge*, T462667, standing in splendid isolation.

The Great Glen to Kyle of Lochalsh

The A87 is one of the main Highland tourist routes, connecting the Great Glen with the west coast and the Isle of Skye. It runs west from Invergarry, between Fort Augustus and Fort William, through Glen Moriston and Glen Shiel to Shiel Bridge, at the head of Loch Duich, and on to Kyle. At Shiel Bridge, a road branches off to Glenelg, from where you can sail across to Skye. It's a beautiful journey and by far the best way to reach the island.

The Highlands

Glen Shiel

The journey from Invergarry to **Shiel Bridge** is worth it for the views alone. Glen Shiel is a spectacular sight, with 3,000ft-high peaks soaring up on either side. This is one of the most popular hiking areas in Scotland, with the magnificent and much-photographed **Five Sisters of Kintail** on the north side of the glen, and the equally beautiful **South Glen Shiel Ridge** on the other. There's a **tourist office** in Shiel Bridge. ■ *Apr-Oct.*

Colour map 3, grid A5

There are several excellent hiking routes in Glen Shiel but these mountains are to be treated with great respect. They require fitness, experience and proper equipment and planning. None of the routes should be attempted without a map, compass and detailed route instructions. You should be aware of the notoriously unpredictable weather conditions and also check locally about deer stalking. The season runs from August to October, but for more details contact the local stalkers (T01599-511282 or 01320-340262). A good trekking guide is the SMC's *Hill Walks in Northwest Scotland*.

OS Landranger No 33

The **Five Sisters Traverse** is a classic ridge route. It starts at the first fire break on the left as you head southeast down the glen from Shiel Bridge and finishes at Morvich, on the other side of the ridge. Allow a full day (8-10 hours). You can also hike from Morvich to Glen Affric Youth Hostel at Cannich. It's a strenuous 20-mile walk, but you can stop off midway at the remote *Allt Beithe* Youth Hostel (see page 414).

The magnificent **South Glen Shiel Ridge** is one of the world's great hikes. It starts from above the *Cluanie Inn* (see below). From here, follow the old public road to Tomdoun which meets up with a good stalking path which climbs to the summit of the first Munro, **Creag a' Mhaim** (3,108ft). The ridge then runs west for almost nine miles and gives you the chance to pick off no fewer than seven Munros. Allow a full day for the walk (9-10 hours), and you'll need to set off early.

Sleeping About 9 miles east of Shiel Bridge is one of the Highlands' classic hotels, the **C** *Cluanie Inn*, T01463-798200. It's a firm favourite with hikers and climbers and it's easy to see why. After a hard day's ridge walking, what could be better than jumping into the jacuzzi, then having a hot dinner and a good pint beside a log fire. You can also camp nearby, but why deny yourself the pleasure if you can afford it?

A less salubrious option is the *Ratagan Youth Hostel*, T01599-511243, just outside Shiel Bridge. It's also popular with hikers and is open all year, except Jan. You can **camp** at *Morvich Caravan Club Site*, T01599-511354, open late Mar to late Oct, or at Shiel Bridge, T01599-511211.

Transport *Citylink* buses between Fort William, Inverness and Skye pass through Glen Shiel several times daily in each direction. There's a *Postbus* service between Kyle and Glenelg (see below) and *Highland Country Buses* run from Ratagan Youth Hostel to Kyle (30 mins) and on to Plockton (50 mins), on schooldays only, departing at 0755 and returning at 1640.

Glenelg

Phone code: 01599
Colour map 3, grid A5

One of the most beautiful journeys in Scotland is the road from Shiel Bridge to the picturesque little village of Glenelg on the Sound of Sleat, only a short distance opposite Kylerhea on Skye.

The unclassified single-track road turns off the A87 and climbs steeply and dramatically through a series of sharp switchbacks to the top of the **Mam Ratagan Pass** (1,115ft). From here the view back across Loch Duich to the Five Sisters of Kintail is simply amazing and the all-time classic calendar shot.

The road then drops down through Glen More to **Glenelg**, the main settlement on the peninsula, which lies on the old drover's route from Skye to the markets in the south. This little-known corner of the Western Highlands is Gavin Maxwell country and was featured in *Ring of Bright Water*, his novel about otters. He disguised the identity of this beautiful, unspoiled stretch of coastline, calling it Camusfearna, and today it remains a quiet backwater. You can see the famous otters at **Sandaig**, on the road running from Glenelg, where Gavin Maxwell lived. The site of his cottage is now marked with a cairn. As well as otters, you can see numerous seabirds, seals and porpoises in the Sound of Sleat, and around the peninsula you may be lucky enough to catch a glimpse of wildcats, pine martens, golden eagles and the recently reintroduced sea eagles.

The village itself consists of a row of whitewashed cottages surrounded by trees and overlooked by the ruins of the 18th-century Bernera Barracks. It's worth stopping in Glenelg, if you've got the time, to experience a night in the wonderfully cosy **E** *Glenelg Inn*, T522273. Even if you can't spend the night, at least spend an hour or two enjoying the atmosphere, good ale and fine seafood. It's one of those places that almost makes you glad it's raining.

Just before the village the road forks. The right turning leads to the **Glenelg-Kylerhea ferry**, which makes the five-minute crossing to Skye. The tiny six-car ferry runs from April to October and is the most scenic and romantic route to the misty isle. For more details, see the Skye chapter (page 496).

A road runs south from Glenelg to Arnisdale. About a mile and a half along this road, a branch left leads to the **Glenelg Brochs** – Dun Telve and Dun Dun Troddan – two of the best-preserved Iron Age buildings in the country. Dun Telve stands to a height of over 30ft and the internal passages are almost intact.

The road south from Glenelg continues past Sandaig Bay and runs along the north shore of unearthly Loch Hourn with great views across the mountains of Knoydart. The road ends at the impossibly cute little fishing hamlet of **Arnsidale**, from where you can take a boat across the loch to Barrisdale on the Knoydart peninsula. For details, see page 444. A bit further along the coast, the road ends at the even tinier hamlet of **Corran**, where there's B&B accommodation at **E-F** *Mrs Nash*.

There's a *Postbus* service from **Kyle of Lochalsh** to **Arnisdale** and **Corran** via Glenelg   **Transport**
at 0945 Mon-Sat. It takes 3 hrs 45 mins. The return bus from Corran departs at 0725.

Eilean Donan Castle

One of Scotland's most photographed sights is the stunningly located Eilean   *Phone code: 01599*
Donan, 10 miles west of Shiel Bridge on the A87. It stands on a tiny islet at the   *Colour map 3, grid A5*
confluence of Loch Duich and Loch Alsh, joined to the shore by a narrow stone bridge and backed by high mountains. This great calendar favourite has also featured in several movies, including *Highlander*, which starred Sean Connery.

The original castle dates from 1230 when Alexander III had it built to protect the area from marauding Vikings. It was destroyed by King George in 1719 during its occupation by Spanish Jacobite forces sent to help the 'Old Pretender', James Stuart. It then lay in ruins, until one of the Macraes had it rebuilt between 1912 and 1932. Inside, the Banqueting Hall with its Pipers' Gallery is most impressive and there's an exhibition of military regalia and interesting displays of the castle's history. The views from the battlements are also worthwhile. ■ *T555202. Daily Apr-Oct 0900-1700. £3.*

There are several places to stay in the nearby village of **Dornie**. **D** *Dornie Hotel*,   **Sleeping &**
T555205, is a good option and serves very good, moderately priced food. Just across   **eating**
the bridge is **D** *Loch Duich Hotel*, T555213. It offers comfortable accommodation, meals and live music in the bar on a Sun evening. There are several good **B&Bs**, including **E** *Tigh Tasgaidh*, T555242, and **F** *Fasgadale*, T588238. A cheaper place to stay is the 6-bed *Silver Fir Bunkhouse*, Carndubh, T555264.

Aside from the hotels listed above, there are a couple of places in Dornie serving decent food. Across the bridge is *Jenny Js*, T555362, which is moderately priced but can be variable. There's also the *Clachan Pub* where you can enjoy a good value 3-course evening meal.

Across the bridge is the turning right for Killilan, a tiny hamlet at the head of Loch Long. About ¾ of a mile up this road is the **C-D** *Conchra House Hotel*, T555233, conchra@aol.com. 6 rooms, this historic 18th-century hunting lodge is peaceful, has lovely views and boasts a reputation for good food. At the end of this road, at Camas-luinie, is *Tigh Iseabeal*, T588205, a 10-bed independent hostel.

Citylink buses between **Fort William** and **Inverness** and **Skye** stop by the castle.   **Transport**

Kyle of Lochalsh

Phone code: 01599
Colour map 3, grid A5
Before the coming of the controversial Skye Bridge a mile to the north (see page 496), the little town of Kyle, as it is known, was the main ferry crossing to Skye and consequently a place which attracted a busy tourist trade. Now, though, the tourist traffic bypasses Kyle, which is probably the most sensible thing to do as it's not the most attractive of places.

There are a couple of interesting boat trips which you can take from Kyle. One is on board the *Seaprobe Atlantis*, a unique boat fitted with underwater windows allowing you to watch 'the world beneath the waves'. Check sailing times at the pier, or at the tourist information centre or call freephone T0800-9804846. The **tourist office** is at the main seafront car park. ■ *T534276. Apr, May and mid-Sept-late Oct Mon-Sat 0930-1730; Jun-mid-Jul and late Aug-mid-Sept Mon-Sat 0930-1900; mid-Jul-late Aug Mon-Sat 0930-2100, Sun 1230-1630.*

Or, if you prefer, you could take a **seafood cruise** – a 2½ hour wildlife-spotting and seafood-eating boat trip. Contact Neil MacRae, T577230.

Sleeping   It's a good idea to get the tourist office to book a room for you, as there's not a lot to choose from. There are a couple of hotels, most luxurious of which is the **B** *Lochalsh Hotel*, T534202, with great views across to Skye and good food. Three miles north, at Erbusaig, is the very comfortable **D** *Old Schoolhouse*, T534369, a B&B with a highly rated restaurant. A mile and a half north of Kyle is **E** *Crowlin View*, T534286. There's also cheap hostel accommodation at *Cuchulainn's*, T534492, on Station Rd. Four miles east of Kyle, at **Balmacara**, you can camp at *Reraig Caravan Site*, T566215.

Eating   Kyle has 2 very good restaurants. Just outside the village, on the road to Plockton, is the *Seagreen Restaurant & Bookshop*, T534388, a bistro-cum-bookshop and gallery serving wholefood and local seafood throughout the day (mid-range to expensive). At the railway station is *The Seafood Restaurant*, T534813, which has a good reputation for seafood (mid-range to expensive), it's open Easter-Oct 1000-1500 and 1830-2100.

Transport   **Bus** *Scottish Citylink* buses, T0990-505050, run to Kyle from **Inverness** (3 daily, 2 hrs); **Glasgow** via **Fort William** (4 daily, 5 hrs, £14.80); and **Edinburgh** via **Fort William** (1 daily, 6 hrs 30 mins). These buses continue to **Portree** (a further hour, £5.80) and **Uig** (1½ hrs, £6.80), for ferries to Tarbert on Harris and Lochmaddy on North Uist. There's also a regular shuttle service across the bridge to **Kyleakin** (every 30 mins, 80p).

Train   The train journey from Inverness to Kyle, though not as spectacular as the West Highland line, is very scenic. It runs 3-4 times Mon-Sat (2 hrs 30 mins, £14.30) and once or twice on Sun from May to Sept. There's also an observation car and dining car in the summer.

Directory   There are a couple of banks with ATMs, 2 small supermarkets and a post office in the village.

Plockton

Phone code: 01599
Colour map 3, grid A4
If there were a poll taken of visitors' favourite Highland villages then you can bet your bottom dollar that Plockton would come top with most folk. If you look for a definition of picturesque in your dictionary, it'll say "see Plockton". Well, maybe not – but it should.

Plockton's neat little painted cottages are ranged around the curve of a wooded bay, with flowering gardens and palm trees. Yachts bob up and down in the harbour and there are views across the island-studded waters of Loch

Carron to the hills beyond. Even on the telly Plockton's charms proved irresistible and millions of viewers tuned in each week to watch the TV series *Hamish Macbeth*, which featured Robert Carlyle as the local bobby.

There are lots of good walks around the village. One of the best ways to appreciate it is to head up to Frithard Hill, from where there are great views of the bay. Another good walk is along the beach, starting from the High School playing fields at the top of the village.

Plockton's a popular place with artists who are drawn by the village's setting and the wonderful light. A good place to find some of their work, as well as other souvenirs, is *The Studio Craft Shop*, on the corner of the seafront and the road leading out of town.

Sleeping & eating

The best place to stay, and eat, is **C-D** *The Haven Hotel*, T544223, on Innes St. 15 rooms, open Feb-Dec. Good value and the food in the restaurant is quite superb (5-course dinner; expensive). Nearby is the cosy and comfortable **E** *Creag-nan-Daroch Hotel*, T544222. There are quite a few places on Harbour St along the waterfront, including the **D** *Plockton Hotel*, T544274. It also serves decent (and cheap) pub food and has a great little beer garden at the front where you can sit and enjoy a drink on a balmy summer evening.

There are lots of **B&Bs** to choose from and one of the nicest is the **E-F** *Shieling*, T544282, at the far end of the harbour. Also on the seafront is **E-F** *An Caladh*, T544356. There's cheaper accommodation at the **F** *Plockton Station Bunkhouse*, Nessun Dorma, Burnside, T544235.

A few miles out of Plockton, on the road to Achmore, is the *Craig Highland Farm*, T544205, which offers B&B accommodation (**E**) and self-catering cottages from £235 per week. The farm is also a conservation centre, where you can see, and feed, rare and ancient breeds of domestic animals (£1.50).

Apart from the hotels listed above, a good place to eat in Plockton is *Off the Rails*, T544423, at the railway station. It's open from 0830 for breakfast, snacks, lunch and evening meals (cheap to mid-range).

Tours

A good way to see the local wildlife is to take a boat trip. *Leisure Marine*, T544306, runs one-hour seal and otter-watching cruises in the summer for £3.50 per person. They also hire out boats. Similar trips are run by *Sea Trek Marine*, T544346.

Wester Ross

From Loch Carron north to Ullapool, is the region of Wester Ross, an area of dramatic mountain massifs, fjord-like sea lochs and remote coastal villages. Here lies some of Europe's most spectacular scenery, from the isolated peninsula of **Applecross** to the mighty peaks of **Torridon**, which offer some of Scotland's best climbing and hill walking. There are also gentler attractions such as the magnificent gardens at **Inverewe** and the beautiful pink sands of **Gruinard Bay**.

East from Plockton

The road from Plockton meets the A890 at **Stromeferry**, which doesn't have a ferry but does have the **West Highland Dairy**, where you can pick up some good local cheese for a picnic (if the weather's fine). The road continues along the east shore of Loch Carron to **Strathcarron**, at its northeastern end, on the Inverness to Kyle of Lochalsh rail line. There's **B&B** accommodation at E *The Shieling*, T01520-722364, open April-October, by the rail station, and at F *Achnashellach Hostel*, T01520-766232. There's a **postbus** service from Strathcarron to **Shieldaig** and **Torridon** twice a day Mon-Sat.

The Highlands

About a mile further on you come to a road junction. The A890 heads right (east) through Glen Carron to **Achnasheen**, where it meets the A832, nine miles east of **Kinlochewe**. The A832 then continues east till it meets the main A835 which connects **Ullapool** with the A9 north of **Inverness**. The A896 meanwhile heads left (west) to Lochcarron.

Lochcarron

Phone code: 01520
Colour map 1, grid C4
Population: 870

Lochcarron village consists of little more than a main street along the shore of the loch, but it has more facilities and services than most other places in these parts. Here you should take the opportunity to withdraw cash at the *Bank of Scotland* ATM, fill up with petrol and buy some supplies at the supermarket. There's also a **tourist office**, which will provide details of the many excellent walks in the surrounding hills. ■ *T722357. Apr-Oct*. For guided walks around Lochcarron, contact *Island Horizons*, Kirkton Rd, T722238/2.

Two miles south of the village, on the road to the 15th-century ruins of **Strome Castle** is Lochcarron Weavers, where you can see tartan being made.

Sleeping & eating

There's a wide range of accommodation and several places to eat. Best of the bunch is the **D-E** *Rockvilla Hotel & Restaurant*, T722379, rockvilla@btinternet.com. This small, family-run hotel offers very good food at cheap-mid-range prices. There are lots of **B&Bs** including **E-D** *Corrack Cottage*, T722797, **E** *Kinloch House*, T722417, and **E-F** *Bank House*, T722332, in the same building as the Bank of Scotland.

Applecross

Phone code: 01520
Colour map 1, grid C4

West of Lochcarron, at Loch Kishorn, a side road leaves the A896 and heads to Applecross. There are many scenic routes in the Highlands but this one beats them all. The **Bealach na Ba** ('Pass of the Cattle') is the highest road in Scotland and is often closed during the winter snows. It climbs relentlessly and dramatically through a series of tortuous switchbacks – both spectacular and terrifying in equal measure. The high plateau, at 2,053ft, is cold and desolate but from here you have the most stunning views; from Ardnamurchan peninsula to Loch Torridon and taking in Eigg, Rum, the Cuillins of Skye, the Old Man of Storr and the Quirang.

The narrow, single-track road then begins its gradual descent to the isolated little village of **Applecross**, site of one Scotland's first Christian monasteries, in 673 AD. The village consists of a row of whitewashed fishermen's cottages looking across to the island of Raasay and backed by wooded slopes. It's a beautifully tranquil place where you can explore beaches and rock pools or enjoy a stroll along sylvan lanes.

Sleeping & eating

The reason many people make the long detour is to savour the delights of the venerable **E** *Applecross Hotel*, T744262. There are, sadly, too few authentic Highland hosteries where you could quite happily while away a few hours, or even an entire afternoon, but if you have to be holed up somewhere to escape the rotten weather, then this place is as good as any and better than most. The welcome is warm, the crack is good and the seafood is fresh and affordable (try a half pint of prawns for a fiver or scallops for £7.50). The rooms upstairs are nothing fancy but comfortable, with sea views. If there's no room at the *Applecross Hotel* there are a few **B&Bs** a mile to the south in the villages of **Camusteel** and **Camusterrach**: **E** *Mrs Cross*, 'Seawinds', Camusteel, T744373, **E-F** *Mrs Dickens*, 'Brackenhill', Camusterrach, T744206, and **F** *Mrs Thompson*, 'Raon-Mor', Camusteel, T744260, open Apr-Oct.

It's possible to reach Applecross by public transport, but only just. A *Postbus* service **Transport** leaves Strathcarron train station daily (except Sun) at 0955, arriving in **Shieldaig** at 1040. Another Postbus then leaves Shieldaig at 1130 and arrives in Applecross at 1300, via the beautiful and winding coast road. No buses run over the Bealach na Ba. A postbus leaves Applecross at 0915 and arrives in Shieldaig at 1010. It continues to **Torridon** (see below) and arrives at 1030. Another postbus leaves Shieldaig at 1045 and arrives at Strathcarron train station at 1130. There are train connections from Strathcarron to Inverness and Kyle (for times T0345-484950).

Torridon

Torridon is perhaps the most striking skyline in the Scottish Highlands. The *Phone code: 01445* multi-peaked mountains of **Beinn Alligin**, **Liathach** (pronounced *Colour map 1, grid C4/5* '*Lee*-ahakh') and **Beinn Eighe** ('Ben-*eay*') form a massive fortress of turrets, spires and pinnacles that provides an awesome backdrop to Loch Torridon as well as the most exhilarating walking and climbing on the Scottish mainland (see below).

The coast road from Applecross meets the A896 from Lochcarron at the lovely little village of **Shieldaig**, on the southern shore of **Loch Torridon**. There's a shop, a post office, a campsite, a couple of B&Bs and the **B** *Tigh-an-Eilean Hotel*, T01520-755251, where you can get reasonable meals.

Several miles east, a side road turns off the A896 by **Torridon** village and winds its way along the northern shore of the loch, then climbs through dramatic scenery before dropping to the beautiful little village of **Diabaig** (pronounced 'Jee-a-beg'), 10 miles from Torridon village. It's a worthwhile side trip, as the views across to the Applecross peninsula and Raasay are fantastic. There's also a great seven-mile coastal walk from Diabaig to Redpoint (see 'Walks around Torridon' below).

Much of the Torridon massif is in the care of the NTS and just before Torridon village is the **NTS countryside centre**, T791221, where you can get information and advice on walks in the area, as well as books and maps. 400 yards past the centre is the **Deer Museum**, which has a small display describing the management of red deer in the Highlands and some live specimens outside.

There are a couple of *SYHA hostels*. One is in Torridon village, T791284, open 29 Jan-31 **Sleeping** Oct, with an adjacent campsite. The other is much smaller and more basic, 4 miles north of Diabaig, on the trail to Redpoint, at the disused crofting township of Craig (no phone; open 14 May-3 Oct). There are several **B&Bs**, including the excellent **E-F** *Upper Diabaig Farm*, T790227, open Apr-Sept, in Upper Diabaig. About a mile south of the turn-off to Torridon village is the magnificent **L** *Loch Torridon Hotel*, T791242, F791296, www.lochtorridonhotel.com. 22 rooms. This elegant former hunting lodge sits on the lochside surrounded by majestic mountains and offers the ultimate in style and comfort, it also boasts one of the finest restaurants in the area (expensive).

The *Postbus* from Applecross to Shieldaig continues to Torridon village (see above). **Transport** There's a postbus from Strathcarron station at 0955 which arrives in Shieldaig at 1040. *Duncan Maclennan* buses (T01520-755239) have a service which leaves Strathcarron at 1230 and arrives in Torridon at 1330 (daily except Sun). There's also a daily (Mon-Sat) *Postbus* service from Diabaig to Kinlochewe and Achnasheen, via Torridon, at 0955. There are also *Duncan Maclennan* buses between Torridon and Shieldaig and Strathcarron.

The Highlands

🐾 Walking around Torridon

Torridon offers some of the most spectacular walking on the Scottish mainland but also presents some of the most serious challenges. You need to be fit, experienced and well prepared and also be aware of the notoriously unpredictable weather (see page 56). You should have a compass and the relevant map. **Beinn Eighe** (3,309ft) has nine peaks and is the largest of the Torridon mountains. To traverse its ridge is a mighty undertaking and can take two days. A much shorter and easier walk around the base of the mountain is described below, under **Beinn Eighe National Nature Reserve**.

For those who are not experienced hill walkers, there's a Ranger Service for visitors. During July and August the ranger, Seamus McNally, takes guided walks up into the mountains three times a week. For more details call T791221/791261. A recommended local mountain guide is Steve Chadwick, T712455).

Beinn Alligin Beinn Alligin (3,232ft) is the most westerly of the Torridon peaks and probably the least demanding. The **Allt a'Bhealaich Walk** is a steep but short walk of about two hours. It starts from the car park just beyond the stone bridge that crosses the Abhainn Coire Mhic Nobuil. Follow the path that runs beside the river gorge until you reach the first bridge, cross it and follow the east bank of the Allt a' Bhealaich burn. Higher up, cross the second bridge and continue to follow the track up to the 380-m contour line, then turn back retracing your steps. This walk doesn't include the ascent of peak but the views are magnificent.

Those who wish to climb the three Horns of Beinn Alligin can continue from the 380-m contour line above the second bridge. The track that follows their ridge is exposed and requires rock scrambling experience.

Liathach Seven-peaked Liathach (3,460ft) stretches over five miles and the magnificent **ridge walk** is considered by many to be the most impressive in Britain. This walk requires a high level of stamina and will take at least seven to eight hours. It also helps of you have a car waiting at the end.

A good place to start this long and strenuous challenge is about half a mile or so east of Glen Cottage, which is just over two miles east of the Countryside Centre. A steep climb takes you to a point just west of Stuc a'Choire Dhuibh Bhig (3,000ft). Then retrace your route to climb the twin tops of Bidein Toll a'Mhuic (3,200ft), linked by a narrow ridge. The path from here descends to the head of a deep ravine and keeps to the crest of the ridge around the rim of Coireag Dubh Beag which plunges steeply to the north. The ridge then rises across a field of huge and unstable boulders to the highest peak – Spidean a'Choire Leith. The view from this point is stunning, with Coire na Caime before you, surrounded by 2,000ft sheer cliffs. From here, the path follows a narrow exposed ridge for over a mile towards Mullach an Rathain (3,358ft). Unless you are an experienced scrambler with a good head for heights, the best way from here is to take the path to the south, below the sharp pinnacles. Beyond the pinnacles the climb to Mullach an Rathain is straightforward. The track from here to Sgorr a'Chadail is a long but fairly easy walk and ends on the path in Coire Mhic Nobuil (see Beinn Alligin above).

Coire Walk A less difficult walk, but still requiring a fair degree of fitness and taking most of the day, is the Coire Walk. It follows the river Coire Mhic Nobuil to its watershed and down again by the Allt a'Choire Dhuibh Mhoir to the main road in Glen Torridon. Again, two cars will shorten the distance considerably.

The walk starts at the same point as the Beinn Alligin walk above. It follows the path up to the first bridge then branches east and continues on the path that runs north of the river, all the way to its source in the pass between Liathach and Beinn Dearg. Here the ground is boggy between the string of pools and lochans and the path is less distinct, but it becomes clear again in the upper reaches of the Coire Dubh Mor, a huge gully that separates Liathach from Beinn Eighe. A little further on, the track joins a stalker's path which curves round Sail Mhor to the famous Coire Mhic Fhearchair, considered to be the most spectacular corrie in Scotland (see Beinn Eighe below). The Coire path leads to a ford, which is crossed by stepping stones, then descends following the west side of the burn down to the car park on the Torridon road, from where it's about 4½ miles to Torridon village.

An excellent low-level coastal walk is from Diabaig to Redpoint. It is far less strenuous or daunting than the others described above and there is a clear path. It starts at the wooden gate to the right of the post office in Diabaig and ends at Red Point Farm, seven miles away.

Diabaig to Red Point Walk
OS Landranger No 19

After four miles, the coastal path reaches the derelict croft houses in the Craig valley. One of these has been converted into a *SYHA* Hostel (see 'Sleeping' above). There are two possible routes from here. You can follow the footpath above the coastline, or leave the footpath after crossing the wooden bridge over the Craig River and climb through an area of woodland. Take a reference from your OS map and you'll reach the highest point, Meall na h-Uamha, from where there are superb views. You can then descend to rejoin the coastal path and continue till you reach the glorious golden sands of Red Point, with wonderful views across to Skye and Raasay. Keep to the path through the farm till you reach the car park. Unless you've arranged your own transport here, you'll have to walk back the way you came, or catch the schoolbus to Gairloch (see page 456).

Loch Maree

On the north side of the Torridon mountains is beautiful Loch Maree, dotted with islands and bordered by the mass of **Slioch** (3,215ft) to the north and ancient Caledonian pine forest to the south. Running along its northern shore, from Slioch almost as far as Poolewe, is the remote Letterewe Estate, one of Scotland's great deer forests. The A832 skirts the south shore of the loch, running northwest from **Kinlochewe**, and passes the **Victoria Falls**, a mile or so beyond **Talladale**. The falls commemorate Queen Victoria's visit in 1877. To find them, look for the 'Hydro Power' signs.

Phone code: 01445
Colour map 1, grid C5

The village of **Kinlochewe** is a good base for walking in this area. It has a post office, shop, garage and accommodation. The **E** *Kinlochewe Hotel*, T760253, offers B&B as well as cheaper bunkhouse beds and cheap bar meals. There's also **B&B** at **E** Cromasaig, on the Torridon road, T760234, cromasaig@msn.com, and a basic campsite a few miles northwest, at *Taangan Farm*, at the head of Loch Maree.

Sleeping

The best accommodation, though, is at **Talladale**, halfway between Kinlochewe and Gairloch. **B** *The Old Mill Highland Lodge*, T760271, open mid-Dec to mid-Oct, is a converted mill set in its own gardens. It's friendly and comfortable, offers great food (price includes dinner), seclusion and great views. **B-C** *Loch Maree Hotel*, T760288, lochmaree@easynet.co.uk. This beautifully located hotel is being returned to its former glory. Queen Victoria was here! It also offers superb cuisine (**A** including dinner).

The Highlands

Transport Kinlochewe is 9 miles west of **Achnasheen** rail station which is on the Inverness-Kyle line. There's a daily (except Sun) *Postbus* service. There's also a *Postbus* (Mon-Sat) from Kinlochewe to **Torridon** and **Diabaig** and a bus to Torridon and **Shieldaig**, T01520-755239. Buses between Gairloch and Inverness (see below) stop in Kinlochewe.

Beinn Eighe National Nature Reserve

While most of the Torridon massif is managed by the NTS, Beinn Eighe (which means 'File Peak' in Gaelic) is under the control of Scottish Natural Heritage. It is Britain's oldest National Nature Reserve, set up in 1951 to protect the ancient Caledonain pine forest west of Kinlochewe. It has since been designated an International Biosphere Reserve and extended to cover 30 square miles. The reserve is the home of a great variety of rare Highland wildlife, including pine martens, wildcats, buzzards, Scottish crossbills and golden eagles. There's also a wide range of flora which can best be appreciated on the excellent mountain trail described below. The trail climbs from the ancient pine woods through alpine vegetation to the tundra-like upper slopes.

About half a mile northwest of Kinlochewe on the A832, is the **Beinn Eighe Visitor Centre**, which has information on the flora and fauna in the reserve and sells pamphlets on the trails described below. Note that camping is restricted to the official campsite at Taangan Farm (see 'Sleeping' above).

The mountain & woodland trails Both trails start and end in the car park at the side of Loch Maree, about two miles beyond the visitor centre. The **woodland trail** heads west along the lochside then crosses the road and climbs for about a mile up to the Conservation cabin before descending back to the starting point. It should take about an hour and is easy to follow, though quite steep in parts, and you'll need a good pair of walking boots.

The **mountain trail** is four miles long and rough and steep in parts. You should be well equipped with good walking boots, waterproofs, food and warm clothing. It should take around three to four hours. The route is well marked with cairns and you should not stray from the path.

The trail heads south from the car park and begins a gentle ascent through woodland to a boggy area and then begins to zigzag up a very steep and rugged section, climbing to over 1,000ft in less than half a mile. This is the steepest section of the trail but the views back across Loch Maree to Slioch are fabulous. The summit of the mountain trail is **Conservation cairn** (1,800ft) from where you can see the tops of 31 Munros on a clear day and enjoy a close-up view of the impressive Beinn Eighe ridge a few miles to the south.

The trail now begins to descend as it heads northwest towards An t-Allt (1,000ft), turns northwards down to a small enclosure, then heads east to the deep Allt na h-Airidhe gorge. From here the trail continues down to the treeline and runs through woodland to join up with the top of the Woodland Trail. Follow the path to the right and this takes you back to the car park.

Gairloch and around

Phone code: 01445
Colour map 1, grid C4

Gairloch consists of a string of tiny crofting townships scattered around the northeastern shore of the loch of the same name. It's a great place which attracts a large number of visitors who come for the many beautiful beaches, excellent walks, golf and fishing and the chance of seeing seals, porpoises, dolphins and whales in the surrounding waters.

If the weather's bad (as it sometimes can be) or if you're interested in local history, then visit the **Gairloch Heritage Museum**, which is beside the tourist office, on the A832 to Poolewe, a few yards beyond the turn-off to Strath. Included are archaeological finds, a mock-up of a crofthouse room, schoolroom and shop, the interior of the local lighthouse and an archive of old photographs. ■ *T712287. Apr-mid-Oct Mon-Sat 1000-1700. £1.50, 50p children.*

The waters around Gairloch are home to a wide variety of marine mammals such as seals, otters, porpoises, dolphins, minke whales and even killer whales. You can take a wildlife-spotting cruise with *Sail Gairloch*, T712636. The cruise lasts two hours and leaves daily from Gairloch Pier (subject to weather conditions). It can be booked at the Gairloch Marine Life Centre by the pier. For information on **sea angling trips**, contact the chandlery shop at the harbour, T712458.

For those who prefer dry land, try a **quad bike tour** of the Flowerdale Deer Forest with *Highland Trails*. Book at *The Anchorage* post office/craft shop at the harbour or at Flowerdale estate office, T712378.

The **tourist office** is at the car park in Auchtercairn, where the road branches off to Strath. They will book accommodation for you and sell a wide range of books and maps. ■ *T712130. Jan-Mar, Nov and Dec Mon-Thur 0900-1230 and 1300-1700, Fri 0900-1230 and 1300-1630; Apr and May, Sept and Oct Mon-Sat 0900-1730, Sun 1300-1800; Jun-Aug Mon-Fri 0900-1800, Sat 1000-1800, Sun 1300-1800.*

Around Gairloch

The beach at Gairloch, by the golf course, is nice but the beach at **Big Sand**, a few miles northwest of Strath, is better, and quieter. Further north is Melvaig, from where you can walk to **Rubha Reidh Lighthouse** (see 'Sleeping' below). Around the headland from the lighthouse is the beautiful, secluded beach at **Camas Mor**. This is a good place for spotting sea birds, and there's a great walk from here, on a marked footpath, to **Midtown**, four miles northwest of Poolewe. You'll have to walk or hitch from here as there's no public transport to Poolewe.

Many of the roads in the area were built during the Potato Famine of 1840 in order to give men work, with funds supplied by Dowager Lady Mackenzie of Gairloch. These became know as the 'Destitution Roads', and one of these is the narrow B8056 which runs west for nine miles to **Red Point** from the junction three miles south of Gairloch, at Kerrysdale. This is a lovely little side trip and well worth it, especially on a clear evening to enjoy the magnificent sunsets at Red Point beach. The beach itself is extremely beautiful, backed by steep dunes and looking across to the Trotternish peninsula on Skye. Red Point is also the start or finish point for the excellent coastal walk to or from **Diabaig** (see page 453). On the road to Red Point is the picturesque little hamlet of **Badachro**, tucked away in a wooded, sheltered bay with fishing boats moored in its natural harbour. It's worth stopping off here on the way back from Red Point for a wee dram at the *Badachro Inn*. What finer way could there be to end the day?

There are lots of other good walks in the area, including to **Flowerdale Falls** and the **Fairy Lochs** and the **USAAF Liberator**. The tourist office (see below) has a selection of walking guides and OS maps.

Sleeping

Gairloch has a wide range of accommodation. The tourist office will help you find a room. **C** *Myrtle Bank Hotel*, T712004, F712214. 12 rooms. Modern hotel in the centre of Gairloch overlooking the loch, very good food and service in the restaurant (expensive dinner and cheap bar meals). An excellent **guesthouse** is the **B** *Little Lodge*, T771237, a converted crofthouse at North Erradale, 6 miles north of Gairloch. Price includes dinner, award-winning hospitality and cooking, wonderful views and immaculate rooms, open Apr-Oct. Another delightful place is **C** *Birchwood Guest House*, T712011, by the harbour. It is also recommended for its excellent food. Dinner is available to non-residents (mid-range to expensive). Open Mar-Nov.

The Highlands

There are numerous cheaper **B&Bs** scattered throughout the area. Most of the owners will provide maps and information on local walks. On the main street in Strath, near the shops, is **E-F** *Bains House*, T712472, which is friendly and great value. On the road that turns off to the right by the *Millcroft Hotel*, beyond the fire station, is **E-F** *Duisary*, T712252, open Apr-Oct. Also in Strath is **E-F** *Burnbridge House*, T712167. In Charleston, by the harbour, is **E** *Mrs A MacIver*, T712388, open Feb-Nov.

Further afield, at Badachro, south of Gairloch on the road to Red Point, is **E** *Lochside*, T741295. Also at Badachro is **F** *Badachro Bunkhouse*, T741291/741255. 13 miles north of Gairloch, at the end of the road, is the ***Rubha Reidh Lighthouse***, T/F771263, ruareidh@netcomuk.co.uk, which offers comfortable B&B (**E-F** or **D** including dinner) and hostel accommodation (**F**). It's best to book ahead in the high season. They also have a tearoom serving home baking, snacks and light lunches; open Sun, Tue and Thur 1100-1700, Easter-Oct. There are buses from Gairloch as far as Melvaig (see below), then it's a 3-mile hike along the road to the lighthouse.

There are a couple of **hostels** in Gairloch. *Auchtercairn Hostel*, T712131, open Mar-Nov, is at Gairloch Sands Apartments, just before the turn-off to Strath. Three miles beyond Gairloch, on the road to Melvaig, is *Carn Dearg Youth Hostel*, T712219, open 15 May-3 Oct.

There are a couple of **campsites**: *Gairloch Caravan & Camping Park*, T712373, is at Strath, with full facilities and close to all amenities; *Sands Holiday Centre*, T712152, open Easter-Oct, is at Big Sand, about a mile beyond Strath.

Eating   The *Myrtle Bank Hotel* (see above) serves very good, expensive, meals, though its bar lunches are good value. The *Scottish Seafood Restaurant*, T712137, next to Gairloch filling station, is good for seafood at mid-range prices (unlicensed). There's also *The Steading Restaurant*, T712449, next to the Heritage Museum, which is open daily 0930-2100. For a lite bite, or tea and scones, try the *Conservatory Coffee Shop*, on the square in Strath. For cheap pasta, there's *Gino's Italian Restaurant* at the friendly *Millcroft Hotel* in Strath, T712376. The best place for a good pint of real ale and some hearty pub grub is *The Old Inn*, T712006, near the harbour.

Transport   There's a **bus** from **Inverness** to Gairloch 3 times a week (Mon, Wed and Sat) at 1705 with *Westerbus*, T712255. The return bus is at 0805. Westerbus also have services to **Kinlochewe** (Mon-Sat at 0730) and to **Mellon Charles/Laide**, via **Poolewe** (Mon-Sat). There's a **Melvaig-Gairloch-Red Point postbus** service Mon-Sat which leaves Gairloch at 0820 heading north to Melvaig and leaves Gairloch heading south to **Red Point** at 1035. On Fri only there's a subsidized taxi service between Gairloch and Melvaig 1030-1230 (to book T712559/712497).

Directory   There are shops and takeaways in Strath and Auchtercairn, a petrol station in Auchtercairn and a bank with ATM near the harbour at Charleston.

Poolewe

Phone code: 01445
Colour map 1, grid B4

Five miles east of Gairloch on the other side of the peninsula is the neat little village of Poolewe, beautifully set at the mouth of the river Ewe, where it cascades into sheltered Loch Ewe.

There are some good walks around Poolewe, including the one around **Loch Kernsary** described below. There's also a nice little drive up the side road running along the west shore of Loch Ewe to **Cove**. You can walk from **Midtown**, midway along the road, to **Rubha Reidh**, north of Gairloch (see above).

The reason most people come here is to visit Inverewe Garden where you'll find an astonishing collection of exotic subtropical plants growing on the same latitude as Siberia, thanks to the mild climate created by the North Atlantic Drift. This wonderful 50-acre oasis of colour is a mecca for garden lovers, but even those who flinch at the mere sight of a lawn-mower will be bowled over the sheer scale and diversity of plants and flowers on view.

Inverewe Garden

The garden was created from a treeless wilderness by Osgood Mackenzie, starting in 1862. By the time of his death, in 1922, he had produced an internationally renowned walled and woodland garden. His work was continued by his daughter, who then gave the garden to the NTS in 1952. Since then, the plant collection has diversified even more and an intricate maze of paths leads you through ever-changing displays of Himalayan rhododendrons, Tasmanian eucalyptus, many Chilean and South African species, together with a large collection of New Zealand plants.

The garden is well worth visiting, in any weather, but especially from the end of April through the summer when the rhododendrons are in bloom. You should allow at least a couple of hours to do it justice. The garden is about a mile north of Poolewe, on the main A832. There's a visitor centre and gift shop and a good restaurant, which serves snacks and hot meals. ■ *T781200. Garden open 15 Mar to 31 Oct daily 0930-2100; Nov to 14 Mar daily 0930-1700. Visitor Centre open 15 Mar to 31 Oct 0930-1730. Guided garden walks 15 Apr to 15 Sept Mon-Thur at 1330. £5, £3.40 child/concession.*

This straightforward but rewarding walk covers six miles and should take around 2½-3 hours. The track is very boggy underfoot in places, especially after rain, so you'll need good boots.

Walk around Loch Kernsary

OS Landranger No 19

Start in Poolewe, from the car park by the school near the bridge over the Ewe. Head up the single-track road with the river on your right. Go through the gate, then the track heads away from the river and up into woodland. At the Letterewe Estate gate cross the stile and continue to the next fork. Turn left here to Kernsary Estate, with views of Loch Maree and Beinn Eighe to the south. Follow the track to the next gate, go through and cross the wooden bridge. Continue along the track and you'll see Loch Kernsary on your left. At the next fork, turn left over the bridge and pass Kernsary Cottage on the right. Beyond the cottage, go through the gate and immediately head left down towards the burn where the ground may be boggy. There's no path here, but cross the wooden footbridge and continue straight on, past the piles of stones on your left. Cross the stile, and the path follows the length of Loch Kernsary. At the head of the loch, the path climbs to give you views down to Poolewe. Follow the path down till it eventually takes you to the main road. Turn left and follow the road back to the car park.

The Highlands

och Kernsary

There are several places to stay in and around **Poolewe** and the tourist office in Gairloch will help you find accommodation. On the Cove road by the lochside is the former home of Osgood Mackenzie, the **B-C** *Pool House Hotel*, T781272, poolhouse@inverewe.co.uk, open Mar-Dec. It enjoys great views and serves good food. At **Inverasdale**, a few miles up the Cove road, is **E** *Bruach Ard*, T781214, open Apr-Oct. Further up this road, near Cove, is **E** *Mrs MacDonald*, T781354, open Apr-Oct. Above Poolewe,

Sleeping & eating

reached by a path that leads from the road beside the campsite, is **F** *Mrs MacIver*, T781389, open Apr-Oct. The excellent *Camping and Caravan Club Site*, T781249, is between Poolewe village and Inverewe Garden.

If you need to grab a quick snack, or fancy a coffee, try the *Bridge Cottage Café*, which is on the left at the turn-off to Cove.

Gruinard Bay to Loch Broom

Around Laide
Phone code: 01445
Colour map 1, grid B5

North of Poolewe, the A832 passes **Aultbea** on its way to **Laide**, where it then skirts the shores of Gruinard Bay, with its lovely coves of pink sand. From Laide Post Office a side road branches north to **Mellon Udrigle** and **Opinan**, both with great beaches. Between Laide and Mellon Udrigle, at **Achgarve**, a road branches left for about half a mile. From the end of this road you can walk all the way to **Slaggan**, a ruined village on the other side of the peninsula. It's a nice spot for a picnic but don't be tempted to swim in the sea as the tidal race makes it dangerous.

Gruinard Bay is a very beautiful part of the northwest coast but will always be synonymous with **Gruinard Island**, standing ominously in the middle of the bay. The island was used as a testing ground for biological warfare during the Second World War and was contaminated with anthrax spores. The Ministry of Defence finally agreed to decontaminate it in 1990 and it has now been declared 'safe'.

Sleeping There are a couple of really good places to stay around here. At the very end of the road that branches north to **Opinan**, standing on its own by the shore is **B** *Obinan Croft*, T731548, rj&mc.beeson@obinan.co.uk, open Mar-Oct. A remote family-run croft with amazing sea views and great food. The perfect place to get away from it all. In the village of **Laide** is the **D-E** *Old Smiddy Guest House*, T731425, oldsmiddy@aol.com, open Apr-Oct. Its excellent restaurant is also open to non-residents, but it's best to book well in advance (expensive). There's also a **campsite** in Laide, the *Gruinard Bay Caravan Park*, T731225, open Apr-Oct.

Transport There are daily **buses** to Laide from **Gairloch** with *Westerbus*, T712255. Some of them continue to Mellon Udrigle. There are buses between Laide and **Inverness** three times a week (Tue, Thur and Fri), leaving at 0805 and returning at 1705. There are also buses on other days between **Gairloch** and **Inverness** which stop at Laide (see above under Gairloch).

Dundonnell
Phone code: 01854
Colour map 1, grid B5

The road heads inland then runs along the southern shore of **Little Loch Broom** to **Dundonnell**, from where there are spectacular views of awesome **An Teallach** (3,483ft), a mountain of almost mythical status amongst Scottish climbers and spoken of in hushed, reverential tones. The path to the highest of its summits is clear and begins southeast of the *Dundonell Hotel*. It will take a full day and you'll need to be well prepared (OS map No 19) and heed the usual advice. You can stay at the **B-C** *Dundonnell Hotel*, T633204, selbie@ dundonnellhotel.co.uk, open February-December, which does good meals (cheap to mid-range bar meals; expensive three-course dinner). Alternatively there's **B&B** at **E-F** *Mrs Ross*, T633237, in Camusnagaul, a few miles back up the loch. Also in Camusnagaul is the *Sail Mhor Croft Independent Hostel*, T633224, sailmhor@btinternet.com, but you should call before arriving.

A few miles beyond Dundonnell, a side road branches left and runs for seven miles to the tiny, remote hamlet of **Badrallach**, where you can stay at the *Badrallach Bothy & Camp Site*, T633281.

The A832 coastal road from Gairloch and Poolewe meets the A835 **Falls of Measach**
Ullapool-Inverness main road at **Braemore junction**, 12 miles south of
Ullapool. Before heading on to Ullapool it's worth stopping at the very impressive Falls of Measach, just by the junction. The falls plunge 150ft into the spectacular **Corrieshalloch Gorge** (or 'ugly/fearsome gorge' in Gaelic) and can be
crossed by a distinctly wobbly suspension bridge (not for vertigo sufferers).
The falls can be reached from the A835 but the most dramatic approach is
from the A832 Gairloch road.

Ullapool

The attractive little fishing port of Ullapool, on the shores of Loch Broom, is the   Phone code: 01854
largest settlement in Wester Ross. The grid-pattern village, created in 1788 at the   Colour map 1, grid B5
height of the herring boom by the British Fisheries Society, is still an important   Population: 1,800
fishing centre as well as being the major tourist centre in the northwest of Scotland
and one of the main ferry terminals for the Outer Hebrides. At the height of the
busy summer season the town is swamped by visitors passing through on their
way to or from Stornoway on Lewis, heading north into the wilds, or south to
Inverness. It has excellent tourist amenities and services and relatively good
transport links, making it the ideal base for those exploring the northwest coast
and a good place to be if the weather is bad.

Ins and outs

Ullapool is the mainland terminal for **ferries** to Stornoway (Lewis). *Scottish Citylink*   **Getting there**
buses, T0990-505050, to and from Inverness (2-3 daily Mon-Sat, 1 hr 20 mins, £7)   *See also 'Transport',*
connect with the ferry to and from Stornoway. For further details of ferries, see the   *page 462*
Outer Hebrides chapter (page 521), or contact the local *CalMac* office on Shore St,
opposite the pier, T612358. There are also buses to places further north, and south
along the coast. Buses stop at the pier near the ferry dock.

Sights

Ullapool's attractions are very much of the outdoor variety and include the
Falls of Measach, **Achiltibuie** and **Stac Pollaidh**. There are also many good
local walks (see 'Walks around Ullapool' below) and cruises to the **Summer
Isles** (see 'Tours' below). It's worth taking a stroll around the **harbour** to
watch the comings and goings of the fishing fleet and you might even see the
occasional seal or otter swimming close to the shore.

The only real 'sight' as such is the **Ullapool Museum and Visitor Centre** in
a converted church in West Argyle Street. It has some interesting displays on
local history, including the story of those who set sail from here, in 1773, on
board *The Hector*, the first ship to carry emigrants from the Highlands to Nova
Scotia in Canada. ■ *T612987. Apr-Oct Mon-Sat 0930-1730; Jul and Aug also
1930-2130; Nov-Mar 1200-1600. £2, £1.50 child.*

The **tourist office** is at 6 Argyle St. It is well run and provides an accommodation booking service as well as information on local walks and trips and has a
good stock of books and maps. ■ *T612135. Easter-Jun and Sept-Nov, Mon-Sat
0900-1800, Sun 1300-1800; Jul and Aug, Mon-Sat 0900-1900, Sun 1300-1800.*

The Highlands

Essentials

Sleeping
■ *on map*
Price codes:
see inside front cover

There is no shortage of places to stay in Ullapool, ranging from one of the very finest hotels in the UK to numerous guesthouses and B&Bs, a couple of good youth hostels and a campsite.

L *Altnaharrie Inn*, T633230. 8 rooms, Open Apr-Oct, this world-renowned hotel is on the other side of Loch Broom and you'll be picked up from town in their own launch. The ultimate Highland retreat, if you can afford it, and unique in every sense, their restaurant is one of most highly acclaimed in the UK.

B *The Ceilidh Place*, 14 West Argyle Pl, T612103, F612886, reservations@ ceilidh.demon.co.uk. 23 rooms. This former boat-shed has grown over the years to become one of the most refreshingly different hotels in the country with comfortable bedrooms, cosy lounge, bookshop, restaurant, bar and coffee shop. They also host a varied programme of arts events such as live music, plays, poetry readings, exhibitions and ceilidhs (see below), a great place to relax and soak up some local culture. Across the road is their clubhouse, with basic but comfortable dorms (**E-F**).

D-C *Harbour Lights Hotel*, Garve Rd (on the left, heading into Ullapool on the A835), T612222, harbour@vacations-scotland.co.uk. 22 rooms, open 1 Mar-31 Oct. Modern hotel offering good service and very good food available all day (mid-range). **D** *Ferry Boat Inn*, Shore St, T612103. On the lochside, decent accommodation and food and the best pub in town. **D-E** *Morefield Hotel*, North Rd, T612161. Open May-Oct. On the edge of town heading north, in the middle of a housing estate, motel-style accommodation and a superb seafood restaurant.

On the other side of Loch Broom, 12 miles from Ullapool, is **C-D** *Tigh-na-Mara*, T01854-655282. Price includes dinner, completely remote and acclaimed vegetarian guesthouse. An absolute must for nature lovers.

E *Brae Guest House*, Shore St, T612421. 8 rooms, open May-Oct, comfortable guesthouse on the loch-front. **E** *Eilean Donan Guest House*, 14 Market St, T612524. Friendly and central. **E** *Point Cottage Guest House*, 22 West Shore St, T612494, smacrae@globalnet.co.uk. Lovely old fishing cottage at the quieter end of the loch-front. **E** *Strathmore House*, Strathmore, Morefield (1 mile north of town), T612423. Open Apr-Oct, friendly, comfortable and good value. There are more **guesthouses** on Garve Rd, heading south out of town, and lots of **B&Bs** along Seaforth Rd and Pulteney St.

Ullapool has a very good *SYHA* **youth hostel** on Shore St, T612254, open Feb-Dec, where you can pick up some good information on local walks. There's an independent hostel, *West House*, on West Argyle St, T613126, which has the full range of facilities and hires out mountain bikes. The only **campsite** is at *Broomfield Holiday Park*, T6120020/612664, on Shore St, at the west end of the village with great views across to the Summer Isles and a laundrette on site. It's open Easter-Sept.

Eating
There's plenty of choice across the range, from one of the UK's top hotel/restaurants to the humble seafront chippie. The *Altnaharrie Inn* (see above) is considered perhaps the finest in the country and Gunn Erkison's cooking is of world renown. Expensive, and non-residents will need to book well in advance. *Mariner's Restaurant* is part of the *Morefield Hotel* (see above). The setting may be a little incongruous but there's nothing wrong with the food. The seafood is sensational, which is why people travel from miles around and it's always busy. Moderate prices and not-so-moderate

portions. *The Ceilidh Place* (see above) is one of those places that tourists seem to hang around for hours or even days. It exudes a laid-back, cultured ambience. The self-service coffee shop does cheap wholefood all day during the summer while the restaurant serves more expensive full meals, with an emphasis on vegetarian and seafood, at night. There's even outdoor seating. Open 1100-2300. Also live music and various other events (see below). *Scottish Larder*, Ladysmith St, T612185. Should be called 'Pies-R-Us'. They have a huge selection, as well as vegetarian options and local seafood. Great value. You can also get decent, cheap pub food at lunchtime and early evening in the *Ferry Boat Inn*, the *Seaforth Inn* and the *Arch Inn* (see below).

Ullapool

© Crown copyright

The Highlands

■ **Sleeping**		● **Eating**
1 Brae Guest House	6 Harbour Lights	1 Arch Inn
2 Broomfield Holiday Park	7 Morefield Hotel & Mariner's Restaurant	2 Scottish Larder
3 The Ceilidh Place	8 Point Cottage Guest House	3 Seaforth Inn
4 Eilean Donan Guest House	9 SYHA Youth Hostel	
5 Ferry Boat Inn	10 West House Hostel	

N

0 metres 100
0 yards 100

Entertainment Ullapool's favourite pub has to be the *Ferry Boat Inn* (or 'FBI' as it's known locally), on Shore St. It has regular live music sessions through the week and during the summer you sit outside on the sea wall and watch the sun go down as you drain your glass. Another good place for a drink is the *Arch Inn*, at the other end of Shore St. The bar of the *Seaforth Inn* has live music at weekends, which has been described by one local as 'raucous'. For something a wee bit more sedate and civilized, head for *The Ceilidh Place*, where you can enjoy a quiet drink in the cosy *Parlour Bar* or take advantage of their varied programme of events. There's live music nightly (except Sun) throughout the summer, ceilidhs and poetry readings, and the clubhouse opposite stages plays.

Shopping The town is well supplied with shops. *Boots* the chemist is on Shore St by the pier, and there's a *Safeway* supermarket next to the car park north of Seafield Rd. A good outdoor equipment shop is *Mountain Man Supplies*, opposite the museum, on West Argyle St.

The best **bookshop** in the northwest is the one at *The Ceilidh Place* (see above). The *Captain's Cabin*, on the corner of Quay St and Shore St, also sells books, as well as crafts and souvenirs.

An excellent **jewellers** is the *Knockan Studio*, opposite the tourist office on Argyle St, T613365, open Mar-Oct, Mon-Sat 0900-1800. For **pottery**, look no further than *Highland Stoneware*, T612980, on Mill St heading north towards Morefield. You can wander round the studios before browsing in their gift shop, which is pricey but you may have luck in their bargain baskets. They also have a factory in Lochinver (see page 465). Open Mon-Fri 0900-1800 (also Sat 0900-1700 Easter-Oct).

Tours During the summer the MV *Summer Queen* runs 4-hour cruises to the **Summer Isles**, with a 45-minute landing on Tanera Mór. These leave Mon-Sat at 1000 from the pier and cost £14 per person. There are also two-hour wildlife cruises around **Loch Broom**, **Annat Bay** and **Isle Martin**, which leave daily at 1415 and also on Sun at 1100, and cost £8 per person. Cruises can be booked at the booth by the pier or by calling T612472.

Transport *Scottish Citylink* **buses** run 2-3 times daily (except Sun) between Ullapool and **Inverness**, connecting with the ferry to Stornoway. There are also buses daily (except Sun) to and from Inverness with *Rapson's Coaches*, T01463-710555, and *Spa Coaches*, T01997-421311. There's a service to **Lochinver** (1-2 times daily except Sun, 1 hr) with *Spa Coaches* and *Rapson's of Brora*, T01408-621245, and to **Achilitibuie** (twice daily Mon-Thur, once on Sat, 1 hr) with *Spa Coaches*. There's also a daily bus to and from **Gairloch**, which continues to Inverness, during the summer only. **Cycle hire** At *West House* independent hostel (see 'Sleeping' above); £10 per day.

Directory **Banks** The only bank is the *Royal Bank of Scotland* in Ladysmith St.

✺ Walks around Ullapool

OS Nos 15, 19 & 20 There are several good walking trails which start in Ullapool. One of these is to the top of **Ullapool Hill**, or Meall Mhor (886ft). Starting from the tourist office, head to the end of Argyle Street, turn left onto North Road and then cross the road at the Far Isles Restaurant. Walk down the lane between Broom Court and the Hydro sub-station and then follow the path which zig-zags up the hillside. There's a good cairned path up to the top of the hill. The views from the top over Glen Achall and, on a clear day, the mountains of Sutherland, are superb. You can return by traversing the hillside to the top of the Braes, or take a track leading to **Loch Achall** and follow the Ullapool River through the quarry road back to the village. The return trip takes 1-2 hours.

The Highlands

A relatively easy, but much longer walk, of 5-6 hours, is to **Rhidorroch Estate**. Take the A835 north out of Ullapool. Opposite the petrol station and before the bridge, take the road on the right signed 'Quarry'. Go through the quarry keeping to the left, and follow the Ullapool River till you see Loch Achall. Continue along the north bank of the loch for another six miles. **East Rhidorroch Lodge** is on the right; cross the bridge to get there, then skirt the lodge fences and cross to the track which leads up the southwestern hill. This brings you out to **Leckmelm**, about four miles south of Ullapool on the A835. This last section offers wonderful views across Loch Broom to An Teallach. From Leckmelm you can also climb **Beinn Eilideach** (1,837ft).

A good coastal walk is to **Rhue Lighthouse** and back. From the north end of Quay Street go down the steps to the river. Cross the bridges and head left by the football field. Follow the path to the left by the duck pond and cross in front of the bungalow. Then follow the shoreline north for about two miles, climbing up the hillside when the tide is high. Follow the path till you reach the little white lighthouse at Rhue Point. To return, take the single-track road out of Rhue back to the main road and up over the hill to Ullapool. It's about six miles in total.

There are many more strenuous hiking routes around Ullapool. The A835 south of town gives access to **Beinn Dearg** (3,556ft) and the **Fannichs**, a range of hills on the southern side of Dirrie More. There's also **An Teallach**, a favourite with Scottish climbers (see page 458). North of Ullapool are the mountains within the **Inverpolly National Nature Reserve** (see below). These include **Ben Mór Coigach** (2,438ft), **Stac Pollaidh** (2,011ft), **Cul Beag** (2,523ft) and **Cul Mór** (2,786ft). These all require hill-walking experience and you should be well prepared for the unpredictable weather conditions. A good climbing guidebook is *The Northern Highlands, SMC District Guide*, by Tom Strang. *North West Frontiers* is an Ullapool-based tour company offering guided walking tours around Ullapool and throughout the Northwest Highlands. Contact them at: 18A Braes, Ullapool, IV26 2SZ, T/F612628, NWF@ compuserve.com, ourworld.compuserve.com/homepages/NWF.

North of Ullapool

Colour map 1, grid B5/6

North of Ullapool you enter a different world. The landscape becomes ever more dramatic and unreal – a huge emptiness of bleak moorland punctuated by isolated peaks and shimmering lochs. A narrow and tortuously twisting road winds its way up the coast, past deserted beaches of sparkling white sand washed by turquoise sea. There's not much tourist traffic this far north and once you get off the main road and on to the backroads, you can enjoy the wonderful sensation of having all this astonishingly beautiful scenery to yourself.

The region immediately north of Ullapool is called **Assynt** and is heaven for serious hill walkers and climbers. Though most are not Munros, and not particularly difficult by Scottish standards, they can attract some of the worst weather imaginable, even in the height of summer. Also remember to check locally regarding access during the deer-stalking season which runs from mid-August to mid-October. (See also 'Safety in the Scottish Mountains', page 56.) Amongst the most spectacular of Assynt's distinctive 'island peaks' are **Suilven** (2,398ft), **Ben More Assynt** (3,275ft), **Quinag** (2,650ft) and **Canisp** (2,775ft).

Much of this region is protected in the **Inverpolly** and **Inchnadamph National Nature Reserves**, home to an extremely rich and diverse wildlife.

The Highlands

Inverpolly National Nature Reserve

Phone code: 01854
Colour map 1, grid B5

About 12 miles north of Ullapool, on the main A835, is the SNH visitor centre at **Knockan Crag**, which gives a good introduction to the diverse flora and fauna in the area. ■ *T666234. Mid-May to mid-Sept daily 1000-1700.* From the visitor centre there's a marked trail which leads up to the Crag and the views from the clifftop are excellent, across to Inverpolly's 'island' peaks of **Cul Mór**, **Cul Beag** and **Stac Pollaidh**.

A few miles north of here is the village of **Knockan**, with accommodation at **E** *Assynt Guided Holidays*, T666215, open mid-May to mid-Oct. Nearby, at **Elphin**, is the *Highland and Rare Breeds Farm* (open mid-May to end of September, daily 1000-1700). Beyond Elphin is **Ledmore**, where the A837 branches east towards **Lairg** and **Bonar Bridge**. There's a good craft shop at Ledmore where you can buy hand-knitted sweaters.

Stac Pollaidh
OS Landrayer No 15

Between Ullapool and Knockan Crag is the turn-off west (left) to the distinctive craggy peak of Stac Pollaidh. The climb up and down takes around four hours. The well-worn path starts from the car park beside Loch Lurgainn and leads to the lowest point on the ridge. The summit lies to the west and the huge buttress which bars the way should be turned on the right when the track along the ridge can be taken. You'll need a head for heights to reach the summit as much of the route is exposed. The summit lies beyond a little tower of rock which requires great care. The descent can be made by way of the big scree gully on the south side, but great care and sure-footedness is needed.

Stac Pollaidh is a very rewarding climb, hence its enduring popularity, but please consider the damage inflicted by tens of thousands of pairs of boots every year. The damage caused has resulted in serious erosion on the south face.

Achiltibuie

Phone code: 01854
Colour map 1, grid B5

The unclassified single-track road winds its way west past Stac Pollaidh to the turn-off for Achiltibuie. This old crofting village, with whitewashed cottages set back from the sea views across to the beautiful **Summer Isles**, is home to one of the northwest's main tourist attractions. The **Hydroponicum**, or 'Garden of the Future', is a gigantic greenhouse which is pioneering the system of hydroponics to grow plants from all over the world. Hydroponics uses water instead of soil to carry nutrients to the plants and can be carried out anywhere. Here you can see an incredible variety of subtropical trees, orchids, flowers, vegetables, herbs and fruits. A guided tour takes you through the different climatic zones and you can taste their produce, including the famous strawberries, in the *Lilypond Café*, which serves meals and snacks. ■ *T622202, www.race.co.uk/hydroponicum. Daily Easter to end of Sept 1000-1800. Guided tours every hour on the hour (£4).*

Another worthwhile attraction is the **Achiltibuie Smokehouse**, 5 miles to the north, at Altandhu. Here, you can watch the salmon, herring, trout and other fish being cured before buying some afterwards. ■ *T622353. May-Sept Mon-Sat 0930-1700. Free.*

Sleeping & eating

Near the Hydroponicum is the **B-C** *Summer Isles Hotel*, T622282, F622251; open Easter-Oct, which enjoys magnificent views across to the Summer Isles. It also boasts an excellent restaurant (expensive). Even if you're not staying or eating here, it's worth stopping to have a drink on the terrace and watch the sun set over the islands. The basic but very cheap *SYHA Youth Hostel* is a few miles south at Achininver, T622254; open mid-May to early Oct. There are also several **B&Bs** in Achiltibuie.

Those inviting **Summer Isles** lying offshore can be visited from Achiltibuie pier on board | **Tours**
the *Hectoria*. **Cruises** leave Mon-Sat at 1030 and 1415 and last 3½ hours, with one hour
ashore on the islands. To book, contact *I. Macleod* at Achiltibuie Post Office, T622200, or
at home, T622315 Cruises cost £12 per person (half price for children). There are also
deep-sea angling trips (1800-2100) which cost £6 per person and £15 per rod.

There are 2 **buses** daily (Mon-Thur) to **Ullapool** with *Spa Coaches*, T01997-421311, | **Transport**
leaving Achiltibuie Post Office at 0800 and 1300. The early bus starts in Reiff (at 0740)
and the other one leaves from Badenscallie. The journey takes an hour. There's also a
bus on Sat, leaving at 0751.

Lochinver

The road from Achiltibuie north to Lochinver is known locally as the 'wee mad | *Phone code: 01571*
road' and you'd be mad to miss this thrilling route which twists and winds its | *Colour map 1, grid B5*
way through some the northwest's most stunning scenery. The village of
Lochinver is a working fishing port and the last sizeable village before Thurso.
It has a good tourist office (see below), lots of accommodation, a bank with
ATM, post office and petrol station.

The best place to start is the **Assynt Visitor Centre**, which houses the **tourist office**. It has displays on the local geology, history and wildlife and there's
also a ranger service with guided walks throughout the summer. ■ *T844330.*
The centre is open Apr-Oct, Mon-Fri 1000-1700 and Sun 1000-1600. Those
looking for local souvenirs should head for **Highland Stoneware**, T844376,
www.highlandtrail.co.uk/stoneware.html, a local pottery factory just outside
the village on the road north.

A few miles south of Lochinver, beyond **Inverkirkaig**, is the trail along the
river to the **Kirkaig Falls**. The path starts near the *Achins Bookshop*, T844262,
which has a good stock of Scottish titles and a café. Follow the path for about two
miles till it branches right to the falls in the gorge below. Continue along the main
path for about another ¾ mile till you reach Fionn Loch with superb views of
mighty **Suilven**. The walk up to the falls and back should take around 1½ hours.
This is one of the main approaches to the foot of the mountain.

L *Inver Lodge Hotel*, Iolaire Rd, T844496, F844395, inverlodge@compuserve.com. 20 | **Sleeping &**
rooms, open Apr-Oct, a modern luxury hotel standing above the village with great | **eating**
views and excellent restaurant (lunch mid-range; dinner expensive). **A** *The
Albannach Hotel*, at Baddidaroch, T844407, F844285. This wonderful 18th-century
house overlooking Loch Inver is one of the very best places to stay in the northwest
and the food offered in the award-winning restaurant is sublime, the price includes
dinner, non-residents are also welcome but booking is essential.

There are many comfortable **guesthouses** and **B&Bs**, including **E** *Ardglas Guest
House*, T844257, amunro@cix.co.uk, and **E** *Polcraig*, T844429, cathelmac@aol.com,
E *Davar*, T844501, open Mar-Oct, and **E** *Tigh-Na-Sith*, T844740; open Apr-Sept.

Apart from the hotels listed above, the best food can be found at *Lochinver's Larder Riverside Bistro*, T844356, on the way into town on the A837. You can eat in or takeaway
and prices are mid-range. Nearby is the cheap and cheerful *Caberfeidh*, T844321.

There's a *Postbus* service from Lochinver to and from **Drumbeg**, via the coast road, | **Transport**
which continues to **Lairg**. It runs once a day, Mon-Sat. There are also buses to and
from Drumbeg and on to **Ullapool**, once or twice daily except Sun, with *Rapsons of
Brora*, T01408-621245, and *Spa Coaches*, T01997-421311.

The Highlands

Loch Assynt and Inchnadamph

Phone code: 01571
Colour map 1, grid B5/6

The area east of Lochinver is a remote wilderness of mountains and moorland dotted with lochs and lochans. As well as being a favourite haunt of hardy climbers and walkers, Assynt is a paradise for anglers. Most of the lochs are teeming with brown trout, and fishing permits are readily available throughout the area from the tourist office in Lochinver or at local hotels, guesthouses and B&Bs. There's also salmon fishing on the river Kirkaig, available through the *Inver Lodge Hotel* (see above), and on Loch Assynt through the *Inchnadamph Hotel* (see below).

The A837 Lochinver-Lairg road meets the A894 to Durness 10 miles east of Lochinver at **Skiag Bridge** by Loch Assynt. Half a mile south of here, by the loch, are the ruins of **Ardvreck Castle**. The castle dates from 1597 and was the stronghold of the Macleods of Assynt until a siege of the castle in 1691, when it was taken by the Seaforth Mackenzies. Before that, the Marquis of Montrose had been imprisoned here following his defeat at Carbisdale in 1650. Access to the castle is free but the ruins are in a dangerous state and should be approached with care.

To the east of the road lies the **Inchnadamph National Nature Reserve**, dominated by the massive peaks of **Ben More Assynt** and **Conival**, which should only be attempted by experienced hill walkers. A few miles south of the village of **Inchnadamph**, at the fish farm, is a steep, but well-marked footpath up to the **Bone Caves**. This is one of Scotland's oldest historical sites, where the bones of humans and animals such as lynx and bear were found together with sawn-off deer antlers dating from over 8,000 years ago.

Sleeping   **C** *Inchnadamph Hotel*, T822202, is an old-fashioned Highland hotel on the shores of Loch Assynt catering for the hunting and fishing fraternity (see above). Nearby is the **F** *Inchnadamph Lodge*, T822218, assynt@presence.co.uk, or *Assynt Field Centre*, which offers basic hostel accommodation in bunk rooms, as well as twin, double and family rooms. Continental breakfast is included. It's open all year but phone ahead between Nov and Mar. It's ideally situated for climbing Ben More Assynt and guides are available.

Lochinver to Kylesku: the coast road

Phone code: 01571
Colour map 1, grid B5

The quickest way north from Lochinver is the A837 east to the junction with the A894 which heads to Kylesku. But by far the most scenic route is the B869 coast road that passes moorland, lochs and beautiful sandy bays. It's best travelled from north to south, giving you the most fantastic views of Suilven. Untypically, most of the land in this part of Assynt is owned by local crofters, who under the aegis of the *Assynt Crofters' Trust*, bought 21,000 acres of the North Assynt Estate, thus setting a precedent for change in the history of land ownership in the Highlands.

The trust now owns the fishing rights to the area and sells permits through local post offices and the tourist office in Lochinver. It has also undertaken a number of conservation projects, including one at **Achmelvich**, a few miles north of Lochinver, at the end of a side road which branches off the coast road. It's worth a detour to see one of the loveliest beaches on the west coast, with sparkling white sand and clear turquoise sea straight out of a Caribbean tourist brochure. You can stay here, at the *SYHA Hostel*, T844480, open mid-May to early October, or camp at the *Shore Caravan Site*, T844393, open April-September.

The Highlands

From the beach car park below the hostel a path leads northwest along the coast. Bear left off the sandy path shortly after the white cottage on the hill ahead comes into view and follow the footpath until the road is reached at **Alltan na Bradhan**, where there are remains of an old meal mill. Continue north from here along the coast for about a mile till you reach a small bay just before **Clachtoll**, the Split Rock. Close by are the remains of an Iron Age Broch, but don't cause further damage by clambering over the ruins. Return to the beach by the same path. The walk there and back should take about 1½ hours.

A side road turns left off the B869 north of **Stoer** and runs out to **Stoer lighthouse**. From here you can walk across the Stoer peninsula to the **Old Man of Stoer**, a dramatic rock pillar standing offshore, surrounded by sheer cliffs. Allow about three hours for the circular walk which starts and ends in the lighthouse car park. There is no public transport to the lighthouse, but the Lochinver-Drumbeg postbus runs to Raffin, one mile away.

Old Man of
Stoer

OS Landranger No 15

A clear path runs from the car park to the cliffs then follows the line of the cliffs northwards. The path heads inland for a short distance as it bypasses a deep gully then meets the clifftop again and after a mile or so you can see the Old Man tucked away in a shallow bay, battered by huge waves.

Beyond the Old Man the path continues to the headland, the **Point of Stoer**, from where it turns back on itself and climbs **Sidhean Mór** (532ft). The views from here are fantastic, across to Harris and Lewis and south to the mountains of Assynt. From here, follow the faint path south, back towards the lighthouse, passing a small loch below Sidhean Beag on your left and an obvious cairn on your right. Then you pass a radio mast and follow the clear track back to the lighthouse car park.

Nine miles further on, in beautiful **Eddrachillis Bay**, is **Drumbeg**, a popular place for anglers who come to fish in the many lochs of North Assynt. There's not much accommodation around here other than self-catering cottages, but you can spend the night at D *Taigh Druimbeag*, T833209; open Easter-end October.

Old Man of Stoer

© Crown copyright

Old Man of Stoer

Sidhean Mór
(532ft)

Small Loch

Stoer
lighthouse

Sidhean Beag
(407ft)

Loch Cúl Fráioch

Parking

Raffin

RUBHA STOER

Culkein

N

km   1
miles   1

Balchladich

B869

To Drumbeg

To Lochinvar ▼

Kylesku

Phone code: 01971
Colour map 1, grid B5

The road runs east from Drumbeg, under the shadow of towering **Quinag** (2,654ft), to meet the A894 heading north to **Kylesku**, site of the sweeping modern road bridge over Loch a'Cháirn Bháin. From Kylesku you can visit Britain's highest waterfall, the 650-ft high **Eas a'Chùal Aluinn**, near the head of Loch Glencoul. **Cruises** leave from the old ferry jetty below the *Kylesku Hotel* to the falls on board the *MV Statesman*, T01571-844446. You can also see porpoises, seals and minke whales *en route*. You may be able to get closer to the falls by getting off the boat and walking to the bottom, then getting on the next boat. ■ *The two-hour round trip runs daily Apr-Sept at 1100 and 1400 (also at 1600 in Jul and Aug), and costs £9, £3 children.*

The Highlands

There's also a trail to the top of the falls. It starts at the south end of Loch na Gainmhich, about three miles north of Skiag Bridge. Skirting the loch follow the track in a southeasterly direction up to the head of the **Bealach a Bhuirich** (the Roaring Pass). Continue until you meet a stream, with several small lochans on your right. Follow this stream until it plunges over the **Cliffs of Dubh** (the Dark Cliffs). You can get a better view of the falls by walking to the right about 100yd and descending a heather slope for a short distance. Allow about three to four hours for the round trip.

Sleeping & eating
Before you leave on the boat trip, pop into the **B** *Kylesku Hotel*, T502231, for some delicious and great-value pub seafood or for B&B, open Mar-Oct. There's also a more formal and expensive restaurant next door. If you want to spend the night here, a cheaper option is the **D** *Newton Lodge*, T/F502070, newtonlge@aol.com, open mid-Mar to mid-Oct. There's also a small hostel at **F** *Kylesku Lodges*, T502003, open Easter-Oct.

Scourie and Handa Island

Phone code: 01971
Colour map 1, grid A5

Ten miles north of Kylesku is the little crofting community of Scourie, sitting above a sandy bay. Anyone remotely interested in wildlife is strongly advised to make a stop here to visit Handa Island, a sea bird reserve run by the Scottish Wildlife Trust, and one of the best places in the country for bird life. The island is now deserted, except for the warden, but once supported a thriving community of crofters, until the potato famine of 1846 forced them to leave, most emigrating to Canada's Cape Breton. Now it's home to huge colonies of shags, fulmars, razorbills, guillemots and puffins. The best time to visit is during the summer breeding season, from late May to August. There's a footpath right round the island, which is detailed in the free SWT leaflet available at the warden's office when you arrive. You should allow three to four hours.

There's a **ferry service** to the island from **Tarbet Beach**, three miles northwest off the A894, about three miles north of Scourie. It sails continuously, depending on demand. ■ *T502077/340. From 0930 to 1700 Mon-Sat during Apr-Sept. The 15-minute crossing costs £6 return.*

Another excellent wildlife boat trip leaves from **Fanagmore**, a mile from Tarbet on the other side of the peninsula, with *Laxford Cruises*, T502251. They sail around beautiful Loch Laxford, where you can see lots of birds from nearby Handa Island, as well as seals, porpoises and otters. ■ *Trips leave at 1000, 1200 and 1400 daily except Sun from Easter till the end of Sept (also at 1600 in Jul and Aug). The trips last one hour 45 minutes and cost £7.50, £3.75 children.*

For bookings contact Julian Pearce, who also runs the wonderful *Seafood Restaurant*, just above the jetty at Tarbet. If you're up this way, don't miss a visit to this moderately priced restaurant serving seafood caught by Julian during his boat trips! It's a great place and you can even stay here, in the self-catering caravan next door, which sleeps up to six.

Sleeping
There is lots of accommodation in and around Scourie. Best of all is the **C** *Eddrachilles Hotel*, a few miles south in Badcall Bay, T502080, F502477, eddrachilles@compuserve.com. 11 rooms, open Mar-Oct, this is one of the most magnificently situated hotels in the country, the 200 year-old building stands in 300 acres of grounds overlooking the bay, the food on offer is superb, though the atmosphere is a little stuffy (their Eddrachilles heel, you might say). Another excellent place to eat is the **C-D** *Scourie Hotel*, T502396; open 1 Apr-mid-Oct, a 17th-century former coaching inn popular with anglers (lunch mid-range; dinner expensive). There are several **B&Bs** in the village, but none better than the welcoming **E** *Scourie Lodge*, T502248, open Mar-Oct, which also does good evening meals. There's also a **campsite**, T502060, on Harbour Rd.

Transport

There's a *Postbus* service to Scourie from Durness and Lairg once a day, Mon-Sat. It leaves Durness at 0820 and arrives at 0935 and continues to Lairg. It returns at 1245 and arrives at 1420. There's also a *Postbus* service between Scourie and **Elphin**, with connections to **Lochinver**.

Kinlochbervie and around

The road north from Scourie passes **Laxford Bridge**, where it meets the A838 running southeast to **Lairg** (see page 481). The A838 also runs north to Durness, on the north coast (see below). At **Rhiconich**, the B801 branches northwest to Kinlochbervie, a small village with a very big fish market. This is one of the west coast's major fishing ports and huge container lorries thunder along the narrow single-track roads carrying frozen fish and seafood to all corners of Europe. It's worth heading down to the fish market in the evenings to see the day's catch being landed and sold.

Phone code: 01971
Colour map 1, grid A5

A few miles beyond Kinlochbervie is **Oldshoremore**, a tiny crofters' village scattered around a stunning white beach and a great place to swim. The less hardy can instead explore the hidden rocky coves nearby.

At the end of the road is **Blairmore**, from where a footpath leads to **Sandwood Bay**, the most stunning and beautiful beach on the west coast. It's a long walk but because of its isolation you'll probably have this glorious mile-long stretch of white sand all to yourself. The beach is flanked at one end by a spectacular rock pinnacle and is said to be haunted by the ghost of an ancient shipwrecked mariner. Allow three hours for the walk there and back, plus time at the beach. You could take a tent and watch the sunset. Sandwood Bay can also be reached from **Cape Wrath**, a day's hike to the north (see page 470).

Sleeping

In Kinlochbervie village is **B** *The Kinlochbervie Hotel*, T521275, F521438. A nicer place to stay is the **D** *Old School Hotel*, T/F521383, half way between Kinlochbervie and the A838 at Rhiconich. It used to be a school, as the name implies, and this only adds to the charm. They also serve great food at mid-range prices, daily 1200-1400 and 1800-2000. In Rhiconich is the **D** *Rhiconich Hotel*, T521224, rhiconichhotel@compuserve.com, and also **B&B** at **E-F** *Benview*, T521242, open Apr-Sept. There's a good **campsite** at Oldshoremore, T521281.

Transport

A *Postbus* leaves Kinlochbervie harbour at 0900 and goes to **Scourie** (35 mins) and on to **Lairg** (1 hr 50 mins) from where there are connections to **Inverness**. The same postbus returns from Lairg at 1245, arrives in Kinlochbervie at 1448, then continues to **Durness** (35 mins).

The North Coast

Scotland's rugged north coast attracts few visitors, but those who do venture this far find that's there's plenty to write home about. This is some of Britain's most spectacular and undisturbed coastline, from the wild and remote **Cape Wrath** in the far northwest, to **John O'Groats**, that perennial favourite of sponsored walkers, in the far northeast. In between lies over 100 miles of storm-lashed cliffs, sheer rocky headlands and deserted sandy coves, all waiting to be explored. It's also great place for birdwatching, with vast colonies of seabirds, and there's a good chance of seeing seals, porpoises and minke whales in the more sheltered estuaries.

Getting around the far north without your own transport can be a slow process. Getting to **Thurso**, the main town, by bus or train is easy, but beyond that things get more difficult. Details of what little public transport there is are given under the relevant destination.

Durness and around

Phone code: 01971
Colour map 1, grid A6

Durness is not only the most northwesterly village on the British mainland but also one of the most attractively located, surrounded by sheltered coves of sparkling white sand and machair-covered limestone cliffs. It's worth stopping here for a few days to explore the area. The **tourist office** arranges guided walks and has a small visitor centre with displays on local history, flora and fauna and geology. ■ *T511259. Apr-Oct Mon-Sat 0900-1800; also Sun 1100-1900 in Jul and Aug.*

A mile east of the village is the vast 200ft-long **Smoo Cave**. A path from near the youth hostel leads down to the cave entrance which is hidden away at the end of a steep, narrow inlet. Plunging through the roof of the cathedral-like cavern is an 80-ft waterfall which can be seen from the entrance, but the more adventurous can take a boat trip into the floodlit interior.

A few miles east of the Smoo Cave are a couple of excellent beaches, at **Sangobeg** and **Rispond**, where the road leaves the coast and heads south along the west shore of stunning **Loch Eriboll**, Britain's deepest sea loch, which was used by the Royal Navy during the Second World War as a base for protecting Russian convoys.

About a mile northwest of Durness is the tiny hamlet of **Balnakeil**, overlooked by a ruined 17th-century church. In the south wall is a graveslab with carved skull-and-crossbones marking the grave of the notorious highwayman Donald MacMurchow. If you're looking for souvenirs, or an escape from the rat race, then head for the **Balnakeil Craft Village**, an alternative artists' community set up in the 1960s, in a former RAF radar station. Here you can buy weavings, pottery, paintings, leatherwork and woodwork in the little prefab huts. There's also a café. ■ *Apr-Oct daily 1000-1800.* Balnakeil has also become well-known in golfing circles. The nine-hole course, T511364, is the most northerly in mainland Britain and its famous ninth hole involves a drive over the Atlantic Ocean.

The beach here is glorious, especially in fine weather when the sea turns a brilliant shade of turquoise. Even better, walk north along the bay to **Faraid Head**, where you can see puffin colonies in early summer. The views from here, across to Cape Wrath in the west and Loch Eriboll in the east, are stupendous.

Cape Wrath There are several excellent trips around Durness, but the most spectacular is to Cape Wrath, Britain's most northwesterly point. It's a wild place and the name seems entirely appropriate, though it actually derives from the Norse word *hwarf*, meaning 'turning place'. Viking ships used it as a navigation point during their raids on the Scottish west coast. Now, a lighthouse stands on the cape, above the 1,000ft-high **Clo Mor Cliffs**, the highest on the mainland and breeding ground for huge colonies of seabirds.

You can walk south from here to Sandwood Bay (see page 469). It's an exhilarating, but long coastal walk, and will take around eight hours. It's safer doing this walk from north to south as the area around the headland is a military firing range and access may be restricted, which could leave you stranded.

Sleeping & A good place to stay is the **D** *Cape Wrath Hotel*, T511212, which is just off the A838 on
eating the road to the ferry at Keoldale. It overlooks the loch and is popular with fishermen and passing tourists who stop here to enjoy the great food and superb views. The best value around Durness has to be the **E** *Port-Na-Con Guest House*, T511367,

shm@capetech.co.uk, on the west shore of Loch Eriboll, 7 miles from Durness. It's popular with anglers and divers so you'll need to book ahead to take advantage of such comfort amidst all this great scenery. The food in the adjoining restaurant is superb and also great value, especially the seafood. Non-residents are welcome but should book. There are also several **B&Bs** in Durness, best of which is **E** *Puffin Cottage*, T511208; open Apr-Sept. There's a basic *SYHA Youth Hostel*, at Smoo, to the east of the village, T511244; open mid-Mar to early Oct. There's also **camping** at *Salgo Sands Caravan Park*, T511222.

A daily bus runs to and from **Thurso**, via Tongue and Bettyhill (Jun-Aug, Mon-Sat) **Transport** with *Highland Country Buses*, T01847-893123, leaving Thurso at 1130 and Durness at 1500. There's also a daily bus service (May to early Oct) to and from **Inverness** via Ullapool and Lochinver, with *Bluebird/Inverness Traction*, T01463-239292. There's a *Postbus* service to **Lairg** via **Tongue** and **Altnaharra**, daily Mon-Sat at 1115; also via **Kinlochbervie** and **Scourie** daily Mon-Sat at 0820.

To get to **Cape Wrath**, first take the passenger ferry across the Kyle of Durness from Keoldale, three miles south of Durness, T511376. It runs from May-Sept, hourly 0930-1630; £2.25 return. The ferry connects with a minibus, T511287, for the 11 miles to the cape (40 minutes; £6 return).

Durness to Thurso

The road east from Durness runs around Loch Eriboll on its way to the lovely **Tongue** little village of Tongue. A causeway runs across the beautiful **Kyle of Tongue**, *Phone code: 01847* but a much more scenic route is the single-track road around its southern side, *Colour map 2, grid A1* with great views of **Ben Hope** (3,041ft) looming to the southwest. The village of Tongue is overlooked by the 14th-century ruins of **Varick Castle** and there's a great beach at **Coldbackie**, two miles northeast.

Sleeping There are several places to stay in Tongue. The **B-C** *Tongue Hotel*, T611206, is a former hunting lodge of the Duke of Sutherland. It overlooks the Kyle of Tongue and does good food. Also recommended for its food is the excellent **C** *Ben Loyal Hotel*, T611216. There are cheaper options, such as the excellent-value **E** *Rhian Cottage*, T611257. There's also a good *SYHA Youth Hostel*, T611301, open mid-Mar to late Oct, beautifully situated at the east end of the causeway, and a couple of **campsites**; one is at Talmine, T601225, five miles north of Tongue by the beach, and the other is *Kincraig Camping and Caravan Site*, T611218, just to the south of the village. Also at Talmine is the lovely 19th-century **E** *Cloisters*, T601286.

The A836 runs south from Tongue, through **Altnaharra**, to **Lairg** (see page **Bettyhill** 481). It also continues east to the crofting community of **Bettyhill**, named after *Phone code: 01641* the Countess of Sutherland who ruthlessly evicted her tenants from their homes *Colour map 2, grid A2* in Strathnaver to make way for more profitable sheep. The whole sorry saga is told in the interesting **Strathnaver Museum**, housed in an old church in the village. There are also Pictish stones in the churchyard behind the museum.
■ *T521418. Apr-Oct Mon-Sat 1000-1300 and 1400-1700. £1.90, £1.20 children.*

The museum sells a leaflet detailing the many prehistoric sites in the Strathnaver valley which runs due south from Bettyhill. The B871 then branches southeast to meet the A897 to Helmsdale. There are a couple of great beaches around Bettyhill, at **Farr Bay** and at **Torrisdale Bay**, which is the more impressive of the two and forms part of the **Invernaver Nature Reserve**.

There's a small **tourist office** in Bettyhill and several places to stay and eat.
■ *Tourist office T521342. Mon-Sat Easter-Sept.*

The Highlands

Sleeping and eating The **E** *Farr Bay Inn*, T521230, does decent bar food. A good value **B&B** is **F** *Bruachmor*, T521265, open Apr-Oct.

Melvich & East from Bettyhill the hills of Sutherland begin to give way to the fields of
Dournreay Caithness. The road passes the turn-off to **Strathy Point** before reaching
Colour map 2, grid 2/3 **Melvich**, another wee crofting settlement overlooking a lovely sandy bay.

South from Melvich the A897 heads to Helmsdale (see page 483) through the **Flow Country**, a vast expanse of bleak bog of major ecological importance. About 15 miles south of Melvich, at **Forsinard**, is an **RSPB Visitor Centre**. ■ *T01641-571225; Easter-Oct daily 0900-1800. Guided walks through the nature reserve leave from the visitor centre.*

The north coast of Scotland is ideally suited to the more active type of tourist, and 10 miles west of Thurso you might say that the radioactive tourist is catered for at the **Dounreay Nuclear Power Station**. Though its fast breeder reactors were decommissioned in 1994, the plant is still a major local employer and now reprocesses spent nuclear fuel. There's a permanent exhibition at the **visitor centre**, where you learn all about the 'benefits' of nuclear power. ■ *T01847-802572. Easter-Sept daily 1000-1700. Free.*

Sleeping There's some excellent accommodation in **Melvich**, including **D** *Bighouse Lodge*, T01641-531207, open May-Oct, an 18th-century mansion sitting at the mouth of the Halladale River in four acres of its own grounds. Also recommended is **E** *Shieling Guest House*, T/F01641-531256, open Apr-Oct.

Thurso

Phone code: 01847 Thurso is the most northerly town on the British mainland and by far the larg-
Colour map 2, grid A3 est settlement on the north coast. In medieval times it was Scotland's chief port
Population: 9,000 for trade with Scandinavia, though most of the town dates from the late 18th century when Sir John Sinclair built the 'new' extension to the old fishing port. The town increased in size to accommodate the workforce of the new nuclear power plant at nearby **Dounreay**, but the plant's demise has threatened the local economy. Today, Thurso is a fairly nondescript place, mostly visited by people catching the ferry to Stromness in Orkney.

Thurso is also known to keen surfers who come here for the unbeatable surf. To the east of town, at **Dunnet Bay**, is a three-mile-long beach with an excellent reef break and there's another good reef break at **Brims Ness** to the west. Further west, at **Strathy Bay** (see above) you'll find rollers that can match anything in Hawaii (though the water's a lot colder).

Sights There's little of real interest in the town centre. Near the harbour are the 17th-century ruins of **Old St Peter's Church**, which stand on the site of the original 13th-century church founded by the Bishop of Caithness. In the town hall on the High Street is the **Heritage Museum**, which features some Pictish carved stones. ■ *T892459. Jun-Sept Mon-Sat 1000-1300 and 1400-1700. 50p.* The **tourist office** is on Riverside Rd. ■ *T892371. Apr-Oct Mon-Sat 0900-1800, also Sun 1000-1800 in Jul and Aug. They have a leaflet on local surfing beaches.*

Sleeping Thurso boasts a wide variety of accommodation, most of it fairly average. A reasonable bet is the huge **C-D** *Royal Hotel*, Traill St, T893191. 102 rooms. Upgraded to include indoor pool and leisure facilities and central. The nicest place to stay, though, is the **B** *Forss Country House Hotel*, T861201, 4 miles out of town at Bridge of Forss. This small family-run hotel is set in 20 acres of lovely woodland and has an excellent restaurant, open to non-residents (mid-range to expensive).

There are lots of cheap **B&Bs**, including: **E** *Murray House*, 1 Campbell St, T895759, **E** *Annandale*, 2 Rendel Govan Rd, T893942, and **E** *Mrs C Murray*, 1 Granville Cresent, T892993. Thurso also has 3 **independent hostels**: *Sandra's Backpackers*, 24-26 Princes St, T894575, *Thurso Hostel*, Ormlie Lodge, Ormlie Rd, T/F896888, and *Thurso Youth Club*, Old Mill, Millbank, T892964, open 1 Jul-30 Aug. The nearest **campsite** is *Thurso Camping Site*, T607771, north of town on the road to Scrabster.

The best place to eat in town is *The Upper Deck* in Scrabster, T892814, by the harbour. **Eating** It has a moderately priced surf'n'turf menu (seafood and meat). Other than that, your best bet is a bar meal at the *Pentland Hotel*, T893202. A decent café is *Johnston's* on Traill St. There are also the ubiquitous Indian and Chinese restaurants and fish and chip shops.

Out of town is the *Forss Country House Hotel* (see above) and *The Bower Inn*, T01955-661292, between Thurso and Wick. To get there, turn off the coast road at Castletown and follow the B876 till you see the sign for Gillock.

Cinema At *Viking Bowl*. **Bowling** *Viking Bowl*, Ormlie Rd, T895050. **Entertainment**
Swimming Millbank Rd, T893260.

Bus *Citylink* buses run to and from **Inverness** (3 hrs 30 mins; £9 single) 4 times daily, **Transport** T0990-505050, continuing to Scrabster to connect with the ferries to and from Stromness in Orkney. *Citylink* buses to Inverness connect with buses to **Edinburgh** (£16.50). *Highland Country Buses*, T01847-893123, run local services to **Bettyhill** (3 times daily Mon-Thur, twice on Sat; 1 hr 10 mins) and to **Reay** (4 times daily Mon-Thur, 3 times on Sat). There are regular daily buses to and from **Wick** via **Halkirk** or Castletown. *Highland Country Buses* also run the service between **Thurso train station** and **Scrabster ferry pier** (5-10 mins). *Harrold Coaches*, T01955-631295, runs a service to and from **John O'Groats** (4 times daily Mon-Thur, twice on Sat; 1 hr). There's also a *Postbus* service to **Wick airport**, leaving Riverside Rd at 0920 and arriving at 1000. Buses arrive at Sir George's St Port Office and depart from Sir George's St Church.

Trains Three trains leave daily from **Inverness** (3 hrs 30 mins; £12.20), 2 of them connecting with the ferries from Scrabster to **Stromness** in Orkney. Trains continue to **Wick** (30 mins) and return trains to Inverness leave from Wick. The train station is at the south end of Princes St, 500 yards from the tourist office.

Ferries To **Stromness** in Orkney leave from Scrabster, 2 miles north of Thurso. For details, see page 554.

Car hire *William Dunnett & Co*, T893101. **Cycle hire** *The Bike & Camping Shop*, the Arcade, 34 High St, T896124, rents mountain bikes for £8 per day.

Dunnett Head and John O'Groats

About 10 miles northeast of Thurso is the most northerly point on the British mainland. No, not John O'Groats, but Dunnet Head. It's reached by turning off the Thurso-John O'Groats road at Dunnett, at the east end of **Dunnett Bay**, a three-mile-long sandy beach that's popular with surfers who come to tackle the gigantic waves of the **Pentland Firth**, the wild and treacherous strait between the mainland and Orkney.

Dunnett
Phone code: 01847
Colour map 2, grid A3/4

It's a much nicer place than John O'Groats, with marvellous views across to Orkney and along the entire north coast (on a clear day). There's a Victorian lighthouse out at the point and the dramatic seacliffs are teeming with seabirds. There's also a great little café, the *Dunnett Head Tearoom*, T851774, a few miles from the lighthouse, which serves cheap snacks and meals (open daily April-October 1500-2000).

John O'Groats
Phone code: 01955
Colour map 2, grid A4

If you still feel inclined to visit this dreary tourist trap, then that's your prerogative, but don't say we didn't warn you. It's boring at best and pretty miserable most of the time. It gets its name from the Dutchman Jan de Groot, who was commissioned by King James IV to run a ferry service to Orkney in 1496.

Ferries still operate from here to Burwick in Orkney, daily from May to September (45 minutes, £15 one way). There are also **Orkney Islands Day Tours**, which leave daily 1 May to 30 September at 0900, and return at 1945 (£31 per person, under 16 half price). A shorter day tour departs daily from 1 June to 5 September at 1030, and returns at 1800 (£28 per person, under 16 £8). Contact: *John O'Groats Ferries*, Ferry Office, John O'Groats, T611353, F611301, www.jogferry.co.uk. Tours also leave from Inverness.

There's a **tourist office** here as well as a post office, craft shops and a chippie. ■ *Tourist office T611373. Apr-Oct Mon-Sat 0900-1700.*

Two miles east of John O'Groats is **Duncansby Head**, which is far more rewarding. South of the headland a path leads to the spectacular **Duncansby Stacks**, a series of dramatic rock formations. The 200-ft cliffs are home to countless seabirds and you can see the narrow, sheer-sided inlets known locally as *geos*.

Sleeping D *John O'Groats Hotel*, T611203, which has a restaurant. There are also several **B&Bs**, including the very decent E *Bencorragh House*, at Upper Gills in Canisbay, a few miles west, T611449; open Mar-Oct. Also in Canisbay is the *SYHA Youth Hostel*, T611424, open 19 Mar-31 Oct. There are a couple of **campsites**, at John O'Groats and further west by the beach at Huna. The tourist office will help you find accommodation.

Transport There are buses to John O'Groats from Thurso (see above under Thurso), and from **Wick** (5 daily Mon-Fri, 4 on Sat) with *Highland Country Buses*.

The East Coast

The east coast of the Highlands, from Inverness north to Wick, doesn't have the same draw as the west coast and attracts far fewer visitors, but it has its own, gentler appeal, and there are many lovely little seaside towns to explore. The sea lochs and estuaries of the inner **Moray Firth** are fringed with fields and woods, a fertile lowland landscape dotted with farms and crofts. Fast-flowing rivers drop from the hills through deep, wooded straths. The bulk of **Ben Wyvis** dominates the horizon northwest of Dingwall.

Across the **Dornoch Firth** is Sutherland – the south land of the Norsemen – where the coastal strip of fertile land narrows towards Helmsdale, backed by heather-clad hills deep blue in the reflective sea light. Prehistoric sites are abundant throughout East Sutherland as are Pictish sculptured stones in Easter Ross. The seagoing Norsemen of Orkney used the firths to extend Viking influence into the Pictish lands, lured by good land and timber for shipbuilding. Dingwall was their *Thingvallr* – or place of assembly. Many existing villages grew up around Celtic Christian missions of the seventh or eighth centuries. From the 11th century **Tain** was an important place of pilgrimage, and the cathedrals at **Dornoch** and **Fortrose**, and **Fearn Abbey**, date from the 13th century.

Few roads existed before the late 18th century. Land routes, like the road over Struie, were drove roads on which cattle, the mainstay of the Highland economy, were walked to market. Travel by sea was easier and firths were crossed by ferry. The fast track across bridges and causeways is a recent phenomenon, although the building of the **Kessock Bridge**, linking Inverness and the Black Isle, was foreseen in the 17th century by the Brahan Seer, a local prophet (see below).

Diverse sea life flourishes in an offshoot of the Gulf Stream, attracting seals, whales, porpoises and a diminishing colony of dolphins, which is carefully monitored and researched. The sea has long provided a living from salmon netting around the river mouths, fishing for herring and cod, shipping and, most recently, oil.

The Black Isle

Across the Kessock Bridge from Inverness is the Black Isle, which is neither an island nor black. It shares with the Moray coast long hours of sunshine and low rainfall, rolling acres of barley and stately woods of oak and beech dropping down to the shores. It also has a compelling atmosphere – a combination perhaps of its soft microclimate, lush vegetation and attractive architecture. Its main attractions are the picturesque town of **Cromarty** and **Chanonry Point**, on the southern side near Rosemarkie, which is one of the best **dolphin-spotting** sites in Europe.

Phone code: 01381
Colour map 2, grid C2

On the north side of the Kessock Bridge is the **North Kessock Tourist Information Centre**. ■ *T01463-731505. Daily from Easter to Oct.* Next door is the **Dolphin and Seal Visitor Centre**, which gives details of accredited dolphin cruises. You can see dolphins from the village of **North Kessock** just to the south.

One of the many sacred wells (and caves) in the area is the unmissable **Clootie Well**, on the verge of the main road between Tore and Munlochy Bay Nature Reserve. It was once blessed by St Curitan (see below under Rosemarkie) and is thought to cure sick children. Thousands of rags still flutter from the surrounding trees, though well-worshippers are in danger of being mown down by traffic. Despite the presence of traffic, it's an eerie place. Go at night, if you dare.

Further east on this road, beyond **Munlochy** and **Avoch** (pronounced 'Och') is the village of **Fortrose**, on the east shore. The magnificent **cathedral** at Fortrose is now largely a ruin where rainwashed carved faces of rose-coloured sandstone peer down from roof bosses, and snapped-off stumps of window tracery are redolent of Reformation vandalism. On **Chanonry Point**, overlooking the Moray Firth, a plaque marks the spot where the **Brahan Seer** was boiled in a barrel of tar in 1660, but not before he had foretold the building of the Caledonian Canal and Kessock Bridge, the Highland Clearances and the Second World War. He also predicted the demise of the local lairds, the Seaforths, not surprisingly, perhaps given that it was Lady Seaforth who ordered his execution, after the seer had a vision of her husband in the arms of another woman. Apparently the precise spot where he met his end is now the 13th hole of the golf course, which just goes to prove that it is indeed unlucky for some. Chanonry Point is also a great place for seeing **dolphins**. They come close to shore at high tide and there's a good chance of seeing them leaping above the waves.

A few miles from Fortrose on the north side of Chanonry Point is the tiny village of **Rosemarkie**. Celtic saints Curitan and Boniface selected this sheltered spot on the southern shore for their Christian mission in the seventh century. St Boniface is remembered at nearby St Bennet's Well. **Groam Museum** houses a superb collection of Pictish sculptured stones found locally, imaginatively displayed alongside contemporary artwork inspired by them. A year-round programme of events and lectures is devoted to the study of Pictish culture. ■ *T620961. Easter-Sept Mon-Sat 1000-1700, Sun 1400-1630; Oct-Apr Sat and Sun 1400-1600. £1.50, 50p children.*

Beware of fairies, last sighted in the 1970's in **Fairy Glen**, now a nature reserve. A lovely marked trail leads into the glen from the top end of the High Street, through a wooded gorge.

A couple of places to eat in Rosemarkie are *Crofters*, T620844, on the seafront, which does cheap bar meals, and the *Plough Inn*, near the museum.

Cromarty

Phone code: 01381
Cromarty has its own website:
www.cali.co.uk/highexp
/Cromarty

On the northeastern tip of the Black Isle peninsula, at the mouth of the Cromarty Firth, is the gorgeous village of Cromarty, one of the east coast's major attractions. Its neat white-harled houses interspersed with gracious merchants' residences are almost unchanged since the 18th century when it was a sea port thriving on trade as far afield as Russia and the Baltic. Many emigrants bound for the New World embarked here. A prosperity based on textiles and fishing led to decline and dereliction. Although restored and much inhabited, it now has the atmosphere of a backwater, but a very attractive one at that, where you feel as if you're stepping back in time, in stark contrast to the numerous oil rigs moored on the opposite shore in **Nigg Bay** (see below).

For a fascinating insight into the history of the area, visit the 18th-century **Cromarty Courthouse**, in Church Street, which houses the town's museum. ■ *T600418. Apr-Oct daily 1000-1700; Nov, Dec and Mar daily 1200-1600. £3, £2 children, includes loan of headset for recorded tour of the town's other historic buildings.*

Next to the courthouse is the thatch-roofed **Hugh Miller's Cottage**, birthplace of the eminent local geologist and author. ■ *T600245. 1 May-30 Sept daily 1100-1300 and 1400-1700 (Sun afternoon only). £2, £1.30 children.* Also worth seeing is the elegant 17th-century **East Church**.

There's a good walk along a coastal path from the east end of the village through woodland to the top of the South Sutor headland, one of the two steep headlands guarding the narrow entrance to the Cromarty Firth. There are excellent views from here across the Moray Firth. Leaflets describing this and other local walks are available at the Cromarty Courthouse.

One of Cromarty's main attractions is its **dolphins**. They can be seen from the shore, or with a **boat trip**, but make sure you go with an accredited operator, such as *Dolphin Ecosse*, T600323. Full-day or half-day trips leave from the harbour and you can see porpoises and seals as well as dolphins, and perhaps even killer whales further out.

To the west, the mudflats of **Udale Bay**, are an RSPB reserve and a haven for wading birds and wintering duck and geese. **Poyntzfield Herb Garden** is an organic plant nursery specializing in rare and native medicinal herbs. Worth visiting if only for a glimpse of the house and the view from the car park over the Cromarty Firth through massive beech trees.

Sleeping & eating

For such an appealing place, there's precious little accommodation. It's advisable to book ahead during the summer. The best place to stay is the **D** *Royal Hotel*, T600217, on Marine Terr. It has a good restaurant and cheaper meals are available in the bar. There are a couple of **B&Bs**, including the very good **E** *Beechfield House* at 4 Urquhart Court, T600308, ricketts@cali.co.uk. Another good place to eat is *Thistle's Restaurant* on Church St, T600471, which has a moderately priced and imaginative menu, including interesting vegetarian dishes. A great place for tea and scones is *Binnie's Tearoom* on Church St. For cheap bar food try the *Cromarty Arms*, opposite the Cromarty Courthouse, which also has live music some nights.

A 2-car **ferry** crosses to **Nigg** every half hour from Apr to Oct, 0900-1800. *Highland Bus* **Transport**
& Coach, T01463-233371, runs a **bus** service from **Inverness** to Fortrose and Cromarty
(4-7 times daily Mon-Sat). There is also a bus service to and from *Dingwall* on Wed
and Thur.

Strathpeffer

The little village of Strathpeffer gained recognition in 1819 when Dr Morrison,   *Phone code: 01997*
a physician from Aberdeen bathed in its sulphur springs and cured himself of   *Colour map 2, grid C1*
rheumatoid arthritis. He quickly spread the word and Strathpeffer became a   *Population: 1,384*
fashionable spa resort attracting thousands of visitors. Two World Wars inter-
vened and the town's popularity declined. Today the only reminder of its past
is the **Water Sampling Pavilion** in the square where you can test the waters.
There's a seasonal **tourist office** on the main square. ■ *T421415. Easter-Nov
Mon-Sat 1000-1700.*

Just outside Strathpeffer on the road to Dingwall is the **Highland Museum
of Childhood** which has many historical displays on childhood in the highlands, as well as collections of dolls, toys and games. ■ *T421031. Mar-Oct
Mon-Sat 1000-1700, Sun 1400-1700; Jul and Aug Mon-Thur 1000-1700 and
1900-2100, Sat 1000-1700, Sun 1400-1700.*

Strathpeffer gets busy in the summer with coach parties but it's a pleasant place
and there are some excellent walks in the surrounding hills. One of these is to
Knock Farrel and the Touchstone Maze, site of an Iron Age vitrified fort   *OS Landranger No 26*
which lies at the north end of a ridge known locally as the **Cat's Back**. A
marked trail starts from Blackmuir Wood car park. Head up the hill from
town, turn left up a road immediately before the youth hostel, and the car park
is on the left. The walk is six miles in total and takes about three hours. Aside
from OS Landranger sheet 26, the route is also described in a Forestry Commission leaflet *Forests of Easter Ross*, available from tourist offices.

Another excellent side trip is to **Rogie Falls**, near Contin, which is three miles
southwest of Strathpeffer on the main A835 Inverness-Ullapool road. The short
walk up to the falls starts from the car park three miles north of Contin on the
A835. There are also some pleasant woodland walks around here. Experienced
hikers can tackle magnificent **Ben Wyvis** (3,432ft). The route to the summit
starts four miles north of **Garve**, seven miles northwest of Contin.

The best accommodation is in **Contin**, 3 miles southwest of Strathpeffer. Top of the   **Sleeping**
list is the excellent **B** *Coull House Hotel*, T421487, www.milford.co.uk/go/
coulhouse.html, an elegant 19th-century country house offering fine food. There are
several **B&Bs** in Contin, including the very grand-looking **E** *Taigh an Eilein*, T421009,
open Apr-Sept. In Strathpeffer itself is the **D** *Brunstane Lodge Hotel*, on Golf Course
Rd, T421261, open Mar-Dec, which serves decent cheap bar meals. There are many
good value B&Bs in Strathpeffer, including: **E** *Inver Lodge*, T421392, open Mar-Dec,
E *White Lodge*, T421730, open Apr-Oct, and the elegant **D-E** *Craigvar*, T421622,
m.s.@gilsmith.demon.co.uk, on the Square.

There are regular **buses** between Strathpeffer and **Dingwall** (see below).   **Transport**

The Highlands

Dingwall and the Cromarty Firth

Phone code: 01349
Colour map 2, grid C1

Dingwall, at the head of the Cromarty Firth, has two major claims to fame. Not only is it believed to be the birthplace of Macbeth, it was also the home for many years of **Neil Gunn** (1891-1973), perhaps the Highlands' greatest literary figure (see also page 483). It's a fairly dull, though functional town, with good shops and banks (with ATMs) lining its long main street. The **Dingwall Museum** tells the history of this Royal Burgh. ■ *T865366. May-Sept Mon-Sat 1000-1700.*

East of Dingwall, before **Evanton**, is **Clanland and Sealpoint**, which has history and wildlife exhibitions and offers the chance to see the local seal population. ■ *T830033. Daily all year 0930-1730.* Standing on a hill above Evanton is the **Fyrish Monument**, a replica of the Gate of Negapatam in India, built by local men and funded by local military hero, Sir Hector Munro, to commemorate his capture of the Indian town, in 1781. To get there, turn off the B9176 towards Boath. It's a stiff two-hour climb up to the top.

The Cromarty Firth is a centre for repairing North Sea oil rigs and many of the villages along its north shore have benefited from the oil industry. One of these is **Invergordon**, just west of Nigg Bay, which has suffered in recent years due to the closure of the local aluminium factory.

Beyond Invergordon, a road branches south to **Nigg Ferry**. The ferry from Cromarty to Nigg was once a major thoroughfare, and now a tiny two-car ferry makes the 20-minute crossing in the summer months (see **Cromarty** above). From the ferry you get a good view of **Nigg Bay**, a vast natural harbour used in both world wars by the Royal Navy. Its entry is guarded by the dramatic headlands of the Sutors, identified in folklore as friendly giants. Also gigantic are the oil rigs ranged along the firth and the oil terminal at Nigg, a dramatic and not unpleasant contrast with Lilliputian Cromarty. Away from the shore, in **Nigg Old Church** (1626) is an old Pictish cross slab. ■ *Daily Easter-Oct 1000-1630.*

Sleeping

If you need to stay in **Dingwall**, the smartest place around is **D** *Tulloch Castle Hotel*, T861325, a castle dating from the 12th century. There's hostel accommodation in **Evanton** at the *Blackrock Bunkhouse*, T830917, open 1 Apr-31 Oct.

Transport

Dingwall is on the rail line between **Inverness** and **Kyle of Lochalsh** and **Thurso**. There are several **trains** daily in each direction (30 mins to Inverness; £3.50 single). There are hourly **buses** between **Inverness** and **Invergordon**, via Dingwall. There are also hourly buses between Inverness and Dingwall via **Muir of Ord**. There are buses between Dingwall and **Rosemarkie** (twice a day Mon-Thur) and between Dingwall and **Cromarty** (Wed and Thur).

Tain

Phone code: 01862
Colour map 2, grid B2
Population: 4,110

Squeezed between the Cromarty Firth to the south and the Dornoch Firth to the north is the **Tain peninsula**, whose largest town is Tain, a place with a 1950's time-warp feel. It's also a place with an impressive historical portfolio. Its backstreets are an intriguing jigsaw of imposing merchants' houses, steep vennels, secret gardens and dormer windows.

Tain was the birthplace of the 11th-century missionary **St Duthac**. Pilgrims flocked here in the Middle Ages to his shrine and a ruin near the links is thought to be the original **chapel**. His head and heart, encapsulated in gold and silver reliquaries, were later kept in the still extant medieval **Collegiate church** until their disappearance during the Reformation. The shrine was much favoured by the Stewart kings, notably James IV who on one of his frequent pilgrimages reputedly approached walking penitentially barefoot along the King's Causeway. Tain's status as a place of sanctuary probably explains why Bruce's family fled here during the Wars of Independence.

The Collegiate church is on Castle Brae, just off the High Street, and inside is a 17th-century panel painted with the badges of the trade guilds, a reminder of the town's busy international trade. Another reminder is the imposing 16th-century **Tolbooth** in the High Street. Next to the church is a **museum** housed in the Pilgrimage which charts the town's medieval history in the **Tain through Time** exhibition. ■ *T894089. Apr-Oct daily 1000-1800; Nov, Dec and Mar 1200-1600. £3.50, £2 children.*

One of Tain's main attractions is the **Glenmorangie whisky distillery**, just off the A9 to the north of town, where you can see how the world-famous whisky is made and try a sample. ■ *T892477. All year Mon-Thur 0900-1700; Jun-Aug also Sat 1000-1600 and Sun 1200-1600. Tours from 1030-1530.*

Also out of town, just to the south off the A9, is the **Aldie Water Mill**, a restored 16th-century mill in working order, with various high-quality craft shops attached. Nearby is **The Tain Pottery**, which you can also visit. ■ *T893786. Daily 1000-1700.*

There are several grand hotels in and around Tain. **A** *Mansfield House Hotel*, Scotsburn Rd, T892052, mansfield@cali.co.uk. 19th-century baronial splendour and superb cuisine. Restaurant also open to non-residents (mid-range to expensive). There's the excellent value **C** *Morangie House Hotel*, on Morangie Rd, T892281. It's popular locally for its food (mid-range) and is open for lunch and dinner. There are also more modest **B&B** options, such as **E** *Golf View House*, at 13 Knockbreck Rd, T892856.

Sleeping & eating

Brown's Gallery, Castle Brae. Showcases work by Highland artists. Local mussels can be bought from *Bannerman's*, a fish and seafood wholesalers.

Shopping

Tain is on the **Inverness-Thurso** rail line and there are 3 **trains** daily in each direction. *Citylink* **buses** between Inverness and Thurso pass through Tain 4 times a day. There are also buses to **Portmahomack** (4 times daily Mon-Thur), **Balintore** (5-6 times daily Mon-Sat), **Lairg** via **Bonar Bridge** (3 times daily Mon-Sat) and **Dornoch** via **Bonar Bridge** (once a day Mon-Thur) with *Inverness Traction*, T01463-239292, and *Rapson's of Brora*, T01408-621245.

Transport

Around Tain

The town of Tain serves a vast hinterland. Inland the hills are little-visited backwoods and farm towns, narrow valleys lined with crofts where cattle graze in boggy haughs and, to the west, glens and moorland. Along the seaboard are the windswept fields of the **Tarbat peninsula**. Good sea angling is to be had from the harbours of the otherwise dull coastal villages such as **Balintore**, and at **Shandwick** is a massive Pictish stone. It is said that unbaptized children were buried near the stone which is now in the Museum of Scotland in Edinburgh.

The seaside village of Portnahomack, or 'port of Colman', is named after the missionary who was keen as mustard to found a religious settlement here. Archaeological work is revealing the importance of this area in Pictish times. The **Tarbat Discovery Centre**, T871790, in Tarbat Old Church displays recently discovered Pictish stonecarving. From the harbour, with its 18th-century girnals (grain warehouses) and sheltered sandy beach, you can see a huge stretch of the Sutherland coast, and the great sandbanks – the 'gizzen brigs' – at the mouth of the Dornoch Firth. Boat trips are available from

Portnahomack
Colour map 2, grid B2

The Highlands

the harbour for sea angling. A worthwhile trip is out to **Tarbat Ness lighthouse**, about three miles north.

Eating A great place to eat out here is *The Oyster Catcher*, T871560, small café-restaurant serving snacks and lunches and dinner from 1930 (if booked). Crêpes are a speciality, but it also does pasta, seafood and fish.

Hill of Fearn
Colour map 2, grid C2

South from Portnahomack, just west of the junction of the B9165 and the B9166, is Hill of Fearn. **Fearn Abbey** was moved here around 1250 from its original site near Edderton, where it was too vulnerable to sea raiders. It later became the parish church, but in 1742 lightning struck the roof which fell in, killing 38 Sunday worshippers. A tragedy was preceded by a fairy harbinger sighted at nearby Loch Eye. In Hill of Fearn is the excellent **Anta Factory Shop**, one of the very best places in the country for classy tartan furnishing fabrics, as well as tartan rugs and throws, and pottery. ■ *Mon-Sat 1000-1700 (also Sun 1000-1600 Jun-Sept).*

The Dornoch Firth

Colour map 2, grid B2

Fairies were said to cross the Dornoch Firth on cockle shells and were once seen building a bridge of fairy gold, perhaps a forerunner of the Dornoch Bridge which carries the A9 across the firth just north of Tain. A more pleasant and interesting route is to follow the A836 along the south shore. From **The Struie**, reached by the B9176 which branches south at Easter Fearn, there's a panoramic view over the Dornoch Firth and the Sutherland hills. In the churches of **Edderton** and **Kincardine** are Pictish stones. Another stands in a field northwest of Edderton, but don't disturb the crops or livestock. A quartz boulder at **Ardgay**, the 'Clach Eiteag', commemorates the cattle tryst and fair which once took place locally.

Ten miles from Ardgay, at the end of lovely **Strathcarron**, is the isolated **Croick church**, one of most poignant reminders of the infamous Clearances. Here, in 1845, 90 local folk took refuge in the churchyard after they had been evicted from their homes in Glencalvie by the Duke of Sutherland to make way for flocks of sheep. A reporter from *The Times* described the 'wretched spectacle' as men, women and children were carted off, many never to return, and the report is there to read. Far more evocative and harrowing, though, are the names and messages the people scratched in spidery copperplate in the window panes.

North of Ardgay is the **Kyle of Sutherland**, where several rivers converge to flood into the sea through lush water meadows. Montrose was defeated here, at **Carbisdale**, in 1651. Overlooking the Kyle, at **Culrain**, is the 19th-century **Carbisdale Castle**, once home of the exiled King of Norway, which now houses the largest and most sumptuous **youth hostel** in Scotland, and possibly anywhere else. ■ *T01549-421232. 26 Feb-31 Oct (except the first two weeks in May). Trains between Inverness and Thurso stop at Ardgay and Culrain. The youth hostel is half a mile up a steep hill from the station. Buses between Inverness and Lairg (see below) stop in Ardgay and Bonar Bridge.*

After the Dornoch Ferry disaster of 1809, a bridge was built over the Kyle at **Bonar Bridge**, from where the A949 runs eastwards to join the main A9 just before Dornoch, while the A836 continues north to Lairg (see below). A few miles north of **Invershin** are the **Falls of Shin**, an excellent place to watch salmon battling upstream on their way to spawning grounds (best seen June-September). A visitor centre and café/restaurant/shop, has information about six easy walks in the immediate area; all under an hour long. The café/restaurant serves good, cheap food daily till 1730.

The Highlands

Lairg

Eleven miles north of Bonar Bridge is the uninspiring village of **Lairg**, the region's main transport hub. Lairg is best known for its annual lamb sale, when young sheep from all over the north of Scotland are bought and sold. There are several interesting walks around the village, some of which lead to prehistoric sites such as the Neolithic hut circles at nearby **Ord Hill**.

Phone code: 01549
Colour map 2, grid B1

These walks, and many others in the region, are described, with maps, in the Forestry Commission's leaflet *Forests of the Far North* (50p), which is available at the Ferrycroft Countryside Centre and **tourist office**. ■ *T402160. Mon-Sat 0900-1700 and Sun 1300-1700.*

There's a bank with ATM in the village and several places to stay, including **E** *The Nip Inn*, on the main street, T402243, which also does bar meals. There are several **B&Bs** and a **campsite** too, but the most interesting place to stay is 9 miles east at **Rogart** train station, where you can get cheap hostel accommodation at the *Rogart Railway Carriages*, T01408-641343, rogmail@globalnet.co.uk. Two old rail carriages have been converted to sleep 16 people and there's a 10% discount for bike or train users.

Sleeping

It is said that all roads meet at Lairg and it's certainly a hard place to avoid. From here, the A839 heads east to meet the A9 between Dornoch and Golspie, and west to meet the A837 which runs out to Lochinver. The A836 heads north to Tongue, and south to Bonar Bridge. The A838 meanwhile heads northwest to Laxford Bridge and on to Durness, near Cape Wrath. **Trains** between **Inverness** and **Thurso** stop at Lairg and Rogart stations 3 times daily. *Inverness Traction* **buses**, T01463-239292, run from here to **Ullapool**, with connections to **Lochinver** and **Durness**, from May to early Oct (Mon-Sat). Lairg is also the central point for several *Postbus* routes, T01463-256228.

Transport

Dornoch

Dornoch is another architectural gem with its deep, golden sandstone houses and leafy cathedral square. Bishop Gilbert of Moravia (Moray) built the cathedral circa 1245. His family's success in gaining a foothold in Northeast Scotland against the Norsemen was rewarded with the Earldom of Sutherland. It was trouble with the Jarls which prompted Gilbert to move his power base here from Caithness, mindful that his predecessor had been boiled in butter by the locals.

Phone code: 01862
Colour map 2, grid B2

The **tourist office** is on the main square. ■ *T810400. Mon-Sat 0900-1300 and 1400-1700.*

The 13th-century **cathedral** was badly damaged in 1570, then subjected to an ill-conceived 'restoration' by the Countess of Sutherland in 1835. Among the few surviving features is a series of gargoyles, including a green man, and the effigy of an unknown knight. ■ *Mon-Fri 0730-2000. You can climb the cathedral tower during Jul and Aug.* Opposite the cathedral is the 16th-century **Bishop's Palace**, now a hotel (see below).

Sights

Nowadays, Dornoch is famous for its links **golf course**, rated as one of the world's finest and relatively easy to get on. It overlooks miles of dunes and pristine sandy beach. A stone near the links marks the spot where the last **witch** in Scotland was burned, in 1722. Folklore recounts a bloody battle on the beach at **Embo**, just to the north, against raiding Vikings in 1259 in which Sir Richard Murray was killed. The battle is commemorated at the **Earl's Cross**. Trout fishing is available on Dornoch Lochans; enquire locally.

Straggling crofting townships such as **Rogart** (see above) are scattered through the glens and around the coast, all occupied and worked vigorously.

The Highlands

The coastal population was swollen in the 19th century by tenants evicted from the inland glens, resettled here and encouraged to try fishing at such villages as **Embo**. Others joined the eager flood of emigrants to the New World already under way. Crofting tenancies still exist but crofters now enjoy more protection (see the 'Outer Hebrides' chapter, page 531).

North of Dornoch is **Loch Fleet**, a river estuary with a ferocious tide race at its mouth and an SNH reserve protecting rare birds and plants. The rotting skeletons of the fishing fleet abandoned in the First World War lie in the sand on the south shore west of the car park. At **Skelbo Castle**, Scottish and English commissioners waited in vain in 1290 for the arrival by ship of the three-year-old Maid of Norway. Her death *en route* sparked off the Wars of Independence. There are several walks in the forestry plantations in the area. Details are available from Dornoch tourist office.

Sleeping There's plenty of accommodation in Dornoch, which can be booked at the tourist office. **C** *Dornoch Castle Hotel*, T810216, open Apr-Oct. Formerly the Bishop's Palace, this 16th-century building is full of character and boasts excellent food (expensive). Another fine hotel is **B** *The Royal Golf Hotel*, T/F810283, scotland@morton-hotels.demon.co.uk, next to the first tee. There are also lots of good **B&Bs** and a **campsite**.

Eating Apart from the hotels listed above, a good place to dine is *The Two Quails*, on Castle St, where you can enjoy an expensive but top-class dinner cooked by a chef trained at the Ritz. Next door is Luigi's, for excellent coffee and a range of exotic ice creams.

Shopping **Bookshops** *The Dornoch Bookshop* on Cathedral Square stocks local books.

Transport There are **buses** to and from **Inverness** (hourly Mon-Sat, 5 times on Sun). *Citylink* buses between Inverness and **Thurso** also stop in Dornoch 4 times daily.

Golspie

Phone code: 01408
Colour map 2, grid B2
Population: 1,650

There is little to recommend the dull little town of Golspie, though it does have a couple of banks and supermarkets. There's an 18-hole golf course and the *Orcadian Stone Company* has a large display of fossils and geological specimens from the Highlands and beyond.

The town lives in the dark shadow of the Sutherlands. On **Beinn a'Bhraggaidh** (1,293ft), to the southwest, is a huge, 100ft-high **monument** to the Duke of Sutherland. Those who make it up to the monument and who know something of the Duke's many despicable acts may find the inscription risible, as it describes him as "a judicious, kind and liberal landlord". There's no reference to the fact that he forcibly evicted 15,000 tenants from his estate. Not surprisingly, locals would like to see this eyesore removed from the landscape, broken into tiny pieces and then scattered far and wide. Unfortunately, they have thus far been unsuccessful.

Dunrobin Castle Dunrobin Castle, one mile north of the village, is the ancient seat of the Dukes of Sutherland, who once owned more land than anyone else in the British Empire. Much enlarged and aggrandized in the 19th century with fairy-tale turrets, the enormous 189-room castle, the largest house in the Highlands, is stuffed full of fine furniture, paintings, tapestries and *objets d'art* and bears witness to their obscene wealth. The castle overlooks beautiful gardens laid out with box hedges, ornamental trees and fountains. In stormy weather you should listen to the sea crashing on the beach beyond the walls. The **museum** is an animal-lover's nightmare and almost a caricature of the aristocracy, with

The Highlands (side margin text)

a spectacular Victorian taxidermy collection. There are also local antiquities, some from ancient brochs, and Pictish stonecarvings. ■ *T633177. 1 Apr-31 May and 1-15 Oct Mon-Sat 1030-1630, Sun 1200-1630; 1 Jun-30 Sept Mon-Sat 1030-1730, Sun 1200-1730. £4.80.*

Brora

Brora sits at the mouth of the river Brora, which as everywhere on this coast, is the site of a once lucrative salmon netting industry. At the harbour, the ice house is a relic of the herring boom. Coal mines, opened in the 16th century, salt pans and a brickworks are all defunct. Still very much alive, however, is *Hunter's*, the local weavers of heavyweight traditional tweeds and a good place to invest in some natty headwear. A mile or so north of town is the **Clynelish distillery**. ■ *T623000. All year Mon-Thur 0930-1630. £2.*

Phone code: 01408
Colour map 2, grid B2
Population: 1,860

Castle Cole in lovely **Strath Brora**, eight miles northwest, is one of several ruined brochs. Another, **Carn Liath** (signposted) is by the main road, three miles south of Brora.

Next to each other, overlooking Brora's golf course are **B** *The Links & Royal Marine Hotels*, T621252, highlandescape@btinternet.com. Among the many **B&Bs** is **D-E** *Glenaveron*, on Golf Rd, T/F621601. If you're staying or just passing through don't miss *Capaldi's*, on the High St, for exquisite home-made Italian ice cream.

Sleeping & eating

Helmsdale

North of Brora is the former herring port of Helmsdale, which gets busy in the summer. The village is most notable for its excellent **Timespan Heritage Centre**, which brings the history of the Highlands to life through a series of high-tech displays, sound effects and an audiovisual programme. ■ *T821327. Easter-Oct Mon-Sat 0930-1700, Sun 1400-1700. £3, £2.40 children.*

Phone code: 01431
Colour map 2, grid B2

The centre also includes a model of Barbara Cartland, which may seem incongruous, until you venture across the road to the *La Mirage* tearoom and see the lady herself in the flesh (pink, of course) – or so it seems. The proprietrix is the inimitable Nancy Sinclair, who has modelled herself, and her tearoom, on the queen of romantic novels. The whole effect is pure kitsch and you never know who might pop in for a plate of fish and chips. Barabara Cartland has been holidaying in Helmsdale for over 60 years. ■ *Daily 1200-2045 (till 1900 Dec-Apr).* The **tourist office** is on the south side of the village, by the A9. ■ *T821640. Apr-Sept Mon-Sat 1000-1700.*

Another good place to eat is the **C** *Navidale House Hotel*, T821258, open Feb-Nov. There are also several **B&Bs**, including **E** *Broomhill House*, T821259, with its distinctive turret, and **E** *Torbuie*, T821424, in Navidale, about a mile south. There's also an *SYHA Youth Hostel*, T821577, open mid-May to early Oct.

Sleeping & eating

Helmsdale is on the Inverness-Wick/Thurso rail line. Buses and trains are the same as for Wick (see below).

Transport

Helmsdale to Wick

North from Helmsdale the A9 climbs spectacularly up the **Ord of Caithness** and over the pass enters a desolate, treeless landscape; an area devastated during the Clearances. To get some idea of the hardships people had to endure, stop at the ruined crofting village of **Badbea**, just beyond **Ousdale**.

The Highlands

👉 *After the Gold Rush*

A short drive from Helmsdale, up the **Strath of Kildonan** (or Strath Ullie), is **Baile an Or** (Gaelic for 'goldfield'), site of the great Sutherland Gold Rush of 1869. It all started after local man Robert Gilchrist returned home from the Australian gold fields only to discover gold here, on his doorstep. His success brought others rushing to Kildonan and soon a shanty town had sprung up to accommodate them.

Within a year the gold rush was over, but small amounts are still found today. Anyone who fancies their luck can try a bit of gold panning in the Kildonan Burn at Baile an Or, about a mile from Kildonan train station. You can rent out gold panning kits at Strath Ullie Crafts & Fishing Tackle, T821343, opposite the Timespan Heritage Centre in Helmsdale, for £2.50 per day, and licences are free.

At **Berriedale**, a farm track leads west to the **Wag**, from where you can climb **Morven** (2,313 feet), the highest hill in Caithness, with amazing views across the whole county.

The A9 coast road then drops down into **Dunbeath**, a pleasant little village at the mouth of a small strath (or glen). This was the birthplace of one of Scotland's foremost writers, **Neil Gunn** (1891-1973). His finest works such as *The Silver Darlings* and *Highland River* reflect his experiences of growing up in the northeast and are fascinating accounts of life here during the days of the herring boom, though the sleepy harbour of today is barely recognizable as the erstwhile bustling fishing port. The villages of Dunbeath, and **Latherton** to the north, are included on the *Neil Gunn Trail*, as is the beautiful walk up the glen, described in the leaflet available at the **Dunbeath Heritage Centre**. Here, you can learn all about the life and works of the famous novelist as well as the history of Caithness. ■ *T01593-731233. Apr-Sept daily 1100-1700. £1.50, 50p children*. If you fancy something to eat, the **D** *Dunbeath Hotel*, T01593-731208, does good, cheap bar meals.

Just outside the village is the **Laidhay Croft Museum**, a restored traditional longhouse with stable, house and byre all under the same roof. ■ *T01593-731370. Daily Apr-Oct 1000-1800. £1, 50p children*.

Between here and Wick are some of the most fascinating archaeological sites in the north. Just beyond **Lybster**, is the turning to the **Grey Cairns of Camster**, five miles north of the A9. These two enormous prehistoric burial chambers date from 2500 BC and are amazingly complete, with corbelled ceilings, and can be entered on hands and knees through narrow passageways.

A few miles to the north of the turn-off, at East Clyth, a path leads to the **Hill o' Many Stanes**, a curious fan-shaped configuration of Bronze Age standing stones; 200 of them in 22 rows. No one yet knows their precise purpose but studies have shown that there were once 600 stones here. Before Wick, at **Ulbster**, is the **Cairn o' Get**. Opposite the sign, are the precipitous **Whaligoe Steps**, which lead down to a tiny, picturesque harbour.

Wick

Phone code: 01955
Colour map 2, grid A4
Population: 8,000

A century ago Wick was Europe's busiest herring port, its harbour jam-packed with fishing boats and larger ships exporting tons of salted fish to Russia, Scandinavia and the West Indian slave plantations. Now, it's a sad, soulless place – "…the meanest of man's towns", as Robert Louis Stevenson once described it.

Wick is actually two towns. On one side of the river is Wick proper and on the other is **Pulteneytown**, the model town planned by Thomas Telford for the British Fisheries Society in 1806 to house evicted crofters who came to

work here. Now it's one great living museum of fishermen's cottages and derelict sheds and stores around the near-deserted quays. It gives a good idea of the
scale of the herring trade during its heyday in the mid-19th century, when over
1,000 boats set sail to catch the 'silver darlings'. Here, on Bank Row is the
superb **Wick Heritage Centre**. The highlight of the centre is its massive photographic collection dating from the late 19th century. ■ *T605393. May-Sept
Mon-Sat 1000-1700. £2, 50p children.*

Three miles north of Wick are the impressive 15th-century clifftop ruins of
Sinclair and Girnigoe Castle. On the A99 heading north out of town is the
Caithness Glass Visitors Centre, where you can watch the famous glass being
blown. ■ *T602286. Mon-Thur 0900-1630. The shop is open till 1700.*

There is a good **walk** along the rocky shore east of town to **The Trinkie**, and
about a mile further on to the **Brig o' Trams**. Ask for details at the **tourist
office** on Whitechapel Road (just off the High Street). ■ *T602596. All year
Mon-Fri 0900-1700, Sun 0900-1300.*

If you have to stay in Wick, there's a reasonable selection of hotels such as **D** *Mackay's* | **Sleeping**
Hotel, Union St, T602323, mackays.hotel@caithness-mm.co.uk, by the roundabout
just across the bridge from the town centre. But you are better off going for the excellent **B** *Portland Arms Hotel*, about 15 miles south, in Lybster, T01593-721208. A
19th-century coaching inn, full of character and offering great food (mid-range to
expensive). The best of the **guesthouses** and **B&Bs** are **E** *Wellington Guest House*,
41-43 High St, T603287, open Mar-Oct, and **E** *The Clachan*, on South Rd, T605384.
Also good value is **E-F** *Greenvoe*, George St, near the town centre, T603942.

The best places to eat are also out of town. These include *The Bower Inn* (see page | **Eating**
473), and the *Old Smiddy Inn*, in Thrumster, 5 miles south of Wick, T651256, open
daily 1200-2100. Probably the best place in town is the *Queen's Hotel*, on Francis St,
T602992, which has a varied menu (mid-range). Alternatively, try *Cabrelli's*, 134 High
St, a great caff serving pizza and fish and chips. A few yards away is *Carter's Bar*, which
does pub food and is an okay place for a drink at night.

Air Wick has an **airport**, a few miles north of town, with daily direct flights to and | **Transport**
from **Kirkwall** (Orkney), **Sumburgh** (Shetland), **Aberdeen** and **Edinburgh** with connections south. Flights are with *Gill Air*, T603914, and *British Airways Express*,
T0345-222111). **Train** The train and bus stations are next to each other behind the
hospital. Trains leave for **Inverness** (3 daily Mon-Sat, 2 on Sun; 3 hrs 45 mins) via
Thurso, **Helmsdale**, **Golspie**, **Lairg** and **Dingwall**. **Bus** *Scottish Citylink*,
T0990-505050, **buses** between **Inverness** and **Thurso** stop *en route* in Wick (3 times
daily). There are also regular local buses to Thurso, via Halkirk or Castletown, and
buses to **Helmsdale** (2-6 times daily Mon-Sat, 1-4 on Sun) and **John O'Groats** (5 daily
Mon-Sat, 4 on Sun). There's a *Postbus* service to **Wick airport** Mon-Sat at 1015.
Car/bike hire *Richard's Garage*, Francis St, T604123.

The Highlands

Strathspey and the Cairngorms

One of Scotland's busiest tourist areas is Strathspey, the broad valley of the river Spey, Scotland's second longest river, which rises high in the hills above Loch Laggan and flows northeast to its mouth on the Moray Firth. The lower reaches are famous for salmon fishing and whisky and are covered in the Speyside section of the 'Northeast Scotland' chapter (see page 382), while the upper reaches attract outdoor sports enthusiasts in droves. Hemmed in between the mighty Monadhliath Mountains to the north and the magnificent Cairngorms, Britain's second highest range, to the south, this is an area which offers excellent hiking, watersports, mountain biking and above all, winter skiing.

The main focus of the area is the tourist resort of Aviemore, a name synonymous with winter sports. It's a fairly tawdry place, but people don't come here for the architecture. Aviemore is surrounded by towering peaks, lochs, rivers and forests of native Caledonian pine which are home to rare wildlife such as pine martens, wildcats, red squirrels, ospryes and capercaillie, and Britian's only herd of wild reindeer. Most of upper Strathspey is privately owned by the Glen More Forest Park and Rothiemurchus Estate which has been in the possession of the Grant family since the 16th century, but both owners allow free access to their lands and provide generous outdoor facilities.

Outdoor Sports

Skiing

Phone code: 01479
For latest snow conditions call the Ski Hotline T0900-1654655

Cairngorm is Scotland's longest-established ski resort and though it cannot compare to anything in the Alps or North America, it remains Scotland's largest ski area, with 28 runs and over 20 miles of pistes. When the sun shines, the snowfall is good and the crowds are thin, it can be a very satisfying experience. The season normally runs from January until the snow disappears, which can be as late as April.

The **Cairngorm Ski Area** is about nine miles southeast of Aviemore, above Loch Morlich in Glen More Forest Park and reached by a frequent bus service. You can rent skis and other equipment from the Day Lodge at the foot of the ski area (T861261), where you can also buy a lift pass (£20 per day). Ski hire (skis, poles and boots) costs £13 per day, and snowboard hire is £16. There are plans to replace the chair-lift with a funicular railway, much to the anger of environmentalists, but this may be a few years away.

If there's enough snow, the area around **Loch Morlich** and **Rothiemurchus Estate** provides good **cross-country** skiing, though in recent years snowfall has been below average. For more information, see page 58. The tourist office provides a free *Cairngorm Piste Map & Ride Guide* leaflet and a *Ski Scotland* brochure which lists ski schools and rental facilities.

Walking

The walks around Strathspey are covered by OS Landranger map No 36 (1:50,000 scale) or OS Outdoor Leisure Map No 3 (1:25,000 scale)

The Cairngorms provide some of Scotland's most challenging walking, with no fewer than 49 Munros and half of Britain's eight mountains over 4,000 feet (**Ben MacDrui**, **Braeriach**, **Cairn Toul** and **Cairn Gorm**). These mountains come into their own in winter, providing experienced climbers with a wide range of classic ice climbs. They should not be taken lightly, in other words, and require a high degree of fitness, experience and preparation (see page 56 for safety precautions).

The summit of Cairn Gorm (4,084 feet) is readily accessible as you take the chair-lift up to the Day Lodge (see above) and from there it's a relatively short climb to the top, though you should be prepared for a sudden change in weather conditions.

The Highlands

As well as the many tough hill walks, there are some excellent **low-level walks**. An easy circular walk of about an hour around **Loch an Eilean** in Rothiemurchus Estate starts from the end of the side road which turns east off the B970 two miles south of Aviemore. There are 50 miles of footpaths through this area, including some lovely walks through the forests. There are also ranger-led guided walks. You can find out more at the **Rothiemurchus Estate Visitor Centre**, T810858, which is a mile from Aviemore along the Ski Road. It's open daily 0900-1700 and can provide a free *Visitor Guide and Footpath Map*. Another good area for walking is around **Glen More Forest Park**. The **visitor centre**, T861220, near Loch Morlich has a *Glen More Forest Guide Map* which details local walks.

The best known of the long-distance trails is the **Lairig Ghru**, a 25-mile hike from Aviemore over the Lairig Ghru Pass to Braemar. The trail is well marked but can take at least eight hours and is very tough in parts, so you'll need to be properly equipped and prepared.

Watersports In summer, the main activities are watersports and there are two centres which offer sailing, canoeing and windsurfing tuition and equipment hire. The **Loch Morlich Watersports Centre** (T861221, lochmorlichw-s@sol.co.uk; open Apr-Oct) is five miles east of Aviemore. The **Loch Insh Watersports Centre**, T651272, user@lochinsh.dial.netmedia.co.uk, open Apr-Oct, offers the same facilities, plus fishing, mountain bike hire and ski instruction on a dry ski slope.

Fishing Fishing is a major pursuit in the area. You can fish for trout and salmon on the **River Spey** and the Rothiemurchus Estate has trout fishing on its stocked loch at **Inverdruie**, where you can hire rods. Fishing permits cost around £10-15 per day for the stocked lochs and £20-30 per day for the River Spey. They are sold at local shops such as *Speyside Sports* in Aviemore, and at *Loch Morlich Watersports Centre* which also hires out rods and tackle. **Alvie Estate**, T01540-651255, near Kingussie also hires rods.

Mountain biking Rothiemurchus and Glen More estates are great areas for mountain biking with lots of excellent forest trails. The **Rothiemurchus Visitor Centre** (see above) at Inverdruie has route maps and you can also hire bikes. Bike hire and good advice on routes is also available at *Bothy Bikes*, Unit 7, Grampian Rd, Aviemore, T810111, open daily 0900-1800. *Aviemore Mountain Bikes*, T811007, at 45a Grampian Rd, organises guided bike tours.

Horse riding Horse riding and pony trekking are on offer at various places throughout Strathspey. There's *Alvie Stables*, at Alvie near Kincraig, T01540-651409, mobile T0831-495397, *Carrbridge Trekking Centre*, Station Rd, Carrbridge, T841602, and *Strathspey Highland Pony Centre*, Rowanlea, Faebuie, Grantown-on-Spey, T873073.

Aviemore

In the 1960s Aviemore was transformed from a sleepy Highland village into the jumble of concrete buildings, tacky gift shops and sprawling coach parks that it is today. The extent of the tourist tat here is so awful it makes Fort William seem charmingly understated by comparison, and there can be few more depressing and hideous sights than Santa Claus Land children's theme park on a drizzly afternoon in November. In saying that, however, the town is the most important tourist centre in the area and has a wide range of facilities.

Phone code: 01479
Colour map 4, grid A3
Population: 2,500

The town lies just off the A9, 33 miles south of Inverness. The train station, banks, restaurants and pretty much everything else are all found along Grampian Road. Buses stop here too (see 'Transport' below).

The **tourist office** is also on Grampian Road, about 400 yards south of the train station. They will book accommodation as well as provide free maps and leaflets on local attractions and change foreign currency. ■ *T810363. Apr-Oct Mon-Fri 0900-1800, Sat 1000-1700, Sun 1000-1600; Nov-Mar Mon-Fri 0900-1700, Sat 1000-1700.*

Sleeping & eating
There's no shortage of accommodation around Aviemore. The best choice in the area is the **C** *Corrour House Hotel*, at Inverdruie, 2 miles southeast of Aviemore, T810220, open Dec-Oct. This Victorian country house oozes charm, enjoys wonderful views and offers superb cuisine. Also recommended is the **D** *Rowan Tree Restaurant & Guest House*, at Loch Alvie, 1½ miles south of Aviemore on the B9152, T810207, open Dec-Oct. This is one of the oldest hotels in the area and offers excellent food (lunch cheap; dinner moderate). One mile south of Aviemore, at Lynwilg, is the beautiful **D** *Lynwilg House*, T811685, a charming, friendly guesthouse with a reputation for good food. There are lots of **B&Bs** in Aviemore itself, including **E** *Ravenscraig Guest House*, T810278, and **E** *Vermont Guest House*, T810470, both on Grampian Rd.

There are a couple of good **hostels** in Aviemore. The large *SYHA hostel*, T810345, is on Grampian Rd near the tourist office and open all year. There's also the *Aviemore Independent Bunkhouse and Backpackers Hostel*, T811137, on Dalfaber Rd. There are several good **campsites**, including the *Rothiemurchus Camping & Caravan Park*, T812800, at Coylumbridge, and a *Forest Enterprise* site at Glenmore, T861271.

Eating
Apart from the hotels and guesthouses listed above, the best place to eat in Aviemore is the *Old Bridge Inn*, T811137, on Dalfaber Rd. This lovely old pub serves excellent value food and hosts ceilidhs and Highland dinner dances in the summer months. There's a good lochside restaurant at the *Loch Insh Watersports Centre* at Kincraig, between Aviemore and Kingussie, which doubles as a café during the day.

Transport
There are *Scottish Citylink* **buses**, T0990-505050, between Aviemore and **Inverness** (45 mins; £4), **Kingussie** (20 min; £3), **Pitlochry** (1 hr 15 mins; £5.50), **Perth** (2 hrs; £7.80), **Glasgow** (3 hrs 30 mins; £9.80) and **Edinburgh** (3 hrs 30 mins; £11.30). For **Aberdeen**, change at Inverness.

There are direct **trains** to and from **Glasgow** and **Edinburgh** (3 hrs) and **Inverness** (40 mins; £8.80). For details T0345-484950. The *Strathspey Steam Railway*, T810725, runs between Aviemore, Boat of Garten and Nethy Bridge. The station is just to the east of the main train station. The *Cairngorm Chairlift Company*, T861261, runs daily buses between Aviemore and Cairngorm Ski Centre from late Oct to Apr.

Car hire from *MacDonald's Self Drive*, 13 Muirton, T811444.

Around Aviemore

There's nothing of real interest in Aviemore. The real enjoyment lies in the surrounding mountains and forests and there are a few interesting places close at hand. A great place for kids is the **Cairngorm Reindeer Centre**, T861228, in Glen More Forest Park, on the road from Coylumbridge, seven miles from Aviemore. Guided walks to see the herd and feed them leave daily at 1100 and also at 1430 during the summer and cost £3 (£4 for adults).

Boat of Garten
Phone code: 01479
Colour map 4, grid A3

Eight miles northeast of Aviemore is the tiny village of Boat of Garten which suddenly shot to fame when a pair of **ospreys**, which had disappeared from these shores, reappeared on nearby **Loch Garten**, two miles east of the village. Now these beautiful birds of prey have established themselves here and elsewhere and there are thought be well over 100 pairs throughout the Highlands. The **Abernethy Forest RSPB Reserve** on the shore of Loch Garten is best visited during the nesting season, between late April and August when the RSPB opens an **observation centre.** ■ *Daily in season 1000-1800. £2.50 for non-members.* You can also see ospreys at the Rothiemurchus trout loch at Inverdruie, and maybe even on Loch Morlich and Loch Insh. The reserve is also home to several other rare species such as capercaillie, whooper swans and red squirrels. Guided walks leave from the observation centre at 0930 on Wednesdays.

Sleeping and eating There's a good selection of accommodation in the village. **C-D** *Heathbank – The Victorian House*, T831234, is a must for Art Nouveau lovers and offers good French cuisine, while the **C-D** *Boat Hotel*, T831258, offers cheap and tasty meals. **D-E** *Glenavon House*, T831213, open Apr-Oct, is a lovely guesthouse on Kinchurdy Rd, and **D-E** *Moorfield House*, on Deshar Rd, T831646, moorfieldhouse@ msn.com, is also a good choice. You can also **camp** at *Campgrounds of Scotland*, T831652.

Transport The best way to get to Boat of Garten is on the *Strathspey Steam Railway* which runs at least 5 times daily from Aviemore, T810725. Loch Garten is not easy to reach without your own transport, but check with one of the local tourist offices about tours.

At Carrbridge, a pleasant little village seven miles north of Aviemore, is the **Landmark Forest Heritage Park**, a woodland theme park which combines entertainment, education and shopping. There's a raised Treetop Trail for viewing wildlife, a fire tower, maze and various nature trails and fun rides. It manages to avoid being tacky and is good fun for kids. ■ *T841614. Daily Apr to mid-Jul 0930-1800; mid-Jul to Aug 0930-2000; Sept and Oct 0930-1730; Nov-Mar 1000-1700. £6.40, £20.10 family ticket.* In the village itself is the decidedly fragile-looking 18th-century **Bridge of Carr**, which is not for vertigo sufferers.

Carrbridge

Sleeping There are several places to stay in Carrbridge. Top of the range is the stylish **C** *Dalrachney Lodge Hotel*, T841252, grantswan@msn.com, a former Victorian hunting lodge with a good restaurant. More down to earth, but nonetheless comfortable is the **E** *Cairn Hotel*, T841212, which serves good-value bar meals. There's also the much cheaper option of the *Carrbridge Bunkhouse Hostel*, T841250, at Dalrachney House, half a mile north of the village on the road to Inverness.

Transport There are several **buses** daily (except Sun) to Carrbridge from **Inverness** and **Grantown-on-Spey** with *Highland Country Buses*, T01463-233371.

Kingussie

The quiet village of Kingussie (pronounced King-yoosie) lies 12 miles southwest of Aviemore and makes a pleasant alternative as a place to stay. The **tourist office** (T661297) is housed in the Folk Museum (see below) and has the same opening hours.

Phone code 01540
Colour map 4, grid A2
Population: 1,500

The main attraction here is the excellent **Highland Folk Museum** which contains a fascinating collection of traditional highland artefacts, as well as a farming museum, an old smokehouse, a water mill and traditional Hebridean 'blackhouse'. During the summer there are also demonstrations of spinning,

Sights

The Highlands

woodcarving and peat-fire baking. ■ *T661307. May-Aug Mon-Fri 0930-1730, Sat and Sun 1300-1700; Apr, Sept and Oct guided tours only Mon-Fri 1030-1630. £3.50.*

Another worthwhile attraction is **Ruthven Barracks**, standing on a hillock across the river. This former barracks was built by the English Redcoats as part of their campaign to tame the Highlands after the first Jacobite rising in 1715. It was destroyed by the Jacobites in the wake of defeat at Culloden to prevent it from falling into enemy hands and it was from here that Bonnie Prince Charlie sent his final order which signalled the end of his doomed cause. Access is free and the ruins are particularly attractive at night when floodlit.

At nearby **Kincraig** village, between Kingussie and Aviemore, is the **Highland Wildlife Park**, which has a captive collection of rare native animals. ■ *T651270. Daily Apr, May, Sept and Oct 1000-1800; Jun-Aug till 1900; Nov-Mar 1000-1600. £6.30.* Those who mourn the loss of the hit TV show, *One Man and His Dog*, will be excited at the prospect of visiting the **Working Sheepdogs Show** at the nearby Leault Farm, where you can see demonstrations of dogs rounding up a flock of sheep. ■ *T651310. Daily. £3.50.*

Sleeping **D** *The Osprey Hotel*, Ruthven Rd, T661510, is a comfortable little hotel with a very good restaurant (expensive). The **D** *Scot House Hotel*, Newtonmore Rd, T661351, is another good choice and also offers great food (lunch cheap; dinner moderate to expensive). There are several good guesthouses, all on Newtonmore Rd, including: **E** *Arden House*, T661369, **E** *Avondale House*, T661731, and **E** *Homewood Lodge*, T661507, homewood@kingussie.ndirect.co.uk. There's also **B&B** at **E** *Glengarry*, T661386, on East Terrace, and **E** *Greystones*, on Acres Rd, T661052, greystones@lineone.net.

There are several decent **hostels** in the area: *The Laird's Bothy*, T661334, is on the High St next to the *Tipsy Laird* pub; *Bothan Airigh Bunkhouse*, T661051, is at Insh, a few miles east of Ruthven Barracks on the B970; *Kirkbeag Hostel*, T651298, is in Kincraig, between Kingussie and Aviemore; and at Balachroick House in Glen Feshie, near Kincraig, is *Glen Feshie Hostel*, T651323. In Newtonmore, a few miles west of Kingussie on the A86, is the *Newtonmore Independent Hostel*, T673360, hostel.newtonmore@dial.pipex.com, and at Laggan Bridge, 8 miles further west on the A86, is the *Pottery Bunkhouse*, T01528-544231, attached to the *Caoldair Pottery*.

Eating The *Osprey Hotel* and *Scot House Hotel* both have very good restaurants, but the outstanding place to eat in this area is the award-winning *The Cross*, T661166, on Tweed Mill Brae, a private drive leading off Ardbroilach Rd. This restaurant with rooms (**L** for dinner, B&B) is expensive but well worth it. Open Mar-Nov & Christmas; closed Tue. The *Tipsy Laird* pub serves good meals and real ales and *La Cafetière* is a nice café.

Transport Kingussie is on the main Inverness to Perth/Glasgow/Edinburgh routes. All **Perth-Inverness trains** stop here and most *Citylink* **buses**. For rail enquiries, T0345-484950. There's also an infrequent school bus service run by *Highland Country Buses* between Kingussie, **Aviemore**, **Newtonmore** and **Dalwhinnie**.

Grantown-on-Spey

Phone code: 01479
Colour map 4, grid A3
Population: 3,250

This genteel Georgian holiday town is 15 miles northeast of Aviemore and attracts the more mature tourist by the coach-load. Everything here is geared towards fishing and anyone wishing to get kitted out in proper style should get themselves down to either *Mortimers* or *Ritchies* on the High Street. The **tourist office** is also here. ■ *T872773. Daily from Apr to Oct 0900-1800.*

As you'd expect in such a respectable place, there's a wide range of upmarket accommodation and a number of very good places to eat. The best places in town are all on Woodlands Terr: **B** Culdearn House, T872106, culdearn@globalnet.co.uk, **D** *Ardconnell House*, T872104, and **D-E** *The Ardlarig*, T873245, theardlarig@ sierra.globalnet.co.uk. They all offer excellent food, though *The Ardlarig* is the only one which caters for non-residents (booking essential). At **Dulnain Bridge**, a few miles southwest of town, is the elegant **C-D** *Auchendean Lodge Hotel*, T851347, and the handsome **B-C** *Muckrach Lodge Hotel & Restaurant*, T851257, muckrachlodge@ sol.co.uk, both of which have superb restaurants. There are lots of other very good **guesthouses** and **B&Bs** to choose from, as well as the *Speyside Backpackers*, T873514, an **independent hostel**, also known as *The Stop-Over*, at 16 The Square.

Sleeping & eating

There are several **buses** daily (Mon-Sat) between Grantown and **Aviemore** (35 minutes) and two or three buses daily, except Sun, to and from **Inverness** (1 hour 15 minutes).

Transport

The Highlands

Skye

11

Skye

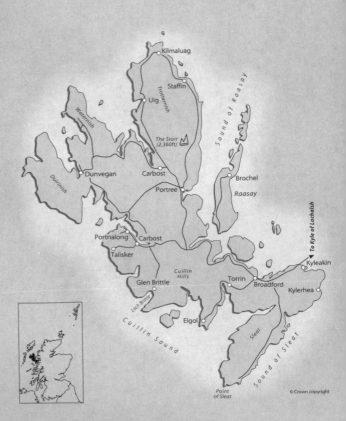

© Crown copyright

The Isle of Skye (An t-Eilean Sgitheanach), the most scenically spectacular of all the Scottish islands, gets its name from the Norse word for cloud (skuy) and it is commonly known as Eilean a Cheo (the Misty Isle), so it obviously rains a lot here. But when the rain and mist clear, the views make the heart soar.

Despite the unpredictable weather, tourism is an important part of the island's economy, and has been since Victorian times when climbers returned home extolling its beauty. In the busy summer months, the main roads become choked with coach tours and caravans, but the island is large enough to escape the worst of the crowds if you take the time to explore it.

The most popular destination is the **Cuillins**, the greatest concentration of peaks in Britain. They provide Scotland's best climbing and have become a mecca for all serious and experienced walkers. Equally spectacular are the bizarre rock formations of the **Trotternish** peninsula, in the north.

Trotternish is also inextricably linked with one of the most significant characters from the island's colourful past, Flora MacDonald, who is buried at **Kilmuir**. More of the island's fascinating history can be discovered at **Dunvegan Castle**, ancient seat of the Macleods and a major tourist landmark.

The island's main settlement, **Portree**, is a pleasant base from which to explore most of the island, though **Broadford** is ideally situated for the south of the island. If you really want to get away from it all, then you should head for the island of **Raasay**, just off the east coast, or the remote **Duirinish** and **Waternish** peninsulas.

Skye

Ins and outs

Getting there   The most popular, and quickest, route to Skye is across the new **bridge** (£5 toll), from Kyle of Lochalsh to Kyleakin. **Coach** services run to Skye from Glasgow and Inverness, with connections to all main cities in the UK (*Citylink*, T0990505050; *National Express*, T0990-808080). There is also a **train** service from Kyle of Lochalsh to Inverness (see page 448).

A more scenic approach is by **ferry** from Mallaig **to Armadale**, on the southern Sleat peninsula. The car and passenger ferry makes the 30-minute crossing 7 times daily each way (first one leaves Mallaig at 0900, Armadale at 0945, and the last one at 1815 and 1900) Mon-Sat from Mar to Oct, and Sun end of May to mid-Sept. The ferry is passenger only during the winter; for details contact Mallaig, T01687-462403, or Armadale, T01471-844248. Booking is recommended during the summer months, T0990- 650000. The one-way trip costs £2.60 per passenger and £14.85 per car. Trains to and from Fort William and Glasgow Queen St connect with some of the ferries (see page 443).

The best way to Skye is from Glenelg **to Kylerhea**, south of Kyleakin. The tiny private car ferry makes the 10-minute crossing when required, from Easter to Oct (Mon-Sat 0900-1800 till mid-May; Mon-Sat 0900-2000, Sun 1000-1800 from mid-May to end-Aug; Mon-Sat 0900-1800, Sun 1000-1800 end-Aug to end Oct). Cost per car with up to 4 passengers, £5.50; day return £9. T01599-511302.

Skye

© Crown copyright

Ferries leave from **Uig**, in the north of Skye, to Lochmaddy on North Uist (1 h 50 min) and to Tarbert on Harris (1 hr 45 min). To Lochmaddy on Mon, Wed and Fri at 0940 and 1820, Tue, Thur and Sat at 1400 and Sun at 0940 and 1400; for return times, see page 521. The return trip costs £13.80 per passenger and £65 per car. To Tarbert on Mon, Wed and Fri at 0515 and 1400, Tue, Thur and Sat at 0940 and 1820 (no service on Sun); for return times, see page 521. Return trip costs the same as for Lochmaddy. For more details, contact Uig, T01470-542219.

Getting around

Skye is the largest of the Hebridean islands at almost 50 miles long, and between 7 and 25 miles wide. It is possible to run up a hefty mileage as the extensive road system penetrates to all but the most remote corners of its many peninsulas. It is possible to get around by public transport midweek, with post buses supplementing the normal services, but as everywhere in the Highlands and Islands, buses are few and far between at weekends, especially Sun, and during the winter months. **Buses** run between Portree, Broadford, Uig (for ferries to the Western Isles), Kyleakin, Armadale (for ferries to Mallaig), Dunvegan and Carbost, and a more limited service runs from Broadford to Elgol and Portree to Glen Brittle. For full details, contact the local tourist office.

Information

Skye is well served by all types of accommodation: B&Bs, guesthouses, hostels, bunkhouses, campsites and some very fine hotels. During the peak summer months advance bookings are recommended. These can be made directly or through the island's **tourist offices**; in Portree (open all year), Broadford, Uig and Dunvegan (see relevant section).

Portree

Portree is the island's capital and main settlement. It's a fairly attractive little fishing port, built around a natural harbour, with a row of brightly-painted houses along the shorefront and the rest of the town rising steeply up to the central Somerled square.

Phone code: 01478
Colour map 1, grid C3

Ins and outs

Portree is ideally placed for trips to all parts of the island. **Buses** leave from the bus station in Somerled Square to Dunvegan, Uig, Broadford, Kyleakin, Armadale, the Talisker Distillery and Glenbrittle. There are also services to the mainland. The *Calmac* **ferry** office is on Park Rd, just off Somerled Square, T612075, F613090. The town is compact enough to get around easily on foot, though there is a regular town bus service for those needing to get into the centre from the outskirts.

Getting there & around
See 'Transport',
page 501 for details

History

The town was so named (*Port Righ* means 'King's Harbour' in Gaelic) to commemorate a visit by King James V in 1540. He came with his fleet to quell a long-standing and bitter feud between the island's main clans, the Macleods and the MacDonalds. The town's other notable royal occasion, in 1746, one of the most poignant moments in Scottish history, was when Prince Charlie bade farewell to Flora MacDonald in MacNab's hostelry, now the *Royal Hotel*.

Almost a quarter of a century later, the town was visited by Dr Johnson and Boswell, who dined in MacNab's, believing it to be 'the only inn on the island'. That may or may not have been the case in those days, but today Portree offers a wide range of places to eat, hotels, B&Bs, pubs, shops and banks to cater for the huge numbers of tourists that come here in the summer.

Gaelic culture

Outside of the Western Isles, Skye is the most important centre of Gaelic culture, with a large proportion of the island's population speaking the Gaelic language in everyday life. This in itself is remarkable given the significant drop in population during the Clearances and the continued undermining of the Gaelic culture ever since, especially through the State education system.

Today, as in other parts of the Hebrides, the native culture is again under threat, this time from the huge influx of 'white settlers' from the south, but there is also a

new-found pride and interest in the Gaelic language. This has been helped by the existence of the Gaelic college on Sleat, through Gaelic writers such as the late Sorley Maclean, a radical local newspaper (The West Highland Free Press), economic support from Highlands and Islands Enterprise and spiritual underpinning from the Sabbatarian Free Church. Gaelic is being taught again in schools and can be heard on television. The ancient heritage of the Highlands and Islands is fighting back and reasserting itself as a major European culture.

Sights

The Aros Experience, on Viewfield Road, half a mile from the town centre on the road to Broadford, is an exhibition and audio-visual display of the island's history and cultural heritage. The island's only theatre is housed here and features a varied programme of events, including drama, traditional music and movies (see 'Entertainment' below). There's also a restaurant serving good value snacks and main meals, a gift shop and a network of forest trails to explore. ■ *T613649. Daily 0900-2100 (off season 0900-1800), aros@demon.co.uk. £3.50, £2.50 child/concession.*

The **An Tuireann Arts Centre**, on Struan Road, hosts contemporary exhibitions of contemporary visual arts and crafts. It has a fine café (see 'Eating' below). ■ *T613306. norahcampbell@antuireann.demon.co.uk. Open Mon-Sat 1000- 1800. Free.*

If the weather's good, Portree offers many opportunities for a wide variety of outdoor activities. **Boat trips** can be made to the island of Rona, north of Raasay, with the *M.V. Brigadoon.* ■ *T613718, or ask for Peter Urquhart at the pier. Trips leave from the pier and cost from £5-15 per person. Full-day charters are also available for £75-150 (12 passengers).* For **horse riding**, *Portree Riding and Trekking Stables are a couple of miles from the town centre.* ■ *T612945. Follow the Struan Road (B885) for 2 miles, then bear right at the fork towards Peiness.* Four miles north of Portree, at Borve, on the road to Uig is the *Skye Riding Centre,* T01470-532439. **Mountain bikes** can be hired at *Island Cycles,* on The Green. ■ *T613121. Mon-Sat 1000-1700.*

The **tourist office** is just off Bridge St. They have bus timetables and a good selection of books and maps. ■ *T612137. Apr to mid-May Mon-Sat 0900-1730; mid-May to Aug Mon-Sat 0900-1900, Sun 1000-1700; Sept Mon-Sat 0900-1800; Oct Mon-Sat 0900-1730, Sun 1100-1600; Nov-Mar Mon-Fri 0900-1730, Sat 1100-1600.*

Essentials

Sleeping
■ *on map page 500*
Price codes:
see inside front cover

There are numerous hotels, guesthouses and B&Bs in Portree, but accommodation can be hard to find in the busy summer season. For a small fee the tourist office will book accommodation for you. Prices tend to be slightly higher in Portree than the rest of the island, though B&Bs on the outskirts of town are usually cheaper.

Things to do on Skye when it's raining

Just in case you didn't know, it can rain quite often on Skye and unless you're one of those hardy souls who's prepared to brave the elements, you'll need to know about the island's main indoor attractions. There are numerous opportunities to shelter from the rain, but most of them cost money, and many will leave you regretting it, so here's our list of top ten things to do. Details of opening times and admission prices are given under each relevant destination.

Beginning in **Portree**, there's the **Aros Experience**, which gives a good introduction to the island's history. North of Uig, at **Kilmuir** on the **Trotternish** peninsula, is the **Skye Museum of Island Life**, which pretty much does what it says on the sign. Northwest from Portree is **Dunvegan Castle**, home of the Clan Maclead and top of most visitors' itineraries. On the road to Dunvegan, is **Edinbane Pottery**, where you can buy pots of every shape and size and watch them being made.

Travelling south from Dunvegan, you'll reach the turn-off to the **Talisker Distillery**, the island's only whisky distillery, where you can sample the distinctive peaty taste. While you're there you can visit nearby **Carbostcraft Pottery**, in the village of **Carbost**, and indulge in some more gift buying. If you're in need of some refreshment after all that culture and shopping, you could do a lot worse than the bar at the **Sligachan Hotel**, which boasts an impressive array of whiskies and climbers' beards. In the southern peninsula of **Sleat**, near the Armadale ferry terminal, is the **Clan Donald Visitor Centre**, a visitor centre that is actually worth visiting. Nearby is one of the branches of **Skye Batiks**, with a huge selection of these 'new age' style fabrics in a range of original Celtic designs (the other branch is in Portree). And for that final drink before boarding the ferry to Mallaig, why not pop in to the cosy bar of the **Hotel Eilean Iarmain**, which also happens to serve wonderful food.

B *Rosedale Hotel*, Beaumont Cres, T613131. 23 rooms, Open May-Sept. Cosy little hotel by the harbour, converted from fishermen's houses. **C-B** *Bosville Hotel*, Bosville Terr, T612846, F613434, bosville@macleodhotels.co.uk. 18 rooms. Comfortable and stylish accommodation with friendly service. Boasts two award-winning restaurants (see 'Eating' below). **C-B** *Viewfield House Hotel*, on the road into Portree from the south, T612217, F613517. 9 rooms. Open mid-Apr to mid-Oct. Grand old country house full of antiques set in 20 acres of woodland garden. Log fire adds to the welcoming atmosphere, great value.

There are also several **guesthouses** on Bosville Terr and many **B&Bs** on Stormyhill Rd and the streets running off it. There are also lots of places to stay on Viewfield Rd heading south out of town. These include: **E** *Mrs MacAlpine*, 'Balloch', Viewfield Rd, T612093; **E** *Mrs Montgomery*, 'Foreland', Stormyhill Rd, T612752; and particularly good value is **E-F** *Mr & Mrs Mathieson*, 'Grenitote', 9 Martin Cres, T612808.

There are a couple of options for budget travellers. *Portree Independent Hostel*, Old Post Office, The Green, T613737. 60 beds. Right in the centre of town, with laundrette (£5 per wash) and email facilities (£5 per hour). *Portree Backpackers Hostel*, 6 Woodpark, Dunvegan Rd, T613641, F613643. 26 beds. There's a **campsite** at Torvaig, just outside the town, T612209, open Apr-Oct.

Expensive *Chandlery Seafood Restaurant*, next door to the *Bosville Hotel* (see under 'Sleeping' for details). Superb French/Scottish cuisine using local produce. Seafood a speciality. *Lower Deck Seafood Restaurant*, on the harbour front at the foot of Quay Brae, T613611. Freshest of seafood and a contender with the *Chandlery* for the

Eating

Skye

best food in town. Open daily Apr-Oct, 1100-2200. For a budget treat try the excellent fish and chips from their takeaway next door. *Skeabost House Hotel*, 4 miles north of Portree on the Dunvegan road, T01470-532202, F532454, skeabost@sol.co.uk. This peaceful country house in lovely grounds on the shores of Loch Snizort has a reputation for fine food using the best local produce.

Mid-range *Ben Tianavaig*, 5 Bosville Terr, T612152. Excellent vegetarian bistro. Seating is limited so you'll need to book. Open lunchtimes at weekends and Tue-Sun 1800-2130. *Bosville Restaurant*, in the *Bosville Hotel* (see 'Sleeping' above). Also recommended. They offer a lunchtime special (soup, sandwich and coffee for £5) which is great value.

Cheaper *Tuireann Café*, part of the arts centre (see 'Sights' above). Natural whole-foods and organic produce, home-made bread, cakes and pastries. Excellent quality and value. Open Mon-Tue 1000-1800, Wed-Sat 1000-2300, Sun 1200-1700 (in the summer). *Spicehut*, Bayfield Rd, T612681. Indian restaurant and takeaway. Open

Portree

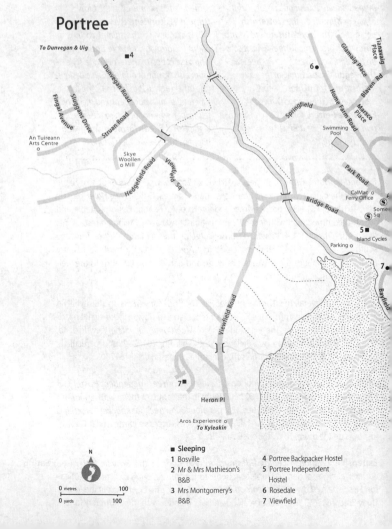

Skye

N

| 0 metres | 100 |
| 0 yards | 100 |

■ **Sleeping**

1 Bosville
2 Mr & Mrs Mathieson's B&B
3 Mrs Montgomery's B&B
4 Portree Backpacker Hostel
5 Portree Independent Hostel
6 Rosedale
7 Viewfield

daily 1200-1430 and 1700-2400. For cheap Chinese takeaway food, there's *Steve's Kitchen Takeaway*, on Bayfield Rd, opposite the library. For cheap bar lunches try the *Portree House*, Home Farm Rd, T613713 (1200-1545).

The town's nightlife is mainly confined to eating and drinking. The bar of the *Pier Hotel* by the harbour is a real fishermen's drinking den. Also popular is the *Royal Hotel*. If you fancy a wild Fri night ceilidh, try the *Portree Community Centre*, Camanachd Square, T613736. The *Aros Experience* (see 'Sights' above) has a theatre which shows drama, movies and live music. Call the box office for details of their monthly programme; T613750. The **swimming pool** is at Camanachd Square, T612655. **Entertainment**

The island's annual **Highland Games** are a one day event held in Portree in early **Aug**. **Festivals**

Most of the shops are within a few streets of Somerled Square. There's a *Safeway* supermarket diagonally opposite the *Bosville Hotel* and a wholefood store, *Jackson's Wholefoods*, at Park Pl, opposite the council offices. *Skye Batiks*, The Green (near the tourist office), T613331. Sells handmade 'batiks' (colourful cotton fabrics), which are pricey but unique souvenirs of Skye (see also under Armadale, page 514). A good pottery is *Carbostcraft Pottery*, on Bayfield Rd, which sells a huge variety of designs (they also have a shop near the Talisker Distillery, see page 509). A good place to buy woollens is *Over the Rainbow*, at the top of Quay Brae, T612555. Open 0900-2200 in the high season. Knitwear and tartan souvenirs can be found at the *Skye Woollen Mill*, Dunvegan Rd, T612889. **Shopping**

There are 4 **buses** daily Mon-Fri (2 on Sat) around the **Trotternish peninsula**, in each direction, via **Uig**. There are daily buses (4 Mon-Sat, 3 on Sun) to **Kyleakin**, and 3 buses daily Mon-Sat to **Armadale** (£8 return) via **Broadford** (£6 return). There are 2 daily buses to **Carbost** (for the Talisker Distillery) and **Fiskavaig** Mon-Fri (one on Sat), and 2 daily buses to **Glenbrittle** (in the summer only). There are 3 buses daily Mon-Fri to **Glendale** via **Dunvegan** (one on Sat), and 3 buses to **Waternish** via **Dunvegan** (Mon-Sat). There's a Scottish Citylink service from **Inverness** (3 Mon-Sat, 2 on Sun, 3 hrs, £10.50) and also from **Glasgow** via **Fort William** to **Kyleakin**, **Portree** and **Uig** 3-4 times daily (3 hrs from Fort William to Portree, £12). **Taxis**: *Ace Taxis*, T613600; *A2B Taxis*, T613456. **Transport**

To Torvaig Campsite & Staffin

To Start of Walk Around Portree

Fraser Crescent

Mill Park

Staffin Road

Budhmor Place

Stormyhill Road

Kitson Cres

moral d

dsor Cr

Martin Crescent

Coolin Drive

Mill Road

Scorrybreac

2

3

th St

Safeway Supermarket

Bosville Terr

Over the Rainbow

Beaumont Cres

Bank Street

Douglas Row

Quay St

kye tiks

The Lump

Pier

Skye

- **Eating**
1 Ben Tianavaig
2 Chandlery Seafood
3 Lower Deck Seafood
4 Pier Hotel
5 Royal Hotel
6 Portree House
7 Spicehut
8 Steve's Kitchen Takeaway

Directory **Banks** *Bank of Scotland* and *Clydesdale Bank* both on Somerled Square. *Royal Bank of Scotland* is on Bank St. All have ATMs. **Communications** Post office: at the top of Quay Brae. **Internet:** at the *Portree Independent Hostel* (see 'Sleeping' above). **Laundry** also at the *Portree Independent Hostel.*

The Trotternish peninsula

Colour map 1, grid C3

North from Portree is the 30-mile long Trotternish peninsula, sticking out like a giant thumb. The interior of the peninsula is a basaltic lava wilderness full of bizarre rock formations. A 20-mile long escarpment of sheer cliffs and towering pinnacles dominates the landscape. The best known of these strange formations, the **Quiraing** and **Old Man of Storr**, can be explored on foot. The A855 and A87 roads follow the coast around the peninsula and a spectacular minor road bisects the ridge from Staffin Bay to Uig. Trotternish is best explored with your own transport, but there a few daily buses covering the circular route from Portree (see Portree Transport).

Uig

Phone code: 01470
Colour map 1, grid C3

The A87 runs northwest from Portree to the tiny ferry port of Uig, dramatically set in a horseshoe bay and the departure point for ferries to **Tarbert** (Harris) and **Lochmaddy** (North Uist). Everything in the village revolves around the ferry timetables and the regular bus service to and from Portree coincides with the arrival and departure of the ferries (for ferry times, see page 496). *Scottish Citylink* runs a service to/from Inverness, Fort William and Glasgow.

The **tourist office** is inside the *CalMac* office at the ferry pier and will book accommodation anywhere on the island. ■ *T542404. 1 Apr-31 Oct, Mon-Sat 0845-1830, also Sun 0845-1400 Jul-Sept.*

Sights Just outside the village is the magical **Fairy Glen**. Turn right just before the *Uig Hotel* coming down the hill from the Portree direction. About a mile up the single track road you enter an eerie, mysterious world of perfect conical hills, some up to 60 feet high. It's almost inconceivable that these are natural formations and the inevitable mist only adds to the spooky strangeness of the place.

Sleeping **B** *Uig Hotel*, on the right of the road into the village from Portree, beside a white church and opposite a round tower, T542205, F542308, all@bestloved.com 17 rooms. Open Apr-Oct. Classy accommodation with great views across the bay, good food and a friendly island welcome. Offers a wide range of outdoor activities including nature walks, off-road Landrover tours, clay pigeon shooting, fly fishing and pony treks into the Fairy Glen. A cheaper options is **D** *The Ferry Inn*, T542242, F542377, stay@ferryinn.demon.co.uk. Amongst the good value **B&Bs** is **E** *Idrigill House*, T542398, F542447. The **F** *SYHA Youth Hostel*, T542211, is high above the port on the south side of the village and is open mid-Mar to Oct.

Eating The *Pub on the Pier* (open till 2300) serves cheap bar meals and the famous Cuillin ales are brewed at the nearby Skye Brewery (tours by appointment, T542477). You can also change foreign currency here. *The Ferry Inn* serves bar meals and there's also *The Norseman*, a self-service café next to the *CalMac* office (open Mon-Sat 0800-2200, Sun 1000-2200).

Flora MacDonald

In Kilmuir graveyard is the memorial which marks the grave of Flora MacDonald, one of the most famous characters in Skye's long history. The memorial bears Dr Johnson's fitting epitaph: "A name that will be mentioned in history, and if courage and fidelity be virtues, mentioned with honour".

It was Flora Macdonald who helped Bonnie Prince Charlie to escape capture following the Jacobite defeat at Culloden in 1746. Pursued by government troops, the prince fled from South Uist 'over the sea to Skye' aboard Flora's boat, disguised as an Irish servant girl by the name of Betty Burke.

He then made his way to Portree, where he bade his farewell to the young woman who had risked her own life to protect his.

When Flora's part in the prince's escape became known, she was immediately arrested and sent to the Tower of London. She was released a year later, married a Skye man and then emigrated to North Carolina where she spent the next 12 years of her life. They returned to her husband's house in Kingsburgh in 1786. Flora died in Skye in 1790, and it is said that her funeral was the largest ever witnessed in the Highlands.

Uig to Duntulm

A few miles north of Uig, on the A855, at **Linicro**, is *Whitewave Activities*, where you can try windsurfing and sea kayaking. There's also B&B and a café. T542414, activities@whiteact.demon.co.uk

Phone code: 01470

Further north, at **Kilmuir**, is **The Skye Museum of Island Life**. The group of thatched houses give a fascinating insight into the way of life of a crofting community at the end of the last century and is the most authentic of several such museums on Skye. ■ *Easter to Oct Mon-Sat 0930-1700. £2, child £1.*

Behind the museum, at the end of the road is **Flora MacDonald's Monument**, which marks the grave of Skye's most famous daughter, with her husband buried alongside. The rather austere memorial is inscribed with Dr Johnson's poignant tribute.

At the northwest tip of the peninsula, 15 minutes' drive from Uig, is **Duntulm Castle**, a fairy-tale ruin dramatically perched on a steep cliff. This 15th century structure, built on the site of an ancient Norse stronghold, became the chief Skye residence of the powerful MacDonalds and was the most imposing castle in the Hebrides. According to local legend, the castle was abandoned around 1732 when a nursemaid accidentally let the baby heir fall from a window onto the cliffs below.

Sleeping Near the castle is **C-D** *Duntulm Castle Hotel*, T552213, F552292. Open Mar-Nov. Friendly and homely with great views across the Minch to the Outer Hebrides. Idyllic and good value.

Duntulm to Portree

Beyond Duntulm the A855 heads across the tip of the peninsula to the east coast, where the famous bizarre rock scenery is found. Here, a few miles north of Staffin and 20 miles north of Portree, is **A** *Flodigarry Country House Hotel*, T01470-552203, F552301. Beautifully located at the foot of the mighty **Quiraing** and with stunning views across Staffin Bay, this is one of the great country house hotels, with a relaxing old-world atmosphere and excellent restaurant. Flora MacDonald's actual cottage is in the grounds and has been tastefully refurbished, giving the chance to stay in a place steeped in the island's history. The lively bar is a good place to enjoy a laugh and a jig.

For full details of the routes for the Quiraing and Old Man of Storr walks, see 'Walks on Skye', page 515.

Skye

Old Man of Storr

Those that can't afford such luxury can always opt for the more modest **F** *Dun Flodigarry Backpackers Hostel*, T/F552212. 66 beds. Laundry facilities, breakfast for £1.20 and only 100 yards from the bar of the *Flodigarry Country House Hotel*.

At the north end of **Staffin Bay**, a minor road cuts across the peninsula to Uig. This road is the access point for the **Quiraing**, the famous jumble of strangely-shaped hills and rocks that is one of the island's classic walks. Even if you don't attempt the walk, the road over the back of the Trotternish ridge from Uig makes a worthwhile detour.

A few miles south of Staffin Bay is **Kilt Rock**, an impressive sea cliff which gets its name from the vertical columnar basalt strata overlying horizontal ones beneath. A rather tenuous comparison perhaps, but the cliffs south of Staffin are particularly spectacular, as are the **Lealt Falls**, a torrent of mountain water at the head of a gorge, a few miles south of Kilt Rock. The falls are signposted by the road, so all you have to do is park the car and peer over.

There's a **campsite** south of Staffin Bay, T562213, open mid-April-end September. A good place for food is the *Oystercatcher Restaurant* in the village of Staffin, T562384, closed Sunday. At **Culnacnoc**, just north of the Lealt Falls, is **D** *Glenview Inn and Restaurant*, T562248, F562211. Five rooms. Cosy and relaxed accommodation with a very fine restaurant.

A few miles further south, and 7 miles north of Portree, is a car park which is the starting point for another of Skye's famous walks; up to the **Old Man of Storr**, the distinctive pinnacle of rock which has detached itself from the cliffs of the Storr behind.

Dunvegan, Waternish and Duirinish

Phone code: 01470 In the northwest of Skye the peninsulas of Waternish (or Vaternish) and Duirinish point out into the Minch towards the Western Isles. The larger Duirinish peninsula holds more interest for the visitor, featuring the beautiful green valley of **Glendale**, an area brimming with history, the dramatic walk to **Neist Point** and **Dunvegan Castle**, Skye's most famous landmark.

Edinbane The turn-off to this much-visited part of the island is 4 miles northwest of Portree. The A850 swings west towards Dunvegan, by-passing the tiny village

Clan warfare

Violent conflict between neighbouring clan chiefs was so commonplace on Skye and the rest of the Western Highlands that it was almost accepted as part of the very fabric of society. One particular gruesome example took place on Eigg, in 1577. The Macleod's had taken refuge in a cave but their presence was discovered by the MacDonalds, who piled brushwood at the entrance and set fire to it, burning alive the 395 people sheltering inside, almost the entire population of the island. Revenge came the following year, at Trumpan church in Ardmore Bay. The Macleods landed under cover of the early morning fog and set light to the church, burning the congregation inside.

of Edinbane. There's a campsite, two hotels, several B&Bs, petrol station, Land Rover tours with *Skyetrak Safari* , T582224, and the renowned *Edinbane Pottery* workshop and showroom, which is a must for souvenir hunters. ■ *T582234. Daily Easter-Oct 0900-1800.*

Waternish Peninsula

The A850 continues west and those with their own transport and time on their hands might wish to make an interesting little detour at the **Fairy Bridge**, where the B886 runs north to **Trumpan**, near the tip of the Waternish peninsula. If the weather's good (and it is, occasionally) this is the best place to watch the sun set, in a blaze of red over the Outer Hebrides. If there's no sunset, then you could always visit *Skyeskins*, the country's only traditional exhibition tannery, at Loch Bay, T592237, or pop into the island's oldest pub, at **Stein**. Either way, you should finish off the day with a meal at the wonderful *Lochbay Seafood*, T592235 for reservations, where you can almost see your dinner being landed. Mid-range prices, open April-October for lunch and till 2030 (closed Sat).

Colour map 1, grid C2/3

The ruined church at Trumpan, at the end of the road, has some grisly skeletons in its cupboard (see 'Clan Warfare' box). In the graveyard is the 'trial stone'. A hole in the stone was used to test whether or not an accused person was telling the truth. If they could quickly find the hole and stick their arm through it while blindfolded, they were found innocent, but if not, they were guilty. The church is also the starting point for the strenuous 8-mile **walk** out to **Waternish point** and back.

Skye

Dunvegan

A few miles further on from the turn-off to Waternish is the little village of Dunvegan. Just to the north of the village is proud Dunvegan Castle, the island's most important tourist attraction. This is the home of the chiefs of the Clan Macleod who have lived here for over seven centuries, making it the oldest inhabited castle in Britain. The present structure dates from the 15th and 16th centuries, and though the Victorian restoration has left it looking more like a baronial house, a look inside reveals its true age. Among the many relics on display is Rory Mor's horn, a huge drinking vessel which the chief's heir must drain 'without setting down or falling down', when filled with claret (about one and a half bottles). There's also a lock of Bonnie Prince Charlie's hair, clipped from his head by Flora MacDonald as a keepsake, but pride of place goes to the **Fairy Flag**. The flag has been dated to between the fourth and seventh centuries and is made of Middle Eastern silk. It is said to have been given to the clan chief by a fairy and has the power to ensure victory in battle for

Dunvegan Castle
Colour map 1, grid C2

the clan, on three occasions. It has so far been used twice. The lovely castle gardens lead down to the lochside jetty, from where you can take seal-spotting cruise (£8, £6 concession) or a boat trip around the loch (£3.80/£2.50). There's also a busy restaurant and gift shop by the castle gates. ■ *Mid-Mar-Oct daily 1000-1730, £5 (£4 concession). A bus leaves Portree at 1000, arrives at the castle at 1048 and returns at 1252.*

In the village itself is the **Giant Angus MacAskill Museum**, housed in thatched whitewashed cottage, which relates the life story of the tallest ever Scotsman, Angus MacAskill, who grew to 7ft and 9in tall. He emigrated to Novia Scotia and toured the United States with the midget General Tom Thumb, who is said to have danced on his outstretched hand. More interesting than the museum, though, are the stories of its owner, Peter MacAskill, in particular the one about the replica coffin, which is worth the admission fee alone. Peter is a descendent of Angus and also runs the museum at Colbost (see below). ■ *T521296. Daily 0930-1830, £1.*

Sleeping & eating There are numerous places to stay in and around Dunvegan, and the **tourist office** in the village will arrange accommodation for you, T521581. There are several hotels including the very comfortable **C** *Atholl House Hotel*, T521219, F521481, reservations@athollhotel.demon.co.uk. A recommended guesthouse is **D** *Roskhill House*, 3 miles south of Dunvegan Castle on the A863, T521317, F521761, stay@roskhill. demon.co.uk. 5 cosy rooms, peaceful setting, great food. Just beyond Roskhill is a turning south off the A863 to **B** *Harlosh House Hotel*, T/F521367, harlosh.house@virgin.net. 6 rooms. Open Easter to mid-Oct. Cosy, comfortable, great views and a reputation for superb food (evenings only). There are also over a dozen **B&Bs**, mostly in the **E** price range, including the beautifully situated *Silverdale*, at Skinidin, just before Colbost, T/F521251, open Mar-Nov.

The Duirinish peninsula

Colour map 1, grid C2 West of Dunvegan is the Duirinish peninsula. The northern half is populated along the western shores of **Loch Dunvegan** and in the beautiful and green **Glendale**, an area brimming with history but with hardly an island family left. Glendale is now dubbed 'Little England', owing to the large number of incoming settlers from the south. The area is famed throughout the Highlands and Islands, for it was here in 1882 that local crofters, spurred on by the 'Battle of the Braes' (see page 512), resisted the cruel and petty tyranny of their estate manager. The authorities sent a gunboat to deal with the uprising and arrested the ringleaders, some of whom were imprisoned in Edinburgh and became known as 'the Glendale Martyrs'. This episode sparked a radical movement throughout the Highlands and led to the Crofter's Holdings Act of 1886 which gave the crofters a more secure tenure and fair rent (see 'History', page 665). The uninhabited southern half of the peninsula is dominated by the flat-topped hills, Healabhal Bheag (1,601ft) and Healabhal Mhor (1,538ft), known as **Macleod's Tables**.

The **Glendale Visitor Route** is sign posted from just before Dunvegan village and leads westwards along the shores of the loch and across the peninsula. There are several interesting little sights along the way. Those interested in finding out more about crofting on the island should head for **Colbost Croft Museum**, housed in a restored 'black house' and with a peat fire burning and an illicit still out the back. ■ *T521296. Daily 1000-1830. £1, children free. The museum is 4 miles from Dunvegan on the B884 to Glendale.* A little further on is *Skye Silver*, where you can buy silver jewellery in traditional Celtic designs. ■ *T511263, www.SkyeSilver.com. Daily 1000-1800.* Further north is the

Borreraig Park Exhibition Croft, which features a huge display of farm equipment from days gone by. ■ *Daily 0900-1800. £1.50.*

At **Borreraig** is the **MacCrimmon Piping Heritage Centre**, a fascinating place which is more of a shrine to the famous MacCrimmons, who were hereditary pipers to the Macleod Chiefs and the first composers, players and teachers of *piobaireachd* (pibroch), which can be heard in the museum (there's an annual recital at Dunvegan Castle in early August). Opposite are the ruins of the ancient piping college. ■ *T511369. Easter to late May daily (except Mon) 1100-1730; late May to end Aug daily 1100-1730; Sept to early Oct daily (except Mon) 1100-1730. £1.50.* Moving from the sublime to the ridiculous, in the village of **Glendale** is a **Toy Museum**, which should appeal to kids of all ages. ■ *T511240. Mon-Sat 1000-1800. £2.*

The B884 continues west, then a road turns off left for Waterstein. At the end of this road (just over 2 miles) is a car park which is the starting point for the walk out to the lighthouse at **Neist Point**, the most westerly point on Skye and one of the most pleasant walks on the island. It's about 1½ miles there and back and well worth the effort. The path is easy to follow and the views of the sea cliffs are wonderful. There are lots of nesting seabirds around and you might even spot whales offshore. The **lighthouse**, built in 1909, is now unmanned, and you can stay in one of the self-catering cottages, T/F511200. You can also join a guided walk to the lighthouse with a local naturalist. ■ *T511265. Walks leave from the road-end at 1400, 1515 and 1630 most days.* The graveyard at the lighthouse looks real enough but take a closer look and you'll see the names of the film crew who worked on the superb 1997 film, *Breaking the Waves*.

Eating

Next to the Colbost Croft Museum is *The Three Chimneys* (T01470-511258), considered by many to be the best restaurant in the north of Scotland and, judging by the numerous awards they've won, that judgement can't be far wrong. Local seafood, meat, veg and dairy produce and a great wine list. Open daily 1230-1430 (except Sun) and 1830-2130. They also now have accommodation a few yards away at *The House Over-By* (6 rooms).

Transport

There are 3 **buses** daily (Mon-Fri) from Glendale to and from Portree via Dunvegan (see above), and 1 bus on Sat and a daily bus from Dunvegan to Glendale (not Sun).

The Cuillins and Minginish

Colour map 3, grid A3/4

The district of Minginish is the wildest and least populated part of the island but for many it is the greatest attraction, for this is where the Cuillins are to be found. This hugely impressive mountain range, often shrouded in rain or cloud, is the spiritual heartland of the island, and when it's clear their heart-aching grandeur can be appreciated from every other peninsula on Skye.

OS Landranger No 32
OS Outdoor Leisure No 8

Though officially called the Cuillin 'Hills', these are the most untamed mountains in Britain. The magnificent scenery and vast range of walks and scrambles have attracted climbers and walkers for centuries but have also claimed many lives. It cannot be stressed too strongly that the Cuillins are the most dangerous mountains in Britain and only for experienced climbers (for more on safety, see page 56).

There are three routes into the Cuillins: from the *Sligachan Hotel* (see below); from Glen Brittle (see below); and from Elgol (see below). The eastern part of the range is known as the **Red Cuillins**. Their smoother, conical granite peaks contrast sharply with the older, darker gabbro of the jagged-edged

Black Cuillins to the west. The latter are particularly suitable for rock climbing and best approached from Glen Brittle, while the former are accessed from the *Sligachan Hotel*. There are 20 'Munros' (mountains over 3,000ft in height) in the Cuillins, with the highest being Sgurr Alasdair, at 3,251ft. Though the sheer majesty of the mountains can only be appreciated at close quarters by the climber, there are impressive views from Elgol, from the road into Glen Brittle and, more distantly, from the west coast of Sleat.

Glen Sligachan is one of the most popular routes into the Cuillin range and the main access point for the more forgiving Red Cuillins, the walk to **Loch Coruisk**, or the ascent of **Marsco**. Every year there's a hill race up nearby **Glamaig**, which was climbed in 55 minutes (up and down) in 1899 by a Gurkha soldier, in bare feet! The legendary rallying point for climbers who come to Skye for the Cuillins is C *Sligachan Hotel*, 7 miles south of Portree, where the A87 Kyleakin-Portree road meets the A863 to Dunvegan, T01471-8650204, F650207. The hotel's *Seamus* bar stocks an impressive selection of malts and also serves the island's real ales and meals. The **campsite** opposite is the most popular place to stay in the area.

Guides & equipment

The following guides have all been recommended. *Skye Highs*, Mike Lates, 3 Luib, Broadford, T01471-822116. *Cuillin Guides*, Gerry Achroyd, Stac Lee, Glen Brittle, T01478-640289. *Hugh Evans*, 4d Wentworth St, Portree, T01478-612682. *Richard MacGuire*, 4 Matheson Place, Portree, T01478-613180. *Colin Threlfall*, at *Outdoor Sports* (see below).

Two good shops for mountain gear are *Cioch Direct*, 4 Ullinish, Struan, T01470-572307, and *Outdoor Sports*, on Bridge Road (next to *Skye Batiks*), Portree.

Elgol

Phone code: 01471
Colour map 3, grid A4

One of the most rewarding drives on Skye is the 14-mile single-track road from Broadford to Elgol (Ealaghol), a tiny settlement near the tip of the Strathaird peninsula, from where you can enjoy the classic view of the Cuillins from across Loch Scavaig and of the islands of Soay, Rum and Canna. It was from here, on 4 July 1746, that the Young Pretender finally left the Hebrides. Before leaving, he was given a farewell banquet by the MacKinnons in what is now called **Prince Charlie's Cave**. There's also the added attraction of a dramatic boat trip to the mouth of **Loch Coruisk**, in the heart of the Black Cuillin. The glacial sea loch, romanticized by Walter Scott and painted by Turner, is over two miles long but only a few hundred yards wide, closed in by the sheer cliffs on either side and overshadowed by the towering mountains of black basalt and gabbro. Elgol is also the starting point for the walk to Camasunary (see 'Walks on Skye', page 516). The road to Elgol also gives great views of Bla Bheinn (pronounced *Blaven*), best seen from Torrin, at the head of Loch Slapin.

■ *For details of sailing times on the Bella Jane, T866244, to book T0800-7313089 (freephone). Return boat trips take 3 hours, including about 1½ hours ashore, and cost £12.50, £6 child. You should be able to see seals and porpoises en route. There's also a one-way trip for experienced walkers/climbers who wish to make the return journey on foot or to explore the Cuillins (costs £9). There are also trips on the Nicola, T866236.*

Sleeping & transport

There are several B&Bs in Elgol, but a more attractive option is **E** *Rowan Cottage*, T/F866287; open Apr-Nov, a mile east at Glasnakille. The only public transport is the *Postbus* from Broadford, which runs twice Mon-Sat and once on Sun and takes 2 hrs.

Skye

Glen Brittle

Six miles along the A863 to Dunvegan from Sligachan is a turning left to Portnalong, Carbost and the Talisker Distillery (B8009), which soon leads to the entrance to Glen Brittle. The road down Glen Brittle affords great views of the western side of the imposing Black Cuillins, until it ends at the campsite and shore at the foot of the glen.

Phone code: 01478
Colour map 3, grid A3

From Glen Brittle there are numerous paths leading up to the corries of the Black Cuillins. There are many alternative options for those wishing to continue up to upper corries or to the Main Ridge. One of the finest of the Cuillin corries is **Coire Lagan**. This walk starts from the beach at Glen Brittle village and takes you up to the lochan in the upper coire, with Sgurr Alasdair, the most difficult of the Munros, towering overhead. A fine Cuillin sampler is the short walk to the spectacular **Eas Mor** waterfall.

Apart from the campsite by the shore, T640404, the only accommodation is at the SYHA Hostel, T640278, in the village. It's open mid-Mar to end of Oct, has 39 beds and costs £8 per night.

Sleeping

There are two daily **buses** from Portree to Glen Brittle Mon-Sat during the summer only. Otherwise, take the Portree-Carbost-Fiscavaig bus, which leaves twice Mon-Fri and once on Sat, and get off at the turn-off, then walk the remaining 7 miles, or hitch, though it can be slow.

Transport

Talisker

A recommended trip for whisky drinkers, or if it's raining, is to the **Talisker Distillery**, at **Carbost** on the shores of Loch Harport, on the B8009 (not in the village of Talisker itself, which is on the west coast). This is Skye's only whisky distillery and produces a very smoky, peaty single malt. The informative tours last around 20-30 minutes and begin with a complimentary dram. ■ *T640314, F640401, large groups need to book in advance. Apr-Jun Mon-Fri 0900-1630; Jul-Sept Mon-Sat 0900-1630; Oct Mon-Fri 0900-1630; Nov-Mar Mon-Fri 1400-1630. £3 (includes discount voucher), .*

Phone code: 01478
Colour map 3, grid A3

Near the distillery is *Carbostcraft Pottery* , which produces a wide range of traditional and original pottery, including the famous 'torn pots'. ■ *T640259. Mon-Sat 0900-1700 from Feb-Dec (also Sun in summer). They also have a shop in Portree.*

There are a few places to stay in and around **Carbost**. Further west, in the village of **Talisker**, is **C** *Talisker House*, T640245, F640214, jon_and_ros.wathen@virgin.net 4 rooms. This excellent guesthouse makes an ideal retreat from the summer hordes and serves fine food. North of Carbost, near **Portnalong**, are two hostels. **F** *Croft Bunkhouse & Bothies*, T/F640254, pete@ skyehostel.free-online.co.uk. Sleeps 26. Also room for camping, transport from Sligachan or Portree, rents mountain bikes, pub and shop nearby. *Skyewalker Independent Hostel*, T640250, F640420, skyewalker@ easynet.co.uk. In a converted school beyond Portnalong on the road to Fiscavaig. 32 beds.

Sleeping & transport

There's a regular bus service (weekdays only) from Portree and Sligachan to Portnalong, T01470-532240.

Skye

Kyleakin to Portree

Kyleakin and Kylerhea

Phone code: 01599
Colour map 3, grid A5

The opening of the Skye Bridge, linking the island with the Kyle of Lochalsh (see page 448), has turned the former ferry terminal of Kyleakin (Caol Acain) into something of a backwater, as well as infuriating the locals with its £5 per car toll. The absence of road traffic, though, makes it a quiet place to stay and it's now a favourite with backpackers, judging by the number of hostels. There's precious little to do here, other than look at the small ruin of **Castle Moil**, but you could take one of the seal cruises organized by *Castle Moil Seal Cruises*, which leave from the ferry pier, taking you to see the seal colony on **Eilean Mahl**. ■ *T544235. Cruises last 1¼ hours and cost £5.50.*

Sleeping   The large, modern *SYHA Hostel*, T534585) is a few hundred yards from the pier, is open all year. Nearby is the *Skye Backpackers Hostel*, T/F534510, open all year, and offers breakfast for £1.40. There's also the *Dun Caan Hostel*, T534087, T/F534795, near the old ferry quay, which is open all year and also hires bikes for £5 per day. There are also several **B&Bs**.

Eating   The backpacker's pub, *Saucy Mary's* serves cheap meals, but the best place to eat is *The Crofter's Kitchen*, outside the village on the road to Broadford, T534134. It serves 3-course meals and snacks (mid-range). Open Mon-Sat 1000-2100, Sun 1230-2100.

Transport   There are **buses** from Kyleakin to **Portree** via Broadford (4 daily), to **Armadale** and **Ardvasar** via Broadford (3 daily Mon-Sat) and half hourly to **Kyle** via the Skye Bridge. *Kyleakin Private Hire* (T534452) run a **taxi** service and guided tours of the island.

Kylerhea   About four miles out of Kyleakin a road turns left off the A87 and heads southeast to Kylerhea (pronounced Kile-ray). The bridge may be the most convenient route to Skye but the best way to cross is on the small car and passenger ferry that makes the 10-minute crossing to Kylerhea from Glenelg (see page 446). For full details of times and prices, see page 496. Near Kylerhea is the Forestry Commission **Otter Haven**. An hour long nature trail takes you to an observation hide where you can look out for these elusive creatures. ■ *T01320-366322. Daily 0900 till one hour before dusk. Free.*

Broadford

Phone code: 01471
Colour map 3, grid A4

Eight miles west of Kyleakin is Broadford (An t-Ath Leathann), Skye's second largest village, which basically consists of a mile-long main street strung out along a wide bay. Broadford may be low on charm but it's high on tourist facilities, with plenty accommodation and places to eat, a tourist office, garage, supermarket and bank (with ATM). There are also a few interesting, and unusual, things to do when it rains, which is always a bonus. The **tourist office** is by the Esso petrol station. ■ *T822361. Apr-Oct Mon-Sat 0930-1730, Mon-Sat 0900-1900, Sun 1000-1700 in Jul/Aug.*

Sights   One of the most incongruous attractions on the island, or elsewhere in the Highlands, is the **Skye Serpentarium**, where you can see, and touch, all kinds of snakes, lizards and other reptiles. ■ *T822209/822533. Easter-Oct, Mon-Sat 1000-1700 (also Sun in Jul/Aug). £2.50, 1.50 concession.* More familiar but also interesting is the **International Otter Survival Fund** visitor centre. ■ *Daily*

The Battle of the Braes

One of the most significant incidents in the island's history took place in April, 1882, when a group of around 100 local crofters and their families fought a pitched battle against a force of 60 police sent by the government from Glasgow. The 'Battle of the Braes', as it became known, was caused, like many other such uprisings throughout the Highlands and Islands (see page 506), by threatened evictions. The local crofters were so incensed by the injustice of the eviction notices served on them that they destroyed the offending documents, leading the government to dispatch its police force. The defeat of the government forces of law and order by a bunch of men, women and children with sticks and stones, is often described as the last battle fought on British soil, and led eventually to the setting up of a Royal Commission to look into the crofters' grievances.

Mar-Oct 0930-1700. £1.50. At the north end of the village, near the post office, is **World of Wood**, where you can find out everything you ever wanted to know about wood and buy all sorts of souvenirs.

When the weather's clear you can take a boat trip to the island of **Pabay** with *Family's Pride II.* ■ *T822037. Trips last 1½ hours, cost £9 and leave daily from the main pier.*

Sleeping There are lots of B&Bs and a couple of hotels in Broadford, so finding a room shouldn't be a problem, except maybe in the peak months. Two notable places are **E** *Lime Stone Cottage*, 4 Lime Park (behind the Serpentarium), T822142, which is full of rustic charm, and **E** *Ptarmigan*, overlooking the bay, T822744, F822745. The *SYHA Hostel* is by the new pier, T822422. Open all year. A mile or so south of the village, at Lower Breakish, off the A87 to Kyleakin, is the *Fossil Bothy*, T822644 (weekdays), T822297, which has 8 beds and charges £7.50, open Easter-Oct, book in advance.

Eating The best place to eat is the *Seagull Restaurant*, at Breakish, south of Broadford on the main road to Kyleakin, T822001. It serves excellent local food with a European twist. Mid-range. For cheap to mid-range bar meals, try the *Claymore Bar-Restaurant*, at the south end of the village, T822333.

Transport Daily *Citylink* **buses** run to and from **Portree**, **Inverness** and **Fort William**. *Waterloo* buses run daily to and from Kyleakin, Portree (£6 return) and Armadale/Ardvasar. For **car hire** try *Sutherlands* at the Esso Garage, T822225, F822759, they charge from £30 per day. You can rent **mountain bikes** from *Fairwinds Bicycle Hire*, just past the Broadford Hotel, T822270, for £7 per day.

Directory *Bank of Scotland* with ATM by the shops opposite the road to the new pier. Next to the Esso station is a Co-op **supermarket**, and there's a **laundrette** in the petrol station shop (open 24 hrs).

Broadford to Portree

The road north to Portree runs between the fringes of the Red Cuillins and the coast, giving good views across to the **Isle of Scalpay**. The road then turns west along the shores of Loch Ainort to the turn-off for the **Luib Folk Museum**, another of Peter MacAskill's island museum's. The restored croft house has a smoky atmosphere and has old newspaper cuttings telling of the 'Battle of the Braes' and the 'Glendale Martyrs'. ■ *Daily 0900-1800. £1.*

Colour map 3, grid A4
Colour map 1, grid C3

The road runs north to **Sconser**, departure point for the ferry to Raasay (see below), then runs around Loch Sligachan and heads north to Portree. On the opposite side of the loch from Sconser are the crofting communities known as **The Braes**, who successfully opposed their landlords' eviction notices and brought the crofters' cause to the public's attention.

Isle of Raasay

Phone code: 01478
Colour map 1, grid C3/4

OS Landranger No 24

The lush and beautiful island of Raasay lies only a few miles off the east coast of Skye yet remains well and truly off the tourist trail. Its hilly terrain and superb cliff scenery offer numerous walking opportunities and the views from the highest point, **Dun Caan** (1,456ft), with the Cuillins on one side and Torridon on the other, are, quite simply, beyond compare. The walk to the distinctive flat-topped summit of this extinct volcano, via an old iron mine, is relatively straightforward and one of the most rewarding anywhere in the islands. So much so, in fact, that Boswell was inspired to dance a Highland jig on reaching the top, in 1773. Another excellent walk starts from North Fearns, at the end of a road running east from **Inverarish**, to the deserted township of **Hallaig**, down the side of Beinn na Leac and back to North Fearns. The circular route is 5 miles long. The island is a nature conservancy, and you may see seals, eagles and otters.

Raasay was for much of its history the property of the Macleods of Lewis, whose chief residence was the ruined **Brochel Castle**, before moving to **Clachan**, where **Raasay House** is now located (see below). The original Raasay House was torched by government troops after Culloden, along with all the island's houses and its boats, as punishment for the Macleods giving refuge to Bonnie Prince Charlie. After the Macleods sold the island, in 1843, the Clearances began in earnest and Raasay suffered a long period of emigration, depopulation and poverty. It is not surprising, then, that the island's most famous son, the great poet **Sorley Maclean**, writes so passionately about this lost society. Born in Oskaig in 1911, he writes in his native Gaelic, as well as in English, and is highly regarded internationally. Raasay's population now numbers around 150 and the island is a bastion of the Free Church, whose strict Sabbatarian beliefs should be respected by visitors.

Those who make it to the north of the island may wish to note that the two miles of road linking **Brochel** to **Arnish** was the work of one man, Calum Macleod. He decided to build the road himself after the council turned down his requests for proper access to his home. He spent between 10 and 15 years building it with the aid of a pick, a shovel and a wheelbarrow and a road-making manual which cost him three shillings. He died in 1988, soon after its completion, and to this day it is known as 'Calum's Road'.

Sleeping The main settlement on the island is **Inverarish**, a 15-min walk from the ferry dock. Half a mile further on is the *Raasay Outdoor Centre*, housed in the huge Georgian mansion that was Raasay House, which runs many and various adventure courses, from climbing to windsurfing, as well as offering basic accommodation from Mar to mid-Oct and a **campsite**, T660266. Nearby are **D** *Isle of Raasay Hotel*, T/F660222, and **E** *Churchton House*, T660260, both of which are open all year.

Further north along the coast, at **Oskaig**, B&B is available at **E** *Mrs Mackay*, T660207, including dinner. A rough track leads up a steep hill from the tiny village to the island's *SYHA Hostel*, T660240, open mid-Mar to end-Oct.

Transport The *CalMac* car and passenger ferry runs from Sconser daily Mon-Sat every hour from 0830 till 1800 (2130 in Jul/Aug). Last return is at 1735 (2100 in Jul/Aug). It takes 15 mins and costs £3.65 per person return, plus £15.70 per car and £1 per bicycle (so leave the car behind!).

The Sleat peninsula

East of Broadford is the turn-off to peninsula of Sleat (pronouned 'slate'), a part of the island so uncharacteristically green and fertile that it's known as 'The Garden of Skye'. Sleat is another entry point to the island. Ferries cross from Mallaig on the mainland to **Armadale** on the southeastern shore of the peninsula. (For details of ferry crossings, see page 496).

Phone code: 01471
Colour map 3, grid A4

While the rest of the island is the preserve of the Macleods, Sleat is **MacDonald country**. The MacDonalds of Sleat are one of the major surviving branches of Clan Donald and have the right to use the title Lord MacDonald (but not Lord of the Isles, which is now used by the heir to the throne).

The clan seat is Armadale Castle, which now houses the Clan Donald Visitor Centre (see below), but the home of the present Lord MacDonald is *Kinloch Lodge*, T833214, F833277, kinloch@dial.pipex.com, at the head of **Loch na Dal**. Lord and Lady MacDonald's family home is also an award-winning restaurant, offering the rare chance to enjoy superb food in the grandest of settings. The track that leads to the 19th century Sporting Lodge turns off the A851 about 8 miles south of Broadford. Lady Claire MacDonald is one of the best known cooks in Scotland and author of several cookbooks, and if you do decide to treat yourself make sure you leave enough room for their exquisite puddings. The 5 course fixed menu is in our expensive range, but well worth it. Accommodation (in our **L** range) is also available in 10 en suite rooms. Open Mar-Nov.

Eating & sleeping

A little further on is **B** *Duisdale Hotel*, T833202, F833404, marie@duisdalehotel.demon.co.uk. 19 rooms (two with four poster beds). Country house hotel set in lovely grounds with great views across the Sound of Sleat. The restaurant serves good traditional Scottish cooking, and a 5-course meal is in our expensive range.

South of Duisdale is the signed turning for Isle Ornsay, or**Eilean Iarmain** (pronounced eelan yarman) in Gaelic, a very beautiful place in a small rocky bay overlooking the tidal Isle of Ornsay with the mountains of Knoydart in the background. This was once Skye's main fishing port and the neat whitewashed cottages and tiny harbour are still there. It is also largely Gaelic-speaking, thanks mainly to the efforts of its landlord, Sir Iain Noble, who owns the hotel and his own local Gaelic whisky company as well as the northern half of the peninsula, which is known as *Fearan Eilean Iarmain*.

Isle Ornsay

Skye

L *Hotel Eilean Iarmain*, T833332, F833275. 12 rooms. Award-winning Victorian hotel full of charm and old-world character, with wonderful views. It is utterly lovely and romantic and an absolute must if you're in the area and can afford it. Award-winning restaurant features local shellfish landed only yards away. A cheaper option is to eat in the cosy **bar** next door, which serves pub grub of an impossibly high standard in a more informal atmosphere. The hotel also offers winter shooting on the local estate and you can enjoy a tasting of the local whisky, T833266.

A few miles further on is a turn-off to the left to the villages of **Ord**, **Tokavaig** and **Tarskavaig**, on the west coast of the peninsula and from where, on a clear day, the views across to the Cuillins. Near Tokavaig is the ruin of **Dunsgaith Castle**, home of the MacDonalds of Sleat until the 17th century. Tarskavaig is a typical crofting township. In the early 19th century the MacDonalds wanted the more fertile glens inland for their sheep farms and so evicted the people to coastal townships like Tarskavaig. Just beyond the turn-off to Ord are the remains of **Knock Castle**, yet another MacDonald stronghold.

West Sleat

Nearby, in Toravaig House, is the *Hairy Coo Backpacker Hotel*, T833231, F833393, stotty@hairycooskye.freeserve.co.uk. 30 beds, open all year, breakfast on request, also serves bar meals. A few miles further on, at Kilmore, is the *Sleat Independent Hostel*, T844440, F844272. Newly-refurbished with all facilities, 24 beds, open all year, free transport to and from Armadale Pier.

At **Ostaig** is the Gaelic College, *Sabhal Mor Ostaig*, where all subjects are taught in Gaelic, including full-time courses in business studies and media, as well as short courses in Gaelic music and culture during the summer months, T844373. The bookshop has a good selection of books and tapes for those wishing to learn the language. The college was founded by Sir Iain Noble (see above). Ostaig is also the beginning or end (depending on which direction you're heading) of the detour to Tarskavaig, Tokavaig and Ord.

Just before the ferry pier at Armadale is the **Clan Donald Visitor Centre**, housed in Armadale Castle which was built in 1815 as the main residence of the MacDonalds of Sleat. Most of the castle is now a roofless ruin but the servants' quarters now contain an excellent exhibition and accompanying video explaining the history of the Lordship of the Isles. The Clan Donald Lords of the Isles took over from their Norse predecessors in ruling the Hebrides, until their power was broken in 1493. The former stables at the entrance comprise offices, a restaurant and bookshop, while the estate manager's house has been converted to accommodate an extensive library and archives. The castle is surrounded by 40 acres of handsome gardens and woodland and there are ranger-led walks along nature trails with fine views across to the mainland. ■ *T844305, 844275, office@cland.demon.co.uk. Daily Apr to end-Oct 0930-1730. £3.80.*

Just beyond the Clan Donald Centre is the turn-off to the Armadale *SYHA Hostel*, T844260. 42 beds. Open mid-March to end October, rents bikes. There's also **B&B** accommodation in the tiny village of **Armadale** which is strung out along the wooded shoreline, but the best bet is in the neighbouring village of **Ardvasar** (pronounced Ard-*vaa*-sar), which has a post office, general store and the lovely C *Ardvasar Hotel*, T844223, F844495, a traditional whitewashed coaching in with nine rooms, an excellent restaurant and the liveliest pub in the vicinity. At the turn-off to the pier is *Skye Batiks* , which also has a shop in Portree (see page 501). Here you'll find the colourful cotton garments which make a unique souvenir of the island, T844396. They also now have B&B accommodation.

On the **ferry pier** is *Ragamuffin*, T844217, which sells a wide range of knitwear and is open daily 0900-1800. Next door is *Pasta Shed*, which does good eat-in or takeaway pizzas. A few hundred yards away is the *Gallery* café/restaurant which serves cheap fish and seafood dishes.

About four or five miles past the ferry port, at the end of the road, is **Aird of Sleat**, a crofting township, from where you walk out to the lighthouse at the **Point of Sleat**. It's a five mile walk on a clear path across moorland with fine coastal scenery.

Transport For full details of **ferry crossings to Mallaig**, see page 496. There are 3 **buses** daily, except Sun, from Armadale Pier to **Portree** (1 hr 20 min) and **Kyleakin** (1 hr) via **Broadford** (40 min). The first bus leaves at 0935.

Walks on Skye

Skye is one of the best places in Scotland for walking. The walks described below range from easy low-level routes to harder walks requiring a reasonably good level of fitness and a detailed map. As in the rest of the Highlands, you should be prepared for the worst and be properly equipped to cope with the wind and rain, even in the height of summer. Good hiking boots are also essential as the ground underfoot is likely to be boggy once off roads and tracks. See also the safety precautions outlined in the Walking section, on page 56.

OS Landranger Nos 23 and 32

For the Cuillin Ridge, a good book is *Black Cuillin Ridge – A Scrambler's Guide*, by SP Bull (Scottish Mountaineering Trust). Also good are the Charles Rhodes books, such as *Introductory Scrambles from Glen Brittle*. For less strenuous walks, try *Selected Walks on North (and South) Skye*, at £3.75. All these books are available in local bookshops and the tourist office in Portree.

Recommended reading

Around Portree

A nice, gentle introduction to walking in the area, and an opportunity to stretch your legs before tackling more strenuous routes such as the Old Man of Storr or the Quiraing, starts out from Bosville Terrace. Follow the street as it curves round then take the right fork at the first junction, down towards the shore. Just after the car park to the right the road splits: follow the path to the right along the northern shore of the bay. The path follows the shore and passes a viewpoint and flagpole. It then becomes rougher as it swings round the headland and reaches a gate in a dyke. Go through the gate and cross the muddy field, then follow the fence up to the left till you reach another gate. Go over the gate and continue along the edge of the next field, then cross a stile at the top of the field. Climb up the slope to the clear track and follow this left as it heads uphill. You'll then see some houses; take the track beyond the house on the left and follow it down between two large farm buildings. The path heads down across rough moorland towards Portree. Cross the stile and continue downhill through some woods, then you'll see a hotel on your left before rejoining the original road near the car park. It's about 2½ miles in total and takes about an hour and a half at an easy pace. The path can get very muddy in places.

The Old Man of Storr

This dramatic basalt finger of rock, 165ft high, stands beneath the steep cliffs of The Storr (2,360ft) and is visible from the A855. The starting point for the 3½ mile walk up and back (1½ hours) is the car park on the left, just over six miles north of Portree, near the northern end of Loch Leathan, which can be reached by bus from Portree.

Cross the stile over the wall by the Forestry Commission sign and follow the clear track up through the conifer plantation. The track is a gradual uphill climb until you come out into open grassland. Go through the gate in the fence and then it's a steep climb up the grassy slope with the massive pinnacle towering overhead. Once at the top you enter an area of weird and impressive rock formations. You can follow any of the dozens of paths that lead between the rocks, or just enjoy the fantastic views across to Raasay and the mainland beyond. You can follow the same path back down to the car park.

Skye

The Quiraing

This four mile walk is quite demanding but the dramatic scenery more than compensates. To get to the starting point, drive 19 miles north from Portree on the A855. At Brogaig, just north of Staffin, take the single-track road to Uig. Follow this for about 2½ miles and, just after the road has zig-zagged its way up the face of the ridge, park in the car park to the left.

Cross the road and follow the well-defined path along the base of the cliffs, with a steep grassy slope down to the right. After about one mile you'll start to see some of the well-known rocky features on the far side of a rough valley. The most imposing of these is **The Prison**, a huge, tilted square block. On the left, among the towering cliffs, is **The Needle**, a shaft of rock about 120 feet high. Scramble up the narrow gully to the left of The Needle to reach **The Table**, an area of flat grassland surrounded by high cliffs (local shinty teams used to play here!). From The Table continue along the path at the foot of the cliffs, past a small lochan on the right and through a stone dyke, until you reach the lowest point of the ridge on your left. Scramble up onto the ridge and make your way back along the tops of the cliffs (take care at this point). There's a hard climb up the slopes of Meall na Suirmamach, but the views from the top are spectacular. Continue along the top of the cliffs for just over a mile and you'll see the car park.

Elgol to Camasunary Bay

This nine mile coastal walk is quite demanding but on a clear day the views of the Cuillins make it well worth the effort. It starts from the car park in Elgol. From the car park, walk back up the road for a short distance, then turn left along a track behind some houses, signposted for 'Garsbheinn'. Beside the last of these houses is a sign for the path to Coruisk. Follow this path along a steep grassy slope. The views across Loch Scavaig to the island of Soay and the Cuillins behind are marvellous. The slope get seven steeper beneath Ben Cleat, then comes the point where vertigo sufferers may wish they hadn't started. This is the notorious 'bad step', an overhanging rock with a 30ft drop to the sea below. Once you negotiate this, you then continue along the foot of Glen Scaladal and cross a burn, which can be tricky if its in spate. Then it's on along the path beyond Beinn Leacach to Camasunary Bay. The shortest way back to Elgol is to retrace your steps (including bad ones), but as an alternative, follow the clear track from Camasunary up the right side of Abhainn nan Lean over the hills to the east until it joins the B8083 from Broadford. From here it's about 3½ miles back along the road to Elgol.

Outer Hebrides

12

Outer Hebrides

The Outer Hebrides – or Western Isles as they are also known – consist of a narrow 130-mile long chain of islands, lying 40 miles off the northwest coast of the Scottish mainland. Relentlessly battered by fierce Atlantic winds the islands can seem a hostile environment and an unappealing proposition, particularly if you happen to be stuck there on a wet Sunday without your own means of transport. Much of the interior is bleak peat bog, rocks and endless tiny lochs, and the long, straggling crofting communities only add to the feeling of desolation. But there are also miles of superb beaches, wild mountain scenery, numerous archaeological treasures and long hours of summer daylight in which to appreciate it all.

Despite the frequency of transport connections with the mainland, the Outer Hebrides remain remote in every sense. Unlike Skye, tourism is of far less importance to the local economy. In many ways, the islands are the last bastion of the old Highland life. Though newer industries such as fish farming have been introduced, the traditional occupations of crofting, fishing and weaving still dominate, and outside Stornoway on Lewis (the only decent-sized town in the islands) life is very much a traditional one, revolving around the seasons and the tides. Almost every islander has more than one occupation, so don't be surprised if the landlady of your guesthouse also weaves Harris Tweed, or if her husband drives the Postbus as well as doing a bit of fishing on the side. This creates a network of relationships where everyone knows everyone else.

The islands are the 'Gaidhealtachd', the land of the Gael. The Gaelic culture has remained more prominent here than in any other part of Scotland and the way of life and philosophy of the islanders will seem totally alien and fascinating to many visitors. Gaelic is the first language for the majority of the islanders – and the only one for the older generation – but the all-pervading influence of the English media has taken its toll and the language is under threat. Though Gaelic is still taught in schools, the younger generation tend to speak to each other in English. Visitors will not have any language problems, as the Gaelic-speaking inhabitants are so polite they will always change to English when visitors are present, though place names and signposts are in Gaelic (see Getting around the islands in Gaelic).

The church is also an important factor in preserving the language, and services are usually held in Gaelic. In fact, religion is one of the most pervasive influences of Hebridean life and the islanders' faith is as strong as the winds that pound their shores. The islands are split between the Presbyterian Lewis, Harris and North Uist, and the predominantly Roman Catholic South Uist and Barra. Benbecula, meanwhile, has a foot in either camp. On Lewis and Harris, the Free Church is immensely powerful and the Sabbath is strictly observed. Don't expect to travel anywhere by public transport, shops and petrol stations will be closed and you'll be hard pressed to find a place to eat, except perhaps in a hotel. Even the swings in the playgrounds are padlocked! On the Roman Catholic islands, however, things are a bit more relaxed.

Ins and outs

By air *British Airways Express*, T0345-222111, flies daily, except Sun, from Glasgow to Stornoway on Lewis (1 hr 45 mins), Barra (1 hr 20 mins) and Benbecula on North Uist (1 hr). There are also from Inverness to Stornoway (45 mins) daily except Sun, and to Benbecula (2 hrs 30 mins) Mon-Fri. Note that weather conditions are so changeable that flights are prone to delay and can be very bumpy. Flights to Barra have an added complication in that they land on the beach, meaning that the runway disappears twice a day under the incoming tide.

Getting there

By boat *CalMac* car and passenger ferries sail to and from Stornoway (Lewis), Tarbert (Harris), Lochmaddy (North Uist), South Uist and Barra. Ferry times change according to the day of the week and time of the year, so they aren't listed in full below. For full details see the *CalMac Ferry Guide* or call *CalMac*, T0990-650000, reservations@calmac.co.uk, for reservations and T01475-650100, www.calmac.co.uk for general enquiries. See also 'Essentials', page 41. Car space is limited during the

Lewis & Harris

Outer Hebrides

© Crown copyright

Festivals in the Outer Hebrides

As the heartland of Gaelic culture, the Outer Hebrides are host to many music events throughout the year, ranging from a spontaneous ceilidh to one of the three local mods. Mods usually consist of three days of competition in piping, singing, instrumental music, drama and poetry and are an opportunity to see the best of the local talent. More information can be obtained from An Comunn Gaidhealach, T01851-703487. Also listed below are the various Highland Games and agricultural shows, where you can also see piping competitions and highland dancing.

25-27 March: Feis nan Coisir, Stornoway, Lewis.

1st Friday in April: Donald Macleod Memorial Piping Competition, Stornoway, Lewis.

21 May-5 June: Highland Festival, held in various locations.

Early June: Harris Mod, Tarbert, Harris.

2nd week in June: Lewis Mod, Stornoway, Lewis.

Mid June: Uist Mod, Iochdar, South Uist.

18-19 June: Lochmaddy Boat Festival, Lochmaddy, North Uist.

Mid July: Berneray Week, Bearnaraigh (Berneray), North Uist.

July: Ceolas Music School, South Uist.

Early July (2 weeks): Barra Festival.

Early/mid July (1 week): Feis Tir an Eorna, Paibeil, North Uist; Barra Highland Games, Borgh (Borve), Barra.

14-17 July: Hebridean Celtic Music Festival, Stornoway, Lewis.

Mid July: North Uist Highland Games, Hosta, North Uist.

Mid/late July: Harris Gala; South Uist Highland Games, Aisgeirnis (Askernish), South Uist; Lewis Highland Games, Tong, Lewis.

3rd week July: Harris Festival

Late July: Barra Live, Barra; West Side Agricultural Show, Barabhas (Barvas), Lewis; South Uist Agricultural Show, Iochdar, South Uist; South Harris Agricultural Show, Leverburgh, Harris.

26-30 July: Feis Eilean an Fhraoich, Stornoway, Lewis.

Late July/early August: North Uist Agricultural Show, Hosta, North Uist.

Early August: Carloway Agricultural Show, Càrlabhagh (Carloway), Lewis; Fies Tir a Mhurain, Lionacleit, Benbecula; Lewis Carnival, Stornoway; Fish Festival, Stornoway.

2nd week August: Harris Arts Festival, Tarbert.

summer months, so it's advisable to book ahead. For details of bus connections on Skye and on the mainland, contact Scottish Citylink, T0990-505050.

To Lewis: CalMac ferry from Ullapool to Stornoway (2 hrs 40 minutes) 2-3 times daily Mon-Sat in the summer (Jun-Sept) and twice daily Mon-Sat in the winter. One-way ticket costs £12.35 per passenger and £56 per car. CalMac offices: Ullapool (T01854-612358) and Stornoway (T01851-702361).

To Harris: from Uig (Skye) to Tarbert (1 hr 45 mins) twice daily Mon-Sat. One-way ticket £8.10 per passenger, £38 per car. Contact Uig (T01470-542219) or Tarbert (T01859-502444).

To North Uist: from Uig to Lochmaddy (1 hr 50 mins) 1-2 times daily. One-way ticket £8.10 per passenger, £38 per car. Contact Lochmaddy (T5000337).

To Barra and South Uist: from Oban to Castlebay (5 hrs) and Lochboisdale (6 hrs 40 mins) once daily except Tue and Sun. One-way ticket £17.80 per passenger, £63 per car. From Mallaig to Castlebay (3 hrs 45 mins) on Sun only, and to Lochboisdale (3 hrs 30 mins) on Tue only. One-way ticket £13.15 per passenger, £46.50 per car. From Castlebay to Lochboisdale (1 hr 50 mins) on Mon, Wed, Thur and Sat, and from Lochboisdale to Castlebay on Tue, Thur, Fri and Sun. One-way ticket £5 per passenger, £28.50 per car.

To North Uist and Harris: a ferry sails to Otternish (North Uist) from Leverburgh (Harris) 3 or 4 times daily. The trip takes 1 hr 10 mins and a one-way ticket costs £4.45 per passenger, £20.80 per car.

Getting around the islands in Gaelic

Aside from the fact that nothing moves on a Sunday, the biggest problem facing visitors to the Outer Hebrides is that road signs and place names are almost exclusively in Gaelic; except for English-speaking Stornoway and Benbecula, where signs are also in English. This means that it's essential, particularly if you're driving, to buy the tourist board's bilingual 'Official Map of the Western Isles', which is available at most tourist offices and many tourist sight gift shops. Also note that the brown tourist sight signs are in both languages, but the Gaelic spelling is much more prominent, so you'll need to be attentive!

In order to reflect the Gaelic-only policy, place names in the text are in Gaelic first, with the English spelling in brackets, and thereafter the names appear in Gaelic only. The exceptions to this are the names of the islands and ferry terminals, which are in English after they are first mentioned in both English and Gaelic.

Island Hopscotch Tickets: a much cheaper way to get around the islands with a car is with one of *CalMac's* Island Hopscotch tickets. There are various route options and tickets give you 30 days unlimited travel on each route. For example, a ticket for the Oban- Castlebay- Lochboisdale- Otternish- Leverburgh- Stornoway- Ullapool route, allows you to visit all the main islands and costs £36 per passenger and £152 per car. See the *CalMac* guide or call the numbers above for full details of the Island Hopscotch Tickets, and the **Island Rover Ticket**, which gives unlimited travel on most CalMac routes for 8 or 15 days.

Getting around

You should allow plenty of time to fully explore the islands. With your own transport and travelling from top to bottom, a week would be enough time for a whistle-stop tour but not enough to explore in any depth or scratch beneath the surface. You will need to allow for the lack of public transport on Sun on most islands and for the fact that weather conditions frequently affect ferry and flight timetables.

By air *Loganair* (operating as *British Airways Express*) fly between Barra, Benbecula and Stornoway Mon-Fri. For full details, T0345-222111.

By boat Passenger ferries run regularly between Ludag in South Uist to both Eoligarry in Barra and to the island of Eriskay, T01878-720238/265. **Car ferries** also connect Eriskay with South Uist, T08178-720261. There are also *CalMac* ferries between Harris and North Uist, and South Uist and Barra (see above for details).

By bus Bus services have improved and now run regularly to most main towns and villages on the islands. Details of local services are given under each destination. You should also invest in a copy of the *Skye & Western Isles Travel Guide* (£1) which is available from the local Tourist Information Centres.

By car Most of the islands' roads are single track but in good condition and, unlike other parts of the Highlands and Islands, not too busy. On Sun you'll barely meet another soul, save for the occasional perplexed tourist looking in vain for somewhere to go. Drivers should note that petrol stations are few and far between, expensive and closed on Sun. The normal rules for single track roads apply and, as elsewhere in the Highlands, you need to look out for wandering sheep. Also note that distances are greater than most people imagine. For example, the distance from Nis (Ness), at the northern tip of Lewis, to Leverburgh in the south of Harris, is 85 miles. From Stornoway to Tarbert is 37 miles. And the distance from Otternish, in the north of North Uist, to Lochboisdale, the main ferry port on South Uist, is 50 miles. Several local

👉 *Things to do when it's raining*

The climate is mild due to the effect of the Gulf Stream, but also moist. You can expect it to rain on an average of two out of every three days, even in summer. The wind is constant and weather fronts come and go with such speed that there's little chance for mist or fog to settle and few problems with that scourge of many a Scottish holiday, the midge.

So what is there to do in the Outer Hebrides when it's raining? That's easy –

there ain't much. There are a few museums and heritage centres dotted around, but you can only look at old black and white photographs for so long. The delights of the islands are very much of the outdoor variety, so unless you're fortunate with the weather, get out there and brave the elements. And if it's a Sunday on one of the northerly Presbyterian islands, you'll have no choice, as everything will be closed.

car hire agencies offer reasonable rental deals. Expect to pay around £15-25 per day, depending on the size of engine and age of the car. Note that you cannot take a rented car off the islands.

By bicycle Cycling is a great way to explore the islands. You can fully appreciate the amazing scenery around you without the risk of driving over the edge of a cliff, and it only costs a few pounds to transport a bike by ferry. There is, of course, the major problem of strong winds, which can leave you frustrated and exhausted. **Bike hire** agencies are also given under the relevant town.

Orientation & information The Outer Hebrides is made up of more than two hundred islands, only ten of which are populated: Lewis and Harris (which are actually one island); Scalpay; Berneray; North Uist; Benbecula; South Uist; Eriskay; Barra; and Vatersay, giving a total population of just under 30,000. The main population centre is Stornoway on Lewis, the only major town in the islands. The rest of the population is scattered throughout the islands in much smaller villages, mostly strung out along the coast.

Lewis and Harris are actually one island, divided by history and a line of high hills that runs between them. The northern part of Lewis is mostly bleak, flat peat moor, while the south and Harris are more rugged, with rocky peaks and superb beaches. The more southerly islands of North Uist, Benbecula and South Uist, joined together by bridges and causeways, are mostly low and flat and peppered with so many lochs they resemble a giant sieve. Toll-free road bridges connect the island of Scalpay with Harris and Great Bernera with Lewis and a causeway connects Berneray with North Uist.

There are **tourist offices** in Stornoway and Tarbert which are open all year round, and also in Lochmaddy, Lochboisdale and Castlebay which are open early Apr to mid Oct. Full details are given under each destination.

The **Western Isles Tourist Board** produces an accommodation brochure as well as the essential *Western Isles Official Tourist Map* (Estate Publications; £3.95), which gives place names in English and Gaelic. They also have their own website (www.witb.co.uk) which provides lots of information on the islands, including up and coming events such as The Royal National Mod, to be held in 2001. Information about the islands can also be obtained at www.hebrides.com. The *Outer Hebrides Handbook and Guide* (£7.95) is written by local experts and is useful on history, culture, and flora and fauna.

Religion in the Outer Hebrides

Religion plays a vitally important role in the islanders' lives and priests and ministers still wield considerable power in the community, particularly in the Calvinist Protestant islands of North Uist, Harris and Lewis, which still strictly adhere to the creed of Sabbatariansim. Here, Sunday is the Lord's Day and the whole community stops work. But despite the fact that the Outer Hebrides are sharply divided between the Protestant northern islands and the Roman Catholic southern islands of Benbecula, Barra and South Uist, there has been little confrontation.

The only conflict has arisen within the Presbyterian Church of Scotland (or Kirk) itself, which has split into various factions over the years. The main split had its roots in the 1712 Patronage act, which allowed a landlord the right to choose the parish minister, thus breaking the fundamental rule of the church ministers and elders. In 1843, in protest at the state's refusal to change the Patronage act, a third of Scottish ministers walked out of the established Church of Scotland to form the Free Church of Scotland – the so-called 1843 Disruption. In 1893 a second disruption occurred, this time within the Free Church of Scotland itself when a minority seceded and formed the Free Presbyterian Church.

Now it becomes really confusing. In 1900 most congregations in the Free Church of Scotland and the United Presbyterian Church joined together to form the United Free Church of Scotland. However, a large proportion of people in Lewis were opposed to this union and the largest congregations decided to continue as the Free Church of Scotland, or 'Wee Frees' as they are popularly known. Later, in 1929, the United Free Church joined with the Established Church of Scotland. And it doesn't end there. As recently as 1988, the Wee Frees split over the threatened expulsion of a minister who attended a requiem mass during the Catholic funeral of a friend. He and his supporters have since formed the breakaway Associated Presbyterian Churches.

Now all this may seem pedantic in the extreme to many outsiders, but to the people of Lewis, Harris and North Uist (and also much of Skye and Raasay), the Free Church is of enormous social and cultural, as well as spiritual, importance. Not only did it organize resistance to the infamous Highland Clearances but it has also done the most to preserve the Gaelic language.

Sleeping

Accommodation on the islands is generally not difficult to find, except perhaps at the height of the summer, when you should book in advance, either directly or through the local tourist office. There are plenty of **B&Bs** and **guesthouses** scattered throughout the islands, many of which offer better value than the hotels. Most don't have private bathrooms, but they're comfortable, very welcoming and will offer evening meals. It's a good idea to book ahead if you're staying on a Sun. If you're staying in the countryside, you should check if there's a convenient pub or hotel to eat in, and if not, make arrangements to eat at your B&B.

There are also several official **youth hostels**, in converted crofts scattered around the islands in isolated locations. Most are difficult to get to without your own transport, but you can always hitchhike. They are run by the **SYHA** or the **Gatliff Hebridean Hostels Trust**. They are basic and adequate, but take a sleeping bag and eating utensils. None of them have phones, so you can't book in advance, and try not to arrive or leave on a Sun. The trust has 8 hostels throughout the islands. Contact them at 71-77 Cromwell Street, Stornoway. There are also several new independent hostels, which are clean and modern and more expensive.

Leodhas (Lewis)

Phone code: 01851
Colour map 1, grid A3

Lewis constitutes the northern two thirds of the most northerly island in the Outer Hebrides (which includes Harris to the south). It is by far the most populous of the Outer Hebridean islands, and with over 20,000 inhabitants, makes up two thirds of the total population. Just over 8,000 people live in Stornoway, the largest town in the Hebrides and the administrative capital of the Western Isles.

The majority of the rest of the population live in the long line of crofting town-ships strung out along the west coast between Port Nis (Ness) and Càrlabhagh (Carloway). The west coast is also where you'll find the island's most interesting sites, the prehistoric remains of Dùn Chàrlabhaigh (Carloway) Broch and the impressive Calanais (Callanish) Standing Stones, and the Arnol Blackhouse. These can all be visited as a day trip from Stornoway, either as an organized tour or using the regular 'West Side Circular' bus service.

The interior of the northern half is flat peat bog, hence the island's name which means 'marshy' in Gaelic. Further south, where Lewis becomes Harris, the scen-ery is more dramatic as the relentlessly flat landscape gives way to rocky hills, pro-viding the backdrop to the sea-lochs that cut deep into the coast and the beautiful beaches around Uig.

History

Lewis was dominated by the Vikings, and the Norse influence can be seen in many of the place names, such as Uig (which is Norse for 'a bay'). After the end of Norwegian sovereignty in 1266, the island was ruled by the Macleods, said to be descendants of early settlers from Iceland. Control of the island was wrested from them by the Mackenzies, who then proceeded to sell it, in 1844, to Sir James Matheson. The new owner built Lews Castle in Stornoway and began to develop the infrastructure of the island as well as investing in new industries. Though many crofts were cleared and families sent to Canada, the people of Lewis fared well and certainly much better than their counterparts in the Southern Isles.

The next proprietor was Lord Leverhulme, founder of Lever Brothers, who bought the island (along with Harris) in 1918. He planned to turn Lewis into a major fishing centre and ploughed money into developing the infrastructure. He was forced to abandon his plans, however, partly because of the decline of the fishing industry, and partly owing to the growing conflict between him and the islanders returning from the war who wanted land of their own to farm. As a final benevolent gesture, Lord Leverhulme offered Lewis to the islanders, but only Stornoway Council accepted. The island was then divided into estates and sold, and hundreds emigrated.

Today, the economy of Lewis is still based on the traditional industries of crofting, fishing and weaving, though there are other economic activities such as fish farming, which is now a major employer, service industries, tourism, construction and the onshore oil yard at Stornoway.

Steòrnabhagh (Stornoway)

Phone code: 01851
Colour map B1, grid B3
Population: 8,132

The fishing port of Stornoway, the only town in the Outer Hebrides, is the islands' commercial capital and as such boasts more services and facilities than you might expect in any town of comparable size. It has the full range of banks, shops, hotels, guesthouses, pubs and restaurants, garages, car hire firms, sports facilities, an airport and ferry terminal, and for the visiting tourist it presents a rare opportunity to stock up on supplies.

Stornoway is also the administrative capital and home to the *Comhairle nan Eilean* (The Western Isles Council), which has done much to broaden the local economy and to promote and protect Gaelic language and culture, but is probably best known for its disastrous financial dealings with the Bank of Credit and Commerce International (BCCI), which collapsed in 1991, losing the islands a cool £23 million.

The **tourist office** is at 26 Cromwell St. They stock maps, bus timetables and various books and brochures and sell tickets for minibus tours to Calanais and for wildlife trips round Lewis and Harris. ■ *T703088. Apr-May and Sept-Oct, Mon-Fri 0900-1800, Sat 0900-1700; Jun-Aug, Mon-Fri 0900-2000; Oct-Mar Mon-Fri 0900-1700.*

Stornoway is the island's transport hub. The **airport** is four miles east of the town centre, a £5 taxi ride away. For details of flights to the other islands and the mainland, see Ins and outs (page 521). The *CalMac* **ferry terminal** is just beyond the **bus station**, which is on South Beach, a short walk from the town centre. Full ferry details are also given in Ins and outs. Buses leave from Stornoway to all parts of the island and also to Tarbert and Levenburgh on Harris. Bus timetables are available from the **tourist office**. See also Transport on page 529.

Getting there & around

The town is compact and most of what you need is within easy walking distance of the tourist office. Some of the B&Bs in the residential areas are a quite a distance from the centre, but there's an hourly town bus service, or hire a **taxi** from *Central Cabs* (T706900).

Stornoway is short on conventional tourist sights and once you've been to the tourist office and bought the necessities from the local supermarkets, there's not much else to do. The focal point of the town has always been its sheltered deep-water **harbour**, and though the fishing industry has declined since its peak at the end of the last century, there's still a fair amount of activity, especially at the fish market on North Beach on Tuesday and Thursday evenings. The harbour is usually full of seals, giving the town its nickname of Portrona (port of seals). There's a good view across the harbour to **Lews Castle**, a 19th-century edifice built by Sir James Matheson with money earned from opium and tea. The castle now houses a college and its real attraction is the wooded grounds, the only place you'll see trees on the islands.

Sights

The **Museum nan Eilean**, on Francis Street, features a range of temporary exhibitions on island life and history. ■ *T703773. Mon-Sat 1000-1730 Apr to Sept; Tue 1000-1700 and Sat 1000-1300 Oct-Mar. Free.*

Anyone remotely interested in Harris Tweed should visit the **Lewis Loom Centre**, housed in the Old Grainstore at the northern end of Cromwell Street, just off Bayhead. The 40-minute guided tour includes demonstrations of traditional methods of warping, dyeing and spinning and a detailed lecture on the history of Harris Tweed. There's also a craft shop. ■ *T703117. Mon-Sat 1000-1700. £2.*

The impressive baronial Town Hall on South Beach currently houses the **An Lanntair Art Gallery**, though plans are afoot to move the gallery into a new arts centre. The gallery features the work of local, national and international artists and also stages various musical events. The coffee shop serves home baking and tasty snacks. ■ *T703307, lanntair@sol.co.uk. Mon-Sat 1000-1730. Free.*

As the largest settlement on the islands, Stornoway has a good selection of accommodation from which to choose, though you should book in advance in the peak summer season. The tourist office will do this for you, for a small fee.

Sleeping

Outer Hebrides

Stornoway

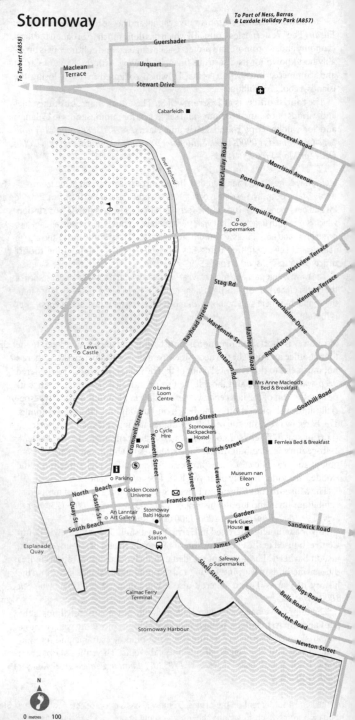

To Port of Ness, Barras
& Laxdale Holiday Park (A857)

To Tarbert (A858)

Guershader

Maclean
Terrace

Urquart

Stewart Drive

Cabarfeidh

Perceval Road

Morrison Avenue

Macaulay Road

Portrona Drive

Torquil Terrace

Co-op
Supermarket

Westview Terrace

River Bayhead

Stag Rd

Kennedy Terrace

Leverhulme Drive

Lews
Castle

Bayhead Street

MacKenzie St

Matheson Road

Robertson

Plantation Rd

Mrs Anne Macleod's
Bed & Breakfast

Goathill Road

Lewis
Loom
Centre

Scotland Street

Cromwell Street

Cycle
Hire

Stornoway
Backpackers
Hostel

Fernlea Bed & Breakfast

Royal

Kenneth Street

Church Street

Keith Street

Lewis Street

Museum nan
Eilean

Parking

North Beach

Golden Ocean
Universe

Francis Street

Quay St

Castle St

An Lanntair
Art Gallery

Stornoway
Balti House

Garden

Park Guest
House

Sandwick Road

South Beach

Bus
Station

James Street

Safeway
Supermarket

Esplanade
Quay

Shell Street

Rigs Road

Calmac Ferry
Terminal

Bells Road

Inaclete Road

Stornoway Harbour

Newton Street

N

0 metres 100
0 yards 100

There are several centrally-located hotels, the best of which is **B** *Royal Hotel*, Cromwell St, T702109, F702142. 24 rooms, good value and good food in the its restaurant and bistro (see 'Eating' below). On the outskirts of town is **B** *Cabarfeidh Hotel*, Manor Park, T702604, F705572. 46 rooms, not as convenient as the *Royal* but with the full range of facilities and a decent restaurant. **B** *Park Guest House*, 30 James St, T702485, T/F703482. 10 rooms, this Victorian town house is comfortable, only 500yd from the ferry terminal, and the best of the guesthouses. It also has an excellent restaurant which is recommended even if you're not staying.

There are many **B&Bs** in and around the town centre, most of which offer a 'room only' rate for those requiring an early start to catch the first ferry. There are several along Matheson Rd, which is close to the town centre and the ferry terminal, including, **E** *Mrs Anne Maclead*, at No 12, T702673, and **E** (**F** room only) *Mrs M MacMillan*, 'Fernlea' No 9, T702125.

The basic **F** *Stornoway Backpackers Hostel* is at 47 Keith St, T703628. Includes breakfast, open all year. There's also a Bunkhouse Hostel at **F** *Laxdale Holiday Park*, on Laxdale Lane, about a mile out of town on the road to Barabhas, T703234/706966. It has 16 beds, basic facilities and is open all year.

Eating

The pubs and hotels serve the usual range of bar meals, but note that pubs are closed on Sun and hotels cater only for residents. Probably the best restaurant in town is at the *Park Guest House* (see 'Sleeping' above), which offers top class modern Scottish cooking using local fish, lamb and venison. It also caters for vegetarians and is open Tue-Sat. Mid-range to expensive. Also recommended is *The Boatshed*, in the *Royal Hotel* (see 'Sleeping' above), which specializes in seafood. Expensive. Less upmarket and cheaper is their *Barnacle Bistro*.

A good place cheap for snacks and light lunches is the café at the *Ann Lantair Gallery* (see 'Sights' above). Cheap business lunches are available at the *Stornoway Balti House*, near the bus station on South Beach, and at the *Golden Ocean Universe*, on north Beach, diagonally opposite the tourist office. The cheapest option is the all-day breakfast for £1.60 served in the *Co-op* supermarket (see map). For a cheap lunch try the *cafeteria* in the *Deep Sea Fishermen's Mission* on North Beach.

There are 2 large supermarkets in town. *Safeway* is beside the ferry terminal and the *Co-op* is by the first roundabout on the road out to Barabhas. There's also a smaller supermarket opposite the tourist office.

Transport

Buses leave from Stornoway to all parts of the island. Note that buses do not run on Sun. To **Port Niss (Ness)** via **Barabhas (Barvas)** 4-6 times per day; to **Arnol, Siabost (Shawbost)**, **Càrlabhagh (Carloway)** , **Calanais (Callanish)**, and back to Stornoway ('West Side Circular') 4-6 times per day; to **Bearnaraigh (Great Bernera)** via **Gearraidh na h-Aibhne (Garynahine)** 4 per day; to **Uig District** 3 per day; to **Ranais (Ranish)** 6-8 times per day. For full details, T840269. There are also buses from Stornoway to **Tarbert** and on to **Leverburgh** (for the ferry to North Uist) 4-5 times per day (T01859-502441). **Car rental** is available at good rates from *Lewis Car Rentals*, 52 Bayhead St, T703760, F705860. Also *Arnol Motors*, in Arnol (see page 530), T01851-710548 (0831-823318 mobile), F710248. You can **rent bikes** at *Alex Dan's Cycle Centre*, 67 Kenneth St, T704025, F701712.

Directory

Banks The *Bank of Scotland* is directly opposite the tourist office and has an ATM. The other major banks are also in the centre of town and also have ATMs. **Communications** The post office is on Francis St. The islands' only **internet café** is *Captions*, 27 Church St, T702238, F706782, bayble@captions.co.uk, www.captions.co.uk. Open Mon-Sat till late in the summer months. **Tour companies** *MacDonald's Coaches*, at the Ferry Terminal, T706267. Coach tours. *Hebridean Exploration*, 19 Westview Tce, T705655 (T0374-292746 mobile). Sea kayak tours. *Elena C*, 5a Knock, Point, T870537, F706384. Wildlife trips from Stornoway harbour.

The West Coast

Phone code: 01851
Colour map 1, grid A3

The west coast of Lewis contains most of what you'll want to see and can be covered in a day trip from Stornoway, either with your own transport, by public bus or as part of a minibus tour.

At **Barabhas (Barvas)** the road forks. The A857 bears right (north) and continues all the way to **Nis (Ness)** (see page 533), but the road you want to take is the A858, which bears left (west). A few miles along this road is the turn-off for **Arnol**. At the end of the village is the **Blackhouse Museum**, one of the best surviving examples of an original blackhouse in Scotland and well worth visiting. These traditional thatched houses were once common throughout the Highlands and Islands and inhabited until the 1960s. They were built in the tradition of 'longhouses' which can be traced back 1,000 years to the time of the Viking invaders. The name 'blackhouses' dates back to the 1850s when modern buildings were introduced. These were known as 'white houses' and the older style houses were called 'blackhouses'. The blackhouses were well adapted to the harsh local climate. They had no windows or chimney and were built with local materials – stone, turf and thatch of oat, barley or marram grass, and with a peat fire burning continually in the central hearth – and attached to the living quarters was the cattle byre. This particular blackhouse was built in 1885 and lived in until 1964. ■ *T710395. Apr-Sept Mon-Sat 0930-1830, Oct-Mar Mon-Sat (closed Fri), 0930-1830. £2, concession £1.50, child £1.*

Two miles south of the Arnol turn-off, at **Bragar**, look out for an archway, formed from the jawbone of a blue whale which was washed up on the coast nearby, in 1920. A few miles further on is the township of **Siabost (Shawbost)**, where the charmingly ramshackle **folk museum**, which was started originally as a project by local schoolchildren, now contains an interesting collection of Hebridean artefacts. ■ *Mon-Sat 0900-1800, free.* Behind the museum is a **campsite**, T710504, March-October.

Just south of Siabost, beside a small loch, is the sign for the newly-restored **Norse Mill and Kiln**, which are a half-mile walk over the hill from the car park. There's not much to see as yet, but it's worth getting out of the car if you want to stretch your legs. A little further on is the turning for **Dail Beag (Dalbeg)**, a lovely secluded beach. Overlooking a small lochan surrounded by hills beside the car park is the *Copper Kettle*, T710592, an unassuming little house which is actually a superb **restaurant**. Meals must be booked at least 24 hours in advance and are moderately priced (last booking 2000). Open 1030 till 1730 for tea, coffee, snacks and home baking (all year, Mon-Sat). Next door is a self-catering bungalow for rent (same phone number).

The landscape gradually becomes more undulating and scenically interesting as the road then passes through the village of **Càrlabhagh (Carloway)**, Lord Leverhume's proposed fishing port. Here, a branch road leads to the ruined and deserted 'blackhouse' village of **Gearrannan (Garenin)**. Several of the thatched houses have been restored and one, run by the Gatliff Trust, provides cheap hostel accommodation with 14 beds and basic facilities. It's open all year, but has no phone. Even if you're not planning to stay a detour is worth it for the beautiful beach and great views across the ocean.

A little further on, standing a few hundred yards from the main road, is the **Dùn Chàrlabhaigh (Doune Carloway) Broch**, the best preserved building of its type in the Outer Hebrides. The impressive 2,000 year-old drystone habitation is beautifully situated on a rocky outcrop, commanding great views across Loch Carloway to the sea beyond. The remaining outer wall is 30ft high and slopes inwards, with an inner wall which rises vertically, leaving chambers between the walls. Parts of the inner wall have collapsed, revealing the interior

Outer Hebrides

Crofting

The word 'croft' is derived from the Gaelic croit, meaning a small area of land, and crofting has been the traditional way of life in the Scottish Highlands for many centuries. Its emotive hold on the psyche of the Highlander comes from the long, hard struggle for security of tenure (see page 665).

A croft is aptly described as a parcel of land entirely surrounded by regulations. Most crofts consist of a few acres of arable land with a proportion of grazing land shared with other crofts. Each crofter is, in effect, a kind of small tenant-farmer, the distinction being that he has almost absolute security of tenure and has the right to assign the croft to a member of his family whether the landlord agrees or not. In fact, over the years, the crofter has managed to acquire most of the rights of ownership with few of the disadvantages.

The croft is the area of land involved and not the house which is called the `croft house'. Crofts can vary in size, from a quarter of an acre upwards. Those on Lewis are small and relatively unproductive, with an average size of only about five acres, while on the Uists, where the land is more fertile, crofts are up to 50 acres or more.

As well as having the sole tenancy of the croft, the crofter usually also has a share in a huge area of 'common grazing' along with the other members of the crofting community – commonly called a township. They also work together in such activities as fencing, sheep dipping or cutting peat.

In reality, crofting does not provide a viable means of living. Very few crofters rely solely on their smallholding for an income and most need to have several occupations (including running a Bed & Breakfast establishment) to make ends meet. But without the family croft, whole communities would just pack up and leave, and so crofting functions as a means of preventing the depopulation of remote rural areas.

---

stairs and galleries. There's also the **Doune Broch Visitor Centre** by the car park, which tastefully complements the architectural style of the site, and which gives a good audio-visual description of how life must have been in one of these structures around 50 BC. ■ *T643338. Doune Broch Centre Apr-Oct, Mon-Sat 1000-1800. Free.*

Calanais (Callanish)

Five miles south of Dun Chàrlabhaigh is the jewel in the islands' prehistoric crown, the **Calanais Standing Stones**, which are unique in Scotland and the equal of Stonehenge in historical value. The stones are in a beautiful setting overlooking Loch Roag and are very atmospheric, especially at sunset or at night, when no one's around. They are in the form of a Celtic cross and in the centre is a circle of 13 stones with a central monolith over 12ft tall, and a chambered burial cairn. The oldest part of this great ceremonial site – probably the stone circle – dates from around 3,000 BC (older than Stonehenge) and continued in use until about 800 BC. The full significance of the site is not yet known, though it probably is connected to the seasonal cycle as many of the stones are aligned with the rising and setting moon. There are also a number of smaller and more isolated stone circles a few miles south of Calanais, on the road to Gearraidh na h-Aibhne (Garynahine).

Phone code: 01851
Colour map 1, grid B2

Next to the stones is the Calanais Visitor Centre, which features 'The Story of the Stones' exhibition, a restaurant and gift shop. On the other side of the stones is the *Blackhouse tearoom and craft shop*, run by the MacBears and better value if you fancy a bite to eat. ■ *Visitor Centre, T621422, calanais.centre@btinternet.com. Mon-Sat, 1000-1900 Apr-Sept, 1000-1600 Oct-Mar. Exhibition £1.50, concession £1, child 50p,*

Outer Hebrides

Sleeping & eating If you want to stay near the stones and visit them after dark, there are several inexpensive B&Bs in the village of Calanais, including the friendly **E-F** *Mrs Morrison*, 27 Callanish (200yd from the site), T621392 (open Mar-Sept). A few miles north, in Tolastadh a' Chaolais (Tolsta Chalois) is the recommended vegetarian B&B run by *Debbie Nash*, 19 Tolsta Chaolais, T621321, **E**.

Aside from the Calanais Visitor Centre or Blackhouse tearoom, places to eat are few and far between, but try *Tigh Mealros*, a few miles south, at Gearraidh na h-Aibhne, T621333. They serve good local grub, with scallops a speciality (closes at 2100).

Transport Local **buses** travel from Stornoway. Contact the tourist office, T703088, in Stornoway, or the bus station, T704327, for details. There are also day trips to Calanais with *Galson Motors*, T840269, leaving from Stornoway bus station, and *W. MacDonald*, T706267, leaving from the pier.

The Uig peninsula

Phone code: 01851
Colour map 1, grid B2

From Gearraidh na h-Aibhne the main A858 runs back to Stornoway, while the B8011 forks west to the remote Uig peninsula in the southwest of the island. Four miles down this road is a turning to the right onto the B8059, which leads to the island of **Bearnaraigh (Great Bernera)**, now connected to the mainland of Lewis by a single-track road bridge. The main settlement on the island is **Breacleit (Breaclete)**, where you can find out about the island's history in the Bernera Museum. ■ *Apr-Sept, Mon-Sat 1100-1800*. The rest of the island is fairly interesting with tiny fishing villages and one or two brochs and some standing stones. The nicest part, though, is on the north coast, near the tiny hamlet of **Bostadh (Bosta)**, where a lovely little sandy bay looks out to the nearby island of **Bearnaraigh Beag (Little Bernera)**. There are a couple of good B&Bs on the island which both offer evening meals, one in **Tobson**, on the west coast, and the other in **Circebost (Kirkibost)**, on the east coast.

Calanais
Standing Stones

Outer Hebrides

The B8011 continues across bleak moorland, then cuts north to **West Loch Roag**, which is fringed by some fine sandy beaches and backed by a much hillier landscape. Just beyond **Miabhag (Miavaig)** is the turn-off right to **Cliobh (Cliff)**, with its picturesque beach which is unsafe for swimming. A mile further on is the little village of **Cnip (Kneep)**, to the east of which is the beautiful **Traigh na Berie**, a long sandy beach backed by flat machair which is ideal for camping.

The road beyond Miabhag leads to **Timsgearraidh (Timsgarry)** and the **Traigh Chapadail (Uig sands)** at the village of **Eadar Dha Fhadhail (Adroil)**. This is the loveliest of all the beaches on Lewis, with miles of sand dunes and machair, but it is famous for an entirely different reason. It was here, in 1831, that a crofter dug up the 'Lewis Chessmen', 78 pieces carved from walrus ivory and belonging to at least eight incomplete chess sets from 12th century Scandinavia. Some are now in the Museum of Scotland in Edinburgh but most can be found in the British Museum in London.

There are a few places to stay around the Uig bay, the best of which is the beautifully-located **D** *Baile Na Cille Guest House*, in Timsgarry, T672242, F672241, RandJGollin @compuserve.com. It's open Apr-Sept, offers dinner for residents and non-residents alike and one of the warmest welcomes in the islands. North of Timsgarry, at Aird Uig, is the *Smugglers* restaurant, T672351, which serves lunch and dinner.

Sleeping & eating

For details of public transport from Stornoway, see page 529.

North to Nis (Ness)

The A857 leaves Stornoway and runs northwest through barren, treeless and relentlessly bleak moorland to **Barabhas (Barvas)**. The landscape is scarred by deep gashes caused by peat digging and the unfamiliar smell you detect in your nostrils is peat burning – a strange mixture of burning grass, whisky and coffee. Peat is the main source of domestic fuel used on the islands and outside most houses, you'll see large stacks of peat, or '*cruachs*'.

Colour map 1, grid A3

The road from Barabhas northeast to Nis runs through a series of forlorn-looking, scrawny settlements that all look identical and merge into one. They consist of modern, characterless grey pebble-dash cottages with the ubiquitous piles of peat in the gardens, and the abandoned cars and vans scattered around everywhere only adds to the ugly and depressing scene.

Just beyond Barabhas a sign points left to the **Morvern Art Gallery**, which has a café, making it a welcome refuge in bad weather. A few miles further on is a turning right to **Baile an Trùiseil (Ballantrushel)**, site of the huge **Clach an Trùiseil**, a 20 feet monolith (the largest in Europe), which was the scene of the last major battle on the island, fought between the Morrisons of Nis and the MacAuleys of Uig. This is the first of a number of prehistoric sights between here and **Siadar (Shader)**, which may be of interest to the keen archaeologist, but otherwise there's little of note on the road north to Nis as it passes through the typical crofting townships of **Coig Peighinnean Buirgh (Five Penny Borve)**, **Gàbhsann bho Dheas (South Galson)**, **Dail (Dell)**, **Suainebost (Swainbost)**, **Tàbost (Habost)** and **Lìonal (Lionel)**. In saying that, those interested in buying souvenirs should look in at the *Borgh Pottery*, by the bridge at Coig Peighinnean. Here you'll find a wide range of beautiful and original domestic and decorative ware. ■ *T850345. Mon-Sat 0930-1800.*

The road continues north, passing through a number of straggling villages that collectively make up **Nis (Ness)**, until it ends at the fishing village of **Port Nis (Port of Ness)**. It's a lovely spot, with a picturesque little harbour and golden sweep of beach enclosed by steep cliffs. Each September the locals head

Outer Hebrides

out to the island of **Sula Sgeir**, 30 miles to the north, for the annual cull of young gannets (or *gugas*), which are considered something of a delicacy by the people of Lewis.

Just before Port Nis, is Lìonal, where the B8015 turns off right and leads to the start of the 10 mile **coastal trail** that works it way round to **Tòlstadh (Tolsta North)** and the beautiful beaches of Traigh Mhor and Garry. These can be reached much more easily by road north from Stornoway. For details of the coastal walk, see the tourist office in Stornoway.

Another minor road heads northwest to the tiny hamlet of **Eòropaidh (Eoropie)** (pronounced 'Yor-erpee'). By the road junction that leads to Rubha Robhanais is the ancient **Teampull Mholuaidh (St Moluag's Church)**, thought to date from the 12th century and restored to its present state in 1912. It is now used on certain Sundays by Stornoway's Episcopal Church. From Eòropaidh a narrow road runs to the lighthouse at **Rubha Robhanais (Butt of Lewis)**, which marks the nothernmost tip of the Outer Hebrides. It's a great place for spotting seabirds or whales and dolphins, but also very wild and windy. Half a mile back down the road, a path leads down to the tiny beach of **Port Sto**, which is more sheltered.

Sleeping There are several options should you wish to stay in this part of the island. There's the *Harbour View Gallery & Café*, T810735, which also offers B&B accommodation. At Gàbhsann bho Deas (South Galson), halfway between Barabhas and Port Nis, is the beautifully-restored 18th-century **D** *Galson Farm Guest House*, T850492. Cheaper, more basic accommodation is available in the *Galson Farm Bunkhouse* (same phone number). At Coig Peighinnean Buirgh (Five Penny Borve) there's B&B with **D** *Ms Catriona Macleod*, T810240.

Na Hearadh (Harris)

Phone code: 01859
Colour map 1, grid B2

Harris is not an island, but together with Lewis forms the largest of the Outer Hebrides, with Harris taking up the southern third. The two parts are divided by the long sea lochs of Loch Seaforth in the east and Loch Resort in the west, though this division is rarely shown on maps. Though joined, the two are very different in terms of geography. Harris is largely mountain and rock whereas Lewis is flat moorland.

Harris itself is almost split in two by the sea, at An Tairbeart (Tarbert), the largest town and ferry terminal. To the north are the highest peaks in the Outer Hebrides, surrounded by some of the finest unspoilt wilderness in the whole country, while to the south are miles of wonderful sandy beaches and, on the east coast, an almost indescribably strange landscape straight out of a science fiction film.

With your own transport you could 'do' Harris in a day quite comfortably, but if the weather's good enough you'll want to spend more time and appreciate its precious natural beauty. There's a regular bus service between Tarbert and Stornoway, and a less frequent one that travels right round South Harris (see transport, Tarbert, on page 536).

History

The separation of Harris and Lewis dates back to Norse times, when the island was divided between the two sons of Leod, progenitor of the Macleods. Harris remained in Macleod hands until 1834. The recent history of Harris is closely bound up with that of Lewis. Both were bought by the soap magnate, Lord

Leverhulme (see page 526), whose grandiose schemes for Lewis came to nothing. Leverhulme then turned his attentions to Harris, where the peaceful little village of An t-Ob (Obbe) was renamed Leverburgh and transformed into a bustling port with all manner of public works programmes under development. His death in 1925 brought an end to all his plans for Harris and instead of becoming a town with a projected population of 10,000, Leverburgh reverted to being a sleepy village, with only the harbour, the roads and the change of name to show for it all.

Since the Leverhulme era there has been no main source of employment for the population of 2,400 on Harris, though a successful fishing industry continues on Scalpaigh (Scalpay). There is still some crofting supplemented by the Harris Tweed industry, though most production is now in Lewis, and whatever employment can be found: road-works, crafts and tourism. The most recent project proposed for Harris, to create one of Europe's largest superquarries, is highly controversial and would involve destroying an area of outstanding natural beauty for the sake of perhaps only a few dozen jobs (see page 539).

An Tairbeart (Tarbert)

Tarbert, the largest settlement on Harris, lies in a sheltered bay on the narrow isthmus that joins North and South Harris. It's a tiny place and there's not much to do, but as it's the main ferry port for Harris, it has more facilities than anywhere else, such as shops, a bank, post office and tourist office. Tarbert's relatively wide range of accommodation and location make it the ideal base from which to explore the delights on offer.

Phone code: 01859
Colour map 1, grid B2
Population: 500

The **tourist office** is close to the ferry terminal. They can arrange accommodation and are a good source of information on local walks. ■ *T502011. Apr-Oct Mon-Sat 0900-1700. It also opens in the winter (check times) and when the ferry arrives.*

C *Harris Hotel*, on the main road from Stornoway on the left before the turning for the ferry, T502154, F502281. An old established favourite, but more importantly, the only place serving food on a Sun (see below). The bar next door also serves meals and is the social hub of the village. **C** *Leachin House*, 1 mile out of Tarbert on the Stornoway road, T/F502157. **B** including dinner. Luxurious Victorian home with great views and superb home cooking (for residents only), only 2 rooms so book ahead. **D** *Allan Guest House*, on the left after the turning into the village, T502146. Open Apr-Sept. Close to the ferry, very comfortable rooms and exceptional food. **B** including dinner. Book ahead. **E** *Macleod Motel*, right beside the ferry pier, T502364. Very handy for the early morning ferry, also has room-only rate.

Sleeping

There are also several B&Bs within 5 mins walk of the ferry pier, including the very friendly and welcoming **E-F** *Mrs Flora Morrison*, Tigh na Mara, T502270. A cheaper option is the new **F** *Rockview Bunkhouse*, on the main street, T/F5022211/502626. Open all year.

Options on places to eat are limited. Most guesthouses and B&Bs will provide dinner on request but check in advance if they do so on a Sun. Aside from those guesthouses mentioned above, probably the best food in the village is the *Firstfruits Tearoom*, T502349, down by the ferry pier. Open Mon-Sat 1030-1630 Apr, May and Sept and till 1830 in Jun, Jul and Aug. Otherwise it's the *Harris Hotel* (see above) which serves food every day till around 2030. They do a 3-course fixed menu (mid-range) or basic and cheap bar meals, as does the bar next door Mon-Sat. The only other option is the chippy next door to the *Rockview Bunkhouse*, where you can get a carry out for £2-3.

Eating

Outer Hebrides

Transport **Ferry** details are given in the Ins and outs section on page 521. There's a **bus** service 4-5 times per day from **Stornoway** to Tarbert (1 hr 15 mins), which continues to **Leverburgh** (for the ferry to North Uist) via the west coast of South Harris. There's also a service 3-4 times per day from Tarbert to Leverburgh via the east coast (45 mins), along the so-called 'Golden Road'. There are also services to **Huisinis** (2-4 per day on schooldays, 45 mins), to **Reinigeadal** (2 per day on schooldays) and to **Scalpaigh** (2-5 per day, 10 mins). Bus timetables are available at the tourist office (see above).

Ceann a Tuath na Hearadh (North Harris)

Phone code: 01859
Colour map 1, grid B2

North Harris is the most mountainous part of the Outer Hebrides and its wild, rugged peaks are ideal for hill walking. The A859 south from Lewis gets progressively more scenic as it skirts **Loch Siophort (Seaforth)** and the mountains rise before you like a giant barrier. The road then climbs past **Bogha Glas (Bowglass)** and **Aird a Mhulaidh (Ardvourlie)** with **Clisham** (2,619ft), the highest peak in the Outer Hebrides, and **Sgaoth Aird** (1,829ft) towering overhead on either side. Just off the A859 near Ardvourlie is **B** *Ardvourlie Castle Guest House*, T502307, F502348. 4 rooms. Open April-October. This lovingly-restored Victorian hunting lodge on the shores of Loch Seaforth just oozes charm and elegance and can't be recommended highly enough. As if that weren't enough, they also happen to serve excellent food. There can be no better end to a day spent walking in the surrounding mountains.

If you can't afford such luxury but still crave the isolation, then carry on south until you reach the turn-off to **Reinigeadal (Rhenigidale)**, which was the most remote community on Harris and accessible only by sea or by a rough hill track until the access road was built. Here you'll find a Gatliff Trust **youth hostel**, a converted croft house (no phone) which sleeps 11 and is open all year (for details on how to get there on foot, see below).

The A859 continues west across the crest of the craggy hills then drops down to the turn-off for the single-track B887 which winds its way all the way out to **Huisinis (Hushinish)** between the impressive mountains of the Forest of Harris on one side and the northern shore of West Loch Tarbert on the other, with views across to the Sound of Taransay and the beaches of South Harris. Immediately beyond the turn-off you pass through **Bun Abhainn Eadarra (Bunavoneadar)**, which was a thriving whaling station until 1930 and one of Lord Leverhulme's many schemes for the island (the slipways and chimney can still be seen). Just before the village of **Miabhag (Meavaig)** a defined footpath heads north into the hills up Glen Meavaig to Loch Voshimid. Further on, though, is a better opportunity for walking. Just before the gates of **Amhuinnsuidhe Castle** (pronounced 'Avan-soo-ee') is a signpost for Chliostair Power Station. From here you can walk two miles up to the dam, then follow the right-hand track round the reservoir and the left-hand track round the upper loch, before you arrive in wild and remote glen.

Just beyond the castle gates you'll see a beautiful waterfall spilling straight into the sea. The road then runs right past the front door of the castle, built in 1868 by the Earl of Dunmore, and which is still a private residence, before passing through an archway and continuing to the tiny crofting township of **Huisinis**, beautifully situated in a sandy bay. This is where the road ends; next stop the USA! Follow the track to the right across the machair to a small jetty from where there are views across to the nearby rocky island of **Scarp**, rising to over 1,000ft. It supported a population of more than 100 as late as the 1940s but was abandoned in 1971 and now the crofters' cottages are used as holiday homes. The island was the scene of a bizarre experiment in 1934, when a German rocket scientist, Gerhard Zucher, tried to prove that rockets could be used

Harris Tweed

Few visitors to Harris will not have heard of its most famous export, Harris Tweed. But how did it emerge from its humble origins to become a product synonymous with high quality craftsmanship and a de rigeur item of clothing for any self-respecting aristocrat?

Traditionally the tweed was made by fishermen's wives to clothe their own families using wool from their own sheep. They carried out the whole process themselves by hand. First the wool was washed, then dyed using native plants and bushes, tree bark and lichen, then carded, spun, warped, woven and finally waulked, or made soft, by beating it on a table. Many women could produce more than they needed and the surplus was available for sale or barter. The cloth was made throughout the Outer Hebrides and originally was not known as Harris Tweed, but simply as clo mòr (or big cloth).

All that changed in 1842 when the Countess of Dunmore, who owned a large part of Harris, took great interest and introduced many of her aristocratic friends to Harris Tweed. Very soon, much of the surplus tweed was being sold and becoming quite a fashion statement in high places. By the beginning of the 20th

century demand was exceeding supply, stimulated by Royal patronage, and faster and more efficient ways of carrying out the ancillary processes were being developed by some of the larger producers. This led, in 1909, to the setting up of the Harris Tweed Association Ltd, to ensure quality control and to protect the interests of the independent crofter/ weavers. So Harris Tweed came officially into being, with its famous Orb trademark, originating from the Coat of Arms of the Countess of Dunmore.

To earn this official stamp of authenticity Harris Tweed must be made from pure Scottish wool, dyed, spun and finished in the Outer Hebrides and hand woven by the islanders in their own homes. There are now about 750 independent weavers and about 400 millworkers employed in the islands, and each weaver can produce three webs of tweed a week (a web measures 80-90 yards in length). In total the industry produces around five million yards of tweed annually, depending on demand. The main production centre is now Lewis but all over the island you can see the woven tweed lying at the gates of crofts waiting to be collected and sent all over the world.

to transport mail and medical supplies to remote communities. His theory went up in smoke, however, when the rocket exploded before it even got off the ground, with 30,000 letters on board.

An interesting little excursion from Tarbert is the 10 mile return route that runs east through the tiny villages of **Urgha** and **Caolas Scalpaigh** to **Carnach** at the end of the road. Just beyond Urgha, on the north side of the road, is a path which leads across the hills to the **Reinigeadal** (see above). Details of the route are available at the tourist office in Tarbert.

The island of **Scalpaigh (Scalpay)**, now connected to Harris by a road bridge, is a thriving fishing community with a population of over 400. It's a pleasant three-mile walk across the island to Eilean Glas Lighthouse, built by the Stevensons and the first ever on the Outer Hebrides. Those who wish to stay on Scalpay can do so at **E** *Suil-na-Mara*, T540278, or **F** *Seafield*, T540250. If you'd like to do some diving, contact *Scalpay Diving Services*, T540328.

Ceann a Deas na Hearadh (South Harris)

An absolute must while you're in the Outer Hebrides is the 45-mile circular route around South Harris. If you only do one thing while you're here, then make sure this is it, for the change in scenery from the west coast to the east is utterly fascinating. One thing you're sure to puzzle over as you travel round is the fact that most people live on the harsh and inhospitable east coast, known as **Na Baigh (Bays)**, while the beautiful west coast with its miles of glorious golden sands is scarcely populated. This is not through choice. The fertile west coast once housed most of the population until the end of the 18th century when they were cleared to make way for sheep farms. Some emigrated to Cape Breton, while others chose instead to stay in Harris and moved to the east side.

The west coast The main road from Tarbert runs south, skirting East Loch Tarbert, then cuts inland and heads west through a dramatic lunar landscape of rocks dotted with tiny lochans. It then begins to descend towards the sea and you can see the vast expanse of **Losgaintir (Luskentyre)** beach directly ahead. A single-track road turns off to the right and runs out to the tiny settlement of Losgaintir. The road cuts through the rich machair as it follows the magnificent stretch of bleached white sand that fills the entire bay, washed by turquoise sea and backed by steep dunes. All this set against the backdrop of the mountains to the north. A short distance offshore is the island of **Tarasaigh (Taransay)**, which was well populated at the beginning of the 1900s but was recently abandoned.

Sleeping You can **camp** on the machair, but ask for permission at the first house. There are a couple of B&Bs **E-F** *Moravia*, T550262, open Mar-Oct, and **E-F** *Seaview*, T550263, open Apr-Oct.

The road follows the coast, passing through the tiny settlements of **Seilebost**, **Horgabost** and **Burgh (Borve)**. There's B&B accommodation at Seilebost and Horgabost, but a few miles further on is another beautiful stretch of white sands at **Sgarasta Bheag (Scaristabeg)**.

Sleeping Overlooking the beach in a wonderful setting is **B** *Scarista House*, T550238, F550277, ian@scaristahouse.demon.co.uk. 5 rooms, open May-Sept. To add to the peace and quiet, there's no TV, only an extensive library and drawing room with open fires. The food on offer is amongst the best on the islands, particularly the seafood. Even if you're not staying, you should treat yourself to dinner here. Expensive but well worth it. There are also self-catering rooms in a separate annexe. The golf course over the road is so scenic the views may put you off your swing.

Beyond Sgarasta Bheag is a turning to the village of **Taobh Tuath (Northton)**, where you can learn about the local machair at the MacGillivary Machair Centre. From here you can walk out to the headland, over Chaipaval hill, with great views all around, to St Kilda to the west, North Uist, the Cuillins of Skye and the hills of North Harris.

The road then runs along the south shore till it reaches the sprawling village of **An t-Ob (Leverburgh)**, site of Lord Leverhulme's ambitious plan to turn a sleepy crofting township into a major fishing port (see page 534). A few of the original buildings can be seen near the pier, which is the departure point for *CalMac's* **car ferry** to Otternish on North Uist (for details, see Ins and outs, page 521).

Sleeping The present village consists of little more than a row of incongruous Scandinavian-style wooden houses, but there are several B&Bs within a couple of miles of the ferry port. One of the best is **E-F** *Caberfeidh House*, T520276, which is close to the ferry and offers room only (**F**). More secluded is **E** *Shieldaig House*, T520378, kwhettall@aol.com, with free cycle hire. Also **E** *Mrs Paula Williams*, T520319, F520146, who caters for vegetarians. A cheaper option is **F** *Am Bothan Bunkhouse*,

T520251, which is close to the ferry, has full facilities and also space for tents. There's a café/restaurant and shop not far from the bunkhouse. For **buses** to Leverburgh see under Tarbert.

Three miles east of Leverburgh, at the southeastern tip of Harris, is **Ròghadal (Rodel)**, dominated by the beautiful 12th century **St Clement's Church**, something of an unusual sight in such a remote spot and one of the most impressive religious building in the Hebrides (only the Benedictine abbey on Iona is larger). The church stands on a site which goes back 1,500 years and was built by Alastair Crotach (Hunchback) Macleod of Harris in the 1520s. Though impressive from the outside, particularly the huge tower, the real interest lies inside, with a collection of remarkable carved wall tombs. There are three tombs, the most notable of which is that of the founder, Alastair Crotach. The one in the south wall of the choir is also worth a close look.

Running north from Roghadal up the east coast of South Harris is the **Golden Road**, so named by the locals because the of the huge expense of building it. This twisting, tortuous single-track road runs through a bizarre and striking moonscape and driving through it is a unique experience (but keep your eyes on the road or you'll end up in one of the many narrow sea lochs). It seems inconceivable that anyone could survive in such an environment, but the road passes through a string of townships created last century by the people evicted from the west coast (see page 537). People here have spent years eking a meagre living from the thin soil by building 'lazy beds' (thin strips of piled-up earth between the rocks) for planting potatoes. Weaving and fishing also provide much-needed income.

Na Baigh (Bays)

At **Lingreabhagh (Lingarabay)** the road skirts the foot **Roinebhal**, the proposed site of one of the largest superquarries in Europe, which would demolish virtually the entire mountain over many decades. Local people and environmentalists are up in arms at the prospect of losing precious fishing grounds not to mention a unique and precious natural asset.

The road passes through a succession of tiny settlements before joining the A859 just south of Tarbert.

Sleeping Accommodation on this coast is limited. There's a *Gatliff Trust hostel* at Caolas Stocinis (Kyles Stockinish), seven miles south of Tarbert (open end Mar to end Sept). There's also the independent *Drinishader Bunkhouse*, at Drinisiader (Drinishader), three miles south of Tarbert, T511255, open all year. Or there's **B&B** at **E-F** *Hillhead*, T511226, at Scadabhagh (Scadabay), between Stocinis and Drinisiadar.

Uibhist a Tuath (North Uist)

North Uist is the largest of the southern chain of the Outer Hebrides, about 13 miles from north to south and 18 miles east to west at its widest point. At first sight it comes as something of a disappointment after the dramatic landscapes of Harris. In fact, it's barely a landscape at all, as over a third of the island's surface is covered by water. The east coast around Lochmaddy, the main settlement, is so peppered with lochs it resembles a giant sieve. But heading west from Lochmaddy the island's attractions become apparent, particularly the magnificent beaches on the north and west coast. Also on the west coast, the Balranald Nature Reserve is the ideal place for bird watching. You're also likely to see otters. There are numerous prehistoric sites scattered across the island, and with all that water around there's obviously plenty of good fishing to be had.

Phone code: 01876
Colour map 1, grid C1
Population: 1,815

Outer Hebrides

Ins and outs

Getting there There are 3 **car ferry** services to North Uist. One is to Otternish from Leverburgh on South Harris, the others are to Lochmaddy, from Uig on Skye, and from Tarbert on Harris. For more details, see page 521. North Uist is joined to the islands of Benbecula and South Uist to the south by causeway and bridge. There are several **buses** daily (Mon-Sat) from Otternish to Lochmaddy and on to Lochboisdale on South Uist.

Getting around There are 4-6 **buses** per day (not Sun) from Otternish to Lochmaddy. These buses continue to Baile a Mhanaich (Balivanich) on Benbecula, where there is an airport (see page 543) and Lochboisdale and Ludag on South Uist (see page 544). There are 4-7 buses per day from Lochmaddy to Otternish. These continue via the new causeway to the island of Bearnaraigh (Berneray) just off the north coast in the sound of Harris. There are 3 buses per day from Lochmaddy to Clachan na Luib (Clachan-a-Luib) which run in an anti-clockwise direction around the north and west coasts. Two buses per day connect Clachan-a-Luib with Baile Sear (Baleshare) and also with Saighdinis (Sidinish). There are also Royal Mail post buses linking the main settlements. Local bus timetables are available at the tourist office in Lochmaddy (see below).

Sights

There are a number of interesting archaeological sites of different periods dotted around the island. The most notable is **Barpa Langass**, seven miles southwest of Lochmaddy, on the slope of Ben Langass, just off the A867 which cuts across the bleak peaty hinterland of North Uist. This is a huge chambered burial cairn dating from around 3,000 BC. Unfortunately, it is now too dangerous to enter. About a mile away, on the southern side of Ben Langass, is the small stone circle known as **Pobull Fhinn**, standing on the edge of Loch Langass. Nearby is **B** *Langass Lodge* (T580285, F580385), whose restaurant specialises in local seafood and game. Three miles northwest of Lochmaddy on the A865 are three bronze age standing stones called **Na Fir Bhreige** (The False Men), said to be the graves of three spies who were buried alive.

Loch nam Madadh (Lochmaddy)

Colour map 1, grid C1   Lochmaddy, the island's main village and ferry port, is a tiny place, so small you're almost through it before you realize. Though it's on the east coast and not close to the beaches, it is the best base for exploring the island as it boasts most facilities. It has a bank, a hotel and pub, a tourist office, a few shops, post office, hospital (T500325) and petrol station. If you have time the **Taigh Chearsabhagh Museum and Arts Centre** (T/F500293, www.taigh-chearsabhagh.com) is worth visiting and has a café.

The **tourist office** is near the ferry pier. ■ *T500321. Mid-Apr to mid-Oct, Mon-Sat 0900-1700, and for the arrival of the evening ferry). They'll provide transport timetables.*

Sleeping &   **C** *Lochmaddy Hotel*, T500332, F500210. Right by the ferry terminal. Open all year.
eating   Their restaurant serves great seafood and the lively bar serves snacks. This is also the place to ask about fishing (see below). There are a couple of good B&Bs: **D-E** *The Old Courthouse*, T500358, and **E** *The Old Bank House*, T500275/324, both of which are open all year. There's also a *SYHA Youth Hostal* at Ostram House, T500368, which is open mid-May to Sept. Half a mile from the ferry pier is an independent hostel, the *Uist Outdoor Centre*, T500480; open all year. The *Stag House* restaurant, T500364, F500417, also does B&B (**D-E**).

The Uists, Benbecula and Barra

© Crown copyright

Sports The *Uist Outdoor Centre* offers a wide range of outdoor activities including kayaking, windsurfing and rock climbing. *Lochmaddy Hotel* (see above) rents out boats for fishing and sells permits for trout and salmon fishing.

Directory **Banks** *Bank of Scotland* is next to the tourist office.

Bearnaraigh (Berneray)

Colour map 1, grid B1 The low-lying island of Bearnaraigh, now connected by a new causeway, is famous as the place where Prince Charles spent a holiday helping out on a croft. It's also the birthplace of the giant Angus MacAskill (see 'Skye', page 506). Its real attraction, though, apart from the splendid isolation, is the three-mile-long sandy beach along its north and west coast.

Sleeping There are a couple of options for those wishing to stay. You can share the prince's crofting experience at **E** *Burnside Croft*, T540235, which also offers cycle hire and stories round the fire for evening entertainment. There's also a *Gatliff Trust Hostel* (no phone; open all year) in 2 restored blackhouses overlooking a lovely sandy beach about a mile up the east coast from the old ferry pier.

Around the island

The real charms of North Uist are its fabulous beaches on the north and west coasts. Heading anti-clockwise from Lochmaddy, the A865 runs northwest, passing the turning for Otternish and **Bearnaraigh** (see above) which is now connected to North Uist by a causeway. It continues west through the township of **Sollas (Solas)**, where there are a couple of **B&Bs**, and then past the beautiful sands of **Bhalaigh (Vallay) Strand**. Near the northwestern tip of the island is **Scolpaig Tower**, standing on an islet in Loch Scolpaig, a 'folly' built for famine relief in the 19th century.

Three miles south of here is the turning to **Balranald RSPB Reserve,** an area of rocky coast, sandy beaches and dunes, machair and lochs. The reserve is ideal for bird watching, especially waders. A two-hour guided walk along the headland allows you to see Manx shearwaters, gannets, skuas, storm petrels and during the summer you can listen out for the distinctive rasping call of the corncrake, one of the rarest birds in Britain. There's a basic visitor centre, which is open April-September. There are a couple of places to stay near Balranald: in **Hogha Gearraidh (Houghgarry)**, overlooking the beautiful beach, is **E** *Mrs Kathy Simpson*, T510312; and in **Ceann a Bhaigh (Bayhead)**, a few miles to the south, is **E-F** *Mrs Morag Nicholson*, T510395. Also in Ceann a Bhaigh is the **Uist Animal Visitors Centre**, where you can see Highland cattle and other rare native breeds as well as more exotic species such as llamas. ■ *Mon-Sat 1000-2200, £2.*

The road continues south to **Clachan na Luib**, at the crossroads of the A865 and A867 which heads east back to Lochmaddy. There's a post office and general store, and a few miles south, at **Cladach a Bhaile Shear (Claddach-baleshare)** is **F** *Taigh Mo Sheannair*, T580246, a renovated crofthouse which offers good hostel accommodation all year round, rents out bicycles and has space for camping

Offshore is the tidal island of **Baile Sear (Baleshare)**, now connected by a causeway to North Uist, with its three-mile long beach on the west coast. A further five miles west are the **Monach Isles** (also known by their old Norse name of Heisker), which were once connected to North Uist at low tide, until the

16th century when a huge tidal wave swept away the sand bridge, thus isolating them. Even so, the islands were still populated until as recently as the 1930s. Now they are populated by the largest breeding colony of grey seals in Europe.

South of Clachan, the road runs past **Cairinis (Carinish)** (where there's B&B accommodation at **E** *Bonnieview*, T580211, over a series of causeways to the little-visited lobster-fishing island of **Griomasaigh (Grimsay)** before heading across another causeway to Benbecula. Near Cairinis is *Feith na Fala*, or Field of Blood, site of the last battle fought in Scotland solely with swords and bows and arrows, in 1601, between the MacDonalds of Sleat and Macleods of Harris. The bloodshed was provoked by one of the MacDonalds divorcing his Macleod wife. When 60 Skye Macleods set off to North Uist to wreak revenge, they were met by sixteen MacDonalds who literally chopped them to pieces, proving that divorce was a messy affair even then.

Beinn na Faoghla (Benbecula)

Tiny Benbecula may be suffering from delusions of stature. Its Gaelic name means 'mountain of the fords' but the highest point is a mere 407ft, with the rest of the island as flat as a pancake. It lies between Protestant North Uist and Catholic South Uist and most visitors use it solely as a means of getting from one to the other via the A865 which cuts straight through the middle.

Phone code: 01870
Colour map 1, grid C1
Population: 1,803

Benbecula's **airport** is at Balivanich (see below) and there are direct flights to Glasgow, Barra and Stornoway (see page 521). The island is connected by causeways to both North and South Uist and **buses** travelling to and from Lochmaddy and Lochboisdale pass through the villages of Balivanich, Lionacleit (Liniclate) and Creag Ghoraidh (Creagorry). There are also regular island buses which run between these settlements.

Getting there & around

Like North Uist, the east of the island is so pitted with lochs that most people live on the west coast. A large percentage of the population are Royal Artillery personnel and their families stationed at **Baile a Mhanaich (Balivanich)**, a sprawling army base of utilitarian buildings in the northwest of the island. The influx of so many English-speakers has had a less than positive impact on Gaelic culture and the military facilities have blighted much of the island's natural beauty, but Benbecula has benefited economically from the army's presence. Not only is there an airport here but also a relatively large number of shops and amenities, including the only NAAFI supermarket in the UK that's open to the public, a Bank of Scotland (with ATM) and post office. There are worries, however, that the base may be run down or closed, which would have a devastating effect on the local economy.

Sights

South of Balivanich the B892 runs around the west coast before joining the main A865 at the southern end of the island. It runs past **Culla Bay**, overlooked by **Baille nan Cailleach (Nunton)**. It was from here in 1746 that Bonnie Prince Charlie set off with Flora MacDonald over the sea to Skye, disguised as her maid (see also page 503). To the south is **Poll-na-Crann**, better known as 'stinky bay' because of the piles of seaweed deposited there by fierce Atlantic storms. From the mid-18th century this kelp was used extensively in making glass and provided a source of income for many communities. By 1820, the so-called kelp boom was over, though it is still gathered today and used for fertilizer.

The B892 ends at **Lionacleit (Liniclate)**, where the new community school serves the Uists and Benbecula. It has extensive facilities, including a swimming pool, library, theatre and even a small local history **museum**. ■ *Mon,*

👉 *A Fishy Tale*

In the 1820s, a dead body was washed up in Culla Bay, near Griminish on Benbecula. It was said to have had the upper body of a well-developed four-year-old child, with long, dark glossy hair, and the lower half was like a salmon, but without scales. Many people came from all around to look at the bizarre creature, before the landlord of the estate ordered a coffin and shroud and it was given a decent burial on the shore of Culla Bay. What exactly this creature was has remained a mystery to this day.

Tue and Thur 0900-1600, Wed 0900-1230 and 1330-1600, Fri 0900-2000, Sat 1100-1300 and 1400-1600.

Sleeping & eating
Most accommodation is in **Lioncleit**, including the ominous-sounding, functional **A** *Dark Island Hotel*, T603030, F602347, which is a lot nicer inside and has a good restaurant. There's also **D** *Inchyra Guest House*, T602176, as well as a couple of **B&Bs** (both **E**) and the *Shellbay campsite*, T602447; open Apr-Oct. In **Balinavich** is a new hostel, **F** *Tigh-na-Cille Bunkhouse*, T602522, which is open all year and sleeps 10 in 2 dorms and 2 twin rooms.

By far the best place to eat on the island is the *Stepping Stone Restaurant* in Balivanich, T603377, F603121, which offers good wholesome Scottish food every day from 1000 till 2100. Snacks, sandwiches, takeaways and home baking are all available, as well as 3- or 5-course meals (mid-range to expensive).

Transport
Car hire *Maclennan Motors*, Balivanich (T602191, F603191); *Ask Car Hire*, Lionacleit (T602818, F602933).

Uibhist a Deas (South Uist)

Phone code: 01870
Colour map 3, grid A1
Population: 2,285

South Uist is the largest of the southern chain of Outer Hebridean islands and the most scenically attractive. Like its southern neighbour, Barra, South Uist is Roman Catholic and generally more relaxed about Sunday openings.

Its 20 miles of west coast is one long sandy beach, backed by dunes with a mile or two of beautiful, flowering machair behind. To the east of the main A865 that runs the length of the island rises a central mountainous spine of rock and peat dotted with numerous lochs. Its two highest peaks, Beinn Mhor (2,034ft) and Hecla (1,988ft), tower over the rocky cliffs of an eastern coastline indented by sea lochs.

Ins and outs

Getting there
The island's main **ferry port** is Loch Baghasdail (Lochboisdale), which is reached from Oban and Mallaig via Castlebay on Barra (it arrives late at night). There are also inter-island ferries from Ludag, at the southern tip of South Uist: a **car ferry** sails the short distance across to the island of Eriskay; and a private **passenger-only** ferry sails to Barra. There are passenger ferry sailings on Sun to and from Barra and a car ferry to Castlebay and Oban, but no ferry arrival from Oban, Mallaig or Castlebay and no bus services. For more details, see page 521.

Getting around
A causeway connects South Uist to Benbecula by road and regular **buses** (4-6 per day Mon-Sat) run between Lochboisdale and Lochmaddy on North Uist, stopping en route at Dalabrog (Daliburgh), Tobha Mòr (Howmore) and Lionacleit and Balinavich on Benbecula. There is also a regular bus service between Lochboisdale and Ludag

Outer Hebrides

Out to lunch

Travelling in the Outer Hebrides can be a very different experience from visiting other parts of Scotland. The pace of life is very different here and the needs of tourists have to come second to the ways of local people.

Take the example of a passenger flight from Glasgow to Benbecula, which was delayed for 30 minutes when the plane had to circle because the air traffic controller was out to lunch!

(for ferries to Eriskay and Barra). For **car hire**, there's *Laing Motors* in Lochboisdale (T700267) and you can **rent bikes** at *Rothan Cycles* (T01870-620283) .

History

The dominant family in South Uist was Clan Ranald, who also owned Benbecula. They were descendants of the first Lord of the Isles, who was a MacDonald. The island's connections with Clanranald came to a sorry end, however, in 1837 when it was sold, along with Benbecula, to pay off bad debts, and became the property of the infamous Lieutenant-Colonel John Gordon Cluny. Though all the southern isles suffered during the brutal clearances of the 19th century, the experiences of people on South Uist were particularly cruel and inhumane. Between 1849 and 1851, over 2,000 were forcibly shipped to Quebec in Canada. Those who refused to board the transport ships were hunted down by dogs and bound before being thrown on board and shipped to Canada, where they were left to starve.

At the north of the island a causeway leads across **Loch Bi** (pronounced 'Bee') to the distinctive modern statue of Our Lady of the Isles, standing by the main road on the lower slopes of **Rueval** hill. Further up the hill is the Royal Artillery control centre, known by the locals as 'Space City', due to its forest of aerials and 'golf balls', which tracks the missiles fired from a range on the northwestern corner of the island out into the Atlantic. Near here, at **Loch a' Chairnain (Lochcarnan)**, is the small, modern **D** *Orosay Inn* (T01870-610298, F610390, orosayinn@ btinternet.com), which is open all year and offers fine Scottish cooking (cheap to mid-range).

Just to the south of here is **Loch Druidibeag Nature Reserve**, on the site of the large freshwater loch, one of the largest breeding grounds in the British Isles for greylag geese and also a favourite haunt for mute swans (there's a warden nearby at Groigearraidh (Grogarry) Lodge). From here the main road runs down the spine of the island, and all along the way little tracks branch off to the west, leading down to lovely beaches. Not far south of Loch Druidibeag is the turning to the tiny village of **Tobha Mòr (Howmore)**, where you can see a collection of the old traditional thatched 'blackhouses' beside the seemingly-endless stretch of golden sand. One of the houses has been converted into a *Gatliff Trust Youth Hostel* (open all year; no phone) which overlooks the ruins of an ancient church and graveyard. The warden lives at Ben More House, at the junction with the main road.

This minor road rejoins the main road near **Bornais (Bornish)**. A few miles south, at **Gearraidh Bhailteas (Milton)**, a cairn marks the birthplace of that famous Heridean lass, **Flora MacDonald** (see page 503). Nearby is the **Kildonan Museum** (T01878-710343) which has a tearoom.

The A865 continues south for a few miles to the village of **Dalabrog (Daliburgh)**, then heads east to the island's main ferry port, **Lochboisdale**.

Machair

Machair is the name given to the strips of land that lie behind the many wonderful beaches of northwest Scotland and the islands. Machair is notable for its fertility, in sharp contrast to the poor, acid peat of the interior. In summer these strips are transformed into a blaze of colour when a multitude of wild flowers bloom – primroses, buttercup, orchid, gentian and wild iris – and this provides good grazing for sheep. The fertility of the machair comes from the calcium-rich shell sand which is blown inshore from the beaches and neutralises the acidity of the peaty soil.

Loch Baghasdail (Lochboisdale)

Phone code: 01878
Colour map 3, grid A1
Population: 300

South Uists's largest settlement is set on a rocky promontory in a beautiful island-dotted sea loch. The imposing entrance is guarded by Calvay island with its 13th century castle ruin. Lochboisdale is a tiny place, with little in the way of tourist sights, though it does have a hotel, bank, post office and **tourist office**, at Pier Rd. ■ *T700286. Open early Apr to mid-Oct.*

Sleeping   You should book accommodation in advance, as the ferry arrives in Lochboisdale late in the evening. **C** *Lochboisdale Hotel*, T700332, F700367. This fishing hotel is right by the ferry terminal and the best place to stay and the only place to have a drink or a meal. There's also **B&B** accommodation by the terminal at **E** *Bayview*, T700329, and **F-E** *Lochside Cottage*, T700472. About a mile from the terminal is **D** *Brae Lea Guest House*, T/F700497, who will collect you from the ferry.

About 10 miles south of Lochboisdale, on the southern coast of the island, is **Ludag jetty**, the departure point for the small private passenger ferry to **Eòlaigearraidh (Eoligarry)** on Barra and the car ferry to Eriskay. A few miles to the west of Ludag, at **Pol a' Charra (Pollachar)** is the charming **C** *Polachar Inn*, T01878-700215, F700768, which has great views across the Sound of Barra and its own beach close by. At **Cille Bhríghde (West Kilbride)** nearby is *Hebridean Croft Originals*, which has a wide range of local crafts on show, as well as a photographic display of local history. It's open daily and has a tearoom.

Eirisgeidh (Eriskay)

Colour map 3, grid A1

The tiny island of Eriskay, with a population of less than 200, gives its name to the native breed of pony, said to have been ridden by King Robert the Bruce at the Battle of Bannockburn in 1314 (see page 289). In the late 1970s it nearly became extinct but one surviving stallion saved the breed and numbers are growing.

Most people come to Eriskay to pay a visit to **Coilleag a' Phrionnsa (Prince's beach)**, the sandy beach on the west coast. This is where Bonnie Prince Charlie first stepped on to Scottish soil, on July 23, 1745, at the start of the ill-fated Jacobite Rebellion. The rare pink convolvulus which grows there today is said to have been planted by the Prince himself from seeds brought from France.

Between Eriskay and South Uist is the wreck of the famous *SS Politician*, the island's other claim to fame. In 1941, the 12,000 ton ship went aground just off the island of Calvey and sank with its cargo, which included 20,000 cases of whisky. This not only provided many islanders with a supply of whisky for many years, but also provided the plot for Compton Mackenzie's book *Whisky Galore!*, which was later made into the famous Ealing comedy of the same name (it was called *Tight Little Island* in the US) and filmed on Barra. Part of the wreck can be seen at low tide and there's more information on the famous incident on display in the appropriately named *Am Politician* pub (open 1230-1430), in the main settlement of **Baile (Balla)**. Also worth a look is **St Michael's**, the Roman Catholic church, built in 1903 and funded by the local fishing fleet.

A series of paths take you round the island in about three hours. For more details, see the *Cuairt Eirisgeidh* leaflet published by the Western Isles Tourist Board.

Eriskay is reached by a frequent car ferry from Ludag (Mon-Sat only; for times, T01878-720261), which lands at the ferry jetty at **Haun**.

Getting there

There's a **B&B** on the island (T01878-720232), or you can camp, though there are few amenities, other than a shop and post office.

Sleeping

Bharraigh (Barra)

It may be tempting to overlook the little island of Barra, only about eight miles long by five miles wide, but this would be a great mistake, as it's one of the most beautiful of all the islands in the Outer Hebrides. Here you'll find the best of the islands in miniature – beaches, machair, peat-covered hills, tiny crofting communities and neolithic remains – and a couple of days spent on Barra gives a real taster of Hebridean life. Gaelic culture is also strong here, but with its Catholic tradition, Barra is a bit more laid-back than many of the other islands in the Outer Hebrides and doesn't follow the others' strict Sabbatrianism.

Population: 1,316
Phone code: 01871
Colour map 3, grid A1

Ins and outs

The best way to arrive by **air** at Tràigh Mhòr ('Cockle Strand'), the famous airstrip on the beach at the north end of the island. This is the only airport in the UK where flight schedules are shown as 'subject to tides'. For flight details see page 521. Barra is reached by **car ferry** from Oban and Mallaig on the mainland (for more details, see page 521) and also by car ferry from Lochboisdale on South Uist, and by passenger-only ferry from Ludag on South Uist (see page 523).

Getting there

There is a regular bus/postbus service (5-8 times per day Mon-Sat) that runs from Castlebay to the ferry port of Eòlaigearraidh, via the **aiport**. There are also buses (3-4 per day Mon-Sat) from Castlebay to Bhatarsaigh (Vatersay). You can also hire a car or a bicycle to tour the island at your leisure (see below).

Getting around

Bàgh a' Chaisteil (Castlebay)

The main settlement is Castlebay, on the southern side of the island, situated in a wide sheltered bay and overlooked by the highest peak, **Sheabhal** (1,260ft), on top of which is a marble statue of the Blessed Virgin and Child. It's an easy walk up to the top and the views are well worth it. The once-thriving herring port is also overlooked by the large Roman Catholic church, Our Lady, Star of the Sea.

Colour map 3, grid A1

The **tourist office** is on the main street near the ferry terminal. It has information on local walks and will book accommodation. ■ *T810223. Apr to mid-Oct Mon-Sat 0900-1700; also open for the arrival of the evening ferry.*

Outer Hebrides

Sights Castlebay's most notable feature is the impressive 15th-century **Kisimul Castle**, built on an island in the middle of the harbour. This was the ancient home of the Chief of the MacNeils, one of the oldest Scottish clans, who owned the island from 1427 till 1838. It was then sold to the notorious Colonel Gordon of Cluny, along with neighbouring South Uist and Benbecula (see page 545), and the poor people of Barra suffered the same cruel fate, 600 of them being shipped to Canada to starve. One hundred years later the castle and much of the island was bought back for the MacNeils by an American architect, Robert Lister MacNeil, who became the 45th Clan Chief and restored the castle to its present state before his death in 1970. His son, the new Clan Chief, uses it as his residence when visiting. ■ *T810449. The castle can be visited by boat from pier on Monday, Wednesday and Saturday afternoons for £3.*

If you're interested in finding out about the island's history, you should visit the **Barra Heritage Centre**. ■ *T810403. Apr-Sept Mon-Fri 1100-1700. £1.*

Sleeping & It's a good idea to book in advance if arriving on the evening ferry from Oban or
eating Mallaig. The best place to stay is the **D** *Castlebay Hotel*, by the ferry terminal (T810223, F810445). 12 rooms, friendly, good food, good value and a great bar. A few miles west of Castlebay is the modern, purpose-built **B-C** *Isle of Barra Hotel* (T810383, F810385, BarraHotel@aol.com). 30 rooms, open Apr-Oct, overlooking a lovely beach with fantastic sea views.

There are also several guesthouses and B&Bs in and around Castlebay, including **E** *Tigh-Na-Mara Guest House*, T810304, 2 mins walk from the ferry, and **E** *Grianamul*, T810416, F810319, ronnie.macneil@virgin.net, open Apr to Oct and also close to the ferry. There's no official campsite, though you can camp rough with permission. A new *Gatliff Trust Youth Hostel* is due to open this year in Breibhig (Brevig), a few miles to the east. Check at the tourist office for details.

The best food is available at the *Castelbay Hotel* and *Isle of Barra Hotel*, both of which offer excellent local fish and seafood at mid-range prices. For something a lot cheaper, try the *Kismul Galley* on the main street, T810645, which offers all-day breakfasts, stovies and home baking and is open Mon-Sat 0900-2100 and Sun 1000-1800. There's also a tearoom at the airport.

Transport **Car hire** is available from £20 per day at *Barra Car Hire*, T810243, and *MacMillan Self Drive*, T890366. **Bicycles** can be hired at *Barra Cycle Hire*, T810284. **Taxi services** and **island tours** with *Hatcher's Taxis*, T810486, and *Nellie's Taxi*, T810302.

As the main ferry port, Castlebay provides the full range of services: hotels, B&Bs, shops, a bank (but no ATM) and post office.

Around Bharraigh

The A888 makes a circular route of 14 miles around the island, making an ideal day's bike tour from Castlebay. Heading west, it passes the turning for the causeway to **Vatersay** (see below), then runs northwest between two hills (**Sheabhal** to the east and **Beinn Tangabhal** to the west) to the west coast, where you'll find the nicest beaches. One of these is at **Halaman Bay**, near the village of **Tangasdal (Tangasdale)**, overlooked by the *Isle of Barra Hotel* (see above). At the turning for **Borgh (Borve)** there are standing stones. Next is the turning for the small settlement of **Baile Na Creige (Craigston)**, where you'll find the **Thatched Cottage Museum**, an original 'blackhouse' and the chambered burial cairn of **Dun Bharpa**. ■ *Museum open Easter-Oct, Mon-Fri 1100-1700. £1.* North of the turning, near **Allathsdal (Allasdale)** is another lovely beach, and just beyond are the remains of **Dun Cuier**, an Iron-age fort.

The A888 then heads east to **Bagh a Tuath (Northbay)**, where a branch left leads to the village of **Eòlaigearraidh (Eoligarry)**, near the northern tip surrounded by sandy bays. A private passenger ferry leaves from here to Ludag on South Uist. The road to Eoligarry passes the island's airport at **Tràigh Mhòr**, the 'cockle strand', which once provided 100 to 200 cartloads of delicious cockles each day. Now, the cockleshells are gathered and used for harling, the roughcast wall covering used on many Scottish houses. By the beach is the house that was once the home of Compton MacKnzie, author of *Whisky Galore!* (see page 546). He lies buried at **Cille Bhara**, to the west of the village of Eòlaigearraidh, along with members of the MacNeil clan. This was one of the most important religious complexes in the Outer Hebrides, built in the 12th century, and consists of a church and two chapels. One of these, St Mary's, has been re-roofed and houses several carved medieval tombstones and a copy of a runic stone. The original is in the Museum of Scotland in Edinburgh (see page 87).

Bhatarsaigh (Vatersay)

A worthwhile trip from Castlebay is to the island of Vatersay, now linked to Barra by a causeway built in an effort to stabilise the island community (the present population is around 70). The island boasts two lovely shell-sand beaches backed by beautiful machair, only a few hundred yards apart on either side of the narrow isthmus that leads to the main settlement of Vatersay. On the west beach, Bagh Siar, is the **Annie Jane Monument**, which commemorates the terrible tragedy in 1853, when the emigrant ship *Annie Jane* was wrecked off the coast of Vatersay, with the loss of 333 lives, many of them islanders.

On a clear day from Vatersay you can enjoy the view of the smaller islands to the south – Sandray, Pabbay and **Mingulay**. The latter was inhabited until 1912, but can still be visited from Barra. This is particularly recommended during the puffin season from June to early August. To arrange a **boat trip**, contact *Mr Campbell*, T01871-810303, or ask at the tourist office in Castlebay.

St Kilda

Over 40 miles west of the Outer Hebrides lie the spectacular and isolated islands of St Kilda, Scotland's first UNESCO World Heritage Site. The largest of the islands, **Hirta**, was the remotest community in Britain, if not Europe, until 1930, when the remaining 36 Gaelic-speaking inhabitants were evacuated at their own request, in one of the most poignant episodes of Scottish history.

In 1957 the islands become the property of the National Trust for Scotland, who in turn leased them to the Nature Conservancy (the forerunner of Scottish Natural Heritage) as a National Nature Reserve. St Kilda is the most important seabird breeding station in northwest Europe. The islands are home to the largest colony of gannets in the world, the largest colony of fulmars in Britain and the largest colony of puffins. These huge numbers of seabirds were vital to the islanders' survival. Their eggs provided food in the summer and gannets and fulmers were caught each season to be plucked, dried and stored for the winter. Their feathers and oil were kept for export to generate income, whilst their bones were shaped into useful tools and skins into shoes.

Today, Hirta is partly occupied by the army as a radar-tracking station for the rocket range on South Uist. The Royal Artillery personnel look over the islands in the winter and help provide services for the volunteers who come in the summer to carry out archaeological and conservation work in and around the old village on Hirta. For more information, contact Scottish Natural Heritage, 135 Stilligarry, South Uist, HS8 5RS, T01870-620238. There are organised tours to the islands, though these are expensive, and usually it's only possible to land on Hirta, where you can visit the museum in the old village or climb up to the highest sea cliffs in the British Isles, at Conachair (1,410ft). For details of tours, ask at one of the main tourist offices in the Outer Hebrides.

Orkney and Shetland

13

Orkney and Shetland

To some these two archipelagos will never be anything more than distant and overlooked specks of land peppering the wild north Atlantic, above an already remote north coast of mainland Scotland. It is true – they are remote and they have maintained a social and political, as well as geographical, distance from the rest of Scotland which goes a long way to explaining the relatively few numbers of visitors each year.

Orkney was under Norse rule until the mid-13th century, and Shetland was only 'given' (as part of a princess' dowry) to Scotland in 1469. Somehow, seeing them as a part of Scotland can be very misleading and each must be seen within the context of its own unique cultural background and unusual geography.

It is these two qualities that make the islands worth visiting and the ones that the tourist boards are keen to plug. Both Orkney and Shetland are littered with outstanding archaeological evidence, not just of Norse occupation, such as at Jarlshof at the very southern tip of Shetland, but also of life back in 3000BC at Skara Brae and the Knap of Howar in the Orkneys. They are also the best places in Britain to see wildlife as yet untamed by the 21st century. Here you can sail alongside porpoises and seals and watch a million migratory seabirds nest and bring up their young during the summer months. And, thanks to fast and frequent transport links, it doesn't take an Arctic expedition to get here!

Orkney

Orkney may only be a short step away from John O' Groats, but to the fiercely independent Orcadians, 'Mainland' means the largest of the Orkney islands and not the Scottish mainland.

Mainland is the largest of the Orkney islands and site of the two main towns and ferry terminals; the capital Kirkwall and the beautiful, old fishing port of Stromness. Here, you'll also find many of Orkney's most precious archaeological treasures: the Stones of Stenness; Maes Howe; the Broch of Gurness; and the remarkable Neolithic village of Skara Brae.

Aside from Mainland, there are a dozen smaller islands to explore, including Hoy, with its wild, spectacular coastal scenery. The even more remote northerly islands offer miles of deserted beaches, and nothing but the calls of myriad birds to shatter the all-pervading peace and quiet.

Ins and outs

Getting there **Air** There are direct flights to **Kirkwall** airport daily except Sunday from Aberdeen, Edinburgh, Glasgow, Inverness and Shetland, with connections to London Heathrow, Birmingham, Manchester and Belfast.

All these flights are operated by *Loganair/British Regional Airlines* and can be booked through *British Airways*, T0345-222111.

Boat There are several ferry routes to Orkney from the mainland. *P&O Scottish Ferries*, T01856-850655, sail from **Aberdeen** to **Stromness** (8 hrs) twice weekly (Tue and Sat) in 'standard season' (Jun-Aug) and once a week (Sat) the rest of the year. From Aberdeen a standard season passenger fare costs £41 single and a car costs £104.50. There's a 20% discount on passenger fares, and 50% on vehicle fares, for midweek sailings. Cars should be booked in advance.

P&O also sail from Scrabster to **Stromness** (2 hrs) twice a day (Mon-Sat; once on Sun) from Apr-Oct and twice a day (Mon-Fri; once on Sat) from Nov-Mar. A standard season passenger fare costs £15.50 single and a car costs £46. A shuttle bus links Scrabster with the nearby town of Thurso, on the north coast. There are regular bus and train services to Thurso from Inverness (see page 473).

P&O sail from Lerwick (Shetland) to **Stromness** (8 hrs) on Fri (all year) and Wed (Jun-Aug), returning on Sun (all year) and Tue (Jun-Aug). A passenger fare costs £38 single and a car costs £86.50. There is a 10% student/senior citizen discount on all P&O ferries to Orkney.

John o'Groats Ferries, T01955-611353, www.jogferry.co.uk, operate a passenger-only (and bicycles) ferry service from John o' Groats to **Burwick** (2-4 times per day; 45 mins) on South Ronaldsay, from May to Sept. A single fare costs £15 (bicycles an extra £3). An **off-peak return** from John o' Groats to **Kirkwall**, departing at 1600 or 1800 costs £23. No bookings required. A free bus meets the afternoon train from Thurso at 1430 and connects with the 1600 or 1800 ferry to Orkney. There are bus connections between Burwick and Kirkwall (45 mins) for all ferry sailings. They also operate the **Orkney Bus**, a daily direct bus/ferry/bus service between **Inverness** and Kirkwall, via John o' Groats. It leaves Inverness at 0730 and 1420 from Jun-Sept (at 1420 only in May). It costs £38 return. Journey time 5 hrs. Advance booking is essential.

Getting around **Air** There are **inter-island flights** which are operated by *Loganair*, T01856-872494. Eight-seater aircraft fly from Kirkwall daily except Sun to **Stronsay, Sanday, North Ronaldsay, Westray** and **Papa Westray**, and on Wed to **Eday**. To Papa Westray and North Ronaldsay costs only £15 single, and to the other islands listed costs £30 single.

Viking heritage

The history of Orkney and Shetland is bound up with the history of the Vikings, who first came to the islands in the latter half of the ninth century and stayed for about 650 years. This was part of a great Viking expansion westwards and in less than a century emigrants from Norway and Denmark settled in Orkney, Shetland, Iceland, Greenland, Caithness, the Western Isles, Isle of Man and parts of Ireland and the northern half of England.

In 872, the king of Norway set up a Norse earldom in Orkney, from which the Vikings ruled Orkney, Shetland and the Western Isles and took part in raids around Britain and Europe, creating the popular image of Vikings as aggressive, bloodthirsty invaders. At home, however, they lived a peaceful life, adhering to the laws of their parliament, the ting, and many converted to Christianity.

In the late 14th century, Norway, Denmark and Sweden were united under a Danish king. In 1469, the Royal estates and prerogatives in Orkney and Shetland were pledged to Scotland as part of the marriage dowry of Margaret, daughter of the King of Denmark, on her marriage to Prince James of Scotland, later to become King James III. Orkney and Shetland were to revert to rule by the kings of Norway when the debt was paid, but the pledge was never redeemed and the islands remained under Scottish control.

Soon after assuming control, the Scots began to change the old Norse laws which they had agreed to maintain and Scottish influence grew. In 1564, Mary, Queen of Scots granted the control and revenues from Orkney and Shetland to her half-brother, Robert Stewart. His prime motivation however was to extract as much money as possible through taxes. He was succeeded by his son, the infamous Patrick Stewart, who demanded even more rents, dues and fines. Earl Patrick eventually got his come-uppance when he was executed in Edinburgh for treason, but the changes he had made continued and Scots and English gradually began to usurp Old Norse as the native language of the islands.

Inter-island flights not leaving from Kirkwall cost £14. There are **sightseeing flights** in Jul and Aug which fly over all these islands and cost £30. There's also an *Orkney Adventure ticket* which allows you to fly to three islands for £66. Flight schedules are given under each relevant destination in this chapter.

Bus Buses on the Orkney islands are very limited. Apart from the daily service between **Burwick** and **Kirkwall** which connects with the ferry, there are buses from Kirkwall to **Stromness, Evie/Tingwall, Dounby, St Margaret's Hope, Deerness** and **East Holm**. There's also a bus to **Houton** (Hoy) which connects with the ferry. Bus details are given under each relevant destination and on page 561.

Boat *Orkney Ferries*, T01856-872044, operates daily car and passenger **ferries** to **Rousay, Egilsay** and **Wyre** from Tingwall; to **Shapinsay, Eday, Stronsay, Sanday, Westray** and **Papa Westray** from Kirkwall; to **Graemsay** and **Hoy** from Stromness; and to **Hoy** and **Flotta** from Houton. There's a ferry on Fri to **North Ronaldsay** from Kirkwall.

Fares: to **Rousay, Egilsay, Wyre, Shapinsay, Hoy, Graemsay** and **Flotta** costs £2.40 per passenger one-way and £7.20 per car. Inter-island fares are £1.20 per passenger. A round-trip costs £4.80. To **Eday, Stronsay, Sanday, Westray, Papa Westray** and **North Ronaldsay** costs £4.80 per passenger one-way and £10.80 per car. An inter-island fare is £2.40, and round-trip costs £9.60. There are also additional Sun sailings in summer (May-Sept); contact Orkney Ferries or the tourist board for the latest schedules. Those travelling by car should book all ferry journeys in advance. Ferry details are given under the relevant destination.

Orkney

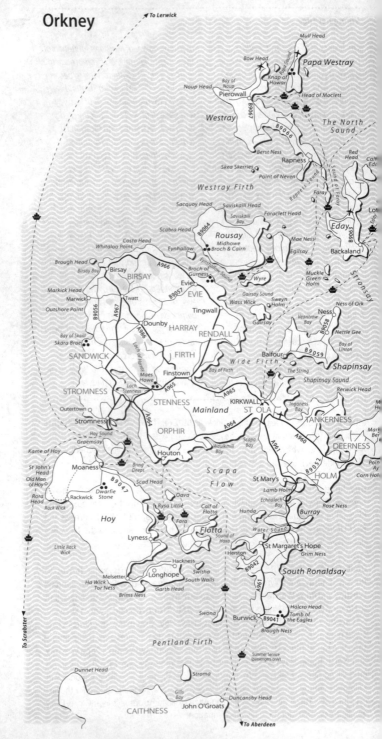

Car Only the main population centres on Mainland are served by public transport and having a car is essential to visit many of the most interesting sights. Bringing a car to Orkney is expensive, but there are several **car hire** firms on the Mainland and on the other islands. Car hire firms are listed under each particular town.

Bicycle Orkney is relatively flat and most of its roads are quiet which makes it ideal for touring by bike, though the wind can make it difficult if it's blowing in the wrong direction. Bicycles can be hired in Kirkwall, Stromness and on many of the other islands. Details are given in the relevant section.

Organized tours Those with limited time may prefer to book a tour of the islands. Both general sightseeing tours and special interest tours are available. *Go-Orkney*, South Cannigall, St Ola, T01856-871871, www.orknet.co.uk/ork-ney-tours, runs a series of tours of Mainland and also to Hoy and Rousay. *Wildabout Orkney*, 5 Clouston corner, Stenness, T01856-851011, www.wildabout.orknet.co.uk, offers highly-rated wildlife, historical, folklore and environmental tours of Mainland for around £16 per person for a full day. *Discover Orkney Tours*, T/F01856-872865, also offer tours of Mainland as well as trips to Westray and Papa Westray.

The **Orkney Tourist Board** (www.orkney.com, orkneytb@csi.com) has tourist offices in Kirkwall and Stromness. They will book accommodation for you, or provide a list of what's available, though many B&Bs are not included in the tourist board scheme. They can also provide information on various sights, walks and the islands' wildlife. Those wishing to leave Mainland and visit the smaller islands should pick up a free copy of the tourist board's excellent information and travel guide, *The Islands of Orkney*. For more background reading, see the *Orkney Guide Book* by Dr C Tait (£14.95).

Tourist information

Orkney and Shetland

N

0 km   5

0 miles   5

© Crown copyright

Viking place names

Despite the disappearance of the Norse language, many of the Viking place names have survived. Here are some of the most common Old Norse elements which will help explain the meaning of many place names:

		geo	creek
		grind	gate
		ham(n)	anchorage
		holm	small island
		houb	lagoon
		howe	mound
		kirk	church
a(y)	island	lax	salmon
a, o	stream	ler	mud, clay
aith	isthmus	lyng	heather
ayre	beach	minn	mouth
bard	headland	mool, noup	headland
bister	farm	setter	farm
brae, brei	broad	ting	parliament
fell, field	hill	toft	house site
fors	waterfall	voe	sea inlet
garth	farm	wick	bay

Kirkwall

Phone code: 01856
Population: 7,000

Orkney's capital is built around a wide sheltered bay and is the main departure point for ferries to the northern islands. First impressions are a little misleading, as the harbour area has been blighted by modern development. More appealing, however, are the narrow winding streets and lanes of the old town, which has not changed much over the centuries. There are many houses dating from the 16th, 17th and 18th centuries, as well as Kirkwall's greatest attraction, its magnificent cathedral, the finest medieval building in northern Scotland.

Getting around The town is compact and it's easy to get around on foot. The **bus station** is 5 mins walk west of the town centre. The **airport**, T872421, is 3 miles southeast of Kirkwall on the A960. There are no buses to and from town. A taxi will cost around £6.

The **main street** changes its name from Bridge St, to Albert St, to Broad St and Victoria St as it twists its way south from the busy harbour. The cathedral is on Broad St and most of the shops and banks are on Broad St and Albert St.

Sights On Broad St, near the cathedral, is the very helpful **tourist office**. They will book accommodation and change money and also provide various useful free leaflets including *The Islands of Orkney* and the *Kirkwall Heritage Guide*. They also stock a wide range of guide books and maps and have details of forthcoming events. Another good source is the weekly newspaper *The Orcadian*. ■ T872856, www.orkneyislands.com. Open Apr-Sept daily 0830-2000; Oct-Mar Mon-Sat 0930-1700.

The town's outstanding sight is the huge and impressive red sandstone **St Magnus Cathedral**, built by masons who had worked on Durham Cathedral in the north of England. It was founded in 1137 by Rognvald Kolson, Earl of Orkney, in memory of his uncle, Magnus Erlendson, who was slain by his cousin, Haakon Paulson, on Egilsay, in 1115. Magnus was buried at Birsay and it is said that heavenly light was seen over his grave. It soon became a shrine, attracting pilgrims from as far afield as Norway. Magnus was canonized in 1133, and four years later his nephew commissioned construction of the cathedral. The building wasn't completed until the 14th century and major additions were made during the intervening centuries. The most recent addition was a new west window for the nave, in 1987 to celebrate the cathedral's 850th anniversary.

The bones of St Magnus now lie in the north choir pillar, while those of St Rognvald lie in the south one. There's also a memorial to John Rae, the 19th-century Arctic explorer, who is buried in the graveyard, as well as a monument to the 833 men of the HMS *Royal Oak* who died when it was torpedoed in Scapa Flow in 1939. ■ *Apr-Sept Mon-Sat 0900-1800, Sun 1400-1800; Oct-Mar Mon-Sat 0900-1300 and 1400-1700, Sun service at 1115.*

Looming impressively nearby are the ruins of the **Bishop's Palace**, built in the 12th century as the first Kirkwall residence of the Bishop of Orkney. Here King Haakon of Norway died in 1263 after his defeat at the Battle of Largs. The palace was repaired and extended in the mid-16th century by Bishop Reid and most of what you see dates from that period. There's a good view of the town from the top of the '*Moosie Too'r*'. The adjacent **Earl's Palace** was built around 1600 by the notorious Patrick Stewart, Earl of Orkney using forced labour. Still very much intact, it is one of Scotland's most elegant Renaissance buildings and was occupied by the tyrannical Stewart only for a very short time, until he was imprisoned and later executed. Wandering around both these spectacularly impressive, and solid, buildings is a very good way to get a feel for a period of Orkney's history that is very often ignored, with the likes of Skara Brae just up the road. ■ *Both buildings are managed by Historic Scotland. Apr-Sept daily 0930-1830. Admission £1.80, £1.30 concession. A joint ticket for all Orkney HS monuments, covering the Broch of Gurness, Maes Howe and Skara Brae, costs £9, £7 concession.*

Opposite St Magnus Cathedral is **Tankerness House and Gardens**, a 16th-century former manse which has been restored and now houses the **Orkney Museum**, which features various archaeological artefacts from Neolithic times to the Vikings. If you are spending any time in Kirkwall at the beginning of your stay, then this is an exceedingly worthwhile exhibition. It is a great way to whet your appetite for the archaeological gems that are lying in wait for you all over the islands, and it also puts them all into a useful chronological context. ■ *T873191. Mon-Sat 1030-1700; May-Sept also Sun 1400-1700. Free.* Old radio buffs should not miss the **Orkney Wireless Museum**, at Kiln Corner, at the harbour end of Junction Road, which houses a jumble of domestic and wartime communications equipment from the 1930s onwards. ■ *Apr-Sept Mon-Sat 1000-1630, Sun 1400-1630. Admission £2.*

A mile south of the town centre on the road to South Ronaldsay is the 200-year-old **Highland Park Distillery**, the most northerly of Scotland's whisky distilleries. There are guided tours of the distillery, one of the few that still has its own floor maltings, and a wee dram of this particularly fine single malt at the end. ■ *T874619. Tours every half hour Apr-Oct Mon-Fri 1000-1700 (last tour at 1600); Jul and Aug also Sat and Sun 1200-1700; Nov, Dec and Mar Mon-Fri at 1400 and 1530 only. Admission £3.*

The top hotel in Kirkwall is the very comfortable **B-C** *Ayre Hotel*, T873001, www.orkneyislands.com/ayre, on the harbour front. Another good option is the **B-D** *Albert Hotel*, T876000, on Mounthoolie Lane in the centre of town. It also has a restaurant and a couple of lively bars (see below). Two miles from town on the A964 Orphir road at St Ola is the **D** *Foveran Hotel*, T872389, overlooking Scapa Flow. It is friendly and comfortable and also offers very good food, including vegetarian. The **D** *West End Hotel*, Main St, T872368, is central and serves good bar meals.

There are also plenty of cheap **B&Bs**, though most rooms are small and don't have en suite facilities. **E-F** *Whiteclett*, St Catherine's Pl, T874193. A 200-year-old listed house near the harbour, and **E-F** *Arundel*, Inganess Rd, T873148. A modern bungalow

Sleeping

Orkney and Shetland

Kirkwall

HATSTON INDUSTRIAL ESTATE

Starrowhawk Rd

Crowness Cres

Grainshore

Scott's Rd

Ayre Road

To Stromness

Peerie Sea Loan

Caravan Park

Peerie Sea

Pickaquoy Liesure Centre

Pickaquoy Road

Car Park

Muddiesdale Rd

Car Park

Pickaquoy Loan

Bus station

W Tankerness La

Great Western Rd

Junction St

Car Park

Burnmouth Rd

Castle St

Car Park

Car Park

West Castle St

Road

Albert St

Broad St

Castle St

Car Park

Harbour St
Wireless Museum

Ayre

Albert

Kirkwall

Bridge St

Shore St

St Catherine's Pl

Cromwell Rd

Comm

Cromw

Garden St

Queen St

Willowbu

Laing St

The Strynd

King St

School Pl

Arts Theatre

Mill St

P & O Ferries

Orkney Ferries Ltd

Car Park

Qn Sonja Kloss

Kingharald Kloss

The Crafty

Car Park

Car Park

Tankerness House

Earl's Palace

St Magnus Cathedral

Palace Rd

Bishop's Palace

St Rognald St

Dundas

George

Car Park

Pol

Victoria St

Victoria Rd

Vict La

Union Rd

Buttquoy Pl

Buttquoy Cres

Eunson Kloss

Glaitness Rd

Viking Pl

St Rognvald Way

High St

Wellington St

Hornersquoy

Union St

Main St

West End

Clay Loan

Junction Rd

Manse Rd

Broad St

Sands Rd

Lavarock Rd

Pipersquoy Dr

Earl Thorfinn St

King Haakon St

Earl Sigurd St

Park Lo

Corse Loan

Nicolson St

Hospital Health Centre

Pipersquoy Rd

Kirklands Rd

Warrenfield Ct

Craigie Cres

Summerdale Dry

Quoy Bnks

Quoy Pl

Holm

CORSE FARM

SYHA Youth Hostel

Scapa Ct

Inis Way

Scapa Cres

Quoybanks Cres

Royal Oak Rd

Old Scapa Road

New Scapa Rd

Holm Branch Rd

To Orphir & Foveran Hotel

Lyni

Holm Road

Lynn

N

0 metres 200
0 yards 200

To Scapa Bay

Highland Park Distillery & Visitor Centre

on a quiet road about a mile from the town centre.

SYHA Youth Hostel, T872243, open Apr-Sept. This large, well-equipped youth hostel is on Old Scapa Rd, about 15 mins walk from the town centre. There's also **camping** at *Pickaquoy Caravan & Camping Site*, T873535. Open May-Sept, on the western outskirts of Kirkwall, off the A965.

Eating

Kirkwall is no gastronome's paradise and you'll be hard-pushed to find somewhere decent to eat in town. The best place to eat is probably the *Foveran Hotel* (see above). Otherwise, the *Albert Hotel* (see above) serves bar meals (made with home-grown produce, cheap to mid-range) as does the *West End Hotel*. The islands' only Indian restaurant is the *Mumtaz*, on Bridge St. The best place for a snack is the *St Magnus Café*, opposite the cathedral. This is a true cafeteria-style café, serving substantial soups and rolls in a bustling and very friendly atmosphere.

Bars & nighlife

Nightlife is Kirkwall revolves around its lively pubs. The *Bothy Bar* at the *Albert Hotel* is a good place for a drink and sometimes has live folk music. The hotel's *Matchmakers Bar* has a disco at weekends. The *Ayre Hotel* also stages folk music nights. Check details in *The Orcadian*. The town's *New Phoenix* **cinema** is housed in the *Pickaquoy Leisure Centre*, T879900, on Pickaquoy Rd. It also has **sports** and fitness facilities and a café and bar.

Transport

For details of flights and ferries to Orkney, see 'Getting there', page 554. Details of inter-island flights and ferries are given in the relevant island sections.

There's a limited **bus** service around the Mainland. *Peace Coaches*, T872866, runs regular buses Mon-Sat from Kirkwall bus station to **Stromness** 30 mins, £2.20. They also run 3-5 buses a day, Mon-Sat, to **Houton**, 30 mins, £1.40, which connect with ferries to Hoy; and a daily bus, Mon-Sat, to **East Holm**, 25 mins, £1, and **Stromness via Dounby**, 55 mins. *Causeway Coaches*, T831444, runs 2-4 buses a day, Mon-Sat, to **St Margaret's Hope**, 30

Orkney and Shetland

Events on Orkney

There are numerous events which take place throughout the year.

Amongst the best-known annual events is **The Ba'** (ball), held on Christmas Day and New Year's Day in Kirkwall. It is a bit like rugby, basketball and a full-scale riot all rolled into one and is contested between two sides – the Uppies and the Doonies – representing different districts of the town. As many as 200 'players' may be involved and a game can last up to seven hours as both sides attempt to jostle the ball along the streets until one reaches their 'goal' to win the prized ba'.

One of the most entertaining events on Orkney is the excellent **Orkney Folk Festival**, which takes place at various locations throughout the islands over three days at the end of May.

The most prestigious and popular event is the acclaimed **St Magnus Festival**, held in June in Kirkwall. It consists of six days of music, drama, literature and the visual arts and features many internationally renowned performers.

During July there are several **regattas** held on most of the islands, while August is marked by numerous **agricultural shows**, culminating in the **Festival of the Horse and Boys' Ploughing Match** on South Ronaldsay (see page 569).

The **Orkney Science Festival** is held in the first week in September, T01856-876214.

For details of what's going on and when, buy a copy of The Orcadian, which comes out on Thursdays.

---

mins, £2.20. *Rosie Coaches*, T751227, runs buses to **Tingwall** and **Evie**. The bus service between Kirkwall and **Burwick** is run by *Shalders Coaches*, T850809. Note that there is no Sun bus service on Orkney.

Car hire *Scarth Car Hire*, Great Western Rd, T872125. *WR Tullock*, Castle St, T876262, and Kirkwall airport, T875500. **Cycle hire** *Bobby's Cycle Centre*, Tankerness Lane, T/F875777. Mountain bikes from £8 per day.

Directory **Banks** Branches of the 3 main Scottish banks with cash machines are on Broad St and Albert St. Exchange also at the tourist office. **Communications** Post office: Junction Rd. Open Mon-Fri 0900-1700, Sat 0930-1230. **Laundry** *The Launderama*, Albert St, T872982. Open Mon-Fri 0830-1730, Sat 0900-1700. **Medical facilities** Balfour Hospital, Health Centre and Dental Clinic, New Scapa Rd, T885400.

West Mainland

Phone code: 01856 Everything west of Kirkwall is known as West Mainland, an area of rich farmland, rolling hills and moorland, fringed by spectacular cliffs along the Atlantic coastline and with the greatest concentration of pre-historic monuments in Britain. Here you'll find, amongst many others, the well-preserved Neolithic village of **Skara Brae**, silent monuments to human endeavour in the form of the standing **Stones of Stenness** and the **Ring of Brodgar**, and the chambered tomb of **Maes Howe**, with its many still unresolved mysteries. The sights below are listed in an anti-clockwise direction starting from Kirkwall.

Evie & the Broch of Gurness Nine miles northwest of Kirkwall is the tiny village of Evie. A track leads from the village towards the coast, past a sandy beach, to the **Broch of Gurness**. Standing on a lonely, exposed headland on the north coast with warm, gentle views across towards the island of Rousay, this is the best-preserved broch on Orkney, thought to date from around 100 BC. It is surrounded by an Iron Age village whose houses are also remarkably well-preserved, with the original hearths, beds, cupboards and even a toilet still in evidence. The broch and village were occupied by the Picts right up till Viking times, around 900 AD. Many Pictish artefacts have been found on the site and the grave of a ninth-century Norse woman was also discovered. ■ *Apr-Sept daily 0930-1830, £2.50, £1.90 concession, T751414 (HS).*

To the southwest of Evie is the **Birsay Moors RSPB Reserve** and at **Lowrie's Water** on Burgar Hill there's a bird-hide from where you can watch breeding red-throated divers. Also on Burgar Hill you'll see several huge aerogenerators built to take advantage of Orkney's fierce winds.

Sleeping D *Woodwick House*, T751330, a very comfortable country house hotel offering good food and occasional cultural events. Good value. The *Eviedale Centre* beside the junction of the road to Dounby, T751270, open April-October, has a small **bothy** and **campsite**. *The Mistra* is the local village shop, post office and pub.

At the far northwestern corner of the Mainland is the parish of Birsay which **Birsay** was a favourite residence of the Earls of Orkney in Viking times as well as the first seat of the Bishop, before the building of St Magnus Cathedral in Kirkwall. Earl Thorfinn the Mighty lived here (1014-64) and built Orkney's first cathedral, **Christchurch**, for the new Bishop.

In the centre of the village are the ruins of the **Earl's Palace**, built by the infamous Earl Robert Stewart in the late 16th century and once described as "a sumptuous and stately dwelling". Not much remains today but enough to give some idea of the sheer scale of the place. ■ *Open at all times. Free.* Close by is **St Magnus church**, built in 1760 on the site of an earlier church, which in turn was built on the foundations of what is believed to be the original Christchurch. Also in Birsay, just south of the A966 and A967 junction, is **Barony Mills**, the last working water-powered mill in Orkney. ■ *Apr-Sept daily 1000-1300 and 1400-1700. Admission £1.50.*

Lying half a mile off the coast near the village is the **Brough of Birsay**, a tidal island, jutting out into the north Atlantic and visible from several other points all the way down the west cost of the mainland. It is only accessible for a couple of hours at low tide (times available from Kirkwall and Stromness tourist offices) but, if possible, it is best seen at the end of the day, as the sun sets - and you'll probably have the whole island to yourself. Pick your way over the shell and bladderack-strewn causeway and wander at your leisure (but don't forget the tide!) amongst the remnants of a Pictish, and then Viking, community. The island was an important Pictish settlement from around the sixth century and many artefacts have been found here. Some of these can be seen at the small ticket office at the entrance to the island (entrance fee £1). The Brough was also the site of an important Viking settlement and there are extensive remains, including the 12th-century **St Peter's church**, where St Magnus was buried after his murder on Egilsay. You can also walk out to the island's **lighthouse** along the top of the cliffs and see puffins (amongst other migrating seabirds) and possibly Minke whales, Pilot whales and Killer whales.

At the southern end of Birsay Bay are the wild and spectacular 300ft-high cliffs **Markwick Head** of Marwick Head, topped by the distinctive **Kitchener Memorial**, erected after the First World War to commemorate Lord Kitchener and the crew of the *HMS Hampshire*, which was sunk by a German mine off the coast in 1916 with the loss of all but 12 of her crew. Marwick Head is also an **RSPB Reserve** and during the nesting season in early summer is home to many thousands of guillemots, razorbills, kittiwakes and fulmars, as well as a few puffins.

A mile inland, by the Loch of Isibister, is another RSPB reserve, **The Loons**, an area of marshland where you can see breeding and migrating wildfowl and waders. Further east, between Boarhouse Loch and Hundland Loch, is the **Kirbuster Farm Museum**, the last surviving Orkney 'black-house' which was lived-in till the 1960s and gives an insight into 19th-century rural life on the islands. ■ *Apr-Sept Mon-Sat 1030-1300 and 1400-1700, Sun 1400-1900. Admission £2.*

Sleeping Accommodation is limited to the **D-E** *Barony Hotel*, T721327, baronyhotel@btinternet.com. Open May-Sept, on the north shore of Boardhouse Loch. It specializes in fishing holidays and is about the only place to offering **food** in these parts. There's also **E-F** *Primrose Cottage*, T/F721384. A comfortable **B&B** overlooking Marwick Bay.

Transport On Mon there's a **bus** between Kirkwall and Birsay with *Shalder Coaches*, T850809.

Skara Brae & South of Birsay, eight miles north of Stromness, in the magnificent setting of
Skaill House the dazzling white sands of the Bay of Skaill, is Skara Brae, the best preserved Stone Age village in northern Europe. First revealed in 1850 after a violent storm blew away the dunes, the site dates from around 5,000 years ago and was occupied for about 600 years. The houses contain stone furniture, fireplaces, drains, beds, dressers and even have damp-proof coursing in the foundations. The whole complex presents a unique picture of the lifestyle of its inhabitants and there's also a replica 'house' that you can enter, and wander around in through the gloom, empathizing with that 3000BC lifestyle! The swish, modern visitor centre has a useful introductory video and exhibition which is definitely worth seeing before you look round the site (and it's also worth buying their guidebook). After leaving the visitor centre, you walk down a 'path of time', which takes you back through landmark achievements of the last seven millennia, gradually building up the suspense and putting the achievements of Skara Brae in perspective - they may only be rudimentary buildings that once had turf for their rooves, but they were built 2000 years before the pyramids of Egypt, and in one of the world's most northerly outposts.

During the summer, a ticket to Skara Brae includes admission to nearby **Skaill House**, an early 17th-century mansion which contains a few old artefacts, including Captain Cook's dinner service from the *Resolution*, but is a bit of a let-down after what you will have just witnessed, not 300 yards away at Skara Brae. ■ *Skara Brae and Skaill House Apr-Sept daily 0930-1830; Skara Brae only also Oct-Mar Mon-Sat till 1630 and Sun 1400-1630. Admission £4 in summer, £3 concession; £3.20 in winter, £2.40 concession.*

A short distance inland from here, at **Sandwick**, is Orkney's only brewery, housed in the old Quoyloo School. It brews the island's *Raven Ale* and various bottled beers, including *Skull-splitter*, named after the Viking Earl, Thorfinn Skull-splitter.

South of the Bay of Skaill is **Yesnaby**, one of the most spectacular places on the islands, where the cliffs have been eroded into a series of stacks and *geos* by the fierce Atlantic seas. An exhilarating, and precarious, half mile walk south from the car park and old Second World War lookout post brings you to **Yesnaby Castle**, a huge sea stack similar to the Old Man of Hoy. It's a dramatic sight, especially in a full force gale.

Ring of Brodgar

There are a few **B&Bs** close to Skara Brae, including **E** *Kierfiold House*, T/F841583, near Loch Harray, and **E-F** *Netherstove*, T/F841625, overlooking the Bay of Skaill. To get to Skara Brae you'll need your own transport, or you can visit as part of a guided tour (see page 554), or walk north along the coast from Stromness, via Yesnaby.

Standing Stones of Stenness & the Ring of Brodgar

Northeast of Stromness, on the road to Kirkwall, is the tiny village of **Stenness**, near some of Orkney's most interesting prehistoric sites. The Standing Stones of Stenness comprise the four remaining stones from an original circle of 12 stones, dating from 3000 BC. The largest of the stones stands over 15ft high. A path leads from the stones to the nearby **Barnhouse Settlement**, a recently-excavated Neolithic village.

About a mile northwest of Stenness is another stone circle, the Ring of Brodgar. This is a particularly impressive henge monument. It is over 100yds in diameter and 27 of the original 60 stones are still standing, some of them up to 15ft high. Given the importance of these sites it is particularly refreshing to realize when you get there that you can walk about amongst the stones in the still calm of a summer evening, with only a few oyster catchers for company, but both do get busy with coach parties during the day. ■ *Admission free.*

Maes Howe

Less than a mile northeast of the Stones of Stenness is Maes Howe, the finest Neolithic burial chamber in Europe. It was built around 2750 BC, making it contemporary with the Standing Stones and Skara Brae, and is amazingly well preserved. A huge mound covers a stone-built entrance passage which leads into a central chamber – over 12ft square and the same in height – with three smaller cells built into the walls of the tomb. A fascinating feature of the site is that the winter solstice sun sets directly over the Barnhouse Stone, half a mile away, and shines down the entrance passage of Maes Howe and onto the back wall of one of the cells. When it was opened, in 1861, no human remains or artefacts were found, giving no clues as to its usage. However, in the 12th century, Vikings returning from the Crusades broke into the tomb searching for treasure. They found nothing but left behind one of the largest collections of runic graffiti anywhere in the world, as well as carvings of a dragon, serpent and walrus. Many of the inscriptions are pretty basic, along the lines of "Thorfinn wrote these runes" but some are more intriguing, such as "Many a woman has come stooping in here no matter how pompous a person she was". A guide gives you an excellent overview of the chamber's mysterious architectural attributes, but the fact remains that the history of this extraordinary place is still largely unsolved – something that obviously adds to the site's attraction. Unfortunately, you do not get the chance to spend very much time in the chamber, so you are unlikely to uncover any great secrets. ■ *Tickets to Maes Howe from Tormiston Mill, on the other side of the road, where there's a an exhibition, introductory video and café, T761606. Apr-Sept daily 0930-1830; Oct-Mar Mon-Wed and Sat 0930-1630, Thur 0930-1200, Fri and Sun 1430-1630. £2.50, £1.90 concession. Also combined ticket for £9 including Skara Brae and Skaill House, Broch of Gurness, Earl's Palace and Bishop's Palace.*

Sleeping There are a few places to stay around **Stenness**. On the shores of Loch Harray is the **C-D** *Merkister Hotel*, T771366, which is a favourite with anglers. It has a very good restaurant and a popular bar. On the shores of Loch Stenness is the **D-C** *Standing Stones Hotel*, T850449, standingstones@sol.co.uk. There's also the lovely **E** *Mill of Eyreland*, T850136, www.orknet.co.uk/mill, a converted mill three miles from Stromness.

Orphir On the southern shores of West Mainland, overlooking Scapa Flow, is the scattered community of Orphir, which has a few sights worth visiting, especially if you're heading across to Hoy from the ferry terminal at **Houton**, a little further west.

The main point of interest in Orphir is the **Orkneyinga Saga Centre**, where a small exhibition and video introduces the saga, written c1200, possibly by an Icelander, which tells the history of the Viking Earls of Orkney from around 900 AD to 1200 AD, when the islands became a part of Scotland rather than Norway. As you would expect, there's plenty of gore and Machievellian carryings on, including an assassination attempt that went disastrously wrong, when a poinsoned shirt meant for Earl Harold was unwittingly and fatally worn by his brother Paul instead. ■ *All year daily 0900-1700, free.* Behind the centre is **The Earl's Bu**, looking out across Orphir Bay south to Cava Island. These are the 12th-century foundations of the home of the Norse Earls of Orkney written about in the saga. Inside the cemetery gates is a section of the circular church built by Haakon and modelled on the rotunda of the Church of the Holy Sepulchre in Jerusalem.

Transport For details of **ferries** to **Hoy** and **Flotta**, see page 571. For details of **buses** to **Houton**, see page 561.

Stromness

Phone code: 01856
Population: 2,500

Stromness is one of the classic Scottish fishing villages and a perfect introduction to Orkney. Ferries from Scrabster arrive here and the newcomer is greeted by rows of stone-built houses hugging the shore, each with their own jetty. Stromness is a much more attractive than Kirkwall and its narrow, winding main street, its wynds and closes, its fascinating shops, and its unique atmosphere make it the ideal base for exploring the West Mainland.

Though referred to in the Viking Saga as Hamnavoe, the town dates from the 17th century. Its importance as a trading port grew in the 18th century when wars and privateers made the English Channel too dangerous and ships used the northern route across the Atlantic, calling in at Stromness to take on food and water and to hire local men as crew. Until the late 19th-century ships of the Hudson Bay Company made Stromness their main base for supplies and used **Login's Well** as a source of fresh water. Whaling ships bound for Greenland also hired local labour. By the late 19th century the herring boom had reached Stromness and there were 400 boats using its harbour, but within two decades the boom was over due to over-fishing. Today, Stromness remains a fishing port, as well as Orkney's main ferry terminal and the headquarters of the Northern Lighthouse Board.

The **tourist office** is at the new the ferry terminal. Its exhibition *This Place Called Orkney* is a useful introduction to the islands and its free *Stromness Heritage Guide* takes you round all the buildings of interest in the town. ■ *T850716. Apr-Oct Mon-Sat 0800-1800, Sun 0900-1600; Nov-Mar Mon-Fri 0900-1700.*

Stromness consists largely of one narrow, winding main street, paved with **Sights**
flagstones, which hugs the shoreline. Running off the street are numerous little
lanes and alleyways, many with fascinating names such as **Khyber Pass**, and
full of interesting buildings which reflect the town's proud maritime heritage.
The houses on the seaward side of the street are gable end to the waterfront and
each has its own jetty. The town is not designed for the motor car, so you'll
have to park by the harbour and explore its delights on foot. The main street
changes its name from Victoria Street to Graham Place, Dundas Street, Alfred
Street and South End as it runs south from the harbour.

The **Stromness Museum**, 52 Albert Street, has exhibitions on natural and
maritime history and contains artefacts from Scapa Flow and the days of the
Hudson Bay company. ■ *T850925. May-Sept daily 1000-1700; Oct-Apr*
Mon-Sat 1030-1230 and 1330-1700. £2. Opposite the museum is the house
where **George Mackay Brown** (1921-96), Orkney's most famous poet and
story-writer, spent the last two decades of his life.

On a jetty to the south of the new harbour is the excellent **Pier Arts Centre**,
housing a permanent collection of works of the St Ives school, including
Barbara Hepworth, Ben Nicholson and Patrick Heron amongst others in a
lovely gallery. ■ *Tue-Sat 1030-1230 and 1330-1700; Jul and Aug also Sun*
1400-1700. Free.

The best hotel in town is the **C-D** *Stromness Hotel*, T850298, www.orkneyislands.com/ **Sleeping**
stromnessghotel. An imposing old building overlooking the harbour, recently refurbished and offering good value meals. Also near the ferry terminal, on John St, is the
E *Ferry Inn*, T850280, m&m@ferryinn.com. Serves food and has a lively bar. There are
several B&B options, including **E-D** *Stenigar*, T850438. Open Apr-Oct, a converted
boatyard on Ness Rd, just before the campsite, with views of Hoy, and **E** *Mrs*
Worthington, T850215. Open Apr-Oct, a traditional gable-ended house at 2 South End.
On Victoria St near the harbour is **E** *Oakleigh Guest House*, T850447. Also has a restaurant serving good food, including vegetarian. A few miles behind Stromness, at
Innertown, is **E** *Thira*, T851181. A comfortable, friendly and non-smoking modern bungalow with spectacular views of Hoy. Also serves an excellent cooked breakfast and will
provide a fantastic dinner made from the finest local ingredients on request.

Brown's Hostel, 45 Victoria St, T850661. This popular independent hostel has no
curfew and is open all year round unlike the *SYHA Hostel*, on Hellihole Rd, a 10-min
walk south from the ferry terminal, T850589. Open Mar-Oct. There's a **campsite**,
T873535, open May to mid-Sept, at Ness Point, a mile south of the ferry terminal. It's
well equipped and has incomparable views but is very exposed.

The best place to eat is the *Hamnavoe Restaurant*, at 35 Graham Pl, T850606. It spe- **Eating &**
cializes in local seafood but also offers good vegetarian dishes. Mid-range. Open **drinking**
Mar-Oct Tue-Sun from 1900. The *Stromness Hotel* bar serves good, cheap meals. The
Ferry Inn also serves cheap bar food. The *Oakleigh Guest House* (see above) has a
good cellar restaurant. Near the ferry terminal on John St, is the popular *Coffee Shop*
which serves good, cheap grub. Open Mon-Sat 0900-1830, Sun 0900-1700 (Mon-Sat
till 1700 in winter). The best places for a drink are the downstairs bar of the *Stromness*
Hotel, the *Ferry Inn* and the bar of the *Royal Hotel*.

Diving *The Diving Cellar*, 4 Victoria St, T850055. Offers diving packages, equipment **Sports**
rental and boat charters. Open Mon-Fri 1100-1400 and 1700-1900, Sat 1300-1700.
Scapa Scuba, 13 Ness Rd, T/F851218. Diving course, guided dives, night dives and
boat charters.

Orkney and Shetland

Scapa Flow

The huge natural harbour of Scapa Flow has been used since Viking times and in the years leading up to the First World War the Royal Navy held exercises there, sometimes involving up to 100 ships. But Scapa was vulnerable to attack and over the course of the war defences were improved with 21 blockships sunk at the eastern approaches. Scapa Flow continued to be used as the main naval base in the Second World War, but the blockships were not enough to prevent a German U-boat from torpedoing HMS Royal Oak and the huge task of building the Churchill Barriers began (see page 569).

Scapa Flow's most famous incident happened at the end of the First World War, when, under the terms of the Armistice, Germany agreed to surrender most of her navy. Seventy-four German ships were interred in Scapa Flow, awaiting the final decision, but as the deadline approached the German commander, Admiral Von Reuter gave the order for all the ships to be scuttled and every ship was beached or sank.

*The scuttled German fleet, however, proved a hazard for fishing and a massive salvage operation began. Today, seven German ships remain at the bottom of Scapa Flow – three battleships and four light cruisers – along with four destroyers and a U-boat and the Royal Navy battleships HMS Royal Oak and HMS Vanguard, which blew up in 1917. This makes Scapa Flow one of the world's great **scuba diving** sites. Two companies in Stromness (see page 568) offer diving courses for beginners and wreck diving for experienced divers.*

Transport For details of **ferries** to Scrabster, Aberdeen and Lerwick, see page 554. For ferries to Hoy, see page 571. There are several **buses** daily (Mon-Sat) between Stromness and Kirkwall, 30 mins, £2.20. There's also a bus from Stromness to **Birsay** on Mon only, with *Shalder Coaches*, T850809. **Car hire** *Brass's Car Hire*, Blue Star Garage, North End Rd, T850850. **Cycle hire** *Orkney Cycle Hire*, 54 Dundas St, T850255. £4.50-8.50 per day.

Directory **Banks** There are branches of *Bank of Scotland* and *Royal Bank of Scotland*, both with cash machines, on Victoria St. **Laundry** Next to the *Coffee Shop*, T850904. Self-service or service washes.

East Mainland and South Ronaldsay

Phone code: 01856 The East Mainland is mainly agricultural land, and though it contains little of the amazing archaeological wealth of its western counterpart, there are some attractive fishing villages, fine coastal walks and many poignant reminders of Orkney's important wartime role.

Deerness There is not much to see inland on the road running southeast from Kirkwall past the airport, but head on towards the Deerness peninsula and you will be richly rewarded by a truly serene, gentle beauty. There are sandy bays, which make for very pleasant short walks and picnics (if you can find a sheltered spot), jutting cliffs and a great variety of birdlife. The peninsula makes the West Mainland seem like a mad, hectic whirl by comparison and is one of the best places on the Mainland to 'get away from it all'. When the weather's good, the view southwest from Sandside Bay to the Isle of **Copinsay** (an RSPB reserve) is glorious, and, as it emerges slowly and gracefully from the wild North Sea, is a perfect example of the whale-like properties that have been attributed to the Orkneys by the islands' most famous peot George Mackay Brown. There is a **footpath** following the coast from Sandside Bay to Mull Head (a Nature Reserve) and round the tip of the peninsula to the Covenanters Memorial (1679), a five mile circular walk.

If you continue along the B9050, the road ends at The Gloup car park at Skaill Bay, from where it's a 200yd-walk to **The Gloup**, a dramatic collapsed sea cave, separated from the sea by a land bridge about 80 yards wide. The word comes from the Old Norse *'gluppa'* meaning chasm, the local name for a blow-hole. A network of signposted footpaths cover the northeastern part of the peninsula and there are circular walks of between two to five miles which start from The Gloup car park. At the northeastern tip is **Mull Head**, a clifftop nature reserve which is home to guillemots, shags, fulmars, razorbills, terns and skuas.

On the south coast of East Mainland, near the northern end of the Churchill Barriers, is the old fishing village of **St Mary's**, once a busy little place but largely forgotten since the building of the causeways. To the east of the village is the **Norwood Museum**, which features the large and eclectic antique collection of local stonemason Norris Wood. ■ *T781217. May-Sept Tue-Thur and Sun 1400-1700 and 1800-2000, £3.*

Sleeping and eating The only place to stay or eat around here is the **E** *Commodore Motel*, T781319.

East Mainland is linked to a string of islands to the south by four causeways, known as the Churchill Barriers, built on the orders of Prime Minister Winston Churchill during the Second World War as anti-submarine barriers to protect the British Navy which was based in Scapa Flow at the time. His decision was prompted by the sinking of the battleship *HMS Royal Oak* in October 1939 by a German U-boat which had slipped between the old blockships, deliberately sunk during the First World War to protect Scapa Flow, and the shore. After the war, a road was built on top of the causeways, linking the islands of Lamb Holm, Glimps Holm, Burray and South Ronaldsay to Mainland. **The Churchill Barriers**

On the island of Lamb Holm camps were built to accommodate the men working on the construction of the barriers, many of whom were Italian Prisoners of War. The camps have long since gone but the Italians left behind the remarkable **Italian Chapel**, fittingly known as 'The Miracle of Camp 60'. It is difficult to believe that such a beautiful building could have been made using two Nissen huts, concrete and bits of scrap metal and the chapel's enduring popularity with visitors is a tribute to the considerable artistic skill of the men involved. One of them, Domenico Chiochetti, returned in 1960 to restore the interior paintwork. ■ *Open all year during daylight hours. Free.*

On the island of Burray the road passes the **Orkney Fossil and Vintage Centre**, which houses a bizarre collection of old furniture, various relics and 350 million-year-old fish fossils found locally. There's also an archive room where you can browse through old books and photographs, and a coffee shop. Not really something to go out of your way for, but worth a look if its raining. ■ *Apr-Sept daily 1000-1800; Oct Wed-Sun 1030-1800. £2.* **Burray**

Sleeping and eating In Burray village, on the south coast of the island, there's **B&B** accommodation at **E** *Vestlaybanks*, T731305, vestlaybanks@btinternet.com, which also provides evening meals. Alternatively, you can eat at the *Sands Motel*, T731298.

South Ronaldsay is the southernmost of the Orkney islands, only six miles from the Scottish mainland, across the stormy Pentland Firth, the most dangerous stretch of water in the British Isles. A small passenger ferry crosses to **Burwick** on the southern tip of the island from John O' Groats (for details see page 554). **South Ronaldsay**

The main settlement is the picturesque little village of **St Margaret's Hope** on the north coast. It is said to be named after Margaret, Maid of Norway, who died near here in 1290 at the age of seven while on her way to marry Prince Edward, later Edward II of England. She had already been proclaimed Queen of Scotland and her premature death was a major factor in the long Wars of Independence with England. The word 'hope' comes from the Old Norse word '*hjop*' meaning bay.

The village smithy has been turned into the **Smiddy Museum**, with lots of old blacksmith's tools to try out. ■ *Open May and Sept daily 1400-1600; Jun-Aug 1200-1600; Oct Sun 1400-1600. Free.* The museum also features a small exhibition on the annual **Boys' Ploughing Match**, a hugely popular event first held in c1860. Each year in August, boys from the village (and now girls as well) dress up as horses and parade in the village square (prizes are given for the best costume). Afterwards the boys and their fathers, or grandfathers, head for the **Sand of Wright** a few miles west and have a ploughing match with miniature ploughs, which are usually family heirlooms. The categories are: best ploughed ring, best *feering* or guiding furrow, neatest ends and best kept plough. This sheltered beach is well worth a visit anyway, ploughing or no ploughing. The views stretch in a spectacular 180 degree panorama, south across the Pentland Firth to Caithness on mainland Scotland, west to South Walls and Cantick Head on Hoy and northwest to Flotta and the west Mainland. It is also yet another good place to spot snipe, lapwing, curlew and redshank. Arctic terns also nest nearby and you can spot them diving dramatically as they fish in the bay.

To the north of the beach is the **Howe of Hoxa**, a ruined broch where Earl Thorfinn Skull-Splitter was buried in AD 963, according to the Orkneyinga saga. South Ronaldsay is a good place to buy local arts and crafts and there are several workshops dotted around the island. One of these is the **Hoxa Tapestry Gallery**, three miles west of the village, on the way to Hoxa Head. Local artist Leila Thompson's huge tapestries are well worth a visit, you may not like the style, but you cannot help but marvel at the extraordinary amount of work and dedication involved in their creation; many of them take years to finish. ■ *T/F831395. Apr-Sept Mon-Fri 1000-1730, Sat and Sun 1400-1800. £2.*

Sleeping and eating There's a good selection of accommodation in St Margaret's Hope. Best of the lot is the award-winning **D** *Creel Restaurant & Rooms*, T831311, on Front Rd. It offers comfortable rooms and superb, though expensive, food using deliciously fresh, locally grown ingredients. Dinner only. For cheaper meals, try the bar of the **E** *Murray Arms Hotel*, T831205, on Back Rd. For a good **B&B** try **E** *Bellevue Guest House*, T831294, or **E** *The Fisher's Gill*, T831711, which also offers seafood dishes. For cheap and basic **hostel** accommodation, head for the *Wheems Bothy*, T831537, open Apr-Oct, which is now an organic farm at Wheems, Eastside, a few miles southeast of St Margaret's Hope.

Transport Details of **buses** between Kirkwall and St Margaret's Hope on page 366.

At the southeastern corner of South Ronaldsay is the recently-excavated **Tomb of the Eagles**, one of the most interesting archaeological sights on Orkney. The 5,000-year-old chambered cairn was discovered by local farmer and amateur archaeologist, Ronald Simison, whose family now runs the privately-owned site and museum. The interior contents of the tomb were practically intact and there were up to 340 people buried here, along with carcasses and talons of sea eagles, hence the name. Various objects were also found outside the tomb, including stone tools and polished stone axes. Before visiting the tomb you can handle the skulls and various other artefacts at the small 'museum' in the family home, which actually means, their front porch! Then you walk for about five to 10 minutes through a field to visit a **burnt mound**, a kind of Bronze Age kitchen, where Ronald Simison will regail you with all manner of fascinating insider information about the excavation process, before walking out along the cliff edge to the spectacularly-sited tomb which you must enter by lying on a trolley and pulling yourself in using an overhead rope. It is particularly eerie being here because there is generally no-one else around, and as you haul yourself into the tomb, with the sound of the North Sea crashing into the cliffs nearby, you wonder to yourself how those buried here met their fate. There is also a lovely, but generally wild and windy, walk back along the cliffs, via a different route back to the car park. ■ *Apr-Oct daily 1000-2000; Nov-Mar 1000-1200. Admission £2.50.*

Hoy

To the southwest of the Mainland is Hoy, the second largest of the Orkney islands. The name is derived from the Norse *Ha-ey*, meaning High Island, which is appropriate as much of the island is more reminiscent of the Scottish highlands than Orkney, with only the southern end being typically low and fertile. Orkney's highest point, **Ward Hill** (1,571ft) is in the north of the island and the north and west coasts are bounded by spectacular cliffs. At **St John's Head** the sheer cliffs rise out of the sea to a height of 1,150ft, the highest vertical cliffs in Britain. The island is most famous for its **Old Man of Hoy**, a great rock stack rising to 450ft. This northern part of Hoy forms the **North Hoy RSPB Reserve** which has a variety of habitats ranging from woodland to tundra-like hill-tops and sea cliffs. The reserve is home to a huge variety of birds including great skuas and Arctic skuas, Manx shearwaters and puffins. On the hills there are red grouse, curlews, golden plovers and dunlins, as well as peregrine falcons, merlins, kestrels and even golden eagles. Mountain hares are quite common and if you are very lucky, you can also see otters along the Scapa Flow coastline.

Phone code: 01856

Hoy's great attraction is its many excellent **walking** opportunities. A minibus runs between **Moaness Pier**, where the ferry from Stromness docks (see 'Transport' below) and **Rackwick**, on the opposite side of the island, but it's a lovely two-hour walk by road through beautiful **Rackwick Glen**, once populated by crofters and fishermen, but now quiet and isolated. On the way you'll pass the **Dwarfie Stone**, a huge, lonely block of sandstone which is the only rock-cut tomb in Britain, dating from around 3000 BC. Be careful, though, because according to Sir Walter Scott, this is the residence of the *Trolld*, a dwarf from Norse legend. On your return you can take a different route through a narrow valley between the **Cuilags** (1,421ft) and **Ward Hill** and **Berriedale Wood**, the most northerly woodland in Britain. The most popular walk on Hoy is the spectacular three-hour hike from Rackwick to the cliffs facing the **Old Man of Hoy**. The path climbs steeply westwards from the old crofting township then turns northwards before gradually descending to the cliff edge.

Lyness & South Walls

On the southeast coast of the island is Lyness, site of a large naval base during both world wars when the British fleet was based in Scapa Flow. Many of the old dilapidated buildings have gone but the harbour area is still scarred with the scattered remains of concrete structures and there's also the unattractive sight of the huge oil terminal on **Flotta**. Lyness has a large **Naval Cemetery**, last resting place of those who died at Jutland, of Germans killed during the scuttle and of the crew of *HMS Royal Oak*. The old pump house opposite the new ferry terminal is now the **Scapa Flow Visitor Centre**, a fascinating naval museum with old photographs, various wartime artefacts, a section devoted to the scuttling of the German Fleet and an audio-visual feature on the history of Scapa Flow. Well worth a visit. ■ *T791300. Mid-May to mid-Sept Mon-Sat 0900-1630, Sun 1030-1545; Jul and Aug Mon-Sat 0900-1630, Sun 0945-1800; mid-Sept to mid-May Mon-Fri 0900-1630. Admission £2.*

At South Walls overlooking Longhope Bay, is **Hackness Martello Tower and Battery** which, along with another tower on the north side at Crockness, was built in 1815 to protect British ships in Longhope Bay against attack by American and French privateers while they waited for a Royal Navy escort on their journey to Baltic ports. ■ *The tower is open to the public. If locked, a sign on the door will tell you where to get the key from.*

Sleeping & eating There's not much accommodation in the north of the island, except for the two SYHA hostels. The larger of the two, *Hoy Youth Hostel* is about a mile from Moaness Pier. It's open from May-Sept. The smaller hostel is *Rackwick Youth Hostel* in Rackwick Glen (open mid-Mar to mid-Sept). To book ahead for both hostels, contact Orkney Council, T873535, ext 2404. Near the pier and post office is the *Hoy Inn*, T791313, a bar and restaurant which serves good seafood (closed Mon). There's also an RSPB information centre here.

There are a few very good **B&Bs** in the south of the island. South of **Lyness** is E *Stoneyquoy*, T/F791234. The owner Louise Budge also runs guided tours of the island for £40 for up to four people, including lunch. On the other side of the bay in Longhope is **E-F** *Burnhouse*, T701263. Also in Longhope is the **E-F** *Old Custom House*, T701358. Near the ferry terminal in Lyness is **E-D** *The Hoy Hotel*, T791377. Open Apr-Oct, which serves meals. The *Anchor Bar*, T791356, in Lyness serves lunches. There are shops/petrol stations in Lyness and Longhope. **Car and bike hire** is available from *Halyel Car Hire* in Lyness, T791240.

Transport There are 2 **ferry** services to Hoy, both run by *Orkney Ferries*, T850624. A passenger ferry sails between **Stromness** and Moaness Pier in the north (30 mins) 3 times a day Mon-Fri and twice on Fri evenings, twice daily Sat and Sun. There's a reduced winter service (mid-Sept to mid-May). There's also a car and passenger service between **Houton** and Lyness and Longhope (45 mins) up to 6 times daily (Mon-Sat). There's a limited Sun service from mid-May to mid-Sept.

Transport on Hoy is very limited. *North Hoy Transport*, T791315, runs a **minibus** service between Moaness Pier and Rackwick, which meets the 1000 ferry from Stromness. Call the same number for a taxi around the island.

Rousay, Egilsay and Wyre

Phone code: 01856 These three islands lie a short distance off the northeast coast of Mainland and, together with Shapinsay to the southeast, are the closest of Orkney's North Isles to Kirkwall.

Rousay is a hilly island about five miles in diameter and known as the 'Egypt of the North' due to the large number archaeological sites. It also has the important **Trumland RSPB Reserve**, home to merlins, hen harriers, peregrine falcons, short-eared owls and red-throated divers, and its three lochs offer good trout fishing,

A road runs right around the island, and makes a pleasant 13 mile bike run, but most of the sights are within walking distance of the ferry pier on the southeast side of the island where most of the 200 inhabitants live. A short distance west of the pier by the road is **Tavershoe Tuick**, an unusual two-storey burial cairn, which was discovered in the late 19th century by Mrs Burroughs, wife of

General Traill Burroughs who lived at nearby Trumland House. A mile further west, to the north of the road, is **Blackhammer**, a stalled Neolithic burial cairn. Further west, and a steep climb up from the road, is **Knowe of Yarso**, another stalled cairn, which contained the remains of at least 21 people. The tomb dates from around 2900 BC.

Most of the island's archaeological sights are to be found along the **Westness Walk**, a mile-long walk which starts from Westness Farm, about four miles west of the ferry pier, and ends at the remarkable Midhowe Cairn. The walk is described in detail in a leaflet available from the tourist offices on Mainland. **Midhowe Cairn** is the largest and longest thus far excavated on Orkney – over 100ft long and 40ft wide – and like the others, dates from around 3000 BC. Housed in a large building to protect it, the 'Great Ship of Death', as it is known, contained the remains of 25 people, in crouched position on or under the eastern shelves of the chamber which is divided into 12 sections. Standing nearby, with fine views across to Eynehallow island, is **Midhowe Broch**, one of the best-preserved brochs on Orkney, occupied from around 200 BC to AD 200. The outer walls are about 60ft in diameter and up to 14ft high in places.

Another fine walk on the island is around the **RSPB Reserve**. A footpath leads from beside Trumland House and heads up towards the island's highest point, **Blotchnie Field** (821ft). A leaflet describing the walk is available from the tourist offices on Mainland or the **Trumland Orientation Centre** by the pier.

Sleeping Accommodation on Rousay is very limited. Near Knowe of Yarso, about 2 miles west of the pier, is the **E-D Taversoe Hotel**, T821325, which offers excellent value meals. The seafood is particularly recommended (closed Mon to non-residents). The only other option is the *Rousay Hostel* at Trumland Organic Farm, T821252, open all year and half a mile from the ferry. It has laundry facilities and you can also camp. The *Pier Restaurant* beside the pier serves food at lunchtime (cheap to mid-range).

Transport A small car **ferry** sails from **Tingwall** (20 mins) to **Rousay** 6 times a day (Mon-Sat; 5 times on Sun). Most of the ferries call in at **Egilsay** and **Wyre** but some are on demand only and should be booked in advance, T751360. A bus connects Tingwall and Kirkwall (see page 561).

You can take one of the very informative **minibus tours** run by *Rousay Traveller*, T821234. These run from Jun-early Sept, Tue-Fri, meeting the 1040 ferry from Tingwall and lasting 6 hrs. Tours cost £14 per person (£12 students). **Bike hire** is available from *Arts, Crafts & Bike Hire* at the pier, T821398.

Egilsay & Wyre These two small islands lie to the east of Rousay and have a couple of interesting sights of their own. Egilsay's claim to fame is the murder here of St Magnus, in 1115, and a **cenotaph** marks the spot where he was slain. The island is dominated by the 12th-century **St Magnus church**, built on the site of an earlier church, possibly as a shrine to St Magnus. It is the only surviving example on Orkney of a round-towered Viking church.

Much of Egilsay has been bought by the RSPB as a reserve to preserve the habitat of the very rare **corncrake**, whose distinctive rasping call may be heard.

Tiny **Wyre** features strongly in the Viking saga as the domain of Kolbein Hruga and the remains of his 12th-century stronghold, **Cubbie Roo's Castle**, and nearby **St Mary's chapel** can be still be seen. Kolbein's home, or *Bu*, was on the site of the nearby **Bu Farm**, where the poet **Edwin Muir** (1887-1959) spent part of his childhood. The far westerly point of the island, known as **the Taing**, is a favourite haunt of seals and a great place to enjoy a summer sunset.

Shapinsay

Phone code: 01856 Less than 30 minutes by ferry from Kirkwall is the fertile, low-lying island of Shapinsay. The main attraction is **Balfour Castle**, an imposing baronial pile which is in fact a Victorian extension to a much older house called 'Cliffdale'. The house, and the rest of the island, was bought by successive generations of the Balfour family who had made their fortune in India. Today, the castle is the home of the Zawadski family and can only be visited as part of an inclusive half-day tour. ■ *T872856. Tour leaves from Kirkwall on Wed and Sun May-Sept, on the 1415 ferry. Tours must be arranged in advance at the tourist office in Kirkwall. They cost £14.50 per person which includes ferry ticket, guided tour of the castle and gardens (at 1500) and complimentary tea and cakes in the servants' quarters. You can take an earlier ferry if you wish to explore the island.*

In the village, built by the Balfours to house their estate workers, is the **Shapinsay Heritage Centre**, in the old Smithy. It has displays on the island's history and a tearoom upstairs. ■ *T711258. Mon, Tue and Thur-Sat 1200-1630, Wed and Sun till 1730. Free.*

A mile north of the village is the **Mill Dam RSPB Reserve**, where there's a hide overlooking a loch from which you can see many species of wildfowl and waders. Four miles from the pier, at the far northeast corner of the island, is the well-preserved **Burroughston Broch** with good views of seals sunning themselves on the nearby rocks. West of here, at **Quholme**, is the original birthplace of the father of **Washington Irving**, author of *Rip Van Winkle*.

Sleeping & You can stay at **L** *Balfour Castle*, T711282, and enjoy all that Victorian splendour. The
eating price includes dinner. The castle has a private chapel and a boat is available for bird watching and fishing trips for residents. Alternatively, there's comfortable B&B in the humbler surroundings of **E** *Girnigoe*, T711256, near the northern end of Veantro Bay. It also offers evening meals. There's a pub in the village, in the old gatehouse. Also 2 shops and a post office.

Transport The small car **ferry** makes 6 sailings daily (including Sun in summer) from **Kirkwall** (25 mins).

Eday

Phone code: 01857 The long, thin and sparsely-populated island of Eday lies at the centre of the North Isles group. It is less fertile than the other islands but its heather-covered hills in the centre have provided peat for the other peatless Orkney islands. Eday's sandstone has also been quarried and was used in the building of St Magnus Cathedral in Kirkwall.

The island has numerous chambered cairns and these, along with the other attractions, are concentrated in the northern part. These are all covered in the signposted five-mile **Eday Heritage Walk** which starts from Community Enterprises Shop and leads up to the Cliffs of Red Head at the northern tip. The walk takes about three hours to complete and it's worth picking up the *Eday Heritage Walk* leaflet.

The walk starts at Mill Bay and heads past **Mill Loch** where an RSPB hide allows you to watch rare red-throated divers breeding in spring and summer. Further north is the huge, 15ft tall **Stone of Setter**, the largest standing stone in Orkney and visible from most of the chambered cairns. Close by are the **Fold of Setter**, a circular enclosure dating back to 2000 BC, and the **Braeside** and **Huntersquoy** chambered cairns. Further north along the path is **Vinquoy Chambered Cairn**, one of the finest in Orkney and similar to the better-known tomb at Maes Howe, dating from around the same time. An acrylic dome provides light to the main chamber, which can be entered by a narrow underground passage.

The path continues to the summit of **Vinquoy Hill**, which commands excellent views of the surrounding islands of Westray and Sanday. From here you can continue north to the spectacular red sandstone cliffs at **Red Head**, home to nesting guillemots, razorbills and puffins in summer, or head southeast along the coast to **Carrick House**. Built for Lord Kinclaven, Earl of Carrick, in 1633, the house is best known for its associations with the pirate, John Gow, whose ship ran aground during a failed attack on the house. He was captured and taken to London for trial and hanged. Sir Walter Scott's novel, *The Pirate*, is based on this story. ■ *T622260. Mid-Jun to mid-Sept, guided tour at 1400. Admission £2.*

Sleeping There's B&B at **E** *Mrs Poppelwell's*, T622248, at Blett, Carrick Bay, opposite the Calf of Eday. She also provides evening meal and packed lunch, and has a self-catering cottage nearby for up to 3. Also **D** *Mrs Cockram*, T622271. Open Jun-Mar, at Skaill Farm, just south of the airport. Price includes dinner. There's a basic *Youth Hostel*, T622206, open Apr-Sept, run by Eday Community Enterprises, just north of the airport.

Transport There are **flights** from **Kirkwall** to Eday airport (called London Airport) with *Loganair*, T872494, on Wed only. There are **ferries** from **Kirkwall** (1 hr 15 mins to 2 hrs) twice daily via **Sanday** or **Stronsay**. The ferry pier is at Backaland, on the southeast of the island, a long way from the main sights.

Orkney Ferries, T872044, also run the **Eday Heritage Tour** every Sun from mid-Jun to mid-Sept. It leaves Kirkwall at 0920 and return at 1955 and costs £28.50 per person, which includes ferries, guided walks or minibus tour, entry to Carrick House and lunch. Book with *Orkney Ferries* or at the tourist office in Kirkwall. You can hire a **taxi** from Mr A Stewart by the pier, T622206, or **hire bikes** from Mr Burkett at Hamarr, near the Post Office south of Mill Loch.

Sanday

Sanday is the largest of the North Isles, 12 miles long, and flat as a pancake except for the cliffs at Spurness. It is well-named, as its most notable feature is its sweeping bays of sparkling white sand backed by machair, and turquoise seas.

Phone code: 01857

There are numerous burial mounds all over the island, the most impressive being **Quoyness Chambered Cairn**, a 5,000 year-old tomb similar to Maes Howe. The 13ft-high structure contains a large main chamber with six smaller cells opening through low entrances. Most of the burial tombs remain unexcavated, such as those at **Tofts Ness**, at the far northeastern tip, where there are over 500 cairns, making it potentially one of the most important prehistoric sites in Britain. At **Scar**, in Burness, a spectacular Viking find was made recently, and at **Pool** a major excavation has uncovered the remains of at least 14 Stone-age houses.

Sanday is known for its **knitwear**, though the factory unfortunately closed down recently. You can still visit **Orkney Angora** craft shop, in Upper Breckan, near the northern tip of the island, T600421.

Sleeping & eating There are a couple of hotels, the **E** *Belsair Hotel*, T600206, which serves meals, and the **E** *Kettletoft Hotel*, T/F600217, which also serves meals and has a lively bar. Both are in Kettletoft, where the ferry used to dock. There's also a handful of **B&Bs** including **E-F** *Quivals*, T600467, run by Tina and Bernie Flett. Tina also runs the ferry bus service

Orkney and Shetland

and Bernie runs a **car and bike hire** service, T600418. Bernie also runs full-day **tours** of the island, on Wed and Fri, from mid-May to early Sept, departing from **Kirkwall** pier at 1010 and returning at 1940 (£28 per person, minimum of 4 people).

There are *Loganair* **flights** to Sanday from **Kirkwall** twice daily Mon-Fri and once on Sat. There's a **ferry** service twice daily from **Kirkwall** (1 hr 30 mins). The ferry arrives at **Loth**, at the southern tip of the island, and is met by a **minibus** which will take you to most places (see *Quivals* above).

Stronsay

Phone code: 01857

The peaceful, low-lying island of Stronsay has some fine sandy beaches and cliffs which attract large colonies of grey seals and nesting seabirds. There are few real sights on this largely agricultural island but the coastline has some pleasant walks. One of the best is to the **Vat of Kirbister** in the southeast, a spectacular '*gloup*' or blow-hole spanned by the finest natural arch in Orkney. To the south of here, at **Burgh Head**, you'll find nesting puffins and the remains of a ruined broch, and at the southeastern tip, at **Lamb Head**, is a large colony of grey seals, lots of seabirds and several archaeological sites.

The main settlement is the quiet village of **Whitehall**, on the northeast coast where the ferry arrives. It's hard to believe it now but this was one of the largest herring ports in Europe. During the boom years of the early 20th century 300 steam drifters were working out of Whitehall and nearly 4,000 fishing crew and shore workers were employed. In the peak year of 1924 over 12,000 tons of herring were landed here, to be cured (salted) and exported to Russia and Eastern Europe. Whitehall developed considerably and *Stronsay Hotel* was said to have the longest bar in Scotland. On Sundays during July and August there were so many boats tied up that it was possible to walk across them to the little island of **Papa Stronsay**. By the 1930s, however, herring stocks were severely depleted and the industry was in decline. The old **Fish Mart** by the pier now houses a **heritage centre** with photos and artefacts from the herring boom days. It also has a café and hostel (see below). ■ *May-Sept 1100-1700, free, T616360.*

Prior to the herring boom, Stronsay's economic mainstay was the **kelp industry**. By the end of the 18th century 3,000 people were employed in the collection of seaweed and production of kelp for export to be used in making iodine, soap and glass.

Sleeping & eating

The new **F** *Stronsay Fish Mart Hostel*, T616360. Open all year, is well-equipped and comfortable. It's run by the **F-E** *Stronsay Hotel*, T616213, margareth@pain-demon.co.uk. The hotel is being refurbished and offers cheap bar food. There's **B&B** at **F-E** *Stronsay Bird Reserve*, T616363. On Mill Bay to the south of Whitehall, where you can also **camp** overlooking the wide sandy bay. At the southern end of the island is the very basic and very cheap *Torness Camping Barn*, T616314, on the shore of Holland Bay near Lea-shun Loch. They also organize nature walks to the nearby seal-hide. Phone for pick-up from the ferry. Other eating options are the café at the Fish Mart, which does cheap meals, and the *Woodlea Takeaway* along the shore (open Wed 2130-2300, Fri-Sun 1630-1830 and 2100-2300).

Transport

There are *Loganair* **flights** to Stronsay from Kirkwall, twice daily Mon-Fri. A **ferry** service runs from **Kirkwall** (1 hr 30 mins) twice daily Mon-Sat (once on Sun) and once daily Mon-Sat from Eday (35 mins).

Car hire and **taxis** are available from *DS Peace*, T616335. Taxis and **island minibus tours** are available from M Williamson, T616255.

Westray

Westray is the second largest of the North Isles with a varied landscape of farmland, hilly moorland, sandy beaches and dramatic cliffs. It is also the most prosperous of the North Isles, producing beef, fish and seafood and supports a population of 700. The main settlement is **Pierowall**, in the north of the island, but though it has one of the best harbours in Orkney, the main ferry terminal is at **Rapness**, on the south coast.

Phone code: 01857

Pierowall is a relatively large village for the North Isles and there are several shops, a post office, a hotel and the **Westray Heritage Centre**, with displays on local and natural history and a tearoom. ■ *Early May to late Sept Tue-Sat 0930-1230 and 1400-1700. £2*. Also in the village is the ruined 17th-century **St Mary's church**. Westray's most notable ruin is the impressive **Notland Castle**, a fine example of a 16th-century fortified Z-plan tower-house.

There are some great coastal **walks** on the island, particularly to the spectacular sea cliffs at **Noup Head**, at the far northwestern tip, which are an **RSPB Reserve** and second only to St Kilda in terms of breeding seabirds, with huge colonies of guillemots, razorbills, kittiwakes and fulmars, as well as puffins. The cliffs on the west coast of Westray are five miles long and there's an excellent walk down the coast from Noup Head, past **Gentleman's Cave**, used as a hiding place by four Jacobite lairds in 1746. Near the southern end of the walk is **Fitty Hill** (554ft), the highest point on the island, which you can climb for great views, and the walk ends at **Inga Ness**, where you can also see puffins. The best place to see puffins is at **Castle o' Burrian**, a sea stack on **Stanger Head**, on the southeastern coast near the Rapness ferry terminal.

Sleeping The best place to stay is **D** *Cleaton House Hotel*, T677508, www.orknet.co.uk/cleaton. A converted Victorian manse about 2 miles southeast of Pierowall. It serves excellent meals in the restaurant (1900-2100) and in the bar (1200-1400, 1800-2100). In the village is the **E** *Pierowall Hotel*, T677208, which is less stylish but comfortable and friendly. It also serves good value bar meals. There are also several B&Bs, including **E-F** *Sand o' Gill*, T677374, where you can also camp or hire their self-catering caravan.

Transport **Flights** to Westray with *Loganair* depart Kirkwall twice daily Mon-Fri and once on Sat. The airport is in the far northeastern corner of the island. There's a **car ferry** service from **Kirkwall** to Rapness, on the south coast of the island (1 hr 30 mins). It sails twice daily in summer (mid-May to mid-Sept) and once daily in winter. There's also a **passenger ferry** from Pierowall to **Papa Westray** (see below).

There are **guided minibus tours** of Westray with Alex Costie of *Island Explorer*, T677355, which connect with ferry at Rapness and cost £20 for a full day. J & M Marcus at Pierowall also run bus tours and offer **car hire**. For **cycle hire** contact Mrs Groat at *Sand o' Gill* (see above) or Mrs Bain at *Twiness*, T677319. For **boat trips** to Papa Westray contact Tom Rendall, T677216. *Discover Orkney*, T/F01856-872865, run **day tours** on a Sun to Westray from Kirkwall, leaving at 0940 and returning at 2015, and costing £29 per person including ferry. The also run a day tour on a Mon to Papa Westray for £26 per person including ferry.

Papa Westray

Tiny Papa Westray, known locally as 'Papay', can be reached on the world's shortest scheduled flight – all of two minutes – from Westray, but there are other reasons to visit this little island, one of the most remote of the Orkney group. Papay is home to Europe's oldest house, the **Knap of Howar**, which

Phone code: 01857

was built around 5,500 years ago and is still standing (they knew how to build 'em in those days). It's on the west coast, just south of the airport. Half a mile north is **St Boniface Kirk**, one of the oldest Christian sites in the north of Scotland, founded in the 8th century, though most of the recently-restored building dates from the 12th century. Inland from the Knap of Howar is **Holland Farm**, former home of the lairds of the island, where you can rummage around the farm buildings and the small **museum**. ■ *Open at all times. Free.*

Papay is famous for its birds and **North Hill**, on the north of the island, is an important **RSPB Reserve**. The cliffs are home to many thousands of breeding seabirds and at Fowl Craig, on the east coast you can see nesting puffins. The interior is home to the largest arctic tern colony in Europe as well as many arctic skuas. If you wish to explore you have to contact the warden at Rose Cottage, T644240, who runs regular guided walks.

It's worth taking a boat trip to the even tinier, deserted **Holm of Papay**, off the east coast. This is the site of several Neolithic burial cairns, including one of the largest **chambered cairns** on Orkney. You enter the tomb down a ladder into the main chamber which is nearly 70ft long, with a dozen side-cells. ■ *Contact Jim Davidson, T644259, for boat trips between May and Sept.*

Sleeping & eating There are few options for sleeping. One is the **D-E** *Beltane House Guest House*, T644267, a row of converted farm workers' cottages to the east of Holland House. It offers dinner (mid-range). It's run by the island community Co-operative, as is the 16-bed *Papa Westray Hostel*, T644267. Open all year, housed in the same complex at Beltane. The co-operative also runs a shop and restaurant serving lunch and evening meals. They have a **minibus** which takes ferry passengers from the pier to anywhere on the island.

Transport The above-mentioned 2-minute **flight** from Westray leaves twice daily Mon-Sat (£14 one-way). There is also a direct flight to Papay from **Kirkwall** daily Mon-Sat, except Fri (£15 one-way). There's a **passenger ferry** from **Pierowall** on Westray 3-6 times daily (25 mins). The **car ferry** from **Kirkwall** to Westray continues to Papa Westray on Tue and Fri (2 hrs 15 mins).

North Ronaldsay

Remote and storm-battered North Ronaldsay is the most northerly of the Orkney islands and a place where old Orcadian traditions remain. It seems remarkable that anyone should live here at all in these extreme conditions but 'North Ron' as it is known locally has been inhabited for many centuries and continues to be heavily farmed. The island's sheep are a hardy lot and live exclusively off the seaweed on a narrow strip of beach, outside a 13-mile stone dyke which surrounds the island. This gives their meat a unique, 'gamey' flavour.

This small, flat island, only three miles long, has few real attractions, except to keen ornithologists who flock here to catch a glimpse of its rare migrants. From late March to early June and mid-August to early November there are huge numbers of migratory birds. The **Bird Observatory**, in the southwest corner of the island by the ferry pier, gives information on which species have been sighted, as well as providing accommodation. There are also colonies of grey seals and cormorants at **Seal Skerry**, on the northeast tip of the island.

Sleeping & eating You can stay at the **D-E** *North Ronaldsay Bird Observatory*, T633200, alison@ nrbo.prestel.co.uk. It offers wind and solar-powered full-board accommodation in private rooms or dorms. Full-board accommodation is also available at **D-E** *Garso House*, T633244, christine.muir@virgin.net, about 3 miles from the ferry pier. They also have a self-catering cottage (up to 5 people) and can arrange **car hire, taxis** or **minibus tours**. The *Burrian Inn and Restaurant* is the island's pub and also serves **food**. **Camping** is possible on the island, contact, T633222.

There are *Loganair* **flights** from **Kirkwall** twice daily Mon-Sat, T01856-872494. There's a car and passenger **ferry** which sails from **Kirkwall** (2 hrs 40 mins) once a week (usually Fri) and also on some Sun between May and Sept. Contact *Orkney Ferries* for details, T01856-872044.

Shetland

Shetland is so far removed from the rest of Scotland, it can only be shown as an inset on maps. In fact, it is easier and quicker to get there from Norway than it is from London. This seems entirely appropriate, for Shetland is historically and culturally closer to Scandinavia than Britain. Many of its place-names are of Norse origin and people still celebrate ancient Viking festivals, such as Up Helly-Aa.

Modern day visitors tend to come by plane rather than longboat and usually bring binoculars, for Shetland is a birdwatchers' paradise. It is home to countless bird species, many of them seeking refuge from the madding crowds. And let's face it, there's no better place than here to really get away from it all.

Ins and outs

Getting there

By air Shetland has good air connections with the rest of the UK. There are regular flights to and from several mainland airports which are operated by *British Airways* franchise partners *Loganair* and *British Regional Airlines*, T0345-222111. Shetland's main airport is at **Sumburgh**, 25 miles south of Lerwick, T01950-460654.

There are direct daily flights from **Aberdeen** (4 Mon-Fri; 2 on Sat and Sun), which has frequent services to all other major British airports (see page 357). There are also direct flights from **Glasgow** (daily), **Edinburgh** (daily except Sun), **London Heathrow** (daily), **Inverness** (Mon-Fri), **Orkney** (daily except Sun), **Wick** (Mon-Sat) and **Belfast** (daily except Sat). There are also international flights to and from **Bergen** and **Oslo** (Norway) on Thur and Sun.

Flying to Shetland is expensive. From Aberdeen a special return fare costs £110-179 and a standard one-way ticket is £122. A special tourist fare of £84 return is available between Orkney and Shetland. For details of the excellent value **Highland Rover Pass**, see page 39.

By boat *P&O Scottish Ferries*, T01224-572615, passenger@poscottishferries.co.uk, operate car ferries to **Lerwick** from **Aberdeen** and **Stromness** (Orkney). There are sailings from Aberdeen once a day Mon-Fri; the journey takes 14 hrs. Passenger fares for a seat with no accommodation cost from £50.50-56.50 one-way (return costs double), depending on the times of year. Cars cost from £160-175 return. For details of ferries from Stromness, see page 554. There are also ferries from **Norway**, **Iceland** and the **Faroe Isles** (see page 32).

Getting around

A **Shetland Transport Timetable**, published by Shetland Islands Council (price 70p), contains details of all air, sea and bus services throughout the islands. It is available from the tourist office in Lerwick.

By air There is a regular scheduled inter-island service from **Tingwall Airport** near Lerwick, T01595-840246, to the islands of **Foula** (£20.50 one-way), **Fair Isle** (£36), **Papa Stour** (£15.50), **Unst** (£20.50) and **Out Skerries** (£17.50). There are also flights from **Sumburgh** to **Fair Isle** and **Unst**.

Shetland

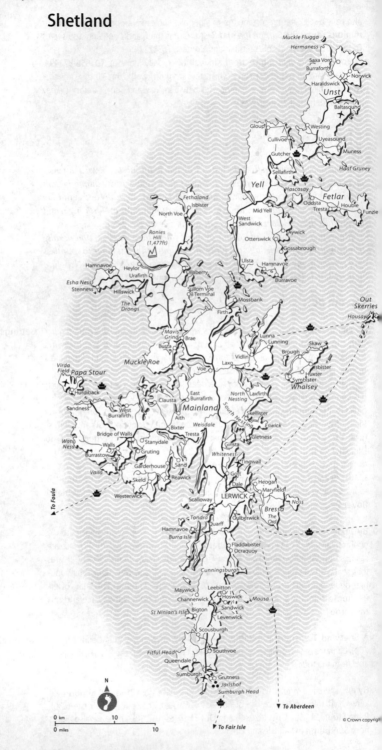

© Crown copyright

By boat A frequent ferry service links the larger islands with the Shetland Mainland. There are regular daily car ferries between **Lerwick** and **Bressay** (5 mins), **East Mainland** and **Whalsay** (30 mins), **North Mainland** and **Yell** (20 mins), **Yell** and **Unst** (10 mins) and **Yell** and **Fetlar** (25 mins). Fares on all these routes are £1.20 per passenger and £2.90 per car. There's a less frequent car ferry service between **East Mainland** and **Skerries** (Mon, Fri, Sat and Sun; 1 hr 30 mins), and **Lerwick** and **Skerries** (Tue and Thur; 2 hrs 30 mins). Fares on these routes are £2.10 per passenger and £2.90 per car. Bookings are essential. There's also a passenger/cargo ferry service between **West Mainland** and **Papa Stour** (Mon, Wed, Fri, Sat and Sun; 40 mins), **West Mainland** and **Foula** (Tue, Sat and alternate Thur; 2 hrs), **Scalloway** and **Foula** (alternate Thur; 3 hrs), **South Mainland** and **Fair Isle** (Tue, Sat and alternate Thur; 2 hrs 30 mins) and **Lerwick** and **Fair Isle** (alternate Thur; 4 hrs 30 mins). Fares on these routes are £2.20 and bookings are also essential.

By road Shetland has around 500 miles of good roads and an extensive public **bus service** links Lerwick with all towns, villages and tourist sights. There are several bus operators. For detailed information on all bus services, call 01595-694100 (Mon-Sat 0900-1715).

The best way to explore the islands is with your own **private car**. It is cheaper to **hire** a car in Lerwick rather than at the airport. For a list of car hire firms see page 584. **Cycling** is a good way to experience the islands, though most places are very exposed and the winds can be strong. **Hitching** is also a feasible way to get around and is relatively safe.

Lerwick

Lerwick is the capital and administrative centre of Shetland and the only sizeable town. Though the islands have been inhabited for many centuries, Lerwick only dates from the 17th century, when it began to grow as a trading port for Dutch herring fishermen, thanks to its superb natural sheltered harbour, the Bressay Sound. The town spread along the waterfront, where merchants built their *lodberries*, which were houses and warehouses with their own piers so that they could trade directly with visiting ships. By the late 19th century, Lerwick had become the main herring port in northern Europe.

Phone code: 01595
Population: 7,600

Lerwick has continued to grow and is now home to a third of Shetland's population. The discovery of **oil** in the North Sea in the early 1970s led to building of the **Sullom Voe Oil Terminal** and the effect on Lerwick has been dramatic. It is now the main transit point to the North Sea oil rigs and there have been major extensions to the harbour area, bringing increased shipping and prosperity to the town.

Ferries from Aberdeen arrive at the main Holmsgarth terminal, which is about a mile north of the old harbour. There's a regular **bus** service between Lerwick and **Sumburgh airport** (50 mins; £1.70) run by *John Leask & Son*, T693162. **Taxis** (around £25) and car hire are also available. All island bus services start and end at the Viking bus station, which is on Commercial Road, a short distance north of the town centre. The town is small and everything is within easy walking distance.

Getting there & around

The town's heart is the attractive **Commercial Street**, which runs parallel to the Esplanade. At the southern end are many old houses and *lodberries* and you can continue south along the cliffs to the **Knab** or to the lovely **Bain's beach**. *Lerwick Walks* is a leaflet detailing many interesting walks in and around town. The main **tourist office** is at Market Cross, on Commercial St. As well as booking accommodation, they are an excellent source of information, books, maps and leaflets and will change foreign currency. ■ *T693434,*

Sights

Orkney and Shetland

👉 **Böds**

There is only one youth hostel in Shetland, but budget travellers shouldn't panic. The Shetland Camping Böd project has developed a network of **camping böds** (pronounced 'burd') which provide basic and cheap accommodation throughout the islands.

A Böd was a building used to house fishermen and their gear during the fishing season and the name has been used to describe these types of accommodation which are similar to English 'camping barns'. They are all located in scenically attractive places and each has its own fascinating history.

They are very basic and the more remote ones have no electricity or lighting. You'll need to bring a stove, cooking and eating utensils, sleeping bag and torch (flashlight). All böds must be booked in advance through the tourist office in Lerwick. They cost £5 per person per night, though they can also be booked for exclusive use by large groups. They are open from the beginning of April till the end of September. There are at present six camping böds on Shetland and these are listed in the relevant places.

www.shetland-tourism.co.uk. *Open May-Sept Mon-Fri 0800-1800, Sat 0800-1600, Sun 1000-1300; Oct-Apr Mon-Fri 0900-1700.*

Overlooking the north end of Commercial Street is **Fort Charlotte**, built in 1665 and later rebuilt in 1780 and named after Queen Charlotte, George III's consort. It has since been used as a prison and Royal Naval Reserve base and though there's little to see in the fort there are fine views of the harbour from the battlements. ■ *Jun-Sept daily 0900-2200; Oct-May 0900-1600. Free.* One of Lerwick's most impressive buildings is the Victorian **town hall**, on Hillhead. The stained glass windows of the main hall depict episodes from Shetland's history. ■ *Mon-Fri 1000-1200 and 1400-1530. Free.*

Opposite the town hall, above the library, is the **Shetland Museum**, which gives a useful introduction to the islands' history. Amongst the artefacts on display is a replica of the St Ninian's Isle treasure. ■ *T695057. Mon, Wed and Fri 1000-1900; Tue, Thur and Sat till 1700. Free.*

Lerwick

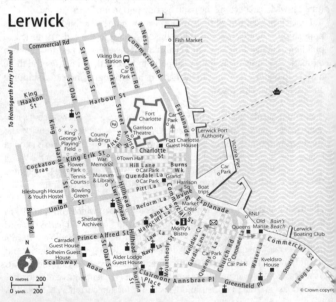

Boat trips and tours

Shetland Wildlife Tours, T01950-422483, www.shetland-wildlife-tours.zetnet.co.uk. Offer a number of guided tours to see the islands' outstandingly rich selection of wildlife; ranging from the excellent value £20 trip around Noss & Bressay, where , if you go at the right time of year, you are almost guaranteed to see seals, porpoises and the astounding gannetry on the spectacular cliffs of Noss' east coast to the more upmarket week-long 'Ultimate Shetland' tour (£675).

There are also Noss & Bressay Wildlife Cruises with **Bressaboats**, T01595-693434, and **Shetland Sea Charters** (same phone number) which costs £20. Bressaboats and Shetland Wildlife Tours both run a full-day Hermaness and Muckle Flugga Cruise which costs £70 per person.

A variety of **bus tours** are available with **John Leask & Son**, The Esplanade, Lerwick, T01595-693162. These cost from £8 up to £18 depending on the destination.

Also in town is the **Up Helly-Aa Exhibition**, in the Galley Shed off St Sunniva Street. This gives a taste of the famous Viking fire festival held annually in Lerwick on the last Tuesday in January when a torch-lit procession through the town by hundreds of people dressed in Viking costumes (*guizers*) is followed by a replica Viking longship built especially for the event. At the end of the procession the ship is set ablaze when the *guizers* throw their flaming torches onto it. ■ *Mid-May to mid-Sept Tue 1400-1600 and 1700-1900, Fri 1700-1900, Sat 1400-1600. Admission £2.*

A mile west of town are the substantial remains of **Clickimin Broch**, a fortified site occupied from 700 BC to around the fifth or sixth century AD. A path leads to the site from opposite the *Safeway* supermarket on the A970. ■ *Always open. Free.*

About a mile north of the ferry terminal is the **Böd of Gremista**, a restored 18th-century fishing *böd* (booth) which was the birthplace of Arthur Anderson (1791-1868), co-founder of the Peninsular and Oriental Steam Navigation Company, now P&O. One of the rooms features an exhibition on Anderson's life and involvement with P&O. ■ *Jun to mid-Sept, Wed and Sun 1000-1300 and 1400-1700. Admission £2.*

Sleeping

Shetland's best accommodation is outside Lerwick, whose hotels are mostly geared towards the oil industry. During the peak months of Jul and Aug and the Folk Festival in Apr, it's a good idea to book in advance.

The most luxurious hotel in town is the **B-C** *Kveldsro House Hotel*, Greenfield Pl, T692195. Pronounced 'kel-ro', it overlooks the harbour and has an upmarket (and expensive) restaurant as well as cheaper bar food. Directly opposite the ferry terminal is the modern **B-C** *Shetland Hotel*, T695515, and 10 mins from the centre is the **B-C** *Lerwick Hotel*, 15 South Rd, T692166, which has a reputation for fine cuisine. In the centre is the refurbished **B-C** *Grand Hotel*, Commercial St, T692826, which features Shetland's only nightclub, and by the harbour is the rather faded **B-C** *Queen's Hotel*, Commercial St, T692826.

There are several pleasant guest houses and B&Bs, including **D-E** *Fort Charlotte Guest House*, 1 Charlotte St, T695956, **D-E** *The Old Manse*, 9 Commercial St, T696301, **D-E** *Alder Lodge Guest House*, 6 Clairmont Pl, T695705, **E** *Carradel Guest House*, 36 King Harald St, T692251, and next door, **E** *Solheim Guest House*, T695275.

Lerwick's clean, well-run *SYHA* **hostel** is at Islesburgh House, King Harald St, T692114, open Apr-Sept. There's **camping** at *Clickimin Caravan & Camp Site*, T741000, near Clickimin Leisure Centre and loch on the western edge of town.

Orkney and Shetland

Eating Despite a ready supply of fresh local produce, Shetland is a gastronomic desert. The best place to eat in Lerwick is *Monty's Bistro & Deli*, 5 Mounthooly St, T696655. It offers good modern Scottish cooking in a cosy, informal setting. Lunch cheap; dinner mid-range. Closed Sun. The next best choice is dinner or bar lunch at the *Kveldsro Hotel* and *Lerwick Hotel* (see above). Best place for a curry is the moderately-priced *Raba* Indian Restaurant, 26 Commercial Rd, T695585. *Osla's Café*, T696005, on Mounthooly St, is a cosy café serving a wide range of coffees, pancakes and other snacks and boasting the islands' only beer garden. Open Mon-Sat till at least 1900, Sun 1200-1600.

Entertainment The best place for a drink is the upstairs bar in the *Lounge*, on Mounthooly St near the tourist office, where local musicians usually play on Sat lunchtimes and some evenings. The town's only **nightclub** is *Posers*, at the *Grand Hotel*.

Folk music has a strong following in Shetland and the islands play host to 2 of Scotland's top folk events. In mid-Apr the islands are alive with the sound of music as musicians from around the globe come to play at the **Shetland Folk Festival**. Later, in mid-Oct, is the **Shetland Accordion and Fiddle Festival**. For details of both events, contact the Folk Festival office, 5 Burns Lane, Lerwick, T694757. To find out what's going on, buy a copy of the *Shetland Times* on Fri, or check out their website, www.shetland-times.co.uk. Also check the tourist board's **Events phoneline**, T694200.

Sport *Clickimin Centre*, Lochside, T741000. Sports and fitness centre open daily 0800-2300.

Transport See 'Ins and outs' at the start of this chapter for details of ferries and flights to and from Lerwick. There are regular daily **buses** (Nos 3 and 4) to and from **Sumburgh airport** which connect with flights. These buses also stop at several main sights, including **Jarlshof**, **Sandwick** (for Mousa Broch) and **St Ninian's Isle**. Bus No 2 runs to **Scalloway** (Mon-Sat). There are also buses (daily except Sun) to **Walls**, **Sandness**, **Aith**, **Skeld**, **North Roe**, **Hillswick**, **Vidlin**, **Toft** and **Mossbank**. Buses depart from the Viking bus station. Full details are given in the *Shetland Transport Timetable*.

There are several **taxi** companies in Lerwick: *6050 Cabs*, T696050; *Sheilds Taxis*, T695276; *Abbys Taxis*, T696666.

Car hire *Bolts Car Hire*, Toll clock Shopping Centre, 26 North Rd, T693636. *John Leask & Son*, Esplanade, T693162. *Star Rent-a-Car*, 22 Commercial Rd, T692075. Both also have offices at Sumburgh Airport. **Cycle hire** *Grantfield Garage*, North Rd, T692709, Mon-Sat 0800-1300 and 1400-1700.

Directory **Banks** *Bank of Scotland*, Clydesdale and Royal are on Commercial St. *Lloyds TSB* is on the Esplanade. **Communications** Post office Commercial St (open Mon-Fri 0900-1700, Sat 0900-1200), also in Toll clock Shopping Centre, 26 North Rd. **Embassies & consulates** Denmark, Iceland, Netherlands and Sweden at *Hay & Company*, 66 Commercial Rd, T692533); Finland, France, Germany and Norway at *Shearer Shipping Services*, Garthspool, T692556. **Laundry** *Lerwick Laundry*, 36 Market St, T693043, closed Sun. Service washes only. **Medical facilities** *Gilbert Bain Hospital*, Scalloway Rd, T743000. Opposite is the *Lerwick Health Centre*, T693201. **Travel agents** *John Leask & Son*, Esplanade, T693162.

Around Lerwick

Bressay & Noss Lying to the east of Lerwick across the Bressay Sound is the island of Bressay (pronounced 'bressah'), which creates a sheltered harbour for the capital and led to its establishment as a major trading port. Bressay is only seven miles long by three miles wide and makes an ideal day trip for **cyclists**. Another good way to get around is on foot and there's a fine walk to the top of **Ward Hill** (742ft), the highest point, from where you get great views of the island and as far afield as Foula and Out Skerries. There are also some good coastal walks, particularly along the cliffs from Noss Sound south to **Bard Head**, **The Ord** and **Bressay Lighthouse**, where you can see large colonies of seabirds.

Serious birdwatchers should head for **Noss**, a tiny, uninhabited island off the east coast of Bressay which is a **National Nature Reserve** with over 100,000 pairs of breeding seabirds. A walk around the perimeter of the island takes at least three hours but is highly recommended. At the east side is the **Noup of Noss**, where the 600ft cliffs are packed full of nesting gannets. The reserve is managed by Scottish Natural Heritage who have a small **visitor centre** at Gungstie.

Sleeping **D-E** *Maryfield House Hotel*, T820207, near the ferry terminal.

Transport Noss can only be visited from late May to late Aug daily except Mon and Thur, from 1000-1700. There are regular car **ferries** from the old harbour in Lerwick to Bressay (see page 581). From the 'Wait here' sign overlooking Noss sound on the east side of Bressay an inflatable dinghy shuttles back and forth to Noss during the island's opening hours (see above). The trip costs £2.50 return. In bad weather, call the tourist office, T693434, to check if it's sailing. A **post car** service runs once a day (except Sunday) from Maryfield ferry terminal to Noss Sound, T820200.

Central Mainland

The Central Mainland is Shetland's slim waist and only a few miles of land separates the east and west coast. Six miles from Lerwick, on the west coast, is Scalloway, once the capital of Shetland and now a fishing port and fish-processing centre. In 1942, during The Second World War, Scalloway became the headquarters of the **Shetland Bus** operations. This was the name given to the Norwegian fishing boats which sailed to Shetland during the night from German-occupied Norway bringing refugees to safety and returning with ammunition and resistance fighters. An interesting exhibition on the 'Shetland Bus' can be seen at **Scalloway Museum** on Main Street. ■ *May to Sept Tue-Thur 1400-1630, Sat 1000-1230 and 1400-1630. Donation requested.*

Scalloway
Phone code: 01595

The harbour is dominated by the ruins of **Scalloway Castle**, built in 1600 by the notorious Earl Patrick Stewart using local slave labour (see page 555). After his execution the castle fell into disrepair though the four-storey main block and one wing remain. Inside, an interpretative display explains its history. Next to the castle is the **Shetland Woollen Company**, T880243, where you can buy the famous Shetland wool and Fair Isle sweaters.

South of Scalloway lie the islands of **Trondra** and **Burra**, now connected to the Mainland by bridges. At Burland on Trondra is the **Spirit of Shetland**, T880437, where you buy Shetland knitwear, while on West Burra is the attractive little fishing village of **Hamnavoe**.

Sleeping There are a few places to stay in Scalloway. In the upper part of the village are **E** *Broch Guest House*, T880767, and **E** *Hildasay Guest House*, T880822. The latter had disabled facilities and arranges fishing trips. Eating options are limited to a bar meal at the *Scalloway Hotel* or *Kiln Bar*, or *Da Haaf Restaurant*, T880328, which is a canteen-style restaurant in the North Atlantic Fisheries college and specializes in (yes, you guessed it) seafood. Does a good fish supper, as well as having a more up market menu for the evenings. Open Mon-Fri 0900-2000.

Transport There are several daily **buses** (except Sun) between Lerwick and Scalloway, operated by *Shalder Coaches*, T880217.

👉 *Birdwatching in Shetland*

Shetland is famous for its birds. As well its huge seabird colonies, the islands attract Arctic species and are an important crossroads for migrating birds. Over 340 species have been recorded on Fair Isle, including rare and exotic birds from Asia and America. Twenty-one out of the 24 seabirds common to Britian breed in Shetland. These can be found around the coastline but the largest colonies are at the **Hermaness** and **Noss** reserves.

Amongst the many species which can be seen are the puffin. About one fifth of Scotland's puffins breed in Shetland. Its cousins in the auk family, guillemots, and razorbills, are also here in abundance during the summer months, along with kittiwakes, shags and that most common of seabirds, the fulmar. Britain's largest seabird, the gannet, can be seen diving spectacularly for fish at Hermaness, Noss, Fair Isle and Foula, while its smallest seabird, the storm petrel, is best seen around dusk on the tiny island of Mousa.

Summer heralds the return of the Arctic tern which breeds along low coastlines, as do the eider, oystercatcher, ringed plover and black guillemot, or tystie, which stays here all year round. The best place to see waders and shelduck are the nutrient-rich tidal mudflats at the Pool of Virkie in the South Mainland.

Many birds breed on agricultural land and these include the lapwing, skylark, meadow pipit and wheater. The hills and moorland provide breeding grounds for many summer visitors such as that pirate of the skies, the great skua, or bonxie, and the Arctic skua. Another Arcitc species, the whimbrel, also nests here, mainly in Unst, Yell and Fetlar. Moorland habitats are also favoured by the curlew, golden plover and merlin, Shetland's only bird of prey, while the lochs are home to large numbers of red-throated divers. Fetlar is home to 90 percent of the population of one of Britain's rarest birds, the red-necked phalarope.

Many of Shetland's bird habitats are protected as **RSPB Reserves** and **National Nature Reserves** and it is an offence to disturb the birds and their young at or near their nests. You also risk being dive-bombed by some of the more aggressively protective species. For a full list of all species recorded on the islands and more practical birdwatching information, be sure to get a copy of the **Shetland Bird Chart** (30p), by Joyce Gammack, available from the tourist office in Lerwick.

Tingwall
Phone code: 01595

North of Scalloway the B9074 runs through the fertile Tingwall Valley, past a nine-hole **golf course** at Asta, and the **Loch of Tingwall**, which is good for brown trout fishing and also home to swans and otters. At the northern end of the loch is a promontory called **Law Ting Holm**, which was the site of the *Althing*, or parliament, during the period of Norse rule. Overlooking the loch is **Tingwall Kirk**, built in the late 18th century on the site of the earlier church of St Magnus which dated back to the early period of Norse Christianity. In the graveyard is the old burial vault with several interesting old grave slabs. Nearby is **Tingwall Agricultural Museum**, which houses a collection of old crofting implements. ■ *Jun-Aug Mon-Sat 1000-1300 and 1400-1700. Admission £1.50.*

Sleeping Near the airport, by the crossroads, is the **D** *Herrislea House Hotel*, T840208, which offers good home cooking daily till 2100 and live music in its *Starboard Tack* bar. In nearby Wormadale is the modern **C** *Westings Hotel*, T840242, which is a good place to stop for lunch.

North of the museum is **Tingwall Airport**, T840246, which has flights to most of the smaller islands (see page 579). Getting to and from the airport is straightforward as regular buses between Lerwick and Westside (see below) stop in Tingwall.

The A971 continues northwest towards Weisdale. At the head of **Weisdale Voe** the B9075 branches north to **Weisdale Mill** which now houses the **Bonhoga Gallery**, a purpose-built art gallery featuring varied exhibitions of local, national and international works. There's also a nice café serving snacks. ■ *T830400. Wed-Sat 1030-1630, Sun 1200-1630.* Weisdale Mill was part of the Kergord estate, known until 1945 as Flemington, and was built from the stones of evacuated crofthouses. Over 300 crofters were forcibly evicted in the mid-19th century during the 'Clearances' when lairds expanded their more profitable sheep-farming activities. In 1940 the mill was requisitioned as the intelligence and administrative HQ for the 'Shetland Bus' operations (see Scalloway above). The Kergord estate today is largest area of woodland in Shetland and attracts a variety of migratory birds.

Weisdale
Phone code: 01595

On the west shore of Weisdale Voe, south of the mill, are the ruins of the house where **John Clunies Ross** (1786-1854) was born. He settled in the Cocos Islands in the Indian Ocean in 1827 and proclaimed himself 'King'. After his death, the islands were ruled by his offspring until they became Australian territory, no doubt to the relief of the islanders.

The Westside

The western Mainland of Shetland, stretching west from Weisdale to Sandness, is known as The Westside. This part of Shetland is notable for its varied landscape of spectacular sea cliffs, rolling green hills, bleak moorland, peaty freshwater lochs and numerous long sea lochs, or *voes*. This is excellent **walking** country, with many fine coastal routes, especially around **Culswick** and **Dale of Walls** (OS Landranger maps Nos 3 and 4). It is also great for **birdwatching** and **trout fishing** and there are many opportunities for spotting **whales, dolphins** and **otters**.

Walls
Phone code: 01595

There are a few interesting archaeological sites here, too. At **Stanydale**, signposted from the road between the villages of **Bixter** and **Walls**, is the site of a Neolothic settlement with the remains of houses, field boundaries and clearance cairns. Near the **Brig o' Waas**, just north of Walls, is the **Scord of Brouster**, prehistoric farm site which has been excavated.

The pretty little village **Walls** (pronounced 'waas') is set around a sheltered natural harbour and is a popular spot with visiting yachts. It also attracts many visitors during its Agricultural Show in August, the biggest such event on Shetland.

Sleeping Walls also boasts the best accommodation on the Westside. Two miles southwest of the village is **B-C** *Burrastow House*, T809307, a restored 18th-century house overlooking Vaila Sound. It's full of character and has a reputation for serving superb cuisine (some say the best on the islands, so you'll need to book ahead). There's a **camping böd** in Walls, at *Voe House*, a restored 18th-century house overlooking the village. Open Apr-Sept. Book through Lerwick tourist office. A mile or so north of the village is **E** *Skeoverick*, T803349, a friendly B&B. At Gruting, east of Brig o' Waas is **E-F** *Pomona*, T810438.

Transport There are daily **buses** to Walls from Lerwick, Mon-Sat, with *Shalder Coaches*, T01595-880217. A **minibus** runs to Sandness from Walls once a day (except Sun). Contact Mr P Isbister, T809268.

Northwest of Walls, the A971 crosses bleak moorland before descending to the crofting township of Sandness (pronounced 'saa-ness'), surrounded by fertile land and facing little Papa Stour, about a mile offshore. There's a good **beach**

Sandness

Orkney and Shetland

here and also a **woollen spinning mill**, where you can watch how they spin the famously fine wool into yarn. ■ *Mon-Fri 0800-1700, free.*

Foula Walls is the departure point for **ferries** to the remote island of Foula, whose name derives from the Norse *fugl ey*, meaning 'bird island'. Lying 15 miles west of the Shetland Mainland, tiny Foula is the second most remote inhabited island after Fair Isle. It supports a population of around 40 people, who are greatly outnumbered by many thousands of seabirds, including a small colony of gannets and the rare Leach's petrel. There are also about 2,500 pairs of great skuas, the largest colony in the UK.

The island is dominated by its sheer cliffs which reach their most awe-inspiring peak at **The Kame** (1,220ft), the second highest sea cliffs in Britain after St Kilda.

An interesting feature of the island's people is that they still observe the old **Julian calendar**, replaced in 1752 in Britain by the present Gregorian system which deleted 11 days from the year. Remote areas of the country kept to the old calendar, adding an extra day in 1800, which was a leap year, and some parts of Shetland continued to observe festivals 12 days after the dates in the new calendar. The most remote areas kept to the old calendar longest, and the people of Foula still celebrate Christmas on 6 January and New Year's Day on 13 January.

Sleeping Those wishing to celebrate two Christmases or New Year's Days, or to stay and admire the bird life, can stay on the island at **E** *Leraback*, T753226, which includes dinner in the price. There is also self catering accommodation available on the island £90-£150 per week for a cottage sleeping 4-6 people. Contact Mr R Holbourn, T753232.

Transport For details of **ferries** and **flights** to Foula, see page 579.

Papa Stour A ferry sails from **West Burrafirth** on the Westside, near Sandness, to the little island of Papa Stour, only a mile offshore. The island, which has a population of around 30, is mostly made up of volcanic rock which has been eroded to form an amazing coastline of stacks, arches and caves, most spectacular of which is **Kirstan's Hole**. The island is home large colonies of auks, terns and skuas and also has a fascinating history of its own. Pick up the island trails leaflet from the tourist office in Lerwick.

Sleeping You can stay on the island at **E** *North House*, T873238, which offers B&B or full board. There's no shop on the island. For details of **ferries** and **flights** to Papa Stour, see page 579. Ferries should be booked with *W Clark*, T810460.

South Mainland

Phone code: 01950 From Lerwick a long, narrow finger of land points south. The main road runs down the east coast for 25 miles till it ends at **Sumburgh Head**, near Shetland's main airport. This southern part of the Shetland Mainland holds the islands' two most important archaeological sights and main tourist attractions.

About 10 miles south of Lerwick, just to the south of **Cunningsburgh**, is the **Catpund Quarries**, where soft soapstone was quarried from Neolithic to medieval times and made into a variety of stone implements and utensils.

Mousa Fifteen miles south of Lerwick, the scattered crofting communities of **Sandwick** look across to the **Isle of Mousa**, site of the best-preserved broch in Scotland. This fortified tower was built around 2,000 years ago and still stands close to its original height of 45ft. It's a very impressive structure when you see it from the inside and has chambers, galleries, an internal staircase and a parapet. The broch features in a Viking saga of the 12th century when the mother of Harald, Earl of Orkney, took refuge there with her lover. The Earl, who did not approve of the liaison, laid siege to the broch but it proved impregnable and he gave up. Entry to the broch is free.

Mousa island is also home to many seabirds and waders, most notably the Storm Petrel, which is best seen at dusk as they return to their nests amongst the beach rocks. You can also see seals on the white-sand beach at West Voe. If you have time, it's a good idea to walk right around the coast, starting from the landing stage at West Ham and first heading south to the broch. Allow about two hours and watch out for dive-bombing terns! A **passenger ferry** sails to the island from **Leebitton harbour** in Sandwick daily from mid-April to mid-September, weather permitting, at 0930, 1230 and 1400, allowing visitors 2½ hours to see the island. The trip takes 15 minutes and costs £6.50 per adult. For bookings, call Tom Jamieson.

Sleeping There's accommodation in Sandwick at the **B-C** *Barclay Arms Hotel*, T431226, which offers evening meals, and **F-E** *Solbrekke*, T431410.

Transport There are several daily **buses** (Mon-Sat; 2-3 on Sun) between Lerwick, Sandwick and Sumburgh Airport.

At Hoswick, between Sandwick and Levenwick, is **Da Warp and Weft Visitor Centre**, which houses an exhibition on weaving, crofting, fishing and island life. ■ *May-Sept Mon-Sat 1000-1700, Sun 1200-1700, free.* Next door is the **Shetland Woollen Company**, where you can buy knitwear. | **South of Sandwick**

Further south on the east coast, at Boddam, is the **Shetland Crofthouse Museum**, a restored thatched crofthouse with 19th-century furniture and utensils. ■ *May-Sept daily 1000-1300 and 1400-1700. £2.*

On the west coast, near Bigton village, a signposted track leads to the spectacular sandy causeway (known as a tombolo) which leads to St Ninian's Isle. The tombolo is the best example of its kind in Britain and you can walk across to the island which is best known for the hoard of Pictish treasure which was discovered in 1958 in the ruins of the 12th-century church. The 28 silver objects included bowls, a spoon and brooches, probably dating from around 800 AD and are now on display in the Royal Scottish Museum in Edinburgh, though you can see replicas in the Shetland Museum in Lerwick. Two daily **buses** (not Sunday) run to Bigton from Lerwick, though you have to change at Channerwick junction. | **St Ninian's Isle to Quendale**

The west coast south of Bigton is beautiful with long, sandy beaches interspersed with dramatic cliff scenery. On the other side of the road from the long, sheltered beach at **Scousburgh Sands** is the **Loch of Spiggie RSPB Reserve**. The loch is an important winter wildfowl refuge, particularly for Whooper Swans and during the summer you can see various ducks, waders, gulls, terns and skuas. There's a hide on the northern shore with an information board. Nearby is the *Spiggie Hotel*, T01950-460409, which offers bar meals, afternoon tea or dinner.

A few miles south of the loch is the village of **Quendale** overlooking a wide, sandy bay. Here you'll find the beautifully-restored and fully working 19th-century **Quendale Mill**, the last of Shetland's watermills. ■ *May-Sept daily 1000-1700. Admission £1.50.*

Orkney and Shetland

Not far from here, between Garth's Ness and Fitful Head, lies the wreck of the *Braer* oil tanker which ran onto the rocks in 1993. A disaster of epic proportions was averted by the hurricane-force gales which dispersed the huge oil spillage. Two **buses** daily (Monday-Saturday) run to Quendale from Lerwick, with a change at Channerwick junction.

Sumburgh & At the southern tip of Mainland is the village of Sumburgh, site of Shetland's
Jarlshof main **airport** for external passenger flights and for helicopters and planes servicing the North Sea oil industry. South of the airport is Shetland's prime archaeological site, Jarlshof, a hugely impressive place which spans 4,000 years of occupation, from Neolithic times through Norse settlement to the 16th century. The original Stone Age dwellings are topped by a medieval broch, Pictish wheelhouses, Viking longhouses and, towering over the whole complex, the ruins of a 16th-century mansion. This remarkable site was only discovered at the end of the 19th century when a violent storm ripped off the top layer of turf. Jarlshof is, in fact, not a genuine name, but the exotic invention of Sir Walter Scott in his novel *The Pirate*. A helpful guidebook available from the visitor centre helps to bring the place to life. ■ *T460112 (HS). Apr-Sept daily 0930-1830. Admission £2.50, £1.90 concession.*

South of Jarlshof is the Mainland ends abruptly at **Sumburgh Head**, an RSPB Reserve. The **lighthouse** on top of the cliff was built by Robert Stevenson in 1821 and the keepers' cottages are now rented out as self-catering accommodation. The lighthouse isn't open to the public but from its grounds you can see many nesting seabirds such as puffins, kittiwakes, fulmars, guillemots and razorbills. Just to the east of the airport is **Pool of Virkie**, another good birdwatching area.

Sleeping Accommodation is limited. There's the **C** *Sumburgh Hotel*, T460201, next to Jarlshof in a converted laird's house. It has a bar and restaurant. There's also a **camping böd** in *Betty Mouat's Cottage*, next to a recently-excavated site at Scatness next to the airport. It sleeps up to 8 and is open Apr-Sept. Book through Lerwick tourist office. Betty Mouat was quite a woman. In 1886, at the age of 60, she was on a boat heading for Lerwick when the captain was swept overboard and the 2 crewmen went to rescue him, leaving Betty alone. They were unable to get back to the boat which drifted for 9 days before ending up in Norway. Betty survived the ordeal.

Transport There are regular daily **buses** from **Lerwick**, which stop at the hotel, **Scatness** and **Grutness Pier** (for Fair Isle) en route to the airport.

Fair Isle

Phone code: 01595 Twenty-four miles southwest of Sumburgh and 27 miles northeast of North Ronaldsay in Orkney, is Fair Isle, the most isolated of Britain's inhabited islands. Only three miles long by 1½ miles wide, the island has a population of around 70 and is best known for its intricately-patterned knitwear, which is still produced by a co-operative, *Fair Isle Crafts*. Co-operative could be said to sum up the friendly islanders, whose lifestyle is based on mutual help and community effort.

Fair Isle is a paradise for **birdwatchers** and keen ornithologists form the majority of the island's visitors. It stands in the flight path of many thousands of migrating birds and over 340 species have been recorded here at the **Fair Isle Bird Observatory** which also offers accommodation and where visitors are welcome to take part. As well as the almost obscenely rich birdlife there are around 240 species of flowering plants, making the island an especially beautiful haven for naturalists. Fair Isle's coastline, especially in the north and west, also boasts some outstanding cliff scenery.

The bird observatory was the brainchild of George Waterston, an ornithologist who first visited in 1935 and then bought the island in 1948 to begin his task of building the observatory. The island was given to the National Trust for Scotland in 1954 and declared a National Scenic Area. It was recently designated a place of outstanding natural beauty and cultural heritage by the Council of Europe. The **George Waterston Memorial Centre** has exhibits and photographs detailing the island's natural history as well as the history of crofting, fishing, archaeology and knitwear. ■ *May to mid-Sept Mon and Fri 1400-1600, Wed 1030-1200. Donations welcome.*

Sleeping There are a few places to stay on the island, but accommodation must be booked in advance and includes meals. The **D** *Fair Isle Lodge and Bird Observatory*, T760258, fairisle.birdobs@zetnet.co.uk, offers full board accommodation in private rooms or in a dormitory (**E**). Alternatively, there's B&B with evening meal and packed lunch at **D-E** *Schoolton*, T760250, and **D-E** *Upper Leogh*, T760248.

Transport For details of **ferries** to Fair Isle from **Grutness** (near Sumburgh) or Lerwick, and **flights** from **Tingwall Airport**, see page 581. A day return flight (£72) allows about 6 hours on the island. You can also fly from **Kirkwall** on Orkney for £69 return, which allows 2½ hrs on the island, T01856-872420. Ferries should be booked with *J W Stout*, T760222.

North Mainland

The main road north from Lerwick branches at **Voe**, a peaceful and colourful little village nestling in a bay at the head of the Olna Firth. One branch leads to the Yell car and passenger ferry terminal at **Toft**, past the turn-off to the massive **Sullom Voe Oil Terminal**, the largest oil and liquefied gas terminal in Europe. The other road heads northwest to Brae (see below). *Phone code: 01806*

Sleeping You can stay in Voe at the *Sail Loft* by the pier. This former fishing store is now Shetland's largest **camping böd**, open Apr-Sept. Food is available at the *Pierhead Restaurant and Bar*, T588332.

Transport Regular **buses** from **Lerwick** to Brae and Hillswick to the northwest, and Toft and Mossbank to the north, pass through Voe daily except Sun.

Brae is not a very pretty place and was built to accommodate workers at the nearby Sullom Voe oil terminal. It does boast a good selection of accommodation and decent facilities, though, and makes a good base from which to explore the wild and wonderful coastal scenery around the Northmavine peninsula to the north. There's also good walking and spectacularly good westerly views around the island of **Muckle Roe** to the southwest and up the island's small hill, South Ward (554ft). Be careful of the overly protective bonxies, though. The island is attached to the mainland by a bridge. **Brae**

Sleeping The best place to stay around Brae, or anywhere else on Shetland, is the **B** *Busta House Hotel*, T522506, www.mes.co.uk/busta, a luxurious and wonderfully-atmospheric 16th-century country house overlooking Busta Voe about 1½ miles from Brae village. The superb restaurant (mid-range to expensive) is the finest on Shetland with a selection of malts to match, and there are also meals in the bar. There are also several B&Bs to choose from, including **E-D** *Valleyfield Guest House*,

T522563, and **E** *Drumquin Guest House*, T522621, both with dinner available. On Muckle Roe is **E** *Westayre*, T522368, which is a working croft. A good place to **eat**, other than *Busta House* is the *Mid Brae Inn* which serves great food daily till 2100.

Transport **Buses** from **Lerwick** to Hillswick (see below) and to **Toft/Mossbank** (see under Yell below) stop in Brae.

Northmavine   **Mavis Grind**, the narrow isthmus where it's claimed you can throw a stone from the Atlantic to the North Sea, leads into Northmavine, the northwest peninsula of North Mainland which is one of Shetland's most dramatic and beautiful areas, with rugged scenery, spectacular coastline and wide empty spaces. This is excellent **walking** country and it's a good idea to abandon the car and explore it on foot. **Hillswick Ness**, to the south of **Hillswick** village, is a nice walk but further west, around the coastline of **Eshaness**, is the most spectacular cliff scenery and amazing natural features, all with unusual and evocative names. North of the lighthouse are the **Holes of Scraada**, **Grind o' da Navir** and the **Villians of Hamnavoe**, which is not a local gang but eroded lava cliffs with blowholes, arches and caves. East of Eshaness are the **Heads of Grocken** and **The Drongs**, a series of exposed sea stacks, which offer superb diving. Further north, overlooking the deep sea inlet of **Ronies Voe**, is the dramatic red granite bulk of **Ronies Hill** (1,477ft), with a well-preserved burial cairn at the summit. The coastal scenery to the north and west of here is even more breathtaking but very remote and exposed. You should be well equipped before setting out. A useful guide is *Walking the Coastline of Northmavine* by Peter Guy.

Between Eshaness and Hillswick, a side road leads south to the **Tangwick Haa Museum**, which features displays and photographs on the history of fishing and whaling and the hardships of life in these parts. ■ *May-Sept Mon-Fri 1300-1700, Sat and Sun 1100-1900. Free.*

Sleeping Accommodation is available in **Hillswick** at the **D** *St Magnus Hotel*, T503372, or B&B at **E-F** *Almara*, T503261, at Upper Urafirth. Also in Hillswick is *The Booth*, Shetland's oldest pub, which serves food daily in summer.

In **Hamnavoe**, reached by a side road which branches north from the road between Hillswick and Eshaness, you can stay at *Johnny Notion's Camping Böd*, birthplace of John Williamson, known as 'Johnny Notions', an 18th-century craftsman who developed an effective innoculation against smallpox. It's open Apr-Sept and has no electricity. Book through Lerwick tourist office.

Transport There is a daily **bus** service from **Lerwick** to Hillswick (Mon-Sat; £1.90), departing at 1710 and arriving at 1825. From there, a feeder service continues to **Eshaness** (20 minutes). Contact *Whites Coaches*, T809443.

Whalsay and Out Skerries

Phone code: 01806   South of Voe, the B9071 branches east to **Laxo**, the ferry terminal for the island of **Whalsay**, one of Shetland's most prosperous small islands owing to its thriving fishing industry which helps support a population of around 1,000. The fleet is based at **Symbister**, the island's main settlement. Beside the harbour at Symbister is the **Pier House**, a restored böd which was used by the Hanseatic League, a commercial association of German merchants who traded in Shetland from the Middle Ages to the early 18th century. Inside is an exhibition explaining the history of the Hanseatic trade and general information on the island. ■ *Mon-Sat 0900-1300 and 1400-1700, Sun 1400-1700. 50p.*

In the seas around Whalsay you can see porpoises, dolphins, minke whales and orcas, hence its Viking name which means 'island of whales'. One of Scotland's great poets **Hugh McDiarmid** (Christopher Grieve) spent most of the 1930s in Whalsay, where he wrote much of his finest poetry, until he was called for war work in 1942, never to return. His former home, at Sodom, near Symbister, is now a **camping böd**. It's open April-September and has no electricity.

Transport There are regular daily car and passenger **ferries** between **Laxo** and **Symbister** (see page 581). To book, call T566259. There are daily **buses** to **Laxo** and and **Vidlin** (see below) from Lerwick, run by *Whites Coaches*, T01595-809443).

The Out Skerries are a small group of rocky islands about five miles from **Out Skerries** Whalsay and 10 miles east of Shetland Mainland. It's made up of three main islands: the larger islands of **Housay** and **Bruray**, which are connected by a road bridge; and the uninhabited island of **Grunay**. The Skerries boast some spectacular and rugged sea cliffs which are home to many rare migrant sea-birds in spring and autumn.

Transport There are **ferries** to the Skerries from **Lerwick** and also from **Vidlin**, about three miles northeast of Laxo (see page 581). For bookings, call *G W Henderson*, T515226. There are also **flights** from **Tingwall Airport** (see page 579).

The North Isles

Yell, the second largest of the Shetland islands, was described rather **Yell** damningly by Shetland-born writer Eric Linklater as 'dull and dark'. And it's *Phone code: 01957* true that the interior is consistently desolate peat moorland. But the coastline is greener and more pleasant and provides an ideal habitat for the island's large **otter** population. Yell is also home a rich variety of birds and offers some good coastal and hill walks, especially around the rugged coastline of **The Herra**, a peninsula about half way up the west coast.

At **Burravoe**, about five miles east of the ferry terminal at **Ulsta**, is the **Old Haa Museum**, housed in Yell's oldest building which dates from 1672. It contains an interesting display on local flora and fauna and history. ■ *T722339. Late Apr-Sept Tue-Thur and Sat 1000-1600, Sun 1400-1700. Free.*

The island's largest village, **Mid Yell**, has a couple of shops, a pub and a leisure centre with a good swimming pool. About a mile northwest, on the hillside above the main road, are the reputedly haunted ruins of **Windhouse**, dating from 1707. To the north is the **RSPB Lumbister Reserve**, where red-throated divers, merlins, great and Arctic skuas and many other bird species come to breed. The reserve is also home to a large number of otters. A pleasant walk leads along the nearby steep and narrow gorge, known as the **Daal of Lumbister**, filled with many colourful flowers. The area to the north of the reserve provides good walking over remote moorland and coastline.

The road continues north past the reserve and around **Basta Voe** where you can see otters. North of **Gutcher**, the ferry port for Unst, is the village of **Cullivoe**, with some good walks along the attractive coastline.

Sleeping There's accommodation on Yell at **E** *Hillhead*, T722274, in Burravoe; at **E** *Pinewood Guest House*, T702427, in South Aywick, between Burravoe and Mid Yell; and at the friendly **E-F** *Post Office*, T744201, in Gutcher. You can also stay at *Windhouse Lodge*, which is a **camping böd** below the ruins of haunted Windhouse. It's well-equipped and open Apr-Sept. **Eating** options are limited to the café in the

Old Haa Museum, the *Seaview Café* in Gutcher, or the *Hilltop Restaurant and Bar* in Mid Yell.

Transport There are frequent car and passenger **ferries** from **Toft** on North Mainland to **Ulsta** on the south coast of Yell (see page 581). It's not essential, but a good idea to book in advance, T722259. 3 **buses** daily (Mon-Fri; 2 on Sat, 1 on Sun) run between Lerwick and Toft (1 hr; £1.90). There's a bus service on Yell which runs between Ulsta and Cullivoe and stops at villages in between, T744214.

Fetlar

Phone code: 01957

Fetlar is the smallest of the North Isles but the most fertile, and known as 'the garden of Shetland'. Indeed, the name derives from Norse meaning 'fat land' as there is good grazing and croftland and a rich variety of plant and bird life. The whole island is good for birdwatching but the prime place is the 1,700 acres of **North Fetlar RSPB Reserve** around Vord Hill (522ft) in the north of the island. This area has restricted access during the summer months and visitors should contact the warden at Bealance, T733246. The warden will also let you know if and when you can see the one or two female Snowy Owls which sometimes visit. The north cliffs of the reserve are home to large colonies of breeding seabirds, including auks, gulls and shags, and you can also see common and grey seals on the beaches in late autumn. Fetlar is home to one of Britain's rarest birds, the **red-necked phalarope**, which breeds in the loch near **Funzie** (pronounced 'finnie') in the east of the island. You can watch them from the RSPB hide in the nearby marshes. Red-throated divers and whimbrel also breed here. The island is also good for **walking** and a leaflet describing some of the walks is available from the tourist office in Lerwick.

The main settlement on the island is **Houbie**, on the south coast. Here you'll see a house called Leagarth, which was built by the island's most famous son, Sir William Watson Cheyne, who with Lord Lister pioneered antiseptic surgery. Nearby is the excellent **Fetlar Interpretive Centre** which presents the island's history and gives information on its bounteous birdlife. ■ *May-Sept Tue-Sun 1200-1700. Free.*

Sleeping There's **B&B** at **E-F** *The Gord*, T733227, in Houbie, and at **E-F** *The Glebe*, T733242, a lovely old house overlooking Papil Water. You can also **camp** at *Gerth's Campsite*, T733227, which overlooks the beach at Tresta and has good facilities.

Transport There are regular car and passenger **ferries** between **Oddsta** in the northwest of the island and **Gutcher** on Yell and **Belmont** on Unst (see page 581). There's a **post car** service which runs around the island from the ferry once a day on Mon, Wed and Fri, T733227.

Unst

Phone code: 01957

Unst is the most northerly inhabited island in Britain but there is more to the island than its many 'most northerly' attractions. It is scenically one of the most varied of the Shetland islands with spectacular cliffs, sea stacks, sheltered inlets, sandy beaches, heather-clad hills, fertile farmland, freshwater lochs and even a sub-arctic desert. Such a variety of habitats supports over 400 plant species and a rich variety of wildlife. Unst is a major breeding site for gannets, puffins, guillemots, razorbills, kittiwakes, shags, Arctic and great skuas and whimbrels amongst others and in the surrounding waters you can see seals, porpoises, otters and even killer whales.

In the east of the island, north of **Baltasound**, is the **Keen of Hamar National Nature Reserve**, 74 acres of serpentine rock which breaks into tiny fragments known as 'debris', giving the landscape a strange, lunar-like appearance. This bleak 'desert' is actually home to some of the rarest plants in Britain.

Baltasound is the island's main settlement, with an airport, hotel, pub, post office, leisure centre with pool and Britain's most northerly brewery, the **Valhalla Brewery** which can be visited by appointment, T711348.

To the north of here is the village of **Haroldswick**, home of Britain's most northerly post office, where your postcards are sent with a special stamp to inform everyone of this fact. Here also is **Unst Boat Haven**, where you can see a beautifully-presented collection of traditional boats and fishing artefacts. ■ *May-Sept daily 1400-1700. Free.* A little way further north is the **Unst Heritage Centre**, which has a museum of local history and island life. ■ *Same opening hours as Boat Haven and also free.* Nearby is an RAF radar tracking station at Saxa Vord. The road ends at Skaw, where there's a lovely beach and Britain's most northerly house. The road northwest from Haroldswick leads to the head of **Burra Firth**, a sea inlet flanked by high cliffs and site of Britain's most northerly golf course.

To the west of Burra Firth is the remote **Hermaness National Nature Reserve**, 2,422 acres of dramatic coastal scenery and wild moorland which is home to over 100,000 nesting seabirds including gannets, and the largest number of puffins and great skuas (or 'bonxies') in Shetland. There's an excellent **visitor centre** in the former lighthouse keeper's shore station where you can pick up a leaflet which shows the marked route into the reserve, and see the local artistic efforts of many of Unst's children. Whilst in the reserve, make sure you keep to the marked paths to avoid being attacked by bonxies, they are highly protective and rest assured that they will attack if they think that their territory is being threatened. ■ *T711278. Open daily late Apr to mid-Sept 0830-1800.*

The views from Hermaness are wonderful, out to the offshore stacks and skerries including **Muckle Flugga**, and then to the wide open north Atlantic ocean. Muckle Flugga is the site of the most northerly lighthouse in Britain, built in 1857-58 by Thomas Stevenson, father of Robert Louis Stevenson. The writer visited the island in 1869 and the illustrated map in his novel *Treasure Island* bears a striking similarity to the outline of Unst. Beyond the lighthouse is **Out Stack**, which marks the most northerly point on the British Isles. With nothing between you and the North Pole but water, this is the place to sit and contemplate what it feels like to be at the end of the world.

Sleeping There's a decent selection of accommodation on Unst. Top choice has to be **C** *Buness House*, T711315, buness@zetnet.co.uk, a lovely old 17th-century Haa in Baltasound. Staying here is a bizarre and rather surreal experience, given that you are on the most northerly island in Britain. The house is crammed full of Indian Raj relics, and the stuffed eagle, tiger and leopard skins hanging in the hallway is a wildlife close-up almost as impressive, though considerably more unsettling and un-'PC', as the Hermaness Nature Reserve in the north of the island that the family own. The food is excellent and the accommodation comfortable. Another good place is **E** *Prestegaard*, T755234, a Victorian house at Uyeasound on the south coast near the ferry. Also in Baltasound is the **E** *Cligera Guest House*, T711579, and the independent *Gardiesfauld Hostel*, T755259; open Apr-Sept, which also **hires bikes**. There's also **B&B** in Haroldswick at **E-F** *Gerratoun*, T711323. **Eating** options are limited, though all the B&Bs serve evening meals on request. The *Baltasound Hotel*, T711334, serves meals and drinks to non-residents.

Transport There are twice daily **flights** (Mon-Fri) to Unst from **Tingwall** and **Sumburgh** airports. There are regular car and passenger **ferries** to Belmont from **Gutcher** on Yell. Booking is advised, T722259. There's an island **bus** service which runs a few times daily (except Sun) between **Baltasound**, **Belmont** and **Haroldswick**, T711666.

Southern Scotland

14

Southern Scotland

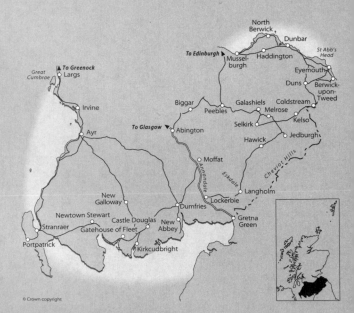

© Crown copyright

The vast swathe of Southern Scotland covered in this chapter comprises East Lothian, the Scottish Borders, Dumfries and Galloway and Ayrshire. It's an area usually overlooked by those on their way to Glasgow, Edinburgh or further north, and consequently relatively free from the litter-strewn lay-bys and crowded beauty spots of more favoured parts.

Despite its proximity to the English border, the south of Scotland is in many ways at the very heart of the country. Under constant threat during the long wars with England, its people were at the front line in the defence of Scottish nationhood. It is, therefore, no coincidence that Scotland's two greatest literary figures, **Robert Burns** and **Sir Walter Scott**, were born and lived here.

Southern Scotland is divided neatly by the A74(M), the main route from England to Scotland. To the east of this line the main tourist focus is the Borders region, with its peaceful little mill towns, in particular the lovely little town of **Melrose**. To the north are the narrow ranges of the **Lammermuir**, **Moorfoot** and **Pentland Hills**. North of the Lammermuirs is **East Lothian**, with its sandy bays and rugged coastline.

The landscape becomes ever more wild and mountainous as you head west from the Tweed Valley across the **Southern Uplands**. The most spectacular scenery is west of Dumfries, in the **Galloway Forest Park**. The **Solway coast**, from Dumfries to the Mull of Galloway, is equally appealing. North of Galloway is the **Ayrshire** coast, lined with seaside resorts and some great golf courses and best known for its associations with Robert Burns, especially Alloway, where he was born.

Ins and outs

Getting around **Bus** services are good around Ayrshire, East Lothian and between the main towns in the Borders, and there are also regular services between Dumfries and Stranraer, along the A75, but services to more remote parts are limited.

Train services are limited to the line north from Berwick-upon-Tweed to Edinburgh on the east coast, and lines from Dumfries and Stranraer to Ayrshire in the west, with links to Glasgow.

Details of all **public transport services** are given under the relevant towns and villages. Phone numbers of travel information lines and the main operators are also given. Bus timetables are available at local tourist offices.

Walking The south of Scotland is excellent walking country and there are numerous marked trails through the forests and hills and circular walks around the towns, especially in the Tweed Valley. The tourist offices have leaflets detailing all the main routes. There are also a number of Ranger-led walks, details of which are also available at tourist offices.

For the more ambitious hiker there are two long-distance trails. The 62-mile **St Cuthbert's Way** is a cross-border trail which links several places associated with St Cuthbert, who started his ministry at Melrose in the mid-seventh-century and ended it at Lindisfarne (Holy Island), on the Northumberland coast. The waymarked route starts at **Melrose Abbey** and climbs across the Eildon Hills before joining the river Tweed. Highlights include Dere Street, a Roman Road, the Cheviot foothills, St Cuthbert's Cave and the causeway crossing to Lindisfarne. Free route leaflets are available from the Scottish Borders Tourist Board (address given on page 607). They can also provide a trail pack which includes maps and route descriptions (£13.50 including P&P).

The most famous and demanding of walks is the 212-mile **Southern Upland Way**, which runs from Portpatrick on the west coast, near Stranraer, to Cockburnspath on the Berwickshire coast in the east, south of Dunbar. The route passes through a great variety of scenery, from the Rhinns of Galloway to the wild heartland of Southern Scotland to the gentler eastern Borders. The most picturesque sections are the beginning and the end, but in between the highlights include Glen Trool, the Lowther Hills, St Mary's Loch and the river Tweed. A route leaflet is available from the *Countryside Ranger Service*, Scottish Borders Council, Harestanes Visitor Centre, Ancrum, Jedburgh TD8 6UQ, T/F01835-830281. The various local tourist offices have leaflets on their own section of the walk. There is also a trail pack (£18 including P&P), available from the Dumfries & Galloway or Scottish Borders tourist boards.

Cycling The quiet backroads of southern Scotland also make it ideal for exploring by bike, especially the Tweed Valley, Galloway Forest Park and around The Machars peninsula. The **Tweed Cycleway** is a waymarked 90-mile route which follows minor roads through the beautiful Tweed Valley, from Biggar to Berwick-upon-Tweed. The tourist office provides a free guide *Cycling in the Scottish Borders* which features over 20 routes, including the Tweed Cycleway. Another route is the **Four Abbeys Cycle Route**, a 55-mile circular tour which takes in Melrose, Dryburgh, Jedburgh and Kelso. It is described in the *Four Abbeys Cycle Way* guide (£2 including P&P) available from tourist offices.

East Lothian

East Lothian stretches east from Musselburgh, to the east of Edinburgh, along the coast to North Berwick and Dunbar. This is real golfing country, with a string of excellent courses running the length of the coast, and there are miles of sandy beaches. The East Lothian coast is also home to huge colonies of seabirds, especially on the Bass Rock, a dramatic volcanic islet off North Berwick. Inland is the attractive historic market town of Haddington and further south the village of Gifford is the gateway to the Lammermuir Hills, which form the boundary with the Borders region and offer good walking opportunities.

Ins and outs

There are good transport links with Edinburgh and most of the main sights can be visited in a few day trips from the capital. **Trains** from Edinburgh stop in Musselburgh, Prestonpans, North Berwick and Dunbar. There are also regular **buses** to all the main towns. For public transport information call the East and Midlothian Traveline (T0800-232323). See also under Edinburgh Transport (page 67).

Getting around

For more information on East Lothian and for a free accommodation, contact **Edinburgh & Lothians Tourist Office** (T0131-4733800, F4733881, www.edinburgh.org), or East Lothian tourist information centres in Musselburgh, North Berwick and Dunbar.

Information

Musselburgh to North Berwick

Six miles east of Edinburgh, across the river Esk, is the town of **Musselburgh**. It's a fairly humdrum place, but may be of interest to golfing enthusiasts as the original home of golf and Royal Musselbugh is one of the oldest clubs in the country. It is also a target for naturalists who come to see the huge populations of migrating waders, ducks and seabirds which flock to the mouth of the river Esk. Ice cream lovers may also be interested to note that *Luca's* on the High Street has most of the competition licked and is definitely worth a stop if you're passing by. There's also a **tourist office**, at Old Craighall. ■ *T6536172.*

Phone code: 0131
Colour map 6, grid A2

Ten miles east of Musselburgh is the conservation village of **Aberlady**, at the mouth of the River Peffer. A row of Georgian cottages line the main street and there's a lovely old church which hints at Aberlady's erstwhile importance as a port. The old harbour is silted up and now forms part of the mudflats and salt marshes of the **Aberlady Bay Nature Reserve**, which is the home of numerous seabirds.

A couple of miles north of Aberlady is **Gullane**, a resort town with an exclusive air which is hopelessly devoted to **golf**. There are no fewer than four golf courses surrounding Gullane; Nos 1, 2 and 3 and the world-famous **Muirfield**, where you need an introduction to play. Golf may be Gullane's *raison d'être*, but **windsurfing** has recently been gaining in popularity.

Between Gullane and North Berwick is the attractive little village of **Dirleton**, dominated by the ruins of **Dirleton Castle**. The original castle dates from the 12th century and was added to over the following three centuries, until it was destroyed by Cromwell's army. The very lovely **gardens**, which date from the 16th century, are well worth a visit. ■ *T01620-850330 (HS). Apr-Sept daily 0930-1830; Oct-Mar Mon-Sat 0930-1630, Sun 1400-1630. £2.50, £1.90 concession.* At the eastern end of the village a road runs north for a mile or so to **Yellowcraigs**, where there's a lovely clean beach and views across to **Fidra island**.

Southern Scotland

**Sleeping &
eating**

In **Aberlady** is the **D-C** *Old Aberlady Inn*, T01875-870503, on the main street. A cosy wee place to stay, with good food and ales in its traditional bar. There's also a **campsite**, T01875-870666, open Mar-Oct, on the Haddington Rd.

There are several hotels and B&Bs in **Gullane** but pick of the bunch is undoubtedly the **L** *Greywalls Hotel*, T01620-810240, open Apr-Oct, a supremely charming and elegant Edwardian country house designed by Sir Edwin Lutyens. It overlooks Muirfied golf course and has an enviable reputation for superb cuisine (expensive). The best place to eat in Gullane, or anywhere else in Southeast Scotland outside Edinburgh, is *La Pontiniere*, T01620-843214, on the main street. This cosy French bistro is *sans pareil* and expensive, but its massive popularity means it's booked up well in advance. Open for lunch Tue-Sat, dinner Fri and Sat only. Disappointed gastronomes can always head for *The Old Clubhouse*, T01620-842008, a pleasant bar/bistro just off the main street. Open till 2200; mid-range prices.

In **Dirleton** is the enticingly-named **A** *Open Arms Hotel*, T01620-850241. A traditional country house hotel opposite the castle, it's a friendly and comfortable place with a highly-rated, and expensive, restaurant. Across the Green is the much cheaper **D** *Castle Inn*, T01620-850221.

North Berwick

Phone code: 01620
Colour map 6, grid A2
Population: 4,850

The dignified and slightly faded Victorian seaside resort of North Berwick is 23 miles east of Edinburgh and easily visited as a day trip from the capital. The town's chief attractions are its fine sandy **beaches** and the two excellent **golf courses**, the West Links and the Glen, but there are several other points of interest for visitors.

The **tourist office** is on Quality Street. ■ *T892197. Apr and May Mon-Sat 0900-1800; Jun and Sept Mon-Sat 0900-1800, Sun 1100-1600; Jul Mon-Sat 0900-1900, Sun 1100-1800; Aug Mon-Sat 0900-2000, Sun 1100-1800; Oct-Mar Mon-Fri 0900-1700.*

Sights

Next to the harbour are the remains of the **Auld Kirk**, the 12th-century Church of St Andrews, scene of one of the strangest events in Scottish history. In 1590, while King James VI was returning from Europe with his new wife, Anne of Denmark, Francis Stewart, Earl of Bothwell was plotting against him. The Earl summoned the witches of East Lothian to the church to meet the 'Devil' (actually Bothwell in disguise) and attempted by means of witchcraft to cause a storm in the Firth of Forth in order to drown King James and his new wife. The attempt failed and when James got wind of this satanic treachery, several witches were tried and executed. Bothwell himself was imprisoned but later escaped.

North Berwick is overlooked by **Berwick Law**, a 613ft volcanic crag, topped by the ruins of a watchtower built during the Napoleonic Wars, and an arch made from a whale's jawbone. It's an easy walk to the top and the views on a clear day are rewarding. Take Law Road out of town and then follow the signs.

Three miles east of town, off the A198, are the mid-14th-century ruins of **Tantallon Castle**, perched dramatically on the edge of the cliffs, looking out to the Bass Rock. This formidable fortress was the stronghold of the 'Red Douglases', Earls of Angus, until Cromwell's attack in 1651, which left only the massive 50ft high curtain wall intact. ■ *T892727 (HS). Apr-Sept daily 0930-1830; Oct-Mar Mon-Wed and Sat 0930-1630, Thur 0930-1200, Fri and Sun 1400-1630. £2.50, £1.90 concession. To get there, take the Dunbar bus from North Berwick (see below).*

There's a great **beach** a few miles south of Tantallon which is well worth the slight detour. Turn left off the A198 at Auldhame farm, follow the road for about a mile to the gate (small toll charge) and beyond to the car park, then walk.

Southern Scotland

Three miles offshore is the 350ft high **Bass Rock**, a massive, guano-covered lump of basalt, used as a prison in the 17th century but now home to millions of nesting gannets and other seabirds including guillemots, razorbills and fulmars. There are also puffins nesting on the nearby island of **Fidra**.

There are lots of places to stay in North Berwick but it's advisable to book ahead at weekends and in the busy season as it's very popular with golfers. **Sleeping**

A-B *The Marine Hotel*, Cromwell Rd, T892406, F894480. 83 rooms, North Berwick's premier hotel, overlooking the seafront and with an open-air pool. There are many excellent **guesthouses** and **B&Bs** to choose from, including: **D** *The Glebe House*, on Law Rd, T/F892608; **E** The Studio, T895150, on Grange Rd; **E** *Tantallon House*, T892873, open Apr-Oct; at 2 West Bay Rd and **E** *Palmerston*, T892884, at 28b St Andrew St. There's a **campsite** at *Tantallan Caravan Park*, T893348; open Mar-Oct, a few miles east of town on Dunbar Rd, overlooking the Glen golf course.

There are several very good places to eat in North Berwick. *The Grange*, 35 High St, T895894. Good contemporary Scottish cuisine in classy surroundings, mid-range-expensive prices. *Quadrant*, 7-9 Quality St, T895110. Surprising to find such a hip café-bar in this corner of East Lothian, stylish design and the food ain't bad either. Open daily till 2300. *The Joypur Restaurant*, 114 High St (T895649) serves good Indian food, and *Poonthais*, at 7 High St, is a good Thai restaurant. **Eating**

There are **boat trips** from North Berwick, weather permitting, to the Bass Rock and Fidra, daily between May and Sept with *Fred Marr*, T892838. Trips cost £4.60 per person and last about an hour and 15 minutes. You can also be dropped off on Bass Rock and picked up three hours later for £10 per person, but you'll need to be dedicated birdwatcher to put up with the stench of guano. **Tours**

The **train station** is a 10-min walk east of the town centre. There's a frequent rail service to and from **Edinburgh** (30 mins). There are also regular **buses** from Edinburgh (every 30 mins), via Aberlady and Gullane. These stop on the High St. There are hourly buses from **Haddington** and from **Dunbar** (several daily Mon-Sat, 2 on Sun), which stop outside the tourist office. **Transport**

Dunbar

Twelve miles southeast of North Berwick, just off the main A1 from Edinburgh to the south, is the little fishing port of Dunbar. The town's claim to fame is as the birthplace of **John Muir**, the explorer naturalist who founded Yellowstone National Park in the US and became known as the father of the Conservation movement. **John Muir House**, 128 High Street, is his childhood home. It has been refurbished in period detail and contains a small museum dedicated to the man's life and work. ■ *T862595. Jun-Sept Mon-Sat 1100-1300 and 1400-1700, Sun 1400-1700. Free.* Also on the High Street is the 16th-century **Town House Museum**, one of the oldest of Dunbar's houses, formerly a prison and now a small local history and archaeology museum. ■ *T863734. Apr-Oct daily 1230-1630. Free.*

Phone code: 01368
Colour map 4, grid C2
Population: 5,800

The scant remains of **Dunbar Castle** stand beside the old **harbour**. A two-mile clifftop trail leads west from the castle to **John Muir Country Park**, a vast area comprising the Tyne estuary and Belhaven Bay and covering a variety of habitats which are home to numerous bird species. As well as the excellent beachcombing possibilities, there's also fishing and horse riding in the park. For more details contact the tourist office in town, or phone, T863886. Dunbar

Southern Scotland

is also well known as the home of **Belhaven beers**, which are still brewed on the original site (signposted off the Edinburgh road). Guided tours can be arranged, T864488. There are also opportunities for some shallow, shore-based **diving**, with *Cromwell Mariner*, T863354, on Shore Street.

The **tourist office** is at 143 High Street. ■ *T863353. May Mon-Sat 0900-1800; Jun, Jul and Sept Mon-Sat 0900-1900, Sun 1100-1800; Aug Mon-Sat 0900-2000, Sun 1100-1800.*

Sleeping & eating There are several **guesthouses** and **B&Bs**. A popular choice is **E-D** *Overcliff Guest House*, 11 Bayswell Park, T864004, a short walk west of the harbour. Also good is **E** *Muirfield House*, 40 Belhaven Rd, T/F862289, open Mar-Oct. There's also the *Belhaven Bay Caravan & Camping Park* in John Muir Country Park, just off the A1087 to the west of town, T893348.

The best place to eat in town is *The Creel*, near the harbour, T863279, which serves good, moderately-priced seafood and other dishes. Open Tue-Sun.

Transport There are regular **buses** from Edinburgh. Dunbar is on the main London-Edinburgh rail line and there are regular **trains** to and from Edinburgh (40 mins) and south to England.

Haddington and around

Phone code: 01620
Colour map 6, grid A2
Population: 8,000

Handsome Haddington is the archetypal prosperous country town. It sits on the river Tyne, only 15 miles east of Edinburgh, making it ideal for a pleasant day out from the rigours of city life. The town dates from the 12th century but most of it was built during the 17th to 19th centuries, when Haddington benefited from its role as the driving force behind the Agricultural Revolution which transformed farming in East Lothian. Haddington was also the birthplace of firebrand preacher **John Knox**, founder of the Presbyterian Church in Scotland, whose famous tract entitled *The First Blast of the Trumpet Against the Monstrous Regiment of Women* did little to endear him to either Mary of Guise, regent of Scotland, Mary, Queen of England or Elizabeth I (see page 663). Also born here were Alexander II of Scotland, in 1198, and Samuel Smiles (1812-1904) author of *Self-Help*.

There's no tourist office in Haddington, but there are information boards at places of interest, and a booklet, *A Walk Around Haddington* (£1) is available from newsagents.

Sights The compact town centre is very attractive and makes for a pleasant stroll. No fewer than 129 buildings have been listed as historically interesting, including the graceful **Town House**, in tree-lined Court Street, which was built in 1748 by William Adam, father of Robert. At the east end of the High Street, Church Street leads to **St Mary's Collegiate Church**, the largest parish church in Scotland, dating from the 14th century and restored in the 1970s. It's a particularly beautiful ecclesiastical building, with lots of interesting nooks and crannies and enjoys a lovely setting on the river. There are public services, brass rubbings on Saturday, concerts on Sunday afternoons in the summer and also a tearoom. ■ *T825111. Apr-Sept Mon-Sat 1100-1600, Sun 1400-1630. Free (donations welcome).* Nearby at Haddington House are the peaceful medicinal gardens of **St Mary's Pleasance**, which are free and open during daylight hours.

Buried in the churchyard is Jane Welsh (1801-66) wife of essayist and historian Thomas Carlyle. The **Jane Welsh Carlyle House**, at 2 Lodge Street, was her home until her marriage, and part of it is open to the public. ■ *T823738. Apr-Sept Wed-Sat 1400-1700. £1.50.*

A mile south of Haddington is **Lennoxlove House**, seat of the Duke of Hamilton. The sprawling confection of styles consists of a medieval tower house with gradual extensions and additions over the centuries. Inside the house are some fine paintings and furniture, but the *pièce de resistance* is the death mask of Mary, Queen of Scots, and a silver casket in which she kept her letters, given to her by her first husband, Francis II of France. ■ *T823720. Easter-Oct Wed, Thur and some Sats and Sun 1400-1630. £3.50, £1.75 concession.*

About four miles northeast of Haddington, on the B1347 at East Fortune, is the excellent **Museum of Flight**, Scotland's National Museum of Aviation. Housed in a complex of the Second World War hangars and nissen huts is a vast and impressive collection of old aircraft – from the Tigermoth to the Vulcan bomber – and wartime memorabilia. ■ *T880308. Apr-Jun, Sept and Oct daily 1030-1700; Jul and Aug daily 1030-1800; Nov-Mar Mon-Fri 1100-1500. £3, children free.*

Six miles east of Haddington, at **East Linton**, is the very photogenic **Preston Mill**, an 18th-century water wheel and grain mill, which includes an exhibition on milling. ■ *T860426. Easter and May-Sept Mon-Sat 1100-1300 and 1400-1700, Sun 1330-1700; weekends in Oct 1330-1600. £2, £1.30 concession. First Edinburgh bus No 106 from Edinburgh to East Linton (T0131-6639233).* Just to the south of East Linton is **Traprain Law**, which offers fantastic views of the coast and hinterland of East Lothian as well as being the site of a prehistoric hillfort. Near the foot of Traprain Law are the extensive 13th-15th century ruins of **Hailes Castle**.

Five miles south of Haddington, on the B6369, is the pretty little village of **Gifford**, birthplace of the Reverend John Witherspoon (in 1723), who was a signatory to the American Declaration of Independence. Gifford makes a good base for hiking in the **Lammermuir Hills** to the south. It's possible to follow trails across the hills and meet up with the Southern Upland Way (see page 600).

Sleeping & eating

There are some top-class hotels in and around town, such as the **B** *Maitlandfield House Hotel*, 24 Sidegate, T826513, which boasts 2 very fine restaurants, and **C** *Browns Hotel*, 1 West Rd, T/F822254, an elegant Regency town house. About 9 miles south of town, at Humbie on the B6368, is **A-B** *Johnstonbourn House Hotel*, T01875-833696, a superb 17th-century country mansion.

A cheaper option is the **E-D** *Plough Tavern*, at 11 Court St, T823326, a traditional inn serving decent food, or **B&B** at **E** *Schiehallion*, 19 Church St, T825663.

There are several very good places to eat, including vegetarian-friendly *The Waterside*, T825764, by the river near Nungate Bridge, where you can enjoy excellent French bistro-style food at mid-range prices. Also good is *Poldrate's*, T826882, in a converted mill on the road to Gifford (mid-range). Perhaps the best of the bunch is *Bonar's*, on the main street in **Gifford**, T810264, an intimate little restaurant with a big reputation (expensive). Also in Gifford is the *Goblin Ha' Hotel*, T810244, which serves good food and ales in the lounge (food till 2100). A great place for a pub lunch is the *Drover's Inn* in **East Linton**, T860298, where you can sit outside on a sunny day, or stay inside on the cosy bistro. Either way, the food is excellent and worth the trip alone. The *Victoria Inn* on Court St, also does decent bar meals as well as hosting the Haddington Folk Club on Wed nights.

Transport

First Edinburgh run regular **buses** to and from Edinburgh, T0131-6639233. There are also hourly buses to **North Berwick** (Mon-Sat, less frequently on Sun; 45 mins) and hourly buses to **Gifford** (20 mins).

The Borders

The Scottish Borders covers a huge swathe of southern Scotland to the east of the M74. It's an unspoiled wilderness of green hills, rushing rivers and bleak, barren moors, and it has an austere beauty which would surprise those who think that real Scotland starts somewhere north of Perth. The Borders' proximity to England also gives it a romantic edge and makes it even more essentially Scottish. This is a region which is drenched in the blood of countless battles with the English and its many ruined castles and abbeys bear witness to Scotland's long, turbulent relationship with its belligerent southern neighbour.

It should come as no surprise then, that this southern corner of Scotland has so inspired the country's greatest poets and writers. Robert Burns and John Buchan often spoke of its rare charms, but it is Sir Walter Scott, inspired not only by the stark beauty of the countryside but also by its lore and legends, who is most closely associated with the region.

The wildest and most spectacular scenery is to be found in the southern part of the region, along the Yarrow Water, between Selkirk and Moffat, the upper reaches of the Tweed valley, south of Peebles, and in Liddesdale, southwest of Jedburgh. But it is along the central valley of the river Tweed, between Peebles in the west and Kelso in the east, where you'll find most of the historic attractions, including the fascinating Traquair House, Sir Walter Scott's mansion at Abbotsford. Together with Selkirk, and the textile-producing towns of Galashiels and Hawick, these towns form the heart of the Borders.

Ins and outs

Getting around　There's a good network of **buses** serving the region's main towns. Bus timetables are available from local tourist offices. For all bus information, call the *Borders Council Transport Division*, T01835-825200. The main operator is *First Edinburgh*, T01896-752237. There are numerous buses running between the main towns of **Galashiels**, **Melrose**, **Peebles**, **Hawick**, **Selkirk**, **Jedburgh** and **Kelso**. There are also buses connecting the Border towns with **Edinburgh** and **Berwick-upon-Tweed**. *Swan's Coaches*, T01289-306436, has regular buses from Berwick-upon-Tweed. *National Express*, T0990-808080, runs services from Newcastle to Edinburgh via **Jedburgh**, **Galashiels** and **Melrose**.

The regular bus service is supplemented during the summer months (Jul-Sept) by the *Harrier Scenic Bus Services*. Buses make round-trip tours once a week on the following routes: **Melrose-Moffat**, via Galashiels, Selkirk, Bowhill House, Yarrow, St Mary's Loch (on Thur); **Selkirk-Eyemouth** via Galashiels, Melrose, Kelso, Coldstream, Berwick-upon-Tweed (on Tue); **Hawick-Eyemouth** via Jedburgh, Town Yetholm, Berwick-upon-Tweed (on Fri). Current timetables are available at local tourist offices.

The main London-Edinburgh **railway line** follows the east coast from **Berwick-upon-Tweed** north to **Dunbar** in East Lothian. There is no rail link with the Border towns, so you'll have to get off at Berwick and take a bus from there.

There's a good **road network** which allows to explore the region easily by car. The best way to see the Borders, though, is on foot or by bike. The 90-mile **Tweed Cycleway** runs past the most important sights, while the **Southern Uplands Way** takes you through the region's most beautiful and spectacular scenery (see page 600).

There are plenty of opportunities for **walking** in the Borders, whether it's a gentle stroll or a serious hike across open country. There's a comprehensive network of paths and

The Riding of the Marches

The Border people's passion for rugby is matched only by their enthusiastic celebration of the Riding of the Marches, which takes place throughout the early summer months in each of the major towns. This ancient ritual dates back to the Middle Ages, when the young men – or 'Callants' – would ride out to check to the boundaries of common lands owned by the town.

Each town has its own variations of the Riding ceremonies, and have other activities including concerts, balls, pageants and various festivities lasting several days. Others also commemorate local historical events. For instance, the Selkirk Gathering, which is the oldest and largest of the Ridings, ends with the Casting of the Colours, which commemorates Scotland's humiliating defeat at the Battle of Flodden.

forest trails plus a programme of Ranger-led walks. For more details see the *Walking in the Scottish Borders* and *Ranger-led Walks*, both available free at tourist offices.

There are nine tourist information centres throughout the region. The ones in Jedburgh and Peebles are open all year, and the others (in Coldstream, Eyemouth, Galashiels, Hawick, Kelso, Melrose and Selkirk) are open from Apr to Oct. Details are given under each town. The Borders Tourist Board has a **website**: www. scot-borders.co.uk, or call the information line, T01835-863435. For any of their free publications call T0870-6070250, and for information on Borders festivals, such as the Melrose Rugby Sevens or the Ridings, call the Events Line, T01750-20054.

Information

Peebles

Due south of Edinburgh is the pleasant little town of Peebles, on the banks of the river Tweed, surrounded by wooded hills. The river here is wide and fast, whereas the pace of life on the town's wide High Street is altogether more sedate. Things liven up somewhat during the week-long **Beltane Fair**, the great Celtic festival of the sun which is held in June and marks the beginning of summer. Another good time to visit is during the **Peebles Arts Festival**, which is held over two weeks at the end of August and beginning of September. Peebles is only a 45-minute drive from Edinburgh and makes a convenient base for a tour of the Tweed valley.

Phone code: 01721
Colour map 6, grid B1
Population: 7,000

The town's **tourist office** is on the High Street. ■ *T720138, peebles@ scot-borders.co.uk. Apr and May Mon-Sat 1000-1700, Sun 1000-1400; Jun Mon-Sat 1000-1730, Sun 1000-1600; Jul and Aug Mon-Sat 0900-1900, Sun 1000-1800; Sept Mon-Sat 1000-1730, Sun 1300-1600; Oct Mon-Sat 1000-1630, Sun 1000-1400; Nov and Dec Mon-Sat 1000-1230 and 1330-1630.*

The **Tweeddale Museum** on the High Street is housed in the Chambers Institute, which was a gift to the town from William Chambers, a native of Peebles and founding publisher of the Chambers Encyclopaedia. It houses two notable friezes: one is a copy of the Elgin marbles taken from the Parthenon in Athens (and yet to be returned to their rightful home); the other is the 19th-century Triumph of Alexander. ■ *Apr-Oct Mon-Fri 1000-1200 and 1400-1700, Sat 1000-1200, Sun 1400-1600; Nov-Mar Mon-Fri only. Free.*

Sights

Just to the west of town, on the A72, is **Neidpath Castle**, perched high on a rocky bluff overlooking the Tweed. The medieval Tower House enjoys an impressive setting but there's little to see inside which would justify the entrance fee. ■ *Easter-Sept Mon-Sat 0930-1830, Sun 1400-1830. £2.50.* The castle can be reached by following the trail along the river Tweed from Hay

Southern Scotland

Cycling around Peebles

There are many graded cycle routes through the Glentress, Cardrona and Elibank and Traquair forests. At Walkerburn, east of Innerleithen, you can link up to the fully signposted 90-mile **Tweed Cycleway**. See the tourist board leaflet Cycling in the Scottish Borders. For bike hire try **Scottish Border Trails**, T720336, open Apr-Oct, at Glentress, a mile or so east of town on the A72. Mountain and Touring bikes cost from £12 per day during peak season. They also organize bicycle tours. Bikes can also be hired from **Crossburn Caravan Cycle Hire**, T/F720501, on the Edinburgh Road. Mountain bikes cost from £8-14 per day.

Lodge Park in town. The walk passes a beautiful picnic spot beneath the castle and you can swim in the river (but take care). The trail continues through lovely wooded countryside and you can cross the river and return at Manor Bror (a three mile round trip) or further on at Lyne footbridge (an eight mile round trip). Details of this and other local walks can be found in the *Popular Walks around Peebles* leaflet available at the tourist office.

Two other good woodland walks are in **Glentress Forest**, just over a mile east of town on the A72, and **Cardona Forest**, on the south side of the Tweed, four miles out of town on the B7062. Also on the B7062 to Traquair (see below), about two miles from town, is **Kailzie Gardens** with a walled garden, greenhouses, woodland walks, trout fishing pond and excellent courtyard tea-room. ■ *T720007. Easter-Oct daily 1100-1730. £2.*

Eight miles southwest of Peebles, a mile beyond the village of Stobo, on the B712 is **Dawyck Botanic Gardens**, an outstation of Edinburgh's Royal Botanic Gardens, which contains a fine collection of trees and shrubs and landscaped wooded paths. ■ *T760254. Daily Mar-Oct 1000-1800.*

Sleeping There's no shortage of accommodation in and around Peebles, from upmarket hotels to modest B&Bs. **A** *Cringletie House Hotel*, T730233, F730244, 2 miles north of town just off the A703 to Edinburgh. Lovely 19th-century baronial house set in 28 acres of grounds with an excellent restaurant and friendly service. **A** *Peebles Hotel Hydro*, Innerleithen Rd, T720602, hydro@scotborders.co.uk. Large resort hotel with excellent sports facilities and a whole host of activities for kids, good restaurant. Also good is **B-C** *Castle Venlaw Hotel*, on the Edinburgh Rd, T720384, enquiries@venlaw.co.uk. A lovely old baronial castle with good views over the town; and the **C-D** *Kingsmuir Hotel*, T720151, chrisburn@kingsmuir.scotborders.co.uk, which does good bar meals. Amongst the dozens of **guesthouses** and B&Bs is the lovely **E-D** *Minniebank Guest House*, at Greenside, beside the river to the west of the bridge, T722093; the excellent **E** *Rowanbrae*, on Northgate, which runs off the east end of the High St, T721630; and **E** *Grey Gables*, on Springwood Rd, T721252, which uses organic produce and can provide vegetarian breakfasts. There's **camping** at Rosetta Caravan & Camping Park, on Rosetta Rd, a 15 min walk north of the High St, T720770. Open Apr-Oct.

Eating Apart from the hotels listed above, the best place to eat is the *Horse Shoe Inn*, T730225, at Eddleston, about 5 miles north of Peebles on the A703. It serves very good, moderately-priced food throughout the day and evening. An excellent deli in town is *The Olive Tree*, at 7 High St. It sells a wide selection of continental delicacies and local produce and specializes in cheeses.

Transport There are hourly **buses** to **Edinburgh** (1 hr), **Galashiels** and **Melrose** and, less frequently, to **Selkirk** and **Biggar**, with *First Edinburgh*, T720181. Buses stop outside the post office, near the tourist office, on Eastgate.

Biggar and around

Eighteen miles west of Peebles, via the A72, A701 and A702, is the old market town of Biggar, just across the regional border, in South Lanarkshire. Biggar stands on the A702, the main route from the M74 to Edinburgh, and makes a pleasant and convenient stopping-point for those driving to the capital from the south. The town centre has had a recent makeover and there are enough places to interest to warrant a few hours here.

Phone code: 01899
Colour map 5, grid B6

The **tourist office** is at 155 High Street. ■ *T221066. Easter-Oct daily 1000-1700.*

The **Moat Park Heritage Centre** is housed in a renovated church near the foot of Kirkstyle, off the High Street. It includes displays on local history, archaeology and geology as well as some very interesting tablecloths. ■ *Easter-Oct Mon-Sat 1000-1230 and 1400-1700, Sun 1400-1700. £2.40, £1.90.* Ask here about details of **Hugh McDiarmid's Cottage**, which is three miles north of town.

Sights

There are four other museums in Biggar. Close by, on North Back Road, is **Gladstone Court Museum**, which features a Victorian street, with shops, a bank and schoolroom preserved just as they were 150 years ago. ■ *Apr-Oct Mon-Sat 1000-1230 and 1400-1700, Sun 1400-1700. £1.80, £1.30.* The Gladstone family, ancestors of the 19th-century Liberal Prime Minister, William Ewart Gladstone, are buried in the churchyard of **St Mary's Church**.

The **Greenhill Covenanters' Museum**, on Burnbrae, traces the development of the Covenanting movement. ■ *Apr-Oct daily 1400-1700. £1, 70p concession.* Nearby is the **Gasworks Museum**, the only surviving coal-fired gasworks in Scotland. ■ *Jun-Sept daily 1400-1700. £1, concession 50p.*

On Broughton Street is the **International Puppet Museum**, set up by Purves Puppets, a touring theatre company. The museum features puppets from all over the world, including some very strange ones indeed. There are also regular workshops and shows are held all year round in the Victorian theatre. ■ *T220631. Museum open Easter-Sept Mon-Sat 1000-1700, Sun 1400-1700. £4.40, £3.30 children.*

Biggar is overlooked by **Tinto Hill** (2,333ft), near the village of Symington, four miles southwest of town, at the junction of the A72 and A73. It's a fairly easy walk from the village to the summit, from where the views are fantastic. There's also a Druidic Circle and Bronze Age burial cairn. A good track starts from near the Tinto Hills farm shop on the A73. Allow about three hours. Regular Biggar-Lanark buses pass through Symington.

An excellent place to stay and eat is the **B-C** *Hartree House Hotel*, just off the A702 on the western outskirts of town, T221027. Open Mar-Dec. Also recommended is **D** *Skirling House*, at **Skirling**, about 3 miles northeast of Biggar, T860274, skirlinghouse@dial.pipex.com, open Mar-Dec, a wonderful B&B with superb home cooking. Another excellent B&B is **D-E** *Lindsaylands House*, 1 mile west of Biggar, T220033. The hotels in town serve bar meals, and there's the usual selection of cafés and takeaways along the High Street. Don't miss the wonderful ice cream at *The Chocolate Box* on the High St (open daily 0900-1700, Sun from 1300).

Sleeping & eating

There are **buses** to Edinburgh several times daily with *Stagecoach*, T01387-253496. There are also regular daily buses to **Lanark**, T01555-870344. A *Postbus* service, T01463-256200, runs to **Tweedsmuir**, **Abington** and **Wanlockhead** (see page 631).

Transport

Five miles east of Biggar, at the junction of the B7016 and A701, is the village of **Broughton**, childhood home of novelist, John Buchan, who wrote the classic

Around Biggar

Southern Scotland

best-seller *The Thirty Nine Steps*. Just to the south of the village is the **John Buchan Centre**, a small museum dedicated to the life and work of the man who went on to become Governor General of Canada. ■ *T01899-221050. Easter and May to mid-Oct daily 1400-1700. £1.50.*

About 10 miles south of Broughton, on the A701 to Moffat, is the historic **D** *Crook Inn*, just to the north of tiny **Tweedsmuir**, T01899-880272. The old country inn has strong literary associations. **Robert Burns** wrote his poem 'Willie Wastle's Wife' in what is now the bar, and Sir Walter Scott used to pay the occasional visit. From the inn you can climb *Broad Law* (2,756ft), the second highest hill in southern Scotland. A steep and winding single-track road climbs east from Tweedsmuir, past the Talla Reservoir, to meet the A708 from Moffat to Selkirk by the shores of **St Mary's Loch** (see 'Around Moffat', page 616).

The Tweed Valley: Peebles to Galashiels

Innerleithen
Phone code: 01896
Colour map 6, grid B1

Seven miles east of Peebles is the village of Innerleithen, home of **Robert Smail's Printing Works**, on the main street, where you can see how printing was done at the beginning of the 20th century. You can watch the printer at work on the original machinery and even try your hand at typesetting. ■ *T830206 (NTS). Easter and 1 May-30 Sept, Mon-Sat 1000-1300 and 1400-1700, Sun 1400-1700; weekends only in Oct, Sat 1000-1300 and 1400-1700, Sun 1400-1700. £2.40, £1.60.*

Sleeping and eating There are some excellent places to stay and eat in Innerleithen, including the superb guesthouse **C** *The Ley*, a few miles north, beyond the golf course, on the B709, T/F830240. Open mid-Feb to Dec. There's also the **D** *Traquair Arms Hotel & Restaurant*, on the Traquair Road, T830229, traquair. arms@scotborders.co.uk. A local favourite for its fine food and real ales. **E-D** *Caddon View Guest House*, 14 Pirn Road, T830208. There's a **campsite** at *Tweedside Caravan Park* on Montgomery Street, T831271, open Apr-Oct. Note that accommodation is usually fully booked during the Traquair Fair in August (see below). For great ice cream, head for *Caldwell's* on the High Street.

Transport *First Edinburgh*, T01721-720181, bus No 62 runs regularly to Innerleithen and Peebles from **Edinburgh**.

Traquair House

The big attraction in these parts is the amazing Traquair House, one of Scotland's great country houses. It lies about a mile south of Innerleithen, on the south side of the Tweed. Traquair is the oldest continually inhabited house in the country and is still owned by the Maxwell Stuarts, who have been living here since 1491. Its history goes much further back, however, and parts of the house are believed to date from the 12th century. The original Tower House was added to over the next five centuries and most of what you see today dates from the mid-17th century. It has been visited by no fewer than 27 monarchs, including Mary, Queen of Scots, who stayed here with her husband Darnley, in 1566. The place is steeped in Jacobite history but the family paid for its Catholic principles. The fifth earl served two years in the Tower of London for his support of Bonnie Prince Charlie in 1745. The fourth earl was also imprisoned in the tower, and sentenced to death, for his part in the Jacobite rising of 1715, but managed to escape with the help of his wife who smuggled him out disguised as a maid. By the turn of the 18th century the family had lost most of its estates and had neither the money nor the motivation to undertake any major rebuilding.

As a result, visiting Traquair is genuinely like stepping back in time and there's a uniquely nostalgic and spooky atmosphere missing from so many other historic houses. One of the most interesting rooms is the **priest's room**, where a succession of resident priests lived in hiding until the Catholic Emancipation Act of 1829 allowed them to give mass. Amongst the many fascinating relics is the cradle used by Mary, Queen of Scots for her son, James VI, and some letters written by the Stuart pretenders.

Also worth seeing are the **gardens**, where you'll find a maze, craft shops, a cottage tearoom and an 18th-century working **brewery** producing *Bear Ale*, which can be purchased in the tearoom and gift shop. A **craft and music fair** is held in the grounds of the house every August.

■ *T830323. Apr, May and Sept daily 1230-1730; Jun-Aug daily 1030-1730; Oct Fri-Sun only 1400-1700. £4.50 (£2.25). Bus No C1 runs once a day to Traquair from Peebles.*

Galashiels

At the junction of the A72 and A7 Edinburgh-Carlisle road, is the gritty, workmanlike textile town of Galashiels, strung out along the banks of the Gala River for more than two miles. Galashiels is one the largest towns in the Borders region and a transport hub, but there's precious little to detain passing tourists.

Phone code: 01896
Colour map 6, grid B2
Population: 13,700

Galashiels has played a vital role in the Borders economy for over 700 years as a major weaving town, producing tartans, tweeds and woollens, and is the home of the Scottish College of Textiles, though the industry has gone into decline in recent times. The only real attraction is **Lochcarron of Scotland** in Huddersfield Street, a working mill with a visitor centre, textiles museum and reasonable mill shop. ■ *Open daily for guided tours all year round, phone for times, T752091.*

Galashiels **tourist office** is at 3 St John's Street, T755551. ■ *Apr-Jun and Sept Mon-Sat 1000-1700, Sun 1400-1600; Jul and Aug Mon-Sat 1000-1800, Sun 1300-1700; Oct Mon-Sat 1000-1230 and 1330-1630.*

There are frequent **buses** to and from **Edinburgh** (hourly; 1 hr 25 mins); **Peebles**, **Melrose, Hawick** (hourly; 40 mins), **Selkirk** (every 30 mins; 15 mins) **Kelso, Berwick-upon-Tweed** (hourly; 1 hr 45 mins), **Langholm** (1 hr 15 mins) and **Carlisle** (2 hrs). The main operator is *First Edinburgh*, T758484.

Melrose

Nestled at the foot of the mystical Eildon Hills, by the banks of the Tweed, is little Melrose, the loveliest of all the Border towns. It's an engaging mix of cute little shops and cottages and dignified Georgian and Victorian houses and boasts one of the most famous ruins in Scotland (see below). The normally soporific atmosphere is shattered every April during the week-long **Melrose Sevens**, when the town is taken over by rugby fans from all over the world for the acclaimed seven-a-side rugby tournament which has been going since 1883.

Phone code: 01896
Colour map 6, grid B2
Population: 2,300

The **tourist office** is next to the abbey ruins in Abbey Street. ■ *T822555. Mar-May Mon-Sat 1000-1700, Sun 1000-1300; Jun Mon-Sat 1000-1800, Sun 1000-1400; Jul and Aug Mon-Sat 0930-1830, Sun 1000-1800; Sept Mon-Sat 1000-1800, Sun 1000-1400; Oct Mon-Sat 1000-1700, Sun 1000-1300.*

The bitter wars that ravaged the Scottish borders for centuries did irrevocable damage to Melrose Abbey but even in ruins it remains toweringly beautiful and impressive. It was founded in 1136 by the prolific David I, who helped to found all four of the great Border Abbeys, and was the first Cistercian monastery in Scotland. It was attacked in 1322 by Edward II but soon restored,

Sights

Southern Scotland

thanks to the financial assistance of Robert the Bruce. In 1385 it was largely destroyed by Richard II of England, then completely rebuilt, only to be ravaged again, this time by Henry VIII, in the mid-16th century. The abbey as it stands today dates from the 14th and 15th centuries and was preserved by the money of the Duke of Buccleuch and the energy and talent of Sir Walter Scott. His great narrative poem *The Lay of the Last Minstrel* painted an eloquent picture of the abbey and helped him on the road to fame.

The red sandstone ruins show an elaborate Gothic style and some of the finest figure sculpture in Scotland. Of particular note are the humorous gargoyles, which include a pig playing the bagpipes on the roof of the south side of the nave. The abbey's real claim to fame is that the **heart of Robert the Bruce** was buried here, at his request, after it had been taken to the Holy Land to help in the Crusades. The lead casket containing the heart was finally excavated in 1996 and now takes pride of place in the abbey museum, in the **Commendator's House**, next to the church. ■ *T822562 (HS). Apr-Sept daily 0930-1830; Oct-Mar Mon-Sat 0930-1630, Sun 1400-1630. £3, £2.30 concession.*

Next to the abbey is **Priorwood Garden**, where plants are grown specifically for dried flower arrangements. There's also a dried flower shop on site. ■ *T822493 (NTS). Apr-Sept Mon-Sat 1000-1730, Sun 1330-1730; Oct-Dec Mon-Sat 1000-1600, Sun 1330-1600. £1 (honesty box).*

On Market Square is the **Trimontium Exhibition**, a small but interesting centre which tells the story of the Roman occupation of the area and includes some archaeological finds. ■ *T822651. Apr-Oct daily 1030-1630. £1.40.* The more adventurous can follow the **Trimontium Walk**, a four-mile guided tour of Roman sites in the area, including the site of the Trimontium (Three Hills) fort at Newstead. ■ *T822651. Mar-Oct Thur 1330-1645. £2.50.*

The most unusual attraction is the **Teddy Bear Museum**, or Teddy Melrose, where you can relive your childhood, or keep the kids entertained, with a display of teddies through the ages, including Rupert, Pooh and other celebrity bears. You can also see them being made and even commission your own tailor-made teddy. There's a gift shop and courtyard tearoom. ■ *T822464. Daily 1000-1700. £1.50.*

Walks around Melrose The three peaks of the **Eildon Hills** can be seen from all parts of the Central Borders region and can be climbed quite easily from Melrose. Starting from Market Square, head along the B6359 to Lilliesleaf, and after 100yd the path is signed to the left and leads to the saddle between the North and Mid hills (Mid Hill is the highest, at 1,385ft). The path leads to the summit of North Hill, then Mid Hill, and finally West Hill, to the south. There are several routes back to town, but heading via the golf course makes a nice circular walk of two miles. Allow about 1½ hours. The route is detailed in the *Eildon Hills Walk* leaflet available from the tourist office.

Melrose is the starting point for the **St Cuthbert's Way**, a 60-mile walk which finishes at **Lindisfarne** (the Holy Isle). The much longer **Southern Upland Way** also passes through the town (for more details see page 600).

Sleeping There's not a huge amount of accommodation in Melrose, considering its appeal, so it's best to book in advance during the summer and especially during the Melrose Sevens in mid-Apr. There are several hotels in Melrose, best of which is **C** *Burts Hotel*, on Market Square, T822285, burtshotel@aol.com. This refurbished traditional 18th-century inn is very comfortable and renowned locally for its excellent modern Scottish cuisine (lunch mid-range; dinner expensive). Also on the square is the small, comfortable **C-D** *Bon Accord Hotel*, T822645. Pick of the **B&Bs** and **guesthouses** is the excellent **E-D** *Dunfermline Guest House*, on Buccleuch St, T822148. Best of the

The Legends of the Eildons

The three-peaked Eildon Hills were considered a sacred place by the ancient Celts and have long been shrouded in mystery and associated with a number of legends. For a start, they are believed to have been created by the wizard/alchemist Michael Scott, and it was here that the mystic Thomas the Rhymer was given the gift of prophecy by the Faerie Queen. Most startling of all, though, is the claim that King Arthur and his knights lie asleep beneath the hills, victims of a terrible spell.

rest are **E** *Braidwood*, also on Buccleuch St, T822488; **E** *Little Fordel*, T822206, on Abbey St; and **E** *Collingwood*, on Waverley Rd, T822670, open Apr-Oct, on the outskirts of town. No smoking.

There's a very good and very popular **youth hostel**, in a large mansion on the edge of town, overlooking the abbey from beside the A6091 bypass, T822521, open all year. There's also a **campsite** at *Gibson Park*, T822969, at end of the High St, opposite the Greenyards rugby ground.

Finding a good place to eat isn't too difficult. Best of all is *Burt's Hotel* (see above), where you can dine in style in the dining room or opt for their excellent pub grub. Another hotel recommended for food is the moderately-priced *King's Arms*, on the High St, T822143. On the other side of the river, in the village of Gattonside, is the *Hoebridge Inn Restaurant*, T823082, which offers good quality Scottish fare at mid-range prices and is well worth the walk. Two very good French-style bistros are the *Melrose Station Restaurant*, T822456, in the old train station near the square (open Wed-Sat); and *Marmions*, T822245, on Buccleuch St near the abbey (closed Sun). Both have mid-range prices. **Eating**

Behind the teddy bear museum is a tiny **theatre**, which stages regular drama productions and musical events, T823854. Check at the tourist office for the current programme. **Entertainment**

There are regular buses to Galashiels (hourly; 15 mins), **Kelso** (several daily; 35 mins), **Jedburgh** (hourly; 30 mins), **Peebles** (several daily; 1 hr 10 mins), **Duns** (several daily; 45 mins) and **Selkirk** (hourly Mon-Sat, less frequently on Sun; 40 mins). To get to **Hawick**, it's easier to catch a bus to Galashiels and then change (see page 677). Buses to Melrose stop in Market Square, close to the abbey and tourist office. **Transport**

Around Melrose

Melrose makes a great base for exploring the beautiful landscapes of the middle stretch of the Tweed, which so inspired Sir Walter Scott, the famous son of the Borders. Two of the area's main sights, **Dryburgh Abbey** and **Abbotsford House**, are inextricably linked with the writer's life and work. The places listed below can all be reached by public transport, but you'll need your own transport if you want to get off the beaten track. Those who wish to explore the area by bike can **hire cycles** in Galashiels, at *Gala Cycles*, T757587, at 58 High Street.

One of the Borders' top tourist attractions is Abbotsford House, home of Sir Walter Scott from 1811 to 1832 and a Mecca for the great novelist's many admirers. For an account of his life, see page 677. **Abbotsford House**

Scott spent a small fortune transforming the original farmhouse into a huge country mansion befitting a man of his status, and though Abbotsford may not be to everyone's taste, the house is an intriguing mix of styles and enjoys a beautiful setting. The house is still lived in by Scott's descendants and the

Southern Scotland

library and study have been preserved much as they were when he lived here, including the collection of over 9,000 antiquarian books. There's also an amazing assortment of Scottish memorabilia, including Rob Roy's purse, Bonnie Prince Charlie's drinking cup and Flora MacDonald's pocketbook.

The house is well worth visiting and sits in pleasant grounds, about three miles west of Melrose, between the Tweed and the B6360. Take the Melrose-Galashiels bus and get off at the Tweedbank traffic island. From there it's a 15-minute walk. ■ *T750043. Mid-Mar to May and Oct Mon-Sat 1000-1700, Sun 1400-1700; Jun-Sept daily 1000-1700. £3.50, £1.80 concession.*

Dryburgh Abbey

Five miles southeast of Melrose on the B6404, near the village of St Boswells, is Dryburgh Abbey. Its setting amongst ancient cedars on the banks of the Tweed, also make it the most beautifully idyllic, romantic and evocative of the Border abbeys. It dates from around 1150, when it was founded by Hugh de Morville for Premonstratensian monks from Alnwick in Northumberland.

The 12th-and 13th-century ruin is remarkably well-preserved and complete, and was chosen as the burial place for Sir Walter Scott. His final resting place is in the north transept of the church. Close by lies Field Marshal Earl Haig, the disastrous First World War commander. ■ *T01835-822381. Apr-Sept 0930-1830; Oct-Mar Mon-Sat 0930-1630, Sun 1400-1630. £2.50, concession £1.90.*

If you're travelling by public transport from Melrose, take the **Jedburgh** bus as far as St Boswells (10 minutes), then walk north from the village for about a mile. If you're driving, make sure you pass **Scott's View**, on the B6356, which offers a sweeping view of the Eildon Hills and Tweed valley. Scott came here many times to enjoy the view (hence its name) and to seek inspiration. There's an even better view from the hill on the other side of the road. In the abbey grounds is the peaceful, secluded **B-C** *Dryburgh Abbey Hotel* (01835-822261).

Thirlestane Castle

North of Melrose, on the main A68, is the stolid market town of **Lauder**, which merits inclusion because of Thirlestane Castle, one of Scotland's oldest and finest castles, which stands on the eastern edge of town. The castellated baronial house is the seat of the Earls of Lauderdale and has been owned by the Maitland family since the 16th century. Inside the 17th-century plaster ceilings are particularly notable. ■ *T01578-722430. May, Jun and Sept Mon, Wed, Thur and Sun 1400-1700; Jul and Aug Mon-Fri and Sun 1400-1700. £4.50.*

Selkirk

Phone code: 01750
Colour map 6, grid B2
Population: 6,000

About six miles southwest of Melrose, on the A7 to Hawick, is the little town of Selkirk, standing on the edge of the Ettrick Forest which rises steeply from the Ettrick Water. Selkirk has been a textile centre since the early 19th century when the growing demand for tweed could no longer be met by the mills of Galashiels. Those mills are closed now and Selkirk is a quiet, unassuming place that only comes to life during the **Selkirk Gathering** in June, the largest of the Border Ridings (see page 607). Selkirk is handily placed for visiting the other Border towns and sights and makes a good base for touring the area.

The **tourist office** is next to Halliwell's House (see below) on Market Square. ■ *T20054. Apr-Oct Mon-Sat 1000-1700, Sun 1400-1700; Jul and Aug Mon-Sat 1000-1800, Sun 1400-1700.*

Sights

Halliwell's House Museum and Robson Gallery, features an 18th-century ironmongers and tells the story of the town and its industry. The gallery has a changing programme of temporary exhibitions. ■ *T20096. Same opening*

Thirlestane Castle

hours as the tourist office. Free. Also on Market Square is **Walter Scott's Courtroom**, where Sir Walter Scott served as Sheriff of Selkirk from 1799 to 1832. It houses an exhibition on his life and writings. ■ *Apr-Oct Mon-Sat 1000-1600, Sun 1400-1600. Free.* Outside the courtroom is a statue of the great novelist, and at the other end of the High Street is a statue of **Mungo Park** (1771-1805) the famous explorer and anti-slavery campaigner who was born in Selkirkshire. At the northern end of town, on the A7 to Galashiels, is **Selkirk Glass**, a thriving local industry, where you can see glass-blowing displays. ■ *T20954. Mon-Fri 0900-1630. Free.*

A-B *Philipburn Country House Hotel*, Linglie Rd, T720747, 100414.1237@ **Sleeping** compuserve.com. Upmarket accommodation and good food. There are also cheaper hotels in town, such as the dependable, family-run **D** *Glen Hotel*, Yarrow Terr, T/F20259, and the **D-E** *Heatherlie House Hotel*, at Heatherlie Park, T21200. There are some good value B&Bs, including **E** *Hillholm*, 36 Hillside Terr, T21293, and **E** *Sunnybrae House*, 75 Tower St, T21156. The cheapest place around is the *SYHA Broadmeadows Youth Hostel* is at Yarrowford, T76262; open mid-Mar to early Oct), 5 miles west of Selkirk on the A708, beyond Bowhill (see below). There's a **campsite** at *Victoria Park Caravan & Camping Site*, T20897, beside the river next to the indoor swimming pool.

Possibilities for eating are limited. The County Hotel, T21233, on the High St serves **Eating** decent bar meals, and the *Court House Coffee Shop* on Market Square does snacks and high teas. Or you can try the local speciality, Bannock bread, from the nearby *Selkirk Bannock Shop*.

The A7 runs south to Hawick and north to Galashiels and Melrose, while the A699 **Transport** heads east to Kelso, via St Boswells. The A708 runs southwest towards Moffat (see below) and the A707 takes you northwest to meet the A72 to Innerleithen and Peebles. *First Edinburgh* bus No 95 runs frequently to and from **Edinburgh** and **Hawick**, via Selkirk and Galashiels. There are also regular daily buses to **Langholm** and **Carlisle**. There's a bus to **Moffat**, on Sat only, leaving at 1150, arriving at 1315, with *McCall's Coaches*. All buses leave from Market Square.

Around Selkirk

Three miles west of Selkirk, where the B7009 turns south off the A708, is the **Bowhill House &** entrance to Bowhill House and Country Park, home of the Scotts of Buccleuch **Country Park** and Queensberry since 1812. They were once the largest landowners in the Borders and fabulously wealthy, a fact made evident by the fantastic collection of French antiques and European paintings on display. There are works by

Southern Scotland

Canaletto, Guardi, Reynolds, Gainsborough and Leandro Bassano. The wooded hills of the Country Park can be explored via a network of footpaths and cycle trails. Bikes can be rented from the visitor centre. There's no public transport to Bowhill. You can take the Selkirk-Moffat bus on Saturday and get off at the turning, then walk. There's the weekly *Harrier Scenic Bus Service* to Bowhill from Selkirk and Melrose in the morning, returning in the afternoon. It runs from July to September (see page 606). ■ *House open daily in Jul, 1300-1630. £4.50. Country Park Apr-Jun and Aug daily except Fri 1200-1700; Jul daily 1200-1700. £1.20.*

Yarrow Water &
Ettrick Water
The A707 heads southwest from Selkirk to Moffat, following the beautiful **Yarrow Water** to **St Mary's Loch**, where the road is crossed by the **Southern Upland Way**. A few miles west of Selkirk is the turning south onto the B7009 which follows the course of the Ettrick Water to meet the B709, which continues south, past the village of **Ettrick**, to **Eskdalemuir** and on to **Langholm** (see page 629).

OS Landranger Nos
73 and 79

This is one of the most remote and beautiful parts of Scotland and an area inextricably linked with **James Hogg** (1770-1835), 'The Ettrick Shepherd', who was a great friend of Sir Walter Scott. Hogg was a notable writer himself and his most famous work, *The Confessions of a Justified Sinner*, is important in Scottish literature. Hogg was born in Ettrick and spent his entire life in the Ettrick and Yarrow valleys. He and Scott would often meet in **E-D** *Tibbie Shiels Inn*, T01750-42231, on the narrow strip of land separating **St Mary's Loch** from the ethereal **Loch of the Lowes**. It's still a famous watering hole and popular stop along the Southern Upland Way. It also serves bar meals. From *Tibbie Shiels Inn* you can follow the Southern Upland Way south to Ettrick Water, where an unclassified road leads east to the village of Ettrick, or continue southwest all the way down to Moffat (see page 630). Alternatively, head north along the eastern shore of St Mary's Loch, to the A708, then continue north to Traquair House (see page 610), then east towards Yair Hill Forest, where you can turn south to the *Broadmeadows Youth Hostel* (see above). These are strenuous hikes and you should be fit and well equipped (see 'Essentials' section, page 53).

At Cappercleuch, on the west shore of St Mary's Loch, a spectacular single-track road twists and turns its way up to the Megget Reservoir and then down past the Talla Reservoir to the tiny village of **Tweedsmuir**, on the A701 (see page 609). East of St Mary's Loch, the A708 is crossed by the B709 which runs north to Innerleithen and south and then east to Hawick. At the road junction is the **E** *Gordon Arms Hotel* (T01750-82232), said to be the last meeting place of Scott and Hogg. It's a popular stopping point for walkers and offers bar food and local ales.

Jedburgh

Phone code: 01835
Colour map 6, grid B2
Population: 4,000

Ten miles from the English border is the attractive little town of Jedburgh, straddling the Jed Water at the edge of the northern slopes of the wild, barren Cheviot Hills. Jeburgh was strategically the most important of the Border towns, due to its proximity to England, and as a result received the full brunt of invading English armies. These days the only invaders are tourists. Jedburgh is the most visited of the Border towns and there are a number of interesting sights. The town's **tourist office** is on Murray's Green. It's a large and well-stocked office with leaflets detailing local walks. ■ *T863435, info@scot-borders.co.uk. Apr, May and Oct Mon-Sat 1000-1700, Sun 1200-1600; Jun and Sept Mon-Sat 0930-1800, Sun 1200-1600; Jul and Aug Mon-Fri 0900-2030, Sat 0900-1900, Sun 1000-1900; Nov-Mar Mon-Fri 1000-1630.*

The town is dominated by **Jedburgh Abbey**, founded in 1138 by David I for **Sights**
Augustinian canons from northern France. The site had much older religious
significance, however, and stonework in the abbey's museum dates from the
first millennium AD. Malcolm IV was crowned here and Alexander III married his second wife in the abbey in 1285. Their wedding feast was held at
nearby Jedburgh Castle (see below), and like the castle, the abbey came under
attack during the many English invasions, most devastatingly in 1523 when it
was bombarded and burned. Despite this, the abbey church is remarkably
complete, particularly the tower. Excavations have recently uncovered the
remains of the cloister buildings and among the finds is the priceless
12th-century 'Jedburgh comb', which is on display in the excellent **visitor
centre** which brilliantly tells the story abbey's long and fascinating history.
■ *T863925. Apr-Sept daily 0930-1830; Oct-Mar Mon-Sat 0930-1630, Sun
1400-1630. £3, £2.30 concession, £1 child.*

Nearby, at the top of the Castlegate, is **Jedburgh Castle Jail and Museum**,
which was formerly the county jail. It was built in 1823 on the site of the
12th-century castle, which changed hands many times, until it was destroyed
by the Scots because of its value to the English. The displays in the cell blocks
depict prison life in the 19th century and there's an exhibition on the town's
history. ■ *T863254. Mar-Nov daily 1000-1600. £1.25, £1 concession.*

At the other end of the town centre is **Mary, Queen of Scots House**, a beautiful 16th-century building of rough-hewn stone which contains a small bedroom occupied by Mary during her stay at Jedburgh in 1566. She spent several
weeks here recovering from illness after her famous 30-mile ride to Hermitage
Castle (see page 619) to visit her injured lover, the Earl of Bothwell. The ensuing scandal was only exacerbated by the murder of her husband Darnley the
following year, at Holyrood Palace in Edinburgh. Many years later, during her
long incarceration, Mary regretted the fact that she hadn't died while staying in
Jedburgh. This episode in Scottish history is told through a series of displays
and there are various artefacts associated with Mary. ■ *T863331. Apr-Nov
Mon-Sat 1000-1645, Sun till 1630. £2, £1 concession.*

There are a few hotels in town, but the most luxurious place to stay is the **Sleeping**
B *Jedforest Hotel*, in the village of Camptown, 6 miles south of Jedburgh, on the
A68, and only 5 miles from the border, T840222. The self-proclaimed 'First Hotel in
Scotland' is very comfortable, with a fine restaurant. Also recommended is the
D *Glenfriars Hotel*, The Friars, T862000. A lovely Georgian house near the north end
of the High St. There are several **B&Bs** in and around town, but few can match the
sheer style and value-for-money of **E-D** *Hunalee House*, T/F863011, sheila.
whittaker@btinternet.com. Open Mar-Oct). This early 17th-century house is a mile
south of town on the A68, set in 10 acres of gardens and woodlands. Also out of town
and great value is **E-D** *Ancrum Craig*, T/F830280, ancrumcraig@clara.net. Open
Jan-Oct, a quiet 19-century country house 2 miles from the A68 near the village of
Ancrum. In town is the **E** *Kenmore Guest House* on Oxnam Rd, T862369, overlooking the Jed Water, and the more characterful **E** *Meadhon House*, 48 Castlegate,
T/F862504.

There are a few **campsites** close to Jedburgh. 4 miles south of town on the A68 is
the *Jedwater Caravan Park*, T840219, open Apr-Oct. 5 miles to the north of Jedburgh
is *Lilliardsedge Park*, T830271, open Easter-Sept; while the *Elliot Park Camping &
Caravanning Club*, T86339, open Mar-early Nov, is a mile north of town.

There's not a great deal of choice for eating in Jedburgh. Best of all is *Simply Scottish*, **Eating**
T864696, on the High St, which offers modern, bistro-style Scottish fare all day at
cheap-mid-range prices. There's also the *Castlegate Restaurant*, T862552, on the

corner of the High St and Abbey Close, which serves traditional meals and snacks. On the High St is the *Wayfarer*, T863503, which does a moderately-priced 3-course evening meal. Eleven miles south of Jedburgh, is the *Carter Bar*, the first/last pub in Scotland, standing on the border with England, in the Cheviot Hills.

Sport & festivals Jedburgh's Common Riding, the **Callant's Festival**, takes place in late Jun/early Jul (see also 'Borders Festivals', on page 607). In early Feb is the **Jedburgh Hand Ba'** game, a bruising and exhausting contest between the 'uppies' (those born above the Market Place) and the 'downies' (those born below), who endeavour to get a leather ball from one end of the town to the other. Visitors from south of the border may wish to note that the game used to be played with the heads of vanquished Englishmen. **Horse riding** is available for experienced riders at *Ferniehurst Mill Lodge*, T863279, 2 miles south of Jedburgh on the A68. They offer accommodation and tailor-made riding holidays.

Transport The bus station is close to the abbey and there are good connections around the Borders. *First Edinburgh*, T01896-752237, runs frequent daily **buses** to **Hawick**, **Kelso** and **Galashiels**. There is also a bus to and from **Berwick-upon-Tweed** and 3 buses daily to and from **Edinburgh**.

Hawick

Phone code: 01450
Colour map 6, grid B2
Population: 15,700

Fourteen miles southwest of Jedburgh and 12 miles south of Selkirk is Hawick (pronounced 'Hoyk'), the largest town in the Borders and centre of the region's knitwear and hosiery industry for over 200 years. Hawick is not a place noted for its great beauty but it does attract lots of visitors who come to shop at its many factory outlets where you can buy all the classic brand names in knitwear.

A list of knitwear suppliers is available at the **tourist office**, in **Drumlanrig Tower** on the High Street. ■ *T372547. Easter-May and Oct Mon-Sat 1000-1700; Jun and Sept Mon-Sat 1000-1730, Sun 1200-1730; Jul and Aug Mon-Sat 1000-1800, Sun 1200-1800.* In the same building is a **museum**, which outlines the tower's role in Anglo-Scottish wars from the 16th century. ■ *Same opening hours as the tourist office. £2.50.*

In Wilton Lodge Park is the **Hawick Museum and Scott Art Gallery**, which has an interesting collection of mostly 19th-century textile exhibits. ■ *Apr-Sept Mon-Fri 1000-1200 and 1300-1700, Sat and Sun 1400-1600. £1.25.*

Sleeping & eating A mile from town, on the A698 to Kelso, is the **C** *Mansfield House Hotel*, T373988, ian@mansfield-house.com. A traditional mansion house hotel offering good food (lunch cheap; dinner mid-range). Also good is **C** *Kirklands Hotel*, West Stewart Pl, T372263. There are plenty of cheaper B&B alternatives, including **E** *Oakwood House*, Buccleuch Rd, T372814. Eating options are pretty much confined to the hotel bars and restaurants.

Transport There are hourly **buses** to and from **Jedburgh** (35 mins) and **Galashiels** (40 mins) and regular daily buses to and from **Selkirk** (20 mins), **Edinburgh** (2 hrs) and **Carlisle** (1 hr 15 mins). There's also a direct service to **Melrose** (40 mins) but it may be quicker to go to Galashiels and change there.

South of Hawick

The A7 runs southwest from Hawick through the dramatic scenery of **Teviotdale** to the tiny village of **Teviothead**, where it then exchanges the valley of the river Teviot for the **Ewes Water**. The Ewes then meets the river Esk at **Langholm**, in Dumfries and Galloway. The A7 continues its route south, to meet the A74(M) just north of **Carlisle**.

A much more beautiful route south is to take the A698 northeast out of Hawick, then turn off onto the A6088 which heads southeast. Just beyond the tiny village of **Bonchester Bridge**, take the B6357 which leads you into lovely **Liddesdale**. The B6357 follows the course of the Liddel Water all the way south to the village of **Canonbie** (see page 629), where it meets the A7.

A few miles north of **Newcastleton**, the B6357 meets the B6399 which runs north back to Hawick. Four miles north of the junction is the turning to **Hermitage Castle**, one of the great Border strongholds. The oldest part of the castle dates from the 13th century and it was in the hands of the Earls of Douglas, until 1492, when it passed to the Earls of Bothwell. The fourth Earl of Bothwell, James Hepburn, was the third husband of Mary, Queen of Scots, following the murder of her second husband, Darnley, and is thought to have been behind the plot to murder him. It was to Hermitage that Mary made her famous ride to visit her future husband who had been injured in a border raid. Mary's marriage to Bothwell in 1566 was ill-advised and only succeeded in uniting their enemies and led ultimately to her imprisonment in Lochleven Castle. Bothwell meanwhile fled to Norway, where he was captured and later died a prisoner himself, in 1578. Hermitage became largely irrelevant following the Union of Crowns in 1603 and fell into disrepair. Much of what you see today dates from the 19th century when the Duke of Buccluech ordered its repair. The vast and eerie ruin is said to be haunted, which is not surprising given its grisly past. One owner, William Douglas, starved his prisoners to death in the ghoulish dungeons, which can still be seen. ■ *T01387-376222 (HS). Apr-Sept daily 0930-1830. £1.80, £1.30 concession. There is no public transport service from Hawick.*

There are a couple of places to stay in the village of **Newcastleton**, 5½ miles south of Hermitage. The **E** *Liddlesdale Hotel*, T/F01387-375255, also serves local specialities such as pheasant and salmon, and there's also the very pleasant **E-D** *Borders Honey Farm*, T/F01387-376737, 4 miles north Newcastleton, on the B6357. | **Sleeping**

Kelso

The little market town of Kelso, at the confluence of the Tweed and Teviot rivers, is one of the most picturesque of the Border towns, with its cobbled streets leading into a wide market square bounded by elegant, three-story 18th and 19th-century town houses.

Kelso's **tourist office** is in the Town House, on The Square. ■ *T223464. Apr-Jun and Sept Mon-Sat 1000-1700, Sun 1000-1300; Jul and Aug Mon-Sat 0930-1830, Sun 1000-1800; Oct Mon-Sat 1000-1630, Sun 1000-1300.* The main **festivals** are the **Border Union Agricultural Show** and the town's **Riding of the Marches**, both of which take place in July. Kelso also hosts its own Rugby Sevens in early September.

Phone code: 01573
Colour map 6, grid B3
Population: 6,000

Kelso Abbey was once the largest and richest of the Border abbeys but suffered the same fate as its counterparts; Jedburgh, Dryburgh and Melrose. Kelso was a strategic point in the Border wars between the Scots and the English and the abbey, founded in 1138 by King David, was laid to waste by successive English invasions, most devastatingly in 1545 by the Earl of Hertford. This latter attack was part of the Henry VIII's so-called 'Rough Wooing', when the king took exception to the Scots' refusal to ratify a marriage treaty between his son and the infant Mary Stuart. Today, little remains of the abbey, and it is the least complete of those in the Borders. The nearby octagonal **Old Parish Church**, built in 1773, is unusual. ■ *Apr-Sept Mon-Sat 0930-1800, Sun 1400-1800;* | **Sights**

Southern Scotland

Oct-Mar Mon-Fri 0930-1600, Sun 1400-1600. Free.

Aside from the abbey, the town's only other major attraction is the pleasant **Cobby Riverside Walk**, which leads along the banks of the Tweed to Floors Castle (see below). Leave The Square by Roxburgh Street, and follow the signposted alley to the start of the walk. The route passes the junction of the Tweed and Teviot rivers, a spot famous for its salmon fishing.

Floors Castle, the vast ancestral home of the Duke of Roxburghe, stands imperiously overlooking the Tweed, about a mile northwest of the town centre. The original Georgian mansion was designed by Robert Adam and built in 1721-26, though it was later remodelled by William Playfair in the 1840s, with the addition of many flamboyant features. Only 10 rooms are open to the public but they are undeniably elegant and palatial, and amongst the many priceless family items on display are outstanding collections of European furniture, porcelain and paintings by Picasso, Matisse and Augustus John, and a 15th-century Brussels tapestry. Floors is the largest inhabited castle in Scotland and the current occupier, the 10th Duke of Roxburghe, is a close personal friend of the royal family. ■ *T223333. Easter to late Oct daily 1000-1630; Oct Sun-Wed 1000-1630. £4.50.*

Sleeping   The most luxurious place to stay hereabouts is **L** *The Roxburghe Hotel & Golf Course*, at the village of **Heiton**, a few miles from town on the A698 to Hawick, T450331, sunlaws.roxgc@virgin.net. This country mansion owned by the Duke of Roxburgh stands in hundreds of acres of park and woodlands on the banks of the Teviot and offers grand style, superb cuisine and a championship golf course. Less salubrious but nevertheless highly recommended is the slightly more affordable **B** *Ednam House Hotel*, on Bridge St, T224168, F226319. A family-run Georgian mansion overlooking the Tweed and close to the town centre. Excellent food served all day (lunch cheap; dinner mid-range) in a restaurant with great views over the river. There are also some fine guesthouses and B&Bs, including **E** *The Old Priory & Coach House*, at 12 Abbey Row, T223030, an 18th-century town house within its own walled garden and offering fine food all day (lunch cheap; dinner mid-range). Also good is **E** *Inglestone House*, Abbey Row, T225800; and the non-smoking **E-D** *Bellevue House*, Bowmont St, T/F224588. The nearest **youth hostel** is at Kirk Yetholm (see below). There's a **campsite** at *Springwood Caravan Park*, T224596, open Mar-Oct, overlooking the Tweed on the A699 heading west towards St Boswells.

Eating   The best places to eat are the *Roxburghe* and *Ednam House Hotels* listed above. The other hotels in town also offer food, most notably the ***Queens Head Hotel*** (T224636) at 24 Bridge St, and the ***Black Swan Hotel*** (T224563) on Horsemarket. Both are just off The Square and offer cheap bar meals. There's also the ***Cottage Garden*** opposite the abbey, which offers tea, coffee and light lunches.

Transport   The **bus station** is on Roxburgh St, a short walk from The Square. There are regular **buses** to and from **Galashiels**, **Melrose**, **Jedburgh**, **Hawick**, **Coldstream** and **Kirk Yetholm**. Services are less frequent on Sun. For more details, contact the main bus operator *First Edinburgh*, T224141. There are also several buses (Mon-Sat) to and from **Berwick-upon-Tweed** via Coldstream (see below).

Around Kelso

Six miles northwest of Kelso on the B6397 is the village of Smailholm, where a turning leads to Smailholm Tower, a classic Scottish tower house and an evocative place full of history and romance. The 15th-century fortified farmhouse, built by the Pringles, squires to the Earls of Douglas, stands on a rocky pinnacle above a small lake. Sir Walter Scott's grandfather owned the nearby farm and the young Scott came here as a sickly child in the 1770s to improve his health. So began the writer's long love affair with the lore and landscapes of the Scottish Borders which inspired so much of his poetry and prose. Scott would write a ballad about this gaunt tower house – *The Eve of St John* – as part of deal with the owner to save it. Today, Smailholm houses a small, unremarkable museum relating to some of Scott's works, but the views from top of the tower are rewarding. ■ *T460365. Apr-Sept daily 0930-1830. £1.80, £1.30 concession.*

Smailholm Tower

Northwest of Kelso, on the A6089 to Gordon, is the signpost for Mellerstain House, home of the Earl of Haddington and one of the Scotland's great Georgian houses. This 18th-century architectural masterpiece was designed by William Adam and his son Robert and perfectly characterizes the elegant symmetry of the period. The superb exterior is more than matched by the exquisitely ornate interiors. There is also furniture by Chippendale and Hepplewhite, as well as paintings by Constable, Gainsborough, Veronese and Van Dyck. The formal Italian gardens, laid out in the early 20th century are equally impressive. ■ *T410225. May-Sept Sun-Fri 1230-1630. £4.50.*

Mellerstain House

Six miles southeast of Kelso on the B6352, are the twin villages of Kirk Yetholm and Town Yetholm, lying within a stone's throw of the English border one the edge of the Cheviot Hills, at the northern end of the **Pennine Way** which runs up the spine of northern England. The villages are also on **St Cuthbert's Way**, which runs from Melrose to Lindisfarne in Northumberland (see page 600).

Kirk Yetholm & Town Yetholm

Sleeping There's accommodation in Kirk Yetholm, at the **C-D** *Border Hotel*, T420237, overlooking the village Green, which marks the end of the Pennine Way. It serves a welcome pint of ale and good food, too. There are several B&Bs, including **D-E** *Valleydene*, T420286, on the High Street, and **D-E** *Spring Valley*, T420253, on The Green. There's also a **youth hostel** in Kirk Yetholm, T420631, open mid-Mar to end Oct. There's **camping** at *Kirkfield Caravan Park*, on Grafton Road in Town Yetholm, T420346, open Apr-Oct.

Transport There are regular **buses** to and from **Kelso**, 20 minutes away.

Coldstream

Standing on the north bank of the river Tweed, which marks the border with England, is the little town of Coldstream. The busy A697 linking Newcastle-upon-Tyne with Edinburgh runs through the centre of town, but Coldstream has little to offer visitors other than history. The well-stocked **tourist office** is in the Town Hall on the High Street. ■ *T882607. Apr-Jun and Sept Mon-Sat 1000-1700, Sun 1000-1300; Jul and Aug Mon-Sat 1000-1800, Sun 1000-1400; Oct Mon-Sat 1000-1230 and 1330-1630.*

Phone code: 01890
Colour map 6, grid B3

The town gave its name to the famous regiment of Coldstream Guards, formed by General Monck in 1659 before he marched south to support the restoration of the Stuart monarchy a year later. The regiment had originally been sent to

Sights

Southern Scotland

Scotland as part of Cromwell's New Model Army, but Monck was persuaded to change allegiance. No doubt the offer of the title, first Duke of Albermarle had something to do with his decision. The Guards remain the oldest regiment in continuous existence in the British army and you can find out all about their proud history in the **Coldstream Museum**, on Market Square, off the High Street. ■ *T882630. Easter-Oct Mon-Sat 1000-1700, Sun 1400-1700. £1.*

Near the handsome five-arched bridge which spans the river at the east end of town is the 18th-century **Toll House**, where eloping couples from England were once granted 'irregular marriages'. On the western edge of town is the 3,000-acre **Hirsel Country Park**, seat of the Earls of Home. Hirsel House isn't open to the *hoi polloi* but you can wander around the grounds. ■ *Open all year during daylight hours.*

Four miles southeast of Coldstream, across the border near the village of Branxton, is **Flodden Field**. In 1513 James IV crossed the Tweed at Coldstream to attack the English, while Henry VIII was busy fighting in France. The invasion was a diversion to assist the French, but Henry sent an army north to meet the threat and James IV's army was routed. The king, his son, and some 9,000 men were slain in one of Scotland's greatest military disasters.

Sleeping & eating The best places to stay are outside the town. **D** *Stainrigg*, T885200, in **Leitholm**, about 4 miles northwest of Coldstream on the B6461. A beautiful country house set in 30 acres of gardens and parkland and offering excellent food. **D-E** *Homebank House*, T830285, is a comfortable country house near the village of **Birgham**, a few miles west of Coldstream on the A698. In town is **E** *Garth House*, 7 Market St, T882477, and **E-F** *Attadale*, 1 Leet St, T883047. The *Coldstream Caravan & Camping Park* is at the southern edge of town (T883376).

Transport There are several **buses** daily (Mon-Sat) between **Kelso** and **Berwick-upon-Tweed** which pass through Coldstream, T01289-306436.

Duns

Phone code: 01361
Colour map 6, grid B3
The quiet market town of Duns lies in the middle of Berwickshire, surrounded by the fertile farmland of the Merse. Duns is best known as the birthplace of Jim Clark (1936-68), a former farmer who went on to become world motor racing champion twice in the 1960s and who remains one of Britain's greatest ever racing drivers. His successful career was tragically cut short when he was killed in a crash while practising at Hockenheim in Germany. The **Jim Clark Room**, 44 Newton Street, is a museum dedicated to his life. ■ *T883960. Easter-Oct Mon-Sat 1000-1300 and 1400-1630, Sun 1400-1630. £1.*

There are some good **local walks**, detailed in the leaflet *Walks Around Duns*, which is available, along with other **tourist information**, at the *Cherry Tree Tearoom*, on Market Square. ■ *Mon-Sat 0900-1645 and Sun from 1100.* The best walk is to the top of **Duns Law** (714ft), from where there are terrific views of the Merse and the Lammermuir Hills to the north. Also at the top is the **Covenanter's Stone**, which marks the spot where the Covenanting army camped in 1639, awaiting the arrival of Charles I's troops.

Sleeping The best place to stay, if you can afford it, is the **B** *Chirnside Hall Hotel*, T818219, F818231, a mile east of Chirnside, on the road to Berwick. This Victorian mansion house offers luxurious accommodation and excellent food all day at mid-range prices (booking essential). A cheaper alternative is **D** *Wellfield House*, Preston Rd, T883189, a traditional Georgian house offering great value (no smoking). Also recommended is the non-smoking **E** *St Albans*, T883285, on Clouds lane behind the police station.

Duns was also the birthplace of John Duns Scotus (1266-1308), a medieval scholar and theologian of some note, who taught at the universities of Oxford and Paris. He opposed the orthodox views of Thomas Aquinas and his teachings divided the Fransicans and Dominicans. After his death his ideas quickly fell out of favour and those who held them were derided as being stupid, and so we now have the word 'dunce', derived from the heterodox views of John Duns Scotus.

The best place to eat in the area is the award-winning *Wheatsheaf Hotel* in the village of Swinton, about 5 miles south of Duns on the A6112, T860257. The food is 1st-class but expensive. Alternatively, you can get cheap bar meals at the *Whip and Saddle*, on Market Square. **Eating**

There are several **buses** daily (fewer on Sun) to and from **Kelso** and **Berwick-upon-Tweed**. **Transport**

Duns lies only a few miles south of the **Lammermuir Hills**, a low-lying range running east to west and acting as a natural boundary between the Borders and East Lothian. The hills are criss-crossed by numerous paths and ancient droving trails, including the easterly section of the **Southern Upland Way**, from **Lauder**, on the A68, to **Cockburnspath** by the A1 on the coast. You can walk the final 10 miles of the route, starting from the hamlet of **Abbey St Bathans**, northwest of Duns on the Whiteadder Water. There's a tiny **youth hostel** in Abbey St Bathans, T01361-840245. **Around Duns**

Two miles east of Duns, on the A6015, is **Manderston House**, described as the finest Edwardian country house in Scotland. No expense has been spared in the design and decoration and the whole effect, from the silver staircase to the inlaid marble floor in the hall, is one of quite staggering opulence. The 56 acres of beautiful gardens should not be missed. ■ *T01361-883450. Mid-May to Sept Thur and Sun 1400-1730. £5.*

Twelve miles east of Duns, and five miles west of Berwick-upon-Tweed, off the B6461 to Swinton, is **Paxton House**, a grand neo-Palladian mansion designed by John and James Adam, the less-famous brothers of Robert, for Patrick Home, who had designs on Frederick the Great's daughter as his wife-to-be, though she jilted him. Inside there's an impressive display of Chippendale and Regency furniture, and the Picture Gallery is an outstation of the National Gallery of Scotland. In the 80 acres of grounds beside the river Tweed is a Victorian boathouse and a salmon-fishing museum. ■ *House open Apr-Oct daily 1100-1700. £4. Grounds open Apr-Oct 1000 till sunset.*

Eyemouth

Five miles north of the border, on the Berwickshire coast, is the busy fishing port of Eyemouth. Fishing has been the life and soul of Eyemouth since the 13th century and the **Eyemouth Museum**, in the Auld Kirk on Market Place, has displays on the town's fishing heritage. The centrepiece is the Eyemouth Tapestry, made by local people in 1981 to mark the centenary of the Great Disaster of 1881, when 189 local fishermen were drowned during a violent storm. ■ *Same opening hours as tourist office. £1.75.* In the same building as the museum is the **tourist office**. ■ *T50678. Apr-Jun and Sept, Mon-Sat 1000-1700 and Sun 1400-1600; Jul and Aug, Mon-Sat 1000-1800, Sun 1300-1800; Oct, Mon-Sat 1000-1230 and 1330-1630.*

Phone code: 018907
Colour map 6, grid B3
Population: 3,500

Southern Scotland

There are a number of excellent coastal **walks** around Eyemouth, particularly the seven-mile **Burnmouth to St Abbs walk** described below. There are also shorter walks, which are described in the *Walks in and around Eyemouth* leaflet, available at the tourist office.

The waters around Eyemouth are excellent for **scuba diving**. They form part of the **St Abbs and Eyemouth Voluntary Marine Reserve**, one of the best dive sites in Scotland, with a wide variety of marine life and the spectacular Cathedral Rock. Divers should head for the *Eyemouth Diving Centre*, T51202, at Eyemouth Holiday Park, on Fort Road, north of town. They rent out diving equipment, charter boats and run diving courses.

The two main events in Eyemouth's calendar naturally have a fishing theme. The week-long **Herring Queen Festival** takes place in late July, while the **Seafood Festival** is held over a weekend in mid-June.

Sleeping   There are several **B&Bs** in and around town, including **E** *Hillcrest*, Coldingham Rd, T50463, and **E** *Ebba House*, Upper Houndlaw, T50350. A couple of miles south, in the village of Ayton, is **E** *Ash House*, T781219. There's also a **campsite** at the *Eyemouth Holiday Park* , T751050, overlooking the beach at the north end of town.

Eating   Eating options are fairly limited. There's a string of pubs and hotels along the harbour serving fresh fish and standard bar meals, or the *Old Bakehouse*, opposite the tourist office, which serves cheap snacks and meals all day.

Transport   There are several **buses** daily to and from **Edinburgh** (1 hr 40 mins), and there are a couple of daily buses (Mon-Fri) to and from **Kelso**, via **Duns**. There's also a daily service to and from **Melrose** and **Berwick-upon-Tweed**. If you're driving, the best route north is the scenic A1107 which joins the fast A1 near Cockburnspath.

St Abb's Head

Phone code: 01890
Colour map 6, grid B3

Three miles north of Eyemouth on the A1107 is the village of **Coldingham**, notable only for its medieval **priory**, founded by King Edgar in 1098, then rebuilt in the 13th century before suffering further attacks in 1545 and 1648. The remaining sections have been incorporated into the present parish church.

Here, the B6438 turns north and winds its way down to the picturesque little fishing village of **St Abbs**, nestled beneath steep cliffs. St Abbs is also a good base for visiting the **St Abbs and Eyemouth Voluntary Marine Reserve** (see above). Divers can charter boats from *D&J Charters* , T771377, or *St Abbs Boat Charter*, T771681. The latter also runs birdwatching **boat trips**.

Just north of the village is the **St Abb's Head National Nature Reserve** (NTS), which comprises almost 200 acres of wild coastline with sheer cliffs inhabited by large colonies of guillemots, kittiwakes, fulmars and razorbills. To get to the reserve, follow the trail from the car park at Northfield Farm, on the road into St Abbs. The path ends at the lighthouse, about a mile from the car park. An excellent coastal walk, from Burnmouth, south of Eyemouth, to St Abbs is described below.

A side road turns off the B6438 at Coldingham and leads a mile down to the coast at **Coldingham Sands**, a tiny resort with a fine sandy beach. It's a popular spot for **surfing** and **diving**. The dive shop at *Scoutscroft Holiday Centre* (see below) rents out equipment and runs diving courses.

In St Abbs there's the excellent **E-D** *Castle Rock Guest House*, Murrayfield, on the cliffs above the harbour, T771715, and nearby is **E** *Wilma Wilson's B&B*, 7 Murrayfield, T771468. **At Coldingham Sands** is **C** *Dunlaverock Country House Hotel*, T771450, a small, comfortable hotel offering excellent food. There's also the 17th century **C** *Press Castle*, T771257, pcstle@globalnet.co.uk. A cheaper option is **D-E** *Cul-Na-Sithe*, T771565, culnasithe@clara.co.uk, which also does meals. Vegetarians may want to head for **E** *Wheaters*, T/F771375, open Feb-Oct, a few miles west of Coldingham, at Lumsdaine. This remote vegetarian guesthouse uses home grown produce. There's also a **youth hostel** at Coldingham Sands, on the cliffs above the south end of the bay, T771298, open mid-Mar to end Oct. There are a few **campsites**, including *Scoutscroft Holiday Centre*, T771338, open Mar-Nov, which also rents diving equipment and offers courses.

Sleeping & eating

Buses between **Edinburgh** and **Berwick-upon-Tweed** pass through Coldingham several times daily. There's also an hourly service between St Abbs, Coldingham, Eyemouth and Berwick.

Transport

Burnmouth to St Abbs walk

Southern Scotland

Burnmouth to
St Abbs coastal
walk

OS Landranger No 67
See map previous page

The Berwickshire coast offers some good walking opportunities along high cliffs with lots of birdlife to see. This walk starts at **Burnmouth**, a few miles south of Eyemouth. To get there, take the hourly bus service from Coldingham, which connects in Berwick with services to other Border towns. The seven-mile route is waymarked and is mostly on good paths, though there is some rough ground. Allow about four hours and take care at some points along the clifftop.

To get to the cliff path, get off the bus at Burnmouth primary school, go through the gate by the houses and walk up the side of the field. Continue along the path towards Eyemouth, past some dramatic scenery at **Fancove Head**, the highest point of the cliffs, at 338ft. When you reach the golf course, follow the signs around the seaward edge and then left across the golf course, then right towards **Eyemouth harbour**.

Cross the bridge near the lifeboat mooring and walk along the quayside to the end of the promenade, where you cross a short section of beach and then climb the steps to the headland and the remains of Eyemouth Fort. Walk around the seaward side of the Caravan Park and turn right to cross the fields and then return to the cliff path. The path descends to **Linkum Shore** and crosses the beach. Follow it around Yellow Craig to reach **Coldingham Bay**. At the far end of the bay, climb the steps and then follow the tarmac path which leads to the village of **St Abbs**. From here you can follow Creel Path to reach the B6438 and from there it's a short walk into Coldingham.

Berwick-upon-Tweed

Phone code: 01289

Yes, we know, Berwick-upon-Tweed is in England, but the town has strong historical ties with Scotland, and its football team plays in the Scottish league. It also makes a convenient stopping point if you've had a long journey north. The town, which takes its name from a river which has its source in Scotland, wasn't always in England. It changed hands more than a dozen times between 1147 and 1482, when it was finally taken for England by Richard, Duke of Gloucester, later Richard III. Berwick was a strategic base for English attacks on the Borders and large sections of the town wall, built by Edward I to repel the Scots, still survive. It has also retained its medieval street plan and many of its steep, cobbled streets are worth exploring.

Sleeping   There is plentiful accommodation. The highly recommended **B** *Marshall Meadows Country House Hotel*, T331133, is a Georgian mansion set in 15 acres of grounds only a few hundred yards from the border. Rather more central is the **D-E** *Dervaig Guest House*, 1 North Rd, T307378, only a few mins from the train station. Also close to the station is **E** *Whyteside House*, 46 Castlegate, T/F331019.

Transport   There are regular **buses** to and from **Edinburgh** (2 hrs), **Kelso** via **Duns**, **Galashiels** and **Eyemouth** with *First Edinburgh*, T01896-752237, and *Swan's Coaches*, T01289-306436. Berwick is on the main London-Aberdeen **rail line** and there are fast and frequent trains to and from **Edinburgh**. For rail information, T0345-484950.

Southern Scotland

Dumfries and Galloway

Dumfries and Galloway is one of Scotland's forgotten corners, forsaken by most visitors for the cities of Edinburgh and Glasgow or the grandeur of the Highlands. But the southwest has much to offer those prepared to leave the more-beaten track. Away from the main routes west from Dumfries to Stranraer and north to Glasgow, traffic and people are notable by their absence, leaving most of the region free from the tourist crush of more popular parts.

Some of the most beautiful scenery is to be found along the Solway coast, west from Dumfries to the Mull of Galloway. Here you'll find the romantic ruins of Caerlaverock Castle, Threave Castle and Sweetheart Abbey, along with Whithorn Priory, known as the 'Cradle of Christianity' in Scotland. Also on this lovely coast is the beguiling town of Kirkcudbright, inspiration for some of Scotland's most famous artists and still a thriving artistic colony. Rising behind the coastline are the Galloway Hills which form part of the 150,000-acre Galloway Forest Park, a vast area of mountains, moors, lochs and rivers, criss-crossed by numerous trails and footpaths suitable for all levels of fitness. Running right through the heart of the Galloway Hills is the 212-mile Southern Upland Way, one of the country's great long-distance walks (see page 600). The southwest also has strong literary associations. The great poet, Robert Burns, lived and died here, in Dumfries, and the town boasts several important Burns sights.

Ins and outs

Getting around The region has a good network of **buses**. The main operators are *Stagecoach Western*, T01387-253496, and *McEwan's*, T01387-710357. *National Express*, T0990-808080, has long-distance coaches from London, Birmingham, Glasgow and Edinburgh to Stranraer, for the **ferry** crossing to Belfast and Larne in Northern Ireland. There are 2 **train** routes from Carlisle to Glasgow, via Dumfries and Moffat. There's also a line from Stranraer to Glasgow. For rail information, T0345-484950. Dumfries & Galloway council has a **travel information line**, T0345-090510, for all public transport services. Open Mon-Fri 0900-1700.

Information The **Dumfries & Galloway Tourist Board** has its head office in Dumfries, at 64 Whitesands, T01387-253862, info@dgtb.demon.co.uk, www.galloway.co.uk. They have a range of free brochures and guide books for the region, including Accommodation, Birdwatching, Cycling, Fishing, Walking and Golfing. There are also tourist offices in Stranraer, Castle Douglas, Gatehouse of Fleet, Gretna Green, Kirkcudbright, Moffat and Newton Stewart.

Annandale

Cutting through Annandale is the A74(M), the congested main route from England to Scotland. Most people whizz straight through this eastern part of Dumfries & Galloway on their way north, but away from the main roads, there are a few interesting places to visit.

Gretna Green The first place you encounter across the border is the nondescript little village of Gretna Green. It's not a particularly interesting place to visit, but Gretna Green has been synonymous with marriage ceremonies for many years and thousands of couples still come here to tie the knot.

Phone code: 01461
Colour map 6, grid C1

The **World Famous Old Blacksmith's Shop** houses a visitor centre with a small exhibition on Gretna Green's history as well as gift shops. ■ *T338224.*

Southern Scotland

Gretna Green weddings

In Scotland, a marriage declaration made before two witnesses was legally binding, and anyone could perform the ceremony. This meant that eloping couples from south of the border came to Scotland to have their weddings witnessed by whomever came to hand. As Gretna Green was the first available community on the main route north, it became the most popular destination for the runaway lovers. In their desperation, many tied the knot at the first place to hand after getting off the stagecoach and in Gretna this happened to be the local blacksmith's shop, situated at the crossroads.

The marriage business boomed in the village, until 1940, when marriage by declaration was made illegal. However, under Scots law young couples can still marry at 16 without parental consent and Gretna Green still attracts its fair share of Romeos and Juliets.

Jan-Mar and Nov/Dec daily 0900-1700; Apr-May and Oct daily 0900-1800; Jun and Sept daily 0900-1900; Jul and Aug daily till 2000. £2, £1.50 concession. Opposite is the **tourist office**. ■ *T337834. Apr-Jun and Sept/Oct daily 1000-1630; Jul and Aug till 1800.* Tourist information is also available from the Gretna Gateway service area (T338500) on the A74(M). There's also a rival blacksmith's shop, the **Gretna Hall Blacksmith's Shop**, at the **B-C** *Gretna Hall Hotel*, T338257. This was where better-off runaway couples would come to maintain a class distinction. ■ *T337635. Apr-Oct daily 0900-2000; Nov-Mar daily 0900-1700. 80p, children free.*

Transport *Stagecoach Western*, T01387-253496, bus No 382 between **Moffat** and **Carlisle** passes through Gretna Green, and No 79 runs to and from **Dumfries**. Gretna Green is also on the Dumfries-Carlisle rail line and there are regular **trains** in either direction. For train information, T0345-484950.

Ecclefechan &
Lockerbie
Phone code: 01576
Colour map 6, grid C1

Nine miles northwest of Gretna Green on the A74(M) is the neat little village of Ecclefechan, birthplace of the great writer and historian **Thomas Carlyle** (1795-1881), one of the most powerful and influential thinkers in 19th-century Britain. His old home, The Arched House, is now a tiny museum known as **Carlyle's Birthplace** and features a collection of personal memorabilia. ■ *T300666. 1 May-30 Sept Fri-Mon 1330-1700. £2, £1.30.*

About eight miles north of Ecclefechan is **Lockerbie**, a quiet, unassuming little town which hit the headlines on 21 December 1988 when a Pan-Am jumbo jet, flying from Frankfurt to New York, was blown up by a terrorist bomb, killing all 196 passengers and crew. The plane's fragments fell on the town, killing a further 11 people. After many months of exhausting diplomatic efforts, the two suspects were extradited from Libya and at the time of writing are being tried in a Scottish court set up in the Netherlands. But for the people of Lockerbie life will never be the same.

Sleeping There are several places to stay in **Ecclefechan**, including the refurbished 18th century **B** *Kirkconnel Hall*, T300277, kirkconnelhall@dial.pipex.com, and **F** *Carlyle House*, opposite Carlyle's Birthplace, T/F300332. There's also a **campsite** at *Cressfield Caravan Park*, T300702, open all year, at the southern end of the village, and also at *Hoddom Castle Caravan Park*, T300251, open Apr-Oct, 3 miles west of Ecclefechan in the grounds of Hoddom Castle.

Transport Ecclefechan is served by **bus** Nos 382 (Moffat-Carlisle) and 383 (Lockerbie-Annan).

Langholm and around

Langholm sits at the confluence of three rivers – the Esk, Lewes and Wauchope – on the A7, one of the main routes north to Edinburgh and a less stressful alternative to the A74(M). During the 18th century, Langholm became a thriving textile town and is still a major centre of the Scottish tweed industry.

Phone code: 01387
Colour map 6, grid C2

Langholm was the birthplace of **Hugh McDiarmid** (1892-1978), poet and co-founder of the Scottish National Party. He is also buried here, against the wishes of the local nobs, who took great exception to his radical views. On the hill above the town is the **McDiarmid Memorial**, a stunning modern sculpture which looks like a giant metallic open book. A path leads for about half a mile to another memorial, from where there are wonderful views across the Southern uplands and the Solway Firth. A signed single-track road leads off the A7, about half a mile north of Langholm, to a path which leads to the memorials.

This is clan Armstrong country and the **Clan Armstrong Trust Museum** is a must for anyone with that particular surname. Neil was here, but we don't know if Gary has ever been. ■ *T381610. Easter-Oct Tue-Sun 1330-1630. £1.50.*

The **tourist office** is north of the town centre on the main road into town. ■ *T380976. Apr, May and Sept Mon-Sat 1030-1630; Jun-Aug daily 1000-1700.* They can provide a full list of accommodation, as well as information on local walks and fishing, and on local festivals such as the town's **Common Riding**, which takes place on the last weekend in July. In the last week in August is the **Langholm & Eskdale Festival of Music and Arts** and at the end of September is the **Eskdale Agricultural Show**.

Sleeping & eating

There are a couple of hotels in town. **D-E** *The Reivers Rest*, 81 High St, T381343, paul@reiversrest.demon.co.uk. Serves bar meals and real ales. There are several **B&Bs**, including **E** *Border House*, 28 High St, T380376. There's also a **campsite** at *Ewes Water Caravan & Camping Park*, T380386, open Apr-Sept, close to town.

Transport

Langholm is on the No 195 **bus** route between **Carlisle** and **Galashiels** bus route and buses pass through several times daily. Bus No 112 runs to and from **Lockerbie**, via **Eskdelmuir** (Mon-Sat).

Around Langholm

The A7 runs north to Hawick and on to Edinburgh. It also runs south to Carlisle, via **Canonbie**, through an area known as the Debatable Land, until the border was settled in 1552. From Canonbie the B6357 provides a more scenic alternative route to the Borders, running through lovely **Liddesdale** towards Hawick and Jedburgh (see page 618). A shorter route to Liddesdale is to take the single-track road heading east off the A7 just to the north of Langholm, which joins the B6357 at **Newcastleton**. The best place to eat in this area is the *Riverside Inn* in Canonbie, T371512, which serves superb pub food.

Another scenic route from Langholm to the Borders region is the B709. It runs northwest to the tiny village of **Eskdalemuir**, 14 miles from Langholm, then north through the Eskdalemuir and Craik forests to **Ettrick**, where it follows the valley of the Ettrick Water to Selkirk (see page 616). About 1½ miles north of Eskdalemuir is one of the **Kagyu Samye Ling Tibetan Monsetery**. This Tibetan Buddhist centre was founded in 1967 for study, retreat and meditation and incorporates the Samye Temple, the first Tibetan Buddhist monastery in the west. There are free guided tours for visitors, regardless of faith, and a programme of weekend courses and teachings. There's also a café and shops on site and pleasant walks through the gardens. ■ *T373232. Daily 0900-1800. Free. Bus No 112 from Langholm to Galashiels stops at the centre.*

Southern Scotland

Moffat

Phone code: 01683
Colour map 6, grid C1
Population: 2,000

Just to the east of the A74(M) at the northern end of Annandale, is the attractive market town of Moffat, with its wide High Street and long, eventful history. Moffat was once something of a fashionable spa town and its sulphur springs attracted the great and the good. Now it's a centre for the local woollen industry (from spa town to 'baa' town, you might say).

The **tourist office** is on Churchgate, at the end of the High Street. ■ *T220620. Apr, May, Sept and Oct daily 1000-1700; Jun-Aug 0930-1830.* Next to the tourist office is the **Moffat Woollen Mill**, where you can see a demonstration of traditional weaving and trace your Scottish ancestry. There's also a shop selling woollens and tartans. ■ *T220134. Mar-Oct daily 0900-1730; Nov-Feb daily till 1700. Free.* Nearby is the **Moffat Museum**, which tells the town's history. ■ *T220868. Easter to end Sept Mon, Tue and Thur-Sat 1030-1300 and 1430-1700, Sun 1430-1700. £1.*

The tourist office has a selection of leaflets detailing the many local walks. For a pleasant short stroll along the River Annan follow the 'Waterside Walk' sign from the High Street. There are more strenuous walks in the Lowther Hills and along the Southern Upland Way (see 'Around Moffat' below).

Amongst the local festivals is the **Moffat Agricultural Show**, held on the last Sat in August, and the **Tweedhope Sheepdog Trials**, at Granton Farm, Beechgrove, on the first Sunday in August.

Sleeping There's plenty of accommodation in Moffat and you should have no problems finding a room. Of the several hotels lining the High St, the best is the very fine **C** *Moffat House Hotel*, T220039. Also on the High St is the **D** *Star Hotel*, T220156, the narrowest hotel in the UK. Overlooking the town is the **C** *Wellview Hotel*, Ballplay Rd, T220184. A Victorian house with an excellent restaurant which offers a 6-course dinner using the best of local produce (expensive). Amongst the many **guesthouses** and **B&Bs** is the highly-rated **D-E** *Hartfell House*, Hartfell Cres, T220153, open Mar-Nov. Many of the B&Bs are on Beechgrove, which is a 5-min walk from the town centre. These include **E** *Gilbert House*, T/F220050, **D-E** *Alba House*, T220418, open Apr-Oct, and **E** *Queensberry House*, T220538, open Mar to mid-Jan. There's also a **campsite** at *Hammerlands Farm*, T220436, open Mar-Nov, about a mile east of town by the A708.

Eating The *Wellview* and *Moffat House Hotels* are the best places to eat in town. The hotels and pubs along the High St all serve **bar meals**, including the *Buccleuch Arms Hotel* and the historic *Black Bull Hotel*. Alternatively, try *Claudio's Restaurant*, T220958, in the old police station at Burnside, which serves a wide range of Italian dishes. Open Mon-Thu and Sun till 2130, Fri/Sat till 2200. There are also a couple of cafés on the High St.

Transport There are frequent **buses** to **Edinburgh** (No X73), **Glasgow** (No X74) and **Dumfries** (Nos 114 and 199). Bus No 199 also runs to Edinburgh, via the A708, on Fri and Sat. Bus No 382 runs to **Carlisle**, via **Lockerbie** and **Gretna Green** and bus No 130 runs to **Galashiels**, via **Selkirk**, along the scenic A708. The main operator is *Stagecoach Western Buses*, T01387-253496. Buses between Moffat and Dumfries are also run by *James Gibson & Son*, T01683-220200. There's also the Harrier Scenic Bus Service, which runs between Moffat and Selkirk on Thur between Jul and Sept (see also page 606). For *Harrier Service* bus times call *First Edinburgh*, T01573-224141.

Around Moffat

Moffat makes a convenient base from which to explore the Lowther Hills to the west and the wild and barren southwest Borders to the east, either by car or on foot. The Southern Upland Way passes only about a mile east of town, by the A708, which runs northeast for 22 miles to Selkirk, in the Borders (see page 614).

Stagecoach Western bus No 130 from Moffat to Galashiels runs along this very beautiful route which passes through the most stunning parts of the Southern Uplands. Ten miles northeast of Moffat on the A708 is the spectacular **Grey Mare's Tail** waterfall, which plunges 200ft from a hanging valley. The base of the falls can be reached from the road by a steep footpath, which continues past the head of the falls to the remote **Loch Skeen**, from where experienced walkers can climb to the summit of **White Coomb** (2,696ft). This is also a popular birdwatching area. The A708 carries on into the Borders region and passes the famous **Tibbie Shiels Inn**, on the shores of **St Mary's Loch** (see page 616).

Another scenic route from Moffat is the A701 which runs north towards Edinburgh. *En route* it meets the A72, which heads east to Peebles and along the Tweed valley (see page 607). Six miles north of Moffat, on the A701, you get a great view of the **Devil's Beef Tub**, a vast, deep natural bowl once used by Border Reivers (rustlers) for hiding stolen cattle (hence the name). The Tub was also used as a hide-out by persecuted Covenanters during Charles II's 'killing times'.

Further north the road enters **Tweeddale** and passes through tiny **Tweedsmuir**, where a spectacular side road climbs up into the hills to meet the A708 at St Mary's Loch (see page 610). *Stagecoach Western* bus No 199 runs along this route to Edinburgh, but only on Fridays and Saturdays, T01387-253496.

West of Moffat, between the A74(M) and Nithsdale, are the wild and bare **The Lowther** Lowther Hills. About 13 miles north of Moffat, at **Elvanfoot**, the B7040 leaves **Hills** the A74(M) and crosses the hills, passing through the old lead-mining villages of **Leadhills** and **Wanlockhead** to meet the A76 a few miles south of **Sanquhar** (see page 635).

Leadhills is a rather forlorn-looking place but a few miles south is Wanlockhead, the highest village in Scotland at 1,500ft and home of the **Museum of Lead Mining**. The visitor centre gives an introduction to the mining industry and then there's a **guided tour** of an old lead mine, miners' cottages and the 18th-century library. ■ *T01659-74387. 1 Apr-31 Oct daily 1000-1630. £3.95*. Wanlockhead was also a gold mining centre and you can try your hand at gold panning at the museum. The **Open Gold Panning Championships** are held there during the second last weekend in May, and during the last weekend in May is the **British Gold Panning Championships**.

Sleeping Wanlockhead is on the Southern Upland Way and there's a youth hostel in the village, at *Lotus Lodge*, T01659-74252, open Apr-Oct.

There's a **bus** (No 223) to Leadhills from Sanquhar which passes through Wanlockhead. For times call the Travel Information Line, T0345-090510.

Southern Scotland

Dumfries

Phone code: 01387
Colour map 5, grid C6
Population: 31,000

Dumfries is the largest town in southwest Scotland, straddling the river Nith, a few miles from the Solway Firth. Known as the 'Queen of the South', Dumfries has long been a thriving market town and seaport for a large agricultural hinterland and its strategic position made it a prime target for English armies. Its long history of successive invasions began in 1306, when Robert the Bruce committed the first act of rebellion against Edward I by capturing Dumfries Castle, which led to the Wars of Independence.

But it was town planners in the 1960s who did more to destroy the town centre than invading armies. Nevertheless, Dumfries is a pleasant and convenient base from which to explore the beautiful Solway coast, and its associations with Robert Burns, who spent the last years of his life here, also make it worth a visit in its own right.

The **tourist office** is at 64 Whitesands, on the corner of Bank Street. ■ *T253862. Apr, May and Oct daily 1000-1700; Jun-Sept daily 0930-1800.*

Sights Most of the town's attractions and facilities are on the east side of the river. A tour of the main sights should begin on the pedestrianized High Street, at the **Burns Statue**, at its northern end. It shows the great bard sitting on a tree stump with his faithful dog at his feet. A few minutes walk along the High Street is the **Midsteeple**, built in 1707 to serve as a courthouse and prison. Nearby, at 56 High Street, is the **Globe Inn**, one of Burns' regular drinking haunts, where you can sit in the poet's favourite chair and enjoy a drink (see 'Eating' below). Continue down the High Street and follow the signs for **Burns' House**, in Burns Street, where the poet spent the last few years of his life and died, in 1796. It contains some interesting memorabilia, including original letters and manuscripts. ■ *T255297. Apr-Sept Mon-Sat 1000-1700, Sun 1400-1700; Oct-Mar Tue-Sat 1000-1700. Free.* Just to the south is the red sandstone **St Michael's Church**. In the churchyard is the **mausoleum** where Burns lies buried.

On the other side of the river, on Mill Road, is the award-winning **Robert Burns Centre**, housed in an old water mill. It tells the story of Burns' last years in the town. ■ *T264808. Apr-Sept Mon-Sat 1000-2000, Sun 1400-1700; Oct-Mar Tue-Sat 1000-1300 and 1400-1700, Sun 1400-1700.* On the hill above, centred around an 18th-century windmill tower, is **Dumfries Museum**, which has good local history, natural history and anthropology displays. ■ *T253374. Apr-Sept Mon-Sat 1000-1700, Sun 1400-1700; Oct-Mar Tue-Sat 1000-1300 and 1400-1700. Free.* On the top floor of the windmill tower is a **Camera Obscura**. ■ *Apr-Sept only. £1.50, concession 75p.*

Also on the west bank of the river, at the west end of the 15th-century Devorgilla Bridge, is the **Old Bridge House**, built in 1660 and the town's oldest house. It is now a museum of town life over the centuries. ■ *T256904. Apr-Sept Mon-Sat 1000-1700, Sun 1400-1700. Free.*

Sleeping There's no shortage of accommodation in Dumfries, though some of the nicest places are out of town (see 'Around Dumfries' below). Among the many hotels is the **B** *Cairndale Hotel*, English St, T254111. 76 rooms, it's popular with business visitors and boasts a full range of leisure facilities as well as hosting a ceilidh on Sun nights. Also good is the newly-refurbished **B** *Station Hotel*, 49 Lovers Walk, T254316. 32 rooms, it's very handy for the train station and has a good restaurant. A short walk west of the town centre is Laurieknowe, where you'll several places to stay, including **D** *Edenbank Hotel* (T252759), and **D** *Dalston House Hotel* (T/F254422).

There are lots of good **guesthouses** and **B&Bs** near the train station, on Lovers Walk, such as **E** *Morton Villa*, at No 28, T255825, **E** *Fulwood Hotel*, at No 30, T252262, and **E-F** *Torbay Lodge*, at No 31, T253922. Also near the train station is **E** *Hazeldean House*, 4 Moffat Rd, T266178. There are also some nice places on the west side of the river, including **E-F** *Merlin*, 2 Kenmure Terr, T261002, near the Burns Centre.

Apart from the hotels listed above, the best place to eat is *Wisharts*, on Mill Rd, T259679, which offers expensive, high quality modern Scottish cuisine in a converted old water mill. Open Tue-Sat. For good Italian food try *Bruno's*, at 3 Balmoral Rd, T255757. Next door and run by the same family is the *Balmoral Fish & Chicken Bar*, which is reputed to sell the best chips in southwest Scotland. Open Wed-Mon 1800-2200. Another good Italian-style restaurant is the moderately-priced *Benvenuto*, at 42 Eastfield Rd, T259890. *Pierre*, 113 Queensbury St, T265888, does a cheap set lunch and is good for fish and seafood. For **vegetarian** food try *Opus*, 95 Queensbury St, T255752. Cheap-mid-range prices. Open Mon-Sat 0900-1700. The pubs in town all serve cheap bar meals, but the most atmospheric place is the *Globe Inn*, 56 High St, once frequented by a certain poet of this parish.

Eating

Dumfries hosts quite a few festivals throughout the year, including the **Dumfries Book Fair**, at the beginning of **May**, and **Guid Nychburris Festival**, in the middle of **Jun**, which features a week of entertainment and ceremonies. On the **2nd Sat in Aug** is the **Dumfries & Lockerbie Agricultural Show**. For a full list of dates for this year, check with the tourist office.

Festivals

The **bus station** is only a short walk west of the High Street, at the top of Whitesands beside the river. There are regular **buses** to Kirkudbright (Nos 500, 501, 502 and 505). No 500 continues twice daily to **Newton Stewart** (1 hr 20 mins) and **Stranraer** (2 hrs), for the ferry to Belfast. *National Express*, T0990-808080, runs a daily service between

Transport

Dumfries

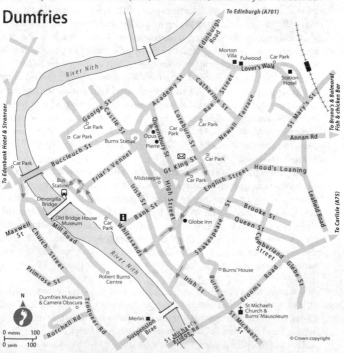

© Crown copyright

London and **Belfast**, via Dumfries and **Stranraer** and towns in between. *Stagecoach Western*, T253496, has a 2 buses daily to and from **Edinburgh** (No 199; 2 hrs 20 mins). There are also regular buses to **Carlisle** (No 79; 50 mins) and to **Moffat** (No 114; 1 hr). Bus No 503 runs to **Castle Douglas** (45 mins) and No 246 to **Cumnock**, via **Sanquhar** (50 mins). There are also buses to **Thornhill**, **Dalbeattie**, via **Rockcliffe**, **Moniaive**, **Glencaple/Caerlaverock Castle** and **Annan** via **Ruthwell**. For all bus times, call the Travel Information Line, T0345-090510.

The **train station** is on the east side of town, a 5-min walk from the centre. There are frequent **trains** Mon-Sat to and from **Carlisle** (35 mins; £6.40) and several daily (Mon-Sat) to and from **Glasgow** (1 hr 30 mins; £16.40), via **Kilmarnock**, where you change for trains to Stranraer. There's a reduced service on Sun. For all rail enquiries, T0345-484950.

Car hire *Arnold Clark*, New Abbey Rd, T247151. Open Mon-Fri 0800-1800, Sat 0830-1700, Sun 1100-1700. From £18 per day. **Cycle hire** *Grierson & Graham*, 10 Academy St, T259483. *Nithsdale Cycle Centre*, 46 Brooms Rd, T254870. For bike repairs and parts, *Kirkpatrick Cycles*, 13-15 Queen St, T254011.

Around Dumfries

There are many interesting sights lying within easy distance of Dumfries, including **Caerlaverock Castle** to the southeast, and **Ellisland Farm** and **Drumlanrig Castle** to the north, in Nithsdale. Bus No 246 travels the A76 through Nithsdale as far as Cumnock.

Caerlaverock Castle Eight miles from Dumfries, on the east bank of the Nith estuary where it enters the Solway Firth, is Caerlaverock Castle, everyone's idea of the perfect medieval fortress and one the best-preserved ruins in Scotland. The unusual triangular-shaped castle, which dates from around 1277, was the stronghold of the Maxwells, the Wardens of the Western Marches. But though surrounded by a moat and impregnable-looking, it has fallen several times over the course of its long history. It was first besieged in 1300 by Edward I of England during the Wars of Independence and soon captured, then destroyed by Robert the Bruce. It was repaired in the 1330s, then 300 years later refurbished in the trendy Renaissance style by Robert Maxwell, first Earl of Nithsdale. But several years later it was attacked again, this time by the Covenanters, who captured it after a 13-week siege and proceeded to trash the place. Caerlaverock was never occupied again. ■ *T770244 (HS). Apr-Sept 0930-1830; Oct-Mar Mon-Sat 0930-1630, Sun 1400-1630. £2.50. To get there, take Stagecoach Western bus No 371 from Dumfries.*

A few miles further on is the **Caerlaverock Wildlife and Wetlands Centre**, an absolute must-see attraction for birdwatchers, and also recommended for those with only a passing interest in our feathered friends. The 1,350 acres of salt marsh and mudflats attract many thousands of birds, most notably barnacle geese, migrating here in the winter. A series of hides and observation towers allow you to get very close to the birds and during the summer months there are nature trails through flower meadows, where you may see the rare natterjack toad. ■ *T770200. Daily 1000-1700. £3.50, children £2.25.*

The Ruthwell Cross About seven miles east of Caerlaverock, along the B724, is the turning to the little village of **Ruthwell**. Inside the village church is the remarkable **Ruthwell Cross**, which dates from the late seventh century when the whole of southern Scotland and northern England, from the Humber-Mersey line to the Forth, was controlled by the Angles. The two main faces of 18-ft high cross are carved

···

An American hero

John Paul Jones (1747-92) was a hero to
the Americans, but the British saw him as
a pirate. Early on in his nautical career, as
plain John Paul, he was imprisoned in
Kirkudbright Tolbooth for the
manslaughter of his ship's carpenter. His
fortunes changed, along with his name, in
later life when he joined the US fleet in

1775. Four years later, during the
American War of Independence, in
command of a few American and French
ships, he won a dramatic victory against a
powerful British force off the English coast
and became an American hero. He is
generally regarded as the father of the
modern US Navy.

···

with religious and secular figures and bears inscriptions in both Latin and
runes. ■ *T870249. Free. Key to church from Mrs Coulthard. Take bus No 79
from Dumfries.*

Sleeping If you want to stay, the very comfortable, family-run **D-E** *Kirkland Country
House Hotel*, T870284, is right next to the church. For something a bit more luxurious,
try **A-B** *Comlongon Castle*, T870283, a 14th-century, family-owned castle and adjacent mansion house hotel, which is very popular for weddings. To get there, head
north from Ruthwell for about a mile to Clarencefield, where a signposted road turns
left (west) for another mile to the castle.

The A76 runs northwest from Dumfries, all the way to Kilmarnock, in Ayrshire. **Nithsdale**
Along the way are several places of interest, starting with **Ellisland Farm**, six
miles from Dumfries. This was the home of Robert Burns from 1788 to 1791,
during which time he built the farmhouse and tried to introduce new farming
methods. Ultimately, this venture collapsed and he moved to Dumfries, but not
before writing his famous ghost story, *Tam o' Shanter*, and Hogmanay favourite,
Auld Lang Syne. The farmhouse is now a museum displaying various personal
items. ■ *T740426. Apr-Sept Mon-Sat 1000-1300 and 1400-1700, Sun
1400-1700; Oct-Mar Tue-Sat 1000-1600. £1.50, concession 75p.*

Eight miles further north is **Thornhill**, where the A702 heads eight miles
west to the peaceful little conservation village of **Moniaive**. There are a couple
of **B&Bs** in the village, including **E-F** *Bainoon*, on the High Street,
T01848-200266. Bus No 202 runs to Moniaive from Dumfries.

Three miles north of Thornhill is the turning for **Drumlanrig Castle**, more
French château than Scottish castle. This sumptuous stately home of the Duke
of Buccleuch and Queensberry is renowned for its superb art collection, which
reflects the mind-boggling wealth of its owners. Included are works by such
luminaries as Rembrandt, Leonardo Da Vinci, Holbein, Breughel and Van
Dyck, as well as numerous family portraits by Allan Ramsay and Godfrey
Kneller. After all that you may need to clear your head with a stroll round the
extensive **country park**. You can also hire mountain bikes and explore a network of cycle trails. There's also a **bicycle museum**, commemorating the fact
that the bicycle was invented nearby, at Keir Mill. ■ *T01848-330248. May to
mid-Aug Mon-Sat 1100-1600, Sun 1200-1600, £4.50. Drumlanrig is 1½ miles
from the A76.*

Seven miles north of Drumlanrig, the B797 turns right (east) off the A76 and
climbs up to **Wanlockhead**, the highest village in Scotland (see 631). A few
miles further, on the A76, is the neat little town of **Sanquhar**, which lies on the
Southern Upland Way. There's a **tourist office**, housed in the oldest working
post office in the world. ■ *T01659-50185. Easter-May and Sept daily
1030-1630; Jun-Aug 1000-1700.*

South of Dumfries

South of Dumfries are some of the area's loveliest sights. The A710 runs past New Abbey and the ruins of **Sweetheart Abbey**, then follows the Solway Coast, past the quiet little coastal villages of **Rockcliffe** and **Kippford**, before looping around to Dalbeattie, where it meets the A711 which runs from Dumfries to Kirkudbright. Bus No 372 runs from Dumfries to Dalbeattie, stopping in New Abbey, Kirkbean, Rockcliffe and Kippford, T710357.

Four miles south of Dumfries is the turn-off to **Mabie Forest**, a large area criss-crossed by forest paths and cycle trails. You can hire bikes at *Riks Bike Shed*, T270275. ■ *Daily 1000-1800 during the summer, and Mon and Fri-Sun 1000-1800 during the winter. Bikes cost £10 per person per day.*

New Abbey
Phone code: 01387
Colou rmap 5, grid C6

Seven miles south of Dumfries, in the pretty little village of New Abbey, are the graceful red sandstone ruins of **Sweetheart Abbey**, founded by Cistercian monks in 1273. They abbey gets its name from the extreme marital devotion of its patron, Lady Devorgilla de Balliol, wife of John, who founded of Balliol College, Oxford. On his death she had his heart embalmed and carried it around with her, until her own death, in 1290. Now both she and the heart are buried in the presbytery. ■ *T01387-850397 (HS). Apr-Sept daily 0930-1830; Oct-Mar Mon-Wed and Sat 0930-1630, Thur 0930-1200, Fri and Sun 1400-1630. £2.80, concession £2.10.*

Just north of the village is **Shambellie House Museum of Costume**, a Victorian country house set in beautiful gardens and which houses a collection of period costumes from the late 18th to the early 20th centuries. ■ *T01387-850375. Apr-Oct daily 1100-1700. £2.50, concession £1.50.*

New Abbey is dominated by **Criffel Hill** (1,867ft). One and a half miles south of the village, take the turning for Ardwell Mains Farm, from where a track leads to the summit. The views from the top are magnificent, stretching all the way south to the lakes and across to the Borders.

A few miles south of New Abbey, at **Kirkbean**, is the turning for the **John Paul Jones Cottage**, birthplace of the US naval hero. It's now a small museum and includes an exhibition and audio visual of his amazing life. ■ *T01387-880613. Apr-Jun Tue-Sun 1000-1700; Jul and Aug daily 1000-1700. £2 (£1).* South of Kirkbean, at **Southerness**, there's an excellent championship **golf course**.

Sleeping There are a couple of places to stay on the village square; the **D-E** *Abbey Arms Hotel*, T01387-850489, and **D-E** *Criffel Inn*, T01387-850305. Both are also great village pubs and serve bar meals.

Rockcliffe &
Kippford
Phone code: 01556
Colour map 5, grid C6

The A710 turns west south of Kirkbean and parallels the Solway Coast, past the wide **Sandyhills Bay** to **Colvend**. About a mile beyond, a side road turns off to the little village of Rockcliffe, nestled in a beautiful rocky cove at the mouth of the Urr estuary. From Rockcliffe you can walk about 1½ miles to neighbouring, Kippford, a popular sailing centre, along the **Jubilee Path** (NTS). The path passes the **Mote of Mark**, an ancient Celtic hillfort. Another path runs south from Rockcliffe, along the cliff tops, to **Castlehill Point**. From Kippford, at low tide, you can walk across the causeway to **Rough Island**, a 20-acre off-shore bird sanctuary owned by the NTS. During May and June, when the terns and oystercatchers are nesting, it's out of bounds.

Sleeping There's a decent choice of accommodation along this stretch of coast. In **Rockcliffe** is the very fine **B** *Barons Craig Hotel*, T630225, and the more modest

E *Millbrae House*, T630217. In **Kippford** is the **D-E** *Anchor Hotel*, T620205, which also serves superb pub food and is the perfect spot for a great pint of real ale after the walk from Rockcliffe. Also in Kippford is **E** *Rosemount Guest House*, T620214. At **Sandyhills**, a couple of miles east, on the A710, is the baronial splendour of **D-E** *Craigbittern House*, T01387-780247, and the comfortable **D-E** *Cairngill House Hotel*, T01387-780681. There are also a few **campsites** in the area, including *Kippford Caravan Park*, T/F620636, open Mar-Oct; the *Sandyhills Bay Leisure Park* T01387-780257, open Apr-Oct; and *Castle Point Caravan Site*, T630248, open Mar-Oct, near Rockcliffe.

Beyond the turnings to Rockcliffe and Kippford is the town of Dalbeattie, where there's a **tourist office** . ■ *T01556-610117. Apr, May and Sept Mon-Sat 1030-1630; Jun-Aug daily 1000-1700.* There's also a decent range of shops. **Dalbeattie & around**

Three miles north of town is the **Mote of Urr**, a 12th-century motte-and-bailey castle. About four miles south, near **Palnackie** is the turn-off for the 15th-century **Orchardton Tower**, the only circular tower house in Scotland. On the first Sat in August Palnackie hosts the **World Flounder Tramping Championships**, an unusual event which involves trying to catch the biggest flounder – with your feet!

From Dalbeattie, the A711 runs southwest to Kirkcudbright and the A745 heads west to Castle Douglas, about five miles away.

Castle Douglas and around

The neat little town of Castle Douglas, standing on the edge of lovely little **Carlingwark Loch**, was laid out in the 18th century by Sir William Douglas, a local lad who made his fortune in the Americas. There's nothing of note in the town itself, but there are a few worthwhile attractions in the surrounding area. You can find out all about these, and other local sights, at the **tourist office**, King Street. ■ *T502611. Apr-Jun, Sept and Oct daily 1000-1630; Jul and Aug daily 1000-1800.* A good way to explore the area is by bike and you can **rent bikes** at *Ace Cycles*, 11 Church Street, T504542. Mountain bikes cost £10 per person per day. *Phone code: 01556 / Colour map 5, grid C5 / Population: 3,500*

A mile southwest of town, off the A75, or reached by the lochside road, is **Threave Garden**, the NTS horticultural school's magnificent floral extravaganza. The best time to visit is early spring when over 200 types of daffodils burst into bloom, but it's a very colourful experience at any time of the year. ■ *T502575. Gardens open daily all year from 0930 till sunset. Visitor Centre open Easter-31 Oct daily 0930-1730. £4.50, £2.90 concession.* **Sights**

Two miles farther west, at Bridge of Dee, a country lane branches north (right) and leads for about a mile to the start of a footpath which takes you to the gaunt tower of **Threave Castle**, standing alone on an island in the middle of the river Dee. Threave was built in the 14th century by Archibald 'the grim', third Earl of Douglas, and head of the 'Black' Douglas line. The Douglases were one of Scotland's most powerful baronial families and the main line, the 'Black' Douglases, were descended from 'the Good' Sir James, trusted friend of Robert the Bruce. The outer wall of the castle was added in 1450 in an unsuccessful attempt to defend it against King James II, who was determined to break the power of the maverick Border family. The Covenanters reduced Threave to its present ruinous state in 1640 and little remains of the interior. It's a romantic ruin nevertheless, especially as you have to be ferried across to the island. It's a 10-minute walk from the car park, then ring the bell for the custodian to take you across in a small rowing boat. ■ *T0131-6688800 (HS). 1 Apr-30 Sept daily 0930-1830. £1.80, concession £1.30.*

The A713 runs north from Castle Douglas along the shores of long and skinny **Loch Ken** to New Galloway (see page 641). The loch is a popular watersports centre, with sailing, windsurfing, water-skiing, canoeing, rowing and fishing. There's also an RSPB nature reserve on the west bank and walking trails. *Loch Ken Marina*, T01644-470220, at the village of **Parton**, on the east bank, eight miles north of Castle Douglas, hires motor boats for water-skiing. It's open Easter-31 October daily 0900-1700. *Galloway Sailing Centre*, T01644-420626, also at Parton, offers watersports tuition and hire, as well as other activities such as quad biking and gorge scrambling, and basic dormitory accommodation (**F**). It's open 1 April-31 October daily 0900-1900; November-March daily till 1700. Fishing permits and boats are available at the marinas and the caravan parks. The village of Parton hosts the **Scottish Alternative Games** on the first Sunday in August. The various traditional Scottish games include the world finals of the Gird'n'Cleek competition, whatever that may be.

Sleeping There's lots of accommodation in Castle Douglas, including **C-D** *Crown Hotel*, T502031, crown@jfs.globalnet.co.uk, the pleasant **D** *Douglas Arms Hotel*, T502331, and **D** *Inperial Hotel*, T502086. All are on King St and serve decent food. There are also many good value **B&Bs** and **guesthouses**. Try **E** *Craigvar House*, 60 St Andrew St, T503515, open Mar-Oct, or **E** *Albion House*, 49 Ernespie Rd, T502360, open Feb-Oct. There are several other places to stay along Ernespie Rd. A few miles northeast of town, at Haugh of Urr, is the peaceful and attractive **E** *Corbieton Cottage*, T660413. Thirteen mile south of Castle Douglas, on the A711, is the village of **Auchencairn**, overlooking a lovely bay. There's a range of accommodation here, including the luxurious, award-winning **B** *Balcary Bay Hotel*, T640217, which has an excellent restaurant. There's also a **campsite** at *Lochside Caravan & Camping Site*, beside the loch, T502521, open Easter-late Oct, and at *Loch Ken Holiday Park*, by the village of Parton, T01644-470282, open late Mar-early Nov.

Eating Apart from the hotels listed above, the best place to eat in Castle Douglas is *Carlo's*, 211 King St, T503977, a moderately-priced Italian restaurant. Eleven miles out of town, on the A712 near Crockettford, is *Craigadam*, T/F650233, where you can enjoy good home cooking at mid-range prices. They also offer B&B (**D-E**).

Transport *McEwan's* bus Nos 501, 502 and 505 run frequently (Mon-Sat; 3 times on Sun) from Dumfries to **Kirkudbright**, stopping in Castle Douglas. Bus No 520 runs north along the east shore of Loch Ken from Castle Douglas to **New Galloway** and **Dalry**.

Kirkcudbright

Phone code: 01557
Colour map 5, grid C5
Population: 3,500

Kirkcudbright (pronounced 'kir-koo-bree') sits at the mouth of the river Dee, 10 miles southwest of Castle Douglas. With its colourful waterfront and streets of elegant Georgian villas and Victorian town houses, it is without doubt the most attractive town in the southwest and makes the ideal base from which to explore the beautiful Solway coast. The Glasgow Boys (see below) started to come here in the late 19th century and established an artists' colony, and ever since then Kirkcudbright has been a favourite haunt of artists. The town's name comes from the now-vanished Kirk of Cuthbert, which relates to St Cuthbert, who converted much of southern Scotland to Christianity.

The town's **tourist office** is beside the harbour. They will book accommodation for you during the busy summer season and sell the leaflet *Walks Around Kirkcudbright*, which details many local walks. ■ *T330494. Apr-Jun, Sept and Oct daily 1000-1700; Jul and Aug daily 0930-1800.*

You can appreciate the glories of Kirkudbright Bay as part of a one-hour **cruise** aboard the *Lady Angela*. Contact *Kirkudbright Bay Cruises* at Four Gables, Silvercraigs Road. ■ *T331838. Cruises daily Apr-Oct. Times vary so check at the tourist office. £5.50, children £3.50.*

Near the harbour is **MacLellan's Castle**, which is a castellated town house **Sights** rather than a defensive fortress. It was built in the 1570s by the then-provost, Thomas MacLellan of Bombie, using stone from the adjoining ruined monastery. The castle is relatively complete, except for the roof, and inside there's a warren of rooms to explore. ■ *T331856 (HS). Apr-Sept daily 0930-1830. £1.50, concession £1.10.*

Nearby, at 12 High Street, is the wonderful **Broughton House**, the Georgian town house which was bought in 1901 by E A Hornel, the renowned artist and member of the 'Glasgow Boys', an influential late 19th-century group of painters who established an artists' colony in Kirkcudbright (see also page 154). Many of Hornel's works are on display here, in the excellent Hornel Gallery. The artist also designed the beautiful **Japanese Garden**, which leads from the house down to the river. ■ *T330437 (NTS). House and Garden open Apr-Oct daily 1300-1730. £2.50, concession 1.70.*

Only a few minutes walk along the High Street is the early 17th-century **tolbooth**, which now houses the **Tolbooth Art Centre**. As well as featuring a display of works by Hornel and his fellow 'colonists', including local artist Jessie King, the centre also tells the story of the town's artists colony from the late 19th century to the present day, and there are temporary exhibitions of local arts and crafts and photography. ■ *T331556. All year Mon-Sat 1100-1600 and Sun 1400-1700 Jun-Sept. £1.50, concession 75p.* Another of the town's art galleries is the **Harbour Cottage Gallery**, which hosts a variety of shows throughout the year. ■ *Mar-Nov daily 1030-1230 and 1400-1700.* Both are among the venues used during the **Kirkcudbright Arts Festival**, which takes place over two weeks in late August and early September.

One of the town's most interesting sights is the **Stewatry Museum**, on St Mary Street, which boasts an extraordinarily diverse collection of exhibits reflecting the social and natural history of this part of the Solway coast, once known as the Kirkcudbright Stewatry, because it was administered by the kings' stewards during the 14th and 15th centuries. ■ *T331643. Same opening hours and admission charge as Tolbooth Art Centre.*

About seven miles southeast of Kirkcudbright is the lovely wee village of **Dundrennan**, site of the ruins of **Dundrennan Abbey**, a 12th-century Cistercian establishment standing in a beautifully bucolic setting in a secluded valley. You may not be too surprised to learn that the abbey has associations with Mary, Queen of Scots. She spent her last night on Scottish soil here. Bus No 505 between Kirkcudbright and Dumfries passes through Dundrennan, or if you're feeling energetic it's a lovely five-mile walk along quiet country roads. ■ *T500262. Apr-Sept daily 0930-1830; Oct-Mar Sat 0930-1630 and Sun 1400-1630. £1.50, concession £1.10.*

There's a wide range of accommodation available in and around town, but it's best to **Sleeping** book in advance during the summer months. The top hotel is the **C** *Selkirk Arms Hotel*, on the High St, T330402. 17 rooms. This beautifully-refurbished Georgian hotel in the old part of town has attractive rooms and also has the town's finest restaurant (see below). Another cracking place to stay is **D** *Gladstone House*, at 48 High St, T331734. 3 rooms, this wonderful, superior guesthouse has a secluded garden and also offers afternoon tea. No smoking. Fantastic value. A cheaper alternative is **E** *Gordon House Hotel*, 116 High St, T/F330670.

Southern Scotland

There are many **B&Bs**, including the very fine **D** *Baytree House*, 110 High St, T330824. A restored Georgian town house. Also worth trying is **D-E** *Mrs Black*, at 1 Gordon Pl, T330472, **E** *Mrs Caygill*, at 'The Marks', T330854, and **E** *Mrs Durok*, at 109a High St, T331279, open Mar-Sept. A few miles north of town, in the village of Twynholm, is the excellent **D-E** *Fresh Fields*, on Arden Rd, T860221, open Jan-Oct.

There are also a couple of **campsites** near the town. *Silvercraigs Caravan & Camping Site*, T502521, open Easter to late-Oct, is on an elevated site overlooking the town, about a 10 min walk from the centre, and *Seaward Caravan Park*, T870267, open Mar-Oct, is part of a new leisure complex at Brighouse Bay with a wide range of facilities including heated pool, 9-hole golf course and pony trekking.

Eating   The best place to eat is the *Selkirk Arms Hotel* (see 'Sleeping' above), whose highly-skilled chef is something of local celebrity. Food is served daily 1200-1400 and 1800-2130 (dinner expensive; lunch cheap-mid-range). Another good place to try is the *Auld Alliance Restaurant*, 5 Castle St, T330569. As the name suggests, it's a mixture of Scottish and French culinary styles, and features Solway scallops and local salmon. Open Easter-Oct Mon-Sat 1830-2130, Sun also 1200-1400 (dinner expensive; lunch cheap).

Transport   Kirkcudbright is 25 miles west of Dumfries and can be reached via the A75 or A711. It is 50 miles east of Stranraer on the A75. **Bus** Nos X75 and 500 between **Dumfries** and **Stranraer** pass through Kirkcudbright, **Castle Douglas** and **Newton Stewart**. Bus Nos 501, 502 and 505 run between Kirkcudbright and Dumfries.

Gatehouse of Fleet and around

Phone code: 01557
Colour map 5, grid C5

The quiet little town of Gatehouse of Fleet lies 10 miles west of Kirkcudbright, a mile or so north of the A75. It's an attractive place on the banks of the Water of Fleet, surrounded by forested hills. The town's **tourist office** is on the High Street. ■ *T814212. Mar, Apr and Oct, daily 1000-1630; Jun and Sept till 1700; Jul and Aug till 1800.* Nearby is the **Mill on the Fleet Museum**, housed in a restored 18th-century cotton mill complete with working water wheel. The museum traces the history of the town's cotton industry which lasted from the mid-18th century until the early 19th century. There's also a pleasant café with riverside terrace. ■ *T814099. Apr-Oct daily 1030-1730. £4, concession £2.*

There are several pleasant walks in the surrounding countryside, including to **Cardoness Castle**, about 1½ miles to the south, standing on a hill overlooking the B796 which connects Gatehouse with the main A75. The remarkably well-preserved ruin was the home of the MacCullochs and is a classic example of a 15th-century tower house. There are excellent views across Fleet Bay from the top floor. ■ *T814427 (HS). Apr-Sept daily 0930-1830; Oct-Mar Sat 0930-1630 and Sun 1400-1630. £1.80, concession £1.30.* Details of other local walks are given in a leaflet which is on sale at the tourist office.

Sleeping   Set in 500 acres of its own grounds is **A** *Cally Palace Hotel*, T814341, cally@ cphotel.demon.co.uk. A very exclusive Georgian mansion and former home of local laird James Murray who amassed a massive fortune from the cotton industry, it now offers impeccable luxury and top-class facilities. Rather more down-to-earth is the **B-C** *Murray Arms Hotel*, on Ann St, T814207. Also serves good bar meals, and **E** *The Bobbin Guest House*, at 36 High St, T814229. **B&B** accommodation is on offer at **D-E** *The Bay Horse*, T814073, at 9 Ann St. A little way out of town is the highly recommended **D-E** *High Auchterlonie Farmhouse*, T840231, open Mar-Oct.

Transport   **Bus** No 500 between **Dumfries** and **Stranraer** stops in Gatehouse of Fleet. No 431 runs between Gatehouse of Fleet and **Newton Stewart**.

The A75 runs west from Gatehouse to **Creetown**, standing on the east shore of Wigtown Bay, overlooked by the distinctive bulk of Cairnsmore of Fleet hill (2,330ft). It's lovely stretch of road as it hugs the shore, with good views across the bay. In Creetown is the **Gem Rock Museum**, which has a wide range of precious stones on display. ■ *Easter-Sept daily 0930-1800; Oct and Nov daily 1000-1600; Dec-Feb Sat and Sun 1000-1600, £2.75, T01671-820357.*

New Galloway and around

Nestled in the valley of **The Glenkens**, which runs north from Loch Ken, is New Galloway, a pleasant little village of whitewashed houses surrounded by beautiful countryside and close to the Galloway Forest Park. A few miles north of New Galloway is the village of **Dalry**, or St John's town of Dalry, to give it it's full name, sitting beside the Water of Ken and giving access to the Southern Upland Way. About five miles farther north on the A713 is the turning to **Polmaddy Settlement**, a reconstructed Galloway village dating from before the Clearances of the 18th and 19th centuries.

Phone code: 01644
Colour map 5, grid C5

To the west of New Galloway lies Galloway Forest Park, the largest forest park in Britain, covering 300 square miles of forested hills, wild and rugged moorland and numerous lochs. It's a vast and beautiful area criss-crossed by waymarked Forestry Commission trails and longer routes such as the Southern Upland Way (see page 600). It's also home to a rich variety of fauna, such as feral goats, red deer, falcons and even golden eagles. Those wishing to hike in the park should be properly equipped and buy the relevant Ordnance survey maps. The OS Outdoor Leisure Map No 32 covers Galloway Forest Park. Also useful is *The Galloway Hills: A Walker's Paradise*, by George Brittain. See also under **Newton Stewart** below.

Galloway Forest Park

The A712 runs southwest from New Galloway, cutting through the southern section of the Galloway Forest Park, to Newton Stewart. This 19 mile stretch of scenic road is known as **The Queen's Way**. Seven miles southwest of New Galloway the road skirts **Clatteringshaws Loch**, hidden amongst the pine trees, with a 14-mile footpath running round it. This path joins the Southern Upland Way which winds its way north towards the **Rhinns of Kells**, a range of hills around 2,600ft that form the park's eastern boundary. On the shores of the loch is the **Clatteringshaws Forest Wildlife Centre**, which gives an introduction to the park's flora and fauna. ■ *T420285. Easter-Oct daily 1000-1700. Free.* From the centre you can follow the lochside trail to **Bruce's Stone**, a huge boulder marking the spot where Robert the Bruce is said to have rested after yet another victory over those troublesome southern neighbours.

About a mile southwest of the Forest Wildlife Centre is the **Raiders' Road**, a 10-mile timber road and erstwhile cattle rustlers' route which runs from the A712 and follows the Water of Dee river southeast to Stroan Loch and then turns north to meet the A762 just north of Mossdale. About halfway along the trail is **the otter's pool**, in a clearing in the forest, a great place for paddling or swimming. The Raider's Road is only open between April and October and there's a toll charge. The A762 heads north along the western shore of Loch Ken back to New Galloway, making a circuit of about 20 miles, starting and ending in New Galloway.

About three miles southwest of Clatteringshaws Loch along The Queen's Way is the **Galloway Deer Range**, where you can get close up to the deer, stroke them and take photos. ■ *T420285. End of Jun to mid-Sept Tue and Thur 1100 and 1400, Sun 1430. £2.50, children £1.*

Southern Scotland

Sleeping & eating There are several hotels and B&Bs in the village. On the High Street, there's the small and comfortable **E** *Leamington Hotel*, T420327, www.smoothounds.co.uk, which does evening meals, and the **D-E** *Cross Keys Hotel*, T420494, where you can also get bar food. A few miles to the east, in the village of Balmaclellan, is **E-F** *High Park*, T420298, a farmhouse B&B. There's also a **youth hostel** at Kendoon, T01644-460680, 5 miles north of Dalry on the B7000, close to the Southern Upland Way and the A713. It's open mid-Mar to early Oct. Take the Castle Douglas-Ayr bus and ask to get off near the hostel. At the bottom of the High St is **E-F** *The Smithy*, T420269, which offers B&B accommodation and is also a café/restaurant/bookshop and **tourist office**. It provides essential information on walks in the forest park, **rents bikes** and also serves home cooked meals and tasty snacks (try their oatcakes). It's open daily Mar, Apr and Sept 1000-2000, May-Aug till 2100 and Oct till 1800.

Transport *McEwan's*, T01387-710357, bus No 520 **Castle Douglas** to **Dalry** stops in New Galloway several times daily (Mon-Sat) and once on Sun. Some of these buses continue to Ayr. There's also a twice weekly bus to Dumfries.

Newton Stewart

Phone code: 01671
Colour map 5, grid C4
Population: 3,200

The town of Newton Stewart is set on the west bank of the river Cree at the junction of the main A75 and the A714, amidst beautiful wooded countryside. It's a popular base for **hiking** in the hills of Galloway Forest Park, especially around **Glen Trool** (see below). Newton Stewart is also a major centre for **salmon and trout fishing**. The season runs from March till mid-October. Permits, guides and the hire of fishing gear can all be arranged at the *Creebridge House Hotel* (see below).

The **tourist office** is on Dashwood Square, just off the main street and opposite the bus station. They can book accommodation for you as well as provide lots of information on walking in Galloway Forest Park. ■ *T402431. Apr and Oct daily 1000-1630; May, Jun and Sept till 1700; Jul and Aug till 1800.* The **Forestry Commission**, T402121, also produces a series of leaflets on its various marked trails through the forest park. See also **Galloway Forest Park** above.

Sleeping As a major walking and fishing centre, Newton Stewart has plenty accommodation across the range. Top of the list is the fabulous **A** *Kirroughtree House*, T402141, mcmhotel@mcmhotel.demon.co.uk. 17 rooms. This grand 18th-century country mansion is set in its own grounds and offers impeccable standards of comfort and service, it's superb restaurant (expensive) has a well-deserved reputation for its gourmet Scottish cuisine. Another fine choice, and a lot cheaper, is the charming **B** *Creebridge House Hotel*, across the river in the village of Minnigaff, T402121, www.creebridge.co.uk. 19 rooms. Arranges fishing permits and offers very good food at mid-range prices.

There are also lots of **B&Bs** to choose from. Many of these are on Corsbie Rd and include **D** *Rowallen House*, T402520, **E** *Oakbank*, T402822, open Feb-Nov, and **E** *Stables Guest House*, T402157. Also good is the friendly **E-F** *Kilwarlin*, 4 Corvisel Rd, T403047, open Apr-Oct. There's a SYHA Youth Hostel, T402211, open mid-Mar to end-Oct, in the village of **Minnigaff**, which is on the other side of the river, across the bridge.

There are a couple of Forestry Commission **campsites** in **Glen Trool** (see below). There's the *Caldons Caravan & Camping Site*, on the western shore of Loch Trool, T840218, open Apr-Sept, and *Talnotry Campsite*, T402420, open Apr-Sept, a picturesque wild campsite about 7 miles from Newton Stewart, close to The Queen's Way and several excellent Forestry Commission trails. There's also the *Glen Trool Holiday Park*, T840280, open Mar-Oct, near Glen Trool village, just off the A714.

The best places to eat are *Kirroughtree House* and *Creebridge House Hotel*. The latter   **Eating**
also serves fine ales. Alternatively, try *The Brig End Pantry*, a tearoom and restaurant
overlooking the Cree bridge, T402003.

Newton Stewart is on the main A75 between **Dumfries** and **Stranraer** and there are   **Transport**
regular **buses** to and from each of these destinations, including Nos X75, 500 and the
National Express No 920. There's also a No 430 bus to Stranraer and No 431 to
Gatehouse of Fleet. Newton Stewart is the departure point for buses south to
Wigtown and **Whithorn**, No 415. There's a service (No 359) north along the A714 to
Girvan, via Bargrennan and **Glen Trool village** several times a day (Mon-Sat; less fre-
quently on Sun).

Around Newton Stewart

Newton Stewart lies at the heart of the most scenically stunning part of Galloway and makes an ideal base for exploring this most beautiful part of the country. About three miles east, near Palnure, is the **Kirroughtree Visitor Centre**,
the southern gateway to Galloway Forest Park. A series of waymarked trails
and cycle routes lead from here into the forest. ■ *T402165. Apr-Sept daily
1200-1730*. You can **hire bikes** at the centre from *Forest Park Cycles*.
■ *T404800. Mar-Oct Mon-Wed and Fri-Sun 0930-1700*.

Four miles north of town, reached via the A714, is the **Wood of Cree
Nature Reserve**, T402861, the largest ancient woodland in southern Scotland.
This RSPB reserve is home to a huge variety of birdlife, including pied
flycatchers, redstarts and wood warblers. There are nature trails running for
two miles through the forest in the Cree Valley.

The prime attraction around Newton Stewart is Glen Trool, one of the most   **Glen Trool**
accessible and loveliest parts of Galloway Forest Park. Ten miles north of Newton Stewart, at **Bargrennan**, on the A714, a narrow road winds its way for five
miles past Glen Trool village to **Loch Trool**, hemmed in by the wooded slopes
of the glen. Halfway up the loch is **Bruce's Stone**, which marks the spot where
Robert the Bruce's guerrilla band ambushed the pursuing English force in
1307, after they had routed the main army at Solway Moss.

There are a number of excellent **hiking trails** which start out from here,
including the one to the summit of **Merrick** (2,766ft), the highest peak in
southern Scotland. It's a tough climb of about four hours, but fairly straightforward and well worth the effort. There are also numerous Forestry Commission trails for the less fit/experienced/adventurous. Part of the **Southern
Upland Way** (see page 600) runs through Glen Trool and along the southern
shores of Loch Trool, then continues east towards Clatteringshaws Loch (see
page 641). On the road to Loch Trool, about a mile from the village, is the **Glen
Trool Visitor Centre**. ■ *T840302. Apr-Oct daily 1030-1730*.

The Machars

South of the A75 is the peninsula of fertile rolling farmland known as the
Machars. It's a somewhat neglected corner of the southwest but has strong
early Christian associations and there are many important sites. The
Machars is served by *Stagecoach Western* (T01776-704484) **bus** No 415
which runs regularly between **Newton Stewart** and **Isle of Whithorn**, via
Whithorn and Wigtown.

Wigtown
Phone code: 01988
Colour map 5, grid C4

The disconsolate little town of Wigotwn sits on the northwesterly shore of Wigtown Bay and is notable for its large number of bookshops. If you need to buy a book in the southwest, then this is the place to do it. The town overlooks the salt marshes and sands of Wigtown Bay which attract thousands of birds, including greylag and pinkfoot geese, ducks and waders in the winter. In 1685 two female Covenanters – Scottish Presbyterians persecuted by Charles II – were drowned at the stake by the rising tide on Wigtown Sands. The **Martyr's Stake** marks the site of their death. About three miles northwest is **Torhouse Stone Circle**, a Bronze Age site of 19 standing stones forming a ring 60ft across.

Sleeping There are a couple of **B&Bs** in town: **E-F** *Glaisnock House*, 20 South Main St, T/F402249, and **E-F** *Craigenlee*, 8 Bank St, T402498.

Whithorn
Phone code: 01988
Colour map 5, grid C4/5

Eleven miles south from Wigtown is Whithorn, a remote and forlorn village but one which occupies an important place in Scotland's history. It was here, in the late fourth century, that **St Ninian** established a mission and built the first Christian church north of Hadrian's Wall. The tiny church, which he called **Candida Casa** (the White House), has not survived but after Ninian's death a priory was built to house his tomb. This became a famous seat of learning and an important place of pilgrimage for penitents from England and Ireland, as well as from Scotland.

The ruins of the 12th-century priory are being excavated and can be visited as part of the **Whithorn Visitor Centre and Dig**, on George Street. In the visitor centre there are exhibitions and an audio-visual display. You can visit the excavations going on behind the visitor centre but there's not much to see and you won't be able to make much sense of the ruins without the help of the complimentary guiding service. The adjacent **Priory Museum** contains some important interesting archaeological finds and early Christian sculpture including the Latinus Stone, which dates from 450 AD and is the earliest Christian memorial in Scotland. ■ *T500508. Apr-Oct daily 1030-1700. £2.70, concession £1.50.*

The 25-mile **Pilgrim's Way** is a route developed by the Whithorn Pilgrimage Trust which follows quiet country lanes and tracks from the abbey at **Glenluce** (see below) southwards to Whithorn. The route is waymarked with Celtic cross symbols. For more details see *A Way to Whithorn: A Guide to the Whithorn Pilgrims Way*, by Andrew Patterson (St Andrews Press).

Isle of Whithorn
Phone code: 01988
Colour map 5, grid C5

Four miles away is the misnamed Isle of Whithorn, which isn't an island at all but an atmospheric old fishing village built around a natural harbour. The entire community was devastated early in the new millennium when one its trawlers, the *Solway Harvester*, went down off the Isle of Man, with the loss of all seven crew members. The village is the site of the ruined 13th-century **St Ninian's Chapel**, built for pilgrims who landed here from England and Ireland. Along the coast, to the west of the village, is **St Ninian's Cave**, said to have been used by the saint as a private place of prayer. It is reached via a footpath off the A747 before entering the Isle of Whithorn.

Sleeping There are a couple of places to stay in the village. Try the **D-E** *Steam Packet Inn*, T500354, a popular fishermen's pub with rooms on the quayside which serves good, cheap bar meals. There's also B&B at **F** *Dunbar House*, on Tonderghie Rd, T500336. About 11 miles west of Whithorn, near the village **Port William**, is the sumptuous **B** *Corsemalzie House Hotel*, T860254, a highly-rated hotel and restaurant.

From Whithorn the A747 heads west to meet the coast and then runs north-west along the east shore of **Luce Bay** for 15 miles till it meets the A75 at the pretty little village of Glenluce. Two miles north of the village, signposted off the A75, is **Glenluce Abbey**, founded in 1192 by Roland, Earl of Galloway for the Cistercian order. The remains, set in beautiful and peaceful valley, include a handsome early 16th-century Chapter House with a vaulted ceiling noted for its excellent acoustics. The abbey was visited by Robert the Bruce, James IV and, you guessed it, Mary, Queen of Scots. It was also the home of the 13th-century wizard and alchemist, **Michael Scott**, who appears in Dante's *Inferno* and who, according to legend, cast a spell on King Arthur and his knights and sent them to sleep under the Eildon Hills overlooking Melrose (see page 613). Buses 430 and 500 between Newton Stewart and Stranraer stop in Glenluce village and you can walk from there.

Glenluce
Colour map 5, grid C4

Stranraer

Stranraer wins no prizes for beauty or tourist appeal but as Scotland's main ferry port for Northern Ireland it's an important town which sees a lot of through traffic. It sits on the shores of sheltered Loch Ryan on the **Rhinns of Galloway**, a windswept peninsula shaped like the head of pick-axe at the end of the Solway coast.

Phone code: 01776
Colour map 5, grid C3
Population: 10,700

Transport links are all conveniently located close to each other. The **train station** is on the ferry pier, close to the Stena Line **ferry terminal** (T0990-707070), from where car and passenger ferries leave for Larne and Belfast. A few minutes' walk south is the **bus station** and further round the bay, on West Pier, is the Seacat **catamaran terminal** (T08705-523523) from where fast car and passenger catamarans depart for Belfast. P&O ferries to Larne (T0990-980666) leave from **Cairnryan**, 5 miles north of Stranraer on the A77. Bus No 303 runs to Cairnryan from Stranraer 4 times daily Mon-Sat. For details on services to Northern Ireland, see 'Essentials', page 32. For information on buses and trains, see 'Transport' below.

Ins & outs

The **tourist office** is at 28 Harbour Street. ■ *T702595. Apr-Jun, Oct and Nov Mon-Sat 0930-1730, Sun 1000-1600; Jul-Sept daily 0930-1800; Dec-Mar Mon-Sat 1000-1600.* The main attraction is the medieval tower which is all that remains of the 16th-century **Castle of St John**, one of the main headquarters of Graham of Claverhouse, the fanatical persecutor of the Protestant Covenanters in the late 17th century. Many of them died in the castle dungeons. It was later used as a prison in the 19th century. Inside an exhibition

Sights

Stranraer

Southern Scotland

traces the castle's history. ■ *T705544. Apr-Sept Mon-Sat 1000-1300 and 1400-1700. £1.20, concession 60p.*

Also worth a peek is the **Stranraer Museum** on George Street, which features displays on local history and has a section devoted to the life of Arctic explorer Sir John Ross (1777-1856), whose expeditions to find the Northwest Passage to the Pacific lead to the discovery, in 1831, of the North Magnetic Pole. His house, called North West Castle, is now a hotel (see below). ■ *T705088. Mon-Sat 1000-1700. Free.*

Three miles east of Stranraer are **Castle Kennedy Gardens**, famous for their riotous rhododendrons and magnificent monkey puzzle trees. The 75 acres of landscaped gardens are set on a peninsula between two lochs and two castles (Castle Kennedy and Lochinch Castle). ■ *T702024. Apr-Sept daily 1000-1700. £3, concession £2.*

Loch Ryan, the huge inlet which protects Stranraer from the stormy Irish Sea, is a haven for a variety of birdlife. The mudflats of **Wig Bay**, on the western shore, offer good opportunities for birdwatching and is also a popular **sailing centre**, T703535.

Sleeping As you'd expect in a major ferry port, there's no shortage of places to stay. The most unusual choice has to be the **L** *Corsewall Lighthouse Hotel*, 11 miles northwest of town at Corsewall Point, T853220, Jim-Neilson@msn.com. 6 rooms. This cosy hotel is housed in a working lighthouse, set in 20 acres of its own grounds on the wild and windy clifftops, a surreal experience, the owners can arrange transport from Stranraer. The most luxurious choice is the superb **B** *North West Castle Hotel*, T704413, NorthWestCastle@mcmhotel.demon.co.uk. 73 rooms. The former home of Sir John Ross (see 'Sights' above) also offers full leisure facilities and excellent cuisine.

There are lots of cheaper **B&Bs** and **guesthouses** to choose from, including the centrally-located **E** *Windyridge Villa*, 5 Royal Cres, T889900, and **E** *Fernlea*, Lewis St, T703037. Also good is **E** *Glen Otter*, Leswalt Rd, T703199. Close to Castle Kennedy is the lovely **D-E** *Chlenry Farmhouse*, T705316. There's also **hostel** accommodation at Sally's Hoose, Balyet Farm, Cairnryan Rd, T703395. It only has 6 beds but is open all year.

There's a **campsite** at *Aird Donald Caravan Park*, T702025, open all year, 1 mile from town, and *Wig Bay Holiday Park*, T853233, 4 miles to the north, open Mar-Oct.

Eating The best place to eat is the expensive *North West Castle Hotel* (see above). A bit cheaper is *L'Aperitif*, on London Rd, T702991. It serves good Italian food Mon-Sat 1200-1400 and 1730-2100. There's also *Bar Pazzerello*, 57 George St, T706585. A café-bar which doubles as a nightclub. Otherwise, you can try the hotel bar meals or the numerous fast food outlets.

Transport For details on **ferry** services to Northern Ireland, see 'Ins and outs' above. **Bus** *National Express* No 920 runs between **London** and **Belfast** via Stranraer 3 times daily. *Stagecoach Western* has an hourly service to **Glasgow** (3 hrs; £7 single). There are regular buses to **Newton Stewart**, **Kirkcudbright** and **Dumfries** and other towns along the A75. There are also regular daily buses to **Ayr** (2 hrs), and daily buses to **Portpatrick** (25 mins), **Port Logan** (35 mins) and **Drummore** (45 mins). **Train** There are several trains daily to **Belfast** via Larne. There's also a daily service to and from **Glasgow** (2 hrs; £19.50) and **Ayr** (1 hr 20 mins). For all rail enquiries call T0345-484950.

Portpatrick

Nine miles southwest of Stranraer on the beautiful and rugged west coast of the Rhinns is the picturesque old port of Portpatrick. Until the mid-19th century it was the main departure point for Northern Ireland but is now peaceful little holiday resort and a good base from which to explore the southern part of the peninsula. Portpatrick is also the starting point for the **Southern Upland Way**, the 212-mile coast-to-coast route which ends at Cockburnspath on the Berwickshire coast (see page 600). The whole route may be beyond most mortals, but you can walk the first section to Stranraer (nine miles), or continue for a further four miles to Castle Kennedy Gardens and return to Portpatrick by bus, via Stranraer. You can arrange **sea fishing trips** from Portpatrick. These cost £8 for a half day, T810468.

Population: 600
Phone code: 01776
Colour map 5, grid C3

Sleeping

By far the best place to stay in this area is the very wonderful **L** *Knockinaam Lodge Hotel*, T810471, which offers great sea views, exquisite and unmatched cuisine (expensive) and impeccable service. It is rated as one of the best hotels in the south of Scotland. Those without the means to enjoy such splendour can try the **B** *Fernhill Hotel*, T810220, which overlooks the village. Its reputation has a fine reputation (lunch cheap to mid-range; dinner mid-range).

There's also plenty of cheaper accommodation, such as: **E** *Carlton Guest House*, South Cres, T810253; **E** *The Knowe*, North Cres, T810441; **E-F** *Ard Choille Guest House*, 1 Blair Terr, T810313; and nearby **E-F** *Albony Guest House*, 4 Blair Terr, T810568. There are a few **campsites** on the hill above the village: *Galloway Point Holiday Park*, T/F810562, open Easter-Oct; *Castle Bay Caravan Park*, T810462, open Mar-Oct, and *Sunnymede Caravan Park*, T/F810293, open Mar-Oct. All have good facilities and enjoy good views.

Eating

The best places to eat are the *Knockinaam Lodge* and *Ferhill Hotels*. Cheaper options include the *Mount Stewart Hotel* and the *Harbour House Hotel*, both on the seafront and both of which serve decent bar meals.

Transport

Stagecoach Western, T01387-253496, **bus** No 367 runs regularly between Portpatrick and **Stranraer**.

South of Portpatrick

From Portpatrick the road runs south to the Mull of Galloway through lush, green farmland which receive high average rainfall. The Rhinns are also warmed by the Gulf Stream which gives the peninsula the mildest climate in Scotland and means it's almost frost-free. This is beautifully-demonstrated at **Logan Botanic Garden**, an outpost of Edinburgh's Royal Botanic Garden, about a mile north of the tiny village of **Port Logan**. The garden boasts a vast array of exotic, subtropical flora from the southern hemisphere, including tree ferns and cabbage palms. ■ *T860231. Mar-Oct daily 0930-1800, £3, concession £2.50.*

Bus No 407 from Stranraer passes through Port Logan on its way to **Drummore**, a fishing village on the east coast of the Rhinns. Five miles further south is the **Mull of Galloway**, a dramatic, storm-lashed headland and Scotland's most southerly point, only 25 miles from Ireland and the Isle of Man. The narrow isthmus is an **RSPB nature reserve** and the home of thousands of seabirds such as guillemots, razorbills and puffins. There's a small information centre. ■ *T01671-402861. Late May-Aug.*

Southern Scotland

Ayrshire

The region of Ayrshire is best known as the birthplace of Robert Burns, Scotland's great poet, loved and revered the world over. The vast majority of visitors come here to visit the many sights associated with the great bard, but the Ayrshire coast is also famed for its excellent golf courses, such as Turnberry, Troon and Prestwick. There are a few other reasons for visiting Ayrshire, most notably Culzean Castle to the south of Ayr, one of Scotland's top tourist attractions. One of the region's main attractions is the beautiful Isle of Arran, but it is covered elsewhere in the Argyll chapter (see page 224).

The most attractive part of Ayrshire is the south, from the main town, Ayr, south to Girvan. North of Ayr is a series of low-key resorts interspersed with ports and industrialized towns stretching to the mouth of the Clyde.

Ins and outs

Getting around South Ayrshire is served by a reasonable bus service along the coast and there's also a train line from Stranraer to Ayr, via Girvan and Maybole. The busy A77 runs north from Stranraer along the coast to Turnberry, where it turns inland to Maybole and bypasses Ayr, before heading northeast towards Glasgow. Near Prestwick it meets the A78 which runs north along the Firth of Clyde coast before turning east towards Glasgow.

Information Ayrshire's tourist services are run by the **Ayrshire and Arran Tourist Board**, whose head office is in Ayr, T01292-262555, ayr@ayrshire-arran.com, www.ayrshire-arran.com. There are also regional offices in Irvine, Kilmarnock, Largs, Girvan, Troon and Millport.

South Ayrshire

Girvan & Ailsa Craig
Phone code: 01465
Colour map 5, grid B4

Between Stranraer and Ayr is the seaside resort of Girvan, where there's a seasonal **tourist office** on Bridge Street, near the harbour, they have a full list of accommodation. ■ *T714950. Easter-May Mon-Fri 1100-1300 and 1400-1700, Sat and Sun 1100-1700; Jun daily 1100-1800; Jul and Aug daily 1000-1900; Sept daily 1100-1700; first half of Oct daily 1200-1600.*

Ten miles west of Girvan is Ailsa Craig, a huge uninhabited lump of granite, 1,114 feet high and two miles in circumference, which resembles a giant floating muffin. It's now a **bird sanctuary** and home to thousands of gannets. It earned the nickname, '**Paddy's Milestone**' as it's halfway between Belfast and Glasgow.

Sleeping **D-E** *Glendrissaig Guest House*, on Newton Stewart Road, T714631, open Apr-Oct, which offers vegetarian meals. **E** *St Oswalds*, 5 Golf Course Road, T713786. Or if you want to play the famous **Turnberry Championship Golf Course**, you can stay at the luxurious **L** *Turnberry Hotel*, T01655-331000, 5miles north of Girvan.

Tours Boats leave from Girvan harbour for the trip to Ailsa Craig at least once a day between May and September. Several companies sail around the rock but only the *MV Glorious* is allowed to land (weather permitting). It's necessary to book at least a week in advance, T713219. A 4 hr trip costs £9 per person, a 6 hr trip costs £10 per person. There are also trips to Ailsa Craig from Troon, on board the paddle steamer *Waverley* (see also under Ayr below).

Transport There are several daily **trains** to and from **Ayr** and **Stranraer**. There's an hourly **bus** service (No X77) between **Glasgow** and **Stranraer** which passes through Girvan.

Twelve mile south of Ayr is Culzean (pronounced 'cullane'), one of Scotland's great castles and the National Trust for Scotland's most visited property. It is one of Ayrshire's few non-Burnsian attractions and well worth a detour of you're in the vicinity. Culzean enjoys a magnificent setting, perched high on a clifftop above a rocky shore and surrounded by 563 acres of country park. The scale of the house and the country park is overwhelming and you should allow more than a few hours to do it justice.

Culzean was designed by Robert Adam and built in 1772-90 for David Kennedy, 10th Earl of Cassilis, as a replacement for the original 15th-century castle. The grand exterior gives no hint of the almost overweening opulence inside. Adam's customary meticulous attention to detail and love of Classical embellishment reaches its zenith here. The magnificent oval staircase is regarded as one of his greatest achievements and the perfect symmetry circular saloon is a deliberate counter-balance to the seascapes on view from the windows. The castle contains a collection of paintings and 18th-century furniture and an armoury and there's an Eisenhower Room, which celebrates the former US President's military career and his association with Culzean. He stayed several times as a guest of the Kennedys, and the top floor was given to him by the erstwhile owners.

The vast **country park** is also well worth exploring and was Scotland's first, created in 1969. It features a network of woodland paths, clifftop trails and the shoreline below, formal gardens, the ice house, pagoda and the beautiful Swan Pond. The best place to start is the **visitor centre** housed in the Home Farm buildings, with a café, shop and exhibits. Here you can pick up free leaflets and maps to help you find your way around, or you can take a guided tour. ■ *T01655-760274. Castle and visitor centre open Easter-Oct daily 1030-1730. Country Park open all year daily 0930-sunset. Castle and park £7, concession £5; park only £3.50, concession £2.50. Guided tours of castle daily at 1530, also at 1100 in Jul and Aug; tours of grounds Apr-Jun daily at 1430, and Jul-Sept daily at 1100 and 1430.* **Accommodation** is available (**L**) in six double bedrooms on the top floor. There's also a top-class, and very expensive, **restaurant** for residents.

Culzean Castle & Country Park
Colour map 5, grid B4

A few miles inland from Culzean, on the A77, is the tiny village of Kirkoswald, is the refurbished thatched cottage which was the home of John Davidson, village souter (shoemaker), who was the original Souter Johnnie of Robert Burns' *Tam o' Shanter*. Life-sized stone figures of the souter, Tam himself, the innkeeper and his wife are in the restored ale-house in the garden, and there are Burns relics in the cottage. ■ *T760603. Easter to early Oct daily 1130-1700; also weekends in Oct 1130-1700. £2, comncession £1.30. There's hourly bus service between Ayr and Girvan which stops in Kirkoswald.*

Kirkoswald & Crossraguel Abbey
Phone code: 01655
Colour map 5, grid B4

Two miles south of **Maybole** on the A77 are the ruins of **Crossraguel Abbey**, a Clunaic establishment founded in the 13th century by the Earl of Carrick much rebuilt during the next three centuries. The remarkably complete remains include the church, cloister, chapter house and much of the domestic premises. ■ *T883113. Apr-Sept daily 0930-1830. £1.80, concession £1.30.* About five miles northwest of Maybole, on the A719 coastal road to Ayr, you'll pass a curious local phenomenon known as the **Electric Brae**. Because of an optical illusion, it appears that you're travelling uphill rather than down.

Sleeping There are a few places to stay in and around Maybole. On the B7023 heading west of town towards Culzean is **E** *Homelea*, T882736. There are also a couple of **campsites**. The *Culzean Bay Holiday Park*, T01292-500444, open Mar-Oct, is 8 miles south of Ayr on the A719 coast road, and the *Walled Garden Camping & Caravan Park*, T740323, open Apr-Oct, is at Kilkerran Estate, 7 miles south of Maybole, off the B741.

Southern Scotland

Ayr

Phone code: 01292
Colour map 5, grid B4
Population: 50,000

The largest town in southwest Scotland and looking west out onto the Firth of Clyde and Arran, Ayr has been a popular seaside resort since Victorian times. The town's 2½ miles of sandy beach, together with Scotland's most important racecourse, continue to attract hordes of visitors from nearby Glasgow. Ayr is best known for its many connections with Scotland's national poet, **Robert Burns**, who was born in the neighbouring village of **Alloway** and who famously praised the town for its 'honest men and bonnie lasses'. For information on Burns' life and work, see **Scottish Writers** (page 675).

Getting around The **bus station** is in the centre of town, at the foot of Sandgate, close to the post office. The **train station** is a 10 min walk east, on Station Rd. There are frequent buses and trains to and from Glasgow, Dumfries and Stranraer. For a **taxi**, call *Central Taxis*, T267655.

Sights The **tourist office** is close to the train station, on Burns Statue Square. ■ *T288688, ayr@ayrshire-arran.com, www.ayrshire-arran.com. Jun and Sept to early Oct Mon-Sat 0915-1800, Sun 1000-1800; Jul and Aug Mon-Sat 0915-1900, Sun 1000-1900; Oct-May Mon-Sat 0915-1700.*

Most of Ayr's important sights are contained within the **Burns National Heritage Park** in Alloway (see below) but there are a few places of interest dotted around the cramped streets of Ayr's **old town**, to the south of the river Ayr. To the west of Sandgate, off Bruce Terrace, is **St John's Tower**, the only surviving part of the 12th-century Church of St John the Baptist. It was here, in 1315, that Robert the Bruce called a meeting of the Scots parliament to decide his successor to the throne. In 1652, Cromwell's army incorporated the church into a fort which they built. The key to the tower is available from the South Ayrshire Council's Parks & Environment department, on Burns Statue Square (£2 deposit required).

As compensation for taking over the Church of St John, in 1654 Cromwell donated money to build the **Auld Kirk**, at the end of Kirk Port, a narrow lane leading off the High Street. The church retains its original canopied pulpit and in the lych gate you can see iron grave-covers used to protect corpses from the body snatchers who sold them to medical schools. A short distance away is the **Auld Brig**, the 13th-century bridge immortalized by Burns in his poem *Twa Brigs*. He described it as "a poor, narrow footpath of a street", but indirectly ensured its survival. It was restored in 1907 and now carries pedestrians. Its near neighbour, the New Bridge, was built in 1788 and rebuilt in 1878. At number 230 High Street is the **Tam o' Shanter Inn**, an ancient thatched pub where the eponymous hero enjoyed an evening of alcoholic excess before mounting his trusty mare, Meg, and setting off on his near-disastrous journey home to Kirkoswald. The pub is now a shrine to the bard and its walls are covered with many of his greatest quotes. A few yards away on the High Street is the **Wallace Tower**, which commemorates the Scottish patriot, William Wallace, who was imprisoned in the town, in 1297, for setting fire to a barn with 500 English soldiers inside.

At the top of the High Street, where it meets Sandgate, is the impressive spire of the **Town Buildings** and opposite is the **Loudon Hall**, which dates from 1534. Turn left before you reach New Bridge and head along South Harbour Street to reach the **harbour**, where you can arrange a **cruise** on board the *Waverley*, the world's last ocean-going paddle steamer. They leave on Tuesday and Wednesday only from early July to the end of August. For bookings or further information, T0141-2218152, or check at the tourist office. Also ask at the tourist office for details of other boat trips from Ayr harbour.

The **beach** lies to the southwest of the town centre, overlooked by the long Esplanande and backed by a grid-iron of streets lined with elegant Victorian villas. This where you'll find most of the guesthouses, particularly around Wellington Square.

The heart of Burns country is Alloway, formerly a separate village a few miles **Alloway** south of Ayr, but now swallowed by its spreading suburbs. All the Burns sights are within easy walking distance of each other and are all part of the **Burns National Heritage Park**. For details of transport to Alloway, see below under **Transport**.

The best place to start is the **Burns Cottage and Museum**, the low, thatched whitewashed 'auld clay biggin' where the poet was born, on 25 January, 1759, and spent the first seven years of his life. The museum contains original manuscripts, books, paintings and other memorabilia, plus a brief history of his life. ■ *T441215. Apr-Oct daily 0900-1800; Nov-Mar Mon-Sat 1000-1600, Sun 1200-1600. £2.50, concession £1.25, ticket also allows entry to the Burns Monument and Gardens; a combined ticket costing £4.25 (£2) includes the Tam o' Shanter Experience.*

Nearby is the **Tam o' Shanter Experience**, a modern building housing two audio-visual theatres, one giving an introduction to Burns' life and the other telling the story of *Tam o' Shanter*, a funny and frightening poem and a cautionary tale of the consequences of alcoholic over-indulgence. There's also a well-stocked gift shop and a restaurant. ■ *T443700. Apr-Oct daily 0900-1800; Nov-Mar daily 0900-1700. £2.80 for each viewing, or included on combined ticket with Burns Cottage and Museum (see above).*

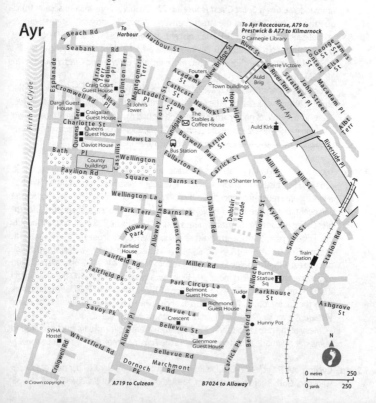

Ayr

Across the road are the ruins of **Alloway Kirk**, where Robert Burns' father, William, is buried. This was the setting for the famous scene in *Tam o' Shanter* when Tam stumbles across a wild orgy of witches, warlocks and demons. When he gets carried away watching one particularly winsome witch, Nannie, and screams out his encouragement, the ghouls give chase and Tam and his mare, Meg, narrowly escape, minus Meg's tail, across the **Brig o' Doon**, the 13th-century humpbacked bridge which still stands nearby, spanning the river Doon. Overlooking the bridge is the ostentatious **Burns Monument**, a Neo-classical temple which houses another museum. There are statues of various Burns characters in the gardens. ■ *Same opening hours as the Burns Cottage and Museum.*

Sleeping There's plenty of accommodation but during the busy high season and important race meetings it's a good idea to book in advance. No arguments about the best hotel in town, it's the **L** *Fairfield House Hotel*, 12 Fairfield Rd, T267461, res@ fairfield.house.demon.co.uk. 45 rooms. Near the seafront, luxury facilities and excellent restaurant and conservatory brasserie. In Alloway is the **B-C** *Northpark House Hotel*, T445572. 5 rooms. This comfortable country mansion is convenient for the Burns Trail and has a good restaurant. Another high-class hotel is the **B-C** *Savoy Park Hotel*, 16 Racecourse Rd, T266112, savoy@ayrcoll.ac.uk, www.savoypark.com.

There are numerous comfortable **guesthouses** and B&Bs in the Victorian new town, in the streets and squares between Alloway Pl and the Esplanade. On Queens Terr are: **E** *Craigallan Guest House* at No 8, T264998, wgham@easynet.co.uk; **E-F** *Dargil Guest House* at No 7, T261955; **E** *Daviot House* at No 12, T269678; and **E** *Queens Guest House* at No 10, T265618. Further north, on Eglinton Terr is the recommended **E** *Craig Court Guest House*, No 22, T261028. There are also several small guesthouses and B&Bs on the streets between Alloway Pl and Burns Statue Square. On Bellevue Crescent are **D-E** *The Crescent*, at No 26, T287329, and **E-D** *Glenmore Guest House* at No 35, T269830. On Park Circus are **E** *Belmont Guest House* at No 15, T265588, belmontguesthouse@bt.internet.com, and **E** *Richmond Guest House* at No 38, T265153.

Cheaper accommodation is available at the *SYHA Youth Hostel*, at 5 Craigweil Rd, about a 20-min walk south of the town centre, off Alloway Pl, T262322, open Mar-Dec. There are a couple of good **campsites** in and around Ayr. *Craigie Gardens Caravan Club Site*, is only a 10-min walk from the centre, T264909, open all year, and *Heads of Ayr Caravan Park*, 5 miles south of town on the A719 to Culzean, T442269, open Mar-Nov.

Eating There are several eating places which stand out. Best of all is *Fouters*, 2a Academy St, T261391. This bistro/restaurant in a converted bank basement opposite the town hall offers superb French-influenced cuisine using the very best of local fish, seafood, game and beef. Lunch cheap; dinner expensive. Open Tue-Sat. Also recommended is *The Stables Coffee House & Restaurant*, Queens Court, 41 Sandgate, T283704. A small, friendly place offering traditional Scottish dishes and excellent cakes, scones and ice cream, all at cheap prices. No smoking. Open daily till 1700 (closed Sun during winter). Another fine place to eat is the *Tudor Restaurant*, 8 Beresford Terr, T261404. More of a café really and serves great home cooked meals and high teas. Open daily 0900-2000 (Jul and Aug till 2100). Another great caff is the *Hunny Pot*, at 37 Beresford Terr, T263239, a short walk from the tourist office. For standard French-style fare try the Ayr branch of *Pierre Victoire*, 4 River St, T282087, which does a good value set lunch.

Many of the pubs also serve cheap lunches. There are many bars clustered around Burns statue Square, and of course there's the *Tam o' Shanter Inn* (see 'Sights' above).

Sport **Cycling** *AMG Cycles*, 55 Dalblair Rd, T287580. Rents bikes for £10 per day, or £17 per weekend. **Golf** There's an excellent 18-hole public course at *Belleisle Park*, T441258.

Horse racing Ayr Racecourse is at 2 Whitletts Rd, T264179, www.ayr-racecourse.co.uk. It's the premier racecourse in Scotland and holds 25 days of racing throughout the year, including the Scottish Grand National in mid-Apr. **Horse riding** Ayrshire Equestrian Centre, South Mains, Corton Rd, T266267. Cross country course, hacks and lessons from £10 per hr.

To get to and from **Alloway**, take a No 1 bus (marked 'Tam o' Shanter') from Burns **Transport** Statue Square. They leave every 30 mins. There's an open-topped bus, 'The Burns Country Tour', which leaves Ayr bus station hourly 1000-1700 from Jun-Sept. It makes a round trip to Alloway and back along the coast. Tickets cost £3 per person and you can get on and off as you please.

Western Buses, T613500, runs hourly **buses** to and from **Glasgow** (1 hr; £3), **Culzean Castle** (30 mins) and **Largs** (1 hr 10 mins). There are buses every 30 mins to **Girvan** and regular buses to **Stranraer** (2 hrs). There are also 2 buses daily (Mon-Sat; 1 hr 20 mins) to **New Galloway** and **Castle Douglas** (2 hrs).

There are **trains** every 30 mins to and from Glasgow Central (50 mins; £4.80), and several daily to **Stranraer** (1 hr 15 mins; £13.70). For all rail enquiries, call T0345-484950.

Communications Internet: there's a cybercafé at Carnegie Library, 12 Main St, T286385, **Directory** jcastle@lib.south.ayrshire.gov.uk.

North and East Ayrshire

Immediately north of Ayr is **Prestwick**, home of another fine Ayrshire golf course and which also has an **international airport**, with flights from Paris, Dublin, Belfast and London Stansted (see 'Getting there; on page 27). North of Prestwick, the A77 turns northeast towards Glasgow, bypassing the distinctly uninspiring industrial town of **Kilmarnock**, best known as the home of Johnnie Walker whisky. From Kilmarnock the A76 heads southeast to Dumfries, passing through **Mauchline**, where Robert Burns married Jean Armour and where their cottage is now another Burns Museum. The A78 meanwhile runs northwards, passing the quiet, staid resort of **Troon**, famous amongst the golfing fraternity for its excellent **golf course**, T01292-311555.

The next town heading north is Irvine, once one of Glasgow's main trading **Irvine** ports and now redeveloped as a new town. Down at the old harbour, on *Phone code: 01294* Gottries Road, is the **Scottish Maritime Museum**, a genuinely interesting *Colour map 5, grid B4* exhibition of various ships which you can board. Amongst the assorted vessels moored at the museum docks is a Clyde 'puffer', an old tug and the *Carrick*, the world's oldest clipper (still undergoing restoration). There's also a reconstructed shipyard worker's tenement flat, a coffee shop and souvenir shop, and regular guided tours. ■ *T278283. Apr-Oct daily 1000-1700. £2, concession £1.* Nearby is the **Magnum Leisure Centre**, the largest in Scotland, with a pool, cinemas, ice rinks and much more besides. ■ *Daily 0900-2200.*

Between Irvine and Kilmarnock on the A759 is **Dundonald Castle**. This was the first home of the Stuart kings, built in 1371 by Robert II and much restored since. ■ *T01563-851489 (HS). Apr-Sept daily 1000-1700. £1.50, concession 75p.*

Irvine's **tourist office** is on New Street near the **train station** and the huge shopping centre. They can arrange **accommodation** in the unlikely event that you'll want to stay. ■ *T313886. Jul and Aug Mon-Sat 0900-1800, Sun 1200-1700; Sept-Jun Mon-Sat 0900-1700, Sun 1200-1700.*

Sleeping E *Harbourside Hotel*, 86 Montgomery Street, T275515, is at the harbourside and handy for transport and pubs and restaurants.

Transport There are regular **trains** to Glasgow and Ayr. *Stagecoach* **buses**, T607007, leave from Irvine Cross on the High Street to Ayr, Glasgow, Kilmarnock and Largs. 7 miles north of Irvine is the dismal town of **Ardrossan**, from where *Caledonian MacBrayne*, T0990-650000, **ferries** depart for Brodick on the Isle of **Arran**. For details of ferry sailings see page 224). **Trains** leave **Glasgow Central** (one hr; £4.10) 5 times daily (4 on Sun) during the high season (Apr-Oct) to connect with the ferries.

Largs

Phone code: 01475
Colour map 5, grid A4
Population: 10,000

The most attractive town on the North Ayrshire coast is the resort of Largs, backed by high wooded hills and facing the island of **Great Cumbrae**, a few miles offshore and reached by ferry from Largs. The town is not only a traditional family holiday centre, but its extensive **marina** is popular with yachties and the **Scottish National Sports Centre** at Inverclyde, T674666, hosts numerous national indoor competitions.

Getting around The **bus** and **train stations** are next to each other on Main St, a short walk from the **ferry pier**. For details of ferry sailings, see under Great Cumbrae below.

Sights The **tourist office**, T673765, is on the seafront promenade next to the ferry pier. ■ *Easter-Jun Mon-Sat 0915-1700, Sun 1000-1700; Jul and Aug till 1800; Sept and Oct Mon-Sat 0915-1700, Sun 1100-1600; Oct-Easter Mon-Fri 0915-1700, Sat 0915-1300 and 1400-1700.*

The award-winning **Vikingar!**, at the north end of the promenade is a multi-media exhibition which fully describes the Viking influence in Scotland, which ended with the Battle of Largs in 1263 (see below). Other facilities include a theatre and cinema, swimming pool, café, bar and gift shop. ■ *T689777, www.vikingar.co.uk. Daily 1030-1800. £3.50, children £2.50.* The Battle of Largs is commemorated by the **Pencil Monument**, about a mile south of town along the shoreline footpath. The defeat of the Vikings by the Scots effectively marked the end of Norse sovereignty over the mainland and Western Isles.

Hidden away in Largs Old Kirk on Bellman's Close, just off the High Street, is **Skelmorlie Aisle**, an absolute gem of Renaissance architecture unique in Scotland. Built in 1636 as a mausoleum for Sir Robert Montgomerie of Skelmorlie and his wife, the burial vault sits within an aisle with a richly-painted timber barrel-vaulted roof. The decoration features the family coat of arms, biblical scenes and representations of the four seasons. The tomb was decorated by Scottish masons following Italian patterns and also includes the coat of arms. ■ *Jun-Aug Mon-Fri 1400-1700, keys from museum next door. Free.*

A few miles south of Largs on the A78 is **Kelburn Castle and Country Centre**, the 13th-century home of the Earls of Glasgow, which boasts a vast range of activities designed for kids. As well as the castle itself, there's a walled garden, secret forest, horse riding, adventure playground, Marine assault course and a woodland glen with a network of trails leading past waterfalls. ■ *T568685, www.kelburncountrycentre.com. End-Mar to end-Oct daily 1000-1800. £4.50, concession £3. Guided tours of castle every afternoon from Jul to Sept an extra £1.50 per person. Free minibuses from Largs station at 1145 and 1345 every weekend from May-Sept, and daily in Jul and Aug.*

Largs is surrounded by the **Clyde Muirshiel Regional Park**, over 100 square miles of countryside with lots of opportunities for walks or just for a picnic with great views across the Firth of Clyde. Contact the tourist office for

Southern Scotland

more information. You can also take a **boat trip** from Largs to Rothesay and the Kyles of Bute with *Clyde Marine Cruises* of Greenock, T01475-721281. The old paddle steamer *Waverley* departs from Largs on Tuesdays during the summer, T0141-2218152, to Arran and Bute. Details also from the tourist office.

Those who wish to splash out can try the **B** *Brisbane House Hotel*, on the seafront promenade, T687200, www.maksu-group.co.uk. It is comfortable and offers very fine Scottish cuisine at mid-range prices. A few miles north town on the A78 is the **B** *Manor Park Hotel*, an elegant Victorian country mansion set in 15 acres of grounds overlooking the Firth of Clyde, T520832.
 There are lots of **guesthouses** and **B&Bs** in town, including: **E-D** *Belmont House*, 2 Broomfield Pl, T676264, open May-Oct; **E-F** *St Leonards Guest House*, 9 Irvine Rd, T673318; and **E-D** *Tigh-Na-Ligh Guest House*, 104 Brisbane Rd, T/F673975. The cheapest place to stay is **F** *Biscayne House*, 110 Irvine Rd, T672851, open all year, an independent hostel with dormitory accommodation. There's a **campsite** about 4 miles north on the A78 at *Skelmorlie Mains Caravan Park*, T520794, open Easter-Oct.

Sleeping

The *Brisbane House Hotel* (see above) is the best place in town for a full-blown meal. Also good is *Fins Seafood Restaurant*, T568989, about 5 miles south of Largs on the A78. It serves great fish and seafood daily except Mon (lunch mid-range; dinner expensive). Don't leave town without visiting the legendary *Nardini's*, T674555, on the promenade. This authentic 1950s Italian café is an institution and is reckoned by some to be the best café in Scotland. The décor alone is worth the detour, but the ice cream makes this a truly magical experience. Also good Italian food and coffee. Open daily 2230 in summer.

Eating

There are hourly **trains** to and from **Glasgow Central** (1 hr; £4.50). There are also hourly **buses** to **Glasgow**, and to **Ayr**, **Ardrossan** and **Irvine** with *Stagecoach*, T01294-607007.

Transport

There are **banks** with ATMs and shops on Main St. The **post office** is just off Main St, on Aitken St.

Directory

Only a few minutes from Largs by ferry is the hilly island of Great Cumbrae. At only four miles long and a couple of miles wide, it's ideally suited for a day or half-day trip from Largs and is best explored on foot or by bike. Great Cumbrae is a major water sports centre and Millport beach is a popular place for **windsurfing**.
 The only settlement of any size is **Millport**, which curves round a bay on the south coast and unfortunately looks across to the great ugly hulk of Hunterston nuclear power station on the mainland. Millport is home to Europe's smallest cathedral, the beautiful **Cathedral of the Isles**, built in the mid-19th century to a design by the renowned architect William Butterfield whose other works include Kebble College, Oxford. ■ *Daily 1100-1600 except during services.* About a mile east of town is the **Marine Life Museum**, part of Glasgow University Marine Biology department, which contains an excellent aquarium. ■ *T530353. Mon-Fri 0930-1215 and 1400-1645; Jul-Sept also Sat. £1.50.*
 The nicest parts of the island are away from Millport and are best explored by bike. The 14-mile main road runs right round the edge of the island, or there's a narrow Inner Circle Road which passes **The Glaidstone** (417ft), the highest point on the island. More information on these cycle routes is available from the **tourist office** at 28 Stuart Street in Millport. ■ *T530753. Easter-May Sat and Sun 1000-1700; Jun and Sept daily 1100-1700; Jul and Aug daily 1000-1800; first two weeks in Oct Sat and Sun 1100-1600.* **Bike hire** is available in Millport at *Mapes & Son*, 3-5 Guildford Street, T530444, for £3.50 per day.

Great Cumbrae Island

Southern Scotland

Sleeping There's no need to stay on the island, as there are frequent daily ferries (see below), but should you wish to, there are a couple of accommodation options. Next to the cathedral is **E** *College of the Holy Spirit*, T530353, tccumbrae@argyll.anglican.org, an Anglican retreat which offers comfortable B&B, dinner and B&B (**D-E**) or full board (**D**). There's also **E-F** *Cir Mhor*, 35 West Bay, T530723.

Eating You are limited to *Minstrels Wine Bar & Restaurant*, T530934, on Clyde St, or the wonderful *Ritz Café* which has been serving great ice cream, chips and cappuccino for almost a century.

Ferries leave **Largs** every 15 mins during the summer (Apr-Oct) and every 30 mins in winter for the 10-mins sailing to the slip on the northeast shore. **Buses** meet the ferry for the 4-mile trip to Millport. The return far is £2.95 per person and £12.65 per car, or £3.40 and £14.90 respectively at peak times. Bikes cost £2 return. For more information, contact *CalMac*, T0990-650000, or at Largs pier, T674134.

Background

15

658

Background

History

Prehistoric times

The rubbish dumps of shellfish-eating cave dwellers on the islands of Oronsay and Kerrera in the Outer Hebrides have provided rich pickings for archaeologists who conclude that these hunter-gatherers of around 6000-5000BC are Scotland's earliest known inhabitants. By 2000-1500 BC these Mesolithic people had been joined by **Beaker folk**, so named from their distinctive pottery, and grain cultivating Megalithic people, arriving by sea via Spain and Portugal, who were tempted to settle by a then prevailing near-Mediterranean climate. Several climate changes for the worse triggered much population movement and also, along with extensive deforestation, caused the formation of peaty soil, now characteristic of much of Scotland, by around 1000 BC.

The pottery and other artefacts of the Beaker people have been found in burial mounds or cairns, such as **Maeshowe** on Orkney Mainland (see page 565) from around this time and suggest a complex social structure and perhaps, more importantly, a belief in the afterlife, as do the prehistoric settlements and monuments in Caithness, Orkney, Shetland and the Outer Hebrides, notably at **Skara Brae** (page 564), **Stenness**, and the **Ring of Brodgar** on Orkney Mainland and **Callanish** on Lewis (see page 531). But throughout Scotland there are hundreds of standing stones and circles, a legacy of the megalithic peoples. In Aberdeenshire surveys reveal precise orientations indicating their use as observatories charting lunar cycles and eclipses. The layout of **Clava Cairns**, near Inverness (see page 215), bears similarities to the great temple at Newgrange in Ireland. And at **Kilmartin**, in Argyll (see page 410), cup and ring marks, stone alignments and burial cairns, formed in a complete 'landscape temple', suggest a geomantic sophistication that has now been forgotten.

At the beginning of the first millenium BC, **Bronze Age** traders from far afield were busy around the coasts. Celts arrived from Germany, bringing with them new agricultural technology and weaponry, such as swords and shields, which in turn necessitated impressive earthwork defences in the form of hillforts and crannogs (see page 672) as competition for land increased. In about 200-100 BC more Celts arrived with superior iron working skills and consequently, more fortifications were also built. The **brochs**, or towers, the remains of many of which can still be seen dotted along the west coast and in the islands, date from this time, see also page 672.

The Picts and the Romans

Indigenous iron age tribes, or as myth relates, Scythians who arrived via Ireland, inhabited most of the country and were identified by the Romans as 'Picts' – possibly meaning 'painted, or tattooed, people'. They thwarted Roman imperial ambition in Alba, the land north of the Forth and Clyde, in around 80AD and a string of Roman military outposts along the highland line remain from this abandoned campaign.

At **Fortingall** near Aberfeldy, the ancient yew tree is said to mark the birthplace of Pontius Pilate, possibly the son of a Roman soldier, and cousin of King Caractacus, who later found preferment in Rome. To add credence to this theory, a gravestone marked 'PP' was found.

Defensive **walls** built by Emperors **Hadrian** (built c123AD from the Solway Firth to the Tyne) and **Antoninus** (from the Clyde to the Forth c143AD) against the Picts inadvertently set a precedent for the eventual polarization of Scotland and England, beginning around the ninth century, out of the mass of tribal kingdoms. An endlessly disputed border led to centuries of retaliatory raids and devastation on either side.

Picts south of the Antonine wall became semi-Romanized and were known as **Britons**, kin to the Welsh. Their kingdom of Strathclyde, with a stronghold on **Dumbarton Rock**, near Glasgow (see page 186), once extended into Lancashire and retained a separate identity into the 11th century. The Lothians, territory of the British Gododdin, was overrun by Anglians from Northumbria. In the seventh century the Anglians challenged the Picts in Alba and were finally defeated at Dunnichen.

Meanwhile an Irish tribe, **the Scots**, who claimed descent from an Egyptian Pharaoh's daughter, had been settling in Pictish territory in Argyll from around the fourth century. Once in Argyll, the sons of the Scots' leader, Erc, established a kingdom called **Dalriada**, sharing it between themselves under a high king at **Dunadd** (see page 216). When their fellow countryman, **Columba**, arrived in the sixth century on **Iona**, they were aided in their cause by his diplomatic skills at the hostile Pictish court of King Brude, in Inverness. In the ninth century, the Scots under **Kenneth MacAlpin** took over the Picts. Although their written records were destroyed, or falsified by the conquering Scots, they left a rich legacy of unique sculptured stones denoting a civilized and artistic culture. When Kenneth set up at **Scone** (see page 272), and Alba became Scotland, the seven kingdoms of Pictland in the north and east survived as great earldoms.

The early Church

Some claim Joseph of Arimathea brought Christianity to **Whithorn** in Galloway (see page 644), which had been a religious centre since the first century. Around 397 AD **Ninian** founded a Christian Mission in Whithorn, at Candida Casa, along eastern Mediterranean monastic lines vastly different from the Roman model. From here he and countless missionaries such as Kentigern, Moluag and Comgan went north to convert the Picts, as far as St Ninian's Isle in Shetland. Their communities, oak churches and cells are remembered in innumerable place names, wells and simple cross-marked stones, often established on pre-Christian sacred sites.

Columba's later mission on **Iona** (see page 248), starting in 563, was restricted geographically by language and political differences with Dalriada. Ties with Ireland were thus closer, but the arrival of the Vikings inhibited sea travel and the monks were driven from Iona. About this time, the Scots took over the Pictish nation and the Columban church moved to **Dunkeld**, with Columba's relics transported in the *breacbannoch*, or Monymusk reliquary. This was carried at Bannockburn and is now in the Museum of Scotland in Edinburgh.

St Andrews (see page 326), later became the principal seat of the church, although Iona retained special status. Communities of Culdees (one of which was at St Andrews) survived into the 13th century, outwith the Columban and later Roman church. These were thought to be adherents of Ninian's church, preserving elements of pre-Christian druid religion.

A common origin for the cross symbol found on both the **Pictish cross slabs** and the free standing crosses of **Iona and Islay** is the chi-ro, or wheeled cross, as found at Whithorn. However the enigmatic symbols, vivid hunting scenes and mythical beasts of the Pictish stones found throughout Pictland are unique, and their function remains a mystery. There are good collections at **Meigle and St Vigeans** in Angus, near Dundee.

Another mystery is the brief flourishing in the early 13th century of an accomplished school of sculptors around Loch Awe, in Argyll. In ancient burial grounds throughout **Knapdale** are found grave slabs depicting swords, warriors, and foreign ships thought to mark the graves of the **Knights Templar** who fled here from France.

The Vikings

Pagan Norsemen in dragonships are first heard of in Argyll in 795 AD, the first of many such coastal raids of unimaginable savagery, which included ritual killings. Colonies of monks were not spared; 68 suffered the 'red martyrdom' on Iona in 807, and its library, 'a shop window crammed with the loot of centuries' was a magnet for raiders.

By the late ninth century, Norsemen had colonized **Orkney** (see page 555), and from Birsay Palace Earl Sigurd wielded power as far south as Moray. A renegade bunch of mixed Norse and Gaelic ancestry, the **Gall-Gaels**, appeared in the Hebrides and Galloway. Some of these, like chieftain Ketil Flatnose's family, became early settlers of Iceland.

Once surrounded by aggressive Norse colonies, now also in Dublin and York, the newly formed 'Scotland' survived through a combination of fighting spirit and a network of shifting alliances with the various Norse powers. Some of these alliances were enduring. In the ninth century 'Torf' Einar, credited with introducing peat cutting, founded a dynasty from which sprang the Earls of Angus.

After the Dublin colony collapsed in 1014, a Viking kingdom of 'Man and the Sudreys' (Hebrides) filled the vacuum, and the isles continued to be ravaged by warring Norsemen. By around 1100 Norwegian king Magnus Barelegs' empire included the entire northern and western seaboard. Against this backdrop, pursuing his own interests, appears **Somerled,** Hebridean hero of Norse-Gaelic blood, progenitor of Clan Donald and the powerful Lordship of the Isles. In 1153, he supported a rebellion against the Scottish crown. Later, in the early 13th century he built a series of castles around the coast, such as Sween, Tioram, Mingary and Dunstaffnage, which foiled the intermittent attempts made by the Scottish crown to assert control.

· The last of the great Norse kings, Hakon, was defeated by the Scots in 1263 at Largs, with the aid of bad winter weather. Orkney and Shetland were only returned to Scotland in the 15th century. A Norse dialect was spoken there into the 18th century and vestiges of Norwegian law still survive, as does the Viking St Magnus Cathedral, in Kirkwall.

Macbeth and the battle for kingship

Macbeth, the earl-king of the vast land of Moray, rose to high kingship with popular support, reigning for a relatively long (1040-1057) and peaceful time with his queen Gruoch, grand-daughter of Kenneth III of Scots. He was vilified by Shakespeare to please James VI, who claimed descent from Duncan. The latter was, in fact, a nasty piece of work, slain not at Glamis but on the battlefield, while invading Macbeth's territory and remembered in the Orkneyinga saga as Karl Hundason, 'low-born son of the hound'.

Competition for the high kingship was nothing new. A suitable 'tanist' or candidate was elected from anyone whose great-grandfather had been king: in practice survival of the fittest. Pictish custom was complicated by the ancient dynastic rivalry among the Dalriadic Scots and perpetuated when they merged with the Picts under Kenneth MacAlpin. This later precipitated the Wars of Independence.

Half-brother to Earl Thorfinn of Orkney, and one of the most able early kings, Macbeth was the first to establish and implement a fair legal system. A firm supporter of the Celtic church, he went on pilgrimage to Rome where an Irish monk observed him liberally scattering money to the poor.

Shakespeare's Birnam Wood incident is, however, historic fact: Malcolm and his Northumbrian allies used tree branches as camouflage to advance on Macbeth in his Dunsinnan stronghold near Perth. This last truly Celtic king was later hunted down and slain at Lumphanan by Malcolm's ally, MacDuff, Earl of Fife, and is buried on Iona.

The Canmores and the Norman conquest

The victor, the uncouth **Malcolm III**, Canmore (meaning 'big head'), was an illegitimate son of Duncan and a miller's daughter. One of his many raids into Northumberland provoked a visit from William the Conqueror, to whom Malcolm was forced to swear fealty: an oath he didn't take too seriously, but which was to be a nail in Scotland's constitutional coffin.

Malcolm married a Saxon-Hungarian princess, who energetically set about Romanizing the Church, for which she was later canonized. **Margaret** founded **Dunfermline Abbey** (see page 311) and introduced southern manners to the Scottish court. Her private chapel survives in Edinburgh castle.

Primogeniture rather than traditional tanistry ensured a dynasty of increasing entanglement with England, lasting over 200 years. **Normans** were granted land as far as the Highland fringes, establishing a feudal system based on loyalty to the crown. The traditional patriarchal tribal culture was eroded, causing constant rebellions in the North and Galloway.

The Norman successor, **David I**, like many of his Norman friends, had English estates, acquired through his wife. This wealth built the great Border abbeys and established the Roman church more fully. New parishes and dioceses revolutionized administration, and burghs were founded to develop international trade, attracting **Flemish** settlers. Society in Medieval Scotland became more typically European than England or even France.

But southern interests became the Achilles heel of a nobility unwilling to resist English ambitions towards Scotland. The crisis came in 1290, when the new child queen died en route from Norway and 13 rival contestants materialized. Two main factions emerged: the Balliols and Comyns against the Bruces. But instead of reverting to 'natural selection', the Scots appealed to Edward I of England to adjudicate.

Wallace and Bruce: the Wars of Succession

Edward chose John Balliol as king. In the ensuing chaos, Edward garrisoned the country with troops and, shrewdly, helped himself to a selection of symbols of nationhood, including ancient records. Resistance found a leader in **William Wallace**, son of a Renfrew laird (see also page 289). A small but strategic victory against English forces at **Stirling Bridge** galvanized support and he was quickly declared 'Guardian of the Realm'. Following his defeat at Falkirk he was betrayed to Edward by one of the Scots noblemen and condemned to suffer an appalling 'traitor's' death in London. This stirred **Robert Bruce** to take up the cause of independence. Encountering his treacherous rival, Red Comyn, in a Dumfries church, he seized the initiative, stabbing him at the altar. With Comyn dead, patriotic church leaders hurried to get Bruce crowned king with full ceremony at Scone before the inevitable blow of Papal excommunication fell. For the next seven years Bruce was a virtual outlaw fighting a guerrilla campaign from hiding in the west, during which time the indomitable Edward I died, stipulating his own epitaph: 'Hammer of the Scots'.

Not until 1314 was Bruce forced to confront Edward II's vastly superior army at **Bannockburn** in pitched battle. His incredible victory was aided by Angus Og of the Isles, and a number of Knights Templar recently arrived seeking sanctuary from persecution in France.

Bannockburn was merely the turning point in a long and sorry tale in which only temporary peace with England came in 1328. The **Declaration of Arbroath**, manifesto of Scotland's independence, was signed in 1320. Bruce was finally recognized as king by the Pope, before he died in 1329. His friend Douglas, as requested, took Bruce's heart on pilgrimage to the Holy Land but when Douglas died en route it was returned to **Melrose Abbey**.

The Stewart Dynasty

From Robert Bruce's title of 'High Steward' sprang the dynasty of Stewart kings. The early Jameses (of whom there were seven in all) all followed a tragic pattern: succeeding as infant kings, imprisoned throughout childhood, and suffering untimely deaths. James I and III were both murdered, and James II blew himself up accidentally with a cannon. Unscrupulous regents frequently took charge and hugely powerful nobles like the house of Douglas competed both amongst themselves and against the king. James II hot-bloodedly murdered the earl of Douglas over dinner at Stirling Castle by throwing him out the window. The Lords of the Isles were put down by the Earl of Mar and his followers in one of the bloodiest battles of all, 'Red Harlaw' near Inverurie. Like the Douglases, they, too, were finally forfeited, in 1543.

However, the early Stewarts made progress towards rescuing the country from anarchy, by laying the foundations for a modern state through a series of constitutional reforms. They embodied the democratic 'Kings of Scots', answerable first to the common people. Mostly cultured and progressive, they found time to write poetry (James I wrote the *King's Quair*), to build Renaissance palaces, and to father sufficient illegitimate 'James Stewarts' to fill numerous ecclesiastical sinecures (James IV and V). James IV was a true Renaissance prince with a glittering court, but a self-destructive streak led to his early death along with most of the nobility at Flodden, in 1513, sacrificed for the long-standing 'Auld Alliance' with France.

Mary, Queen of Scots

There is no more tragic and romantic figure in Scottish history than Mary, Queen of Scots. Raised in France for safekeeping as a Catholic, her brief reign was dogged by bad luck, bad judgement and bad timing. She arrived back in Scotland in 1561, a young widow, at the height of Reformation turmoil in which both France and Catholicism were inimical. Something of a loose cannon, she was embroiled in a power struggle not helped by her disastrous choice of husbands. Implicated in the celebrated murder of the first one, her cousin, Henry Lord Darnley, she then swiftly married one of the chief suspects, the Earl of Bothwell, incurring the fury of everyone else (see also page 617). Imprisoned after the Battle of Carberry on the island fortress of Loch Leven, she escaped only to throw herself on the mercy of her cousin Queen Elizabeth I, who, mindful that in Catholic eyes Mary had the better claim to the English throne, locked her up at Fotheringhay for 19 years before deciding to do away with her altogether. After Elizabeth's death, Mary's son, already James VI of Scotland, ascended to the English throne as James I in 1603, with the **Union of Crowns**.

Reformation and the roots of Scottish education

The Reformation came relatively late to Scotland and the motives were as much political as religious, though, of course, in 16th-century terms the two were inextricably linked. A pro-English Protestant faction had grown over decades, opposing the French Catholic Regent, Mary of Guise, and a rebel parliament in 1560 banned Catholic Mass. Thus shattering for good the Auld Alliance with France, first formalized in 1295.

The casualties of the Reformation were countless and included religious buildings, works of art and even whole libraries. It amounted to a complete obliteration of the past over which even today amnesia prevails, though unlike England, there were very few martyrs. So began 100 years of bitter struggle to establish the reformed church. Cue the Protestant exile, **John Knox**, a Calvinist rabble-rouser of dubious character and little diplomacy who was prone to blasting his trumpet off against the 'monstrous regiment of women,' namely Mary, Queen of Scots. Knox's skills as a colourful orator, and his self-appointed role as official historian of the Reformation have allowed him to eclipse the real hero, **Andrew Melville**, who sacrificed his career of reforming university education, to devote himself to the nuts and bolts of church reform.

Schooling for all as a passport to intellectual freedom and moral probity was a dream of the reformers. While grammar and song schools already existed, by the end of the 17th century most parishes had schools using the bible as textbook. The 'Dominie' (schoolmaster) was until recently a hugely influential community figure. Prior to the Reformation the **Universities** of St Andrews (1412), Glasgow (1451) and Aberdeen (1495) had been established and Edinburgh University was added to the list in the 1580's.

Jacobean Scotland was vibrant and vigorously European. Religious extremists were checked by James VI, the 'Wisest fool in Christendom,' and unprecedented peace allowed Renaissance culture to blossom, but trouble was brewing.

The Covenanters

The struggle of the kirk (church) against the king erupted in the 17th century into full scale civil war, with hostility towards bishops the recurrent theme. A riot in St Giles in Edinburgh expressed public feeling and resulted in **The National Covenant**, signed in Edinburgh in 1638, pledging faith to 'the true religion' and affirming the authority of the powerful General Assembly of the Church of Scotland in all matters spiritual. Covenanters and king came to blows, followed by an extremist group of Presbyterians allying with the English parliament against the king, in the **Solemn League and Covenant**. Battle-hardened Scots flooded back from European campaigns to take up arms.

A supporter of the original Covenant, **Montrose**, led a spirited but doomed campaign for the king against the extremists. At Ardvreck, in Assynt, he was betrayed to his arch-enemy 'King Campbell', Duke of Argyll, who gave him a traitor's death in Edinburgh. After the Restoration Argyll found himself on the wrong side and met the same end on the same spot.

Throughout the 17th century the dark side of religious idealism – fanaticism and paranoia – were epitomized by the 'kirk sessions', courts in which the church conducted an orgy of scapegoating and witch-hunts. Fundamental differences of ideology, constitution and culture between two countries only recently 'twinned', opened cracks in the alliance with the Parliamentarians. When **Charles I** was beheaded in 1649 the Scots were appalled and appointed Charles II king, despite falling under Cromwell's military 'Protectorate'.

Although Charles II's **Restoration** in 1660 was greeted with wild rejoicing, the reinstatement of the bishops once gain proved problematic. Some unconsenting ministers of the church were outlawed and finding a loyal following, especially in the southwest, they held illegal services, 'Conventicles', in the open air. Crippling fines and brutal persecution from officers of the crown, including Graham of Claverhouse merely increased their resistance, and many died in the 'Killing Times' as martyrs to high principle.

The Union of Parliaments

While all were united in their opposition to the determinedly Papist James II who fled ignominiously in 1689, the terms of the **Revolution Settlement** to establish William of Orange in Scotland led to 'Seven III Years' of increasing political friction, during which one third of the populace died of famine and pestilence.

William's foreign policy forced Scotland into war with her traditional ally, France, and matters came to a head over trade. After a brief heyday of free trade with English New World colonies under Cromwell, restrictions were again in force after 1660. Funds were therefore raised to establish a Scots colony in Panama; the **Darien Scheme**. It collapsed disastrously and with great loss of life, owing to obstruction by William and last minute withdrawal of English support. Investors great and small were bankrupted.

Meanwhile, haunted by the spectre of the Stuarts (or Stewarts), in exile at St Germain in France, and without consultation, England excluded Scotland from the succession in an **Act of Settlement** in 1701. Weary of a contentious Scots Parliament with power to decide succession in Scotland, the English proposed complete economic and political union between the two realms.

Without free trade with England, economic ruin threatened and the **Act of Union** was hammered out over six years to completion. The Scottish Parliament was dissolved in 1707. Despite vigorous opposition, threats and bribery assured that a bankrupt and exhausted Scotland was, in popular mythology, sold to England for £398,085 – part compensation for Darien, part wages for the Commissioners who closed the deal.

Jacobite rebellion and the Clearances

William's government redcoats first clashed with supporters of James II (the Jacobites) at **Killiecrankie** in 1689. They were led by Graham of Claverhouse, 'Bonnie Dundee', who was killed in the battle. In 1692, an expedition to weed out the Jacobites in the Highlands resulted in the **Glencoe massacre**, which provoked unprecedented public outcry (see page 437).

The Act of Settlement was not forgotten and dwindling trade and increased taxation fuelled dissatisfaction with the Union. A lively underground resistance, aided by long-standing French connections, revolved around the Jacobite court in exile at St Germain. Sympathy also came from English quarters.

Four attempts ensued to reinstate a Stewart monarchy, supported erratically by France, and culminating at **Culloden**, in 1746 (see page 409). Much support came from north of the Tay, which was Catholic and Episcopalian country. The term 'Jacobite' popularly denoted anti-establishment and Episcopalian. Also, pejoratively, Highlander, and was evocative of a linguistic, social and cultural divide between Lowlander and Highlander whihch had grown since the 15th century. **Highland culture** and independence was not diminished after the demise of the Lords of the Isles, hence the rise of the Campbells to enormous power as government agents, dealing for instance with the troublesome MacGregors. Claiming descent from Kenneth MacAlpin, the MacGregors were almost annihilated in 1603, and outlawed until 1774. They played a significant part in the Jacobite rebellions (see also page 299).

Although traditionally indifferent to the monarchy, many clans came out in support for the Prince Charles (of 'Bonnie Prince Charlie' fame) in 1745. After defeat at Culloden, savage reprisals were led by the 'Butcher' Cumberland. Rebels were beheaded or hanged, estates confiscated and the pipes and Highland dress proscribed until 1782. Clansmen were enlisted into Highland regiments and 1,150 were exiled, swelling the ranks of emigrants to the colonies. Gaelic culture was effectively expunged and Scotland as a whole suffered disgrace.

Background

Rise and fall of Bonnie Prince Charlie

Charles Edward Stuart, the 'Young Pretender', grandson of James II was born in Italy. First setting foot on Scottish soil, aged 23, with seven companions (the Seven Men of Moidart), his forceful personality persuaded reluctant clan chiefs to join him in raising the Standard at Glenfinnan for his father in 1745. Inadequately prepared government troops under 'Johnny Cope' (of ballad fame) enabled his swift progress to Edinburgh, where he held court at Holyrood, dazzling the populace with a grand ball. Edinburgh was charmed but embarrassed.

With sights set on the English throne, he reached Derby. Encouraging reports about panic in London were offset by news of advancing government troops which prompted retreat. The pursuing redcoats were outwitted as far as Inverness, and the ensuing bloodbath at **Culloden**, though Charles' only defeat, was decisive. Fleeing to the Hebrides, he was given shelter by **Flora MacDonald** (see page 503) and then spent a summer as a lone fugitive. Despite a £30,000 reward for his capture, he managed to escape on a French frigate in 1746. Too late by a fortnight, 40,000 louis d'ors then arrived from France, enough to revive the whole campaign.

This failure has been ascribed to a fatal weakness of character and a collapse of resolve at Derby. He ended his days a degenerate and broken man, ensuring the complete collapse of the Jacobite cause. But Bonnie Prince Charlie is remembered in numerous nostalgic songs, a toast to 'the King over the Water' and a host of memorabilia.

The Enlightenment

Intellectual life flourished in late 18th century Scotland. Embracing all the arts, its roots lay in the philosophical nature, shaped by European thought, underlying Scots law, education and the church. The sceptic **David Hume** (1711-76) was the foremost of a school of philosophers, best known for his *Treatise on Human Nature* and *Essays, Moral and Political*. Kirkcaldy born **Adam Smith** pioneered political economy in his *Wealth of Nations* (1776), a powerful impetus to later political reform.

An emphasis on research and practicality in the sciences fostered inventiveness in applied science, contributing much to industry and agriculture. **James Watt** (1736-1819) developed the steam engine which powered the machinery of the Industrial Revolution, medicine flourished at Edinburgh university, and further generations spawned engineers and inventors like **Alexander Graham Bell** and **John Logie Baird**, inventors of the telephone and television respectively.

Classicism was espoused in architecture and by painters like **Allan Ramsay, Raeburn** and **Nasymth**, and gave way in literature to the Romanticism of **Robert Burns** whose work profoundly influenced popular culture and notions of democracy.

Sir Walter Scott's best selling historical novels worked miracles for Scotland's public image. It was he who stage-managed the visit of George IV, who sportingly donned a kilt and, for modesty's sake, pink tights for the occasion. Later on, Queen Victoria was inspired to adopt a Highland home, and with the craze for 'Balmorality', the Highlands assumed a romantic glamour, becoming a fashionable resort for southern sportsmen.

Industrial revolution

Until around 1750, half of Scotland's population lived north of the Clyde and Tay. **Emigration** to the lowlands or North America was already a problem as a money economy threatened traditional ways of life. The decision of landlords to resettle their tenants on the coasts, replacing black cattle with sheep, was a disastrous economic and social experiment, with brutal evictions in some areas – although

Clans and tartans

Before Culloden and the Clearances, Highland tradition decreed that a person's loyalty lay first and foremost with their own particular clan, or family group. There were two classes of clan: clansmen of the clan who were related by blood and shared the same family name, and individuals and groups who sought and obtained the protection of the clan. This resulted in a clan having septs, or sub-groups, of different surnames. Most Scottish surnames can be traced to a clan name, each with their own particular tartan.

Clan tartans are patterns for general use by clanspeople, but there are also variations of clan tartans which are used for specific purposes. Dress tartans were originally worn by the women of the clan who preferred light-coloured patterns, and were woven on a white background. Hunting tartans are worn for sport and outdoor activities, with brown or some other dark hue as the predominant colour, in order to give some form of camouflage. Rather confusingly, ancient clan tartan does not signify an older pattern, but is merely a term used to describe a tartan woven in lighter-coloured shades.

For a comprehensive history of Scottish clans and families, see Scottish Family History, by Margaret Stuart and James Balfour Paul (Edinburgh, 1930), or The Surnames of Scotland: their origin, meaning and history by George Black (New York, 1940). These books are available in most public libraries. Those wishing to trace their Scottish ancestry should start at the Scots Ancestry Research Society, 20 York Place, Edinburgh.

popular myth forgets that famine, disease and overpopulation were rife and many went willingly. Eventually, in 1886, crofters' rights were to some extent recognized (see also page 511).

The gap between Highland and Lowland life continued to widen as overgrazing, deforestation for industry, and deer 'forests', led to desolation in the Highlands, while improvements and drainage transformed lowland agriculture.

At the same time **industrialization** was soon to bring a massive population shift. Wool cloth and linen, long established as cottage industries, were undergoing mechanization. By 1820 mills were established in the coalfields of Lanark, Renfrew, and Ayr. Linen declined in favour of cotton spun and woven in Paisley and New Lanark, while tweed was first woven in Galashiels, in 1830. Dundee substituted jute for linen and Kirkcaldy developed linoleum. Thriving on trade with America, Glasgow's population mushroomed, absorbing many from the Highlands, also thousands of Irish refugees from the potato famine of the 1840's. Poor housing, overcrowding and disease became chronic.

20th-century Scotland

By 1900 iron and later steel, mainly in the west, had become manufacturing mainstays, serviced by new canals, railways and roads. As well as emigrants, Scotland supplied goods to North America: locomotives, girders, bridges, textile machinery and tools.

Shipyards flourished on the **Clyde**. The first iron steam ships were launched around 1800, although fast wooden clippers like the Cutty Sark were still competitive in the mid-19th century, when major shipping companies such as Cunard came to the fore. From 1880, skilled labour built steel ships for world markets as well as for the Royal Navy. Business boomed during the First World War, when political activity among skilled workers inspired by the Bolshevik revolution, led by Marxist and Scottish Nationalist **John Maclean**, gave rise to the myth of 'Red Clydeside'.

Post-war slump hit all industries in the 1920's from which they never really recovered. A dangerous dependency on mining, metalworking and heavy

Background

engineering was a crucial factor in industrial decline and the innovative spirit of the 19th century is only now re-emerging among pioneering computer software development companies in the central belt.

The rise of nationalism and the new Parliament

In a long Liberal tradition dedicated to political reform, the issue of Home Rule reared its head repeatedly after the 1880's. Nationalist sentiments voiced by writers in the 1920's, such as Lewis Spence, Hugh MacDiarmid, Grassic Gibbon and Neil Gunn, took political shape as the **Scottish National Party** in 1934.

Support grew through the 1950s and 1960s until nationalist fervour reached its height in the 1970s, roused by expectations that revenue from the **oil and gas** recently discovered in the North Sea would reverse economic decline. These hopes were dashed by oil revenues disappearing into the British Treasury at Westminster, and consequently, a 1979 referendum demonstrated only lukewarm support for devolution.

Twenty years on, the Scots voted emphatically in favour of devolution and the **Scottish Parliament** reconvened after 292 years on 12 May, 1999. Members of the Scottish Parliament (known as MSPs) were elected by proportional representation, a novel voting system for a country used to the 'first-past-the-post' system in elections to the UK parliament. This resulted in a coalition government between the Labour and Liberal-Democrat parties, who are trying to come to terms with the idea of government by compromise, an alien concept in British politics. The thorny issue of student tuition fees almost proved an early stumbling block and many detractors saw the final settlement as a "fudge", but more optimistic observers are hopeful of a more mature attitude of government and a move away from the old confrontational style of party politics.

However, the political future is fraught with potential problems and great uncertainty. The nationalists see devolved government merely as a means to their desired end of full independence, and only time will tell if the Scots get a taste for greater self-determination. Perhaps the most immmediate issue, though, is the so-called 'West Lothian question'. This refers to the matter of MSPs in the UK parliament having a say in the running of English affairs while English MP s have no say over matters dealt with by the Scottish parliament. This could yet lead to devolved regional government in England, or it could push Scotland further down the road towards full independence.

Scotland's political seas may be choppy, but culturally, the country is in great shape, with writers, artists and film-makers attracting international acclaim, and with Glasgow and Edinburgh established as major European cultural cities. As the notion of 'Britishness' recedes ever further and European integration looms on the horizon, Scotland appears to be embracing the future with a new-found confidence, healthy optimism and a strong sense of identity.

Land and environment

Geographically, Scotland can be divided into three areas: Southern Uplands, Central Lowlands and Highlands. The **Southern Uplands** is the area south from Edinburgh and Glasgow to the English border, and consists of a series of hill ranges sandwiched between fertile coastal plains. The **Central Lowlands**, the triangle formed by Edinburgh, Glasgow and Dundee to the north, contains most of the population and is the country's industrial heartland. The Highland Boundary Fault is the geographical division running northeast from Helensburgh (west of Glasgow) to Stonehaven (south of Aberdeen). To the north of this line lie the **Highlands and Islands**, which comprise roughly two-thirds of the country. This is an area of high mountain ranges punctuated by steep-sided valleys, or glens, and deep lochs. The northwest coastline is indented by numerous steep, fjord-like sea lochs and offshore are some 790 islands, 130 of which are inhabited. These are grouped into the Outer Hebrides, or Western Isles, the Inner Hebrides, and, to the north, the Orkney and Shetland Islands.

Much of Scotland was long ago covered by the **Caledonian forest**, which consisted mainly of the **Scots pine**, along with **oak**, **birch** and other hardwoods. Over the centuries, the trees were felled for timber and to accommodate livestock and now only around one percent of this ancient forest still remains. Small pockets of native Scots pine can be found scattered around the Highlands, at Rothiemurchus, near Aviemore, at Glen Tanar, near Ballater in Deeside, around Braemar, at Strathyre near Callander and Achray Forest near Aberfoyle, at Rowardennan on Loch Lomond, in Glen Affric and on the shores of Loch Maree.

Several decades ago, the **Forestry Commission**, a government body, set about fencing off large areas of moorland for reforestation. Now much of the landscape is dominated by regimented rows of fast-growing sitka spruce, which are not particularly attractive. There are also serious concerns over the damage coniferization causes to the unique habitats in many areas, in particular to large areas of bogland in the "Flow Country" of Caithness and Sutherland, a unique natural environment as precious as any tropical rainforest. This and other endangered habitats are registered as an SSSI – a site of Special Scientific Interest – but this has proved less than adequate. The only real guarantee of protection is for such areas to be owned or managed by environmental organizations such as *Scottish Natural Heritage*, the *Scottish Wildlife Trust*, the *Royal Society for the Protection of Birds*, the *Woodland Trust* and *John Muir Trust* (see page 59).

Tourism can also have a damaging effect on the fragile ecology of the Highlands. The unique alpine flora of the Cairngorms is threatened by the hordes of summer visitors using the ski lifts, and controversy rages over proposals to replace the Cairngorm ski lift with a funicular railway.

Background

Scottish wildlife

Scotland has many of Britain's remotest areas and wildest scenery. As a result it is also home to many of the country's rarest animals and its most exotic wildlife. For example, **pine martens**, golden and sea **eagles**, **ospreys**, **killer whales** or **orcas**, **red deer** and **red squirrels**, amongst others, are all best seen in Scotland.

As for the **wildcat**, it is debatable whether or not such a thing really exists now because of interbreeding with feral domestic cats. The **water-vole** (best known as "Ratty" in The Wind in the Willows) is now a threatened species throughout Britain but has its last strongholds in the northwest of Scotland in areas not yet colonised by the invading American mink. Both the harbour or **common seal** and the larger **grey seal** can be found living and breeding in Scottish waters. The latter is especially friendly and curious so will often be seen following small boats.

Red deer occur in large numbers through out Scotland and are of great importance to the local economies of many parts of the Highlands where stalking estates cover much of the land. Males (stags) are larger than the females (hinds) and are characterized by impressive antlers, which are used in the autumn rut to compete for mates. Each year in late winter the antlers are cast and stags must grow a new pair during the summer. Whilst growing, the antlers appear soft and velvety. During the rut, the glens resound with the sound of roaring stags, their antlers clashing, each trying to out-do his neighbouring rival. Red deer are most easily seen in winter, when they are forced down off the mountains in search of food. Large numbers can be seen on Rannoch Moor and between Blair Atholl and Drumochter Pass from the A9 Perth-Inverness road.

Sika deer which are slightly smaller than red deer and spotted in summer can now also been seen in some places, having escaped from deer parks. They have even been known to hybridize with red deer. **Roe deer**, meanwhile, are widespread.

Golden eagles can be seen throughout the Highlands and Islands, especially on Skye, Mull, the Outer Hebrides, around Aviemore and Deeside and in the northwest. Far less prevalent is the **sea eagle**, recently re-introduced after having been extinct for much of this century. Much larger even the golden eagle, the sea eagle eats fish, but also takes large mammals including domestic livestock, which ultimately led to its persecution. Sea eagles can be seen on the Hebridean islands of Rùm and C anna, as well as parts of the west coast, around Argyll and Loch Maree.

The **osprey**, known in North America as the "fish hawk" and also a member of the eagle family, has a famous nesting site at the RSPB reserve at **Loch Garten**, near Aviemore in Strathspey (see page 488). Also in the reserve, which is a lovely example of Caledonian pine forest, can be found other Scottish specialities such as **crossbills**, so called because of the shape of their beaks, designed for extracting seeds from pine cones. **Capercaillie**, the largest member of the grouse family and the size of a large turkey, is now very rare and runs the risk of extinction largely due to loss of habitat. Male capercaillies display at "leks", where groups of courting males fan their tails and try to attract females.

The Caledonian forest is also home to pine-martens and red squirrels. The **pine-marten** is a giant tree weasel, about the size of a cat, and reddish in colour with a white throat. It now has a very limited distribution, being most abundant in **Beinn Eighe Nature Reserve** in Wester Ross (see page 454). **Red squirrels** are much more widespread and common throughout natural and plantation coniferous forests in Scotland, especially on Speyside and Deeside. They are smaller than the invading north American grey squirrel, and have tufts on their ears, and sometimes whitish tails.

Like red deer, **grouse** are very important to the local economy, and so responsible for the land management of much of southern, central and northeastern Scotland. Grouse moors can be recognized from a distance by the mosaic of burnt, young and mature heather patches providing an environment to maximize the number of breeding territories.

Grouse moors are also home to other species, the most notable of which are perhaps the **ptarmigan** and **mountain hare**, both of which turn white in winter. The ptarmigan is another species of grouse which tends to live at a higher altitude, in snowy areas. However, it may often be seen looking very out of place when the snow has melted. Mountain hares, with shorter ears than brown hares and without black on the tail, will always run uphill when disturbed. Both ptarmigan and mountain hares are abundant in the **Cairngorms** and can be seen easily from **Glen Shee**.

Otters, live both on rivers and along the coast and are most easily seen on the islands and the west coast. The best place to see them is **Skye**, especially at the Otter Haven at **Kylerhea**. Otters eat fish and other marine life, and can be seen swimming or scampering along the shore. Their droppings which are usually found on prominent places along the shore, have a very characteristic smell.

Many species such as foxes and badgers, common in England, can be found throughout Scotland as well, although they haven't reached some of the islands. However, in some cases animals have been introduced to the islands to the detriment of the local wildlife. For example, the hedgehog is regarded by some as a pest in the Outer Hebrides where it eats the eggs of many ground-nesting birds, especially waders, which have evolved in the absence of such predators. And one mammal which is soon to be re-introduced to the Highlands of Scotland is the European **beaver**.

The seas around the north of Scotland are some of the best places in Europe to see **whales, dolphins** and **porpoises**. The best area is the **Moray** and **Cromarty Firths**, near Inverness, which are home to Europe's largest population of **bottlenose dolphins**. Dolphins can be seen all year round, but the best months are between May and September. Other good places for sighting dolphins, porpoises and whales is the coast around **Gairloch**, in Wester Ross, where you may see **minke whales**, and if you're lucky, **killer whales**, and around **Bressay, Noss** and **Mousa** on **Shetland**.

For details of where to see seabirds, and other birdlife, see the **Birdwatching** section, in Essentials (page 59).

Background

Culture

Architecture

Early structures:
from brochs to
towers
A thousand years before Stonehenge, a Neolithic architect was supervising the construction of **Maes Howe** (see page 565) in Orkney. Dramatically accompanied by two stone circles, its massive precision-cut stonework houses a tomb. Religious architecture evolved into the Bronze Age and over 22 centuries of chambered tombs survive, notably at **Camster** and **Kilmartin**. Henges and stone circles, as at Cairnpapple also abound. At **Skara Brae** (see page 564) is a 5,000 year-old village, a Neolithic Pompeii where stone furniture and utensils survive in rooms straight out of the 'Flintstones'.

Brochs, fortresses not dissimilar to diminutive industrial cooling towers such as at **Mousa** on Shetland (see page 590), appeared around 75 BC. A staircase ascended within double walls and a well often provided water for the besieged within. On duns and hilltops, timber laced forts, built from 700 BC into the Middle Ages, are sometimes found to have been fired to such an extent that stonework fused solid or vitrified. Whether this was intentional, or the result of attack, remains a mystery.

Ninth century wheelhouses, with stone piers radiating from a central hearth, are visible at **Jarlshof** on Shetland, and appeared later in the Hebrides. Timber began to be used for Pictish hall houses, **crannogs** – lake dwellings on wooden rafts – and early churches (such as at Whithorn).

In the 11th century, **round towers**, such as those at Brechin and Abernethy, were used for defence and as belfries by Culdee communities. Around this time the first cathedrals were built. The one at Birsay on Orkney, founded in 1050 by Earl Thorfinn, was soon replaced by another in Kirkwall commemorating the Norse **St Magnus** (see page 558). This was built by masons from Durham cathedral after working at Dunfermline Abbey, also Romanesque, built for St Margaret. She also commissioned St Rule's in St Andrews, whose tall square tower suggests Northumbrian influence, echoed in those at Muthill, Dunning (in Strathearn) and Dunblane.

Abbeys &
cathedrals
David I (1124-53) granted land to Roman monastic orders and two centuries of abbey and cathedral building ensued, mostly in the lowlands, with **St Andrews** (see page 326) being finally consecrated in 1318. Years of neglect and depredations by English troops and iconoclastic reformers leave many as picturesque ruins, stripped of magnificent wood and stone carving, stained glass and wallpainting. Stone carving at **Rosslyn** (see page 130) and wallpaintings at Fowlis Easter, both 15th-century collegiate churches, are rare survivors. The ruins of St Andrews Cathedral, Oronsay Priory and the Valerian clad cloisters of **Iona's** nunnery (see page 249) are all legacy of the Augustinians.

Ambitious reconstruction of **Melrose**, never completed owing to lack of funds, was overseen by a Parisian master mason in the 14th century and Benedictines built Kelso and Arbroath. Cluniacs settled at Crossraguel, near Ayr, and Paisley. **Elgin cathedral**, repaired after vengeful destruction in 1390 by the Wolf of Badenoch, was considered 'the ornament of the realm', while **Inchcolm Abbey** in the Firth of Forth (see page 133) is the best preserved of all the ecclesiastical buildings of this period.

Symbols of feudalism built by Norman settlers appear in the form of timber motte and bailey fortresses – timber towers with defensive earthworks, found mostly south of the Forth and Clyde.

Medieval castles

The advent of siege warfare during the Wars of Independence necessitated building in stone, pioneered by Edward I's masons at Kildrummy, where a high curtain wall with towers, a keep and gatehouse encircles a courtyard. The fairytale moated **Caerlaverock**, near Dumfries (see page 634), was besieged by Edward in 1300 during the Wars of Independence.

Square or oblong tower houses, with a defensive entry at first floor level, barrel vaulting and great hall were to be an enduring form of dwelling, evolving from the 14th century into the 17th. More elaborate are L-plan and Z-plan versions, with one or two towers added at corners to defend the entry. An exotic deviation is the spectacular double L-plan at Borthwick.

While ordinary folk lived in thatched turf and stone hovels (some into the 20th century), the cosmopolitan and cultured Stewart kings set about building new palaces and improving existing residences. **Holyroodhouse** (see page 82) underwent a long evolution from the 1530's into the 17th century.

Renaissance Palaces

The old castle at **Linlithgow** (see page 292) had emerged by 1540 a wholly residential Renaissance palace ranged around a quadrangle, which even impressed the French Mary of Guise. While the Great Hall at **Stirling** (see page 285) is a triumph of late Gothic, the later Palace block (1540-42) reveals many Renaissance features, such as the recessed bays along the exterior with sculpted figures, and the famous carved wooden ceiling medallions, the 'Stirling Heads'. The classical façade at the royal hunting seat, **Falkland** (see page 318), added by French masons employed by James V is the earliest example of Renaissance architecture in Britain (1537-41).

A minor building boom in the late 16th century was a result of church land being transferred over a long period into private hands. The old tower house formula found favour, preferred over earlier royal examples of Renaissance innovation. Everyone from nobility to minor gentry was afforded both defence against troublesome neighbours as well as gracious living. **Claypotts** in Dundee is a good example of 'the castle with a country house built on top', while at **Craigievar** (see page 380), finished as late as 1626, idiosyncratic inventiveness reaches its apogée where the roofline explodes in a flurry of fairytale turrets. Families of masons developed individual styles detectable in Aberdeenshire where many tower houses, great and small, are still inhabited or have been recently revived. Defensive features like gun loops (apertures for guns) survived less of necessity than as status symbols, and interiors, especially timber ceilings, were vividly painted, with exuberant imagery, as at **Crathes** (see page 372).

The Tower house

'New towns' to promote trade were established by David I and settled with English and Flemish merchants, with a strict hierarchy of trading rights and privileges. Stone houses first replaced wood in the east coast burghs in the 16th century, setting a precedent for future urban design. Every burgh had its symbols of commerce and government at its centre: the Mercat (market) cross and the Tolbooth (town hall).

16th-century townhouses

Culross (see page 309) is typical, with its white harled houses and crow steps. Its terracotta pantiles are characteristic of Fife and the Lothians, first arriving into the ports as ships' ballast, these were later produced locally.

At **Cromarty**, in Easter Ross, two centuries later, the spirit of vernacular architecture had not changed dramatically. Nor had urban layout, many houses still being built gable end on to the street. The multi-storey tenement became a distinctive feature of urban living, pioneered in Edinburgh's **Canongate**, where many buildings such as **Gladstone's Land** are still intact.

William Bruce & Less defensive and more comfortable was the country mansion, a concept
the 17th- pioneered by Alexander Seton, paragon of a new kind of architectural patron, at
century **Pinkie House** in Musselburgh, a daring essay in elegance and erudition. In an urban
mansion setting, **Culross Palace** and **Argyll's Ludgings** in Stirling, are outstanding examples
of grand town houses.

Post Restoration, William Bruce exemplifies a new concept: the architect.
Introducing classical symmetry to existing buildings such as Holyrood and
Thirlestane, he also designed **Hopetoun** in 1699-1703 (see page 133). The
innovative oblong shape and hipped roof of Kinross are characteristic of his many
other country house designs with their Anglo-Dutch interiors and plasterwork. He
also revolutionized garden and landscape design.

Bruce's protege, James Smith, was a pioneer of British Palladianism. Rising from
master mason to King's Master of Works and private architect, his own house,
Newhailes (c1690), was the inspiration for countless lairds' houses, both grand and
humble, built throughout Scotland in the 18th century.

The Adams: Despite economic uncertainty in the early 18th century, William Adam's talent and
Edinburgh shrewd business ability won him many influential patrons. He set a new fashion in
New Town modestly sized but elegant country houses with Palladian influences and
extravagant stucco work, like the **House of Dun** (1730) near Montrose (see page
351) and paved the way for his talented sons. John, although competent, was
eclipsed by Robert, who achieved an international reputation.

Cornering the market in Scotland for a series of Georgian Gothic castles, such as
Mellerstain and **Culzean**, he also designed numerous neo-Classical public
buildings in Edinburgh, where increasing prosperity mid-century inspired the vision
of a 'New Athens'. The layout and design of the **Georgian New Town** involved a
host of architects such as Playfair and Reid over nearly 70 years, culminating in the
19th century with Greek Revival monuments such as Calton Hill, and Thomas
Hamilton's **Royal High School** (1825), considered the finest.

Victorian Not content with Classicism, architects raided the Gothic, Tudor, Jacobean and
Baronial Scottish past, even Asia and Europe, for ideas. Late 18th-century country houses by
Gillespie Graham were assymetrial and castellated. Inspired by the picturesque
movement, they are the harbingers of the High Victorian revival of Scottish baronial
which reached its peak in the 1860's. New and unprecedented wealth found
industrial tycoons and landowners beating a path to the doors of fashionable
architects like Burn and Bryce, to build colossal and fantastic country seats with
room for entertaining on a huge scale and the latest in comforts, like plumbing.
Some followed Queen Victoria's example at Balmoral, building extravagant Highland
shooting lodges. Most eclectic of all is **Mount Stuart** on Bute (1870's) a
neo-Gothic/Renaissance palace whose sumptuous interior even includes details
from Charlemagne's tomb (see page 198).

Flamboyant design extended to monumental industrial buildings like textile
mills and foundries, also railway stations, viaducts and bridges.

Glasgow's Glasgow grew phenomenally through the 19th century to become the 'Second City
heyday: of the Empire'. While acres of tenements housed artisans and middle class families,
Thomson & earlier Georgian suburbs were abandoned for commodious villas for the prosperous,
Mackintosh designed by leading architects in areas like Kelvingrove. Many, especially on the
south side, were designed by Alexander 'Greek' Thomson using Classical Greece and
Egypt as inspiration. The best known of his public works is the Greek Revival church
in St Vincent St (1858). The originality of his work is itself currently enjoying an
long-overdue revival.

While **Glasgow University** (1870) by Gilbert Scott was inspired by medieval Flemish cloth halls, banks were modelled on Renaissance palazzos. Thomson designed Egyptian-style warehouses, and Burnet in the 1890's returned from New York to design tall, narrow-fronted buildings with steel frames. By 1896 and Charles Rennie Mackintosh's debut, Glasgow had the most exciting architecture in Europe.

The forward-looking Beaux-Arts rationalism of Burnet and company was challenged by Traditionalists reacting against aggressive modernity and advocating traditional building materials and craftsmanship, and referring back to 16th- and 17th-century vernacular architecture. **Rennie Mackintosh** was a leading, if independent exponent, as exemplified at **Hill House** in Helensburgh (see page 192) while a more mainstream Arts and Crafts aesthetic was adopted by **Robert Lorimer** who 'restored' many early houses such as Earlshall in Fife, as well as designing anew.

20th century: Traditionalism and Modernism

Background

In contrast, Art Déco was favoured by architects such as Glasgow's **Jack Coia**, and by the mid-century, **Basil Spence** was a champion of Modernism. Traditionalism versus Modernism was to become an enduring theme.

Economic depression and dramatic social change brought an urgent need for solutions to both rural depopulation, and urban overpopulation and decay. Already by the 1930's two contrasting visions of social progress were being proposed: restoration of organic unity, versus modernist utopia.

A desperate need for housing resulted in massive building projects into the 1970's transforming cities. Many historic buildings were demolished and city centres gutted in an effort to remedy post-war dereliction. Edinburgh had the worst slums in Europe where overpopulated tenements were literally collapsing. The first residential tower-blocks, the epitome of the Modern Functionalist brave new world, appeared, most notoriously in Glasgow's Gorbals. Urban over-spill was re-housed in New Towns such as Cumbernauld, which although internationally acclaimed in the 1960's, was unpopular with its inhabitants.

Post-war to present day

Traditionalists meanwhile continued to advocate experiments in vernacular style and a move was made to protect historic buildings.

Most prominent of recent public buildings is the new wing of the **Museum of Scotland in Edinburgh**. Completed at a time of renewed national confidence and cultural awareness, historical references are foremost. The sandstone-clad exterior is reminiscent of a medieval fortress, and from within the view over the adjacent Greyfriar's church, scene of the signing of the National Covenant in 1638, has been emphasized.

With the building of the **Scottish Parliament** at Holyrood by Eric Miralles still under way, it is not inappropriate that its temporary home is in the Assembly Rooms of the Church of Scotland, that most democratic of institutions.

Scottish writers and poets

Any overview, no matter how brief, of Scotland's literary tradition must begin with a poet who has become inextricably linked with the image of Scotland and all things Scottish across the globe. Robert Burns was born on 25 January 1759, in a small cottage in Alloway, Ayrshire, where he lived until the age of eight. His father was a market gardener and Burns later referred to himself as 'a very poor man's son'. During this time, he and his brother were placed under the instruction of a village tutor but, following the family's move to a farm a few miles away, Robert's attendance at school was interrupted by the need to work the farm. But his father was keen that his son's education continue, be it from a brief spell with a tutor or under his own instruction.

Robert Burns

Background

☞ **Great Scots**

For such a small country, Scotland has produced a remarkable number of intellectual geniuses who have been peculiarly influential. Many of them were great scientists, like **James Clerk Maxwell**, described by Einstein as the most important physicist after Newton, who by paving the way for Einstein's theory of relativity, practically invented the modern world. There was also **John Napier**, the inventor of logarithms, **Lord Kelvin**, who devised the second law of thermodynamics, and **James Hutton**, **Roderick Murchison** and **Charles Lyell**, who together created modern geology.

In medicine, Scotland led the world. **Robert Liston** and **James Young Simpson** discovered the benefits of chloroform and **Alexander Fleming** discovered penicillin, the most effective antibiotic ever devised. The number of technologists is incredible and includes **James Watt**, who developed the steam engine, **R W Thomson** who invented the fountain pen and pneumatic tyre, **John Macadam**, who gave the world the metalled road, **Charles Mackintosh** who invented waterproof fabric, **Alexander Graham Bell** who invented the telephone and not forgetting **John Logie Baird**, the father of television.

Scotland has also given the world the Bank of England, the decimal point, colour photographs, the fax machine, the photocopier, the bicycle, the bus, the thermos flask, the thermometer, the gas mask, the gravitating compass, interferon, insulin and Dolly, the cloned sheep.

Another move and a few weeks at school in Kirkoswald followed, while Robert continued to labour for his father, although in this time he had shown signs of his talent in a succession of love poems and poems based on day-to-day incidents of his life.

Following the death of their father in 1784, Robert and Gilbert rented another farm but luck wasn't on their side, as they fought against failing crops and an increasing struggle to provide for the family. To combat the anxiety of this situation, Burns found a refuge in his writing. Within the next two years, he had composed poetry which encompassed many subjects but mainly concerned itself with life as he was living it. He was also keen to point out what he saw as a kinship between all living things, such as in his famous 'To A Mouse', which was written, 'On turning her up in her nest with the plough, November, 1785'. The most frequently quoted lines of this poem; 'The best laid schemes o' mice an' men – Gang aft a-gley,' has entered the language, as have many sayings originated by Burns, and is a perfect summing up of his point.

Burns wrote in the dialect of plain country people and about the lives they led, but the emotions he described were so genuine that they appealed to all classes. The first three shilling volume of his poetry was released in July, 1786, by a publisher in Kilmarnock and his wife, Jean Armour, but only got as far as Greenock. However, by this time he had made a reputation for himself in Edinburgh and changed course for the capital to seek his fortune.

The 'ploughman-poet' was fêted by the cultured Edinburgh society. But, despite these attentions and his growing popularity, he remained a son of the soil at heart, unimpressed by the fuss his presence caused. In a letter of March, 1787, he wrote, "Scottish themes and Scottish story are the themes I could wish to sing," and while expressing a desire "to make leisurely pilgrimages through Caledonia," he preferred "to return to my old acquaintance the plough; and, if I can meet with a lease by which I can live, to commence a farmer".

In 1788 Burns and his wife set up a home at Ellisland, but given his previous lack of success as a farmer, he accepted a job as an Exciseman in Dumfriesshire, seizing contraband and checking on licences for the sale of alcohol. It was during this

Classic horror stories

An interesting side point is the Scottish connection with three other classics of the horror genre. **Mary Shelley**, *author of* Frankenstein, *spent much of her childhood in Tayside, while* Dracula, **Bram Stoker's** *definitive vampire novel was partly written in Cruden Bay, Aberdeenshire. Stoker is said to have borrowed much of the atmosphere for his tale from the jagged, storm lashed rocks of the bay. The third story is* The Hound Of The Baskervilles.

period, possibly inspired by coming into contact with so many people through his job, that he wrote of the joys of human companionship in what is perhaps his most celebrated work, *Auld Lang Syne*. Sung or spoken, this poem stands to this day as a symbol of friendship and is practically an anthem when friends gather to celebrate New Year around the world. His love of the companionship of friends is also a focus of *Tam O'Shanter*, which also serves as a cautionary warning against overindulgence and is a ghost story in the tradition of the mythic, while his irritation against the assumed superiority of some was put into words in *A Man's A Man For A' That*, which also returns to his theme of kinship:

"It's coming yet, for a' that,
That man to man, the world o'er.
Shall brothers be for a' that".

In 1791, Burns quit farming and moved to Dumfries. His poems of this period were a return to the form of traditional ballads, such as *Bannockburn* (often mistakenly referred to as *Scots, Wha Hae*) which celebrates the resolute spirit of his ancestors during the battle.

After a period of ill health, Burns died on 21 July 1796, and was buried in St Michael's Churchyard, Dumfries. A statue was erected in his honour by the citizens of Dumfries in 1822 and, to this day, visitors may still be shown around Burns' Cottage in Alloway and view the poet's birthplace, while his memory is celebrated every year on 25 January, his date of birth, now referred to as Burns Night.

Burns was famously described as having eyes which "were large and glowed… when he spoke with such feeling and interest. I have never seen such eyes in a human head," by another man regarded as one of the nation's greatest literary figures, Sir Walter Scott. The two men had met while Scott was still in his teens and it was to have a profound effect on him which lasted throughout his life.

Sir Walter Scott

Scott was the son of a wealthy Edinburgh lawyer and was born there in 1771, the sixth surviving child of 12. He contracted polio as a child, leaving him lame in the right leg, the Old Town at the time being disease-ridden. His parents then moved to the New Town, while young Scott was sent to his uncle's farm at Sandyknowe in the Borders for a period of recuperation. This period was to last five years, during which time he immersed himself in tales and ballads of Jacobites and Border heroes, giving him a passion for history which would infuse his later work.

Following spells at Edinburgh High School and University, Scott became a solicitor in his father's firm before becoming an advocate in 1792, while devoting his spare time to the love of poetry and literature which had seen him writing verse at the age of 11 and translating poems from their original German.

In 1797, he married Charlotte Carpenter and the marriage was to last for the rest of her life. At the time, he had been collecting local material which would eventually become poems in his three volumes of *Minstrelsy Of The Scottish Border'* which established his name as a literary figure. Other romantic poetic works followed, such as *The Lady Of The Lake*, as with Burns, employing the Scottish dialect.

Apart from these works, he also acted as editor on others' works, wrote contemporary history, biographies and collected historical documents. He was appointed Clerk to the Court of Session in 1806.

In 1811, Scott purchased Abbotsford, a farmhouse near Melrose, and his alterations and rebuilding were to drain his finances over the next 14 years. It was during this period that he would find the style which would remain his best remembered contribution to literature, the historical novel. Collectively known as the *Waverley* novels, these included *Old Mortality*, *Rob Roy* and *The Heart Of Midlothian*.

The original *Waverley* was a romantic tale of the Jacobite Rebellion of 1745 and the Highland society of the time. By 1819, Scott had moved beyond purely Scottish history and wrote *Ivanhoe*, set in 12th-century England. It remains his most enduring work and he followed it with *Kenilworth*, *Redgauntlet* and *The Talisman*.

Scott's fascination with history went beyond his fictional work and, in 1817, he and some friends discovered the ancient Honours of Scotland, the royal sword, crown and sceptre, which had remained hidden behind a sealed door at Edinburgh Castle since the days of Charles II.

In 1825, Scott was the victim of multiple tragedies. His publishers and a printing company in which he was a partner collapsed with disastrous financial consequences. Added to that, his beloved Charlotte died and he threw himself into his work so ferociously that he suffered four strokes.

Trips to Malta and Italy didn't succeed in improving his health and he died at Abbotsford on 21 September 1832. His huge popularity was believed to have kept the spirit of Scotland alive and he is commemorated by the Scott Monument in Princes Street, Edinburgh. This is an impressive architectural achievement and, if you have the stamina, affords a breathtaking view of Scott's native city.

Robert Louis Stevenson
Scott is best remembered for his romantic historical adventures. This tradition was to continue in the work of another of the nation's most famous authors. Robert Louis Stevenson was born at 8 Howard Place, Edinburgh, on November 13th, 1850. Like Scott, he was trained in law. He was also fond of travel.

It was these travels which led to his employment as a writer of travel articles and essays. However, while staying in Braemar in 1881, his young stepson, Lloyd Osbourne, asked him 'to try to write something interesting instead'. The rented house had a playroom, where Stevenson drew pirate maps of an island. These became the basis of his tale, which had the working title of *The Sea Cook*. When he offered it to *Young Folks* magazine, the editor suggested a new title and so, in the autumn of 1881, *Treasure Island* appeared in serial form, written by one 'Captain George North', a suitably seafaring pseudonym for Stevenson.

Two years after the serial appeared, it was released as a novel, under Stevenson's own name this time, and sold out almost immediately. For Stevenson, it was just the first of the many adventure tales, including *Kidnapped*, its sequel, *Catriona* and *The Master of Ballantrae*, he wrote before his death in Samoa on 3 December 1894.

Apart from adventure stories, he was also fond of the macabre, as shown in stories like *The Bottle Imp* and *The Bodysnatcher*, and he was responsible for one of the classics of horror literature, *The Strange Case of Doctor Jeckyll and Mister Hyde*, at once an update of the werewolf myth of man-turning-beast as well as exploration of the dual nature of man. The tale was inspired by Edinburgh's notorious Deacon Brodie, a respectable pillar of the community by day and a robber and highwayman by night. Stevenson wrote the first draft in a few days but it shocked his wife to such an extent that he burned it and rewrote it, injecting some moral points to appease his spouse.

Arthur Conan Doyle
Sherlock Holmes is regarded by many as the quintessential English detective, even though his creator, Sir Arthur Conan Doyle, was very much a Scot. Born at Picardy Place, Edinburgh, on 22 May 1859, Conan Doyle was schooled in Lancashire before

returning to study medicine at Edinburgh University in 1876. It was while serving as an out-patient clerk at Edinburgh Royal Infirmary that Doyle met the man who was to influence most the creation of his famous character, Doctor Joseph Bell. "His strong point", Doyle later noted, "was diagnosis, not only of disease, but of occupation and character".

Doyle was living in London and had published several short stories and essays when memories of his former mentor, combined with a love of the detective fiction of Edgar Allan Poe, inspired him to write *A Study In Scarlet*, which first appeared in the 1887 edition of *Beeton's Christmas Annual*. Doctor Watson recounted Sherlock Holmes' unique detective skills in this, followed by a further three novels and 56 short stories, with all but *The Sign Of Four* making their initial appearance in *The Strand Magazine*.

Holmes became a phenomenon that not even Doyle could control. In fact, by 1893 he was so annoyed that his more serious literary endeavours were being neglected that he achieved what many criminals had failed to do. He killed Holmes.

Following publication of *The Final Problem*, in which Holmes and his mortal foe, Professor Moriarty plunged over the Reichenbach Falls, there were public displays of grief and mourning. It was clear that the public were not going to let Holmes rest in peace and eventually Doyle was forced to find an ingenious way of reviving the character. He penned his last Holmes story in 1927, a mere three years before his own death. In memory of a much loved son and his famous creation, a statue of Holmes was recently erected in Edinburgh.

Despite Doyle's reluctance to continue with the character, Holmes has taken on a life of his own. Of all fictional characters, he has been the subject of most films. He has also been played on stage, radio, television, in musicals and has been the subject, or victim, of countless parodies or pastiches by numerous authors, from Agatha Christie to Stephen King.

Doyle's personal favourites of these parodies were written by his 'older literary friend', **JM Barrie**. Born in Kirriemuir in 1860, James Matthew Barrie was the son of a weaver. Educated at Glasgow Academy and Edinburgh University, Barrie spent some years in Nottingham as a journalist before returning to Kirriemuir to write.

Other Scottish writers

He moved to London in 1885, and it was there that he wrote his first novel, *Better Dead*. More novels and plays followed, best known of which is *Peter Pan, or The Boy Who Wouldn't Grow Old*. First published in 1904, it was written for the children of a friend, Llewlyn Davis. Barrie returned to Kirriemuir. Before his death in 1937, he bequeathed the copyright for *Peter Pan* to Great Ormond Street Hospital in London.

The tradition of the adventure story has continued throughout the 20th century, in the works of Perth-born **John Buchan,** author of *The Thirty-Nine Steps*. It was also the major theme in Glasgow-born **Alistair MacLean's** many novels, of which the most famous are *The Guns of Navarone*, *Ice Station Zebra* and *Where Eagles Dare*.

Other important Scottish books include: *The House with the Green Shutters*, by **George Douglas Brown**, *Sunset Song* by **Lewis Grassic Gibbon**, *The Silver Darlings* by **Neil Gunn**, *The Prime of Miss Jean Brodie* by **Muriel Spark** and **James Hogg's** *Confessions of a Justified Sinner*. Aside from Robert Burns, there are many fine **poets**, and the Selected Poems of **Norman McCaig**, **Hugh McDiarmid** and **George Mackay Brown** are all recommended.

Many of the writers living and working in Scotland today use their environment for inspiration. **Iain Banks**, author of *The Wasp Factory*, *The Crow Road* and many others (as well as science fiction novels written under the name Iain M Banks) based his fantasy, *The Bridge*, on the structure of the Forth Railway Bridge. **Irvine Welsh** has explored the capital's drug culture in the likes of *Trainspotting*, while **Ian Rankin's** crime novels take place in the real streets and bars of Edinburgh. Other notable contemporary works of fiction include *Lanark*, by **Alisdair Gray**, **William MacIlvanney's** *Docherty*, **James Kelman's** Booker prize-winning *How Late It Was,*

How Late, **Janice Galloway's** *The Trick is to Keep Breathing*, **A L Kennedy's** *Night Geometry and the Garscadden Trains*, and **Alan Warner's** *Morvern Caller*.

Scottish music

It could easily be argued that, in its music, Scotland produces the finest and clearest expression of its culture. All tastes are currently catered for within its music scene, reflecting the cosmopolitan nature of a country standing at the threshold of a new era with its own parliament and a deep sense of love of its history and traditions, while keeping a weather eye on the future. Although the words 'Scottish music' often conjure up images of a tartan-clad piper on a mist-covered moor, that same piper is just as likely to be found supplying stirring melodies to the decidedly nineties edge of 'drums and bass' styles heard in clubs around the country. And that's not all – the sheer number of options available to those seeking any style of music, ranging from folk to funk, from 'Tattoo' to 'T In The Park', is truly remarkable.

Yet, despite the fact a new millennium has come and gone, bringing with it so many changes in music and technology, Scotland as a nation still responds, virtually as one, to the skirl of a full set of highland **bagpipes**. Little wonder the pipes have been a dominant instrument for centuries, in celebration, in battle, in mourning, and are never far from the traveller's notion of all things Scottish. Indeed, in practically all the major cities and towns – Edinburgh, Dundee and Aberdeen on the east coast, Glasgow to the west, Perth at the foot of the beautiful Highlands and to the north, Inverness – 364 days a year, a piper can be found busking on the main thoroughfares, come rain or shine.

The pipes' unique sound is enjoyed the world over, not just in Scotland – witness the large numbers of pipe bands in the USA, Canada, across Europe, Australia and New Zealand. However, perhaps the best way to enjoy the pipes is to visit the country in summer when, accompanied by a full complement of drummers, many pipe bands can be seen taking part in competitions or playing at Highland Games in the open air – a real treat for the traveller from near or far.

It would also be totally remiss not to mention the **Edinburgh Military Tattoo**, now in its fortieth year. This takes place annually during August at the world-renowned Edinburgh Festival on the esplanade of Edinburgh Castle (see page 121). Pipe bands and military units from all over the world take part in a display guaranteed to impress and stir the blood in equal measure.

Indoors, unfortunately, acoustic bagpipes are a little too loud for the average music fan, and another instrument comes to the fore – the violin, or 'fiddle'. Whichever way one hears it, solo or accompanied by guitar, accordion, voice or best of all more violins – fewer sweeter sounds can be heard than a well-played fiddle. Traditional Scottish music can be passionate or jocular, mournful or joyous. In the hands of a good player, few instruments compare to the fiddle's wealth of expression. For confirmation, simply seek out the work of **Ally Bain**. With **The Boys Of The Lough**, **Phil Cunningham** or solo, his handling of all traditional Scottish styles is superb. Your Discman will never be the same again!

Delving a little deeper into Scotland's music, one may come across **Strathspey and Reel societies**. These are groups of fiddlers, large or small, which are well attended across the length and breadth of Scotland, regardless of the size of town. Most welcome visitors to their meetings to enjoy the music and, as most of these take place in pubs, and hotels, to enjoy the local brew, too! If this turns out to be impractical, a night spent at a ceilidh can be even more entertaining.

A **ceilidh** (pronounced '*kay*-lee') is an evening of Scottish music and dancing, the music provided by a ceilidh band, which normally consists of a fiddler, an accordionist, a drummer and a singer. One can then spend the evening sampling the delights of Gay Gordons or Dashing White Sergeants. In case you're wondering,

Scottish Pop, Rock and Dance Music

There's more to Scottish music than fiddles and bagpipes and many of the top Scottish pop and rock acts have had a major influence on the international music scene. Some of the best known names include Lonnie Donegan, Donovan, Lulu, The Average White Band, The Skids, Simple Minds, Big Country, Annie Lennox, Edwyn Collins, Aztec Camera, The Cocteau Twins, Love & Money, Altered Images, Texas, Del Amitri,

Blue Nile, Lloyd Cole & the Commotions, Billy Mackenzie, Waterboys, The Jesus & Mary Chain, Soup Dragons, Teenage Fanclub, Bronski Beat, The KLF, The Orb, The Shamen, Primal Scream, Finlay Quaye and Howie B. Glasgow's fecund indie scene continues to produce contenders such as Arab Strap and Belle and Sebastian while this year's Brit Awards were dominated by the hugely successful Travis.

Background

these aren't people who frequent these events – they are actually Scottish country dances which, along with eightsome reels, figure prominently in the ceilidh dance-band repertoire. Beware the well-meaning local lad or lassie bearing gifts of whisky, however – an excellent evening enjoying the music can often lead to a spectacular hangover the following morning!

In a similar vein (though with a slightly less frenetic style), folk music clubs still thrive in Scotland although, sadly, seem to be restricted to an 'early-in-the-week' slot of a Monday or Tuesday evening in bars around Scotland as landlords attempt to bring in customers on what are generally quieter nights for business. Even the Scots, with their fearsome (and well earned) reputation for partying, can't do it *every* night of the week!

Thankfully, this does not take away from the enthusiasm shown by the participants as fiddles, whistles, guitars, mandolins and bhodrans are produced and traditional songs and tunes are belted out by lusty voices and nimble fingers. Visiting the larger cities, look out for boards outside pubs which proclaim 'Live Music Tonight' or 'Folk Music Session – All Welcome', as the venues occasionally change from one week to the next, although the musicians tend to remain the same and are relatively easy to be found in both Edinburgh and Glasgow.

In **Edinburgh**, honourable mentions must go to *Whistle Blinkey's* at Tron Square, Edinburgh, T0131-5575114, which, despite its (dare I say it) slightly less salubrious air, hosts a folk session every night of the week. *Ensign Ewart's*, T0131-2257440, at the top of the Royal Mile hosts folk sessions on a Tuesday and Thursday; and sessions also take place in *Finnegan's Wake*, Victoria Street, T0131-2263816, and *Biddy Mulligan's* in the Grassmarket area of the city. A monthly gig guide is also available from pubs in Edinburgh for further, up-to-the-minute details.

Where to hear folk music

In **Glasgow**, the *Scotia Bar*, Stockwell Street, T0141-5528681, hosts sessions on a Wednesday night and a Saturday afternoon and serves a superb pint of a very well known brand of Irish stout, and *Clutha Vault*, Clydeside, T0141-5527520, hosts folk nights on Mondays and Tuesdays. In **Dunkeld**, Perthshire, is *Maclean's Real Music Bar*, in the *Taybank Hotel*, T01350-727340. Best night for a rousing folk session is a Thursday, with other sessions on Wednesday, Friday, Saturday and Sunday. Further east, in the city of **Dundee**, an excellent folk session can be enjoyed in the *Westport Bar*, not far from the city centre in the Hawkhilll area. This takes place on Monday night and 'The Westie', as it is popularly known, has long been a supporter of live music in the area. The folk club meets in the main bar. Other, larger gigs (ie ones which may cost money to attend) take place upstairs and cover all styles of music, not just folk.

Folk festivals Thankfully, folk music is not just confined to pubs on Monday evenings in Scotland. Folk festivals take place all over the country, from Arran to Shetland, and are great fun. Musicians from all over Scotland gather to play the tunes, sing the songs and maybe, just maybe, drink the odd beer or two. Amongst the best of the folk festivals is the **Celtic Connections**, held in Glasgow over three weeks in January, and the **Shetland Folk Festival Shetland** held over a long weekend in mid-April. Also recommended are those held in **Edinburgh** before Easter, in **Inverness** in July and August, **Stonehaven** in mid-July, **Auchtermuchty** in mid-August, **Girvan** in early May, **Killin** at the end of June, **Islay** during the last two weeks in May, **Arran** in early June, **Skye** at the end of July and **Kirriemuir** on the first weekend in September. Details of these festivals, and many others, are available from the Scottish Area Tourist Boards (see page 21).

Other music festivals Finally, for the younger (and young at heart) traveller, a few words on what has become the biggest annual music event in Britain, (north of Glastonbury!) – *T In The Park*. Held at Batado airfield, near **Kinross**, this is a festival which truly does reflect the breadth of musical tastes in Scotland. The main stage attracts some of the biggest names in pop (Blur and the Manic Street Preachers last year) but other attractions such as an 'acoustic' tent, a 'dance' tent and a 'folk' tent mean that no-one is left out and everyone has a place to shelter if it starts raining! This is a two-day event with one or two day tickets available, and a very large campsite! Check press for more details.

Language

Though the vast majority of Scots speak English, to the untutored ear, the Scottish dialect can be hard to understand, as many words and expressions are derived not from English but from **Lowland Scots**, or *lallans*, which is now recognized as a separate language as opposed to simply a regional dialect. The greatest exponent of the old Scots tongue was the great bard, Robert Burns, but it enjoyed something of a revival in the 20th century, led by great literary figures such as the poet Hugh McDiarmid. But though Lowland Scots has found its way onto the school curriculum in recent years, most Scots only use it in its most diluted form.

Scottish Gaelic Another ancient Scottish language which survives is Scottish Gaelic (*Gaidhlig*, pronounced 'Gallic'). It is spoken by about 85,000 people in Scotland (about two percent of the population) in the *Gaidhealtachd*, the Gaelic-speaking areas of the Outer Hebrides, parts of Skye and a few of the smaller Hebridean islands. Gaelic is one of the Celtic languages which has included Irish Gaelic, Manx, Welsh, Cornish and Breton. Today, only Scottish and Irish Gaelic, Welsh and Breton survive.

Scottish Gaelic is most closely related to Irish Gaelic and was introduced to Scotland from Ireland around the third century BC. Gaelic expanded greatly from the fifth century to around the 12th century and became the national language, spoken throughout most of the country, with the exception of the Norse-speaking Orkney and Shetland isles.

From that point, however, Gaelic began a steady decline over the following centuries and even before Union with England was being usurped by English as more and more wealth and power passed into non-Gaelic hands. This transfer of power was given a major boost by the Reformation in the mid-16th century as strong anti-Gaelic feeling was a major feature of the Church of Scotland.

Gaelic culture still flourished in the Highlands but the failure of two successive Jacobite rebellions in the 18th century helped seal its fate. In the wake of Culloden, all features of traditional Gaelic culture were proscribed and ethnic cleansing by government and landlords culminated in the Highland Clearances of the 19th century. The final nail in the coffin came in 1872 with the Education Act which gave no official recognition to Gaelic.

After two centuries of decline, Gaelic is now staging a comeback, thanks to financial help from government agencies and the EU which has enabled the introduction of bilingual primary and nursery schools and a massive increase in broadcasting time given to Gaelic-language programmes. This Renaissance can also be seen, and heard, in the fields of music and literature, and the recent return of the Scottish Parliament can surely only help to strengthen the position of Gaelic in Scottish society.

Those wishing to **teach themselves Gaelic** could start with the BBC *Can Seo* cassette and book. The best phrasebook is *Everyday Gaelic* by Morag MacNeill (Gairm).

Background

Footnotes

16

686

Footnotes

Index

Note: The code in italics after certain place names refers to the colour map, grid reference. Thus Aberdeen can found on map 4, square A6.

Shorts

Special interest pieces on
and about Scotland

694

Footnotes

Advertisers

Footnotes

Will you help us?

We try as hard as we can to make each Footprint Handbook as up-to-date and accurate as possible but, of course, things always change. Many people write to us - with corrections, new information, or simply comments.

If you want to let us know about an experience or adventure - hair-raising or mundane, good or bad, exciting or boring or simply something rather special - we would be delighted to hear from you. Please give us as precise information as possible, quoting the edition number (you'll find it on the front cover) and page number of the Handbook you are using.

Your help will be greatly appreciated, especially by other travellers. In return we will send you details about our special guidebook offer.

Write to Elizabeth Taylor
Footprint Handbooks
6 Riverside Court
Lower Bristol Road
Bath
BA2 3DZ
England
or email info@footprintbooks.com

PRODUCT OF SCOTLAND

Walkers

· ESTABLISHED 1898 ·

The world's **classic** *pure butter* **shortbread**

Map index

Scotland

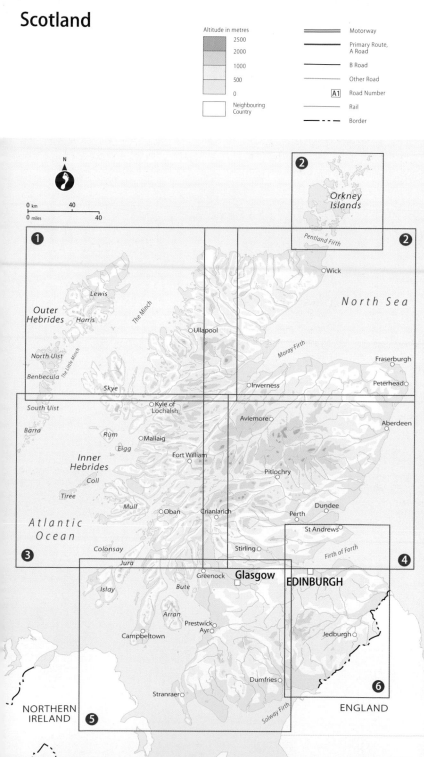

Altitude in metres
2500
2000
1000
500
0

Neighbouring Country

Motorway

Primary Route, A Road

B Road

Other Road

A1 Road Number

Rail

Border

N

0 km 40
0 miles 40

❶

Outer Hebrides

Lewis

Harris

The Minch

North Uist

The Little Minch

Benbecula

Skye

South Uist

Barra

Rùm

Eigg

Inner Hebrides

Coll

Tiree

Mull

Colonsay

Jura

Islay

Bute

Arran

Campbeltown

Atlantic Ocean

Kyle of Lochalsh

Mallaig

Fort William

Oban

Crianlarich

Greenock

Prestwick

Ayr

Stranraer

Dumfries

NORTHERN IRELAND

❺

Ullapool

Inverness

Aviemore

Pitlochry

Perth

Stirling

Glasgow

EDINBURGH

Jedburgh

Solway Firth

❷

Orkney Islands

Pentland Firth

Wick

North Sea

Moray Firth

Fraserburgh

Peterhead

Aberdeen

Dundee

St Andrews

Firth of Forth

❸

❹

❻

ENGLAND

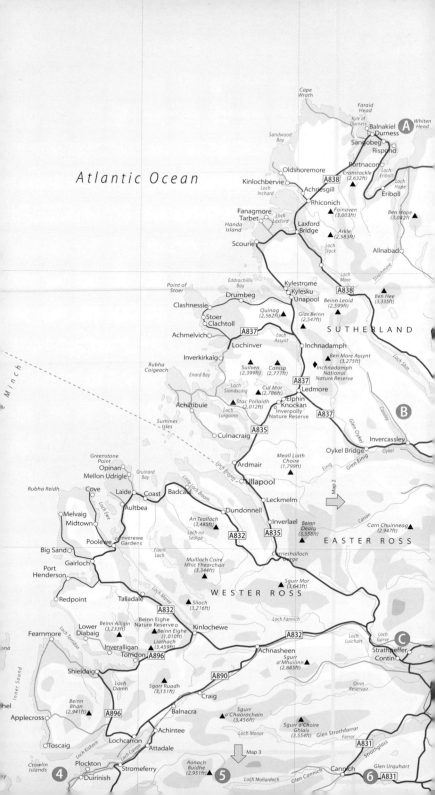

Map 2

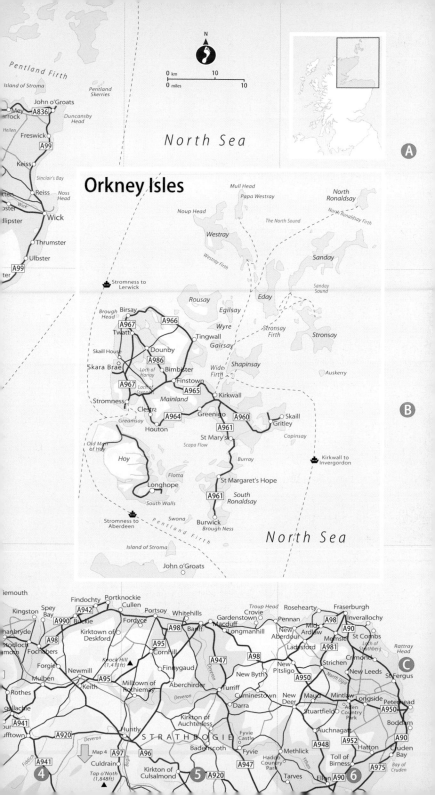

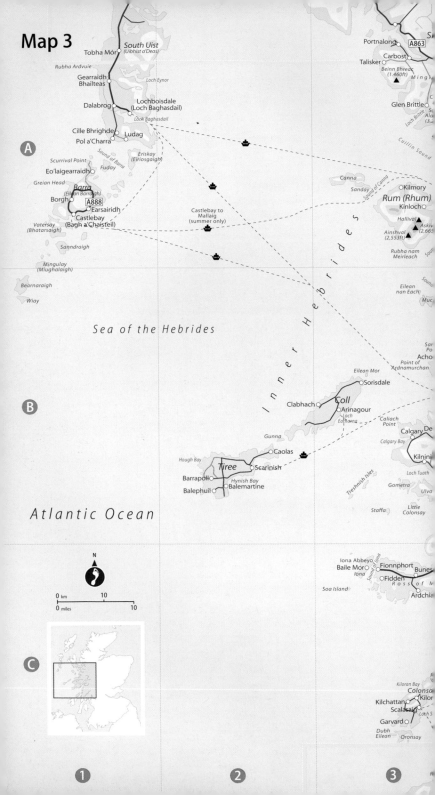

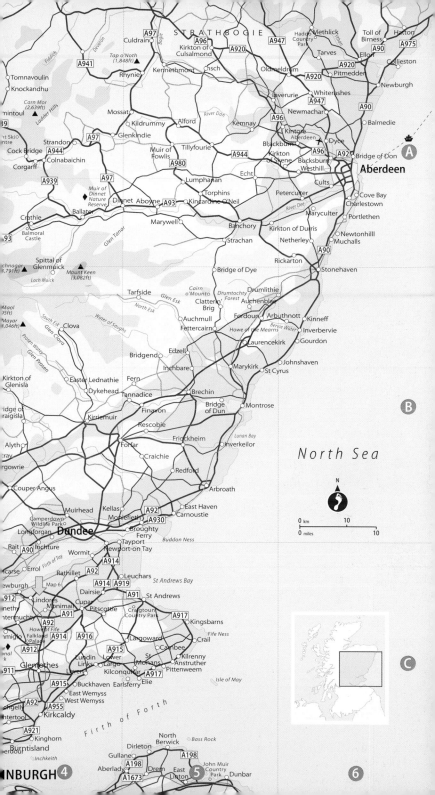

Map 5

Jura
Shian Bay
Loch Righ Mor
Ardlussa
Rubh' an t-Sailein
Loch Tarbert
Rubh a' Mhail
Nave Island
Sanaigmore
Loch Gruinart
Ardnave
Adradh
Port Askaig
Ben an Oir (2,576ft)
Sgarbh Breac (1,195ft)
Feolin Ferry
Ballygrant
A846
Bridgend
Bowmore
Islay
Beinn Bheigeir (1,611ft)
A847
Loch Indaal
A846
Kintour
Glenegedale
Kintra
The Oa
Lower Killeyan
Port Ellen
Mull of Oa
Rubha nan Leacan
Texa

Tarbert
Keillmore
Sound of Jura
Small Isles
Kilmory
Danna Island
Point of Knap
Druimdrishaig
Kilberry
Rubha na Traille
Ardpatrick Point
Clachan
Claggain Bay
Gigha
Ardminish
Cara Island
Glenacardoch Point
Tayinloan
Killean
Kintyre
Bellochantuy Bay
Glenbarr
Dippen
Saddell
Lussa Loch
Machrihanish Bay
Kilchenzie
Peninver
Ardnacross Bay
Campbeltown
Machrihanish
Davaar Island
Corrie Glen
Macharioch
Southend
Mull of Kintyre
Sanda Island

Atlantic Ocean

Tayvallich
Lochgilphead
Ardrishaig
A83
Otter Ferry
Clachan of Glendaruel
Craignure
Auchenbrec
A886
Map 3
A83
Kilfinan
A8003
Port Driseach
Tighnabruaich
Kames
Millhouse
A886
Port Bannatyne
A884
Rothes
Bute
Kingarth
Loch Caolisport
Knapdale
Loch Fyne
West Loch Tarbert
Tarbert
West Tarbert
Kennacraig
Skipness
Kilberry
Ballochroy
Crossaig
Claonaig
Cock of Arran
Lochranza
A841
Pirnmill
Casteal Abhail (2,819ft)
Goat Fell (2,868ft)
Corrie
Brodick Castle & Garden
Arran
Carradale
Dougarrie
Brodick
Ard Bheinn (1,680ft)
Tormore
Lamlash
Blackwaterfoot
Whiting
Ardlamont Point
Meikle Kilmory
Sound of Bute
Kilbrannan Sound
Garroch Head
Lagg
A841
Bennan Head
Pladda
Campbeltown to Ballycastle (Northern Ireland) (summer only)
Ailsa Craig

NORTHERN IRELAND

Ballantrae
Milleur Point
Cairnryan to Larne (Northern Ireland) (summer only)
Kirkcolm
Cairnryan
A718
Leswalt
Loch Ryan
A77
Stranraer
Stranraer to Belfast (summer only)
A77
Ca...ker
Portpatrick
A77
A716
Stoneykirk
Sandhead
Port Logan
Drumm...
Mull of Ge...

N

0 km 10
0 miles 10

① ② ③

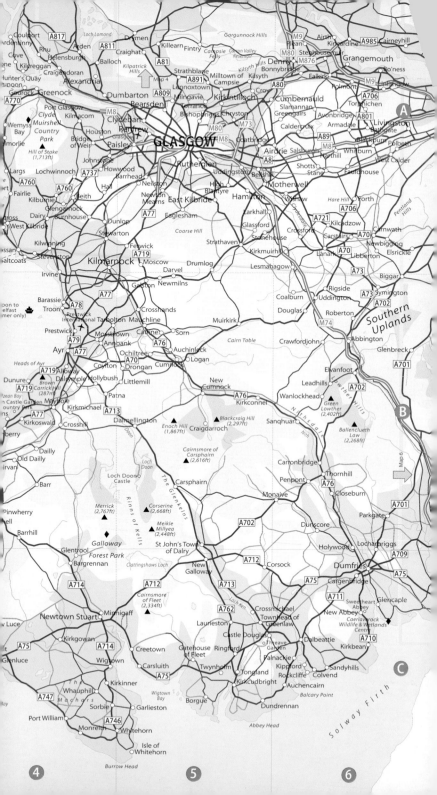

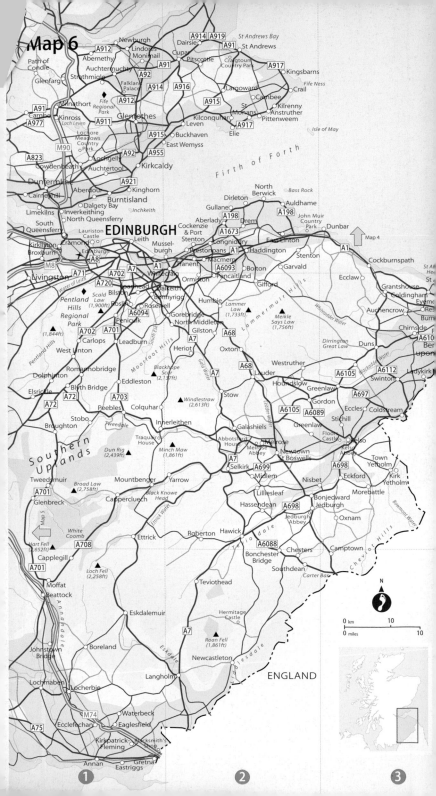

Acknowledgements

Alan Murphy would like to thank those who contributed to this book: Suzy Kennard for the History and Architecture sections, William Clyde for the History of Golf, Duncan Lindsay for Music, Jos Milner for Wildlife and Frank Nicholas for Scottish Writers. Thanks to those who helped with the research of the travelling text: Suzy Kennard for the Northeast Highlands; William Clyde for Dundee; Duncan Lindsay for Perth; Norma Rowlerson for Aberdeen and Deeside; Sarah Thorowgood for Orkney and Shetland and John Murphy for Edinburgh.

Thanks also go to the staff of the many local and regional tourist offices for their invaluable advice and assistance, in particular to Moira Dyer and Jennifer Mclean at Glasgow Tourist Board and Sally Monro at Highland Tourist Board. Also thanks to Mike Blair at Caledonian McBrayne, Ann Johnstone at the National Trust for Scotland, Jane Ferguson at Historic Scotland and all at the Festival Fringe office in Edinburgh.

Finally, a special thanks to all at Footprint for their support and hard work, especially Sarah Thorowgood and Rachel Fielding. And to Philippa, for her patience and understanding.